P9-DEV-789

1954	1956	1958	1960	1962	1964	1965	1966	1967	1968	1969	1970	1971	1972	1973
240.7	271.9	296.3	332.2	363.4	411.4	444.3	481.9	509.5	559.8	604.7	648.1	702.5	770.7	851.6
53.8	72.2	64.5	78.8	87.9	101.7	118.0	130.4	128.0	139.9	155.0	150.2	176.0	205.6	242.9
86.4	91.6	106.1	113.2	131.4	144.4	153.0	173.6	194.6	212.1	223.8	236.1	249.9	268.9	287.6
0.3	2.3	0.4	2.4	2.4	5.5	3.9	1.9	1.4	−1.3	−1.2	1.2	−3.0	−8.0	0.6
381.3	438.0	467.3	526.6	585.2	663.0	719.1	787.8	833.6	910.6	982.2	1,035.6	1,125.4	1,237.3	1,382.6
40.5	47.1	52.5	56.6	60.4	66.0	70.2	75.9	82.3	89.8	98.3	107.0	116.5	127.6	140.0
340.8	390.9	414.8	470.0	524.8	597.0	648.9	711.9	751.3	820.8	883.9	928.6	1,008.9	1,109.7	1,242.6
−2.2	−2.5	−2.7	−3.2	−4.3	−5.0	−5.4	−5.2	−5.5	−6.2	−6.1	−6.4	−7.7	−8.7	−12.7
33.2	32.8	38.0	43.7	50.1	57.9	62.3	68.2	71.3	79.7	84.6	94.4	108.0	113.1	123.0
309.8	360.6	379.5	429.8	479.0	544.1	592.0	648.9	685.5	747.3	805.4	840.6	908.6	1,005.3	1,132.3
10.6	13.5	15.9	21.9	25.4	30.1	31.6	40.6	45.5	50.4	57.8	62.0	69.6	79.5	97.9
17.6	22.0	19.0	22.7	24.0	28.0	30.9	33.7	32.7	39.4	39.7	34.4	37.7	41.9	49.3
12.3	16.9	12.1	15.0	17.4	22.0	27.8	30.5	27.1	26.6	24.1	20.3	28.6	36.9	53.5
26.4	32.3	37.8	42.3	44.8	50.5	55.0	61.6	70.5	83.6	95.5	113.2	127.5	141.8	175.9
295.7	340.5	370.3	412.5	457.0	514.5	556.7	605.7	650.7	714.5	779.3	837.1	900.2	988.8	1,107.5
31.8	38.7	40.9	48.7	54.8	56.0	61.9	71.0	77.9	92.1	109.9	109.0	108.7	132.0	140.6
263.9	301.8	329.4	363.8	402.2	458.5	494.8	534.7	572.9	622.5	669.4	728.1	791.5	856.8	967.0
1954	1956	1958	1960	1962	1964	1965	1966	1967	1968	1969	1970	1971	1972	1973
1,868.2	2,040.2	2,057.5	2,262.9	2,454.8	2,708.4	2,881.1	3,069.2	3,147.2	3,293.9	3,393.6	3,397.6	3,510.0	3,702.3	3,916.3
−0.7	2.0	−1.0	2.4	6.1	5.8	6.4	6.5	2.5	4.7	3.0	0.1	3.3	5.5	5.8
7,822	8,432	8,421	8,681	9,098	9,825	10,311	10,735	11,081	11,468	11,726	12,039	12,366	12,794	13,566
26.9	27.2	28.9	29.6	30.2	31.0	31.5	32.4	33.4	34.8	36.7	38.8	40.5	41.8	44.4
0.7	1.5	2.8	1.7	1.0	1.3	1.6	2.9	3.1	4.2	5.5	5.7	4.4	3.2	6.2
28.6	33.6	31.9	36.5	39.8	45.0	49.5	53.8	55.0	58.1	60.7	58.7	59.5	65.3	70.6
130.3	136.0	138.4	140.7	147.8	160.3	167.8	172.0	183.3	197.4	203.9	214.4	228.3	249.2	262.8
3.05	3.77	3.83	4.82	4.50	4.50	4.54	5.63	5.61	6.30	7.96	7.91	5.72	5.25	8.03
163.0	168.9	174.9	180.7	186.5	191.9	194.3	196.6	198.7	200.7	202.7	205.1	207.7	209.9	211.9
62.3	66.6	67.6	69.6	70.6	73.1	74.5	75.8	77.3	78.7	80.7	82.8	84.4	87.0	89.4
3.5	2.8	4.6	3.9	3.9	3.8	3.4	2.9	3.0	2.8	2.8	4.1	5.0	4.9	4.4
5.5	4.1	6.8	5.5	5.5	5.2	4.5	3.8	3.8	3.6	3.5	4.9	5.9	5.6	4.9
43.9	45.8	50.5	51.4	55.7	60.5	62.7	65.2	66.6	68.9	69.2	70.5	73.6	76.0	78.4
2.2	0.1	2.8	1.7	4.7	4.6	3.5	4.0	2.2	3.4	0.4	2.0	4.3	3.3	3.2
0.2	2.7	0.8	2.8	3.4	6.8	5.4	3.0	2.6	0.6	0.4	2.3	−1.4	−5.8	7.1
270.8	272.7	279.7	290.5	302.9	316.1	322.3	328.5	340.4	368.7	365.8	380.9	408.2	435.9	466.3

(Continued)

ECONOMICS

ECONOMICS

Principles, Problems, and Policies

Fourteenth Edition

CAMPBELL R. McCONNELL
PROFESSOR OF ECONOMICS, EMERITUS
UNIVERSITY OF NEBRASKA

STANLEY L. BRUE
PROFESSOR OF ECONOMICS
PACIFIC LUTHERAN UNIVERSITY

Irwin
McGraw-Hill

Boston   Burr Ridge, IL   Dubuque, IA   Madison, WI   New York   San Francisco   St. Louis
Bangkok   Bogotá   Caracas   Lisbon   London   Madrid
Mexico City   Milan   New Delhi   Seoul   Singapore   Sydney   Taipei   Toronto

Irwin/McGraw-Hill

A Division of The McGraw·Hill Companies

Economics
Principles, Problems, and Policies

domestic   3 4 5 6 7 8 9 0   VNH   VNH   9 4 3 2 1 0 9
international   3 4 5 6 7 8 9 0   VNH   VNH   9 4 3 2 1 0 9

ISBN 0-07-047094-4
ISBN 0-07-366215-1 (*Wall Street Journal* edition)

Editorial director: Michael Junior
Publisher: Gary Burke
Sponsoring editor: Lucille Sutton
Developmental editor: Marilea Fried
Marketing manager: Nelson Black
Project manager: Eva Marie Strock
Production supervisors: Diane Renda, Pam Augspurger

Supplements coordinator: Louis Swaim
Designer: Amanda Kavenagh
Cover designer: Francis Owens
Editorial assistant: Lee Hertel
Compositor: York Graphic Services, Inc.
Typeface: Janson Text
Printer: Von Hoffmann Press, Inc.

Last Word illustrations and back cover illustration by Jacques Cournoyer

Library of Congress Cataloging-in-Publication Data
McConnell, Campbell R.
    Economics: principles, problems, and policies / Campbell R.
McConnell, Stanley L. Brue. — 14th ed.
      p.   cm.
    Includes index.
    ISBN 0-07-047094-4
    1. Economics.   I. Brue, Stanley L., 1945–   . II. Title.
HB171.5.M47   1998
330—dc21   98–23775
                                                      CIP

http://www.mhhe.com

Campbell R. McConnell earned his Ph.D. from the University of Iowa after receiving degrees from Cornell College and the University of Illinois. He taught at the University of Nebraska–Lincoln from 1953 until his retirement in 1990. He is also coauthor of *Contemporary Labor Economics*, 5th ed. (McGraw-Hill) and has edited readers for the principles and labor economics courses. He is a recipient of both the University of Nebraska Distinguished Teaching Award and the James A. Lake Academic Freedom Award and is past president of the Midwest Economics Association. Professor McConnell was awarded an honorary Doctor of Laws degree from Cornell College in 1973 and received its Distinguished Achievement Award in 1994. His primary areas of interest are labor economics and economic education. He has an extensive collection of jazz recordings and enjoys reading jazz history.

Stanley L. Brue did his undergraduate work at Augustana College (SD) and received his Ph.D. from the University of Nebraska–Lincoln. He teaches at Pacific Lutheran University, where he has been honored as recipient of the Burlington Northern Faculty Achievement Award. He has also received the national Leavey Award for excellence in economic education. Professor Brue is past president and a current member of the International Executive Board of Omicron Delta Epsilon International Economics Honorary. He is coauthor of *Economic Scenes*, 5th ed. (Prentice-Hall) and *Contemporary Labor Economics*, 5th ed. (McGraw-Hill) and author of *The Evolution of Economic Thought*, 5th ed. (HB/Dryden). For relaxation, he enjoys boating on Puget Sound and skiing trips with his family.

. . . .

**To Mem
and to Terri
and Craig**

. . . .

CONTENTS IN BRIEF

CONTENTS

LIST OF KEY GRAPHS

Welcome to the fourteenth edition of *Economics* (and its companion editions of *Macroeconomics* and *Microeconomics*), the nation's best-selling economics textbook. About $4\frac{1}{2}$ million U.S. students have used this book. It has been adapted into Canadian, Australian, Italian, and Russian editions and translated into French, Spanish, and several other languages.

The resurging U.S. economy, changes in the focus of monetary policy, economic turmoil in Southeast Asia, dynamic new technologies, an overhaul of U.S. farm and welfare policies, swings in exchange rates, capitalism in Russia—what an interesting time to teach and learn economics! Clearly, those who understand economic principles will have a distinct advantage in making sense of the economy and successfully participating in it.

WHAT'S NEW?

We thoroughly revised, polished, and updated this edition. (Using a software analogy, this is version 14.0, not 13.1 or 13.2.) The comments of over 100 reviewers and survey respondents motivated many of the changes and helped us create a text full of energy and innovation.

New or Highly Revised Chapters

One chapter is totally new to this edition, and three other chapters contain much new content.

- *Chapter 26: Technology, R&D, and Efficiency.* This entirely new chapter is an explicit and cohesive discussion of the microeconomics of technological advance. We think that topics such as invention, innovation, R&D decision making, and creative destruction are exciting and simply too important to ignore or set into sidebars, so we devote an entire chapter to them. (To make room for this new content, we consolidated the discussions of monopolistic competition and oligopoly into a single chapter [Chapter 25].)
- *Chapter 16: Extending the Analysis of Aggregate Supply.* In this greatly revised chapter we introduce

the distinction between short-run and long-run aggregate supply and then use that distinction to develop an "extended aggregate demand and aggregate supply model." We use that model to analyze demand-pull inflation, cost-push inflation, and recession. In the remainder of the chapter we look at other aggregate supply topics such as the Phillips Curve and supply-side economics.

- *Chapter 17: Disputes in Macro Theory and Policy.* In this nearly new chapter we broaden the ideas developed in Chapter 16 to discuss modern disputes in macro theory and policy. We now use the classic-Keynesian discussion of previous editions as a historical backdrop for an examination of modern debates on (1) the sources of macro instability, (2) the extent of "self-correction" in the economy, and (3) the debate over "rules" versus "discretion." The chapter systematically examines new classical economics and introduces ideas such as misperceptions theory, coordination failures, efficiency wages, and insider-outsider relationships.
- *Chapter 40: Transition Economies: Russia and China.* We added a discussion of China to the previous edition's material on Russia. We look briefly at Marxian ideology and the institutions, goals, and major problems of central planning, and then turn to the collapse of the Soviet economy, the elements of the Russian reform, and contemporary outcomes. Finally, we discuss the main features of market reform in China, including rapid economic growth and remaining difficulties.

New Pedagogy

- *Quick Quizzes.* We added 4 multiple-choice questions as Quick Quizzes to each of the 24 Key Graphs. Each quiz relates to the content of the specific Key Graph and is written in the same style and at the same level of difficulty as the test bank questions. The correct answers are provided upside down so students can instantly measure their understanding of key concepts.
- *Internet Questions.* Each chapter contains two

Web-Based Questions which require students to access specified Internet addresses. These questions help students apply specific economic concepts and introduce them to relevant *Economics* Internet sites.

A Building-Block Approach to Macro

With the changes in this edition, we created a fully integrated building-block approach to macro theory, policy, and issues. Specifically, we

- Build the aggregate expenditures model (AE model)
- Derive aggregate demand from the AE model and develop the aggregate demand–aggregate supply model (AD-AS model)
- Use the AD-AS model to discuss fiscal policy
- Introduce monetary considerations into the AD-AS model
- Use the AD-AS model to discuss monetary policy
- Extend the AD-AS model by distinguishing between short-run and long-run aggregate supply
- Apply the "extended AD-AS model" to macroeconomic instability, modern macroeconomic disputes, and economic growth

Added Content on Women, Minorities, and Discrimination

In text and vignettes, this edition includes new information on women, minorities, and discrimination. For example, in Chapter 2 we added a Last Word on the rise of women's participation in the labor force. A new Last Word in Chapter 28 deals with the impact of occupational licensing on African-style hairbraiders. Chapter 36 develops the taste for discrimination model, the idea of statistical discrimination, and the theory of occupational crowding. The new Last Word in Chapter 36 looks at the effects of "blind" auditions on the gender composition of major symphony orchestras.

Greater Emphasis on the Economic Perspective

Newly organized Chapter 1 now begins with a discussion of scarcity and choice, rational behavior, and marginal analysis. In Chapter 2 we use the ideas of marginal benefits and marginal costs to determine the optimal position on the production possibilities curve. We continue to reinforce the economic perspective in the remainder of the book in a number of discussions, including those on investment decisions, sunk costs, rational R&D decisions, and immigration policy.

Added Directness, Reduced Formalism, Extra Human Interest Material

Our line-by-line editing adds directness and reduces formalism, but we were careful to *not* reduce the thoroughness of our explanations. Where needed, the "extra sentence of explanation" remains a distinguishing characteristic of *Economics*. Students will especially enjoy our new Last Words in Chapters 4, Pink Flamingos and "Dollar Votes"; Chapter 26, On the Path to the Personal Computer and Internet; and Chapter 28, Of African-Style Hairbraiders and Stodgy Economists. All 40 Last Words present interesting applications with attractive modern art.

Other New Topics and Revised Discussions

Along with the changes just discussed, there are many other revisions. Here are just a few examples.

- *Part 1.* *Chapter 1:* Figure 1-1 and its discussion revised; new, livelier examples. *Chapter 2:* Improved discussion of the economic rationale for increasing costs; new applications (land-use controversies, devastation from war, and emerging technologies); consolidated discussion of economic systems. *Chapter 3:* New examples: increased demand for sports-utility vehicles; improved fuel efficiency of aircraft engines; increased demand for salsa; buyout of haddock fishing boats; the decline in the price of pink salmon. *Chapter 4:* Improved discussion of consumer sovereignty; improvements to Table 4-1 on least-cost production; new Global Perspective on the Index of Economic Freedom. *Chapter 5:* New explicit definitions of stocks and bonds; new discussion of the principal-agent problem; new Global Perspective on government employment as a percentage of total employment for various countries. *Chapter 6:* Improved explanation of the most-favored-nation clause.
- *Part 2.* *Chapter 7:* Changed terminology relating to Figure 7-2 (from "expanding, static, and de-

clining economy" to "expanding, static, and declining production capacity"); simplification of the explanation of the GDP price index (new Tables 7-5 and 7-6); fuller discussion of the CPI. *Chapter 8:* Improved discussion of structural unemployment; revision of the discussion of Okun's law; addition to Table 8-2 of unemployment rates by level of education. *Chapter 9:* Figure 9-5 (investment demand) is now a Key Graph; new Figure 9-6 shows shifts in the investment-demand curve; new Figure 9-7 links the real interest rate, the investment-demand curve, and the economy's investment schedule. *Chapter 10:* Figure 10-8 on recessionary and inflationary gaps is now a Key Graph. *Chapter 11:* Improved discussion of possible causes of downward price and wage inflexibility. *Chapter 12:* New discussion of the proposed balanced-budget requirement; clarified discussion of the crowding-out effect of fiscal policy, including criticisms of the idea.

- **Part 3.** *Chapter 13:* "Unit of account" replaces the term "measure of value"; new section on recent developments in money and banking (relative decline of banks and thrifts, globalization of financial markets, and electronic money and smart cards). *Chapter 15:* Expanded discussion of the Fed's targeting of the Federal funds rate; new Global Perspective 15-1 lists the names (including nicknames) of the central banks of selected nations.
- **Part 4.** *Chapter 16:* "New" chapter extends the analysis of aggregate supply. *Chapter 17:* "New" chapter contrasts contemporary views on macro theory and policy. *Chapter 18:* Covers economic growth (Chapter 19 in the thirteenth edition); discusses the weak productivity gains in services; discusses the controversial idea of a "new economy." *Chapter 19:* Updated section on the policy responses to budget deficits, including the deficit reduction legislation of 1992 and the line-item veto.
- **Part 5.** *Chapter 20:* Revised discussion (based on new research) of the price elasticity of illegal drugs. *Chapter 21:* Figure 21-1 is now a Key Graph; new Figure 21-2 shows the demand curve derived from a change in product price in the utility-maximizing model. *Chapter 22:* Explicit definitions of marginal, average, and total product now precede the discussion of diminishing returns; substantially revised Table 22-1 and Figure 22-2; new example of scale economies ("extraordinarily large stamping ma-

chine"). *Chapter 23:* Figure 23-2 now includes the firm's total profit curve; the graphical discussion of the TR-TC approach is confined to profit maximization; section on qualifications of the pure competition model is consolidated. *Chapter 24:* New Table 24-2 lays out the steps for determining profit-maximizing output, price, and profit (if any) in pure monopoly; new graphical comparison of outcomes under pure monopoly and pure competition (Figure 24-6); "discount coupons" added as an example of price discrimination. *Chapter 25:* The discussion of monopolistic competition and oligopoly is now combined into a single chapter; kinked demand model as a Key Graph added; several new examples. *Chapter 26:* New chapter on technology, R&D, and efficiency.

- **Part 6.** *Chapter 27:* Table 27-3 summarizes the differences between substitute resources and complementary resources; updated labor demand examples; revised discussion of least-cost and profit-maximizing combinations of resources. *Chapter 28:* Discussions of real wage stagnation and pitfalls of pay-for-performance plans; rewritten section on labor market imperfections. *Chapter 29:* The loanable funds model is now used in this micro chapter in both the micro split *and* the hardbound book.
- **Part 7.** *Chapter 30:* New hypothetical example (enterprising artist and his public art) to highlight the free-rider problem and public goods characteristics; new discussion of the "tragedy of the commons." *Chapter 31:* Expanded discussion of pork-barrel politics and bureaucratic inefficiency; new material on VAT and flat tax proposals, including criticisms.
- **Part 8.** *Chapter 32:* Discussion of Microsoft and tying contracts; new examples of price-fixing cases; updated and reorganized section on industrial policy. *Chapter 33:* New discussion of the reform of farm policy (the end of price supports for grain commodities). *Chapter 34:* Updated data on income mobility; revised discussions on causes of increasing inequality; new section on welfare reform. *Chapter 35:* Expanded discussion of managed health care (preferred provider organizations and health maintenance organizations). *Chapter 36:* Consolidated and revised discussion of unionism; much new content on discrimination, including discussion of the affirmative action debate; updated discussion of immigration.
- **Part 9.** *Chapter 37:* Chapter on international trade tightened. *Chapter 38:* Improved explanation of

the balance of payments; major consolidation of the discussion of past exchange-rate systems and the section on U.S. trade deficits. *Chapter 39:* New world map indicating industrially advanced nations, middle-income developing nations, and low-income developing nations (Figure 39-1); revised discussion of international debt difficulties, including mention of the recent IMF bailouts of the Southeast Asian economies; entirely new policy section on development. *Chapter 40:* Extensively revised chapter now includes discussion of the transition to markets in China as well as in Russia.

New Last Words

Several Last Words are new; others have been revised and updated. All 40 Last Words are accompanied by new art. We continue to place these boxes at the ends of chapters, where they are less likely to interrupt readers' concentration.

The new Last Word topics are women and production possibilities (Chapter 2); consumer sovereignty, dollar votes, and plastic pink flamingos (Chapter 4); the demise of wage and price controls (Chapter 16); the irrelevancy of sunk costs (Chapter 22); maximization of consumer surplus in pure competition (Chapter 23); a brief history of the personal computer and Internet (Chapter 26); the substitution of ATMs for bank tellers (Chapter 27); the impact of occupational licensing on African-style hairbraiders; (Chapter 28); social security reform (Chapter 34); the shortage of human organs for transplant (Chapter 35); the impact of blind auditions on the employment of women in major orchestras (Chapter 36); enterprise transition to capitalism in Russia (Chapter 40).

FUNDAMENTAL GOALS

Although the fourteenth edition only modestly resembles the first one, our intention remains the same: to introduce beginning economics students to principles essential to understanding the basic economizing problem, specific economic issues, and policy alternatives available for dealing with them. Two fortunate by-products of this objective are an ability to reason accurately and dispassionately about economic matters and a lasting interest in economics. As always, we present the principles and problems of economics in a straightforward, logical fashion. *We continue to stress clarity of presentation, step-by-step organization, and a consistent level of analysis.*

DISTINGUISHING FEATURES

- *Comprehensive Explanations at an Appropriate Level.* *Economics* is comprehensive, analytical, and challenging yet accessible to a wide range of students. Its thoroughness and accessibility enable instructors to select topics for special classroom emphasis with confidence that students can read and comprehend independently other assigned material in the book.
- *Comprehensive Definition of Economics.* Because students must first understand the fundamentals, we devote nearly all of Chapter 2 to a careful statement and development of the economizing problem and an exploration of its implications. This foundation will help put into proper perspective essential economic concepts.
- *Fundamentals of the Market System.* Economies throughout the world are making difficult transitions from planning to markets. Our detailed description of the institutions and operation of the *market system* in Chapter 4 is even more relevant than before. We pay particular attention to property rights, freedom of enterprise and choice, competition, and the role of profits because these concepts are poorly understood by beginning students.
- *Early Integration of International Economics.* We give the principles and institutions of the global economy early treatment. Chapter 6 examines the growth of world trade, the major participants in world trade, specialization and comparative advantage, the foreign exchange market, tariffs and subsidies, and various trade agreements. This strong introduction to international economics permits "globalization" of later macroeconomics and microeconomics discussions.
- *Early and Extensive Treatment of Government.* Government is an integral component of modern capitalism. This book introduces the economic functions of government early and systematically treats them in Chapter 5. Chapter 30 examines government and market failure in further detail, and Chapter

31 looks at salient facets of public choice theory and public finance. Both the macroeconomics and microeconomics sections of the text include problem- and policy-oriented chapters.

- ***Emphasis on Economic Growth.*** This edition continues to emphasize economic growth. Chapter 2 uses the production possibilities curve to show the basic ingredients of growth. Chapter 18 discusses the rate and causes of growth, in addition to some of the controversies surrounding it. Chapter 39 focuses on the developing countries and the growth obstacles they confront. Chapter 40 looks at growth in the transition economies of the Soviet Union and China. Our new micro chapter on technology, R&D, and efficiency lays the micro foundation for understanding economic growth.

- ***Emphasis on the Theory of the Firm.*** We give much attention to microeconomics in general and to the theory of the firm in particular, for two reasons. First, the concepts of microeconomics are difficult for most beginning students; too-brief expositions usually compound these difficulties by raising more questions than they answer. Second, we wanted to couple analysis of the various market structures with a discussion of the impact of each market arrangement on price, output levels, resource allocation, and the rate of technological advance.

- ***Emphasis on Economic Issues.*** For many students, Part 4 (macroeconomic issues) and Part 7 (micro-oriented problems) are where the action is. We sought to guide that action along logical lines through the application of appropriate analytical tools. In these parts we favor inclusiveness; instructors can effectively omit whatever chapters they choose.

ORGANIZATION AND CONTENT

Economics reflects the challenge specific topics and concepts will likely pose for average students. For instance, the theory of the firm and macro output and price-level determination are carefully treated. Here, simplicity is correlated with comprehensiveness, not brevity.

Our experience suggests that in treating each basic topic—aggregate demand and aggregate supply, money and banking, theory of the firm, and international economics—it is desirable to couple analysis with policy. Generally, we use a three-step development of analytical tools: (1) verbal descriptions and illustrations, (2) numerical examples, and (3) graphical presentation based on these numerical illustrations.

All these considerations caused us to organize the book into nine parts: Part 1: An Introduction to Economics and the Economy; Part 2: National Income, Employment, and Fiscal Policy; Part 3: Money, Banking, and Monetary Policy; Part 4: Problems and Controversies in Macroeconomics; Part 5: Microeconomics of Product Markets; Part 6: Microeconomics of Resource Markets; Part 7: Microeconomics of Government; Part 8: Microeconomic Issues and Policy; and Part 9: International Economics and the World Economy.

ORGANIZATIONAL ALTERNATIVES

Although instructors generally agree on the content of the principles of economics course, they often differ as how to arrange the material; *Economics* provides considerable organizational flexibility. Previous users tell us they often substantially rearrange chapters with little sacrifice of continuity.

We chose to move from macro- to microeconomics, but the introductory material of Part 1 can be followed immediately by the microeconomic analysis of Parts 5 and 6. Similarly, the AD-AS model appears after two chapters on aggregate expenditures analysis. Those who want to rely exclusively on AD-AS can omit these two chapters, supplementing the AD discussion with discussion of investment demand and the multiplier implicit within shifts of the AD curve.

Some instructors will prefer to intersperse the microeconomics of Parts 5 and 6 with the problems chapters of Part 8. Chapter 33 on agriculture may follow Chapter 23 on pure competition; Chapter 32 on antitrust, regulation, and industrial policy may follow Chapters 24 to 26 on imperfect competition models and technological advance. Chapter 36 on labor market issues (unions, discrimination, and immigration) may follow Chapter 28 on wages; and Chapter 34 on income inequality may follow Chapters 28 and 29 on distributive shares of national income.

Instructors who teach the typical two-semester course and feel comfortable with the book's organization will find that by putting Parts 1 to 4 in the first semester and Parts 5 through 9 in the second, the material is divided logically between the two semesters. For those instructors who choose to emphasize international economics, Parts 1, 2, 3, and 9 may be covered the first semester, Parts 4 through 8 the second.

For a course based on three quarters of work, we suggest Chapters 1 through 12 for the first quarter, 13 through 29 for the second, and 31 through 40 for the third.

Those teaching a one-semester course will discern several possible chapter groupings. At the end of this Preface we suggest outlines for three one-semester courses, emphasizing macroeconomics, microeconomics, or a survey of micro and macro theory, and two one-quarter course options.

PEDAGOGICAL AIDS

Economics has always been student-oriented. The To the Student statement at the beginning of Part 1 details the book's many pedagogical aids. The fourteenth edition is also accompanied by a variety of high-quality supplements.

The Supplements

- **Study Guide.** William Walstad—one of the world's foremost experts on economic education—prepared the fourteenth edition of the *Study Guide*, which many students find indispensable. Each chapter has an introductory statement, a checklist of behavioral objectives, an outline, a list of important terms, fill-in questions, problems and projects, objective questions, and discussion questions. The answers to *Economics'* end-of-chapter Key Questions appear at the end of the *Study Guide*, along with the text's Glossary.

The *Guide* is a superb "portable tutor" for the principles student. Separate *Study Guides* are available for the individual macro and micro paperback editions of the text.

- **Instructor's Resource Manual** Professor Arienne Turner of Fullerton College revised and updated the *Instructor's Resource Manual*. It includes chapter summaries, listings of "what's new" in each chapter, new teaching tips and suggestions, learning objectives, chapter outlines, data and visual aid sources with suggestions for classroom use, and questions and problems. Answers to the text's end-of-chapter Key Questions are also included.

The *Manual* is again available for use with IBM-PC compatibles and MacIntosh computers. The PC version is also available in CD-ROM format. Users can print out portions of the *Manual's* contents, complete with their own additions and alterations, for use as student handouts or in whatever ways they wish.

Three Test Banks

Two test banks of objective, predominately multiple-choice questions and a third test bank of short-answer essay questions and problems supplement this edition of *Economics*.

- **Test Bank I.** This test bank includes more than 5200 questions, most written by the text authors.
- **Test Bank II.** Written by William Walstad, this test bank contains more than 5000 questions. All Test Bank II questions are now categorized according to level of difficulty: easy, moderate, or difficult.
- **Test Bank III.** Also prepared by William Walstad, Test Bank III contains "constructive response" testing to evaluate student understanding in a manner different from conventional multiple-choice and true-false questions. Suggested answers to the essay and problem questions are included.

For all test items in Test Banks I and II, the nature of each question is identified (for example, G = graphical; C = complex analysis; etc.), as are the numbers of the text pages that are the basis for each question. Also, each chapter in Test Banks I and II includes an outline or table of contents that groups questions by topics. In all, more than 10,000 questions of equal quality give instructors maximum testing flexibility while assuring the fullest possible text correlation.

Additional Supplements

- **Computerized Testing.** Test Banks I, II, and III are available in computerized versions, both for IBM-PC and compatibles and MacIntosh computers. These systems generate multiple tests, scrambled tests, and high-quality graphs. Developed by the Brownstone Research group, this software meets the needs of the widest spectrum of computer users.

- *Color Transparencies (Figures and Tables).* We offer over 300 full-color transparencies for overhead projectors. They include most text figures and are available on request to adopters.
- *PowerPoint Presentation.* Norman Hollingsworth of DeKalb College once again created our PowerPoint slides, which consist of over 2000 audio-enhanced images.
- *Student Software.* *DiscoverEcon* is available for both *Microeconomics* and *Macroeconomics*. This menu-driven software, which was developed by Gerald Nelson at the University of Illinois, gives students a complete tutorial linked to the text. Each chapter features two essay questions and a multiple-choice test. Whenever relevant, interactive graphing problems let students observe how the economic picture is altered when they select different data. Links to the Glossary and text references clarify key concepts.

Two additional interactive tutorials are available with this edition: *Microeconomics and Macroeconomics Interactive CD-ROM* and *WinEcon*.

Developed by Charles Link and Jeffrey Miller at the University of Delaware, the *Microeconomics and Macroeconomics Interactive CD-ROM* gives students a rich, easy-to-use menu covering core topics in introductory economics with an audio component that makes it an excellent tool for reviewing basic concepts. Both tutorials have a real-world focus: Newspaper and magazine articles highlight economic concepts, and interactive videos allow students to "interview" business leaders.

WinEcon is an interactive software package offering over 75 hours of tutorial material. It includes self-assessment questions and exams, economic databases, and an economic glossary and references to leading economic texts. It is the first computer-based learning package to cover the entire first-year economics syllabus. *WinEcon* combines two products in one: teaching software and student tools, and *WinEcon* Lecturer with tests, exams, course management, and customization program. It was developed at the University of Bristol with the help of the Teaching and Learning Technology Programme Economics Consortium (TLTP), a group of eight United Kingdom university economics departments.
- *Website for Students and Instructors.* Our dynamic text Website can be found at http://www.mhhe.com/economics/mcconnell. At the Website, students can find learning support, including answers to the text's Key Questions.
- *MHLA.* McGraw-Hill Learning Architecture is our on-line student tutorial and course-management program, which includes materials directly linked to McConnell & Brue, *Economics*, fourteenth edition.

ACKNOWLEDGMENTS

We give special thanks to James Reese of the University of South Carolina at Spartansburg, who wrote the 80 end-of-chapter Internet exercises.

Our colleagues at the University of Nebraska–Lincoln and Pacific Lutheran University generously shared knowledge of their specialties with us and provided encouragement.

As indicated, the fourteenth edition benefited from a number of perceptive reviews. In both quantity and quality, the reviewers were a rich source of suggestions for this revision. These contributors are listed at the end of this Preface.

Professor Thomas Barbiero of Ryerson Polytechnical Institute provided helpful ideas in his role as coauthor of the Canadian edition of *Economics*. Also, we greatly appreciate the suggestions for improvement provided by Professor Walstad, the author of the *Study Guide*. Thanks also to Robert Jensen, who proofread the entire manuscript (twice), and William Harris of the University of Delaware, who supplied a number of new questions for Test Bank I.

We are greatly indebted to the many professionals at McGraw-Hill—in particular Gary Burke, Lucille Sutton, Marilea Fried, Lee Hertel, Nelson Black, Marty Quinn, Miller Murray, Eve Strock, Francis Owens, Diane Renda, and Pam Augspurger—for their publishing expertise.

We thank Ed Millman and Susan Gottfried for their thorough and sensitive editing, Amanda Kavanagh for her creative design, and Jacques Cournoyer for his vivid Last Word illustrations.

We also strongly acknowledge the newly integrated Irwin/McGraw-Hill sales staff, who greeted this edition with wholehearted enthusiasm.

Campbell R. McConnell
Stanley L. Brue

CONTRIBUTORS

REVIEWERS

David Allen, University of Alabama–Huntsville

Kevin Baird, Montgomery County Community College

Joe A. Bell, Southwest Missouri State University

Dixie Blackley, LeMoyne College

John Boffoe-Bonnie, Pennsylvania State University–Media

Carol Condon, Kean College of New Jersey

Betsy Crowell, University of Michigan–Dearborn

Norman Cure, Macomb Community College

Chris Duelfer, Cedar Crest College

Robert Eggleston, Shippensburg University

Ron Elkins, Central Washington University

Arthur Friedberg, Mohawk Valley Community College

Jeff D. Gibbs, Abraham Baldwin College

Sadie Gregory, Virginia State University

Medhi Haririan, Bloomsburg University of Pennsylvania

Paul Harris, Camden County College

Gus Herring, Brookhaven College

Calvin Hoerneman, Delta College

John Hill, Northeastern State University

Katherine M. Huger, Charleston Southern University

Mashid Jalilvand, University of Wisconsin–Stout

Zeinholm Kabis, St. Ambrose University

James Kahiga, DeKalb College

Demetri Kantarelis, Assumption College

Mehmet Karaaslan, Alfred University

Elizabeth Kelly, University of Wisconsin–Madison

Vani Kotcherlokota, University of Nebraska–Kearny

Ross LaRoe, Denison University

Mark S. LeClair, Fairfield University

Judy Lee, Leeward Community College

Jon G. Lindgren, North Dakota State University

Patrick Litzinger, Robert Morris College

Elizabeth J. Lott, Pace University

William C. O'Connor, Western Montana College

Martha L. Olney, University of California–Berkeley

Lucjan Orlowski, Sacred Heart University

Joseph Prinzinger, Lynchburg College

Janet M. Rives, University of Northern Iowa

Henry Ryder, Gloucester County Community College

John Saussey, Harrisburg Area Community College

Charlene Schick, Cypress College

Teresa Sherrouse, Augusta College

Dorothy Siden, Salem State College

Victor Ukpolo, Austin Peay State University

Janet West, University of Nebraska–Omaha

Fred E. Williams, Montreat College

Study Guide Student Reviewers from Anne Arundel Community College, Arnold, Maryland:

Erica Beisler

John Botwright

Pam Newman

Chris Rzepkowski

Laureen Thomas

Kathy Van Liew

and their instructor, Professor Raymond F. Turner

FOCUS GROUP PARTICIPANTS

Vinod Agarwal, Old Dominion University

Hamid Azari, Alabama State University

Dan Berkowitz, University of Pittsburgh

Larry Biacci, Pennsylvania State University–Hazelton

Michael Brandl, West Texas A & M University

Christopher Brown, Arkansas State University–Mountain Home

Lindsey Calkins, John Carroll University

James Cobbe, Florida State University

David Connell, University of Nebraska at Omaha

Arifeen M. Daneshyan, Kutztown University

Allen Dickes, Washburn University

Michael Gootzeit, University of Memphis

Linda Harris Dobkins, Emory and Henry College

Robert Ebert, Baldwin-Wallace College

Jill Herndon, Hamline University

Julie Hotchkiss, Georgia State University

Christopher Lingle, Case Western Reserve University

Darryl Lowry, Roanoke College

Larry Mack, North Highland Community College

Bart Macomber, Highland Community College

Richard McGrath, College of William and Mary

Dennis O'Toole, Virginia Commonwealth University

Walter Park, The American University

C. S. Pyun, University of Memphis

Charles Roberts, Western Kentucky University

Steve Rockland, San Diego State University

Julie Ryan, Beaver College

Ken Scalet, York College

Chuck Slusher, University of North Carolina–Chapel Hill

Gerald Stollman, Oakland Community College

Robert Tansky, St. Clair County Community College

Roy Townsend, Greenville Technical College

Arienne Turner, Fullerton College

David Vernon, Lubbock Christian University

Eugene Williams, McMurry University

Hamid Zangeneh, Widener University

QUESTIONNAIRE RESPONDENTS

Emmanuel Asigbee, Kirkwood Community College

Jan E. Christopher, Delaware State University

Betty Chu, San Jose State University

John Connelly, Corning Community College

Larry DeBrock, University of Illinois

Floyd Allen DeCook, Broward Community College

John W. Dorsey, University of Maryland at College Park

Rodney D. Green, Howard University

Barnali Gupta, Miami University

Ruby Hargrove, St. Augustine's College

Michael N. Hayes, Radford University

Mark L. Huston, San Diego Mesa College

Patti J. Impink, Macon College

Mark Karscig, Central Missouri State University

Erwin L. Kelly, Jr., California State University–Sacramento

Philip J. Lane, Fairfield University

Saul Mekies, Kirkwood Community College

John R. Moroney, Texas A&M University

Dennis L. Nelson, University of Minnesota–Duluth

Mehdi Pousti, Kansas State University

David L. Priddy, Piedmont Virginia Community College

Michael Reclam, Virginia Military Institute

David Roe, Furman University

Richard Rosenberg, Pennsylvania State University

Nancy Short, Chandler-Gilbert Community College

Mary Huff Stevenson, University of Massachusetts–Boston

Robert Vowels, Tennessee State University

Robert B. Wagner, Houston Community College

Mike M. Williams, Bethune Cookman/Daytona Beach Community College

Edgar W. Wood, University of Mississippi

Wendy V. Wysocki, Monroe County Community College

Janice Yee, Wartburg College

Armand Zottola, Central Connecticut State University

SUGGESTED ONE-SEMESTER AND ONE-QUARTER COURSE OUTLINES
(Core chapters are indicated by "c"; optional chapters by "o"

Chapter	One-semester course			One-quarter course	
	Macro emphasis	*Micro* emphasis	*Macro-Micro* survey	*Macro* emphasis	*Micro* emphasis
1	c	c	c	c	c
2	c	c	c	c	c
3	c	c	c	c	c
4	c	c	c	c	c
5	c	c		c	c
6	c	c		c	c
7	c		c	c	
8	c		c	c	
9	c		c	c	
10	c		c	c	
11	c		c	c	
12	c		c	c	
13	c		c	c	
14	c		c	c	
15	c		c	c	
16	c		o	o	
17	c		o	o	
18	c		o		
19	c		o		
20		c	c		c
21		c			
22		c	c		c
23		c	c		c
24		c	c		c
25		c	o		c
26		c	o		c
27		c			c
28		c			c
29		c			c
30		o			o
31		o			
32		o[1]			
33		o[2]			
34		o[3]			
35		o			
36		o[4]			
37	o	o			
38	o	o			
39	o				
40	o				

[1] If used, Chapter 32 may follow Chapter 26.
[2] If used, Chapter 33 may follow Chapter 23.
[3] If used, Chapter 34 may follow Chapter 28 or 29.
[4] If used, Chapter 36 may follow Chapter 28.

ECONOMICS ON THE WORLD WIDE WEB*

PART 1

Bob Parks' A Random Walk Around Economics on the Net
wuecon.wustl.edu/~bob/econwalknet.html
NetEc netec.wustl.edu/local/NetEc.html
Resources for Economists on the Internet
econwpa.wustl.edu/EconFAQ/EconFAQ.html
Dismal Sciences www.dismal.com/
The Mining Company economics.miningco.com/
Classroom Expernomics
www.marietta.edu/~delemeeg/expernom.html
Computer Aided Instruction in Economics
userwww.sfsu.edu/~bjblecha/cai.htm
Economic Education, EcEdWeb
http://ecedweb.unomaha.edu/
Econ Teaching Resources
woodrow.mpls.frb.fed.us/econed/class/econsite.html
AmosWorld amos.bus.okstate.edu/
Economics Working Paper Archive (EconWPA)
econwpa.wustl.edu/wpawelcome.html
Journal of Economic Literature and EconLit (JEL)
www.econlit.org/
CARL's UnCover uncweb.carl.org/
sci.finance.abstracts
www.public.iastate.edu/~arnie/sci-finance-abstracts.htm
Economics Research Network (ERN) (part of SSRN)
www.ssrn.Com/
Student Economic Review www.bess.tcd.ie/ser.html
IDEAL (Academic Press)
www.apnet.com/www/ap/aboutid.htm
Applied Economics www.chapmanhall.com/ae/
B>Quest (Business Quest) www.westga.edu/~bquest/
**Roland's Overview of Conferences and Meetings on
Economic Theory**
www.wiwiss.fu-berlin.de/w3/w3bester/roland/econ_co.htm
**Economics Departments, Institutes and Research Centers
in the World (EDIRC)—Associations and Societies**
www.er.uqam.ca/nobel/r14160/economics/assocs.html
American Economic Association (AEA)
www.vanderbilt.edu/AEA/
History of Economics Society
cs.muohio.edu/~HisEcSoc/other_resources.shtml
History of Economics Internet References
cfec.vub.ac.be/cfec/hope.htm
Regional Science Association (RSA)
gopher://olymp.wu-wien.ac.at:70/11/.inst/.iir/.rsa
International Association for Feminist Economics
www.bucknell.edu/~jshackel/iaffe
International Economics and Philosophy Society
www.bath.ac.uk/Centres/Ethical/ieps.htm
American Law and Economics Association (ALEA)
webserver.law.yale.edu/alea/alea.htm
Southern Economic Association (SEA)
bubba.ucc.okstate.edu/economics/journal/south1.html
Eastern Economic Association www.iona.edu/orgs/eea.htm

Western Economic Association International
www.weainternational.org/
National Association of Business Economists (NABE)
www.nabe.com/

PART 2

EconData
www.inform.umd.edu:8080/EdRes/Topic/Economics/ EconData/
Bureau of Economic Analysis www.bea.doc.gov/
NBER's Macro-Historical Database
www.nber.org/databases/macrohistory/contents/index.html
National Economic Research & Data Services (NERDS)
www.econ-line.com/
Centre for Policy Modelling www.fmb.mmu.ac.uk/cpm/
**County and City Databooks, Interactive Data Resources,
University of Virginia Social Sciences Data Center**
www.lib.virginia.edu/socsci/ccdb/
Economic Time Series Page
bos.business.uab.edu/data/data.htm
WEFA Group www.wefa.com/
Panel Study on Income Dynamics www.umich.edu/~psid
**Economic History Services Operated By the Cliometric
Society** cs.muohio.edu/
Society of Italian Economic Historians
italia.hum.utah.edu/gruppo/vasta/welcome.htm

PART 3

Board of Governors of the Federal Reserve System
www.bog.frb.fed.us
All Other Federal Reserve Banks
www.bog.frb.fed.us/otherfrb.htm
Central Bank Resource Center
www.patriot.net/users/bernkopf
Banking on the WWW www.wiso.gwdg.de/ifbg/banking.html
Federal Deposit Insurance Corporation (FDIC)
www.fdic.gov/
World Bank www.worldbank.org/
Inter-American Development Bank www.iadb.org/
Bank of Japan www.boj.or.jp/en/index.htm
FINWeb www.finweb.com/
NETworth networth.galt.com/
**Market Broadcasting Corporation—Real Time FX, Fixed
Income, and Money Market Data** www.pctrader.com/
Financial Data Finder at Ohio State
www.cob.ohio-state.edu/dept/fin/osudata.htm
Wall Street Research Net www.wsrn.com/
Briefing by Charter Media www.briefing.com
Security APL QuoteServer www.secapl.com/cgi-bin/qs
New Zealand Investment Center www.nzinvest.com
Iowa Electronic Markets www.biz.uiowa.edu/iem
The Virtual Stock Market Game virtualstockexchange.com/

PART 4

Dr. Ed Yardeni's Economics Network www.yardeni.com
Economic Growth Resources
www.nuff.ox.ac.uk/Economics/Growth/
**UK Chapter of the Society for the Advancement of Socio-
economics (SASE)** www.bath.ac.uk/Centres/BUCEP/SASE
**Centre for Economic Performance (CEP), London School
of Economics** cep.lse.ac.uk/
IKE Group (Aalborg University, Denmark)
www.business.auc.dk/ike/ike.html

---

*Web addresses change often. Consult our Web site (http://www.
mhhe.com/economics/mcconnell) for timely updates.

The Quantitative Macroeconomics and Real Business
Cycle Home Page www.er.uqam.ca/noble/r14160/rbc/
Economic Chart Dispense bos.business.uab.edu/charts.htm
ESRC Macroeconomic Modelling Bureau (U.K.)
www.csv.warwick.ac.uk/~mbras/
FAIRMODEL fairmodel.econ.yale.edu/

PART 5

Economic Science Association www.econlab.arizona.edu/esa/
Inter-university Consortium for Political and Social
Research (ICPSR) www.icpsr.umich.edu/
Centre for Economic Learning and Social Evolution
(ELSE) ada.econ.ucl.ac.uk/
Pool Listing Service in Game Theory
fismat.dima.unige.it/citg/citg.htm
Economic Science Laboratory, Univ. of Arizona
www.econlab.arizona.edu/
Center for Rationality www.ma.huji.ac.il/~ranb
The Information Economy (by Hal Varian)
www.sims.berkeley.edu/resources/infoecon
Openair-Market Net: The World Wide Guide to Farmers'
Markets, Street Markets, Flea Markets and Street Vendors
www.openair.org/

PART 6

Bureau of Labor Statistics (LABSTAT)
stats.bls.gov/blshome.html
Model User Group International (CGE Modeling)
watarts.uwaterloo.ca/~mug/index.html
Communications for a Sustainable Future csf.colorado.edu/

PART 7

FEDSTATS www.fedstats.gov/
The Federal Web Locator www.law.vill.edu/fed-agency/
EDGAR (SEC) www.sec.gov/edgarhp.htm
U.S.Department of Commerce (STAT-USA) www.stat-usa.gov
Government Information Sharing Project
govinfo.kerr.orst.edu/
Economic Statistics Briefing Room (ESBR)—White House
www.whitehouse.gov/fsbr/esbr.html
CIA Publications and Handbooks
www.odci.gov/cia/publications/pubs.html
National Transportation Statistics www.bts.gov
Energy Resources Board (DOE) www.eia.doe.gov/energy/
U.S. Census Bureau www.census.gov
Integrated Public Use Microdata Sample (IPUMS)
www.hist.umn.edu/~ipums
International Society for Ecological Economics
kabir.umd.edu/ISEE/ISEEhome.html
Centre for Economic and Social Studies for the
Environment (CESSE) www.ulb.ac.be/ceese/french/ceese.html

PART 8

Antitrust Policy: An online resource linking economic
research, policy issues, and cases www.antitrust.org
USDA Economics and Statistics System (Cornell
University) usda.mannlib.cornell.edu/usda
Agricultural Economics Virtual Library
www.aeco.ttv.edu/aecovl

Food and Agricultural Organization of the UN www.fao.org/
American Agricultural Economics Association (AAEA)
www.aaea.org/
USDA Agriculture Economic Research Service
www.econ.ag.gov/
Australian Agricultural and Resource Economics Society
Inc. (AARES) yarra.vicnet.net.au/~archa/aares/aares.htm
Social Security Administration (OSS-IS) www.ssa.gov/
The Health and Retirement Study (HRS) and Asset and
Health Dynamics Among the Oldest Old (AHEAD)
www.umich.edu/~hrswww/

PART 9

The Office of the United States Trade Representative
www.ustr.gov/
United States International Trade Commission (USITC)
www.usitc.gov/
International Monetary Fund (IMF) www.imf.org
PACIFIC Exchange Rate Service Retrieval Interface
pacific.commerce.ubc.ca/xr/
Getting Around the Planet
www.olsen.ch/cgi-bin/exmenu/pathfinder/
International Trade & Business WWW Reference Pages
pacific.commerce.ubc.ca/trade/
The Global Trade Analysis Project (GTAP)
www.agecon.purdue.edu/gtap/index.htm
Global Financial Data www.globalfindata.com
QuoteCom Data Service www.quote.com/
Statistics Canada www.statcan.ca/
Canadian Economics Association (CEA) economics.ca
AmchamNet—American Chamber of Commerce–Brazil
www.amcham.com.br
Bank of Hawaii Economic Research Center
www.boh.com/econ/
Australian Bureau of Statistics www.statistics.gov.au/
New Zealand Treasury www.treasury.govt.nz/
InTechTra's Hong Kong Stocks Reports
www.asiawind.com/pub/hksr/
Turkish Economics Page www.siue.edu/~itanris/econtr.html
Israel Central Bureau of Statistics
www.cbs.gov.il/engindex.htm
Finnish Society for Economic Research
www.hkkk.fi/~fecons/
The Research Institute of the Finnish Economy (ETLA)
www.etla.fi
Eurostat europa.eu.int/eurostat.html
European Economic Association
www.hec.unil.ch/prague/eea/premier.htm
Euro Internet fgr.wu-wien.ac.at/nentwich/euroint2.htm
Carolina Population Center (UNC—Chapel Hill)
www.cpc.unc.edu/
Central European Regional Research Organization
(CERRO) gopher://olymp.wu-wien.ac.at:70/11/.cerro.ind
German Federal Statistical Office
www.statistik-bund.de/e_home.htm
REESweb: Russian and East European Studies—Business,
Economics, and Law Resources www.pitt.edu/~cjp/rees.html

1

An Introduction to Economics and the Economy

TO THE STUDENT

Economics is largely concerned with efficiency—accomplishing goals using the best methods. Several features of this book and its ancillaries are designed to improve your efficiency in learning economics (and therefore your course grade):

- *Appendix on graphs* Being comfortable with graphical analysis and a few quantitative concepts is a big advantage in understanding principles of economics. The appendix to Chapter 1 reviews graphing, line slopes, and linear equations. Be sure to not skip it.

- *Introductions* The introductory paragraphs of each chapter place the chapter in the proper context, state its main objectives, and tell you how it is organized. These introductions lead you into the economic analysis.

- *Terminology* A significant portion of any introductory course is terminology. Key terms are set in **boldface type,** listed at the end of each chapter, and defined in the glossary at the end of the book.

- *Reviews* Important things should be said more than once. Each chapter contains a summary and two or three Quick Reviews. These reviews will help you focus on essential ideas and study for exams. If any review statement seems unclear, you should reread the corresponding section of the text.

- *Key Graphs* Graphs that have special relevance are labeled Key Graphs, and each includes a multiple-choice Quick Quiz. Your instructor may or may not emphasize all these figures, but you should pay special attention to those that are discussed in class; you can be certain that there will be exam questions on them.

- *Figure legends* The legends accompanying the figures in this book are self-contained analyses of the figures. Study these legends carefully—they are quick synopses of important ideas.

- *Globalization* The economics of individual nations are becoming part of an overall global economy. To gain appreciation of this wider economic environment, be sure to take a look at the Global Perspectives, which compare the United States to other selected nations.

- *Last Words* Each chapter concludes with a Last Word minireading. While it is tempting to ignore these sections, don't. Some of them are revealing applications of economic concepts; others are short case studies. A few present views which contrast with mainstream thinking; and most are fun to read. All will broaden your grasp of economics.

- *Questions* A comprehensive list of questions is located at the end of each chapter. The old cliché that you "learn by doing" is very relevant to economics. Answering these questions will enhance your understanding. Several of the questions are designated as Key Questions and are answered in the *Study Guide* and the *Instructor's Resource Manual,* and they can also be found at our Website, http://www.mhhe.com/economics/mcconnell. You can turn to these particular questions when they are cited in each chapter, or later, after you have read the full chapter.

- *Study Guide* We enthusiastically recommend the *Study Guide* accompanying this text. This "portable tutor" contains not only a broad sampling of various kinds of questions but a host of useful learning aids.

You will find in Chapter 1 that economics involves a special way of thinking—a unique approach to analyzing problems. The overriding goal of this book is to help you acquire that skill. If our cooperative efforts—yours, ours, and your instructor's—are successful, you will be able to comprehend a whole range of economic, social, and political problems that otherwise would have remained murky and elusive.

The Nature and Method of Economics

Human beings, those unfortunate creatures, are plagued with wants. We want, among other things, love, social recognition, and the material necessities and comforts of life. Our efforts to meet our material wants, that is, to improve our well-being or "make a living," are the concern of economics.

Biologically, we need only air, water, food, clothing, and shelter. But, in contemporary society, we also seek the many goods and services associated with a comfortable or affluent standard of living. Fortunately, society is blessed with productive resources—labor and managerial talent, tools and machinery, land and mineral deposits—which are used to produce goods and services. This production satisfies many of our material wants and occurs through the organizational mechanism called the *economic system* or, more simply, *the economy*.

The blunt reality, however, is that the total of all our material wants is many times greater than the productive capacity of our limited resources. Thus, the complete satisfaction of material wants is impossible. This unyielding reality provides our definition of **economics:** *the social science concerned with the efficient use of limited or scarce resources to achieve maximum satisfaction of human material wants.*

Although it may not be evident, most of the headline-grabbing issues of our time—inflation, unemployment, health care, social security, budget deficits, discrimination, tax reform, poverty and inequality, pollution, and government regulation and deregulation of business—are rooted in the one challenge of using scarce resources efficiently.

In this first chapter, however, we will not plunge into problems and issues; instead, we will discuss some important preliminaries. Specifically, we first look at the economic perspective—how economists think about problems. Next, we state some of the benefits of studying economics. Then we consider the specific methods economists use to examine economic behavior and the economy, distinguishing between macroeconomics and microeconomics. Finally, we examine the problems, limitations, and pitfalls that hinder sound economic reasoning.

THE ECONOMIC PERSPECTIVE

Economists view things through a unique perspective. This **economic perspective** or *economic way of thinking* has several critical and closely interrelated features.

Scarcity and Choice

From our definition of economics, it is easy to see why economists view the world through the lens of scarcity. Since human and property resources are scarce (limited), it follows that the goods and services we produce must also be scarce. Scarcity limits our options and necessitates that we make choices. Because we "can't have it all," we must decide what we will have.

At the core of economics is the idea that "there is no free lunch." You may get treated to lunch, making it "free" to you, but there is a cost to someone—ultimately to society. Scarce inputs of land, equipment, farm labor, the labor of cooks and waiters, and managerial talent are required. Because these resources could be used in alternative production activities, they and the other goods and services they could have produced are sacrificed in making the "free" lunch available. Economists call these sacrifices *opportunity costs*.

Rational Behavior

Economics is grounded on the assumption of "rational self-interest." That is, individuals make rational decisions to achieve the greatest satisfaction or the maximum fulfillment of their goals. For instance, they spend their incomes to get the greatest benefit from the goods and services they can afford.

Rational behavior means that different people will make different choices because their preferences, circumstances, and available information differ. You may have decided that it is in your best interest to attend college before entering the full-time labor force, while a high school classmate has chosen to forgo additional schooling and go to work. Why the different choices? Your academic abilities, along with your family's income, may be greater than your classmate's. You may also know that college-educated workers have better job opportunities and lower unemployment rates than less educated workers. Hence, you opted for college, while your former classmate—the one with less academic ability, less money, and less information—chose a job. Both choices reflect the pursuit of self-interest and are rational, but they are based on differing circumstances and information.

Of course, rational decisions may change as circumstances change. Suppose the Federal government decides it is in the national interest to increase the supply of college-educated workers. It might offer 2 years of "free" community college to all low-income students. Under these new conditions, your high school classmate might now opt for college rather than a job.

It is important to remember that rational self-interest is not the same as selfishness. People make personal sacrifices to help family members or friends, and they contribute to charities because they derive pleasure from doing so. Parents help pay for their children's education for the same reason. These self-interested, but unselfish, acts help maximize the givers' satisfaction as much as any personal purchase of goods or services.

Marginalism: Benefits and Costs

The economic perspective focuses largely on **marginal analysis**—comparisons of marginal benefits and marginal costs. (Used this way, "marginal" means "extra," "additional," or "a change in.") Most choices or decisions involve changes in the status quo. Should you go to school for another year or not? Should you spend more or less money on compact discs each month? Similarly, businesses regularly must decide whether to employ more or fewer workers or to produce more or less output.

Each option involves marginal benefits and, because of scarcity, marginal costs. In making choices rationally, the decision maker must compare these two amounts. Example: Your time is scarce. What will you do with 2 "free" hours on a Saturday afternoon? You could watch Gigantic State University's Fighting Aardvarks play basketball on television. The *marginal benefit* to you would be the pleasure of seeing the game. The *marginal cost* would be the benefit from the other things you have to sacrifice to watch the game, including perhaps studying, jogging, or taking a nap. If the marginal benefit exceeds the marginal cost, then it is rational to watch the game. But if you determine that the marginal cost of watching the game is greater than the marginal benefit, then you should select one of the other options.

On the national level, government regularly makes decisions involving marginal benefits and marginal costs. More spending on health care may mean less spending on libraries, aid to the poor, or military security. In a world of scarcity, the decision to obtain the marginal benefit associated with some specific option always includes the marginal cost of forgoing something else. Again, there is no free lunch.

One somewhat surprising implication of decisions based on marginal analysis is that there *can* be too much of a good thing. Although certain goods and services seem inherently desirable—education, health care, a clean environment—we can in fact have too much of them. "Too much" occurs when we keep producing them beyond the point where their marginal cost (the value of the forgone options) equals their marginal benefit.

If we choose to produce so much health care that its marginal cost to society exceeds its marginal benefit, we are providing "too much" of it even though we all agree that health care is a good thing. When the marginal costs of health care exceed the marginal benefits, we are sacrificing alternative products (for example, education and pollution reduction) which are more valuable than health care *at the margin*—the place where we consider the very last units of each. **(Key Question 1)**

This chapter's Last Word provides an everyday application of the economic perspective.

WHY STUDY ECONOMICS?

Is studying economics worth your time and effort? More than half a century ago John Maynard Keynes (1883–1946), one of the most influential economists of this century, said:

> The ideas of economists and political philosophers, both when they are right and when they are wrong, are more powerful than is commonly understood. Indeed the world is ruled by little else. Practical men, who believe themselves to be quite exempt from any intellectual influences, are usually the slaves of some defunct economist.

Most of the ideologies of the modern world have been shaped by prominent economists of the past—Adam Smith, David Ricardo, John Stuart Mill, Karl Marx, and John Maynard Keynes. And current world leaders routinely solicit the advice and policy suggestions of today's economists.

For example, the President of the United States benefits from the recommendations of his Council of Economic Advisers. The broad range of economic issues facing political leaders is suggested by the contents of the annual *Economic Report of the President.*

Areas covered typically include unemployment, inflation, economic growth, taxation, poverty, international trade, health care, pollution, discrimination, immigration, regulation, and education, among others.

Economics for Citizenship

A basic understanding of economics is essential if we are to be well-informed citizens. Most of today's political problems have important economic aspects: How important is it that we balance the Federal budget? How can we make the social security retirement program financially secure? Why do we continue to have large international trade deficits? How can we best reduce pollution? What must we do to keep inflation in check? What can be done to boost U.S. productivity and economic growth? Are existing welfare programs effective and justifiable? Do we need to reform our tax system? How should we respond to growing market dominance by a few firms in some high-technology sectors of the economy?

As voters, we can influence the decisions of our elected officials in responding to such questions. But intelligence at the polls requires a basic working knowledge of economics. And a sound grasp of economics is even more helpful to the politicians themselves.

A survey by the National Center for Research in Economic Education suggests that economic illiteracy is widespread in the United States. The public, high school seniors, and college seniors show a broad lack of knowledge of the basic economics needed to understand economic events and changes in the national economy. When asked questions about fundamental economics, only 39 percent of the general public, 35 percent of high school seniors, and 51 percent of college seniors gave correct answers.

Professional and Personal Applications

Economics lays great stress on precise, systematic analysis. Thus, studying economics invariably helps students improve their analytical skills, which are in great demand in the workplace. Also, the study of economics helps us make sense of the everyday activity we observe around us. How is it that so many different people, in so many different places, doing so many different things, produce exactly the goods and services we want to buy? Economics provides an answer.

Economics is also vital to business. An understanding of the basics of economic decision making and the operation of the economic system enables business managers and executives to increase profit. The executive who understands when to use new technology, when to merge with another firm, when to expand employment, and so on, will outperform the executive who is less deft at such decision making. The manager who understands the causes and consequences of recessions (downturns in the overall economy) can make more intelligent business decisions during these periods.

Economics helps consumers and workers make better buying and employment decisions. How can you spend your limited money income to maximize your satisfaction? How can you hedge against the reduction in the dollar's purchasing power that accompanies inflation? Is it more economical to buy or lease a car? Should you use a credit card or pay cash? Which occupations pay well; which are most immune to unemployment?

Similarly, an understanding of economics makes for better financial decisions. Someone who understands the relationship between budget deficits and interest rates, between foreign exchange rates and exports, between interest rates and bond prices, is in a better position to successfully allocate personal savings. So, too, is someone who understands the business implications of emerging new technologies.

In spite of these practical benefits, however, you should know that economics is *mainly* an academic, not a vocational, subject. Unlike accounting, advertising, corporate finance, and marketing, economics is not primarily a how-to-make-money area of study. Knowledge of economics and mastery of the economic perspective will help you run a business or manage your personal finances, but that is not its primary objective. Instead, economics ultimately examines problems and decisions from the *social*, rather than the *personal*, point of view. The production, exchange, and consumption of goods and services are discussed from the viewpoint of society's best interest, not strictly from the standpoint of one's own pocketbook.

QUICK REVIEW 1-1

■ Economics is concerned with obtaining maximum satisfaction through the efficient use of scarce resources.

■ The economic perspective stresses **(a)** resource scarcity and the necessity of making choices, **(b)** the assumption of rational behavior, and **(c)** comparisons of marginal benefit and marginal cost.

■ Your study of economics will help you as a voting citizen as well as benefit you professionally and personally.

ECONOMIC METHODOLOGY

The tasks and procedures involved in economics are summarized in Figure 1-1.

Theoretical Economics

All sciences are based on observable and verifiable behavior, realities, or facts. As a social science, economics examines the observable and verifiable behavior of individuals (consumers, workers) and institutions (business, government) engaged in the production, exchange, and consumption of goods and services.

Fact gathering about economic activity and economic outcomes can be a complex process. Because

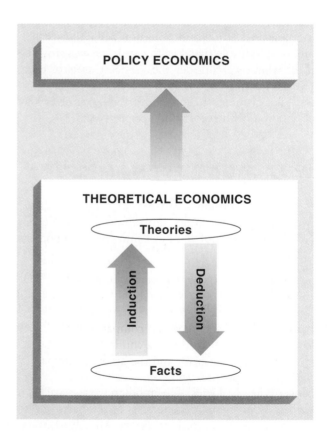

FIGURE 1-1 The relationship between facts, principles, and policies in economics In analyzing problems or aspects of the economy, economists may use the inductive method, through which they gather, systematically arrange, and generalize from facts. Alternatively, they may use the deductive method, in which they develop hypotheses which are then tested against facts. Generalizations derived from either method are useful not only in explaining economic behavior but also as a basis for formulating economic policies.

the world of reality is cluttered with innumerable interrelated facts, economists, like all scientists, must be highly selective in gathering information. They must determine which facts are relevant to the problem under consideration. But even when this sorting process is complete, the relevant information may at first seem random and unrelated.

The economist thus seeks *principles*—generalizations about the way individuals and institutions behave. The process of deriving principles is called **theoretical economics** or *economic analysis* (see the lower box in Figure 1-1). *The role of economic theorizing or economic analysis is to systematically arrange facts, interpret them, and generalize from them.* Principles and theories, the end result of economic analysis, bring order and meaning to facts by putting them in correct relationship to one another. As economist Kenneth Boulding states, "Theories without facts may be barren, but facts without theories are meaningless."[1]

As seen in Figure 1-1, economists are as likely to move from theories to facts in studying economic behavior as they are to move from facts to theories. That is, economists use both deductive and inductive methods. **Induction** moves from facts to theory, from the particular to the general. In this approach, an accumulation of facts is arranged systematically and analyzed to derive the underlying principle. The left, upward arrow from "facts" to "theories" in the figure suggests the inductive method.

Usually, economists create generalizations through **deduction.** They draw on casual observation, insight, logic, or intuition to frame a tentative, untested principle called a *hypothesis.* For example, they may conjecture, based on "armchair logic," that consumers will buy more of a product when its price falls. To test this hypothesis, economists must subject it to systematic and repeated comparison with relevant facts. Do real-world data confirm an inverse relationship between price and the amount purchased? This testing process, sometimes called *empirical economics*, is implied by the right, downward arrow from "theories" to "facts" in Figure 1-1.

Deduction and induction are complementary, rather than opposing, techniques of investigation. A hypothesis formed by deduction provides guidelines for the economist in gathering and organizing factual data. Conversely, some understanding of factual, real-world evidence is required to formulate meaningful hypotheses.

Economic **principles** and theories are *meaningful statements about economic behavior or the economy.* They are drawn from facts, while facts themselves help prove the validity of principles already established. Good theories are supported by facts concerning how individuals and institutions actually behave in producing, exchanging, and consuming goods and services. Since these facts may change in time, economists must continually check principles and theories against the shifting economic environment.

Several other points relating to economic principles are important to know.

Terminology Economists speak of *laws, principles, theories,* and *models.* These terms are sometimes confusing to students, but they all mean essentially the same thing: They are generalizations about the economic behavior of individuals and institutions. The terms "economic laws" and "principles" are useful, but they are somewhat misleading because they imply a high degree of exactness, universal application, and even moral rightness that is rare in social science. The word "theory" is often used in economics even though many people incorrectly believe theories have nothing to do with real-world applications. Economists often use the term "model," which refers to a simplified picture of reality, an abstract generalization of how relevant facts actually relate to one another.

In this book we use these four terms synonymously. Custom or convenience will govern each particular choice. Thus, the relationship between the price of a product and the amount of the product consumers purchase will be called the *law of demand,* rather than the theory or principle of demand, simply because this is the custom.

Generalizations As we have already mentioned, economic principles are **generalizations** relating to economic behavior or to the economy itself. They are imprecise because economic facts are usually diverse; no two individuals or institutions act in exactly the same way. *Economic principles are expressed as the tendencies of typical, or average consumers, workers, or business firms.* For example, when economists say that consumer spending rises when personal income increases, they are well aware that some households may save *all* of an increase in their incomes. But, on average, and for the full economy, spending goes up when income increases. Similarly, economists say that consumers buy more of a particular product when its price falls. Some consumers may increase their purchases by a large amount, others by a small amount,

---

[1]Kenneth E. Boulding, *Economic Analysis: Microeconomics*, 4th ed. (New York: Harper & Row, 1966), p. 5.

and a few not at all. This "price-quantity" principle, however, holds for the typical consumer and for consumers as a group.

"Other-Things-Equal" Assumption

Like other scientists, economists use the *ceteris paribus* or **other-things-equal assumption** to construct their generalizations. They assume that all other variables except those under immediate consideration are held constant for a particular analysis. For example, consider the relationship between the price of Pepsi and the amount purchased. It helps to assume that, of all the factors which might influence the amount of Pepsi purchased (for example, the price of Pepsi, the price of Coca-Cola, and consumer incomes and preferences), only the price of Pepsi varies. The economist can then focus on the "price of Pepsi–purchases of Pepsi" relationship without being confused by changes in other variables.

Natural scientists such as chemists or physicists can usually conduct controlled experiments where "all other things" are in fact held constant (or virtually so). They can test with great precision the assumed relationship between two variables. For example, they might examine the height from which an object is dropped and the length of time it takes to hit the ground. But economics is not a laboratory science. Economists test their theories using real-world data, which are generated by the actual operation of the economy. In this rather bewildering environment, "other things" *do* change. Despite the development of complex statistical techniques designed to hold other things equal, controls are less than perfect. As a result, economic principles are less certain and less precise than those of laboratory sciences.

Abstractions

Economic principles, or theories, are *abstractions*—simplifications which omit irrelevant facts and circumstances. These models do *not* mirror the full complexity of the real world. The very process of sorting out and analyzing facts involves simplification and removal of clutter. Unfortunately, this "abstraction" leads some people to consider economic theory impractical and unrealistic. This is nonsense! Economic theories are practical precisely because they *are* abstractions. The full scope of economic reality itself is too complex and bewildering to be understood as a whole. Economists abstract, that is, build models, to give meaning to an otherwise overwhelming and confusing maze of facts. Theorizing for this purpose is highly practical.

Graphical Expression

Many of the economic models in this book are expressed graphically; the most important are labeled Key Graphs. We strongly urge you to read the appendix to this chapter as a review of graphs.

Policy Economics

Applied economics or **policy economics** recognizes the principles and data which can be used to formulate policies, as shown in the upper part of Figure 1-1. Economic theories are the foundation of economic policy—a course of action based on economic principles and intended to resolve a specific problem or further a nation's economic goals. Economic policy normally is applied to problems after they arise. However, if economic analysis can predict some undesirable event such as unemployment, inflation, or an increase in poverty, then it may be possible to avoid or moderate that event through economic policy.

Economic Policy

The creation of policies to achieve specific goals is no simple matter. Here are the basic steps in policymaking:

1. *State the goal.* The first step is to make a clear statement of the economic goal. If we say that we want "full employment," do we mean that everyone between, say, 16 and 65 years of age should have a job? Or do we mean that everyone who wants to work should have a job? Should we allow for some unemployment caused by inevitable changes in the structure of industry and workers voluntarily changing jobs? The goal must be specific.

2. *Determine the policy options.* The next step is to formulate alternative policies designed to achieve the goal, and determine the possible effects of each policy. This requires a detailed assessment of the economic impact, benefits, costs, and political feasibility of the alternative policies. For example, to achieve full employment, should government use fiscal policy (which involves changing government spending and taxes), monetary policy (which entails altering the supply of money), an education and training policy which enhances worker employability, or a policy of wage subsidies to firms that hire disadvantaged workers?

3. *Implement and evaluate the policy which was selected.* After implementing the policy, we need to evaluate how well it worked. Only through unbiased evaluation can we improve on economic policy. Did a specific change in taxes or the money supply alter the level of employment to the extent predicted? Did deregulation of a particular industry (for example, the airlines) yield the predicted beneficial results? If not, why not? **(Key Question 5)**

Economic Goals If economic policies are designed to achieve certain economic goals, then we need to recognize a number of goals which are widely accepted in the United States and many other countries. They include:

1. *Economic growth* Produce more and better goods and services, or, more simply, develop a higher standard of living.
2. *Full employment* Provide suitable jobs for all citizens who are willing and able to work.
3. *Economic efficiency* Achieve the maximum fulfillment of wants using the available productive resources.
4. *Price-level stability* Avoid large upswings and downswings in the general price level; that is, avoid inflation and deflation.
5. *Economic freedom* Guarantee that businesses, workers, and consumers have a high degree of freedom in their economic activities.
6. *Equitable distribution of income* Ensure that no group of citizens faces stark poverty while others enjoy extreme luxury.
7. *Economic security* Provide for those who are chronically ill, disabled, handicapped, laid off, aged, or otherwise unable to earn minimal levels of income.
8. *Balance of trade* Seek a reasonable overall balance with the rest of the world in international trade and financial transactions.

Although most of us might accept these goals as generally stated, we might also disagree substantially on their specific meanings. What are "large" changes in the price level? What is a "high degree" of economic freedom? What is an "equitable" distribution of income? How can we measure precisely such abstract goals as "economic freedom"? These objectives are often the subject of spirited public debate.

Also, some of these goals are complementary; when one is achieved, some other one will also be realized. For example, achieving full employment means eliminating unemployment, which is a basic cause of inequitable income distribution. But other goals may conflict or even be mutually exclusive. They may en-

tail **tradeoffs,** meaning that to achieve one we must sacrifice another. For example, efforts to equalize the distribution of income may weaken incentives to work, invest, innovate, and take business risks, all of which promote economic growth. Taxing high-income people heavily and transferring the tax revenues to low-income people is one way to equalize the distribution of income. But then the incentives to high-income individuals may diminish because higher taxes reduce their rewards for working. Similarly, low-income individuals may be less motivated to work when government stands ready to subsidize them.

When goals conflict, society must develop a system of priorities for the objectives it seeks. If more economic freedom is accompanied by less economic security and more economic security allows less economic freedom, society must assess the tradeoffs and decide on the optimal (best) balance between them.

QUICK REVIEW 1-2

■ Economic theories (laws, principles, or models) are generalizations relating to the economic behavior of individuals and institutions; good theories are supported by facts.

■ Induction observes facts and generalizes from them; deduction uses logic to create hypotheses and then tests them with factual data.

■ Policymaking requires a clear statement of goals, a thorough assessment of options, and an unbiased evaluation of results.

■ Some of society's economic goals are complementary, while others conflict; where conflicts exist, tradeoffs arise.

MACROECONOMICS AND MICROECONOMICS

Economists derive and apply principles about economic behavior at two levels.

Macroeconomics

Macroeconomics examines either the economy as a whole or its basic subdivisions or aggregates such as the government, household, and business sectors. An **aggregate** is a collection of specific economic units treated as if they were one unit. Therefore, we might lump together the millions of consumers in the U.S. economy and treat them as if they were one huge unit called "consumers."

In using aggregates, macroeconomics seeks to obtain an overview, or general outline, of the structure of the economy and the relationships of its major aggregates. Macroeconomics speaks of such economic measures as *total* output, *total* employment, *total* income, *aggregate* expenditures, and the *general* level of prices in analyzing various economic problems. No or very little attention is given to specific units making up the various aggregates. Macroeconomics examines the forest, not the trees.

Microeconomics

Microeconomics looks at specific economic units. At this level of analysis, the economist observes the details of an economic unit, or very small segment of the economy, under the figurative microscope. In microeconomics we talk of an individual industry, firm, or household. We measure the price of a *specific* product, the number of workers employed by a *single* firm, the revenue or income of a *particular* firm or household, or the expenditures of a *specific* firm, government entity, or family. In microeconomics, we examine the trees, not the forest.

The macro-micro distinction does not mean that economics is so highly compartmentalized that every topic can be readily labeled as either macro or micro; many topics and subdivisions of economics are rooted in both. Example: While the problem of unemployment is usually treated as a macroeconomic topic (because unemployment relates to *aggregate* spending), economists recognize that the decisions made by *individual* workers in searching for jobs and the way *specific* product and labor markets operate are also critical in determining the unemployment rate. **(Key Question 7)**

Positive and Normative Economics

Both macroeconomics and microeconomics involve facts, theories, and policies. Each contains elements of *positive* economics and *normative* economics. **Positive economics** focuses on facts (once removed at the level of theory) and avoids value judgments. It tries to establish scientific statements about economic behavior. Positive economics deals with what the economy is actually like. Such factually based analysis is critical to good policy analysis.

In contrast, **normative economics** involves value judgments about what the economy should be like or what particular policy actions should be recommended to get it to be that way. Normative economics looks at the desirability of certain aspects of the economy. It underlies expressions of support for particular economic policies.

Positive economics concerns *what is*, while normative economics embodies subjective feelings about *what ought to be*. Examples: Positive statement: "The unemployment rate in several European nations is higher than that in the United States." Normative statement: "European nations ought to undertake policies to reduce their unemployment rates." A second positive statement: "Other things equal, if tuition is increased, enrollment at Gigantic State University will fall." Normative statement: "Tuition should be lowered at GSU so that more students can obtain an education." Whenever words such as "ought" or "should" appear in a sentence, there is a strong chance you are encountering a normative statement.

As you can imagine, most of the disagreement among economists involves normative, value-based policy questions. Of course, there is often some disagreement about which theories or models best represent the economy and its parts. But most economic controversy reflects differing opinions or value judgments about what society itself should be like. **(Key Question 8)**

QUICK REVIEW 1-3

■ Macroeconomics examines the economy as a whole; microeconomics focuses on specific units of the economy.

■ Positive economics deals with factual statements ("what is"); normative economics involves value judgments ("what ought to be").

PITFALLS TO OBJECTIVE THINKING

Because they affect us so personally, we often have difficulty thinking objectively about economic issues. Here are some common pitfalls to avoid in successfully applying the economic perspective.

Biases

Most people bring a bundle of biases and preconceptions to the field of economics. For example, you might think that corporate profits are excessive or that lending money is always superior to borrowing money. Perhaps you believe that government is necessarily less efficient than businesses or that more government regulation is always better than less. Biases cloud thinking and interfere with objective analysis. The beginning economics student must be willing to shed biases and preconceptions which are not supported by facts.

Loaded Terminology

The economic terminology used in newspapers and popular magazines is sometimes emotionally biased, or loaded. The writer or the interest group he or she represents may have a cause to promote or an ax to grind and may slant an article accordingly. High profits may be labeled "obscene," low wages may be called "exploitive," or self-interested behavior may be "greed." Government workers may be referred to as "mindless bureaucrats," and those favoring stronger government regulations may be called "socialists." To objectively analyze economic issues, you must be prepared to reject or discount such terminology.

Definitions

Some of the terms used in economics have precise technical definitions which are quite different from those implied by their common usage. This is generally not a problem if everyone understands these definitions and uses them consistently. For example, "investment" to the average citizen means the purchase of stocks and bonds in security markets, as when someone "invests" in Microsoft stock or government bonds. But to the economist, "investment" means the purchase of real capital assets such as machinery and equipment or the construction of a new factory building. It does not mean the purely financial transaction of swapping cash for securities.

Fallacy of Composition

Another pitfall in economic thinking is the assumption that what is true for one individual or part of a whole is necessarily true for a group of individuals or the whole. This is a logical fallacy called the **fallacy of composition;** the assumption is *not* correct. A statement which is valid for an individual or part is *not* necessarily valid for the larger group or whole.

Consider the following example from outside of economics. You are at a football game and the home team makes an outstanding play. In the excitement, you leap to your feet to get a better view. A valid statement: "If you, *an individual,* stand, your view of the game is improved." But is this also true for the

group—for everyone watching the play? Not necessarily. If *everyone* stands to watch the play, everyone—including you—will probably have a worse view than when all remain seated.

A second example comes from economics: An *individual* farmer who reaps a particularly large crop is likely to realize a sharp gain in income. But this statement cannot be generalized to farmers as a *group*. The individual farmer's large or "bumper" crop will not influence (reduce) crop prices because each farmer produces a negligible fraction of the total farm output. But for *all* farmers as a group, prices decline when total output increases. Thus, if all farmers reap bumper crops, the total output of farm products will rise, depressing crop prices. If the price declines are relatively large, total farm income might actually *fall*.

Recall our earlier distinction between macroeconomics and microeconomics: *The fallacy of composition reminds us that generalizations valid at one of these levels of analysis may or may not be valid at the other.*

Causation Fallacies

Causation is sometimes difficult to identify in economics. Two important fallacies often interfere with economic thinking.

Post Hoc Fallacy You must think very carefully before concluding that because event A precedes event B, A is the cause of B. This kind of faulty reasoning is known as the *post hoc, ergo propter hoc,* or **"after this, therefore because of this" fallacy.**

Example: Suppose that early each spring the medicine man of a tribe performs a special dance. A week or so later the trees and grass turn green. Can we safely conclude that event A, the medicine man's dance, has caused event B, the landscape's turning green? Obviously not. The rooster crows before dawn, but this does not mean the rooster is responsible for the sunrise!

Gigantic State University hires a new basketball coach and the team's record improves. Is the new coach the cause? Maybe. But perhaps the presence of more experienced players or an easier schedule is the true cause.

Correlation versus Causation Do not confuse correlation, or connection, with causation. Correlation between two events or two sets of data indicates they are associated in some systematic and dependable way. For example, we may find that when variable X increases, Y also increases. But this corre-

Fast-Food Lines: An Economic Perspective

How can the economic perspective help us understand the behavior of fast-food consumers?

You enter a fast-food restaurant. Do you immediately look to see which line is the shortest? What do you do when you are in the middle of a long line and a new station opens? Have you ever gone to a fast-food restaurant, seen very long lines, and then left? Have you ever become annoyed when someone in front of you in line placed an order that took a long time to fill?

The economic perspective is useful in analyzing the behavior of fast-food customers. These customers are at the restaurant because they expect the marginal benefit from the food they buy to match or exceed its marginal cost. When customers enter the restaurant, they scurry to the *shortest* line, believing that the shortest line will reduce their time cost of obtaining their food. They are acting purposefully; time is limited and people prefer using it in some way other than standing in line.

If one fast-food line is temporarily shorter than other lines, some people will move toward that line. These movers apparently view the time saving associated with the shorter line to exceed the cost of moving from their present line. The line changing tends to equalize line lengths. No further movement of customers between lines occurs once all lines are about equal.

Fast-food customers face another cost-benefit decision when a clerk opens a new station at the counter. Should they move to the new station or stay put? Those who shift to the new line decide that the time saving from the move exceeds the extra cost of physically moving. In so deciding, customers must also consider just how quickly they can get to the new station compared with others who may be contemplating the same move. (Those who hesitate in this situation are lost!)

Customers at the fast-food establishment select lines without having perfect information. For example, they do not first survey those in the lines to determine what they are ordering before deciding which line to enter. There are two reasons for this. First, most customers would tell them "It's none of your business," and therefore no information would be forthcoming. Second, even if they could obtain the information, the amount of time necessary to get it (a cost) would most certainly exceed any time saving associated with finding the best line (the benefit). Because information is costly to obtain, fast-food patrons select lines without perfect information. Thus, not all decisions turn out as expected. For example, you might enter a short line and find that the person in front of you is ordering hamburgers and fries for 40 people in the Greyhound bus parked out back! Nevertheless, at the time you made your decision, you thought it was optimal.

Imperfect information also explains why some people who arrive at a fast-food restaurant and observe long lines decide to leave. These people conclude that the marginal cost (monetary plus time costs) of obtaining the fast food is too large relative to the marginal benefit. They would not have come to the restaurant in the first place had they known the lines would be so long. But getting that information by, say, employing an advance scout with a cellular phone would cost more than the perceived benefit.

Finally, customers must decide what to order when they arrive at the counter. In making their choices they again compare marginal costs and marginal benefits in attempting to obtain the greatest personal satisfaction or well-being for their expenditure.

Economists believe that what is true for the behavior of customers at fast-food restaurants is true for economic behavior in general. Faced with an array of choices, consumers, workers, and businesses rationally compare marginal costs and marginal benefits in making decisions.

lation does not necessarily mean that there is causation—that an increase in X is the cause of an increase in Y. The relationship could be purely coincidental or dependent on some other factor, Z, not included in the analysis.

Here is an economic example: Economists have found a positive correlation between education and income. In general, people with more education earn higher incomes than people with less education. Common sense suggests education is the cause and higher incomes are the effect; more education implies a more knowledgeable and productive worker, and such workers receive larger salaries.

But causation could also partly run the other way. People with higher incomes could buy more education, just as they buy more furniture and steaks. Or is part of the relationship explainable in still other ways? Are education and income correlated because the characteristics—ability, motivation, personal habit—required to succeed in education are the same ones required to be a productive and highly paid worker? If so, then people with those traits will probably obtain more education *and* earn higher incomes. But greater education will not be the sole cause of the higher income. **(Key Question 9)**

A LOOK AHEAD

The ideas in this chapter will come into much sharper focus as you advance through Part 1, where we develop specific economic principles and models. Specifically, in Chapter 2 we build a model of the production choices facing an economy. In Chapter 3 we develop a model that will help you understand how prices and quantities of goods and services are established in individual markets. In Chapter 4 we combine all markets in the economy to see how the so-called *market system* works. Finally, in Chapters 5 and 6 we examine important sectors (components) of the economy, specifically, the private sector, the government sector, and the international sector.

CHAPTER SUMMARY

1. Economics is the study of the efficient use of scarce resources in the production of goods and services to satisfy as many wants as possible.

2. The economic perspective includes three elements: scarcity and choice, rational behavior, and marginalism. It sees individuals and institutions making rational decisions based on comparisons of marginal costs and marginal benefits.

3. A knowledge of economics contributes to effective citizenship and provides useful insights for politicians, consumers, and workers.

4. The tasks of empirical economics are **(a)** gathering economic facts relevant to a particular problem or specific segment of the economy, and **(b)** testing hypotheses against the facts to validate theories.

5. Generalizations stated by economists are called principles, theories, laws, or models. The derivation of these principles is the object of theoretical economics.

6. Induction distills theories from facts; deduction uses logic to derive hypotheses that are then tested against facts.

7. Economic principles are valuable predictors. They are the bases for economic policy, which is designed to identify and solve problems and control undesirable events.

8. Our society accepts certain shared economic goals, including economic growth, full employment, economic efficiency, price-level stability, economic freedom, equity in the distribution of income, economic security, and a reasonable balance in our international trade and finance. Some of these goals are complementary; others entail tradeoffs.

9. Macroeconomics looks at the economy as a whole or its major aggregates; microeconomics examines specific economic units or institutions.

10. Positive statements state facts ("what is"); normative statements express value judgments ("what ought to be").

11. In studying economics we encounter such pitfalls as biases and preconceptions, unfamiliar or confusing terminology, the fallacy of composition, and the difficulty of establishing clear cause-effect relationships.

TERMS AND CONCEPTS

economics	induction	policy economics	positive economics
economic perspective	deduction	tradeoffs	normative economics
marginal analysis	generalizations	macroeconomics	fallacy of composition
theoretical economics	"other-things-equal"	aggregate	"after this, therefore
principles	assumption	microeconomics	because of this" fallacy

STUDY QUESTIONS

1. **KEY QUESTION** Use the economic perspective to explain why someone who is normally a light eater at a standard restaurant may become somewhat of a glutton at a buffet-style restaurant which charges a single price for all you can eat.

2. Distinguish between the inductive and deductive methods for establishing economic principles. Why must both methods ultimately involve gathering facts?

3. Why is it significant that economics is not a laboratory science? What problems may be involved in deriving and applying economic principles?

4. Explain the following statements:
   a. Good economic policy requires good economic theory.
   b. Generalization and abstraction are nearly synonymous.
   c. Facts serve to sort out good and bad theories.
   d. The *other things equal assumption* helps isolate key economic relationships.

5. **KEY QUESTION** Explain in detail the interrelationships between economic facts, theory, and policy. Critically evaluate this statement: "The trouble with economic theory is that it is not practical. It is detached from the real world."

6. To what extent do you accept the eight economic goals stated and described in this chapter? What priorities do you assign to them?

7. **KEY QUESTION** Indicate whether each of the following statements applies to microeconomics or macroeconomics:
   a. The unemployment rate in the United States was 4.9 percent in August 1997.
   b. The Alpo dogfood plant in Bowser, Iowa, laid off 15 workers last month.
   c. An unexpected freeze in central Florida reduced the citrus crop and caused the price of oranges to rise.
   d. Our national output, adjusted for inflation, grew by 2 percent in 1995.
   e. Last week Wells Fargo Bank lowered its interest rate on business loans by one-half of 1 percentage point.
   f. The consumer price index rose by 2.3 percent in 1997.

8. **KEY QUESTION** Identify each of the following as either a positive or a normative statement:
   a. The high temperature today was 89 degrees.
   b. It was too hot today.
   c. The general price level rose by 4.4 percent last year.
   d. Inflation eroded living standards last year and should be reduced by government policies.

9. **KEY QUESTION** Explain and give an example of (a) the fallacy of composition, and (b) the "after this, therefore because of this" fallacy. Why are cause-and-effect relationships difficult to isolate in economics?

10. Suppose studies show that students who study more hours receive higher grades. Does this relationship guarantee that any particular student who studies longer will get higher grades?

11. Studies indicate that married men on average earn more income than unmarried men of the same age. Why must we be cautious in concluding that marriage is the *cause* and higher income is the *effect*?

12. **(Last Word)** Use the economic perspective to explain the behavior of the *workers* (rather than the customers) observed at a fast-food restaurant. Why are these workers there, rather than, say, cruising around in their cars? Why do they work so diligently? Why do so many of them quit these jobs once they have graduated from high school?

13. **WEB-BASED QUESTION** Economic Goals— Are They Being Achieved? The three primary economic goals are economic growth, full employment, and price-level stability. The White House http://www.whitehouse.gov/fsbr/esbr.html provides links to economic information produced by a number of federal agencies. Visit their links for Output, Income, Expenditures, and Wealth, and Employment, Unemployment, and Earnings.

14. **WEB-BASED QUESTION** Normative Economics—Republicans versus Democrats Many economic policy statements made by both the Republicans http://www.rnc.org/ and the Democrats http://www.democrats.org/ are normative rather than positive economic statements. Visit both the Republican and Democratic Web sites and compare and contrast their views on how to achieve economic goals. How much of the rhetoric is based on positive statements compared with normative statements?

Graphs and Their Meaning

If you glance quickly through this text, you will find many graphs. Some seem simple, while others seem more formidable. All are important. They are included to help you visualize and understand economic relationships. Physicists and chemists sometimes illustrate their theories by building arrangements of multicolored wooden balls, representing protons, neutrons, and electrons, which are held in proper relation to one another by wires or sticks. Economists most often use graphs to illustrate their models. By understanding these "pictures," you can more readily comprehend economic relationships. Most of our principles or models explain relationships between just two sets of economic facts, which can be conveniently represented with two-dimensional graphs.

Construction of a Graph

A graph is a visual representation of the relationship between two variables. Table 1 is a hypothetical illustration showing the relationship between income and consumption for the economy as a whole. Without even studying economics, we would expect intuitively that people would buy more goods and services when their incomes go up. Thus we are not surprised to find in Table 1 that total consumption in the economy increases as total income rises.

The information in Table 1 is expressed graphically in Figure 1. Here is how it is done: We want to show visually or graphically how consumption changes as income changes. Since income is the determining factor, we represent it on the **horizontal axis** of the graph, as is customary. And because consumption depends on income, we represent it on the **vertical axis** of the graph, as is also customary. Actually, what we are doing is representing the *independent variable* on the horizontal axis and the *dependent variable* on the vertical axis.

Now we arrange the vertical and horizontal scales of the graph to reflect the ranges of values of consumption and income, and we mark the scales in convenient increments. As you can see, the values marked on the scales cover all the values in Table 1. The increments on both scales are $100 for approximately each $\frac{1}{2}$ inch.

Because the graph has two dimensions, each point within it represents an income value and its associated consumption value. To find a point that represents one of the five income-consumption combinations in Table 1, we draw perpendiculars from the appropriate values on the vertical and horizontal axes. For example, to plot point *c* (the $200 income–$150 consumption point), perpendiculars are drawn up from the horizontal (income) axis at $200 and across from the vertical (consumption) axis at $150. These perpendiculars intersect at point *c*, which represents this particular income-consumption combination. You should verify that the other income-consumption combinations shown in Table 1 are properly located in Figure 1. Finally, by assuming that the same general relationship between income and consumption prevails for all other incomes, we draw a line or smooth curve to connect these points. That line or curve represents the income-consumption relationship.

If the graph is a straight line, as in Figure 1, we say the relationship is *linear*.

Direct and Inverse Relationships

The line in Figure 1 slopes upward to the right, so it depicts a direct relationship between income and con-

TABLE 1 The relationship between income and consumption

Income per week	Consumption per week	Point
$ 0	$ 50	a
100	100	b
200	150	c
300	200	d
400	250	e

TABLE 2 The relationship between ticket prices and attendance

Ticket price	Attendance, thousands	Point
$25	0	a
20	4	b
15	8	c
10	12	d
5	16	e
0	20	f

sumption. By a **direct relationship** (or positive relationship) we mean that two variables—in this case, consumption and income—change in the *same* direction. An increase in consumption is associated with an increase in income; a decrease in consumption accompanies a decrease in income. When two sets of data are positively or directly related, they always graph as an *upsloping* line, as in Figure 1.

In contrast, two sets of data may be inversely related. Consider Table 2, which shows the relationship between the price of basketball tickets and game attendance at Gigantic State University. Here we have a negative or **inverse relationship** because the two variables change in *opposite* directions. When ticket prices decrease, attendance increases. When ticket prices increase, attendance decreases. The six data points in Table 2 are plotted in Figure 2. Observe that an inverse relationship always graphs as a *downsloping* line.

Dependent and Independent Variables

Although it is not always easy, economists seek to determine which variable is the "cause" and which is the "effect." Or, more formally, they seek the independent variable and the dependent variable. The **independent variable** is the cause or source; it is the variable that changes first. The **dependent variable** is the effect or outcome; it is the variable which changes because of the change in the independent variable. As noted in our income-consumption example, income generally is the independent variable and consumption the dependent variable. Income causes consumption to be what it is rather than the other way around. Similarly, ticket

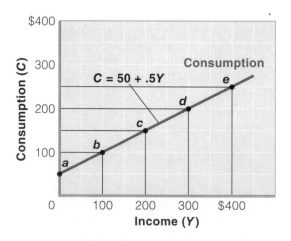

FIGURE 1 Graphing the direct relationship between consumption and income Two sets of data which are positively or directly related, such as consumption and income, graph as an upsloping line.

FIGURE 2 Graphing the inverse relationship between ticket prices and game attendance Two sets of data which are negatively or inversely related, such as ticket price and the attendance at basketball games, graph as a downsloping line.

prices determine attendance at GSU basketball games; attendance does not determine ticket prices. Ticket price is the independent variable, and the quantity of tickets purchased is the dependent variable.

You may recall from your high school courses that mathematicians always put the independent variable (cause) on the horizontal axis and the dependent variable (effect) on the vertical axis. Economists are less tidy; their graphing of independent and dependent variables is more arbitrary. Their conventional graphing of the income-consumption relationship is consistent with mathematical presentation, but economists put price and cost data on the vertical axis. Hence, economists' graphing of GSU's ticket price–attendance data conflicts with normal mathematical procedure.

Other Things Equal

Our simple two-variable graphs purposely ignore many other factors which might affect the amount of consumption occurring at each income level or the number of people who attend GSU basketball games at each possible ticket price. When economists plot the relationship between any two variables, they invoke the *ceteris paribus* (other things equal) assumption. Thus, in Figure 1 all factors other than income which might affect the amount of consumption are presumed to be constant or unchanged. Similarly, in Figure 2 all factors other than ticket price which might influence attendance at GSU basketball games are assumed constant. In reality, "other things" are not equal; they often change, and when they do, the relationship represented in our two tables and graphs will change. Specifically, the lines we have plotted would shift to new locations.

Consider a stock market "crash." The dramatic drop in the value of stocks might cause people to feel less wealthy and therefore less willing to consume at each level of income. The result might be a downward shift of the consumption line. To see this, you should plot a new consumption line in Figure 1, assuming that consumption is, say, $20 less at each income level. Note that the relationship remains direct; the line merely shifts downward to reflect less consumption spending at each income level.

Similarly, factors other than ticket prices might affect GSU game attendance. If a professional basketball team locates in the same city as GSU, attendance at GSU games might be less at each ticket price. To see this, redraw Figure 2, assuming that 2000 fewer students attend GSU games at each ticket price. **(Key Appendix Question 2)**

Slope of a Line

Lines can be described in terms of their slopes. The **slope of a straight line** is the ratio of the vertical change (the rise or drop) to the horizontal change (the run) between any two points of the line.

Positive Slope   Between point b and point c in Figure 1 the rise or vertical change (the change in consumption) is +$50 and the run or horizontal change (the change in income) is +$100. Therefore:

$$\text{Slope} = \frac{\text{vertical change}}{\text{horizontal change}} = \frac{+50}{+100} = \frac{1}{2} = .5$$

Note that our slope of $\frac{1}{2}$ or .5 is positive because consumption and income change in the same direction; that is, consumption and income are directly or positively related.

The slope of .5 tells us there will be a $1 increase in consumption for every $2 increase in income. Similarly, it indicates that for every $2 decrease in income there will be a $1 decrease in consumption.

Negative Slope   Between any two of the identified points in Figure 2, say, point c and point d, the vertical change is −5 (the drop) and the horizontal change is +4 (the run). Therefore:

$$\text{Slope} = \frac{\text{vertical change}}{\text{horizontal change}} = \frac{-5}{+4} = -1\frac{1}{4} = -1.25$$

This slope is negative because ticket price and attendance have an inverse relationship.

Note that on the horizontal axis attendance is stated in thousands of people. So the slope of −5/+4 or −1.25 means that lowering the price by $5 will increase attendance by 4000 people. This is the same as saying that a $1.25 price reduction will increase attendance by 1000 persons.

Slopes and Measurement Units   The slope of a line will be affected by the choice of units for either variable. If, in our ticket price illustration, we had chosen to measure attendance in individual people, our horizontal change would have been 4000 and the slope would have been

$$\text{Slope} = \frac{-5}{+4000} = \frac{-1}{+800} = -.00125$$

The slope depends on the way the relevant variables are measured.

Slopes and Marginal Analysis   Recall that economics is largely concerned with changes from the status quo. The concept of slope is important in economics because it reflects marginal changes—those involving 1 more (or 1 less) unit. For example, in Figure 1 the .5 slope shows that $.50 of extra or marginal consumption is associated with each $1 increase in income. In this example, people collectively will consume $.50 of any $1 increase in their incomes and reduce their consumption by $.50 for each $1 decline in income.

Infinite and Zero Slopes   Many variables are unrelated or independent of one another. For example, the quantity of wristwatches purchased is not related to the price of bananas. In Figure 3a we represent the price of bananas on the vertical axis and the quantity of watches demanded on the horizontal axis. The graph of their relationship is the line parallel to the vertical axis, indicating that the same quantity of watches is purchased no matter what the price of bananas. The slope of such a line is *infinite*.

Similarly, aggregate consumption is completely unrelated to the nation's divorce rate. In Figure 3b we put consumption on the vertical axis and the divorce rate on the horizontal axis. The line parallel to the horizontal axis represents this lack of relatedness. This line has a slope of *zero*.

Vertical Intercept

A line can be located on a graph (without plotting points) if we know its slope and its vertical intercept. The **vertical intercept** of a line is the point where the line meets the vertical axis. In Figure 1 the intercept is $50. This intercept means that if current income were zero, consumers would still spend $50. They might do this through borrowing or by selling off some of their assets. Similarly, the vertical intercept in Figure 2 shows that at a $25 ticket price, GSU's basketball team would be playing in an empty arena.

Equation of a Linear Relationship

If we know the vertical intercept and slope, we can describe a line succinctly in equation form. In its general form, the equation of a line is

$y = a + bx$

where y = dependent variable
   a = vertical intercept
   b = slope of line
   x = independent variable

For our income-consumption example, if C represents consumption (the dependent variable) and Y represents income (the independent variable), we can write $C = a + bY$. By substituting the known values of the intercept and the slope, we get

$C = 50 + .5Y$

This equation also allows us to determine the amount of consumption C at any specific level of income. You should use it to confirm that at the $250 income level, consumption is $175.

When economists reverse mathematical convention by putting the independent variable on the vertical axis and the dependent variable on the horizontal axis, then y stands for the independent variable, rather than the dependent variable in the general form. We noted previously that this case is relevant for our GSU ticket price–attendance data. If P represents the ticket price (independent variable) and Q represents attendance (dependent variable), their relationship is given by

$P = 25 - 1.25Q$

(a)   (b)

FIGURE 3 Infinite and zero slopes
(a) A line parallel to the vertical axis has an infinite slope. Here, purchases of watches remain the same no matter what happens to the price of bananas. (b) A line parallel to the horizontal axis has a slope of zero. Here, consumption remains the same no matter what happens to the divorce rate. In both (a) and (b), the two variables are totally unrelated to one another.

where the vertical intercept is 25 and the negative slope is $-1\frac{1}{4}$ or -1.25. Knowing the value of P lets us solve for Q, our dependent variable. You should use this equation to predict GSU ticket sales when the ticket price is $7.50. **(Key Appendix Question 3)**

Slope of a Nonlinear Curve

We now move from the simple world of linear relationships (straight lines) to the more complex world of nonlinear relationships. The slope of a straight line is the same at all its points. The slope of a line representing a nonlinear relationship changes from one point to another. Such lines are referred to as *curves*. (It is also permissible to refer to a straight line as a "curve.")

Consider the downsloping curve in Figure 4. Its slope is negative throughout, but the curve flattens as we move down along it. Thus, its slope constantly changes; the curve has a different slope at each point.

To measure the slope at a specific point, we draw a straight line tangent to the curve at that point. A line is *tangent* at a point if it touches, but does not intersect, the curve at that point. Thus line *aa* is tangent to the curve in Figure 4 at point A. The slope of the curve at that point is equal to the slope of the tangent line. Specifically, the total vertical change (drop) in the tangent line *aa* is -20 and the total horizontal change (run) is $+5$. Because the slope of the tangent

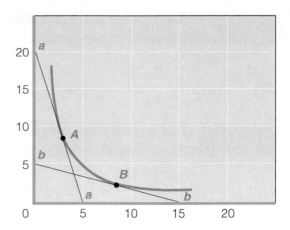

FIGURE 4 **Determining the slopes of curves** The slope of a nonlinear curve changes from point to point on the curve. The slope at any point (say, B) can be determined by drawing a straight line tangent to that point (line *bb*) and calculating the slope of that line.

line *aa* is $-20/+5$, or -4, the slope of the curve at point A is also -4.

Line *bb* in Figure 4 is tangent to the curve at point B. Following the same procedure, we find the slope at B to be $-5/+15$, or $-\frac{1}{3}$. Thus, in this flatter part of the curve, the slope is less negative. **(Key Appendix Question 6)**

APPENDIX SUMMARY

1. Graphs are a convenient and revealing way to represent economic relationships.

2. Two variables are positively or directly related when their values change in the same direction. The line (curve) representing two directly related variables slopes upward.

3. Two variables are negatively or inversely related when their values change in opposite directions. The curve representing two inversely related variables slopes downward.

4. The value of the dependent variable (the "effect") is determined by the value of the independent variable (the "cause").

5. When the "other factors" which might affect a two-variable relationship are allowed to change, the graph of the relationship will likely shift to a new location.

6. The slope of a straight line is the ratio of the vertical change to the horizontal change between any two points. The slope of an upsloping line is positive; the slope of a downsloping line is negative.

7. The slope of a line or curve depends on the units used in measuring the variables. It is especially relevant for economics because it measures marginal changes.

8. The slope of a horizontal line is zero; the slope of a vertical line is infinite.

9. The vertical intercept and slope of a line determine its location; they are used in expressing the line—and the relationship between the two variables—as an equation.

10. The slope of a curve at any point is determined by calculating the slope of a straight line tangent to the curve at that point.

APPENDIX TERMS AND CONCEPTS   -

horizontal axis   direct relationship   independent variable   slope of a straight line
vertical axis   inverse relationship   dependent variable   vertical intercept

APPENDIX STUDY QUESTIONS   -

1. Briefly explain the use of graphs as a way to represent economic relationships. What is an inverse relationship? How does it graph? What is a direct relationship? How does it graph? Graph and explain the relationships you would expect to find between **(a)** the number of inches of rainfall per month and the sale of umbrellas, **(b)** the amount of tuition and the level of enrollment at a university, and **(c)** the size of a university's athletic scholarships and the number of games won by its football team.

   In each case cite and explain how variables other than those specifically mentioned might upset the expected relationship. Is your graph in part b, above, consistent with the fact that, historically, enrollments and tuition have both increased? If so, explain any difference.

2. KEY APPENDIX QUESTION   Indicate how each of the following might affect the data shown in Table 2 and Figure 2 of this appendix:
   a. GSU's athletic director schedules higher-quality opponents.
   b. GSU's Fighting Aardvarks experience three losing seasons.
   c. GSU contracts to have all its home games televised.

3. KEY APPENDIX QUESTION   The following table contains data on the relationship between saving and income. Rearrange these data into a meaningful order and graph them on the accompanying grid. What is the slope of the line? The vertical intercept? Interpret the meaning of both the slope and the intercept. Write the equation which represents this line. What would you predict saving to be at the $12,500 level of income?

Income (per year)	Saving (per year)
$15,000	$1,000
0	−500
10,000	500
5,000	0
20,000	1,500

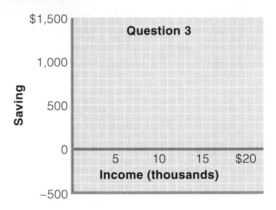

4. Construct a table from the data shown on the graph below. Which is the dependent variable and which the independent variable? Summarize the data in equation form.

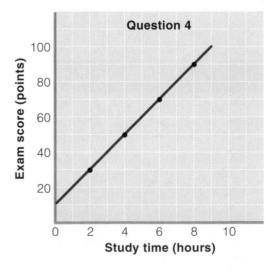

5. Suppose that when the interest rate which must be paid to borrow funds is 16 percent, businesses find it unprofitable to invest in machinery and equipment. However, when the interest rate is 14 percent, $5 billion worth of investment is profitable. At 12 percent interest, a total of $10 billion of investment is profitable. Similarly, total investment increases by $5 billion for each successive 2-percentage-point decline in the interest rate. Describe the relevant relationship between the interest rate and investment in words, in a table, graphically, and as an equation. Put the interest rate on the vertical axis and investment on the horizontal axis. In your equation use the form $i = a + bI$, where i is the interest rate, a is the vertical intercept, b is the slope of the line (which is negative), and I is the level of investment. Comment on the advantages and disadvantages of the verbal, tabular, graphical, and equation forms of description.

6. **KEY APPENDIX QUESTION** The accompanying graph shows curve XX' and tangents at points A, B, and C. Calculate the slope of the curve at these three points.

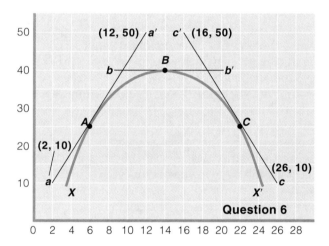

Question 6

7. In the accompanying graph, is the slope of curve AA' positive or negative? Does the slope increase or decrease as we move along the curve from A to A'? Answer the same two questions for curve BB'.

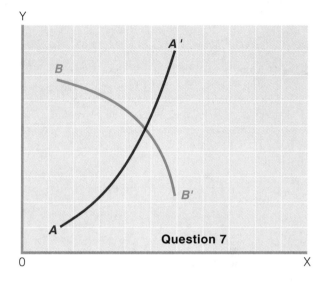

Question 7

2

The Economizing Problem

You make decisions every day that capture the essence of economics. Suppose you have $40 and are deciding how to spend it. Should you buy a pair of new jeans? Two or three compact discs? A ticket for a music concert?

Similarly, what should you do with your time between 3 and 6 o'clock on, say, a Thursday afternoon? Should you work extra hours at your part-time job? Do research on a term project? Prepare for an economics quiz? Watch TV? Take a nap?

Money and time are both scarce, and making decisions in the context of scarcity always means there are costs. If you choose the jeans, the cost is the forgone CDs or concert. If you nap or watch TV, the cost might be a low score on your quiz.

Scarcity, choices, and costs—these are the key elements of this chapter. Here we introduce and explore the fundamentals of economic science. We first illustrate, extend, and modify our definition of economics and explore the so-called *economizing problem* by means of a model. Next, we briefly survey the ways diverse economies respond to the economizing problem. Finally, we develop an overview of the market system in the form of the circular flow model.

THE FOUNDATION OF ECONOMICS

Two fundamental facts together constitute the **economizing problem** and provide a foundation for the field of economics:

1. *Society's material wants, that is, the material wants of its citizens and institutions, are virtually unlimited and insatiable.*
2. *Economic resources—the means of producing goods and services—are limited or scarce.*

You must fully understand these two facts because all that follows depends directly on them.

Unlimited Wants

In stating the first fact, what do we mean by "material wants?" We mean, first, the desires of consumers to obtain and use various goods and services that provide **utility,** meaning pleasure or satisfaction.[1] An amazingly wide range of products accomplishes this, from houses and automobiles to toothpaste, pizzas, sweaters, and hamburgers. Innumerable prod-

---

[1]This definition leaves a variety of wants—recognition, status, love, and so forth—for the other social sciences to examine and study.

ucts sometimes classified as *necessities* (food, shelter, and clothing) and *luxuries* (perfumes, yachts, racecars) can satisfy human wants. Of course, what is a luxury to Smith may be a necessity to Jones, and what is a necessity today may have been a luxury a few years ago.

Services satisfy our wants as much as products do. Repair work on a car, the removal of an inflamed appendix, legal and accounting advice, and haircuts and hairstyling all satisfy human wants. Actually, we buy many goods, such as automobiles and washing machines, for the services they render. Thus, the differences between goods and services are often smaller than they would appear to be.

"Wants" also include the desires of businesses and units of government to satisfy material goals. Businesses want factory buildings, machinery, trucks, warehouses, communication systems, and other things that help them achieve their production goals. Government, reflecting the collective wants of its citizenry or goals of its own, seeks highways, mass transit systems, schools, and military equipment.

We say that, as a group, these wants are *insatiable*, or *unlimited*, meaning that our desires for goods and services cannot be completely satisfied. Our desires for a *particular* good or service can be satisfied; over a short period of time we can surely get enough toothpaste or pasta. And one appendicitis operation is plenty.

But goods *in general* are another story. We do not, and presumably cannot, get enough. A simple mental experiment can help verify this: Suppose all members of society were asked to list the goods and services they would buy if they had unlimited income. Do you imagine that their list would ever end?

Furthermore, over time, wants multiply. As we fill some of the wants on the list, new ones pop up. Material wants have a high reproduction rate. The rapid introduction of new products whets our appetites, and extensive advertising persuades us that we need items we might not otherwise have desired. Not long ago, we did not want personal computers, Internet service, video recorders, fax machines, and compact discs because they did not exist. Also, we often cannot stop with simple satisfaction: The acquisition of an Escort or Geo has been known to whet the appetite for a Porsche or Mercedes.

At any specific time the individuals and institutions constituting society have innumerable unfulfilled material wants. Some wants—food, clothing, shelter—have biological roots. But some are also in-fluenced by the conventions and customs of society. The specific kinds of food, clothing, and shelter we seek are frequently determined by the general social and cultural environment in which we live. Over time, wants change and multiply, fueled by the development of new products and extensive promotion.

The overall objective of all economic activity is to satisfy these diverse material wants.

Scarce Resources

In stating the second fundamental fact—*economic resources are limited or scarce*—what do we mean by **economic resources?** In general, we mean all natural, human, and manufactured resources which go into the production of goods and services. This covers a lot of ground: all the factory and farm buildings and all the equipment, tools, and machinery used to produce manufactured goods and agricultural products; all transportation and communication facilities; the innumerable types of labor; and land and mineral resources of all kinds. Economists broadly classify these as either *property* resources—land or raw materials and capital—or *human* resources—labor and entrepreneurial ability.

Resource Categories   Let's examine four specific categories of resources.

Land   Land means much more to the economist than to most people. Land is all natural resources—all "gifts of nature"—usable in the production process. Such resources as arable land, forests, mineral and oil deposits, and water resources come under this classification.

Capital   Capital (or *capital goods* or *investment goods*) includes all manufactured aids to production, that is, all tools, machinery, equipment, and factory, storage, transportation, and distribution facilities used in producing goods and services and getting them to the ultimate consumer. The process of producing and purchasing capital goods is known as **investment.**

Two other points are pertinent. First, *capital goods* differ from *consumer goods* since the latter satisfy wants directly, while the former do so indirectly by aiding production of consumer goods. Second, the term "capital" as here defined does *not* refer to money. True, business executives and economists often talk of "money capital," meaning money available to purchase machinery, equipment, and other productive facilities. But money, as such, produces nothing, so it is not an economic resource. *Real capital*—tools, machinery, and other productive equipment—is an economic resource; *money* or *financial capital* is not.

Labor   Labor is a broad term for all the physical and mental talents of individuals available and usable in producing goods and services. (This *excludes* a special set of talents—entrepreneurial ability—which, because of its special significance in a capitalistic economy, we consider separately.) The services of a logger, retail clerk, machinist, teacher, professional football player, and nuclear physicist all fall under the general heading "labor."

Entrepreneurial Ability   Finally, there is the special human resource we label **entrepreneurial ability** or, simply, *enterprise.* The entrepreneur performs four related functions:

1. The entrepreneur *takes the initiative* in combining the resources of land, capital, and labor to produce a good or service. Both a sparkplug and a catalyst, the entrepreneur is the driving force behind production and the agent who combines the other resources in what is hoped will be a successful business venture.
2. The entrepreneur *makes basic business-policy decisions*, that is, those nonroutine decisions which set the course of a business enterprise.
3. The entrepreneur *is an innovator*—the one who attempts to introduce on a commercial basis new products, new productive techniques, or even new forms of business organization.
4. The entrepreneur *is a risk bearer.* This is apparent from a close examination of the other three entrepreneurial functions. The entrepreneur in a capitalistic system has no guarantee of profit. The reward for his or her time, efforts, and abilities may be profits *or* losses and eventual bankruptcy. The entrepreneur risks not only time, effort, and business reputation but his or her invested funds and those of associates or stockholders.

Since these four resources—land, labor, capital, and entrepreneurial ability—are combined to *produce* goods and services, they are called the **factors of production.**

Resource Payments   The income received from supplying raw materials and capital equipment (the property resources) is called *rental income* and *interest income*, respectively. The income accruing to those who supply labor is called *wages*, which includes salaries and all wage and salary supplements such as bonuses, commissions, and royalties. Entrepreneurial income is called *profits*, which may be negative—that is, losses.

Relative Scarcity   The four types of economic resources, or factors of production, or *inputs*, have one fundamental characteristic in common: *They are scarce or limited in supply.* Our "spaceship earth" contains only limited amounts of resources to use in producing goods and services. Quantities of arable land, mineral deposits, capital equipment, and labor (time) are all limited; they are available only in finite amounts. Because of the scarcity of productive resources and the constraint that this scarcity puts on productive activity, output itself is limited. Society is not able to produce and consume all the goods and services it wants. Thus, in the United States, one of the most affluent nations, output per person was limited to $28,500 in 1996. In the poorest nations, annual output per person is as low as $200 or $300!

ECONOMICS: EMPLOYMENT AND EFFICIENCY

The economizing problem is thus at the heart of the definition of economics, first stated in Chapter 1: *Economics is the social science concerned with the problem of using scarce resources to attain the maximum fulfillment of society's unlimited wants.* Economics is concerned with "doing the best with what we have." Because our resources are scarce, we cannot satisfy all our unlimited wants. The next best thing is to achieve the greatest possible satisfaction of those wants.

Economics is thus a science of efficiency—the best use of scarce resources. Society wants to use its limited resources efficiently; it desires to produce as many goods and services as possible from its available resources, so that it maximizes total satisfaction. To realize this outcome, it must achieve both full employment and full production.

Full Employment: Using Available Resources

By **full employment** we mean the use of all available resources. No workers should be involuntarily out of work; the economy should provide employment for all who are willing and able to work. Nor should capital equipment or arable land sit idle. But note that we say all *available* resources should be employed. Each society has certain customs and practices which determine what particular resources are available for employment. For example, in most countries legislation and custom provide that children and the very aged should not be employed. Similarly, to maintain productivity, it is desirable to allow farmland to lie fallow periodically. And it is desirable to "conserve" some resources for use by future generations.

Full Production: Using Resources Efficiently

The employment of all available resources is not enough to achieve efficiency. Full production must also be realized. By **full production** we mean that all employed resources should be used so that they provide the maximum possible satisfaction of our material wants. If we fail to realize full production, economists say our resources are *underemployed*.

Full production implies two kinds of efficiency—productive and allocative efficiency:

1. **Productive efficiency** is the production of *any particular mix of goods and services in the least costly way*. When we produce, say, compact discs at the lowest achievable unit cost, we are expending the smallest amount of resources to produce CDs and therefore making available the largest amount of resources to produce other desired products. Suppose society has only $100 of resources available. If we can produce a CD for only $5 of resources, then $95 of resources will be available to produce other goods. This is clearly better than producing the CD for $10 and having only $90 of resources for alternative uses.

    In real-world terms, productive efficiency requires that Ford pickups and Dodge vans be produced with computerized and roboticized assembly techniques. It would be wasteful of scarce resources—that is, inefficient—to use the primitive assembly lines of the 1920s. Similarly, it would be inefficient to have farmers harvesting wheat with scythes or picking corn by hand since mechanical harvesting equipment is available to do the job at a much lower cost per unit.

2. **Allocative efficiency** is the production of *that particular mix of goods and services most wanted by society*. For example, society wants resources allocated to compact discs and cassettes, not to 45

rpm records. We want personal computers (PCs), not manual typewriters. Furthermore, we do not want to devote *all* our resources to producing CDs and PCs; we want to assign some of them to producing automobiles and office buildings. Allocative efficiency requires that the "right" mix of goods and services be produced—each item at least unit cost. It means apportioning limited resources among firms and industries in such a way that society obtains the combination of goods and services which it wants the most. **(Key Question 5)**

QUICK REVIEW 2-1

■ Human material wants are virtually unlimited.

■ Economic resources—land, capital, labor, and entrepreneurial ability—are scarce.

■ Economics is concerned with the efficient allocation of scarce resources to achieve the maximum fulfillment of society's material wants.

■ Economic efficiency embodies full employment and full production; the latter requires both productive and allocative efficiency.

Production Possibilities Table

Because resources are scarce, a full-employment, full-production economy cannot have an unlimited output of goods and services. Therefore, people must choose which goods and services to produce and which to forgo. The necessity and consequences of these choices can best be understood through a production possibilities model. Let's examine the model first as a table, then as a graph.

Assumptions We begin our discussion with four simplifying assumptions:

1. *Full employment and productive efficiency* The economy is employing all its available resources (full employment) and producing goods and services at least cost (productive efficiency). We will consider allocative efficiency later.

2. *Fixed resources* The available supplies of the factors of production are fixed in both quantity and quality. Nevertheless, they can be reallocated, within limits, among different uses; for example, land can be used for factory sites or for food production.

3. *Fixed technology* The state of technology—the methods used to produce output—does not change during our analysis. This assumption and the previous one imply that we are looking at an economy at one specific time or over a very short period of time. Later in the analysis, we will examine the situation over a longer period.

4. *Two goods* The economy is producing only two goods: pizzas and industrial robots. Pizza symbolizes **consumer goods,** products which satisfy our wants *directly*; industrial robots symbolize **capital goods,** products which satisfy our wants *indirectly* by enabling more efficient production of consumer goods.

The Need for Choice From our assumptions, we see that society must choose among alternatives. Limited resources mean limited outputs of pizza and robots. And since all available resources are fully employed, to increase the production of robots we must shift resources away from the production of pizza. The reverse is also true: To increase the production of pizza, we must take resources from the production of robots. There is no such thing as a free pizza. This, recall, is the essence of the economizing problem.

A **production possibilities table** lists the different combinations of two products which can be produced with a specific set of resources (and with full employment *and* productive efficiency). Table 2-1 is such a table for a pizza-robot economy; the data are, of course, hypothetical. At alternative A, this economy would be devoting all its available resources to the production of robots (capital goods); at alternative E, all resources would go to pizza production (consumer goods). Those alternatives are unrealistic extremes; an economy typically produces both capital and consumer goods, as in B, C, and D. As we move

from alternative A to E, we increase the production of pizza at the expense of robot production.

Because consumer goods satisfy our wants directly, any movement toward E looks tempting. In producing more pizzas, society increases the current satisfaction of its wants. But there is a cost: fewer robots. This shift of resources to consumer goods catches up with society over time as the stock of capital goods dwindles—or at least ceases to expand at the current rate—with the result that some potential for greater production is lost. By moving toward alternative E, society chooses "more now" at the expense of "much more later."

By moving toward A, society chooses to forgo current consumption. The sacrifice of current consumption frees resources which can be used to increase the production of capital goods. By building up its stock of capital this way, society will have greater future production and, therefore, greater future consumption. By moving toward A, society is choosing "more later" at the cost of "less now."

Generalization: *At any point in time, an economy achieving full employment and productive efficiency must sacrifice some of one good to obtain more of another good. Scarce resources prohibit such an economy from having more of both goods.*

Production Possibilities Curve

The data and ideas of a production possibilities table can also be shown graphically. We use a simple two-dimensional graph, arbitrarily representing the output of capital goods (here, robots) on the vertical axis and the output of consumer goods (here, pizza) on the horizontal axis, as shown in **Figure 2-1 (Key Graph).** Following the procedure given in the appendix to Chapter 1, we graph a **production possibilities curve.**

Each point on the production possibilities curve represents some maximum output of the two products. The curve is a production *frontier* because it shows the limit of attainable outputs. To obtain the various combinations of pizza and robots that fall *on* the production possibilities curve, society must achieve both full employment and productive efficiency. Points lying *inside* (to the left of) the curve are also attainable but not as desirable as points on the curve. Points inside the curve imply that the economy could have more of both robots and pizza if it achieved full employment and productive efficiency. Points lying *outside* (to the right of) the production possibilities

TABLE 2-1 Production possibilities of pizza and robots with full employment and productive efficiency

Type of product	Production alternatives				
	A	B	C	D	E
Pizza (in hundred thousands)	0	1	2	3	4
Robots (in thousands)	10	9	7	4	0

FIGURE 2-1 The production possibilities curve Each point on the production possibilities curve represents some maximum combination of two products which can be produced if full employment and full production are achieved. When operating on the curve, more robots means less pizza, and vice versa. Limited resources and a fixed technology make any combination of robots and pizza lying outside the curve (such as at *W*) unattainable. Points inside the curve are attainable, but they indicate that full employment and productive efficiency are not being realized.

QUICK QUIZ 2-1

1. **Production possibilities curve *ABCDE* is concave because:**
   a. the marginal benefit of pizza declines as more pizza is consumed.
   b. the curve gets steeper as we move from *E* to *A*.
   c. it reflects the law of increasing opportunity costs.
   d. resources are scarce.

2. **The *marginal* opportunity cost of the second unit of pizza is:**
   a. 2 units of robots.
   b. 3 units of robots.
   c. 7 units of robots.
   d. 9 units of robots.

3. **The *total* opportunity cost of 7 units of robots is:**
   a. 1 unit of pizza.
   b. 2 units of pizza.
   c. 3 units of pizza.
   d. 4 units of pizza.

4. **All points on this production possibilities curve necessarily represent:**
   a. allocative efficiency.
   b. less than full use of resources.
   c. unattainable levels of output.
   d. productive efficiency.

Answers: 1. c; 2. a; 3. b; 4. d

---

curve, like point *W*, would represent a greater output than that at any point on the curve, but such points are unattainable with the current supplies of resources and technology.

Law of Increasing Opportunity Cost

Because resources are scarce relative to the virtually unlimited wants which they can be used to satisfy, people must choose among alternatives. More of pizza means less of robots. The amount of other products which must be forgone or sacrificed to obtain 1 unit of a specific good is called the **opportunity cost** of

that good. In our case, the amount of robots which must be given up to get another unit of pizza is the *opportunity cost*, or simply the *cost*, of that unit of pizza.

In moving from alternative A to B in Table 2-1, we find that the cost of 1 additional unit of pizza is 1 less unit of robots. But as we now pursue the concept of cost through the additional production possibilities—B to C, C to D, and D to E—an important economic principle is revealed: The opportunity cost of each additional unit of pizza is greater than that of the previous one. When we move from A to B, just 1 unit of robots is sacrificed for 1 more unit of pizza; but going from B to C sacrifices 2 additional units of robots for 1 more unit of pizza; then 3 more of robots for 1 more of pizza; and finally 4 for 1. Conversely, you should confirm that as we move from E to A, the cost of an additional robot is $\frac{1}{4}$, $\frac{1}{3}$, $\frac{1}{2}$, and 1 unit of pizza, respectively, for the four successive moves.

Note two points about these opportunity costs:

1. Our costs are measured in *real* terms, that is, in actual goods rather than money. We will shift to monetary comparisons in a moment.

2. We are discussing *marginal* (meaning "extra") opportunity costs, rather than cumulative or total opportunity costs. For example, the marginal opportunity cost of the third unit of pizza in Table 2-1 is 3 units of robots (= 7 − 4). But the *total* opportunity cost of 3 units of pizza is 6 units of robots (= 1 unit of robots for the first unit of pizza *plus* 2 units of robots for the second unit of pizza *plus* 3 units of robots for the third unit of pizza).

The **law of increasing opportunity costs** generalizes our example: The more of a product which is produced, the greater is its opportunity cost ("marginal" being implied).

Concavity The law of increasing opportunity costs is reflected in the shape of the production possibilities curve: The curve is *concave*, or bowed out, from the origin. In Figure 2-1, you can see that when the economy moves from *A* to *E*, it must give up successively larger amounts of robots (1, 2, 3, and 4) to acquire equal increments of pizza (1, 1, 1, and 1). This reality is evidenced in the slope of the production possibilities curve, which becomes steeper as we move from *A* to *E*. A curve that gets steeper as you move down along it is always concave as viewed from the origin.

Economic Rationale What is the economic rationale for the law of increasing opportunity costs? Why does the sacrifice of robots increase as we produce more pizza? The answer is that *economic resources are not completely adaptable to alternative uses.* Many resources are better at producing one good than at producing others. Fertile farmland is highly conducive to producing the ingredients needed to make pizza, while land containing rich mineral deposits is highly suited to producing the materials needed to make robots. As we step up pizza production, resources that are less and less adaptable to making pizza must be "pushed" into pizza production. If we start at *A* and move to *B*, we can shift the resources whose productivity of pizza is greatest in relation to their productivity of robots. But as we move from *B* to *C*, *C* to *D*, and so on, resources highly productive of pizza become increas-

ingly scarce. To get more pizza, resources whose productivity in robots is great in relation to their productivity in pizza will be needed. It will take more and more of such resources, and hence a greater sacrifice of robots, to achieve each increase of 1 unit in the production of pizza. This lack of perfect flexibility, or interchangeability, on the part of resources is the cause of increasing opportunity costs. **(Key Question 6)**

Allocative Efficiency Revisited

Our analysis has assumed full employment and productive efficiency, both of which are necessary to produce at *any point* on an economy's production possibilities curve. We now turn to allocative efficiency, which requires that the economy produce at the most valued, or *optimal*, point on the production possibilities curve. Of all the attainable combinations of pizza and robots on the curve in Figure 2-1, which is best? That is, what specific quantities of resources should be allocated to pizza and what specific quantities to robots?

Our discussion of the *economic perspective* in Chapter 1 puts us on the right track. Recall that economic decisions center on comparisons of marginal benefits and marginal costs. Any economic activity— for example, production or consumption—should be expanded as long as marginal benefits exceed marginal costs and should be reduced if marginal costs are greater than marginal benefits. The optimal amount of the activity occurs where MB = MC.

Consider pizza. We already know from the law of increasing opportunity costs that the marginal cost (MC) of additional units of pizza will rise as more units are produced. This can be shown with an upsloping MC curve, as in Figure 2-2. We are also aware that we obtain extra or marginal benefits (MB) from additional units of pizza. However, although material wants in the aggregate are insatiable, the second unit of a particular product yields less additional utility or benefit to you than the first. And a third will provide even less MB than the second. So it is for society as a whole. Therefore, we can portray the marginal benefits from pizza with a downsloping MB curve, as in Figure 2-2.

The optimal quantity of pizza production is indicated by the intersection of the MB and MC curves: 200,000 units in Figure 2-2. Why is this the optimal quantity? If only 100,000 pizzas were produced, the marginal benefit of pizza would exceed its marginal cost. In money terms, MB might be $15, while MC

FIGURE 2-2 Allocative efficiency: MB = MC Resources are being allocated efficiently to a product when its output quantity is such that its marginal benefit (MB) equals its marginal cost (MC). Here, the optimal quantity of pizza is 200,000.

----

is only $5. This suggests that society would be *under-allocating* resources to pizza production; more of it should be produced.

How do we know? Because society values an additional pizza as being worth $15, while the alternative products which the required resources could produce are worth only $5. Society benefits—it is better off in the sense of having a higher-valued output to enjoy—whenever it can gain something worth $15 by forgoing something worth only $5. A reallocating of resources from other products to pizza would mean society is using its resources more efficiently. Each additional pizza up to 200,000 would provide such a gain, indicating that allocative efficiency would be improved by this production. But when MB = MC, the benefits of producing pizza or alternative products with the available resources are equal. Allocative efficiency is achieved where MB = MC.

The production of 300,000 pizzas would represent an *overallocation* of resources to their production. Here the MC of pizza is $15 and its MB is only $5. This means 1 unit of pizza is worth only $5 to society, while the alternative products which the required resources could otherwise produce are valued at $15. By producing 1 less unit, society loses a pizza worth $5. But by reallocating the freed resources, it gains other products worth $15. When society gains some-

thing worth $15 by forgoing something worth only $5, it is better off. In Figure 2-2, such net gains can be realized until pizza production has been reduced to 200,000.

Generalization: *Resources are being efficiently allocated to any product when its output is such that its marginal benefit equals its marginal cost (MB = MC).* Suppose that by applying the above analysis to robots, we find their optimal (MB = MC) output is 7000. This would mean that alternative C on our production possibilities curve—200,000 pizzas and 7000 robots—would result in allocative efficiency for our hypothetical economy. **(Key Question 9)**

QUICK REVIEW 2-2

■ The production possibilities curve illustrates four concepts: **(a)** *scarcity* of resources is implied by the area of unattainable combinations of output lying outside the production possibilities curve; **(b)** *choice* among outputs is reflected in the variety of attainable combinations of goods lying along the curve; **(c)** *opportunity cost* is illustrated by the downward slope of the curve; **(d)** the law of *increasing opportunity costs* is implied by the concavity of the curve.

■ Full employment and productive efficiency must be realized for the economy to operate on its production possibilities curve.

■ A comparison of marginal benefits and marginal costs is needed to determine allocative efficiency—the best or optimal output mix on the curve.

UNEMPLOYMENT, GROWTH, AND THE FUTURE

Let's now release the first three assumptions underlying the production possibilities curve to see what happens.

Unemployment and Productive Inefficiency

The first assumption was that our economy was achieving full employment and productive efficiency. Our analysis and conclusions change if some resources are idle (unemployment) or if least-cost production is not realized. The five alternatives in Table 2-1 represent maximum outputs; they illustrate the combinations of robots and pizzas which can be produced when the economy is operating at full capacity—with full employment and productive efficiency. With unemployment or inefficient production, the economy would produce less than each alternative shown in the table.

Graphically, situations of unemployment or productive inefficiency are represented by points *inside* the original production possibilities curve (reproduced in Figure 2-3). Point *U* is one such point. Here the economy is falling short of the various maximum combinations of pizza and robots reflected by the points *on* the production possibilities curve. The arrows in Figure 2-3 indicate three possible paths back to full employment and least-cost production. A move toward full employment and productive efficiency would yield a greater output of one or both products.

A Growing Economy

When we drop the assumptions that the quantity and quality of resources and technology are fixed, the production possibilities curve shifts positions; that is, the potential maximum output of the economy changes.

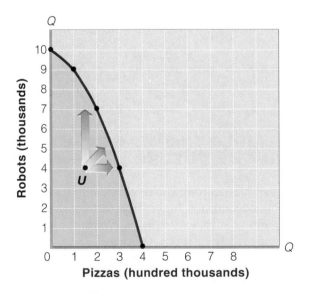

FIGURE 2-3 Unemployment, productive inefficiency, and the production possibilities curve   Any point inside the production possibilities curve, such as *U*, represents unemployment or a failure to achieve productive efficiency. The arrows indicate that, by realizing full employment and productive efficiency, the economy could operate on the curve. This means it could produce more of one or both products than it is producing at point *U*.

Increases in Resource Supplies   Let's first abandon the assumption that total supplies of land, labor, capital, and entrepreneurial ability are fixed in both quantity and quality. Common sense tells us that over time a nation's growing population will bring about increases in the supplies of labor and entrepreneurial ability. Also, labor quality usually improves over time. Historically, our stock of capital has increased at a significant, though unsteady, rate. And although we are depleting some of our energy and mineral resources, new sources are being discovered. The drainage of swamps and the development of irrigation programs add to our supply of arable land.

The net result of these increased supplies of the factors of production is the ability to produce more of both pizza and robots. Thus 20 years from now, the production possibilities in Table 2-1 may be superseded by those shown in Table 2-2. The greater abundance of resources would result in a greater potential output of one or both products at each alternative. Economic growth in the sense of an expanded potential output will have occurred.

But such a favorable change in the production possibilities data does not *guarantee* that the economy will actually operate at a point on its new production possibilities curve. Some 130 million jobs will give the United States full employment now, but 10 or 20 years from now its labor force will be larger, and 130 million jobs will not be sufficient for full employment. The production possibilities curve may shift, but at the future date the economy may fail to produce at a point on that new curve.

Advances in Technology   Our second assumption is that we have constant or unchanging technology. Actually, though, technology has progressed greatly over time. An advancing technology involves both

TABLE 2-2   Production possibilities of pizza and robots with full employment and productive efficiency

Type of product	Production alternatives				
	A′	B′	C′	D′	E′
Pizza (in hundred thousands)	0	2	4	6	8
Robots (in thousands)	14	12	9	5	0

new and better goods *and* improved ways of producing them. For now, let's think of technological advances as being only improvements in capital facilities—more efficient machinery and equipment. Such technological advances alter our previous discussion of the economizing problem by improving productive efficiency, allowing society to produce more goods with fixed resources. As with increases in resource supplies, technological advances enable the production of more robots *and* more pizza.

Thus, when either supplies of resources increase or an improvement in technology occurs, the production possibilities curve in Figure 2-3 shifts outward and to the right, as illustrated by curve *A'*, *B'*, *C'*, *D'*, *E'* in Figure 2-4. Such an outward shift of the production possibilities curve represents growth of economic capacity or, simply, **economic growth:** *the ability to produce a larger total output.* This growth is the result of (1) increases in supplies of resources, (2) improvements in resource quality, and (3) technological advance.

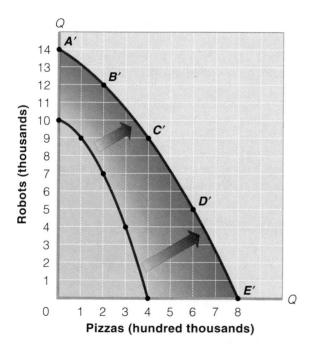

FIGURE 2-4 Economic growth and the production possibilities curve The expanding resource supplies, improved resource quality, and technological advances which occur in a dynamic economy move the production possibilities outward and to the right, allowing the economy to have larger quantities of both types of goods.

The consequence of growth is that our full-employment economy can enjoy a greater output of both robots and pizza. *While a static, no-growth economy must sacrifice some of one product to get more of another, a dynamic, growing economy can have larger quantities of both products.*

Economic growth does *not* typically mean proportionate increases in a nation's capacity to produce all its products. Note in Figure 2-4 that at the maximums, the economy can produce twice as much pizza as before but only 40 percent more robots. You should sketch in two new production possibilities curves: one showing the situation where a better technique for producing robots has been developed while the technology for producing pizza is unchanged, and the other illustrating an improved technology for pizza while the technology for producing robots remains constant.

Present Choices and Future Possibilities An economy's current choice of positions on its production possibilities curve is a basic determinant of the future location of that curve. Let's designate the two axes of the production possibilities curve as *goods for the future* and *goods for the present*, as in Figure 2-5. Goods for the future are such things as capital goods, research and education, and preventive medicine. They increase the quantity and quality of property resources, enlarge the stock of technological information, and improve the quality of human resources. As we have already seen, goods for the future, like industrial robots, are the ingredients of economic growth. Goods for the present are pure consumer goods such as pizza, clothing, soft drinks, and boom boxes.

Now suppose there are two economies, Alta and Zorn, which are initially identical in every respect except one: Alta's current choice of positions on its production possibilities curve strongly favors present goods rather than future goods. Point *A* in Figure 2-5a indicates this choice. It is located quite far down the curve to the right, indicating a high priority for goods for the present, at the expense of fewer goods for the future. Zorn, in contrast, makes a current choice that stresses larger amounts of future goods and lesser amounts of present goods, as shown by point *Z* in Figure 2-5b.

Now, other things equal, we can expect the future production possibilities curve of Zorn to be farther to the right than Alta's curve. By currently choosing an output more favorable to technological advance and to increases in the quantity and quality of resources,

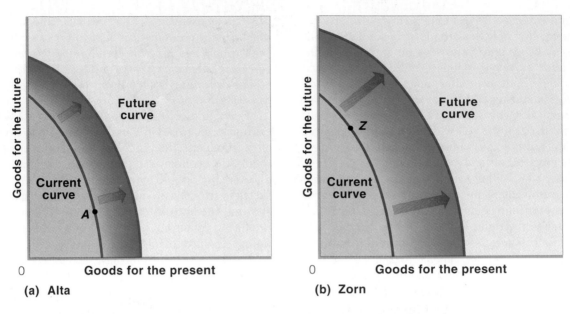

FIGURE 2-5 An economy's present choice of positions on its production possibilities curve helps determine the curve's future location A nation's current choice favoring "present goods," as made by Alta in (a), will cause a modest outward shift of the curve in the future. A nation's current choice favoring "future goods," as made by Zorn in (b), will result in a greater outward shift in the curve in the future.

Zorn will achieve greater economic growth than Alta. In terms of capital goods, Zorn is choosing to make larger current additions to its "national factory"—to invest more of its current output—than Alta. The payoff from this choice for Zorn is more rapid growth—greater future production capacity. The opportunity cost is fewer consumer goods in the present for Zorn to enjoy. **(Key Questions 10 and 11)**

A Qualification: International Trade

The message of the production possibilities curve is that an individual nation is limited to the combinations of output indicated by its production possibilities curve. *But this message must be modified when international specialization and trade exist.*

You will see in later chapters that a nation can avoid the output limits imposed by its domestic production possibilities curve through international specialization and trade. *International specialization* means directing domestic resources to output which a nation is highly efficient at producing. *International trade* involves the exchange of these goods for goods produced abroad. Specialization and trade enable a na-

tion to get more of a desired good at less sacrifice of some other good. Rather than sacrifice 3 robots to get a third unit of pizza, as in Table 2-1, a nation might be able to obtain the third unit of pizza by trading only 2 units of robots for it. Specialization and trade have the same effect as having more and better resources or discovering improved production techniques; both increase the quantities of capital and consumer goods available to society. The output gains

QUICK REVIEW 2-3

■ Unemployment and the failure to achieve productive efficiency cause the economy to operate at a point inside its production possibilities curve.

■ Increases in resource supplies, improvements in resource quality, and technological advance cause economic growth, depicted as an outward shift of the production possibilities curve.

■ An economy's present choice of capital and consumer goods helps determine the future location of its production possibilities curve. (See Global Perspective 2-1.)

■ International specialization and trade enable a nation to obtain more goods than indicated by its production possibilities curve.

from greater international specialization and trade are the equivalent of economic growth.

Applications

There are many possible applications of production possibilities analysis. Here are a few examples.

1. Wartime Production At the beginning of World War II (1939–1945), the United States had considerable unemployment. By quickly employing its idle resources, the U.S. economy was able to produce an almost unbelievably large quantity of war goods and at the same time increase the output of consumer goods (as shown in Figure 2-3). The Soviet Union, in contrast, entered World War II at almost capacity production; it was operating close to full employment. Its military preparations required considerable shifting of resources from the production of civilian goods, and its standard of living dropped substantially.

The U.S. position during the Vietnam conflict was similar to that of the Soviet Union during World War II. The U.S. economy was fully employed in the mid-1960s, and the government accelerated military spending for Vietnam while simultaneously increasing expenditures on domestic "war on poverty" programs. This attempt to achieve both more pizza and more robots, or more guns and more butter, at the same time in a full-employment economy was doomed to failure. The attempt to spend beyond our capacity to produce—to realize a point like W in Figure 2-1—contributed to the high inflation of the 1970s.

2. Discrimination Discrimination based on race, gender, age, sexual orientation, or ethnic background impedes the efficient employment of human resources, keeping the economy operating at some point inside its production possibilities curve. Discrimination prevents blacks, women, and others from obtaining jobs in which society can use their skills and talents efficiently. Elimination of discrimination would help move the economy from some point inside the production possibilities curve toward a point on the curve.

3. Land-Use Controversies The tradeoffs portrayed in the production possibilities curve are part of many controversies relating to alternative uses of publicly owned land. One example is the conflict between the logging industry in the Pacific Northwest

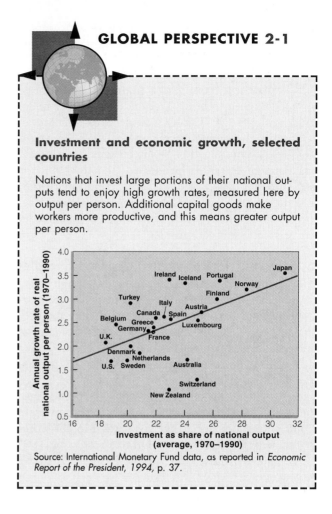

GLOBAL PERSPECTIVE 2-1

Investment and economic growth, selected countries

Nations that invest large portions of their national outputs tend to enjoy high growth rates, measured here by output per person. Additional capital goods make workers more productive, and this means greater output per person.

Source: International Monetary Fund data, as reported in *Economic Report of the President, 1994*, p. 37.

and environmentalists trying to save that area's spotted owls. Envision a production possibilities curve with "lumber production" on one axis and "spotted owls" on the other. It so happens that the spotted owl depends on the mature trees in national forests for nests and survival. Increasing the output of lumber limits the owl's habitat, destroys the species, and thus reduces environmental quality. Maintaining the mature forests preserves the owl but destroys thousands of jobs in the logging and lumber industry.

A second land-use example is the continuing debate on whether more Federal land in Alaska and the southwest should be included in the nation's system of national parks and monuments. Some of the land under question contains sizable oil, natural gas, and mineral deposits, but usually no drilling or mining is allowed in national parks and monuments. Here, the relevant production possibilities curve has "national parks and monuments" on one axis and "minerals" on the other. The concepts of resource scarcity, opportunity costs, and the necessity of choice again become quite apparent.

4. Destruction from War

In the early 1990s, Iraq invaded Kuwait to bring Kuwait's oil resources under Iraqi control. But a quick and decisive military response by the United States and its allies devastated Iraq's economy. Allied bombing inflicted great physical damage on Iraq's production facilities and its system of roads, bridges, and communications. Devastation of Iraq's human resources was also severe. Consequently, Iraq's production possibilities curve swiftly shifted inward.

5. Growth: Japan versus the United States

Since the 1950s, Japan has been investing more than 25 percent of its domestic output in productive machinery and equipment, compared with only about 10 percent for the United States. The consequences are in accord with our previous discussion. From 1960 to 1990, domestic output expanded at about 6.4 percent per year in Japan but only 3.2 percent in the United States. (Japan's production possibilities curve shifted outward twice as rapidly as did the U.S. curve.) In 1980 output per person in Japan was $16,711, compared with $17,643 in the United States; by 1995 these figures had changed to $39,640 and $26,980, respectively.

6. Famine in Africa

Modern industrial societies take economic growth—rightward shifts of the production possibilities curve—for granted. But periodic catastrophic famines in sub-Saharan nations of Africa show that in some circumstances the production possibilities curve may shift leftward. In addition to drought, a cause of African famines is ecological degradation—poor land-use practices. Land has been deforested, overfarmed, and overgrazed, causing the production possibilities of these highly agriculturally oriented countries to diminish. In fact, the per capita domestic outputs of most of these nations declined in the past decade or so.

7. Emerging Technologies

The world economies are experiencing a spurt of new technologies relating to computers, communications, and biotechnology. Technological advances have dropped the prices of computers and greatly enhanced their speed. Cellular phones, the Internet, and fax machines have increased communication capability, enhancing production and improving the efficiency of markets. Advances in biotechnology, specifically genetic engineering, have resulted in important agricultural and medical discoveries. Some observers believe that these new technologies are of such significance that they will ultimately contribute to faster economic growth than has occurred in the recent past (faster rightward shifts in nations' production possibilities curves).

ECONOMIC SYSTEMS

A society needs to select an **economic system**—*a particular set of institutional arrangements and a coordinating mechanism*—to respond to the economizing problem. Economic systems can differ as to (1) who owns the factors of production and (2) the method used to coordinate and direct economic activity.

Pure Capitalism

The private ownership of resources and the use of a system of markets and prices to coordinate and direct economic activity characterize *laissez-faire capitalism*, or **pure capitalism.** In such **market systems** each participant acts in his or her own self-interest; each individual or business seeks to maximize its satisfaction or profit through its own decisions regarding consumption or production. The system allows for the private ownership of capital, communicates through prices, and coordinates economic activity through *markets*—places where buyers and sellers come together. Goods and services are produced and resources are supplied by whomever is willing and able to do so. The result is competition among many small, independently acting buyers and sellers of each product and resource. Thus, economic power is widely dispersed.

Advocates of pure capitalism argue that such an economy promotes efficiency in the use of resources, stability of output and employment, and rapid economic growth. Hence, there is little or no need for government planning, control, or intervention. The term "laissez-faire" means "let it be," that is, keep government from interfering with the economy. The idea is that such interference will disturb the efficient working of the market system. Government's role is therefore limited to protecting private property and establishing an environment appropriate to the operation of the market system.

The Command Economy

The polar alternative to pure capitalism is the **command economy** or *communism*, characterized by public (government) ownership of virtually all property resources and economic decision making through central economic planning. All major decisions concerning the level of resource use, the composition and distribution of output, and the organization of production are determined by a central planning board appointed by government. Business firms are governmentally owned and produce according to government directives. The planning board determines production goals for each enterprise, and the plan specifies the amounts of resources to be allocated to each enterprise so that it can reach its production goals. The division of output between capital and consumer goods is centrally decided, and capital goods are allocated among industries on the basis of the central planning board's long-term priorities.

Mixed Systems

Pure capitalism and the command economy are extremes; real-world economies fall between the two. The U.S. economy leans toward pure capitalism, but with important differences. Government actively participates in the economy by promoting economic stability and growth, providing certain goods and services which would be underproduced or not produced at all by the market system, and modifying the distribution of income. In contrast to wide dispersion of economic power among many small units, as implied by pure capitalism, U.S. capitalism has spawned a number of very powerful economic organizations in the form of large corporations and labor unions. The ability of these power blocs to manipulate some markets to their advantage is a further reason for government involvement in the economy.

While the former Soviet Union historically approximated the command economy, it relied to some extent on market-determined prices and had some private ownership. Recent reforms in the former Soviet Union, China, and most of the eastern European nations have moved these economies toward more capitalistic, market-oriented systems.

North Korea and Cuba are the best remaining examples of centrally planned economies.

But private ownership and reliance on the market system do not always go together, nor do state ownership and central planning. For example, the fascism of Hitler's Nazi Germany has been dubbed *authoritarian capitalism* because the economy had a high degree of governmental control and direction but property was privately owned. In contrast, the present economic system of China might be called *market socialism.* It is characterized by extensive government ownership of natural resources and capital coupled with considerable reliance on free markets to organize and coordinate some parts of economic activity. The Swedish economy is also a hybrid system. Although more than 90 percent of Sweden's business activity is in private hands, government is deeply involved in redistributing income. Similarly, the capitalistic Japanese economy involves much planning and coordination between government and the business sector.

The Traditional Economy

Some developing countries have customary or **traditional economies,** in which production methods, exchange of goods, and distribution of income are all sanctioned by custom. Heredity and caste dictate the economic roles of individuals, and changes in socioeconomic status are rare. Technological change may also be constrained because it clashes with tradition and threatens the social fabric. Economic activity is often secondary to religious and cultural values and society's desire to perpetuate the status quo.

The main point here is that there is no unique or universally accepted way to respond to the economizing problem. Various societies, having different cultural and historical backgrounds, different mores and customs, and contrasting ideological frameworks—not to mention a great diversity of resources—use different institutions to deal with the reality of scarcity. The best method for responding to this reality in one society may or may not be appropriate in another society.

THE CIRCULAR FLOW MODEL

Because market systems now dominate the world economy, our focus in the remainder of this chapter, and the two following, is on how nations use markets to respond to the economizing problem. Our goal in this last section is modest: We want to identify the major groups of decision makers and the major markets in the market system. Our tool is the circular flow diagram.

Resource and Product Markets

Figure 2-6 (Key Graph) shows two groups of decision makers: households and businesses. (Government will be added as a third decision maker in Chapter 5.) The coordinating mechanism which aligns the decisions of households and businesses is the market system, in particular resource and product markets.

The upper half of the diagram portrays the **resource market,** *the place where resources or the services of resource suppliers are bought and sold.* Households (that is, people) either own all economic resources directly or own them indirectly through their ownership of business corporations. These households *supply* their resources to businesses. Businesses *demand* resources because resources are necessary for producing goods and services. The interaction of the demand for and supply of the immense variety of human and property resources establishes the price of each resource. The payments which businesses make to obtain resources are costs to businesses, but those payments simultaneously are flows of wage, rent, interest, and profit income to the households supplying the resources. Thus resources flow from households to businesses, and money flows from businesses to households.

Now consider the **product market,** *the place where goods and services of businesses are bought and sold,* depicted in the bottom half of the diagram. The money income received by households from the sale of resources does not, as such, have real value. Consumers cannot eat or wear coins and paper money. But they can spend their money for goods and services. And by their willingness to spend money income, households express their *demand* for a vast variety of goods and services. Simultaneously, businesses combine the resources they have obtained to produce and *supply* these goods and services. The interaction of consumer demand and business supply decisions determines product prices. The flow of consumer expenditures for goods and services constitutes sales revenues for businesses.

This **circular flow model** suggests a complex, interrelated web of decision making and economic activity. Note that households and businesses participate in both basic markets, but on different sides of each. Businesses are on the buying or demand side of resource markets, and households (as resource owners and suppliers) are on the selling or supply side. In the product market, these positions are reversed; households are on the buying or demand side, and businesses on the selling or supply side. Each group of economic units both buys and sells.

Moreover, the specter of scarcity haunts these transactions. Because households have only limited amounts of resources to supply to businesses, consumers' money incomes are limited, which means that each consumer's income will go only so far. A limited amount of money income clearly will not permit the purchase of all the goods and services the consumer might like to buy. Similarly, because resources are scarce, the output of finished goods and services is also necessarily limited.

To summarize: In a monetary economy, households, as resource owners, sell their resources to businesses and, as consumers, spend the resource income by buying goods and services. Businesses must buy resources to produce goods and services; their finished products are then sold to households in exchange for consumption expenditures or, as business sees it, revenues. These revenues are used to purchase additional resources to maintain the circular flow. The net result is, in Figure 2-6, a counterclockwise *real flow* of economic resources and finished goods and services, and a clockwise *money flow* of income and consumption expenditures. These flows are simultaneous and repetitive.

Limitations

Our model simplifies in many ways. Transactions between households and between businesses are concealed. Government and the "rest of the world" are ignored as decision makers. The model implies constant flows of output and income, while in fact these flows vary over time. Nor is the circular flow a perpetual-motion machine; production exhausts human energies and absorbs physical resources, the latter creating potential problems of environmental pollution. Finally, our model does not explain how product and resource prices are actually determined. We turn to this last topic in Chapter 3.

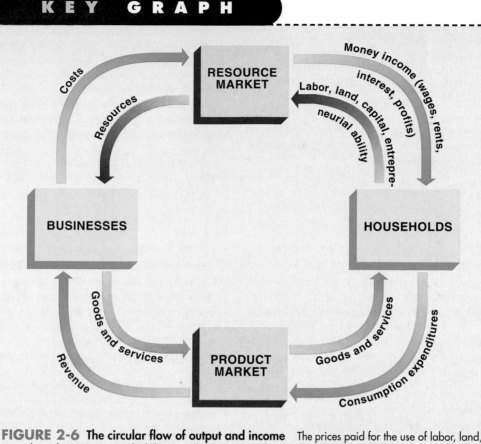

FIGURE 2-6 The circular flow of output and income The prices paid for the use of labor, land, capital, and entrepreneurial ability are determined in the resource market shown in the upper loop. Businesses are on the demand side and households are on the supply side of this market. The prices of finished goods and services are determined in the product market shown in the lower loop. Households are on the demand side and businesses are on the supply side of this market.

Q U I C K   Q U I Z   2 - 6

1. The resource market is where:
   a. households sell products and businesses buy products.
   b. businesses sell resources and households sell products.
   c. households sell resources and businesses buy resources (or the services of resources).
   d. businesses sell resources and households buy resources (or the services of resources).

2. Which of the following would be determined in the product market?
   a. a manager's salary.
   b. the price of equipment used in a bottling plant.
   c. the price of 80 acres of farmland.
   d. the price of a new pair of athletic shoes.

3. In this circular flow diagram:
   a. money flows counterclockwise.
   b. resources flow counterclockwise.
   c. goods and services flow clockwise.
   d. households are on the supply side of the product market.

4. In this circular flow diagram:
   a. households spend income in the product market.
   b. firms supply resources to households.
   c. households receive income through the product market.
   d. households produce goods.

Answers: 1. c; 2. d; 3. b; 4. a

Women and Expanded Production Possibilities

A large increase in the number of employed women has shifted the U.S. production possibilities curve outward.

One of the more remarkable trends of the past half-century in the United States has been the substantial rise in the number of women working in the paid workforce. Today, nearly 60 percent of women work full- or part-time in paid jobs, compared to only 40 percent in 1965. There are many reasons for this increase.

1. Women's Rising Wage Rates Women have acquired more education and skill training, which have greatly increased their productivity in the workplace. As a result, the wages women can earn in the labor market have increased rapidly over time. These higher wages have boosted women's opportunity costs—the forgone wage earnings—of staying at home. In response, women have substituted labor market employment for now more "expensive" home activities. This substitution has been particularly pronounced for married women.

Higher wages for women have produced other reallocations of time and purchasing patterns to facilitate labor market work. Day care services have partly replaced personal childcare. Restaurant meals, fast food, prepared take-home meals, and pizza delivery now substitute for elaborate homemade family meals. Convenience stores

and catalog sales have proliferated, as have lawn-care and in-home cleaning services. Shorter family vacations by airplane have replaced longer cross-country trips by car. Microwave ovens, dishwashers, automatic washers and dryers, and other household "capital goods" are now commonly used to enhance productivity in the home. These and similar household adjustments have helped make labor force participation more attractive for women.

2. Expanded Job Accessibility Greater accessibility to jobs, as distinct from higher pay, is a second factor boosting the employment of women. Service industries which traditionally have employed mainly women have expanded both absolutely and relatively in the past several decades. A growing demand for teachers, nurses, secretarial workers, salesclerks, and other service jobs has attracted many women to the labor market. Also, population has shifted from farms and rural regions to urban areas, where jobs for women are more abundant and geographically accessible. Finally, the decline in the average length of the workweek, together with an increased availability of part-time jobs, have made it easier for women to combine labor market employment with child-rearing and household activities.

3. Changing Preferences and Attitudes Women as a group have changed their preferences from household activities to labor market employment. An increasing number of women have found personal fulfillment in jobs, careers, and earnings. More broadly, most industrial societies now widely accept and encourage labor force participation by married women, including women with preschool children. Today about 60 percent of American mothers with preschool children participate in the labor force, compared to only 30 percent in 1970. More than

CHAPTER SUMMARY

1. Economics is grounded on two basic facts: **(a)** human material wants are virtually unlimited; **(b)** economic resources are scarce.

2. Economic resources may be classified as property resources—raw materials and capital—or as human resources—labor and entrepreneurial ability. These resources (land, capital, labor, and entrepreneurial ability) are the factors of production.

3. Economics is concerned with the problem of using or managing scarce resources to produce goods and services which fulfill the material wants of society. Both full em-

ployment and efficient use of available resources are essential to maximize want satisfaction.

4. Efficient use of resources consists of productive efficiency (producing all output combinations in the least costly way) and allocative efficiency (producing the specific output mix most desired by society).

5. An economy which is achieving full employment and productive efficiency—that is, operating on its production possibilities curve—must sacrifice the output of some types of goods and services to achieve increased production of others. Because resources are not equally produc-half of today's employed mothers return to work before their youngest child is 2 years old.

4. Declining Birthrates There were 3.8 lifetime births per woman in 1957 at the peak of the baby boom, but that number is less than 2 today. This marked decline in the typical family size has freed up time for greater labor force participation since child rearing and associated homemaking activities are time-consuming. Not only do women now have fewer children, but these children are also spaced closer together in age. Thus, women who leave their jobs during their children's early years can return to the labor force sooner.

The decline in birthrates has resulted from the widespread availability and use of birth control methods, coupled with changing lifestyles. But higher wage rates have also been at work. Women with relatively high wage earnings, on average, have fewer children than women with lower earnings. The opportunity cost of children—the income sacrificed by not being employed—rises as wage earnings rise. In the language of economics, the higher "price" associated with children has reduced the "quantity of children demanded."

5. Rising Divorce Rates Marital instability, as evidenced by high divorce rates in the 1970s and 1980s, may have motivated many women to establish and maintain labor market ties. The economic impact of divorce on nonworking women is often disastrous because alimony and child support are not always forthcoming. Most previously nonworking women enter the labor force following divorce. And married women—perhaps even women contemplating marriage—increasingly may have participated in the labor force to protect themselves against the financial difficulties of potential divorce.

6. Stagnating Male Earnings A final factor explaining the rise in the women's labor force participation rate is that men's real earnings have risen very slowly in the past two decades, particularly for men without college degrees. This stagnation has motivated many wives to enter the labor force to maintain family living standards. If wives had not entered the labor force in record numbers in the past two decades, many households would have suffered absolute or relative declines in their real incomes.

Together, these factors have produced a rapid rise in the availability of women workers in the United States. This increase in the *quantity of resources* has helped push the U.S. production possibilities curve outward. That is, it has greatly contributed to U.S. economic growth.

---

tive in all possible uses, shifting resources from one use to another brings the law of increasing opportunity costs into play. The production of additional units of a product entails the sacrifice of *increasing* amounts of the other product.

6. Allocative efficiency means operating at the optimal point on the production possibilities curve. That point represents the highest-valued mix of goods and is determined by expanding the production of each good until its marginal benefit (MB) equals its marginal cost (MC).

7. Over time, technological advance and increases in the quantity and quality of resources allow the economy to produce more of all goods and services—to experience economic growth. Society's choice as to the mix of con-

sumer goods and capital goods in current output is a major determinant of the future location of the production possibilities curve and thus of economic growth.

8. The various economic systems of the world differ in their ideologies and also in their responses to the economizing problem. Basic differences center on **(a)** whether most resources are owned by government or held privately and **(b)** whether economic activity is coordinated mainly by a market system or by central planning.

9. The circular flow model provides an overview of the operation of the capitalist system. This simple model locates the product and resource markets and shows the major income-expenditure flows and resource-output flows that constitute the lifeblood of the capitalistic economy.

TERMS AND CONCEPTS

economizing problem
utility
economic resources
land
capital
investment
labor
entrepreneurial ability

factors of
    production
full employment
full production
productive efficiency
allocative efficiency
consumer goods
capital goods

production possibilities
    table
production possibilities
    curve
opportunity cost
law of increasing
    opportunity costs
economic growth

economic system
pure capitalism
market systems
command economy
traditional economies
resource market
product market
circular flow model

STUDY QUESTIONS

1. Explain this statement: "If resources were unlimited and freely available, there would be no subject called *economics*."

2. Comment on the following statement from a newspaper article: "Our junior high school serves a splendid hot meal for $1 without costing the taxpayers anything, thanks in part to a government subsidy."

3. Critically analyze: "Wants aren't insatiable. I can prove it. I get all the coffee I want to drink every morning at breakfast." Explain: "Goods and services are scarce because resources are scarce." Analyze: "It is the nature of all economic problems that absolute solutions are denied to us."

4. What are economic resources? What are the major functions of the entrepreneur?

5. KEY QUESTION Why is the problem of unemployment part of the subject matter of economics? Distinguish between productive efficiency and allocative efficiency. Give an illustration of achieving productive, but not allocative, efficiency.

6. KEY QUESTION Here is a production possibilities table for war goods and civilian goods:

	Production alternatives				
Type of production	A	B	C	D	E
Automobiles	0	2	4	6	8
Rockets	30	27	21	12	0

   a. Show these data graphically. Upon what specific assumptions is this production possibilities curve based?

   b. If the economy is at point C, what is the cost of one more automobile? One more rocket? Explain how the production possibilities curve reflects the law of increasing opportunity costs.

   c. What must the economy do to operate at some point on the production possibilities curve?

7. What is the opportunity cost of attending college?

8. Suppose you arrive at a store expecting to pay $100 for an item but learn that a store 2 miles away is charging $50 for it. Would you drive there and buy it? How does your decision benefit you? What is the opportunity cost of your decision? Now suppose that you arrive at a store expecting to pay $6000 for an item but learn that it costs $5950 at the other store. Do you make the same decision as before? Perhaps surprisingly, you should! Explain why.

9. KEY QUESTION Specify and explain the shapes of the marginal-benefit and marginal-cost curves. How are these curves used to determine the optimal allocation of resources to a particular product? If current output is such that marginal cost exceeds marginal benefit, should more or fewer resources be allocated to this product? Explain.

10. KEY QUESTION Label point G inside the production possibilities curve you drew in question 6. What does it indicate? Label point H outside the curve. What does that point represent? What must occur before the economy can attain the level of production shown by point H?

11. KEY QUESTION Referring again to question 6, suppose improvement occurs in the technology of producing rockets but not in the production of automobiles. Draw the new production possibilities curve. Now assume that a technological advance occurs in producing automobiles but not in producing rockets. Draw the new production possibilities curve. Now draw a production possibilities curve which reflects technological improvement in the production of both products.

12. Explain how, if at all, each of the following affects the location of the production possibilities curve:

    a. Standardized examination scores of high school and college students decline.

    b. The unemployment rate falls from 9 to 6 percent of the labor force.

    c. Defense spending is reduced to allow government to spend more on health care.

    d. Society decides it wants compact discs rather than long-playing records.

    e. A new technique improves the efficiency of extracting copper from ore.

    f. A new baby boom increases the size of the nation's workforce.

13. Explain: "Affluence tomorrow requires sacrifice today."

14. Suppose that, based on a nation's production possibilities curve, an economy must sacrifice 10,000 pizzas domestically to get the 1 additional industrial robot it desires but that it can get the robot from another country in exchange for 9000 pizzas. Relate this information to the following statement: "Through international specialization and trade, a nation can reduce its opportunity cost of obtaining goods and thus 'get outside its production possibilities curve.'"

15. Contrast how pure capitalism and a command economy try to cope with economic scarcity.

16. Explain this statement: "Although the United States has a capitalist economy, *not* a traditional economy,

traditions (for example, weddings, Christmas, and Halloween) play an important role in determining what goods get produced."

17. Portray the major features of the circular flow model. In what way are businesses and households both *suppliers* and *demanders* in this model? Explain how scarcity enters the model.

18. **(Last Word)** Which *two* of the six reasons listed in the Last Word do you think are the *most important* in explaining the rise in participation of women in the workplace? Explain your reasoning.

19. **WEB-BASED QUESTION** Different Geographical Areas and Outputs—Japan and the United States Compared to the United States, Japan has 4 percent of the geographical area (slightly smaller than California) and 47 percent of the population (1996 estimates). Other things equal, Japan should have far less than 47 percent of the U.S. output. Visit the OECD (Organization for Economic Cooperation and Development) http://www.oecd.org/std/gdp.htm and calculate the ratio of Japan's gross domestic product (a measure of national output) to the gross domestic product of the United States. Is the ratio above or below 47 percent? What might explain this difference?

20. **WEB-BASED QUESTION** Increasing Productivity in Hong Kong The Hong Kong Productivity Council http://hkpcms.hkpc.org/ was established in 1967 to promote increased productivity. Its mission is "to achieve a more effective utilization of available resources and to enhance the value-added content of products and services. The aim is to increase efficiency and competitiveness, thereby contributing to raising the standard of living of people in Hong Kong." How does the Council define productivity, and how does it try to increase it?

3

Understanding Individual Markets: Demand and Supply

According to an old joke, if you teach a parrot to say "Demand and supply," you have an economist. There is an element of truth in this quip. The tools of demand and supply can take us far in understanding not only specific economic issues but also how the entire economy works.

Our circular flow model in Chapter 2 identified the participants in the product and resource markets. There, we asserted that prices were determined by the "interaction" between demand and supply in these markets. In this chapter we examine that interaction in detail, explaining how prices and output quantities are determined.

MARKETS

Recall from Chapter 2 that a **market** is *an institution or mechanism which brings together buyers ("demanders") and sellers ("suppliers") of particular goods, services, or resources.* Markets exist in many forms. The corner gas station, the fast-food outlet, the local music store, a farmer's roadside stand—all are familiar markets. The New York Stock Exchange and the Chicago Board of Trade are markets where buyers and sellers of stocks and bonds and farm commodities from all over the world communicate with one another and buy and sell. Auctioneers bring together potential buyers and sellers of art, livestock, used farm equipment, and, sometimes, real estate. The all-American quarterback and his agent bargain with the owner of an NFL team. A graduating finance major interviews with Citicorp or Wells Fargo at the university placement office.

All these situations which link potential buyers with potential sellers are markets. As our examples imply, some markets are local, while others are national or international. Some are highly personal, involving face-to-face contact between demander and supplier; others are impersonal, with buyer and seller never seeing or knowing each other.

To keep things simple, this chapter focuses on markets consisting of large numbers of independently acting buyers and sellers exchanging a standardized product. These are the highly competitive markets such as a central grain exchange, a stock market, or a market for foreign currencies in which the equilibrium price is "discovered" by the interacting decisions of buyers and sellers. They are *not* the markets in which one or a handful of producers "set" prices, such as the markets for commercial airplanes or greeting cards.

DEMAND

Demand is *a schedule or a curve showing the various amounts of a product consumers are willing and able to purchase at each of a series of possible prices during a specified period of time.*[1] Demand, therefore, shows the quantities of a product which will be purchased at various possible prices, *other things equal.* Demand can easily be shown in table form. Table 3-1 is a hypothetical **demand schedule** for a single consumer purchasing bushels of corn.

The portrayal of demand in Table 3-1 reflects the relationship between the possible prices of corn and the quantity of corn the consumer would be willing and able to purchase at each of these prices. We say willing and *able* because willingness alone is not effective in the market. You may be willing to buy a Porsche, but if this willingness is not backed by the necessary dollars, it will not be effective and, therefore, not be reflected in the market. In Table 3-1, if the price of corn were $5 per bushel, our consumer would be willing and able to buy 10 bushels per week; if it were $4, the consumer would be willing and able to buy 20 bushels per week; and so forth.

The table showing demand does not tell us which of the five possible prices will actually exist in the corn market. This depends on demand *and supply.* Demand is simply a statement of a buyer's plans, or intentions, with respect to the purchase of a product.

To be meaningful, the quantities demanded at each price must relate to a specific period—a day, a week, a month. Saying "A consumer will buy 10 bushels of corn at $5 per bushel" is meaningless. Saying "A consumer will buy 10 bushels of corn *per week* at $5 per bushel" is clear and meaningful. Without a specific time period we would not know whether demand for a product was large or small.

Law of Demand

A fundamental characteristic of demand is this: *All else equal, as price falls, the quantity demanded rises, and as price rises, the corresponding quantity demanded falls.* In short, there is a negative or *inverse* relationship between price and quantity demanded. Economists call this inverse relationship the **law of demand.**

---

[1]This definition obviously is worded to apply to product markets. To adjust it to apply to resource markets, substitute the word "resource" for "product" and the word "businesses" for "consumers."

TABLE 3-1   An individual buyer's demand for corn

Price per bushel	Quantity demanded per week
$5	10
4	20
3	35
2	55
1	80

The "other things equal" assumption is critical here. Many factors other than the price of the product being considered affect the amount purchased. The quantity of Nikes purchased will depend not only on the price of Nikes but also on the prices of such substitutes as Reeboks, Adidas, and Filas. The law of demand in this case says that fewer Nikes will be purchased if the price of Nikes rises *and the prices of Reeboks, Adidas, and Filas all remain constant.* In short, if the *relative price* of Nikes increases, fewer Nikes will be bought. However, if the price of Nikes and all other competing shoes increase by some amount— say, $5—consumers might buy more, less, or the same amount of Nikes.

What is the foundation for the law of demand? There are several levels of analysis on which to argue the case. Let's look at three of them:

1. Common sense and simple observation are consistent with the law of demand. People ordinarily *do* buy more of a product at a low price than at a high price. Price is an obstacle which deters consumers from buying. The higher this obstacle, the less of a product they will buy; the lower price obstacle, the more they will buy. The fact that businesses have "sales" is evidence of their belief in the law of demand. Businesses reduce their inventories by lowering prices, not by raising them.

2. In any specific time period, each buyer of a product will derive less satisfaction (or benefit or utility) from each successive unit of the good consumed. The second Big Mac will yield less satisfaction to the consumer than the first, and the third still less satisfaction than the second. That is, consumption is subject to **diminishing marginal utility.** And because successive units of a particular product yield less and less marginal utility, consumers will buy additional units only if the price of those units is reduced.

3. The law of demand can also be explained in terms of income and substitution effects. The **income effect** indicates that a lower price increases the purchasing power of a buyer's money income, enabling the buyer to purchase more of the product than she or he could buy before. A higher price has the opposite effect.

   The **substitution effect** suggests that at a lower price, buyers have the incentive to substitute the now cheaper good for similar goods which are now relatively more expensive. Consumers tend to substitute cheap products for dear products.

   For example, a decline in the price of beef will increase the purchasing power of consumer incomes, enabling them to buy more beef (the income effect). At a lower price, beef is relatively more attractive and is substituted for pork, mutton, chicken, and fish (the substitution effect). The income and substitution effects combine to make consumers able and willing to buy more of a product at a low price than at a high price.

The Demand Curve

The inverse relationship between price and quantity demanded for any product can be represented on a simple graph, in which, by convention, we measure *quantity demanded* on the horizontal axis and *price* on the vertical axis. In Figure 3-1 we have plotted the five price-quantity data points in Table 3-1 and con-nected them with a smooth curve, labeled *D*. Such a curve is called a **demand curve.** It slopes downward and to the right because the relationship it portrays between price and quantity demanded is inverse. The law of demand—people buy more at a low price than at a high price—is reflected in the downward slope of the demand curve.

   Table 3-1 and Figure 3-1 contain exactly the same data and reflect the same relationship between price and quantity demanded. But the advantage of a graph is that it shows the relationship more simply and clearly than a table or a description in words. Moreover, graphs allow us to very easily show the effects of *changes* in variables. Graphs are thus valuable tools in economic analysis.

Individual and Market Demand

Until now we have concentrated on just one consumer. But competition requires that many buyers are in each market. We can get from *individual* demand to *market* demand by adding the quantities demanded by all consumers at each of the various possible prices. If there are just three buyers in the market, as represented in Table 3-2, it is relatively easy to determine the total quantity demanded at each price. Figure 3-2 shows the graphical summing procedure: At each price we add the individual quantities demanded to obtain the total quantity demanded for that price; we then plot the price and total quantity as one point of the market demand curve.

FIGURE 3-1 An individual buyer's demand for corn An individual's demand schedule graphs as a downsloping curve such as *D* because price and quantity demanded are inversely related. Specifically, the law of demand generalizes that, other things equal, consumers will buy more of a product as its price declines. Here and in later figures, *P* stands for price, and *Q* stands for quantity (either demanded or supplied.)

TABLE 3-2   Market demand for corn, three buyers

Price per bushel	Quantity demanded			Total quantity demanded per week
	First buyer	Second buyer	Third buyer	
$5	10 +	12 +	8 =	30
4	20 +	23 +	17 =	60
3	35 +	39 +	26 =	100
2	55 +	60 +	39 =	154
1	80 +	87 +	54 =	221

Competition, of course, entails many more than three buyers of a product. To avoid hundreds or thousands or millions of additions, we suppose that all the buyers in a market are willing and able to buy the same amounts at each of the possible prices. Then we just multiply those amounts by the number of buyers to obtain the market demand. Curve D_1 in Figure 3-3 was obtained this way, for a market with 200 corn buyers whose demand is that in Table 3-1. Table 3-3 shows the calculations.

Determinants of Demand

An economist constructing a demand curve such as D_1 in Figure 3-3 assumes that price is the most important influence on the amount of any product purchased. But the economist knows that other factors can and do affect purchases. These factors are called **determinants of demand,** and they are assumed to be constant when a demand curve like D_1 is drawn. They are the "other things equal" in the relationship between price and quantity demanded. When any of these determinants changes, the location of the demand curve will shift to the right or left. For this reason, determinants of demand are sometimes referred to as *demand shifters.*

The basic determinants of demand are (1) consumers' tastes and preferences, (2) the number of consumers in the market, (3) consumers' money incomes, (4) the prices of related goods, and (5) consumer expectations about future prices and incomes.

Change in Demand

A change in one or more of the determinants of demand will change the demand data (the demand schedule) in Table 3-3 and therefore the location of the demand curve in Figure 3-3. A change in the demand schedule or, graphically, a shift in the location of the demand curve is called a *change in demand.*

If consumers become willing and able to buy more corn at each possible price than is reflected in column 4 in Table 3-3, this *increase in demand* means a shift of the demand curve to the *right,* say, from D_1 to D_2. Conversely, a *decrease in demand* occurs when consumers buy less corn at each possible price than is indicated in column 4, Table 3-3. Graphically, a decrease in demand is shown as a shift of the demand curve to the *left,* say, from D_1 to D_3 in Figure 3-3.

Let's now examine how changes in each determinant affect demand.

Tastes   A favorable change in consumer tastes or preferences for a product—one which makes the product more desirable—means that more of it will be demanded at each price. Demand will increase; the

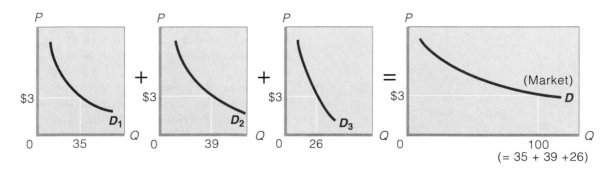

FIGURE 3-2 Market demand for corn, three buyers   The market demand curve *D* is found by adding horizontally the individual demand curves (D_1, D_2, and D_3) of all consumers in the market. At the price of $3, for example, the three individual curves yield a total quantity demanded of 100 bushels.

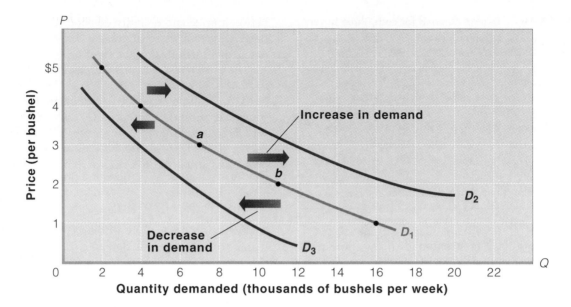

FIGURE 3-3 Changes in the demand for corn A change in one or more of the determinants of demand causes a change in demand. An increase in demand is shown as a shift of the demand curve to the right, as from D_1 to D_2. A decrease in demand is shown as a shift of the demand curve to the left, as from D_1 to D_3. These changes in demand are distinguished from a change in quantity demanded, which is caused by a change in the price of the product, as shown by a movement from, say, point a to point b on fixed demand curve D_1.

demand curve will shift rightward. An unfavorable change in consumer preferences will decrease demand, shifting the demand curve to the left.

New products can affect consumer tastes; for example, the introduction of compact discs has greatly decreased the demand for cassette tapes. Consumers concern about the health hazards of cholesterol and obesity have increased the demands for broccoli, low-calorie sweeteners, and fresh fruit while decreasing the demands for beef, veal, eggs, and whole milk. Over the past several years, the demands for light

trucks and sports utility vehicles have greatly increased, driven by a change in tastes. So, too, has the demand for bagels.

Number of Buyers An increase in the number of consumers in a market increases demand. A decrease in the number of consumers decreases demand. For example, improvements in communications have given financial markets international range, increasing demand for stocks and bonds. And the baby boom after World War II increased demand for diapers, baby lotion, and the services of obstetricians. When the baby boomers reached their 20s in the 1970s, the demand for housing increased. Conversely, the aging of the baby boomers in the 1980s and 1990s has been a factor in the relative slump in housing demand. Also, increasing life expectancy has increased demands for medical care, retirement communities, and nursing homes. And international trade agreements such as the North American Free Trade Agreement (NAFTA) and the General Agreement on Tariffs and Trade (GATT) have reduced foreign trade barriers to American farm products, increasing the demands for those products.

Income How changes in money income affect demand is more complex. For most commodities, a rise

TABLE 3-3   Market demand for corn, 200 buyers

(1) Price per bushel	(2) Quantity demanded per week, single buyer		(3) Number of buyers in the market		(4) Total quantity demanded per week
$5	10	×	200	=	2,000
4	20	×	200	=	4,000
3	35	×	200	=	7,000
2	55	×	200	=	11,000
1	80	×	200	=	16,000

in income causes an increase in demand. Consumers typically buy more steaks, sunscreen, and stereos as their incomes increase. Conversely, the demands for such products decline as incomes fall. Commodities whose demand varies *directly* with money income are called *superior*, or **normal, goods.**

Although most products are normal goods, there are a few exceptions. As incomes increase beyond some point, the amount of bread or lard or cabbages purchased at each price may diminish because higher incomes allow consumers to buy more high-protein foods, such as dairy products and meat. Rising incomes may also decrease the demands for used clothing and third-hand automobiles. Similarly, rising incomes may cause demands for hamburger and charcoal grilles to decline as wealthier consumers switch to T-bones and gas grilles. Goods whose demand varies *inversely* with money income are called **inferior goods.**

Prices of Related Goods A change in the price of a related good may increase or decrease the demand for a product, depending on whether the related good is a substitute or a complement. A **substitute good** is one that can be used in place of another good. A **complementary good** is one used together with another good.

Substitutes Beef and chicken are examples of substitute goods. When the price of beef rises, consumers buy less beef, increasing the demand for chicken. Conversely, as the price of beef falls, consumers buy more beef, decreasing the demand for chicken. *When two products are substitutes, the price of one and the demand for the other move in the same direction.* So it is with Nikes and Reeboks, sweaters and jackets, Toyotas and Hondas, and Coke and Pepsi.

Complements Complementary goods are used together and are usually demanded together. If the price of gasoline falls and, as a result, you drive your car more, this extra driving increases your demand for motor oil. Thus, gas and oil are jointly demanded; they are complements. So it is with ham and eggs, tuition and textbooks, movies and popcorn, cameras and film. *When two products are complements, the price of one good and the demand for the other good move in opposite directions.*

Unrelated Goods Many goods are not related to one another; they are *independent goods*. Examples are such pairs of goods as butter and golf balls, potatoes and automobiles, bananas and wristwatches. A change

in the price of one has little or no impact on the demand for the other.

Expectations Consumer expectations about future product prices, product availability, and future income can shift demand. Consumer expectations of higher future prices may prompt them to buy now to "beat" anticipated price rises, thus increasing today's demand. Similarly, the expectations of rising incomes may induce consumers to be freer in current spending. In contrast, the expectation of falling prices or falling income will decrease current demand for products.

First example: If freezing weather destroys much of Florida's citrus crop, consumers may reason that the price of orange juice will rise. They may stock up on orange juice by purchasing large quantities now.

Second example: In late 1993 there was a substantial increase in the demand for guns. Reason? The expectation that Congress would pass more stringent gun control laws.

Third example: A first-round NFL draft choice might splurge for a new Mercedes in anticipation of a lucrative professional football contract.

In summary, an *increase* in demand—the decision by consumers to buy larger quantities of a product at each possible price—can be caused by:

1. A favorable change in consumer tastes
2. An increase in the number of buyers
3. Rising incomes if the product is a normal good
4. Falling incomes if the product is an inferior good
5. An increase in the price of a substitute good
6. A decrease in the price of a complementary good
7. Consumer expectations of higher future prices and incomes

Be sure you can "reverse" these generalizations to explain a *decrease* in demand. Table 3-4 provides additional illustrations to reinforce your understanding of the determinants of demand. **(Key Question 2)**

Changes in Quantity Demanded

A *change in demand* must not be confused with a *change in quantity demanded.* A **change in demand** is a shift of the entire curve to the right (an increase in demand) or to the left (a decrease in demand). It occurs because the consumer's state of mind about purchasing the product has been altered. The cause is a change in one or more of the determinants of demand. Recall that "demand" is a schedule or curve; therefore, a "change in demand" means a change in the entire schedule and a shift of the entire curve.

TABLE 3-4   Determinants of demand: factors which shift the demand curve

Determinant	Examples
Change in buyer tastes	Physical fitness increases in popularity, increasing the demand for jogging shoes and bicycles.
Change in number of buyers	Japan reduces import quotas on U.S. telecommunications equipment, increasing the demand for it; a birthrate decline reduces the demand for education.
Change in income	An increase in incomes increases the demand for such normal goods as butter, lobster, and filet mignon while reducing the demand for such inferior goods as cabbage, turnips, retreaded tires, and used clothing.
Change in the prices of related goods	A reduction in airfares reduces the demand for bus transportation (substitute goods); a decline in the price of compact disc players increases the demand for compact discs (complementary goods).
Change in expectations	Inclement weather in South America causes the expectation of higher future coffee prices, thereby increasing the current demand for coffee.

In contrast, a **change in quantity demanded** designates the movement from one point to another point—from one price-quantity combination to another—on a fixed demand schedule or demand curve. The cause of such a change is an increase or decrease in the price of the product being considered. In Table 3-3, for example, a decline in the price from $5 to $4 will increase the quantity of corn demanded from 2000 to 4000 bushels.

In Figure 3-3 the shift of the demand curve D_1 to either D_2 or D_3 is a change in demand. But the movement from point a to point b on curve D_1 represents a change in quantity demanded: demand has not changed; it is the entire curve, and it remains fixed in place.

QUICK REVIEW 3-1

■ A market is any arrangement which facilitates the purchase and sale of goods, services, and resources.

■ Demand is a schedule or a curve showing the amount of a product buyers are willing and able to purchase at each potential price in a series of prices.

■ The law of demand states that, other things equal, the quantity of a good purchased varies inversely with its price.

■ The demand curve shifts because of changes in **(a)** consumer tastes, **(b)** the number of buyers in the market, **(c)** incomes, **(d)** the prices of substitute or complementary goods, and **(e)** expectations.

■ A change in demand is a shift of the entire demand curve; a change in quantity demanded is a movement from one point to another on a firm's stable demand curve.

SUPPLY

Supply is *a schedule or curve showing the amounts of a product a producer is willing and able to produce and make available for sale at each of a series of possible prices during a specific period.*[2] Table 3-5 is a hypothetical **supply schedule** for a single producer of corn. It shows the quantities of corn which will be supplied at various prices, other things equal.

---

[2]This definition is worded to apply to product markets. To adjust it to apply to resource markets, substitute "resource" for "product" and change "owner" to "producer."

TABLE 3-5   An individual producer's supply of corn

Price per bushel	Quantity supplied per week
$5	60
4	50
3	35
2	20
1	5

Law of Supply

Table 3-5 shows a positive or direct relationship between price and quantity supplied. *As price rises, the corresponding quantity supplied rises; as price falls, the quantity supplied falls.* This particular relationship is called the **law of supply.** A supply schedule tells us that firms will produce and offer for sale more of their product at a high price than at a low price. This, again, is basically common sense.

Price is an obstacle from the standpoint of the consumer, who is on the paying end. The higher the price, the less the consumer will buy. But the supplier is on the receiving end of the product's price. To a supplier, price represents *revenue* and thus is an incentive to produce and sell a product. The higher the price, the greater this incentive and the greater the quantity supplied.

Consider a farmer who can shift resources among alternative products. As price moves up in Table 3-5, the farmer finds it profitable to take land out of wheat, oats, and soybean production and put it into corn. And the higher corn prices allow the farmer to cover the increased costs associated with more intensive cultivation and the use of more seed, fertilizer, and pesticides. The overall result is more corn.

Now consider a manufacturer. Beyond some production quantity, manufacturers usually encounter increasing costs per added unit of output. Certain productive resources—in particular, the firm's plant and machinery—cannot be expanded quickly. So the firm uses more of the other resources, such as labor, to produce more output. But at some point the existing plant becomes increasingly crowded and congested, meaning that each added worker produces less added output. As a result, the cost of successive units of output rises. The firm will not produce these more costly units unless it receives a higher price for them. Again, price and quantity supplied are directly related.

The Supply Curve

As with demand, it is convenient to represent supply graphically. In Figure 3-4, curve S_1 is a graph of the market supply data in Table 3-6. Those data assume there are 200 suppliers in the market, each willing and able to supply corn according to Table 3-5. That is, we obtain the market **supply curve** by horizontally adding the supply curves of the individual producers. Note that the axes in Figure 3-4 are the same as those used in our graph of market demand, except for the change from "quantity demanded" to "quantity supplied" on the horizontal axis.

Determinants of Supply

In constructing a supply curve, the economist assumes that price is the most significant influence on the quantity supplied of any product. But other factors (the "other things equal") can and do affect supply. The supply curve is drawn assuming that these other things are fixed and do not change. If any of them does change, a *change in supply* will occur—the entire supply curve will shift.

The basic **determinants of supply** are (1) resource prices, (2) the technique of production, (3) taxes and subsidies, (4) prices of other goods, (5) price expectations, and (6) the number of sellers in the market. A change in any one or more of these determinants of supply, or *supply shifters*, will move the supply curve for a product either to the right or to the left. A shift to the *right*, as from S_1 to S_2 in Figure 3-4, designates an *increase* in supply: Producers supply larger quantities of the product at each possible price. A shift to the *left*, as from S_1 to S_3, indicates a *decrease* in supply: Suppliers offer less output at each price.

Changes in Supply

Let's consider how changes in each of the determinants affect supply. As our discussion proceeds, remember that costs are a major factor underlying supply curves; anything that affects costs (other than changes in output itself) usually shifts the supply curve.

Resource Prices   The prices of the resources used in the production process help determine the costs of production incurred by firms. Higher *resource* prices raise production costs and, assuming a particular *product* price, squeeze profits. This reduction in profits reduces the incentive for firms to supply output at each product price. In contrast, lower resource prices

FIGURE 3-4 Changes in the supply of corn A change in one or more of the determinants of supply causes a change in supply. An increase in supply is shown as a rightward shift of the supply curve, as from S_1 to S_2. A decrease in supply is depicted as a leftward shift of the curve, as from S_1 to S_3. In contrast, a change in the quantity supplied is caused by a change in the product's price and is shown by a movement from one point to another, as from a to b, on a fixed supply curve.

----

induce firms to supply more output at each product price since production costs fall and profits expand.

It follows that a decrease in resource prices will increase supply, shifting the supply curve to the right. If prices of seed and fertilizer decrease, we can expect the supply of corn to increase. Conversely, an increase in resource prices will raise production costs and reduce supply, shifting the supply curve to the left. Increases in the prices of iron ore and coke will increase the cost of producing steel and reduce its supply.

Technology Improvements in technology enable firms to produce units of output with fewer resources. Because resources are costly, using fewer of them lowers production costs and increases supply. Example: Recent improvements in the fuel efficiency of aircraft engines have reduced the cost of providing passenger

air service. Thus, airlines now offer more air service than previously at each ticket price; the supply of air service has increased.

Taxes and Subsidies Businesses treat most taxes as costs. An increase in sales or property taxes will increase production costs and reduce supply. In contrast, subsidies are "taxes in reverse." If government subsidizes the production of a good, it in effect lowers production costs and increases supply.

Prices of Other Goods Firms producing a particular product, say, soccer balls, can sometimes use their plant and equipment to produce alternative goods, say, basketballs and volleyballs. Higher prices of these "other goods" may entice soccer ball producers to switch production to them in order to increase profits. This *substitution in production* results in a decline in the supply of soccer balls. Alternatively, lower prices of basketballs and volleyballs may entice producers of these goods to produce more soccer balls, increasing their supply.

Expectations Expectations about the future price of a product can affect the producer's current willingness to supply that product. It is difficult, however, to generalize about how the expectation of higher prices affects the present supply of a product. Farmers anticipating a higher corn price in the future might withhold some of their current corn harvest from the market, which would cause a decrease in the current supply of corn. Similarly, if the price of Intel stock is expected to rise significantly in the near future, the supply offered for sale today might decrease. In contrast, in many types of manufacturing industries, ex-

TABLE 3-6   Market supply of corn, 200 producers

(1) Price per bushel	(2) Quantity supplied per week, single producer		(3) Number of sellers in the market		(4) Total quantity supplied per week
$5	60	×	200	=	12,000
4	50	×	200	=	10,000
3	35	×	200	=	7,000
2	20	×	200	=	4,000
1	5	×	200	=	1,000

pected price increases may induce firms to add another shift of workers or expand their production facilities, causing current supply to increase.

Number of Sellers   Other things equal, the larger the number of suppliers, the greater the market supply. As more firms enter an industry, the supply curve shifts to the right. Conversely, the smaller the number of firms in the industry, the less the market supply. This means that as firms leave an industry, the supply curve shifts to the left. Example: The United States and Canada have imposed restrictions on haddock fishing to replenish dwindling stocks. As part of that policy, the Federal government has bought the boats of some of the haddock fishermen as a way of putting them out of business and decreasing the catch. The result has been a decline in the market supply of haddock.

Table 3-7 is a checklist of the determinants of supply, along with further illustrations. **(Key Question 5)**

Changes in Quantity Supplied

The distinction between a *change in supply* and a *change in quantity supplied* parallels that between a change in demand and a change in quantity demanded. Because supply is a schedule or curve, a **change in supply** means a change in the entire schedule and a shift of the entire curve. An increase in supply shifts the curve to the right; a decrease in supply shifts it to the left. The cause of a change in supply is a change in one or more of the determinants of supply.

In contrast, a **change in quantity supplied** is a movement from one point to another on a fixed supply curve. The cause of such a movement is a change in the price of the specific product being considered. In Table 3-6, a decline in the price of corn from $5 to $4 decreases the quantity of corn supplied from 12,000 to 10,000 bushels. This is a change in quantity supplied, not a change in supply. Supply is the full schedule of prices and quantities shown, and this schedule does not change when price changes.

QUICK REVIEW 3-2

■ A supply schedule or curve shows that, other things equal, the quantity of a good supplied varies directly with its price.

■ The supply curve shifts because of changes in **(a)** resources prices, **(b)** technology, **(c)** taxes or subsidies, **(d)** prices of other goods, **(e)** expectations of future prices, and **(f)** the number of suppliers.

■ A change in supply is a shift of the supply curve; a change in quantity supplied is a movement from one point to another on a fixed supply curve.

TABLE 3-7   Determinants of supply: factors which shift the supply curve

Determinant	Examples
Change in resource prices	A decline in the price of fertilizer increases the supply of wheat; an increase in the price of irrigation equipment reduces the supply of corn.
Change in technology	The development of a more effective insecticide for corn rootworm increases the supply of corn.
Changes in taxes and subsidies	An increase in the excise tax on cigarettes reduces the supply of cigarettes; a decline in subsidies to state universities reduces the supply of higher education.
Change in prices of other goods	A decline in the prices of mutton and pork increases the supply of beef.
Change in expectations	Expectations of substantial declines in future oil prices cause oil companies to increase current supply.
Change in number of suppliers	An increase in the number of firms producing personal computers increases the supply of personal computers; formation of women's professional basketball leagues increases the supply of women's professional basketball games.

SUPPLY AND DEMAND: MARKET EQUILIBRIUM

We can now bring together supply and demand to see how the buying decisions of households and the selling decisions of businesses interact to determine the price of a product and the quantity actually bought and sold. In Table 3-8, columns 1 and 2 repeat the market supply of corn (from Table 3-6), and columns 2 and 3 repeat the market demand for corn (from Table 3-3). Note that column 2 lists a common set of prices. We assume competition—a large number of buyers and sellers.

Surpluses

We have limited our examples to only five possible prices. Of these, which will actually prevail as the market price for corn? We can find an answer through trial and error; for no particular reason, let's start with $5. We immediately see that this cannot be the prevailing market price. At the $5 price, producers are willing to produce and offer for sale 12,000 bushels of corn, but buyers are willing to buy only 2000 bushels. The $5 price encourages farmers to produce lots of corn but discourages most consumers from buying it. The result is a 10,000-bushel **surplus** or *excess supply* of corn. This surplus, shown in column 4 in Table 3-8, is the excess of quantity supplied over quantity demanded at $5. Corn farmers would find themselves with 10,000 unsold bushels of output.

A price of $5—even if it existed temporarily in the corn market—could not persist over a period of time. The very large surplus of corn would prompt com-

peting sellers to lower the price to encourage buyers to take the surplus off their hands.

Suppose the price goes down to $4. The lower price encourages consumers to buy more corn and, at the same time, induces farmers to offer less of it for sale. The surplus diminishes to 6000 bushels. Nevertheless, since there is still a surplus, competition among sellers will once again reduce the price. Clearly, then, the prices of $5 and $4 are unstable—they will not survive—because they are "too high." The market price of corn must be less than $4.

Shortages

Let's jump now to $1 as the possible market price of corn. Observe in column 4 in Table 3-8 that at this price, quantity demanded exceeds quantity supplied by 15,000 units. The $1 price discourages farmers from devoting resources to corn production and encourages consumers to attempt to buy more than is available. The result is a 15,000-bushel **shortage** of, or *excess demand* for, corn. The $1 price cannot persist as the market price. Many consumers who are willing and able to buy at this price will not get corn. They will express a willingness to pay more than $1 to get some of the available output. Competition among these buyers will drive up the price to something greater than $1.

Suppose the competition among buyers boosts the price to $2. This higher price reduces, but does not eliminate, the shortage of corn. For $2, farmers devote more resources to corn production, and some buyers who were willing to pay $1 per bushel choose not to buy corn at $2. But a shortage of 7000 bushels still exists at $2. This shortage will push the market price above $2.

Equilibrium Price and Quantity

By trial and error we have eliminated every price but $3. At $3, *and only at this price*, the quantity of corn that farmers are willing to produce and supply is identical with the quantity consumers are willing and able to buy. There is neither a shortage nor a surplus of corn at that price.

With no shortage or surplus at $3, there is no reason for the price of corn to change. Economists call this price the *market-clearing* or **equilibrium price,** equilibrium meaning "in balance" or "at rest." At $3, quantity supplied and quantity demanded are in balance at the **equilibrium quantity** of 7000 bushels. So

TABLE 3-8   Market supply of and demand for corn

(1) Total quantity supplied per week	(2) Price per bushel	(3) Total quantity demanded per week	(4) Surplus (+) or shortage (−)
12,000	$5	2,000	+10,000↓
10,000	4	4,000	+6,000↓
7,000	3	7,000	0
4,000	2	11,000	−7,000↑
1,000	1	16,000	−15,000↑

Arrows indicate effect on price.

$3 is the only stable price of corn under the supply and demand conditions shown in Table 3-8.

The price of corn—or of any other product bought and sold in competitive markets—will be established where the supply decisions of producers and the demand decisions of buyers are mutually consistent. Such decisions are consistent only at the equilibrium price (here, $3) and equilibrium quantity (here, 7000 bushels). At a higher price, suppliers want to sell more than consumers want to buy and a surplus results; at any lower price, consumers want to buy more than producers make available for sale and a shortage results. Such discrepancies between the supply and demand intentions of sellers and buyers then prompt price changes that bring the two sets of intentions into accord.

A graphical analysis of supply and demand should yield these same conclusions. **Figure 3-5 (Key Graph)** shows the market supply and demand curves for corn on the same graph. (The horizontal axis now measures both quantity demanded and quantity supplied.)

Graphically, the intersection of the supply curve and demand curve for a product indicates the market equilibrium. Here, equilibrium price and quantity are $3 per bushel and 7000 bushels. At any above-equilibrium price, quantity supplied exceeds quantity demanded This surplus of corn causes price reductions by sellers who are eager to rid themselves of their surplus. The falling price causes less corn to be offered and simultaneously encourages consumers to buy more. The market moves to its equilibrium.

Any price below the equilibrium price creates a shortage; quantity demanded now exceeds quantity supplied. Buyers try to obtain the product by offering to pay more for it; this drives the price upward toward its equilibrium level. The rising price simultaneously causes producers to increase the quantity supplied and many buyers to leave the market, eliminating the shortage. Again the market moves to its equilibrium.

Rationing Function of Prices

The ability of the competitive forces of supply and demand to establish a price at which selling and buying decisions are consistent is called the **rationing function of prices.** In our case, the equilibrium price of $3 clears the market, leaving no burdensome surplus for sellers and no inconvenient shortage for potential buyers. And it is the combination of freely made individual decisions that sets this market-clearing price. In effect, the market mechanism of supply and demand says that any buyer willing and able to pay $3 for a bushel of corn will be able to acquire one; buyers who are not, will not. Similarly, any seller willing and able to produce bushels of corn and offer them for sale at $3 will be able to do so; sellers who are not, will not. **(Key Question 7)**

Changes in Supply, Demand, and Equilibrium

We know that demand might change because of fluctuations in consumer tastes or incomes, changes in consumer expectations, or variations in the prices of related goods. Supply might change in response to changes in resource prices, technology, or taxes. What effects will such changes in supply and demand have on equilibrium price and quantity?

Changes in Demand   Suppose that supply is constant and demand increases, as shown in Figure 3-6a. As a result, the new intersection of the supply and demand curves is at higher values on both the price and quantity axes. Clearly, an increase in demand raises both equilibrium price and equilibrium quantity. Conversely, a decrease in demand, such as that shown in Figure 3-6b, reduces both equilibrium price and equilibrium quantity. (The value of graphical analysis is now apparent: We need not fumble with columns of figures to determine the outcomes, but only compare the new and the old points of intersection on the graph.)

Changes in Supply   Let's now suppose demand is constant but supply increases, as in Figure 3-6c. The new intersection of supply and demand is located at a lower equilibrium price but at a higher equilibrium quantity. An increase in supply reduces equilibrium price but increases equilibrium quantity. In contrast, if supply decreases, as in Figure 3-6d, the equilibrium price rises while the equilibrium quantity declines.

Complex Cases   When both supply and demand change, the effect is a combination of the individual effects.

1. Supply Increase; Demand Decrease   What effect will a supply increase and a demand decrease have on equilibrium price? Both changes decrease price, so the net result is a price drop greater than that resulting from either change alone.

What about equilibrium quantity? Here the effects of the changes in supply and demand are op-

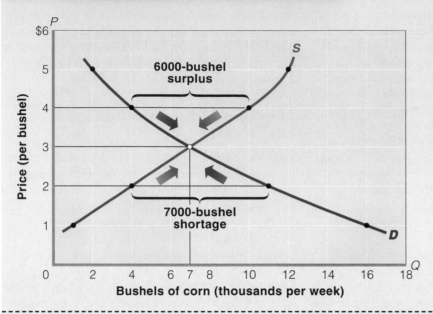

FIGURE 3-5 Equilibrium price and quantity The intersection of the downsloping demand curve *D* and the upsloping supply curve *S* indicates the equilibrium price and quantity, here $3 and 7000 bushels of corn. The shortages of corn at below-equilibrium prices, for example, 7000 bushels at $2, drive up price. These higher prices increase the quantity supplied and reduce the quantity demanded until equilibrium is achieved. The surpluses caused by above-equilibrium prices, for example, 6000 bushels at $4, push price down. As price drops, the quantity demanded rises and the quantity supplied falls until equilibrium is established. At the equilibrium price and quantity, there are neither shortages nor surpluses of corn.

QUICK QUIZ 3-5

1. Demand curve *D* is downsloping because:
 a. producers offer less of a product for sale as the price of the product falls.
 b. lower prices of a product create income and substitution effects which lead consumers to purchase more of it.
 c. the larger the number of buyers in a market, the lower the product price.
 d. price and quantity demanded are directly (positively) related.

2. Supply curve *S*:
 a. reflects an inverse (negative) relationship between price and quantity supplied.
 b. reflects a direct (positive) relationship between price and quantity supplied.
 c. depicts the collective behavior of buyers in this market.

 d. shows that producers will offer more of a product for sale at a low product price than at a high product price.

3. At the $3 price:
 a. quantity supplied exceeds quantity demanded.
 b. quantity demanded exceeds quantity supplied.
 c. the product is abundant and a surplus exists.
 d. there is no pressure on price to rise or fall.

4. At price $5 in this market:
 a. there will be a shortage of 10,000 units.
 b. there will be a surplus of 10,000 units.
 c. quantity demanded will be 12,000 units.
 d. quantity demanded will equal quantity supplied.

Answers: 1. b; 2. b; 3. d; 4. b

---

posed: The increase in supply increases equilibrium quantity, but the decrease in demand reduces it. The direction of the change in quantity depends on the relative sizes of the changes in supply and demand. If the increase in supply is larger than the decrease in demand, the equilibrium quantity will increase. But if the decrease in demand is greater than the increase in supply, the equilibrium quantity will decrease.

2. Supply Decrease; Demand Increase A decrease in supply and an increase in demand both increase price. Their combined effect is an increase in equilibrium price greater than that caused by either change separately. But their effect on equilibrium quantity is again indeterminate, depending on the relative sizes of the changes in supply and demand. If the decrease in supply is larger than the increase in de-

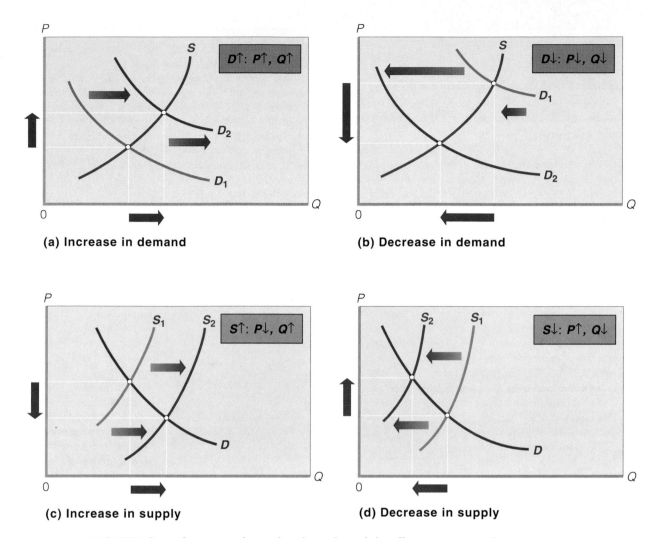

FIGURE 3-6 Changes in demand and supply and the effects on price and quantity The increase in demand from D_1 to D_2 in (a) increases both equilibrium price and quantity. The decrease in demand from D_1 to D_2 in (b) decreases both equilibrium price and quantity. The increase in supply from S_1 to S_2 in (c) decreases equilibrium price and increases equilibrium quantity. The decline in supply from S_1 to S_2 in (d) increases equilibrium price and reduces equilibrium quantity. The boxes in the top right corners summarize the respective changes and outcomes. The upward arrows in the boxes signify increases in demand (D), supply (S), equilibrium price (P), and equilibrium quantity (Q); the downward arrows signify decreases in these items.

----

mand, the equilibrium quantity will decrease. In contrast, if the increase in demand is greater than the decrease in supply, the equilibrium quantity will increase.

3. Supply Increase; Demand Increase What if supply and demand both increase? A supply increase drops equilibrium price, while a demand increase

boosts it. If the increase in supply is greater than the increase in demand, the equilibrium price will fall. If the opposite holds, the equilibrium price will rise.

The effect on equilibrium quantity is certain: The increases in supply and in demand each raise equilibrium quantity. Therefore, the equilibrium quantity will increase by an amount greater than that caused by either change alone.

Ticket Scalping: A Bum Rap?

Some market transactions get a bad name that is not warranted.

Tickets to athletic and artistic events are sometimes resold at higher-than-original prices—a market transaction known by the unsavory term "scalping." For example, a $40 ticket to a college bowl game may be resold by the original buyer for $200, $250, or more. The media often denounce scalpers for "ripping off" buyers by charging "exorbitant" prices. Scalping and extortion are synonymous in some people's minds.

But is scalping really sinful? We must first recognize that such ticket resales are voluntary—not coerced—transactions. This implies that both buyer and seller expect to gain from the exchange or it would not occur. The seller must value the $200 more than seeing the game, and the buyer must

value seeing the game more than the $200. So there are no losers or victims here: Both buyer and seller benefit from the transaction. The "scalping" market simply redis-

tributes assets (game tickets) from those who value them less to those who value them more.

Does scalping impose losses or injury on other parties—in particular, the sponsors of the event? If the sponsors are injured, it is because they initially priced tickets below the equilibrium level. In so doing they suffer an economic loss in the form of less revenue and profit than they might have otherwise received. But the loss is self-inflicted because of their pricing error. That mistake is quite separate and distinct from the fact that some tickets were later resold at a higher price.

What about spectators? Does scalping somehow impose losses by deteriorating the quality of the game's audience? No! People who most want to see the game—generally those with the greatest interest in and understanding of the game—will pay the scalper's high prices. Ticket scalping also benefits the athletic teams and performing artists—they will appear before more dedicated and perhaps more appreciative audiences.

So, is ticket scalping undesirable? Not on economic grounds. Both seller and buyer of a "scalped" ticket benefit, and a more interested and appreciative audience results. Game sponsors may sacrifice revenue and profits, but that stems from their own misjudgment of the equilibrium price.

---

4. Supply Decrease; Demand Decrease What of decreases in both supply and demand? If the decrease in supply is greater than the decrease in demand, equilibrium price will rise. If the reverse is true, equilibrium price will fall. Because decreases in supply and in demand each reduce equilibrium quantity, we can be sure that equilibrium quantity will fall.

Table 3-9 summarizes these four cases. To understand them fully you should draw supply and demand diagrams for each case to confirm the effects listed in the table.

Special cases might arise where a decrease in demand and a decrease in supply, or an increase in demand and an increase in supply, exactly cancel out. In

both cases, the net effect on equilibrium price will be zero; price will not change. **(Key Question 8)**

TABLE 3-9   Effects of changes in both supply and demand

Change in supply	Change in demand	Effect on equilibrium price	Effect on equilibrium quantity
1 Increase	Decrease	Decrease	Indeterminate
2 Decrease	Increase	Increase	Indeterminate
3 Increase	Increase	Indeterminate	Increase
4 Decrease	Decrease	Indeterminate	Decrease

A Reminder: "Other Things Equal"

We must stress once again that specific demand and supply curves (such as those in Figure 3-6) show relationships between prices and quantities demanded and supplied, *other things equal*. The downsloping demand curves tell us that price and quantity demanded are inversely related, other things equal. The upsloping supply curves imply that price and quantity supplied are directly related, other things equal.

If you forget the other-things-equal assumption, you can encounter situations which *seem* to be in conflict with these basic principles. For example, suppose salsa manufacturers sell 1 million bottles of salsa at $4 a bottle in 1 year; 2 million bottles at $5 in the next year; and 3 million at $6 in the year thereafter. Price and quantity purchased vary directly, and these data seem to be at odds with the law of demand. But there is no conflict here; these data do *not* refute the law of demand. The catch is that the law of demand's other-things-equal assumption has been violated over the 3 years in the example. Specifically, because of changing tastes and growing incomes, the demand for salsa has increased sharply, as in Figure 3-6a. The result is higher prices *and* larger quantities purchased.

As another example, the price of coffee occasionally has shot upward at the same time that the quantity of coffee produced has declined. These events seemingly contradict the direct relationship between price and quantity denoted by supply. The catch again is that the other-things-equal assumption underlying the upsloping supply curve was violated. Poor coffee harvests decreased supply, as in Figure 3-6d, increasing the equilibrium price of coffee and reducing the equilibrium quantity.

These examples also emphasize the importance of our earlier distinction between a change in quantity demanded (or supplied) and a change in demand (supply). In Figure 3-6a a change in demand caused a change in the quantity supplied. In Figure 3-6d a change in supply caused a change in quantity demanded.

Application: Pink Salmon

To reinforce the concepts we just discussed, let's briefly examine the real-world market for pink salmon—a market in which price has dramatically changed.

In the early 1970s, fishermen earned today's equivalent of $.60 for each pound of pink salmon delivered

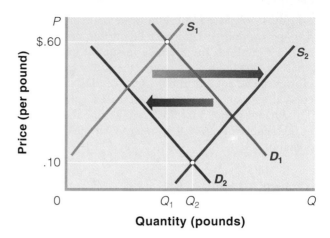

FIGURE 3-7 The market for pink salmon Since the early 1970s, the supply of pink salmon has increased and the demand for pink salmon has decreased. As a result, the price of pink salmon has declined, here from $.60 to $.10 a pound. Since supply has increased more than demand has declined, the equilibrium quantity of pink salmon has increased, here from Q_1 to Q_2.

to the docks. This equilibrium price is shown in Figure 3-7 at the intersection of supply curve S_1 and demand curve D_1. The corresponding equilibrium quantity of pink salmon—the type most often used for canning—was Q_1 pounds. (The actual "quantity numbers" are unimportant to our analysis.)

Between the early 1970s and late 1990s, changes in supply and demand occurred in the market for pink salmon. On the supply side, improved technology in the form of larger, more efficient fishing boats greatly increased the catch and lowered the cost of obtaining the fish. Also, the then-high profits at the $.60 price encouraged many new fishermen to enter the industry. As a result of these changes, the supply of pink salmon greatly increased and the supply curve shifted to the right, as from S_1 to S_2 in Figure 3-7.

Over the same years, the demand for pink salmon declined, as represented by the shift from demand curve D_1 to D_2 in Figure 3-7. The decline in demand resulted mainly from changes in consumer tastes, together with increases in consumer income: Buyers shifted their preferences away from canned fish and toward higher-quality fresh or frozen fish, including higher-quality species of salmon such as Chinook and Coho.

These supply and demand changes had a sizable effect on the price of pink salmon, as shown in Figure

3-7. By 1997 the equilibrium price had fallen to just $.10 per pound—83 percent below the price in the early 1970s. Both the increase in supply and the decrease in demand helped reduce the equilibrium price. However, the equilibrium *quantity* of pink salmon increased, as represented by the increase from Q_1 to Q_2. This change in quantity occurred because the increase in the supply of pink salmon exceeded the decline in demand.

QUICK REVIEW 3-3

■ In competitive markets, prices adjust to the equilibrium level at which quantity demanded equals quantity supplied.

■ The equilibrium price and quantity are those indicated by the intersection of the supply and demand curves for any product or resource.

■ An increase in demand increases equilibrium price and quantity; a decrease in demand decreases equilibrium price and quantity.

■ An increase in supply reduces equilibrium price but increases equilibrium quantity; a decrease in supply increases equilibrium price but reduces equilibrium quantity.

■ Over time, equilibrium price and quantity may change in directions which seem at odds with the laws of demand and supply because the other-things-equal assumption is violated.

CHAPTER SUMMARY

1. A market is any institution or arrangement which brings together buyers and sellers of a product, service, or resource.

2. Demand is a schedule or curve representing the willingness of buyers in a specific period to purchase a particular product at each of various prices. The law of demand implies that consumers will buy more of a product at a low price than at a high price. Therefore, other things equal, the relationship between price and quantity demanded is negative or inverse and is graphed as a downsloping curve. Market demand curves are found by adding horizontally the demand curves of the many individual consumers in the market.

3. Changes in one or more of the determinants of demand—consumer tastes, the number of buyers in the market, the money incomes of consumers, the prices of related goods, and consumer expectations—shift the market demand curve. A shift to the right is an increase in demand; a shift to the left is a decrease in demand. A change in demand is different from a change in the quantity demanded, the latter being a movement from one point to another point on a fixed demand curve because of a change in the product's price.

4. Supply is a schedule or curve showing the amounts of a product which producers are willing to offer in the market at each possible price during a specific period. The law of supply states that, other things equal, producers will offer more of a product at a high price than at a low price. Thus, the relationship between price and quantity supplied is positive or direct, and supply is graphed as an upsloping curve. The market supply curve is the horizontal summation of the supply curves of individual producers of the product.

5. Changes in one or more of the determinants of supply—resource prices, production techniques, taxes or subsidies, the prices of other goods, price expectations, or the number of sellers in the market—shift the supply curve of a product. A shift to the right is an increase in supply; a shift to the left is a decrease in supply. In contrast, a change in the price of the product being considered causes a change in the quantity supplied, which is shown as a movement from one point to another point on a fixed supply curve.

6. The equilibrium price and quantity are those indicated by the intersection of the supply and demand curves. The interaction of market demand and market supply adjusts the price to the point at which quantity demanded and quantity supplied are equal. This is the equilibrium price. The corresponding quantity is the equilibrium quantity.

7. The ability of market forces to synchronize selling and buying decisions to eliminate potential surpluses and shortages is known as the rationing function of prices.

8. A change in either demand or supply changes the equilibrium price and quantity. Increases in demand raise both equilibrium price and equilibrium quantity; decreases in demand reduce both equilibrium price and equilibrium quantity. Increases in supply reduce equilibrium price and increase equilibrium quantity; decreases in supply raise equilibrium price and reduce equilibrium quantity.

9. Simultaneous changes in demand and supply affect equilibrium price and quantity in various ways, depending on their direction and relative magnitudes.

TERMS AND CONCEPTS

market
demand
demand schedule
law of demand
diminishing marginal
  utility
income effect
substitution effect
demand curve

determinants of demand
normal good
inferior good
substitute good
complementary good
change in demand
change in quantity
  demanded
supply

supply schedule
law of supply
supply curve
determinants of supply
change in supply
change in quantity
  supplied
surplus
shortage

equilibrium price
equilibrium quantity
rationing function of
  prices

STUDY QUESTIONS

1. Explain the law of demand. Why does a demand curve slope downward? What are the determinants of demand? What happens to the demand curve when each of these determinants changes? Distinguish between a change in demand and a change in the quantity demanded, noting the cause(s) of each.

2. KEY QUESTION What effect will each of the following have on the demand for product B?
  a. Product B becomes more fashionable.
  b. The price of substitute product C falls.
  c. Income declines and B is an inferior good.
  d. Consumers anticipate the price of B will be lower in the near future.
  e. The price of complementary product D falls.
  f. Foreign tariff barriers on B are eliminated.

3. Explain the following news dispatch from Hull, England: "The fish market here slumped today to what local commentators called 'a disastrous level'— all because of a shortage of potatoes. The potatoes are one of the main ingredients in a dish that figures on almost every café-menu—fish and chips."

4. Explain the law of supply. Why does the supply curve slope upward? What are the determinants of supply? What happens to the supply curve when each of these determinants changes? Distinguish between a change in supply and a change in the quantity supplied, noting the cause(s) of each.

5. KEY QUESTION What effect will each of the following have on the supply of product B?
  a. A technological advance in the methods of producing B.
  b. A decline in the number of firms in industry B.
  c. An increase in the prices of resources required in the production of B.

  d. The expectation that the equilibrium price of B will be lower in the future than it is currently.
  e. A decline in the price of product A, a good whose production requires substantially the same techniques and resources as does the production of B.
  f. The levying of a specific sales tax on B.
  g. The granting of a 50-cent per-unit subsidy for each unit of B produced.

6. "In the corn market, demand often exceeds supply and supply sometimes exceeds demand." "The price of corn rises and falls in response to changes in supply and demand." In which of these two statements are the terms "supply" and "demand" used correctly? Explain.

7. KEY QUESTION Suppose the total demand for wheat and the total supply of wheat per month in the Kansas City grain market are as follows:

Thousands of bushels demanded	Price per bushel	Thousands of bushels supplied	Surplus (+) or shortage (−)
85	$3.40	72	_____
80	3.70	73	_____
75	4.00	75	_____
70	4.30	77	_____
65	4.60	79	_____
60	4.90	81	_____

  a. What is the equilibrium price? What is the equilibrium quantity? Fill in the surplus-shortage column and use it to explain why your answers are correct.
  b. Graph the demand for wheat and the supply of wheat. Be sure to label the axes of your graph correctly. Label equilibrium price P and equilibrium quantity Q.

c. Why will $3.40 not be the equilibrium price in this market? Why not $4.90? "Surpluses drive prices up; shortages drive them down." Do you agree?

d. Now suppose that the government establishes a ceiling (maximum legal) price of, say, $3.70 for wheat. Explain carefully the effects of this ceiling price. Demonstrate your answer graphically. What might prompt government to establish a ceiling price?

8. KEY QUESTION   How will each of the following changes in demand and/or supply affect equilibrium price and equilibrium quantity in a competitive market; that is, do price and quantity rise, fall, or remain unchanged, or are the answers indeterminate because they depend on the magnitudes of the shifts? You should use supply and demand diagrams to verify the answers.

a. Supply decreases and demand is constant.
b. Demand decreases and supply is constant.
c. Supply increases and demand is constant.
d. Demand increases and supply increases.
e. Demand increases and supply is constant.
f. Supply increases and demand decreases.
g. Demand increases and supply decreases.
h. Demand decreases and supply decreases.

9. "Prices are the automatic regulator which tends to keep production and consumption in line with each other." Explain.

10. Explain: "Even though parking meters may yield little or no net revenue, they should nevertheless be retained because of the rationing function they perform."

11. Use two market diagrams to explain how an increase in state subsidies to public colleges might affect tuition and enrollments in both public and private colleges.

12. Critically evaluate: "In comparing the two equilibrium positions in Figure 3-6a, I note that a larger amount is actually purchased at a higher price. This refutes the law of demand."

13. Suppose you go to a recycling center and are paid $.25 per pound for your aluminum cans. However, the recycler charges you $.20 per bundle to accept your old newspapers. Use demand and supply diagrams to portray both markets. Explain how differ-

ent government policies with respect to the recycling of aluminum and paper might account for these different market outcomes.

14. Advanced analysis: Assume that demand for a commodity is represented by the equation $P = 10 - .2Q_d$ and supply by the equation $P = 2 + .2Q_s$, where Q_d and Q_s are quantity demanded and quantity supplied, respectively, and P is price. Using the equilibrium condition $Q_s = Q_d$, solve the equations to determine equilibrium price. Now determine equilibrium quantity. Graph the two equations to substantiate your answers.

15. (Last Word)   Discuss the economic aspects of ticket scalping, specifying gainers and losers.

16. WEB-BASED QUESTION   Changes in Supply— USDA's Weekly Weather and Crop Bulletin   The USDA (United States Department of Agriculture) http://www.usda.gov/nass/ publishes a weekly weather and crop bulletin, found under Today's Reports at their home page. Select a crop to analyze (corn, soybeans, cotton, rice, sorghum, or winter wheat), and then predict whether there will be an increase or a decrease in the supply of that crop based on the report. Assuming that demand remains unchanged, do you expect prices to increase or decrease within the next month? To check your price forecast, visit USDA's Market News http:/www.ams.usda.gov/marketnews.htm during the next month.

17. WEB-BASED QUESTION   Changes in Demand—Baby Diapers and Retirement Villages Other things equal, an increase in the number of buyers for a product or service will increase demand. Baby diapers and retirement villages are two products designed for different population groups. The U.S. Census http://www.census.gov/ipc/www/idbpyr.html provides population pyramids (graphs which show the distribution of population by age and sex) for countries for the current year, 2025, and 2050. View the population pyramids for Mexico, Japan, and the United States. Which country would you expect to have the greatest percentage increase in demand for baby diapers in the year 2050? For retirement villages? Which country would you expect to have the greatest absolute increase in demand for baby diapers? For retirement villages?

CHAPTER FOUR

Pure Capitalism and the Market System

In Chapter 3 we saw how equilibrium prices and quantities are established in individual product and resource markets. We now widen our focus to take in all product and resource markets—the *competitive market system,* also known as the *private enterprise system* or, simply, *capitalism.* The press and television regularly report on the progress of Russia, the eastern European nations, and China in their transitions from command economies to capitalism. Precisely what are the features of capitalism these nations are trying to emulate?

In this chapter, we describe the capitalist ideology and explain how pure, or laissez-faire, capitalism would operate. Although it has never actually existed, pure capitalism provides a useful approximation to the economies of the United States and many other industrially advanced nations. We will modify this approximation in later chapters to correspond more closely to the reality of modern capitalism.

In examining pure capitalism, we first discuss its basic assumptions and institutions—the significant practices, relationships, and organizations. We then consider certain other institutions common to all advanced industrial economies. Finally, we explain how a market system coordinates economic activity and contributes to the efficient use of scarce resources. In achieving this third goal, we rely heavily on Chapter 3's explanation of supply and demand in individual markets.

CAPITALIST IDEOLOGY

Let's begin by examining in some detail the basic tenets that define capitalism: (1) private property, (2) freedom of enterprise and choice, (3) self-interest as the dominant motive, (4) competition, (5) reliance on the market system, and (6) a limited role for government.

Private Property

In a capitalist system, property resources (land, capital) are usually owned by private individuals and firms, not by government. In fact, the private ownership of capital is what gives capitalism its name. This right of **private property,** coupled with the freedom to negotiate binding legal contracts, allows private persons or businesses to obtain, control, employ, and dispose of property resources as they see fit. The right to bequeath—the right of a property owner to designate who receives his or her property at the time of death—sustains the institution of private property.

Property rights are significant because they encourage investment, innovation, exchange, and economic growth. Why would anyone stock a store, construct a factory, or clear land for farming if someone else, including government, could take that property for his or her own benefit?

Property rights also apply to intellectual property via patents and copyrights. These long-term protections encourage people to write books, music, and computer programs and to invent new products and production processes without fear that others will steal them and the rewards they may bring.

Another important role of property rights is that they facilitate exchange. A title to an automobile or deed to a cattle ranch assures the buyer that the seller is the legitimate owner. Finally, with property rights, people can spend their time, energy, and resources producing more goods and services, rather than using them to protect and retain the property they have already produced and acquired.

There are broad legal limits to this right of private ownership. For example, the use of private property to produce illegal drugs is prohibited. And even in pure capitalism, government ownership of certain property resources may be essential to produce "public goods": national defense, basic education, and courtrooms and prisons, for instance.

Freedom of Enterprise and Choice

Closely related to private ownership of property is freedom of enterprise and choice. Capitalism requires that various economic units make certain choices, which are expressed and implemented through the free markets of the economy.

Freedom of enterprise means that private businesses are free to obtain economic resources, to organize those resources in the production of goods and services of the firm's own choosing, and to sell them in the markets of their choice. In pure capitalism no artificial obstacles or restrictions imposed by government or other producers block an entrepreneur's decision to enter or leave a particular industry.

Freedom of choice means that owners can employ or dispose of their property and money as they see fit. It also means that workers are free to enter any lines of work for which they are qualified. Finally, it means that consumers are at liberty, within the limits of their incomes, to buy that collection of goods and services which best satisfies their wants.

Freedom of *consumer* choice in a capitalist economy is perhaps the most profound of these freedoms. The consumer is in a particularly strategic position;

in a sense, the consumer is sovereign. Consumers ultimately decide via their choices what the capitalist economy should produce. Businesses and resource suppliers then make their free choices within these constraints. They are not really "free" to produce goods and services consumers do not desire because producing such items would be unprofitable.

Again, all these choices are free only within broad legal limitations. Illegal choices are punished through fines and imprisonment. (The degree of economic freedom varies greatly from nation to nation, as indicated in Global Perspective 4-1.)

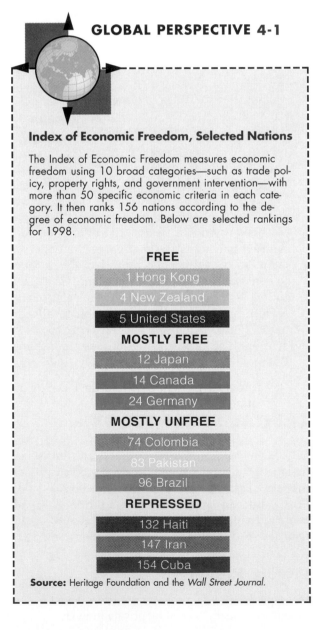

GLOBAL PERSPECTIVE 4-1

Index of Economic Freedom, Selected Nations

The Index of Economic Freedom measures economic freedom using 10 broad categories—such as trade policy, property rights, and government intervention—with more than 50 specific economic criteria in each category. It then ranks 156 nations according to the degree of economic freedom. Below are selected rankings for 1998.

FREE
1 Hong Kong
4 New Zealand
5 United States

MOSTLY FREE
12 Japan
14 Canada
24 Germany

MOSTLY UNFREE
74 Colombia
83 Pakistan
96 Brazil

REPRESSED
132 Haiti
147 Iran
154 Cuba

Source: Heritage Foundation and the *Wall Street Journal*.

Self-Interest

The primary driving force of capitalism is **self-interest.** Each economic unit attempts to do what is best for itself. Entrepreneurs aim to maximize their firm's profit or, in adverse circumstances, minimize losses. Property owners attempt to get the highest price for the sale or rent of their resources. Workers attempt to maximize their utility (satisfaction) by finding jobs which offer the best combination of wages, fringe benefits, and working conditions. Consumers, in purchasing a specific product, seek to obtain it at the lowest possible price. Consumers also apportion their expenditures to maximize their utility. In brief, capitalism presumes self-interest as the *modus operandi* for the various economic units as they express their free choices. The motive of self-interest gives direction and consistency to what might otherwise be an extremely chaotic economy.

Pursuit of self-interest should not be confused with selfishness. A stockholder may invest to receive the best available corporate dividends but then donate much of it to the United Way or give it to grandchildren. A worker may take a second job to help pay college tuition for her or his children. An entrepreneur may make a fortune and donate much of it to a charitable foundation.

Competition

Freedom of choice exercised in promotion of one's own monetary returns is the basis for competition. In its pure form, **competition** requires:

1. Large numbers of independently acting buyers and sellers operating in the market for any particular product or resource

2. Freedom of buyers and sellers to enter or leave any particular market, based on their economic self-interest

Large Numbers The essence of competition is the widespread diffusion of economic power within the two major aggregates—businesses and households—that comprise the economy. When many buyers and many sellers are in a particular market, no one buyer or seller is able to demand or supply a quantity of the product sufficiently large to affect its price. Let's examine this statement in terms of the supply side of the product market.

We know that when a product becomes unusually scarce, its price rises. An unseasonable frost in Florida may seriously reduce the supply of citrus crops and sharply increase the price of oranges. Similarly, if a single producer or a small group of producers acting together can somehow restrict the total output of a product, then it can raise the price to the seller's advantage. By controlling supply, a firm can "rig the market" on its own behalf. In its purest form, competition means there are so many independently acting firms that each has virtually no influence over the market supply or, therefore, over price *because it is contributing an almost negligible fraction of the total output.*

Suppose there are 10,000 farmers, each producing and selling 100 bushels of corn in the Kansas City grain market when the price of corn is $4 per bushel. Could a single farmer who feels dissatisfied with that price cause an artificial scarcity of corn to boost the price above $4? The answer is "no." Even if Farmer Jones withheld his output completely, he would reduce the total amount supplied only from 1,000,000 to 999,900 bushels. This is not much of a shortage! Supply would be virtually unchanged, and the $4 price would persist.

Competition means that each seller is providing a minuscule amount of the market supply. Individual sellers can make no noticeable impact on total output; thus a seller cannot as an individual producer manipulate product price, which is why economists say that an individual competitive seller is "at the mercy of the market."

The same reasoning applies to the demand side of the market. Buyers are plentiful and act independently. Thus single buyers cannot manipulate the market to their advantage by refusing to buy at the market price.

The widespread diffusion of economic power underlying competition controls the use and limits the potential abuse of that power. A producer charging more than the equilibrium price will lose sales to other producers. An employer paying less than the equilibrium wage rate will lose workers to other employers. Competition is the basic regulatory force in pure capitalism.

Easy Entry and Exit Competition also implies that it is simple for producers to enter or leave an industry; there are no artificial barriers to the expansion or contraction of specific industries. This freedom of an industry to expand or contract provides a competitive economy with the flexibility needed to remain efficient over time. Freedom of entry and exit allows the economy to adjust to changes in consumer tastes, technology, and resource availability.

Markets and Prices

The basic coordinating mechanism of a capitalist economy is the market system. Without a market economy, there is no capitalism. Decisions made by buyers and sellers of products and resources become effective through a system of markets. We know from Chapters 2 and 3 that a market is a mechanism or arrangement which brings buyers (demanders) and sellers (suppliers) into contact with one another. The preferences of sellers and buyers are registered on the supply and demand sides of various markets, and the outcome of these choices is a set of product and resource prices. These prices are guideposts on which resource owners, entrepreneurs, and consumers make and revise their free choices as they pursue their self-interests.

Just as competition is the controlling mechanism, so a system of markets and prices is the basic organizing force. The market system is an elaborate communication system through which innumerable individual free choices are recorded, summarized, and balanced against one another. Those who obey the dictates of the market system are rewarded; those who ignore them are penalized by the system. Through this communication system, society decides what the economy should produce, how production can be efficiently organized, and how the fruits of productive effort are distributed among the individual economic units which make up capitalism.

Not only is the market system the mechanism through which society decides how it allocates its resources and distributes the resulting output, but it is through the market system that these decisions are carried out. All this will be detailed in the final sections of this chapter.

Limited Government

A pure capitalist economy promotes a high degree of efficiency in the use of its resources. There is little need for governmental intervention in the operation of such an economy beyond its role of imposing broad legal limits on the exercise of individual choices and the use of private property. The concept of pure capitalism as a self-regulating and self-adjusting economy precludes any extensive economic role for government. However, as you will find in Chapter 5, a number of limitations and potentially undesirable outcomes associated with capitalism and the market system have resulted in active government participation in the economy.

QUICK REVIEW 4-1

- Pure capitalism rests on the private ownership of property and freedom of enterprise and choice.

- Pure capitalism permits economic entities—businesses, resource suppliers, and consumers—to pursue and further their own self-interests. Competition prevents any single economic entity from dictating product or resource prices.

- The coordinating mechanism of capitalism is a system of markets and prices.

- The efficient operation of the market system under capitalism allegedly makes significant government intervention unnecessary.

OTHER CHARACTERISTICS

Private property, freedom of enterprise and choice, self-interest as a motivating force, competition, and reliance on a market system are more or less exclusively associated with pure capitalism.

In addition, certain institutions and practices are characteristic of all modern economies, including those with much central command: (1) the use of advanced technology and large amounts of capital goods, (2) specialization, and (3) the use of money. Advanced technology and specialization are prerequisites to efficient employment of an economy's resources. The use of money helps society specialize and use advanced technology.

Extensive Use of Technology and Capital Goods

All advanced industrial economies are based on state-of-the-art technology and the extensive use of capital goods. In pure capitalism, the opportunity and motivation for technological advance are created by competition, freedom of choice, self-interest, and the fact that monetary rewards for new products or production techniques accrue directly to the innovator. Pure capitalism therefore encourages extensive use and rapid development of complex capital goods: tools, machinery, large-scale factories, and facilities for storage, communication, transportation, and marketing. In the command economy, in contrast, the motivation for technological advance is weak; it must come through the directive of the central plan.

Why are advanced technology and capital goods important? Because the most direct method of producing a product is usually the least efficient. The inefficiencies of direct production can be avoided through **roundabout production**—the construction and use of capital to aid in the production of consumer goods. It would be ridiculous for a farmer to go at production with bare hands. There are huge benefits—in the form of more efficient production and, therefore, a more abundant output—from creating tools of production (capital equipment) and using them in the production process. The farmer's output will increase with the use of a plow, a tractor, storage bins, and so on. There is a better way for the farmer to get water out of a well than to dive in after it!

But there is a hitch. Recall the main message of the production possibilities curve: For an economy operating on its production possibilities curve, resources used to produce capital goods must be diverted from the production of consumer goods. Society must sacrifice some consumer goods today to produce the capital goods which will give it more consumer goods tomorrow. Greater abundance tomorrow requires sacrifices today. **(Key Question 2)**

Specialization

The extent to which society relies on **specialization** is astounding. The majority of consumers produce virtually none of the goods and services they consume, and they consume little or nothing of what they produce. The worker who spends most of a lifetime machining parts for marine engines may never "consume" an ocean cruise. The worker who devotes 8 hours a day to installing windows in Fords may own a Honda. Few households seriously consider producing their own food, shelter, and clothing. Many farmers sell their milk to the local dairy and then buy margarine at the local general store. Society learned long ago that self-sufficiency breeds inefficiency. The jack-of-all-trades may be a very colorful individual but is certainly not efficient.

Division of Labor In what ways does human specialization—called the **division of labor**—enhance a society's output?

1. *Makes use of ability differences* Specialization enables individuals to take advantage of existing differences in their abilities and skills. If caveman A is strong, swift, and accurate with a spear, and caveman B is weak and slow but patient, their distribution of talents can be most efficiently used if A hunts and B fishes.

2. *Allows learning by doing* Even if the abilities of A and B are identical, specialization may be ad-

vantageous. By devoting all your time to a single task, you are more likely to develop the appropriate skills and to discover improved techniques than by apportioning your time among a number of diverse tasks. You learn to be a good hunter by hunting!

3. *Saves time* Specialization—devoting all one's time to, say, a single task—avoids the loss of time involved in shifting from one job to another.

For all these reasons the division of labor results in greater total output from society's limited human resources.

Geographic Specialization Specialization also works on a regional and international basis. Oranges could be grown in Nebraska, but because of the unsuitability of the land, rainfall, and temperature, the costs would be very high. Florida could achieve some success in the production of wheat, but for similar reasons such production would be costly. That is why Nebraskans produce those products—wheat in particular—for which their resources are best adapted, and Floridians do the same, producing oranges and other citrus fruits. In specializing, both produce more than is needed locally. Then, very sensibly, Nebraskans and Floridians swap some of their surpluses—wheat for oranges. Specialization thus enables each area to make the goods it can most efficiently produce, and it permits both to enjoy a larger amount of all goods than would otherwise be available.

Similarly, on an international basis the United States specializes in such items as commercial aircraft and computers, which it sells abroad in exchange for video recorders from Japan, bananas from Honduras, and woven baskets from Thailand. Both human specialization and geographical specialization are essential in achieving efficiency in the use of resources.

Use of Money

Virtually all economies, advanced or primitive, use money. Money performs several functions, but first and foremost it is a **medium of exchange;** it makes trade easier.

In our example, Nebraskans must exchange wheat for Florida's oranges if both states are to share in the benefits of specialization. If trade were highly inconvenient or prohibited for some reason, the gains from their specialization would be lost. Nebraska and Florida would then be forced to be more self-sufficient—to produce both wheat and oranges and whatever else their consumers desire. *A convenient means of exchanging goods is a prerequisite of specialization.*

Exchange can, and sometimes does, occur on the basis of **barter,** that is, swapping goods for goods, say, wheat for oranges. But barter can pose serious problems for the economy because it requires a *coincidence of wants* between the two transactors. In our example, we assumed that Nebraskans had excess wheat to trade and wanted oranges. And we assumed Floridians had excess oranges to swap and wanted wheat. So exchange occurred. But if this coincidence of wants does not exist, trade is stymied.

Suppose Nebraska does not want any of Florida's oranges but is interested in buying potatoes from Idaho. Ironically, Idaho wants Florida's oranges but not Nebraska's wheat. And, to complicate matters, suppose that Florida wants some of Nebraska's wheat but none of Idaho's potatoes. The situation is summarized in Figure 4-1.

In no case do we find a coincidence of wants. Trade by barter clearly would be difficult. To overcome such a stalemate, economies use **money,** which is simply a convenient social invention to facilitate exchanges of goods and services. Historically, cattle, cigarettes, shells, stones, pieces of metal, and many other commodities have been used, with varying degrees of success, as a medium for facilitating exchange. But to be money, an item needs to pass only one test: *It must be generally acceptable to sellers in exchange for*

goods and services. Money is socially defined; whatever society accepts as a medium of exchange *is* money.

Most economies use pieces of paper as money. This is true with the Nebraska-Florida-Idaho economy; the three states use paper dollars as money. The use of dollars as a medium of exchange allows them to overcome their trade stalemate, as demonstrated in Table 4-1.

Specifically:

1. Floridians exchange money for some of Nebraska's wheat.
2. Nebraskans exchange the money earned from the sale of wheat for some of Idaho's potatoes.
3. Idahoans exchange the money received from the sale of potatoes for some of Florida's surplus oranges.

The willingness to accept paper money (or any other kind of money) as a medium of exchange has permitted a three-way trade which allows each state to specialize in one product and obtain the other product(s) its residents desire, despite the absence of a coincidence of wants between any two of the parties. Barter, resting as it does on a coincidence of wants, would not have permitted this exchange and so would not have allowed the three states to specialize. The efficiencies of specialization would then have been lost to those states.

On a global basis the fact that different nations have different currencies complicates international

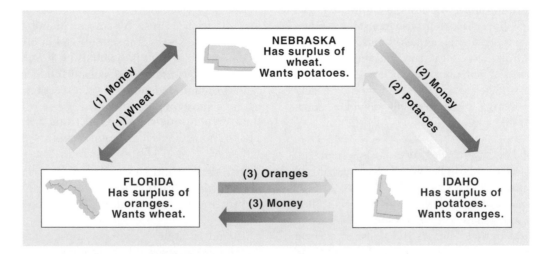

FIGURE 4-1 Money facilitates trade where wants do not coincide By the use of money as a medium of exchange, trade can be accomplished despite a noncoincidence of wants. (1) Nebraska trades the wheat that Florida wants for money from Floridians; (2) Nebraska trades the money for the potatoes it wants from Idaho; (3) Idaho trades the money to Florida for the oranges it wants.

specialization and exchange. However, foreign exchange markets permit U.S. residents, Japanese, Germans, Britons, and Mexicans to exchange dollars, yen, marks, pounds, and pesos for one another to complete international exchanges of goods and services.

A final example: Imagine a Detroit laborer producing crankshafts for Oldsmobiles. At the end of the week, instead of receiving a piece of paper endorsed by the company comptroller, or a few pieces of paper engraved in green and black, the worker receives from the company paymaster four Oldsmobile crankshafts. With no desire to hoard crankshafts, the worker ventures into the Detroit business district to spend this income on a bag of groceries, a pair of jeans, and a movie. Obviously, the worker is faced with some inconvenient and time-consuming trading, and may not be able to negotiate any exchanges at all. Finding a clothier with jeans who happens to be in the market for an Oldsmobile crankshaft can be a formidable task. And if the jeans do not trade evenly for crankshafts, how do the transactors "make change"? It is fair to say that money is one of the great social inventions of civilization.

QUICK REVIEW 4-2

■ Advanced economies achieve greater efficiency in production through the use of large quantities of technologically advanced capital goods.

■ Specialization enhances efficiency by allowing individuals, regions, and nations to produce those goods and services for which their resources are best suited.

■ The use of money facilitates the exchange of goods and services which specialization requires.

THE COMPETITIVE MARKET SYSTEM

We noted earlier that a fundamental feature of capitalism is its reliance on a market system. We have also stressed that a capitalistic system is characterized by competition, freedom of enterprise, and choice. Consumers are free to buy what they choose; businesses, to produce and sell what they choose; and resource suppliers, to make their property and human resources available in whatever occupations they choose. We may wonder why such an economy does not collapse in chaos. If consumers want breakfast cereal, businesses choose to produce aerobic shoes, and resource suppliers want to offer their services in man-

ufacturing computer software, production would seem to be deadlocked because of the apparent inconsistency of these free choices.

In reality, the millions of decisions made by households and businesses are highly consistent. Firms *do* produce those particular goods and services which consumers want. Households *do* provide the kinds of labor which businesses want to hire. In the next two sections you will see how a competitive market system constitutes a coordinating mechanism which overcomes the potential chaos suggested by freedom of enterprise and choice. The competitive market system is a mechanism both for communicating decisions of consumers, producers, and resource suppliers to one another and for synchronizing those decisions toward consistent production objectives.

The Five Fundamental Questions

To understand the operation of a market economy, we must first recognize that every economy must respond to these Five Fundamental Questions:

1. *How much of a society's resources should be used?* What proportion of available resources should be used in producing goods and services?

2. *What is to be produced?* What collection of goods and services will best satisfy society's material wants?

3. *How is that output to be produced?* How should production be organized? What firms should do the producing, and what production techniques should they use?

4. *Who is to receive the output?* How should households share the output of the economy?

5. *Can the system adapt to change?* Can it adjust to changes in consumer wants, resource supplies, and technology?

The **Five Fundamental Questions** are merely an elaboration of the economic choices underlying Chapter 2's production possibilities curve. These questions would be irrelevant were it not for the economizing problem: scarce resources in a world of unlimited wants.

THE MARKET SYSTEM AT WORK

We will defer the "how much" question until we discuss macroeconomics, which deals in detail with the complex question of levels of resource usage. Chapter

2's circular flow diagram (Figure 2-6) provides the setting for our discussion of the remaining questions. In examining how the market system answers these questions, we must draw upon our understanding of supply and demand (Chapter 3).

Determining What Is to Be Produced

With product and resource prices in place—established by competing buyers and sellers in both the product and resource markets—how would a purely capitalist economy decide on the specific types and quantities of goods to be produced? Knowing that businesses seek profits and want to avoid losses, we can generalize that those goods and services which can be produced at a profit will be produced and those whose production entail a loss will not. Two things determine profits and losses:

1. The total revenue a firm receives when it sells its product
2. The total cost of producing the product

Both total revenue and total cost are price-times-quantity figures. Total revenue is found by multiplying product price by the quantity of the product sold. Total cost is found by multiplying the price of each resource used by the amount employed and summing the results.

Economic Costs and Profits To say that those products which can be produced profitably *will* be produced and those which cannot *will not* is an accurate generalization only if the meaning of **economic costs** is clearly understood.

Let's again think of businesses as simply organizational charts, that is, businesses "on paper," distinct from the capital, raw materials, labor, and entrepreneurial ability which make them going concerns. To become actual producing firms, these "on paper" businesses must secure all four types of resources. *Economic costs are the payments which must be made to secure and retain the needed amounts of these resources.* The per-unit size of these costs—that is, the resource prices—will be determined by supply and demand in the resource market. Like land, labor, and capital, entrepreneurial ability is a scarce resource and has a price tag on it. Costs therefore must include not only wage and salary payments to labor and interest and rental payments for capital and land but also payments to the entrepreneur for the functions he or she performs in organizing and combining the other resources to produce

a commodity. The payment for these contributions of the entrepreneur is called **normal profit.**

A product will be produced only when total revenue is large enough to pay wages, interest, rent, and a normal profit to the entrepreneur. However, if the total revenue from the sale of a product exceeds all these economic costs, the remainder will go to the entrepreneur as an added reward. This return above all economic costs is called *pure profit* or **economic profit.** Economic profit is *not* an economic cost because it need not be realized for the business to acquire and retain the entrepreneurial resource. But economic profit *is* the profit which lures other producers to a particular industry.

Profits and Expanding Industries An example will explain how the market system determines what goods will be produced. With current technology, suppose the most favorable relationship between total revenue and total cost in producing product X occurs when the firm's output is 15 units. Assume, too, that the least-cost combination of resources in producing 15 units of X is 2 units of labor, 3 units of land, 1 of capital, and 1 of entrepreneurial ability, selling at prices of $2, $1, $3, and $3, respectively. Finally, suppose that the 15 units of X which these resources produce can be sold for $1 per unit, or $15 total. Will firms produce X? Yes, because each firm will be able to pay wage, rent, interest, and normal profit costs of $13 [= $(2 \times \$2) + (3 \times \$1) + (1 \times \$3) + (1 \times \$3)$]. The difference between total revenue of $15 and total cost of $13 is an economic profit of $2.

This economic profit is evidence that industry X is prosperous. It will become an **expanding industry** as new firms, attracted by these above-normal profits, are formed or shift from less profitable industries.

But the entry of new firms will be self-limiting. As new firms enter industry X, the market supply of product X will increase relative to the market demand. This will lower the market price of X (as in Figure 3-6c), and economic profit will in time diminish and then disappear. The market supply and demand conditions prevailing when economic profit becomes zero will determine the total amount of X produced. At this point the industry will be at its "equilibrium size," at least until a further change in market demand or supply upsets that equilibrium.

Losses and Declining Industries But what if the initial market situation for product X were less favorable? Suppose conditions in the product market were such that the firm could sell the 15 units of X at a price of just $.75 per unit. Total revenue would then be $11.25 (= 15 × $0.75). After paying wage, rental, and interest costs of $10, the firm would obtain a below-normal profit of $1.25. In other words, *losses* of $1.75 (= $11.25 − $13) would be incurred.

Certainly, firms would not be attracted to this unprosperous **declining industry.** On the contrary, if these losses persisted, some of the firms in industry X would go out of business or migrate to more prosperous industries where normal or even economic profits prevailed. However, as this happened, the market supply of X would fall relative to the market demand. Product price would rise (as in Figure 3-6d), and the losses would eventually disappear. Industry X would then stop shrinking. The supply and demand situation which prevailed when economic profit became zero would determine the total output of product X. Again, the industry would for the moment have reached its equilibrium size.

Consumer Sovereignty and "Dollar Votes"

In the market system, consumers are sovereign; they have the ultimate authority in determining the types and quantities of goods produced. **Consumer sovereignty** works through consumer demand. Consumer demand is crucial in determining the types and quantities of goods produced. Consumers, unrestrained by government and with money incomes from the sale of their resources, spend their dollars on those goods they are most willing and able to buy. These expenditures are **dollar votes** through which consumers register their wants via the demand side of the product market. If the dollar votes for a certain product are great enough to provide a normal profit, businesses will produce that product. If there is an increase in consumer demand, so that enough dollar votes are cast to provide an economic profit, that profit will cause an expansion of the industry and an increase in the output of the product.

Conversely, a decrease in consumer demand, that is, fewer dollar votes cast for the product, will result in losses and, in time, contraction of the industry. As firms leave the industry, the output of the product will decline. Indeed, the industry may cease to exist. Again, the consumers are sovereign; they collectively direct resources away from industries which are not meeting their wants.

The dollar votes of consumers determine not only which industries continue to exist but also which individual products survive or fail. Example: In 1991,

responding to doctors and nutritionists, McDonald's introduced its low-fat McLean burger. Good idea? Not really. Most consumers found the new product "too dry" and "not tasty," so sales were meager. In 1996 McDonald's quietly dropped the McLean burger from its menu at the same time that it introduced its higher-fat Arch Deluxe burger. In effect, consumers had collectively "voted out" the McLean burger.

Market Restraints on Freedom From the viewpoint of businesses, we now see that firms are not really free to produce what they wish. Consumers' buying decisions make the production of some products profitable and others not, thus restricting the choice of businesses in deciding what to produce. Businesses must match their production choices with consumer choices or face losses and eventual bankruptcy.

It is the same for resource suppliers. The demand for resources is a **derived demand**—derived, that is, from the demand for the goods and services which the resources help produce. There is a demand for autoworkers because there is a demand for automobiles. There is no demand for buggy-whip braiders because there is no demand for buggy whips. Resource suppliers are not free to allocate their resources to the production of goods which consumers do not value highly. Firms do not produce such products because consumer demand is not sufficient to make them profitable.

In brief: Consumers register their preferences on the demand side of the product market; producers and resource suppliers respond appropriately in seeking to further their own self-interests. The market system communicates the wants of consumers to businesses and resource suppliers and elicits appropriate responses.

Organizing Production

How is production to be organized in a market economy? This Fundamental Question is composed of three subquestions:

1. How should resources be allocated among specific industries?
2. What specific firms should do the producing in each industry?
3. What combinations of resources—what technology—should each firm employ?

The preceding section answered the first two subquestions. The market system steers resources to those industries whose products consumers want—simply because those industries survive, are profitable, and pay for resources. It simultaneously deprives unwanted industries of profits and hence of scarce resources.

The second and third subquestions are closely intertwined. In a competitive market economy, the firms which survive to do the producing are the ones willing and able to employ the most economically efficient technique of production. And the most efficient technique depends on:

1. The available technology, that is, the alternative combinations of resources which will produce the desired results

2. The prices of the needed resources

The combination of resources which is most efficient economically depends not only on the state of available technology but on the relative worth of the required resources as measured by their market prices. A technique which requires just a few physical inputs of resources to produce a specific output may be highly *in*efficient economically *if* the required resources are valued very highly in the market. *Economic efficiency means obtaining a particular output of product with the least input of scarce resources, when both output and resource inputs are measured in dollars and cents.* That combination of resources which will produce, say, $15 worth of product X at the lowest possible money cost is the most efficient.

Suppose there are three possible techniques for producing the desired $15 worth of product X. Suppose also that the quantity of each resource required by each production technique and the prices of the required resources are as shown in Table 4-1. By multiplying the required quantities of each resource by its price in each of the three techniques, the total cost of producing $15 worth of X by each technique is determined.

Technique 2 is economically the most efficient because it is the least costly. It permits society to obtain $15 worth of output by using a smaller amount of resources—$13 worth—than the $15 worth required by the two other techniques.

But will firms actually use technique 2? The answer is "yes." Firms will want to use the most efficient technique because it yields the greatest profit.

A change in either technology *or* resource prices, however, may cause the firm to shift from the technology it is using. If the price of labor falls to $.50, technique 1 becomes superior to technique 2. Businesses will find they can lower their costs by shifting to a technology which uses more of the resource whose price has fallen. Exercise: Would a new technique involving 1 unit of labor, 4 of land, 1 of capital, and 1 of entrepreneurial ability be preferable to the techniques listed in Table 4-1, assuming the resource prices shown there? **(Key Question 8)**

Distributing Total Output

The market system enters the picture in two ways in solving the problem of distributing total output. Generally, any specific product will be distributed to consumers on the basis of their ability and willingness to pay the existing market price for it. If the price of some product, say, a pocket calculator, is $15, then those buyers who are able and willing to pay that price will get a pocket calculator; those who are not, will not. This is the rationing function of equilibrium prices.

The sizes of consumers' money incomes determines their ability to pay the equilibrium prices for pocket calculators and other products. And con-

TABLE 4-1 Three techniques for producing $15 worth of product X

Resource	Price per unit of resource	Technique 1 Units	Technique 1 Cost	Technique 2 Units	Technique 2 Cost	Technique 3 Units	Technique 3 Cost
Labor	$2	4	$ 8	2	$ 4	1	$ 2
Land	1	1	1	3	3	4	4
Capital	3	1	3	1	3	2	6
Entrepreneurial ability	3	1	3	1	3	1	3
Total cost of $15 worth of X			$15		$13		$15

sumers' money incomes depend on the quantities of the various property and human resources they supply and on the prices in the resource market. Resource prices are key in determining the size of each household's claim against the total output of society. Within the limits of a consumer's money income, however, it is a person's willingness to pay the equilibrium price for a pocket calculator which determines whether or not a unit of this product is distributed to her or him. And this willingness to buy the calculator depends on that consumer's preference for it compared with other available products and their relative prices. Thus, product price is not only key in determining how output is distributed, it also is central in determining the spending patterns of consumers.

There is nothing particularly ethical about the market system as a mechanism for distributing output. Households which accumulate large amounts of property resources by inheritance, through hard work and frugality, through business acumen, or by illegal activities will receive large incomes and thus command large shares of the economy's total output. Others, offering unskilled and relatively unproductive labor resources which elicit low wages, will receive meager money incomes and small portions of total output.

Accommodating Change

Industrial societies are dynamic: Consumer preferences, technology, and supplies of resources all change. This means that the particular allocation of resources which is *now* the most efficient for a *specific* pattern of consumer tastes, for a *specific* range of technological alternatives, and for *specific* supplies of resources will become obsolete and inefficient as consumer preferences change, new techniques of production are discovered, and resource supplies change over time. Can the market economy adjust to these changes so that resources are still used efficiently?

Guiding Function of Prices   Suppose consumer tastes change. Specifically, assume that, because of greater health consciousness, consumers decide they want more exercise bikes and fewer cigarettes than the economy currently provides. This change in consumer tastes will be communicated to producers through an increase in demand for bikes and a decline in demand for cigarettes. Bike prices will rise and cigarette prices will fall. Now, assuming firms in both industries were enjoying precisely normal profits before

these changes in consumer demand, higher exercise bike prices mean economic profit for the bike industry, and lower cigarette prices mean losses for the cigarette industry. Self-interest induces new competitors to enter the prosperous bike industry. Losses in time force firms to leave the depressed cigarette industry.

These adjustments in the business sector are appropriate for the assumed changes in consumer tastes. Society—meaning consumers—wants more exercise bikes and fewer cigarettes, and that is precisely what it is getting as the bike industry expands and the cigarette industry contracts. This is consumer sovereignty at work.

But will resource *suppliers* be agreeable to these adjustments? Will the market system prompt resource suppliers to shift their human and property resources from the cigarette to the bike industry, permitting the output of bikes to expand at the expense of cigarette production? The answer is "yes."

The economic profit which initially follows the increase in demand for bikes not only will induce that industry to expand but also will give it the revenue needed to obtain the resources essential to its growth. Higher bike prices will permit firms in that industry to pay higher prices for resources, increasing resource demand and drawing resources from less urgent alternative employments.

The reverse occurs in the adversely affected cigarette industry. The losses following the decline in consumer demand will cause a decline in the demand for resources in that industry. Workers and other resources will be released from the shrinking cigarette industry but will find employment in the expanding bike industry. Furthermore, the increased demand for resources in the bike industry will mean higher resource prices in that industry than those being paid in the cigarette industry, where declines in resource demand have lowered resource prices. The resulting differential in resource prices will provide the incentive for resource owners to further their self-interests by shifting their resources from the cigarette to the bike industry. And this is the precise shift needed to permit the bike industry to expand and the cigarette industry to contract.

The ability of the market system to communicate changes in such basic data as consumer tastes and to elicit appropriate responses from businesses and resource suppliers is called the *directing* or **guiding function of prices.** By affecting product prices and profits, changes in consumer tastes direct the expansion of some industries and the contraction of others. These

Pink Flamingos and "Dollar Votes"

After 40 years, consumer sovereignty and "dollar votes" still support continued production of plastic pink flamingos. Lovers of the icon say that critics do not have a leg to stand on.

LEOMINSTER, Mass.–One of the icons of the American landscape–not the bald eagle or the bison, but the plastic pink flamingo–is approaching 40. And it's still not getting any respect.

Despite its enduring appeal (15 million to 20 million have been sold), the lawn ornament can't seem to escape the T-word, a fate that ruffles the feathers of flamingo fans.

"People say they're tacky, but all great art began as tacky," said Don Featherstone, the Union Products vice president and artist whose signature is molded in every flamingo body. "Art Deco in New York was torn down. But now, they're putting it back up."

Featherstone himself is a bit of a strange bird. A sculptor with a classical art background, he and his wife of 20 years dress alike every day. He attends many flamingo-themed social events sponsored by groups such as the Society for the Preservation of the Plastic Lawn Flamingo.

His plastic company's catalog pictures page after page of adornments suited for any gardener's fancy: a 22-inch black-and-white penguin, a blue-headed pheasant, a green-chested rooster.

All nice, but just not the same thing.

"I tried to put some ducks out there because this is duck country," said Mary-Elizabeth Buckham, who has a flock of pink plastic birds on the lawn of her Victorian home in Centreville, Md. "But nobody wanted to see what they were doing."

Buckham dresses her 34 birds—curving pink necks, spindly wire legs and hollow bodies with molding feather detail—in homemade clothes and rearranges them every week for an adoring public.

At Christmas there was a nativity scene with flamingo wise men and a flamingo baby Jesus. At Thanksgiving there was a "flurkey flock," and at Halloween, flamingo ghosts. Even lawn jockeys aren't that versatile.

The first pink flamingo ornaments, in 1952, were flat, made of plywood. They were made of foam a few years later, but dogs tended to eat them. They've been made of plastic since 1957.

Some versions just didn't fly. A movable-leg model some years back was a flop.

Half a million of the birds move off store shelves in America, Mexico and South America every year, at $9.95 a pair. With numbers like that, Featherstone says he'll suffer the sarcasm.

"As long as they keep buying them, I really don't care," he said with a smile.

Source: Carolyn Thompson, "Flamingo Sales still In the Pink," Associated Press, May 28, 1996. Printed by permission of the Associated Press.

---

adjustments carry through to the resource market as expanding industries demand more resources and contracting industries demand fewer; the resulting changes in resource prices guide resources from the contracting to the expanding industries. Without a market system, some administrative agency, presumably a government planning board, would have to direct businesses and resources into appropriate industries.

Similar analyses show that the system can and does adjust to other fundamental changes—for example, to changes in technology and in the available supplies of various resources.

Role in Promoting Progress Adjusting to changes is one thing; initiating desirable changes is another. Does the competitive market system promote technological improvements and capital accumulation—the two changes that lead to greater productivity and a higher level of material well-being for society?

Technological Progress The market system provides a strong incentive for technological advance. This advance may occur as improved production methods or as new products. A firm developing a new cost-cutting technique has a temporary advantage over its rivals. By passing part of its cost reduction to the consumer through a lower product price, the firm can increase sales and obtain economic profit at the expense of rival firms. Similarly, a firm which successfully introduces a popular new product gains revenue and enhances economic profit at the expense of rival firms. Moreover, the market system is conducive to the rapid spread of technological advance throughout the industry. Rival firms must follow the lead of the most progressive firm or suffer immediate losses and eventual failure.

The lower product price or improved product which a technological advance permits will cause the innovating industry to expand. The expansion may result when existing firms increase their output or when new firms enter the industry, lured by economic profit created by the technological advance. As the industry expands, resources are shifted from less progressive industries to more progressive industries. And so it should be. Efficiency in the use of scarce resources demands that resources be continually reallocated from less efficient industries to those which become relatively more efficient in fulfilling society's wants.

Capital Accumulation A technological advance typically requires additional capital goods. The market system provides the resources necessary to produce those capital goods by adjusting the product market and resource market through increased dollar votes for capital goods. That is, the market system acknowledges dollar voting for capital goods as well as for consumer goods.

But who will register votes for capital goods? First, the entrepreneur, as a receiver of profit income, can be expected to apportion part of that income to the purchase of capital goods. Doing so will yield an even greater profit income in the future if the innovation is successful. Moreover, by paying interest, the entrepreneur can borrow portions of the incomes of households and use the borrowed funds to cast dollar votes for the production of more capital goods. **(Key Question 10)**

COMPETITION AND THE "INVISIBLE HAND"

In capitalism the market system is the organizational mechanism and competition is the mechanism of control. Supply and demand communicate the wants of

consumers (society) to businesses and, through businesses, to resource suppliers. It is competition, however, which forces businesses and resource suppliers to make appropriate responses.

But competition does more than guarantee responses appropriate to the wishes of society. It also forces firms to adopt the most efficient production techniques, keeping costs and prices at their lowest levels. In a competitive market, more efficient firms will eventually eliminate a firm which fails to use the least-costly production technique. And we have seen that competition provides an environment conducive to such technological advance.

In 1776 Adam Smith, in his book *The Wealth of Nations*, first noted that the operation of a competitive market system creates a curious and important unity between private and social interests. Firms and resource suppliers, seeking to further their own self-interests and operating within the framework of a highly competitive market system, will simultaneously, as though guided by an **"invisible hand,"** promote the public or social interest. For example, we have seen that in a competitive environment, businesses use the least-costly combination of resources to produce a specific output because it is in their private self-interests to do so. To act otherwise would be to forgo profit or even to risk business failure. But, at the same time, it is clearly also in the social interest to use scarce resources in the least-costly (most efficient) way.

In our more-bikes–fewer-cigarettes illustration, it is self-interest, awakened and guided by the competitive market system, which induces responses appropriate to the change in society's wants. Businesses seeking to make higher profits and to avoid losses, and resource suppliers pursuing greater monetary awards, negotiate changes in the allocation of resources and end up with the output that society demands. The force of competition controls or guides self-interest in such a way that it automatically, and quite unintentionally, furthers the best interests of society. The "invisible hand" tells us that when firms maximize their profits, society's domestic output is also maximized.

The virtues of the market system are thus implicit in our discussion. Three merit emphasis:

1. *Efficiency* The basic economic argument for the market system is that it promotes the efficient use of resources. The competitive market system guides resources into the production of those goods and services most wanted by society. It forces the use of the most efficient techniques in

organizing resources for production, and it leads to the development and adoption of new and more efficient production techniques.

2. Incentives The market system provides incentives for improvement and innovation. Greater work effort means higher money incomes, which can be translated into a higher standard of living. Similarly, the assuming of risks by entrepreneurs can result in substantial profit incomes. Successful innovations may also generate economic rewards.

3. Freedom The major noneconomic argument for the market system is its great emphasis on personal freedom. In contrast to central planning, the market system can coordinate economic activity without coercion. The market system permits—indeed, it thrives on—freedom of enterprise and choice. Entrepreneurs and workers are not herded from industry to industry by government directives to meet production targets established by some governmental agency. On the contrary, they are free to further their own self-interests, subject to the rewards and penalties imposed by the market system itself.

QUICK REVIEW 4-3

■ The output mix of the market system is determined by profits, which in turn depend heavily on consumer preferences. Profits cause preferred, efficient industries to expand; losses cause inefficient industries to contract.

■ Competition forces industries to use the least-costly (most efficient) production methods.

■ Consumer incomes and product prices determine the distribution of output among households in a market economy.

■ Competitive markets reallocate resources in response to changes in consumer tastes, technological advances, and changes in supplies of resources.

■ The "invisible hand" of the market system channels the pursuit of self-interest to the good of society.

CHAPTER SUMMARY

1. The capitalist system is characterized by private ownership of resources, including capital, and the freedom of individuals to engage in economic activities of their choice to advance their own material well-being. Self-interest is the driving force of such an economy, and competition functions as a regulatory or control mechanism.

2. In the capitalist system, markets and prices organize and make effective the many millions of individual decisions which determine what is produced, the methods of production, and the sharing of output. The capitalist ideology envisions government playing a minor and relatively passive economic role.

3. Specialization and an advanced technology based on the extensive use of capital goods are common to all advanced industrial economies.

4. Functioning as a medium of exchange, money circumvents problems of bartering and thus permits easy trade and greater specialization, both domestically and internationally.

5. Every economy faces Five Fundamental Questions: (a) How much of available resources should be employed to produce goods? (b) What goods and services are to be produced? (c) How should they be produced? (d) To whom should the output be distributed? (e) Can the system adapt to changes in consumer tastes, resource supplies, and technology?

6. In a market economy those products whose production and sale yield total revenue sufficient to cover all costs, including a normal profit, are produced. Those whose production does not yield a normal profit, or more, are not produced.

7. Economic profit designates an industry as prosperous and promotes its expansion. Losses mean an industry is unprosperous and result in contraction of that industry.

8. Consumer sovereignty means that both businesses and resource suppliers channel their efforts in accordance with the wants of consumers.

9. Competition forces firms to use the least-costly, and therefore the most economically efficient, production techniques.

10. The prices commanded by the resources owned and supplied by each household will determine that household's claim on the economy's output. Within the limit of each household's money income, consumer preferences and the relative prices of products determine the distribution of total output.

11. The competitive market system can communicate changes in consumer tastes to resource suppliers and entrepreneurs, prompting appropriate adjustments in the allocation of the economy's resources. The competitive market system also provides an environment conducive to technological advance and capital accumulation.

12. Competition, the primary mechanism of control in the market economy, promotes a unity of private and social interests; as though directed by an "invisible hand," competition harnesses the self-interest motives of businesses and resource suppliers to simultaneously further the social interest in using scarce resources efficiently.

TERMS AND CONCEPTS

private property
freedom of enterprise
freedom of choice
self-interest
competition
roundabout production
specialization

division of labor
medium of exchange
barter
money
Five Fundamental
  Questions
economic costs

normal profit
economic profit
expanding industry
declining industry
consumer sovereignty
dollar votes
derived demand

guiding function of
  prices
"invisible hand"

STUDY QUESTIONS

1. Explain each of these statements:
  a. Capitalism not only *accepts* self-interest as a fact of human existence; it *relies* on self-interest to achieve society's material goals.
  b. Where there is private property, property rights, and economic freedom, there will be capitalism; unlike the command economy, capitalism emerges spontaneously.

2. KEY QUESTION What advantages result from "roundabout" production? What problem is involved in increasing a full-employment economy's stock of capital goods? Illustrate this problem using the production possibilities curve. Does an economy with unemployed resources face the same problem?

3. What are the advantages of specialization in the use of human and material resources? Explain: "Exchange is the necessary consequence of specialization."

4. What problems does barter entail? Indicate the economic significance of money as a medium of exchange. "Money is the only commodity that is good for nothing but to be gotten rid of. It will not feed you, clothe you, shelter you, or amuse you unless you spend or invest it. It imparts value only in parting."[1] Explain this statement.

5. Briefly describe how the market system answers the Fundamental Questions. Why must economic choices be made?

6. Evaluate and explain the following statements:
  a. The capitalistic system is a profit and loss economy.
  b. Competition is the indispensable disciplinarian of the market economy.
  c. Production methods which are inferior in the engineering sense may be the most efficient methods in the economic sense.

7. Explain the meaning and implications of the following quotation.

The beautiful consequence of the market is that it is its own guardian. If output prices or certain kinds of remuneration stray away from their socially ordained levels, forces are set into motion to bring them back to the fold. It is a curious paradox which thus ensues: the market, which is the acme of individual economic freedom, is the strictest taskmaster of all. One may appeal the ruling of a planning board or win the dispensation of a minister; but there is no appeal, no dispensation, from the anonymous pressures of the market mechanism. Economic freedom is thus more illusory than at first appears. One can do as one pleases in the market. But

---

[1]Federal Reserve Bank of Philadelphia, "Creeping Inflation," *Business Review*, August 1957, p. 3.

if one pleases to do what the market disapproves, the price of individual freedom is economic ruination.[2]

8. KEY QUESTION Assume that a business firm finds its profit will be at a maximum when it produces $40 worth of product A. Suppose also that each of the three techniques shown in the following table will produce the desired output.

Resource	Price per unit of resource	Resource units required		
		Technique 1	Technique 2	Technique 3
Labor	$3	5	2	3
Land	4	2	4	2
Capital	2	2	4	5
Entrepreneurial ability	2	4	2	4

a. With the resource prices shown, which technique will the firm choose? Why? Will production entail profit or losses? Will the industry expand or contract? When will a new equilibrium output be achieved?

b. Assume now that a new technique, technique 4, is developed. It combines 2 units of labor, 2 of land, 6 of capital, and 3 of entrepreneurial ability. In view of the resource prices in the table, will the firm adopt the new technique? Explain your answer.

c. Suppose now that an increase in the labor supply causes the price of labor to fall to $1.50 per unit, all other resource prices being unchanged. Which technique will the producer now choose? Explain.

d. "The market system causes the economy to conserve most in the use of those resources which are particularly scarce in supply. Resources which are scarcest relative to the demand for them have the highest prices. As a result, producers use these resources as sparingly as is possible." Evaluate this statement. Does your answer to question 8c bear out this contention? Explain.

---

[2]Robert L. Heilbroner, *The Worldly Philosophers*, 3d ed. (New York: Simon & Schuster, 1967), p. 42.

9. Suppose the demand for bagels dramatically rises while the demand for breakfast cereal plummets. Explain how the competitive market economy will make the needed adjustments to reestablish an efficient allocation of society's scarce resources?

10. KEY QUESTION Some large hardware stores such as Home Depot boast of carrying as many as 20,000 different products in each store. What motivated the producers of these particular items—everything from screwdrivers to ladders to water heaters—to make them and offer them for sale? How did producers decide on the best combinations of resources to use? Who made these resources available, and why? Who decides whether these specific hardware products should continue to get produced and offered for sale?

11. In a single sentence, describe the meaning of the phrase "invisible hand."

12. (Last Word) Relate the human-interest story about the plastic pink flamingo to (a) consumer sovereignty and dollar votes, (b) freedom of enterprise, and (c) the role of profit in allocating society's scarce resources.

13. WEB-BASED QUESTION The United Nations' Virtual Marketplace The United Nations http://urgento.gse.rmit.edu.au/untpdc/eto has set up an Electronic Trade Opportunity (ETO), a large-scale virtual marketplace for trade offers (ETOs) from around the world. ETOs are received by millions of companies every week in one of several electronic forms. How does this new virtual marketplace improve the efficient use of resources and increase the freedom of enterprise and choice? Does it increase competition? How does it help firms in developing countries? Why would the United Nations set up such a virtual marketplace?

14. WEB-BASED QUESTION Barter and the IRS Bartering occurs when goods or services are exchanged without the exchange of money. For some, barter's popularity is that it enables them to avoid paying taxes to the government. How might such avoidance occur? Does the Internal Revenue Service (IRS) http://www.irs.ustreas.gov/tax_edu/teletax/tx420.html treat barter as taxable or nontaxable income? How is the value of a barter transaction determined? What are some IRS barter examples? What does the IRS require of so-called barter exchanges with regard to their members?

CHAPTER FIVE

The Mixed Economy: Private and Public Sectors

Let's now move from the model of pure capitalism closer to the reality of the U.S. economy. For convenience, we divide the economy into sectors (major parts). We first describe the *private sector,* comprising the *household* sector and *business* sector, and then introduce and analyze the *public sector* (government). Because government is new to our discussion, it will get most of our attention.

Our purpose is to provide some facts and analysis about households, businesses, and governmental units since they are the primary decision makers of our mixed economy. Here, our focus is inward; we look at the domestic economy. In Chapter 6 we look outward, examining how the domestic economy relates to the rest of the world.

HOUSEHOLDS AS INCOME RECEIVERS

The household sector of the United States economy is currently composed of about 101 million households, which are the ultimate suppliers of all economic resources and, simultaneously, the major spenders in the economy.

Let's first consider households as income receivers. Two ways of looking at the income received by households are (1) according to the functions which earned it and (2) according to the households which received it.

The Functional Distribution of Income

The **functional distribution of income** indicates how total money income is divided among wages, rents, interest, and profits, that is, according to the function performed by the income receiver. Wages are paid to labor, rents and interest to owners of property resources, and profits to the owners of corporations and unincorporated businesses.

The functional distribution of total U.S. income for 1997 is shown in Figure 5-1. The largest source of income for households is the wages and salaries paid to workers by the business and government units hiring them. In our mixed economy, the bulk of total income goes to labor, not to capital. Proprietors' income—the incomes of doctors, lawyers, small-business owners, farmers, and owners of other unincorporated enterprises—is in fact a combination of wage and profit incomes. Some of this income is payment for one's own labor, and some of it is profit from one's own business.

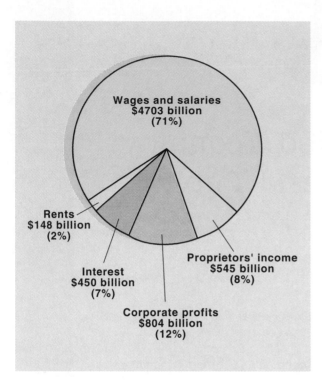

FIGURE 5-1 The functional distribution of U.S. income, 1997 Almost three-fourths of national income is received as wages and salaries. Capitalist income—corporate profit, interest, and rents—accounts for about one-fifth of total income. (*Source: Survey of Current Business*, February 1998.)

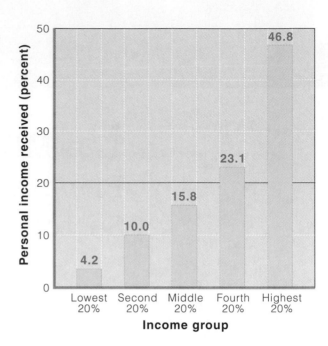

FIGURE 5-2 The distribution of income among U.S. families, 1996 Personal income is quite unequally distributed in the United States, with the top 20 percent of families receiving nearly one-half of the total income. In an equal distribution, all five vertical bars would be as high as the horizontal line drawn at 20 percent; then each 20 percent of families would get 20 percent of total income.

The other three types of earnings are self-evident: Some households own corporate stock and receive dividend incomes on their holdings. Many households also own bonds and savings accounts which yield interest income. Rental income results from households' providing buildings and natural resources (including land) to businesses.

The Personal Distribution of Income

The **personal distribution of income** indicates how total money income is divided among individual households. Figure 5-2 shows one way to present that distribution. There, households (families) are divided into five numerically equal groups or quintiles, and the heights of the bars show the percentage of total income received by each group. In 1996 the poorest 20 percent of all families received about 4 percent of

total personal income in contrast to the 20 percent they would have received if income were equally distributed. In comparison, the richest 20 percent of all families received 47 percent of personal income. On the basis of such data, most economists agree there is considerable inequality in the personal distribution of American income. **(Key Question 2)**

HOUSEHOLDS AS SPENDERS

How do households dispose of their income? Part flows to government as taxes, and the rest is divided between personal consumption expenditures and personal saving. In 1997, households disposed of their total personal income as shown in Figure 5-3.

Personal Taxes

Personal taxes, of which the Federal personal income tax is the major component, have risen in both ab-

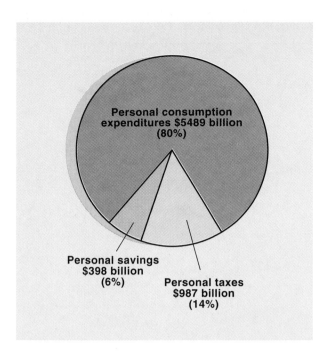

FIGURE 5-3 **The disposition of household income, 1997** Household income is apportioned among taxes, saving, and consumption, with consumption being the major use of income. [*Source: Survey of Current Business,* February 1998. (The income concept in this figure differs from that used in Figure 5-1, accounting for the quantitative discrepancies between "total income" in the two figures.)]

solute and relative terms since World War II. In 1941, households paid $3.3 billion, or 3 percent of their $95.3 billion total income, in personal taxes, compared with $987 billion, or 14 percent of $6874 billion total income, in 1997.

Personal Saving

Economists define "saving" as that part of after-tax income which is not spent; hence, households have just two choices of what to do with their incomes after taxes—use it to consume or save it. Saving is the portion of income which is not paid in taxes or used to purchase consumers goods but which flows into bank accounts, insurance policies, bonds and stocks, mutual funds, and other financial assets.

Reasons for saving center on *security* and *speculation.* Households save to provide a nest egg for unforeseen contingencies (sickness, accident, unemploy-

ment), for retirement from the workforce, to finance the education of children, or simply for financial security. Also, people save for speculation. You might channel part of your income to purchase stocks, speculating that they will increase in value.

The desire to save is not enough. You must be *able* to save, and that depends on the size of your income. If your income is low, you may not be able to save any money. If your income is lower yet, you may *dissave,* that is, consume in excess of your after-tax income. You do this by borrowing and by digging into savings you may have accumulated in years when your income was higher.

Both saving and consumption vary directly with income; as households get more income, they save more and consume more. In fact, the top 10 percent of income receivers account for most of the personal saving in the U.S. economy.

Personal Consumption Expenditures

Figure 5-3 shows that four-fifths of total income flows from income receivers back into the business sector as personal consumption expenditures—money spent on consumer goods.

The size and composition of the economy's total output of goods and services depend on the size and composition of consumer spending. As indicated in Table 5-1, household spending is classified as expenditures on (1) durable goods, (2) nondurable goods, and (3) services.

If a product generally has an expected life of 3 years or more, it is called a **durable good;** if its life is less than 3 years, it is labeled a **nondurable good.** Automobiles, personal computers, washing machines, and most furniture are durables. Most food and clothing items are nondurables. **Services** consist of the work done for consumers by lawyers, barbers, doctors, mechanics, and so on. Observe in Table 5-1 that *the United States is a service-oriented economy in that more than one-half of consumer spending is for services.*

QUICK REVIEW 5-1

■ The functional distribution of income indicates how income is divided among wages, rents, interest, and profits; the personal distribution of income shows how income is apportioned among households.

TABLE 5-1 The composition of personal consumption expenditures, 1997*

Types of consumption	Amount, billions	Percentage of total
Durable goods	**$ 659**	**12**
Motor vehicles and parts	$263	5
Furniture and household equipment	268	5
All others	129	2
Nondurable goods	**1593**	**29**
Food	776	14
Clothing and shoes	278	5
Gasoline and oil	125	2
Fuel oil and coal	11	0
All others	403	7
Services	**3237**	**59**
Housing	826	15
Household operations	329	6
Medical care	855	16
Transportation	236	4
Personal services, recreation, and others	991	18
Total personal consumption expenditures	**$5489**	**100**

*Excludes interest paid to businesses.

Source: Survey of Current Business, February 1998. Details may not add to totals because of rounding.

■ Wages and salaries are the major component of the functional distribution of income. The personal distribution reveals considerable inequality.

■ Eighty percent of household income is consumed; the rest is saved or paid in taxes.

■ More than half of consumer spending is for services.

THE BUSINESS POPULATION

Businesses constitute the second major part of the private sector. To avoid confusion, we must start by distinguishing among a plant, a firm, and an industry.

A **plant** is a physical establishment—a factory, farm, mine, store, or warehouse—which performs one or more functions in fabricating and distributing goods and services.

A business **firm** is a business organization which owns and operates plants. Most firms operate only one plant, but many own and operate several. Multiplant firms may own horizontal, vertical, or conglomerate combinations of plants. A **vertical combi-**

nation of plants is a group of plants, with each performing a different function in the various stages of the production process. As an example, every large steel firm—USX, Bethlehem Steel, Republic Steel, and others—owns iron ore and coal mines, limestone quarries, metal refineries, rolling mills, foundries, and, in some cases, fabricating shops.

A **horizontal combination** of plants is one in which all plants perform the same function. The large chain stores in the retail field—JC Penney, Foot Locker, Toys "Я" Us, Wal-Mart—are examples.

A **conglomerate combination** is made up of plants which operate across several different markets and industries. For example, Warner-Lambert Company owns plants involved in such diverse fields as chewing gum (Trident), razors (Shick), cough drops (Halls), breath mints (Certs), and antacids (Rolaids). Firms such as these are called *conglomerates*.

An **industry** is a group of firms producing the same, or similar, products. This seems to be a simple concept, but industries are usually difficult to identify in practice. For example, how do we identify the automobile industry? The simplest answer is "all firms producing automobiles." But how should we account for small trucks? Certainly, small pickup trucks are similar in many respects to vans and station wagons. And what about firms which make parts for cars, say, airbags? What industry are they in? Is it better to speak of the "motor vehicle industry" rather than the "automobile industry?" If so, where should we then place motorcycles?

Delineating an industry becomes even more complex because most businesses are multiproduct firms. Automobile manufacturers in the United States also make such diverse products as diesel locomotives, buses, refrigerators, guided missiles, and air conditioners. For these reasons, industry classifications are usually somewhat arbitrary.

LEGAL FORMS OF BUSINESSES

The business population is extremely diverse, ranging from giant corporations such as General Motors with 1996 sales of $168 billion and 648,000 employees to neighborhood specialty shops and "mom-and-pop" groceries with 1 or 2 employees and sales of only $200 to $300 per day. This diversity makes it necessary to classify business firms by some criterion such as legal

structure, industry or product, or size. Figure 5-4a shows how the business population is distributed among the three major legal forms: (1) the sole proprietorship, (2) the partnership, and (3) the corporation.

Sole Proprietorship

A **sole proprietorship** is a business owned and operated by one person. Usually, the proprietor (the owner) personally supervises its operation.

Advantages   This simple type of business organization has two major advantages:

1. A sole proprietorship is easy to organize; there is virtually no legal red tape or expense.
2. The proprietor is his or her own boss and has substantial freedom of action. Since the proprietor's profit income depends on the enterprise's success, there is a strong and immediate incentive to manage the business efficiently.

Disadvantages   The disadvantages of this form of business organization are several:

1. With rare exceptions, the financial resources of a sole proprietorship are insufficient to permit the firm to grow into a large enterprise. Finances are

(a) Percentage of firms   (b) Percentage of sales

The business population by form of legal organization

Form	Number of firms
Sale proprietorships*	16,154,000
Partnerships	1,493,000
Corporations	3,965,000
Total	21,612,000

*Excludes farmers.

FIGURE 5-4 **The business population and shares of domestic output**   (a) Sole proprietorships dominate the business population numerically, but (b) corporations account for 90 percent of total sales (output). The table shows the population numbers.

usually limited to what the proprietor has in the bank and to what he or she can borrow. Since proprietorships often fail, commercial banks are not eager to extend them credit.

2. Being in complete control of an enterprise forces the proprietor to carry out all management functions. A proprietor must make decisions concerning buying, selling, and the hiring and training of personnel, as well as producing, advertising, and distributing the firm's product. In short, the potential benefits of specialization in business management are not available to the typical small-scale proprietorship.

3. Most important, the proprietor is subject to *unlimited liability*. Individuals in business for themselves risk not only the assets of the firm but also their personal assets. If the assets of an unsuccessful sole proprietorship are insufficient to pay the firm's bills, creditors can file claims against the proprietor's personal property.

Partnership

The **partnership** form of business organization is a natural outgrowth of the sole proprietorship. Partnerships were developed to overcome some of the shortcomings of proprietorships. In a partnership, two or more individuals (the partners) agree to own and operate a business together. Usually they pool their financial resources and business skills. Similarly, they share the risks and the profits or losses.

Advantages   What are the advantages of a partnership?

1. Like the sole proprietorship, it is easy to organize. Although a written agreement is almost invariably involved, there is not much legal red tape.

2. Greater specialization in management is possible because there are more participants.

3. Because there are several owners the odds are that the financial resources of a partnership are greater than those of a sole proprietorship. Partners can pool their financial capital and are usually somewhat better risks in the eyes of lending institutions.

Disadvantages   Partnerships may have some of the shortcomings of the proprietorship and some of their own as well:

1. Whenever several people participate in management, the division of authority can lead to inconsistent policies or to inaction when action is required. Worse, partners may disagree on basic policy.

2. The finances of partnerships are still limited, although they are generally superior to those of a sole proprietorship. But the financial resources of three or four partners may still not be enough to ensure the growth of a successful enterprise.

3. The continuity of a partnership is precarious. Generally, when a partner dies or withdraws, the partnership must be dissolved and completely reorganized, which can disrupt its operations.

4. Unlimited liability plagues a partnership, just as it does a proprietorship. In fact, each partner is liable for all business debts incurred, not only as a result of each partner's own management decisions but also as a consequence of the actions of any other partner. A wealthy partner risks money on the prudence of less affluent partners.

Corporation

A **corporation** is a legal creation which can acquire resources, own assets, produce and sell products, incur debts, extend credit, sue and be sued, and perform the functions of any other type of enterprise. This "legal person" is distinct and separate from the individuals who own it. Hired managers operate most corporations.

Advantages   The advantages of the corporate form of business enterprise have catapulted it into a dominant position in modern U.S. capitalism. Although corporations are relatively small in number, they are frequently large in size and scale of operations. As Figure 5-4 indicates, less than 20 percent of all businesses are corporations, but they account for roughly 90 percent of all business sales.

1. The corporation is by far the most effective form of business organization for raising financial capital (money). As this chapter's Last Word reveals, the corporation features unique methods of finance—the selling of stocks and bonds—which allow the firm to pool the financial resources of extremely large numbers of people.

Financing via sales of stocks and bonds also provides advantages to the purchasers of these securities. **Stocks** are shares of ownership of a corporation. **Bonds** are promises to repay a loan, usually with a set rate of interest. Financing through stocks and bonds allows households to participate in business and share the expected monetary reward without actively engaging in management. In addition, an individual can spread any risks by buying the securities of several corporations. Finally, it is usually easy for holders of corporate securities to sell those holdings. Organized stock exchanges simplify the transfer of securities from sellers to buyers. This "ease of sale" increases the willingness of savers to make financial investments in corporate securities.

In addition, corporations have easier access to bank credit than other types of business organizations. Corporations are better risks and are more likely to become profitable clients of banks.

2. Corporations have the distinct advantage of **limited liability.** The owners (stockholders) of a corporation risk *only* what they paid for their stock. Their personal assets are not at stake if the corporation cannot pay its debts. Creditors can sue the corporation as a legal person but cannot sue the owners of the corporation as individuals. Limited liability clearly makes it easier for the corporation to sell its stock.

3. Because of their advantage in attracting financial capital, successful corporations find it easier to expand the size and scope of their operations and to realize the benefits of expansion. They can take advantage of mass-production technologies and greater specialization in the use of human resources. While the manager of a sole proprietorship may be forced to share her or his time among production, accounting, and marketing functions, a corporation can hire specialists in each of these areas and achieve greater efficiency.

4. As a legal entity, the corporation has a life independent of its owners and its officers. Sole proprietorships and partnerships are subject to sudden and unpredictable demise, but legally at least, corporations are immortal. The transfer of corporate ownership through inheritance or the sale of stock does not disrupt the continuity of the corporation. Corporations have a permanence, lacking in other forms of business organization, which is conducive to long-range planning and growth.

Disadvantages The corporation's advantages are of tremendous significance and typically override any accompanying disadvantages. Yet there are drawbacks to the corporate form:

1. Some red tape and legal expenses are involved in obtaining a corporate charter.

2. From the social point of view, the corporate form of enterprise lends itself to certain abuses. Because the corporation is a legal entity, unscrupulous business owners sometimes can avoid personal responsibility for questionable business activities by adopting the corporate form of enterprise.

3. A further disadvantage of corporations is the **double taxation** of some corporate income. Corporate profit that is shared among stockholders as *dividends* is taxed twice—once as corporate profit and again as stockholders' personal income.

4. In sole proprietorships and partnerships, the owner of the real and financial assets of the firm also directly controls those assets. In large corporations in which ownership is widely diffused over tens or hundreds of thousands of stockholders, there is *separation of ownership and control.* That is, the people who own a corporation usually do not manage it—others are hired to do so.

This reality may create a so-called **principal-agent problem.** The *principals,* in this case, are the stockholders who own the corporation. These owners hire managers as their *agents* to run the business on their behalf. But the interests of the managers (agents) and the wishes of the owners (principals) are not always in accord. The owners typically want maximum profit. Management, however, seeking the power and prestige which accompany control over a large enterprise, may favor unprofitable expansion of the firm's operations. Or a conflict of interest can develop over dividend policies, such as what portion of corporate earnings after taxes should be paid out as dividends and what portion reinvested by the firm. And corporation officials may vote themselves large salaries, pensions, and so forth out of corporate earnings which might otherwise be used for increased dividend payments.

Postscript: A number of states have passed legislation authorizing "hybrid" business structures which allow some of the advantages of corporations to firms with one or relatively few owners. Two such structures are the *limited-liability company* (LLC) and the *S corporation.*

The LLC is like an ordinary partnership for tax purposes but resembles a corporation on liability issues. Like a partnership, an LLC distributes all profit directly to owners and investors. But like a corporation, an LLC shields the personal assets of owners from liability claims. LLCs have a limited life, typically 30 or 40 years.

The S corporation is a corporation with 35 or fewer employees. The profit from the corporation passes directly through to the owners as if the firm were a sole proprietorship or partnership, so the owners avoid the double taxation on distributed profit. The owners also get the benefit of limited liability. **(Key Question 4)**

Large Corporations

A glance back at Figure 5-4 reminds us that, although relatively small in number, corporations are the major source of production in the U.S. economy. The fact that corporations constitute less than 20 percent of the business population yet produce 90 percent of total business output suggests that many corporations are very large. In 1996 some 45 corporations in the United States had annual sales over $20 billion; 143 firms realized sales over $10 billion. General Motors alone had sales of $168 billion. Remarkably, there are only 22 nations in the world whose annual domestic outputs are more than GM's sales!

But the influence of large corporations varies significantly from industry to industry. They dominate manufacturing and are strong in the transportation, communication, power utilities, and banking and financial industries. At the other extreme are some 2 million farmers whose combined sales in 1996 were less than those of the economy's two largest industrial corporations. In between are a variety of retail and service industries characterized by relatively small firms. Nevertheless, large firms do dominate the U.S. business landscape, and in terms of total output, the United States clearly is a "big business" economy.

QUICK REVIEW 5-2

■ A plant is a physical establishment which contributes to the production of goods and services; a firm is a business organization which owns and operates plants; plants may be arranged in vertical, horizontal, or conglomerate combinations.

■ The three basic legal forms of business are the sole proprietorship, the partnership, and the corporation; while sole proprietorships make up nearly three-fourths of all firms, corporations account for about nine-tenths of total sales.

■ The major advantages of corporations which have led to their popularity are a superior ability to raise financial

capital, the limited liability they convey to owners, and their life beyond that of their owners and officers.

■ Very large corporations dominate many U.S. industries.

ECONOMIC FUNCTIONS OF GOVERNMENT

All economies in the real world are "mixed": Government and the market system share the responsibility of responding to the Five Fundamental Questions. The U.S. economy is predominantly a market economy, yet the economic activities of government are of great significance.

In the next several sections we discuss the major economic functions of government—the public sector. These functions are (1) providing a legal and social framework, (2) maintaining competition within markets, (3) redistributing income as necessary for equity, (4) reallocating resources, and (5) stabilizing the economy.

The first two of these economic functions strengthen and facilitate the working of the market system; the last three modify pure capitalism to achieve economic and social goals.

LEGAL AND SOCIAL FRAMEWORK

Government provides the legal framework and the services needed for a market economy to operate effectively. The legal framework sets the legal status of business enterprises, ensures the rights of private ownership, and allows the making and enforcement of contracts. Government also establishes the legal "rules of the game" governing the relationships of businesses, resource suppliers, and consumers with one another. Units of government can referee economic relationships, seek out foul play, and exercise authority in imposing appropriate penalties.

Services provided by government include police powers to maintain internal order, a system of standards for measuring the weight and quality of products, and a system of money to facilitate exchanges of goods and services.

The Pure Food and Drug Act of 1906 is an example of how government has strengthened the market system. This act sets rules of conduct governing producers in their relationships with consumers. It prohibits the sale of adulterated and misbranded foods and drugs, requires net weights and ingredients of products to be specified on their containers, establishes quality standards which must be stated on labels of packaged foods, and prohibits deceptive claims on patent-medicine labels. These measures are designed to prevent fraudulent activities by producers and to increase the public's confidence in the integrity of the market system. Similar legislation pertains to labor-management relations and relations of business firms to one another.

This type of government activity is presumed to improve resource allocation. Supplying a medium of exchange, ensuring product quality, defining ownership rights, and enforcing contracts increase the volume and safety of exchange. This widens markets and permits greater specialization in the use of property and human resources. Such specialization means a more efficient allocation of resources. However, some argue that government overregulates the interactions of businesses, consumers, and workers and say that this stifles economic incentives and impairs efficiency.

MAINTAINING COMPETITION

Competition is the basic regulatory mechanism in a capitalist economy. It is the force which subjects producers and resource suppliers to the dictates of consumer sovereignty. With competition, buyers are the boss, the market is their agent, and businesses are their servants.

It is a different story where there is only a single seller—a **monopoly**—or a small handful of sellers with *monopoly power.* Monopolists are not regulated by competition. When the number of sellers becomes so small that each seller can influence total supply, the seller or sellers have the power to set the product price. By restricting supply, these firms can charge above-competitive prices. Also, because entry to these industries is blocked, monopolists can enjoy persistent economic profits. The restricted output and the high prices and profits directly conflict with the interests of consumers. In fact, producer sovereignty supplants consumer sovereignty, and monopoly supplants competition. Where there is monopoly, the pursuit of self-interest does *not* lead to the social good. Rather, society's economic resources are *underallocated* to the monopolized product.

In the United States, government has attempted to control monopoly primarily in two ways:

1. ***Regulation and ownership***   In a few situations, industries are *natural monopolies*—industries in which technology is such that only a single seller can achieve the lowest possible costs. Government has allowed these monopolies to exist but has also created public commissions to regulate their prices and set their service standards. Some aspects of transportation, communications, electricity, and other utilities are natural monopolies which government regulates in varying degrees. Sometimes, especially at the local level of government, public ownership replaces regulation.

2. ***Antimonopoly laws***   In nearly all markets, efficient production can best be attained with a high degree of competition. The Federal government has therefore enacted a series of antitrust (antimonopoly) laws, beginning with the Sherman Act of 1890, to maintain and strengthen competition.

REDISTRIBUTION OF INCOME

The market system is impersonal. It may distribute income with more inequality than society desires. The market system yields very large incomes to those whose labor, by virtue of inherent ability and acquired education and skills, commands high wages. Similarly, those who, through hard work or easy inheritance, possess valuable capital and land receive large property incomes.

But others in society have less productive ability, have received only modest amounts of education and training, and have accumulated or inherited no property resources. Moreover, many of the aged, the physically and mentally handicapped, and female-headed families earn only very small incomes, or, like the unemployed, no incomes at all. Thus, in the market system there is considerable inequality in the distribution of income and therefore in the distribution of output among individual households. Poverty amidst overall plenty in the economy persists.

Thus, society chooses to redistribute income through a variety of government policies and programs:

1. ***Transfers***   *Transfer payments*, for example, in the form of welfare checks and food stamps, provide relief to the destitute, the dependent, the handicapped, and older citizens; unemployment compensation payments provide aid to the unemployed.

2. *Market intervention* Government also alters the distribution of income by *market intervention*, that is, by acting to modify the prices which are or would be established by market forces. Providing farmers with above-market prices for their outputs and requiring that firms pay minimum wages are illustrations of government price fixing designed to raise incomes of specific groups.

3. *Taxation* The personal income tax has been used historically to take a larger proportion of the incomes of the rich than of the incomes of the poor, thus narrowing the after-tax income gap between high- and low-income earners.

The *extent* to which government should redistribute income is subject to many debates. Redistribution involves both benefits and costs. The alleged benefits are greater "fairness," or "economic justice"; the alleged costs are reduced incentives to work, save, invest, and produce, and therefore less total output and income.

REALLOCATION OF RESOURCES

Market failure occurs when the competitive market system (1) produces the "wrong" amounts of certain goods and services or (2) fails to allocate any resources whatsoever to the production of certain goods and services whose output is economically justified. The first type of failure results from what economists call *spillovers*, and the second type involves *public goods*. Both kinds of market failure can be corrected by government action.

Spillovers or Externalities

When we say that competitive markets automatically bring about efficient resource use, we assume that all the benefits and costs for each product are fully reflected in the market demand and supply curves. This is not always so in real markets; certain benefits or costs may escape the buyer or seller.

A spillover occurs when some of the costs or the benefits of a good are passed on to or "spill over to" parties other than the immediate buyer or seller. Spillovers are also called *externalities* because they are benefits or costs accruing to some third party which is external to the market transaction.

Spillover Costs Production or consumption costs inflicted on a third party without compensation are called **spillover costs.** Many spillover costs are in the form of environmental pollution. When a chemical manufacturer or meatpacking plant dumps its wastes into a lake or river, swimmers, fishermen, and boaters—and perhaps drinking-water supplies—suffer spillover costs. When a petroleum refinery pollutes the air with smoke or a paper mill creates distressing odors, the community bears spillover costs for which it is not compensated.

What are the economic effects? Recall that costs determine the position of the firm's supply curve. When a firm avoids some costs by polluting, its supply curve lies farther to the right than it does when the firm bears the full costs of production. This results in a larger output than is socially desirable—a market failure in the form of an *overallocation* of resources to the production of the good.

Correcting for Spillover Costs Government can do two things to correct the overallocation of resources. Both solutions are designed to internalize the external costs, that is, to make the offending firm pay the costs rather than shift them to others:

1. *Legislation* In our examples of air and water pollution, the most direct action is legislation prohibiting or limiting pollution. Such legislation forces potential polluters to pay for the proper disposal of industrial wastes—here, by installing smoke-abatement equipment or water-purification facilities. The idea is to force potential offenders, under the threat of legal action, to bear all the costs associated with production.

2. *Specific taxes* A less direct action is based on the fact that taxes are a cost and therefore a determinant of a firm's supply curve. Government might levy a *specific tax*—a tax confined to a particular product—on each unit of the polluting firm's output. The amount of this tax would roughly equal the estimated amount of the spillover cost arising from the production of each unit of output. Through this tax, government would pass back to the offending firm a cost equivalent to the spillover cost which the firm is avoiding. This would shift the firm's supply curve to the left, reducing equilibrium output and eliminating the overallocation of resources.

Spillover Benefits But spillovers may also appear as benefits. Production or consumption of certain goods and services may confer spillover or external benefits on third parties or on the community at large without compensating payment. Measles and polio immunization result in direct benefits to the immedi-

ate consumer of those vaccines. But immunization against contagious diseases yields widespread and substantial spillover benefits to the entire community. Discovery of an AIDS vaccine would benefit society far beyond the persons vaccinated. Unvaccinated individuals would clearly benefit by the slowing of the spread of the disease.

Education is another example of **spillover benefits.** Education benefits individual consumers: "More educated" people generally achieve higher incomes than "less educated" people. But education also provides benefits to society. The economy as a whole benefits from a more versatile and more productive labor force, on the one hand, and smaller outlays for crime prevention, law enforcement, and welfare programs, on the other. There is evidence indicating that any worker with a *specific* educational or skill level will be more productive if associated workers have more education. In other words, worker Crum becomes more productive simply because coworkers Jones and Green are more educated.

Spillover benefits mean that the market demand curve, which reflects only private benefits, understates total benefits. The demand curve for the product lies farther to the left than it would if all benefits were taken into account by the market. This means that a smaller amount of the product will be produced or, alternatively, that there will be an *underallocation* of resources to the product—again a market failure.

Correcting for Spillover Benefits

How might the underallocation of resources associated with spillover benefits be corrected? The answer is to either subsidize consumers (to increase demand), subsidize producers (to increase supply), or, in the extreme, have government produce the product.

1. *Subsidize consumers* To correct the underallocation of resources to higher education, the U.S. government provides low-interest loans to students so that they can afford more education. These loans increase the demand for higher education.

Here's a more complex example: The Food Stamp Program is designed to improve the diets of low-income families. The food stamps the government gives to these families can be exchanged only for food. Stores accepting the stamps are reimbursed with money by the government. This program thus purposely increases the demand for food. Part of the rationale is that improved nutrition helps disadvantaged children perform better in school and disadvantaged adults be better employees. In helping people

become more productive, some of the benefits of the extra food consumption spill over to the society as a whole.

2. *Subsidize suppliers* In some cases government might find it more convenient and administratively simpler to correct an underallocation by subsidizing producers. This is done in higher education, where state governments provide substantial portions of the budgets of public colleges and universities. These subsidies lower the costs of producing higher education and increase its supply. Publicly subsidized immunization programs, hospitals, and medical research are other examples.

3. *Provide goods via government* A third policy option may be used where spillover benefits are extremely large: Government may finance or, in the extreme, own and operate all industries which are involved.

Public Goods and Services

Private goods, which are produced through the competitive market system, are said to be *divisible* because they are produced in units small enough to be purchased and used by individual buyers. Private goods are also subject to the **exclusion principle.** Buyers who are willing and able to pay the equilibrium price of the product obtain it, but those who are unable or unwilling to pay are *excluded* from the product and its benefits.

Certain other goods and services called **public goods** are not produced by the market system because they have the opposite characteristics. Public goods are *indivisible;* they must be produced in such large units that they cannot ordinarily be sold to individual buyers. Individuals can buy hamburgers, computers, and automobiles through the market but cannot buy aircraft carriers, highways, space telescopes, and air-traffic control.

More important, *the exclusion principle does not apply to public goods;* there is no effective way of excluding individuals from their benefits once those goods come into existence. Obtaining the benefits of private goods requires that they be *purchased;* obtaining benefits from public goods requires only that they be *available.*

The classic public goods example is a proposed lighthouse on a treacherous coast. The construction of the lighthouse would be economically justified if its benefits (fewer shipwrecks) exceeded its cost. But the benefits accruing to one user would not be great enough to justify the purchase of such an indivisible product. Moreover, once it was in operation, the warning light would be a guide to all ships; there would be no practical way to exclude any captain from using the light. Economists call this the **free-rider-problem:** people receiving benefits from a good without contributing to its cost.

Because the exclusion principle does not apply to the lighthouse, private enterprises have no economic incentive to supply it. Since the services of the lighthouse cannot be priced and sold, it would be unprofitable for a private firm to devote resources to it. So here we have a service that could yield substantial benefits but to which the market would allocate no resources. It is a public good, much like national defense, flood control, public health, satellite navigation systems, and insect-abatement programs. If society requires such goods, they must be provided by the public sector and financed by compulsory charges in the form of taxes.

Quasipublic Goods

The applicability of the exclusion principle distinguishes private from public goods, and government may provide the latter. However, many other goods and services are provided by government even though they could be made exclusive. Such goods, called **quasipublic goods,** include education, streets and highways, police and fire protection, libraries and museums, preventive medicine, and sewage disposal. These goods or services could be produced and delivered in such a way that the exclusion principle applied. All could be priced and provided by private firms through the market system. But, as noted earlier, these services have substantial spillover benefits, so they would be underproduced by the market system. Therefore, government may provide them to avoid the underallocation of resources which would otherwise occur.

Since quasipublic goods can be produced in either the private or the public sector—and because spillover benefits are difficult to measure—we can understand the continuing controversy surrounding the status of medical care and low-income housing. Are these private goods to be produced through the market system, or are they quasipublic goods to be provided by government?

Allocation of Resources to Public and Quasipublic Goods

The market system fails to allocate resources for public goods and underallocates resources for quasipublic goods. What then, is the mechanism by which such goods get produced?

Public and quasipublic goods are purchased through the government on the basis of group, or collective, choices. (Contrast this with private goods, which are purchased from private enterprises on the basis of individual choices.) The types and qualities of goods to be produced by government are determined in a democracy by political voting. That is, the members of a society vote for particular political candidates. Each candidate represents certain public policies, and those policies determine the quantities of the various public and quasipublic goods to be produced and consumed. The group choices made in the political arena supplement the choices of households and businesses in answering the Five Fundamental Questions.

How are resources reallocated from the production of private goods to the production of public and quasipublic goods? In an economy whose resources are fully employed, government must free resources from private goods production to make them available for production of public and quasipublic goods. The means of releasing resources from private uses is to reduce private demand for them. This is accomplished by levying taxes on households and businesses, taking some of their income out of the circular flow. With lower incomes and hence less purchasing power, households and businesses must curtail their consumption and investment spending. Taxes diminish the private demand for goods and services, which in turn reduces the private demand for resources. So by diverting purchasing power from private spenders to government, taxes remove resources from private uses. (Global Perspective 5-1 shows the extent to which various countries divert labor from private sector to public sector employment.)

Government expenditures of tax proceeds can then reallocate the resources to the provision of public and quasipublic goods and services. Personal and corporate income taxation releases resources from the production of consumer goods (food, clothing, television sets) and investment goods (printing presses, boxcars, warehouses). Government expenditures shift these resources to the production of public and quasipublic goods (post offices, submarines, parks). Government purposely reallocates resources to bring about significant changes in the composition of the economy's total output. **(Key Questions 9 and 10)**

STABILIZATION

Historically, the most recent function of government is that of stabilizing the economy—helping the pri-

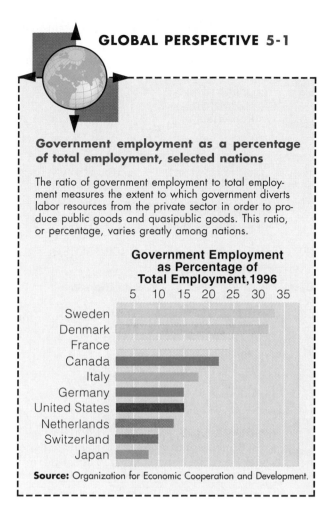

GLOBAL PERSPECTIVE 5-1

Government employment as a percentage of total employment, selected nations

The ratio of government employment to total employment measures the extent to which government diverts labor resources from the private sector in order to produce public goods and quasipublic goods. This ratio, or percentage, varies greatly among nations.

Government Employment as Percentage of Total Employment, 1996

Nation	
Sweden	
Denmark	
France	
Canada	
Italy	
Germany	
United States	
Netherlands	
Switzerland	
Japan	

Source: Organization for Economic Cooperation and Development.

vate economy achieve full employment of resources and stable prices. Here we will only outline (rather than fully explain) how government tries to do this; macroeconomics goes into this topic in great detail.

An economy's level of output depends directly on total or aggregate expenditure. A high level of total spending means it is profitable for industries to produce large outputs, which in turn ensures that both property and human resources will be employed at high levels. But aggregate spending may either fall short of or exceed the particular level necessary for full employment and price stability. Either of two possibilities, unemployment and inflation, may then occur:

1. *Unemployment* The level of total spending in the private sector may be too low to employ all available resources. Then government may choose to augment private spending so that total spending—private *plus* public—will be sufficient to generate full employment. Government can

do this by adjusting government spending and taxation. Specifically, it might increase its own spending on public goods and services or reduce taxes to stimulate private spending. It might also reduce interest rates to promote more private borrowing and spending.

2. *Inflation* Inflation is a rising general level of prices and is undesirable because it makes goods and services less attainable for many households. Prices of goods and services rise when the economy attempts to spend more than its capacity to produce. If aggregate spending exceeds the economy's output, prices will rise as consumers bid for available goods. That is, excessive aggregate spending is inflationary. Government's appropriate response is to eliminate the excess spending. It can do this by cutting its own expenditures, raising taxes to curtail private spending, or increasing interest rates to reduce private borrowing and spending.

QUICK REVIEW 5-3

■ Government enhances the operation of the market system by providing an appropriate legal foundation and promoting competition.

■ Transfer payments, direct market intervention, and taxation are ways government can lessen income inequality.

■ Government can correct for the overallocation of resources associated with spillover costs through legislation or specific taxes; the underallocation of resources associated with spillover benefits can be offset by government subsidies.

■ Government (rather than private firms) must provide desired public goods because such goods are indivisible and the exclusion principle does not apply to them; government also provides many quasipublic goods because of their large spillover benefits.

■ Government spending, tax revenues, and interest rates can be manipulated to stabilize the economy.

THE CIRCULAR FLOW REVISITED

Government is thoroughly integrated into the real and monetary flows that make up the economy. In Figure 5-5 we integrated government into the circular flow model of Chapter 2. In that figure flows (1) through (4) restate Figure 2-6. Flows (1) and (2) show business expenditures for the resources provided by households. These expenditures are costs to

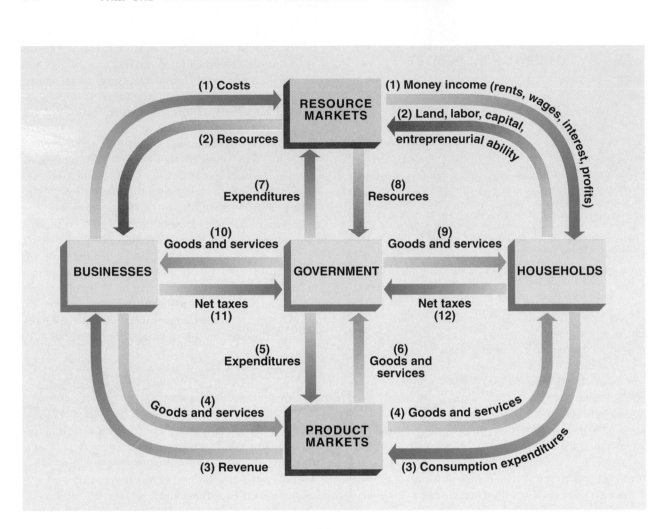

FIGURE 5-5 The circular flow and the public sector Government expenditures, taxes, and transfer payments affect the distribution of income, the allocation of resources, and the level of economic activity.

----

businesses but represent wage, rent, interest, and profit income to households. Flows (3) and (4) portray households' consumer expenditures for the goods and services produced by businesses.

Now consider the modifications resulting from the addition of government. Flows (5) through (8) tell us that government makes purchases in both product and resource markets. Specifically, flows (5) and (6) represent government purchases of such things as paper, computers, and military hardware from private businesses. Flows (7) and (8) reflect government purchases of resources. The Federal government employs and pays salaries to members of Congress, the armed forces, Justice Department lawyers, meat inspectors, and so on. State and local governments hire and pay teachers, bus drivers, police, and firefighters. The Federal government might also lease or purchase land to expand a military base;

a city may buy land on which to build a new elementary school.

Government then provides public goods and services to both households and businesses as shown by flows (9) and (10). Financing public goods and services requires tax payments by businesses and households as reflected in flows (11) and (12). These flows are labeled as *net* taxes to acknowledge that they also include "taxes in reverse" in the form of transfer payments to households and subsidies to businesses. Thus, flow (11) entails not merely corporate income, sales, and excise taxes flowing from businesses to government but also various subsidies to farmers, shipbuilders, and some airlines. Most business subsidies are "concealed" in the form of low-interest loans, loan guarantees, tax concessions, or public facilities provided at prices below their cost. Similarly, flow (12) includes both taxes (personal income taxes, payroll taxes) collected by government directly from households and transfer payments, for example, welfare payments and social security benefits, paid to households.

Our circular flow model shows how government can alter the distribution of income, reallocate resources, and change the level of economic activity. The structure of taxes and transfer payments can have a significant impact on income distribution. In flow (12) a tax structure which draws tax revenues primarily from well-to-do households, combined with a system of transfer payments to low-income households, will result in greater equality in the distribution of income.

Flows (6) and (8) imply an allocation of resources different from that of a purely private economy. Government buys goods and labor resources which differ from those purchased by households.

Finally, all the governmental flows suggest ways government might try to stabilize the economy. If the economy were experiencing unemployment, an increase in government spending with taxes and transfers held constant would increase total spending, output, and employment. Similarly, with the level of government expenditures constant, a decline in taxes or an increase in transfer payments would increase spendable incomes and boost private spending and employment. To fight inflation, the opposite policies would be in order: reduced government spending, increased taxes, and reduced transfers.

GOVERNMENT FINANCE

How large is the public sector? What are the main economic programs of Federal, state, and local gov-

ernments? How are these programs financed? We examine these questions in the remainder of the chapter.

Government Growth: Purchases and Transfers

We can get a general impression of the size of government's economic role and how it has grown by examining government purchases of goods and services and government transfer payments. The distinction between these two kinds of outlays is significant:

1. **Government purchases** are *exhaustive;* the products purchased directly absorb (require the use of) resources and are part of the domestic output. For example, the purchase of a missile absorbs the labor of physicists and engineers along with steel, explosives, and a host of other inputs.

2. **Transfer payments** are *nonexhaustive;* they do not directly absorb resources or account for production. Social security benefits, welfare payments, veterans' benefits, and unemployment compensation are examples of transfer payments. Their key characteristic is that recipients make no current contribution to domestic output in return for these payments.

Figure 5-6 shows that government purchases of goods and services have been approximately 20 percent of domestic output over the past 35 years. Of course, domestic output has increased greatly during that time so that the *absolute* volume of government purchases has increased substantially. Government purchases were $113 billion in 1960 as compared with $1,454 billion in 1997.

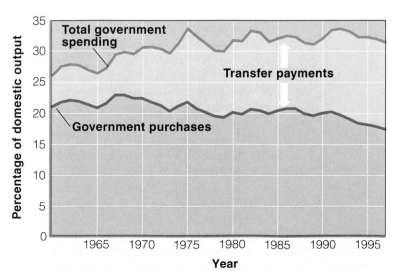

FIGURE 5-6 Government purchases, transfers, and total spending as a percentage of domestic output, 1960–1997   Government purchases have stayed close to 20 percent of domestic output since 1950. Transfer payments, however, have increased as a percentage of domestic output so that total government spending (purchases plus transfers) has grown and is now nearly one-third of domestic output.

But if we now look at transfer payments we get a different impression of government's role and growth. As Figure 5-6 reveals, transfers have grown significantly since the 1960s, rising from 5 percent of domestic output in 1960 to over 13 percent in 1997. The net result is that tax revenues required to finance total government spending—purchases plus transfers—now equal about one-third of domestic output.

In 1997 the so-called Tax Freedom Day in the United States was May 9. By this day the average worker had earned enough (from the start of the year) to pay the taxes required to finance government purchases and transfers for the year. Tax Freedom Day arrives later in several other countries, as implied in Global Perspective 5-2.

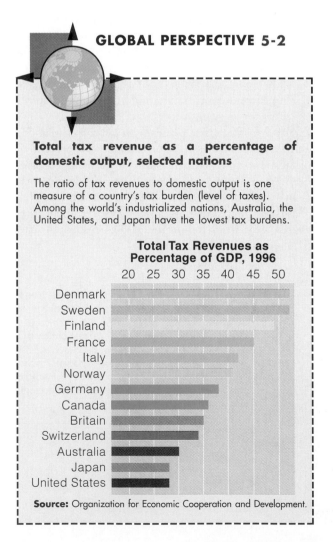

GLOBAL PERSPECTIVE 5-2

Total tax revenue as a percentage of domestic output, selected nations

The ratio of tax revenues to domestic output is one measure of a country's tax burden (level of taxes). Among the world's industrialized nations, Australia, the United States, and Japan have the lowest tax burdens.

Total Tax Revenues as Percentage of GDP, 1996

20   25   30   35   40   45   50

Denmark
Sweden
Finland
France
Italy
Norway
Germany
Canada
Britain
Switzerland
Australia
Japan
United States

Source: Organization for Economic Cooperation and Development.

FEDERAL FINANCE

Now let's look separately at the Federal, state, and local units of government to compare their expenditures and taxes. Figure 5-7 tells the story for the Federal government.

Federal Expenditures

Four important areas of Federal spending stand out: (1) pensions and income security, (2) national defense, (3) health, and (4) interest on the public debt. The *pensions and income security* category includes the many income-maintenance programs for the aged, persons with disabilities or handicaps, the unemployed, and families with no breadwinner. *National defense* constitutes about one-fifth of the Federal budget and thus underscores the high cost of military preparedness. *Health* reflects the high cost of government health programs for the retired and poor. *Interest on the public debt* is high because the public debt itself is extremely large.

Federal Tax Revenues

The revenue side of Figure 5-7 clearly shows that the personal income tax, payroll taxes, and the corporate income tax are the basic revenue getters, accounting for 45, 35, and 12 cents of each dollar collected.

Personal Income Tax   The **personal income tax** is the kingpin of our national tax system and merits special comment. This tax is levied on *taxable income*, that is, on the incomes of households and unincorporated businesses after certain exemptions ($2450 for each household member) and deductions (business expenses, charitable contributions, home mortgage interest payments, certain state and local taxes) are taken into account.

The Federal personal income tax is a *progressive tax*, meaning that people with higher incomes pay a larger percentage of that income as taxes than do persons with lower incomes. The progressivity is achieved by applying higher tax rates to successive layers or brackets of income.

Columns 1 and 2 in Table 5-2 portray the mechanics of the income tax for a married couple filing a joint return in 1997. Note that a 15 percent tax rate applies to all taxable income up to $41,200, a 28 percent rate applies to additional income up to $99,600, and even greater rates apply for three more layers of additional income, the highest rate being 39.6 percent.

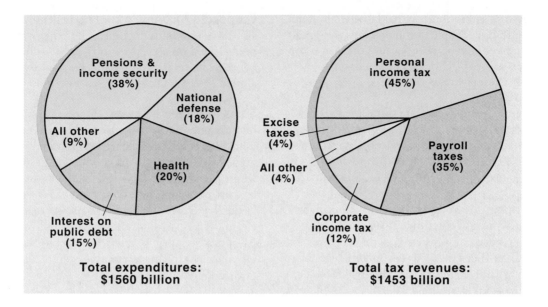

Total expenditures:
$1560 billion

Total tax revenues:
$1453 billion

FIGURE 5-7 **Federal expenditures and tax revenues, 1996**   Federal expenditures are dominated by spending for pensions and income security and spending for national defense. A full 80 percent of Federal tax revenue is derived from just two sources: the personal income tax and payroll taxes. (*Source:* U.S. Office of Management and Budget.)

The tax rates shown in column 2 in Table 5-2 are marginal tax rates. A **marginal tax rate** is the rate at which the tax is paid on each *additional* unit of taxable income. Thus, if a couple's taxable income is $50,000, they will pay the marginal tax rate of 15 percent on each dollar from $1 to $41,200 and the marginal tax rate of 28 percent on each dollar from $41,201 to $50,000. You should be able to show that their total income tax will be $8644.

The marginal tax rates in column 2 overstate the personal income tax bite because the rising rates in that column apply only to the income within each successive tax bracket. To get a better picture of the tax burden, we must consider average tax rates. The

TABLE 5-2   **Federal personal income tax rates, 1997***

(1) Total taxable income	(2) Marginal tax rate, %	(3) Total tax on highest income in bracket	(4) Average tax rate on highest income in bracket, % (3) ÷ (1)
$1 to $41,200	15.0	$ 6,180	15.0
$41,201 to $99,600	28.0	22,532	22.6
$99,601 to $151,750	31.0	38,699	25.5
$151,751 to $271,050	36.0	$81,647	30.1
Over 271,050	39.6	—	—

*Data are for a married couple filing a joint return.

average tax rate is the total tax paid divided by total taxable income. The couple in the previous paragraph is in the 28 percent tax bracket because they pay a top marginal tax rate of 28 percent on some of their income. But their average tax rate is 17.3 percent (= $8644/$50,000).

A tax whose average tax rate rises as income increases is progressive. Such a tax claims both a larger absolute amount and a larger proportion of income as income rises. Thus we can say that the Federal personal income tax is progressive. **(Key Question 15)**

Payroll Taxes Social security contributions are **payroll taxes**—taxes based on wages and salaries—used to finance two compulsory Federal programs for retired workers: social security (an income-enhancement program) and Medicare (which pays for medical services). These taxes are paid equally by employers and employees. Improvements in, and extensions of, the social security programs, plus growth of the labor force, have resulted in very significant increases in these payroll taxes in recent years. In 1998, employees and employers each paid 7.65 percent on the first $68,400 of an employee's annual earnings and 1.45 percent on all additional earnings.

Corporate Income Tax The Federal government also taxes corporate income. The **corporate income tax** is levied on a corporation's profit—the difference between its total revenue and its total expenses. For almost all corporations, the tax rate is 35 percent.

Sales and Excise Taxes Taxes on commodities or on purchases take the form of **sales and excise taxes.** The difference between the two is mainly one of coverage. Sales taxes fall on a wide range of products, whereas excises are levied individually on a small, select list of commodities. As Figure 5-7 suggests, the Federal government collects excise taxes (on such commodities as alcoholic beverages, tobacco, and gasoline) but does not levy a general sales tax; sales taxes are the primary revenue source of most state governments.

STATE AND LOCAL FINANCE

Note in Figure 5-8 that the basic sources of tax revenue for state governments are sales and excise taxes, which account for about 49 percent of all tax revenue.

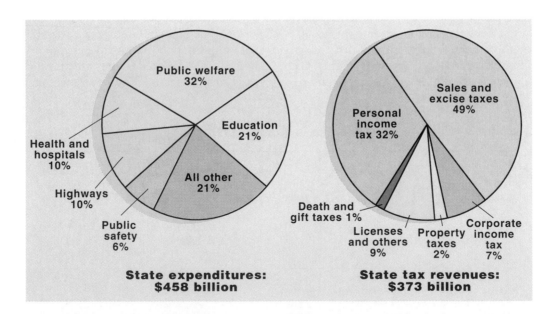

FIGURE 5-8 State expenditures and tax revenues, 1994 State governments spend mainly on public welfare and education. Their primary source of tax revenue is sales and excise taxes. (*Source:* U.S. Bureau of the Census.)

State personal income taxes, which have much more modest rates than does the Federal income tax, are the second most important source of state revenue. A tax on corporate income and license fees account for most of the remainder of state tax revenue.

The major outlays of state governments are for (1) public welfare, (2) education, (3) health and hospitals, and (4) highway maintenance and construction.

Figure 5-8 contains aggregated data, so it tells us little about the finances of individual states. And states vary significantly in the taxes levied. Thus, although personal income taxes are a major source of revenue for all state governments combined, seven states do not have a personal income tax. Also, there are great variations in the size of tax receipts and disbursements among the states.

The receipts and expenditures shown in Figure 5-9 are for all units of local government, including not only cities and towns but also counties, municipalities, townships, and school districts. One source of revenue and one use of revenue stand out: The bulk of the revenue received by local government comes from **property taxes.** And most local revenue is spent for education.

The gaping deficit found by comparing revenues and expenditures in Figure 5-9 is largely removed when nontax sources of income are taken into account: In 1994 the tax revenues of local governments were supplemented by some $242 billion in intergovernmental grants from Federal and state governments. Furthermore, local governments received an additional $93 billion as proprietary income, that is, as revenue from government-owned hospitals and utilities.

Fiscal Federalism

Historically, the tax collections of both state and local governments have fallen substantially short of their expenditures. These revenue shortfalls are largely filled by Federal transfers or grants. It is not uncommon for 15 to 20 percent of all revenue received by state and local governments to come from the Federal government. In addition to Federal grants to state and local governments, the states also make grants to local governmental units. This system of intergovernmental transfers is called **fiscal federalism.** Because the Federal budget has suffered large and persistent deficits, Federal grants in recent years have

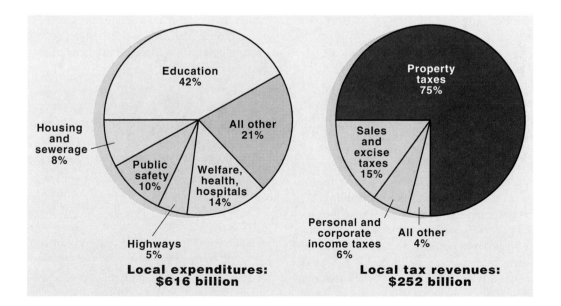

FIGURE 5-9 Local expenditures and tax revenues, 1994 The expenditures of local governments are largely for education and are financed by property taxes. (*Source:* U.S. Bureau of the Census.)

The Financing of Corporate Activity

One advantage of corporations is their ability to finance their operations through the sale of stocks and bonds. It is informative to examine the nature of corporate finance in more detail.

Generally, corporations finance their activities in three different ways. First, a very large portion of a corporation's activity is financed internally out of undistributed corporate profits. Second, as do individuals or unincorporated businesses, corporations may borrow from financial institutions. For example, a small corporation planning to build a new plant may obtain the funds from a commercial bank, a savings and loan association, or an insurance company. Third, unique to corporations, they can issue common stocks and bonds.

Stocks versus Bonds A common stock is an ownership share. The purchaser of a stock certificate has the right to vote for corporate officers and to share in dividends. If you buy 1000 of the 100,000 shares issued by Specific

Motors, Inc. (hereafter SM), then you own 1 percent of the company, are entitled to 1 percent of any dividends declared by the board of directors, and control 1 percent of the votes in the annual election of corporate officials.

In contrast, a bond is not an ownership share. A bond purchaser is simply lending money to a corporation. A bond is merely an IOU, in acknowledgment of a loan, whereby the corporation promises to pay the holder a fixed amount at some specified future date and other fixed amounts (interest payments) every year up to the bond's maturity date. For example, you might purchase a 10-year SM bond with a face value of $1000 with a 10 percent stated rate of interest. This means that, in exchange for your $1000, SM guarantees you a $100 interest payment for each of the next 10 years and then repays your $1000 principal at the end of that period.

Differences There are clearly important differences between stocks and bonds. First, as noted, the bondholder is not an owner of the company but is only a lender. Second, bonds are considered to be less risky than stocks for two reasons. On the one hand, bondholders have a "legal prior claim" upon a corporation's earnings. Dividends cannot be paid to stockholders until all interest payments that are due to bondholders have been paid. On the other hand, holders of SM stock do not know how much their

declined. That has caused state and local governments to increase tax rates, impose new taxes, and restrain expenditures.

Lotteries

Both state and local governments have increasingly turned to **lotteries** as a means of closing the gaps between their tax receipts and expenditures. In 1996 some 36 states had lotteries that sold $34 billion of tickets.

Lotteries are controversial. Critics argue that (1) it is morally wrong for states to sponsor gambling; (2) lotteries generate compulsive gamblers who impoverish themselves and their families; (3) low-income families spend a larger proportion of their incomes on lotteries than do high-income families; (4) as a cash business, lotteries attract criminals and other undesirables; and (5) lotteries send the message that luck and fate—rather than education, hard work, and saving and investing—are the route to wealth.

Defenders contend that (1) lotteries are preferable to taxes because they are voluntary rather than com-

pulsory; (2) they are a painless way to finance government services such as education, medical care, and welfare; and (3) lotteries are competitive with illegal gambling and thus socially beneficial in curtailing organized crime.

QUICK REVIEW 5-4

■ Government purchases account for about 20 percent of U.S. output; the addition of transfers increases government spending to almost one-third of domestic output.

■ Income security and national defense are the main areas of Federal spending; personal income, payroll, and corporate income taxes are the primary sources of revenue.

■ States rely on sales and excise taxes for revenue; their spending is largely for public welfare and education.

■ Education is the main expenditure for local governments, and most of their revenue comes from property taxes.

dividends will be or how much they might obtain for their stock if they decide to sell. If Specific Motors falls on hard times, stockholders may receive no dividends at all and the value of their stock may plummet. Provided the corporation does not go bankrupt, the holder of an SM bond is guaranteed a $100 interest payment each year and the return of his or her $1000 at the end of 10 years.

Bond Risks This is not to imply that the purchase of corporate bonds is riskless. The market value of your SM bond may vary over time in accordance with the financial health of the corporation. If SM encounters economic misfortunes which raise questions about its financial integrity, the market value of your bond may fall. Should you sell the bond prior to maturity, you may receive only $600 or $700 for it (rather than $1000) and thereby incur a capital loss.

Changes in interest rates also affect the market prices of bonds. Specifically, increases in interest rates cause bond prices to fall and vice versa. Assume you purchase a $1000 ten-year SM bond this year (1999) when the interest rate is 10 percent. This obviously means that your bond provides a $100 fixed interest payment each year. But now suppose that by next year the interest rate has jumped to 15 percent and SM must now guarantee a $150 fixed annual payment on its new (year-2000) $1000 ten-year bonds. Clearly, no sensible person will pay you $1000 for your bond, which pays only $100 of interest income per year when new bonds can be purchased for $1000 which pay the holder $150 per year. Hence, if you sell your 1999 bond before maturity, you will suffer a capital loss.

Bondholders face another element of risk due to inflation. If substantial inflation occurs over the 10-year period during which you hold an SM bond, the $1000 principal repaid to you at the end of that period will represent substantially less purchasing power than the $1000 you loaned to SM 10 years earlier. You will have lent "dear" dollars but will be repaid in "cheap" dollars.

CHAPTER SUMMARY

1. The functional distribution of income shows how society's total income is divided among wages, rents, interest, and profit; the personal distribution of income shows how total income is divided among individual households.

2. Households use their total incomes to pay personal taxes, for saving, and to buy consumer goods. Over half of their consumption expenditures are for services.

3. Sole proprietorships are firms owned and usually operated by single individuals. Partnerships are firms owned and usually operated by just a handful of individuals. Corporations are legal entities, distinct and separate from the individuals who own them. They often have thousands, or even millions, of owners—the stockholders of the firm.

4. Government enhances the operation of the market system by **(a)** providing an appropriate legal and social framework, and **(b)** acting to maintain competition.

5. Government alters the distribution of income through the tax-transfer system and by market intervention.

6. Spillovers or externalities cause the equilibrium output of certain goods to vary from the socially efficient output. Spillover costs result in an overallocation of resources, which can be corrected by legislation or specific taxes. Spillover benefits are accompanied by an underallocation of resources, which can be corrected by subsidies to consumers or producers.

7. Only government is willing to provide public goods because such goods are indivisible and entail benefits from which nonpaying consumers (free riders) cannot be excluded; private firms will not produce these goods. Quasipublic goods have some characteristics of public goods and some of private goods; they are provided by government because the private sector would underallocate resources to their production.

8. Government can reduce unemployment or inflation by altering its taxation, spending, and interest-rate policies.

9. Government purchases exhaust (use up or absorb) resources; transfer payments do not. Government purchases have been about 20 percent of domestic output since 1960. However, transfers have grown significantly, so total government spending is now nearly one-third of domestic output.

10. The main categories of Federal spending are pensions and income security, national defense, health, and interest on the public debt; revenues come primarily from personal income, payroll, and corporate income taxes.

11. The primary sources of revenue for the states are sales and excise taxes and personal income taxes; major state expenditures go to public welfare, education, health and hospitals, and highways.

12. At the local level, most revenue comes from the property tax, and education is the most important expenditure.

13. Under the U.S. system of fiscal federalism, state and local tax revenues are supplemented by sizable revenue grants from the Federal government.

TERMS AND CONCEPTS

functional distribution of income	horizontal combination	double taxation	transfer payments
personal distribution of income	conglomerate combination	principal-agent problem	personal income tax
durable good	industry	monopoly	marginal tax rate
nondurable good	sole proprietorship	spillover costs	average tax rate
services	partnership	spillover benefits	payroll taxes
plant	corporation	exclusion principle	corporate income tax
firm	stocks	public goods	sales and excise taxes
vertical combination	bonds	free-rider problem	property taxes
	limited liability	quasipublic goods	fiscal federalism
		government purchases	lotteries

STUDY QUESTIONS

1. Distinguish between functional and personal distributions of income.

2. KEY QUESTION Assume the five residents of Econoville receive incomes of $50, $75, $125, $250, and $500. Present the resulting personal distribution of income as a graph similar to Figure 5-2. Compare the incomes of the lowest and highest fifth of the income receivers.

3. Distinguish clearly between a plant, a firm, and an industry. Why is an "industry" often difficult to define in practice?

4. KEY QUESTION What are the major legal forms of business organization? Briefly state the advantages and disadvantages of each. How do you account for the dominant role of corporations in the U.S. economy?

5. "The legal form an enterprise assumes is dictated primarily by the financial requirements of its particular line of production." Do you agree?

6. Enumerate and briefly discuss the main economic functions of government. Which of these functions

do you think is the most controversial? Explain your reasoning.

7. What divergencies arise between equilibrium and an efficient output when **(a)** spillover costs and **(b)** spillover benefits are present? How might government correct for these discrepancies? "The presence of spillover costs suggests underallocation of resources to that product and the need for governmental subsidies." Do you agree? Why or why not? Explain how zoning and seat belt laws might be used to deal with a problem of spillover costs.

8. Researchers have concluded that injuries caused by firearms cost more than $500 million a year in hospital expenses alone. Because the majority of those shot are poor and without insurance, roughly 85 percent of these hospital costs must be borne by taxpayers. Use your understanding of externalities to recommend appropriate policies.

9. KEY QUESTION What are the basic characteristics of public goods? Explain the significance of the exclusion principle. By what means does government provide public goods?

10. KEY QUESTION Draw a production possibilities curve with public goods on the vertical axis and private goods on the horizontal axis. Assuming the economy is initially operating on the curve, indicate how the production of public goods might be increased. How might the output of public goods be increased if the economy is initially operating at a point inside the curve?

11. Use your understanding of the characteristics of private and public goods to determine whether the following should be produced through the market system or provided by government: **(a)** bread; **(b)** street lighting; **(c)** bridges; **(d)** parks; **(e)** swimming pools; **(f)** medical care; **(g)** mail delivery; **(h)** housing; **(i)** air traffic control; **(j)** libraries. State why you answered as you did in each case.

12. Explain how government can manipulate its expenditures and tax revenues to reduce **(a)** unemployment and **(b)** the rate of inflation.

13. "Most government actions simultaneously affect the distribution of income, the allocation of resources, and the levels of unemployment and prices." Use the circular flow model to confirm this assertion for each of the following: **(a)** the construction of a new high school in Blackhawk County; **(b)** a 2 percent reduction in the Federal corporate income tax; **(c)** an expansion of preschool programs for disadvantaged children; **(d)** a $50 million increase in spending for space research; **(e)** the levying of a tax on air polluters; and **(f)** a $1 increase in the legally required minimum wage.

14. What is the most important source of revenue and major type of expenditure at the Federal level? At the state level? At the local level?

15. KEY QUESTION Suppose in Fiscalville there is no tax on the first $10,000 of income, but earnings between $10,000 and $20,000 are taxed at 20 percent and income between $20,000 and $30,000 at 30 percent. Any income above $30,000 is taxed at 40 percent. If your income is $50,000, how much will you pay in taxes? Determine your marginal and average tax rates. Is this a progressive tax? Explain.

16. (Last Word) Describe three ways to finance corporate activity. Make a case arguing that stocks are more risky for the financial investor than are bonds.

17. WEB-BASED QUESTION **Personal Distribution of Income—What Is the Trend?** Visit the U.S. Census Bureau http://www.census.gov/hhes/income/midclass/index.html. Since 1969, how has the share of aggregate household income received by the lowest and highest income quintiles (one-fifths) changed?

18. WEB-BASED QUESTION **Federal Expenditures—Historical Tables and 5-Year Estimates** The Office of Management and Budget provides a search page for Federal budget publications at http://www.access.gpo.gov/omb/omb003.html. Search for the current fiscal year outlays estimates by selecting Historical Tables and inserting the search words OUTLAYS BY FUNCTION AND SUBFUNCTION for the previous 25 years to 5 years in the future. Use the data provided to create pie charts for 25 years ago, the current year, and 5 years hence using the following categories: pensions and income security, national defense, health, interest on the public debt, and all other. Which categories are shrinking and which are expanding as a percentage of total expenditures?

6

The United States in the Global Economy

Backpackers in the wilderness like to think they are "leaving the world behind," but, like Atlas, they carry the world on their shoulders. Much of their backpacking equipment is imported—knives from Switzerland, rain gear from South Korea, cameras from Japan, aluminum pots made in England, miniature stoves from Sweden, sleeping bags from China, and compasses from Finland. Some backpackers wear hiking boots from Italy, sunglasses made in France, and watches from Japan. Moreover, they may drive to the trailheads in Japanese-made Toyotas or Swedish-made Volvos, sipping coffee from Brazil or snacking on bananas from Honduras.

International trade and the global economy affect all of us daily, whether we are hiking in the wilderness, driving our cars, listening to music, or working at our jobs. We cannot "leave the world behind." We are enmeshed with the rest of the world in a complex web of economic relationships—trading of goods and services, multinational corporations, cooperative ventures among the world's firms, and ties among the world's financial markets. This web is so complex that it is difficult to determine just what is—or isn't—a U.S. product. RCA television sets are made by a company based in France; a Canadian company owns Tropicana Orange Juice; and the parent company of Gerber baby food is Swiss. The Chevrolet Lumina sedan is manufactured in Canada, and a British corporation owns Burger King. Many "U.S." products are made with components from abroad, and, conversely, many "foreign" products contain numerous U.S.-produced parts. For example, international firms supply major components of the new U.S. Boeing 777 airplane (see Figure 6-1).

This chapter introduces the basic principles underlying the global economy. (A more advanced discussion of international economics is in the last part of this book.) Here, we first look at world trade today, the U.S.' role in it, and some factors which have caused it to grow. Next, we modify Chapter 5's circular flow diagram to account for international trade flows, explore the basis for world trade, and look at the system of exchange rates which facilitate it. Finally, we describe several restrictive trade practices and discuss major efforts to liberalize trade.

Boeing
U.S. suppliers
International suppliers

Trailing edge panels
Fixed trailing edge
Cargo doors
Vertical fin
Dorsal fin
Rudder
Section 48
Section 47
Elevator
Section 46
Fuselage sections and doors
Section 44
Large cargo door
Floor beams
Horizontal stabilizer
Section 43
Wing-to-body fairing
Section 41
Spoilers
Inboard flaps
Flaperon
Spoilers
Wing center section
Flap support fairings
Outboard flap
Aileron
Landing gear doors
Radome
In-spar ribs
Leading edge slats
Wingbox
Fixed leading edge
Wingtip assembly
Nose landing gear
Main landing gear
Primary exhaust cowl assembly
Engine
Nacelles, struts and fairings

FIGURE 6-1 **The Boeing 777: who supplies the parts?** International firms supply major components of the "American" Boeing 777 aircraft. (*Source: Seattle Post Intelligencer.* Reprinted by permission.)

WORLD TRADE

The volume of world trade is so large and its characteristics are so unique that it is difficult to describe except in some general terms.

Volume and Pattern

Table 6-1 provides a rough index of the importance of world trade for several countries. Many nations with restricted resource bases and limited domestic markets cannot efficiently produce the variety of goods they want to consume. Such countries must import the goods they desire from other nations, which in turn means they must export, or sell abroad,

TABLE 6-1 **Exports of goods and services as a percentage of GDP, selected countries, 1996**

Country	Exports as percentage of GDP
Netherlands	56
Canada	38
New Zealand	30
United Kingdom	30
France	24
Italy	24
Germany	23
United States	12
Japan	10

Source: IMF, International Financial Statistics, 1997.

some of their own products. For such countries, exports may run from 25 to 35 percent or more of their domestic output. Other countries, the United States, for example, have rich and diversified resource bases and vast internal markets. They are less dependent on world trade.

Volume For the United States and the world the volume of international trade has been increasing both absolutely and relatively. A comparison of the boxed data in Figure 6-2 reveals substantial growth in the dollar amount of U.S. exports and imports over the past several decades. The lines in the figure show the growth of exports and imports of goods and services as percentages of gross domestic product (GDP)—the dollar value of all goods and services produced within the United States. Exports and imports currently are 12 to 14 percent of GDP, more than double their percentages in 1965.

However, the United States now accounts for a diminished percentage of total world trade. In 1947 it supplied about one-third of the world's total exports, compared with about one-eighth today. World trade has increased more rapidly for other nations than it has for the United States. *But in terms of absolute volumes of imports and exports, the United States is still the world's leading trading nation.*

Dependence There can be no question as to the United States' dependence on the world economy.

The United States is almost entirely dependent on other countries for bananas, cocoa, coffee, spices, tea, raw silk, nickel, tin, natural rubber, and diamonds. Even casual observation suggests that imported goods compete in many of our domestic markets: Japanese cameras and video recorders, French and Italian wines, Swiss and Austrian snow skis, and Japanese motorcycles and autos are a few examples. Even the "great American pastime" of baseball relies heavily on imported gloves and baseballs.

But world trade is a two-way street, and many U.S. industries benefit from foreign markets. Almost all segments of U.S. agriculture rely on sales abroad; for example, exports of rice, wheat, cotton, and tobacco vary from one-fourth to more than one-half of their total output. The U.S. computer, chemical, semiconductor, aircraft, automobile, machine tool, and coal industries, among many others, sell significant portions of their output in international markets. Table 6-2 shows some of the major commodity exports and imports of the United States.

Trade Patterns The following facts provide an overview of the pattern of U.S. international trade:
1. The United States has a *trade deficit* in goods. In 1996 U.S. imports of goods exceeded U.S. exports of goods by $191 billion.
2. The United States has a *trade surplus* in services. In 1996 U.S. exports of services exceeded U.S. imports of services by $80 billion.

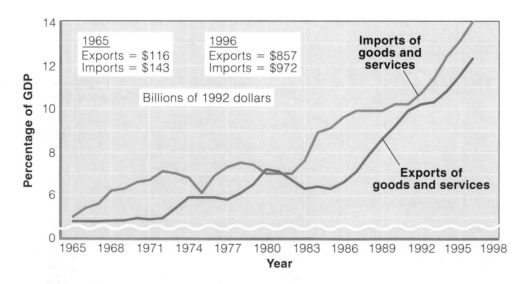

1965
Exports = $116
Imports = $143

1996
Exports = $857
Imports = $972

Billions of 1992 dollars

Imports of goods and services

Exports of goods and services

FIGURE 6-2 U.S. trade as percentage of GDP American imports and exports have increased in volume and have more than doubled as a percentage of GDP since 1965. [*Source: Economic Report of the President, 1997.* Data from national income accounts and adjusted for inflation (1992 dollars).]

TABLE 6-2   Principal U.S. exports and imports of goods, 1996 (in billions of dollars)

Exports	Amount	Imports	Amount
Computers	$43.7	Petroleum	$72.7
Chemicals	42.5	Automobiles	65.9
Semiconductors	35.8	Computers	61.5
Consumer durables	33.2	Clothing	39.6
Aircraft	30.8	Semiconductors	36.7
Generating equipment	24.1	Household appliances	31.1
Grains	21.2	Chemicals	26.9
Telecommunications	20.3	Consumer electronics	18.4
Automobiles	17.0	Iron and steel	17.2
Nonferrous metals	15.5	Toys and sporting goods	15.4

Source: Consolidated from Department of Commerce data.

3. The United States imports some of the same categories of goods that it exports, specifically, automobiles, computers, chemicals, semiconductors, and telecommunications equipment (see Table 6-2).

4. As shown in Table 6-3, most U.S. export and import trade is with other industrially advanced nations, not with developing countries.

5. Canada is the United States' most important trading partner quantitatively. In 1996, 22 percent of U.S. exports were sold to Canadians, who in turn provided 20 percent of U.S. imports (see Table 6-3).

6. There are sizable trade deficits with Japan and China. In 1996, U.S. imports from Japan exceeded U.S. exports to Japan by $49 billion, and U.S. imports from China exceeded exports to China by $44 billion (see Table 6-3).

7. The U.S. dependence on foreign oil is reflected in the excess of imports in our trade with countries belonging to the Organization of Petroleum Exporting Countries (OPEC). In 1996, the United States imported $44 billion of goods (mainly oil) from OPEC members, while exporting $20 billion of goods to those countries (see Table 6-3).

TABLE 6-3   U.S. exports and imports of goods by area, 1996

Exports to	Value, billions of dollars		Percentage of total	Imports from	Value, billions of dollars		Percentage of total
Industrial countries	$354		58	Industrial countries	$443		55
Canada		$135	22	Canada		$159	20
Japan		66	11	Japan		115	14
Western Europe		137	22	Western Europe		162	20
Australia		12	2	Australia		4	1
Other		3	1	Other		3	1
Developing countries	258		42	Developing countries	360		45
Mexico		57	9	Mexico		75	9
China		12	2	China		56	7
Eastern Europe		7	1	Eastern Europe		7	1
OPEC countries		20	3	OPEC countries		44	5
Other		162	26	Other		178	22
Total	**$612**		**100**	**Total**	**$803**		**100**

Note: Data are on international transactions basis and exclude military shipments. Data do not add to totals because of rounding.
Source: Survey of Current Business, October 1997.

Linkages International trade requires complex financial linkages among nations. For example, how does the United States finance its $111 billion trade deficit in goods and services? How does a nation, or a person, obtain more goods from others than it provides to them? The answer is by either borrowing or by selling assets. This is how the United States finances its trade deficit. It borrows from citizens of other nations; the United States is the world's largest debtor nation. Moreover, nations with which the United States has large trade deficits, such as Japan, often "recycle their dollars" by buying U.S. assets.

Rapid Trade Growth

Several factors have propelled the rapid growth of international trade since World War II.

Transportation Technology High transportation costs are a barrier to any type of trade, particularly trade between distant places. But improvements in transportation have shrunk the globe, fostering world trade. Airplanes now transport low-weight, high-value items such as diamonds and semiconductors quickly from one nation to another. We now routinely transport oil in massive tankers, greatly reducing the cost of transportation per barrel. Grain is loaded onto oceangoing ships at modern, efficient grain silos at Great Lakes and coastal ports. Container ships transport self-contained railroad boxes directly to foreign ports, where cranes place the containers onto railroad cars for internal shipment. Natural gas flows through large-diameter pipelines from exporting to importing countries—for instance, from Russia to Germany and from Canada to the United States. Workers clean fish on large processing ships directly on the fishing grounds; refrigerated vessels then transport the fish to overseas ports.

Communications Technology World trade has also expanded because of dramatic improvements in communications technology. Telephones, fax (facsimile) machines, and computers now directly link traders around the world, allowing exporters to assess overseas markets and to complete trade deals. New communications methods enable us to move money around the world in the blink of an eye. Exchange rates, stock prices, and interest rates flash onto computer screens nearly simultaneously in Los Angeles, London, and Lisbon.

In short, exporters and importers today can as easily communicate between Sweden and Australia as between San Francisco and Oakland. A distributor in New York can get a price quote on 1000 woven baskets in Thailand as quickly as a quotation on 1000 laptop computers in New Jersey.

General Decline in Tariffs Tariffs—excise taxes (duties) on imported products—have had their ups and downs, but since 1940 they have generally fallen worldwide. A glance ahead to Figure 6-6 shows that U.S. tariffs as a percentage of imports are now about 5 percent, down from 37 percent in 1940. Many nations still have barriers to free trade, but, on average, tariffs have fallen greatly, increasing international trade.

Peace During World War II powerful industrial countries fought one another, certainly disrupting international trade. Since then, trade has not only been restored but has been bolstered by peaceful relations and by major trade agreements linking most industrial nations. In particular, Japan and Germany—two defeated World War II powers—now are major participants in world trade.

Participants

All nations of the world participate to some extent in international trade.

United States, Japan, and Western Europe As implied in Global Perspective 6-1, the top participants in world trade are the United States, Germany, and Japan. In 1996 these three nations had combined exports of $1.6 trillion. Along with Germany, other western European nations such as France, Britain, and Italy are major exporters and importers. In fact, three major "players"—the United States, Japan, and the western European nations—now dominate world trade. These three areas also form the heart of the world's financial system and headquarter most of the world's large **multinational corporations**—firms which have sizable production and distribution activities in other countries. Among the world's top 25 multinationals are Royal Dutch Shell and Unilever (Britain and the Netherlands); Ford Motor, General Motors, and IBM (United States); British Petroleum (Britain); Nestlé (Switzerland); Fiat (Italy); Siemens and Bayer Chemicals (Germany); Mitsubishi and Mitsui (Japan); and Elf Aquitaine (France).

New Players New, important participants have arrived on the world trade scene. One group of such na-

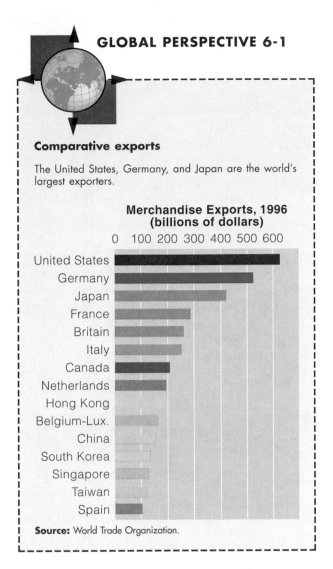

GLOBAL PERSPECTIVE 6-1

Comparative exports

The United States, Germany, and Japan are the world's largest exporters.

Merchandise Exports, 1996 (billions of dollars)

United States, Germany, Japan, France, Britain, Italy, Canada, Netherlands, Hong Kong, Belgium-Lux., China, South Korea, Singapore, Taiwan, Spain

Source: World Trade Organization.

Chinese exports and imports each were about $50 billion. In 1996 they each topped $151 billion, with 33 percent of China's exports going to the United States. Also, China has been attracting much foreign investment (more than $600 billion since 1990). Experts predict China will eventually become one of the world's leading trading nations.

The collapse of communism in eastern Europe and the former Soviet Union has also altered world trade patterns. Before this collapse, the eastern European nations of Poland, Hungary, Czechoslovakia, and East Germany mainly traded with the Soviet Union and such political allies as North Korea and Cuba. Today, East Germany is reunited with West Germany, and Poland, Hungary, and the Czech Republic have established new trade relationships with western Europe and the United States.

Russia itself has initiated far-reaching market reforms, including widespread privatization of industry, and has consummated major trade deals with firms from across the globe. Although its transition to capitalism has been far from smooth, no doubt Russia can be a major trading power. Other former Soviet republics—now independent nations—such as Ukraine and Estonia also are opening their economies to international trade and finance.

BACK TO THE CIRCULAR FLOW

We can easily add "the rest of the world" to Chapter 5's circular flow model. We do so in Figure 6-3 via two adjustments:

1. Our previous "Resource Markets" and "Product Markets" now become "U.S. Resource Markets" and "U.S. Product Markets." Similarly, we add the modifier "U.S." to the "Businesses," "Government," and "Households" sectors.

2. We place the foreign sector—the "Rest of the World"—so that it interacts with "U.S. Product Markets." This sector designates all foreign nations with which the United States deals and the individuals, businesses, and governments they comprise.

Flow (13) in Figure 6-3 shows that people, businesses, and governments abroad buy U.S. products—our exports—from our product market. This goods and services flow of U.S. exports to foreign nations is accompanied by a monetary revenue flow (14) from the rest of the world to the United States. In response to these revenues from abroad, U.S. businesses demand more domestic resources [flow (2)] to produce the

tions is the newly industrializing Asian economies of Hong Kong (now part of China), Singapore, South Korea, and Taiwan. These **"Asian tigers"** have expanded their share of world exports from about 3 percent in 1972 to more than 10 percent today. Together, they export about as much as either Germany or Japan and much more than France, Britain, or Italy. Other countries in southeast Asia, particularly Malaysia and Indonesia, have also expanded their international trade.

China, with its increasing reliance on the market system, is another emerging trading power. Since initiating market reforms in 1978, its annual growth of output has averaged 9 percent (compared with 2 to 3 percent annually in the United States). At this remarkable rate, China's total output nearly doubles every 8 years! An upsurge of exports and imports has accompanied this expansion of output. In 1989

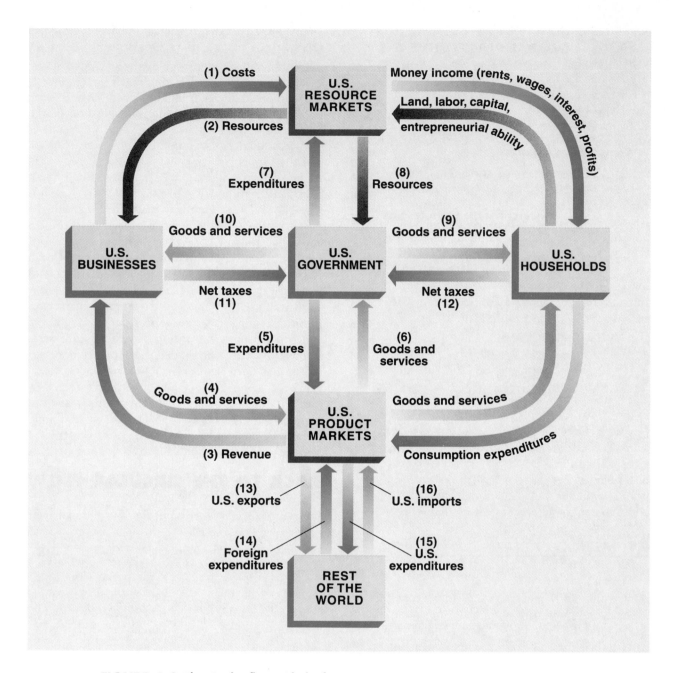

FIGURE 6-3 The circular flow with the foreign sector Flows (13) to (16) in the lower portion of the diagram show how the U.S. economy interacts with the "Rest of the World." People abroad buy U.S. exports, contributing to U.S. business revenues and money incomes. People in the United States, in turn, spend part of their incomes to buy imports from abroad. Income from a nation's exports helps pay for its imports.

goods for export; they pay for these resources with revenue from abroad. Thus, the domestic flow (1) of money income (rents, wages, interest, and profits) to U.S. households rises.

But U.S. exports are only half the picture. Flow (15) shows that U.S. households, businesses, and government spend some of their income on foreign products. These products, of course, are our imports—

flow (16). Purchases of imports, say, autos and electronics, contribute to foreign output and income, which in turn enable foreign households to buy U.S. exports.

Our circular flow model is a simplification which emphasizes product market effects, but a few other U.S.–rest-of-the-world relationships also require comment. Specifically, there are linkages between the U.S. resource markets and the rest of the world.

The United States imports and exports not only products but also resources. For example, the United States imports crude oil and exports raw logs. Moreover, some U.S. firms engage in production abroad, which diverts spending on capital from our domestic resource market to resource markets in other nations. For instance, General Motors might build an auto assembly plant in Canada. Or, flowing in the other direction, Sony might construct a plant for manufacturing CD players in the United States.

There are also international flows of labor. About 1 million legal and illegal immigrants enter the United States each year, expanding the availability of labor resources in the United States and raising total output and income. On the other hand, immigration tends to increase the labor supply in certain U.S. labor markets, reducing wage rates for some types of U.S. labor.

The expanded circular flow model (Figure 6-3) also demonstrates that a nation engaged in world trade risks instability which would not affect a "closed" nation. Recessions and inflation can be highly contagious among trading nations. Suppose the nations of southeast Asia experience a severe recession. As their incomes decline, they purchase fewer U.S. exports. As a result, flows (13) and (14) in Figure 6-3 decline and inventories of unsold U.S. goods rise. U.S. firms respond by reducing their production and employment, which diminishes the flow of money income to U.S. households [flow (1)]. Recession in Asia in this case has contributed to a recession in the United States.

Figure 6-3 also helps us see that the foreign sector alters resource allocation and incomes in the U.S. economy. With a foreign sector, the United States produces more of some goods (exports) and fewer of others (imports) than it would otherwise. Thus, U.S. labor and other resources are shifted toward export industries and away from import industries. The United States uses more resources to make commercial aircraft and to grow wheat and less to make autos and clothing. So we ask: "Do these shifts of resources make economic sense? Do they enhance U.S. total output and thus the U.S. standard of living?" We look at some answers next. **(Key Question 3)**

QUICK REVIEW 6-1

■ World trade has increased globally and nationally. In terms of volume, the United States is the world's leading international trader, with exports and imports of about 12 to 14 percent of GDP.

■ Advances in transportation and communications technology, declines in tariffs, and peaceful relations among major industrial countries all have helped expand world trade.

■ The United States, Japan, and the western European nations dominate world trade. Recent new traders are the "Asian tigers" (Hong Kong, Singapore, South Korea, and Taiwan), China, the eastern European nations, and the newly independent states formerly constituting the Soviet Union.

■ The circular flow model with foreign trade includes flows of exports from our domestic product market, imports to our domestic product market, and the corresponding flows of resources and spending.

SPECIALIZATION AND COMPARATIVE ADVANTAGE

Specialization and trade increase the productivity of a nation's resources and allow for larger total output than otherwise. This notion is not new! According to Adam Smith in 1776:

> It is the maxim of every prudent master of a family, never to attempt to make at home what it will cost him more to make than to buy. The taylor does not attempt to make his own shoes, but buys them of the shoemaker. The shoemaker does not attempt to make his own clothes, but employs a taylor. The farmer attempts to make neither the one nor the other, but employs those different artificers. . . .
>
> What is prudence in the conduct of every private family, can scarce be folly in that of a great kingdom. If a foreign country can supply us with a commodity cheaper than we can make it, better buy it of them with some part of the produce of our own industry, employed in a way in which we have some advantage.[1]

---

[1]Adam Smith, *The Wealth of Nations* (New York: Modern Library, 1937), p. 424. (Originally published in 1776.)

Nations specialize and trade for the same reasons as individuals: Specialization and exchange among individuals, regions, and nations result in greater overall output and income.

Basic Principle

In the early 1800s British economist David Ricardo expanded on Smith's idea, correctly observing that it pays for a person or a country to specialize and exchange even if that person or nation is more productive than a potential trading partner in *all* economic activities.

Consider the certified public accountant (CPA) who is also a skilled house painter. Suppose the CPA can paint her house in less time than the professional painter she is thinking of hiring. Also suppose the CPA can earn $50 per hour doing her accounting and must pay the painter $15 per hour. Let's say that it will take the accountant 30 hours to paint her house and will take the painter 40 hours.

Should the CPA take time from her accounting to paint her own house, or should she hire the painter? The CPA's opportunity cost of painting her house is $1500 (= 30 hours of sacrificed CPA time × $50 per CPA hour). The cost of hiring the painter is only $600 (= 40 hours of painting × $15 per hour of painting). Although the CPA is better at both accounting and painting, she *will get her house painted at lower cost by specializing in accounting and using some of the earnings from accounting to hire a house painter.*

Similarly, the house painter can reduce his cost of obtaining accounting services by specializing in painting and using some of his income to hire the CPA to prepare his income tax forms. Suppose that it would take the painter 10 hours to prepare his tax return, while the CPA could handle this task in 2 hours. The house painter would sacrifice $150 of income (= 10 hours of painting time × $15 per hour) to accomplish a task which he could hire the CPA to do for $100

(= 2 hours of CPA time × $50 per CPA hour). By using the CPA to prepare his tax return, the painter *lowers his cost of getting the tax return completed.*

What is true for our CPA and house painter is also true for nations. Countries can reduce their cost of obtaining desirable goods by specializing.

Comparative Costs

Our simple example clearly shows that specialization is economically desirable because it results in more efficient production. To understand the global economy, let's now put specialization in the context of trading nations, employing the familiar concept of the production possibilities table for our analysis. Suppose production possibilities for two products in Mexico and the United States are as shown in Tables 6-4 and 6-5. In these tables we assume constant costs. Each country must give up a constant amount of one product to secure a particular increment of the other product. (This assumption simplifies our discussion without impairing the validity of our conclusions.)

Specialization and trade are mutually beneficial or "profitable" to the two nations if the comparative costs of the two products within the two nations differ. What are the comparative costs of avocados and soybeans in Mexico? By comparing production alternatives *A* and *B* in Table 6-4, we see that 5 tons of soybeans (= 15 − 10) must be sacrificed to produce 20 tons of avocados (= 20 − 0). Or, more simply, in Mexico it costs 1 ton of soybeans (*S*) to produce 4 tons of avocados (*A*); that is, $1S \equiv 4A$. Because we assumed constant costs, this domestic *comparative-cost ratio* will not change as Mexico expands the output of either product. This is evident from production possibilities *B* and *C*, where we see that 4 more tons of avocados (= 24 − 20) cost 1 unit of soybeans (= 10 − 9).

Similarly, in Table 6-5, comparing U.S. production alternatives *R* and *S* reveals that in the United

TABLE 6-4   Mexico's production possibilities table (in tons)

Product	Production alternatives				
	A	*B*	*C*	*D*	*E*
Avocados	0	20	24	40	60
Soybeans	15	10	9	5	0

TABLE 6-5   U.S. production possibilities table (in tons)

Product	Production alternatives				
	R	*S*	*T*	*U*	*V*
Avocados	0	30	33	60	90
Soybeans	30	20	19	10	0

States it costs 10 tons of soybeans (= 30 − 20) to obtain 30 tons of avocados (= 30 − 0). That is, the domestic comparative-cost ratio for the two products in the United States is $1S \equiv 3A$. Comparing production alternatives S and T reinforces this: an extra 3 tons of avocados (= 33 − 30) comes at the direct sacrifice of 1 ton of soybeans (= 20 − 19).

The comparative costs of the two products within the two nations are clearly different. Economists say that the United States has a domestic comparative advantage or, simply, a **comparative advantage** over Mexico in soybeans. The United States must forgo only 3 tons of avocados to get 1 ton of soybeans, but Mexico must forgo 4 tons of avocados to get 1 ton of soybeans. In terms of domestic opportunity costs, soybeans are relatively cheaper in the United States. *A nation has a comparative advantage in some product when it can produce that product at a lower domestic opportunity cost than can a potential trading partner.* Mexico, in contrast, has a comparative advantage in avocados. While 1 ton of avocados costs $\frac{1}{3}$ ton of soybeans in the United States, it costs only $\frac{1}{4}$ ton of soybeans in Mexico. Comparatively speaking, avocados are cheaper in Mexico.

Because of these differences in domestic comparative costs, if both nations specialize, each according to its comparative advantage, each can achieve a larger total output with the same total input of resources. Together they will be using their scarce resources more efficiently.

Terms of Trade

The United States can shift production between soybeans and avocados at the rate of $1S$ for $3A$. Thus, the United States would specialize in soybeans only if it could obtain *more than* 3 tons of avocados for 1 ton of

soybeans by trading with Mexico. Similarly, Mexico can shift production at the rate of $4A$ for $1S$. So it would be advantageous to Mexico to specialize in avocados if it could get 1 ton of soybeans for *less than* 4 tons of avocados.

Suppose that through negotiation the two nations agree on an exchange rate of 1 ton of soybeans for $3\frac{1}{2}$ tons of avocados. These **terms of trade** are mutually beneficial to both countries since each can "do better" through such trade than by domestic production alone. The United States can get $3\frac{1}{2}$ tons of avocados by sending 1 ton of soybeans to Mexico, while it can get only 3 tons of avocados by shifting resources domestically from soybeans to avocados. Mexico can obtain 1 ton of soybeans at a lower cost of $3\frac{1}{2}$ tons of avocados through trade with the United States, compared to the cost of 4 tons if Mexicans produce the 1 ton of wheat themselves.

Gains from Specialization and Trade

Let's pinpoint the size of the gains in total output from specialization and trade. Suppose that, before specialization and trade, production alternative C in Table 6-4 and alternative T in 6-5 were the optimal product mixes for the two countries. These outputs are shown in column 1 in Table 6-6. That is, Mexico preferred 24 tons of avocados and 9 tons of soybeans (Table 6-4) and the United States preferred 33 tons of avocados and 19 tons of soybeans (Table 6-5) to all other alternatives available within their respective domestic economies.

Now assume both nations specialize according to comparative advantage, Mexico producing 60 tons of avocados and no soybeans (alternative E) and the United States producing no avocados and 30 tons of

TABLE 6-6 Specialization according to comparative advantage and the gains from trade (in tons)

Country	(1) Outputs before specialization	(2) Outputs after specialization	(3) Amounts traded	(4) Outputs available after trade	(5) Gains from specialization and trade (4) − (1)
Mexico	24 avocados	60 avocados	−35 avocados	25 avocados	1 avocados
	9 soybeans	0 soybeans	+10 soybeans	10 soybeans	1 soybeans
United States	33 avocados	0 avocados	+35 avocados	35 avocados	2 avocados
	19 soybeans	30 soybeans	−10 soybeans	20 soybeans	1 soybeans

soybeans (alternative R). These outputs are reflected in column 2 in Table 6-6. Using our $1S \equiv 3\frac{1}{2} A$ terms of trade, assume Mexico exchanges 35 tons of avocados for 10 tons of U.S. soybeans. Column 3 in Table 6-6 shows the quantities exchanged in this trade. As indicated in column 4, after the trade Mexico has 25 tons of avocados and 10 tons of soybeans, while the United States has 35 tons of avocados and 20 tons of soybeans. Compared with their optimum product mixes before specialization and trade (column 1), *both* nations now enjoy more avocados and more soybeans! Specifically, Mexico has gained 1 ton of avocados and 1 ton of soybeans. The United States has gained 2 tons of avocados and 1 ton of soybeans. These gains are shown in column 5, where we have subtracted the *before*-specialization outputs of column 1 from the *after*-specialization outputs in column 4.

Specialization based on comparative advantage improves global resource allocation. The same total inputs of world resources and technology results in a larger global output. If Mexico and the United States allocate all their resources to avocados and soybeans, respectively, the same total inputs of resources can produce more output between them, indicating that resources are being used or allocated more efficiently.

We noted in Chapter 2 that through specialization and international trade a nation can overcome the production constraints imposed by its domestic production possibilities table and curve. Table 6-6 and its discussion show just how this is done. The domestic production possibilities data of the two countries have not changed, meaning that neither nation's production possibilities curve has shifted. But specialization and trade mean that citizens of both countries have enjoyed increased consumption. *Thus, specialization and trade have the same effect as an increase in resources or technological progress: they make more goods available to an economy.* **(Key Question 4)**

FOREIGN EXCHANGE MARKET

People, firms, or nations which specialize in the production of specific goods or services exchange those products for money and then use the money to buy other products or to pay for the use of resources. Within the economy, prices are stated in the domestic currency and buyers use that currency to purchase domestic products. In Mexico, for example, buyers possess pesos, exactly the currency sellers want.

International markets are different. How many dollars does it take to buy a truckload of Mexican av-

ocados selling for 3000 pesos, a German automobile selling for 90,000 marks, or a Japanese motorcycle priced at 300,000 yen? Producers in Mexico, Germany, and Japan want payment in pesos, marks, and yen, respectively, so they can pay their wages, rent, interest, dividends, and taxes. A **foreign exchange market,** a market in which various national currencies are exchanged for one another, serves this need. The equilibrium prices in these markets are called **exchange rates;** an exchange rate is the rate at which the currency of one nation is exchanged for the currency of another nation. (See Global Perspective 6-2.) Two points about the foreign exchange market are particularly noteworthy:

1. *A competitive market*   Real-world foreign exchange markets conform closely to the markets discussed in Chapter 3. They are competitive markets characterized by large numbers of buyers and sellers dealing in standardized products such as the American dollar, the German mark, the British pound, the Swedish krona, and the Japanese yen.

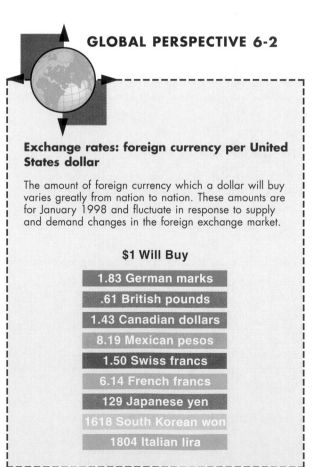

GLOBAL PERSPECTIVE 6-2

Exchange rates: foreign currency per United States dollar

The amount of foreign currency which a dollar will buy varies greatly from nation to nation. These amounts are for January 1998 and fluctuate in response to supply and demand changes in the foreign exchange market.

$1 Will Buy

1.83 German marks

.61 British pounds

1.43 Canadian dollars

8.19 Mexican pesos

1.50 Swiss francs

6.14 French francs

129 Japanese yen

1618 South Korean won

1804 Italian lira

2. *Linkages to all domestic and foreign prices* The market price or exchange rate of a nation's currency is an unusual price; it links all domestic (say, United States) prices with all foreign (say, Japanese or German) prices. Exchange rates enable consumers in one country to translate prices of foreign goods into units of their own currency: they need only multiply the foreign product price by the exchange rate. If the dollar-yen exchange rate is $.01 (1 cent) per yen, a Sony television set priced at ¥20,000 will cost $200 (= 20,000 × $.01) in the United States. If the exchange rate is $.02 (2 cents) per yen, it will cost $400 (= 20,000 × $.02) in the United States. Similarly, all other Japanese products would double in price to U.S. buyers. As you will see, a change in exchange rates has important implications for a nation's level of domestic production and employment.

Dollar-Yen Market

How does the foreign exchange market work? Let's look briefly at the market for dollars and yen, leaving details to a later chapter. U.S. firms exporting to Japan want payment in dollars, not yen; but Japanese importers of U.S. goods possess yen, not dollars. So the Japanese importers are willing to supply their yen in exchange for dollars in the foreign exchange market. At the same time, there are U.S. importers of Japanese goods who need to pay Japanese exporters with yen, not dollars. These importers go to the foreign exchange market as demanders of yen. We then have a market in which the "price" is in dollars and the "product" is yen.

Figure 6-4 shows the supply of yen (by Japanese importers) and the demand for yen (by U.S. importers). The intersection of demand curve D_y and supply curve S_y establishes the equilibrium dollar price of yen. Here the equilibrium price of 1 yen—the dollar-yen exchange rate—is 1 cent per yen, or $.01 = ¥1. At this price, the market for yen clears; there is neither a shortage nor a surplus of yen. The equilibrium $.01 price of 1 yen means that $1 will buy 100 yen or ¥100 worth of Japanese goods. Conversely, 100 yen will buy $1 worth of U.S. goods.

Changing Rates: Depreciation and Appreciation

What might cause the exchange rate to change? The determinants of the demand for and supply of yen are similar to the determinants of demand and supply for almost any product. In the United States, several things might increase the demand for—and therefore the dollar price of—yen. Incomes might rise in the United States, enabling residents to buy not only more domestic goods but also more Sony televisions, Nikon cameras, and Nissan automobiles from Japan. So people in the United States would need more yen and the demand for yen would increase. Or a change in people's tastes might enhance their preferences for Japanese goods. When gas prices soared in the 1970s, many auto buyers in the United States shifted their demands from gas-guzzling domestic cars to gas-efficient Japanese compact cars. The result was an increased demand for yen.

The point is that an increase in the U.S. demand for Japanese goods will increase the demand for yen

FIGURE 6-4 The market for yen U.S. imports from Japan create a demand D_y for yen, while U.S. exports to Japan create a supply S_y of yen. The dollar price of 1 yen—the exchange rate—is determined at the intersection of the supply and demand curves. In this case the equilibrium price is $.01, meaning that 1 cent will buy 1 yen.

112 PART ONE AN INTRODUCTION TO ECONOMICS AND THE ECONOMY

and raise the dollar price of yen. Suppose the dollar price of yen rises from $.01 = ¥1 to $.02 = ¥1. When the dollar price of yen increases, we say a **depreciation** of the dollar relative to the yen has occurred: It then takes more dollars (pennies in this case) to buy a single unit of the foreign currency (a yen). Alternatively stated, the *international value of the dollar* has declined. A depreciated dollar buys fewer yen and therefore fewer Japanese goods; the yen and all Japanese goods have become more expensive to U.S. buyers. Result: Consumers in the United States shift their expenditures from Japanese goods to now less expensive American goods. The Ford Taurus becomes relatively more attractive than the Honda Accord to U.S. consumers. Conversely, because each yen buys more dollars—that is, because the international value of the yen has increased—U.S. goods become cheaper to people in Japan and U.S. exports to them rise.

If the opposite event occurred—if the Japanese demanded more U.S. goods—then they would supply more yen to pay for these goods. The increase in the supply of yen relative to the demand for yen would decrease the equilibrium price of yen in the foreign exchange market. For example, the dollar price of yen might decline from $.01 = ¥1 to $.005 = ¥1. A decrease in the dollar price of yen is called an **appreciation** of the dollar relative to the yen. It means that the international value of the dollar has increased. It then takes fewer dollars (or pennies) to buy a single yen; the dollar is worth more because it can purchase more yen and therefore more Japanese goods. Each Sony Walkman becomes less expensive in terms of dollars, so people in the United States purchase more of them. In general, U.S. imports rise. Meanwhile, because it takes more yen to get a dollar, U.S. exports to Japan fall.

We summarize these currency relationships in Figure 6-5, which you should examine closely. **(Key Question 6)**

QUICK REVIEW 6-2

■ A country has a comparative advantage in a product when it can produce that product at a lower domestic opportunity cost than can a potential trading partner.

■ Specialization based on comparative advantage increases the total output available for nations which trade with one another.

■ The foreign exchange market is the market where the currencies of nations are exchanged for one another.

FIGURE 6-5 Currency appreciation and depreciation An increase in the dollar price of foreign currency is equivalent to a decline in the international value of the dollar (dollar depreciation). An increase in the dollar price of foreign currency also implies a decline in the foreign currency price of dollars. That is, the international value of foreign currency rises relative to the dollar (the foreign currency appreciates).

■ An appreciation of the dollar is an increase in the international value of the dollar relative to the currency of some other nation; a dollar now buys more units of that currency. A depreciation of the dollar is a decrease in the international value of the dollar relative to another currency; a dollar now buys fewer units of that currency.

GOVERNMENT AND TRADE

If people and nations benefit from specialization and international exchange, why do governments sometimes try to restrict the free flow of imports or to bolster exports? What kinds of world trade barriers can governments erect, and why would they do so?

Trade Impediments and Subsidies

There are four usual means by which governments might interfere with free trade:

1. **Protective tariffs** are excise taxes or duties placed on imported goods. Most are designed to shield domestic producers from foreign competition. They impede free trade by increasing the prices of imported goods, shifting demand toward domestic products. An excise tax on imported shoes, for example, would make domestically made shoes more attractive to consumers.

2. **Import quotas** are limits on the quantities or total value of specific items that may be imported. Once a quota is "filled," it chokes off imports of that product. Import quotas can be more effective than tariffs in retarding international commerce. A particular product could be imported in large quantities despite high tariffs; a low import quota completely prohibits imports once the quota is filled.

3. **Nontariff barriers** (and, implicitly, *nonquota* barriers) include licensing requirements, unreasonable standards pertaining to product quality, or simply unnecessary bureaucratic red tape in customs procedures. Some nations require that their domestic importers of foreign goods obtain licenses. By restricting the issuance of licenses, imports can be effectively impeded. Great Britain bars coal importation in this way. Also, some nations impede imports of fruit by insisting that *each* crate be inspected for worms and insects.

4. **Export subsidies** consist of governmental payments to domestic producers of export goods. The payments reduce their production costs, permitting them to charge lower prices and thus sell more exports in world markets. Two examples: Participating European governments have heavily subsidized Airbus Industries, which produces commercial aircraft. These subsidies have helped Airbus compete against Boeing, an American firm. The United States and other nations have subsidized domestic farmers, boosting domestic food supply. This has reduced the market price of food, artificially decreasing export prices on agricultural produce.

Why Government Trade Interventions?

Why would a nation want to send more of its output for consumption abroad than it gains as imported output in return? Why the impulse to impede imports or boost exports through government policy when free trade is beneficial to a nation? There are several reasons—some legitimate, most not. We will look at two here, and examine others in a later chapter.

Misunderstanding of the Gains from Trade It is a commonly accepted myth that the fundamental benefit of international trade is greater domestic employment in the export sector. This suggests that exports are "good" because they increase domestic employment, whereas imports are "bad" because they deprive people of jobs at home. In reality, the true benefit from international trade is the *overall* increase in output obtained through specialization and exchange. A nation can fully employ its resources, including labor, with or without international trade. International trade, however, enables society to use its resources in ways that increase its total output and therefore its overall well-being.

A nation does not need international trade to locate *on* its production possibilities curve. A closed (nontrading) national economy can have full employment without international trade. But through world trade an economy can reach a point *beyond* its domestic production possibilities curve. The gain from trade is the extra output obtained from abroad—the imports gotten for less cost than if they were produced using domestic resources. The only valid reason for exporting part of our domestic output is to obtain imports that are of greater value to us. Specialization and international exchange make this possible.

Political Considerations While a nation as a whole gains from trade, trade may harm particular domestic industries and groups of resource suppliers. In our earlier comparative-advantage example, specialization and trade adversely affected the U.S. avocado industry and the Mexican soybean industry. Those industries might seek to preserve their economic positions by persuading their respective governments to protect them from imports—perhaps through tariffs or import quotas:

> The direct beneficiaries of import relief or export subsidy are usually few in number, but each has a large individual stake in the outcome. Thus, their incentive for vigorous political activity is strong.
>
> But the costs of such policies may far exceed the benefits. It may cost the public [$80,000–$120,000] a year to protect a domestic job that might otherwise pay an employee only half that amount in wages and benefits.

Furthermore, the costs of protection are widely diffused—in the United States, among 50 states and [268] million citizens. Since the cost borne by any one citizen is likely to be quite small, and may even go unnoticed, resistance at the grass-roots level to protectionist measures often is considerably less than pressures for their adoption.[2]

Policymakers often see little public opposition to demands for *protectionism* because tariffs and quotas are buried in the prices of goods. Indeed, the public may be won over by the apparent plausibility ("Cut imports and prevent domestic unemployment") and patriotic ring ("Buy American!") of the protectionist arguments. The alleged benefits of tariffs are immediate and clear-cut to the public, but the adverse effects cited by economists are obscure and dispersed over the entire economy. When political deal making is added in—"You back tariffs for the apparel industry in my state, and I'll back tariffs on the auto industry in your state"—the sum can be a network of protective tariffs, import quotas, and export subsidies.

Costs to Society

Tariffs and quotas benefit domestic producers of the protected products, but they harm domestic consumers, who must pay higher than world prices for the protected goods. They also hurt those domestic firms which use the protected goods as inputs in their production processes. For example, a tariff on imported steel would boost the price of steel girders, hurting firms that construct large buildings. Also, tariffs and quotas reduce competition in the protected industries. With less competition from foreign producers, domestic firms may be slow to design and implement cost-saving production methods and introduce new and improved products.

Study after study has shown that the cost of trade protection to consumers and adversely affected input buyers exceeds the benefit to the protected firms. That is, there is a *net cost* (cost *minus* benefit) to society from trade protection. In the United States this net cost was as much as $50 billion a couple of decades ago but has dropped significantly in recent years along with declines in U.S. tariffs and quotas.

---

[2] *Economic Report of the President, 1982*, p. 177. Updated.

MULTILATERAL TRADE AGREEMENTS AND FREE-TRADE ZONES

When one nation enacts barriers against imports, the nations whose exports suffer may retaliate with trade barriers of their own. In such a *trade war*, tariffs escalate, choking off world trade and reducing everyone's economic well-being. The **Smoot-Hawley Tariff Act** of 1930 is a classic example. Although this act was meant to reduce imports and stimulate U.S. production, its high tariffs prompted affected nations to retaliate with equally high tariffs. International trade across the globe fell, lowering the output, income, and employment levels of all nations. Economic historians generally agree that the Smoot-Hawley Tariff Act was a contributing cause of the Great Depression. In view of this fact, the world's nations have worked to lower tariffs worldwide. Their pursuit of free trade has been aided by powerful domestic interest groups. Specifically, exporters of goods and services, importers of foreign components used in "domestic" products, and domestic sellers of imported products all strongly support lower tariffs worldwide.

Figure 6-6 makes clear that the United States has been a high-tariff nation over much of its history. But it also demonstrates that, in general, U.S. tariffs have declined during the past half-century.

Reciprocal Trade Agreements Act and GATT

The **Reciprocal Trade Agreements Act** of 1934 started the downward trend of tariffs. Specifically aimed at reducing tariffs, this act had two main features.

1. *Negotiating authority* It authorized the President to negotiate with foreign nations agreements reducing U.S. tariffs by up to 50 percent of the existing rates. Tariff reductions hinged on other nations' reciprocating by lowering tariffs on U.S. exports.

2. *Generalized reductions* The specific tariff reductions negotiated between the United States and any particular nation became generalized through **most-favored-nation clauses,** which often accompanied these agreements. These clauses stipulated that any subsequently reduced U.S. tariffs, resulting from negotiation with any other nation, would apply equally to the nation

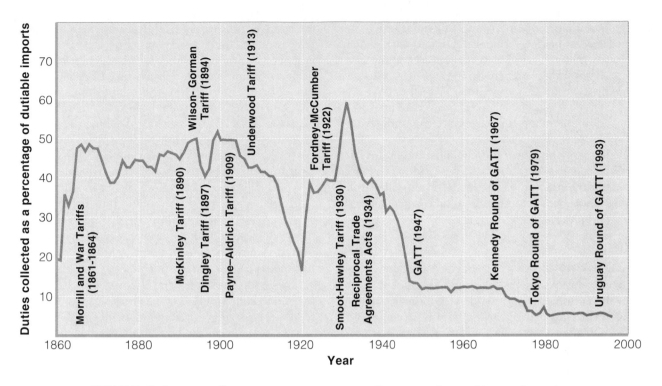

FIGURE 6-6 U.S. tariff rates, 1860–1997 U.S. tariff rates have fluctuated historically. But beginning with the Reciprocal Trade Agreements Act of 1934, the trend has been downward. (*Source:* U.S. Department of Commerce data.)

signing the original agreement. So if the United States negotiated a reduction in tariffs with, say, France, the lower U.S. tariffs on French imports would also apply to the imports of the other nations having most-favored-nation status, say, Sweden and Switzerland. This way, new reductions in U.S. tariffs automatically applied to many other nations.

But the Reciprocal Trade Agreements Act gave rise to only bilateral (between-two-nations) negotiations. Its approach was broadened in 1947 when 23 nations, including the United States, signed the **General Agreement on Tariffs and Trade (GATT).** GATT is based on three cardinal principles: (1) equal, nondiscriminatory trade treatment for all member nations; (2) the reduction of tariffs by multilateral negotiations; and (3) the elimination of import quotas.

Basically, GATT is a forum to negotiate reductions in trade barriers on a multilateral basis among nations. With 125 nations now belonging to GATT, there is little doubt that it has been a positive force in the trend toward liberalized world trade. Under its sponsorship, member nations have completed eight "rounds" of negotiations to reduce trade barriers in the post-World War II period.

GATT's Uruguay Round The eighth and most recent "round" of GATT negotiations began in Uruguay in 1986. After 7 years of wrangling, in 1993 the participant nations reached a new agreement. The agreement took effect on January 1, 1995, and its provisions will be phased in through 2005.

Under this latest GATT agreement, tariffs will be eliminated or reduced on thousands of products, with tariffs dropping overall by 33 percent. The agreement will also liberalize government rules which in the past have impeded the global market for such services as advertising, legal services, tourist services, and financial services. Quotas on imported textiles and apparel will be phased out, to be replaced with tariffs. (Tariffs are preferable to quotas, since tariffs let in an unlimited amount of imported goods; in contrast, quotas block all imports beyond a specified quantity.)

Other important provisions will reduce agricultural subsidies paid to farmers and protect intellectual property (patents, trademarks, copyrights) against piracy. Finally, the Uruguay Round of GATT created the **World Trade Organization (WTO)** as GATT's successor. The WTO has judicial powers to intermediate among members and rule on disputes involving the trade rules.

When fully implemented, the most recent GATT agreement is expected to boost the world's GDP by about $6 trillion, or 8 percent. Consumers in the United States will gain about $30 billion annually.

European Union

Countries have also sought to reduce tariffs by creating regional free-trade zones or trade blocs. The most dramatic example is the **European Union (EU),** formerly called the European Economic Community. Initiated as the Common Market in 1958, the EU now comprises 15 western European nations—France, Germany, Italy, Belgium, the Netherlands, Luxembourg, Denmark, Ireland, United Kingdom, Greece, Spain, Portugal, Austria, Finland, and Sweden.

Goals The original Common Market called for (1) gradual abolition of tariffs and import quotas on all products traded among the participating nations; (2) establishment of a common system of tariffs applicable to all goods received from nations outside the EU; (3) free movement of capital and labor within the Common Market; and (4) creation of common policies in other economic matters of joint concern, such as agriculture, transportation, and restrictive business practices. The EU has achieved most of these goals and is now a strong **trade bloc:** a group of countries having a common identity, set of economic interests, and trade rules.

Results The motives for creating the EU were political and economic. The main economic motive was liberalized trade for members. While it is difficult to determine how much of EU prosperity and growth has resulted from economic integration, that integration clearly has created large markets for EU industries. The resulting economies of large-scale production have enabled European industries to achieve much lower costs than they could in their small, single-nation markets.

The effects of EU success on nonmember nations, such as the United States, are mixed. A peaceful and increasingly prosperous EU makes its members better customers for U.S. exports. But U.S. and other nonmember firms encounter tariffs which make it difficult to compete against firms within the EU trade bloc. For example, before the establishment of the EU, American, German, and French automobile manufacturers all faced the same tariff selling their products in, say, Belgium. However, with the establishment of free internal trading among EU members, Belgian tariffs on German Volkswagens and French Renaults fell to zero, but an external tariff still applies to U.S. Chevrolets and Fords. This puts U.S. firms at a serious disadvantage. Similarly, EU trade restrictions hamper eastern European exports of metals, textiles, and farm products, goods which the eastern Europeans produce in abundance.

By giving preferences to countries within their free-trade zone, trade blocs such as the EU tend to reduce their trade with nonbloc members. Thus, the world loses some of the benefits of a completely open global trading system. Eliminating this disadvantage has been one of the motivations for liberalizing global trade through the World Trade Organization.

North American Free Trade Agreement

In 1993 Canada, Mexico, and the United States formed a trade bloc. The **North American Free Trade Agreement (NAFTA)** established a free-trade zone having about the same combined output of the EU but a much larger geographical area. NAFTA will eliminate tariffs and other trade barriers between Canada, Mexico, and the United States over a 15-year period.

Critics of the agreement fear that one result will be a loss of U.S. jobs as firms move to Mexico to take advantage of lower wages and weaker regulations on pollution and workplace safety. Also, there is concern that Japan and South Korea will build plants in Mexico to transport goods tariff-free to the United States, further hurting U.S. firms and workers.

Defenders of NAFTA reject these concerns. They contend that specialization according to comparative advantage will enable each nation to obtain more total output from its scarce resources. They also argue that NAFTA's free-trade zone will encourage worldwide investment in Mexico, enhancing Mexican productivity and national income. Mexican consumers will use some of that increased income to buy U.S. exports. Any loss of jobs, say defenders of NAFTA, most likely would have occurred anyway to other low-wage countries such as China.

Hostile Trade Blocs or Further Integration?

With the formation of NAFTA, it may appear that the world's nations are separating into potentially hostile trade blocs. But NAFTA is also a means for negotiating reductions in trade barriers with the EU, Japan, and other trading countries. Access to the vast North American market is as important to the EU and Japan as is access to their markets by Canada, Mexico, and the United States. NAFTA gives the United States leverage in future trade negotiations with the EU and Japan. Eventually, direct negotiations between the EU and NAFTA might link the two free-trade zones. Japan and other major trading nations, not wishing to be left out of the world's wealthiest trade markets, would be forced to eliminate their trade barriers, opening their domestic markets to additional imports. Nor do other nations and trade blocs want to be excluded from free-trade zones. Examples:

1. *APEC* The United States and several other nations have agreed to liberalize trade and open investment over the next few decades through the Asian-Pacific Economic Cooperation (APEC) forum. APEC members are Australia, Brunei, Canada, Chile, China (Hong Kong), Indonesia, Japan, Malaysia, Mexico, New Zealand, the Philippines, Papua New Guinea, Singapore, South Korea, Taiwan, Thailand, and the United States.

2. *Chile's potential inclusion in NAFTA* Canada, Mexico, and the United States are negotiating with Chile to become the fourth partner in NAFTA.

3. *Mercosur* The free-trade group encompassing Brazil, Argentina, Uruguay, and Paraguay—called Mercosur—has expressed interest in eventually linking up with NAFTA.

Economists generally agree that the ideal free-trade area would encompass the entire world. **(Key Question 10)**

QUICK REVIEW 6-3

■ Governments promote exports and reduce imports through tariffs, quotas, nontariff barriers, and export subsidies.

■ The various "rounds" of the General Agreement on Tariffs and Trade (GATT) have established multinational reductions in tariffs and import quotas among the 125 member nations.

■ The Uruguay Round of GATT, which went into effect in 1995 and will be fully implemented by 2005, **(a)** reduces tariffs worldwide; **(b)** liberalizes rules impeding barriers to trade in services; **(c)** reduces agricultural subsidies; **(d)** creates new protections for intellectual property; **(e)** phases out quotas on textiles and apparel; and **(f)** sets up the World Trade Organization.

■ The European Union (EU) and the North American Free Trade Agreement (NAFTA) have reduced internal trade barriers among their members by establishing large free-trade zones.

AMERICAN FIRMS IN THE WORLD ECONOMY

Freer international trade has brought with it intense competition in the United States and the world. Not long ago three large U.S. producers dominated the U.S. automobile industry. Imported autos were an oddity, accounting for a tiny portion of auto sales. But General Motors, Ford, and Chrysler now face intense competition as they struggle for sales against Nissan, Honda, Toyota, Hyundai, BMW, and others. Similarly, imports have gained major shares of the U.S. markets for automobile tires, clothing, sporting goods, electronics, motorcycles, outboard motors, and toys.

Nevertheless, thousands of U.S. firms—large and small—have thrived and prospered in the global marketplace. Boeing, McDonald's, Dow Chemicals, Intel, Coca-Cola, 3M, Microsoft, AT&T, Monsanto, Procter & Gamble, and Hewlett-Packard are just a few of them. These and many other firms have continued to retain high market shares at home and have dramatically expanded their sales abroad. Of course, not all firms have been so successful. Some corporations simply have not been able to compete; their international competitors make better-quality products, have lower production costs, or both. Not surprisingly, the U.S. firms which have been hurt most by foreign competition are precisely those which have long enjoyed the protection of tariffs and quotas. These barriers to imports have artificially limited competition, removing the incentive to improve production methods and products. Also, trade barriers have shielded some domestic firms from the gradual changes in output and employment resulting from

Buy American: The Global Refrigerator

Humorist Art Buchwald looks at the logic of the "Buy American" campaign.

"There is only one way the country is going to get on its feet," said Baleful.

"How's that?" I asked, as we drank coffee in his office at the Baleful Refrigerator Company.

"The consumer has to start buying American," he said, slamming his fist down on the desk. "Every time an American buys a foreign refrigerator it costs one of my people his job. And every time one of my people is out of work it means he or she can't buy refrigerators."

"It's a vicious circle," I said.

Baleful's secretary came in. "Mr. Thompson, the steel broker is on the phone."

My friend grabbed the receiver. "Thompson, where is that steel shipment from Japan that was supposed to be in last weekend? . . . I don't care about weather. We're almost out of steel, and I'll have to close down the refrigerator assembly line next week. If you can't deliver when you promise, I'll find myself another broker."

"You get your steel from Japan?" I asked Baleful. "Even with shipping costs, their price is still lower than steel made in Europe. We used to get all our sheets from Belgium, but the Japanese are now giving them a run for their money."

The buzzer on the phone alerted Baleful. He listened for a few moments and then said, "Excuse me, I have a call from Taiwan. Mark Four? Look, R&D designed a new push-button door handle and we're going to send the specs to you. Tell Mr. Chow if his people send us a sample of one and can make it for us at the same price as the old handle, we'll give his company the order."

A man came in with a plastic container and said, "Mr. Baleful, you said you wanted to see one of these before we ordered them. They are the containers for the ice maker in the refrigerator."

Baleful inspected it carefully and banged it on the floor a couple of times. "What's the price on it?"

"Hong Kong can deliver it at $2 a tray, and Dong-Fu Plastics in South Korea said they can make it for $1.70."

"It's just a plastic tray. Take the South Korea bid. We'll let Hong Kong supply us with the shelves for the freezer. Any word on the motors?"

---

national shifts in comparative advantage over time. As trade protection declines under WTO and NAFTA, some U.S. firms will surely discover that they are producing goods for which the United States clearly has a comparative *dis*advantage (perhaps some types of apparel, for example).

Is the greater competition which accompanies the global economy a good thing? Although some domestic producers and their workers do not like it, foreign competition clearly benefits consumers. Imports break down the monopoly power of existing firms, reducing product prices and providing consumers with a greater variety of goods. Foreign competition also forces domestic producers to become more efficient and to improve product quality; this has already happened in several U.S. industries, including steel and autos. Evidence shows that most—but clearly not all—U.S. firms *can* and *do* compete successfully in the global economy.

What about U.S. firms which cannot successfully compete in open markets? The harsh reality is that they should go out of business, much like an unsuccessful corner boutique. Persistent economic losses mean scarce resources are not being used efficiently. Shifting these resources to alternative, profitable uses will increase total U.S. output.

CHAPTER SUMMARY

1. International trade is growing in importance globally and for the United States. World trade is significant to the United States in two respects. **(a)** The absolute volumes of American imports and exports exceed those of any other single nation. **(b)** The United States is completely depen-dent on trade for certain commodities and materials that cannot be obtained domestically.

2. Principal U.S. exports include chemicals, computers, consumer durables, aircraft, and grain; major U.S. imports

"There's a German company in Brazil that just came out with a new motor, and it's passed all our tests, so Johnson has ordered 50,000."

"Call Cleveland Motors and tell them we're sorry, but the price they quoted us was just too high."

"Yes, sir," the man said and departed.

The secretary came in again and said, "Harry telephoned and wanted to let you know the defroster just arrived from Finland. They're unloading the box cars now."

"Good. Any word on the wooden crates from Singapore?"

"They're at the dock in Hoboken."

"Thank heaven. Cancel the order from Boise Cascade."

"What excuse should I give them?"

"Tell them we made a mistake in our inventory, or we're switching to plastic. I don't care what you tell them."

Baleful turned to me. "Where were we?"

"You were saying that if the consumer doesn't start buying American, this country is going to be in a lot of trouble."

"Right. It's not only his patriotic duty, but his livelihood that's at stake. I'm going to Washington next week to tell the Senate Commerce Committee that if they don't get on the stick, there isn't going to be a domestic refrigerator left in this country. We're not going to stay in business for our health."

"Pour it to them," I urged him.

Baleful said, "Come out with me into the showroom."

I followed him. He went to his latest model, and opened the door. "This is an American refrigerator made by the American worker, for the American consumer. What do you have to say to that?"

"It's beautiful," I said. "It puts foreign imports to shame."

Source: Art Buchwald, "Being Bullish on Buying American." Reprinted by permission. We discovered this article in *Master Curriculum Guide in Economics: Teaching Strategies for International Trade* (New York: Joint Council on Economic Education, 1988).

are petroleum, automobiles, clothing, computers, and household appliances. Quantitatively, Canada is the United States' most important trading partner.

3. Global trade has been greatly facilitated by **(a)** improvements in transportation technology, **(b)** improvements in communications technology, **(c)** general declines in tariffs, and **(d)** continuing peaceful relations among major industrial nations. The United States, Japan, and the western European nations dominate the global economy. But the total volume of trade has been increased by several new trade participants, including the "Asian tigers" (Hong Kong, Singapore, South Korea, and Taiwan), China, the eastern European countries, and the newly independent countries of the former Soviet Union.

4. The open-economy circular flow model connects the domestic U.S. economy to the rest of the world. Customers from abroad enter the U.S. product market to buy some U.S. output. These U.S. exports create business revenues and generate income in the United States. U.S. households spend some of their money incomes on products made abroad and imported to the United States.

5. Specialization based on comparative advantage enables nations to achieve higher standards of living through exchange with other countries. A trading partner should specialize in products and services for which its domestic opportunity costs are lowest. The terms of trade must be such that both nations can get more of some output via trade than they can obtain by producing it at home.

6. The foreign exchange market sets exchange rates between nations' currencies. Foreign importers are suppliers of their currency, and domestic importers are demanders of the foreign currency. The resulting supply-demand equilibrium sets an exchange rate; such exchange rates link the price levels of all nations. Depreciation of a nation's currency reduces its imports and increases its exports; appreciation increases its imports and reduces its exports.

7. Governments shape trade flows through **(a)** protective tariffs, **(b)** quotas, **(c)** nontariff barriers, and **(d)** export subsidies. These are impediments to free trade; they result from misunderstandings about the gains to be had from trade and also result from political considerations. By increasing product prices, trade barriers cost U.S. consumers billions of dollars annually.

8. The Reciprocal Trade Agreements Act of 1934 marked the beginning of a trend toward lower U.S. tariffs. In 1947 the General Agreement on Tariffs and Trade (GATT) was formed to encourage nondiscriminatory treatment for all member trading nations, reduce tariffs, and eliminate import quotas.

9. The Uruguay Round of GATT negotiations, completed in 1993 and to be implemented through 2005, **(a)** reduces tariffs, **(b)** liberalizes trade in services, **(c)** reduces agricultural subsidies, **(d)** reduces pirating of intellectual property, **(e)** phases out import quotas on textiles and apparel, and **(f)** establishes the World Trade Organization.

10. Free-trade zones (trade blocs) may liberalize trade within regions but may also impede trade with nonbloc members. Two examples of free-trade arrangements are the European Union (EU), formerly the European Community or "Common Market," and the North American Free Trade Agreement (NAFTA), comprising Canada, Mexico, and the United States.

11. The global economy has created intense foreign competition in many U.S. product markets, but most U.S. firms can compete well both at home and in global markets.

TERMS AND CONCEPTS

multinational
  corporations
"Asian tigers"
comparative advantage
terms of trade
foreign exchange
  market
exchange rates

depreciation
appreciation
protective tariffs
import quotas
nontariff barriers
export subsidies
Smoot-Hawley Tariff
  Act

Reciprocal Trade
  Agreements Act
most-favored-nation
  clauses
General Agreement on
  Tariffs and Trade
  (GATT)

World Trade
  Organization (WTO)
European Union (EU)
trade bloc
North American Free
  Trade Agreement
  (NAFTA)

STUDY QUESTIONS

1. How important is international trade to the U.S. economy? What country is the United States' most important trading partner, quantitatively? How have persistent U.S. trade deficits been financed? "Trade deficits mean we get more merchandise from the rest of the world's nations than we provide them in return. Therefore, trade deficits are economically desirable." Do you agree? Why or why not?

2. What factors account for the rapid growth of world trade since World War II? Who are the major players in international trade today? Who are the "Asian tigers," and how important are they in world trade?

3. KEY QUESTION Use the circular flow model (Figure 6-3) to explain how an increase in exports would affect the revenues of domestic firms, the money incomes of domestic households, and imports from abroad. Use Table 6-3 to find the exact amounts (in 1996) of U.S. exports [flow (13)] and imports [flow (16)] in the circular flow model. What do these amounts imply for flows (14) and (15)?

4. KEY QUESTION The following are production possibilities tables for South Korea and the United States. Assume that before specialization and trade the optimal product mix for South Korea is alternative *B* and for the United States is alternative *U*.

Product	South Korea's production possibilities					
	A	*B*	*C*	*D*	*E*	*F*
Radios (in thousands)	30	24	18	12	6	0
Chemicals (in tons)	0	6	12	18	24	30

Product	U.S. production possibilities					
	R	*S*	*T*	*U*	*V*	*W*
Radios (in thousands)	10	8	6	4	2	0
Chemicals (in tons)	0	4	8	12	16	20

a. Are comparative-cost conditions such that the two areas should specialize? If so, what product should each produce?
b. What is the total gain in radio and chemical output which results from this specialization?
c. What are the limits of the terms of trade? Suppose actual terms of trade are 1 unit of radios

for $1\frac{1}{2}$ units of chemicals and that 4 units of radios are exchanged for 6 units of chemicals. What are the gains from specialization and trade for each area?

d. Can you conclude from this illustration that specialization according to comparative advantage results in more efficient use of world resources? Explain.

5. Suppose that the comparative-cost ratios of two products—baby formula and tuna fish—are as follows in the hypothetical nations of Canswicki and Tunata:

Canswicki: 1 can baby formula $\equiv$ 2 cans tuna fish
Tunata: 1 can baby formula $\equiv$ 4 cans tuna fish

In what product should each nation specialize? Explain why terms of trade of 1 can baby formula $\equiv$ $2\frac{1}{2}$ cans tuna fish would be acceptable to both nations.

6. KEY QUESTION "U.S. exports create a demand for foreign currencies; foreign imports of U.S. goods generate supplies of foreign currencies." Do you agree? Would a decline in U.S. incomes or a weakening of U.S. preferences for foreign products cause the dollar to depreciate or appreciate? What would be the effects of that depreciation or appreciation on U.S. exports and imports?

7. If the French franc declines in value (depreciates) in the foreign exchange market, will it be easier or harder for the French to sell their wine in the United States? Suppose you were planning a trip to Paris. How would depreciation of the franc change the dollar cost of this trip?

8. True or False? "An increase in the American dollar price of the German mark implies that the German mark has depreciated in value." Explain.

9. What tools do governments use to promote exports and restrict imports? Who benefits and who loses from protectionist policies? What is the net outcome for society?

10. KEY QUESTION What is GATT? How does it affect nearly every person in the world? What were the major outcomes of the Uruguay Round of GATT? How is GATT related to the European Union (EU) and the North American Free Trade Agreement (NAFTA)?

11. Explain: "Free-trade zones such as the EU and NAFTA lead a double life: they can promote free trade among members, but pose serious trade obstacles for nonmembers." Do you think the net effects of these trade blocs are good or bad for world trade? Why?

12. What do you see as the competitive strengths of U.S. firms? Competitive weaknesses? Explain: "Even if Japan captured the entire worldwide auto market, that simply would mean that Japan would have to buy a whole lot of other products from abroad. Thus, the United States and other industrial nations would necessarily experience an increase in exports to Japan."

13. (Last Word) What point is Art Buchwald making in his humorous essay on the Baleful Refrigerator Company? Why might Mr. Baleful *oppose* tariffs on imported goods, even though he wants consumers to buy "American" refrigerators?

14. WEB-BASED QUESTION **Trade Balances with Partner Countries** The U.S. Census Bureau http://www.census.gov/foreign-trade/www/javabal.html ranks the top trading partners of the United States (imports and exports added together) as well as the top 10 countries with which the U.S. has a trade surplus and a trade deficit. Using the current year-to-date data, compare the top 10 deficit and surplus countries with the top 10 trading partners. Are deficit and surplus countries equally represented in the top 10 trading partners list, or is the list dominated by one group? The top 10 trade partners represent what percent of U.S. imports, and what percent of U.S. exports?

15. WEB-BASED QUESTION **Foreign Exchange Rates—The Yen for Dollars** The Federal Reserve System http://www.bog.frb.fed.us/releases/H10/hist/ provides historical foreign exchange rate data for a wide variety of currencies. The information is based on data collected by the Federal Reserve Bank of New York from a sample of market participants. Look at the data for the Japanese yen from 1990 to the present. Assume that you were in Tokyo every New Year's since January 1, 1990, to this year and bought a bento (boxed lunch) for 1000 yen. Convert this amount to dollars using the yen/dollar exchange rate for each January since 1990, and plot the dollar price of the bento over time. Has the dollar appreciated or depreciated against the yen? What was the least amount in dollars your box lunch cost? The most?

2

National
Income,
Employment,
and Fiscal
Policy

CHAPTER SEVEN

Measuring Domestic Output, National Income, and the Price Level

"Disposable Income Flat"; "Personal Consumption Surges"; "Net Investment Stagnates"; "Russia's GDP Slide Halted"; "GDP Price Index Rises Less Rapidly Than CPI."

These are typical headlines in the business and economics news. They look like gibberish—unless you know the language of macroeconomics and national income accounting. This chapter will help you learn that language and the ideas it communicates. After studying it, you will have a basic understanding of how government statisticians and accountants measure and record the levels of domestic output, national income, and prices for the economy.

In this chapter we first explain why it is important to measure the performance of an economy. Then we define the key measure of total output—gross domestic product (GDP)—and show how it is actually calculated. We also derive and explain several other important measures of output and income. Next, we turn to the measurement of the overall level of prices—the price level. We then demonstrate how GDP is adjusted for inflation or deflation so that it more accurately reflects the physical amount of a nation's production. Finally, we list and explain some limitations of the measures of domestic output and national income.

MACROECONOMIC MEASUREMENT

Our first goal is to explain the ways the overall production performance of the economy is measured. This is part of *national income accounting*, which does for the economy as a whole what private accounting does for the individual business enterprise or, for that matter, for the household.

A firm measures its flows of income and expenditures to assess its operations over some time period, usually 3 months or a year. With this information the firm can gauge its economic health. If things are going well, the accounting data can be used to explain this success. Costs might be down or output or prices up, resulting in large profit. If things are going badly, accounting measures can help discover why. And by comparing the accounts over several periods, the firm can detect the growth or decline of profit and what caused the change. All this information helps the firm's managers make intelligent business decisions.

National income accounting operates in much the same way for an economy.

1. It allows us to keep a finger on the economic pulse of a nation. A national income accounting system permits us to measure the level of production in an economy in some particular year and explain why it is at that level.

2. By comparing national accounts over a number of years, we can track the long-run course of the economy and see whether it has grown, been steady, or stagnated.

3. Information supplied by national accounts provides a basis for designing and applying public policies to improve the performance of the economy. Without national accounts, economic policy would be based on guesswork. *National income accounting allows us to assess the health of an economy and formulate policies to maintain and improve that health.*

GROSS DOMESTIC PRODUCT

There are many measures of an economy's economic performance. The best available measures, however, are based on the economy's annual total output of goods and services or, as it is sometimes called, its *aggregate output.* An economy's aggregate output is measured by its **gross domestic product** (GDP): *the total market value of all final goods and services produced within a country in 1 year.* GDP includes goods and services produced by citizen-supplied *and* foreign-supplied resources within a particular nation's geographical boundaries. Thus, U.S. GDP includes not only the value of Fords produced at a U.S.-owned factory in Michigan but also the value of Honda autos produced at a Japanese-owned factory in Ohio.

GDP measures the market value of annual output; *it is a monetary measure.* Indeed it must be if we are to compare the heterogeneous collection of goods and services produced in different years and get a meaningful idea of their relative worth.

If the economy produces three sofas and two computers in year 1 and two sofas and three computers in year 2, in which year is output greater? We cannot answer that question until price tags are attached to the various products as indicators of society's evaluation of their relative worth.

In Table 7-1, the money price of sofas is $500 and the price of computers is $2000. Year 2's output of $7000 is greater than year 1's output of $5500 because society values year 2's output more highly; society is willing to pay $1500 more for the collection of goods produced in year 2 than in year 1.

Avoidance of Multiple Counting

To measure total output accurately, all goods and services produced in any specific year must be counted once, but not more than once. Most products go through a series of production stages before reaching a market. As a result, parts of some products may be bought and sold many times. To avoid multiple counting of parts that are sold and resold, GDP includes only the market value of *final goods* and ignores transactions involving *intermediate goods.*

By **final goods** we mean goods and services being purchased for final use by the purchaser, and not for resale or further processing or manufacturing. *They are "purchases not resold."* **Intermediate goods** are goods and services that are purchased for further processing and manufacturing or for resale.

The value of final goods is included in GDP, and the value of intermediate goods is excluded. Why? Because the value of final goods already includes the value of all intermediate goods involved in producing the final goods. Counting intermediate goods separately would be **multiple counting**, which would exaggerate the value of GDP.

TABLE 7-1 Comparing heterogeneous outputs by using money prices

Year	Annual output	Market value
1	3 sofas and 2 computers	3 at $500 + 2 at $2000 = $5500
2	2 sofas and 3 computers	2 at $500 + 3 at $2000 = $7000

To clarify this, suppose there are five stages in manufacturing a wool suit and getting it to the consumer—the ultimate or final user. As Table 7-2 indicates, firm A, a sheep ranch, provides $120 worth of wool to firm B, a wool processor. Firm A receives $120 from B and pays it out in wages, rent, interest, and profit. Firm B processes the wool and sells it to firm C, a suit manufacturer, for $180. What does firm B do with the $180 it receives? As noted, $120 goes to firm A, and the remaining $60 is used by B to pay wages, rent, interest, and profit for the resources needed in processing the wool. The manufacturer sells the suit to firm D, a clothing wholesaler, who sells it to firm E, a retailer, and then, at last, a consumer, the final user, buys it for $350.

At each stage, the difference between what a firm has paid for the product and what it receives for selling the product is paid out as wages, rent, interest, and profit for the resources used by that firm to produce and distribute the suit.

How much of this should we include in GDP to account for the production of the suit? We should include just $350, the value of the final product. This amount includes all the intermediate transactions leading up to the product's final sale. It would be a gross distortion to include the sum of all the intermediate sales, $1140, in GDP. This would be multiple counting: counting the final product *and* the sale and resale of its various parts in the multistage production process. The production and sale of the suit have generated $350, *not* $1140, worth of output and income.

To avoid multiple counting, national income accountants are careful to calculate only the *value added* by each firm. **Value added** is the market value of a firm's output *less* the value of the inputs which it has purchased from others. For example, column 3, Table 7-2, shows that the value added by firm B is $60, the difference between the $180 value of its output and the $120 it paid for the inputs provided by firm A. By adding the values added by the five firms in Table 7-2, the total value of the suit can be accurately determined. Similarly, by calculating and summing the values added by all firms in the economy, we can determine the GDP—the market value of total output.

Exclusion of Nonproduction Transactions

GDP measures the annual production of the economy. Although many monetary transactions in the economy are for currently produced final goods and services, many other transactions are not. These nonproduction transactions must be excluded. *Nonproduction transactions* are of two major types: (1) purely financial transactions and (2) secondhand sales.

Financial Transactions   Purely financial transactions are of three general kinds:

1. *Public transfer payments*   These are the social security payments, welfare payments, and veterans' payments which government makes to particular households. The basic characteristic of public transfer payments is that recipients make no contribution to current production in return for them. To include them in GDP would be to overstate this year's production.

2. *Private transfer payments*   These payments—for example, a university student's monthly sub-

TABLE 7-2   Value added in a five-stage production process

(1) Stage of production	(2) Sales value of materials or product	(3) Value added
	0	
Firm A, sheep ranch	$ 120	$120 (= $120 − $ 0)
Firm B, wool processor	180	60 (= 180 − 120)
Firm C, suit manufacturer	220	40 (= 220 − 180)
Firm D, clothing wholesaler	270	50 (= 270 − 220)
Firm E, retail clothier	**350**	80 (= 350 − 270)
Total sales values	$1140	
Value added (total income)		**$350**

sidy from home or an occasional gift from a wealthy relative—do not entail production but simply the transfer of funds from one private individual to another.

3. *Security transactions*   Buying and selling of stocks and bonds are also excluded from GDP. Stock market transactions involve swapping paper assets. The amount spent on these assets does not directly create current production. Only the services provided by the security broker are included in GDP. However, sales of *new* issues of stocks and bonds transfer money from savers to businesses which often spend the proceeds on capital goods. Thus, these transactions may *indirectly* contribute to spending, which does account for output and hence add to GDP.

Secondhand Sales   Secondhand sales are excluded from GDP because they either reflect no *current* production or involve multiple counting. Suppose you sell your 1965 Ford Mustang to a friend; this transaction should be excluded in determining this year's GDP because it does not represent any current production. Including sales of goods produced some years ago in this year's GDP would exaggerate this year's output. Similarly, if you purchased a brand new Mustang but resold it a week later to your neighbor, the sale to your neighbor would be excluded from current GDP. When you originally bought the new car, that is when its value was included in GDP. To include its resale value at a later time would be to count it twice. **(Key Question 3)**

Two Sides to GDP: Spending and Income

Let's consider how the market value of total output—or for that matter, any single unit of output—is measured. Returning to Table 7-2, how can we measure the market value of a suit?

We can determine how much a consumer, the final user, pays for it; that will tell us the value of the final product. Or we can add up all the wage, rent, interest, and profit incomes created in producing it. This second approach is the value-added technique discussed in Table 7-2.

The final-product and value-added approaches are two ways of looking at the same thing. *What is spent on a product is received as income by those who helped produce it.* Chapter 2's circular flow model demonstrated this. If $350 is spent on the suit, then $350 is the total amount of income derived from its produc-

tion. You can verify this by looking at the incomes generated by firms A, B, C, D, and E in Table 7-2—$120, $60, $40, $50, and $80—which total $350.

This equality of the expenditure for a product and the income derived from its production is guaranteed, because profit balances the two. Profit—or loss—is the income remaining after wage, rent, and interest incomes have been paid by the producer. If the wage, rent, and interest incomes the firm must pay in getting the suit produced are less than the $350 expenditure for the suit, the difference will be the firm's profit.[1] Conversely, if wage, rent, and interest incomes exceed $350, profit will be negative. That is, losses will be incurred, balancing the expenditure on the product and the income derived from its production.

It is the same for the total output of the economy. There are two ways of looking at GDP: One is to see GDP as the sum of all the expenditures in buying that total output. This is the *output*, or **expenditures, approach.** The other views GDP in terms of the income derived or created from producing it. This is the *earnings*, or *allocations*, or **income, approach.**

This year's GDP can be determined either by adding up all that is spent to buy this year's total output or by summing up all the incomes derived from the production of this year's total output. That is,

$$\left.\begin{array}{l}\text{Amount spent to}\\\text{purchase this year's}\\\text{total output}\end{array}\right\} = \left\{\begin{array}{l}\text{money income}\\\text{derived from}\\\text{producing this}\\\text{year's total output}\end{array}\right.$$

This relationship is an *identity*: an equation whose variables are defined and measured such that one side of the equation always equals the other side. Buying (spending money) and selling (receiving money income) are two aspects of the same transaction. *What is spent on a product is income to those who have contributed their human and property resources to getting that product produced and to the market.*

We can expand this identity to read as in Figure 7-1. On the output side of GDP, all final goods produced in an economy are purchased by the three domestic sectors (households, businesses, and government) and by foreign buyers. On the income side of GDP (and aside from a few complicating factors, discussed later in this chapter), the total receipts of businesses acquired from the sale of total output are allocated among resources suppliers as wage, rent, interest, and profit income.

---

[1]The term "profit" is used here in the accounting sense to include both normal profit and economic profit as defined in Chapter 4.

Expenditures, or output, approach

Income, or allocations, approach

Consumption expenditures by households
    plus
Investment expenditures by businesses
    plus
Government purchases of goods
and services
    plus
Expenditures by foreigners

= GDP =

Wages
    plus
Rents
    plus
Interest
    plus
Profits
    plus
Statistical adjustments

FIGURE 7-1 The expenditures and income approaches to GDP   There are two general approaches to measuring gross domestic product. We can determine GDP as the value of output by summing all expenditures on that output. Alternatively, with some modifications, we can determine GDP by adding up the components of income arising from the production of that output.

EXPENDITURES APPROACH

To determine GDP through expenditures, we add up all spending on final goods and services. But national income accountants have more precise terms for the different types of spending than those listed in the left panel in Figure 7-1.

Personal Consumption Expenditures (C)

What we have called "consumption expenditures by households" is **personal consumption expenditures** to national income accountants. It includes expenditures by households on *durable consumer goods* (automobiles, refrigerators, video recorders), *nondurable consumer goods* (bread, milk, vitamins, pencils, toothpaste), and *consumer expenditures for services* (of lawyers, doctors, mechanics, barbers). We will use the letter C to designate this part of GDP.

Gross Private Domestic Investment (I_g)

Under the heading **gross private domestic investment** (I_g), national income accountants combine:
1. All final purchases of machinery, equipment, and tools by business enterprises
2. All construction
3. Changes in inventories

This is more than we have meant by "investment" thus far. The first item simply restates our definition of investment spending as the purchase of tools, machinery, and equipment.

The second item includes such construction as building a new factory, warehouse, or store. But "all construction" also includes residential construction. Why is that investment rather than consumption? Because apartment buildings are investment goods which, like factories and stores, are income-earning assets when they are rented or leased. Other residential units which are rented or leased are, for the same reason, investment goods. And owner-occupied houses are investment goods because they *could* be rented out to yield a money-income return, even though the owners may choose not to do so. For these reasons all residential construction is considered investment.

Finally, changes in inventories are counted as investment because an increase in inventories is, in effect, "unconsumed output." And, as we know from production possibilities analysis, that is what investment is.

Inventory Changes: A Part of Investment   Let's look at inventory changes more carefully. Because GDP measures total current (this year's) output, we must include within it any products produced this year even though they are *not sold* this year. GDP must include the market value of any additions to inventories accruing during the year. A laptop computer produced in 1998 must be counted as GDP in 1998, even though it remains unsold as of February 1999. If we excluded an increase in inventories, GDP would understate the current year's total production. If businesses have more goods on their shelves and in warehouses at year's end than they had at the start, the economy has produced more than was purchased during the year. This increase in inventories must be included in GDP as part of current production, along with the value of goods which were manufactured *and sold* during the year.

What about a decline in inventories? This must be subtracted in figuring GDP. The economy can sell a total output which exceeds its production by dipping into, and thus reducing, its inventories. Then some of this year's purchases reflect not current production but a drawing down of inventories on hand at the beginning of this year. And inventories on hand at the start of any year's production represent the production of previous years. The laptop computer produced in 1998 but sold in 1999 cannot be counted as part of 1999 GDP. Because GDP is a measure of the *current* year's output, we must omit any purchases of past production, that is, any drawing down of inventories, in determining GDP. We do this by subtracting inventory decreases in determining investment expenditures.

Noninvestment Transactions

We have discussed what investment is. Now we need to emphasize what it is not. Investment does *not* include the transfer of financial assets (stocks, bonds) or resale of physical assets. Economists exclude the buying of stocks and bonds from their definition of investment because such purchases merely transfer the ownership of existing assets. The same is true of the resale of existing physical assets.

Investment is the construction or manufacture of *new* capital assets. The production of these assets creates jobs and income; the transfer (sale) of claims to existing capital goods does not.

Gross versus Net Investment

Our category "gross private domestic investment" includes purchases of machinery and equipment, all construction, and changes in inventories. Let's focus for a moment on the modifiers, "gross," "private," and "domestic." "Private" and "domestic" tell us that we are talking about spending by private business enterprises, not government (public) agencies, and that

investment is in the nation itself—rather than abroad.

"Gross" is not as simple. **Gross private domestic investment** includes the production of *all* investment goods—those which replace machinery, equipment, and buildings used up to produce the current year's output *and* any net additions to the economy's stock of capital. Gross investment includes both investment in replacement capital *and* investment in added capital. **Net private domestic investment,** however, refers only to investment in added capital.

To make the distinction clear: In 1997 the U.S. private sector produced and purchased $1238 billion of capital goods. But in producing that output, it used up $717 billion of machinery and equipment. Thus, it added $521 (= $1238 − $717) billion to its stock of capital. Gross private investment in 1997 was $1238 billion; net private investment was $521 billion. The difference is the value of the private capital used up in producing 1997's GDP.

Net Investment and Economic Growth

The amount of a nation's capital worn out or used up in a particular year is called *depreciation*. Other things equal, the relationship between gross investment and depreciation indicates whether an economy's production capacity is expanding, static, or declining. Figure 7–2 illustrates these cases.

1. *Expanding production capacity*   When gross investment exceeds depreciation (Figure 7-2a), the economy's production capacity is expanding; its stock of capital is growing. *Positive net investment expands the production capacity of the economy.* As indicated previously, this was true for the U.S. economy in 1997. It added $521 billion to the size of the "national factory" that year. This increase in capital helped shift the U.S. production possibilities curve outward.

2. *Static production capacity*   When *gross investment and depreciation are equal, a nation's production capacity is static* (Figure 7-2b). Production capacity is standing pat; the economy produces just enough capital to replace what is consumed in producing the year's output—no more, no less. Example: In World War II, the Federal government purposely restricted private investment to free resources for the production of war goods. In 1942, gross private investment and depreciation were each about $10 billion. Thus net investment was roughly zero. At the end of 1942, our stock of capital was about the same as

FIGURE 7-2 Expanding, static, and declining production capacity (a) When gross investment exceeds depreciation, the economy is making a net addition to its stock of capital; all else equal, the economy's production capacity expands. (b) When gross investment precisely replaces the capital facilities depreciated in producing the year's output, the stock of capital goods remains unchanged; all else equal, the economy's production capacity is static. (c) When gross investment is insufficient to replace the capital goods depreciated in the year's production, the economy's stock of capital falls; all else equal, production capacity declines.

it was at the start of that year. The U.S. economy's production capacity was stationary; its production facilities did not expand.

3. *Declining production capacity* *When gross investment is less than depreciation, an economy's production capacity declines.* The economy uses up more capital than it produces (Figure 7-2c). When that situation occurs, net investment is negative; the economy is *disinvesting*. Depressions foster such circumstances. During bad times, when pro-

duction and employment are low, the nation has a greater production capacity than it is currently using. There is no incentive to replace depreciated capital equipment, much less add to the existing stock. Depreciation is likely to exceed gross investment, with the result that the nation's stock of capital is less at the end of each year than it was at the start.

This was the case during the Great Depression. In 1933 gross investment was about

$2 billion, while the capital consumed during that year was $8 billion. Net disinvestment was therefore $6 billion. That is, net investment was a minus $6 billion, indicating that the size of our "national factory" shrunk during that year.

We use the letter I for domestic investment spending, attaching the subscript g to mean gross investment and the subscript n to mean net investment. It is gross investment I_g that is used in determining GDP. **(Key Question 6)**

Government Purchases (G)

Government purchases (of consumption goods and capital goods) include all government spending (Federal, state, and local) on the finished products of businesses and all direct purchases of resources, including labor. It excludes all government transfer payments because such outlays reflect no current production but merely transfers of government receipts to some households. We use the letter G to indicate government purchases, the third part of GDP.

Net Exports (X_n)

A country's international trade transactions enter into national income accounting. Let's use the U.S. economy to show how: On the one hand, we want to include in GDP all spending that accounts for the production of goods and services in the United States. Spending by people abroad on U.S. goods accounts

for U.S. output, just as does spending by U.S. citizens in U.S. markets. Thus, we must include what the rest of the world spends on U.S. goods and services—U.S. exports—when determining GDP by the expenditures approach.

On the other hand, we know that part of the money spent for consumption, investment, and government purchases is spent on imports: goods and services produced abroad. This spending does not reflect production in the United States; it is some other nation's GDP. So we must subtract the value of imports to avoid overstating total production in the United States.

Rather than add exports and subtract imports separately, national income accountants add to GDP the difference "exports less imports." This difference, called **net exports,** is the amount by which foreign spending on a nation's goods and services exceeds that nation's spending on foreign goods and services. It is designated by X_n.

If people abroad buy $45 billion of U.S. exports, and Americans buy $35 billion of foreign imports in a year, U.S. net exports are *plus* $10 billion. If the rest of the world spends $30 billion on U.S. exports and Americans spend $40 billion on foreign imports, U.S. net exports are *minus* $10 billion.

The left side of Table 7-3 shows the computation of U.S. GDP for 1997 via the expenditures approach. Note that in 1997 Americans spent $97 billion more on foreign goods and services than the rest of the world spent on U.S. goods and services.

TABLE 7-3 Accounting statement for the U.S. economy, 1997 (in billions)

Receipts: expenditures approach		Allocations: income approach	
Personal consumption expenditures (C)	$5489	Compensation of employees	$4703
Gross private domestic investment (I_g)	1238	Rents	148
Government purchases (G)	1454	Interest	450
Net exports (X_n)	−97	Proprietors' income	545
		Corporate income taxes	319
		Dividends	336
		Undistributed corporate profits	149
		National income	$6650
		Indirect business taxes	545
		Consumption of fixed capital	868
		Net foreign factor income earned in the U.S.	21
Gross domestic product	$8084	Gross domestic product	$8084

Source: U.S. Department of Commerce data.

The GDP Equation: $C + I_g + G + X_n$

These four categories of expenditures—personal consumption expenditures *(C)*, gross private domestic investment *(I_g)*, government purchases *(G)*, and net exports *(X_n)*—include all possible types of spending. Added together, they measure the market value of the year's output or, in other words, the GDP. That is,

$$C + I_g + G + X_n = \text{GDP}$$

For the United States in 1997 (Table 7-3):

$$\$5489 + \$1238 + \$1454 - \$97 = \$8084$$

Global Perspective 7-1 compares GDPs for selected nations.

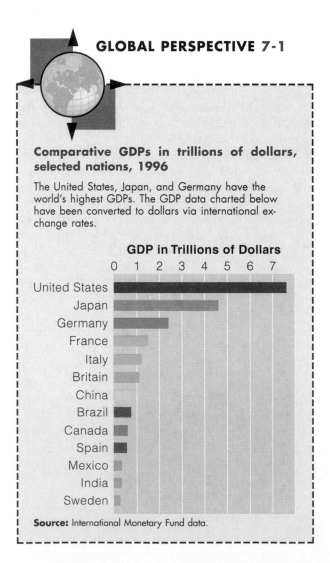

GLOBAL PERSPECTIVE 7-1

Comparative GDPs in trillions of dollars, selected nations, 1996

The United States, Japan, and Germany have the world's highest GDPs. The GDP data charted below have been converted to dollars via international exchange rates.

GDP in Trillions of Dollars

| | 0 | 1 | 2 | 3 | 4 | 5 | 6 | 7 |

United States
Japan
Germany
France
Italy
Britain
China
Brazil
Canada
Spain
Mexico
India
Sweden

Source: International Monetary Fund data.

INCOME APPROACH[2]

The allocations side of Table 7-3 shows how 1997's $8084 of expenditure was distributed as income. It would be simple if we could say that all expenditures on the economy's annual output flowed to U.S. households as wage, rent, interest, and profit incomes. But the picture is complicated by three adjustments which are necessary to balance the expenditures and income sides of the national accounting statement. Let's first look at the various items of national income shown on the right side of Table 7-3. Then we will turn to the three complications.

Compensation of Employees

This largest income category comprises primarily the wages and salaries paid by businesses and government to suppliers of labor. It also includes wage and salary supplements, in particular, payments by employers into social insurance and into a variety of private pension, health, and welfare funds for workers. These wage and salary supplements are part of the employer's cost of obtaining labor and are treated as a component of the firm's total wage payments.

Rents

Rents consist of income payments received by households and businesses which supply property resources. Examples include the monthly payments of renters to landlords and the annual lease payments by corporate tenants for the use of office space. The number in Table 7-3 is *net* rent—gross rental income minus depreciation of rental property. It is the rental income which remains after allowable depreciation (wearing out of the property) is subtracted from gross rental revenues.

Interest

Interest comprises the money-income payments flowing from private businesses to the suppliers of money capital. It includes items such as the interest payments households receive on saving deposits, certificates of deposit (CDs), and corporate bonds.

---

[2]Some instructors may choose to omit this section because the expenditures approach is more relevant for the analysis of Chapters 9 through 12.

Proprietors' Income

What we have loosely termed "profits" until now is broken down in the national income accounts into two accounts: *proprietors' income*, or income of unincorporated businesses, and *corporate profits*. Proprietors' income is the net income of sole proprietorships and partnerships. Corporate profits cannot be described so easily because corporate earnings may be distributed in several ways.

Corporate Profits

Generally, three things can happen to corporate profits:

1. *They may be collected as corporate income taxes.* A portion will be claimed by, and therefore flow to, government as corporate income taxes.

2. *They may be distributed as dividends.* A part of the remaining corporate profits will be paid out to stockholders as dividends. Such payments flow to households, which are the ultimate owners of all corporations.

3. *They may be retained as undistributed corporate profits.* What remains of corporate profits after both corporate income taxes and dividends have been paid is called *undistributed corporate profits.* These retained corporate earnings will be invested, currently or in the future, in new plants and equipment, increasing the real assets of the businesses doing the investing.

By adding employee compensation, rents, interest, proprietors' income, and corporate profits we get U.S. **national income**—all income earned by U.S.-supplied resources, whether here or abroad. But Table 7-3 reveals that national income, shown on the right-hand side of the account, is less than the sum of expenditures, shown on the left-hand side.

Three Adjustments

We can balance both sides of the account by adding three items to national income.

Indirect Business Taxes The first adjustment is to add to national income certain taxes, called **indirect business taxes,** which firms treat as costs of production and therefore add to the prices of the products they sell. Such taxes include general sales taxes, excise taxes, business property taxes, license fees, and custom duties.

To see why we must add indirect business taxes to national income in balancing expenditures and income, assume that a firm produces a good selling at $1. Production of this item creates $1 of wage, rent, interest, and profit income. But now government imposes a 5 percent sales tax on all products sold at retail. The retailer adds this 5 percent to the price of the product, raising its price from $1 to $1.05, and thus shifts the sales tax to consumers. This $.05 is *not* earned income (is *not* part of national income), because government contributes nothing directly to the production of the good in return for the tax receipt. The value of the output is $1.05, but only $1 of this value is paid to households as wage, rent, interest, and profit income. Therefore, we must add the $.05 to the $1 of national income in calculating GDP—the total value of output. In Table 7-3 we make this adjustment for the entire economy.

Depreciation: Consumption of Fixed Capital

The second adjustment involves depreciation. The useful life of capital equipment extends far beyond the year of purchase. Capital may be purchased in 1 year and used productively for many years after that. To avoid gross understatement of profit and therefore of total income in the year of purchase, and overstatement of profit and total income in succeeding years, the total cost of such goods must be allocated over their lives. The annual charge which estimates the amount of capital equipment used up in each year's production is called *depreciation.* Depreciation is a bookkeeping entry designed to yield a more accurate statement of profit and hence total income for a firm in each year.

If profits and total income for the economy are to be stated accurately, a gigantic depreciation charge must be made against the economy's private and public stock of capital. (Public capital includes government buildings, port facilities, and so on.) This depreciation charge is called **consumption of fixed capital**—the allowance for capital goods "consumed" in producing this year's GDP. It is the portion of this year's GDP which must be set aside to replace the capital goods used up in production. That part of this charge which relates to the private sector is the difference between gross private investment, I_g, and net private investment, I_n.

For present purposes, the significance of this charge is that this part of the business sector's receipts is not available for income payments to resource suppliers. This part of receipts—this portion of the value of production—is a cost of production which reduces business profits. But, unlike other costs of production, depreciation *does not add to anyone's income*. We must therefore add consumption of fixed capital to national income in balancing an economy's expenditures and income, as in Table 7-3.

Net Foreign Factor Income   Our last step is to make a slight adjustment relating to "national" versus "domestic." National income (NI) is the total income of Americans, whether earned in the United States or abroad. But GDP measures *domestic* output—the total output produced within the boundaries of the United States, irrespective of the nationality of those providing the resources. In moving from NI to GDP, we must consider the income U.S. citizens gain from supplying resources abroad and the income foreigners gain by supplying resources in the United States. In 1997 foreign-owned resources earned $21 billion more in the United States than U.S.-supplied resources earned abroad. This difference is called *net foreign factor income*. We must *add* it to national income when computing the value of our domestic output because it derives from output produced within the borders of the United States.

Table 7-3 summarizes our discussion of the expenditures and income approaches to GDP. This table is a giant accounting statement for the U.S. economy. The left side shows what the economy produced in 1997 and the total receipts derived from that production. The right side shows how the income derived from the production of 1997's GDP was allocated.

QUICK REVIEW 7-1

■ Gross domestic product (GDP) measures the total market value of all final goods and services produced within a nation in a specific year.

■ The expenditures approach to GDP sums total spending on final goods and services: GDP = $C + I_g + G + X_n$.

■ When net investment is positive, the economy's production capacity expands; when net investment is negative, the economy's production capacity erodes.

■ The income approach to GDP sums the total income earned by a nation's resource suppliers and then adds in indirect business taxes, consumption of fixed capital (depreciation), and net foreign factor income.

OTHER NATIONAL ACCOUNTS

Our discussion has centered on GDP as the measure of an economy's annual output. But there are related national accounts of equal importance which can be derived from GDP. To obtain these other accounts, we can start with GDP and make various adjustments.

Net Domestic Product (NDP)

GDP as a measure of total output has a defect: *It fails to make allowance for replacing the capital goods used up in this year's production*. As a result, it gives an exaggerated value of the output available for consumption and for addition of new capital. For example, we observe in Table 7-3 that $868 billion of 1997's GDP consisted of depreciation (consumption of fixed capital). Thus, 1997's GDP of $8084 does not tell us what that year's production *added* to society's well-being by way of new output available for consumption and additions to the stock of capital. For this purpose it would be much more accurate to subtract from GDP the $868 billion of machinery and equipment which was consumed in producing the GDP and which had to be replaced. This subtraction gives us **net domestic product** (NDP). That is,

NDP = GDP − consumption of fixed capital

In 1997 for the United States:

	Billions
Gross domestic product	$8084
Consumption of fixed capital	− 868
Net domestic product	$7216

NDP is simply GDP adjusted for depreciation. It measures the total annual output which the entire economy—households, businesses, government, and foreigners—can consume without impairing its capacity to produce in ensuing years.

Adjusting Table 7-3 from GDP to NDP is easy on the income side: We just omit consumption of fixed capital. The other items then add up to an NDP of $7216 billion.

Things are not quite so simple on the expenditure side because consumption of fixed capital includes depreciation of both private and public capital goods. In effect, we subtract part of the $868 billion of consumption of fixed capital (specifically,

$717 billion) from gross private investment and the other part ($151 billion) from government purchases. NDP is therefore $7216 billion.

The "net" in NDP alludes to the fact that it includes *net* (not *gross*) investment in the economy. It "nets out" consumption of fixed capital from the total of private and public investment.

National Income (NI)

In analyzing some problems, it is useful to know how much a nation's resource suppliers earned for their contributions of land, labor, capital, and entrepreneurial talent. As we already noted, U.S. national income (NI) includes all income earned by U.S.-owned resources, whether located at home or abroad. To derive national income from NDP, we must make two adjustments to NDP:

1. *Subtract net foreign factor income earned in the United States.* We want a measure of all factor (resource) income earned by people in the United States. We thus need to exclude the factor income earned in the United States by foreigners and add the factor income earned by U.S. citizens abroad. In 1997 foreign-supplied resources earned more income in the United States than U.S.-supplied resources earned abroad. We thus accomplish our goal by subtracting from NDP the net output produced (that is, net foreign factor income earned) by foreign-owned resources in the United States.

2. *Subtract indirect business taxes from NDP.* Government contributes nothing directly to production in return for the indirect business tax revenues it receives; government is not an economic resource. Indirect taxes are not part of payments to resources, and thus not part of national income.

For the United States in 1997:

	Billions
Net domestic product	$7216
Net foreign factor income earned in the U.S.	−21
Indirect business taxes	−545
National income	$6650

We also know that NI can be obtained through the income approach by directly adding up employee compensation, rent, interest, proprietors' income, and corporate profits (Table 7-3).

Personal Income (PI)

Personal income (PI) includes all income *received* whether earned or unearned. It is likely to differ from national income (income *earned*) because some income earned—social security taxes (payroll taxes), corporate income taxes, and undistributed corporate profits—is not actually received by households. Conversely, some income received—transfer payments—is not currently earned. Transfer payments include such items as social security payments, unemployment compensation payments, welfare payments, disability and education payments to veterans, and private pension payments.

In moving from national income to personal income, we must subtract the three types of income which are earned but not received and add the income which is received but not currently earned. Again for the United States in 1997:

	Billions
National income (income earned)	$6650
Social security contributions	−732
Corporate income taxes	−319
Undistributed corporate profits	−149
Transfer payments	+1424
Personal income	$6874

Disposable Income (DI)

Disposable income (DI) is personal income less personal taxes. *Personal taxes* include personal income taxes, personal property taxes, and inheritance taxes, the first of the three being the greatest amount.

	Billions
Personal income (income received before personal taxes)	$6874
Personal taxes	−987
Disposable income (income received after personal taxes)	$5887

Disposable income is the amount of income which households have to dispose of as they see fit. Because economists define saving as "that part of disposable income not spent on consumer goods," it follows that households divide their disposable income between consumption *(C)* and saving *(S)*. That is,

$$DI = C + S$$

■ Net domestic product (NDP) is the market value of annual output less depreciation (consumption of fixed capital).

■ National income (NI) is all income *earned* by citizens of a particular nation for their current contributions to production within the nation or abroad.

■ Personal income (PI) is all income *received* by households whether earned or not.

■ Disposable income (DI) is all income received by households less personal taxes.

Table 7-4 summarizes the relationships between GDP, NDP, NI, PI, and DI. **(Key Question 8)**

The Circular Flow Revisited

Figure 7-3 combines the expenditures and income approaches to GDP. As a more realistic and more complex expression of the circular flow model of the economy (Chapters 2, 5, and 6), this figure deserves your careful study.

Starting at the GDP rectangle in the upper left, the expenditure side of GDP is shown by the green arrows. To the right of the GDP rectangle are the allocations of GDP and the additions and subtractions needed to derive NDP, NI, PI, and DI. Red arrows depict all allocations or income flows. Note the division of DI between consumption and saving in the

TABLE 7-4 The relationships between GDP, NDP, NI, PI, and DI in the United States, 1997

	Billions
Gross domestic product (GDP)	$8084
Consumption of fixed capital	−868
Net domestic product (NDP)	$7216
Net foreign factor income earned in the U.S.	−21
Indirect business taxes	−545
National income (NI)	$6650
Social security contributions	−732
Corporate income taxes	−319
Undistributed corporate profits	−149
Transfer payments	+1424
Personal income (PI)	$6874
Personal taxes	−987
Disposable income (DI)	$5887

household sector. For the government sector, the flows of revenue in the form of types of taxes are denoted on the right; government disbursements in the form of purchases of goods and services and transfers are shown on the left. For the business sector, we have investment expenditures on the left and the three major sources of funds for business investment on the right.

Finally, observe the role of the rest of the world in the flow diagram. Spending by people abroad on U.S. exports adds to U.S. GDP, but U.S. consumption, government, and investment expenditures buy imported products as well as domestically produced goods. The flow emanating from "Rest of the World" shows that the U.S. handles this complication by calculating *net* exports (exports minus imports). This may be a positive or a negative amount. Also, note that *net* foreign factor income earned in the United States is subtracted from NDP in deriving NI.

Figure 7-3 simultaneously portrays the expenditure and income aspects of GDP, fitting the two approaches to one another. These flows of expenditures and income are part of a continuous, repetitive process. Cause and effect are intermingled: Expenditures create income, and from this income arise expenditures, which again flow to resource owners as income.

The table inside the covers of this book contains a useful historical summary of the national accounts and related statistics.

NOMINAL VERSUS REAL GDP

Recall that GDP is the market value of all final goods and services produced in a year. So money or *nominal* values are used as a common denominator to sum a heterogeneous output into a meaningful total. But this raises a problem: The value of different years' outputs (GDPs) can be usefully compared only if the value of money itself does not change because of inflation (rising overall prices) or deflation (falling overall prices).

Inflation or deflation complicates GDP because GDP is a price-times-quantity figure. The direct data used to measure GDP are the total sales revenues of business firms, but these revenues include both output quantities and the level of prices, which means that a change in either the quantity of output or the level of prices will affect the size of the GDP. Identical changes in GDP will occur if there is, say, a 5 percent

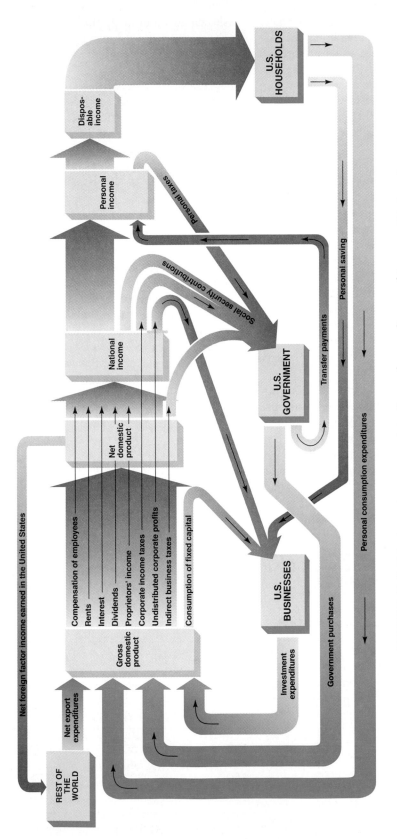

FIGURE 7-3 U.S. domestic output and the flows of expenditure and income This figure is an elaborate circular flow diagram which fits the expenditures and allocations sides of GDP to one another. The income or allocations flows are shown in red; the expenditure flows, in green. You should trace through the income and expenditure flows, relating them to the five basic national income accounting measures.

increase in output with no change in prices *or* a 5 percent increase in prices with no change in output. But it is the quantity of goods produced and distributed to households which affects their standard of living, not the price tags on these goods. The hamburger selling for $2 in 1997 yields the same satisfaction as an identical hamburger of 1970 that sold for 50 cents, *not* four times as much satisfaction, as the nominal value might imply.

Fortunately, we can resolve this difficulty by *deflating* GDP for rising prices and *inflating* it when prices are falling. These adjustments give us a picture of GDP for various years as if prices and the value of the dollar were the same as those in some reference period (or year). A GDP figure which reflects the prices prevailing when the output is produced is called unadjusted GDP, or **nominal GDP.** In contrast, a GDP figure that is deflated or inflated for price-level changes is called adjusted GDP, or **real GDP.**

Adjustment Process in a One-Good Economy

There are two ways we can adjust nominal GDP figures for price changes. Let's consider each using a simplified example. Assume an economy produces only one good, pizza, and in the amounts indicated in Table 7-5 for years 1, 2, and 3. An examination of columns 1 and 2 tells you that the nominal GDPs for years 2 and 3, as shown in column 4, greatly overstate the increases in real output occurring in those 2 years. That is, *the monetary measure of production (nominal GDP) does not accurately reflect the actual changes which have occurred in output (real GDP).* Considerable proportions of the sharp increases in nominal GDP in years 2 and 3 are due to the rather drastic inflation

shown in column 2, the remainder owing to the changes in output shown in column 1. Both increases in output and price increases are reflected in the nominal GDP.

Let's first suppose that we have directly gathered data from financial reports of businesses to derive nominal GDP in various years. In this approach, we will not know *directly* to what extent changes in price and changes in quantity of output have accounted for the observed increases in GDP. At this stage, we do not have before us the data in column 1, but only the data in column 4.

GDP Price Index   So how can we determine real GDP in our pizza-only economy? One method is to determine price changes and then adjust the nominal GDP figures. Once the price changes (as shown in column 2) are discovered, we can derive a price index which compares prices between years and estimates overall changes in the price level. Generally defined, a **price index** *measures the combined price of a particular collection of goods and services, called a "market basket," in a specific period relative to the combined price of an identical (or highly similar) group of goods and services in a reference period.* This point of reference, or benchmark, is called the base period or *base year.* More formally,

$$\text{Price index in given year} = \frac{\text{price of market basket in specific year}}{\text{price of same market basket in base year}} \times 100 \quad (1)$$

By convention, the price ratio between the specific year and the base year is multiplied by 100. For example, a price ratio of 2/1 (= 2) is expressed as an

TABLE 7-5   Calculating real GDP

Year	(1) Units of output	(2) Price of pizza per unit	(3) Price index (year 1 = 100)	(4) Unadjusted, or nominal, GDP (1) × (2)	(5) Adjusted, or real, GDP
1	5	$10	100	$ 50	$50
2	7	20	200	140	70
3	8	25	250	200	80
4	10	30	___	___	___
5	11	28	___	___	___

index number of 200. Similarly, the price ratio of 1/3 (= .33) is expressed as 33.

In our simple example, our market basket consists of only one product: pizza. We see in column 2 in Table 7-5 that the price of pizza was $10 in year 1, $20 in year 2, $25 in year 3, and so on. Selecting year 1 as the base year, we can express the prices of the pizza "market basket" in, say, years 2 and 3 relative to the price of the market basket in year 1 as follows:

$$\text{Price index, year 2} = \frac{\$20}{\$10} \times 100 = 200$$

$$\text{Price index, year 3} = \frac{\$25}{\$10} \times 100 = 250$$

For year 1 the index must be 100 since the specific year and the base year are identical ($10).

These index numbers tell us that the price of pizza increased from year 1 to year 2 by 100 percent $\{=[(200 - 100)/100)] \times 100\}$ and from year 1 to year 3 by 150 percent $\{=[(250 - 100)/100] \times 100\}$.

We can now use the index number in column 3 to deflate the nominal GDP figures in column 4. The simplest and most direct method of deflating is to express these index numbers as hundredths, that is, in decimal form, and divide them into the corresponding nominal GDP. This procedure yields real GDP:

$$\text{Real GDP} = \frac{\text{nominal GDP}}{\text{price index (in hundredths)}} \qquad (2)$$

Column 5 shows the results. These real GDP figures measure the value of total output in years 1, 2, and 3 as if the price of pizza had been constant at $10 throughout the 3-year period. So real GDP shows the market value of each year's output measured in terms

of dollars which have the same purchasing power as in the base year.

To ensure you understand the deflating process, you should complete Table 7-5 for years 4 and 5, using equation (2). Second, you should rework the entire deflating procedure, using year 3 as the base period. You will find that in this case you must *inflate* some of the nominal GDP data, using the same procedure as used in our examples.

An Alternative Method   We could more directly establish real GDP by initially gathering *separate* data on physical outputs (as in column 1) and their prices (as in column 2). Let's again consider our pizza-only economy in Table 7-5. If we first determine the physical outputs for each year, as shown in column 2, we can then see what each of those actual outputs would have sold for *if the base year price (here $10) had prevailed*. In year 2, the 7 units of pizza would be valued at $70 (= 7 units of output *times* the $10 price in the base year). As confirmed in column 5, this $70 of output *is* year 2's real GDP. Similarly, the real GDP of $80 for year 3 is found by multiplying the 8 units of output in year 3 by the $10 price in the base year.

When we determine real GDP through this method, the price index for a specific year is *implied*; it is simply the nominal GDP divided by the real GDP for that year:

$$\frac{\text{Price index}}{\text{(in hundredths)}} = \frac{\text{nominal GDP}}{\text{real GDP}} \qquad (3)$$

Example: In year 2 in Table 7-5, the price index of 200, or, in hundredths, 2.00, equals the nominal GDP of $140 divided by the real GDP of $70. You should note that equation (3) is simply a rearrangement of equation (2). Table 7-6 summarizes the two methods

---

TABLE 7-6   Steps for deriving real GDP from nominal GDP

Method 1
1. Find nominal GDP for each year.
2. Compute a GDP price index.
3. Divide each year's nominal GDP by that year's price index (in hundredths) to determine real GDP.

Method 2
1. Break down nominal GDP into physical quantities of output and prices for each year.
2. Find real GDP for each year by determining the dollar amount which each year's physical output would have sold for if base-year prices had prevailed. (The GDP price index can then be found by dividing nominal GDP by real GDP.)

we have used to determine real GDP in our assumed single-good economy. **(Key Question 11)**

Real-World Considerations and Data

In the real world of many goods and services, the government's determination of real GDP and its actual price index are much more complex than in our pizza-only economy. The government accountants must assign "weights" to various categories of goods and services based on their relative proportions of total output. In the United States, accountants update these weights annually as expenditure patterns change, and they "roll" the base year continuously forward using a moving average. The actual GDP price index in the United States is called the *chain-type annual-weights price index*—a name which hints at its complexity and why we are sparing you the details.

Nevertheless, once real GDP and the GDP price index are established, the relationship between nominal GDP, real GDP, and the GDP price index is clear. Table 7-7 provides some U.S. illustrations of these relationships. Note that the point of reference for the price index is 1992, where the index value is arbitrarily set at 100. Because the long-run trend has been for the price level to rise, the pre-1992 values of real GDP (column 3) are higher than the nominal values (column 2). This upward adjustment acknowledges that prices were lower in the years before 1992. As a result, nominal GDP understated the real output of those years and must be inflated.

The rising price level has caused nominal GDP figures for the post-1992 years to overstate real output. The government accountants therefore reduce, or deflate, these figures to gauge what GDP would have been in 1994, 1996, and so on, if 1992 prices had prevailed. So, since the 1992 reference year, real GDP has been less than nominal GDP.

By inflating the nominal pre-1992 GDP data and deflating the post-1992 data, government accountants determine annual real GDP, which can then be compared to any other year in the series. That is, the real GDP values in column 3 are directly comparable with one another in a meaningful way since they reflect changes in physical output.

Table 7-7 also reminds us that once nominal GDP and real GDP are known, the price index can be calculated, or, alternatively, if nominal GDP and the price index are known, real GDP can be calculated. Example: For 1994 nominal GDP was $6947.0 billion and real GDP was $6610.7. So the price level was 105.09 (= $6947.0/$6610.7 × 100), or 5 percent higher than in 1992. Alternatively, to find real GDP for 1994 we could express the 1994 GDP price index in hundredths (1.0509) and divide it into the nominal GDP of $6947.0.

To test your understanding of the relationships between nominal GDP, real GDP, and the price level, you should (1) determine the price-index values for

TABLE 7-7 Nominal GDP, real GDP, and GDP price index, selected years

(1) Year	(2) Nominal GDP, billions of $	(3) Real GDP, billions of $	(4) GDP price index* (1992 = 100)
1965	719.1	2881.1	24.95
1970	1035.6	3397.6	_____
1975	1630.6	3873.9	42.09
1980	2784.2	_____	60.34
1985	4180.7	5323.5	78.53
1990	5743.8	6136.3	93.64
1992	6244.4	6244.4	100.00
1993	6558.1	6389.6	_____
1994	6947.0	6610.7	105.09
1995	7265.4	_____	107.76
1996	7636.0	6928.4	110.22

*Chain-type annual-weights price index.
Source: U.S. Department of Commerce.

years 1970 and 1993, and (2) determine real GDP for years 1980 and 1995. For each of these years we have purposely left out data in Table 7-7. **(Key Question 12)**

THE CONSUMER PRICE INDEX

The GDP price index in Table 7-7 is *not* the same as the **consumer price index** (CPI), which government uses to report the rate of inflation each month. The CPI measures the prices of a market basket of some 300 consumer goods and services purchased by a typical urban consumer. The GDP index in Table 7-7 is much broader; it includes not only consumer goods and services but also capital goods, goods and services purchased by government, and goods and services entering world trade.

The present composition of the market basket used in the CPI was determined from a survey of the spending patterns of urban consumers in the 1982–1984 period. Thus the CPI in any specific year is as follows:

$$CPI = \frac{\text{price of 1982–1984 market basket in specific year}}{\text{price of same market basket in base period (1982–1984)}} \times 100$$

Unlike the GDP price index, in which the weights (relative purchases) of various goods and services are adjusted continuously, the CPI is a historical, *fixed-weight price index*. If 20 percent of consumer spending was on housing in 1982–1984, the assumption is that 20 percent of spending is still on housing in 1998. The base period is changed roughly every 10 years. The idea behind the historical, fixed-weight approach is to measure changes in the cost of a *constant* standard of living. Changes in the CPI thus allegedly measure the rate of inflation facing consumers. For example, the CPI increased from 156.9 in 1996 to 160.5 in 1997, indicating that 1996's rate of inflation was 2.3 percent [= (160.5 − 156.9)/156.9]. However, many economists believe that the CPI overstates actual inflation. We address this issue in this chapter's Last Word.

GDP AND ECONOMIC WELL-BEING

GDP is a reasonably accurate and extremely useful measure of domestic economic performance. It is not, and was never intended to be, an index of society's overall well-being—its total satisfaction. GDP is merely a measure of the annual volume of goods and services produced. Many things could make a country better off without necessarily raising GDP, such as reduction of crime and violence, greater equality of opportunity, improved racial harmony, better understanding between parents and children, and reductions of drug and alcohol abuse.

Nevertheless, it is widely held that there should be a strong positive correlation between real GDP and economic well-being; that is, greater production should move society toward "the good life." Thus, we must understand some of the shortcomings of GDP—why it might understate or overstate real output, and why more output will not necessarily make society better off.

Nonmarket Transactions

Certain production transactions do not take place in markets. Thus, GDP as a measure of the market value of output fails to include them. Examples include the production services of a homemaker and the work of the carpenter who repairs his or her own home. Such transactions are *not* reflected in the profit and loss statements of business firms and therefore escape the national income accountants, causing GDP to be understated. However, some large nonmarket production transactions, such as the part of farmers' output which farmers consume themselves, *are* estimated by national income accountants.

Leisure

The U.S. workweek has declined significantly over the twentieth century, from about 53 hours at the turn of the century to about 36 hours now. Also, the expanded availability of paid vacations, holidays, and leave time has reduced the work year, which has given us increased leisure time and, thus, has had a positive effect on our well-being. Our system of national income accounting understates our well-being by not directly recognizing the benefits of increased leisure. Nor do national accounts reflect the satisfaction—the "psychic income"—which many people derive from their work.

Improved Product Quality

GDP is a quantitative, not a qualitative, measure. It does not accurately reflect improvements in product quality. There is a fundamental qualitative difference between a $3000 personal computer purchased today and a computer costing the same amount just a few years ago. Today's $3000 computer has far more speed and storage capacity as well as a clearer monitor and improved multimedia capabilities.

Failure to account adequately for quality improvement is a shortcoming of GDP accounting. Quality improvement clearly affects economic well-being as much as does the quantity of goods. Because product quality has improved over time, GDP understates the resulting improvement in our material well-being.

Composition and Distribution of Output

Changes in the composition of total output and its allocation among specific households may influence economic well-being. GDP, however, reflects only the size of output and tells us nothing about whether this collection of goods is "right" for society. A handgun and a set of encyclopedias, both selling for $350, are weighted equally in the GDP. Distribution is also ignored by GDP. Some economists feel that a more equal distribution of total output would increase national economic well-being. If they are correct, a future trend toward a less unequal distribution of GDP would enhance the economic well-being of society. A more unequal distribution—which appears to be occurring—would have the reverse effect.

Per Capita Output

For many purposes the most meaningful measure of economic well-being is *per capita output*, found by dividing real GDP by population. Because GDP measures the size of total output, it may conceal or misrepresent changes in the standard of living of individuals and households. GDP may rise, but if population is also growing rapidly, the per-person standard of living may be constant or even declining.

This is the plight of some developing countries. Madagascar's domestic output grew approximately 1 percent per year from 1985 to 1995. But annual population growth was 3 percent, resulting in a yearly decrease in per capita output slightly above 2 percent.

GDP and the Environment

Undesirable and much publicized "gross domestic by-products," such as dirty air and water, toxic waste, automobile junkyards, congestion, and noise, accompany production and the growth of GDP. The costs of pollution reduce our economic well-being. These spillover costs are associated with production and hence with the GDP but are not deducted from total output; thus GDP overstates our national economic well-being.

Ironically, the final physical product of economic production and consumption is garbage. A rising GDP means more garbage, and it may mean more pollution and a greater divergence between GDP and economic well-being. In fact, under existing accounting procedures, when a manufacturer pollutes a river and government spends to clean it up, the cleanup expense is added to the GDP while the pollution is not subtracted!

The Underground Economy

Economists agree there is a large underground sector in our economy. Some participants in this sector engage in illegal activities such as gambling, loan-sharking, prostitution, and the narcotics trade. These may well be "growth industries." Obviously, persons receiving income from illegal businesses choose to conceal their incomes.

However, most participants in the underground economy are in *legal* activities but do not fully report their incomes to the Internal Revenue Service (IRS).

Does the CPI Overstate Inflation?

A growing number of economists agree that the CPI overstates inflation.

They're back! Each month more than 300 price agents working for the Bureau of Labor Statistics (BLS) personally contact the same 19,000 stores, supermarkets, hospitals, bowling alleys, and other establishments to obtain the current prices of 90,000 items. The agents' task is to price the market basket of goods and services used to calculate the CPI. The prices are then sent to the BLS, where statisticians group them into seven categories: housing, food and drinks, transportation, medical care, apparel and upkeep, entertainment, and "other." The BLS then enters the numbers into its computers, cranks out the new CPI, and releases the results to the press. The next day's news tells us that the CPI rose by, say, 0.2 percent last month. This means the "inflation rate on an annual basis" is roughly 2.4 percent (= 0.2 × 12 months).

Changes in the CPI supposedly measure the rate of inflation facing consumers. But economists point to four problems with the CPI which may cause it to overstate the true rate of inflation, perhaps by as much as 1 percentage point each year.

1. Changing Spending Patterns Although the composition of the market basket remains unchanged, consumers *do* change their spending patterns. In particular, they shift their purchases in response to changes in relative prices. When the price of beef rises while the prices of fish and chicken are steady, consumers substitute fish or chicken for beef. This means that over time consumers are buying a market basket which contains more of the relatively low-priced and less of the relatively high-priced product. Because the historical, fixed-weight CPI does not account for these substitutes, it overstates the actual rate of inflation.

2. New Products Many new products such as digital answering machines, laptop computers, cellular phones, golf clubs with titanium heads, and telephone pagers are either not included or severely underweighted in the market basket used to construct the CPI. Often prices of new products drop dramatically following their introductions. The CPI,

with its historical, fixed-weight market basket, does not account for such price declines and thus overstates inflation.

3. Quality Improvements The CPI does not adequately account for quality improvements. To the extent that product quality has improved since the base period, higher prices are justified. We ought to pay more for medical care today than we did several years ago because it is generally of higher quality. The same occurs with autos, auto tires, electronics equipment, and many other items. But the CPI picks up most increases in the value of the market basket as increases in inflation, not as quality improvements. Again the CPI overstates the true rate of inflation.

4. Sale and Discount Prices In calculating the CPI, the Federal government accounts for price changes only on a same-store basis. If one of these stores raises its price on some good, then the price increase shows up in the CPI. But, in view of the higher price, many consumers may go to lower-price outlets to buy the product. Thus, all consumers do not face the price increase, as the CPI implies. As a related example, the CPI tracks full-price airfares, not discount fares. From 1978 to 1996 full-price fares increased by nearly 9 percent annually, while discount fares increased by only 2 percent annually. Failure to account fully for sale prices means the CPI overstates the true rate of inflation facing consumers.

So what if the CPI overstates inflation? The problem is that the CPI affects nearly everyone. Illustrations are numerous: Government payments to social security receivers are indexed to the CPI; when the CPI rises, social security payments automatically rise in lockstep. Millions of unionized workers have cost-of-living adjustment (COLA) clauses in their labor contracts; such adjustments are tied to increases in the CPI. Moreover, the wage expectations of nearly all workers are linked to the rate of inflation, as measured by the CPI. When the CPI rises, lenders often raise their interest rates on loans to account for inflation. Government's tax revenues may suffer from the overstatement of inflation, since personal income brackets are adjusted upward annually to reflect increases in the CPI. And the nation's economic policymakers base some of their policies on the CPI's rate of change. Finally, since the CPI is used to calculate real (inflation-adjusted) wages, an overstated rate of inflation means that real wages have grown more rapidly than the official statistics suggest.

A bell captain at a hotel or a waiter at a restaurant may underreport tips from customers. A business-person may record only a portion of sales receipts for the tax collector. A worker who wants to retain unemployment compensation benefits may obtain an "off-the-books" or "cash-only" job so there is no record of his or her work activities. A brick mason may agree to remodel a neighbor's fireplace in exchange for the neighbor's doing off-the-books repair work on the mason's boat engine. None of these underground transactions, obviously, are included in GDP.

Although there is no consensus on the size of the underground economy, estimates suggest it is between 7 and 12 percent of the recorded GDP. In 1997, that meant GDP was understated by between $566 and $970 billion.

Global Perspective 7-2 indicates the relative sizes of underground economies in selected nations.

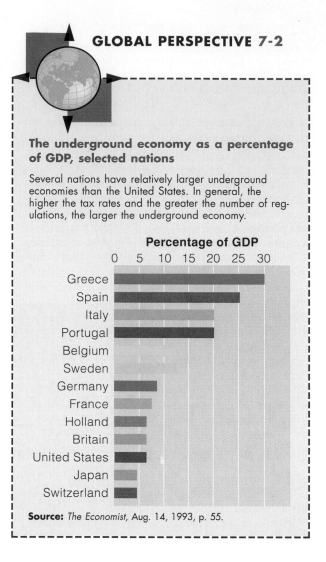

GLOBAL PERSPECTIVE 7-2

The underground economy as a percentage of GDP, selected nations

Several nations have relatively larger underground economies than the United States. In general, the higher the tax rates and the greater the number of regulations, the larger the underground economy.

Percentage of GDP

Source: *The Economist,* Aug. 14, 1993, p. 55.

CHAPTER SUMMARY

1. Gross domestic product (GDP), a basic measure of an economy's economic performance, is the market value of all final goods and services produced within the borders of a nation in a year.

2. Intermediate goods, nonproduction transactions, and secondhand sales are purposely excluded in calculating GDP.

3. GDP may be calculated by summing total expenditures on all final output or by summing the income derived from the production of that output.

4. By the expenditures approach, GDP is determined by adding consumer purchases of goods and services, gross investment spending by businesses, government purchases, and net exports: $GDP = C + I_g + G + X_n$.

5. Gross investment is divided into **(a)** replacement investment (required to maintain the nation's stock of capital at its existing level), and **(b)** net investment (the net increase in the stock of capital). Positive net investment is associated with an expanding production capacity; negative net investment, with a declining production capacity.

6. By the income or allocations approach, GDP is calculated as the sum of compensation to employees, rents, interest, proprietors' income, corporate income taxes, dividends, undistributed corporate profits, *plus* indirect business taxes, consumption of fixed capital, and net foreign factor income earned in the United States.

7. Other national accounts are derived from GDP. Net domestic product (NDP) is GDP less the consumption of fixed capital. National income (NI) is total income earned by a nation's resource suppliers; it is found by subtracting net foreign factor income earned in the United States and indirect business taxes from NDP. Personal income (PI) is the total income paid to households prior to any allowance for personal taxes. Disposable income (DI) is personal income after personal taxes have been paid. DI measures the amount of income households have available to consume or save.

8. Price indexes are computed by dividing the price of a specific collection or "market basket" of output in a particular period by the price of the same market basket in a base period and multiplying the result (the quotient) by 100. The GDP price index is used to adjust nominal GDP for inflation or deflation and thereby obtain real GDP.

9. Nominal (current-dollar) GDP measures each year's output valued in terms of the prices prevailing in that year. Real (constant-dollar) GDP measures each year's output in terms of the prices which prevailed in a selected base year. Because real GDP is adjusted for price-level changes, differences in real GDP are due only to differences in production activity.

10. The consumer price index (CPI) measures changes in the price of a market basket of some 300 goods and services purchased by urban consumers. Unlike the GDP price index, in which the weights of the goods change annually with spending patterns, the CPI is a fixed-weight price index, meaning that each year the items in the market basket remain the same as those in the base period (1982–1984).

11. National income accounting measures exclude nonmarket and illegal transactions, changes in leisure and in product quality, the composition and distribution of output, and the environmental effects of production. Nevertheless, these measures are reasonably accurate and very useful indicators of a nation's economic performance.

TERMS AND CONCEPTS

national income
   accounting
gross domestic product
final goods
intermediate goods
multiple counting
value added
expenditures approach

income approach
personal consumption
   expenditures
gross private domestic
   investment
net private domestic
   investment
government purchases

net exports
national income
indirect business taxes
consumption of fixed
   capital
net domestic product
personal income
disposable income

nominal GDP
real GDP
price index
consumer price index

STUDY QUESTIONS

1. In what ways are national income statistics useful?

2. Explain why an economy's output, in essence, is also its income.

3. KEY QUESTION Why do national income accountants include only final goods in measuring GDP for a particular year? Why don't they include the value of the stocks and bonds bought and sold? Why don't they include the value of the used furniture bought and sold?

4. What is the difference between gross private domestic investment and net private domestic investment?

If you were to determine net domestic product through the expenditures approach, which of these two measures of investment spending would be appropriate? Explain.

5. Why are changes in inventories included as part of investment spending? Suppose inventories declined by $1 billion during 1999. How would this affect the size of gross private domestic investment and gross domestic product in 1999? Explain.

6. KEY QUESTION Use the concepts of gross and net investment to distinguish between economies in which production capacity is expanding, static, and declining. "In 1933 net private domestic investment was minus $6 billion. This means in that particular year the economy produced no capital goods at all." Do you agree? Why or why not? Explain: "Though net investment can be positive, negative, or zero, it is quite impossible for gross investment to be less than zero."

7. Define net exports. Explain how U.S. exports and imports each affect domestic production. Suppose foreigners spend $7 billion on U.S. exports in a given year and Americans spend $5 billion on imports from abroad in the same year. What is the amount of the United States' net exports? Explain how net exports might be a negative amount.

8. KEY QUESTION Below is a list of domestic output and national income figures for a given year. All figures are in billions. The questions which follow ask you to determine the major national income measures by both the expenditures and income methods. Results you obtain with the different methods should be equal.

Personal consumption expenditures	$245
Net foreign factor income earned in the U.S.	4
Transfer payments	12
Rents	14
Consumption of fixed capital (depreciation)	27
Social security contributions	20
Interest	13
Proprietors' income	33
Net exports	11
Dividends	16
Compensation of employees	223
Indirect business taxes	18
Undistributed corporate profits	21
Personal taxes	26
Corporate income taxes	19
Corporate profits	56
Government purchases	72
Net private domestic investment	33
Personal saving	20

   a. Using the above data, determine GDP by both the expenditures and income methods. Then determine NDP.
   b. Now determine NI in two ways: first, by making the required additions or subtractions from NDP; and second, by adding up the types of income which make up NI.
   c. Adjust NI (from part b) as required to obtain PI.
   d. Adjust PI (from part c) as required to obtain DI.

9. Using the following national income accounting data, compute **(a)** GDP, **(b)** NDP, and **(c)** NI. All figures are in billions.

Compensation of employees	$194.2
U.S. exports of goods and services	17.8
Consumption of fixed capital	11.8
Government purchases	59.4
Indirect business taxes	14.4
Net private domestic investment	52.1
Transfer payments	13.9
U.S. imports of goods and services	16.5
Personal taxes	40.5
Net foreign factor income earned in the U.S.	2.2
Personal consumption expenditures	219.1

10. Why do national income accountants compare the market value of the total outputs in various years rather than actual physical volumes of production? What problem is posed by any comparison over time of the market values of various total outputs? How is this problem resolved?

11. KEY QUESTION Suppose that in 1984 the total output in a single-good economy was 7000 buckets of chicken. Also suppose that in 1984 each bucket of chicken was priced at $10. Finally, assume that in 1992 the price per bucket of chicken was $16 and that 22,000 buckets were purchased. Determine the GDP price index for 1984, using 1992 as the base year. By what percentage did the price level, as measured by this index, rise between 1984 and 1992? Use the two methods listed in Table 7-6 to determine real GDP for 1984 and 1992.

12. KEY QUESTION The following table shows nominal GDP and an appropriate price index for a group of selected years. Compute real GDP. Indicate in each calculation whether you are inflating or deflating the nominal GDP data.

Year	Nominal GDP, billions	Price index (1992 = 100)	Real GDP, billions
1959	$ 507.2	23.0	$_____
1964	663.0	24.6	$_____
1967	833.6	26.6	$_____
1973	1382.6	35.4	$_____
1988	5049.6	86.1	$_____
1995	7265.4	107.8	$_____

13. Which of the following are included in this year's GDP? Explain your answer in each case.
   a. Interest on an AT&T bond
   b. Social security payments received by a retired factory worker
   c. The services of a painter in painting the family home
   d. The income of a dentist

e. The money received by Smith when she sells her economics textbook to a book buyer

f. The monthly allowance which a college student receives from home

g. Rent received on a two-bedroom apartment

h. The money received by Mac when he resells this year's model Plymouth Prowler to Stan

i. Interest received on corporate bonds

j. A 2-hour decline in the length of the workweek

k. The purchase of an AT&T bond

l. A $2 billion increase in business inventories

m. The purchase of 100 shares of GM common stock

n. The purchase of an insurance policy

14. **(Last Word)** What is the CPI? What are its shortcomings in accurately measuring inflation?

15. **WEB-BASED QUESTION** **Latest Short-Term Indicators—Rank the Economies** The OECD (Organization for Economic Cooperation and Development) http://www.oecd.org/std/indksti.htm provides the latest short-term indicators of their member countries for the previous year. Of the following five countries (United States, Germany, Japan, France, and Italy), rank them from 5 to 1 for best to worse in the following categories: GDP (percentage change), CPI (percentage change), unemployment rate, and interest rate (assume lowest is best). Which economy received the greatest number of total points? Which received the lowest?

16. **WEB-BASED QUESTION** **Per Capita Gross Domestic Product** The OECD (Organization for Economic Cooperation and Development) http://www.oecd.org/std/nahome.htm provides an annual comparison of levels of GDP per capita based on both exchange rates and on purchasing power parities (PPPs). Rank the current top 10 countries using each method. How do the rankings differ, and which method is a more realistic indicator of "output per person"? What explains the difference in Japan's per capita income when calculated using exchange rates and when calculated using PPPs?

8

Macroeconomic Instability: Unemployment and Inflation

In an ideal economy, real GDP expands over time at a brisk, steady pace. Additionally, the price level remains constant or rises only slowly. The result is neither significant unemployment nor inflation. Several periods of U.S. history fit this pattern, but experience shows that steady economic growth, full employment, and a stable price level are not always achieved. Evidence: (1) The inflation rate skyrocketed to 13.5 percent in 1980. (2) During a 16-month period in the early 1980s, real output fell by 3.3 percent. (3) Three million more people were unemployed in 1982 than in 1980. (4) The annual inflation rate rose from 1.9 percent in 1986 to 4.8 percent in 1989. (5) In 1990–1991, output in the U.S. economy declined for the eighth time since 1950.

Here and in the next several chapters we explore the problem of achieving macroeconomic stability: steady economic growth, full employment, and price stability. The present chapter proceeds as follows: First, we establish an overview of the business cycle—the periodic fluctuations in output, employment, and price level characterizing market economies. Then we look in detail at unemployment: What are the various types of unemployment? How is unemployment measured? Why is unemployment undesirable? Finally, we examine inflation—a problem which plagued the United States throughout the 1970s and into the early 1980s. What are inflation's causes and consequences?

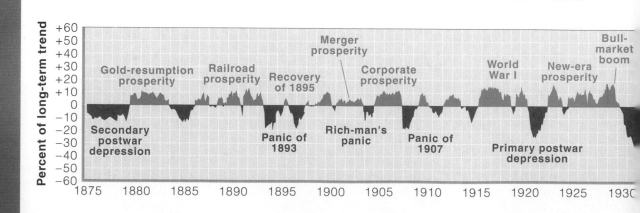

THE BUSINESS CYCLE

Nations seek economic growth, full employment, and price-level stability as their major macroeconomic goals. For the most part, the history of the industrial nations, including the United States, is one of remarkable economic growth. Technological progress, rapid increases in capital, increased skill levels of labor, and other factors have interacted to raise real GDP and real GDP per capita.

But long-run economic growth has not always been steady; it is sometimes interrupted by periods of economic instability, as revealed for the United States in Figure 8-1. In various countries at various times, rapid economic growth has been marred by inflation. At other times, growth has given way to recession and depression, that is, to declines in employment and real output. In short, both unemployment and inflation have interrupted and complicated the long-term trend of economic growth. These difficulties often are associated with *business cycles.*

Phases of the Cycle

The term **business cycle** refers to alternating increases and decreases in the level of economic activity, sometimes extending over several years. Individual business cycles (one "up" and one "down" period) vary substantially in duration and intensity. Yet all display common phases which are variously labeled by different economists. Figure 8-2 shows the four phases of a stylized business cycle.

1. **Peak**   We begin our description with a **peak** at which business activity has reached a temporary maximum, such as the middle peak shown in Figure 8-2. Here the economy is at full employment and the level of real output is at or very close to its capacity. The price level is likely to rise during this phase.

2. **Recession**   The peak is followed by a **recession**—a period of decline in total output, income, employment, and trade, lasting 6 months or longer. This downturn is marked by the widespread contraction of business in many sectors of the economy. But because many prices are downwardly inflexible, the price level is likely to fall only if the recession is severe and prolonged—that is, if a depression occurs.

3. **Trough**   The **trough** of the recession or depression is the phase in which output and employment "bottom out" at their lowest levels. The trough phase of the cycle may be short-lived or quite long.

4. **Recovery**   In the expansion or **recovery** phase, output and employment increase toward full employment. As recovery intensifies, the price level may begin to rise before there is full employment and full-capacity production.

Although they all have the same phases, business cycles vary greatly in duration and intensity. Many economists therefore prefer to talk of business *fluctuations* rather than *cycles* because cycles imply regularity while fluctuations do not. The Great Depression of the 1930s resulted in a 40 percent decline in real GDP

FIGURE 8-1 U.S. business-cycle experience   The horizontal line at 0 represents the long-run growth trend of U.S. economic activity. The alternating periods of prosperity (green) and depressions or recessions (red) indicate deviations from this trend. (*Source:* AmeriTrust Company, Cleveland. Updated.)

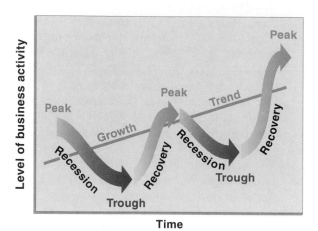

FIGURE 8-2 The business cycle Economists distinguish four phases of the business cycle, with the duration and strength of each phase being highly variable.

over a 3-year period in the United States and seriously impaired business activity for a decade. By comparison, more recent U.S. recessions, detailed in Table 8-1, were relatively minor in both intensity and duration.

Causation: A First Glance

Economists have suggested many theories to explain fluctuations in business activity. Some contend that major innovations, such as the railroad, the automobile, and synthetic fibers, have great impact on investment and consumption spending and therefore on

TABLE 8-1 U.S. recessions since 1950

Period	Duration, months	Depth (decline in real output)
1953–54	10	−3.7%
1957–58	8	−3.9
1960–61	10	−1.6
1969–70	11	−1.0
1973–75	16	−4.9
1980	6	−2.3
1981–82	16	−3.3
1990–91	8	−1.6

Source: Economic Report of the President, 1993. Updated.

output, employment, and the price level. These major innovations occur irregularly and thus contribute to the variability of economic activity.

Other economists have explained the business cycle in terms of political and random events, as suggested by some of the labeling in Figure 8-1. Wars, for example, can be economically disruptive. A virtually insatiable demand for war goods during hostilities can generate a period of overfull employment and sharp inflation, which is followed by an economic slump when peace returns and military spending plummets.

Still other economists view the business cycle as a purely monetary phenomenon. When government creates too much money, they say, an inflationary boom occurs. In contrast, too little money precipitates a decline in output and employment.

Despite these diverse opinions, most economists see changes in the level of total spending as the immediate cause of cyclical changes in the levels of real output and employment. In a market economy, businesses produce goods or services only if they can sell them profitably. If total spending sinks, many businesses find that it is no longer profitable to produce their usual volume of goods and services. Therefore, output, employment, and incomes will fall. In contrast, a higher level of spending means that more production is profitable, and output, employment, and incomes will rise. Once the economy nears full employment, further gains in real output become more difficult to achieve. Still more spending may raise the price level as consumers bid for the limited amount of available goods.

Noncyclical Fluctuations

Not all changes in business activity result from business cycles. For example, there can be **seasonal variations** in business activity. Pre-Christmas and pre-Easter buying surges cause considerable fluctuations in the tempo of business activity each year, particularly in the retail industry. Agriculture, the automobile industry, and construction are also subject to some degree of seasonality.

Business activity also displays a **secular trend**—expansion or contraction over a long period of years, say, 25, 50, or 100 years. The long-run secular trend for U.S. capitalism has been remarkable expansion. For present purposes, the importance of this long-run expansion is that the business cycle fluctuates around a long-run growth trend. Note in Figure 8-1 that cyclical fluctuations are measured as deviations from the secular growth trend. Also, the stylized cycle of Figure 8-2 is drawn against a trend of growth.

Cyclical Impact: Durables and Nondurables

The business cycle is felt in every nook and cranny of the economy. The parts of the economy are related in such a way that few, if any, escape the negative effects of depression or surging inflation. However, the business cycle affects various individuals and segments of the economy in different ways and degrees.

With regard to production and employment, service industries and industries producing nondurable consumer goods are somewhat insulated from the most severe effects of recession. And, of course, recession actually helps some firms, such as pawnbrokers and law firms specializing in bankruptcies! Who is hit hardest by recession? The firms and industries producing capital goods and consumer durables. The construction industry is particularly vulnerable. Industries and workers producing housing and commercial buildings, heavy capital goods, farm implements, automobiles, refrigerators, gas ranges, and similar products bear the brunt of bad times. Conversely, these "hard-goods" industries benefit most from expansion.

Two facts help explain the vulnerability of these industries to the business cycle.

Postponability Within limits, a purchase of hard goods can be postponed. As the economy slips into bad times, producers frequently delay the purchase of more modern production facilities and the construction of new plants. The business outlook simply does not warrant increases in the stock of capital goods. The firm's present capital facilities and buildings will likely see it through the recession. In good times, capital goods are usually replaced before they completely depreciate. When recession strikes, however, business firms patch up their outmoded equipment and make it do. As a result, investment in capital goods declines sharply. Some firms, having excess plant capacity, may not even bother to replace all the capital they are currently consuming. Net investment for them may be negative.

It is much the same for consumer durables. When recession occurs and the household must trim its budget, plans for the purchase of such durables as major appliances and automobiles feel the ax first. People

repair their old appliances and cars rather than buy new ones. Purchases of many consumer nondurables—food and clothing, for instance—are not so easily postponed; people must clothe themselves and eat. The quantity and quality of purchases of nondurables will decline to some extent, but not so much as will purchases of capital goods and consumer durables.

Monopoly Power Many industries producing capital goods and consumer durables are industries of *high concentration*, in which a small number of large firms dominate the market. These firms have monopoly power—the ability to set above-competitive prices to increase their profit. When recession hits, each of these firms is very reluctant to lower its price because doing so would upset the industry price structure. Specifically, each firm fears that its price cut would spark a *price war*—successive rounds of deeper and deeper price cuts by rivals. This reluctance to lower price means that, at least for a time, the effects of a drop in demand are primarily a decline in production and a decrease in employment.

The reverse pattern is true in nondurables, or *low-concentration* "soft-goods" industries, in which prices are established in competitive markets. Firms in such industries are unable to resist the price declines dictated by the market, so their *prices* decline more rapidly than their levels of production and employment.

Figure 8-3 provides evidence from the Great Depression on this point. It shows the percentage declines in price and quantity in 10 selected industries as the economy fell from peak prosperity in 1929 to the depth of depression in 1933. Generally, high-concentration industries make up the top half of the table and low-concentration industries the bottom half. Note the drastic production declines and relatively modest price declines of the high-concentration industries. Contrast those outcomes to the large price declines and relatively small output declines which occurred in the low-concentration industries. (**Key Question 1**)

QUICK REVIEW 8-1

■ The long-term secular trend of real domestic output has been upward in the United States.

■ The typical business cycle has four phases: peak, recession, trough, and recovery.

■ Industries producing capital goods and consumer durables normally suffer greater output and employment

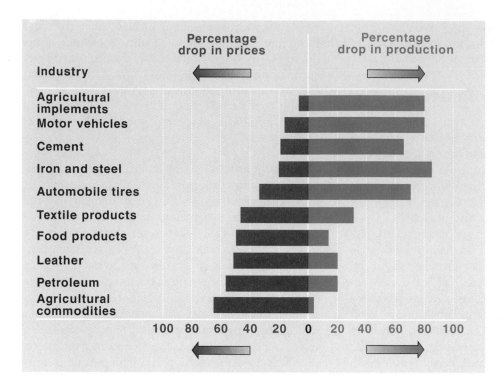

FIGURE 8-3 Relative price and production declines in 10 industries, 1929–1933 The high-concentration (durables) industries shown in the top half had relatively small price declines and large declines in output during the early years of the Great Depression. In the low-concentration (nondurables) industries of the bottom half, price declines were relatively large, and production fell by relatively small amounts. [*Source:* Gardiner C. Means, *Industrial Prices and Their Relative Inflexibility* (U.S. Government Printing Office, 1935), p. 8.]

declines during recession than do service and nondurable consumer goods industries. The latter suffer greater price declines, however.

UNEMPLOYMENT

"Full employment" is hard to define. A person might think it means that everyone in the labor market—100 percent of the labor force—is employed. But that is not so; some unemployment is normal or warranted.

Types of Unemployment

Before defining full employment, let's first introduce three types of unemployment: frictional, structural, and cyclical.

Frictional Unemployment At any time some workers will be "between jobs." With freedom to choose occupations and jobs, some workers will be voluntarily moving from one job to another. Others will have been fired and will be seeking reemployment. Still others will be temporarily laid off from their jobs because of seasonality, for example, bad weather in the construction industry. And there will

be some particularly young workers searching for their first jobs.

As these unemployed people find jobs or are called back from temporary layoffs, other job seekers and temporarily laid-off workers will replace them in the "unemployment pool." Therefore, even though the specific individuals who are unemployed for these reasons change from month to month, this type of unemployment persists.

Economists use the term **frictional unemployment**—consisting of *search unemployment* and *wait unemployment*—for workers who are either searching for jobs or waiting to take jobs in the near future. "Frictional" correctly implies that the labor market does not operate perfectly or instantaneously—without friction—in matching workers and jobs.

Frictional unemployment is inevitable and, at least in part, desirable. Many workers who are voluntarily between jobs are moving from low-paying, low-productivity jobs to higher-paying, higher-productivity positions. This means greater income for workers and a better allocation of labor resources—and therefore a larger real output—for the economy as a whole.

Structural Unemployment Frictional unemployment blurs into a category called **structural unem-**

ployment. Here, economists use "structural" in the sense of "compositional." Changes over time in consumer demand and in technology alter the "structure" of the total demand for labor, both occupationally and geographically.

Occupationally, some skills will be less in demand or may even become obsolete; demand for other skills, including skills not existing earlier, will expand. Unemployment results because the composition of the labor force does not respond quickly or completely to the new structure of job opportunities. Some workers thus find that they have no marketable talents; their skills and experience have become obsolete or unneeded. They are structurally unemployed due to a *mismatch between their skills and the skills required by employers who are hiring workers.*

Geographically, the demand for labor also changes over time. The migration of industry and thus of employment opportunities from the Snow Belt to the Sun Belt over the past few decades is an example. Another example is the movement of jobs from inner-city factories to suburban industrial parks. These shifting job opportunities mean that some workers become structurally unemployed; there is a *mismatch between their location and the location of job openings.*

The following list presents several illustrations of structural unemployment:

1. Many years ago, highly skilled glassblowers were thrown out of work by the invention of bottle-making machines.

2. Historically, mechanization of agriculture in the south dislodged thousands of low-skilled, poorly educated blacks from their jobs. Many migrated to northern cities and suffered prolonged unemployment because of racial bias and insufficient skills.

3. Many oil field workers in U.S. "oil-patch" states found themselves structurally unemployed when the world price of oil nosedived in the 1980s. Less drilling and oil-related activity took place, resulting in widespread layoffs.

4. In the 1980s many pilots, mechanics, flight attendants, and other airline employees became structurally unemployed as a result of mergers following deregulation of the airline industry.

5. Recently, "corporate downsizing" has occurred in several major U.S. manufacturing industries. Many people losing their jobs have been corporate managers who have found it difficult to find new work.

6. Recent closures of military bases and other defense cutbacks have displaced many workers, adding them to the roles of the structurally unemployed.

The distinction between frictional and structural unemployment is hazy. The key difference is that frictionally unemployed workers have salable skills and either are located where jobs exist or are able to move to where jobs exist. Structurally unemployed workers cannot easily be reemployed without retraining, additional education, or geographic relocation. Frictional unemployment is short-term; structural unemployment is more long-term and therefore is regarded as more serious.

Cyclical Unemployment **Cyclical unemployment** occurs in the recession phase of the business cycle. It is caused by a deficiency of total spending. As the overall demand for goods and services decreases, employment falls and unemployment rises. For this reason, cyclical unemployment is sometimes called *deficient-demand unemployment.* During the recession year 1982, for example, the unemployment rate rose to 9.7 percent. This compares with a 6.7 percent unemployment rate in the recession year 1991. Cyclical unemployment at the depth of the Great Depression in 1933 was about 25 percent of the labor force.

Definition of "Full Employment"

Full employment does *not* mean zero unemployment. Economists regard frictional and structural unemployment as essentially unavoidable in a dynamic economy. Thus, "full employment" is something less than 100 percent employment of the labor force. Specifically, the **full-employment unemployment rate** is equal to the total frictional and structural unemployment. Stated differently, the full-employment unemployment rate is achieved when cyclical unemployment is zero.

The full-employment rate of unemployment is also referred to as the **natural rate of unemployment.** The real level of domestic output associated with the natural rate of unemployment is called the economy's **potential output.** The economy's potential output is the real output produced when the economy is "fully employed."

From a slightly different vantage point the full-employment or natural rate of unemployment results when labor markets are in balance in the sense that the number of job seekers equals the number of job vacancies. The natural rate of unemployment is some positive amount because it takes time for frictionally unemployed job seekers to find open jobs they can fill. Also, it takes time for the structurally unemployed to achieve the skills and geographic relocation needed for reemployment. If the number of job seekers exceeds available vacancies, labor markets are not in balance; there is a deficiency of total spending and cyclical unemployment is present. But if total spending is excessive, a shortage of labor will arise; the number of job vacancies will exceed the number of workers seeking employment. Here, the actual rate of unemployment will be below the natural rate. Such unusually "tight" labor markets are normally associated with inflation.

The concept of the natural rate of unemployment merits elaboration in two respects:

1. *Not automatic* "Natural" does not mean the economy will always operate at the natural rate and thus realize its potential output. Our brief discussion of the business cycle demonstrated that the economy sometimes operates at an unemployment rate higher than the natural rate—due to cyclical unemployment. In contrast, the economy may on some occasions achieve an unemployment rate below the natural rate. For example, during World War II, when the natural rate was about 4 percent, the pressure of wartime production resulted in an almost unlimited demand for labor. Overtime work was common, as was "moonlighting" (working at more than one job). And the government mandated that some people working in essential industries remain in these jobs, which helped reduce frictional unemployment. As a result, the actual rate of unemployment was below 2 percent in 1943–1945, and it dropped to 1.2 percent in 1944. The economy was producing beyond its potential output, but it was building up considerable inflationary pressure in the process.

2. *Not immutable* The natural rate of unemployment is not forever fixed. It can change when demographics change or when there are changes in society's laws and customs. In the 1960s this unavoidable minimum of frictional and structural unemployment was about 4 percent of the labor force. That is, full employment meant that 96 percent of the labor force was employed. In the 1980s, economists generally agreed that the natural rate of unemployment was about 6 percent. Today, the consensus is that the rate is about 5.5 percent. Why these changes? First, the demographic makeup of the labor force has changed since the 1960s. In the

1970s and 1980s, younger workers became a larger part of the labor force. Because they traditionally have high unemployment rates, their greater relative numbers increased the natural unemployment rate. Second, laws and customs have changed. For example, the unemployment compensation program in the United States has been expanded both in the number of workers covered and in the size of benefits. By cushioning the economic impact of joblessness, unemployment compensation permits unemployed workers to engage in a more deliberate, lengthy job search, thereby increasing frictional unemployment and the natural unemployment rate.

The recent drop in the natural rate from 6 percent to about 5.5 percent has occurred mainly because the growing proportion of younger workers has reversed itself as the baby-boom generation has aged. The labor force now has a larger proportion of middle-aged workers, who traditionally have lower unemployment rates. Also, increased competition in product and labor markets has limited price and wage increases. A decade ago, a 5.5 percent rate of unemployment might have boosted the inflation rate; today, this lower unemployment rate appears to be consistent with a stable, low rate of inflation.

Measurement of Unemployment

Determining the unemployment rate means first determining who is eligible and available to work. Figure 8-4 is a helpful starting point. It shows the total U.S. population as being divided into three groups. One group is made up of people under 16 years of age and people who are institutionalized, for example, in mental hospitals or correctional institutions. These people are not considered potential members of the labor force.

A second group, labeled "Not in labor force," are adults who are potential workers but for some reason—they are homemakers, in school, or retired—are not employed and are not seeking work.

The third group is the **labor force,** which constituted about 50 percent of the total population in 1997. The labor force is all people who are able and willing to work. *Both those who are employed and those who are unemployed but actively seeking work are counted as being in the labor force.* The **unemployment rate** is the percentage of the labor force unemployed:

$$\text{Unemployment rate} = \frac{\text{unemployed}}{\text{labor force}} \times 100$$

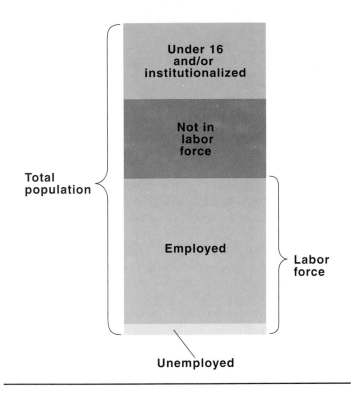

Total population	267,901,000
Less: Under 16 and/or institutionalized	–64,767,000
Less: Not in labor force	–66,837,000
Equals: Labor force	136,297,000
Employed	129,558,000
Unemployed	6,739,000

FIGURE 8-4 The labor force, employment, and unemployment, 1997 The labor force consists of persons 16 years of age or older who are not in institutions and who are (1) employed or (2) unemployed but seeking employment.

The statistics below Figure 8-4 show that in 1997 the unemployment rate averaged

$$\frac{6,739,000}{136,297,000} \times 100 = 4.9\%$$

Unemployment rates for select years between 1929 and 1997 are provided on the inside covers of this book.

The U.S. Bureau of Labor Statistics (BLS) determines who is employed and who is not by a nationwide random survey of some 60,000 households each month. A series of questions is asked as to which members of the household are working, unemployed and looking for work, not looking for work, and so on. From the answers, an unemployment rate is developed for the entire nation. Despite the use of scientific sampling and interviewing techniques, the data collected in this survey are subject to criticism:

1. ***Part-time employment*** The official data include all part-time workers as fully employed. In 1997 about 18.9 million people worked part-time because of personal choice. But another 2.8 million part-time workers either wanted to work full-time and could not find suitable full-time work or worked fewer hours because of a temporary slack in consumer demand. These last two groups were, in effect, partially employed and partially unemployed. By counting them as fully employed, say critics, the official BLS data understate the unemployment rate.

2. ***Discouraged workers*** You must be actively seeking work to be counted as unemployed. An unemployed individual who is not actively seeking employment is classified as "not in the labor force." The problem is that many workers, after unsuccessfully seeking employment for a time,

become discouraged and drop out of the labor force. The number of such **discouraged workers** is larger during recession than prosperity; an estimated 1.25 million people fell into this category in recession-year 1991. By not counting discouraged workers as unemployed, say critics, official data understate the unemployment rate. **(Key Question 3)**

Economic Cost of Unemployment

Unemployment above the natural rate involves great economic and social costs.

GDP Gap and Okun's Law The basic economic cost of unemployment is forgone output. *When the economy fails to create enough jobs for all who are able and willing to work, potential production of goods and services is irretrievably lost.* In terms of Chapter 2's analysis, unemployment means that society is located at some point inside its production possibilities curve. Economists measure this sacrificed output as the **GDP gap**—the amount by which *actual GDP* falls short of *potential GDP.*

Potential GDP is determined by assuming that the natural rate of unemployment exists. The growth of potential GDP is simply projected forward on the basis of the economy's "normal" growth rate of real GDP. Figure 8-5 shows the GDP gap for recent years in the United States. It also indicates the close correlation between the actual unemployment rate (Figure 8-5b) and the GDP gap (Figure 8-5a). The higher the unemployment rate, the larger the GDP gap.

Macroeconomist Arthur Okun quantified the relationship between the unemployment rate and the GDP gap. **Okun's law,** based on recent estimates, indicates that *for every 1 percentage point which the actual unemployment rate exceeds the natural rate, a GDP gap of about 2 percent occurs.* With this information, we can calculate the absolute loss of output associated with any above-natural unemployment rate. For example, in 1992 the unemployment rate was 7.4 percent, or 1.4 percentage points above the 6.0 percent natural rate of unemployment then existing. Multiplying this 1.4 percent by Okun's 2 indicates that 1992's GDP gap was 2.8 percent of potential GDP (in real terms). Then, by applying this 2.8 percent loss to 1992's potential GDP of $6300 billion, we find that the economy sacrificed $176 billion of real output because the natural rate of unemployment was not achieved. **(Key Question 5)**

As you can see in Figure 8-5, sometimes the economy's actual output will exceed its potential output. (We already noted that this happened during World War II when unemployment rates fell below 2 percent. Extra shifts of workers were employed, capital equipment was used beyond its designed capacity, and overtime work and moonlighting were common.) We observe in Figure 8-5 that an economic expansion caused actual GDP to exceed potential GDP in 1988 and 1989, creating a "negative" GDP gap. Potential GDP can occasionally be exceeded, but the excess of actual over potential GDP eventually causes inflation and cannot be sustained indefinitely.

Unequal Burdens An increase in the unemployment rate from 5.5 to, say, 9 or 10 percent might be more tolerable to society if every worker's hours of work and wage income were reduced proportionally. But this is not the case. Part of the burden of unemployment is that its cost is unequally distributed.

Table 8-2 (page 158) examines unemployment rates for various labor market groups for 2 years. The 1990–1991 recession pushed the 1992 unemployment rate to 7.4 percent. In contrast, the economy achieved full employment in 1996, with a 5.4 percent unemployment rate. By observing the large variance in unemployment rates for the different groups *within each year* and comparing the rates *between the 2 years,* we can generalize as follows:

1. *Occupation* White-collar workers enjoy lower unemployment rates than blue-collar workers. White-collar workers generally are employed in less cyclically vulnerable industries (such as services and nondurable goods) or are self-employed. Also, white-collar workers are usually less subject to unemployment during recession than blue-collar workers. Businesses want to retain their more skilled white-collar workers, in whom they have invested the expense of training. But it is not always this way. During the 1990–1991 recession, many firms "downsized" their management structures, discharging more white-collar workers than ever before. The unemployment rate of white-collar workers increased more rapidly than that of blue-collar laborers. Nevertheless, the unemployment rate of white-collar workers remained far below that of blue-collar workers.

2. *Age* Teenagers incur much higher unemployment rates than adults. Teenagers have low skill levels, more frequently quit their jobs, are more frequently discharged from jobs, and have little

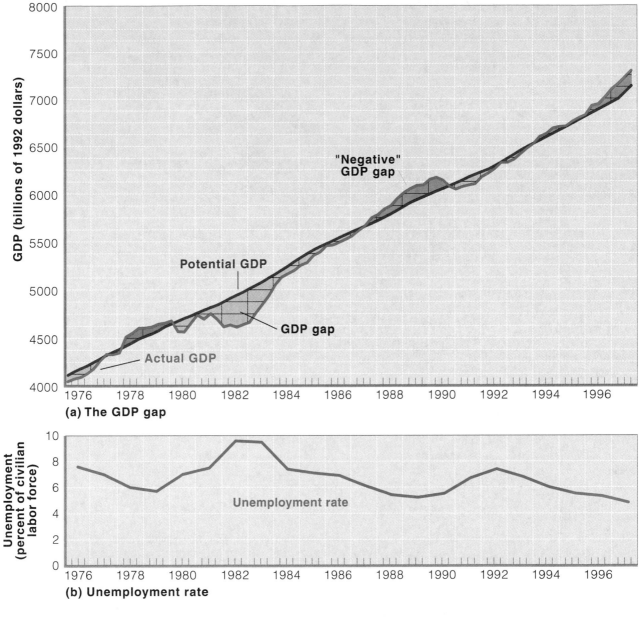

FIGURE 8-5 Potential and actual GDP and the unemployment rate (a) The difference between potential GDP and actual GDP is the GDP gap. The GDP gap measures the output the economy sacrifices because it fails to use fully its production potential. (b) A high unemployment rate means a large GDP gap, and vice versa. [*Source: Economic Report of the President* and Robert J. Gordon, *Macroeconomics,* 7th ed. (New York: Addison-Wesley, 1998). Updated.]

----

geographic mobility. Many unemployed teenagers are new in the labor market, searching for their first job.

3. **Race**   The unemployment rate for blacks—adults and teenagers—has been roughly *twice* that of whites.

Factors explaining this discrepancy include discrimination in education and the labor market, the concentration of blacks in less skilled (blue-collar) occupations, and the geographic isolation of blacks in central-city areas where employment

TABLE 8-2 Unemployment rates by demographic group: recession (1992) and full employment (1996)*

Demographic group	Unemployment rate, 1992	Unemployment rate, 1996
Overall	7.4%	5.4%
Occupation:		
Blue-collar	9.3	7.1
White-collar	4.6	3.4
Age:		
16–19	20.2	18.1
Black, 16–19	39.8	30.6
White, 16–19	17.1	14.2
Male, 20+	7.0	4.6
Female, 20+	6.3	4.8
Race:		
Black	14.1	10.5
White	6.5	4.7
Gender:		
Female	6.9	5.4
Male	7.8	5.4
Education		
Less than high school diploma	13.5	10.9
High school degree only	7.7	5.5
College degree or more	2.9	2.2
Duration:		
15 weeks or more	2.6	1.7

*Civilian labor-force data. In 1992 the economy was suffering the lingering unemployment effects of the 1990–1991 recession.
Sources: Economic Report of the President; Employment and Earnings; Census Bureau.

opportunities for new labor market entrants are minimal.

4. *Gender* Male and female unemployment rates are highly similar. The lower unemployment rate for women in 1992 occurred because there are more male than female workers in such cyclically vulnerable hard-goods industries as automobile, steel, and construction.

5. *Education* Less educated workers, on average, have higher unemployment rates than workers with more education. Less education is usually associated with lower-skilled, less permanent jobs, more time in between jobs, and jobs which are more vulnerable to cyclical layoff.

6. *Duration* The number of persons unemployed for long periods—15 weeks or more—as a percentage of the labor force is much less than the overall unemployment rate. But this percentage rises significantly during recessions. The "long-term" unemployed were only 1.7 percent of the labor force in 1996 compared with the overall 5.4 percent unemployment rate. A large proportion of unemployment is of relatively short duration. But also observe that the long-term unemployed were 2.6 percent of the labor force in 1992, implying more economic hardship when recessions occur.

Noneconomic Costs

Severe cyclical unemployment is more than an economic malady; it is a social catastrophe. Depression means idleness. And idleness means loss of skills, loss of self-respect, a plummeting of morale, family disintegration, and sociopolitical unrest. A job

> . . . gives hope for material and social advancement. It is a way of providing one's children a better start in life. It may mean the only honorable way of escape from the poverty of one's parents. It helps to overcome racial and other social barriers. In short . . . a job is the passport to freedom and to a better life. To deprive people of jobs is to read them out of our society.[1]

History demonstrates that severe unemployment leads to rapid and sometimes violent social and political change. The shift of U.S. political philosophy toward the left during the Depression of the 1930s is an example. The Depression-inspired New Deal was a revolution in U.S. political and economic thinking. Witness also Hitler's ascent to power against a background of unemployment. Furthermore, the high unemployment among some minorities unquestionably has been a cause of the unrest and violence which periodically plague cities in the United States and elsewhere. At the individual level, research links increases in suicide, homicide, cardiovascular mortality, and mental illness to high unemployment.

International Comparisons

Unemployment rates vary greatly among nations at any specific time. One reason for the differences is that nations have different natural rates of unemployment. Another explanation is that nations may be in different phases of their business cycles. Global Perspective 8-1 shows unemployment rates for five industrialized nations in recent years. Historically, the United States has had higher unemployment rates than most industrially advanced nations. But this pattern changed in the 1980s. The U.S. unemployment rate has been below the rates in the United Kingdom, Germany, and France in several years since 1987.

QUICK REVIEW 8-2

■ Unemployment is of three general types: frictional, structural, and cyclical.

■ The natural unemployment rate (frictional plus structural) is presently estimated to be about 5.5 percent.

■ Society loses real GDP when cyclical unemployment occurs; according to Okun's law, for each 1 percentage point of unemployment above the natural rate, the U.S.

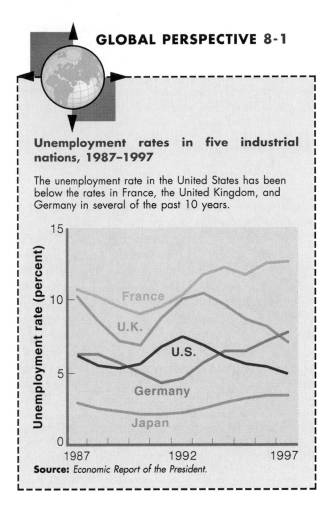

GLOBAL PERSPECTIVE 8-1

Unemployment rates in five industrial nations, 1987–1997

The unemployment rate in the United States has been below the rates in France, the United Kingdom, and Germany in several of the past 10 years.

Source: *Economic Report of the President.*

economy suffers a 2 percent decline in real GDP below potential.

■ Blue-collar workers, teenagers, blacks, and less educated workers bear a disproportionate burden of unemployment.

INFLATION DEFINED AND MEASURED

We now turn to inflation as an aspect of macroeconomic instability. The problems inflation poses are more subtle than those of unemployment.

Meaning of Inflation

Inflation is *a rising general level of prices.* This does not mean that *all* prices are rising. Even during periods of rapid inflation, some prices may be relatively constant and others falling. For example, although the United

---

[1] Henry R. Reuss, *The Critical Decade* (New York: McGraw-Hill Book Company, 1964), p. 133.

States experienced high rates of inflation in the 1970s and early 1980s, the prices of video recorders, digital watches, and personal computers declined. As you will see, one troublesome aspect of inflation is that prices rise unevenly. Some streak upward; others ascend leisurely; still others do not rise at all.

Measurement of Inflation

Inflation is measured by price-index numbers such as those introduced in Chapter 7. Recall that a price index measures the general level of prices in any year relative to prices in a base period.

To illustrate, the consumer price index (CPI) now uses 1982–1984 as the base period, meaning that period's price level is set equal to 100. The 1997 price index was about 161. Thus consumer prices were 61 percent higher in 1997 than in 1982–1984, so a set of goods which cost $100 in 1982–1984 cost $161 in 1997.

The *rate* of inflation can be calculated for any specific year (say, 1997) by subtracting the previous year's (1996) price index from that year's (1997) index, dividing by the previous year's index, and multiplying by 100 to express the result as a percentage. As an example, the CPI was 156.9 in 1996 and 160.5 in 1997, so the rate of inflation for 1997 is calculated as follows:

$$\text{Rate of inflation} = \frac{160.5 - 156.9}{156.9} \times 100 = 2.3\%$$

The so-called **rule of 70** provides a quantitative grasp of inflation's effect. If we divide the number 70 by the annual rate of inflation, the quotient is the number of years it takes for inflation to double the price level:

$$\begin{array}{l}\text{Approximate} \\ \text{number of years} \\ \text{required to double} \\ \text{price level}\end{array} = \frac{70}{\begin{array}{c}\text{annual percentage rate} \\ \text{of inflation}\end{array}}$$

Examples: A 3 percent annual rate of inflation will double the price level in about 23(= 70 ÷ 3) years. Inflation of 8 percent per year will double the price level in about 9(= 70 ÷ 8) years. The rule of 70 is generally applicable. You can use it, for example, to estimate how long it will take for real GDP *or* your savings account to double. **(Key Question 7)**

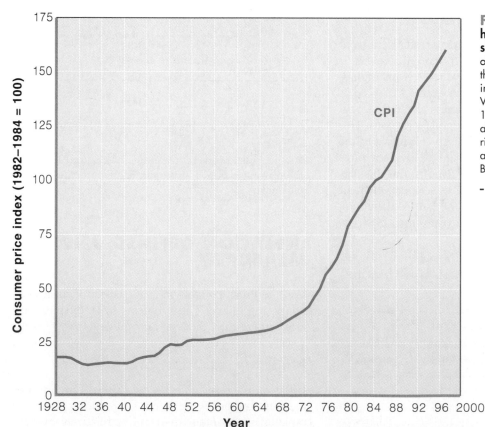

FIGURE 8-6 Price-level behavior in the United States since 1928 The price stability of the 1920s and the deflation of the early 1930s gave way to sharp inflation in the immediate post–World War II period. The 1951–1965 period saw a reasonably stable price level, but the period since 1965 has clearly been an "age of inflation." (*Source:* Bureau of Labor Statistics.)

Facts of Inflation

Figure 8-6 shows inflation in the United States since 1928. The curve represents annual values of the consumer price index relative to the base period (here, 1982–1984). That is, the CPI for the 1982–1984 period is arbitrarily set at 100.

Although the past three decades have been an "age of inflation," the U.S. economy has not always been inflation-prone. The price level was stable in the prosperous 1920s and declined—*deflation* occurred—during the early years of the Great Depression of the 1930s. Prices then rose in the immediate years after World War II (1945–1948). However, overall price stability characterized the 1951–1965 period, when the average annual increase in the price level was less than 1.5 percent. But the price increases which began in the late 1960s and surged in the 1970s introduced Americans to double-digit inflation. In 1979 and 1980 the price level rose 12 to 13 percent annually. However, by the 1990s, the inflation rate had settled back into a 2 to 4 percent annual range. Historical rates of inflation are listed on the inside covers of this textbook.

Inflation is not unique to the United States; all industrial nations have experienced this problem. Global Perspective 8-2 traces the post-1986 annual inflation rates of the United States, the United Kingdom, Japan, France, and Germany. Observe that inflation in the United States has been neither unusually high nor low relative to inflation in these other industrial countries.

Some nations have had double-digit, triple-digit, or even higher annual rates of inflation in recent years. In 1996, for example, the annual inflation rate in Turkey was 82 percent; in Venezuela, 120 percent; and in Bulgaria, 123 percent. A few nations experienced astronomical rates of inflation in 1996: Turkmenistan, 992 percent; and Angola, 4145 percent!

Causes: Theories of Inflation

Economists distinguish between two types of inflation: *demand-pull inflation* and *cost-push inflation*.

Demand-Pull Inflation   Traditionally, changes in the price level are attributed to an excess of total spending beyond the economy's capacity to produce. Because resources are fully employed, the business sector cannot respond to this excess demand by ex-

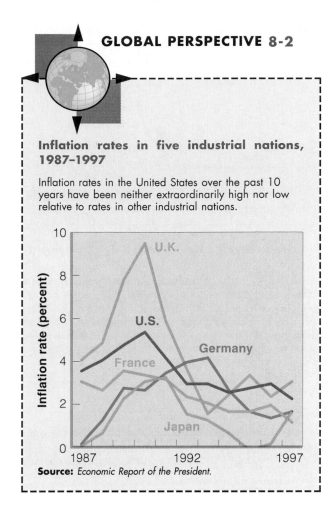

GLOBAL PERSPECTIVE 8-2

Inflation rates in five industrial nations, 1987–1997

Inflation rates in the United States over the past 10 years have been neither extraordinarily high nor low relative to rates in other industrial nations.

Source: *Economic Report of the President.*

panding output, so the excess demand bids up the prices of the limited real output, causing **demand-pull inflation.** The essence of this type of inflation is "too much spending chasing too few goods."

But the relationship between total spending, on the one hand, and output, employment, and the price level, on the other, is not so simple. Figure 8-7 will help us unravel the complications. This figure is a graph of the price level and real domestic output, with the full-employment level of output designated Q_f. The three ranges marked on the curve are ranges of price-level and real-output changes. Let's examine increases in total spending—represented by the left-to-right arrow—to see where demand-pull inflation arises:

1. *Range 1*   Toward the left in range 1, output is very low relative to the economy's full-employment output. This implies a very low level of total spending—the sum of consumption,

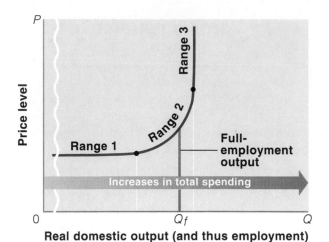

FIGURE 8-7 The price level and the level of real GDP (and thus employment) As total spending increases, the price level first stays constant as real output expands (range 1); then increases as real output approaches, reaches, and exceeds the full-employment level (range 2); and finally jumps sharply as real output nears and attains its maximum capacity (range 3). Demand-pull inflation occurs in ranges 2 and 3.

- -

investment, government, and net export spending—and a substantial GDP gap. Unemployment rates are high and businesses have much idle production capacity.

Assume now that total spending increases. As it does, real domestic output will increase, and the unemployment rate will fall. But there is little or no increase in the price level in range 1. Since firms have excess production capacity, their costs and thus their prices do not rise as they increase their output. Large amounts of idle human and property resources will be put back to work at their *existing* prices. An unemployed worker does not ask for a wage increase when called back to a job.

2. *Range 2* As output continues to expand in response to still further increases in total spending, the economy enters range 2. Here it approaches and will eventually surpass its full-employment output.

Even before full employment is achieved, the price level may begin to rise. As production expands, supplies of idle resources disappear at different rates in various sectors and industries. Bottlenecks develop in some industries, even though most still have room to expand. Some industries are able to reach their full-production

capacity before others and thus cannot respond to further increases in total spending for their products. Consequently, costs and therefore prices rise. Then, as still more labor is hired, workplaces become increasingly congested, and each added worker contributes less to output. Labor costs rise further, forcing up more product prices. As full employment is approached, many firms hire less-qualified workers, and this, too, contributes to rising costs and prices. The price-level increases which occur before Q_f is reached are sometimes called *premature inflation*; it is demand-pull inflation taking place prior to the economy's achieving its full-employment output.

As total spending in range 2 increases *beyond* output Q_f, still higher prices induce some businesses to demand, and some households to supply, resources beyond the full-employment level of output. Firms may employ additional work shifts and use overtime to achieve greater output. Households may supply additional workers such as teenagers and spouses, who previously had chosen not to enter the labor force. In this part of range 2, the part to the right of Q_f, the rate of unemployment falls below the natural rate and the actual GDP exceeds potential GDP. Here, the pace of inflation usually quickens.

3. *Range 3* As total spending increases into range 3, the economy simply cannot supply more resources. Firms cannot respond to increases in demand by increasing output. Real domestic output is at an absolute maximum, so further increases in demand do only one thing: raise the price level. The rate of inflation may be high and growing because total demand greatly exceeds society's absolute capacity to produce. The demand-pull inflation of range 2 becomes the *pure* demand-pull inflation of range 3. There is no increase in real output to absorb some of the increased spending.

Chapter 7's distinction between nominal and real GDP points up another feature of inflation. As long as the price level is constant (range 1), increases in nominal and real GDP are identical. But with inflation in range 2, nominal GDP is rising faster than real GDP, so nominal GDP must be "deflated" to measure changes in physical output. In range 3, nominal GDP is rising—perhaps rapidly due to high inflation—but real GDP is constant. In brief, the demand-pull inflation of ranges 2 and 3 breaks the equality between nominal and real GDP.

Cost-Push or Supply-Side Inflation Inflation may also arise on the supply or cost side of the market. During several periods in our economic history the price level has risen even though aggregate demand was not excessive. These were periods when output and employment were both *declining* (evidence of a deficiency of total demand) while the general price level was *increasing.*

The theory of **cost-push inflation** explains rising prices in terms of factors which raise **per-unit production costs.** A per-unit production cost is the average cost of a particular level of output. This average cost is found by dividing the total cost of all resource inputs by the amount of output produced. That is,

$$\text{Per-unit production cost} = \frac{\text{total input cost}}{\text{units of output}}$$

Rising per-unit production costs squeeze profits and reduce the amount of output firms are willing to supply at the existing price level. As a result, the economy's supply of goods and services declines. This decline in supply drives up the price level. Under this scenario, costs are *pushing* the price level upward, rather than demand *pulling* it upward, as with demand-pull inflation.

Two potential sources of cost-push inflation are increases in nominal wages and increases in the prices of nonwage inputs such as raw materials and energy:

1. *Wage-push variant* One variation of cost-push inflation theory suggests that, under some circumstances, unions may be a source of inflation. Unions exert some control over nominal wage rates through collective bargaining. Suppose they demand and receive large increases in wages. Also suppose that these wage gains set the standard for wage increases paid to nonunion workers. If the economy's wage gains are excessive relative to such offsetting factors as an increase in output per hour worked, then producers' per-unit production costs will rise. Firms will respond by reducing the amount of goods and services they offer for sale. If there is no change in demand, this decline in supply will increase the price level. Because the culprit is an excessive increase in nominal wages, this variation of cost-push inflation is sometimes called *wage-push inflation.*

2. *Supply-shock variant* The *supply-shock* variation of cost-push inflation traces rising production costs—and therefore rising product prices—to abrupt, unanticipated increases in the costs of raw materials or energy inputs. The rocketing prices of imported oil in 1973–1974 and again in 1979–1980 are good illustrations. As energy prices rose during these periods, the costs of producing and transporting virtually every product in the economy increased. Rapid cost-push inflation ensued.

Complexities

The real world is more complex than the distinction between demand-pull and cost-push inflation suggests. It is difficult to distinguish between demand-pull and cost-push inflation unless the original source of inflation is known. For example, suppose a major boost in total spending occurs in a fully employed economy, causing demand-pull inflation. But as the demand-pull stimulus works its way through various product and resource markets, individual firms find their wage costs, material costs, and fuel prices rising. From their perspective they must raise their prices because production costs (someone else's prices) have risen. Although this inflation is clearly demand-pull in origin, it may appear to be cost-push inflation to business firms and to government. Without proper identification of the originating source, government may mistakenly focus public policy on slowing rising costs rather than on reducing excessive total spending.

Another complexity is that cost-push inflation and demand-pull inflation differ in their sustainability. Demand-pull inflation will continue as long as there is excess total spending. Cost-push inflation automatically is self-limiting; it will die out by itself. Increased per-unit costs will lead to reduced supply, which means decreased real output and employment. These decreases will constrain further per-unit cost increases. In other words, cost-push inflation generates a recession. And in a recession, the efforts of workers and other resource suppliers are on keeping their resources employed, not on pushing up the prices of the resources they command.

QUICK REVIEW 8-3

■ Inflation is a rising general level of prices and is measured as a percentage change in a price index such as the CPI.

■ The U.S. inflation rate has been within the middle range of rates of other advanced industrial nations and far below the rates experienced by some nations.

■ Demand-pull inflation occurs when total spending exceeds the economy's ability to provide goods and services at the existing price level; total spending *pulls* the price level upward.

■ Cost-push inflation occurs when factors such as excessive wage increases and rapid increases in raw-material prices drive up per-unit production costs; higher costs *push* the price level upward.

REDISTRIBUTION EFFECTS OF INFLATION

We now turn from the causes of inflation to its effects. In this section we consider how inflation redistributes income; in the next section, we examine the possible effects of rising prices on domestic output.

The historical relationship between the price level and domestic output is ambiguous. Until recently, real output and the price level have risen and fallen together. In the past two decades, however, there have been times when real output has fallen while prices have continued to rise. We will dodge this difficulty by assuming here that real output is constant and at the full-employment level. Holding real output and income constant will allow us to isolate the effects of inflation on the distribution of that income: With a fixed national income pie, how does inflation affect the size of the slices going to different income receivers? Before we can answer, we need to discuss some terminology.

Nominal and Real Income   You must first be clear about the difference between money (or nominal) income and real income. **Nominal income** is the number of dollars received as wages, rent, interest, or profits. **Real income** measures the amount of goods and services nominal income can buy.

If your nominal income increases faster than the price level, your real income will rise. If the price level increases faster than your nominal income, your real income will decline. We can determine approximately how real income changes with this formula:

Percentage   percentage   percentage
change in ≈ change in − change in
real income   nominal income   price level

If your nominal income rises by 10 percent and the price level rises by 6 percent in the same period, your real income will *increase* by about 4 percent. Conversely, a 6 percent increase in nominal income

accompanied by 10 percent inflation will *decrease* your real income by approximately 4 percent.[2]

The main point is this: While inflation reduces the purchasing power of the dollar—the amount of goods and services each dollar will buy—it does not necessarily decrease a person's real income. Your real income (or standard of living) drops only when your nominal income fails to keep pace with inflation.

Anticipations   The redistribution effects of inflation depend on whether or not it is expected. With fully expected or **anticipated inflation,** an income receiver *may* be able to avoid or lessen the adverse effects inflation would otherwise have on real income. The generalizations which immediately follow assume **unanticipated inflation**—inflation whose full extent was *not* expected.

Fixed-Nominal-Income Receivers

Our distinction between nominal and real incomes shows that *inflation penalizes people who receive fixed nominal incomes.* Inflation redistributes real income away from fixed-income receivers and toward others in the economy. The classic case is the elderly couple living on a private pension or annuity providing a fixed amount of nominal income each month. They may have retired in, say, 1984 on what appeared to be an adequate pension. However, by 1998 they will discover that the purchasing power of that pension has been cut by one-half.

Similarly, landlords who receive lease payments of fixed dollar amounts will be hurt by inflation as they receive dollars of declining value over time. To a lesser extent some white-collar workers, some public sector employees whose incomes are dictated by fixed pay scales, and families living on fixed levels of welfare will also be victims of inflation. Note, however, that the United States has *indexed* social security benefits. This means that these payments increase when the

---

[2]A more precise calculation follows Chapter 7's process for changing nominal GDP to real GDP. Thus,

$$\text{Real income} = \frac{\text{nominal income}}{\text{price index (in hundredths)}}$$

In our first illustration, if nominal income rises by 10 percent from $100 to $110 and the price level (index) increases by 6 percent from 100 to 106, then real income has increased as follows:

$$\frac{\$110}{1.06} = \$103.77$$

The 4 percent increase in real income shown by the simple formula in the text is a reasonable approximation of the 3.77 percent yielded by our more precise formula.

consumer price index increases, preventing or lessening erosion from inflation.

Some people living on flexible incomes *may* benefit from inflation. The nominal incomes of such people may spurt ahead of the price level, with the result that their real incomes are enhanced. As an example, workers in expanding industries who are represented by strong unions may keep their nominal wages apace with, or ahead of, the rate of inflation.

Some wage earners are hurt by inflation. Those in declining industries or without strong unions may find that the price level jumps ahead of their money incomes.

Business executives and other profit receivers may benefit from inflation. If product prices rise faster than resource prices, business receipts will grow at a faster rate than costs. Thus some—but not necessarily all—profit incomes will outdistance the rising tide of inflation.

Savers

Inflation hurts savers. *As prices rise, the real value, or purchasing power, of a nest egg of savings deteriorates.* Savings accounts, insurance policies, annuities, and other fixed-value paper assets once adequate to meet rainy-day contingencies or provide for a comfortable retirement decline in real value during inflation. The simplest case is the individual who hoards money as a cash balance. A $1000 cash balance would have lost one-half its real value between 1980 and 1995. Of course, most forms of savings earn interest. But the value of savings will still decline if the rate of inflation exceeds the rate of interest.

Example: A household may save $1000 in a certificate of deposit (CD) in a commercial bank or savings and loan association at 6 percent annual interest. But if inflation is 13 percent (as in 1980), the real value or purchasing power of that $1000 will be cut to about $938 by the end of the year. The saver will receive $1060 (equal to $1000 plus $60 of interest), but deflating that $1060 for 13 percent inflation means that its real value is only about $938 (= $1060 ÷ 1.13).

Debtors and Creditors

Inflation redistributes real income between debtors and creditors. *Unanticipated inflation benefits debtors (borrowers) at the expense of creditors (lenders).* Suppose you borrow $1000 from a bank, to be repaid in 2 years. If in that time the general level of prices dou-

bles, the $1000 which you repay will have only half the purchasing power of the $1000 originally borrowed. True, if we ignore interest charges, the same number of dollars will be repaid as was borrowed. But because of inflation, each of these dollars will buy only half as much as it did when the loan was negotiated. As prices go up, the value of the dollar comes down. Thus, the borrower is loaned "dear" dollars but, because of inflation, pays back "cheap" dollars.

The inflation of the past several decades has been a windfall to those who purchased homes in earlier periods with low, fixed-interest-rate mortgages. Inflation has greatly reduced the real burden of their mortgage indebtedness. They have also benefited because the nominal value of housing has increased more rapidly then the overall price level.

The Federal government, which has amassed $5.4 trillion of public debt over the decades, has also benefited from inflation. Historically, the Federal government has regularly paid off its loans by taking out new ones. Inflation has permitted the Treasury to pay off its loans with dollars which have less purchasing power than the dollars it originally borrowed. Nominal national income and therefore tax collections rise with inflation; the amount of public debt owed does not. Thus, inflation reduces the real burden of the public debt to the Federal government. Because inflation benefits the Federal government in this way, some economists have questioned whether society can really expect government to be zealous in its efforts to halt inflation.

In fact, some nations such as Brazil once used inflation so extensively to reduce the real value of their debt that lenders forced them to borrow money in U.S. dollars or in some other relatively stable currency instead of their own currency. This prevents them from using domestic inflation as a means of subtly "defaulting" on their debt. Any inflation they generate will reduce the value of their own currencies but not the value of the dollar-denominated debt they must pay back.

Anticipated Inflation

The redistribution effects of inflation are less severe or are eliminated if people (1) anticipate inflation and (2) can adjust their nominal incomes to reflect expected price-level changes. The prolonged inflation which began in the late 1960s prompted many unions in the 1970s to insist on labor contracts with **cost-of-living adjustment** (COLA) clauses; such agreements automatically raise workers' nominal incomes when inflation occurs.

Similarly, the redistribution of income from lender to borrower might be altered if inflation is anticipated. Suppose a lender (perhaps a commercial bank or savings and loan institution) and a borrower (a household) both agree that 5 percent is a fair rate of interest on a 1-year loan *provided* the price level is stable. But assume inflation has been occurring and is expected to be 6 percent over the next year. If the bank lends the household $100 at 5 percent interest, the bank will be paid back $105 at the end of the year. But if 6 percent inflation does occur during that year, the purchasing power of the $105 will have been reduced to about $99. The *lender* will in effect have paid the *borrower* $1 to use the lender's money for a year.

The lender can avoid this subsidy by charging an **inflation premium,** that is, by increasing the interest rate by 6 percent, the amount of the anticipated inflation. By charging 11 percent, the lender will receive back $111 at the end of the year. Adjusted for the 6 percent inflation, that amount will have purchasing power of today's $105. The result then will be a mutually agreeable transfer of purchasing power from borrower to lender of $5, or 5 percent, for the use of $100 for 1 year. Financial institutions have also developed variable-interest-rate mortgages to protect themselves from the adverse effects of inflation. (Incidentally, this example points out that, rather than being a cause of inflation, high nominal interest rates are a consequence of inflation.)

Our illustration shows the difference between the real rate of interest and the money or nominal rate of interest. The **real interest rate** is *the percentage increase in purchasing power which the lender receives from the borrower.* In our example the real interest rate is 5 percent. The **nominal interest rate** is *the percentage increase in money which the lender receives.* In our example the nominal rate of interest is 11 percent. The difference in these two concepts is that the real interest rate is adjusted or deflated for the rate of inflation while the nominal interest rate is not. The nominal interest rate is the sum of the real interest rate plus the premium paid to offset the expected rate of inflation. These distinctions are illustrated in Figure 8-8.

Addenda

Three final points must be mentioned:

1. *Deflation* The effects of unanticipated deflation are substantially the reverse of those of inflation. *Assuming no change in total output,* people with fixed money incomes will find their real in-

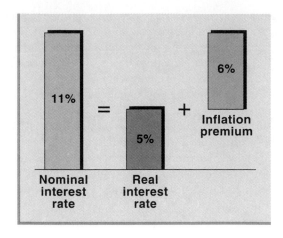

FIGURE 8-8 The inflation premium and nominal and real interest rates The inflation premium—the expected rate of inflation—gets built into the nominal interest rate. Here, the nominal interest rate of 11 percent comprises the real interest rate of 5 percent plus the inflation premium of 6 percent.

comes enhanced. Creditors will benefit at the expense of debtors. And savers will discover the purchasing power of their savings has grown because of the falling prices.

2. *Mixed effects* The fact that any person may be an income earner, a holder of financial assets, and an owner of real assets simultaneously will likely cushion the redistribution impact of inflation. If the individual owns fixed-value monetary assets (savings accounts, bonds, and insurance policies), inflation will lessen their real value. But that same inflation may increase the real value of any property assets (a house, land) which the person owns.

In short, many individuals are simultaneously hurt and benefitted by inflation. All these effects must be considered before we can conclude that any particular person's net position is better or worse because of inflation.

3. *Arbitrariness* The redistribution effects of inflation are *arbitrary;* they occur regardless of society's goals and values. Inflation lacks a social conscience and takes from some and gives to others, whether they be rich, poor, young, old, healthy, or infirm.

QUICK REVIEW 8-4

■ Inflation arbitrarily harms those who receive relatively fixed nominal incomes, and it helps some people who receive flexible nominal incomes.

■ Unanticipated inflation penalizes savers, and it benefits debtors at the expense of creditors.

■ The nominal interest rate exceeds the real interest rate by the expected rate of inflation.

OUTPUT EFFECTS OF INFLATION

We assumed in the last section that the economy's real output is fixed at the full-employment level. In that situation, the redistribution effects of inflation and deflation are that some groups gain real income at the expense of others. If the size of the pie is fixed and inflation causes some groups to get larger slices, other groups must get smaller slices. But, in fact, the level of domestic output—the size of the pie—may vary as the price level changes.

There is uncertainty and disagreement as to whether inflation will be accompanied by a rising or a falling real output. We will consider three scenarios, one associating inflation with an expanding output and two associating it with a declining output.

Stimulus of Demand-Pull Inflation

Some economists argue that full employment can be achieved only if some modest amount of inflation is tolerated. They base their reasoning on the ideas illustrated by Figure 8-7.

We know that the levels of real output and employment depend on total spending. If spending is low, the economy will operate in range 1. In this range the price level is stable, but real output is substantially below its potential and the unemployment rate is high. If total spending increases so that the economy moves into range 2, society must accept a higher price level—some amount of inflation—to achieve greater real output and the accompanying lower unemployment rates.

If further increases in total spending pull the economy into range 3, that spending will be purely inflationary because the full-capacity level of real output will have been reached.

It seems, then, that in range 2 there is a tradeoff between output (and thus employment) and inflation. Some moderate amount of inflation must be accepted if we are to realize high levels of output and employment. The high levels of spending which give us higher levels of output and low unemployment rates also cause some inflation. That implies there is an in-verse relationship between the inflation rate and the unemployment rate.

This perspective has been criticized in recent years. Many economists feel that any tradeoff between the inflation rate and the unemployment rate is transitory and that there is no such tradeoff in the long run. This controversy will be explored in Chapter 16.

Cost-Push Inflation and Unemployment

There is an equally plausible set of circumstances in which inflation might reduce both output and employment. Suppose the level of total spending is initially such that the economy is enjoying full employment *and* price-level stability. If cost-push inflation occurs, the existing level of total spending will now buy less real output because of the higher price level. Thus, real output will soon fall and unemployment will rise.

Economic events of the 1970s are an example of how inflation can reduce real output. In late 1973 the Organization of Petroleum Exporting Countries (OPEC) became very effective in exerting its market power and was able to quadruple the price of oil. The cost-push inflationary effects generated rapid price-level increases in the 1973–1975 period. At the same time the U.S. unemployment rate rose from slightly less than 5 percent in 1973 to 8.5 percent in 1975. Similar outcomes occurred in 1979–1980 in response to a second OPEC oil supply shock.

Hyperinflation and Breakdown

Some economists express anxiety over our first scenario. They are fearful that the mild, "creeping" inflation which might initially accompany an economic recovery phase can snowball into severe **hyperinflation.** This is an extremely rapid inflation whose impact on real output and employment can be devastating. The economists' contention is that as prices persist in creeping upward, households and businesses will expect them to rise further. So, rather than let their idle savings and current incomes depreciate, people will "spend now" to beat anticipated price rises. Businesses will do the same by buying capital goods. Actions based on this "inflationary psychosis" will then intensify the pressure on prices, and inflation will feed on itself.

Wage-Price Inflationary Spiral   Furthermore, as the price level rises, labor will demand and get higher nominal wages. Unions may seek wage increases sufficient not only to cover last year's price increases but also to compensate for inflation anticipated during the future life of their new collective bargaining agreements. Prosperity is not a good time for firms to risk strikes by resisting such demands, so they will agree, expecting to recoup their rising labor costs by boosting their prices. And for good measure, businesses may jack prices up an extra notch to be sure their profits keep up with the inflationary parade. As such price increases raise the general price level further, labor finds it once again has an excellent reason to demand and obtain substantial wage increases. But this triggers another round of price increases. And so on. The net effect is a cumulative *wage-price inflationary spiral*. Nominal wage and price rises feed on each other and transform creeping inflation into galloping inflation.

Potential Economic Collapse

Aside from its disruptive redistribution effects, hyperinflation can cause economic collapse. Severe inflation encourages speculative activity. Businesses may find it increasingly profitable to hoard both materials and finished products, anticipating further price increases. But restricting the availability of materials and products intensifies the inflationary pressure. Also, rather than invest in capital equipment, businesses and individual savers may purchase nonproductive wealth—jewels, gold and other precious metals, real estate, and so forth—as a hedge against inflation.

In the extreme, as prices shoot up sharply and unevenly, normal economic relationships are disrupted. Business owners do not know what to charge for their products. Consumers do not know what to pay. Resource suppliers want to be paid with actual output, rather than with rapidly depreciating money. Creditors avoid debtors to escape the repayment of debts with cheap money. Money eventually becomes almost worthless and ceases to do its job as a medium of exchange. The economy may be thrown into a state of barter. Production and exchange drop dramatically, and the net result is economic, social, and possibly political chaos. The hyperinflation has precipitated monetary collapse, depression, and sociopolitical disorder.

Examples

History reveals a number of examples which fit this scenario. Consider the effects of World War II on price levels in Hungary and Japan:

> The inflation in Hungary exceeded all known records of the past. In August 1946, 828 octillion (1 followed by 27 zeros) depreciated pengös equaled the value of 1 prewar pengö. The price of the American dollar reached a value of 3×10^{22} (3 followed by 22 zeros) pengös. Fishermen and farmers in 1947 Japan used scales to weigh currency and change, rather than bothering to count it. Prices rose some 116 times in Japan, 1938 to 1948.[3]

The German inflation of the 1920s was also catastrophic:

> The German Weimar Republic is an extreme example of a weak government which survived for some time through inflationary finance. On April 27, 1921, the German government was presented with a staggering bill for reparations payments to the Allies of 132 billion gold marks. This sum was far greater than what the Weimar Republic could reasonably expect to raise in taxes. Faced with huge budget deficits, the Weimar government simply ran the printing press to meet its bills.
>
> During 1922, the German price level went up 5,470 percent. In 1923, the situation worsened; the German price level rose 1,300,000,000,000 times. By October of 1923, the postage on the lightest letter sent from Germany to the United States was 200,000 marks. Butter cost 1.5 million marks per pound, meat 2 million marks, a loaf of bread 200,000 marks, and an egg 60,000 marks. Prices increased so rapidly that waiters changed the prices on the menu several times during the course of a lunch. Sometimes customers had to pay double the price listed on the menu when they ordered.[4]

A closing word of caution: Dramatic hyperinflations like these are almost invariably the consequence of imprudent expansion of the money supply by government. Such expansions result in excessive spending and thus demand-pull inflation. With appropriate public policies, however, mild inflation need not become hyperinflation.

---

[3]Theodore Morgan, *Income and Employment*, 2d ed. (Englewood Cliffs, NJ: Prentice-Hall, 1952), p. 361.

[4]Raburn M. Williams, *Inflation! Money, Jobs, and Politicians* (Arlington Heights, IL: AHM Publishing Corporation, 1980), p. 2.

CHAPTER SUMMARY

1. The United States and other industrial economies have gone through periods of fluctuations in domestic output, employment, and the price level. Although they have common phases—peak, recession, trough, recovery—business cycles vary greatly in duration and in intensity.

The Stock Market and Macroeconomic Instability

How, if at all, do changes in stock prices relate to the macroeconomy?

Financial investors daily buy and sell the stock (ownership shares) of thousands of corporations. These corporations pay dividends—a portion of their profits—to the owners of their shares. The price of a particular company's stock is determined by supply and demand. Individual stock prices generally rise and fall in concert with the collective expectations for each firm's profits. Greater profits normally result in higher dividends to the owners of the stock, and in anticipation of these higher dividends, financial investors are willing to pay more for the stock.

Stock market averages such as the Dow Jones Industrial Average—the weighted-average price of the stocks of 30 major U.S. industrial firms—are closely watched and reported. It is common for these price averages to change over time, or even to rise or fall sharply during a single day. On "Black Monday," October 19, 1987, the Dow Jones Industrial Average experienced a record 1-day drop of 20 percent. About $500 billion in stock market wealth evaporated in a single day. A sharp drop in stock prices also occurred in October 1997, mainly in response to rapid declines in stock prices in Hong Kong and other Southeast Asia stock markets.

The volatility of the stock market raises this question: Do changes in stock price averages *cause* macroeconomic instability? There are linkages between the stock market and the economy that might lead us to think the answer is "yes." Consider a sharp decline in stock prices. Feeling poorer, owners of stock may respond by reducing their spending on goods and services. Firms may react by cutting back on their purchases of new capital goods because that is more attractive than raising funds by issuing new shares of stock.

Studies find, however, that the consumption and investment impacts of stock price changes are relatively mild. Therefore, although stock price averages do influence total spending, the stock market is *not* a major cause of recession or inflation.

A related question emerges: Even though changes in stock prices do not *cause* significant changes in domestic output and the price level, might they *predict* such changes? That is, if stock market values are based on expected profits, wouldn't we expect rapid changes in stock price averages to forecast changes in future business conditions? Indeed, stock prices often *do* fall prior to recessions and rise prior to expansions. For this reason stock prices are among a group of 10 variables which constitute an index of leading indicators (Last Word, Chapter 12). Such an index often provides a useful clue to the future direction of the economy. But taken alone, stock market prices are not a reliable predictor of changes in GDP. Stock prices have fallen rapidly in some instances with no recession following. Black Monday itself did not produce a recession during the following 2 years. In other instances, recessions have occurred with no prior decline in stock market prices.

---

2. Although economists explain the business cycle in terms of such ultimate causal factors as major innovations, political events, and money creation, they generally agree that the level of total spending is the immediate determinant of real output and employment.

3. The business cycle affects all sectors of the economy, but in varying ways and degrees. The cycle has greater output and employment effects in the capital goods and durable consumer goods industries than in the services and nondurable goods industries. Over the cycle, price fluctuations are greater in competitive than in monopolistic industries.

4. Economists distinguish between frictional, structural, and cyclical unemployment. The full-employment or natural rate of unemployment, composed of frictional and structural unemployment, is currently about 5.5 percent. Part-time and discouraged workers complicate the accurate measurement of unemployment.

5. The economic cost of unemployment, as measured by the GDP gap, consists of the goods and services forgone by society when its resources are involuntarily idle. Okun's law suggests that every 1 percentage point increase in unemployment above the natural rate causes a 2 percent GDP gap.

6. Unemployment rates and inflation rates vary widely among nations. Unemployment rates differ because nations have different natural rates of unemployment and often are in different phases of their business cycles. Inflation and unemployment rates in the United States recently have been in the middle range compared with rates in other industrial nations.

7. Economists discern both demand-pull and cost-push (supply-side) inflation. Two variants of cost-push inflation are wage-push inflation and inflation caused by supply shocks.

8. Unanticipated inflation arbitrarily redistributes real income at the expense of fixed-income receivers, creditors, and savers. If inflation is anticipated, individuals and businesses may be able to take steps to lessen or eliminate adverse redistribution effects.

9. The demand-pull theory of inflation suggests that some inflation may be necessary for the economy to realize high levels of output and employment. However, the cost-push theory of inflation indicates that inflation may be accompanied by declines in real output and employment. Hyperinflation, usually associated with injudicious government policy, might undermine the monetary system and cause economic collapse.

TERMS AND CONCEPTS

business cycle	cyclical unemployment	GDP gap	anticipated inflation
peak	full-employment	Okun's law	unanticipated inflation
recession	unemployment rate	inflation	cost-of-living adjustment
trough	natural rate of	rule of 70	inflation premium
recovery	unemployment	demand-pull inflation	real interest rate
seasonal variations	potential output	cost-push inflation	nominal interest rate
secular trend	labor force	per-unit production costs	hyperinflation
frictional unemployment	unemployment rate	nominal income	
structural unemployment	discouraged workers	real income	

STUDY QUESTIONS

1. KEY QUESTION What are the four phases of the business cycle? How long do business cycles last? How do seasonal variations and secular trends complicate measurement of the business cycle? Why does the business cycle affect output and employment in capital goods industries and consumer durable goods industries more severely than in industries producing consumer nondurables?

2. What factors make it difficult to determine the unemployment rate? Why is it difficult to distinguish between frictional, structural, and cyclical unemployment? Why is unemployment an economic problem? What are the consequences of a GDP gap? What are the noneconomic effects of unemployment?

3. KEY QUESTION Use the following data to calculate **(a)** the size of the labor force and **(b)** the official unemployment rate: total population, 500; population under 16 years of age or institutionalized, 120; not in labor force, 150; unemployed, 23; part-time workers looking for full-time jobs, 10.

4. Since there is an unemployment compensation program which provides income for those out of work, why worry about unemployment?

5. KEY QUESTION Assume that in a particular year the natural rate of unemployment is 5 percent and the actual rate of unemployment is 9 percent. Use Okun's law to determine the size of the GDP gap in percentage-point terms. If the nominal GDP is $500 billion in that year, how much output is being forgone because of cyclical unemployment?

6. Explain how an *increase* in your nominal income and a *decrease* in your real income might occur simultaneously. Who loses from inflation? Who loses from unemployment? If you had to choose between **(a)** full employment with a 6 percent annual rate of inflation and **(b)** price stability with an 8 percent unemployment rate, which would you select? Why?

7. KEY QUESTION If the price index was 110 last year and is 121 this year, what is this year's rate of inflation? What is the "rule of 70"? How long would it take for the price level to double if inflation persisted at **(a)** 2, **(b)** 5, and **(c)** 10 percent per year?

8. Describe the relationship between total spending and the levels of output and employment. Explain what happens to the price level as increases in total spending move the economy from substantial unemployment to moderate unemployment, to full employment, and finally to full-capacity output.

9. Explain how hyperinflation might lead to a depression.

10. Evaluate as accurately as you can how each of the following individuals would be affected by unanticipated inflation of 10 percent per year:
   a. A pensioned railroad worker
   b. A department store clerk
   c. A UAW assembly line worker
   d. A heavily indebted farmer
   e. A retired business executive whose current income comes entirely from interest on government bonds
   f. The owner of an independent small-town department store

11. A noted television comedian once defined inflation as follows: "Inflation? That means your money today won't buy as much as it would have during the depression when you didn't have any." Is his definition accurate? Explain.

12. (**Last Word**) Suppose that stock prices fall by 10 percent in the stock market. All else equal, are these lower stock prices likely to *cause* a decrease in real GDP? How might these lower prices forecast a decline in real GDP?

13. WEB-BASED QUESTION The Employment Situation—Write the News Release Visit the U.S. Department of Labor http://stats.bls.gov/news.release/empsit.toc.htm and look at the current employment situation summary for the latest month. Then rewrite the following paragraph. See also http://stats.bls.gov/cps_faq.htm for their FAQs (frequently asked questions). Employment (rose/fell/remained unchanged), and the unemployment rate edged (up/down/stayed unchanged) to (?) percent in the latest month. The jobless rate had (risen/fallen/stayed unchanged) from (?) percent in (previous month) to (?) percent in (latest month). The number of payroll jobs (increased/decreased/ were unchanged) by (? thousand) in the latest month, with widespread gains/losses in the (?) sector of the economy. Average weekly hours (declined/increased/ unchanged), and average hourly earnings were (lower/higher/unchanged) over the month.

14. WEB-BASED QUESTION Inflation and the "Official CPI" Each month, BLS releases thousands of detailed CPI numbers to the press. However, the press generally focuses on the broadest, most comprehensive CPI, called the official CPI. Go to the U.S. Department of Labor http://stats.bls.gov/cpi-faq.htm CPI FAQs (frequently asked questions) page. Which index is the official CPI reported in the media? Look at http://stats.bls.gov/news.release/cpi.toc.htm and find the *current* figures for the official CPI: **(a)** index level (for example, July 1992 = 140.5); **(b)** 12-month percentage change (for example, July 1991 to July 1992 = 3.2 percent); **(c)** 1-month percentage change on a seasonally adjusted basis (for example, from June 1992 to July 1992 = 0.1 percent); and **(d)** the annual percentage rate of change so far this year.

9

Building the Aggregate Expenditures Model

Two of the most critical questions in macroeconomics are: (1) What determines the level of GDP, given a nation's production capacity? (2) What factors can cause real GDP to expand in one period and fall in another? To answer these questions, we construct the *aggregate expenditures model*. Recall that to economists "aggregate" means "total" or "combined," so "aggregate expenditures" refers to the economy's total spending. The model is based on the general equality between total spending and output described in Chapter 7. One of its primary uses is in clarifying the occurrence of business fluctuations discussed in Chapter 8.

We begin this chapter with a brief review of the economic thinking and events leading to the development of the aggregate expenditures model. Next we examine the relations between income and consumption and between income and saving, both aspects of the model. Then we focus on investment—specifically how businesses choose the amounts of capital goods to buy. Finally, we combine consumption, saving, and investment into a model which can be used to determine the equilibrium level of GDP for an economy.

The model developed in this chapter applies only to a private (no government), closed (no foreign trade) economy. In the next chapter we complete the model by adding government and the foreign sector.

HISTORICAL BACKDROP

A bit of historical background will help you see how and why the aggregate expenditures model came about.

Classical Economics and Say's Law

Until the Great Depression of the 1930s, many economists of the nineteenth and early twen-tieth centuries—now called classical econo-mists[1]—believed the market system would en-sure full employment of the economy's re-sources. They acknowledged that now and then abnormal circumstances such as wars, po-litical upheavals, droughts, speculative crises, and gold rushes would occur, deflecting the

---

[1]The most prominent classical economists were David Ricardo, John Stuart Mill, F. Y. Edgeworth, Alfred Marshall, and A. C. Pigou.

economy from full-employment status (as seen in Figure 8-1). But when these deviations did occur, automatic adjustments in prices, wages, and interest rates within the market would soon restore the economy to the full-employment level of output. A slump in output and employment would reduce prices, wages, and interest rates. Lower prices would increase consumer spending, lower wages would increase employment, and lower interest rates would boost investment spending. Any excess supply of goods and workers soon would be eliminated.

Classical macroeconomists denied the possibility of long-term underspending—a level of spending insufficient to purchase the entire full-employment output. This denial was based in part on **Say's law,** attributed to the nineteenth-century French economist J. B. Say. Say's law is the seemingly simple notion that the very act of producing goods generates an amount of income equal to the value of the goods produced. The production of any output automatically provides the income needed to take that output off the market— the income needed to buy what's produced. In other words, *supply creates its own demand.*

Say's law can best be understood in terms of a barter economy. A shoemaker, for example, produces or *supplies* shoes as a means of buying or *demanding* the shirts and stockings produced by other workers. The shoemaker's supply of shoes is his income that he will "spend" to satisfy his demand for other goods. The goods he buys (demands) will be exactly equal in value to the goods he produces (supplies). And so it allegedly is for other producers and for the entire economy. Demand must be the same as supply! The circular flow model of the economy and national income accounting both suggest something of this sort. Income generated from the production of any level of output would, when spent, be just sufficient to provide a matching total demand. Assuming the composition of output is in accord with consumer preferences, all markets would be cleared of their outputs. It would seem that what all business owners need to do to sell a full-employment output is to produce that output; Say's law guarantees there will be sufficient consumption spending to buy it all.

Say's law and classical macroeconomics are not simply a historical curiosity. A few modern economists have reformulated, revitalized, and extended the work of the nineteenth- and early twentieth-century economists to generate a "new" classical economics. (We will examine this modern reincarnation in later chapters.)

The Great Depression and Keynes

Two events weakened the theory that supply creates its own demand (Say's law) and led to the realization that underspending or overspending can occur:

The Great Depression

The Depression of the 1930s was worldwide. In the United States, it cut real GDP by 40 percent and raised the unemployment rate to nearly 25 percent. Much the same occurred in other industrial nations. The negative effects of the Depression lingered for a decade. There is, obviously, a blatant inconsistency between a theory which says that unemployment is virtually impossible and the actual occurrence of a 10-year siege of very substantial unemployment.

Keynes and Keynesian Economics

In 1936 British economist John Maynard Keynes (pronounced "Caines") explained why there was cyclical employment in capitalistic economies. In his *General Theory of Employment, Interest, and Money,* Keynes attacked the foundations of classical theory and touched off a major revolution in economic thinking on macroeconomic questions. Keynes disputed Say's law, pointing out that in some periods not all income will get spent on the output which is produced. When widespread underspending occurs, unsold goods will accumulate in producers' warehouses. Producers will respond to rising inventories by reducing their output and cutting their employment. A recession or depression will follow.

Because Keynes developed the ideas underlying the aggregate expenditures model, this kind of analysis is referred to as **Keynesian economics.** But the model reflects contributions of numerous other economists since Keynes. In the aggregate expenditures model, the macroeconomy is inherently unstable; it is subject to periods of recession and inflation. Keynesian economics says that capitalism is not a self-regulating system capable of uninterrupted prosperity. While capitalism is an excellent engine of long-term economic growth, we cannot always depend on it to "run itself."

Furthermore, economic fluctuations are not associated exclusively with external forces such as wars, droughts, and similar abnormalities. Rather, the Keynesian view sees the causes of unemployment and inflation as the failure of certain fundamental economic decisions—in particular, saving and investment decisions—to be completely synchronized. In addition, product prices and wages are downwardly inflexible, meaning that significant declines in prices and wages will occur only after extended and costly periods of recession or depression. Internal factors, in addition to external forces (wars and droughts), contribute to economic instability.

SIMPLIFICATIONS

Four assumptions will help us build the aggregate expenditures model:

1. Initially we will assume a "closed economy" where there are no international trade transactions. Complications arising from exports and imports in the "open economy" will be deferred to Chapter 10.

2. We will also ignore government until Chapter 10, permitting us first to demonstrate that at times laissez-faire capitalism may not achieve and maintain full employment. For now we will deal with a "private" closed economy.

3. Although both businesses and households save, we will for convenience speak as if all saving were personal saving.

4. To keep things simple, we will assume that depreciation and *net* foreign factor income earned in the United States are zero.

We should note two implications of these assumptions. First, recall from Chapter 7 that aggregate spending has four components: consumption, investment, government purchases, and net exports. Assumptions 1 and 2 mean that, for now, we are concerned only with consumption and investment.

Second, assumptions 2 through 4 permit us to treat gross domestic product (GDP), national income (NI), personal income (PI), and disposable income (DI) as being equal to each other. All the items which in practice distinguish them from one another result from depreciation, net foreign factor income earned in the United States, government (taxes and transfer payments), and business saving (see Table 7-4). Our assumptions mean that if $500 billion of goods and services is produced as GDP, exactly $500 billion of DI is received by households to use as either consumption or saving.

TOOLS OF THE AGGREGATE EXPENDITURES MODEL

The aggregate expenditures model embodies the following basic theory regarding the macroeconomy:

The amount of goods and services produced and therefore the level of employment depend directly on the level of total or aggregate expenditures. Businesses will produce a level of output they can profitably sell. Workers and machinery are idled when there are no markets for the goods and services they can produce. Total output and employment decrease when the level of aggregate expenditures decreases, and they increase when it increases.

Our strategy in this chapter is to analyze the consumption and investment components of aggregate expenditures and derive a private sector model of equilibrium GDP and employment. Chapter 10 examines changes in real GDP and adds net exports and government expenditures (along with taxes) to the model.

As we begin our discussion, be sure you understand that we are assuming the economy has substantial excess production capacity and unemployed labor (unless specified otherwise). An increase in aggregate expenditures will thus increase real output and employment but *not* the price level.

QUICK REVIEW 9-1

■ Classical macroeconomics was grounded in Say's law, which asserted that supply creates its own demand and therefore underspending leading to recessions was unlikely.

■ The Great Depression and Keynes' development of an alternative model of the macroeconomy undermined classical macroeconomics and led to the modern aggregate expenditures theory.

■ In the aggregate expenditures model, the level of total or aggregate expenditures determines the amount of output produced which in turn establishes the level of employment.

CONSUMPTION AND SAVING

In terms of absolute size, consumption is the largest component of aggregate expenditures. We therefore need to understand the determinants of consumption spending. Recall that economists define personal saving as "not spending" or "that part of disposable income (DI) not consumed." In other words, saving equals disposable income less consumption. Thus, in examining the determinants of consumption we are also exploring the determinants of saving.

Income-Consumption and Income-Saving Relationships

Many factors influence the level of consumer spending. But the most significant determinant is income—in particular, disposable income. And, since saving is that part of disposable income not consumed, DI is also the basic determinant of personal saving.

Consider some recent historical data. In Figure 9-1 each green dot represents consumption and disposable income for 1 year since 1973. The green line, fitted to these points, shows that consumption is directly related to disposable income; moreover, households clearly spend most of their incomes.

But we can say more. The black 45 degree line is added to the diagram as a reference line. Because this line bisects the 90 degree angle formed by the vertical and horizontal axes of the graph, each point on the line must be equidistant from the two axes. That is, each point on the line represents a situation in which consumption equals disposable income, or C = DI. We can therefore regard the vertical distance from any point on the horizontal axis to the 45 degree line as measuring either consumption *or* disposable income. If we regard it as measuring disposable income, then the vertical distance by which actual consumption in any year falls short of the 45 degree line represents the amount of saving in that year. For example, in 1993 consumption was \$4459 billion, and disposable income was \$4829 billion; hence, saving in 1993 was \$370 billion. Disposable income less consumption equals saving, or DI − C = S. By observing these vertical distances as we move to the left or to the right in Figure 9-1, we see that saving also varies directly with the level of disposable income: As DI increases, saving increases; as DI decreases, saving decreases.

Figure 9-1 thus suggests that (1) households consume most of their disposable incomes, and (2) both consumption and saving are directly related to the income level.

The Consumption Schedule

The dots in Figure 9-1 represent historical data—how much households *actually had as DI* and *actually did consume* (and save) over a period of years. Those data are useful for finding the relationship between DI and consumption and saving. But to build our model, we need a schedule which tells us the various amounts households would *plan* to consume at each

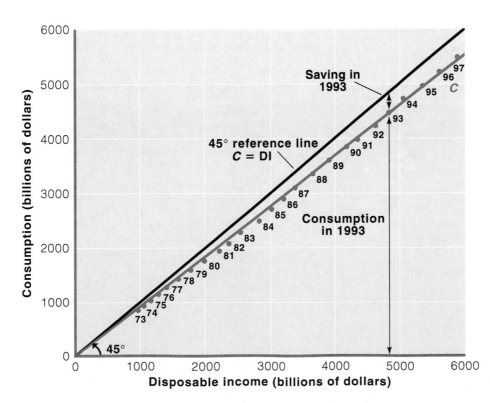

FIGURE 9-1 Consumption and disposable income, 1973–1997 Each dot in this figure shows consumption and disposable income in a specific year. The line C generalizes the relationship between consumption and disposable income. It indicates a direct relationship and shows that households consume the bulk of their incomes.

----

of various levels of disposable income which could prevail at *some specific time*. A hypothetical **consumption schedule** of the type we require is shown in columns 1 and 2, Table 9-1, and is plotted in **Figure 9-2a (Key Graph).** This consumption schedule reflects the direct consumption–disposable income relationship suggested by the empirical data in Figure 9-1, and it is consistent with many empirical household budget studies. Households tend to spend a *larger proportion* of a small disposable income than of a large disposable income.

The Saving Schedule

It is simple to derive a **saving schedule.** Because saving equals disposable income *less* consumption ($S = DI - C$), we need only subtract consumption (Table 9-1, column 2) from disposable income (column 1) to find the amount saved (column 3) at each DI. Thus, columns 1 and 3 in Table 9-1 are the saving schedule, plotted in Figure 9-2b. Note that there is a direct relationship between saving and DI but that saving is a smaller proportion (fraction) of a small DI than of a large DI. If households consume a smaller and smaller proportion of DI as DI increases, then they must save a larger and larger proportion.

Remembering that at each point on the 45 degree line consumption equals DI, we see that *dissaving* (consuming in excess of after-tax income) will occur at relatively low DIs like $370 billion (row 1, Table 9-1), where consumption is actually $375 billion. Households can consume more than their incomes by liquidating (selling for cash) accumulated wealth or by borrowing. Graphically, dissaving is shown as the vertical distance of the consumption schedule *above* the 45 degree line or as the vertical distance of the saving schedule *below* the horizontal axis. Dissaving at the $370 billion level of income is marked in Figure 9-2a and b. Each of the two vertical distances measures the $5 billion of dissaving occurring at the $370 billion income level.

In our example, the **break-even income** is $390 billion (row 2). This is the income level where households plan to consume their entire incomes ($C = DI$). Graphically, the consumption schedule cuts the 45 degree line, and the saving schedule cuts the horizontal axis (saving is zero) at the break-even income level.

At all higher incomes, households plan to save part of their incomes. Graphically, the vertical distance of the consumption schedule *below* the 45 degree line measures this saving, as does the vertical distance of the saving schedule *above* the horizontal axis. For example, at the $410 billion level of income (row 3), both these distances indicate $5 billion worth of saving (see Figure 9-2a and b).

TABLE 9-1 Consumption and saving schedules (in billions) and propensities to consume and save

(1) Level of output and income (GDP = DI)	(2) Consumption (C)	(3) Saving (S) (1) − (2)	(4) Average propensity to consume (APC) (2)/(1)	(5) Average propensity to save (APS) (3)/(1)	(6) Marginal propensity to consume (MPC) Δ(2)/Δ(1)*	(7) Marginal propensity to save (MPS) Δ(3)/Δ(1)*
(1) $370	$375	$−5	1.01	−.01		
(2) 390	390	0	1.00	.00	.75	.25
(3) 410	405	5	.99	.01	.75	.25
(4) 430	420	10	.98	.02	.75	.25
(5) 450	435	15	.97	.03	.75	.25
(6) 470	450	20	.96	.04	.75	.25
(7) 490	465	25	.95	.05	.75	.25
(8) 510	480	30	.94	.06	.75	.25
(9) 530	495	35	.93	.07	.75	.25
(10) 550	510	40	.93	.07	.75	.25

* The Greek letter Δ, delta, means "the change in."

(a) Consumption schedule

(b) Saving schedule

FIGURE 9-2 (a) Consumption and (b) saving schedules The two parts of this figure show the income-consumption and income-saving relationships in Table 9-1 graphically. The saving schedule in (b) is found by subtracting the consumption schedule in (a) vertically from the 45 degree line. Consumption equals disposable income (and saving thus equals zero) at $390 billion for these hypothetical data.

QUICK QUIZ 9-2

1. **The slope of the consumption schedule in this figure is .75. Thus, the**
   a. slope of the saving schedule is 1.33.
   b. marginal propensity to consume is .75.
   c. average propensity to consume is .25.
   d. slope of the saving schedule is also .75.

2. **In this figure, when consumption is a positive amount, saving**
   a. must be a negative amount.
   b. also must be a positive amount.
   c. can be either a positive or a negative amount.
   d. is zero.

3. **In this figure,**
   a. the marginal propensity to consume is constant at all levels of income.

   b. the marginal propensity to save rises as disposable income rises.
   c. consumption is inversely (negatively) related to disposable income.
   d. saving is inversely (negatively) related to disposable income.

4. **When consumption equals disposable income,**
   a. the marginal propensity to consume is zero.
   b. the average propensity to consume is zero.
   c. consumption and saving must be equal.
   d. saving must be zero.

Answers: 1. b; 2. c; 3. a; 4. d

Average and Marginal Propensities

Columns 4 to 7 in Table 9-1 show additional characteristics of the consumption and saving schedules.

APC and APS   The fraction, or percentage, of any total income which is consumed is called the **average propensity to consume** (APC). The fraction of any total income which is saved is the **average propensity to save** (APS). That is,

$$APC = \frac{consumption}{income}$$

and

$$APS = \frac{saving}{income}$$

For example, at the $470 billion level of income (row 6) in Table 9-1, the APC is $\frac{450}{470} = \frac{45}{47}$, or about 96 percent, while the APS is $\frac{20}{470} = \frac{2}{47}$, or about 4 percent. Columns 4 and 5 in Table 9-1 show the APC and APS at each of the 10 levels of DI; note there that the APC falls and the APS rises as DI increases. This is another way of stating a point we just made: The fraction of total DI which is consumed declines as DI rises, and the fraction of DI which is saved rises as DI increases.

Because disposable income is either consumed or saved, the fraction of any DI consumed plus the fraction saved (not consumed) must exhaust that income. Mathematically, APC + APS = 1 at any level of disposable income. Columns 4 and 5 in Table 9-1 illustrate this.

Global Perspective 9-1 shows APCs for several countries.

MPC and MPS   The fact that households consume a certain proportion of some total income—for example, $\frac{45}{47}$ of a $470 billion disposable income—does not guarantee they will consume the same proportion of any *change* in income they might receive. The proportion, or fraction, of any change in income consumed is called the **marginal propensity to consume** (MPC), marginal meaning "extra" or "a change in." Equivalently, the MPC is the ratio of a *change* in consumption to the *change* in income which caused that change in consumption:

$$MPC = \frac{change\ in\ consumption}{change\ in\ income}$$

Similarly, the fraction of any change in income saved is the **marginal propensity to save** (MPS). The MPS

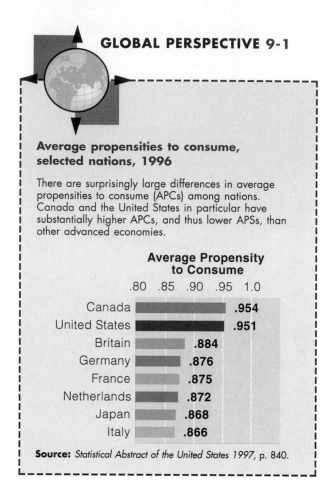

is the ratio of a *change* in saving to the *change* in income bringing it about:

$$MPS = \frac{change\ in\ saving}{change\ in\ income}$$

If disposable income is $470 billion (row 6 in Table 9-1) and household incomes rise by $20 billion to $490 billion (row 7), households will consume $\frac{15}{20}$, or $\frac{3}{4}$, and save $\frac{5}{20}$, or $\frac{1}{4}$, of that *increase in income*. In other words, the MPC is $\frac{3}{4}$ or .75, and the MPS is $\frac{1}{4}$ or .25, as shown in columns 6 and 7.

The sum of the MPC and the MPS for any change in disposable income must always be 1. Consuming and saving out of extra income is an either-or proposition; the fraction of any change in income not consumed is, by definition, saved. Therefore the fraction consumed (MPC) plus the fraction saved (MPS) must exhaust the whole change in income:

MPC + MPS = 1

In our example .75 plus .25 equals 1.

MPC and MPS as Slopes The MPC is the numerical value of the slope of the consumption schedule, and the MPS is the numerical value of the slope of the saving schedule. We know from the appendix to Chapter 1 that the slope of any line is the ratio of the vertical change to the horizontal change involved in moving from one point to another on that line.

In Figure 9-3 we measure the slopes of the consumption and saving lines, using enlarged portions of Figures 9-2a and 9-2b. Observe that consumption changes by $15 billion (vertical change) for each $20 billion change in disposable income (horizontal change); the slope of the consumption line is thus .75 (= $15/$20)—the value of the MPC. Saving changes by $5 billion (vertical change) for every $20 billion change in disposable income (horizontal

change). The slope of the saving line therefore is .25 (= $5/$20), which is the value of the MPS. **(Key Question 6)**

Nonincome Determinants of Consumption and Saving

The level of disposable income is the basic determinant of the amounts households will consume and save, just as price is the basic determinant of the quantity demanded of a single product. Recall that changes in determinants other than price, such as consumer tastes or incomes, will shift the demand curve for a product. Similarly, certain determinants other than income might cause households to consume more or less at each possible level of income and thereby change the locations of the consumption and saving schedules. These other determinants are wealth, expectations, indebtedness, and taxation.

Wealth Generally, the greater the wealth households have accumulated, the larger the amount of consumption and the smaller the amount of saving out of any level of current income. By "wealth" we mean both real assets (a house, automobiles, television sets, and other durables) and financial assets (cash, savings accounts, stocks, bonds, insurance policies, pensions) which households own. Households save—refrain from consumption—to accumulate wealth. The more wealth households have accumulated, the weaker the incentive to save in order to accumulate additional wealth. An increase in wealth thus shifts the saving schedule downward and the consumption schedule upward.

Examples: The dramatic stock market crash of 1929 significantly decreased the financial wealth of many families almost overnight and was a factor in the low levels of consumption in the depressed 1930s. More recently, the general decline in real estate values during 1989 and 1990 eroded household wealth and contributed to a reduction of consumer spending.

For the most part, however, the amount of wealth held by households changes only modestly from year to year and therefore does not account for large shifts in the consumption and saving schedules.

Expectations Household expectations about future prices, money incomes, and the availability of goods may significantly affect current spending and saving. Expectations of rising prices and product shortages tomorrow may trigger more spending and less saving

FIGURE 9-3 The marginal propensity to consume and the marginal propensity to save The MPC is the slope (= ΔC/ΔDI) of the consumption schedule, and the MPS is the slope (= ΔS/ΔDI) of the saving schedule. The Δ means "change in."

today. This shifts the consumption schedule upward and the saving schedule downward.

Household Debt

In drawing a particular consumption schedule, we assume that household debt as a percentage of DI is constant. When consumers as a group increase their household debt, they can increase current consumption. Increased borrowing enables consumers to increase consumption at each level of DI; it shifts the consumption schedule upward. However, when levels of household debt get abnormally high, households may elect to reduce their consumption to pay off some of their loans. At that time, the consumption schedule shifts downward.

Taxation

When we add government to our analysis (Chapter 10), the convenient equality between GDP and DI breaks down. At that stage, we plot consumption and saving against GDP (not DI). You will then see that changes in taxes will shift the consumption and saving schedules. Taxes are paid partly at the expense of consumption and partly at the expense of saving. Therefore, an increase in taxes will shift both the consumption *and* saving schedules downward. Conversely, a tax reduction will be partly consumed and partly saved by households. A tax decrease will shift both the consumption *and* saving schedules upward.

Shifts and Stability

Three final points regarding the consumption and saving schedules are relevant:

1. *Terminology* The movement from one point to another on a stable consumption schedule (for example, from *a* to *b* on C_0 in Figure 9-4a) is called a *change in the amount consumed*. The sole cause of this change in consumption is a change in disposable income (or, later, GDP). On the other hand, a *change in the consumption schedule* refers to an upward or downward shift of the entire schedule—for example, a shift from C_0 to C_1 or C_2 in Figure 9-4a. A shift of the consumption schedule is caused by changes in any one or more of the four nonincome determinants just discussed.

    A similar distinction in terminology applies to the saving schedule in Figure 9-4b.

2. *Schedule shifts* The first three nonincome determinants of consumption (wealth, expectations, and household debt) will shift the consumption

schedule in one direction and the saving schedule in the opposite direction. If households decide to consume more at each possible level of disposable income, they want to save less, and vice versa. (Even when they spend more by borrowing, they are, in effect, reducing their current saving by the amount borrowed.) Graphically, if the consumption schedule shifts upward from C_0 to C_1 in Figure 9-4, the saving schedule will shift downward, from S_0 to S_1. Similarly, a downshift in the

(a) Consumption schedule

(b) Saving schedule

FIGURE 9-4 Shifts in the (a) consumption and (b) saving schedules Normally, if households consume more at each level of DI, they are necessarily saving less. Graphically this means that an upshift of the consumption schedule (C_0 to C_1) entails a downshift of the saving schedule (S_0 to S_1). If households consume less at each level of DI, they are saving more. A downshift of the consumption schedule (C_0 to C_2) is reflected in an upshift of the saving schedule (S_0 to S_2). (This pattern breaks down, however, when increases in consumption result from increased borrowing or when a shift in the consumption schedule results from a change in taxes.)

consumption schedule from C_0 to C_2 means an upshift in the saving schedule from S_0 to S_2.

The exception to the above generalization involves the fourth nonincome determinant: taxation. We have seen that households will consume less *and* save less when they must pay higher taxes. Thus, a tax increase will lower both the consumption *and* saving schedules, while a tax cut will shift both schedules upward.

3. *Stability* Although changes in nonincome determinants can shift the consumption and saving schedules, in practice these schedules are quite stable. Only significant increases or decreases in taxes have a major impact on the location of the schedules. Their stability may be because consumption-saving decisions are strongly influenced by *long-term* considerations such as saving to meet emergencies or saving for retirement. It may also be because changes in the nonincome determinants frequently work in opposite directions and therefore may be self-canceling.

QUICK REVIEW 9-2

■ Consumption spending and saving both rise when disposable income increases; they fall when disposable income decreases.

■ The average propensity to consume (APC) is the fraction of any specific level of disposable income which is spent on consumer goods; the average propensity to save (APS) is the fraction of any specific level of disposable income which is saved. The APC falls and the APS rises as disposable income increases.

■ The marginal propensity to consume (MPC) is the fraction of any change in disposable income which is consumed and is the slope of the consumption schedule; the marginal propensity to save (MPS) is the fraction of any change in disposable income which is saved and is the slope of the saving schedule.

■ Changes in consumer wealth, consumer expectations, household debt, and taxes can shift the consumption and saving schedules.

INVESTMENT

We now turn to investment, the second component of private spending. Recall that investment consists of expenditures on new plants, capital equipment, machinery, and so on. The investment decision is a marginal-benefit–marginal-cost decision: The mar-

ginal benefit from investment is the expected rate of return businesses hope to realize. The marginal cost is the interest rate which must be paid for borrowing funds. We will see that businesses will invest in all projects for which the expected rate of return exceeds the interest rate. Expected returns (profits) and the interest rate therefore are the two basic determinants of investment spending.

Expected Rate of Return

Investment spending is guided by the profit motive; businesses buy capital goods only when they expect such purchases to be profitable. Suppose the owner of a small cabinetmaking shop is considering investing in a new sanding machine costing $1000 and having a useful life of only 1 year. The new machine will presumably increase the firm's output and sales revenue. Suppose the *net* expected revenue from the machine (that is, after such operating costs as power, lumber, labor, and certain taxes have been subtracted) is $1100. Then, after operating costs have been accounted for, the remaining expected net revenue is sufficient to cover the $1000 cost of the machine and leave a profit of $100. Comparing this $100 profit with the $1000 cost of the machine, we find that the **expected rate of return,** r, on the machine is 10 percent (= $100/$1000).

The Real Interest Rate

One important cost associated with investing which our example has so far ignored is interest—the financial cost of borrowing the *money* capital required to purchase the *real* capital (the sanding machine).

To include the interest cost, we note that it is computed by applying the interest rate, i, to the amount borrowed—the cost of the machine. The cost of the machine is the same amount that we used to compute the rate of return, r. Thus, we can generalize as follows: If the expected rate of return (say, 10 percent) exceeds the interest rate (say, 7 percent), the investment will be profitable. But if the interest rate (say, 12 percent) exceeds the expected rate of return (10 percent), the investment will be unprofitable. The firm should undertake all profitable investment projects. That means it should invest to the point where $r = i$, since then it has undertaken all investment for which r exceeds i.

But what if the firm does *not* borrow, instead financing the investment internally out of funds saved from past profits? The role of the interest rate in investing in real capital does not change. When the firm uses money from savings to invest in the sander, it incurs an opportunity cost because it forgoes the interest income it could have earned by lending the funds to someone else.

The *real* rate of interest, rather than the nominal rate, is crucial in making investment decisions. Recall from Chapter 8 that the nominal interest rate is expressed in dollars of current value, while the real interest rate is stated in dollars of constant or inflation-adjusted value. The real interest rate is the nominal rate less the rate of inflation. In our sanding machine illustration we have implicitly assumed a constant price level so that all our data, including the interest rate, are in real terms.

But what if inflation *is* occurring? Suppose a $1000 investment is expected to yield a real (inflation-adjusted) rate of return of 10 percent and the nominal interest rate is 15 percent. At first, we would say the investment will be unprofitable. But assume there is ongoing inflation of 10 percent per year. This means the investing firm will pay back dollars with approximately 10 percent less in purchasing power. While the nominal interest rate is 15 percent, the real rate is only 5 percent (= 15 percent − 10 percent). Comparing this 5 percent real interest rate with the 10 percent expected real rate of return, we find that the investment *is* profitable and should be undertaken.

Investment Demand Curve

We now move from a single firm's investment decision to total demand for investment goods by the entire business sector. Assume every firm has estimated the expected rates of return from all investment projects and these data have been collected. The data can be *cumulated*—successively summed—by asking: How many dollars' worth of investment projects have an expected rate of return of, say, 16 percent or more? Of 14 percent or more? Of 12 percent or more? And so on.

Suppose there are no prospective investments yielding an expected return of 16 percent or more. But there are $5 billion of investment opportunities with expected rates of return between 14 and 16 percent; an *additional* $5 billion yielding between 12 and 14 percent; still an *additional* $5 billion yielding between 10 and 12 percent; and an *additional* $5 billion in each successive 2 percent range of yield down to and including the 0 to 2 percent range.

To cumulate these figures for each rate of return, *r*, we add the amounts of investment which will yield *that particular rate of return* r *or higher.* This way we obtain the data in Table 9-2, shown graphically in **Figure 9-5 (Key Graph).** In Table 9-2 the number opposite 12 percent, for example, tells us there are $10 billion of investment opportunities which yield an expected rate of return of 12 percent *or more.* The $10 billion includes the $5 billion of investment expected to yield a return of 14 percent or more *plus* the $5 billion expected to yield between 12 and 14 percent.

We know from our example of the sanding machine that an investment project will be profitable, and will be undertaken, if its expected rate of return, *r*, exceeds the real interest rate, *i*. Let's first suppose *i* is 12 percent. Businesses will undertake all investments for which *r* exceeds 12 percent. That is, they will invest until the 12 percent rate of return *equals* the 12 percent interest rate. Figure 9-5 reveals that $10 billion of investment spending will be undertaken at a 12 percent interest rate; that means $10 billion of investment projects have an expected rate of return of 12 percent or more.

Put another way: At a financial "price" of 12 percent, $10 billion of investment goods will be demanded. If the interest rate is lower, say, 8 percent, the amount of investment for which *r* equals or exceeds *i* is $20 billion. Thus, firms will demand $20 billion of investment goods at an 8 percent real interest rate. At 6 percent, they will demand $25 billion of investment goods.

TABLE 9-2 **Rates of expected return and investment**

Expected rate of return (r)	Cumulative amount of investment having this rate of return or higher, billions per year
16%	$ 0
14	5
12	10
10	15
8	20
6	25
4	30
2	35
0	40

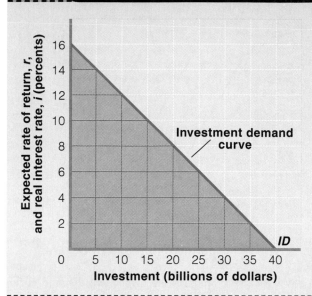

FIGURE 9-5 The investment demand curve The investment demand curve is constructed by arraying all potential investment projects in descending order of their expected rates of return. The curve is downsloping, reflecting an inverse relationship between the real interest rate (the financial "price" of each dollar of investing) and the quantity of investment demanded.

QUICK QUIZ 9-5

1. **The investment demand curve:**
   a. reflects a direct (positive) relationship between the real interest rate and investment.
   b. reflects an inverse (negative) relationship between the real interest rate and investment.
   c. shifts to the right when the real interest rate rises.
   d. shifts to the left when the real interest rate rises.

2. **In this figure:**
   a. greater cumulative amounts of investment are associated with lower expected rates of return on investment.
   b. lesser cumulative amounts of investment are associated with lower expected rates of return on investment.
   c. higher interest rates are associated with higher expected rates of return on investment, and therefore greater amounts of investment.
   d. interest rates and investment move in the same direction.

3. **In this figure, if the real interest rate falls from 6 to 4 percent:**
   a. investment will increase from 0 to $30 billion.
   b. investment will decrease by $5 billion.
   c. the expected rate of return will rise by $5 billion.
   d. investment will increase from $25 billion to $30 billion.

4. **In this figure, investment will be:**
   a. zero if the real interest rate was zero.
   b. $40 billion if the real interest rate was 16 percent.
   c. $30 billion if the real interest rate was 4 percent.
   d. $20 billion if the real interest rate was 12 percent.

Answers: 1. b; 2. a; 3. d; 4. c

By applying the marginal-benefit–marginal-cost rule that investment projects should be undertaken up to the point where $r = i$, we see that we can add the real interest rate to the vertical axis in Figure 9-5. The curve in Figure 9-5 not only shows rates of return, it shows the quantity of investment demanded at each "price" i of investment. Various possible real interest rates are shown on the vertical axis in Figure 9-5 and the corresponding quantities of investment demanded on the horizontal axis. The inverse (downsloping) relationship between the interest rate (price) and dollar quantity of investment demanded is consistent with the *law of demand* discussed in Chapter 3. The curve labeled *ID* in Figure 9-5 is the economy's **investment demand curve.** It shows the amount of investment forthcoming at each real interest rate.

This analysis of investment allows us to anticipate an important aspect of macroeconomic policy. You will find in our discussion of monetary policy (Chapter

15) that by changing the supply of money, government can change the interest rate. It does this primarily to change the level of investment spending. At any time, firms have a variety of investment projects under consideration. If real interest rates are high, only projects with the highest expected rates of return will be undertaken. The level of investment will be low. As the real interest rate is lowered, projects whose expected rates of return are less will also become potentially profitable and investment in them will rise. To fight recession, government reduces interest rates; to fight inflation, government increases interest rates. **(Key Question 8)**

Shifts in the Investment Demand Curve

Figure 9-5 portrays the interest-rate–amount-of-investment relationship, *other things equal*. When these other things change, the investment-demand curve shifts to the right or to the left. In general, any factor which leads businesses collectively to expect greater rates of return on their investments will increase investment demand; that factor will shift the investment demand curve to the right, as from ID_0 to ID_1 in Figure 9-6. Any factor which leads businesses collectively to expect lower rates of return on their investments will shift the curve to the left, as from ID_0 to ID_2. What are these non-interest-rate determinants of investment demand?

Acquisition, Maintenance, and Operating Costs
As the sanding machine example revealed, the initial costs of capital goods, and the estimated costs of operating and maintaining those goods, affect the expected rate of return on investment. When costs fall, the expected rate of return from prospective investment projects will rise, shifting the investment demand curve to the right. Example: Lower electricity costs associated with running equipment would shift the investment demand curve to the right. Higher costs, in contrast, will shift the curve to the left.

Business Taxes
Business owners look to expected returns *after taxes* in making their investment decisions. An increase in business taxes will lower the expected profitability of investments and shift the investment demand curve to the left; a tax reduction will shift it to the right.

Technological Change
Technological progress—the development of new products, improvements in

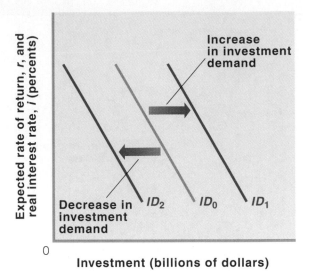

FIGURE 9-6 Shifts in the investment demand curve
Increases in investment demand are shown as rightward shifts in the investment demand curve; decreases in investment demand are shown as leftward shifts in the investment demand curve.

existing products, and the creation of new machinery and production processes—stimulates investment. The development of a more efficient machine, for example, will lower production costs or improve product quality, increasing the expected rate of return from investing in the machine. Profitable new products—mountain bikes, sports utility vehicles, high-resolution televisions, cellular phones, and so on—induce a flurry of investment as firms tool up for expanded production. A rapid rate of technological progress shifts the investment demand curve to the right.

Stock of Capital Goods on Hand
The stock of capital goods on hand, relative to output and sales, influences investment decisions by firms. When the economy is *overstocked* with production facilities and firms have excessive inventories of finished goods, the expected rate of return on new investment declines. Firms with excess production capacity have little incentive to invest in new capital. Therefore, less investment is forthcoming at each real interest rate; the investment demand curve shifts to the left.

When the economy is *understocked* with production facilities and firms are selling their output as fast as it can be produced, the expected rate of return on new investment increases. Firms add to their production facilities to meet the growing demand for their products and services. So the investment demand curve shifts to the right.

Expectations We noted that business investment is based on *expected* returns (expected additions to profit). Capital goods are durable; they have a life expectancy of 10 or 20 years. Thus, the expected rate of return on any capital investment will depend on the firm's expectations of *future* sales, *future* operating costs, and *future* profitability of the product which the capital helps to produce. These expectations are based on forecasts of future business conditions as well as on such elusive and difficult-to-predict factors as changes in the domestic political climate, the thrust of foreign affairs, population growth, and consumer tastes. If executives become more optimistic about future sales, costs, and profits, the investment demand curve will shift to the right; a pessimistic outlook will shift it to the left.

Global Perspective 9-2 compares investment spending relative to GDP for several nations in a recent year. Domestic interest rates and investment demand determine the levels of investment relative to GDP.

QUICK REVIEW 9-3

■ A specific investment will be undertaken if the expected rate of return, *r*, equals or exceeds the real interest rate, *i*.

■ The investment demand curve shows the total monetary amounts which will be invested by an economy at various possible real interest rates.

■ The investment demand curve shifts when changes occur in **(a)** the costs of acquiring, operating, and maintaining capital goods, **(b)** business taxes, **(c)**, technology, **(d)** the stock of capital goods on hand, and **(e)** business expectations.

Investment Schedule

To add the investment decisions of businesses to the consumption plans of households, we must express investment plans in terms of the level of disposable income (DI) or gross domestic product (GDP). That is, we need to construct an **investment schedule** showing the amounts business firms collectively intend to invest at each possible level of GDP. Such a schedule represents the investment plans of businesses in the same way the consumption and saving schedules represent the consumption and saving plans of households. In developing the investment schedule, we will assume that investment is *independent* of the level of current disposable income or real output.

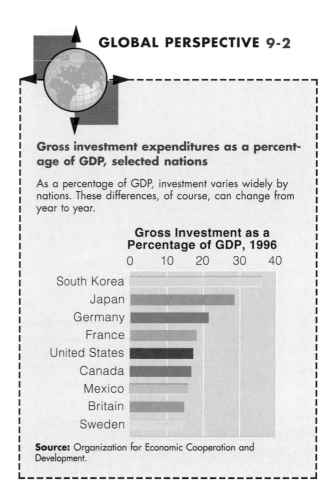

GLOBAL PERSPECTIVE 9-2

Gross investment expenditures as a percentage of GDP, selected nations

As a percentage of GDP, investment varies widely by nations. These differences, of course, can change from year to year.

Gross Investment as a Percentage of GDP, 1996

South Korea
Japan
Germany
France
United States
Canada
Mexico
Britain
Sweden

Source: Organization for Economic Cooperation and Development.

Suppose the investment demand curve is as shown in Figure 9-7a and the current real interest rate is 8 percent. This means that firms will find it profitable to spend $20 billion on investment goods. Our assumption tells us that this $20 billion of investment will occur at both low and high levels of GDP. The line I_g (*gross* investment) in Figure 9-7b shows this graphically; it is the economy's *investment schedule*. You should not confuse this investment schedule I_g with the investment demand curve *ID* in Figure 9-7a. The investment schedule shows the amount of investment forthcoming at each level of GDP. As indicated in Figure 9-7, this amount ($20 billion) is determined by the interest rate together with the location of the investment demand curve. Table 9-3 shows the investment schedule in tabular form for the GDP levels in Table 9-1.

The assumed independence of investment and income is admittedly a simplification. A higher level of

(a) Investment demand curve

(b) Investment schedule

FIGURE 9-7 **(a) The investment demand curve and (b) the investment schedule**   (a) The level of investment spending (here, $20 billion) is determined by the real interest rate (here, 8 percent) together with the investment demand curve ID. (b) The investment schedule I_g relates the amount of investment ($20 billion) determined in (a) to the various levels of GDP.

business activity may *induce* additional spending on capital facilities for at least two reasons:

1. Investment is related to profit; much investment is financed internally out of business profits. Therefore, it is plausible that as GDP rises, so will business profits and therefore the level of investment.

2. At low levels of income and output, the business sector has excess production capacity; many industries have idle machinery and equipment and therefore little incentive to purchase additional capital goods. But, as the level of domestic income and output rises, this excess capacity disappears and firms are inclined to add to their stock of capital goods.

Instability of Investment

In contrast to the consumption schedule, the investment schedule is unstable; it shifts significantly upward or downward quite often. Investment, in fact, is the most volatile component of total spending. Figure 9-8 shows just how volatile investment has been. Note that its swings are much greater than are those of GDP. The figure also suggests that our simplified treatment of investment as independent of GDP (Figure 9-7b) is essentially realistic; investment does not closely follow GDP.

Factors explaining the variability of investment follow:

Durability   Because of their durability, capital goods have an indefinite useful life. Within limits, purchases of capital goods are discretionary and therefore postponable. Older equipment and buildings can be scrapped and replaced, or they can be patched up and

TABLE 9-3   **The investment schedule (in billions)**

(1) Level of real output and income	(2) Investment (I_g)
$370	$20
390	20
410	20
430	20
450	20
470	20
490	20
510	20
530	20
550	20

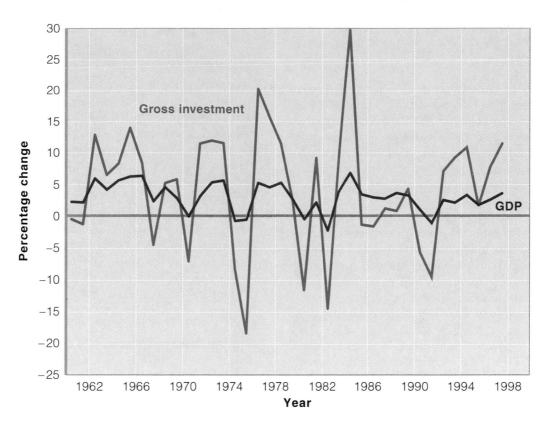

FIGURE 9-8 The volatility of investment Annual percentage changes in investment spending are often several times greater than the percentage changes in GDP. (Data are in real terms.)

used for a few more years. Optimism about the future may prompt firms to replace their older facilities; modernizing their plants will call for a high level of investment. A less optimistic view, however, may lead to very small amounts of investment as older facilities are repaired and kept in use.

Irregularity of Innovation We know that technological progress is a major determinant of investment. New products and processes stimulate investment. But history suggests that major innovations— railroads, electricity, automobiles, fiber optics, and computers—occur quite irregularly. When they do occur, they induce a vast upsurge or "wave" of investment spending which in time recedes.

A classic illustration is the widespread acceptance of the automobile in the 1920s. This event not only substantially increased investment in the automobile industry itself but also induced tremendous investment in such related industries as steel, petroleum, glass, and rubber as well as public investment in streets

and highways. But when investment in these related industries was ultimately "completed"—when enough capital facilities had been created to meet the needs of the automobile industry—total investment leveled off.

Variability of Profits Businesses invest only when they think it will be profitable, and to a significant degree, the expectation of future profitability is influenced by the size of current profits. Current profits, however, are themselves highly variable (line 13 of the table on the inside covers provides information on undistributed corporate profits). Thus, the variability of profits contributes to the volatile nature of the incentive to invest.

The instability of profits may also cause investment fluctuations in a second way. Profits are a major source of funds for business investment. U.S. businesses often prefer this internal source of financing to increases in external debt or stock issue.

In short, expanding profits give firms both greater *incentives* and greater *means* to invest; declining profits have the reverse effects. The fact that actual profits are variable thus adds doubly to the instability of investment.

Variability of Expectations   Firms tend to project current business conditions into the future. But their expectations can change radically and quickly when some event suggests a possible dramatic change in future business conditions. Changes in the domestic political climate, changes in exchange rates, changes in the outlook for international peace, court decisions in key labor or antitrust cases, legislative actions, changes in trade barriers, changes in governmental economic policies, and a host of similar considerations may cause substantial shifts in business optimism or pessimism.

The stock market requires specific comment in this regard. Firms frequently look to the stock market as an indicator of society's overall confidence in future business conditions. Rising stock prices signify public confidence in the business future, while falling stock prices imply a lack of confidence. The stock market, however, is highly speculative. Participants who jump in and buy when stock prices begin to rise, or sell as soon as prices start to fall, can seriously magnify initially modest changes in stock prices. The volatility of this market can produce swings in optimism and pessimism, thus adding to the instability of investment spending. This stock market effect on investment, however, has proved to be relatively mild in the past several decades.

For the reasons we just discussed, changes in investment cause most fluctuations in output and employment. We can think of the volatility of investment shown in Figure 9-8 as being reflected in occasional and substantial upward and downward shifts of the investment schedule in Figure 9-7b, caused by occasional and substantial rightward and leftward shifts of the investment demand schedule in Figure 9-7a.

EQUILIBRIUM GDP: EXPENDITURES-OUTPUT APPROACH

In this and the next section, we use the consumption, saving, and investment schedules to explain the equilibrium levels of output, income, and employment. We will do so first by taking the **aggregate expenditures–domestic output** (or $C + I_g = $ GDP) **approach.**

Tabular Analysis

Columns 2 through 5 in Table 9-4 repeat the consumption and saving schedules in Table 9-1 and the investment schedule in Table 9-3.

Real Domestic Output   Let's look again at column 2, Table 9-4. It lists the various possible levels of total output—of real GDP—the business sector might produce. *Producers are willing to offer any of these 10 levels of output if they can expect to receive an identical level of income from the sale of that output.* For example, the business sector will produce $370 billion of output, incurring $370 billion of costs (wages, rents, interest, and profit) only if firms believe they can sell this output for $370 billion. Some $390 billion of output will be offered for sale if firms think they can sell this output for $390 billion. And so it is for all the other possible levels of output.

Aggregate Expenditures   In our assumed private closed economy in Table 9-4, aggregate expenditures consist of consumption (column 3) plus investment (column 5). Their sum is shown in column 6, which with column 2 makes up the **aggregate expenditures schedule** for the economy. This schedule shows the amount $(C + I_g)$ which will be spent at each possible output or income level.

At this point we are working with *planned investment*—the data in column 5, Table 9-4. These data show the amounts firms *intend* to invest, not the amounts which *actually will be invested* if there are unplanned changes in inventories.

Equilibrium GDP   Of the 10 possible levels of GDP in Table 9-4, which will be the equilibrium level? Which total output will the economy be capable of sustaining?

The equilibrium output is that output whose production will create total spending just sufficient to purchase that output. So the equilibrium level of GDP is the level where the total quantity of goods produced (GDP) equals the total quantity of goods purchased $(C + I_g)$. Look at the domestic output levels in column 2 and the aggregate expenditures levels in column 6 and you will see that this equality exists only at $470 billion of GDP (row 6). That is the only output at which the economy is willing to spend precisely the amount necessary to take that output from the shelves. There, the annual rates of production and spending are in balance. There is no overproduction,

TABLE 9-4   Determination of the equilibrium levels of employment, output, and income: a closed private economy

(1) Possible levels of employment, millions	(2) Real domestic output (and income) (GDP = DI),* billions	(3) Consumption (C), billions	(4) Saving (S), billions	(5) Investment (I_g), billions	(6) Aggregate expenditures (C + I_g), billions	(7) Unintended investment (+) or disinvestment (−) in inventories	(8) Tendency of employment, output, and incomes
(1) 40	$370	$375	$−5	$20	$395	$−25	Increase
(2) 45	390	390	0	20	410	−20	Increase
(3) 50	410	405	5	20	425	−15	Increase
(4) 55	430	420	10	20	440	−10	Increase
(5) 60	450	435	15	20	455	−5	Increase
(6) **65**	**470**	**450**	**20**	**20**	**470**	**0**	**Equilibrium**
(7) 70	490	465	25	20	485	+5	Decrease
(8) 75	510	480	30	20	500	+10	Decrease
(9) 80	530	495	35	20	515	+15	Decrease
(10) 85	550	510	40	20	530	+20	Decrease

*If depreciation and net foreign factor income earned in the United States are zero, government is ignored, and it is assumed that all saving occurs in the household sector of the economy, GDP as a measure of domestic output is equal to NI, PI, and DI. This means that households receive a DI equal to the value of total output.

which would result in a piling up of unsold goods and therefore cutbacks in the production rate. Nor is there an excess of total spending, which would draw down inventories of goods and prompt increases in the rate of production. In short, there is no reason for businesses to alter this rate of production; $470 billion is therefore the **equilibrium GDP.**

Disequilibrium   To better understand the meaning of the equilibrium level of GDP; let's examine other levels of GDP to see why they cannot be sustained.

If businesses produced $410 billion of GDP (row 3 in Table 9-4), they would find that this output yields $405 billion in consumer spending. Supplemented by $20 billion of planned investment, total expenditures $(C + I_g)$ would be $425 billion, as shown in column 6. The economy would provide an annual rate of spending more than sufficient to purchase the $410 billion of annual production. Because buyers would be taking goods off the shelves faster than firms could produce them, an unintended decline in business inventories of $15 billion would occur (column 7) if this situation continued. But businesses can adjust to such an imbalance between aggregate expenditures and real output by stepping up production. Greater output will increase employment and total income. In brief, if aggregate expenditures exceed the domestic

output, those expenditures will drive domestic output upward.

We can make a similar comparison of GDP (column 2) and $C + I_g$ (column 6) at any other level of GDP *below* the $470 billion equilibrium level. In each case we will find that the economy wants to spend in excess of the level at which businesses are willing to produce. The excess of total spending at all these levels of GDP will drive GDP upward to the $470 billion equilibrium level.

The reverse is true at all levels of GDP *above* the $470 billion equilibrium level. Businesses will find that these total outputs fail to generate the spending needed to clear the shelves of goods. Being unable to recover their costs, businesses will cut back on production.

To illustrate: At the $510 billion output (row 8), business managers would find there is insufficient spending to permit the sale of all that output. Of the $510 billion of income which this output creates, $480 billion would be received back by businesses as consumption spending. Though supplemented by $20 billion of planned investment spending, total expenditures ($500 billion) would fall $10 billion short of the $510 billion quantity produced. If this imbalance persisted, $10 billion of inventories would pile up (column 7). But businesses can adjust to this unintended accumulation of unsold goods by cutting back on the rate of production. The resulting decline in output would mean fewer jobs and a decline in total income. You should verify that all other levels of GDP above the $470 billion equilibrium level would also result in insufficient spending.

The equilibrium level of GDP occurs where the total output, measured by GDP, and aggregate expenditures, $C + I_g$, are equal. Any excess of total spending over total output will drive GDP upward. Any deficiency of total spending will pull GDP downward.

Graphical Analysis

The same analysis can be shown in a graph. In **Figure 9-9 (Key Graph)** the **45 degree line** now takes on increased significance. Recall that the special property of this line is that at any point on it, the value of what is being measured on the horizontal axis (in this case GDP) is equal to the value of what is being measured on the vertical axis (here, aggregate expenditures or $C + I_g$). Having discovered in our tabular analysis that the equilibrium level of domestic output is determined where $C + I_g$ equals GDP, we can say that the 45 degree line in Figure 9-9 is a graphical statement of this equilibrium condition.

Now we must graph the aggregate expenditures schedule onto Figure 9-9. One way to do this is to duplicate the consumption schedule C in Figure 9-2a and add to it *vertically* the constant $20 billion amount of investment I_g from Figure 9-7b. This $20 billion is the amount we assumed firms plan to invest at all levels of GDP. Or, more directly, we can plot the $C + I_g$ data in column 6, Table 9-4.

Observe in Figure 9-9 that the aggregate expenditures line $C + I_g$ shows that total spending rises with income and output (GDP), but not as much as income rises, because the marginal propensity to consume—the slope of line C—is less than 1. A part of any increase in income will not be spent; it will be saved. And because the aggregate expenditures line $C + I_g$ is parallel to the consumption line C, the slope of the aggregate expenditures line also equals the MPC for the economy and is less than 1. For our particular data, aggregate expenditures rise by $15 billion for every $20 billion increase in real output and income because $5 billion of each $20 billion increment is saved. Therefore, in numerical terms the slope of the aggregate expenditures line is .75 (= Δ$15/Δ$20).

The equilibrium level of GDP is the GDP which corresponds to the intersection of the aggregate expenditures schedule and the 45 degree line. This intersection locates

the only point at which aggregate expenditures (on the vertical axis) are equal to GDP (on the horizontal axis). Because Figure 9-9 is based on the data in Table 9-4, we once again find that equilibrium output is $470 billion. Observe that consumption at this output is $450 billion and investment is $20 billion.

It is evident from Figure 9-9 that no levels of GDP above the equilibrium level are sustainable because at those levels $C + I_g$ falls short of GDP. Graphically, the aggregate expenditures schedule lies *below* the 45 degree line in those situations. At the $510 billion GDP level, for example, $C + I_g$ is only $500 billion. This underspending causes inventories to rise, prompting firms to readjust production downward in the direction of the $470 billion output level.

Conversely, at levels of GDP below $470 billion, the economy wants to spend in excess of what businesses are producing. Then $C + I_g$ exceeds total output. Graphically, the aggregate expenditures schedule lies *above* the 45 degree line. At the $410 billion GDP level, for example, $C + I_g$ totals $425 billion. This overspending causes inventories to decline, prompting firms to raise production toward the $470 billion GDP. Unless there is some change in the location of the aggregate expenditures line, the $470 billion level of GDP will be sustained indefinitely.

EQUILIBRIUM GDP: LEAKAGES-INJECTIONS APPROACH

The expenditures-output approach to determining GDP spotlights aggregate expenditures as the immediate determinant of the levels of output and income. Though the **leakages-injections** ($S = I_g$) **approach** is less direct, it does have the advantage of underscoring the *reason* $C + I_g$ and GDP are unequal at all levels of output except the equilibrium level.

The idea of the leakages-injections approach is this: Under our simplifying assumptions we know that the production of any level of real output will generate an identical amount of disposable income. But we also know a part of that income may be saved—*not* consumed—by households. Saving therefore represents a **leakage** or withdrawal of spending from the income-expenditures stream. Saving is what keeps consumption short of total output or GDP; as a result of saving, consumption by itself is insufficient to take all domestic output off the shelves, setting the stage, it would seem, for a decline in total output.

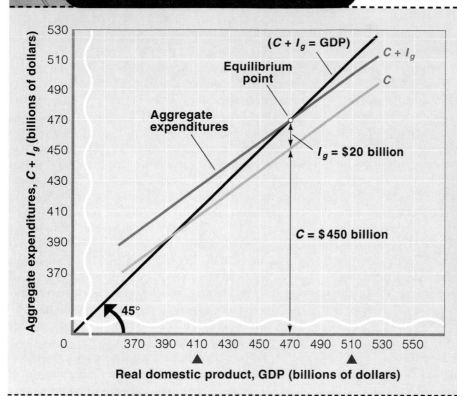

FIGURE 9-9 **The aggregate expenditures–domestic output approach to equilibrium GDP** The aggregate expenditures schedule, $C + I_g$, is determined by adding the investment schedule I_g to the upsloping consumption schedule C. Since investment is assumed to be the same at each level of GDP, the vertical distances between C and $C + I_g$ do not change. Equilibrium GDP is determined where the aggregate expenditures schedule intersects the 45 degree line, in this case at $470 billion.

QUICK QUIZ 9-9

1. In this figure, the slope of the aggregate expenditures schedule $C + I_g$:
   a. increases as real GDP increases.
   b. falls as real GDP increases.
   c. is constant and equals the MPC.
   d. is constant and equals the MPS.

2. At all points on the 45 degree line:
   a. equilibrium GDP is possible.
   b. aggregate expenditures exceed real GDP.
   c. consumption exceeds investment.
   d. aggregate expenditures are less than real GDP.

3. The $490 billion level of real GDP is *not* at equilibrium because:
   a. investment exceeds consumption.

   b. consumption exceeds investment.
   c. planned $C + I_g$ exceeds real GDP.
   d. planned $C + I_g$ is less than real GDP.

4. The $430 billion level of real GDP is *not* at equilibrium because:
   a. investment exceeds consumption.
   b. consumption exceeds investment.
   c. planned $C + I_g$ exceeds real GDP.
   d. planned $C + I_g$ is less than real GDP.

Answers: 1. c; 2. a; 3. d; 4. c

However, the business sector does not intend to sell its entire output to consumers; some domestic output will consist of capital goods sold within the business sector. Investment can therefore be thought of as an **injection** of spending into the income-expenditures stream; investment is an adjunct to consumption. Investment is thus a potential replacement for the leakage of saving.

If, at a certain level of GDP, the leakage of saving exceeds the injection of investment, then $C + I_g$ will fall short of GDP and that level of GDP is too high to be sustained. Any GDP for which saving exceeds investment is an above-equilibrium GDP. Conversely, if the injection of investment exceeds the leakage of saving, then $C + I_g$ will be greater than GDP and GDP will be driven upward. Any GDP for which investment exceeds saving is a below-equilibrium GDP.

Only where $S = I_g$—where the leakage of saving is exactly offset by the injection of investment—will aggregate expenditures equal real output. And that equality is what defines the equilibrium GDP.

In the closed private economy assumed here, there is a single leakage (saving) and a single injection (investment). In more general terms, a *leakage* is any use of income other than to purchase domestically produced output. In the expanded models that follow (in Chapter 10), we will need to incorporate the additional leakages of imports and taxes into our analysis.

Similarly, an *injection* is any supplement to consumer spending on domestic production. Again, in later models we will add injections of exports and government purchases to our discussion. But for now we need only compare the single leakage of saving with the sole injection of investment to obtain the equilibrium GDP.

Tabular Analysis

Our $C + I_g$ = GDP approach has led us to conclude that, in our example, all levels of GDP less than $470 billion are unstable. That is true because then $C + I_g$ exceeds GDP, which drives GDP upward. Now let's look at the saving schedule (columns 2 and 4) and the investment schedule (columns 2 and 5) in Table 9-4. Comparing the amounts households and firms want to save and invest at GDP levels *below* $470 billion explains the excesses of total spending. At each of these lower GDP levels, firms plan to invest more than households want to save.

For example, at a GDP of $410 billion (row 3), households will save only $5 billion but businesses

will invest $20 billion. Hence, investment exceeds saving by $15 billion (= $20 − $5). Columns 6 and 2 show that aggregate expenditures exceed GDP by that same $15 billion (= $425 − $410). The small leakage of saving at this relatively low income level is more than compensated for by the larger injection of investment spending. That causes $C + I_g$ to exceed GDP and drives GDP upward.

In contrast, all levels of GDP *above* $470 billion are unstable because they exceed $C + I_g$. The reason for this insufficient spending is that at all GDP levels above $470 billion, households want to save more than firms plan to invest. The saving leakage is not compensated for by the injection of investment.

For example, households will save $30 billion at a GDP of $510 billion (row 8). Firms, however, will plan to invest only $20 billion. This $10 billion excess of saving over planned investment will reduce total spending to $10 billion below the value of total output. Specifically, aggregate expenditures will be $500 billion and real GDP is $510 billion. This spending deficiency will reduce GDP.

Again we verify that the equilibrium GDP is $470 billion. At this level of GDP the saving desires of households and the investment plans of businesses are the same ($20 billion each). When firms and households attempt to invest and save the same amounts—where leakages equal injections—aggregate expenditures will equal GDP. Here, there will be no unplanned changes in inventories.

Graphical Analysis

The leakages-injections approach to determining equilibrium GDP is demonstrated in Figure 9-10, in which we have again graphed the saving schedule in

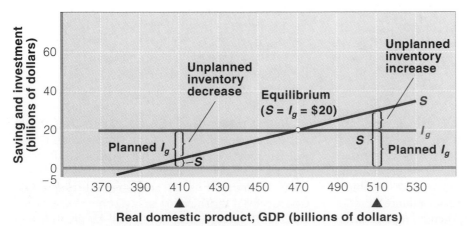

FIGURE 9-10 The leakages-injections approach to equilibrium GDP In this approach the equilibrium GDP is determined by the intersection of the saving (S) and planned investment (I_g) schedules. Only at that point will households plan to save the amount businesses want to invest. At other, nonequilibrium GDPs, overspending or underspending will result in unplanned inventory changes.

Figure 9-2b and the investment schedule in 9-7b. The numerical data for these schedules are in columns 2, 4, and 5, Table 9-4. The two lines S and I_g intersect at the equilibrium GDP, $470 billion. Only here do businesses and households plan to invest and save the same amounts; only here will GDP and $C + I_g$ be the same.

At higher levels of GDP, households will save more than businesses plan to invest. Because the saving leakage will exceed the investment injection, $C + I_g$ will fall short of GDP, driving GDP downward. At the $510 billion GDP, for example, saving of $30 billion will exceed investment of $20 billion by $10 billion, with the result that $C + I_g$ will be $10 billion short of GDP.

At all levels of GDP below the $470 billion equilibrium level, businesses will plan to invest more than households save. Because the injection of investment will exceed the leakage of saving, $C + I_g$ will exceed GDP, driving GDP upward. To illustrate: At the $410 billion level of GDP the $5 billion leakage of saving is more than compensated for by the $20 billion that businesses plan to invest. The result is that $C + I_g$ will exceed GDP by $15 billion. **(Key Question 10)**

PLANNED VERSUS ACTUAL INVESTMENT

We have seen that differences between saving and investment can occur and bring about changes in the equilibrium GDP. Now we must emphasize that, in another sense, saving and investment are always equal. This apparent contradiction concerning the equality of saving and investment is resolved when we distinguish between **planned investment** and saving (which need not be equal) and **actual investment** and saving (which by definition must be equal). The catch is that *actual investment consists of planned investment and unplanned investment (unplanned changes in inventory investment). Unplanned investment acts as a balancing item which equates the actual amounts saved and invested in any period.*

Disequilibrium and Inventories

Consider, as an example, the $490 billion above-equilibrium GDP (row 7 in Table 9-4). What happens if businesses produce this output, thinking they can sell it? At this level, households save $25 billion of their $490 billion DI, so consumption is only $465

billion. *Planned* investment (column 5) is $20 billion; businesses intend to buy $20 billion worth of capital goods. This means aggregate expenditures $(C + I_g)$ are $485 billion, and sales therefore fall short of production by $5 billion. This extra $5 billion of goods is retained by businesses as an *unintended* or *unplanned* increase in inventories (column 7). It is unintended because it results from the failure of total spending to take total output off the shelves. Remembering that, by definition, changes in inventories are a part of investment, we note that *actual* investment is $25 billion ($20 planned *plus* $5 unintended or unplanned). It exactly equals the saving of $25 billion, even though saving exceeds *planned* investment by $5 billion. Since firms cannot earn profits by accumulating unwanted inventories, they will cut back production.

Now look at the below-equilibrium $450 billion output (row 5, Table 9-4). Because households save only $15 billion of their $450 billion DI, consumption is $435 billion. Planned investment by firms is $20 billion, so aggregate expenditures are $455 billion. Sales exceed production by $5 billion. This is so only if an unplanned decrease in business inventories occurs. Firms must unintentionally *dis*invest $5 billion in inventories (column 7). Note again that actual investment is $15 billion ($20 planned minus $5 unplanned) and equal to saving of $15 billion, even though planned investment exceeds saving by $5 billion. The decline in inventories from the excess of sales over production will induce firms to expand production.

Once again: At all *above-equilibrium* GDPs (where saving exceeds planned investment), actual investment and saving are made equal by unintended increases in inventories which are added to planned investment. In Figure 9-9, the vertical distance of the saving schedule above the (planned) investment schedule I_g represents an unintended inventory increase.

At all *below-equilibrium* GDPs (where planned investment exceeds saving), actual investment is made equal to saving by unintended decreases in inventories, which are subtracted from planned investment. An unintended inventory decrease is shown graphically as the vertical distance of the (planned) investment schedule above the saving schedule.

Attainment of Equilibrium

These distinctions are important because they mean that it is the equality of planned investment and saving which determines the equilibrium level of GDP.

John Maynard Keynes (1883–1946)

The British economist John Maynard Keynes is the originator of the central ideas underlying the aggregate expenditures model.

In 1935 George Bernard Shaw received a letter from John Maynard Keynes in which Keynes asserted, "I believe myself to be writing a book on economic theory which will largely revolutionize . . . the way the world thinks about economic problems." And, in fact, Keynes' *General Theory of Employment, Interest, and Money* (1936) did just that: It revolutionized economic analysis and established Keynes as one of the most influential economists of all times.

Keynes was far more than an economist: He was an incredibly active, many-sided man who also played such diverse roles as principal representative of the Treasury at the World War I Paris Peace Conference, deputy for the Chancellor of the Exchequer, a director of the Bank of England, trustee of the National Gallery, chairman of the Council of the Encouragement of Music and the Arts, bursar of King's College, Cambridge, editor of the *Economic Journal,* chairman of the *Nation* and later the *New Statesman* magazines, and chairman of the National Mutual Life Assurance Society. He also ran an investment company, organized the Camargo Ballet (his wife, Lydia Lopokova, was a renowned star of the Russian Imperial Ballet), and built (profitably) the Arts Theatre at Cambridge.*

In addition, Keynes found time to amass a personal fortune by speculating in stocks, international currencies, and commodities. He was also a leading figure in the Bloomsbury group, an avant-garde group of intellectual luminaries who greatly influenced the artistic and literary standards of England.

Most importantly, Keynes was a prolific scholar. His books encompassed such widely ranging topics as probability theory, monetary economics, and the economic consequences of the World War I peace treaty. His magnum opus, however, was the *General Theory of Employment, Interest, and Money,* described by John Kenneth Galbraith as "a work of profound obscurity, badly written and prematurely published." Yet the book established the major insights discussed in the chapter: the consumption function, the investment demand curve, the investment schedule, and the equilibrium GDP.

Moreover, *General Theory* attacked the contention by the classical economists that recessions and depressions are unlikely to occur, and if they do, they will automatically correct themselves. Keynes' analysis suggested that a major decline in investment spending in a capitalist economy results in an even greater decline in total spending, total output, and total income. Further, said Keynes, the economy's slide into recession or depression was unlikely to be reversed by automatic mechanisms. The economy might therefore languish for many years in depression. Indeed, the massive unemployment of the worldwide depression of 1930s seemed to provide sufficient evidence that Keynes was right. His basic policy recommendation—government needed to play an active role in ensuring that the economy stayed fully employed—was controversial in view of the classical position that government intervention in the economy was detrimental. Keynes, a strong critic of socialism, argued that government stabilization policy was needed to ensure the continuance of the market system that classical economists, and Keynes himself, so admired.

*E. Ray Canterberry, *The Making of Economics,* 3d ed. (Belmont, CA: Wadsworth Publishing Company, 1987), p. 126.

We can think of the process by which equilibrium is achieved as follows:

1. A difference between saving and planned investment creates a difference between the production and spending plans of the economy as a whole.

2. The difference between production plans and spending plans results in unintended investment or disinvestment in inventories.

3. As long as unintended investment in inventories persists, firms will revise their production plans downward and reduce GDP. Conversely, as long as unintended disinvestment in inventories exists, firms will revise their production plans upward and increase GDP. Both GDP movements are toward equilibrium because they bring about the equality of planned investment and saving.

4. GDP will reach equilibrium when planned investment and saving are equal. At that GDP, there is no unintended investment or disinvestment in inventories to drive GDP upward or downward. **(Key Question 11)**

QUICK REVIEW 9-4

■ In a private closed economy, equilibrium GDP occurs where aggregate expenditures equal real domestic output ($C + I_g = $ GDP).

■ Alternatively, equilibrium GDP is established where saving equals planned investment ($S = I_g$).

■ Actual investment consists of planned investment plus unplanned changes in inventories and is always equal to saving in a private closed economy.

■ At equilibrium GDP, changes in inventories are zero; no unintended investment or disinvestment occurs.

CHAPTER SUMMARY

1. Classical economists argued that because supply creates its own demand (Say's law), general underspending was improbable. Thus the economy would provide virtually continuous full employment. Even if temporary declines in total spending occurred, these declines would be compensated for by downward price and wage adjustments which would boost spending and employment, restoring the economy to its full-employment level of output.

2. The Great Depression and Keynes' *General Theory of Employment, Interest, and Money* undermined classical macroeconomics. The Great Depression challenged the classical precept that full employment was the norm in a capitalist economy. Keynes' aggregate expenditures analysis showed how periods of underspending or overspending could occur.

3. The basic tools of the aggregate expenditures model are the consumption, saving, and investment schedules, which show the various amounts households intend to consume and save and firms plan to invest at the various income and output levels, assuming a fixed price level.

4. The *average* propensities to consume and save show the fractions of any *total* income that are consumed and saved; APC + APS = 1. The *marginal* propensities to consume and save show the fractions of any *change* in total income that are consumed and saved; MPC + MPS = 1.

5. The locations of the consumption and saving schedules are determined by **(a)** the amount of wealth owned by households; **(b)** expectations of future income, future prices, and product availability; **(c)** the relative size of household debt; and **(d)** taxation. The consumption and saving schedules are relatively stable.

6. The immediate determinants of investment are **(a)** the expected rate of return and **(b)** the real rate of interest. The economy's investment demand curve can be found by

cumulating investment projects, arraying them in descending order according to their expected rates of return, graphing the result, and applying the rule that investment will be profitable up to the point at which the real interest rate, i, equals the expected rate of return, r. The investment demand curve reveals an inverse relationship between the interest rate and the level of aggregate investment.

7. Shifts in the investment demand curve can occur as the result of changes in **(a)** the acquisition, maintenance, and operating costs of capital goods; **(b)** business taxes; **(c)** technology; **(d)** the stocks of capital goods on hand; and **(e)** expectations.

8. For simplicity we assume that the level of investment determined by the current interest rate and the investment demand curve does not vary with the level of real GDP.

9. The durability of capital goods, the irregular occurrence of major innovations, profit volatility, and the variability of expectations all contribute to the instability of investment spending.

10. For a private closed economy the equilibrium level of GDP occurs when aggregate expenditures and real output are equal or, graphically, where the $C + I_g$ line intersects the 45 degree line. At any GDP greater than equilibrium GDP, real output will exceed aggregate spending, resulting in unintended investment in inventories, and eventual declines in output and income (GDP). At any below-equilibrium GDP, aggregate expenditures will exceed real output, resulting in unintended disinvestment in inventories and eventual increases in GDP.

11. The leakages-injections approach determines equilibrium GDP at the point where the amount households save and the amount businesses plan to invest are equal. This is the point where the saving and planned investment schedules intersect. Any excess of saving over planned investment will cause a shortage of total spending, forcing GDP to fall. Any excess of planned investment over saving will cause an excess of total spending, inducing GDP to rise. The change in GDP will in both cases correct the discrepancy between saving and planned investment.

12. Actual investment consists of planned investment plus unplanned changes in inventories. When planned investment diverges from saving, an unintended investment or disinvestment in inventories occurs which equates actual investment and saving. At equilibrium GDP, planned investment equals saving; inventory levels are then constant (there is no unplanned investment or disinvestment).

TERMS AND CONCEPTS

Say's law	average propensity to save	investment schedule	45 degree line
Keynesian economics	marginal propensity to	aggregate expenditures–	leakages-injections
consumption schedule	consume	domestic output	approach
saving schedule	marginal propensity to	approach	leakage
break-even income	save	aggregate expenditures	injection
average propensity to	expected rate of return	schedule	planned investment
consume	investment demand curve	equilibrium GDP	actual investment

STUDY QUESTIONS

1. Relate Say's law to the view held by classical economists that the economy generally will operate at a position *on* its production possibilities curve (Chapter 2). Use production possibilities analysis to demonstrate the Keynesian view on this matter.

2. Explain what relationships are shown by **(a)** the consumption schedule, **(b)** the saving schedule, **(c)** the investment demand curve, and **(d)** the investment schedule.

3. Precisely how are the APC and the MPC different? Why must the sum of the MPC and the MPS equal 1? What are the basic determinants of the consumption and saving schedules? Of your own level of consumption?

4. Explain how each of the following will affect the consumption and saving schedules or the investment schedule:
  a. A decline in the amount of government bonds which consumers are holding
  b. The threat of limited, nonnuclear war, leading the public to expect future shortages of consumer durables
  c. A decline in the real interest rate
  d. A sharp decline in stock prices
  e. An increase in the rate of population growth

  f. The development of a cheaper method of manufacturing pig iron from ore
  g. The announcement that the social security program is to be restricted as to size of benefits
  h. The expectation that mild inflation will persist in the next decade
  i. An increase in the Federal personal income tax

5. Explain why an upshift in the consumption schedule typically involves an equal downshift in the saving schedule. What are the exceptions to this relationship?

6. KEY QUESTION Complete the following table:

Level of output and income (GDP = DI)	Consumption	Saving	APC	APS	MPC	MPS
$240	$_____	$−4	___	___		
260	_____	0	___	___	___	___
280	_____	4	___	___	___	___
300	_____	8	___	___	___	___
320	_____	12	___	___	___	___
340	_____	16	___	___	___	___
360	_____	20	___	___	___	___
380	_____	24	___	___	___	___
400	_____	28	___	___	___	___

a. Show the consumption and saving schedules graphically.

b. Find the break-even level of income. Explain how it is possible for households to dissave at very low income levels.

c. If the proportion of total income consumed (APC) decreases and the proportion saved (APS) increases as income rises, explain both verbally and graphically how the MPC and MPS can be constant at various levels of income.

7. What are the basic determinants of investment? Explain the relationship between the real interest rate and the level of investment. Why is the investment schedule less stable than the consumption and saving schedules?

8. KEY QUESTION Assume there are no investment projects in the economy which yield an expected rate of return of 25 percent or more. But suppose there are $10 billion of investment projects yielding expected returns of between 20 and 25 percent; another $10 billion yielding between 15 and 20 percent; another $10 billion between 10 and 15 percent; and so forth. Cumulate these data and present them graphically, putting the expected rate of return on the vertical axis and the amount of investment on the horizontal axis. What will be the equilibrium level of aggregate investment if the real interest rate is **(a)** 15 percent, **(b)** 10 percent, and **(c)** 5 percent? Explain why this curve is the investment demand curve.

9. Explain graphically the determination of the equilibrium GDP by **(a)** the aggregate expenditures–domestic output approach and **(b)** the leakages-injections approach for a private closed economy. Why must these two approaches always yield the same equilibrium GDP? Explain why the intersection of the aggregate expenditures schedule and the 45 degree line determines the equilibrium GDP.

10. KEY QUESTION Assuming the level of investment is $16 billion and independent of the level of total output, complete the following table and determine the equilibrium levels of output and employment which this private closed economy would provide. What are the sizes of the MPC and MPS?

Possible levels of employment, millions	Real domestic output (GDP = DI), billions	Consumption, billions	Saving, billions
40	$240	$244	$_____
45	260	260	_____
50	280	276	_____
55	300	292	_____
60	320	308	_____
65	340	324	_____
70	360	340	_____
75	380	356	_____
80	400	372	_____

11. KEY QUESTION Using the consumption and saving data in question 10 and assuming investment is $16 billion, what are saving and planned investment at the $380 billion level of domestic output? What are saving and actual investment at that level? What are saving and planned investment at the $300 billion level of domestic output? What are the levels of saving and actual investment? Use the concept of unplanned investment to explain adjustments toward equilibrium from both the $380 and $300 billion levels of domestic output.

12. "Planned investment is equal to saving at all levels of GDP; actual investment equals saving only at the equilibrium GDP." Do you agree? Explain. Critically evaluate: "The fact that households may save more than firms want to invest is of no consequence, because events will in time force households and firms to save and invest at the same rates."

13. Advanced analysis: Linear equations for the consumption and saving schedules take the general form $C = a + bY$ and $S = -a + (1 - b)Y$, where C, S, and Y are consumption, saving, and national income, respectively. The constant a represents the vertical intercept, and b the slope of the consumption schedule.

a. Use the following data to substitute numerical values for a and b in the consumption and saving equations:

National income (Y)	Consumption (C)
$ 0	$ 80
100	140
200	200
300	260
400	320

b. What is the economic meaning of b? Of $(1 - b)$?

c. Suppose the amount of saving which occurs at each level of national income falls by $20, but that the values of b and $(1 - b)$ remain unchanged. Restate the saving and consumption equations for the new numerical values, and cite a factor which might have caused the change.

14. Advanced analysis: Suppose that the linear equation for consumption in a hypothetical economy is $C = 40 + .8Y$. Also suppose that income (Y) is $400. Determine **(a)** the marginal propensity to consume,

(b) the marginal propensity to save, **(c)** the level of consumption, **(d)** the average propensity to consume, **(e)** the level of saving, and **(f)** the average propensity to save.

15. **Advanced analysis:** Assume that the linear equation for consumption in a hypothetical private closed economy is $C = 10 + .9Y$, where Y is total real income (output). Also suppose that the equation for investment is $I_g = I_{g0} = 40$, meaning that I_g is 40 at all levels of total real income. Using the equation $Y = C + I_g$, determine the equilibrium level of Y. What are the total amounts of consumption, saving, and investment at equilibrium Y?

16. **(Last Word)** What is the significance of John Maynard Keynes book, *General Theory of Employment, Interest, and Money*, published in 1936?

17. **WEB-BASED QUESTION** **The Beige Book and Current Consumer Spending** The Beige Book http://www.bog.frb.fed.us/FOMC/BB/Current/ is a report on current economic conditions published eight times a year by the Federal Reserve System. Each Federal Reserve Bank gathers anecdotal information on current economic conditions in its district through reports from bank and branch directors and interviews with key executives, economists, market experts, and other sources. Locate the current Beige Book report. Compare consumer spending for the entire U.S. economy with consumer spending in your Federal Reserve District. What are the economic strengths and weaknesses for both? Are retailers reporting that recent sales have met their expectations? What are the expectations for the future?

18. **WEB-BASED QUESTION** Investment Instability—Changes in Real Private Nonresidential Fixed Investment Investment is the most volatile component of total spending. Real private nonresidential fixed investment is made up of two components: structures and producers' durable equipment. The Bureau of Economic Analysis provides data for real private nonresidential fixed investment in table form http://www.bea.doc.gov/briefrm/tables/ebr2.htm and graphical form http://www.bea.doc.gov/briefrm/nonresfi.htm. Has recent investment been volatile? Which is the largest component of investment, structures or producers' durable equipment? Which component has been more volatile (as measured by percentage change from preceding quarter)? Are recent quarterly percentage changes similar to previous years' changes? Looking at the investment graph, what investment forecast would you make for the forthcoming year?

CHAPTER TEN

Aggregate Expenditures: The Multiplier, Net Exports, and Government

10

You have seen why a particular equilibrium level of real GDP exists, specifically in a private closed economy. But recall from Chapter 8 that the GDP of U.S. capitalism is seldom stable; instead, it experiences long-run growth and is punctuated by cyclical fluctuations. We now turn our attention to why and how the equilibrium real GDP fluctuates. And since the public sector and the foreign sector *do* influence real GDP, later in this chapter we make the aggregate expenditures model more realistic by bringing these two sectors into the model.

We first analyze changes in investment spending and how they affect output, income, and employment. You will discover that a change in investment creates a multiple change in GDP. Then we "open" our simplified "closed" economy to show how exports and imports affect it. Next, we bring government—with its expenditures and taxes—into the model; the "private" economy becomes the "mixed" economy. Finally, we apply our extended model to two historical periods and consider some of the model's deficiencies.

CHANGES IN EQUILIBRIUM GDP AND THE MULTIPLIER

In the private closed economy, the equilibrium GDP will change in response to changes in the investment schedule or the saving and consumption schedules. Because the investment schedule is much less stable than the consumption and saving schedules, we will assume that the investment schedule is what changes.

Figure 10-1 shows the effect of changes in investment. Suppose the expected rate of re-
turn on investment rises (shifting the investment demand curve in Figure 9-7a to the right) or the interest rate falls (now the investment demand curve in Figure 9-7a does not shift; we instead move down the curve). As a result, investment spending increases by, say, $5 billion. This is indicated in Figure 10-1a by an upward shift of the aggregate expenditures schedule from $(C + I_g)_0$ to $(C + I_g)_1$ and in Figure 10-1b by an upward shift in the investment schedule from I_{g0} to I_{g1}. In each graph the result is a rise in the equilibrium GDP from $470 to $490 billion.

(a) Change in aggregate expenditures schedule

(b) Change in investment schedule

FIGURE 10-1 Changes in the equilibrium GDP caused by shifts in the aggregate expenditures schedule and the investment schedule (a) An upshift in the aggregate expenditures schedule from $(C + I_g)_0$ to $(C + I_g)_1$ will increase the equilibrium GDP. Conversely, a downshift from $(C + I_g)_0$ to $(C + I_g)_2$ will lower the equilibrium GDP. (b) An upshift in the investment schedule (I_{g0} to I_{g1}) will raise, and a downshift (I_{g0} to I_{g2}) will lower, the equilibrium GDP.

If the expected rate of return on investment decreases or the interest rate rises, the result is a decline in investment spending of, say, $5 billion. This is shown by the downward shift of the investment schedule from I_{g0} to I_{g2} in Figure 10-1b and the downward shift of the aggregate expenditures schedule from $(C + I_g)_0$ to $(C + I_g)_2$ in Figure 10-1a. In each case, the shift reduces the equilibrium GDP from the original $470 billion to $450 billion.

You should verify these conclusions in Table 9-4 by substituting first $25 billion and then $15 billion

for the $20 billion planned investment amount in column 5. If you do, you will see that $C + I_g$ becomes equal to GDP first at $490 billion (row 7) and then at $450 billion (row 5), the values indicated in Figure 10-1.

At the risk of getting ahead of ourselves, we note that the $5 billion changes in investment may be the direct result of economic policy. Looking back at Figure 9-7a, we see that the initial $20 billion of investment is associated with an 8 percent interest rate. If the economy is in recession at that investment level, monetary authorities may purposely reduce the interest rate to 6 percent (by increasing the supply of money). This will cause a $5 billion increase in investment and in aggregate expenditures to expand the economy's GDP.

Conversely, suppose the initial $20 billion of investment is "too great" and thus is causing demand-pull inflation. The monetary authorities may increase the interest rate (by reducing the money supply), causing a reduction in investment and aggregate expenditures to constrain the inflation. Monetary policy—changing the money supply to alter interest rates and aggregate expenditures—is the subject of Chapter 15.

The Multiplier Effect

You may have noticed above that a $5 billion change in investment spending led to a $20 billion change in output and income. This surprising result is called the *multiplier effect:* a change in a component of aggregate expenditures leads to a larger change in equilibrium GDP. The **multiplier** determines how much larger; it is the ratio of a change in equilibrium GDP to the change in GDP. Stated generally,

$$\text{Multiplier} = \frac{\text{change in real GDP}}{\text{initial change in spending}}$$

Here the multiplier is 4 (= $20/$5). By rearranging the above equation, we can also say that

$$\text{Change in GDP} = \text{multiplier} \times \text{initial change in spending}$$

Three points about the multiplier must be made here:
1. The "initial change in spending" is usually associated with investment spending because of its

volatility. But changes in consumption, net exports, and government purchases also lead to the multiplier effect.
2. The "initial change in spending" refers to an upshift or downshift of the aggregate expenditures schedule due to an upshift or downshift of one of its components. In Figure 10-1b we find that real GDP has increased by $20 billion because the investment schedule has shifted upward by $5 billion from I_{g0} to I_{g1}.
3. Implicit in this second point is that the multiplier works in both directions. An increase in initial spending can create a multiple increase in GDP, or a decrease in spending can be multiplied into a larger decrease in GDP.

Rationale The multiplier effect follows from two facts. First, the economy supports repetitive, continuous flows of expenditures and income through which dollars spent by Smith are received as income by Chin, then spent by Chin and received as income by Gonzales, and so on. Second, any change in income will cause both consumption and saving to vary in the same direction as, and by a fraction of, the change in income.

It follows that an initial change in the rate of spending will cause a spending chain through the economy. That chain of spending, although of diminishing importance at each successive step, will cumulate to a multiple change in GDP.

The rationale underlying the multiplier effect is illustrated numerically in Table 10-1. Suppose a $5 billion increase in investment spending occurs. This is the upshift of the aggregate expenditures schedule by $5 billion in Figure 10-1a and the upshift of the

TABLE 10-1   **The multiplier: a tabular illustration (in billions)**

	(1) Change in income	(2) Change in consumption (MPC = .75)	(3) Change in saving (MPS = .25)
Increase in investment of **_$5.00_**	$ 5.00	$ 3.75	$1.25
Second round	3.75	2.81	0.94
Third round	2.81	2.11	0.70
Fourth round	2.11	1.58	0.53
Fifth round	1.58	1.19	0.39
All other rounds	4.75	3.56	1.19
Total	**_$20.00_**	$15.00	**_$5.00_**

investment schedule from $20 to $25 billion in Figure 10-1b. Because we are still using the data in Table 9-1, we assume that the MPC is .75 and the MPS is .25. Also, we suppose that the economy is initially in equilibrium at $470 billion.

The initial increase in investment spending generates an equal amount of wage, rent, interest, and profit income because spending income and receiving income are two sides of the same transaction. How much consumption will be induced by this $5 billion increase in the incomes of households? The answer is found by applying the marginal propensity to consume of .75 to this change in income. Thus, the $5 billion increase in income initially raises consumption by $3.75 (= .75 × $5) billion and saving by $1.25 (= .25 × $5) billion, as shown in columns 2 and 3 in Table 10-1.

The $3.75 billion of consumption spending is received by other households as income (second round). These households consume .75 of this $3.75 billion, or $2.81 billion, and save .25 of it, or $0.94 billion. The $2.81 billion which is consumed flows to still other households as income to be spent or saved (third round). And the process continues.

Figure 10-2, derived from Table 10-1, shows the cumulative effects of this process. Each round *adds* the orange blocks to national income and GDP. The cumulation of the additional income in each round—the sum of the orange blocks—is the total change in income or GDP. Though the spending and respending effects of the increase in investment diminish with each successive round of spending, the cumulative increase in output and income will be $20 billion. The $5 billion increase in investment will therefore increase the equilibrium GDP by $20 billion, from $470 to $490 billion. Thus, the multiplier is 4 (= $20 billion ÷ $5 billion).

It is no coincidence that the multiplier effect ends at the point where exactly enough saving has been generated to offset the initial $5 billion increase in investment spending. Only then will the disequilibrium created by the investment increase be corrected. In other words, GDP and total incomes *must* rise by $20 billion to create $5 billion in additional saving to balance the $5 billion increase in investment spending. Income must increase by four times the initial excess of investment over saving, because households save one-fourth of any increase in their incomes (that is, the MPS is .25).

The Multiplier and the Marginal Propensities You may have sensed from Table 10-1 a relationship be-

tween the MPS and the multiplier. The fraction of an increase in income saved—the MPS—determines the cumulative respending effects of any initial change in spending and therefore determines the multiplier. *The MPS and the multiplier are inversely related.* The smaller the fraction of any change in income saved, the greater the respending at each round and, therefore, the greater the multiplier. If the MPS is .25, as in our example, the multiplier is 4. If the MPS were .33, the multiplier would be 3. If the MPS were .2, the multiplier would be 5. Let's see why.

Look again at Table 9-4 and Figure 10-1b. Initially the economy is in equilibrium at the $470 billion level of GDP. Now businesses increase investment by $5 billion so that planned investment of $25 billion exceeds saving of $20 billion at the $470 billion level. This means $470 billion is no longer the equilibrium GDP. By how much must output and income rise to restore equilibrium? By enough to generate $5 billion of additional saving to offset the $5 billion increase in investment. Because households save $1 out of every $4 of additional income they receive (MPS = .25),

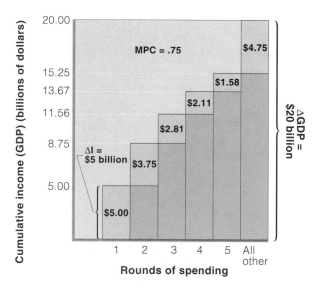

FIGURE 10-2 The multiplier process (MPC = .75) An initial change in investment spending of $5 billion creates an equal $5 billion of new income in round 1. Households spend $3.75 (= .75 × $5) billion of this new income, creating $3.75 of added income in round 2. Of this $3.75 of new income, households spend $2.81 (= .75 × $3.75) billion, and income rises by that amount in round 3. The cumulation of such income increments over the entire process eventually results in a total change of income and GDP of $20 billion. The multiplier therefore is 4 (= $20 billion ÷ $5 billion).

GDP must rise by $20 billion—four times the increase in investment—to create the $5 billion of extra saving necessary to restore equilibrium. Thus, the multiplier is 4.

If the MPS were .33, GDP would have to rise by only $15 billion (three times the increase in investment) to generate $5 billion of additional saving and restore equilibrium, and the multiplier therefore would be 3. But if the MPS were .20, GDP would have to rise by $25 billion for people to save an extra $5 billion and equilibrium to be restored; then the multiplier would be 5.

Also, recall that the MPS measures the slope of the saving schedule. In the leakages-injections ($S = I_g$) approach, this means that if the MPS is relatively large (say, .5) and the slope of the saving schedule is therefore relatively steep (.5), any upward shift in investment spending will be subject to a relatively small multiplier. A $5 billion increase in investment will entail a new point of intersection of the S and I_g schedules only $10 billion to the right of the original equilibrium GDP. The multiplier is only 2.

But if the MPS is relatively small (say, .10), the slope of the saving schedule will be relatively gentle (.10). Therefore, the same $5 billion upward shift in the investment schedule will provide a new intersection point $50 billion to the right of the original equilibrium GDP. The multiplier is 10 in this case. You should verify these two examples by drawing appropriate saving and investment diagrams.

We can summarize by saying *the multiplier is equal to the reciprocal of the MPS*. The reciprocal of any number is the quotient you obtain by dividing 1 by that number:

$$\text{Multiplier} = \frac{1}{\text{MPS}}$$

This formula is a quick way to determine the multiplier. To do so, all you need to know is the MPS.

Recall, too, from Chapter 9 that MPC + MPS = 1; it follows, then, that MPS = 1 − MPC. Therefore, we can also write the multiplier formula as

$$\text{Multiplier} = \frac{1}{1 - \text{MPC}}$$

Significance of the Multiplier The significance of the multiplier is that a small change in the investment plans of businesses or the consumption and saving plans of households can trigger a larger change in the equilibrium GDP. The multiplier magnifies the fluctuations in business activity initiated by changes in spending.

As illustrated in Figure 10-3, the larger the MPC (the smaller the MPS), the greater the multiplier. If the MPC is .75, the multiplier is 4; a $10 billion decline in planned investment will reduce the equilibrium GDP by $40 billion. But if the MPC is only .67, the multiplier is 3; the same $10 billion drop in investment will reduce the equilibrium GDP by only $30 billion. This makes sense intuitively: A large MPC means the succeeding rounds of consumption spending shown in Figure 10-2 diminish slowly and thereby cumulate to a large change in income. Conversely, a small MPC (a large MPS) causes the increases in consumption to decline quickly so the cumulative change in income is small.

Generalizing the Multiplier The multiplier we presented above is called the *simple multiplier* because it is based on a simple model of the economy. When it is computed as 1/MPS, the simple multiplier reflects only the leakage of income into saving. In the real world successive rounds of income and spending can also be diminished by leakages into imports and taxes. As with the leakage into saving, some part of income at each round would be siphoned off as additional taxes, and another part would be used to purchase additional goods from abroad. The result of these added leakages is that the 1/MPS statement of the multiplier can be generalized. Specifically, we can

FIGURE 10-3 The MPC and the multiplier The larger the MPC (the smaller the MPS), the greater the size of the multiplier.

change the denominator to read "fraction of the change in income which is not spent on domestic output" or "fraction of the change in income which leaks, or is diverted, from the income-expenditures stream." The more realistic multiplier which results when all leakages—saving, taxes, and imports—are included is called the *complex multiplier*. The Council of Economic Advisers, which advises the President on economic matters, has estimated the complex multiplier for the United States to be about 2. **(Key Question 2)**

INTERNATIONAL TRADE AND EQUILIBRIUM OUTPUT

Our aggregate expenditures model has ignored international trade by assuming a closed economy. We now acknowledge the existence of exports and imports and note that **net exports** (exports minus imports) may be either positive or negative. Item 4 on the inside covers of this book reveals that net exports in some years have been positive (exports > imports) and in other years negative (imports > exports). In 1975, for example, net exports were a *positive* $14 billion, while in 1987 they were a *negative* $142 billion.

Net Exports and Aggregate Expenditures

Like consumption and investment, exports (X) create domestic production, income, and employment for a nation. Even though U.S. goods and services produced for export are sent abroad, foreign spending on those goods and services increases production and creates jobs and incomes in the United States. Exports must therefore be added as a component of each nation's aggregate expenditures.

Conversely, when an economy is open to international trade, part of its consumption and investment spending will be for imports (M)—goods and services produced abroad rather than in domestic industries. To avoid overstating the value of domestic production, we must reduce the sum of consumption and investment expenditures by the amount expended on imported goods. In measuring aggregate expenditures for domestic goods and services, we must subtract expenditures on imports.

In short, for a private closed economy, aggregate expenditures are $C + I_g$. But for an open economy with international trade, aggregate spending is $C + I_g + (X - M)$. Or, recalling that net exports (X_n) equal

$(X - M)$, we can say that aggregate expenditures for a private open economy are $C + I_g + X_n$.

The Net Export Schedule

Table 10-2 shows two potential net export schedules for the hypothetical economy in Tables 9-1 and 9-4. Similar to consumption and investment schedules, a net export schedule lists the amount of a particular expenditure—in this case net exports—which will occur at each level of GDP. In net export schedule X_{n1} (columns 1 and 2), exports exceed imports by $5 billion at each level of GDP. Perhaps exports are $15 billion while imports are $10 billion. In schedule X_{n2} (columns 1 and 3), imports are $5 billion higher than exports. Perhaps imports are $20 billion while exports are $15 billion. To simplify our discussion, we assume in both schedules that net exports are independent of GDP.[1]

The two net export schedules in Table 10-2 are plotted in Figure 10-4b. Schedule X_{n1} reveals that a *positive* $5 billion of net exports is associated with each level of GDP. Conversely, X_{n2} is below the horizon-

---

[1]In reality, although our *exports* depend on *foreign* incomes and are thus independent of U.S. GDP, our *imports* do vary directly with our own *domestic* national income. Just as our domestic consumption varies directly with our GDP, so do our purchases of foreign goods. As our GDP rises, U.S. households buy not only more Pontiacs and more Pepsi but also more Porsches and Perrier. However, for now we will ignore the complications of the positive relationship between imports and U.S. GDP.

TABLE 10-2 Two net export schedules (in billions)

(1) Level of GDP	(2) Net exports X_{n1} $(X > M)$	(3) Net exports X_{n2} $(X < M)$
$370	$+5	$-5
390	+5	-5
410	+5	-5
430	+5	-5
450	+5	-5
470	+5	-5
490	+5	-5
510	+5	-5
530	+5	-5
550	+5	-5

(a) Aggregate expenditures schedule

(b) Net export schedule, X_n

FIGURE 10-4 Net exports and equilibrium GDP Positive net exports such as shown by the net export schedule X_{n1} in (b) elevate the aggregate expenditures schedule in (a) from the closed-economy level of $C + I_g$ to the open-economy level of $C + I_g + X_{n1}$. Negative net exports such as depicted by the net export schedule X_{n2} in (b) lower the aggregate expenditures schedule in (a) from the closed-economy level of $C + I_g$ to the open-economy level of $C + I_g + X_{n2}$.

tal axis and thus shows net exports of *negative* $5 billion at all GDPs.

Net Exports and Equilibrium GDP

The aggregate expenditures schedule labeled $C + I_g$ in Figure 10-4a is identical to that in Table 9-4 and Figure 9-8. That is, $C + I_g$ reflects the combined consumption and gross investment expenditures occurring at each level of GDP. With no foreign sector, the equilibrium GDP will be $470 billion. This equilibrium real output is determined at the intersection of

the $C + I_g$ schedule and the 45 degree reference line. Only there will aggregate expenditures equal GDP.

But net exports can be either positive or negative. Let's see how each of the net export schedules in Figure 10-4b affects equilibrium GDP.

Positive Net Exports Suppose the net export schedule is X_{n1}. The $5 billion of additional net export expenditures by the rest of the world is accounted for by adding that $5 billion to the $C + I_g$ schedule in Figure 10-4a. Aggregate expenditures at each level of GDP are then $5 billion higher than $C + I_g$ alone.

The aggregate expenditures schedule for the open economy thus becomes $C + I_g + X_{n1}$. It shows that international trade in this case increases equilibrium GDP from $470 billion in the private closed economy to $490 billion in the private open economy.

You should verify that the new equilibrium GDP is $490 billion by adding $X_n = \$5$ billion to each level of aggregate expenditures in Table 9-4 and then determining the GDP for which $C + I_g + X_n$ equals GDP.

Generalization: *Positive net exports increase aggregate expenditures beyond what they would be in a closed economy and thus increase an economy's GDP.* Adding net exports of $5 billion has increased GDP by $20 billion, in this case implying a multiplier of 4.

Negative Net Exports An extension of our reasoning enables us to determine the effect of negative net exports on equilibrium GDP. If net exports are X_{n2} in Figure 10-4b, net exports are a negative $5 billion. This means that our hypothetical economy is importing $5 billion more of goods than it is selling to people abroad. The aggregate expenditures schedule shown as $C + I_g$ in Figure 10-4a therefore overstates the expenditures on *domestic* output at each level of GDP. We must reduce the sum of consumption and investment expenditures by the $5 billion net amount spent on imported goods. We must subtract the $5 billion of *net* imports (= minus $5 billion of net exports) from $C + I_g$.

After we subtract $5 billion from the $C + I_g$ schedule in Figure 10-4a, the relevant aggregate expenditures schedule becomes $C + I_g + X_{n2}$. It shows that equilibrium GDP falls from $470 to $450. Again, a change in net exports of $5 billion has resulted in a fourfold change in GDP, reminding us that the multiplier is 4. Confirmation of the new equilibrium GDP can be obtained by subtracting $X_n = -\$5$ billion from aggregate expenditures at each level of GDP in Table 9-4 and ascertaining the new equilibrium GDP for which $C + I_g + X_n$ equals GDP.

This gives a corollary to our first generalization: *Negative net exports reduce aggregate expenditures below what they would be in a closed economy and therefore decrease an economy's GDP.* Imports add to the stock of goods available in the economy but they diminish real GDP by reducing expenditures on domestically produced products.

Our generalizations of the effects of X_n on GDP mean that a decline in net exports—a decrease in exports or an increase in imports—reduces aggregate expenditures and contracts a nation's GDP.

Conversely, an increase in net exports—the result of either an increase in exports or a decrease in imports—increases aggregate expenditures and expands a nation's GDP.

Net exports vary greatly among the major industrial nations, as is shown in Global Perspective 10-1. **(Key Question 5)**

International Economic Linkages

Our analysis of net exports and real GDP reveals how circumstances or policies abroad can affect our GDP.

Prosperity Abroad A rising level of real output and thus income among a nation's foreign trading partners permits it to sell more goods abroad, thus raising its net exports and increasing its real GDP. We should be interested in the prosperity of our trading partners because their good fortune enables them to buy more of our exports and transfer some of their prosperity to us.

Tariffs Suppose foreign trading partners impose high tariffs on U.S. goods to reduce their imports

GLOBAL PERSPECTIVE 10-1

Net exports of goods, select nations

Some nations, such as Japan and Germany, have positive net exports; other countries, such as the United States and the United Kingdom, have negative net exports.

Source: Organization for Economic Cooperation and Development. Data are for 1996.

from the United States and thus to increase production in their own economies. Their imports are U.S. exports. So when they restrict their imports to stimulate *their* economies, they are reducing our (the United States) exports and depressing *our* economy. We may retaliate by imposing trade barriers on their products. If so, their exports to us will decline and their net exports may fall. It is not at all clear, then, whether tariffs increase or decrease a nation's net exports. In the Great Depression of the 1930s various nations, including the United States, imposed trade barriers as a way of reducing domestic unemployment. But rounds of retaliation simply throttled world trade, worsened the depression, and increased unemployment.

Exchange Rates   Depreciation of the dollar relative to other currencies (discussed in Chapter 6) enables people abroad to obtain more dollars per unit of their own currencies. The price of U.S. goods in terms of these currencies will fall, simulating purchases of U.S. exports. Also, U.S. customers will find they need more dollars to buy foreign goods and, consequently, will reduce their spending on imports. The increased exports and decreased imports will increase U.S. net exports and thus expand the nation's GDP.

Whether depreciation of the dollar will actually raise real GDP or produce inflation depends on the initial position of the economy relative to its full-employment output. If the economy is operating below its full-employment level, depreciation of the dollar and the resulting rise in net exports will increase aggregate expenditures and thus expand real GDP. But if the economy is already fully employed, the increase in net exports and aggregate expenditures will cause demand-pull inflation. Because resources are already fully employed, the increased spending cannot expand real output; but it can and does increase the prices of the existing output.

This last example has been cast only in terms of *depreciation* of the dollar. You should now think through the impact that *appreciation* of the dollar would have on net exports and equilibrium GDP.

QUICK REVIEW 10-1

■ The multiplier effect reveals that an initial change in spending can cause magnified changes in domestic income and output. The multiplier is the factor by which the initial change is magnified: multiplier = change in real GDP/initial change in spending.

■ The higher the marginal propensity to consume (the lower the marginal propensity to save), the larger the simple multiplier: multiplier = 1/MPS.

■ Positive net exports increase aggregate expenditures on domestic output and increase equilibrium GDP; negative net exports decrease aggregate expenditures on domestic output and reduce equilibrium GDP.

ADDING THE PUBLIC SECTOR

Our final step in constructing the aggregate expenditures model is to move the analysis from that of a private (no government) open economy to a mixed economy having a public sector. This means adding government spending and taxes to the model.

Simplifying Assumptions

For clarity, the following simplifying assumptions are made:

1. We continue to use the simplified investment and net export schedules, where levels of investment and net exports are independent of the level of GDP.
2. We suppose government purchases neither depress nor stimulate private spending. They do not cause any upward or downward shifts in the consumption and investment schedules.
3. We assume government's net tax revenues—total tax revenues less "negative taxes" in the form of transfer payments—are derived entirely from personal taxes. Although DI will fall short of PI by the amount of government's tax revenues, GDP, NI, and PI will remain equal.
4. We assume that a fixed amount of taxes is collected regardless of the level of GDP.
5. We continue to suppose that, unless otherwise indicated, the price level is constant.

These assumptions will give us a simple and uncluttered view of how government spending and taxes fit within the aggregate expenditures model. Most of these assumptions will be dropped in Chapter 12 when we discuss how government uses changes in its expenditures and taxes to alter equilibrium GDP and the rate of inflation.

Government Purchases and Equilibrium GDP

Suppose government decides to purchase $20 billion of goods and services regardless of the level of GDP.

Tabular Example   Table 10-3 shows the impact of this purchase on the equilibrium GDP. Columns 1 through 4 are carried over from Table 9-4 for the private closed economy, in which the equilibrium GDP was $470 billion. The only new items are exports and imports in column 5 and government purchases in column 6. (Observe in column 5 that net exports—exports minus imports—are zero). By adding government purchases to private spending $(C + I_g + X_n)$, we get a new, higher level of aggregate expenditures, as shown in column 7. Comparing columns 1 and 7, we find that aggregate expenditures and real output are equal at a higher level of GDP. Without government spending, equilibrium GDP was $470 billion (row 6); with government spending, aggregate expenditures and real output are equal at $550 billion (row 10). *Increases in public spending, like increases in private spending, shift the aggregate expenditures schedule upward and result in a higher equilibrium GDP.*

Note, too, that government spending is subject to the multiplier. A $20 billion increase in government purchases has increased equilibrium GDP by $80 billion (from $470 billion to $550 billion). The multiplier in this example is 4.

This $20 billion increase in government spending is *not* financed by increased taxes. In a moment you will find that increased taxes *reduce* equilibrium GDP.

In the leakages-injections approach, government purchases are an injection of spending. Leakages of saving and imports cause consumption of real output

to fall short of income, creating a potential spending gap. This gap may be filled by injections of investment, exports, and government purchases. In Table 10-3 the $550 billion equilibrium level of GDP (row 10) occurs where leakages equal injections, or where $S + M = I_g + X + G$. That is, when taxes are zero, $40 + 10 = 20 + 10 + 20$.

Graphical Analysis   In Figure 10-5a we add $20 billion of government purchases, G, vertically to the level of private spending, $C + I_g + X_n$. That increases the aggregate expenditures schedule (private plus public) to $C + I_g + X_n + G$, resulting in the $80 billion increase in equilibrium GDP from $470 to $550 billion.

Figure 10-5b shows the same change in equilibrium GDP via the leakages-injections approach. Like investment and exports, government spending is an injection which offsets the leakage of saving and imports. It therefore raises the "injections" schedule as shown. Assuming no taxes, the equilibrium GDP is determined by the intersection of the $S + M$ schedule and the $I_g + X + G$ schedule.

Both the aggregate expenditures and leakages-injections approaches indicate the same $550 billion equilibrium GDP. This is $80 billion more than the $470 billion equilibrium GDP of the private closed economy.

A decline in government spending G will lower the aggregate expenditures schedule in Figure 10-5a

TABLE 10-3   The impact of government purchases on equilibrium GDP

(1) Real domestic output and income (GDP = DI), billions	(2) Consumption (C), billions	(3) Saving (S), billions	(4) Investment (I_g), billions	(5) Net exports (X_n), billions		(6) Government purchases (G), billions	(7) Aggregate expenditures $(C + I_g + X_n + G)$, billions, (2) + (4) + (5) + (6)
				Exports (X)	Imports (M)		
(1) $370	$375	$−5	$20	$10	$10	$20	$415
(2) 390	390	0	20	10	10	20	430
(3) 410	405	5	20	10	10	20	445
(4) 430	420	10	20	10	10	20	460
(5) 450	435	15	20	10	10	20	475
(6) 470	450	20	20	10	10	20	490
(7) 490	465	25	20	10	10	20	505
(8) 510	480	30	20	10	10	20	520
(9) 530	495	35	20	10	10	20	535
(10) **550**	**510**	**40**	**20**	**10**	**10**	**20**	**550**

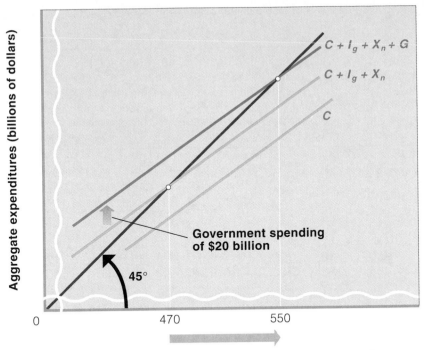

(a) Aggregate expenditures–domestic output approach

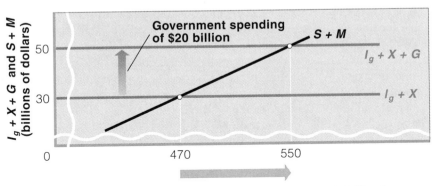

(b) Leakages–injections approach

FIGURE 10-5 Government spending and equilibrium GDP
(a) *Aggregate expenditures–domestic output approach.* The addition of government expenditures of *G* to our analysis raises the aggregate expenditures ($C + I_g + X_n + G$) schedule and increases the equilibrium level of GDP, as would an increase in C, I_g, or X_n. (b) *Leakages-injections approach.* Government spending is an injection which adds to private investment and export spending, raising the injection ($I_g + X + G$) schedule and increasing the equilibrium GDP.

and lower the $I_g + X + G$ schedule in Figure 10-5b. In either case, the result is a multiplied decline in the equilibrium GDP. You should verify in Table 10-3 that if government spending were to decline from $20 billion to $10 billion, the equilibrium GDP would fall by $40 billion, that is, from $550 to $510 billion.

Taxation and Equilibrium GDP

Government also collects taxes. Suppose government imposes a **lump-sum tax,** which is *a tax of a constant amount or, more precisely, a tax yielding the same amount of tax revenue at each level of GDP.* Also, assume this lump-sum tax is $20 billion, so government obtains $20 billion of tax revenue at each level of GDP.

Tabular Example   Table 10-4 continues our example. In it we now find taxes in column 2, and we see in column 3 that disposable (after-tax) income is lower than GDP (column 1) by the $20 billion amount of the tax. Because disposable income is used for consumer spending and saving, the tax lowers both

TABLE 10-4   Determination of the equilibrium levels of employment, output, and income: private and public sectors

(1) Real domestic output and income (GDP = NI = PI), billions	(2) Taxes (T), billions	(3) Disposable income (DI), billions, (1) − (2)	(4) Con-sump-tion (C_a), billions	(5) Saving, (S_a), billions, (3) − (4)	(6) Invest-ment (I_g), billions	(7) Net exports (X_n), billions Exports (X)	Imports (M)	(8) Govern-ment purchases (G), billions	(9) Aggregate expenditures ($C_a + I_g + X_n + G$), billions, (4) + (6) + (7) + (8)
(1) $370	$20	$350	$360	$−10	$20	$10	$10	$20	$400
(2) 390	20	370	375	−5	20	10	10	20	415
(3) 410	20	390	390	0	20	10	10	20	430
(4) 430	20	410	405	5	20	10	10	20	445
(5) 450	20	430	420	10	20	10	10	20	460
(6) 470	20	450	435	15	20	10	10	20	475
(7) **490**	**20**	**470**	**450**	**20**	**20**	**10**	**10**	**20**	**490**
(8) 510	20	490	465	25	20	10	10	20	505
(9) 530	20	510	480	30	20	10	10	20	520
(10) 550	20	530	495	35	20	10	10	20	535

consumption and saving relative to what they would be in the private economy. But by how much will each decline as a result of the $20 billion in taxes? The MPC and MPS hold the answer: The MPC tells us what fraction of a decline in disposable income will come out of consumption, and the MPS indicates what fraction will come out of saving. Since the MPC is .75, if government collects $20 billion in taxes at each possible level of GDP, the amount of consumption at each level of GDP will drop by $15 billion (= .75 × $20 billion). Since the MPS is .25, the amount of saving at each level of GDP will fall by $5 billion (= .25 × $20 billion).

Columns 4 and 5 in Table 10-4 list the amounts of consumption and saving *at each level of GDP;* we see they are $15 and $5 billion smaller, respectively, than those in Table 10-3. For example, before taxes, where GDP equaled DI, consumption was $420 billion and saving $10 billion at the $430 billion level of GDP (row 4 in Table 10-3). After taxes are imposed, DI is $410 billion ($20 billion short of the $430 billion GDP), with the result that consumption is only $405 billion and saving is $5 billion (row 4, Table 10-4).

Taxes cause disposable income to fall short of GDP by the amount of the taxes. This decline in DI reduces both consumption and saving at each level of GDP. The declines in C and S are determined by the MPC and MPS.

What is the effect of taxes on equilibrium GDP? To find out, we calculate aggregate expenditures

again as shown in column 9, Table 10-4. Note there that aggregate spending is $15 billion less at each level of GDP than it was in Table 10-3. The reason is that after-tax consumption, designated by C_a, is $15 billion less at each level of GDP. Comparing real output and aggregate expenditures in columns 1 and 9, we see that the aggregate amounts produced and purchased are equal only at $490 billion of GDP (row 7). The $20 billion lump-sum tax has caused equilibrium GDP to fall by $60 billion from $550 billion (row 10, Table 10-3) to $490 billion (row 7, Table 10-4).

The leakages-injections approach confirms this result. Taxes, like saving and imports, are a leakage from the domestic income-expenditures stream. Saving, importing, and paying taxes are all uses of income which do not involve domestic consumption. Consumption will now fall short of domestic output—creating a potential spending gap—in the amount of after-tax saving and imports *plus* taxes. This gap may be filled by planned investment, exports, and government purchases. Thus, our new equilibrium condition for the leakages-injections approach is this: After-tax saving, S_a, plus imports plus taxes equals planned investment plus exports plus government purchases. Symbolically, $S_a + M + T = I_g + X + G$. You should verify in Table 10-4 that this equality of leakages and injections is fulfilled *only* at the $490 billion GDP (row 7).

Graphical Analysis In Figure 10-6a the $20 billion *increase* in taxes shows up as a $15 (*not* $20) billion *decline* in the aggregate expenditures ($C_a + I_g + X_n + G$) schedule. Under our assumption that all taxes are personal income taxes, this decline in aggregate expenditures results solely from a decline in the consumption C component of the aggregate expenditures schedule. The equilibrium GDP changes from $550 billion to $490 billion because of this tax-caused drop in consumption. *Increases in taxes lower the aggregate expenditures schedule relative to the 45 degree line and reduce the equilibrium GDP.*

Consider now the leakages-injections approach. The analysis here is more complex because the $20 billion in taxes has a twofold effect in Figure 10-6b:

1. The taxes reduce DI by $20 billion and, with the MPS at .25, cause saving to fall by $5 billion at each level of GDP. In Figure 10-6b this is shown as a shift from $S + M$ (saving before taxes plus imports) to $S_a + M$ (saving after taxes plus imports).

2. The $20 billion in taxes is a $20 billion leakage at each GDP level which must be added to $S_a + M$ (not $S + M$), giving us $S_a + M + T$.

(a) Aggregate expenditures–domestic output approach

FIGURE 10-6 **Taxes and equilibrium GDP** (a) *Aggregate expenditures–domestic output approach.* If the MPC is .75, the imposition of $20 billion of taxes will lower the consumption schedule by $15 billion and cause a decline in the equilibrium GDP. (b) *Leakages-injections approach.* Here taxes have a twofold effect. First, with an MPS of .25, the imposition of taxes of $20 billion will reduce disposable income by $20 billion and saving by $5 billion at each level of GDP. This is shown by the shift from S (saving before taxes) + M to S_a (saving after taxes) + M. Second the $20 billion of taxes is an additional $20 billion leakage at each GDP level, giving us $S_a + M + T$. By adding government, the equilibrium condition changes from $S + M = I_g + X$ to $S_a + M + T = I_g + X + G$.

(b) Leakages-injections approach

Equilibrium now exists at the $490 billion GDP, where the total amount which households save plus imports plus the amount of taxes government intends to collect is equal to the total amount businesses plan to invest plus exports plus the amount of government purchases. The equilibrium condition for the leakages-injections approach is $S_a + M + T = I_g + X + G$. Graphically, the intersection of the $S_a + M + T$ and the $I_g + X + G$ schedules determines the equilibrium GDP.

In contrast to our previous case, a *decrease* in existing taxes will raise the aggregate expenditures schedule in Figure 10-6a as a result of an increase in consumption at all GDP levels. In Figure 10-6b a tax cut will lower the $S_a + M + T$ schedule. The result is a magnified *increase* in the equilibrium GDP. You should employ both the expenditures-output and leakages-injections approaches to confirm that a tax reduction of $10 billion (from the present $20 billion to $10 billion) will increase the equilibrium GDP from $490 to $520 billion. **(Key Question 8)**

Balanced-Budget Multiplier

There is a curious thing about our tabular and graphical illustrations. *Equal increases in government spending and taxation increase the equilibrium GDP. If G and T are each increased by a particular amount, the equilibrium level of real output will rise by the same amount.* In our

example the $20 billion increase in G and $20 billion rise in T cause the equilibrium GDP to increase by $20 billion (from $470 to $490 billion).

The rationale for this **balanced-budget multiplier** is revealed in our example. A change in government spending affects aggregate expenditures more powerfully than a tax change of the same size.

Government spending has a *direct* and unadulterated impact on aggregate expenditures. Government spending is a *direct* component of aggregate expenditures. So when government purchases increase by $20 billion, as in our example, the aggregate expenditures schedule shifts upward by the entire $20 billion.

But a change in taxes affects aggregate expenditures *indirectly* by changing disposable income and thereby changing consumption. Specifically, our lump-sum tax increase shifts the aggregate expenditures schedule downward only by the amount of the tax *times* the MPC. A $20 billion tax increase shifts the aggregate expenditures schedule downward by $15 billion (= $20 billion × .75).

The overall result is a *net* upward shift of the aggregate expenditures schedule of $5 billion that, subject to a multiplier of 4, boosts GDP by $20 billion. This $20 billion increase in GDP is equal to the size of the initial increase in government expenditures and taxes. Hence, *the balanced-budget multiplier is 1.*

The fact that the balanced-budget multiplier is 1 is clarified in Figure 10-7. With an MPC of .75, the

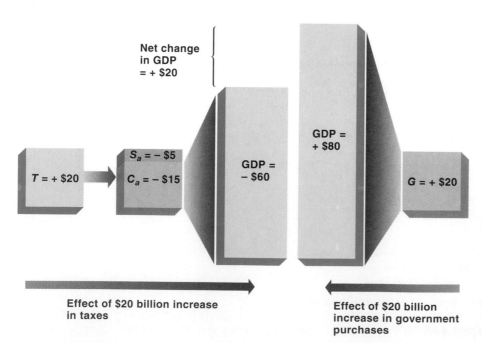

Net change in GDP = + $20

$T = + \$20$

$S_a = -\$5$
$C_a = -\$15$

GDP = − $60

GDP = + $80

$G = + \$20$

Effect of $20 billion increase in taxes

Effect of $20 billion increase in government purchases

FIGURE 10-7 The balanced-budget multiplier The balanced-budget multiplier is 1. An equal increase in taxes and government expenditures will increase GDP by an amount equal to the increase in the amount of government expenditures and taxes. Given an MPC of .75, a tax increase of $20 billion will reduce disposable income by $20 billion and lower consumption expenditures by $15 billion. Because the multiplier is 4, GDP will therefore decline by $60 billion. The $20 billion increase in government expenditures, however, will produce an increase in GDP of $80 billion. The net increase in GDP will be $20 billion, which equals the amount of the increase in government expenditures and taxes.

tax increase of $20 billion reduces disposable income by $20 billion and decreases consumption expenditures by $15 billion. The $15 billion decline in consumption expenditures *reduces* GDP by $60 billion (= $15 billion × the multiplier of 4). But observe in Figure 10-7 that the increase in government expenditures of $20 billion *increases* GDP by $80 billion (= $20 billion × the multiplier of 4). The equal increases of taxes and government expenditures of $20 billion thus yield a *net* increase of GDP of $20 billion (= $80 billion − $60 billion). *Equal increases in G and T expand GDP by an amount equal to those increases.*

This balanced-budget multiplier effect is not limited to situations in which the multiplier is 4. It holds no matter what the multiplier is—a fact you should verify by experimenting with different MPCs and MPSs. The balanced-budget multiplier is always 1.

EQUILIBRIUM VERSUS FULL-EMPLOYMENT GDP

Now that we have the complete aggregate expenditures model at our disposal, we can use it to evaluate the equilibrium GDP.

The $490 billion equilibrium GDP in our complete analysis (Table 10-4 and Figure 10-6) may or may not provide full employment. Indeed, our assumption thus far has been that the economy is operating at less than full employment.

Recessionary Gap

Assume in Figure 10-8a that the full-employment level of GDP is $510 billion and the aggregate expenditures schedule is $(C_a + I_g + X_n + G)_1$. This schedule intersects the 45 degree line to the left of the economy's full-employment output, so the economy's equilibrium GDP of $490 billion is $20 billion short of its full-employment output of $510 billion. According to column 1 in Table 9-4, total employment at the full-employment GDP is 75 million workers. But the economy depicted in Figure 10-8a is employing only 70 million workers; 5 million available workers are not employed. For that reason, the economy is sacrificing $20 billion of output.

The **recessionary gap** is the amount by which aggregate expenditures *at the full-employment GDP* fall short of those required to achieve the full-employment GDP. This deficiency of spending contracts or depresses the economy. Table 10-4, representing the complete economy, shows that at the full-employment level of $510 billion (column 1), the corresponding level of aggregate expenditures is only $505 billion (column 9). The recessionary gap is thus $5 billion, the amount by which the aggregate expenditures curve would have to shift upward to realize equilibrium at the full-employment GDP. Graphically, the recessionary gap is the *vertical* distance (measured at the full-employment GDP) by which the actual aggregate expenditures schedule $(C_a + I_g + X_n + G)_1$ lies below the hypothetical full-employment aggregate expenditures schedule $(C_a + I_g + X_n + G)_0$. Observe in Figure 10-8a that this recessionary gap is $5 billion. Because the multiplier is 4, we observe a $20 billion differential (the recessionary gap of $5 billion times the multiplier of 4) between the equilibrium GDP and the full-employment GDP. This $20 billion difference is the *GDP gap*—a notion we first developed when discussing Figure 8-5.

Inflationary Gap

The **inflationary gap** is the amount by which an economy's aggregate expenditures *at the full-employment GDP* exceed those just necessary to achieve the full-employment GDP. In Figure 10-8b, there is a $5 billion inflationary gap at the $510 billion full-employment GDP. This is shown by the *vertical* distance between the actual aggregate expenditures schedule $(C_a + I_g + X_n + G)_2$ and the hypothetical schedule $(C_a + I_g + X_n + G)_0$ which would be just sufficient to achieve the $510 billion full-employment GDP. Thus, the inflationary gap is the amount by which the aggregate expenditures schedule would have to shift downward to realize equilibrium at the full-employment GDP.

The effect of this inflationary gap—this excessive spending—is that it will pull up output prices. Businesses cannot respond to the $5 billion in excessive spending by expanding their real outputs, so demand-pull inflation will occur. Nominal GDP will rise because of a higher price level, but real GDP will not. Table 10-5 summarizes the steps for determining recessionary and inflationary gaps. **(Key Question 10)**

HISTORICAL APPLICATIONS

Let's see how the concepts of recessionary and inflationary gaps apply to two economic events.

FIGURE 10-8 Recessionary and inflationary gaps The equilibrium and full-employment GDPs may not coincide. (a) A recessionary gap is the amount by which aggregate expenditures at the full-employment GDP fall short of those needed to achieve the full-employment GDP. Here, the $5 billion recessionary gap causes a $20 billion GDP gap. (b) An inflationary gap is the amount by which aggregate expenditures at the full-employment GDP exceed those just sufficient to achieve the full-employment GDP. Here the inflationary gap is $5 billion; this overspending produces demand-pull inflation.

QUICK QUIZ 10-8

1. In the economy depicted:
 a. the MPS is .50.
 b. the MPC is .75.
 c. the full-capacity level of real GDP is $530 billion.
 d. nominal GDP always equals real GDP.

2. The inflationary gap depicted will cause:
 a. demand-pull inflation.
 b. cost-push inflation.
 c. cyclical unemployment.
 d. frictional unemployment.

3. The recessionary gap depicted will cause:
 a. demand-pull inflation.
 b. cost-push inflation.

 c. cyclical unemployment.
 d. frictional unemployment.

4. In the economy depicted, the $5 billion inflationary gap:
 a. expands real GDP to $530 billion.
 b. leaves real GDP at $510 billion but causes inflation.
 c. could be remedied by equal $5 billion increases in taxes and government spending.
 d. implies that real GDP exceeds nominal GDP.

Answers: 1. b; 2. a; 3. c; 4. b

The Great Depression

In October 1929 the stock marked collapsed. At the same time the most severe and prolonged depression of modern times began. In the United States real GDP (in 1992 dollars) plummeted from $791 billion in 1929 to a low of $577 billion in 1933. The unemployment rate rose from 3.2 to 24.9 percent in the same period. As late as 1939, real GDP was only slightly above its level of 10 years earlier and the unemployment rate was still 17.2 percent. (As shown in Global Perspective 10-2, the Great Depression was worldwide.)

A sagging level of investment spending was the major weight which pulled U.S. capitalism into the

TABLE 10-5   Determining the recessionary and inflationary gaps

---

Steps:
1. Determine the economy's full-employment GDP.
2. Look at the economy's current aggregate expenditures schedule, and from that schedule find the amount of expenditure which would be forthcoming at the economy's full-employment GDP.
3. Find the amount of expenditures just necessary to achieve the full-employment GDP.
4. Subtract the amount determined in step 2 from the amount determined in step 3. A negative difference identifies a recessionary gap; a positive difference reflects an inflationary gap.

---

economic chaos of the 1930s. In real terms, gross investment spending shrank from $92 billion in 1929 to $10 billion in 1932—an 89 percent decline. In Figure 10-8, we would depict this decline in investment as a large downward shift in the nation's aggregate expenditures schedule. The outcome in the 1930s was a severe recessionary (depressionary) gap and a historic decline in real GDP.

Several factors caused this steep decline in investment:

Overcapacity and Business Indebtedness

Flush with the prosperity of the 1920s, businesses had over-expanded their production capacity. In particular, there was tremendous expansion of the automobile industry—and the related petroleum, rubber, steel, glass, and textile industries—which ended as the market for new autos became saturated. Business indebtedness also increased rapidly during the 1920s. Furthermore, by the late 1920s much of the income of businesses was committed for the payment of interest and principal on past capital purchases and thus was not available for sustaining expenditures on new capital.

Decline in Residential Construction

The 1920s experienced a boom in residential construction in response to population growth and to housing demand which was deferred because of World War I. This investment spending began to level off as early as 1926, and by the late 1920s the construction industry had virtually collapsed.

Stock Market Crash

The most striking aspect of the Great Depression was the stock market crash of October 1929. The optimism of the prosperous 1920s had elevated stock market speculation to something of a national pastime. This speculation had bid up

stock prices to the point where they did not reflect financial reality; stock prices rose far beyond the profit-making potentials of the firms they represented. A

GLOBAL PERSPECTIVE 10-2

Changes in industrial production, selected countries, 1929–1930 and 1937–1938

The Great Depression of the 1930s was global, with large declines in industrial output occurring in most countries. The Depression began in 1929–1930 for many countries. Precipitous declines in industrial output again occurred in some nations in 1937–1938.

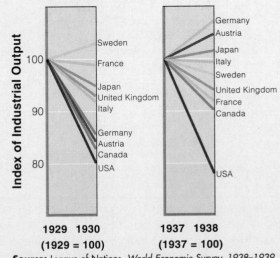

Source: League of Nations, *World Economic Survey, 1938–1939,* p. 107.

Squaring the Economic Circle

Humorist Art Buchwald examines the multiplier.

WASHINGTON—The recession hit so fast that nobody knows exactly how it happened. One day we were the land of milk and honey and the next day we were the land of sour cream and food stamps.

This is one explanation.

Hofberger, the Chevy salesman in Tomcat, Va., a suburb of Washington, called up Littleton, of Littleton Menswear & Haberdashery, and said, "Good news, the new Novas have just come in and I've put one aside for you and your wife."

Littleton said, "I can't, Hofberger, my wife and I are getting a divorce."

"I'm sorry," Littleton said, "but I can't afford a new car this year. After I settle with my wife, I'll be lucky to buy a bicycle."

Hofberger hung up. His phone rang a few minutes later.

"This is Bedcheck the painter," the voice on the other end said. "When do you want us to start painting your house?"

"I changed my mind," said Hofberger, "I'm not going to paint the house."

"But I ordered the paint," Bedcheck said. "Why did you change your mind?"

"Because Littleton is getting a divorce and he can't afford a new car."

That evening when Bedcheck came home his wife said, "The new color television set arrived from Gladstone's TV Shop."

"Take it back," Bedcheck told his wife.

"Why?" she demanded.

"Because Hofberger isn't going to have his house painted now that the Littletons are getting a divorce."

The next day Mrs. Bedcheck dragged the TV set in its carton back to Gladstone. "We don't want it."

Gladstone's face dropped. He immediately called his travel agent, Sandstorm. "You know that trip you had scheduled for me to the Virgin Islands?"

"Right, the tickets are all written up."

"Cancel it. I can't go. Bedcheck just sent back the color TV set because Hofberger didn't sell a car to Littleton because they're going to get a divorce and she wants all his money."

Sandstorm tore up the airline tickets and went over to see his banker, Gripsholm. "I can't pay back the loan this month because Gladstone isn't going to the Virgin Islands."

Gripsholm was furious. When Rudemaker came in to borrow money for a new kitchen he needed for his restaurant, Gripsholm turned him down cold. "How can I loan you money when Sandstorm hasn't repaid the money he borrowed?"

Rudemaker called up the contractor, Eagleton, and said he couldn't put in a new kitchen. Eagleton laid off eight men.

Meanwhile, General Motors announced it was giving a rebate on its new models. Hofberger called up Littleton immediately. "Good news," he said, "even if you are getting a divorce, you can afford a new car."

"I'm not getting a divorce," Littleton said. "It was all a misunderstanding and we've made up."

"That's great," Hofberger said. "Now you can buy the Nova."

"No way," said Littleton. "My business has been so lousy I don't know why I keep the doors open."

"I didn't realize that," Hofberger said.

"Do you realize I haven't seen Bedcheck, Gladstone, Sandstorm, Gripsholm, Rudemaker or Eagleton for more than a month? How can I stay in business if they don't patronize my store?"

Source: Art Buchwald, "Squaring the Economic Circle," *Cleveland Plain Dealer,* Feb. 22, 1975. Reprinted by permission.

downward adjustment was necessary, and it came suddenly and quickly in 1929.

The stock market crash had significant secondary effects. Most important were the psychological repercussions. The buoyant optimism of the 1920s gave way to a wave of crippling pessimism, and the crashing of stock prices created highly unfavorable conditions for acquiring additional money for investment.

Shrinking Money Supply   The nation's money supply plummeted in the early years of the Great Depression, from $27 billion in 1929 down to $20 billion by 1933. This shrinkage resulted from forces operating both abroad and at home, including inappropriate policies of the Federal Reserve Banks. This drastic reduction of the money supply contributed heavily to a sharp decline in aggregate expenditures, including investment, which occurred in the early 1930s.

Vietnam War Inflation

The 1960s was a period of prolonged expansion of real GDP, fueled by increases in consumption spending and investment. One factor in this long expansion was the revolution in economic policy which occurred under the Kennedy and Johnson administrations. This new policy called for government to manipulate its tax collections and expenditures in such a way as to increase aggregate demand, increasing employment and real GDP. For example, in 1962 legislation was enacted which provided for a 7 percent tax credit on investment in new machinery and equipment, thus strengthening the incentives of businesses to invest. In 1964 the government cut personal and corporate income taxes, boosting consumption spending and further increasing investment spending. The unemployment rate fell from 5.2 percent in 1964 to 4.5 percent in 1965.

At this time another expansionary force came into play. The escalation of the war in Vietnam resulted in a 40 percent increase in government spending on national defense between 1965 and 1967. There was another 15 percent increase in war-related spending in 1968. Simultaneously, the draft claimed more and more young people from the ranks of the unemployed.

Remarkably, the unemployment rate fell below 4 percent during the entire 1966–1969 period. But the increased government expenditures, imposed on an already booming economy, also brought about the worst inflation in two decades. Inflation jumped from 1.6 percent in 1965 to 5.7 percent by 1970. In terms of Figure 10-8, the booming investment expenditures and the added government expenditures shifted the aggregate expenditures schedule sharply upward, creating a sizable inflationary gap.

QUICK REVIEW 10-2

■ Government purchases shift the aggregate expenditures schedule upward and raise the equilibrium GDP.

■ Taxes reduce disposable income, lower consumption spending and saving, shift the aggregate expenditures schedule downward, and reduce the equilibrium GDP.

■ The balanced-budget multiplier is 1.

■ A recessionary gap is the amount by which an economy's aggregate expenditures schedule must shift upward to achieve the full-employment GDP; the inflationary gap is the amount by which the economy's aggregate expenditures schedule must shift downward to eliminate demand-pull inflation and still achieve the full-employment GDP.

■ The Great Depression of the 1930s was a period having a large recessionary (depressionary) gap; the years of the Vietnam war (the late 1960s) were characterized by a large inflationary gap.

CRITIQUE AND PREVIEW

Our analysis and examples demonstrate the power of the aggregate expenditures model to help us understand how the economy works, how recessions or depressions can occur, and how demand-pull inflation can arise. But models are only approximations of reality—they have shortcomings. The aggregate expenditures theory has four limitations:

1. ***Does not show price-level changes***   The model can account for demand-pull inflation, as in Figure 10-8b, but it does not indicate how *much* the price level will rise when aggregate expenditures are excessive relative to the economy's capacity. Will the $5 billion inflationary gap of Figure 10-8b cause a 3 percent, 5 percent, 10 percent, or some other rate of inflation? By how much will the GDP price index of Chapter 7 rise for each $1 billion of the inflationary gap? The aggregate expenditures model does not include the price level; it has no way of measuring the rate of inflation.

2. ***Ignores premature demand-pull inflation***   In Chapter 8, specifically Figure 8-7, we noted that demand-pull inflation can occur *before* an actual economy reaches its full-employment level of output. The aggregate expenditures model does not explain why this can happen. In Figure 10-8 the economy could move from $490 billion of expenditures and real GDP to the $510 billion full-employment level of GDP without inflation occurring. In the aggregate expenditures model, inflation occurs only after the economy reaches its full-employment level of output—but that is not what often happens in reality.

3. ***Bars real GDP beyond the full-employment level of output***   We also know from our discussions surrounding Figures 8-5 and 8-7 that for a time an actual economy can expand beyond its full-employment real GDP. The aggregate expenditures model does not allow for this possibility. In Figure 10-8b, the economy's real output cannot expand beyond the full-employment level of $510 billion, even though the aggregate expenditures schedule is $(C_a + I_g + X_n + G)_2$. This high level of spending does *not* generate additional real output; in this model, spending simply drives up inflation.

4. ***Omits cost-push inflation***   We know from Chapter 8 that there are two general types of in-flation: demand-pull inflation and cost-push inflation. The aggregate expenditures model does not address cost-push inflation.

In Chapter 11, we remedy these deficiencies while preserving the insights of the aggregate expenditures model. We use the model to derive aggregate demand—a schedule or curve relating various price levels to the amounts of real GDP which will be demanded at those price levels. When this aggregate demand curve is combined with an aggregate supply curve, we obtain an aggregate expenditures–based model which overcomes the shortcomings just discussed. The better you understand the aggregate expenditures model, the easier it will be to grasp Chapter 11's aggregate demand–aggregate supply model.

CHAPTER SUMMARY

1. A shift in the saving and consumption schedules or in the investment schedule causes the equilibrium output and income level to change by more than the amount of the initial change. This multiplier effect accompanies both increases and decreases in aggregate expenditures.

2. The multiplier is equal to the reciprocal of the marginal propensity to save: The higher the marginal propensity to save, the lower the multiplier. Also, the higher the marginal propensity to consume, the greater the multiplier.

3. The net export schedule relates net exports (exports minus imports) to levels of real GDP. In the aggregate expenditures model we assume that the level of net exports is the same at all levels of real GDP.

4. Positive net exports increase aggregate expenditures to a higher level than would be the case if the economy were a closed one, and they thereby raise equilibrium real GDP by a magnified amount; negative net exports decrease aggregate expenditures relative to those in a closed economy, decreasing equilibrium real GDP. Increases in exports or decreases in imports have an expansionary effect on real GDP, while decreases in exports or increases in imports have a contractionary effect.

5. Government purchases shift the aggregate expenditures schedule upward and raise GDP.

6. Taxation reduces disposable income, lowers both consumption spending and saving, shifts the aggregate expenditures curve downward, and reduces equilibrium GDP.

7. The equilibrium GDP and the full-employment GDP may differ. The recessionary gap is the amount by which aggregate expenditures at the full-employment GDP fall short of those needed to achieve the full-employment GDP. This gap produces a magnified GDP gap. The inflationary gap is the amount by which aggregate expenditures at the full-employment GDP exceed those just sufficient to achieve the full-employment GDP; it causes demand-pull inflation.

8. The Great Depression of the 1930s resulted from a precipitous decline in aggregate expenditures which produced a severe and long-lasting recessionary (depressionary) gap. The Vietnam war period provides a good example of an inflationary gap. An abrupt increase in aggregate demand caused by war spending led to a sizable inflationary gap, with its accompanying demand-pull inflation.

9. The aggregate expenditures model provides many insights about the macroeconomy, but it does not **(a)** show price-level changes, **(b)** account for premature demand-pull inflation, **(c)** allow for real GDP to temporarily expand beyond the full-employment output, or **(d)** account for cost-push inflation.

TERMS AND CONCEPTS

multiplier	balanced-budget	recessionary gap
net exports	multiplier	inflationary gap
lump-sum tax		

STUDY QUESTIONS

- -

1. What effect will each of the changes listed in question 4 of Chapter 9 have on the equilibrium level of GDP? Explain your answers.

2. KEY QUESTION What is the multiplier effect? What relationship does the MPC bear to the size of the multiplier? The MPS? What will the multiplier be when the MPS is 0, .4, .6, and 1? What will it be when the MPC is 1, .90, .67, .50, and 0? How much of a change in GDP will result if firms increase their level of investment by $8 billion and the MPC in the economy is .80? If the MPC is .67? Explain the difference between the simple multiplier and the complex multiplier.

3. Graphically depict the aggregate expenditures model for a private closed economy. Now show a decrease in the aggregate expenditures schedule and explain why the decline in real GDP in your diagram is greater than the initial decline in aggregate expenditures. What would be the ratio of a decline in real GDP to the initial drop in aggregate expenditures if the slope of your aggregate expenditures schedule were .8?

4. Speculate on why a planned increase in saving (an upshift of the saving schedule) by households, *not* accompanied by an increase in investment spending by firms, might result in a decline in real GDP and *no* increase in actual saving. Demonstrate this point graphically, using the leakages-injections approach to equilibrium real GDP. Now assume in your diagram that planned investment instead increases to match the initial increase in desired saving. Using your knowledge from Chapter 2, explain why these *joint* increases in planned saving and planned investment might be desirable for a society.

5. KEY QUESTION The data in columns 1 and 2 in the bottom table are for a private closed economy:
- **a.** Use columns 1 and 2 to determine the equilibrium GDP for this hypothetical economy.
- **b.** Now open this economy to international trade by including the export and import figures of columns 3 and 4. Fill in columns 5 and 6 and determine the equilibrium GDP for the open economy. Explain why this equilibrium GDP differs from that of the closed economy.
- **c.** Given the original $20 billion level of exports, what would be the equilibrium GDP if imports were $10 billion greater at each level of GDP? Or $10 billion less at each level of GDP? What generalization concerning the level of imports and the equilibrium GDP do these examples illustrate?
- **d.** What is the multiplier in these examples?

6. Assume that, without taxes, the consumption schedule of an economy is as shown:

GDP, billions	Consumption, billions
$100	$120
200	200
300	280
400	360
500	440
600	520
700	600

- **a.** Graph this consumption schedule and determine the MPC.
- **b.** Assume now that a lump-sum tax is imposed such that the government collects $10 billion in taxes at all levels of GDP. Graph the resulting con-

(1) Real domestic output (GDP = DI), billions	(2) Aggregate expenditures, private closed economy, billions	(3) Exports, billions	(4) Imports, billions	(5) Net exports, billions	(6) Aggregate expenditures, private open economy, billions
$200	$240	$20	$30	$_____	$_____
250	280	20	30	_____	_____
300	320	20	30	_____	_____
350	360	20	30	_____	_____
400	400	20	30	_____	_____
450	440	20	30	_____	_____
500	480	20	30	_____	_____
550	520	20	30	_____	_____

sumption schedule, and compare the MPC and the multiplier with that of the pretax consumption schedule.

7. Explain graphically the determination of equilibrium GDP for a private economy through the aggregate expenditures approach. Now add government spending (any amount that you choose) to your graph, showing its impact on equilibrium GDP. Finally, add taxation (any amount of lump-sum tax that you choose) to your graph and show its effect on equilibrium GDP. Looking at your graph, determine whether equilibrium GDP has increased, decreased, or stayed the same in view of the sizes of the government spending and taxes that you selected.

8. KEY QUESTION   Refer to columns 1 and 6 in the table for question 5. Incorporate government into the table by assuming that it plans to tax and spend $20 billion at each possible level of GDP. Also assume that all taxes are personal taxes and that government spending does not induce a shift in the private aggregate expenditures schedule. Compute and explain the change in equilibrium GDP caused by the addition of government.

9. What is the balanced-budget multiplier? Demonstrate the balanced-budget multiplier in terms of your answer to question 8. Explain: "Equal increases in government spending and tax revenues of n dollars will increase the equilibrium GDP by n dollars." Does this hold true regardless of the size of the MPS? Why or why not?

10. KEY QUESTION   Refer to the table below in answering the questions which follow:

(1) Possible levels of employment, millions	(2) Real domestic output, billions	(3) Aggregate expenditures $(C_a + I_g + X_n + G)$, billions
90	$500	$520
100	550	560
110	600	600
120	650	640
130	700	680

a. If full employment in this economy is 130 million, will there be an inflationary or a recessionary gap? What will be the consequence of this gap? By how much would aggregate expenditures in column 3 have to change at each level of GDP to eliminate the inflationary or recessionary gap? Explain.

b. Will there be an inflationary or recessionary gap if the full-employment level of output is $500 billion? Explain the consequences. By how much would aggregate expenditures in column 3 have

to change at each level of GDP to eliminate the inflationary or recessionary gap?

c. Assuming that investment, net exports, and government expenditures do not change with changes in real GDP, what are the sizes of the MPC, the MPS, and the multiplier?

11. Advanced analysis: Assume the consumption schedule for a private open economy is such that consumption $C = 50 + 0.8Y$. Assume further that planned investment I_g and net exports X_n are independent of the level of real GDP and constant at $I_g = 30$ and $X_n = 10$. Recall also that, in equilibrium, the real output produced (Y) is equal to aggregate expenditures: $Y = C + I_g + X_n$.

a. Calculate the equilibrium level of income or real GDP for this economy. Check your work by expressing the consumption, investment, and net export schedules in tabular form and determining the equilibrium GDP.

b. What happens to equilibrium Y if I_g changes to 10? What does this reveal about the size of the multiplier?

12. (Last Word) What is the central economic idea humorously illustrated in Art Buchwald's piece, "Squaring the Economic Circle"?

13. WEB-BASED QUESTION   The Multiplier—Calculate a Change in GDP The Bureau of Economic Analysis has current data on national income and product accounts at http://www.bea.doc.gov/briefrm/tables/ebr1.htm. Find the most current values for GDP $= C + I + G + (X - M)$. Assume a MPC of .75, and that for each of the following, the values of the initial variables are those you just discovered. What would be the new value of GDP if: **(a)** Investment increased by 5 percent? **(b)** Imports increased by 5 percent and exports increased by 5 percent? **(c)** Consumption increased by 5 percent? **(d)** Government spending increased by 5 percent? Which 5 percent increase caused GDP to change the most in absolute dollars?

14. WEB-BASED QUESTION   Net Exports—What Is the Current Economic Impact? Positive net exports have an expansionary effect on domestic GDP; negative net exports have a contractionary effect. Check the latest monthly figures at the Bureau of Economic Analysis http://www.census.gov/ftp/pub/indicator/www/ustrade.html for exports and imports of goods and services. Assume a multiplier of 4. Compared to the previous month, how much is GDP increased or decreased by a change in **(a)** net exports of goods, **(b)** net exports of services, and **(c)** net exports of goods and services? Which has the greatest impact? Should services be included or excluded from net exports?

11

Aggregate Demand and Aggregate Supply

The aggregate expenditures model developed in Chapters 9 and 10 is a *fixed-price-level model*—its focus is on changes in real GDP, not on changes in the price level. Moving closer to the real world, we now develop a *variable-price-level model* so that we can simultaneously analyze changes in real GDP *and* the price level. To do this, we need to aggregate all the individual product markets of the economy into a single market. We must combine the thousands of individual equilibrium prices—of pizzas, robots, corn, computers, crankshafts, donuts, new houses, perfume, and legal services—into an aggregate price level. Similarly, we must merge the equilibrium quantities of all the individual products and services into a real GDP. Our new graphical model measures the price level on the vertical axis and real domestic output, or real GDP or real output, on the horizontal axis.

Specifically, in this chapter we introduce the concepts of aggregate demand and aggregate supply, explaining the shapes of the aggregate demand and aggregate supply curves and the forces causing them to shift. Next, we consider the equilibrium levels of prices and real GDP. Finally, we explore the effects of shifts in the aggregate demand and aggregate supply curves on the price level and the size of real GDP.

What you learn in this chapter will help organize your thinking about equilibrium GDP, the price level, and government macroeconomic policies. The tools you acquire here will also help you in later chapters, where we contrast differing views on macroeconomic theory and policy.

AGGREGATE DEMAND

Aggregate demand *is a schedule or a curve showing the various amounts of goods and services—the amounts of real output—that domestic consumers, businesses, government, and foreign buyers collectively desire to purchase at each possible price level.* Other things equal, the lower the price level, the larger the real GDP these buyers will purchase. Conversely, the higher the price level, the smaller the real GDP they will buy. Thus, the relationship between the price level and the amount of real GDP demanded is inverse or negative.

Aggregate Demand Curve

The inverse relationship between the price level and real output is shown in Figure 11-1 where the aggregate demand curve AD slopes

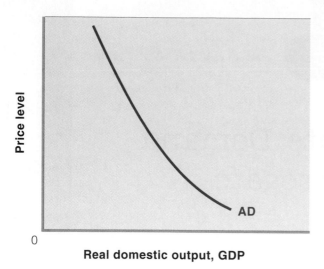

FIGURE 11-1 The aggregate demand curve The downsloping aggregate demand curve AD indicates an inverse relationship between the price level and the amount of real domestic output purchased.

---

downward as does the demand curve for an individual product.

Why the downward slope? The rationale is *not* the same as that for a single product. That explanation centered on income and substitution effects. When the price of an individual product falls, the consumer's (constant) nominal income will enable him or her to purchase more of the product (the income effect). And, as price falls, the consumer wants to buy more of the product because it becomes relatively less expensive than other goods (the substitution effect).

But these explanations do not work for aggregates. In Figure 11-1, when the economy moves down its aggregate demand curve, it moves to lower price levels. But our circular flow model tells us that when consumers pay lower prices for goods and services, less income is likely to flow to resource suppliers in the form of wages, rents, interest, and profits. As a result, a decrease in the price level does *not* necessarily mean an increase in the nominal income of the economy as a whole. Thus, a decline in the price level need not produce an income effect (more of a product is purchased because a decline in its price leaves buyers with more real income).

Similarly, in Figure 11-1 prices in general are falling as we move down the aggregate demand curve, so the rationale for the substitution effect (more of a

product is purchased because it becomes cheaper relative to all other products) is not applicable. There is no overall substitution effect when the price level falls.

If the substitution and income effects do not explain the downsloping aggregate demand curve, what does? The rationale rests on the following three factors.

Wealth Effect The first reason for the downsloping aggregate demand curve involves the **wealth effect.** A higher price level reduces the real value or purchasing power of the public's accumulated financial assets. In particular, the real value of assets with fixed money values, such as savings accounts or bonds, diminishes. Because of the erosion of purchasing power of such assets, the public is poorer in real terms and will reduce its spending. A household might buy a new car or a sailboat if the purchasing power of its financial asset balances is, say, $50,000. But if inflation erodes the purchasing power of the asset balances to $30,000, the family may defer its purchase.

Conversely, a decline in the price level will increase the real value or purchasing power of a household's wealth and increase consumption spending.

Interest-Rate Effect The **interest-rate effect** suggests that the aggregate demand curve is downsloping because of the impact of price-level changes on interest rates and, in turn, on consumption and investment spending. As the price level rises, so do interest rates, and rising interest rates reduce certain kinds of consumption and investment spending.

Elaboration: *The aggregate demand curve assumes the supply of money in the economy is fixed.* When the price level increases, consumers need more money for purchases and businesses similarly require more money to meet their payrolls and to buy other needed resources. In short, a higher price level increases the demand for money.

With a fixed supply of money, this increase in the demand for money drives up the price paid for its use. That price is the interest rate. Higher interest rates curtail interest-sensitive expenditures by businesses and households. A firm expecting a 10 percent return on a potential purchase of capital will find that purchase profitable when the interest rate is, say, only 7 percent. But the purchase is unprofitable and will not be made when the interest rate has risen to, say, 12 percent. Similarly, some consumers will decide *not* to purchase houses or automobiles when the interest rate rises.

Conclusion: A higher price level—by increasing the demand for money and the interest rate—reduces the amount of real output demanded.

Foreign Purchases Effect We found in Chapter 7's discussion of national income accounting that imports and exports are components of total spending. The volumes of our imports and exports depend on, among other things, relative price levels here and abroad. If the price level rises in the United States relative to the levels in foreign countries, U.S. buyers will purchase more imports and fewer domestic goods. Similarly, the rest of the world will buy fewer U.S. goods, reducing U.S. exports. In brief, a rise in the U.S. price level will increase our imports and reduce our exports, reducing the amount of net export (export minus import) spending on U.S.-produced products.

More generally, the **foreign purchases effect** is this: A relative increase in a nation's price level reduces its net exports, resulting in a decline in the aggregate amount of domestic output demanded. Conversely, a relative decline in a nation's price level increases its net exports, thereby increasing the amount of domestic output demanded.

Derivation of the Aggregate Demand Curve from the Aggregate Expenditures Model[1]

We can derive the downsloping aggregate demand curve of Figure 11-1 directly from the aggregate expenditures model of Chapters 9 and 10. To do so, we simply need to relate the various possible price levels to corresponding equilibrium GDPs. Note first that in Figure 11-2 we have stacked the aggregate expenditures model (Figure 11-2a) and the aggregate demand curve (Figure 11-2b) vertically. We can do this because real GDP is measured on the horizontal axes of both models. Now suppose that the economy's price level is P_2 and its aggregate expenditures schedule is $(C_a + I_g + X_n + G)_2$, the middle schedule in Figure 11-2a. The equilibrium GDP is then GDP_2. So in Figure 11-2b we can plot the equilibrium real output GDP_2 and the corresponding price level P_2. This gives us one point—namely, $2'$—in Figure 11-2b.

Now assume the price level drops to P_1. Other things equal, this lower price level will (1) increase

the value of wealth, boosting consumption expenditures; (2) reduce the interest rate, promoting investment expenditures; and (3) reduce imports and increase exports, increasing net export expenditures. The aggregate expenditures schedule will rise from $(C_a + I_g + X_n + G)_2$ to, say, $(C_a + I_g + X_n + G)_1$ in Figure 11-2a, giving us equilibrium at GDP_1. In Figure 11-2b we plot this new price-level–real-output combination, P_1 and GDP_1, as point $1'$.

Now suppose the price level increases from the original P_2 to P_3. The real value of wealth falls, the interest rate rises, exports fall, and imports rise. Consequently, the consumption, investment, and net export schedules fall, shifting the aggregate expenditures schedule downward from $(C_a + I_g + X_n + G)_2$ to, say, $(C_a + I_g + X_n + G)_3$, which gives us equilibrium at GDP_3. This lets us locate a third point in Figure 11-2b, namely, point $3'$, where the price level is P_3 and real output is GDP_3.

In summary, a decrease in the economy's price level shifts its aggregate expenditures schedule upward and increases real GDP. An increase in the price level shifts its aggregate expenditures schedule downward, reducing real GDP. The resulting price-level–real GDP combinations yield various points such as $1'$, $2'$, and $3'$ in Figure 11-2b. Together, such points locate the downsloping aggregate demand curve for the economy.

Determinants of Aggregate Demand

Changes in the price level change the level of aggregate spending (Figure 11-2a); this, in turn, changes the amount of real GDP demanded by the economy. More specifically, an increase in the price level, *other things equal*, will decrease the quantity of real GDP demanded; a decrease in the price level will increase the amount of real GDP demanded. These changes are represented graphically as movements along a fixed aggregate demand curve. However, if one or more of those "other things" change, the entire aggregate demand curve shifts. We refer to those "other things" as **determinants of aggregate demand;** they "determine" the *location* of the aggregate demand curve.

We must then distinguish between *changes in the quantity of real output demanded* (caused by changes in the price level) and *changes in aggregate demand* (caused by changes in one or more of the determinants of aggregate demand). A similar distinction was made in

---

[1]This section presumes knowledge of the aggregate expenditures model discussed in Chapters 9 and 10 and can be skipped by readers who are not assigned those chapters.

Real domestic output, GDP
(a) Aggregate expenditures model

Real domestic output, GDP
(b) Aggregate demand–aggregate supply model

FIGURE 11-2 Deriving the aggregate demand curve from the expenditures-output model Through the wealth, interest-rate, and foreign purchases effects, the consumption, investment, and net export schedules and therefore the aggregate expenditures schedule will rise when the price level declines and fall when the price level increases. If the aggregate expenditures schedule is $(C_a + I_g + X_n + G)_2$ when the price level is P_2, the equilibrium output is GDP_2; then P_2 and GDP_2 determine one point (2') on the aggregate demand curve. A lower price level such as P_1 increases aggregate expenditures to $(C_a + I_g + X_n + G)_1$, providing point 1' on the aggregate demand curve. Similarly, a high price level at P_3 shifts aggregate expenditures down to $(C_a + I_g + X_n + G)_3$, so P_3 and GDP_3 yield another point on the aggregate demand curve at 3'.

Chapter 3 in discussing demand curves for single products.

In Figure 11-3, an increase in aggregate demand is depicted by the rightward movement of the curve from AD_1 to AD_2. This shift indicates that, at each price level, the desired amount of real goods and services is larger than before.

A decrease in aggregate demand is shown as the leftward shift of the curve from AD_1 to AD_3, indicating that people desire to buy less real output at each price level.

To reemphasize: The changes in aggregate demand shown in Figure 11-3 occur when changes happen in any of the factors we have assumed to be constant under the phrase "other things equal." These determinants of aggregate demand, or *aggregate demand shifters*, are listed in Figure 11-3. Let's examine each of them in some detail.

Consumer Spending   Even if the price level is constant, domestic consumers collectively may alter their purchases of U.S.-produced real output. When this happens, the entire aggregate demand curve shifts. It shifts leftward, as from AD_1 to AD_3 in Figure 11-3, when consumers buy less output than before at each possible price level; it moves rightward, as from AD_1 to AD_2, when they buy more at each possible price level.

Several factors other than the price level may change consumer spending, thus shifting the aggregate demand curve. As indicated in Figure 11-3, these factors are real consumer wealth, consumer expectations, household indebtedness, and taxes.

Consumer Wealth   Consumer wealth includes all consumer assets, both financial assets such as stocks and bonds and physical assets such as houses and land.

Price level

0   Real domestic output, GDP

Increase in aggregate demand

Decrease in aggregate demand

AD₃ AD₁ AD₂

Determinants of aggregate demand: factors which shift the aggregate demand curve

1. Change in consumer spending
   a. Consumer wealth
   b. Consumer expectations
   c. Household indebtedness
   d. Taxes
2. Change in investment spending
   a. Interest rates
   b. Profit expectations on investment projects
   c. Business taxes
   d. Technology
   e. Degree of excess capacity
3. Change in government spending
4. Change in net export spending
   a. National income abroad
   b. Exchange rates

FIGURE 11-3 Changes in aggregate demand A change in one or more of the listed determinants of aggregate demand will change aggregate demand. An increase in aggregate demand is shown as a rightward shift of the AD curve, here from AD₁ to AD₂; a decrease in aggregate demand, as a leftward shift, here from AD₁ to AD₃.

A sharp decline in the real value of consumer assets encourages people to save more (buy fewer products) to restore their wealth. The resulting decline in consumer spending will decrease aggregate demand—that is, shift the aggregate demand curve leftward. In contrast, an increase in the real value of consumer wealth will increase consumption spending at each price level; the aggregate demand curve will shift rightward.

Warning: We are *not* referring here to the previously discussed "wealth effect" or "real-balances effect." That assumes a fixed aggregate demand curve and results from a change in the price level. In contrast, the change in real wealth addressed here is independent of a change in the price level; it is a *non-price-level factor* which shifts the entire aggregate demand curve. An example would be a rocketing boost in stock prices which increases consumer wealth, even though the price level has not changed. Similarly, a sharp decline in the real value of houses and land reduces consumer wealth, independent of changes in the general price level.

Consumer Expectations Changes in expectations about the future may alter consumer spending.

When people expect their future real incomes to rise, they spend more of their current incomes. Thus present consumption spending increases (present saving falls), and the aggregate demand curve shifts rightward. An expectation that real income will decline in the future reduces present consumption spending and therefore shifts the aggregate demand curve leftward.

Similarly, a widely held expectation of surging future inflation increases aggregate demand today because consumers want to buy products before prices escalate. Conversely, expectations of lower prices in the near future may reduce present consumption. People may postpone some of their present consumption to take advantage of the future lower prices.

Household Indebtedness Households with high levels of indebtedness from past buying financed by borrowing may be forced to cut present spending to pay off their existing debt. The result is a decline in consumption spending and a leftward shift of the aggregate demand curve. When household indebtedness is low, borrowing and present consumption spending tend to increase. The aggregate demand curve shifts to the right.

Taxes A reduction in personal income tax rates raises take-home income and increases consumer purchases at each possible price level. So tax cuts shift the aggregate demand curve rightward. Tax increases reduce consumption spending and shift the aggregate demand curve to the left.

Investment Spending Investment spending—the purchase of capital goods—is a second major determinant of aggregate demand. A decline in the amount of new capital goods desired by businesses at each price level will shift the aggregate demand curve leftward. An increase in the desired amount of investment goods will increase aggregate demand. Let's consider the individual factors which can alter the level of investment spending, as listed in Figure 11-3.

Interest Rates All else equal, an increase in interest rates caused by a factor other than a change in the price level will lower investment spending and reduce aggregate demand. We are *not* referring here to the so-called "interest-rate effect" due to a change in the price level. Instead, we are identifying a change in the interest rate resulting from, say, a change in the nation's money supply. An increase in the money supply reduces the interest rate, increasing investment and aggregate demand. A decrease in the supply of money increases the interest rate, reducing investment and aggregate demand.

Expected Returns on Investment Projects Higher expected returns on investment projects will increase the demand for capital goods and shift the aggregate demand curve rightward. For example, an anticipated rise in consumer spending can improve the expected returns of possible investment projects. Alternatively, if the profit outlook on possible investment projects dims because of an expected decline in consumer spending, investment spending will decline. Consequently, aggregate demand will also decline.

Business Taxes An increase in business taxes reduces after-tax profits from corporate investment and reduces investment spending and aggregate demand. Conversely, a tax reduction increases after-tax profits from corporate investment, boosts investment spending, and pushes the aggregate demand curve rightward.

Technology New and improved technologies stimulate investment spending and increase aggregate demand. Example: Recent advances in microbiology and electronics have spawned new labs and production facilities to exploit the new technologies.

Degree of Excess Capacity A rise in excess capacity—unused existing capital—will retard the demand for new capital goods and reduce aggregate demand. Other things equal, firms operating factories at well below capacity have little incentive to build new factories. But when firms collectively discover their excess capacity is dwindling, they build new factories and buy more equipment. Thus, investment spending rises and the aggregate demand curve shifts to the right.

Government Spending Government's desire to buy goods and services is a third determinant of aggregate demand. An increase in government purchases of real output at each price level will increase aggregate demand as long as tax collections and interest rates do not change as a result. An example would be a decision by government to expand the interstate highway system. In contrast, a reduction in government spending, such as a cutback in orders for military hardware, will reduce aggregate demand.

Net Export Spending The final determinant of aggregate demand is net export spending. When foreign consumers change their purchases of U.S. goods independently of changes in the U.S. price level, the nation's aggregate demand curve shifts. We specify "independently of changes in price level" to distinguish these changes from spending changes arising from the foreign purchases effect. That effect helps explain why a change in the U.S. price level moves the economy *along* its existing AD curve.

In discussing aggregate demand shifters, we instead address changes in net exports caused by factors other than changes in the price level. Increases in net exports caused by these other factors push the U.S. aggregate demand curve rightward. The logic is as follows: First, a higher level of U.S. exports constitutes an increased *foreign demand* for U.S. goods. Second, a reduction of U.S. imports implies an increased *domestic demand* for U.S.-produced products.

The non-price-level factors which alter net exports are primarily national income abroad and exchange rates.

National Income Abroad Rising national income in a foreign nation increases the foreign demand for U.S. goods, increasing aggregate demand in the United States. As income levels rise in a foreign nation, its citizens can afford to buy both more products made at home *and* more made in the United States. U.S. exports therefore rise in step with increases in the national income of U.S. trading partners. Declines in national income abroad have the opposite effect: U.S. net exports decline, shifting the U.S. aggregate demand curve leftward.

Exchange Rates   A change in the exchange rate (Chapter 6) between the dollar and other currencies also affects net exports and hence aggregate demand. Suppose the dollar price of yen rises, meaning the *dollar depreciates* in terms of the yen. This is the same as saying the yen price of dollars falls—the *yen appreciates*. The new relative values of dollars and yen means consumers in Japan can obtain *more* dollars with any particular number of yen. Consumers in the United States can obtain *fewer* yen for each dollar. Japanese consumers therefore discover that U.S. goods are cheaper in terms of yen. They buy more U.S. goods. Consumers in the United States find that fewer Japanese products can be purchased with a set number of dollars. They buy fewer Japanese goods.

With respect to U.S. *exports*, a $30 pair of U.S.-made blue jeans now might be bought for 2880 yen compared to 3600 yen. And in terms of U.S. *imports*, a Japanese watch might now cost $225 rather than $180. In these circumstances U.S. exports will rise and imports will fall. This increase in net exports translates into a rightward shift of the U.S. aggregate demand curve.

You are urged to think through the opposite scenario in which the dollar appreciates (the yen depreciates).

QUICK REVIEW 11-1

■ Aggregate demand reflects an inverse relationship between the price level and the amount of real domestic output demanded.

■ Changes in the price level produce wealth, interest-rate, and foreign purchases effects which explain the downward slope of the aggregate demand curve.

■ Changes in one or more of the determinants of aggregate demand (Figure 11-3) alter the amounts of real GDP demanded at each price level; they shift the aggregate demand curve.

■ An increase in aggregate demand is shown as a rightward shift of the aggregate demand curve; a decrease, as a leftward shift of the curve.

Aggregate Demand Shifts and the Aggregate Expenditures Model[2]

The determinants of aggregate demand listed in Figure 11-3 are the components of Chapter 10's aggregate expenditures model. When one of these determinants changes, so does the location of the aggregate expenditures schedule. We can easily link shifts in the aggregate expenditures schedule to shifts of the aggregate demand curve.

Let's suppose that the price level is constant. In Figure 11-4 we begin with the aggregate expenditures schedule at $(C_a + I_g + X_n + G)_1$ in the top diagram, yielding real output of GDP_1. Assume now that more optimistic business expectations increase investment spending, so the aggregate expenditures schedule rises from $(C_a + I_g + X_n + G)_1$ to $(C_a + I_g + X_n + G)_2$. (The notation "at P_1" reminds us that the price level is assumed to be constant.) The result will be a multiplied increase in real output from GDP_1 to GDP_2.

In the lower graph the increase in investment spending is reflected in the horizontal distance between AD_1 and the broken curve to its right. The immediate effect of the increase in investment is an increase in aggregate demand by the exact amount of this new spending. But then the multiplier process magnifies the initial increase in investment into successive rounds of consumption spending and an ultimate multiplied increase in aggregate demand from AD_1 to AD_2. Equilibrium real output rises from GDP_1 to GDP_2, the same multiplied increase in real GDP as that in the top graph. *The initial increase in investment in the top graph has shifted the AD curve in the lower graph by a horizontal distance equal to the change in investment times the multiplier.* The change in real GDP is still associated with the constant price level P_1. To generalize,

$$\text{Shift of AD curve} = \text{initial change in spending} \times \text{multiplier}$$

AGGREGATE SUPPLY

Aggregate supply *is a schedule or a curve showing the level of real domestic output which will be produced at each price level.* Higher price levels create an incentive for

---

[2]This section presumes knowledge of the aggregate expenditures model (Chapters 9 and 10). It may be skipped by instructors who wish to rely exclusively on the aggregate demand–aggregate supply framework.

(a) Aggregate expenditures model

(b) Aggregate demand–aggregate supply model

FIGURE 11-4 Shifts in the aggregate expenditures schedule and in the aggregate demand curve   (a) A change in some determinant of consumption, investment, or net exports (other than the price level) shifts the aggregate expenditures schedule upward from $(C_a + I_g + X_n + G)_1$ to $(C_a + I_g + X_n + G)_2$. The multiplier increases real output from GDP_1 to GDP_2. (b) The counterpart of this change is an initial rightward shift of the aggregate demand curve by the amount of initial new spending (from AD_1 to the broken curve). This leads to a multiplied rightward shift of the curve to AD_2, which is just sufficient to show the same increase in GDP as in the aggregate expenditures model.

- -

enterprises to produce and sell more output, while lower price levels reduce output. As a result, the relationship between the price level and the amount of real output businesses offer for sale is direct or positive.

Aggregate Supply Curve

For now, think of the aggregate supply curve as being made up of three distinct segments or ranges: the

(1) horizontal, (2) intermediate (upsloping), and (3) vertical ranges. Let's examine these three ranges and see what each represents. Unless specified otherwise, we assume the aggregate supply curve itself does not shift when the price level changes. You already know from our discussion of Figure 8-7 that the shape of the aggregate supply curve reflects what happens to the per-unit production cost as GDP expands or contracts. You also know from Chapter 8 that the per-unit production cost is found by dividing the total cost of all the resources used in production by the total quantity of output. That is, the per-unit production cost of a particular level of output is the average cost of that output. And the average cost of a particular output establishes the output's price level since the price level must be high enough to cover all the costs of production, including profit "costs."

Horizontal Range   In Figure 11-5 the full-employment real output is designated as Q_f. Recall from Chapter 8 that the natural rate of unemployment occurs at this output. Observe in the figure that the **horizontal range** (*ab*) of aggregate supply includes only real levels of output which are substantially less than the full-employment output Q_f. Thus,

FIGURE 11-5 The aggregate supply curve   The aggregate supply curve shows the level of real domestic output which will be produced at various price levels. It has three ranges: a horizontal range *ab*, where the price level remains constant as domestic output varies; a vertical range *cd*, where real domestic output is constant at the full-capacity level and only the price level can vary; and an intermediate range *bc*, where both real output and the price level are variable.

- -

the horizontal range implies that the economy is in a severe recession or depression and that large amounts of unused machinery and equipment and unemployed workers are available for production. These idle resources—both human and property—can be put back to work with little or no upward pressure on the price level. As output expands over this range from a to b, no shortages or production bottlenecks will be incurred to raise prices. Workers unemployed for 2 or 3 months will hardly expect a wage increase when recalled to their jobs. Because producers can acquire labor and other inputs at stable prices, per-unit production costs do not rise as output is expanded up to Q_u. There is no reason to raise product prices.

This horizontal range also implies that if real output falls, product and resource prices will not move downward. That means real output and employment may fall, but product prices and wages will remain rigid. Indeed, real output and employment will decline in this range *because* prices and wages are inflexible.

Vertical Range At the other extreme, we find that the economy reaches its full-capacity real output at Q_c. Any increase in the price level in this **vertical range** (*cd*) will not produce additional real output because the economy is already operating at its full capacity. Individual firms may try to expand production by bidding resources away from other firms. But the resources and additional production which one firm gains will be lost by some other firm. This bidding will raise resource prices (costs) and ultimately product prices, but real output will remain unchanged.

Intermediate (Upsloping) Range Finally, in the **intermediate range** (*bc*) between Q_u and Q_c, an expansion of real output is accompanied by a rising price level. The aggregate economy is made up of innumerable product and resource markets, and full employment is not reached evenly or simultaneously in the various sectors or industries. Example: As the economy expands in real-output range *bc*, the high-tech computer industry may encounter shortages of skilled workers while the automobile and steel industries still face substantial unemployment. At the same time, in certain industries raw-material shortages or other production bottlenecks may begin to appear. Expansion may also mean some firms will be forced to use older and less efficient machinery as they approach capacity production. And adding employees may create congestion in workplaces. Also, less capable workers may be hired as output expands. All these things tend to decrease productivity, increase costs, and raise prices as production increases in range *bc*.

Once the full-employment level of GDP is reached at Q_f, for a time further price-level increases may bring forth added real output. We know from Chapter 8 that employment and real GDP can expand beyond the full-employment level of output until the economy reaches its maximum capacity. Recall from Figure 8-5 that actual GDP periodically exceeds full-employment GDP. In a prosperous economy the size of the labor force, daily working hours, and the workweek can be extended. Workers can also "moonlight"—hold more than one job. But once the economy's full capacity is reached at Q_c, the aggregate supply curve becomes vertical.

In the intermediate range of aggregate supply, per-unit production costs rise and firms must receive higher product prices for their output to be profitable. In this range rising real output is accompanied by an increasing price level.

Determinants of Aggregate Supply

Our discussion of the shape of the aggregate supply curve reveals that real output increases as the economy moves from left to right through the horizontal and intermediate ranges of aggregate supply. These changes in output result from *movements along* the aggregate supply curve and must be distinguished from *shifts* of the curve itself. An existing aggregate supply curve identifies the relationship between the price level and real output, *other things equal*. But when one or more of these other things change, the curve itself shifts.

The shift of the curve from AS_1 to AS_2 in Figure 11-6 represents an *increase* in aggregate supply. Over the intermediate and vertical ranges this shift is rightward, indicating that businesses collectively will produce more output at each price level. Over the horizontal range of the aggregate supply curve, an increase in aggregate supply can be thought of as a decline in the price level at each level of output (a downward shift of the aggregate supply curve). We will refer to an increase in aggregate supply as a "rightward" shift of the curve. The shift of the curve from AS_1 to AS_3 is a "leftward" shift, depicting a *decrease* in aggregate supply. That means businesses now will produce less output at each price level than before (or charge higher prices at each level of output).

Figure 11-6 lists the other things which shift the aggregate supply curve when they change. Called the

Determinants of aggregate supply: factors which shift the aggregate supply curve

1. Change in input prices
   a. Domestic resource availability
      a_1 Land
      a_2 Labor
      a_3 Capital
      a_4 Entrepreneurial ability
   b. Prices of imported resources
   c. Market power
2. Change in productivity
3. Change in legal-institutional environment
   a. Business taxes and subsidies
   b. Government regulations

FIGURE 11-6 Changes in aggregate supply A change in one or more of the listed determinants of aggregate supply will cause a change in aggregate supply. An increase in aggregate supply is shown as a rightward shift of the AS curve from AS_1 to AS_2; a decrease in aggregate supply, as a leftward shift from AS_1 to AS_3.

determinants of aggregate supply, they collectively determine the *location* of the aggregate supply curve. These determinants have one thing in common: When they change, per-unit production costs also change *at each price level*. This changes profits and causes producers to change their collective output *at each price level*. Hence, when one of the determinants listed in Figure 11-6 changes, the aggregate supply curve shifts. Changes which decrease per-unit production costs shift the aggregate supply curve to the right; changes which increase per-unit production costs shift it to the left. *When per-unit production costs change for reasons other than changes in real output, firms collectively alter the amount of output they produce at each price level.*

Let's examine the aggregate supply shifters in Figure 11-6 in more detail.

Input Prices Input or resource prices—to be distinguished from the output prices that make up the price level—are a major determinant of aggregate supply. All else equal, higher input prices increase per-unit production costs and reduce aggregate supply. Lower input prices do just the opposite. A number of factors influence input prices.

Domestic Resource Availability Increases in the supply of domestic resources lower resource prices and thus decrease per-unit production costs; that shifts the aggregate supply curve to the right. At any specific price level, firms collectively will then produce and offer for sale more real output than before. In contrast, declines in resource supplies increase input prices and shift the aggregate supply curve to the left.

How might changes in the availability of land, labor, capital, and entrepreneurial resources work to shift the aggregate supply curve? We can look at several examples.

1. *Land* Land resources might expand through discoveries of mineral deposits, irrigation of land, or technical innovations, permitting us to transform what were previously "nonresources" into valuable factors of production. An increase in the supply of land resources lowers the price of land inputs, lowering per-unit production costs. For example, the recent discovery that widely available materials at low temperatures can act as superconductors of electricity is expected eventually to reduce per-unit production costs by reducing electricity loss during transmission. This lower price of electricity will increase aggregate supply.

Two examples of reductions in land-resource availability may also be cited: (1) the widespread depletion of the nation's underground water reserves through irrigation, and (2) the nation's loss of topsoil through intensive farming. Eventually, these problems may increase water and land prices and shift the aggregate supply curve leftward.

2. *Labor* About 75 percent of all business costs are wages or salaries. Other things equal, changes in wages have a significant impact on per-unit production costs and on the location of the aggregate supply curve. An increase in the availability of labor resources reduces the price of labor and increases aggregate supply; a decrease has the opposite effect. Examples: The influx of women into the labor force during the past two decades placed a downward pressure on wages and expanded U.S. aggregate supply. Emigration of employable workers from abroad also has historically increased the availability of labor in the United States and reduced wages.

The great loss of life during World War II greatly diminished the postwar availability of labor in the United States, raising per-unit production costs. Currently, the AIDS epidemic has reduced the supply of labor and thus diminished the nation's aggregate supply of real output.

3. *Capital* Aggregate supply usually increases when society adds to its stock of capital. Such an addition would happen if society saved more of its income and used the savings to purchase capital goods. In much the same way, an improvement in the quality of capital reduces production costs and increases aggregate supply. For example, businesses over the years have increased aggregate supply by replacing poor-quality equipment with new, superior equipment.

On the other hand, aggregate supply declines when the quantity and quality of the nation's stock of capital diminishes. Example: In the depths of the Great Depression of the 1930s, the U.S. capital stock deteriorated because new purchases of capital were insufficient to offset the normal wearing out and obsolescence of plant and equipment. Aggregate supply declined.

4. *Entrepreneurial ability* Finally, the amount of entrepreneurial ability available to the economy may change, shifting the aggregate supply curve. Recent media focus on individuals such as Ted Turner and Bill Gates, who have amassed fortunes through entrepreneurial efforts, might con-ceivably increase the number of people who have entrepreneurial aspirations. If so, the aggregate supply curve might shift rightward.

Prices of Imported Resources Just as foreign demand for U.S. goods contributes to U.S. aggregate demand, resources imported from abroad add to U.S. aggregate supply. Whether domestic or imported, resources boost a nation's production capacity. Generally, a decrease in the prices of imported resources expands a nation's aggregate supply; an increase in the prices of these resources reduces a nation's aggregate supply.

Exchange-rate fluctuations are one factor that alters the price of imported resources. Suppose the dollar price of foreign currency falls—the dollar appreciates—enabling U.S. firms to obtain more foreign currency with each dollar. This means that domestic producers face a lower dollar price of imported resources. Under these conditions, U.S. firms would expand their imports of foreign resources and realize reductions in per-unit production costs at each level of output. Falling per-unit production costs of this type shift the U.S. aggregate supply curve to the right.

Also, an increase in the dollar price of foreign currency—dollar depreciation—raises the prices of imported resources. U.S. imports of these resources fall, per-unit production costs jump upward, and the U.S. aggregate supply curve moves leftward.

Market Power A change in the degree of market power or monopoly power held by sellers of resources can also affect input prices and aggregate supply. *Market power* is the ability to set a price above the price that would occur in a competitive situation. The rise and fall of market power held by the Organization of Petroleum Exporting Countries (OPEC) during the past three decades is a good illustration. The tenfold increase in the price of oil that OPEC achieved during the 1970s permeated the economy, drove up per-unit production costs, and jolted the U.S. aggregate supply curve leftward. But then a steep reduction in OPEC's market power during the mid-1980s reduced the cost of manufacturing and transporting products and, as a direct result, increased U.S. aggregate supply.

A change in the market power of labor unions also can affect the location of the aggregate supply curve. Some observers believe that unions experienced growing market power in the 1970s, resulting in union wage increases which widened the gap between union and nonunion workers. This higher pay may have increased per-unit production costs and produced leftward shifts of aggregate supply. But union market power greatly waned during the 1980s. The price of union labor fell in many industries, resulting in lower per-unit production costs. The outcome then was an increase in aggregate supply.

Productivity   Productivity relates a nation's level of real output to the quantity of input used to produce that output. In other words, **productivity** is a measure of average real output, or of real output per unit of input:

$$\text{Productivity} = \frac{\text{total output}}{\text{total inputs}}$$

An increase in productivity means the economy can obtain more real output from its limited resources—its inputs.

How does an increase in productivity affect the aggregate supply curve? We first need to see how a change in productivity alters the per-unit production cost. Suppose real output is 10 units, 5 units of input are needed to produce that quantity, and the price of each input unit is $2. Then

$$\text{Productivity} = \frac{\text{total output}}{\text{total inputs}} = \frac{10}{5} = 2$$

and

$$\text{Per-unit} \atop \text{production cost} = \frac{\text{total input cost}}{\text{total output}} = \frac{\$2 \times 5}{10} = \$1$$

Note that we obtain the total input cost by multiplying the unit input cost by the number of inputs used.

Now suppose productivity increases so that real output doubles to 20 units, while the input unit price and quantity remain constant at $2 and 5 units. You should use the above equations to confirm that productivity rises from 2 to 4 and that the per-unit production cost of the output falls from $1 to $.50. That is, the doubled productivity caused the per-unit production cost to decrease by half.

By reducing the per-unit production cost, an increase in productivity shifts the aggregate supply curve rightward; a decline in productivity increases the per-unit production cost and shifts the aggregate supply curve leftward.

You will see in Chapter 18 that productivity growth is a major factor explaining the long-term expansion of aggregate supply in the United States and the corresponding growth of real GDP. More machinery and equipment per worker, improved production technology, a better-educated and better-trained labor force, and improved forms of business enterprises have raised productivity and increased aggregate supply.

Legal-Institutional Environment   Changes in the legal-institutional setting in which businesses collectively operate may alter the per-unit costs of output and shift the aggregate supply curve. Two changes of this type are (1) changes in taxes and subsidies, and (2) changes in the extent of regulation.

Business Taxes and Subsidies   Higher business taxes, such as sales, excise, and payroll taxes, increase per-unit costs and reduce aggregate supply in much the same way as a wage increase. Example: An increase in payroll taxes paid by businesses will increase production costs and reduce aggregate supply.

Similarly, a business subsidy—a payment or tax break by government to firms—reduces production costs and increases aggregate supply. Example: During the 1970s, the government subsidized firms which produced energy from alternative sources such as wind, oil shale, and solar power. The purpose was to reduce production costs and encourage development of energy sources which might substitute for oil and natural gas. To the extent that these subsidies were successful, the aggregate supply curve moved rightward.

Government Regulation   It is usually costly for businesses to comply with government regulations. Thus, regulation increases per-unit production costs and shifts the aggregate supply curve leftward. "Supply-side" proponents of deregulation of the economy have argued forcefully that, by increasing efficiency and reducing the paperwork associated with complex regulations, deregulation will reduce per-unit costs. In this way the aggregate supply curve purportedly will shift rightward. Conversely, increases in regulation raise production costs and reduce aggregate supply.

QUICK REVIEW 11-2

■ The aggregate supply curve has three distinct ranges: a horizontal range, an upsloping intermediate range, and a vertical range.

■ In the intermediate range, per-unit production costs and therefore the price level rise as output expands toward—and beyond—its full-employment level.

(a) Equilibrium in the intermediate range of aggregate supply

(b) Equilibrium in the horizontal range of aggregate supply

FIGURE 11-7 The equilibrium price level and equilibrium real GDP The intersection of the aggregate demand and supply curves determines the equilibrium price level and equilibrium real output. In (a), where the aggregate demand curve intersects the aggregate supply curve in its intermediate range, the price level will change to eliminate underproduction or overproduction of output; in (b), where the aggregate demand curve intersects the aggregate supply curve in its horizontal range, no change in the price level accompanies the move toward equilibrium real output.

QUICK QUIZ 11-7

1. **The AD curve slopes downward because:**
   a. per-unit production costs fall as real GDP increases.
   b. the income and substitution effects are at work.
   c. changes in the determinants of AD alter the amounts of real GDP demanded at each price level.
   d. decreases in the price level give rise to wealth, interest-rate, and foreign purchases effects which increase the amounts of real GDP demanded.

2. **The AS curve slopes upward in the intermediate range because:**
   a. per-unit production costs rise as real GDP expands toward and beyond its full-employment level.
   b. the income and substitution effects are at work.
   c. changes in the determinants of AS alter the amounts of real GDP supplied at each price level.
   d. increases in the price level give rise to wealth, interest-rate, and foreign purchases effects which increase the amounts of real GDP supplied.

3. **At price level P_1 in graph (a):**
   a. a GDP surplus of Q_2 minus Q_1 occurs which drives the price level up to P_e.
   b. a GDP shortage of Q_2 minus Q_1 occurs which drives the price level up to P_e.
   c. the aggregate amount of real GDP demanded is less than the aggregate amount of GDP supplied.
   d. the economy is in an "unemployment equilibrium."

4. **Suppose the business sector has produced real GDP Q_2 in graph (b). We would expect:**
   a. the price level to fall below P_e.
   b. the AD curve to shift to the right until it intersects AS at real GDP Q_2.
   c. the price level to rise above P_e.
   d. inventories to increase, compelling firms to reduce production to Q_e.

Answers: 1. d; 2. a; 3. b; 4. d

■ By altering the per-unit production cost independent of changes in the level of output, changes in one or more of the determinants of aggregate supply (Figure 11-6) shift the location of the aggregate supply curve.

■ An increase in aggregate supply is shown as a rightward shift of the aggregate supply curve, a decrease as a leftward shift of the curve.

EQUILIBRIUM: REAL OUTPUT AND THE PRICE LEVEL

We found in Chapter 3 that the intersection of a product's demand curve and supply curve determines its equilibrium price and quantity. Similarly, as we see in **Figure 11-7 (Key Graph),** the intersection of the

233

aggregate demand and aggregate supply curves determines the economy's **equilibrium price level** and **equilibrium real domestic output.**

In Figure 11-7a, where the aggregate demand curve crosses the aggregate supply curve in its intermediate range, the equilibrium price level and level of real output are P_e and Q_e, respectively. To illustrate why P_e is the equilibrium price and Q_e is the equilibrium level of output, suppose the price level were P_1 rather than P_e. We observe from the aggregate supply curve that price level P_1 would encourage businesses to produce (at most) real output Q_1. How much real output would domestic consumers, businesses, government, and foreign buyers want to purchase at P_1? The aggregate demand curve tells us the answer is Q_2. Competition among buyers to purchase the lesser available real output Q_1 will drive up the price level to P_e.

As the arrows in Figure 11-7a indicate, the rise in the price level from P_1 to P_e encourages *producers* to increase their real output from Q_1 to Q_e and simultaneously causes *buyers* to scale back their purchases from Q_2 to Q_e. When equality occurs between the amount of real output produced and the amount purchased, as it does at P_e, the economy has achieved equilibrium.

In Figure 11-7b the aggregate demand curve intersects the aggregate supply curve in the range where the aggregate supply curve is perfectly horizontal. Here, the price level does *not* play a role in bringing about the equilibrium level of real output. To understand why, first observe that the equilibrium price and real-output levels in Figure 11-7b are P_e and Q_e. If firms produce a larger output, such as Q_2, they cannot sell it all. Aggregate demand is insufficient to take all that output off the shelves. Faced with unwanted inventories of goods, businesses will reduce their production to Q_e—shown by the leftward-pointing arrow—and the market will then clear.

If firms produce only smaller output Q_1, they will find their inventory of goods quickly diminishing because the quantity of output demanded Q_e exceeds production. They will step up their production and, as shown by the rightward-pointing arrow, output will rise from Q_1 to its equilibrium level Q_e.

CHANGES IN EQUILIBRIUM

Let's now shift the aggregate demand and aggregate supply curves to see the effects on equilibrium real output and the price level.

Shifting of Aggregate Demand

Suppose households, businesses, and government decide to increase their spending—an action which shifts the aggregate demand curve to the right. Our list of determinants of aggregate demand (Figure 11-3) provides several reasons why this shift could occur. Perhaps consumers become more optimistic about future economic conditions. Such favorable expectations might stem from new technological advances which promise to increase the competitiveness of U.S. products in both domestic and world markets and therefore to increase future real income. As a result, consumers would consume more (save less) of their current incomes. Similarly, firms might anticipate enhanced future profits from current investments in new capital. They would therefore increase their investment spending on new equipment and facilities which incorporate the new technology.

As shown in Figure 11-8, the precise effects of an *increase* in aggregate demand depend on whether the economy is currently in the horizontal, intermediate, or vertical range of the aggregate supply curve.

In the horizontal range of Figure 11-8a, where there is high unemployment and much unused production capacity, an increase in aggregate demand (from AD_1 to AD_2) creates a large increase in real output (Q_1 to Q_2) and thus in employment with no increase in the price level (it remains at P_1).

In the vertical range of Figure 11-8b, where labor and capital are at their full capacities, an increase in aggregate demand (AD_5 to AD_6) affects the price level only, increasing it from P_5 to P_6. Real output remains at Q_c.

In the intermediate range of Figure 11-8c an increase in aggregate demand (AD_3 to AD_4) raises both real output (Q_3 to Q_4) *and* the price level (P_3 to P_4).

Price-level increases due to increases in aggregate demand in the vertical and intermediate ranges of the aggregate supply curve (Figure 11-8b and c) constitute *demand-pull inflation.* It results when shifts in aggregate demand *pull up* the price level. **(Key Question 4)**

Multiplier with Price-Level Changes[3]

Close inspection reveals that real GDP does not increase as much in Figure 11-8c as it does in Figure

---

[3]Instructors who do not assign Chapters 9 and 10 may want to use this section as a springboard for introducing the MPC, MPS, and multiplier concepts.

FIGURE 11-8 The effects of increases in aggregate demand The effects of an increase in aggregate demand depend on the range of the aggregate supply curve in which it occurs. (a) An increase in aggregate demand in the horizontal range increases real output but leaves the price level unaffected. (b) In the vertical range, an increase in aggregate demand increases the price level, but real output cannot increase beyond the full-capacity level. (c) An increase in demand in the intermediate range increases both real output and the level of prices.

11-8a, even though the shifts in aggregate demand are of equal magnitudes. In Figure 11-9, which combines Figures 11-8a and 11-8c, we see that the shift in aggregate demand from AD_1 to AD_2 occurs in the horizontal range of the aggregate supply curve. That means the economy is in recession, with excess production capacity and a high unemployment rate. Businesses are willing to produce more output *at existing prices*. In this range, any initial change in spending and resulting multiple change in aggregate demand transmits fully into a change in real GDP and employment. The price level remains constant. In the horizontal range of aggregate supply a "full-strength" multiplier is at work.

If the economy is in either the intermediate or the vertical range of the aggregate supply curve, part or all of any initial increase in aggregate demand will be dissipated in inflation and therefore *not* be reflected in increased real output and employment. In Figure 11-9 the shift of aggregate demand from AD_2 to AD_3 is of the same magnitude as the shift from AD_1 to AD_2. But look what happens. Because we are now in the intermediate range of the aggregate supply curve, a portion of the increase in aggregate demand is absorbed as inflation as the price level rises from P_1 to P_2. Real GDP rises only to GDP′. If the aggregate supply curve had been horizontal, then the shift from AD_2 to AD_3 would have increased real output to

GDP_3. But inflation has reduced the multiplier so that the actual increase is to GDP′, only about half as much as otherwise.

Our conclusion is this: *For any initial increase in aggregate demand, the resulting increase in real GDP will be*

FIGURE 11-9 Inflation and the multiplier The aggregate demand–aggregate supply model shows how inflation reduces the size of the multiplier. For the increase in aggregate demand from AD_1 to AD_2 the price level is constant and the multiplier is at full strength; output increases from GDP_1 to GDP_2. Although the increase in aggregate demand from AD_2 to AD_3 is of the same magnitude, the impact is partly dissipated in inflation (from P_1 to P_2), and real output increases only from GDP_2 to GDP′.

smaller the greater the increase in the price level. Price-level increases weaken the multiplier.

You should sketch an increase in aggregate demand equal to the shift from AD_2 to AD_3 in the vertical range of aggregate supply to confirm that this increase in spending would be entirely absorbed as inflation. The multiplier would be zero because real GDP would be unchanged.

A Ratchet Effect?

What happens when there is a *decrease* in aggregate demand? Our model predicts that in the horizontal range of aggregate supply, real GDP falls and the price level remains unchanged. In the vertical range prices fall and real output remains at the full-capacity level. In the intermediate range the model suggests that both real output and the price level diminish.

But a complicating factor raises doubts about the predicted effects of declines in aggregate demand in the vertical and intermediate ranges. The reverse movements of aggregate demand—from AD_6 to AD_5 in Figure 11-8b and from AD_4 to AD_3 in Figure 11-8c—may *not* restore the initial equilibrium positions, at least in the short term. The complication is that many prices—of both products and resources—rise quickly but are "sticky" or inflexible in a downward direction. Some economists call this the **ratchet effect** (a ratchet is a mechanism which cranks a wheel forward but not backward).

Graphical Depiction   The workings of the ratchet effect are shown in Figure 11-10. If aggregate demand increases from AD_1 to AD_2, the economy moves from the P_1Q_1 equilibrium at point *a* in the horizontal range of aggregate supply to the P_2Q_c equilibrium at *b* in the vertical range. This increase in aggregate demand has increased the price level. The higher product prices in turn result in increases in wages and other resource prices, raising per-unit production costs at each level of available GDP. Thus the aggregate supply curve shifts upward from P_1abAS to P_2cAS.

But while product prices, resource prices, and per-unit production costs easily move upward, they do not so easily come down. If aggregate demand should decrease from AD_2 to AD_1, the economy will *not* return to the original equilibrium position at *a*. Rather, the higher per-unit production costs will remain, meaning that the aggregate supply curve stays in place at P_2cAS. Thus the initial increase in demand has ratcheted up the price level from P_1 to P_2. Any subsequent decline in aggregate demand (as from AD_2 to

FIGURE 11-10 The ratchet effect   An increase in aggregate demand from AD_1 to AD_2 will move the equilibrium position from *a* to *b* with real domestic output rising from Q_1 to Q_c and the price level from P_1 to P_2. But if prices are inflexible downward, then a decline in aggregate demand from AD_2 to AD_1 will not return the economy to its original equilibrium at *a*. Rather, the new equilibrium will be at *c* with the price level remaining at P_2 and real output falling below the original level to Q_2. The ratchet effect means that the aggregate supply curve has changed from P_1abAS to P_2cAS.

AD_1) reduces real output (here, from Q_c to Q_2) but does *not* reduce the price level.

Causes of Downward Price-Level Inflexibility

The reasons for downward price inflexibility are numerous and interrelated.

1. *Wage contracts*   Wage rates often are inflexible downward, at least for a time. It is usually not profitable for firms to cut their product prices when they cannot also cut their wage rates and thus reduce their per-unit production costs. But why are wages inflexible downward? One reason is that part of the labor force works under contracts prohibiting wage cuts for the duration of the contract. (It is not uncommon for collective bargaining agreements in major industries to run for 3 years.) Similarly, wages and salaries of non-union workers are usually adjusted once a year, rather than quarterly or monthly.

2. *Morale, effort, and productivity*   Wage inflexibility downward is reinforced because employers may *not want* to reduce wage rates. Current wages may be so-called **efficiency wages**—*wages which elicit maximum work effort and thus minimize labor*

cost per unit of output. Lower wages may reduce worker morale and work effort, thereby reducing labor productivity (output per worker). While lower wage rates do reduce labor costs per hour of work, lower worker productivity means *less output* per hour of work. If the latter more than counterbalances the former, then a lower wage rate will increase, not reduce, labor costs per unit of production. In these situations, firms will resist lowering wages when faced with a decline in aggregate demand.

3. *Training investments* Most employers have an "investment" in the training and experience of their present workforces. If they cut wage rates and salaries when aggregate demand declines, they may lose workers more or less randomly; some highly trained and some relatively unskilled workers may quit. When highly trained workers find jobs with new firms, the old employer loses any chance of getting a return on that training investment. A better option might be to maintain wages and lay off workers on the basis of seniority. Generally, workers with less seniority who are laid off will also be less skilled workers in whom the employer's training investment is least. Equally qualified less skilled workers will be available to hire when the economy recovers.

4. *Minimum wage* The minimum wage imposes a legal floor under the wages of the least skilled workers. Firms cannot reduce this wage when aggregate demand declines.

5. *Menu costs* Firms that think a recession will be relatively short-lived may be reluctant to cut their prices. One reason is so-called **menu costs,** named after their most obvious example: the cost of printing new menus when a restaurant changes its prices. But there are other costs of changing prices. There are the costs of (1) estimating the magnitude and duration of the shift in demand to determine whether prices should be dropped, (2) repricing items held in inventory, (3) printing and mailing new catalogs, and (4) communicating new prices to customers, perhaps through advertising. When menu costs are substantial, firms may choose to avoid them by retaining current prices. That is, they will wait to see if the decline in aggregate demand is permanent.

6. *Fear of price wars* Some firms may be concerned that if they reduce their prices, rivals not only will match their price cuts but may retaliate by making even deeper cuts. That is, an initial price cut may touch off an unwanted *price war:* successively deeper and deeper rounds of price cuts. In this unwanted situation, all the firms end up with far less profit than if they had simply maintained their prices. For this reason, each firm may resist making the initial price cut, choosing instead to reduce production and lay off workers. A glance back at Figure 8-3 will reveal the extent of downward price inflexibility at the beginning of the Great Depression. Despite the catastrophic decline in aggregate demand which occurred between 1929 and 1933, monopolistic firms in the agricultural implements, motor vehicle, cement, iron and steel, and similar industries had a remarkable capacity to resist price cuts, accepting large declines in production and employment as an alternative.

Controversy Not all economists are persuaded that the ratchet effect is relevant today. They point to the declining power of unions in the United States and large wage cuts in several basic industries following the 1981–1982 recession as evidence of increased downward wage flexibility. They also note that growing foreign competition has undermined monopoly power and the accompanying ability of firms to resist price cuts when faced with falling demand. But defenders of the ratchet effect question whether these recent changes have altered the basic historical pattern. Since 1950 the price level has fallen in only a single year—1955. Meanwhile, in this period the economy has experienced eight recessions (listed in Table 8-1).

Shifting of Aggregate Supply

Two hypothetical situations will help illustrate the effects of a change in aggregate supply on the equilibrium price level and level of real output.

First, suppose that foreign suppliers impose steep increases on the prices of oil imported by the United States, as OPEC did in 1973–1974 and again in 1979–1980. The higher energy prices spread through the world economy, driving up the cost of producing and distributing virtually every domestically produced product and imported resource. Thus, domestic per-unit costs of production rise at each output level. The U.S. aggregate supply curve shifts leftward, say, from AS_1 to AS_2 in Figure 11-11. The price-level increase here is clearly **cost-push inflation** (Chapter 8).

The effects of a leftward shift in aggregate supply are doubly bad. When aggregate supply shifts from AS_1 to AS_2, the economy moves from point *a* to *b.* Real output declines from Q_1 to Q_2, and the price

Why is Unemployment in Europe So High?

Are the high unemployment rates in Europe the result of structural problems or deficient aggregate demand?

Several European economies have had high rates of unemployment in the past several years. For example, in 1996 France had an unemployment rate of 12.6 percent; Great Britain, 8.2 percent; Italy, 12.1 percent; and Germany, 7.2 percent.

There is little dispute that recessions in Europe in the early 1990s contributed to these high rates. Declines in aggregate demand reduced real GDP and increased unemployment. Nevertheless, a mystery remains: Why were unemployment rates in many European nations so high even *before* their recessions? In 1990 the unemployment rate in France was 9.1 percent; in Great Britain, 6.9 percent; and in Italy, 7.0 percent (compared with only 5.5 percent in the United States). And why have European unemployment rates remained far higher than those in the United States during economic recovery? There are two views on these questions.

1. High Natural Rates of Unemployment Many economists believe the high unemployment rates in Europe largely reflect high natural rates of unemployment. They envision a situation as in Figure 11-7a, where aggregate demand and aggregate supply have produced the full-employment level of real output Q_e. But high levels of frictional and structural unemployment accompany this level of output. In this view, the recent extensive unemployment in Europe has resulted from a high natural rate of unemployment, not from deficient aggregate demand. An increase in aggregate demand would push these economies beyond their full-employment levels of output, causing demand-pull inflation.

The alleged sources of the high natural rates of un-

employment are government policies and union contracts which have increased the costs of hiring workers and reduced the cost of being unemployed. Examples: High minimum wages have discouraged employers from hiring low-skilled workers; generous welfare benefits have weakened incentives for people to take available jobs; restrictions against firings have discouraged firms from employing workers; 30 to 40 days per year of paid vacations and holidays have boosted the cost of hiring workers; high worker absenteeism has reduced productivity; and high employer costs of health, pension, disability, and other benefits have discouraged hiring.

2. Deficient Aggregate Demand Not all economists agree that government and union policies have pushed up Europe's natural rate of unemployment. Instead, they point to insufficient aggregate demand as the culprit. They see the European economies in terms of Figure 11-7b, where the equilibrium real output Q_e is less than it would be if aggregate demand were stronger. The argument is that the European governments have been so fearful of inflation that they have not undertaken appropriate fiscal and monetary policies (discussed later in Chapters 12 and 15) to increase aggregate demand. In this view, increases in aggregate demand would not be inflationary, since these economies have considerable excess capacity. If they are operating in the horizontal range of their aggregate supply curves, a rightward shift of their aggregate demand curves would expand output and employment without increasing inflation.

Conclusion: The debate over high unemployment in Europe reflects disagreement on where European aggregate demand curves lie relative to full-employment levels of output. If these curves are *at* the full-employment real GDP, as in Figure 11-7a, then the high levels of unemployment are "natural." Public policies should focus on lowering minimum wages, reducing vacation time, reducing welfare benefits, easing restrictions on layoffs, and so on. But if the aggregate demand curves in the European nations lie to the left of their full-employment levels of output, as in Figure 11-7b, then expansionary government policies such as reduced interest rates or tax cuts may be in order.

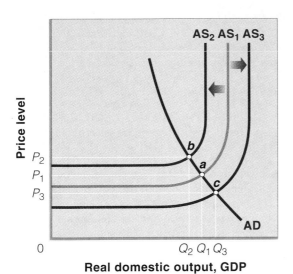

Real domestic output, GDP

FIGURE 11-11 The effects of changes in aggregate supply A leftward shift of aggregate supply from AS_1 to AS_2 will cause cost-push inflation in that the price level increases from P_1 to P_2. Real output will fall from Q_1 to Q_2. A rightward shift of aggregate supply from AS_1 to AS_3 will increase real output from Q_1 to Q_3 and reduce the price level from P_1 to P_3.

- -

level rises from P_1 to P_2. Employment falls and inflation occurs.

Now suppose one of the factors in Figure 11-6 changes so that aggregate supply increases. Maybe the economy experiences a sharp increase in productivity. Or perhaps a liberalization of immigration laws increases the supply of labor and pulls wage rates

down. Or maybe lower business excise tax rates reduce per-unit costs (an excise tax is a cost as viewed by a business), shifting the aggregate supply curve rightward. In Figure 11-11 the shift of aggregate supply from AS_1 to AS_3 moves the economy from a to c. Real output increases from Q_1 to Q_3, and assuming downward price and wage flexibility, the price level falls from P_1 to P_3.

The shift of the aggregate supply curve from AS_1 to AS_3 involves a change in the full-employment *and* full-capacity levels of real output. In particular, this shift signifies economic growth and indicates that the economy's potential output has increased. In terms of Chapter 2, the economy's production possibilities curve has moved outward, reflected in the rightward shift of the aggregate supply curve in Figure 11-11. **(Key Questions 5, 7, and 9)**

QUICK REVIEW 11-3

■ The equilibrium price level and amount of real output are determined at the intersection of the aggregate demand and aggregate supply curves.

■ Increases in aggregate demand in the upsloping and vertical ranges of aggregate supply cause demand-pull inflation.

■ The price level is "sticky" or inflexible in a downward direction, at least for a time.

■ Decreases in aggregate supply cause cost-push inflation.

■ Increases in aggregate supply expand real output; they result in economic growth.

CHAPTER SUMMARY

- - - - - - - - - - - - - - - - - -

1. For purposes of analysis we consolidate—or aggregate—the outcomes from the enormous number of individual product markets into a composite market in which there are two variables—the price level and the level of real output. This is accomplished through an aggregate demand–aggregate supply model.

2. The aggregate demand curve shows the level of real output which the economy will purchase at each price level.

3. The aggregate demand curve is downsloping because of the wealth effect, the interest-rate effect, and the foreign purchases effect. The wealth or real-balances effect indicates that inflation reduces the real value or purchasing power of fixed-value financial assets held by house-

holds, causing them to cut back their consumer spending. The interest-rate effect means that, with a specific supply of money, a higher price level increases the demand for money, raising the interest rate and reducing consumption and investment purchases. The foreign purchases effect suggests that an increase in one country's price level relative to the price levels in other countries reduces the net export component of that nation's aggregate demand.

*4. A change in the price level alters the location of the aggregate expenditures schedule through the wealth,

- -

*Starred summary items presume knowledge of the aggregate expenditures model presented in Chapters 9 and 10.

interest-rate, and foreign purchases effects. The aggregate demand curve is derived from the aggregate expenditures model by allowing the price level to change and observing the effect on the aggregate expenditures schedule and thus on equilibrium GDP.

5. The determinants of aggregate demand are spending by domestic consumers, businesses, government, and foreign buyers. Changes in the factors listed in Figure 11-3 cause changes in spending by these groups and shift the aggregate demand curve.

*6. With the price level held constant, increases in consumption, investment, and net export expenditures shift the aggregate expenditures schedule upward and the aggregate demand curve to the right. Decreases in these spending components produce the opposite effects.

7. The aggregate supply curve shows the levels of real output which businesses will produce at various possible price levels.

8. The shape of the aggregate supply curve depends on what happens to per-unit production costs—and therefore to the prices businesses must receive to cover costs and make a profit—as real output expands. In the horizontal range of aggregate supply, there is substantial unemployment and thus production can be increased without raising per-unit costs or prices. In the intermediate range, per-unit costs increase as production bottlenecks appear and less efficient equipment and workers are employed. Prices must therefore rise as real output is expanded. The vertical range coincides with full capacity; real output is at a maximum and cannot be increased, but the price level will rise in response to an increase in aggregate demand.

9. Figure 11-6 lists the determinants of aggregate supply: input prices, productivity, and the legal-institutional environment. A change in any one of these factors will change per-unit production costs at each level of output and therefore alter the location of the aggregate supply curve.

10. The intersection of the aggregate demand and aggregate supply curves determines an economy's equilibrium price level and real GDP.

11. Increases in aggregate demand **(a)** increase real output and employment but do not alter the price level in the horizontal range of aggregate supply, **(b)** increase both real output and the price level in the intermediate range, and **(c)** increase the price level but do not change real output in the vertical range.

12. In the intermediate and vertical ranges of the aggregate supply curve, the aggregate demand–aggregate supply model shows that the multiplier is weakened because a portion of any increase in aggregate demand is dissipated in inflation.

13. The ratchet effect is at work when prices are flexible upward but inflexible downward. An increase in aggregate demand raises the price level, but the price level does not fall when aggregate demand decreases.

14. Leftward shifts of the aggregate supply curve reflect increases in per-unit production costs and cause cost-push inflation. Rightward shifts of the aggregate supply curve result from decreases in per-unit costs and produce an expansion of real output.

TERMS AND CONCEPTS

aggregate demand
wealth effect
interest-rate effect
foreign purchases effect
determinants of
   aggregate demand
aggregate supply

horizontal range
   (of AS curve)
vertical range
   (of AS curve)
intermediate range
   (of AS curve)

determinants of
   aggregate supply
productivity
equilibrium price level
equilibrium real domestic
   output

ratchet effect
efficiency wages
menu costs

STUDY QUESTIONS

1. Why is the aggregate demand curve downsloping? Specify how your explanation differs from that for the downsloping demand curve for a single product.

2. Explain the shape of the aggregate supply curve, accounting for the horizontal, intermediate, and vertical ranges of the curve.

*3. Explain carefully: "A change in the price level shifts the aggregate expenditures curve but not the aggregate demand curve."

4. KEY QUESTION Suppose that the aggregate demand and supply schedules for a hypothetical economy are as shown below:

Amount of real domestic output demanded, billions	Price level (price index)	Amount of real domestic output supplied, billions
$100	300	$400
200	250	400
300	200	300
400	150	200
500	150	100

a. Use these sets of data to graph the aggregate demand and supply curves. Find the equilibrium price level and level of real output in this hypothetical economy. Is the equilibrium real output also the full-capacity real output? Explain.

b. Why will a price level of 150 not be an equilibrium price level in this economy? Why not 250?

c. Suppose that buyers desire to purchase $200 billion of extra real output at each price level. Sketch in the new aggregate demand curve as AD_1. What factors might cause this change in aggregate demand? What are the new equilibrium price level and level of real output? Over which range of the aggregate supply curve—horizontal, intermediate, or vertical—has equilibrium changed?

5. KEY QUESTION Suppose that the hypothetical economy in question 4 has the following relationship between its real output and the input quantities necessary for producing that output:

Input quantity	Real domestic output
150.0	400
112.5	300
75.0	200

a. What is productivity in this economy?

b. What is the per-unit cost of production if the price of each input unit is $2?

c. Assume that the input price increases from $2 to $3 with no accompanying change in productivity. What is the new per-unit cost of production? In what direction would the $1 increase in input

price push the aggregate supply curve? What effect would this shift in aggregate supply have on the price level and the level of real output?

d. Suppose that the increase in input price does not occur but, instead, that productivity increases by 100 percent. What would be the new per-unit cost of production? What effect would this change in per-unit production cost have on the aggregate supply curve? What effect would this shift of aggregate supply have on the price level and the level of real output?

6. Will an increase in the U.S. price level relative to price levels in other nations shift the U.S. aggregate demand curve? If so, in what direction? Explain. Will a decline in the dollar price of foreign currencies shift the U.S. aggregate supply curve rightward or simply move the economy along an existing aggregate supply curve? Explain.

7. KEY QUESTION What effects would each of the following have on aggregate demand or aggregate supply? In each case use a diagram to show the expected effects on the equilibrium price level and level of real output. Assume all other things remain constant.

a. A widespread fear of depression on the part of consumers

b. A large purchase of wheat by Russia

c. A $1 increase in the excise tax on cigarettes

d. A reduction in interest rates at each price level

e. A cut in Federal spending for health care

f. The expectation of a rapid rise in the price level

g. The complete disintegration of OPEC, causing oil prices to fall by one-half

h. A 10 percent reduction in personal income tax rates

i. An increase in labor productivity

j. A 12 percent increase in nominal wages

k. Depreciation in the international value of the dollar

l. A sharp decline in the national incomes of our western European trading partners

m. A decline in the percentage of the U.S. labor force which is unionized

8. What is the relationship between the production possibilities curve discussed in Chapter 2 and the aggregate supply curve discussed in this chapter?

9. KEY QUESTION Other things equal, what effect will each of the following have on the equilibrium price level and level of real output?

a. An increase in aggregate demand in the vertical range of aggregate supply

b. An increase in aggregate supply (assume prices and wages are flexible)

---

*Questions with an asterisk presume knowledge of the aggregate expenditures model (Chapters 9 and 10).

c. Equal increases in aggregate demand and aggregate supply

d. A reduction in aggregate demand in the horizontal range of aggregate supply

e. An increase in aggregate demand and a decrease in aggregate supply

f. A decrease in aggregate demand in the intermediate range of aggregate supply (assume prices and wages are inflexible downward)

*10. Suppose that the price level is constant and investment spending increases sharply. How would you show this increase in the aggregate expenditures model? What would be the outcome? How would you show this rise in investment in the aggregate demand–aggregate supply model? What range of the aggregate supply curve is involved?

*11. Explain how an upsloping aggregate supply curve weakens the multiplier.

12. In the accompanying diagram assume that the aggregate demand curve shifts from AD_1 in year 1 to AD_2 in year 2, only to fall back to AD_1 in year 3. Locate the new year 3 equilibrium position on the assumption that prices and wages are **(a)** completely flexible and **(b)** completely rigid downward. Which of the two equilibrium positions is more desirable? Which is more realistic? Explain why the price level might be ratcheted upward when aggregate demand increases. Be sure to refer to both *efficiency wages* and *menu costs* in your answer.

13. "Unemployment can be caused by a leftward shift of aggregate demand or a leftward shift of aggregate supply." Do you agree? Explain. In each case, specify price-level effects.

14. (Last Word) State the alternative views on why unemployment in Europe has recently been so high. Discuss the policy implications of each view.

15. WEB-BASED QUESTION The Interest-Rate Effect—Price Levels and Interest Rates The interest-rate effect suggests that as the price level rises, so do interest rates, and rising interest rates reduce certain kinds of consumption and investment spending. Compare price levels http://stats.bls.gov/top20.html (initially select Consumer Price Index—All Urban Consumers) and interest rates http://www.bog.frb.fed.us/releases/h15/data.htm (initially select 1-year U.S. Treasury Bills—monthly averages) over the past decade. Do the data support the link between the price level and interest rates? Alternately, compare the producer price index and other interest-rate data. Is the relationship the same?

16. WEB-BASED QUESTION Aggregate Demand and Supply—Equilibrium Prices and GDPs Actual data showing aggregate demand and supply curves do not exist. However, data for prices (CPI) and GDP http://www.oecd.org/std/fas.htm do exist for several countries. Look at the data for the United States, Japan, and Germany. Assume that these CPI and GDP figures represent the equilibrium price and real GDPs for their respective years. Plot the price/GDP levels for the past 3 years for each country using a graph similar to Figure 11-7. Are there any similarities across countries? What changes in aggregate demand and supply are implied by the equilibrium points?

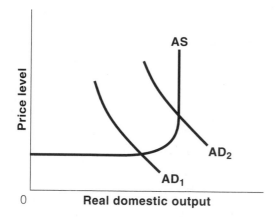

12

Fiscal Policy

$\mathbf{F}$rom time to time, national governments individually take purposeful budget actions to "stimulate their economies" or to "reign in inflation." Here are three examples:

- In the early 1980s, the United States reduced personal income tax rates by some 25 percent, without offsetting decreases in government spending. By expanding aggregate demand, this tax cut helped end the recession of 1980–1981 and promoted growth of output and employment.
- Earlier, during the Vietnam war, the United States placed a 10 percent surcharge—a tax *added* to taxes otherwise owed—on both corporate and personal income taxes. The idea was to reduce private spending and contain the demand-pull inflation it caused.
- In the mid-1990s, Japan instituted a massive government spending program to help move its economy out of recession.

What is the logic of such fiscal actions? Shouldn't government always match any increase in its spending with an increase in taxes, or match any tax cuts with cuts in government spending? Under what circumstances might government purposely change its spending and taxation—engage in so-called *fiscal policy*—to stabilize the economy? Do such policies always work?

This chapter looks briefly at the legislative mandates which give the U.S. government authority to pursue its stabilization role in the economy. It then explores the tools of government fiscal policy in terms of the aggregate demand–aggregate supply model. Next, we examine some factors which automatically adjust government expenditures and tax revenues as GDP rises and falls. Finally, problems, criticisms, and complications of government fiscal policy are addressed.

LEGISLATIVE MANDATES

The idea that government fiscal actions can exert a stabilizing influence on the economy emerged from the Depression of the 1930s. Macroeconomic theory has since played a ma-

jor role in the design of remedial fiscal (budgetary) measures.

Employment Act of 1946 In 1946, when the end of World War II re-created the specter of unemployment, the Federal government formalized its responsibility to promote economic stability. The **Employment Act of 1946** proclaims:

> The Congress hereby declares that it is the continuing policy and responsibility of the Federal Government to use all practicable means consistent with its needs and obligations and other essential considerations of national policy, with assistance and cooperation of industry, agriculture, labor and State and local governments, to coordinate and utilize all its plans, functions, and resources for the purpose of creating and maintaining, in a manner calculated to foster and promote free competitive enterprise and the general welfare, conditions under which there will be afforded useful employment opportunities, including self-employment, for those able, willing, and seeking to work and to promote maximum employment, production, and purchasing power.

The Employment Act of 1946 is a landmark in American socioeconomic legislation because it commits the Federal government to taking action through monetary and fiscal policy to maintain economic stability.

CEA and JEC Responsibility for fulfilling the purposes of the act rests with the executive branch; the President must submit an annual economic report describing the current state of the economy and making policy recommendations to stabilize the economy. The act also established the **Council of Economic Advisers** (CEA) to assist and advise the President on economic matters, and the *Joint Economic Committee* (JEC) of Congress, which has since investigated a wide range of economic problems of national interest. In its advisory capacity as "the president's intelligence arm in the war against the business cycle," the three-member CEA and its staff gather and analyze relevant economic data and use them to make forecasts, to formulate programs and policies designed to fulfill the goals of the Employment Act, and to "educate" the president, Congress, and the general public on problems and policies relevant to the nation's economic health.

DISCRETIONARY FISCAL POLICY

Discretionary fiscal policy is the deliberate manipulation of taxes and government spending by Congress to alter real GDP and employment, control inflation, and stimulate economic growth. "Discretionary" means that the changes in taxes and government

spending are *at the option of* the Federal government. These changes do not occur automatically, independent of specific congressional action.

For clarity, we again assume government spending does not in any way affect planned private spending. Also, we assume fiscal policy affects only the aggregate demand side of the macroeconomy; it has no intended or unintended effects on aggregate supply. Both assumptions will be dropped when we examine the real-world complications and shortcomings of discretionary fiscal policy—or, more simply, *fiscal policy*.

First, we will examine fiscal policy in two situations: recession and demand-pull inflation.

Expansionary Fiscal Policy

When recession occurs, an **expansionary fiscal policy** may be in order. Consider Figure 12-1, where we suppose that a sharp decline in investment spending has shifted the economy's aggregate demand curve leftward from AD_1 to AD_2. (Disregard the arrows and the dashed line for now.) Perhaps profit expectations on investment projects have dimmed, curtailing much investment spending and reducing aggregate demand. Consequently, real GDP has fallen to $485 billion from its near full-employment level of $505 billion. Accompanying this $20 billion decline in real output is an increase in unemployment since fewer workers are needed to produce the diminished output. This economy is experiencing recession and cyclical unemployment.

What should the Federal government do to rev up the economy? It has three main fiscal policy options: (1) increase government spending, (2) reduce taxes, or (3) use some combination of the two. If the Federal budget is balanced at the outset, fiscal policy during a recession or depression should create a government **budget deficit**—government spending in excess of tax revenues.

Increased Government Spending All else equal, an increase in government spending will shift an economy's aggregate demand curve to the right, as from AD_2 to AD_1 in Figure 12-1. To see why, suppose that the recession prompts government to initiate $5 billion of new spending on highways, satellite communications systems, and Federal prisons. We represent this new $5 billion of government spending as the horizontal distance between AD_2 and the dashed line immediately to its right. At *each* price level the amount of real output demanded is now $5 billion greater

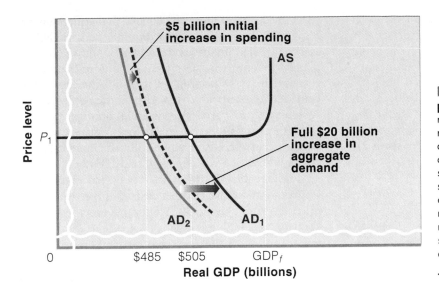

FIGURE 12-1 Expansionary fiscal policy Expansionary fiscal policy, which is represented here, uses increases in government spending or tax cuts to push the economy out of recession. In an economy with an MPC of .75, a $5 billion increase in government spending or a $6.67 billion decrease in personal taxes (producing a $5 billion initial increase in consumption) expands aggregate demand from AD_2 to the dashed curve. The multiplier then magnifies this initial increase in spending to AD_1. Hence, real GDP rises by the desired $20 billion.

than that demanded before the increase in government spending.

But the aggregate demand curve shifts rightward to AD_1; aggregate demand increases by much more than the $5 billion increase in government purchases. This occurs because the multiplier process magnifies the initial change in spending into successive rounds of new consumption spending. If the economy's MPC is .75, then the simple multiplier is 4. The aggregate demand curve thus shifts rightward by four times the distance representing the $5 billion increase in government spending. Because this particular increase in aggregate demand occurs within the horizontal range of aggregate supply, real output rises by the full extent of the multiplier. Observe that real output jumps to $505 billion, up $20 billion from its recessionary level of $485 billion. Concurrently, unemployment falls as firms call back workers laid off during the recession.

Tax Reductions Alternatively, government could reduce taxes to shift the aggregate demand curve rightward, as from AD_2 to AD_1. Suppose government cuts personal income taxes by $6.7 billion, which increases disposable income by the same amount. Consumption will rise by $5 billion (= MPC of .75 × $6.67 billion), and saving will go up by $1.67 billion (= MPS of .25 × $6.67 billion). In this case the horizontal distance between AD_2 and the dashed line in Figure 12-1 represents only the $5 billion initial increase in consumption spending. Again, we call it "initial" consumption spending because the multi-

plier process yields rounds of increased consumption spending. The aggregate demand curve eventually shifts rightward by four times the $5 billion initial increase in consumption produced by the tax cut. Real GDP rises by $20 billion, from $485 billion to $505 billion, implying a multiplier of 4. Employment also increases accordingly.

Undoubtedly you have noted that a tax cut must be somewhat larger than the proposed government spending increase to achieve the same amount of rightward shift in the aggregate demand curve. This is because part of a tax reduction boosts *saving*, not consumption. *To increase initial consumption by a specific amount, government must reduce taxes by more than that amount.* With an MPC of .75, taxes must fall by $6.67 billion for $5 billion of new consumption to be forthcoming, because $1.67 billion is saved (not consumed). If the MPC instead had been, say, .6, an $8.33 billion reduction in tax collections would have been necessary to increase initial consumption by $5 billion. The smaller the MPC, the greater the tax cut needed to accomplish a specific initial increase in consumption and a specific shift in the aggregate demand curve.

Combined Government Spending Increases and Tax Reductions Government can combine spending increases and tax cuts to produce the desired initial increase in spending and eventual increase in aggregate demand and real GDP. In the economy depicted in Figure 12-1, government might increase its spending by $1.25 billion while reducing taxes by $5 billion. You should ascertain why this combination will produce the targeted $5 billion initial increase in new spending.

If you were assigned Chapters 9 and 10, you should think through these three fiscal policy options in terms of the recessionary-gap analysis associated with the aggregate expenditures model (Figure 10-8). Recall from Chapter 11 that rightward shifts of the aggregate demand curve relate directly to upshifts of the aggregate expenditures schedule. **(Key Question 2)**

Contractionary Fiscal Policy

When demand-pull inflation occurs, a restrictive or **contractionary fiscal policy** may help control it. Figure 12-2 emphasizes the vertical range of aggregate supply. Suppose that a shift of the aggregate demand curve from AD_3 to AD_4 in the vertical range of aggregate supply has boosted the price level from P_3 to P_4. (Ignore the dashed line for now.) This increase in aggregate demand might have resulted from a sharp increase in, say, investment or net export spending. If government looks to fiscal policy to control this inflation, its options are opposite those used to combat recession. It can (1) decrease government spending, (2) raise taxes, or (3) use some combination of these two policies. When the economy faces demand-pull inflation, fiscal policy should move toward a government **budget surplus**—tax revenues in excess of government spending.

Decreased Government Spending
Reduced government spending shifts the aggregate demand curve leftward to control demand-pull inflation. In Figure 12-2, the horizontal distance between AD_4 and the dashed line represents a $5 billion reduction in government spending. Once the multiplier process is complete, this spending cut will shift the aggregate demand curve leftward from AD_4 all the way to AD_3. Assuming downward price flexibility, the price level will return to P_3, where it was before demand-pull inflation occurred. Real output will remain at its full-capacity level of $515 billion of real GDP.

In the real world prices are "sticky" downward, so stopping inflation is a matter of halting the rise in the price level, not reducing it to some previous level. Demand-pull inflation usually is experienced as a continual shifting of the aggregate demand curve to the right. Fiscal policy is designed to stop such shifts, not to restore a lower previous price level. Nevertheless, Figure 12-2 displays the basic principle: Reductions in government expenditures can halt demand-pull inflation.

Increased Taxes
Just as government can use tax cuts to increase consumption spending, it can use tax increases to reduce consumption spending. If the economy in Figure 12-2 has an MPC of .75, government must raise taxes by $6.67 billion to reduce consumption by $5. The $6.67 tax reduces saving by $1.67 (= the MPS of .25 × $6.67 billion) and this $1.67 billion reduction in saving, by definition, is not a spending reduction. But the $6.67 billion tax increase also reduces consumption spending by $5 billion (= the MPC of .75 × $6.67), as shown by the

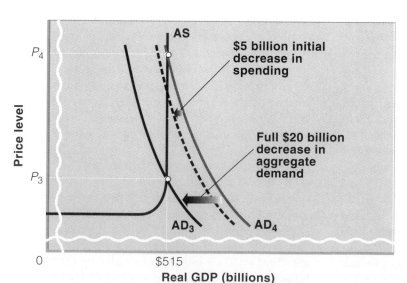

FIGURE 12-2 Contractionary fiscal policy Contractionary fiscal policy, which is represented here, uses decreases in government spending or increases in taxes to reduce demand-pull inflation. In an economy with an MPC of .75, a $5 billion decline in government spending or a $6.67 increase in taxes (producing a $5 billion initial decrease in consumption) shifts the aggregate demand curve from AD_4 to the dashed line. The multiplier effect then shifts the curve further leftward to AD_3. The overall decrease in aggregate demand halts the demand-pull inflation.

distance between AD₄ and the dashed line to its left in Figure 12-2. After the multiplier process, aggregate demand will have shifted leftward by $20 billion at each price level (= multiplier of 4 × $5 billion) and the price level will have fallen from P_4 to P_3. Demand-pull inflation will have been controlled.

Combined Government Spending Decreases and Tax Increases

Government can combine spending decreases and tax increases to reduce aggregate demand and check inflation. To test your understanding, you should determine why a $2 billion decline in government spending *paired* with a $4 billion increase in taxes would shift the aggregate demand curve from AD₄ to AD₃.

Also, if you were assigned Chapters 9 and 10, you should be able to explain the three fiscal policy options for fighting inflation in terms of the inflationary-gap concept developed with the aggregate expenditures model (Figure 10-8). Recall from Chapter 11 that leftward shifts of the aggregate demand curve are associated with downshifts of the aggregate expenditures schedule. **(Key Question 3)**

Financing of Deficits and Disposing of Surpluses

The expansionary effect of deficit spending on the economy depends on the method used to finance the deficit. Similarly, the anti-inflationary impact of the creation of a budget surplus depends on what is done with the surplus.

Borrowing versus New Money

There are two ways the government can finance a deficit: borrowing from (selling interest-bearing bonds to) the public and, with the help of its monetary authorities, issuing new money to its creditors. The impact of each method on aggregate demand is different:

1. *Borrowing* If the government enters the money market and borrows, it will compete with private business borrowers for funds. This added demand for funds might drive up the interest rate and crowd out some private investment spending and interest-sensitive consumer spending. Declines in private spending reduce the expansionary impact of the deficit spending.

2. *Money creation* If the government finances its deficit spending by obtaining newly created money from its monetary authorities, the crowding out of private spending can be avoided.

Federal spending can increase without any adverse effect on investment or consumption. *The creation of new money is a more expansionary (but potentially more inflationary) way of financing deficit spending than is borrowing.*

Debt Retirement versus Idle Surplus

Demand-pull inflation calls for fiscal action which will result in a budget surplus. But the anti-inflationary effect of this surplus depends on what government does with it:

1. *Debt reduction* Since the Federal government has an outstanding debt of $5.4 trillion, it is logical to think that government should use a surplus to retire outstanding debt. Using it to pay off debt, however, may reduce the anti-inflationary impact of the creation of a surplus. To retire its debt, the government buys back some of its bonds; in doing so, it transfers its surplus tax revenues back into the money market. This causes interest rates to fall and thus private borrowing and spending to rise. The increase in private spending somewhat offsets the contractionary fiscal policy which created the budget surplus.

2. *Impounding* Government can realize a greater anti-inflationary effect from its creation of a budgetary surplus by impounding the surplus funds, that is, allowing them to stand idle. When a surplus is impounded, the government is extracting and withholding purchasing power from the economy. If surplus tax revenues are not put back into the economy, no portion of that surplus can be spent. There is no chance that funds will create inflationary pressure to offset the anti-inflationary impact of the contractionary fiscal policy. We conclude that *the impounding of a budget surplus is more anti-inflationary than the use of the surplus to retire public debt.*

Policy Options: *G* or *T*?

Is it preferable to use government spending or taxes to eliminate recession and inflation? The answer depends largely on one's view as to whether the public sector is too large or too small.

"Liberal" economists, who think there are many unmet social and infrastructure needs, usually recommend that government spending be increased during recessions. In times of demand-pull inflation, they tend to recommend tax increases. Both actions either expand or preserve the absolute size of government.

"Conservative" economists, who think the public sector is too large and inefficient, usually advocate tax cuts during recessions and cuts in government spending during times of demand-pull inflation. Both actions either restrain the growth of government or reduce its absolute size.

Discretionary fiscal policy designed to stabilize the economy can be associated with either an expanding or a contracting public sector.

QUICK REVIEW 12-1

■ The Employment Act of 1946 commits the Federal government to promoting "maximum employment, production, and purchasing power."

■ Discretionary fiscal policy is the purposeful change of government expenditures and tax collections by government to promote full employment, price stability, and economic growth.

■ Government uses expansionary fiscal policy to shift the aggregate demand curve rightward—that is, to stimulate spending and expand real output. This policy involves increases in government spending, reductions in taxes, or some combination of the two.

■ Government uses contractionary fiscal policy to shift the aggregate demand curve leftward in an effort to halt demand-pull inflation. This policy entails reductions in government spending, tax increases, or some combination of the two.

■ The expansionary effect of fiscal policy is greater when the budget deficit is financed through money creation rather than via borrowing; the contractionary effect of the creation of a budget surplus is greater when the budget surplus is impounded rather than used for debt reduction.

NONDISCRETIONARY FISCAL POLICY: BUILT-IN STABILIZERS

To some degree government tax revenues change automatically, and in a countercyclical direction, over the course of the business cycle. This automatic response or *built-in stability* results from the makeup of most tax systems. We did not include this built-in stability in our discussion of fiscal policy because we implicitly assumed that the same amount of tax revenue was collected at each level of GDP. That is not actually so. In reality, our net tax system is such that *net tax revenues vary directly with GDP.* (*Net taxes* are tax revenues less transfers and subsidies. From here on, we will use the simpler "taxes" to mean "net taxes.")

Virtually any tax will yield more tax revenue as GDP rises. In particular, personal income taxes have progressive rates and thus yield more than proportionate increases in tax revenues as GDP expands. Furthermore, as GDP increases and more goods and services are purchased, revenues from corporate income taxes and sales and excise taxes also increase. And, similarly, payroll tax payments increase as economic expansion creates more jobs. Conversely, when GDP declines, tax receipts from all these sources also decline.

Transfer payments (or "negative taxes") behave in the opposite way from tax revenues. Unemployment compensation payments, welfare payments, and subsidies to farmers all *decrease* during economic expansion and *increase* during a contraction.

Automatic or Built-In Stabilizers

Figure 12-3 shows how the U.S. tax system creates built-in stability. Government expenditures *G* are fixed and assumed to be independent of the level of GDP; a particular level of spending is decided on by Congress. But Congress does *not* determine the *level* of tax revenues; rather, it establishes tax *rates*. Tax revenues then vary directly with the level of GDP which the economy actually realizes. The direct relationship between tax revenues and GDP is shown by the upsloping line *T*.

Economic Importance   The economic importance of this direct relationship between tax receipts and GDP is revealed when we consider two things:
1. Taxes reduce spending and aggregate demand.
2. It is desirable from the standpoint of stability to reduce spending when the economy is moving toward inflation and to increase spending when the economy is slumping.

In other words, the tax system portrayed in Figure 12-3 builds some stability into the economy. It automatically brings about changes in tax revenues and therefore in the public budget which counter both inflation and recession. A **built-in stabilizer** is *anything which increases the government's budget deficit (or reduces its budget surplus) during a recession and increases its budget surplus (or reduces its budget deficit) during inflation without requiring explicit action by policymakers.* As Figure 12-3 reveals, this is precisely what the U.S. tax system does.

As GDP rises during prosperity, tax revenues *automatically* increase and, because they reduce spend-

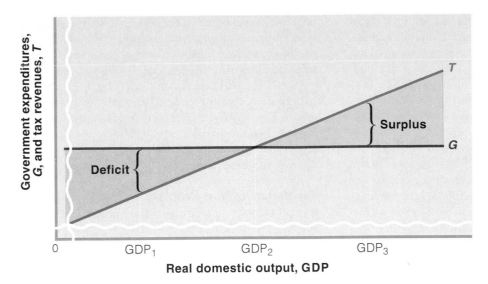

FIGURE 12-3 Built-in stability Tax revenues *T* vary directly with GDP, and government spending *G* is assumed to be independent of GDP. As GDP falls in a recession, deficits will occur automatically and will help alleviate that recession. As GDP rises during expansion, surpluses will occur automatically and will offset possible inflation.

ing, they restrain the economic expansion. That is, as the economy moves toward a higher GDP, tax revenues automatically rise and move the budget from deficit toward surplus.

Conversely, as GDP falls during recession, tax revenues *automatically* decline, increasing spending and cushioning the economic contraction. With a falling GDP, tax receipts decline and move the government's budget from surplus toward deficit. In Figure 12-3, the low level of income GDP_1 will automatically yield an expansionary budget deficit; the high and perhaps inflationary income level GDP_3 will automatically generate a contractionary budget surplus.

Tax Progressivity It is clear from Figure 12-3 that the size of the automatic budget deficits or surpluses—and therefore built-in stability—depends on how responsive tax revenues are to changes in GDP. If tax revenues change sharply as GDP changes, the slope of line *T* in the figure will be steep and the vertical distances between *T* and *G*—the deficits or surpluses—will be large. If tax revenues change very little when GDP changes, the slope will be gentle and built-in stability will be low.

The steepness of *T* in Figure 12-3 depends on the tax system itself. In a **progressive tax system,** the average tax rate (= tax revenue/GDP) rises with GDP. In a **proportional tax system,** the average tax rate remains constant as GDP rises. In a **regressive tax system,** the average tax rate falls as GDP rises. The progressive tax system has the steepest tax line *T* of the three. However, tax revenues will rise with GDP un-

der both the progressive and proportional tax systems, and they may rise, fall, or remain the same under a regressive tax system. But what you should realize is this: *The more progressive the tax system, the greater the economy's built-in stability.*

Changes in public policies or laws which alter the progressivity of the tax system affect the degree of built-in stability. For example, in 1993 the Clinton administration increased the highest marginal tax rate on personal income from 31 to 39.6 percent and boosted the corporate income tax 1 percentage point to 35 percent. These increases in tax rates raise the overall progressivity of the tax system, slightly bolstering the economy's built-in stability.

The built-in stability provided by our tax system has reduced the severity of business fluctuations. But built-in stabilizers can only diminish, *not* correct, major changes in equilibrium GDP. Discretionary fiscal policy—changes in tax rates and expenditures—may be needed to correct inflation or recession of any appreciable magnitude.

Actual versus Full-Employment Budget

We have built-in stability because tax revenues vary directly with GDP. But those automatic increases or decreases in tax revenues mean that the **actual budget** in any particular year does not tell us whether government's current discretionary fiscal policy is expansionary, neutral, or contractionary. Here's why: Suppose an economy is achieving full-employment output at GDP_f in Figure 12-4. But note from the government spending line G and the tax line T that there is an actual budget deficit shown by vertical distance *ab*. Now assume that investment spending plummets, swamping the expansionary effect of this budget deficit and causing a recession to GDP_r. Let's assume that government takes no new discretionary action, so lines G and T remain as shown in the figure. With the economy at GDP_r, tax revenues are lower than before, while government spending remains unaltered. The budget deficit therefore rises to *ec*, expanding from *ab* ($= ed$) by amount *dc*. The added deficit of *dc* is called a **cyclical deficit** because it relates to the business cycle. It is *not* the result of discretionary fiscal actions by government; rather, it is the by-product of the economy's slide into recession.

Note in Figure 12-4 that to find the actual deficit *ec* for year 2, we must know where lines G and T are located *and* the specific level of GDP. The same G and T lines give different deficits or surpluses with different GDPs. Thus, we cannot evaluate the government's fiscal policy—the extent to which it is expansionary, neutral, or contractionary—by looking

only at the size of a current budget deficit or surplus. Because an actual budget deficit or surplus is the result of more than fiscal decisions about spending and taxes (as shown by the locations of lines G and T in Figure 12-4), we must also consider the level of GDP (where the economy is operating on the horizontal axis of Figure 12-4). In the economy represented in Figure 12-4, the actual budget deficit in year 2 (GDP_r) differs from that in year 1 (GDP_f) only because GDP is lower in year 2 than in year 1.

Resolution of the Problem   Economists resolve this problem by standardizing the budget deficits and surpluses for different years in the business cycle; they do this by using the **full-employment budget.** This budget, also called the standardized budget, *measures what the Federal budget deficit or surplus would be with existing tax and government spending structures if the economy were at full employment throughout the year.* The idea is to compare actual government expenditures for each particular year with the tax revenues which would have occurred in that year if the economy had achieved full employment.

Consider Figure 12-4 once again. In full-employment year 1, the full-employment deficit is *ab*, the amount of the actual deficit. In year 2, however, the actual budget deficit of *ec* overstates the full-employment deficit. Specifically, the cyclical part of the deficit *dc* must be subtracted from the actual deficit *ec* to obtain the full-employment deficit, *ed*. We note, then, that the full-employment deficit for year 2 is the same as that for year 1 ($ed = ab$). By comparing these two full-employment deficits, we see that government did not change its fiscal policy between years 1 and 2.

A full-employment budget deficit is also called a **structural deficit** because it reflects the configuration of the G line and T line, *independent of any changes in GDP.* The structural deficits for years 1 and 2 in Figure 12-4 are the same ($ab = ed$). *Discretionary fiscal policy is reflected in deliberate changes in the full-employment deficit (structural deficit).* The actual budget deficit in any particular year is the sum of the structural and cyclical deficits. So changes in the actual budget deficit do not alone tell us whether fiscal policy has become more or less expansionary or contractionary. Changes in the structural deficit (or structural surplus) give us that information.

Historical Comparison   Figure 12-5 compares the deficits and surpluses in the U.S. full-employment budget with the deficits and surpluses in the actual

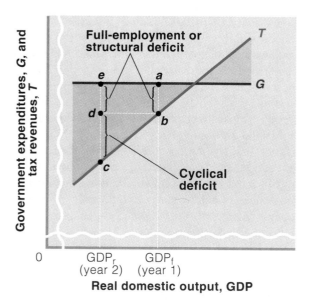

FIGURE 12-4 Full-employment (structural) deficits and cyclical deficits   The actual budget deficit for any specific year is the amount by which government's expenditures exceed its tax revenues. It consists of the structural deficit (or full-employment deficit) and the cyclical deficit. At full-employment output GDP_f, the actual deficit is *ab*, the structural deficit is *ab*, and the cyclical deficit is zero. At recessionary output GDP_r, the actual budget deficit is *ec*, the structural deficit is *ed* (=*ab*), and the cyclical deficit is *dc*.

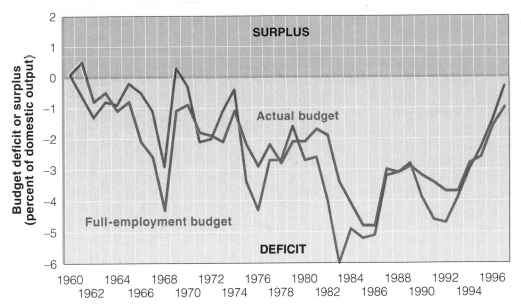

FIGURE 12-5 Actual and full-employment deficits and surpluses in the United States   Full-employment (or structural) budget deficits and surpluses often differ in size from actual budget deficits and surpluses. Changes in full-employment budget deficits or surpluses are better indicators of whether government's fiscal policy is expansionary, neutral, or contractionary than are changes in actual budget deficits or surpluses. (*Source:* Congressional Budget Office.)

budget since 1960. (The deficits and surpluses are shown here as percentages of GDP.) In most years the size of the actual budget deficit or surplus differs from the size of the full-employment deficit or surplus. To reemphasize: The key to assessing discretionary fiscal policy is to disregard the actual budget deficit and instead observe the *change* in the full-employment budget (change in the structural deficit or surplus) from year to year. For example, fiscal policy was very expansionary between 1965 and 1968 and between 1981 and 1986, as reflected in the rapid increases in the full-employment deficit. In contrast, fiscal policy was contractionary in 1969, 1974, 1987, and 1996, as noted by large decreases in the full-employment deficit.

Also, observe in Figure 12-5 that structural deficits have been particularly large since 1981. A big part of the actual deficits during the 1980s and early 1990s was not cyclical (resulting from automatic decreases in tax revenues due to below-full-employment GDP). Rather, the actual deficits reflected structural imbalances between government spending and tax revenues caused by large tax cuts in the 1980s, together with increases in government spending. The year 1989 is an example. Although the economy had achieved full

employment, a sizable structural deficit remained. The same was true in 1995.

Large full-employment-budget deficits persisted through most of the 1990s. During this period the U.S. government largely abandoned discretionary fiscal policy in its attempt to reduce its large structural deficits. These budget deficits were so large that financing them increased real interest rates and undoubtedly crowded out much private investment, a scenario we will elaborate on shortly. Thus, in the 1990s the role of stabilizing the economy has fallen nearly exclusively on the nation's central bank, the Federal Reserve. This institution and its economic policies are the subject of Chapters 13 through 15. **(Key Question 7)**

Global Perspective 12-1 shows that budget deficits are not confined to the United States.

Proposed Balanced-Budget Requirement

The large annual budget deficits in the United States during the past two decades have led some congressional leaders to call for a constitutional amendment requiring that the Federal government balance its

Source: Organization for Economic Cooperation and Development.

GLOBAL PERSPECTIVE 12-1

Budget deficits as a percentage of GDP, selected nations

In 1996 all the major industrial nations had budget deficits, but these deficits varied greatly as a percentage of GDP. In some cases the deficits were largely cyclical; in other instances they were mainly full-employment or structural deficits.

Budget Deficit as a Percentage of GDP, 1996

budget each year. In its strictest form (no exceptions allowed), such a mandate would virtually eliminate discretionary fiscal policy as a tool for stabilizing the economy. Specifically, government could no longer create or increase structural budget deficits as a way to halt and remedy recession.

Of even greater significance, a strict balanced-budget requirement would force government to reduce its spending or increase taxes during recession. To see why, consider Figure 12-6. Suppose that in year 1 the economy is operating at its full-employment level GDP$_f$. Note from the T_1 and G_1 lines that, in this case, the Federal government is balancing its budget: tax revenues equal government spending at GDP$_f$.

Next suppose that in year 2 the economy slides into recession, with real output declining to GDP$_r$. Tax revenues automatically decline, as shown by T_1, and a budget deficit of *ab* emerges. To comply with the balanced-budget requirement, government must

eliminate this cyclical deficit. It can do so in one of three ways:

1. Increasing taxes so that the tax line shifts upward to T_2, intersecting the G_1 line at point *a*
2. Reducing government spending so that the government spending line shifts downward to G_2, intersecting the T_1 line at point *b*
3. Increasing taxes and reducing spending in some *combination* to eliminate the budget deficit shown as distance *ab*

The problem with all three options is that they are aspects of *contractionary* fiscal policy. They all reduce aggregate demand, which *decreases* real GDP. And, as these actions further reduce real GDP, tax revenues decline once again. A new budget deficit therefore arises, requiring greater tax increases or government spending decreases to comply with the balanced-budget requirement. *Rather than stabilizing the economy, a strict balanced-budget requirement may force government to take actions which worsen recession.*

FIGURE 12-6 The effects of a requirement to balance the budget during recession A decline in real output from GDP$_f$ to GDP$_r$ will automatically create a budget deficit of *ab*. If required by law to eliminate this deficit, government will have to (1) shift the tax line upward to T_2 so that it intersects G_1 at point *a*, (2) shift the government spending line downward to G_2 so that it intersects T_1 at point *b*, or (3) enact a combination of tax increases and government spending decreases so that the new tax and government spending lines intersect at GDP$_r$. Each action is contractionary; it will cause a further decline in real GDP.

QUICK REVIEW 12-2

■ Tax revenues automatically increase in economic expansions and decrease in recessions; transfers automatically decrease in expansions and increase in recessions.

■ Automatic changes in taxes and transfers add a degree of built-in stability to the economy.

■ The full-employment budget compares government spending to the tax revenues which would accrue if there were full employment; changes in it are more useful than changes in the actual budget in revealing whether fiscal policy is expansionary, neutral, or contractionary.

■ Full-employment budget deficits are also called structural deficits and are distinct from cyclical deficits.

■ A strict mandate to balance the budget annually would intensify recession by requiring contractionary tax increases and government spending cuts.

PROBLEMS, CRITICISMS, AND COMPLICATIONS

Economists recognize that governments may encounter a number of significant problems in enacting and applying fiscal policy.

Problems of Timing

Several problems of timing may arise in connection with fiscal policy:

1. *Recognition lag* The recognition lag is the time between the beginning of a recession or an inflation and the certain awareness that it is actually happening. This lag arises because of the difficulty in predicting the future course of economic activity. Although forecasting tools such as the index of leading indicators (see this chapter's Last Word) provide clues to the direction of the economy, the economy may be 4 or 6 months into a recession or inflation before that fact appears in relevant statistics and is acknowledged. Meanwhile, the economic downslide or the inflation may become more serious than it would have if the situation had been identified and acted on sooner.

2. *Administrative lag* The wheels of democratic government turn slowly. There will typically be a significant lag between the time the need for fiscal action is recognized and the time action is actually taken. The U.S. Congress has on occasion taken so much time in adjusting fiscal policy that the economic situation has changed in the interim, rendering the belated policy action inappropriate.

3. *Operational lag* There is also a lag between the time fiscal action is taken and the time that action affects output, employment, or the price level. Although changes in tax rates can be put into effect quickly, government spending on public works—the construction of dams, interstate highways, and so on—requires long planning periods and even longer periods of construction. Such spending is of questionable use in offsetting short—for example, 6- to 18-month—periods of recession. Because of such problems, discretionary fiscal policy has increasingly relied on tax changes rather than changes in spending as its main weapon.

Political Problems

Fiscal policy is created in the political arena, and this greatly complicates its use in stabilizing the economy.

Other Goals Economic stability is *not* the sole objective of government spending and taxing policies. Government is also concerned with providing public goods and services and redistributing income. A classic example of conflict of goals occurred during World War II when massive government spending for military goods caused strong and persistent inflationary pressures in the early 1940s. The defeat of Nazi Germany and Japan was simply a higher-priority goal than achieving price stability.

State and Local Finance Fiscal policies of state and local governments are frequently pro-cyclical—they worsen rather than correct recession or inflation. Unlike the Federal government, most state and local governments face constitutional or other legal requirements to balance their budgets. Like households and private businesses, state and local governments increase expenditures during prosperity and cut them during recession. During the Great Depression of the 1930s, most of the increase in Federal spending was offset by decreases in state and local spending. During the recession of 1990–1991, many state and local governments had to increase tax rates, impose new taxes, and reduce spending to offset falling tax revenues resulting from the reduced personal income and spending of their citizens.

Expansionary Bias? Rhetoric to the contrary, deficits may be politically attractive and surpluses politically painful. Fiscal policy may therefore have an expansionary-inflationary bias. Tax reductions are politically popular, and so are increases in government spending, provided the constituents of the politicians promoting them share in the benefits. But both can be inflationary. In contrast, higher taxes upset voters, while reductions in government expenditures can be politically precarious. For example, it might be political suicide for a farm-state senator to vote for tax increases and against agricultural subsidies.

A Political Business Cycle?

Some economists contend the goal of politicians is not to act in the interests of the national economy but, rather, to get reelected. A few economists have suggested the notion of a **political business cycle.** They argue that politicians might manipulate fiscal policy to maximize voter support, even though their fiscal decisions *destabilize* the economy. In this view, fiscal policy, as we have described it, may be corrupted for political purposes and actually *cause* economic fluctuations.

The populace, it is assumed, takes economic conditions into account in voting. Incumbents are penalized at the polls if the economy is depressed; they are rewarded if it is prosperous. As an election approaches, the incumbent administration (aided by an election-minded Congress) cuts taxes and increases government spending. Not only are these actions popular, they push all the critical economic indicators in positive directions. Output and real incomes rise; unemployment falls; and the price level is relatively stable. As a result, incumbents enjoy a very cordial economic environment for reelection.

But after the election, continued expansion of the economy will be reflected increasingly in a rising price level and less in growing real incomes. Growing public concern over inflation prompts politicians to enact a contractionary fiscal policy. Crudely put, a "made-in-Washington" recession is engineered by trimming government spending and increasing taxes to restrain inflation. A mild recession will not hurt an incumbent administration because the next election is still 2 or 3 years away and the critical consideration for most voters is the performance of the economy in the year or so before the election. Indeed, the recession provides a new starting point from which fiscal policy can again be used to generate another expansion in time for the next election campaign.

Such a scenario is difficult to document, and empirical tests of this theory are inconclusive. Nevertheless, there is some evidence to support the political theory of the business cycle.

Crowding-Out Effect

We now move from practical problems in implementing fiscal policy to a basic criticism of fiscal policy itself. This criticism is based on an alleged **crowding-out effect:** *An expansionary fiscal policy (deficit spending) will increase the interest rate and reduce private spending, weakening or canceling the stimulus of the fiscal policy.*

Suppose the economy is in recession and government enacts discretionary fiscal policy in the form of increased government spending. To finance its budget deficit, government borrows funds in the money market. The resulting increase in the demand for money raises the price paid for borrowing money: the interest rate. Because investment spending varies inversely with the interest rate, some investment will be choked off or crowded out. (Some interest-sensitive consumption spending—for example, purchases of automobiles on credit—may also be crowded out.)

Graphical Presentation The crowding-out effect is shown graphically in Figure 12-7. Suppose the economy has a noninflationary full-capacity level of real GDP at $515 billion, as shown in Figure 12-7a. For simplicity our aggregate supply curve here has no real-world intermediate range. Up to the $515 billion full-capacity output, the price level is constant. After the economy achieves full capacity, the vertical range of AS prevails so that any further increase in aggregate demand would be purely inflationary.

We begin in Figure 12-7a with aggregate demand at AD_1, which gives us equilibrium at real GDP of $495 billion. Assume now that government enacts an expansionary fiscal policy that shifts the aggregate demand curve rightward by $20 billion to AD_2. The economy thus achieves full-capacity output without inflation at $515 billion of GDP. Assuming an MPC of .75 and thus a simple multiplier of 4, we know that an increase in government spending of $5 billion or a decrease in taxes of $6.67 billion would create this expansionary effect. With no offsetting or complicating factors, this "pure and simple" expansionary fiscal policy moves the economy from recession to its full-capacity output.

In Figure 12-7b the complication of crowding out is shown. While fiscal policy is expansionary and designed to shift aggregate demand from AD_1 to AD_2, the borrowing needed to finance the deficit spending presumably increases the interest rate and crowds out some investment spending. The aggregate demand curve thus shifts only to AD'_2, not to AD_2.

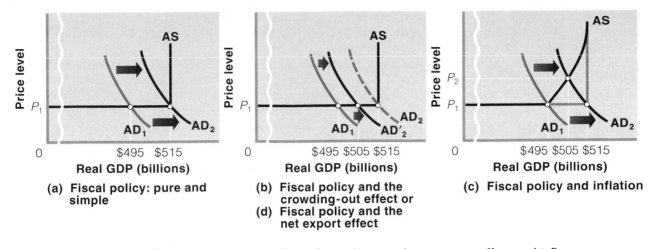

FIGURE 12-7 Fiscal policy: the effects of crowding out, the net export effect, and inflation   With a simplified aggregate supply curve, we observe in (a) that fiscal policy is uncomplicated and works at full strength to produce full employment at a GDP of $515 billion. In (b) it is assumed that some amount of private investment is crowded out by the expansionary fiscal policy so that fiscal policy is weakened, achieving a GDP of only $505 billion. In (c) a more realistic aggregate supply curve reminds us that when the economy is in the intermediate range of the aggregate supply curve, part of the impact of an expansionary fiscal policy will be reflected in inflation (the price level rise to P_2). In (d)—the same graph as (b)—we assume that fiscal policy increases the interest rate, which attracts foreign financial capital to the United States. The dollar therefore appreciates and U.S. net exports fall, weakening the expansionary fiscal policy. GDP again rises only to $505 billion.

Equilibrium real GDP expands to $505 billion, not to the desired $515 billion. Lesson: *The crowding-out effect may weaken expansionary fiscal policy.*

Criticisms of the Crowding-Out Effect   While few would question the logic of the crowding-out effect, there is disagreement as to its existence under all circumstances. Some economists argue that little crowding out will occur when there is recession. They note that the increased government spending will likely improve business profit expectations, and these improved prospects may encourage private investment. Thus, private investment need not fall, even though interest rates rise.

Also, critics of the crowding-out view point out that policymakers can counteract the crowding-out effect. Specifically, the monetary authorities could increase the supply of money by just enough to offset the deficit-caused increase in the demand for money. Then the equilibrium interest rate would not change, and the crowding-out effect would be zero. In the 1980s the monetary authorities did not increase the supply of money to "accommodate" the expansionary fiscal policy; consequently, the crowding-out effect of the large 1980s deficits may have been quite great. In comparison, in the 1960s the monetary authorities

wanted to keep interest rates stable. Hence, they increased the money supply when government borrowing threatened to push up interest rates. As a result, crowding out was less significant.

Fiscal Policy, Aggregate Supply, and Inflation

Our discussion of the complications and criticisms of fiscal policy has thus far been entirely oriented toward aggregate demand. We now consider a complication involving aggregate supply: *With an upsloping aggregate supply curve, some portion of the potential effect of an expansionary fiscal policy on real output may be dissipated in the form of inflation.* Observe in Figure 12-7c that we have switched to a more realistic aggregate supply curve which includes an intermediate range. We ignore the crowding-out effect so that the expansionary fiscal policy is successful in shifting the aggregate demand curve from AD_1 to AD_2. If the aggregate supply were shaped as in Figure 12-7a and b, full employment would now be realized at $515 billion and the price level would remain at P_1. But the upsloping intermediate range of the aggregate supply curve causes part of the increase in aggregate demand to be dissipated in higher prices. As a result, the increase in real GDP is diminished. Specifically, the price level rises from P_1 to P_2, and real GDP increases from $495 billion to $505 billion, not to $515. In the real world, expansionary fiscal policy does not escape the realities imposed by the upsloping portion of the aggregate supply curve.

Fiscal Policy in the Open Economy

Additional complications arise from the fact that each national economy is a component of the world economy.

Shocks Originating from Abroad Events and policies abroad which affect a nation's net exports affect its own economy. Economies are open to unforeseen international *aggregate demand shocks* which can alter domestic GDP and make current domestic fiscal policy inappropriate.

Suppose the United States is in a recession and has enacted an expansionary fiscal policy to increase aggregate demand and GDP without igniting inflation (as from AD_1 to AD_2 in Figure 12-7a). Now suppose the economies of the major trading partners of the United States unexpectedly expand rapidly. Greater employment and rising incomes in those nations mean more purchases of U.S. goods. In the United States, net exports rise, and aggregate demand increases too rapidly; the nation experiences demand-pull inflation. If it had known in advance that its net exports might rise significantly, the United States would have enacted a less expansionary fiscal policy. We see, then, that participation in the world economy brings with it the complications of mutual interdependence along with the gains from specialization and trade.

Net Export Effect The **net export effect** may also work through international trade to reduce the effectiveness of fiscal policy. We concluded in our discussion of the crowding-out effect that an expansionary fiscal policy might boost interest rates, reducing *investment* and weakening fiscal policy. Now we want to know what effect an interest-rate increase might have on a nation's *net exports* (exports minus imports).

Suppose the United States undertakes an expansionary fiscal policy which causes a higher U.S. interest rate. The higher interest rate will attract financial capital from abroad, where interest rates are unchanged. But foreign financial investors must acquire U.S. dollars to invest in U.S. securities. We know that an increase in the demand for a commodity—in this

case, dollars—will raise its price. So the price of dollars rises in terms of foreign currencies; that is, the dollar appreciates.

What will be the impact of this dollar appreciation on U.S. net exports? Because more units of foreign currencies are needed to buy goods from the United States, the rest of the world will see U.S. exports as being more expensive. Hence, U.S. exports will decline. Americans, who can now exchange their dollars for more units of foreign currencies, will buy more imports. Consequently, with U.S. exports falling and imports rising, net export expenditures in the United States will diminish; this is a contractionary change, so the U.S. expansionary fiscal policy will be partially negated.[1]

A return to our aggregate demand and supply analysis in Figure 12-7b, now labeled d, will clarify this point. An expansionary fiscal policy aimed at increasing aggregate demand from AD_1 to AD_2 may hike the domestic interest rate and ultimately reduce net exports through the process just described. The decline in the net export component of aggregate demand will partially offset the expansionary fiscal policy. The aggregate demand curve will shift rightward from AD_1 to AD'_2, *not* to AD_2, and equilibrium GDP will increase from $495 to $505, *not* to $515. Thus, the net export effect of fiscal policy joins the problems of timing, politics, crowding out, and inflation in complicating the "management" of aggregate demand.

Table 12-1 summarizes the net export effect resulting from fiscal policy. Column 1 reviews the analysis just discussed (Figure 12-7d). But note that the net export effect works in both directions. By reducing the domestic interest rate, a *contractionary* fiscal policy *increases* net exports. In this regard, you should follow through the analysis in column 2 in Table 12-1 and relate it to the aggregate demand–aggregate supply model. **(Key Question 9)**

QUICK REVIEW 12-3

■ Time lags and political problems complicate fiscal policy.

■ The crowding-out effect indicates that an expansionary fiscal policy may increase the interest rate and reduce investment spending.

---

[1] The appreciation of the dollar will also reduce the dollar price of foreign resources such as oil imported into the United States. As a result, aggregate supply will increase and part of the contractionary net export effect described here may be offset.

TABLE 12-1 Fiscal policy and the net export effect

(1) Expansionary fiscal policy	(2) Contractionary fiscal policy
Problem: Recession, slow growth ↓	Problem: Inflation ↓
Expansionary fiscal policy ↓	Contractionary fiscal policy ↓
Higher domestic interest rate ↓	Lower domestic interest rate ↓
Increased foreign demand for dollars ↓	Decreased foreign demand for dollars ↓
Dollar appreciates ↓	Dollar depreciates ↓
Net exports decline (aggregate demand decreases, partially offsetting the expansionary fiscal policy)	Net exports increase (aggregate demand increases, partially offsetting the contractionary fiscal policy)

■ The upsloping range of the aggregate supply curve means that part of an expansionary fiscal policy may be dissipated in inflation.

■ Fiscal policy may be weakened by the net export effect, which works through changes in (**a**) the interest rate, (**b**) the international value of the dollar, and (**c**) exports and imports.

Supply-Side Fiscal Policy

We have seen how movements along the aggregate supply curve can complicate the operation of fiscal policy. Let's now turn to the possibility of a more direct link between fiscal policy and aggregate supply—so-called **supply-side fiscal policy.** Economists recognize that fiscal policy—especially tax changes—*may* alter aggregate supply and affect the results of a change in fiscal policy.

Suppose in Figure 12-8 that aggregate demand and aggregate supply are AD_1 and AS_1 so that the

equilibrium level of real GDP is Q_1 and the price level is P_1. Assume further that government concludes the level of unemployment associated with Q_1 is too high and therefore enacts an expansionary fiscal policy in the form of a tax cut. The demand-side effect is an increase in aggregate demand from AD_1 to, say, AD_2. This shift increases real GDP to Q_2 but also boosts the price level to P_2.

How might tax cuts affect aggregate supply? Some economists—labeled "supply-side" economists—contend that tax reductions will shift the aggregate supply curve to the right. They give three main reasons:

1. *Saving and investment* Lower taxes will increase disposable incomes, increasing household saving. Similarly, tax reductions on businesses will increase the profitability of investment. In brief, lower taxes will increase saving and investment, increasing the rate of capital accumulation. The size of our "national factory"—our production capacity—will grow more rapidly.

2. *Work incentives* Lower personal income tax rates also increase after-tax wages from work and thus increase work incentives. Many people not already in the labor force will offer their services because after-tax wages are higher. Those already

FIGURE 12-8 Supply-side effects of fiscal policy The traditional view is that tax cuts will increase aggregate demand, as from AD_1 to AD_2, increasing both real domestic output (Q_1 to Q_2) and the price level (P_1 to P_2). If the tax reductions induce favorable supply-side effects, aggregate supply will shift rightward, as from AS_1 to AS_2. This allows the economy to realize an even larger output (Q_3 compared with Q_2) and a smaller price-level increase (P_3 compared with P_2).

The Leading Indicators

One of several tools policymakers use to forecast the future direction of real GDP is a monthly index of 10 variables which in the past have together provided advance notice of changes in GDP.

"Index of Leading Indicators Falls Sharply for the Third Month—Recession Feared"; "Index of Leading Indicators Surges Again"; "Decline in Stock Market Drags Down Index of Leading Indicators." Headlines such as these appear regularly in newspapers. The focus of the articles is the Conference Board's composite index of 10 economic variables.* This "indicator" has historically reached its peak or trough in advance of the corresponding turns in the business cycle. Changes in the index of leading indicators thus provide a clue to the future direction of the economy and so may shorten the length of the "recognition lag" associated with the implementation of macroeconomic policy.

Here is how each of the 10 components of the index would change if it were predicting a *decline* in GDP. The opposite changes would forecast a *rise* in GDP.

1. Average Workweek Decreases in the length of the average workweek of production workers in manu-

*The Conference Board is a private, nonprofit research and business membership group, with more than 2700 corporate and other members in 60 nations.

facturing foretell declines in future manufacturing output and hence in GDP.

2. Initial Claims for Unemployment Insurance Higher first-time claims for unemployment insurance are associated with falling employment and subsequently sagging GDP.

3. New Orders for Consumer Goods Decreases in the number of orders received by manufacturers for consumer goods portend reduced future production—a decline in GDP.

4. Vendor Performance Somewhat ironically, better on-time delivery by sellers of inputs indicates slackening business demand and potentially falling GDP.

5. New Orders for Capital Goods A drop in orders for capital equipment and other investment goods implies reduced future aggregate demand and thus lower GDP.

6. Building Permits for Houses Decreases in the number of building permits taken out for new homes imply future declines in investment and therefore the possibility that GDP will fall.

7. Stock Prices Declines in stock prices often are reflections of expected declines in corporate sales and profits. Also, lower stock prices diminish consumer wealth, leading to possible cutbacks in consumer spending. Lower stock prices also make it less attractive for firms to issue

in the labor force will want to work more hours and take fewer vacations.
3. *Risk taking* Lower tax rates prod risk takers. Individuals and businesses will be more willing to risk their energies and financial capital on new production methods and new products when lower tax rates promise a larger potential after-tax reward.

Through all these avenues, lower taxes will shift aggregate supply to the right, say, from AS_1 to AS_2 in Figure 12-8, reducing inflation and further increasing real GDP.

Supply-siders also contend that lower tax *rates* need not result in lower tax *revenues*. In fact, they say that lower tax rates that cause a substantial expansion of output and income may generate *increases* in tax

revenues. This enlarged tax base may enhance total tax revenues even though tax rates are lower. (The mainstream view is that a reduction in tax rates will reduce tax revenues and increase budget deficits.)

Mainstream Skepticism Most economists are skeptical about the supply-side effects of tax cuts, particularly in view of evidence from the supply-side tax cuts of the 1980s. First, these critics feel the positive effects of a tax reduction on incentives to work, save and invest, and bear risks are not nearly as strong as supply-siders believe. Second, any rightward shifts of the aggregate supply curve will occur over an extended period of time, while the demand-side impact will be much more immediate.

new shares of stock as a way of raising funds for investment. Thus, declines in stock prices can bring forth declines in aggregate demand and GDP.

8. Money Supply Decreases in the nation's money supply are associated with falling GDP. (This component and the next will make more sense to you after you read Chapters 13 through 15.)

9. Interest-Rate Spread Increases in short-term nominal interest rates typically reflect monetary policies designed to slow the economy. Such policies have much less of an effect on long-term interest rates, which are higher than short-term rates. So a smaller difference between short-term interest rates and long-term interest rates suggests restrictive monetary policies and potentially a future decline in GDP.

10. Consumer Confidence Declines in consumer confidence about the future, measured by an index of consumer expectations, foreshadow lower consumption spending and potential future declines in GDP.

None of these factors *alone* consistently predicts the future course of the economy. It is not unusual in any month, for example, for one or two of the indicators to be decreasing while the other indicators are increasing. Rather, changes in the composite of the 10 components are what in the past have provided advance notice of a change in the direction of GDP. The rule of thumb is that three successive monthly declines or increases in the index indicate the economy will soon turn in that same direction.

Although the composite index has correctly signaled business fluctuations on numerous occasions, it has not been infallible. At times the index has provided false warnings of recessions which never happened. In other instances, recessions have so closely followed the downturn in the index that policymakers have not had sufficient time to make use of the "early" warning. Moreover, changing structural features of the economy have, on occasion, rendered the existing index obsolete and necessitated its revision.

Given these caveats, the index of leading indicators can best be thought of as a useful but not totally reliable signaling device which authorities must employ with considerable caution in formulating macroeconomic policy.

CHAPTER SUMMARY

1. Government responsibility for achieving and maintaining full employment is specified in the Employment Act of 1946. The Council of Economic Advisers (CEA) was established to advise the president on policies to fulfill the goals of the act.

2. Increases in government spending expand, and decreases contract, aggregate demand and equilibrium GDP. Increases in taxes reduce, and decreases expand, aggregate demand and equilibrium GDP. Fiscal policy therefore calls for increases in government spending and decreases in taxes—a budget deficit—to correct for recession. Decreases in government spending and increases in taxes—

a budget surplus—are appropriate fiscal policy for correcting demand-pull inflation.

3. Built-in stability arises from net tax revenues which vary directly with the level of GDP. During recession, the Federal budget automatically moves toward a stabilizing deficit; during expansion, the budget automatically moves toward an anti-inflationary surplus. Built-in stability lessens, but does not fully correct, undesired changes in the GDP.

4. An actual budget deficit consists of two elements: the structural deficit (if any) and the cyclical deficit (if any).

The structural deficit—also known as the full-employment deficit—is that part of an actual deficit which would occur even if the economy were at its full-employment output. The cyclical deficit is that part of an actual deficit which arises when real GDP is less than full-employment GDP.

5. The full-employment budget or standardized budget measures the Federal budget deficit or surplus which would occur if the economy operated at full employment throughout the year. Changes in the full-employment deficit or surplus—also called the structural deficit or surplus—provide meaningful information as to whether government's fiscal policy is expansionary, neutral, or contractionary. Changes in the actual budget deficit or surplus do not, since such deficits or surpluses depend on the state of the economy.

6. The enactment and application of appropriate fiscal policy are subject to certain problems and questions. The important ones are: **(a)** Can fiscal policy be better timed to maximize its effectiveness in heading off economic fluctuations? **(b)** Can the economy rely on Congress to enact appropriate fiscal policy? **(c)** An expansionary fiscal policy may be weakened if it crowds out some private investment spending. **(d)** Some of the effect of an expansionary fiscal policy may be dissipated in inflation. **(e)** Fiscal policy may be rendered ineffective or inappropriate by unforeseen events occurring within the borders of international trading partners. Also, fiscal policy may precipitate changes in exchange rates which weaken its effects. **(f)** Supply-side economists contend that traditional fiscal policy fails to consider the effects of tax changes on aggregate supply.

TERMS AND CONCEPTS

Employment Act of 1946
Council of Economic Advisers
discretionary fiscal policy
expansionary fiscal policy
budget deficit

contractionary fiscal policy
budget surplus
built-in stabilizer
progressive tax system
proportional tax system

regressive tax system
actual budget
cyclical deficit
full-employment budget
structural deficit
political business cycle

crowding-out effect
net export effect
supply-side fiscal policy

STUDY QUESTIONS

1. What is the central thrust of the Employment Act of 1946? What is the role of the Council of Economic Advisers (CEA) in responding to this law? Class assignment: Determine the names and educational backgrounds of the present members of the CEA.

2. KEY QUESTION Assume that a hypothetical economy with an MPC of .8 is experiencing severe recession. By how much would government spending have to increase to shift the aggregate demand curve rightward by $25 billion? How large a tax cut would be needed to achieve this same increase in aggregate demand? Why the difference? Determine one possible combination of government spending increases and tax decreases which would accomplish this same goal.

3. KEY QUESTION What are government's fiscal policy options for ending severe demand-pull inflation? Use the aggregate demand–aggregate supply model to show the impact of these policies on the price level. Which of these fiscal policy options do

you think a "conservative" economist might favor? A "liberal" economist?

4. (For students assigned Chapters 9 and 10) Use the aggregate expenditures model to show how government fiscal policy could eliminate either a recessionary gap or an inflationary gap (Figure 10-8). Use the concept of the balanced-budget multiplier to explain how equal increases in G and T could eliminate a recessionary gap and how equal decreases in G and T could eliminate an inflationary gap.

5. Designate each statement *true* or *false* and justify your answer:
   a. Expansionary fiscal policy during a depression will have a greater positive effect on real GDP if government borrows the money to finance the budget deficit than if it creates new money to finance the deficit.
   b. Contractionary fiscal policy during severe demand-pull inflation will be more effective if government impounds the budget surplus

rather than using the surplus to pay off some of its past debt.

6. Explain how built-in (or automatic) stabilizers work. What are the differences between proportional, progressive, and regressive tax systems as they relate to an economy's built-in stability?

7. KEY QUESTION Define the "full-employment budget," explain its significance, and state how it differs from the "actual budget." What is the difference between a structural deficit and a cyclical deficit? Suppose the economy depicted in Figure 12-4 is operating at its full-employment, noninflationary level of real output, GDP$_f$. What is the size of its structural deficit? Its cyclical deficit? Should government raise taxes or reduce government spending to eliminate this structural deficit? What are the risks of so doing?

8. The actual budget deficit increased significantly in 1990 and 1991, but the full-employment budget deficit remained relatively constant. Can you think of a logical explanation?

9. KEY QUESTION Briefly state and evaluate the problem of time lags in enacting and applying fiscal policy. Explain the notion of a political business cycle. What is the crowding-out effect, and why is it relevant to fiscal policy? In what respect is the net export effect similar to the crowding-out effect?

10. In view of your answers to question 9, explain the following statement: "While fiscal policy clearly is useful in combating the extremes of severe recession and demand-pull inflation, it is impossible to use fiscal policy to fine-tune the economy to the full-employment, noninflationary level of real GDP and keep the economy there indefinitely."

11. Suppose that government engages in deficit spending to push the economy away from recession and that this spending is directed toward new "public capital" such as roads, bridges, dams, harbors, office parks, and industrial sites. How might this spending increase the expected rate of return on some types of potential *private* investment projects? What are the implications for the crowding-out effect?

12. Use Figure 12-4 to explain why a deliberate increase in the structural deficit which causes the economy to expand from GDP$_r$ to GDP$_f$ might reduce the size of the actual deficit. In requesting a tax cut in the early 1960s, President Kennedy said, "It is a paradoxical truth that tax rates are too high today and tax revenues are too low and the soundest way to raise tax revenues in the long run is to cut tax rates now." Relate this quotation to your previous answer.

13. Discuss: "Mainstream economists tend to focus on the aggregate demand effects of tax-rate reductions; supply-side economists emphasize the aggregate supply effects." Identify three routes through which a tax cut might increase aggregate supply. If tax cuts are so good for the economy, why don't we cut taxes to zero?

14. **Advanced analysis:** (For students assigned Chapters 9 and 10) Assume that, without taxes, the consumption schedule for an economy is as shown below:

GDP, billions	Consumption, billions
$100	$120
200	200
300	280
400	360
500	440
600	520
700	600

a. Graph this consumption schedule and determine the size of the MPC.
b. Assume a lump-sum (regressive) tax of $10 billion is imposed at all levels of GDP. Calculate the tax rate at each level of GDP. Graph the resulting consumption schedule, and compare the MPC and the multiplier with that of the pretax consumption schedule.
c. Now suppose a proportional tax with a 10 percent tax rate is imposed instead of the regressive tax. Calculate the new consumption schedule, graph it, and note the MPC and the multiplier.
d. Finally, impose a progressive tax such that the tax rate is 0 percent when GDP is $100, 5 percent at $200, 10 percent at $300, 15 percent at $400, and so forth. Determine and graph the new consumption schedule, noting the effect of this tax system on the MPC and the multiplier.
e. Explain why proportional and progressive taxes contribute to greater economic stability, while a regressive tax does not. Demonstrate using a graph similar to Figure 12-3.

15. **(Last Word)** What is the composite index of leading economic indicators, and how does it relate to discretionary fiscal policy?

16. WEB-BASED QUESTION Latest Economic Indicators—How Goes the Economy? The U.S. Census Bureau http://www.census.gov/econ/www/ constantly tracks the latest economic indicators. Check last month's Economic Indicator Calendar for current indicator values. Assign a +1 to those economic indicators which point to an expansion, a −1 for those indicating contraction, or 0 if indeterminate or neutral. Sum these values for a crude forecast. How goes the economy?

17. WEB-BASED QUESTION   The Federal Budget—What Is the Role of Fiscal Policy in the Budgetary Process? Each year the President, through the Office of Management and Budget http://www.whitehouse.gov/WH/EOP/OMB/html/ombhome.html, sends his proposed budget to Congress. However, the House of Representatives http://www.house.gov/ budget/welcome.htm and the Senate http://www.senate.gov/~budget/ have their own opinions about what the budget should be. Using these links, trace the steps of the Federal budget process from the initial executive proposal to final presidential signature. What role does fiscal policy play in this process? What are the major policy disagreements relating to the current budget?

3

PART THREE

Money,
Banking,
and Monetary
Policy

13

Money and Banking

"**M**oney bewitches people. They fret for it, and they sweat for it. They devise most ingenious ways to get it, and most ingenuous ways to get rid of it. Money is the only commodity that is good for nothing but to be gotten rid of. It will not feed you, clothe you, shelter you, or amuse you unless you spend it or invest it. It imparts value only in parting. People will do almost anything for money, and money will do almost anything for people. Money is a captivating, circulating, masquerading puzzle."[1]

Money. A fascinating aspect of the economy. And a crucial element of economics. Money is more than a tool for facilitating the economy's operation. When it is working properly, the monetary system is the lifeblood of the circular flows of income and expenditure which typify all economies. A well-operating monetary system helps achieve both full employment and efficient resource use. A malfunctioning monetary system can contribute to severe fluctuations in the economy's levels of output, employment, and prices *and* can distort the allocation of resources.

In this chapter we are concerned with the nature and functions of money and the basic institutions of the U.S. banking system. In the next chapter we examine the ways individual commercial banks and the banking system as a whole can vary the money supply. In Chapter 15 we discuss how the central banks of the economy regulate the supply of money to promote full employment and price-level stability.

We begin here with a review of the functions of money. Next, we shift to the supply of money and pose the question: What constitutes money in the United States? Third, we consider what "backs" the supply of money and what is meant by the demand for money. Then we combine the supply of money and the demand for money to portray and explain the market for money. Finally, the institutional structure of the Federal Reserve System is discussed, and recent developments relating to the banking industry are examined.

THE FUNCTIONS OF MONEY

Just what is money? There is an appropriate saying that "money *is* what money *does*."

Anything which performs the functions of money *is* money. So what are these functions?

---

[1]Federal Reserve Bank of Philadelphia, "Creeping Inflation," *Business Review*, August 1957, p. 3.

1. *Medium of exchange* First, and foremost, money is a **medium of exchange;** it is usable for buying and selling goods and services. A worker in a bakery does not want to be paid 200 bagels per week. Nor does the bakery wish to receive, say, tuna fish for its bagels. Money, however, is readily acceptable as payment. It is a social invention with which resource suppliers and producers can be paid and that can be used to buy any of the full range of items available in the marketplace. As such a medium of exchange, money allows society to escape the complications of barter. And because it provides a convenient way of exchanging goods, money allows society to gain the advantages of geographic and human specialization.

2. *Unit of account* Money is also a **unit of account.** Society uses the monetary unit as a yardstick for measuring the relative worth of a wide variety of goods, services, and resources. Just as we measure distance in miles or kilometers, we gauge the value of goods in dollars. With a money system, we need not state the price of each product in terms of all other products for which it can be exchanged; we need not specify the price of cows in terms of corn, crayons, cigars, Chevrolets, and croissants.

This use of money as a common denominator means that the price of each product need be stated *only* in terms of the monetary unit. It permits buyers and sellers to readily compare the prices of various commodities and resources. Such comparisons aid rational decision making. In Chapter 7 we used money as a unit of account in calculating the size of the GDP. Money is also used as a unit of account for transactions involving future payments. Debt obligations of all kinds are measured in the monetary unit.

3. *Store of value* Finally, money serves as a **store of value.** Because money is the most liquid—meaning the most spendable—of all assets, it is a very convenient way to store wealth. The money you place in a safe or checking account will still be available to you months or years later when you wish to use it. Most methods of holding money do not yield monetary returns such as one gets by storing wealth in the form of real assets (property) or paper assets (stocks, bonds, and so forth). However, money does have the advantage of being *immediately* usable by a firm or a household in meeting all financial obligations.

THE SUPPLY OF MONEY

Conceptually, anything generally acceptable as a medium of exchange *is* money. Historically, whales' teeth, elephant tail bristles, circular stones, nails, slaves (yes, human beings), cattle, cigarettes, and pieces of metal have been used as media of exchange. In the United States the debts of governments and of commercial banks and other financial institutions are used as money, as you will see.

Money Definition M1

Neither economists nor public officials agree on how broadly or narrowly the economy's money supply should be defined. In the most narrow useful definition, the money supply is designated *M*1 and composed of two items:

1. Currency, that is, coins and paper money in the hands of the (nonbank) public

2. All checkable deposits, meaning deposits in commercial banks and "thrift" or savings institutions on which checks can be drawn[2]

Coins and paper money are debts of government and governmental agencies. Checking accounts represent debts of the commercial bank or savings institution. Table 13-1 shows the amount of each in the *M*1 money supply.

Currency: Coins + Paper Money From copper pennies to silver dollars, coins are the "small change" of our money supply. Coins, however, are a very small portion of the total money supply; they constitute only 2 or 3 percent of *M*1. Coins are "convenience money" which permits people to make very small purchases.

All coins in circulation in the United States are **token money.** This means the **intrinsic value**—the value of the bullion (metal) contained in the coin itself—is less than the face value of the coin. This is so to avoid the melting down of token money for profitable sale as a "commodity," in this case, bullion. If 50-cent pieces each contained 75 cents' worth of silver bullion, it would be profitable to melt them and sell the metal. Although it is illegal to do this, 50-cent

---

[2]In the ensuing discussion of the definitions of money several of the quantitatively less significant components are not explicitly discussed to sidestep a maze of details. For example, travelers' checks are included in the *M*1 money supply. Reference to the statistical appendix of any recent *Federal Reserve Bulletin* will provide you with more comprehensive definitions.

TABLE 13-1   Alternative money definitions for the United States: M1, M2, and M3

Money definition or concept	Absolute amount, (billions)	Percentage of concept M1	Percentage of concept M2	Percentage of concept M3
Currency (coins and paper money)	$ 414	39%	10%	8%
plus Checkable deposits	643*	61	16	12
equals M1	$1057	100%		
plus Noncheckable savings deposits, including MMDAs	1314		33	25
plus Small time deposits	962*		24	18
plus Money market mutual fund balances (MMMFs)	631		16	12
equals M2	$3964		100%	
plus Large time deposits	1241*			24
equals M3	$5205			100%

*These figures include other quantitatively smaller components. Percentages may not add to 100 percent due to rounding.
Source: Federal Reserve Bulletin, December 1997, p. A12. Data are for September 1997.

pieces would disappear from circulation. This is one of the potential defects of commodity money: Its worth as a commodity may come to exceed its worth as money, ending its function as a medium of exchange.

Paper money constitutes about 37 percent of the economy's *M*1 money supply. All this $391 billion of paper currency is in the form of **Federal Reserve Notes,** issued by the Federal Reserve Banks (the U.S. central banks) with the authorization of Congress. A glance at any bill in your wallet will reveal Federal Reserve Note printed at the top of the face of the bill.

Checkable Deposits   The safety and convenience of using checks have made checking accounts the largest component of the U.S. money supply. You would not think of stuffing $4896.47 in bills and coins in an envelope and dropping it in a mailbox to pay a debt. But to write and mail a check for a large sum is commonplace. A check must be endorsed (signed on the reverse side) by the person cashing it; the writer of the check subsequently receives a record of the canceled check as a receipt attesting to the fulfillment of the obligation. Similarly, because the writing of a check requires endorsement by the person cashing it, the theft or loss of your checkbook is not nearly as calamitous as losing an identical amount of currency. Finally, it is more convenient to write a check than to transport and count out a large sum of currency. For all these reasons, *checkbook money* is the dominant form of money in the U.S. economy. About 60 percent of *M*1 is in the form of **checkable deposits,** on which checks can be drawn.

It might seem strange that checking accounts are part of the money supply. But it is clear why: Checks, which are nothing more than a way to transfer the ownership of deposits in banks and other financial institutions, are generally acceptable as a medium of exchange. True, as a stop at most gas stations will verify, checks are less generally accepted than currency for small purchases. But for major purchases sellers willingly accept checks as payment. Moreover, people can convert checkable deposits into paper money and coins on demand; checks drawn on these deposits are thus the equivalent of currency.

To summarize:

Money, *M*1 = currency + checkable deposits

Institutions Offering Checkable Deposits   In the United States, several types of financial institutions allow customers to write checks on the funds they have deposited:

1. *Commercial banks*   These banks are the primary depository institutions. They accept the deposits of households and businesses; keep the money safe until it is demanded via checks; and in the meantime use it to make available a wide variety of loans. Commercial bank loans provide short-term working capital to businesses and farmers, and they finance consumer purchases of automobiles and other durable goods.

2. *Thrift institutions*   The commercial banks are supplemented by other financial institutions— savings and loan associations (S&Ls), mutual savings banks, and credit unions—collectively desig-

nated as **thrift** or **savings institutions,** or simply "thrifts." **Savings and loan associations** and **mutual savings banks** accept the savings of households and businesses, which are then used to finance housing mortgages and provide other loans. **Credit unions** accept the deposits of their "members"—usually a group of individuals who work for the same company—and lend these funds to finance installment purchases.

The checkable deposits of banks and thrifts are known by various names—demand deposits, NOW (negotiable order of withdrawal) accounts, ATS (automatic transfer service) accounts, and share draft accounts. Nevertheless, they are all similar in that depositors can write checks on them whenever, and in whatever amount, they choose.

Qualification We must qualify our definition of money: Currency and checkable deposits owned by government (the Treasury) and by the Federal Reserve Banks, commercial banks, or other financial institutions are excluded from $M1$ and other money measures.

A paper dollar in the hands of Sally Sorenson obviously constitutes just $1 of the money supply. But if we counted dollars held by banks as part of the money supply, the same $1 would count for $2 when deposited in a bank. It would count for a $1 demand deposit owned by Sorenson and also for $1 of currency resting in the bank's till or vault. This problem of double counting is avoided by excluding currency resting in banks in determining the total money supply.

Excluding currency held by, and checkable deposits owned by, government is more arbitrary. This exclusion permits economists to better gauge the money supply and rate of spending in the private sector of the economy apart from spending initiated by government policy.

Money Definition M2

A second and broader definition of money includes $M1$ plus several near-monies. **Near-monies** are certain highly liquid financial assets which do not directly function as a medium of exchange but can be readily converted into currency or checkable deposits without risk of financial loss. There are four near-monies included along with $M1$ in the $M2$ definition of money:

1. On demand you can withdraw currency from a **noncheckable savings account** at a commercial bank or thrift institution. Or you may request that funds be transferred from a noncheckable savings account to a checkable account.

2. You can also withdraw funds quickly from a **money market deposit account** (MMDA). These are interest-bearing accounts offered by banks and thrifts which pool individual deposits to buy a variety of interest-bearing short-term securities. MMDAs have minimum balance requirements and limit how often money can be withdrawn.

3. **Time deposits** become available to a depositor only at maturity. For example, a 6-month time deposit can only be withdrawn without penalty 6 months or more after it has been deposited. In return for this withdrawal limitation, the financial institution pays a higher interest rate on such deposits than on its MMDA accounts. Although time deposits are less liquid than noncheckable savings accounts, they can be taken as currency or shifted to checkable accounts when they mature.

4. Through a telephone call, a depositor can redeem shares in a **money market mutual fund** (MMMF) offered through a mutual fund company. Such companies use the combined funds of individual shareholders to buy interest-bearing short-term credit instruments such as certificates of deposits and U.S. government securities. Thus, they in turn can offer interest on the money market accounts of their mutual fund customers (depositors).

Thus, in equation form,

$$\text{Money, } M2 = \begin{array}{l} M1 + \text{noncheckable savings} \\ \text{deposits} + \text{MMDAs} + \text{small} \\ \text{(less than \$100,000) time deposits} \\ + \text{MMMFs} \end{array}$$

That is, **M2** includes (1) the medium-of-exchange items (currency and checkable deposits) constituting $M1$ *plus* (2) the four other items which can be quickly converted into currency and checkable deposits without financial loss. Table 13-1 shows that the addition of noncheckable savings deposits, MMDAs, small time deposits, and MMMFs yields an $M2$ money supply of $3964 billion compared to the narrower $M1$ money supply of $1057 billion.

Money Definition M3

A third money supply definition, **M3,** recognizes that large ($100,000 or more) time deposits—usually owned by businesses as certificates of deposit—are also a near-money which can be converted into checkable deposits. There is a market for these certificates, and they can be sold (liquidated) at any time, although perhaps at the risk of a loss. Adding these large time deposits to $M2$ yields the still broader $M3$ definition of money:

$$\text{Money, } M3 = \begin{array}{l} M2 + \text{large (\$100,000 or} \\ \text{more) time deposits} \end{array}$$

Table 13-1 reveals that the $M3$ money supply is \$5205 billion.

Still other slightly less liquid assets such as certain government securities (for example, Treasury bills and U.S. savings bonds) can be easily converted into $M1$ money. Actually, there is an entire spectrum of assets which vary slightly from one another in terms of their liquidity or "moneyness." They are not, however, included in $M1$, $M2$, and $M3$.

Which definition of money shall we use? The simple $M1$ definition includes only items *directly* and *immediately* usable as a medium of exchange. For this reason it is an often-cited statistic in discussions of the money supply. However, for some purposes economists prefer the broader $M2$ definition. For example, $M2$ is used as 1 of the 10 trend variables in the index of leading indicators (Last Word, Chapter 12). And what of $M3$ and still broader definitions of money? These definitions are so inclusive that many economists question their usefulness.

We will use the narrow $M1$ definition of money in our discussion and analysis, unless stated otherwise. The important principles applying to $M1$ are also applicable to $M2$ and $M3$ because $M1$ is the base component in these broader measures.

Near-Monies: Implications

Near-monies are important for several related reasons:
1. *Spending habits*   These highly liquid assets affect people's consumption and saving habits. Usually, the greater the amount of financial wealth people hold as near-monies, the greater their willingness to spend out of their money incomes.
2. *Stability*   Conversion of near-monies into money or vice versa can affect the economy's stability. For example, during the recovery and peak phases of the business cycle, converting noncheckable financial assets into checkable deposits or currency adds to the money supply and could cause inflation. Such conversions can complicate the task of the monetary authorities in

controlling the money supply and the level of economic activity.
3. *Policy*   The specific definition of money used is important for monetary policy. For example, the money supply as measured by $M1$ might be constant, while money defined as $M2$ might be increasing. If the monetary authorities feel it is appropriate to have an expanding supply of money and if they measure the supply with the narrow $M1$ definition, they would likely call for specific actions to increase currency and checkable deposits. But if they used the broader $M2$ definitions, they would see that the desired expansion of the money supply is already taking place and that no specific policy action is needed. **(Key Question 4)**

Credit Cards

You may wonder why we have ignored credit cards—Visa, MasterCard, American Express, Discover, and so forth—in our discussion of how money is defined. After all, credit cards are a convenient way to make purchases. The answer is that a credit card is *not* really money but, rather, a means of obtaining a short-term loan from the commercial bank or other financial institution which has issued the card.

When you purchase a sweatshirt with a credit card, the issuing bank will reimburse the store. Later, you reimburse the bank. You may pay an annual fee for the services provided, and if you repay the bank in installments, you pay a sizable interest charge on the loan. Credit cards are merely a means of deferring or postponing payment for a short period.

However, credit cards and other forms of credit allow individuals and businesses to "economize" in the use of money. Credit cards permit you to have less currency and checkable deposits on hand for transactions. Credit cards help you synchronize your expenditures and your receipt of income, reducing the cash and checkable deposits you must hold.

QUICK REVIEW 13-1

■ Money serves as a medium of exchange, a unit of account, and a store of value.

■ The narrow $M1$ definition of money includes currency held by the public plus checkable deposits in commercial banks and thrift institutions.

■ Thrift institutions as well as commercial banks offer accounts on which checks can be written.

■ The *M2* definition of money includes *M1* plus noncheckable savings deposits, money market deposit accounts, small (less than $100,000) time deposits, and money market mutual fund balances; *M3* consists of *M2* plus large time deposits (more than $100,000).

WHAT "BACKS" THE MONEY SUPPLY?

This heading asks a slippery question. Our answer is at odds with most preconceptions. Essentially what backs money is the government's ability to keep the value of money relatively stable.

Money as Debt

The major components of the money supply—paper money and checkable deposits—are debts, or promises to pay. *In the United States, paper money is the circulating debt of the Federal Reserve Banks. Checkable deposits are the debts of commercial banks and thrift institutions.*

Paper currency and checkable deposits have no intrinsic value. A $5 bill is just a piece of paper. A checkable deposit is merely a bookkeeping entry. And coins, we know, have less intrinsic value than their face value. Nor will government redeem the paper money you hold for anything tangible, such as gold. In effect, the government has chosen to "manage" the nation's money supply. Its monetary authorities attempt to provide the amount of money needed for that particular volume of business activity which will promote full employment, price-level stability, and a healthy rate of economic growth.

Most economists agree that managing the money supply is more sensible than linking it to gold or any other commodity whose supply might arbitrarily and capriciously change. A large increase in the nation's gold stock as the result of a new gold discovery might increase the money supply far beyond the amount needed to transact a full-employment level of business activity. Therefore, rapid inflation might occur. Or a long-lasting decline in domestic gold production could reduce the domestic money supply to the point where economic activity is choked off and unemployment and a retarded growth rate result.

The point is that paper money cannot be converted into a fixed amount of gold or any other precious commodity; it is exchangeable only for other pieces of paper money. The government will swap one paper $5 bill for another bearing a different serial number. That is all you can get if you ask the government to redeem some of your paper money. Similarly, check money cannot be redeemed for gold but only for paper money, which, as you have just seen, will not be redeemed by the government for anything tangible.

Value of Money

If currency and checkable deposits have no intrinsic characteristics giving them value *and* if they are not backed by gold or other precious materials, then why are they money? What gives a $20 bill or a $100 checking account entry its value? The answer to these questions involves three points.

Acceptability Currency and checkable deposits are money because they are accepted as money. By virtue of long-standing business practice, currency and checkable deposits perform the basic function of money; they are acceptable as a medium of exchange. Suppose that you swap a $20 bill for a shirt or blouse at a clothing store. Why does the merchant accept this piece of paper in exchange for that product? The merchant accepts paper money because he or she is confident that others will in turn accept it in exchange for goods, services, and resources. The merchant knows that paper money can purchase the services of clerks, acquire products from wholesalers, and pay the rent on the store. We accept paper money in exchange because we are confident it will be exchangeable for real goods, services, and resources when we spend it.

Legal Tender Our confidence in the acceptability of paper money is partly a matter of law; currency has been designated as **legal tender** by government. This means paper currency *must* be accepted in payment of a debt, or else the creditor forfeits both the privilege of charging interest and the right to sue the debtor for nonpayment. Put bluntly, paper dollars are accepted as money partly because government says they are money. The paper money in our economy is **fiat money;** it is money because the government has declared it so, not because it can be redeemed for precious metal. The general acceptability of currency is also enhanced because government accepts it in payment of taxes and other obligations due the government.

Do not be overimpressed by the power of government, however. Paper currency's general acceptance in exchange is more important than government's decree that money is legal tender. The government has *not* decreed checks to be legal tender, but they successfully perform the vast bulk of the economy's exchanges of goods, services, and resources. It is true, though, that a governmental agency—the Federal Deposit Insurance Corporation (FDIC)—insures the deposits of commercial banks and S&Ls, undoubtedly contributing to the willingness of individuals and businesses to use checkable deposits as a medium of exchange.

Relative Scarcity The value of money, like the economic value of anything else, depends on supply and demand. Money derives its value from its scarcity relative to its utility (want-satisfying power). The utility of money lies in its capacity to be exchanged for goods and services, now or in the future. The economy's demand for money thus depends on the total dollar volume of transactions in any period plus the amount of money individuals and businesses want to hold for possible future transactions. With a reasonably constant demand for money, the supply of money

will determine the value or "purchasing power" of the monetary unit (dollar, pound, peso, or whatever).

Money and Prices

The purchasing power of money is the amount of goods and services a unit of money will buy. When money rapidly loses its purchasing power, it rapidly loses its role as money.

Value of the Dollar The amount a dollar will buy varies inversely with the price level; *a reciprocal relationship exists between the general price level and the value of the dollar.* Figure 13-1 shows this inverse relationship graphically. When the consumer price index or "cost-of-living" index goes up, the purchasing power of the dollar goes down, and vice versa. Higher prices lower the value of the dollar because more dollars will be needed to buy a particular amount of goods, services, and resources. For example, if the price level doubles, the value of the dollar declines by one-half, or 50 percent.

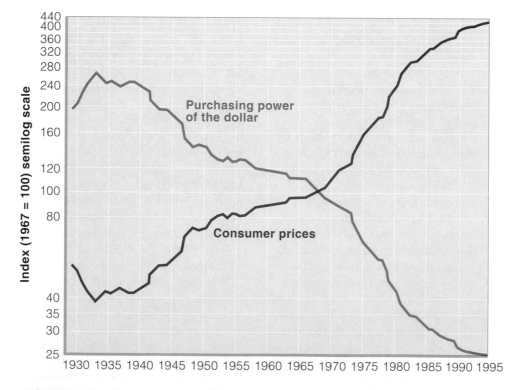

FIGURE 13-1 The price level and the value of money An inverse relationship exists between the general price level and the purchasing power of the dollar. (This graph is called a "semilog chart" because equal vertical distances measure equal percentage changes rather than equal absolute changes.)

Conversely, lower prices increase the purchasing power of the dollar because fewer dollars are needed to obtain a specific quantity of goods and services. If the price level falls by, say, one-half, or 50 percent, the purchasing power of the dollar doubles.

In equation form, the relationship looks like this:

$$D = \frac{1}{P}$$

To find the value of the dollar D, divide 1 by the price level P expressed as an index number (in hundredths). If the price level is 1.0, then the value of the dollar is 1. If the price level rises to, say, 1.20, D falls to .833; a 20 percent increase in the price level reduces the value of the dollar by 16.67 percent. Check your understanding of this reciprocal relationship by determining the value of D and its percentage rise when P falls by 20 percent to 0.80. **(Key Question 6)**

Inflation and Acceptability   In Chapter 8 we noted situations in which a nation's currency became worthless and unacceptable in exchange. These were circumstances in which government issued so many pieces of paper currency that the value of each of these units of money was almost totally undermined. The infamous post-World War I inflation in Germany is an example. In December 1919 there were about 50 billion marks in circulation. Four years later this figure had expanded to 496,585,345,900 billion marks! The result? The German mark in 1923 was worth an infinitesimal fraction of its 1919 value.[3]

How might inflation and the accompanying decreases in the value of a nation's currency affect the acceptability of paper currency as money? Households and businesses will accept paper currency as a medium of exchange as long as they know they can spend it without any noticeable loss in its purchasing power. But this is not the case when there is spiraling inflation. Runaway inflation, such as in Germany in the early 1920s and in several Latin-American nations in the 1980s, may significantly depreciate the value of money between the time it is received and the time it is spent. It is as if the government were constantly taxing away the purchasing power of its currency. Rapid declines in the value of a currency may cause it to cease being used as a medium of exchange. Businesses and households may refuse to accept paper

money in exchange because they do not want to bear the loss in its value which will occur while it is in their possession. (All this despite the fact that government says the paper currency is legal tender!) Without an acceptable domestic medium of exchange, the economy may try to substitute a more stable currency from another nation. Example: Many transactions in Russia and South America now occur in dollars rather than less stable rubles or pesos. At the extreme, the economy may simply revert to inefficient barter.

Similarly, people will use a particular unit of money as a store of value only as long as there is no sizable deterioration in the value of that money because of inflation. And an economy can effectively employ money as a unit of account only when its purchasing power is relatively stable. A measure of value which is subject to drastic shrinkage does not permit buyers and sellers to establish the terms of trade clearly. When the value of the dollar is declining rapidly, sellers will not know what to charge, and buyers will not know what to pay, for goods and services.

Stabilization of Money's Value

Stability of the value of money entails (1) appropriate fiscal policy, as explained in Chapter 12, and (2) intelligent management or regulation of the money supply. Businesses and households accept paper money in exchange for goods, services, and resources only when they expect it to command a roughly equivalent amount of these items when it is spent. In the United States a blending of legislation, government policy, and social practice inhibits imprudent expansion of the money supply which might seriously jeopardize money's value in exchange.

That which is true for paper currency also applies to checking account money—the debt of commercial banks and thrift institutions. Your checking account of $200 means your bank or thrift is indebted to you for that number of dollars. You can collect this debt in one of two ways. You can go to the bank or thrift and demand paper currency for your checkable deposit; this amounts to changing the debts you hold from the debts of a bank or thrift to government-issued debts. Or, and this is more likely, you can "collect" the debt which the bank or savings institution owes you by transferring this claim by check to someone else.

For example, if you buy a $200 leather coat from a store, you can pay for it by writing a check, which transfers your bank's indebtedness from you to the

---

[3]Frank G. Graham, *Exchange, Prices and Production in Hyperinflation Germany, 1920–1923* (Princeton, NJ: Princeton University Press, 1930), p. 13.

store. Your bank now owes the store the $200 it previously owed you. The store accepts this transfer of indebtedness (the check) as a medium of exchange because it can convert it into currency on demand or can transfer the debt to others in making purchases of its choice. Thus, checks, as means of transferring the debts of banks and thrifts, are acceptable as money because we know banks and thrifts will honor these claims.

The ability of banks and thrifts to honor claims against them depends on their not creating too many of these claims. You will see that a decentralized system of private, profit-seeking banks may not contain sufficient safeguards against the creation of too much check money. Thus, the U.S. banking and financial system has substantial centralization and governmental control to guard against the imprudent creation of checkable deposits.

Caution: This does not mean that in practice the monetary authorities have always judiciously controlled the supplies of currency and checkable deposits. Indeed, many economists allege that most of the inflationary woes the United States and other nations have experienced are the consequence of imprudent increases in the money supply by central banks. But that gets us ahead of our story; all you need to know for now is that a nation's monetary authorities control its supply of money. This supply is represented graphically by a vertical money supply curve, such as S_m in Figure 13-2c.

QUICK REVIEW 13-2

■ In the United States, all money is essentially the debts of government, commercial banks, and thrift institutions.

■ These debts efficiently perform the functions of money as long as their value, or purchasing power, is relatively stable.

■ The value of money is rooted not in carefully defined quantities of precious metals but, rather, in the amount of goods, services, and resources that money will purchase.

■ Government's responsibility in stabilizing the value of the monetary unit involves (1) the application of appropriate fiscal policies and (2) effective control over the supply of money.

THE DEMAND FOR MONEY

The public wants to hold some of its wealth as *money* for two basic reasons: to make purchases with it and to hold it as an asset.

Transactions Demand, D_t

People want money because it is a medium of exchange; it is convenient for purchasing goods and services. Households must have enough money on hand to buy groceries and pay mortgage and utility bills until the next paycheck. Businesses need money to pay for labor, materials, power, and other inputs. Money demanded for all such purposes is called the **transactions demand** for money.

The basic determinant of the amount of money demanded for transactions is the level of nominal GDP. The larger the total money value of all goods and services exchanged in the economy, the larger the amount of money needed to negotiate these transactions. *The transactions demand for money varies directly with nominal GDP.* We specify *nominal* GDP because households and firms will want more money for transactions if either prices rise *or* real output increases. In both instances there will be a larger dollar volume of transactions to accomplish.

In **Figure 13-2a (Key Graph)** we graph the quantity of money demanded for transactions against the interest rate. Because the amount demanded depends on the level of nominal GDP and is independent of the interest rate, the transactions demand, D_t, graphs as a vertical line. That is, we assume changes in the interest rate do not affect the amount of money demanded for transactions.

The transactions demand curve is placed at $100 billion on the assumption that each dollar held for transactions purposes is spent on the average three times per year *and* that nominal GDP is $300 billion. Thus the public needs $100 billion (= $300 billion ÷ 3) of money to purchase that GDP.

Asset Demand, D_a

The second reason for holding money derives from money's function as a store of value. People may hold their financial assets in many forms—as corporate stocks, private or government bonds, or as $M1$ money. Thus, there is an **asset demand** for money.

What determines this kind of demand for money? First, we must recognize that each of the various ways to hold financial assets has advantages and disadvantages. To simplify, let's compare holding money as an asset with holding bonds. The advantages of holding money are its liquidity and lack of risk. Money is the most liquid of all assets; it is immediately usable in making purchases. Money is an at-

(a) Transactions demand for money, D_t

(b) Asset demand for money, D_a

(c) Total demand for money, $D_m = D_t + D_a$, and supply

FIGURE 13-2 The demand for money and the money market The total demand for money D_m is determined by horizontally adding the asset demand for money D_a to the transactions demand D_t. The transactions demand is vertical because it is assumed to depend on nominal GDP rather than on the interest rate. The asset demand varies inversely with the interest rate because of the opportunity cost involved in holding currency and checkable deposits which pay no interest or very low interest. Combining the money supply (stock) S_m with total money demand D_m portrays the money market and determines the equilibrium interest rate i_e.

QUICK QUIZ 13-2

1. **In this graph, at the interest rate i_e:**
   a. the amount of money demanded as an asset is $50 billion.
   b. the amount of money demanded for transactions is $200 billion.
   c. bond prices will decline.
   d. $100 billion is demanded for transactions, $100 billion is demanded as an asset, and the money supply is $200 billion.

2. **In this graph, at an interest rate of 10 percent:**
   a. no money will be demanded as an asset.
   b. total money demanded will be $200 billion.
   c. the Federal Reserve will supply $100 billion of money.
   d. there will be a $100 billion shortage of money.

3. **Curve D_a slopes downward because:**
   a. lower interest rates increase the opportunity cost of holding money.
   b. lower interest rates reduce the opportunity cost of holding money.

   c. the asset demand for money varies directly (positively) with the interest rate.
   d. the transactions-demand-for-money curve is perfectly vertical.

4. **Suppose the supply of money declined to $100 billion. The equilibrium interest rate would:**
   a. fall, the amount of money demanded for transactions would rise, and the amount of money demanded as an asset would decline.
   b. rise and the amounts of money demanded for transactions and as an asset would both fall.
   c. fall and the amounts of money demanded for transactions and as an asset would both increase.
   d. rise, the amount of money demanded for transactions would be unchanged, and the amount of money demanded as an asset would decline.

Answers: 1. d; 2. a; 3. b; 4. d

tractive asset to be holding when the prices of goods, services, and other financial assets are expected to decline. When the price of a bond falls, the bond-holder will suffer a loss if the bond must be sold before maturity. There is no such risk with holding money.

The disadvantage of holding money as an asset is that, compared with holding bonds, it does *not* earn interest or, if it is in an interest-bearing checking account, earn as much interest income as bonds or noncheckable deposits. Idle currency, of course, earns no interest at all.

Knowing this, the problem is deciding how much of your financial assets to hold as, say, bonds and how much as money. The solution depends primarily on the rate of interest. A household or business incurs an opportunity cost when holding money; interest income is forgone or sacrificed. If a bond pays 10 percent interest, then it costs $10 per year of forgone income to hold $100 as cash or in a noninterest checkable account.

It is no surprise, then, that *the asset demand for money varies inversely with the rate of interest.* When the interest rate or opportunity cost of holding money as an asset is low, the public will choose to hold a large amount of money as assets. When the interest rate is high, it is costly to "be liquid" and the amount of assets held as money will be small. When it is expensive to hold money as an asset, people hold less of it; when money can be held cheaply, people hold more of it. This inverse relationship between the interest rate and the amount of money people want to hold as an asset is shown by D_a in Figure 13-2b.

Total Money Demand, D_m

As shown in Figure 13-2, the **total demand for money,** D_m, is found by horizontally adding the asset demand to the transactions demand. The resulting downsloping line in Figure 13-2c represents the total amount of money the public wants to hold—for transactions *and* as an asset—at each possible interest rate.

Recall that the transactions demand for money depends mainly on the nominal GDP. A change in the nominal GDP—working through the transactions demand for money—will shift the total money demand curve. Specifically, an increase in nominal GDP means the public wants to hold a larger amount of money for transactions, and this will shift the total money demand curve to the right. A decline in the nominal GDP will shift the total money demand curve to the left. As an example, suppose nominal GDP increases from $300 to $450 billion and the average dollar held for transactions is still spent three times per year. Then the transactions demand curve will shift from $100 billion (= $300 billion ÷ 3) to $150 billion (= $450 billion ÷ 3). The total money demand curve

will then lie $50 billion farther to the right at each possible interest rate.

THE MONEY MARKET

We can combine the demand for money with the supply of money to portray the **money market** and determine the equilibrium rate of interest. In Figure 13-2c the vertical line, S_m, represents the money supply. The money supply is shown as a vertical line because we assume the monetary authorities and financial institutions have provided the economy with some particular *stock* of money, such as the M1 total shown in Table 13-1.

Just as in a product or resource market, the intersection of demand and supply determines equilibrium price. Here, the "price" is the equilibrium interest rate (i_e), that is, the price paid for the use of money.

If disequilibrium existed in the money market, how would the money market achieve equilibrium? Consider Figure 13-3, which repeats Figure 13-2c and adds two alternative supply-of-money curves.

Responses to a Shortage of Money

Suppose the supply of money is reduced from $200 billion, S_m, to $150 billion, S_{m1}. At the previous interest rate of 5 percent, the quantity of money demanded now exceeds the quantity supplied by $50 billion. People will attempt to make up for this shortage of money by selling some of the financial assets they own (we assume for simplicity that these assets are bonds). But one person's receipt of money through the sale of a bond is another person's loss of money through the purchase of that bond. Overall, there is only $150 billion of money available. The collective attempt to get more money by selling bonds will increase the supply of bonds relative to the demand for bonds in the bond market, but it will not increase the amount of money available as a whole. The outcome is that the price of bonds will fall.

Generalization: *Lower bond prices are associated with higher interest rates.* To clarify this, suppose a bond with no expiration date pays a fixed $50 annual interest and is selling for its face value of $1000. The interest yield on this bond is 5 percent:

$$\frac{\$50}{\$1000} = 5\%$$

FIGURE 13-3 Restoring equilibrium in the money market A decrease in the supply of money creates a temporary shortage of money in the money market. People and institutions attempt to gain more money by selling bonds. The supply of bonds therefore increases, which reduces bond prices and raises interest rates. At higher interest rates, people reduce the amount of money they wish to hold. Thus, the amount of money supplied and demanded once again is equal at the higher interest rate. An increase in the supply of money creates a temporary surplus of money, resulting in an increase in the demand for bonds and higher bond prices. Interest rates fall and equilibrium is reestablished in the money market.

- -

Now suppose the price of this bond falls to $667 because of the increased supply of bonds. The $50 fixed annual interest payment will now yield $7\frac{1}{2}$ percent to whomever buys the bond:

$$\frac{\$50}{\$667} = 7\frac{1}{2}\%$$

Because all borrowers must compete by offering to pay lenders interest yields similar to those available on bonds, a higher general interest rate emerges. In Figure 13-3 the interest rate rises from 5 percent with the money supply at $200 billion to $7\frac{1}{2}$ percent when the money supply is $150 billion. This higher interest rate raises the opportunity cost of holding money and reduces the amount of money firms and households want to hold. Specifically, the amount of money demanded declines from $200 billion at the 5 percent interest rate to $150 billion at the $7\frac{1}{2}$ percent interest rate. The money market is back in equilibrium, now with the quantities of money demanded and supplied equaling $150 billion at the new $7\frac{1}{2}$ percent interest rate.

Responses to a Surplus of Money

An increase in the supply of money from $200 billion, S_m, to $250 billion, S_{m2}, results in a surplus of $50 billion at the initial 5 percent interest rate. People will now try to rid themselves of money by purchasing more bonds. But one person's expenditure of money is another person's receipt of money. The collective attempt to buy more bonds will increase the demand for bonds and pull bond prices upward.

Corollary: *Higher bond prices are associated with lower interest rates.* In our example, the $50 interest payment on a bond now priced at, say, $2000, will yield a bond buyer only $2\frac{1}{2}$ percent:

$$\frac{\$50}{\$2000} = 2\frac{1}{2}\%$$

The point is that interest rates in general will fall as people unsuccessfully attempt to reduce their money holdings below $250 billion by buying bonds. In this case, the interest rate will fall to a new equilibrium at $2\frac{1}{2}$ percent. Because the opportunity cost of holding money now is lower—being liquid is less expensive—consumers and businesses will increase the amount of currency and checkable deposits they are willing to hold from $200 billion to $250 billion. Eventually equilibrium in the money market will be restored: The quantities of money demanded and supplied will each be $250 billion at an interest rate of $2\frac{1}{2}$ percent.

In Chapter 15 you will see how monetary policy is used to change the money supply to alter the equilibrium real interest rate. A higher interest rate reduces investment and consumption spending, decreasing aggregate demand. A lower rate increases investment and consumption spending, increasing aggregate demand. Either situation ultimately affects the levels of real output, employment, and prices. **(Key Question 7)**

QUICK REVIEW 13-3

■ People hold money for transaction and asset purposes.

■ The total demand for money is the sum of the transactions and asset demands; it is graphed as an inverse relationship (downsloping line) between the interest rate and the quantity of money demanded.

■ The equilibrium interest rate is determined by money demand and supply; it occurs where people are willing to hold the exact amount of money being supplied by the monetary authorities.

■ Bond prices and interest rates are inversely related.

THE FEDERAL RESERVE AND THE BANKING SYSTEM

In the United States, the "monetary authorities" we mentioned are the members of the Board of Governors of the **Federal Reserve System** (the "Fed"). As shown in Figure 13-4, this Board directs the activities of the 12 Federal Reserve Banks, which in turn control the lending activity of the nation's banks and thrift institutions.

Historical Background

Early in the twentieth century, Congress decided that centralization and public control were essential for an efficient banking system. Decentralized, unregulated banking had fostered the inconvenience and confusion of numerous private bank notes being used as currency. It had also resulted in occasional episodes of monetary mismanagement such that the money supply was inappropriate to the needs of the economy: sometimes "too much" money precipitated rapid in-flation; other times "too little" money stunted the economy's growth by hindering the production and exchange of goods and services. No single entity was charged with creating and implementing nationally consistent banking policies.

An unusually acute 1907 money panic motivated Congress to appoint the National Monetary Commission to study the monetary and banking problems of the economy and to outline a course of action for Congress. The result was the Federal Reserve Act of 1913.

Figure 13-4 represents the monetary system which has developed under the frequently amended Federal Reserve Act. Let's examine the nature and roles of the various parts of the Federal Reserve System and their relationships to one another.

Board of Governors

The kingpin of the U.S. money and banking system is the **Board of Governors** of the Federal Reserve System. The U.S. president, with the confirmation of

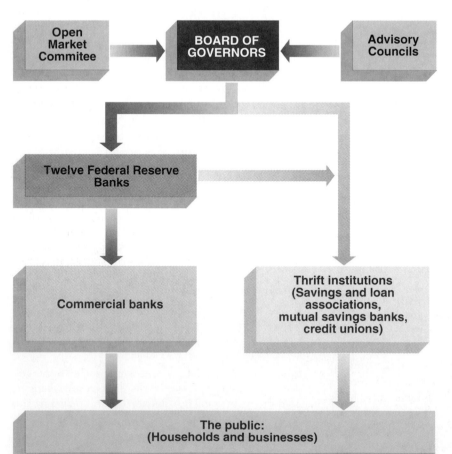

FIGURE 13-4 Framework of the Federal Reserve System and its relationship to the public With the advice of the Open Market Committee and three Advisory Councils, the Board of Governors makes the basic policy decisions providing monetary control of the U.S. money and banking systems. These decisions are made effective through the 12 Federal Reserve Banks.

the Senate, appoints the 7 Board members. Terms are long—14 years—and staggered so that one member is replaced every 2 years. The president selects the chairperson and vice-chairperson of the Board from among the members, and these officers serve 4-year terms. The long-term appointments provide the Board with continuity, experienced membership, and independence from political pressures which could result in inflation.

Assistance and Advice

Several entities assist the Board of Governors in determining banking and monetary policy. The first is clearly the most powerful.

The **Federal Open Market Committee** (FOMC) is made up of the 7 members of the Board of Governors plus 5 of the presidents of the Federal Reserve Banks. The FOMC sets the Fed's monetary policy and directs the purchase and sale of government securities (bills, notes, and bonds) in the open market. As you will see in Chapter 15, these aptly named *open-market operations* are the most significant technique available to the Fed for controlling the money supply.

Three **Advisory Councils** made up of private citizens meet periodically with the Board of Governors to voice their views on banking and monetary policy. The *Federal Advisory Council* is composed of 12 commercial bankers, 1 selected annually by each of the 12 Federal Reserve Banks. The *Thrift Institutions Advisory Council* consists of representatives from savings and loan associations, savings banks, and credit unions. The third advisory group, the 30-member *Consumer Advisory Council*, includes representatives of consumers of financial services and academic and legal specialists in consumer matters. As their names indicate, the councils are purely advisory. They have no policy-making powers, and the Board has no obligation to heed their advice.

The 12 Federal Reserve Banks

The 12 **Federal Reserve Banks** serve as central banks, quasipublic banks, and bankers' banks.

Central Banks   Most nations have one central bank, for example, Britain's Bank of England or Germany's Bundesbank. The United States has, in effect, 12 "central" banks whose policies are coordinated by the Board of Governors. The 12 Federal Reserve Banks partly accommodate the geographical size and economic diversity of the United States and the nation's large number of commercial banks and thrifts. These central banks are also the result of a political compromise between proponents of centralization and those who distrust powerful financial institutions.

Figure 13-5 locates the 12 Federal Reserve Banks and indicates the district each serves. These central banks carry out the basic policy of the Board of Governors. The Federal Reserve Bank in New York City is the most important of the central banks since it carries out most of the Fed's open-market operations.

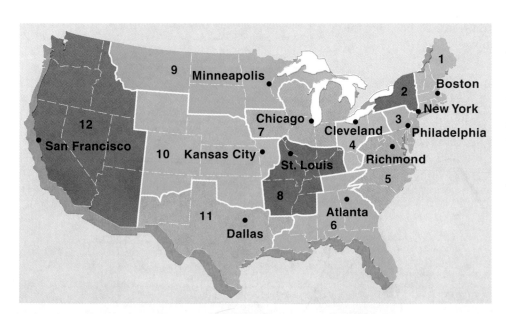

FIGURE 13-5 The 12 Federal Reserve Districts The Federal Reserve System divides the United States into 12 districts, each having one central bank and in some instances one or more branches of the central bank. Hawaii and Alaska are included in the twelfth district. *(Source: Federal Reserve Bulletin.)*

Quasipublic Banks The 12 Federal Reserve Banks are quasigovernmental banks, meaning that they are a blend of private ownership and public control. Each Federal Reserve Bank is owned by the private commercial banks in its district. (Commercial banks are required to purchase shares of stock in the Federal Reserve Bank in their district.) But a governmental body, the Board of Governors, sets the basic policies that the Federal Reserve Banks pursue. The owners of these central banks thus control neither the central bank officials nor their policies.

Despite their private ownership, the Federal Reserve Banks are essentially public institutions. Unlike private firms, they are not motivated by profit. The policies the central banks follow are designed by the Board of Governors to promote the well-being of the economy as a whole. Thus, the activities of the Federal Reserve Banks are frequently at odds with the profit motive.[4] Also, the Federal Reserve Banks do not compete with commercial banks. With rare exceptions, the Federal Reserve Banks do not deal with the public but, rather, deal with the government and the commercial banks and thrifts.

Bankers' Banks The Federal Reserve Banks are "bankers' banks." They perform essentially the same functions for banks and thrifts as those institutions perform for the public. Just as banks and thrifts accept the deposits of and make loans to the public, so the central banks accept the deposits of and make loans to banks and thrifts. But the Federal Reserve Banks have a third function which banks and thrifts do not perform: They issue currency. Congress has authorized the Federal Reserve Banks to put into circulation Federal Reserve Notes, which constitute the economy's paper money supply.

Commercial Banks and Thrifts

The workhorses of the U.S. banking system are its 9500 **commercial banks.** Roughly two-thirds are **state banks,** private banks chartered (authorized) by individual states to operate within those states. One-third are private banks chartered by the Federal government to operate nationally; they are **national**

banks. While some of the U.S. national banks are very large, none of them rank among the world's largest private banks (see Global Perspective 13-1).

The 14,000 thrift institutions are regulated by agencies separate and apart from the Board of Governors and the Federal Reserve Banks. For example, the operation of savings and loan associations is regulated and monitored by the Treasury Department's Office of Thrift Supervision. But the thrifts are subject to monetary control by the Federal Reserve System. In particular, like the banks, thrifts are required to keep a certain percentage of their checkable deposits as "reserves." In Figure 13-4 we use orange arrows to denote that the thrift institutions are partially subject to the

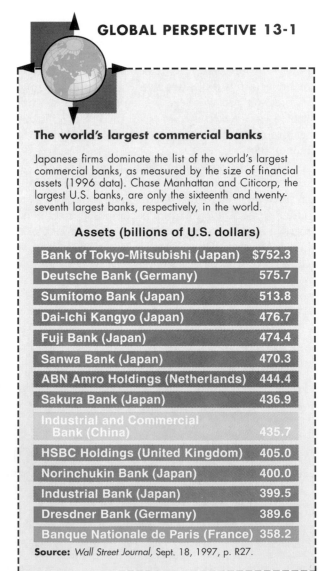

GLOBAL PERSPECTIVE 13-1

The world's largest commercial banks

Japanese firms dominate the list of the world's largest commercial banks, as measured by the size of financial assets (1996 data). Chase Manhattan and Citicorp, the largest U.S. banks, are only the sixteenth and twenty-seventh largest banks, respectively, in the world.

Assets (billions of U.S. dollars)

Bank of Tokyo-Mitsubishi (Japan)	$752.3
Deutsche Bank (Germany)	575.7
Sumitomo Bank (Japan)	513.8
Dai-Ichi Kangyo (Japan)	476.7
Fuji Bank (Japan)	474.4
Sanwa Bank (Japan)	470.3
ABN Amro Holdings (Netherlands)	444.4
Sakura Bank (Japan)	436.9
Industrial and Commercial Bank (China)	435.7
HSBC Holdings (United Kingdom)	405.0
Norinchukin Bank (Japan)	400.0
Industrial Bank (Japan)	399.5
Dresdner Bank (Germany)	389.6
Banque Nationale de Paris (France)	358.2

Source: *Wall Street Journal,* Sept. 18, 1997, p. R27.

---

[4]Although it is not their goal, the Federal Reserve Banks have actually operated profitably, largely as a result of Treasury debts held by them. Part of the profits are used to pay dividends to banks on their holdings of stock; the remaining profit is usually turned over to the U.S. Treasury.

control of the Board of Governors and the central banks. Decisions concerning monetary policy affect the thrifts along with the commercial banks.

Fed Functions and the Money Supply

The Fed performs several functions, some of which we have already identified:

1. *Issuing currency* The Fed issues Federal Reserve Notes, the paper currency used in the U.S. monetary system. (The Federal Reserve Bank which issued a particular bill is named in the circle to the left on the face of the bill. The newly designed $50 and $100 bills, however, identify the bank only by its district number. "A1," for example, identifies the Boston bank, "B2" the New York bank, and so on.)

2. *Setting reserve requirements and holding reserves* The Fed sets reserve requirements. The central banks accept as deposits from the banks and thrifts any portion of their mandated reserves not held as vault cash.

3. *Lending money to banks and thrifts* At times, the Fed lends money to banks and thrifts, charging them an interest rate called the *discount rate.*

4. *Providing for check collection* Another important function of the Fed is to provide the means for the collection of checks. If Sarah writes a check on her Salem bank or thrift to Sam, who deposits it in his San Diego bank or thrift, how does the San Diego bank collect the money represented by the check drawn against the Salem bank? Answer: The Fed handles it in 2 or 3 days by adjusting the reserves (deposits) of the two banks.

5. *Acting as fiscal agent* The Fed acts as the fiscal agent (provider of financial services) for the Federal government. The government collects huge sums through taxation, spends equally large amounts, and sells and redeems bonds. The government uses the Fed's facilities in carrying out these activities.

6. *Supervising banks* The Fed supervises the operation of banks. Periodic bank examinations access bank profitability, ascertain that banks perform in accordance with the myriad regulations to which they are subject, and uncover questionable practices or fraud.[5]

7. *Controlling the money supply* Finally, and most important, the Fed has ultimate responsibility for regulating the supply of money, and this in turn enables it to affect interest rates. The major task of the Fed is to manage the money supply (and thus interest rates) on the basis of the needs of the economy. This involves making an amount of money available that is consistent with high and rising levels of output and employment and a relatively constant price level. While all the other functions are more or less routine or of a service nature, correctly managing the nation's money supply requires making basic but unique policy decisions. (These decisions are discussed in detail in Chapter 15.)

Federal Reserve Independence

The independence of the Fed is a matter of continuing controversy. Opponents of an independent Fed say that it is undemocratic to have a powerful economic agency whose members are not elected and thus not directly subject to the will of the people. They also point out that since the legislative and executive branches of government bear ultimate responsibility for maintaining economic stability and promoting economic growth, they should have available *all* the policy tools essential to the economy's health, including monetary policy. Voters tend to hold Congress and the president responsible for the consequences of Fed policies over which they have no control. Critics cite instances of the Fed using monetary policy to counter the effects of Congress' fiscal policy.

Defenders of Fed independence, including most economists, contend that the Fed must be protected from political pressures so that it can effectively control the money supply and maintain price stability. They point out that countries with less central bank independence, on average, have higher rates of inflation than countries with more central bank independence (see Global Perspective 13-2). It is often politically useful for Congress and the executive branch to enact inflationary fiscal policies, including tax cuts and special-interest spending. Citizens would likely pressure Congress to keep interest rates low, via expansions in the money supply, even though at times high interest rates are necessary to reduce aggregate

---

[5]The Fed is not alone in this task of supervision. The individual states supervise all banks that they charter. The Comptroller of the Currency supervises all national banks, and the Office of Thrift Supervision oversees all thrifts. Also, the Federal Deposit Insurance Corporation supervises all banks and thrifts whose deposits it insures.

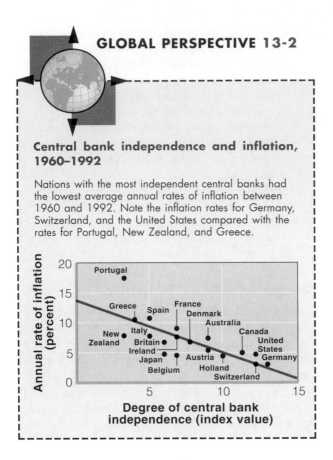

GLOBAL PERSPECTIVE 13-2

Central bank independence and inflation, 1960–1992

Nations with the most independent central banks had the lowest average annual rates of inflation between 1960 and 1992. Note the inflation rates for Germany, Switzerland, and the United States compared with the rates for Portugal, New Zealand, and Greece.

demand and thus to control inflation. Fed defenders argue that an independent monetary authority is needed to control the consequent inflation.

RECENT DEVELOPMENTS IN MONEY AND BANKING

The banking industry is undergoing a series of sweeping changes, spurred by competition from other financial institutions, globalization of banking, and advances in information technology.

The Relative Decline of Banks and Thrifts

Banks and thrifts are just two of several types of firms offering financial services. Table 13-2 identifies and briefly describes the major categories of firms within the U.S. *financial services industry* and lists examples of firms in each category. Although banks and thrifts remain the main institutions offering checkable deposits, their shares of *total* financial assets (value

of things owned) are declining. As shown in Figure 13-6, in 1980 banks and thrifts together held nearly 60 percent of financial assets in the United States. By 1996 that percentage had declined to 30 percent. The share held by thrifts decreased from 23 percent to 7 percent, largely as a result of the financial collapse of the numerous savings and loan associations in the late 1980s and early 1990s. The 37 percent share held by banks in 1980 declined to 24 percent by 1996.

Figure 13-6 reveals that pension funds, insurance companies, securities-related firms, and especially mutual funds have all expanded their shares of financial assets. Clearly, U.S. households and businesses are channeling relatively more saving away from banks and thrifts and toward these other financial institutions, mainly because these other institutions generally offer higher rates of return than do banks and thrifts. They are able to do so largely because they can participate more fully than banks and thrifts in national and international stock and bond markets.

Banks and thrifts have responded to the relative decline in traditional banking in several ways.

Expansion of Services   In recent years, banks and thrifts have begun offering a variety of new services. For example, banks have increased their lending for commercial real estate projects such as housing developments, apartments, and office buildings. Banks and thrifts have developed new loan "products" such as home equity loans (loans based on the value of one's house) and low- or zero-down-payment mortgages. They also now offer a variety of interest-bearing accounts such as money market deposit accounts.

Banks and thrifts have made banking more convenient by opening up full-service branch banks in suburbs and "minibanks" in shopping malls and grocery stores. Supplementing these branches has been an explosion in the number of bank-owned automatic teller machines (ATMs) which allow customers to withdraw cash, deposit checks, move money between accounts, and make other banking transactions. They have also introduced "bank-by-telephone" and, more recently, "bank by Internet" services.

Mergers with Other Banks and Thrifts   During the past two decades, many banks have purchased bankrupt savings and loans and have merged with other banks. Recent examples of large bank mergers include Chase Manhattan's merger with Chemical Bank and Wells Fargo's merger with First Interstate. Major savings and loans have also merged; for exam-

TABLE 13-2 Major U.S. Financial Institutions

Institution	Description	Examples
Commercial banks	State and national banks which provide checking and savings accounts, sell certificates of deposit, and make loans. The Federal Deposit Insurance Corporation (FDIC) insures checking and savings accounts up to $100,000.	Chase Manhattan, Citicorp, BankAmerica, J. P. Morgan, Wells Fargo
Thrifts	Savings and loan associations (S&Ls), mutual savings banks, and credit unions which offer checking and savings accounts and make loans. Historically, S&Ls made mortgage loans for houses while mutual savings banks and credit unions made small personal loans, such as automobile loans. Today, major thrifts offer the same range of banking services as commercial banks. The Federal Deposit Insurance Corporation insures checking and savings deposits up to $100,000.	Home Savings of America, Washington Mutual, Golden West Financial
Insurance companies	Firms which offer policies (contracts) through which individuals pay premiums to insure against some loss, say, disability or death. In some life insurance policies and annuities, the funds are invested for the client in stocks and bonds and paid back after a specified number of years. Thus, insurance sometimes has a saving or financial-investment element.	Prudential, New York Life, Travelers Group, Massachusetts Mutual
Mutual fund companies	Firms which pool deposits by customers to purchase stocks or bonds (or both). Customers thus own a part of a particular set of stocks or bonds, say, stocks in companies expected to grow rapidly (a growth fund) or bonds issued by state governments (a municipal bond fund).	Fidelity, Putnam, Dreyfus, Kemper
Pension funds	For-profit or nonprofit institutions which collect savings from workers (or from employers on their behalf) throughout their working years and then buy stocks and bonds with the proceeds and make monthly retirement payments.	Teachers Insurance and Annuity Association-College Retirement Equity Fund, Teamsters' Union
Securities-related firms	Firms which offer security advice and buy and sell stocks and bonds for clients. More generally known as *stock brokerage firms*.	Merrill-Lynch, Solomon, Leyman Brothers, Charles Schwab

ple, Washington Mutual recently acquired Great Western Financial. The purpose of such mergers is to create large regional or national banks or thrifts which can compete more effectively with the other participants in the financial services industry. Consolidation of traditional banking is expected to continue; there are 4500 fewer banks today than in 1990.

Push for Regulatory Reform In 1994 Congress ended Federal restrictions on banks' branching into other states, and a 1996 reform partially ended the legal separation of the banking industry and the securities-related industry. Banks are now allowed to obtain up to one-fourth of their revenues from security transactions. This change set up a flurry of purchases of small security firms by banks. Banks have pressed for further latitude in engaging in security-related activities. They would like to offer stock accounts, much as mutual fund companies and security-related companies do now.

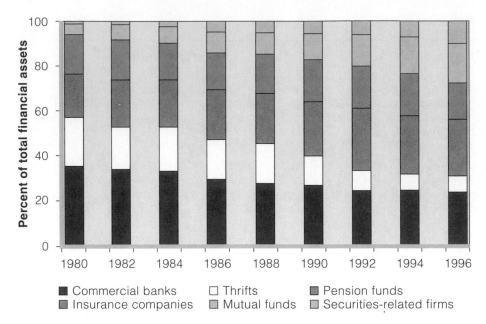

FIGURE 13-6 Financial assets held by major categories of U.S. financial services firms The combined share of total financial assets held in U.S. banks and thrifts has declined significantly since 1980. The shares of pension funds, insurance companies, mutual funds, and securities-related firms have increased. (*Source:* Federal Reserve Bank of Dallas; updated.)

Banks point out that less-regulated firms have invaded traditional banking, while banks have been prohibited from offering nonbanking products. For example, General Motors and AT&T now offer credit cards, and mutual fund companies now offer money market mutual funds, which pay relatively high interest and on which large checks ($500 or more) can be written. To counter such encroachments, banks want changes in the law so that they can own and operate companies in any line of business. With such reform, a bank could merge with, say, an insurance company or even a manufacturer of cash registers.

Critics of these reforms are concerned that increased participation by banks in nonbanking businesses could endanger the stability of the banking system. Losses in other lines of business during times of recession might cause the firms to fail, collapsing their banking operations along with them. Such bank failures might undermine confidence in the entire banking system and in the Fed's ability to maintain an adequate supply of money.

Globalization of Financial Markets

Another significant banking development is the increased integration of world financial markets. Major foreign financial institutions have operations in the United States, and U.S. financial institutions do business abroad. For example, VISA, MasterCard, and American Express offer worldwide credit card services. Moreover, U.S. mutual fund companies now offer a variety of international stock and bond funds. Globally, financial capital increasingly flows in search of the highest risk-adjusted returns. As a result, U.S. banks must increasingly compete with foreign banks for both deposits and loan customers.

Recent advances in computer and communications technology mean the trend toward international financial integration is likely to accelerate. Nevertheless, we must not overstate the extent of this globalization. Studies indicate that the bulk of investment in the major nations is still financed through domestic saving within each nation.

Electronic Money

Technological progress has also led to a new form of money: electronic cash and "smart cards." Although still in their infancies, these innovations potentially are of great significance to commercial banks, thrifts, and central banks.

Electronic money, dubbed **E-cash,** is simply an entry in an electronic file stored in a computer. The Internet and the widespread availability of personal computers have made it possible for individuals to use E-cash instead of checks or currency in making transactions. E-cash is deposited, or "loaded," into the account through Internet payments such as a paycheck,

The Global Greenback

A large amount of U.S. currency is circulating abroad.

Russians use them. So do Argentineans, Brazilians, Poles, Vietnamese, Chinese, and even Cubans. They are U.S. dollars. Like blue jeans, computer software, and movie videos, the dollar has become a major U.S. "export." Billions of dollars of U.S. currency currently are circulating overseas. Russians hold about $30 billion in U.S. cash; Argentineans, $5 to $7 billion. The Polish government estimates that $5 billion of U.S. dollars is circulating in Poland.

The currency leaves the United States when Americans buy imports, travel in other countries, or send dollars to relatives living abroad. The United States profits when the dollars stay in other countries. It costs the government about 4 cents to print a dollar. For someone abroad to obtain this new dollar, $1 worth of resources, goods, or services must be sold to Americans. These commodities are U.S. gains. The dollar goes abroad and, assuming it stays there, presents no claim on U.S. resources or goods or services. Americans in effect make 96 cents on the dollar (= $1 gain in resources, goods, or services *minus* the 4-cent printing cost). It's like American Express selling traveler's checks which never get cashed.

Black markets and other illegal activity undoubtedly fuel some of the demand for U.S. cash abroad. The dollar is king in covert trading in diamonds, weapons, and pirated software. Billions of cash dollars are involved in the narcotics trade. But the illegal use of dollars is only a small part of the story. The massive volume of dollars in other nations reflects a global search for monetary stability. On the basis of past experience, foreign citizens are confident the dollar's purchasing power will remain relatively steady.

Argentina has pegged its peso directly to the dollar, with the central bank issuing new pesos only when it has more dollars or gold on hand. The result has been a remarkable decline in inflation. In Russia and the newly independent countries of eastern Europe, the U.S. dollar has retained its buying power while that of domestic currencies has plummeted. As a result, many Russians hold their savings in dollars. In Brazil, where the inflation rate at times has been more than 1000 percent annually, people have long sought the stability of dollars. In the shopping districts of Beijing and Shanghai, Chinese consumers trade their domestic currency for dollars. In Bolivia half of all bank accounts are denominated in dollars. There is a thriving "dollar economy" in Vietnam, and even Cuba has partially legalized the use of U.S. dollars. The U.S. dollar is the official currency in Panama and Liberia.

There is little risk to the United States in satisfying the world's demand for dollars. If all the dollars came rushing back to the United States at once, the nation's money supply would surge, possibly causing demand-pull inflation. But there is not much chance of that happening. Overall, the global greenback is a positive economic force. It is a reliable medium of exchange, unit of account, and store of value which facilitates transactions that might not otherwise occur. Dollar holdings have helped buyers and sellers abroad overcome special monetary problems. The result has been increased output in those countries and thus greater output and income globally.

retirement benefit, or stock dividend. It is withdrawn, or "unloaded," from the account through Internet payments to others for a wide variety of goods and services.

In the future, account holders will be able to load sums from their E-cash accounts onto so-called *stored-value cards*. These **smart cards** are plastic cards containing computer chips which store information, including the amount the consumer has loaded. The amount of each purchase or other payment is then automatically deducted from the balance in the card's memory. Consumers will be able to transfer traditional money to their smart cards through their computers or telephones or at automatic teller machines. Thus, nearly all payments could be made with a personal computer or a smart card.

You can easily see why banks and thrifts would like to have the exclusive right to issue E-cash and smart cards; these innovations threaten to push banks out of the payment system. Any firm—a telephone company, a group of local merchants, or a hotel chain, for instance—could issue smart cards. Also, computer-related firms such as software producers could get into "banking" by developing and selling E-cash software programs. More likely, however, banks themselves will implement such software and set up E-cash and smart-card systems of their own since they know the banking business better than anyone else. Chase Manhattan, Citibank, VISA, and MasterCard have already teamed up to test a "first-generation" smart-card system in various parts of the country.

It is too early to predict the extent to which E-cash and smart cards will gain widespread public acceptance. If electronic money does catch on, however, it will present special problems for central banks.

Unlike currency, E-cash is "issued" by private firms rather than by government. To control the money supply, the central banks will need to find ways to control the total amount of E-cash, including that created through Internet loans.

QUICK REVIEW 13-4

■ The Federal Reserve System consists of the Board of Governors, 12 Federal Reserve Banks, commercial banks, and thrift institutions.

■ The 12 Federal Reserve Banks are publicly controlled central banks which deal with banks and thrifts rather than the public.

■ The Federal Reserve's major role is to regulate the supply of money in the economy.

■ Three recent developments in banking are the relative decline in traditional banking, the internationalization of banking, and the emergence of E-cash and smart cards.

CHAPTER SUMMARY

1. Anything that is accepted as **(a)** a medium of exchange, **(b)** a unit of monetary account, and **(c)** a store of value can be used as money.

2. The Federal Reserve System recognizes three "official" definitions of the money supply. *M*1 is currency and checkable deposits; *M*2 is *M*1 plus noncheckable savings deposits, money market deposit accounts, small (less than $100,000) time deposits, and money market mutual fund balances; and *M*3 is *M*2 plus large ($100,000 or more) time deposits. In our analysis we concentrate on *M*1 since its components are immediately spendable.

3. Money is the debts of government and depository institutions (commercial banks and thrift institutions) and has value because of the goods, services, and resources it will command in the market. Maintaining the purchasing power of money depends largely on the government's effectiveness in managing the money supply.

4. The total demand for money consists of the transactions and asset demands for money. The transactions demand varies directly with the nominal GDP; the asset demand varies inversely with the interest rate. The money market combines the total demand for money with the money supply to determine the equilibrium interest rate.

5. Disequilibria in the money market are corrected through changes in bond prices. As bond prices change,

interest rates move in the opposite direction. At the equilibrium interest rate, bond prices are stable and the amounts of money demanded and supplied are equal.

6. The U.S. banking system is composed of **(a)** the Board of Governors of the Federal Reserve System, **(b)** the 12 Federal Reserve Banks, and **(c)** some 9500 commercial banks and 14,000 thrift institutions. The Board of Governors is the basic policymaking body for the entire banking system. The directives of the Board are made effective through the 12 Federal Reserve Banks, which are simultaneously **(a)** central banks, **(b)** quasipublic banks, and **(c)** bankers' banks.

7. The major functions of the Fed are to **(a)** issue Federal Reserve Notes, **(b)** set reserve requirements and hold reserves deposited by banks and thrifts, **(c)** lend money to banks and thrifts, **(d)** provide for the rapid collection of checks, **(e)** act as the fiscal agent for the Federal government, **(f)** supervise the operations of the banks, and **(g)** regulate the supply of money in the best interest of the economy.

8. The Fed is essentially an independent institution, meaning that it is under the control of neither the president of the United States nor Congress. Opponents of an independent Fed say that monetary policy should be in the hands of elected officials (the president and Congress).

Defenders of Fed independence say that freedom from political pressure is critical to the Fed's role of providing the economy with an adequate, noninflationary supply of money.

9. Since the 1980s banks and thrifts have lost considerable market share to pension funds, insurance companies, mutual funds, and securities-related firms. Other significant banking developments include globalization of banking services and the emergence of electronic money, including smart cards.

TERMS AND CONCEPTS

medium of exchange
unit of account
store of value
M1, M2, M3
token money
intrinsic value
Federal Reserve Notes
checkable deposits
thrift (savings)
   institutions

savings and loan
   associations
mutual savings banks
credit unions
near-monies
noncheckable savings
   account
money market deposit
   account
time deposits

money market mutual
   fund
legal tender
fiat money
transactions demand
asset demand
total demand for money
money market
Federal Reserve System
Board of Governors

Federal Open Market
   Committee
Advisory Councils
Federal Reserve Banks
commercial banks
state banks
national banks
E-cash
smart cards

STUDY QUESTIONS

1. Describe how rapid inflation can undermine money's ability to perform each of its three basic functions.

2. What are the disadvantages of commodity money (for example, money made from precious metals)? What are the advantages of paper money and check money compared with commodity money?

3. Explain and evaluate the following statements:
   a. The invention of money is one of the great achievements of humankind, for without it the enrichment which comes from broadening trade would have been impossible.
   b. Money is whatever society says it is.
   c. In most economies of the world, the debts of government and commercial banks are used as money.
   d. People often say they would like to have more money, but what they usually mean is that they would like to have more goods and services.
   e. When the prices of everything go up, it is not because everything is worth more but because the currency is worth less.
   f. Any central bank can create money; the trick is to create enough of it, but not too much of it.

4. KEY QUESTION What are the components of the M1 money supply? What is the largest component? Why is the face value of a coin greater than its intrinsic value? Distinguish between M2 and M3.

What are near-monies? Of what significance are they? What arguments can you make for including noncheckable savings deposits in a definition of money?

5. What "backs" the money supply in the United States? What determines the value of money? Who is responsible for maintaining the value of money? Why is it important to be able to alter the money supply? What is meant by **(a)** "sound money" and **(b)** a "52-cent dollar"?

6. KEY QUESTION Suppose the price level and value of the dollar in year 1 are 1.0 and $1, respectively. If the price level rises to 1.25 in year 2, what is the new value of the dollar? If, instead, the price level falls to .50, what is the value of the dollar? What generalization can you draw from your answers?

7. KEY QUESTION What is the basic determinant of **(a)** the transactions demand and **(b)** the asset demand for money? Explain how these two demands might be combined graphically to determine total money demand. How is the equilibrium interest rate in the money market determined? How might **(a)** the expanded use of credit cards, **(b)** a shortening of worker pay periods, and **(c)** an increase in nominal GDP each independently affect the transactions demand for money and the equilibrium interest rate?

8. Suppose the following data characterize a hypothetical economy: money supply = $200 billion; quantity of money demanded for transactions = $150 billion; quantity of money demanded as an asset = $10 billion at 12 percent interest, increasing by $10 billion for each 2-percentage-point fall in the interest rate.
   a. What is the equilibrium interest rate? Explain.
   b. At the equilibrium interest rate, what are the quantity of money supplied, the total quantity of money demanded, the amount of money demanded for transactions, and the amount of money demanded as an asset?

9. Suppose a bond with no expiration date has a face value of $10,000 and annually pays a fixed amount of interest of $800. Compute and enter in the space provided below either the interest rate which the bond would yield to a bond buyer at each of the bond prices listed or the bond price at each of the interest yields shown. What generalization can be drawn from the completed table?

Bond price	Interest yield, %
$ 8,000	_____
_____	8.9
$10,000	_____
$11,000	_____
_____	6.2

10. Assume that the money market is initially in equilibrium and that the money supply is now increased. Explain the adjustments toward a new equilibrium interest rate. Will bond prices be higher or lower at the new equilibrium rate of interest? What effects would you expect the interest-rate change to have on the levels of output, employment, and prices? Answer the same questions for a decrease in the money supply.

11. How is the chair of the Federal Reserve System selected? Describe the relationship between the Board of Governors of the Federal Reserve System and the 12 Federal Reserve Banks. What is meant when economists say that the Federal Reserve Banks are central banks, quasipublic banks, and bankers' banks? What are the seven basic functions of the Federal Reserve System?

12. Following are two hypothetical ways that the Federal Reserve Board might be appointed. Would you favor either of these two methods over the present method? Why or why not?
   a. Upon taking office, the U.S. president appoints 7 people to the Federal Reserve Board, including a chair. Each appointee must be confirmed by a majority vote of the Senate, and each serves the same 4-year term as the president.
   b. Congress selects 7 members from its ranks (4 from the House of Representatives and 3 from the Senate) to serve at its pleasure as the Board of Governors of the Federal Reserve System.

13. What are the major categories of firms which make up the U.S. financial services industry? Which of these categories have experienced a declining share of financial assets since 1980? How have firms in these categories responded?

14. In what way are E-cash accounts and smart cards potentially related? Do you think E-cash and smart cards will dominate transactions sometime within the next 20 years?

15. **(Last Word)** Over the years, the Federal Reserve Banks have printed many billions of dollars more in currency than U.S. households, businesses, and financial institutions now hold. Where is this "missing" money? Why is it there?

16. **WEB-BASED QUESTION** **Board of Governors—Create Some Trading Cards** The Federal Reserve Board http://www.bog.frb.fed.us/BIOS/ provides a detailed biography of the seven members of the Board of Governors. Create "Baseball Card"-types of descriptions and photos (use your Web browser to copy their photos) of the Board members (swapping with your classmates is optional). What is the composition of the Board with regard to age, gender, education, previous employment, and ethnic background? Who are the forthcoming "free agents" near the end of their terms?

17. **WEB-BASED QUESTION** **Everything You Wanted to Know About U.S. Currency but Were Afraid to Ask** U.S. currency is made up of coins and paper money. Visit the Federal Reserve Bank of Atlanta http://www.frbatlanta.org/publica/brochure/fundfac/money.htm and the U.S. Treasury http://www.treas.gov/bep/index.html to answer the following questions. What is the largest denomination note currently in circulation? What has been the largest denomination note in circulation, and when was it last printed? The Federal Reserve Act requires that adequate backing be pledged for all Federal Reserve Notes in circulation. What is this backing? Who owns the notes, The Treasury or the Federal Reserve? What are some tips for spotting counterfeit currency? When was the last silver dollar minted? What have been the largest and smallest U.S. coin denominations since the Coinage Act of 1792?

14

How Banks Create Money

If you visit Washington, D.C., you might enjoy touring the U.S. Bureau of Engraving and Printing. There, each day, more than $25 million of Federal Reserve Notes rolls off the printing presses in large sheets, which are then cut into individual bills and sent to the 12 Federal Reserve Banks for distribution.

Although the government printing presses create some of the nation's money, the bulk of the money in the U.S. economy is checkable deposits of commercial banks and thrifts, *not* currency. Who creates these checkable deposits? The answer is loan officers at commercial banks and thrifts. Although this may sound like something *60 Minutes* and a congressional committee should investigate, banking authorities are well aware that banks and thrifts create checking-deposit money. In fact, the Federal Reserve *relies* on these institutions to create a large part of the nation's money supply.

Because the bulk of all checkable deposits are "demand deposits" of commercial banks, this chapter explains how those banks can create demand-deposit money. Specifically, you will see how money can be created by (1) a *single* commercial bank which is part of a multibank system and (2) the commercial banking *system* as a whole. Keep in mind that thrift institutions also provide checkable deposits. Therefore, when we say "commercial bank," we also mean "thrift institution." And the more inclusive term "checkable deposits" can be substituted for "demand deposits."

THE BALANCE SHEET OF A COMMERCIAL BANK

An understanding of the basic items on a bank's balance sheet, and of how various transactions change these items, will provide the tools for analyzing the workings of the U.S. monetary system.

A **balance sheet** is a statement of assets and claims on assets which summarizes the fi-

nancial position of a firm—in this case a commercial bank (*or* thrift)—at a specific point in time. Every balance sheet must balance, because every known *asset*, being something of economic value, will be claimed by someone. Can you think of an asset—something of monetary value—which no one claims? A balance sheet balances when the value of assets equals the amount of claims against those assets. The claims shown on a balance sheet are divided into two groups: the claims of the owners of the firm against the firm's assets, called *net worth*, and the claims of nonowners, called *liabilities*. Thus, a balance sheet balances because

Assets = liabilities + net worth

A balance-sheet approach to our study of the money-creating ability of commercial banks is valuable in two respects:

1. A bank's balance sheet provides a convenient point of reference from which we can introduce new terms and concepts in an orderly way.
2. The use of balance sheets allows us to quantify certain concepts and relationships which are difficult to comprehend if discussed in words alone.

PROLOGUE: THE GOLDSMITHS

Let's now see how a *fractional reserve system of banking* operates. The characteristics and working of such a system can be better understood by first considering a bit of economic history.

When early traders began to use gold in making transactions, they soon realized that it was both unsafe and inconvenient for consumers and merchants to carry gold and have it weighed and assessed for purity every time a transaction was negotiated. It therefore became commonplace by the sixteenth century to deposit one's gold with goldsmiths whose vaults or strongrooms could be used for a fee. Upon receiving a gold deposit, a goldsmith issued a receipt to the depositor. Soon goods were traded for the goldsmiths' receipts, and the receipts became the first kind of paper money.

At this point the goldsmiths—embryonic bankers—used a 100 percent reserve system; their circulating paper money receipts were fully backed by gold, which was "in reserve" in their vaults. But because of the public's acceptance of the goldsmiths' receipts as paper money, the goldsmiths became aware that the gold they stored was rarely redeemed. In fact, they found themselves in charge of enterprises where the amount of gold deposited with them in any week or month was likely to exceed the amount withdrawn.

Then some adroit goldsmith hit on the idea that paper money could be issued *in excess of* the amount of gold held. Goldsmiths would put these additional "receipts" redeemable in gold—their paper money—into circulation by making interest-earning loans to merchants, producers, and consumers. Borrowers were willing to accept loans in the form of gold receipts because the receipts were accepted as a medium of exchange.

This was the beginning of the **fractional reserve system** of banking, in which only a fraction of the money supply is backed by currency (here, gold) held in reserve in bank vaults. If, for example, our ingenious goldsmith made loans equal to the amount of gold stored, then the total value of paper money in circulation would be twice the value of the gold. Gold reserves would be 50 percent of outstanding paper money.

Fractional reserve banking—the system in the United States and most other countries today—has two significant characteristics:

1. *Money creation and reserves*   Banks in such a system can *create money*. When a goldsmith made loans by giving borrowers paper money not fully backed by gold reserves, money was being created. The quantity of such money the goldsmith could create would depend on the amount of reserves deemed prudent to keep on hand. The smaller the amount of reserves thought necessary, the larger the amount of paper money the goldsmith could create. Although gold is no longer used to "back" the U.S. money supply, bank lending (money creation) today is constrained by the amount of currency reserves banks feel obligated, or are required by law, to keep.
2. *Bank panics and regulation*   Banks which operate on the basis of fractional reserves are vulnerable to bank "panics" or "runs." A goldsmith who issued paper money equal to twice the value of gold reserves could not convert all that paper money into gold in the event all holders of that paper money appeared simultaneously demanding gold. In fact, many European and U.S. banks were once ruined by this unfortunate circumstance. However, a bank panic is highly unlikely *if* the banker's reserve and lending policies are prudent. Indeed, a basic reason why banking systems are highly regulated industries is to prevent bank runs. This is also the reason why the United States has in place a system of deposit insurance.

A SINGLE COMMERCIAL BANK

We need to explore how money can be created by a single bank which is part of a multibank banking system. Here are some questions we will consider: What items make up a commercial bank's balance sheet? How does a single commercial bank create money? If it can create money, can it destroy money too? What factors govern how a bank creates money?

Formation of a Commercial Bank

To answer these questions we must understand what is on a commercial bank's balance sheet and how certain transactions affect it. Let's begin with the organization of a local commercial bank.

Transaction 1: Creating a Bank

Suppose farsighted citizens of the metropolis of Wahoo, Nebraska (yes, there is such a place), decide their town needs a new commercial bank to provide banking services for that growing community. Once these enterprising individuals secure a state or national charter for their bank, they turn to the task of selling, say, $250,000 worth of capital stock (equity shares) to buyers, both in and out of the community. These financing efforts meet with success and the Bank of Wahoo now exists—at least on paper. How does the Wahoo bank's balance statement appear at its birth?

The new owners of the bank have sold $250,000 worth of shares of stock in the bank—some to themselves, some to other people. As a result, the bank now has $250,000 in cash on hand and $250,000 worth of capital stock outstanding. The cash is an asset to the bank. Cash held by a bank is sometimes called **vault cash** or *till money*. The outstanding shares of stock constitute an equal amount of claims which the owners have against the bank's assets. The shares of stock are the net worth of the bank. The bank's balance sheet reads:

CREATING A BANK

BALANCE SHEET 1: WAHOO BANK

Assets		Liabilities and net worth	
Cash	$250,000	Capital stock	$250,000

Each item listed in a balance sheet such as this is called an *account*.

Transaction 2: Acquiring Property and Equipment

The board of directors must now get the newborn bank off the drawing board and make it a reality. First, property and equipment must be acquired. Suppose the directors, confident of the suc-

cess of their venture, purchase a building for $220,000 and buy $20,000 worth of office equipment. This simple transaction changes the composition of the bank's assets. The bank now has $240,000 less in cash and $240,000 of new property assets. Using blue to denote those accounts affected by each transaction, we find that the bank's balance sheet at the end of transaction 2 appears as follows:

ACQUIRING PROPERTY AND EQUIPMENT

BALANCE SHEET 2: WAHOO BANK

Assets		Liabilities and net worth	
Cash	$ 10,000	Capital stock	$250,000
Property	240,000		

Note that the balance sheet still balances, as it must.

Transaction 3: Accepting Deposits

Commercial banks have two basic functions: to accept deposits of money and to make loans. Now that the bank is operating, suppose that the citizens and businesses of Wahoo decide to deposit $100,000 in the Wahoo bank. What happens to the bank's balance sheet?

The bank receives cash, which we know is an asset to the bank. Suppose this money is placed in the bank as demand deposits (checking accounts), rather than time deposits or savings accounts. These newly created demand deposits constitute claims which depositors have against the assets of the Wahoo bank. Thus, the depositing of money in the bank creates a new liability account—demand deposits. The bank's balance sheet now looks like this:

ACCEPTING DEPOSITS

BALANCE SHEET 3: WAHOO BANK

Assets		Liabilities and net worth	
Cash	$110,000	Demand deposits	$100,000
Property	240,000	Capital stock	250,000

There has been no change in the economy's total supply of money, but a change has occurred in the composition of the money supply as a result of transaction 3. Bank money, or demand deposits, has *increased* by $100,000, and currency held by the public has *decreased* by $100,000. Currency held by a bank, you will recall, is *not* part of the economy's money supply.

It is apparent that a withdrawal of cash will reduce the bank's demand-deposit liabilities and its holdings of cash by the amount of the withdrawal. This, too, changes the composition, but not the total supply, of money in the economy.

Transaction 4: Depositing Reserves in a Federal Reserve Bank
All commercial banks and thrift institutions which provide checkable deposits must keep a *legal reserve* or **required reserves**. These required reserves are *an amount of funds equal to a specified percentage of the bank's own deposit liabilities. A member bank must keep these reserves on deposit with the Federal Reserve Bank in its district or as vault cash.* To simplify, we suppose the Bank of Wahoo keeps its required reserves *entirely* as deposits in the Federal Reserve Bank of its district. But remember that vault cash is counted as reserves and real-world banks keep a significant portion of their reserves in their vaults.

The "specified percentage" of its deposit liabilities which the commercial bank must keep as reserves is known as the **reserve ratio**—the ratio of the required reserves the commercial bank must keep to the bank's own outstanding deposit liabilities:

$$\text{Reserve ratio} = \frac{\text{commercial bank's required reserves}}{\text{commercial bank's demand-deposit liabilities}}$$

If the reserve ratio were $\frac{1}{10}$, or 10 percent, the Wahoo bank, having accepted $100,000 in deposits from the public, would have to keep $10,000 as reserves. If the ratio were $\frac{1}{5}$, or 20 percent, $20,000 of reserves would be required. If $\frac{1}{2}$, or 50 percent, $50,000 would be required.

The Fed has the authority to establish and vary the reserve ratio within limits legislated by Congress. The limits now prevailing are shown in Table 14-1. A 3 percent reserve is required on the first $49.3 million of checkable deposits held by an institution. A 10 percent reserve is required on an institution's checkable deposits over $49.3 million, although the Fed can vary this between 8 and 14 percent. Currently, no reserves are required against noncheckable nonpersonal (business) savings and time deposits; up to 9 percent *can* be required. Also, after consultation with appropriate congressional committees, the Fed may impose reserve requirements for 180 days in excess of those specified in Table 14-1.

To simplify our discussion suppose the reserve ratio for commercial banks is $\frac{1}{5}$, or 20 percent, and this requirement applies only to demand deposits.

TABLE 14-1   Reserve requirements (reserve ratios) for banks and thrift institutions

Type of deposit	Current requirement	Statutory limits
Checkable deposits		
$0–49.3 million	3%	3%
Over $49.3 million	10	8–14
Noncheckable nonpersonal savings and time deposits	0	0–9

Source: Federal Reserve. Data are for 1997.

Although it's higher than in reality, 20 percent is convenient for computations. And because we are concerned with checkable (spendable) demand deposits, we ignore reserves on noncheckable savings and time deposits. The main point is that reserve requirements are *fractional*, meaning they are less than 100 percent. This point is vital in our analysis of the lending ability of the banking system.

The Wahoo bank will just be meeting the required 20 percent ratio between its reserves in the Federal Reserve Bank and its own deposit liabilities by depositing $20,000 in the Federal Reserve Bank. We will use "reserves" to mean the funds commercial banks deposit in the Federal Reserve Banks, thereby distinguishing them from the public's *deposits* in commercial banks.

But suppose the Wahoo bank anticipates that its holdings of the public's demand deposits will grow in the future. Thus, instead of sending just the minimum amount, $20,000, it sends an extra $90,000, for a total of $110,000. In so doing, the bank will avoid the inconvenience of sending additional reserves to the Federal Reserve Bank each time its own demand-deposit liabilities increase. And, as you will see, it is on the basis of extra reserves that banks can lend and thereby earn interest income.

Actually, the bank would not deposit *all* its cash in the Federal Reserve Bank. However, because (1) banks as a rule hold vault cash only in the amount of $1\frac{1}{2}$ or 2 percent of their total assets, and (2) vault cash can be counted as reserves, we can assume all the bank's cash is deposited in the Federal Reserve Bank and therefore constitutes the commercial bank's total reserves. Then we do not need to bother adding two assets—"cash" and "deposits in the Federal Reserve Bank"—to determine "reserves."

After Wahoo bank deposits $110,000 of reserves at the Fed, its balance sheet becomes:

DEPOSITING RESERVES AT THE FED
BALANCE SHEET 4: WAHOO BANK

Assets		Liabilities and net worth	
Cash	$ 0	Demand	
Reserves	110,000	deposits	$100,000
Property	240,000	Capital stock	250,000

There are three things you should understand about this latest transaction.

1. Excess Reserves Some terminology: The amount by which the bank's **actual reserves** exceed its *required reserves* is the bank's **excess reserves:**

$$\frac{\text{Actual}}{\text{reserves}} - \frac{\text{required}}{\text{reserves}} = \frac{\text{excess}}{\text{reserves}}$$

In this case,

Actual reserves	$110,000
Required reserves	−20,000
Excess reserves	$90,000

The only reliable way of computing excess reserves is to multiply the bank's demand-deposit liabilities by the reserve ratio to obtain required reserves ($100,000 × 20 percent = $20,000) and then to subtract required reserves from the actual reserves listed on the asset side of the bank's balance sheet.

To make sure you understand this, you should compute the bank's excess reserves from balance sheet 4, assuming that the reserve ratio is (1) 10 percent, (2) $33\frac{1}{3}$ percent, and (3) 50 percent.

We will soon demonstrate that the ability of a commercial bank to make loans depends on the existence of excess reserves. So understanding this concept is crucial in seeing how the banking system creates money.

2. Control What is the rationale underlying the requirement that member banks deposit reserves in the Federal Reserve Bank of their district? You might think the basic purpose of reserves is to enhance the liquidity of a bank and protect commercial bank depositors from losses. Reserves would constitute a ready source of funds from which commercial banks can meet large and unexpected cash withdrawals by depositors.

But this reasoning breaks down under scrutiny. Although historically reserves were seen as a source of liquidity and therefore as protection for depositors, a bank's required reserves are not great enough to meet sudden, massive cash withdrawals. If the banker's nightmare should materialize—everyone with demand deposits appearing at once to demand these deposits in cash—the legal reserves held as vault cash or at the Federal Reserve Bank would be insufficient. The banker simply could not meet this "bank panic." Because reserves are fractional, demand deposits may be 10 to 20 times greater than a bank's required reserves.

Commercial bank deposits must be protected by other means. Periodic bank examinations are one way of promoting prudent commercial banking practices. And banking laws restrict banks as to the kinds of assets they may acquire; for example, banks are generally prohibited from buying common stocks. Furthermore, insurance funds administered by the Federal Deposit Insurance Corporation (FDIC) exist to insure individual deposits in banks and thrifts up to $100,000.

If it is not the purpose of reserves to provide for commercial bank liquidity, then what is their function? *Control* is the basic answer. Required reserves help the Fed influence the lending ability of commercial banks. Chapter 15 will examine how the Fed can take certain actions which either increase or decrease commercial bank reserves and affect the ability of banks to grant credit. The objective is to prevent banks from *over*extending or *under*extending bank credit. To the degree that these policies are successful in influencing the volume of commercial bank credit, the Fed can help the economy avoid business fluctuations. Another function of reserves is to facilitate the collection or "clearing" of checks. **(Key Question 2)**

3. Asset and Liability Transaction 4 brings up another accounting matter. Specifically, the reserves created in transaction 4 are an asset to the depositing commercial bank because they are a claim this bank has against the assets of another institution. But reserves are a liability to the Federal Reserve Bank because they are a claim against it. To the Wahoo bank the reserves are an asset; they are a claim this bank has against assets of another institution—the Federal Reserve Bank. To the Federal Reserve Bank these reserves are a liability, a claim which another institution—the Bank of Wahoo—has against it. The demand deposit you get by depositing money in a commercial bank is an asset to you and a liability to the bank. In the same way, *the reserves which a commercial bank establishes by depositing money in a bankers' bank are an asset to that bank and a liability to the Federal Reserve Bank.*

Transaction 5: Clearing a Check Drawn Against the Bank
Assume that Clem Bradshaw, a Wahoo farmer, deposited a substantial portion of the $100,000 in demand deposits which the Wahoo bank received in transaction 3. Suppose now that Clem buys $50,000 of farm machinery from the Ajax Farm Implement Company of Beaver Crossing, Nebraska. Bradshaw pays for this machinery by writing a $50,000 check, against his deposit in the Wahoo bank, to the Ajax company. We need to know (1) how this check is collected or cleared and (2) the effect the collection of the check has on the balance sheets of the banks involved in the transaction.

To learn this, we must consider the Wahoo bank (Bradshaw's bank), the Beaver Crossing bank (the Ajax Company's bank), and the Federal Reserve Bank of Kansas City. For simplicity, we deal only with changes which occur in the specific accounts affected by this transaction. We trace the transaction in three steps, keyed by letters to Figure 14-1.

a. Bradshaw gives his $50,000 check, drawn against the Wahoo bank, to the Ajax company. Ajax deposits the check in its account with the Beaver Crossing bank. The Beaver Crossing bank increases Ajax's demand deposits by $50,000 when the check is deposited. Ajax is now paid in full. Bradshaw is pleased with his new machinery.

b. Now the Beaver Crossing bank has Bradshaw's check. This check is simply a claim against the assets of the Wahoo bank. The Beaver Crossing bank will collect this claim by sending the check (along with checks drawn on other banks) to the Federal Reserve

FIGURE 14-1 The collection of a check through a Federal Reserve Bank The bank against which a check is drawn and cleared (Wahoo bank) loses both reserves and deposits; the bank in which the check is deposited (Beaver Crossing bank) acquires reserves and deposits.

Bank of Kansas City. Here a clerk will *clear*, or collect, the check for the Beaver Crossing bank by *increasing* Beaver's reserve in the Federal Reserve Bank by $50,000 and *decreasing* Wahoo's reserve by a like amount. The check is collected merely by making bookkeeping notations to the effect that Wahoo's claim against the Federal Reserve Bank has been reduced by $50,000 and Beaver's claim increased by $50,000. Note these changes on the balance sheets in Figure 14-1.

c. Finally, the Federal Reserve Bank sends the cleared check back to the Wahoo bank, and for the first time the Wahoo bank discovers that one of its depositors has drawn a check for $50,000 against his demand deposit. Accordingly, the Wahoo bank reduces Bradshaw's demand deposit by $50,000 and notes that the collection of this check has caused a $50,000 decline in its reserves at the Federal Reserve Bank. Observe that the balance statements of all three banks balance. The Wahoo bank has reduced both its assets and liabilities by $50,000. The Beaver Crossing bank has $50,000 more in reserves and in demand deposits. Ownership of reserves at the Federal Reserve Bank has changed—Wahoo owning $50,000 less, Beaver owning $50,000 more—but total reserves stay the same.

Whenever a check is drawn against one bank and deposited in another bank, collection of that check will reduce both reserves and demand deposits of the bank on which the check is drawn. Conversely, if a bank receives a check drawn on another bank, the bank receiving the check will, in the process of collecting it, have its reserves and deposits *increased* by the amount of the check. In our example, the Wahoo bank loses $50,000 in both reserves and deposits to the Beaver Crossing bank. But there is no loss of reserves or deposits for the banking system as a whole. What one bank loses, another bank gains.

If we bring all the other assets and liabilities back into the picture, the Wahoo bank's balance sheet looks like this at the end of transaction 5:

CLEARING A CHECK			
BALANCE SHEET 5: WAHOO BANK			
Assets		Liabilities and net worth	
Reserves	$ 60,000	Demand deposits	$ 50,000
Property	240,000	Capital stock	250,000

You should verify that with a 20 percent reserve requirement, the bank's *excess* reserves now stand at $50,000.

Transaction 5 is reversible. If a check drawn against another bank is deposited in the Wahoo bank, the Wahoo bank will receive both reserves and deposits equal to the amount of the check when it is collected.

QUICK REVIEW 14-1

■ When a bank accepts deposits of cash, the composition of the money supply is changed but the total supply of money is not directly altered.

■ Commercial banks and thrifts are required to keep required reserves, equal to a specified percentage of their own deposit liabilities, as cash or on deposit with the Federal Reserve Bank of their district.

■ The amount by which a bank's actual reserves exceed its required reserves is called excess reserves.

■ A bank which has a check drawn and collected against it will lose to the recipient bank both reserves and deposits equal to the value of the check.

Money-Creating Transactions of a Commercial Bank

The next three transactions are crucial because they explain (1) how a commercial bank can literally create money by making loans, (2) how money is destroyed when loans are repaid, and (3) how banks create money by purchasing government bonds from the public.

Transaction 6: Granting a Loan In addition to accepting deposits, commercial banks grant loans to borrowers. What effect does lending by a commercial bank have on its balance sheet?

Suppose Grisley Meat Packing Company of Wahoo decides it is time to expand its facilities. Suppose, too, the company needs exactly $50,000— which just happens to be equal to the Wahoo bank's excess reserves—to finance this project.

Grisley goes to the Wahoo bank and requests a loan for this amount. The Wahoo bank knows the Grisley company's fine reputation and financial soundness and is convinced of its ability to repay the loan. So the loan is granted. In return, the president of Grisley hands a promissory note—a fancy IOU—to the Wahoo bank. Grisley wants the convenience and safety of paying its obligations by checks. So, instead of receiving a bushelbasket full of currency from the bank, Grisley gets a $50,000 increase in its demand-deposit account in the Wahoo bank.

The Wahoo bank has acquired an interest-earning asset (the promissory note which it files under "Loans") and has created demand deposits (a liability) to "pay" for this asset. Grisley has swapped an IOU for the right to draw an additional $50,000 worth of checks against its demand deposit in the Wahoo bank. Both parties are pleased.

At the moment the loan is completed, the Wahoo bank's position is shown by balance sheet 6a:

WHEN A LOAN IS NEGOTIATED

BALANCE SHEET 6a: WAHOO BANK

Assets		Liabilities and net worth	
Reserves	$ 60,000	Demand	
Loans	50,000	deposits	$100,000
Property	240,000	Capital stock	250,000

All this looks simple enough. But a close examination of the Wahoo bank's balance statement will reveal a startling fact: *When a bank makes loans, it creates money.* The president of Grisley went to the bank with something which is *not* money—her IOU—and walked out with something that *is* money—a demand deposit.

Contrast transaction 6a with transaction 3, in which demand deposits were created but only by currency going out of circulation. There was a change in the *composition* of the money supply in that situation but no change in the total *supply* of money. But when banks lend, they create demand deposits which *are* money. By extending credit the Wahoo bank has "monetized" an IOU. Grisley and the Wahoo bank have created and then swapped claims. The claim created by Grisley and given to the bank is not money; an individual's IOU is not acceptable as a medium of exchange. But the claim created by the bank and given to Grisley is money; checks drawn against a demand deposit are acceptable as a medium of exchange.

The bulk of the money we use in our economy is created through the extension of credit by commercial banks. This checking account money may be thought of as "debts" of commercial banks and thrift institutions. Checks are bank "debts" in the sense that they are claims which banks and thrifts promise to pay "on demand."

But there are forces limiting the ability of a commercial bank to create demand deposits ("bank money") by lending. The Wahoo bank can expect the newly created demand deposit of $50,000 to be a very active account. Grisley would not borrow $50,000 at, say, 7, 10, or 12 percent interest for the sheer joy of knowing funds were available if needed.

Assume that Grisley awards a $50,000 building contract to the Quickbuck Construction Company of Omaha. Quickbuck, true to its name, completes the expansion job and is paid with a check for $50,000 drawn by Grisley against its demand deposit in the Wahoo bank. Quickbuck, with headquarters in Omaha, does *not* deposit this check in the Wahoo bank but instead deposits it in the Fourth National Bank of Omaha. Fourth National now has a $50,000 claim against the Wahoo bank. This check is collected in the manner described in transaction 5. As a result, the Wahoo bank *loses* both reserves and deposits equal to the amount of the check; Fourth National *acquires* $50,000 of reserves and deposits.

In summary, assuming a check is drawn by the borrower for the entire amount of the loan ($50,000) and given to a firm which deposits it in some other bank, the Wahoo bank's balance sheet will read as follows *after the check has been cleared against it:*

AFTER A CHECK IS DRAWN ON THE LOAN

BALANCE SHEET 6b: WAHOO BANK

Assets		Liabilities and net worth	
Reserves	$ 10,000	Demand	
Loans	50,000	deposits	$ 50,000
Property	240,000	Capital stock	250,000

After the check has been collected, the Wahoo bank just meets the required reserve ratio of 20 percent (= $10,000 ÷ $50,000). The bank has *no excess reserves.* This poses a question: Could the Wahoo bank have lent more than $50,000—an amount greater than its excess reserves—and still have met the 20 percent reserve requirement if a check for the full amount of the loan were cleared against it? The answer is "no"; the bank is "fully loaned up."

Here is why: Suppose the Wahoo bank had loaned $55,000 to the Grisley company. Collection of the check against the Wahoo bank would have lowered its reserves to $5,000 (= $60,000 − $55,000), and deposits would once again stand at $50,000 (= $105,000 − $55,000). The ratio of actual reserves to deposits would then be $5,000/$50,000, or only 10 percent. The Wahoo bank could thus *not* have lent $55,000.

By experimenting with other amounts over $50,000, you will find that the maximum amount the Wahoo bank could lend at the outset of transaction 6 is $50,000. This amount is identical with the amount of excess reserves the bank had available when the loan was negotiated. *A single commercial bank in a multibank banking system can lend only an amount equal to its initial preloan excess reserves.* When it lends, the lending bank faces the likelihood that checks for the entire amount of the loan will be drawn and cleared against it. A lending bank can expect to lose to other banks reserves equal to the amount it lends.[1]

Transaction 7: Repaying a Loan

If commercial banks create demand deposits—money—when they make loans, is money destroyed when loans are repaid? Yes. We see this by noting what happens when Grisley repays the $50,000 it borrowed.

To simplify, we (1) suppose the loan is repaid not in installments but in one lump sum 2 years after it is made and (2) ignore interest charges on the loan. Grisley simply writes a check for $50,000 against its demand deposit, which we assume was $50,000 before the Grisley loan was negotiated. As a result, the Wahoo bank's demand-deposit liabilities decline by $50,000; Grisley has given up $50,000 worth of its claim against the bank's assets. In turn, the bank will surrender Grisley's IOU, which it has been holding these many months. The bank and the company have reswapped claims. But the claim given up by Grisley is money; the claim it is repurchasing—its IOU—is not. The supply of money has therefore been reduced by $50,000; that amount of demand deposits has been destroyed, unaccompanied by an increase in the money supply elsewhere in the economy.

The Grisley company's IOU has been "demonetized," as shown in balance sheet 7. The Wahoo bank's demand deposits and loans have each returned to zero. The decline in demand deposits lowers the bank's required reserves to zero and gives it new excess reserves (= its reserves of $10,000); this provides the basis for new loans to be made. **(Key Questions 4 and 8)**

REPAYING A LOAN

BALANCE SHEET 7: WAHOO BANK

Assets		Liabilities and net worth	
Reserves	$ 10,000	Demand	
Loans	0	deposits	$ 0
Property	240,000	Capital stock	250,000

In the unlikely event Grisley repays the loan with cash, the money supply will still decline by $50,000. In this case, Grisley would repurchase its IOU by handing over $50,000 in cash to the bank. Loan balances decline in the asset column by $50,000 and cash increases by $50,000. Remember, we exclude currency held by banks from the money supply because to include such cash would be double counting; it is apparent that this constitutes a $50,000 reduction in the supply of money.

Transaction 8: Buying Government Securities

When a commercial bank buys government bonds from the public, the effect is substantially the same as lending. New money is created.

Assume that the Wahoo bank's balance sheet initially stands as it did at the end of transaction 5. Now suppose that, instead of making a $50,000 loan, the bank buys $50,000 of government securities from a securities dealer. The bank receives the interest-bearing bonds, which appear on its balance statement as the asset "Securities," and gives the dealer an increase in its demand-deposit account. The Wahoo bank's balance sheet appears as follows:

BUYING GOVERNMENT SECURITIES

BALANCE SHEET 8: WAHOO BANK

Assets		Liabilities and net worth	
Reserves	$ 60,000	Demand	
Securities	50,000	deposits	$100,000
Property	240,000	Capital stock	250,000

Demand deposits, that is, the supply of money, have been increased by $50,000, as in transaction 6. *Bond purchases from the public by commercial banks increase the supply of money in the same way as does lending to the public.* The bank accepts government bonds (which are not money) and gives the securities dealer an increase in its demand deposits (which are money).

---

[1]Qualification: If some of the checks written on a loan are redeposited in the lending bank by their recipients, then that bank will be able to lend an amount somewhat greater than its initial excess reserves.

Of course, when the securities dealer draws and clears a check for $50,000 against the Wahoo bank, the bank loses both reserves and deposits in that amount and then just meets the legal reserve requirement. Its balance sheet now reads precisely as in 6b except that "Securities" is substituted for "Loans" on the asset side.

Finally, the selling of government bonds to the public by a commercial bank—like the repayment of a loan—reduces the supply of money. The securities buyer pays by check, and both "Securities" and "Demand deposits" (the latter being money) decline by the amount of the sale.

Profits, Liquidity, and the Federal Funds Market

The asset items on a commercial bank's balance sheet reflect the banker's pursuit of two conflicting goals:

1. *Profit*   One goal is profit. Commercial banks, like any other business, seek profits, which is why the bank makes loans and buys securities—the two major earning assets of commercial banks.

2. *Liquidity*   The other goal is safety. For a bank, safety lies in liquidity, specifically such liquid assets as cash and excess reserves. A bank must be on guard for depositors' wanting to transform their demand deposits into cash. Similarly, it must guard against more checks clearing against it than are cleared in its favor, causing a net outflow of reserves. Bankers thus seek a balance between prudence and profit. The compromise is between assets that earn high returns and highly liquid assets.

An interesting way banks can partly reconcile the goals of profit and liquidity is to lend temporary excess reserves held at the Federal Reserve Banks to other commercial banks. Normal day-to-day flows of funds to banks rarely leave all banks with their exact levels of legally required reserves. Also, funds held at the Federal Reserve Banks are highly liquid, but they do not draw interest. Banks therefore lend these excess reserves to other banks on an overnight basis as a way to earn additional interest without sacrificing long-term liquidity. Banks which borrow in this *Federal funds market*—the market for immediately available reserve balances at the Federal Reserve—do so because they are temporarily short of required reserves. The interest rate paid on these overnight loans is called the **Federal funds rate.**

In Figure 14-1, we would show an overnight loan of reserves from the Beaver Crossing bank to the

Wahoo bank as a decrease in reserves at the Beaver Crossing bank and an increase in reserves at the Wahoo bank. Ownership of reserves at the Federal Reserve Bank of Kansas City would change, but total reserves would not be affected. Exercise: Determine what other changes would be required on the Wahoo and Beaver Crossing bank balance sheets as a result of the overnight loan.

QUICK REVIEW 14-2

■ Banks create money when they make loans; money vanishes when bank loans are repaid.

■ New money is created when banks buy government bonds from the public; money disappears when banks sell government bonds to the public.

■ Banks balance profitability and safety in determining their mix of earning assets and highly liquid assets.

■ Banks borrow and lend temporary excess reserves on an overnight basis in the Federal funds market; the interest rate on these loans is the Federal funds rate.

THE BANKING SYSTEM: MULTIPLE-DEPOSIT EXPANSION

Thus far we have seen that a single bank in a banking system can lend one dollar for each dollar of its excess reserves. The situation is different for all commercial banks as a group. We will find that *the commercial banking system can lend, that is, can create money, by a multiple of its excess reserves. This multiple lending is accomplished even though each bank in the system can only lend "dollar for dollar" with its excess reserves.*

Our immediate task is to uncover how these seemingly paradoxical results come about. To do this, we must keep our analysis uncluttered. Therefore, we will rely on three simplifying assumptions:

1. The reserve ratio for all commercial banks is 20 percent.

2. Initially all banks are exactly meeting this 20 percent reserve requirement. No excess reserves exist; all banks are "loaned up" (or "loaned out").

3. If any bank can increase its loans as a result of acquiring excess reserves, an amount equal to these excess reserves will be loaned to one borrower, who will write a check for the entire amount of the loan and give it to someone else, who will deposit the check in another bank. This third assumption means the worst thing possible happens

to every lending bank—a check for the entire amount of the loan is drawn and cleared against it in favor of another bank.

The Banking System's Lending Potential

Suppose a junkyard owner finds a $100 bill while dismantling a car which has been on the lot for years. He deposits the $100 in bank A, which adds the $100 to its reserves. We will record only *changes* in the balance sheets of the various commercial banks. The deposit changes bank A's balance sheet as shown by entries (a_1):

MULTIPLE-DEPOSIT EXPANSION PROCESS

BALANCE SHEET: COMMERCIAL BANK A

Assets		Liabilities and net worth	
Reserves	$+100 ($a_1$)	Demand deposits	$+100 ($a_1$)
	− 80 (a_3)		+ 80 (a_2)
Loans	+ 80 (a_2)		− 80 (a_3)

Recall from transaction 3 that this $100 deposit of currency does *not* alter the money supply. While $100 of demand-deposit money comes into being, it is offset by the $100 of currency no longer in the hands of the public (the junkyard owner). What *has* happened is that bank A has acquired *excess reserves* of $80. Of the newly acquired $100 in reserves, 20 percent, or $20, must be earmarked for the required reserves on the new $100 deposit and the remaining $80 is excess reserves. Remembering that a single commercial bank can lend only an amount equal to its excess reserves, we conclude that bank A can lend a maximum of $80. When a loan for this amount is made, bank A's loans increase by $80 and the borrower gets an $80 demand deposit. We add these figures—entries (a_2)—to bank A's balance sheet.

But now we use our third assumption: The borrower draws a check for $80—the entire amount of the loan—and gives it to someone who deposits it in another bank, bank B. As we saw in transaction 6, bank A *loses* both reserves and deposits equal to the amount of the loan, as indicated in entries (a_3). The net result of these transactions is that bank A's reserves now stand at +$20 (= $100 − $80), loans at +$80, and demand deposits at +$100 (= $100 + $80 − $80). When the dust has settled, bank A is just meeting the 20 percent reserve ratio.

Recalling transaction 5, we know that bank B *acquires* both the reserves and the deposits that bank A has lost. Bank B's balance sheet is changed as in entries (b_1):

MULTIPLE-DEPOSIT EXPANSION PROCESS

BALANCE SHEET: COMMERCIAL BANK B

Assets		Liabilities and net worth	
Reserves	$+80 ($b_1$)	Demand deposits	$+80 ($b_1$)
	−64 (b_3)		+64 (b_2)
Loans	+64 (b_2)		−64 (b_3)

When the borrower's check is drawn and cleared, bank A *loses* $80 in reserves and deposits and bank B *gains* $80 in reserves and deposits. But 20 percent, or $16, of bank B's new reserves must be kept as required reserves against the new $80 in demand deposits. This means that bank B has $64 (= $80 − $16) in excess reserves. It can therefore lend $64 [entries ($b_2$)]. When the new borrower draws a check for the entire amount and deposits it in bank C, the reserves and deposits of bank B both fall by the $64 [entries ($b_3$)]. As a result of these transactions, bank B's reserves now stand at +$16 (= $80 − $64), loans at +$64, and demand deposits at +$80 (= $80 + $64 − $64). After all this, bank B is just meeting the 20 percent reserve requirement.

We are off and running again. Bank C acquires the $64 in reserves and deposits lost by bank B. Its balance sheet changes as in entries (c_1):

MULTIPLE-DEPOSIT EXPANSION PROCESS

BALANCE SHEET: COMMERCIAL BANK C

Assets		Liabilities and net worth	
Reserves	$+64.00 ($c_1$)	Demand deposits	$+64.00 ($c_1$)
	−51.20 (c_3)		+51.20 (c_2)
Loans	+51.20 (c_2)		−51.20 (c_3)

Exactly 20 percent, or $12.80, of these new reserves will be required reserves, the remaining $51.20 being excess reserves. Hence, bank C can safely lend a maximum of $51.20. Suppose it does [entries (c_2)]. And suppose the borrower draws a check for the entire amount and gives it to someone who deposits it in another bank [entries (c_3)].

Bank D—the bank receiving the $51.20 in reserves and deposits—now notes these changes on its balance sheet [entries (d_1)]:

MULTIPLE-DEPOSIT EXPANSION PROCESS

BALANCE SHEET: COMMERCIAL BANK D

Assets		Liabilities and net worth	
Reserves	$+51.20 (d_1)	Demand	
	−40.96 (d_3)	deposits	$+51.20 (d_1)
Loans	+40.96 (d_2)		+40.96 (d_2)
			−40.96 (d_3)

It can now lend $40.96 [entries (d_2)]. The newest borrower draws a check for the full amount and deposits it in still another bank [entries (d_3)].

Now, if we wanted to be particularly obnoxious, we could go ahead with this procedure by bringing banks E, F, G, H, . . . , N into the picture. But, we suggest you work through the computations for banks E, F, and G to be sure you understand the procedure.

The entire analysis is summarized in Table 14-2. Data for banks E through N are supplied so that you may check your computations. Our conclusion is star-

tling: On the basis of only $80 in excess reserves (acquired by the banking system when someone deposited $100 of currency in bank A), the *entire commercial banking system* is able to lend $400, the sum of the amounts in column 4. The banking system can lend excess reserves by a multiple of 5 when the reserve ratio is 20 percent. Yet each single bank in the banking system is lending only an amount equal to its own excess reserves. How do we explain this? Why can the *banking system* lend by a multiple of its excess reserves, when *each individual bank* can only lend "dollar for dollar" with its excess reserves?

The answer is that *reserves lost by a single bank are not lost to the banking system as a whole*. The reserves lost by bank A are acquired by bank B. Those lost by B are gained by C. C loses to D, D to E, E to F, and so forth. Although reserves can be, and are, lost by *individual* banks in the banking system, there is no loss of reserves for the banking *system* as a whole.

An individual bank can safely lend only an amount equal to its excess reserves, but the commercial banking system can lend by a multiple of its excess reserves. This contrast, incidentally, is an illustration of why it is imperative that we keep the fallacy of composition (Chapter 1) firmly in mind. Commercial

TABLE 14-2   **Expansion of the money supply by the commercial banking system**

Bank	(1) Acquired reserves and deposits	(2) Required reserves (reserve ratio = .2)	(3) Excess reserves, (1) − (2)	(4) Amount bank can lend; new money created = (3)
Bank A	$100.00 (a_1)	$20.00	**$80.00**	$ 80.00 (a_2)
Bank B	80.00 (a_3, b_1)	16.00	64.00	64.00 (b_2)
Bank C	64.00 (b_3, c_1)	12.80	51.20	51.20 (c_2)
Bank D	51.20 (c_3, d_1)	10.24	40.96	40.96 (d_2)
Bank E	40.96	8.19	32.77	32.77
Bank F	32.77	6.55	26.22	26.22
Bank G	26.22	5.24	20.98	20.98
Bank H	20.98	4.20	16.78	16.78
Bank I	16.78	3.36	13.42	13.42
Bank J	13.42	2.68	10.74	10.74
Bank K	10.74	2.15	8.59	8.59
Bank L	8.59	1.72	6.87	6.87
Bank M	6.87	1.37	5.50	5.50
Bank N	5.50	1.10	4.40	4.40
Other banks	21.97	4.40	17.57	17.57
Total amount of money created (sum of the amounts in column 4)				**$400.00**

banks *as a group* can create money by lending in a manner much different from that of the *individual banks* in that group.

The Monetary Multiplier

The banking system magnifies any original excess reserves into a larger amount of newly created demand-deposit money. The *demand-deposit multiplier*, or **monetary multiplier,** is similar in concept to the spending-income multiplier in Chapter 10. That multiplier exists because the expenditures of one household are received as income by another; it magnifies a change in initial spending into a larger change in GDP. The spending-income multiplier is the reciprocal of the MPS (the leakage into saving which occurs at each round of spending).

In contrast, the monetary multiplier exists because the reserves and deposits lost by one bank are received by another bank. It magnifies excess reserves into a larger creation of demand-deposit money. The monetary multiplier m is the reciprocal of the required reserve ratio R (the leakage into required reserves which occurs at each step in the lending process). In short,

$$\text{Monetary multiplier} = \frac{1}{\text{required reserve ratio}}$$

or, using symbols,

$$m = \frac{1}{R}$$

In this formula, m represents the maximum amount of new demand-deposit money which can be created by a *single dollar* of excess reserves, given the value of R. By multiplying the excess reserves E by m, we can find the maximum amount of new demand-deposit money, D, which can be created by the banking system. That is,

$$\begin{array}{c}\text{Maximum} \\ \text{demand-deposit} \\ \text{creation}\end{array} = \begin{array}{c}\text{excess} \\ \text{reserves}\end{array} \times \begin{array}{c}\text{monetary} \\ \text{multiplier}\end{array}$$

or, more simply,

$$D = E \times m$$

In our example in Table 14-2, R is .20 so m is 5 (= 1/.20). Then

$$D = \$400 = \$80 \times 5$$

Higher reserve ratios mean lower monetary multipliers and therefore less creation of new deposit

money via loans; smaller reserve ratios mean higher monetary multipliers and thus more creation of new deposit money via loans. With a high reserve ratio, say, 50 percent, the monetary multiplier would be 2 (= 1/.5), and in our example the banking system could create only \$160 (= \$80 of excess reserves × 2) of new deposit money. With a low reserve ratio, say, 5 percent, the monetary multiplier would be 20 (= 1/.05), and the banking system could create \$1600 (= \$80 of excess reserves × 20) of new deposit money. Again you should note similarities with the spending-income multiplier, in which higher MPSs mean lower multipliers and lower MPSs mean higher multipliers. Also, like the spending-income multiplier, the monetary multiplier works in both directions. *The monetary multiplier applies to money destruction as well as to money creation.*

But keep in mind that, despite the similar rationales underlying the spending-income and monetary multipliers, the former has to do with changes in income and output and the latter with changes in the supply of money.

Figure 14-2 depicts the final outcome of our example of a multiple-deposit expansion of the money supply. The initial deposit of \$100 of currency into

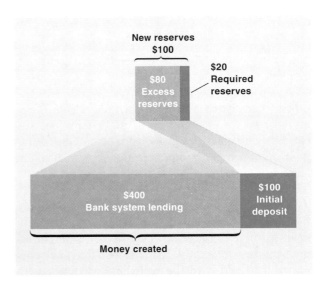

FIGURE 14-2 The outcome of the money expansion process A deposit of \$100 of currency into a checking account creates an initial demand deposit of \$100. If the reserve ratio is 20 percent, only \$20 of reserves is legally required to support the \$100 demand deposit. The \$80 of excess reserves allows the banking system to create \$400 of demand deposits through making loans. The \$100 of reserves supports a total of \$500 of money (\$100 + \$400).

----

the bank (lower right box) creates new reserves of an equal amount (upper box). With a 20 percent reserve ratio, however, only $20 of currency reserves is needed to "back up" this $100 demand deposit. The excess reserves of $80 permit the creation of $400 of new demand deposits via the making of loans, confirming a monetary multiplier of 5. The $100 of new reserves supports a total supply of money of $500, consisting of the $100 initial demand deposit plus $400 of demand deposits created through lending.

You might experiment with the following two brain teasers to test your understanding of multiple credit expansion by the banking system:

1. Rework the analysis in Table 14-2 (at least three or four steps of it) assuming the reserve ratio is 10 percent. What is the maximum amount of money the banking system can create upon acquiring $100 in new reserves and deposits? (The answer is not $800!)

2. Suppose a banking system is "loaned up" and faces a 20 percent reserve ratio. Explain how the banking system might have to *reduce* its outstanding loans by $400 when a $100 cash withdrawal from a demand-deposit account forces one bank to draw down its reserves by $100. **(Key Question 13)**

Some Modifications

There are complications which might modify the preciseness of our analysis.

Other Leakages   Aside from the leakage of required reserves at each step of the lending process, two other leakages of money from commercial banks might dampen the money-creating potential of the banking system:

1. Currency Drains   A borrower might request that part of his or her loan be paid in currency. Or the recipient of a check drawn by a borrower might ask the bank to redeem it partially or wholly in currency rather than add it to the recipient's account. If the person who borrowed the $80 from bank A in our illustration asked for $16 of it in cash and the remaining $64 as a demand deposit, bank B would later receive only $64 in new reserves (of which only $51.20 would be excess) rather than $80 (of which $64 was excess). This decline in excess reserves would reduce the lending potential of the banking system accordingly. In fact, if the first borrower had taken the en-

tire $80 in cash and if this currency remained in circulation, the multiple expansion process would have stopped then and there. But the convenience and safety of demand deposits make this unlikely.

2. Excess Reserves   Our analysis of the commercial banking system's ability to expand the money supply by lending is based on the supposition that commercial banks are willing to meet precisely the legal reserve requirement. To the extent that bankers hold excess reserves, the overall credit expansion potential of the banking system will be reduced. For example, suppose bank A, upon receiving $100 in new cash, decided to add $25, rather than the legal minimum of $20, to its reserves. Then it would lend only $75, rather than $80, and the monetary multiplier would be diminished accordingly.[2] In fact, the amount of excess reserves which banks have held in recent years has been very minimal. The explanation is very simple: Excess reserves earn no interest income for a bank; loans and investments do. Hence, our assumption that a bank will lend an amount equal to its excess reserves is reasonable and generally accurate.

QUICK REVIEW 14-3

■ Whereas a single bank in a multibank system can safely lend (create money) by an amount equal to its excess reserves, the banking system can lend (create money) by a multiple of its excess reserves.

■ The monetary multiplier is the reciprocal of the required reserve ratio; it is the multiple by which the banking system can expand the money supply for each dollar of excess reserves.

■ Currency drains and a desire by banks to hold excess reserves may reduce the size of the monetary multiplier.

Need for Monetary Control

Our illustration of the banking system's ability to create money rests on the assumption that commercial banks are willing to create money by lending and that households and businesses are willing to borrow. In

---

[2]Specifically, in our $m = 1/R$ monetary multiplier, we now add to R, the required reserve ratio, the additional excess reserves which bankers choose to keep. For example, if banks want to hold additional excess reserves equal to 5 percent of any newly acquired demand deposits, then the denominator becomes .25 (equal to the .20 reserve ratio plus the .05 addition to excess reserves). The monetary multiplier is reduced from 5 to 1/.25, or 4.

The Bank Panics of 1930 to 1933

A series of bank panics in the early 1930s resulted in a multiple contraction of the money supply.

In the early months of the Great Depression, before there was deposit insurance, several financially weak banks became insolvent. As word spread that customers of these banks had lost their deposits, a general concern arose that something similar could happen at other banks. Depositors became frightened that their banks did not, in fact, still have all the money they had deposited. And, of course, in a fractional reserve banking system, that is precisely the reality. Acting on their fears, people en masse tried to withdraw currency—that is, "cash out" their accounts—from their banks. They wanted to get their money before it was all gone. This "run on the banks" caused many previously financially sound banks to declare bankruptcy. More than 9000 banks failed within 3 years.

The massive conversion of checkable deposits to currency during 1930 to 1933 reduced the nation's money supply. This might seem strange since a check written for "cash" reduces demand-deposit money and increases currency in the hands of the public by the same amount. So how does the money supply decline? Our discussion of the money-*creation* process provides the answer, but now the story becomes one of money *destruction*.

Suppose that people collectively cash out $10 billion from their checking accounts. As an immediate result, demand-deposit money declines by $10 billion, while currency held by the public increases by $10 billion. But here is the catch: Assuming a reserve ratio of 20 percent, the $10 billion of currency in the banks had been sup-

porting $50 billion of deposit money, the $10 billion of deposits plus $40 billion created through loans. The $10 billion withdrawal of currency forces banks to reduce loans (and thus demand-deposit money) by $40 billion to continue to meet their reserve requirement. In short, a $40 billion destruction of deposit money occurs. This is the scenario which occurred in the early years of the 1930s.

Accompanying this multiple contraction of demand deposits was the banks' "scramble for liquidity" to try to meet further withdrawals of currency. To obtain more currency, they sold many of their holdings of government securities to the public. You know from this chapter that a bank's sale of government securities to the public, like a reduction in loans, reduces the money supply. The public writes checks for the securities, reducing their demand deposits, and the bank uses the currency it obtains to meet the ongoing bank run. In short, the loss of reserves from the banking system, in conjunction with the scramble for security, reduced the amount of demand-deposit money by far more than the increase in currency in the hands of the public. Thus, the money supply collapsed.

In 1933, President Franklin Roosevelt ended the bank panics by declaring a "national bank holiday," which closed all national banks for 1 week and resulted in the federally insured deposit program. Meanwhile, the nation's money supply had plummeted by 25 percent, the largest such drop in U.S. history. This decline in the money supply contributed to the nation's worst and longest depression.

Today, a multiple contraction of the money supply on the 1930–1933 magnitude is unthinkable. FDIC insurance has kept individual bank failures from becoming general panics. Also, while the Fed stood idly by during the bank panics of 1930 to 1933, today it would take immediate and dramatic actions to maintain the banking system's reserves and the nation's money supply. These actions are the subject matter of Chapter 15.

reality the willingness of banks to lend on the basis of excess reserves varies cyclically, and therein lies the rationale for governmental control of the money supply to promote economic stability.

When prosperity reigns, banks will expand credit to the maximum of their ability. Loans are interest-earning assets, and in good economic times there is little fear of borrowers' defaulting. But, as you will find in Chapter 15, the money supply has an effect on aggregate demand. By lending and thereby creating money to the maximum of their ability during prosperity, commercial banks may contribute to excessive aggregate demand and therefore to inflation.

If recession appears on the economic horizon, bankers may hastily withdraw their invitations to borrow, seeking the safety of liquidity (excess reserves) even if it means sacrificing potential interest income. Bankers may fear large-scale withdrawal of deposits by a panicky public and simultaneously doubt the ability of borrowers to repay. It is not too surprising that during some years of the Great Depression of the 1930s, banks had excess reserves but lending was at a low ebb. The point is that during recession banks may decrease the money supply by cutting back on lending. This contraction of the money supply will restrain aggregate demand and intensify the recession. A rapid shrinkage of the money supply did indeed contribute to the Great Depression, as this chapter's Last Word indicates.

We thus conclude that profit-motivated bankers can be expected to vary the money supply in a way that reinforces cyclical fluctuations. For this reason the Federal Reserve System has at its disposal certain monetary tools to alter the money supply in a countercyclical, rather than procyclical, fashion. We turn to an analysis of these tools in Chapter 15.

CHAPTER SUMMARY

1. The operation of a commercial bank can be understood through its balance sheet, where assets equal liabilities plus net worth.

2. Modern banking systems are fractional reserve systems: only a fraction of deposits is backed by currency.

3. Commercial banks must keep required reserves on deposit in a Federal Reserve Bank or as vault cash. These required reserves are equal to a specified percentage of the commercial bank's demand-deposit liabilities. Excess reserves are equal to actual reserves minus required reserves.

4. Banks lose both reserves and demand deposits when checks are drawn against them.

5. Commercial banks create money—create demand deposits, or deposit money—when they make loans. The creation of checkable deposits by bank lending is the most important source of money in our economy. Money is destroyed when bank loans are repaid.

6. The ability of a single commercial bank to create money by lending depends on the size of its *excess* reserves. Generally speaking, a commercial bank can lend only an amount equal to the amount of its excess reserves. Money creation is thus limited because, in all likelihood, checks drawn by borrowers will be deposited in other banks, causing a loss of reserves and deposits to the lending bank equal to the amount it has loaned.

7. Rather than making loans, banks may decide to use excess reserves to buy bonds from the public. In doing so, banks merely credit the demand-deposit accounts of the bond sellers, thus creating demand-deposit money. Money vanishes when banks sell bonds to the public because bond buyers must draw down their demand-deposit balances to pay for the bonds.

8. Banks earn interest by making loans and purchasing bonds; they maintain liquidity by holding cash and excess reserves. Banks having temporary excess reserves often lend them overnight to banks which are short of required reserves. The interest rate paid on loans in this Federal funds market is called the Federal funds rate.

9. The commercial banking system as a whole can lend by a multiple of its excess reserves because the banking *system* cannot lose reserves, although individual banks can lose reserves to other banks in the system.

10. The multiple by which the banking system can lend on the basis of each dollar of excess reserves is the reciprocal of the reserve ratio. This multiple credit expansion process is reversible.

11. The fact that profit-seeking banks would alter the money supply in a procyclical direction underlies the need for the Federal Reserve System to control the money supply.

TERMS AND CONCEPTS

balance sheet	required reserves	actual reserves	Federal funds rate
fractional reserve system	reserve ratio	excess reserves	monetary multiplier
vault cash			

STUDY QUESTIONS

1. Why must a balance sheet always balance? What are the major assets and claims on a commercial bank's balance sheet?

2. KEY QUESTION Why are commercial banks required to have reserves? Explain why reserves are an asset to commercial banks but a liability to the Federal Reserve Banks. What are excess reserves? How do you calculate the amount of excess reserves held by a bank? What is the significance of excess reserves?

3. "Whenever currency is deposited in a commercial bank, cash goes out of circulation and, as a result, the supply of money is reduced." Do you agree? Explain why or why not.

4. KEY QUESTION "When a commercial bank makes loans, it creates money; when loans are repaid, money is destroyed." Explain.

5. Explain why a single commercial bank can safely lend only an amount equal to its excess reserves but the commercial banking system can lend by a multiple of its excess reserves. What is the monetary multiplier, and how does it relate to the reserve ratio?

6. Assume that Jones deposits $500 in currency into her demand-deposit account in First National Bank. A half-hour later Smith obtains a loan for $750 at this bank. By how much and in what direction has the money supply changed? Explain.

7. Suppose the National Bank of Commerce has excess reserves of $8000 and outstanding demand deposits of $150,000. If the reserve ratio is 20 percent, what is the size of the bank's actual reserves?

8. KEY QUESTION Suppose Continental Bank has the following simplified balance sheet and that the reserve ratio is 20 percent:

Assets		(1)	(2)	Liabilities and net worth		(1)	(2)
Reserves	$22,000	__	__	Demand			
Securities	38,000	__	__	deposits	$100,000	__	__
Loans	40,000	__	__				

   a. What is the maximum amount of new loans which this bank can make? Show in column 1 how the bank's balance sheet will appear after the bank has loaned this additional amount.
   b. By how much has the supply of money changed? Explain.

   c. How will the bank's balance sheet appear after checks drawn for the entire amount of the new loans have been cleared against the bank? Show the new balance sheet in column 2.
   d. Answer questions **(a)**, **(b)**, and **(c)** on the assumption that the reserve ratio is 15 percent.

9. Third National Bank has reserves of $20,000 and demand deposits of $100,000. The reserve ratio is 20 percent. Households deposit $5000 in currency into the bank which is added to reserves. How much excess reserves does the bank now have?

10. Suppose again that Third National Bank has reserves of $20,000 and demand deposits of $100,000. The reserve ratio is 20 percent. The bank now sells $5000 in securities to the Federal Reserve Bank in its district, receiving a $5000 increase in reserves in return. How much excess reserves does the bank now have? Why does your answer differ (yes, it does!) from the answer to question 9?

11. Suppose a bank discovers that its reserves will temporarily fall slightly short of those legally required. How might it remedy this situation through the Federal funds market? Now assume the bank finds that its reserves will be substantially and permanently deficient. What remedy is available to this bank? (Hint: Recall your answer to question 4.)

12. Suppose that Bob withdraws $100 of cash from his checking account at Security Bank and uses it to buy a camera from Joe, who deposits the $100 in his checking account in Serenity Bank. Assuming a reserve ratio of 10 percent and no initial excess reserves, determine the extent to which **(a)** Security Bank must reduce its loans and demand deposits because of the cash withdrawal and **(b)** Serenity Bank can safely increase its loans and demand deposits because of the cash deposit. Have the cash withdrawal and deposit changed the money supply?

13. KEY QUESTION Suppose the simplified consolidated balance sheet shown below is for the entire commercial banking system. All figures are in billions. The reserve ratio is 25 percent.

Assets		(1)	Liabilities and net worth		(1)
Reserves	$ 52	__	Demand		
Securities	48	__	deposits	$200	__
Loans	100	__			

a. How much excess reserves does the commercial banking system have? What is the maximum amount the banking system might lend? Show in column 1 how the consolidated balance sheet would look after this amount has been lent. What is the monetary multiplier?

b. Answer the questions in **(a)** assuming the reserve ratio is 20 percent. Explain the resulting difference in the lending ability of the commercial banking system.

14. What are banking "leakages"? How might they affect the money-creating potential of the banking system?

15. Explain why there is a need for the Federal Reserve System to control the money supply.

16. **(Last Word)** Explain how the bank panics of 1930 to 1933 produced a decline in the nation's money supply. Why are such panics highly unlikely today?

17. **WEB-BASED QUESTION**   **How's Your Own Bank Doing?** The FDIC (Federal Deposit Insurance Corporation) http://192.147.69.47/drs/id20/ *Institution Directory (ID)* system provides demographic data and financial profiles for each FDIC-insured institution. The *ID* system can be used to identify and list FDIC-insured institutions and compare individual bank performance and condition ratios with statistics published in the *Quarterly Banking Profile* http://www.fdic.gov/databank/qbp/homepage.html. Look up your own bank's financial statement and see how it has performed over the past year in the following categories: net worth, total assets, total liabilities, short-term liabilities, net income, number of employees, and number of branches. Compare your bank's performance with the banking industry's performance found in the *Quarterly Banking Profile*.

18. **WEB-BASED QUESTION**   Assets and Liabilities of All Commercial Banks in the United States The Federal Reserve http://www.bog.frb.fed.us/releases/h8/about.htm provides an aggregate balance sheet for commercial banks in the United States and for several subgroups of banks: domestically chartered, large domestic, small domestic, and foreign-related. Balance sheet detail is limited mainly to bank loans and investments; estimates of the major deposit and nondeposit liability terms are povided for each bank group. The release is published weekly. Check the current release and look at Loans and leases in bank credit. Rank the following components with regard to size: commercial and industrial, real estate, consumer, security, and other. Over the past 12 months, which has increased by the largest percentage? By absolute amounts? Has the net worth (assets less liabilities) of all commercial banks in the United States increased during the past year?

Monetary Policy

In Chapter 13 you saw that the supply of money and the demand for money determine the economy's equilibrium interest rate. In Chapter 14 you learned that the banking system can create deposit money, thus greatly affecting the supply of money. In this chapter you will see how the Fed can change the supply of money and thus change the equilibrium interest rate. You will also discover the reasons why the Fed might want to do so.

The Fed's variety of techniques for changing the supply of money, and thus interest rates, are reflected in headlines such as "Bank Reserve Requirement Lowered—First Change since 1983," "Fed Aggressively Selling Bonds," and "Fed Increases Discount Rate to 4 Percent." What stories are these and similar headlines telling?

In this chapter, we first discuss the objectives of *monetary policy* and the roles of participating institutions. Next, we look at the combined balance sheet of the Federal Reserve Banks; it is through these central banks that monetary policy is implemented. Third, we analyze in detail the techniques of monetary control, asking what the key instruments of monetary control are and how they work. Fourth, we examine the cause-and-effect chain of monetary policy and evaluate the effectiveness of monetary policy. We end the chapter with a brief recapitulation of mainstream macroeconomic theory and policy.

THE GOAL OF MONETARY POLICY

Recall from Chapter 13 that the Board of Governors of the Federal Reserve System (the "Fed") is responsible for supervising and controlling the operation of the U.S. banking system. (For the names of central banks in various nations, see Global Perspective 15-1.) This Board formulates basic policies which the banking system follows. Because the Board of Governors is a public body, its decisions are made in what it perceives to be the public interest. The 12 Federal Reserve Banks—the U.S. central banks—implement the policy decisions of the Board. As quasipublic banks, the Federal Reserve Banks are not guided by the profit motive but, rather, pursue measures the Board of Governors recommends.

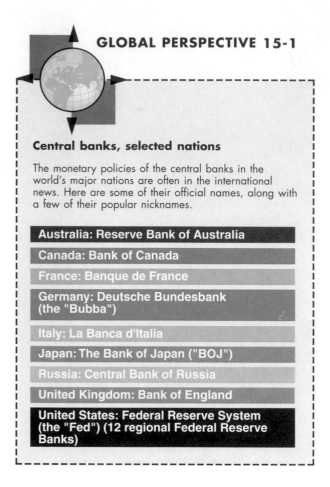

GLOBAL PERSPECTIVE 15-1

Central banks, selected nations

The monetary policies of the central banks in the world's major nations are often in the international news. Here are some of their official names, along with a few of their popular nicknames.

Australia: Reserve Bank of Australia

Canada: Bank of Canada

France: Banque de France

Germany: Deutsche Bundesbank (the "Bubba")

Italy: La Banca d'Italia

Japan: The Bank of Japan ("BOJ")

Russia: Central Bank of Russia

United Kingdom: Bank of England

United States: Federal Reserve System (the "Fed") (12 regional Federal Reserve Banks)

However, to say that the Board follows policies which "promote the public interest" is not enough. We must pinpoint the goal of monetary policy. *The fundamental objective of* **monetary policy** *is to assist the economy in achieving a full-employment, noninflationary level of total output.* Monetary policy consists of altering the economy's money supply to stabilize aggregate output, employment, and the price level. It en-

tails increasing the money supply during a recession to stimulate spending and restricting it during inflation to constrain spending.

The Federal Reserve Board alters the amount of the nation's money supply by manipulating the size of excess reserves held by commercial banks. Excess reserves, you will recall, are critical to the money-creating ability of the banking system. Once you see how the Federal Reserve controls excess reserves and the money supply, we will explain how changes in the stock of money affect interest rates, aggregate demand, and the economy.

CONSOLIDATED BALANCE SHEET OF THE FEDERAL RESERVE BANKS

Because U.S. monetary policy is implemented by the Federal Reserve Banks, we need to consider the balance sheet of these banks. Some of the Fed's assets and liabilities differ from those found on the balance sheet of a commercial bank. Table 15-1 is a simplified consolidated balance sheet showing the pertinent assets and liabilities of the 12 Federal Reserve Banks as of September 30, 1997.

Assets

There are two Fed assets we need to consider.

Securities The securities shown in the table are government bonds which Federal Reserve Banks have purchased. These bonds consist largely of Treasury bills (short-term securities) and Treasury bonds (long-term securities) issued by the U.S. government to finance past and present budget deficits. These securities are part of the public debt—money borrowed and

TABLE 15-1 Twelve Federal Reserve Banks' consolidated balance sheet, September 30, 1997 (in millions)

Assets		Liabilities and net worth	
Securities	$424,518	Reserves of commercial banks	$ 21,791
Loans to commercial banks	313	Treasury deposits	7,692
All other assets	63,257	Federal Reserve Notes (outstanding)	433,581
		All other liabilities and net worth	25,024
Total	$488,088	Total	$488,088

Source: Federal Reserve Bulletin, December 1997.

owed by the Federal government. Some of the bills and bonds may have been purchased directly from the Treasury, but most are bought in the open market from commercial banks or the public. Although these bonds are an important source of income to the Federal Reserve Banks, they are not bought and sold purposely for income. Rather, they are bought and sold primarily to influence the size of commercial bank reserves and, therefore, the banks' ability to create money by lending.

Loans to Commercial Banks For reasons we will discuss soon, commercial banks occasionally borrow from Federal Reserve Banks. The IOUs which commercial banks give to these "bankers' banks" in return for loans are listed as loans to commercial banks. From the Federal Reserve Banks' point of view, these IOUs are assets—they are claims against commercial banks which have borrowed from them. To commercial banks, these IOUs are liabilities. By borrowing in this way, commercial banks obtain increases in their reserves in exchange for IOUs.

Liabilities

On the liability side we find three items.

Reserves of Commercial Banks You are familiar with this account. It is an asset from the viewpoint of member banks but a liability to Federal Reserve Banks.

Treasury Deposits Just as businesses and private individuals find it convenient and desirable to pay their obligations by check, so does the United States Treasury. It keeps deposits in the Federal Reserve Banks and draws checks on them to pay its obligations. To the Treasury such deposits are assets; to the Federal Reserve Banks they are liabilities. The Treasury creates and replenishes these deposits by depositing tax receipts and money borrowed from the public or the banks through the sale of bonds.

Federal Reserve Notes Outstanding The paper money supply in the United States consists of Federal Reserve Notes issued by the Federal Reserve Banks. When it is in circulation, this paper money constitutes claims against assets of Federal Reserve Banks and is thus treated by them as a liability. Just as your own IOU is neither an asset nor a liability to you when it is in your own possession, so Federal Reserve

Notes resting in the vaults of Federal Reserve Banks are neither an asset nor a liability. Only notes in circulation (outstanding) arc liabilities to the bankers' banks. These notes come into circulation through commercial banks and are not part of the money supply until they are in the hands of the public.

TOOLS OF MONETARY POLICY

With this cursory look at the Federal Reserve Banks' balance sheet, we can now explore how the Board of Governors of the Federal Reserve System can influence the money-creating abilities of the commercial banking system. The Board can use three instruments of monetary control to influence commercial bank reserves:

1. Open-market operations
2. The reserve ratio
3. The discount rate

Open-Market Operations

Open-market operations are the most important means the Fed has to control the money supply. **Open-market operations** refers to the *buying and selling of government bonds (securities) by the Federal Reserve Banks in the open market*—that is, the buying of bonds from, or the selling of bonds to, commercial banks and the general public.

Buying Securities Suppose the Board of Governors orders the Federal Reserve Banks to buy government bonds in the open market. The bonds can be purchased from commercial banks or the public. In both cases the overall effect is the same—commercial bank reserves are increased.

From Commercial Banks When Federal Reserve Banks buy government bonds *from commercial banks,*

(a) Commercial banks give up part of their holdings of securities to the Federal Reserve Banks.
(b) The Federal Reserve Banks pay for these securities by increasing the reserves of commercial banks by the amount of the purchase.

A commercial bank may pay for a bond bought from a private individual by increasing the seller's demand deposit; similarly, the bankers' bank may pay for bonds bought from commercial banks by increasing the banks' reserves. The transaction would change the consolidated balance sheets of the commercial banks and the Federal Reserve Banks as shown below.

The upward arrow shows that securities have moved from the commercial banks to the Federal Reserve Banks. Therefore, we write "– Securities" (minus securities) in the asset column of the balance sheet of the commercial banks. For the same reason, we write " + Securities" in the asset column of the balance sheet of the Federal Reserve Banks.

FED BUYS BONDS FROM COMMERCIAL BANKS

FEDERAL RESERVE BANKS

Assets	Liabilities and net worth
+ Securities (a)	+ Reserves of commercial banks (b)
(a) Securities	(b) Reserves

COMMERCIAL BANKS

Assets	Liabilities and net worth
– Securities (a)	
+ Reserves (b)	

The downward arrow indicates that the Federal Reserve Banks have provided reserves to the commercial banks. We therefore write " + Reserves" in the asset column of the balance sheet for the commercial banks. The plus sign in the liability column of the balance sheet of the Federal Reserve Banks indicates that commercial bank reserves have increased; they are a liability to the Federal Reserve Banks.

The important aspect of this transaction is that, when Federal Reserve Banks purchase securities from commercial banks, the reserves—and therefore the lending ability—of the commercial banks are increased.

From the Public   If Federal Reserve Banks purchase securities *from the general public*, the effect on commercial bank reserves is much the same. Suppose the Grisley Meat Packing Company has negotiable government bonds which it sells in the open market to the Federal Reserve Banks. The transaction goes like this:

(a) Grisley gives up securities to the Federal Reserve Banks and gets in payment a check drawn by the Federal Reserve Banks on themselves.
(b) Grisley promptly deposits this check in its account with its Wahoo bank.
(c) The Wahoo bank collects this check against the Federal Reserve Banks by sending it to a Federal Reserve Bank for collection. As a result, the Wahoo bank receives an increase in its reserves.

Balance sheet changes are as follows:

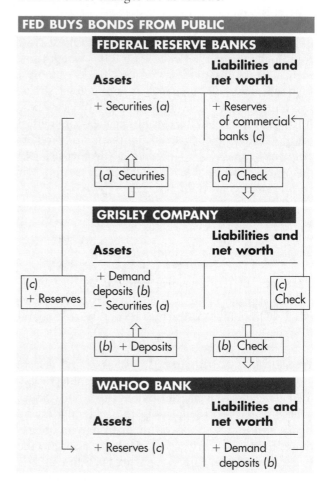

We need to understand two aspects of this transaction.

1. As with Federal Reserve purchases of securities directly from commercial banks, the reserves and lending ability of the commercial banking system have been increased. This is indicated by the " + Reserves," showing an increase in assets of the Wahoo bank.

2. The supply of money is directly increased by the central banks' purchase of government bonds (aside from any expansion of the money supply which may occur from the increase in commercial bank reserves). This direct increase in the money supply has taken the form of an increased amount of checking account money in the economy, as a result of Grisley's deposit; thus the "+ Demand deposits" in the Wahoo bank's balance sheet. Because these demand deposits are an asset as viewed by Grisley, demand deposits have increased (plus sign) on Grisley's balance sheet.

There is a slight difference between the Federal Reserve Banks' purchases of securities from the commercial banking system and those from the public. If we assume all commercial banks are "loaned up" initially, Federal Reserve bond purchases *from commercial banks* increase actual reserves and excess reserves of commercial banks by the entire amount of the bond purchases. As shown in the left panel in Figure 15-1, a $1000 bond purchase from a commercial bank increases both the actual and excess reserves of the commercial bank by $1000.

In contrast, Federal Reserve Bank purchases of bonds *from the public* increase actual reserves but also increase demand deposits. Thus, a $1000 bond pur-

chase from the public would increase demand deposits and hence the actual reserves of the "loaned up" banking system by $1000. But with a 20 percent reserve ratio applied to the demand deposit, the excess reserves of the banking system would only be $800.

However, in both transactions the result is the same: *When Federal Reserve Banks buy securities in the open market, commercial banks' reserves are increased.* When the banks lend out their excess reserves, the nation's money supply will rise. Observe in Figure 15-1 that a $1000 purchase of bonds by the Federal Reserve results in $5000 of additional money, regardless of whether the purchase was made from commercial banks or from the general public.

Selling Securities You should now suspect that Federal Reserve Bank sales of government bonds reduce commercial bank reserves. Let's see why.

To Commercial Banks Suppose the Federal Reserve Banks sell securities in the open market to *commercial banks:*

(a) Federal Reserve Banks give up securities which the commercial banks acquire.

FIGURE 15-1 The Federal Reserve's purchase of bonds and the expansion of the money supply Assuming all banks are "loaned up" initially, a Federal Reserve purchase of a $1000 bond from either a commercial bank or the public can increase the money supply by $5000 when the reserve ratio is 20 percent. In the left panel of the diagram, the purchase of a $1000 bond from a commercial bank creates $1000 of excess reserves which support a $5000 expansion of demand deposits through loans. In the right panel, the purchase of a $1000 bond from the public creates a $1000 demand deposit but only $800 of excess reserves, because $200 of reserves is required to "back up" the $1000 new demand deposit. The commercial banks can therefore expand the money supply by only $4000 by making loans. This $4000 of checking account money *plus* the new demand deposit of $1000 equals $5000 of new money.

(b) Commercial banks pay for these securities by drawing checks against their deposits—that is, against their reserves—in Federal Reserve Banks. The Fed collects these checks by reducing the commercial banks' reserves accordingly.

The balance sheet changes appear as follows:

The reduction in commercial bank reserves is indicated by the minus signs before these entries.

To the Public   If Federal Reserve Banks sell securities *to the public*, the final outcome is the same. Let's put the Grisley company on the buying end of government bonds which the Federal Reserve Banks are selling:

(a) The Federal Reserve Bank sells government bonds to Grisley, which pays with a check drawn on the Wahoo bank.

(b) The Federal Reserve Banks clear this check against the Wahoo bank by reducing Wahoo's reserves.

(c) The Wahoo bank returns the canceled check to Grisley, reducing Grisley's demand deposit accordingly.

The balance sheets change as shown in the right text column.

Federal Reserve bond sales of $1000 to the commercial banking system reduce the system's actual and excess reserves by $1000. But a $1000 bond sale to the public reduces excess reserves by $800 because the public's demand-deposit money is also reduced by $1000 by the sale. Since the commercial banking system's outstanding demand deposits are reduced by $1000, banks need keep $200 less in reserves.

Whether the Fed sells bonds to the public or to commercial banks, the result is the same: *When Federal Reserve Banks sell securities in the open market, commercial bank reserves are reduced.* If all excess reserves are already lent out, this decline in commercial bank reserves produces a decline in the nation's money supply. In our example, a $1000 sale of government securities results in a $5000 decline in the money supply whether the sale is made to commercial banks or to the general public. You can verify this by reexamining Figure 15-1 and tracing the effects of a *sale* of a $1000 bond by the Fed either to commercial banks or to the public.

What makes commercial banks and the public willing to sell government securities to, or buy them from, Federal Reserve Banks? The answer lies in the price of bonds and their interest rates. We know from Chapter 13 that bond prices and interest rates are inversely related. When the Fed buys government bonds, the demand for them increases. Government bond prices rise and their interest rates decline. The higher bond prices and their lower interest rates prompt banks, securities firms, and individual holders of government bonds to sell them to the Federal Reserve Banks.

When the Fed sells government bonds, the additional supply of bonds in the bond market lowers bond prices and raises their interest rates, making government bonds attractive purchases for banks and the public.

The Reserve Ratio

The Fed's Board of Governors can also manipulate the **reserve ratio** to influence the ability of commercial banks to lend. The following example shows how: Suppose a commercial bank's balance sheet shows that reserves are $5000 and demand deposits $20,000. If the legal reserve ratio is 20 percent (row 2, Table 15-2), the bank's *required* reserves are $4000. Since *actual* reserves are $5000, the *excess* reserves of this bank are $1000. On the basis of $1000 of excess reserves, this single bank can lend $1000; however, the banking system as a whole can create a maximum of $5000 in new checking account money by lending (column 7).

Raising the Reserve Ratio Now, what if the Board of Governors raised the reserve ratio from 20 to 25 percent? (See row 3.) Required reserves would jump from $4000 to $5000, shrinking excess reserves from $1000 to zero. *Raising the reserve ratio increases the amount of required reserves banks must keep. Either banks lose excess reserves, diminishing their ability to create money by lending, or they find their reserves deficient and are forced to contract checkable deposits and therefore the money supply.* In the example in Table 15-2, excess reserves are transformed into required reserves, and the money-creating potential of our *single bank* is reduced from $1000 to zero (column 6). Moreover, the *banking system's* money-creating capacity declines from $5000 to zero (column 7).

What if the Board of Governors increases the reserve requirement to 30 percent? (see row 4.) The commercial bank would face the prospect of failing to meet this requirement. To protect itself against such an eventuality, the bank would be forced to lower its demand deposits and at the same time increase its reserves. To reduce its demand deposits, the bank could let outstanding loans mature and be repaid without extending new credit. To increase reserves, the bank might sell some of its bonds, adding the proceeds to its reserves. Both actions would reduce the supply of money (if unclear on this, see Chapter 14, transactions 6 and 8).

Lowering the Reserve Ratio What would happen if the Board of Governors lowered the reserve ratio from the original 20 to 10 percent? (See row 1.) In this case, required reserves would decline from $4000 to $2000, and excess reserves would jump from $1000 to $3000. The single bank's lending (money-creating) ability would increase from $1000 to $3000 (column 6), and the banking system's money-creating potential would expand from $5000 to $30,000 (column 7). *Lowering the reserve ratio changes required reserves to excess reserves and enhances the ability of banks to create new money by lending.*

TABLE 15-2 The effects of changes in the reserve ratio on the lending ability of commercial banks

(1) Reserve ratio, %	(2) Demand deposits	(3) Actual reserves	(4) Required reserves	(5) Excess reserves, (3) − (4)	(6) Money-creating potential of single bank, = (5)	(7) Money-creating potential of banking system
(1) 10	$20,000	$5000	$2000	$ 3000	$ 3000	$30,000
(2) 20	20,000	5000	4000	1000	1000	5,000
(3) 25	20,000	5000	5000	0	0	0
(4) 30	20,000	5000	6000	− 1000	− 1000	− 3,333

From the examples in Table 15-2 we can see that a change in the reserve ratio affects the money-creating ability of the *banking system* in two ways:

1. It changes the amount of excess reserves.

2. It changes the size of the monetary multiplier.

For example, when the legal reserve ratio is raised from 10 to 20 percent, excess reserves are reduced from $3000 to $1000 and the demand-deposit multiplier is reduced from 10 to 5. The money-creating potential of the banking system declines from $30,000 (= $3000 × 10) to $5000 (= $1000 × 5).

Changing the reserve ratio is a powerful technique of monetary control, but it is used infrequently. The last such change was in 1992, when the Fed lowered the reserve ratio from 12 to 10 percent.

The Discount Rate

One of the functions of a central bank is to be a "lender of last resort." Occasionally, commercial banks have unexpected and immediate needs for additional funds. In such cases, each Federal Reserve Bank will make short-term loans to commercial banks in its district.

When a commercial bank borrows, it gives the Federal Reserve Bank a promissory note (IOU) drawn against itself and secured by acceptable collateral—typically U.S. government securities. Just as commercial banks charge interest on their loans, so too Federal Reserve Banks charge interest on loans they grant to commercial banks. The interest rate they charge is called the **discount rate.**

As a claim against the commercial bank, the borrowing bank's promissory note is an asset to the lending Federal Reserve Bank and appears on its balance sheet as "Loans to commercial banks." To the commercial bank the IOU is a liability, appearing as "Loans from the Federal Reserve Banks" on the commercial bank's balance sheet. [See entries (*a*) on the balance sheets in the right-hand column.]

In providing the loan, the Federal Reserve Bank *increases* the reserves of the borrowing commercial bank. Since no required reserves need be kept against loans from Federal Reserve Banks, *all* new reserves acquired by borrowing from Federal Reserve Banks are excess reserves. [These changes are reflected in entries (*b*) on the balance sheets.]

The main point is that *commercial bank borrowing from the Federal Reserve Banks increases the reserves of commercial banks, enhancing their ability to extend credit.*

COMMERCIAL BANK BORROWING FROM THE FED

FEDERAL RESERVE BANKS

Assets	Liabilities and net worth
+ Loans to commercial banks (*a*) ⇧ IOUs	+ Reserves of commercial banks (*b*) ⇩ + Reserves

COMMERCIAL BANKS

Assets	Liabilities and net worth
+ Reserves (*b*)	+ Loans from the Federal Reserve Banks (*a*)

The Fed's Board of Governors has the power to establish and change the discount rate at which commercial banks borrow from Federal Reserve Banks. From the commercial banks' point of view, the discount rate is a cost of acquiring reserves. When the discount rate is decreased, commercial banks are encouraged to obtain additional reserves by borrowing from Federal Reserve Banks. Commercial bank lending based on these new reserves then constitutes an increase in the money supply.

An increase in the discount rate discourages commercial banks from obtaining additional reserves through borrowing from the central banks. An increase in the discount rate therefore is used by the Fed to restrict the money supply. **(Key Question 2)**

Easy Money and Tight Money

Suppose the economy is faced with recession and unemployment. The Fed decides an increase in the supply of money is needed to stimulate aggregate demand so as to employ idle resources. To increase the supply of money, the Board of Governors must expand the excess reserves of commercial banks. What actions will bring this about?

1. *Buy securities* The Board of Governors should order Federal Reserve Banks to buy securities in the open market. These bond purchases will be paid for by increases in commercial bank reserves.

2. *Reduce the reserve ratio* The reserve ratio should be reduced, automatically changing required reserves into excess reserves and increasing the size of the monetary multiplier.

3. *Lower the discount rate* The discount rate should be lowered to induce commercial banks to add to their reserves by borrowing from Federal Reserve Banks.

This set of actions is called an **easy money policy.** Its purpose is to make bank loans cheaply and easily available to increase aggregate demand and employment.

Suppose, on the other hand, excessive spending is pushing the economy into an inflationary spiral. The Board of Governors should attempt to reduce aggregate demand by limiting or contracting the supply of money. The key to this goal lies in reducing the reserves of commercial banks. How is this done?

1. *Sell securities* Federal Reserve Banks should sell government bonds in the open market to reduce commercial bank reserves.

2. *Increase the reserve ratio* Increasing the reserve ratio will automatically strip commercial banks of excess reserves and decrease the monetary multiplier.

3. *Raise the discount rate* A boost in the discount rate will discourage commercial banks from building up their reserves through borrowing at Federal Reserve Banks.

This group of directives is called a **tight money policy.** The objective is to tighten the supply of money to reduce spending and control inflation.

Relative Importance

Of the three instruments of monetary control, open-market operations clearly are the most important.

The discount rate is less important for two interrelated reasons. First, the amount of commercial bank reserves obtained by borrowing from the central banks is typically very small. On average, only 2 or 3 percent of bank reserves are acquired this way. Indeed, open-market operations often lead commercial banks to borrow from Federal Reserve Banks. That is, if Fed sales of bonds to the public leave commercial banks temporarily short of reserves, commercial banks will be prompted to seek loans from the Federal Reserve Banks. Commercial bank borrowing from the Fed occurs largely *in response to open-market operations* and not so much in response to discount-rate changes.

Second, while changes in the reserve ratio and open-market operations are initiated by actions of the Fed, the discount rate depends on actions (borrowing) of commercial banks to be effective. For exam-

ple, if the Fed lowers the discount rate at a time when very few banks are inclined to borrow from Federal Reserve Banks, the lower rate will have little or no impact on bank reserves and the money supply.

Nevertheless, some economists say that a change in the discount rate has an "announcement effect"; it is a clear and explicit way for the Fed to communicate to the financial community and the general economy the intended direction of monetary policy. Other economists dismiss this claim, contending that changes in the discount rate are usually "passive"; the discount rate is changed mainly to keep it in line with other short-term interest rates, not to implement a policy change.

What about changes in reserve requirements? The Fed has used this instrument of monetary control only sparingly. Normally, it can accomplish its monetary goals through open-market operations, without resorting to changes in reserve requirements. The limited use of changes in the reserve ratio undoubtedly is related to the fact that reserves earn no interest. Raising or lowering reserve requirements can have substantial effects on bank profits.

But there are more positive reasons why open-market operations are the primary technique of monetary policy. This mechanism of monetary control has the advantage of flexibility—government securities can be purchased or sold in large or small amounts—and the impact on bank reserves is prompt. Yet, compared with reserve-requirement changes, open-market operations work subtly and less directly. Furthermore, there is no question about the ability of the Federal Reserve Banks to affect commercial bank reserves through bond sales and purchases. A glance at the consolidated balance sheet for the Federal Reserve Banks (Table 15-1) reveals very large holdings of government bonds ($425 billion), the sales of which could theoretically reduce commercial bank reserves from $22 billion to zero.

QUICK REVIEW 15-1

■ The objective of monetary policy is to help the economy achieve a full-employment, noninflationary level of domestic output.

■ The Fed has three main methods of monetary control, each of which works by changing the amount of excess reserves in the banking system:

a. Conducting open-market operations (the Fed's buying and selling of government bonds to the banks and the public)

(a) The money market

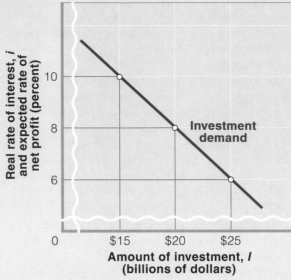

(b) Investment demand

QUICK QUIZ 15-2

1. The *ultimate* objective of an easy money policy is depicted by:
   a. a decrease in the money supply from S_{m3} to S_{m2}.
   b. a reduction of the interest rate from 8 to 6 percent.
   c. an increase in investment from $20 billion to $25 billion.
   d. an increase in real GDP from Q_1 to Q_f.

2. A successful tight money policy is shown as a shift in the money supply curve from:
   a. S_{m3} to S_{m2}, an increase in investment from $20 billion to $25 billion, and a decline in aggregate demand from AD_3 to AD_2.
   b. S_{m1} to S_{m2}, an increase in investment from $20 billion to $25 billion, and an increase in real GDP from Q_1 to Q_f.
   c. S_{m3} to S_{m2}, a decrease in investment from $25 billion to $20 billion, and a decline in the price level from P_3 to P_2.
   d. S_{m3} to S_{m2}, a decrease in investment from $25 billion to $20 billion, and an increase in aggregate demand from AD_2 to AD_3.

b. Changing the reserve ratio (the percentage of commercial bank deposit liabilities required as reserves)
c. Changing the discount rate (the interest rate the Federal Reserve Banks charge on loans to banks and thrifts)

■ Open-market operations are the Fed's most important monetary control mechanism.

MONETARY POLICY, REAL GDP, AND THE PRICE LEVEL

Thus far, we have explained only how the Fed can change the money supply. We next need to link up the money supply, the interest rate, investment spending, and aggregate demand to see how monetary policy affects the economy. How does monetary policy work?

Cause-Effect Chain

The three diagrams in **Figure 15-2 (Key Graph)** will help you understand how monetary policy works toward achieving the goal of full employment and price stability.

Money Market Figure 15-2a represents the money market, in which the demand curve for money and

(c) **Equilibrium real GDP and the price level**

FIGURE 15-2 Monetary policy and equilibrium GDP An easy money policy which shifts the money supply curve rightward from S_{m1} to S_{m2} lowers the interest rate from 10 to 8 percent. As a result, investment spending increases from $15 billion to $20 billion, shifting the aggregate demand curve rightward from AD_1 to AD_2. Real output rises from the recessionary level Q_1 to the full-employment level Q_f. A tight money policy which shifts the money supply curve leftward from S_{m3} to S_{m2} increases the interest rate from 6 to 8 percent. Investment spending thus falls from $25 billion to $20 billion and the aggregate demand curve shifts leftward from AD_3 to AD_2, curtailing inflation.

3. **The Federal Reserve could increase the money supply from S_{m1} to S_{m2} by:**
   a. increasing the discount rate.
   b. reducing taxes.
   c. buying government securities in the open market.
   d. increasing the reserve requirement.

4. **If the spending-income multiplier is 4 in the economy depicted, an increase in the money supply from $125 billion to $150 billion will:**

   a. shift the aggregate demand curve rightward by $20 billion.
   b. increase real GDP by $25 billion.
   c. increase real GDP by $100 billion.
   d. shift the aggregate demand curve leftward by $5 billion.

Answers: 1. d; 2. c; 3. c; 4. a

the supply curve of money are brought together. Recall from Chapter 13 that the total demand for money is made up of the transactions and asset demands. The transactions demand is directly related to the nominal GDP. The asset demand is inversely related to the interest rate. The interest rate is the opportunity cost of holding money as an asset; the higher the cost, the smaller the amount of money the public wants to hold. The total demand for money D_m is thus inversely related to the interest rate, as is indicated in Figure 15-2a. Also, recall that an increase in nominal GDP will shift D_m to the right, and a decline in nominal GDP will shift D_m to the left.

We complete our graphical portrayal of the money market by showing three potential money supply curves, S_{m1}, S_{m2}, and S_{m3}. In each case the money supply is shown as a vertical line representing some fixed amount of money determined by the Fed's Board of Governors. While monetary policy (specifically, the supply of money) helps determine the interest rate, the interest rate does *not* determine the location of the money supply curve.

The equilibrium interest rate is the rate at which the amounts of money demanded and supplied are equal. With money demand D_m in Figure 15-2a, if the supply of money is $125 billion ($S_{m1}$), the equilibrium interest rate is 10 percent. With a money supply of $150 ($S_{m2}$), the interest rate is 8 percent; with a money supply of $175 billion ($S_{m3}$), it is 6 percent.

You know from Chapter 10 that the real, not the nominal, rate of interest is critical for investment decisions. So here we assume Figure 15-2a portrays real interest rates.

Investment   These 10, 8, and 6 percent real interest rates are carried rightward to the investment demand curve in Figure 15-2b. This curve shows the inverse relationship between the interest rate—the cost of borrowing to invest—and the amount of investment spending. At the 10 percent interest rate it will be profitable for the nation's businesses to invest $15 billion; at 8 percent, $20 billion; at 6 percent, $25 billion.

The investment component of total spending is more likely to be affected by changes in the interest rate than is the consumer spending component. Of course, consumer purchases of automobiles, which depend heavily on installment credit, are sensitive to interest rates. But overall the interest rate is *not* a very crucial factor in determining how households divide their disposable incomes between consumption and saving.

The impact of changing interest rates on investment spending is great because of the large cost and long-term nature of capital purchases. Capital equipment, factory buildings, and warehouses are tremendously expensive. In absolute terms, interest charges on funds borrowed for these purchases are considerable.

Similarly, the interest cost on a house purchased on a long-term contract will be very large: A $\frac{1}{2}$ percentage point change in the interest rate could amount to thousands of dollars on the total cost of a home.

Also, changes in the interest rate may affect investment spending by changing the relative attractiveness of purchases of capital equipment versus purchases of bonds. In purchasing capital goods, the interest rate is the *cost* of borrowing the funds to make the investment. In purchasing bonds, the interest rate is the *return* on the financial investment. If the interest rate increases, the cost of buying capital goods increases while the return on bonds increases. Businesses are then more inclined to use business saving to buy securities than to buy equipment. Conversely, a drop in the interest rate makes purchases of capital goods relatively more attractive than bond ownership.

In brief, the impact of changing interest rates is mainly on investment (and, through that, on aggregate demand, output, employment, and the price

level). Moreover, as Figure 15-2b shows, investment spending varies inversely with the interest rate.

Equilibrium GDP   Figure 15-2c shows the impact of our three interest rates and corresponding levels of investment spending on aggregate demand. As noted, aggregate demand curve AD_1 is associated with the $15 billion level of investment, AD_2 with investment of $20 billion, and AD_3 with investment of $25 billion. That is, investment spending is one of the determinants of aggregate demand. Other things equal, the greater this investment spending, the farther to the right lies the aggregate demand curve.

Suppose the money supply in Figure 15-2a is $125 billion ($S_{m1}$), producing an equilibrium interest rate of 10 percent. In Figure 15-2b we see that this 10 percent interest rate will bring forth $15 billion of investment spending. This $15 billion of investment spending joins with consumption spending, net exports, and government spending to yield aggregate demand curve AD_1 in Figure 15-2c. The equilibrium levels of real output and prices are Q_1 and P_1, as determined by the intersection of AD_1 and the aggregate supply curve AS.

To test your understanding of these relationships, you should explain why each of the other two levels of money supply in Figure 15-2a results in a different interest rate, level of investment, aggregate demand curve, and equilibrium real output and price level.

Effects of an Easy Money Policy

We have assumed the money supply is $125 billion ($S_{m1}$) in Figure 15-2a. Because the resulting real output Q_1 in Figure 15-2c is far below the full employment output, Q_f, the economy must be experiencing substantial unemployment. The Fed therefore should institute an *easy money policy*.

To increase the money supply, the Federal Reserve Banks will take some combination of the following actions: (1) Buy government securities from banks and the public in the open market, (2) lower the legal reserve ratio, and (3) lower the discount rate. The result will be an increase in excess reserves in the commercial banking system. Because excess reserves are the basis on which commercial banks and thrifts can earn profit by lending and thereby expand the money supply, the nation's money supply likely will rise. An increase in the money supply will lower the interest rate, increasing investment, aggregate demand, and equilibrium GDP.

For example, an increase in the money supply from $125 billion to $150 billion ($S_{m1}$ to S_{m2}) will reduce the interest rate from 10 to 8 percent, as indicated in Figure 15-2a, and increase investment from $15 billion to $20 billion, as shown in Figure 15-2b. This $5 billion increase in investment spending will shift the aggregate demand curve rightward by more than the increase in investment because of the multiplier effect. If the economy's MPC is .75, the multiplier will be 4, meaning that the $5 billion increase in investment will shift the AD curve rightward by $20 billion (= 4 × $5) at each price level. Specifically, aggregate demand will shift from AD_1 to AD_2 as shown in Figure 15-2c. This rightward shift in the aggregate demand curve will increase GDP from Q_1 to the desired full-employment GDP of Q_f.

Column 1 in Table 15-3 summarizes the chain of events associated with an easy money policy.

Effects of a Tight Money Policy

Now let's assume the money supply and interest rate are $175 billion ($S_{m3}$) in Figure 15-2a. This results in an interest rate of 6 percent, investment spending of $25 billion, and aggregate demand AD_3. As you can see in Figure 15-2c, we have depicted severe demand-pull inflation. Aggregate demand AD_3 is excessive relative to the economy's full-employment level of real output Q_f. To reign in spending, the Fed will institute a *tight money policy*.

The Federal Reserve Board will direct Federal Reserve Banks to undertake some combination of the following actions: (1) Sell government securities to banks and the public in the open market, (2) increase the legal reserve ratio, and (3) increase the discount rate. Banks then will discover their reserves are below those required. They therefore will need to reduce their demand deposits by refraining from issuing new loans as old loans are paid back. This will shrink the money supply and increase the interest rate. The higher interest rate will discourage investment, decreasing aggregate demand and restraining demand-pull inflation.

If the Fed reduces the money supply from $175 billion to $150 billion ($S_{m3}$ to S_{m2} in Figure 15-2a), the interest rate will increase from 6 to 8 percent and investment will decline from $25 billion to $20 billion (Figure 15-2b). This $5 billion decrease in investment, bolstered by the multiplier process, will shift the aggregate demand curve leftward from AD_3 to AD_2. For example, if the MPC is .75, the multiplier

TABLE 15-3   Monetary policies for recession and inflation

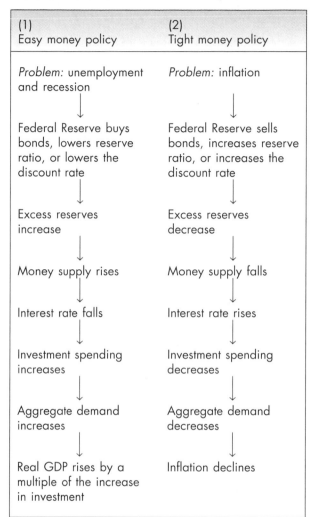

(1) Easy money policy	(2) Tight money policy
Problem: unemployment and recession	*Problem:* inflation
↓	↓
Federal Reserve buys bonds, lowers reserve ratio, or lowers the discount rate	Federal Reserve sells bonds, increases reserve ratio, or increases the discount rate
↓	↓
Excess reserves increase	Excess reserves decrease
↓	↓
Money supply rises	Money supply falls
↓	↓
Interest rate falls	Interest rate rises
↓	↓
Investment spending increases	Investment spending decreases
↓	↓
Aggregate demand increases	Aggregate demand decreases
↓	↓
Real GDP rises by a multiple of the increase in investment	Inflation declines

will be 4 and the aggregate demand curve will shift leftward by $20 billion (= 4 × $5 billion of investment) at each price level. This leftward shift of the aggregate demand curve will eliminate the excessive spending and thus the demand-pull inflation. In the real world, of course, the goal will be to stop inflation—halt further increases in the price level—rather than to actually drive down the price level.

Column 2 in Table 15-3 summarizes the cause-effect chain of a tight money policy. **(Key Question 3)**

Refinements and Feedback

The components in Figure 15-2 let us (1) see some of the factors which determine the effectiveness of monetary policy and (2) note the existence of a "feedback" or "circularity" problem which complicates monetary policy.

Policy Effectiveness

Figure 15-2 reveals the magnitudes by which an easy or tight money policy will change the interest rate, investment, and aggregate demand. These magnitudes are determined by the particular shapes of the money demand and investment demand curves. Pencil in other curves to see that *the steeper the* D_m *curve is, the larger the effect of any change in the money supply on the equilibrium rate of interest. Furthermore, any change in the interest rate will have a larger impact on investment—and hence on aggregate demand and GDP—the flatter the investment demand curve*. A specific change in money supply will be most effective when the demand curve for money is relatively steep and the investment demand curve is relatively flat.

A particular change in the quantity of money will be relatively ineffective when the money demand curve is flat and the investment demand curve is steep. In that case, neither the interest rate nor the level of investment will significantly change.

Feedback Effects

You may have sensed in Figure 15-2 a feedback problem which complicates monetary policy. The problem is this: By reading from Figure 15-2a to 15-2c we discover that the interest rate, working through the investment demand curve, is a determinant of the equilibrium GDP. Now we must recognize that causation also runs the other way. The level of GDP is a determinant of the equilibrium interest rate. This link comes about because the transactions component of the money demand curve is directly related to the level of nominal GDP.

How does this feedback from Figure 15-2c to 15-2a affect monetary policy? It means that the increase in the GDP which an easy money policy brings about will *increase* the demand for money, partially offsetting the interest-rate-reducing effect of the easy money policy. A tight money policy will reduce the nominal GDP. But this will *decrease* the demand for money and slow the interest-rate-increasing effect of the tight money policy. **(Key Question 4)**

Monetary Policy and Aggregate Supply

As is true of fiscal policy, the effect of a specific monetary policy depends on where the initial and subsequent equilibrium points are located on the aggregate supply curve. In Figure 15-2c, if the economy is initially at a leftward point in the horizontal range of AS, then an easy money policy which shifts the aggregate demand curve rightward from AD_1 to AD_2 will have a large impact on real GDP and have little or no impact on the price level.

But if the economy is already near, at, or beyond full employment, an increase in aggregate demand will have little or no effect on real output and employment. It will, however, substantially increase the price level. To see this, observe in Figure 15-2c that an increase in the aggregate demand curve from AD_2 to AD_3 would occur mainly in the vertical range of the aggregate supply curve. Needless to say, an easy money policy would be inappropriate when the economy is already achieving full employment. Figure 15-2c makes clear the reason why: It would be highly inflationary.

Similarly, a tight money policy is appropriate when the economy is fully employed and suffering demand-pull inflation but would be inappropriate when the economy is suffering substantial cyclical unemployment. In the latter case, the main impact of such a policy would be to reduce real output and worsen unemployment.

EFFECTIVENESS OF MONETARY POLICY

In this section we discuss some strengths and weaknesses of monetary policy as a stabilization tool and see how it has worked in the real world.

Strengths of Monetary Policy

Most economists regard monetary policy as an essential component of U.S. national stabilization policy, especially in view of the following features and evidence.

Speed and Flexibility

Compared with fiscal policy, monetary policy can be quickly altered. Recall that the application of fiscal policy may be delayed by congressional deliberations. In contrast, the Open Market Committee of the Federal Reserve System can buy or sell securities on a daily basis and thus affect the money supply and interest rates almost immediately.

Isolation from Political Pressure Since members of the Fed's Board of Governors are appointed for 14-year terms, they are not often subject to lobbying and need not concern themselves with their popularity with voters. Thus the Board, more easily than Congress, can engage in politically unpopular policies which might be necessary for the long-term health of the economy. And, monetary policy itself is a more subtle and more politically conservative measure than fiscal policy. Changes in government spending directly affect the allocation of resources, and changes in taxes can have extensive political ramifications. By contrast, monetary policy works more subtly and therefore is more politically palatable.

Success During the 1980s and 1990s The case for monetary policy has been greatly bolstered by its successful use during the 1980s and 1990s. A tight money policy helped bring the inflation rate down from 13.5 percent in 1980 to 3.2 percent 3 years later.

In the early 1990s, the Fed successfully used monetary policy to help move the economy out of the 1990–1991 recession. This success is noteworthy because the huge budget deficits of the 1980s and early 1990s had put fiscal policy "on the shelf." Congressional budgeting was mainly aimed at reducing the budget deficit, not at stimulating the economy. From a fiscal policy perspective, the tax hikes and government spending reductions during this period were mildly contractionary. But the Fed's easy money policy reduced interest rates on commercial loans from 10 percent in 1990 to 6 percent in 1993. Eventually, these low interest rates had their intended effects: Investment spending and interest-sensitive consumer spending rose rapidly, increasing the economy's real GDP.

The expansion of GDP which began in 1992 has continued, with the unemployment rate falling from 7.5 percent that year to less than 5 percent in 1997. To ensure against renewed inflation, in 1994 and 1995, and then again in early 1997, the Fed reduced reserves in the banking system to increase the interest rate and slow the growth of borrowing and spending. Thus far, the strategy has worked; inflation has been held in check throughout the expansion.

In view of Congress' focus on balancing the Federal budget and the Fed's recent policy successes in controlling inflation and promoting growth, for the time being *monetary policy has assumed the role of primary stabilization tool in the United States.*

Shortcomings and Problems

Despite its recent successes, monetary policy has certain limitations and it encounters real-world complications.

Less Control? Some commentators suggest that changes in banking practices (some of which we discussed in Chapter 13) may reduce, or make less predictable, the Fed's control of the money supply. People can now move near-monies quickly from mutual funds and other financial investments to checking accounts, and vice versa. A particular monetary policy aimed at changing bank reserves might then be rendered less effective by movements of funds within the financial system. For example, people might respond to a tight money policy by quickly converting near-monies in their mutual fund accounts or other liquid financial investments to money in their checking accounts. Bank reserves would then not fall as intended by the Fed, the interest rate would not rise, and aggregate demand might not change. Also, banking and finance are increasingly global. Flows of funds to or from the United States might undermine or render inappropriate a particular domestic monetary policy. Finally, the prospects of E-cash and smart cards might complicate the measurement of money and make its issuance more difficult to control.

How legitimate are these concerns? These financial developments could make the Fed's task of monetary policy more difficult. But recent studies and Fed experience confirm that the traditional central bank tools of monetary policy remain effective in changing the money supply and interest rates.

Cyclical Asymmetry If pursued vigorously, tight money can deplete commercial banking reserves to the point where banks are forced to reduce the volume of loans. This means a contraction of the money supply. But an easy money policy suffers from a "You can lead a horse to water, but you can't make it drink" problem. An easy money policy can ensure only that commercial banks have the excess reserves needed to make loans. It cannot guarantee that the banks will actually make the loans and thus that the supply of money will increase. If commercial banks, seeking liquidity, are unwilling to lend, the efforts of the Board of Governors will be to little avail. Similarly, the public can frustrate the intentions of the Fed by deciding not to borrow excess reserves. Additionally, the money the Fed injects into the system by buying bonds from the public could be used by the public to pay off existing loans.

In short, a potential *cyclical asymmetry* is at work. Monetary policy may be highly effective in slowing expansions and controlling inflation but largely ineffective in moving the economy from a recession or depression toward its full-employment output. This potential cyclical asymmetry, however, has *not* created major difficulties for monetary policy in recent eras. Since the Great Depression, higher excess reserves have generally translated into added lending and therefore into an increase in the money supply.

Changes in Velocity

Total expenditures may be regarded as the money supply *multiplied* by the **velocity of money**—the number of times per year the average dollar is spent on goods and services. If the money supply is $150 billion, total spending will be $600 billion if velocity is 4 but only $450 billion if velocity is 3.

Some economists feel that velocity changes in the opposite direction from the money supply, offsetting or frustrating policy-related changes in the money supply. During inflation, when the money supply is restrained by policy, velocity may increase. Conversely, when measures are taken to increase the money supply during recession, velocity may fall.

Velocity might behave this way because of the asset demand for money. An easy money policy, for example, means an increase in the supply of money relative to the demand for it and therefore a reduction in the interest rate (Figure 15-2a). But when the interest rate—the opportunity cost of holding money as an asset—is lower, the public will hold larger money balances. This means dollars will move from hand to hand—from households to businesses and back again—less rapidly. That is, the velocity of money will decline. A reverse sequence of events may cause a tight money policy to induce an increase in velocity.

The Investment Impact

Some economists doubt that monetary policy has as much impact on investment as Figure 15-2 implies. The combination of a relatively flat money demand curve and a relatively steep investment demand curve will mean that a particular change in the money supply will not cause a very large change in investment and, thus, not a large change in the equilibrium GDP.

Furthermore, the operation of monetary policy as portrayed in Figure 15-2 may be complicated, or temporarily offset, by unfavorable changes in the location of the investment demand curve. For example, a tight money policy designed to drive up interest rates may have little impact on investment spending if the investment demand curve in Figure 15-2b at the same time shifts to the right because of business optimism, technological progress, or expectations of higher future prices of capital. Monetary policy would have to raise interest rates extraordinarily high under these circumstances to be effective in reducing aggregate demand. Conversely, a severe recession may undermine business confidence, push the investment demand curve to the left, and frustrate an easy money policy.

Interest as Income

Monetary policy is based on the idea that expenditures on capital goods and interest-sensitive consumer goods are *inversely* related to interest rates. We must now acknowledge that businesses and households are also *recipients* of interest income. The size of such income and the spending which flows from it vary *directly* with the level of interest rates.

Suppose inflation is intensifying and the Fed raises interest rates to increase the cost of capital goods, housing, and automobiles. The complication is that higher interest rates on a wide range of financial instruments (for example, bonds, certificates of deposits, checking accounts) will increase the incomes and spending of the households and businesses that own them. Such added spending is obviously at odds with the Fed's effort to restrict aggregate demand. Here is an opposite example: In 1991 and 1992 the Fed repeatedly lowered interest rates to stimulate a sluggish economy. One possible reason this strategy took so long to become effective was that households that were receiving 8 or 10 percent on their bonds and CDs in the late 1980s received only 4 or 5 percent in the early 1990s. This diminished interest income undoubtedly lowered their spending.

The point is this: For those who pay interest as an *expense*, a rise in the interest rate reduces spending, while a decline in the interest rate increases spending. But for those who view interest as *income*, a rise in the interest rate increases spending, while a decline in the interest rate reduces spending. The change in spending by interest-income receivers *partly* offsets and weakens the change in spending by purchasers of capital goods, homes, and autos.

Recent Focus: The Federal Funds Rate

In the past few years, the Fed has communicated its changes in monetary policy by announcing changes in its targets for the *Federal funds rate*. (Recall that this rate is the interest rate which banks charge one another on overnight loans.) Statements by the Fed that it intends to increase the Federal funds rate suggest a "tighter" monetary policy is coming, while statements that it intends to reduce the Federal funds rate foretell an "easier" monetary policy. Interest rates, in general, rise and fall with the Federal funds rate. For example, in Figure 15-3 observe that changes in the **prime interest rate**—the interest rate banks charge their most creditworthy customers—generally track changes in the Federal funds rate.

The Fed does not *set* either the Federal funds rate or the prime rate; each is established by the interaction of lenders and borrowers. But because the Fed can change the supply of excess reserves in the banking system and then the money supply, it normally can obtain the market interest rates it desires. To increase the Federal funds interest rate, the Fed *sells* bonds in the open market. Such open-market operations reduce excess reserves in the banking system, lessening the excess reserves available for overnight loans in the Federal funds market. The decreased supply of excess reserves in that market increases the Federal funds interest rate. In addition, reduced excess reserves decrease the amount of bank lending and hence the amount of deposit money. We know that declines in the supply of money lead to increases in interest rates in general, including the prime interest rate.

In contrast, when the Fed wants to reduce the Federal funds rate, it *buys* bonds from banks and the public. As a result, the supply of reserves in the Federal funds market increases and the Federal funds rate declines. The money supply rises because the increased supply of excess reserves leads to greater lending and creation of deposit money. As a result, interest rates in general fall, including the prime interest rate. (**Key Question 5**)

QUICK REVIEW 15-2

■ The Fed is engaging in an easy money policy when it increases the money supply to reduce interest rates and increase investment spending and real GDP; it is engaging in a tight money policy when it reduces the money supply to increase interest rates and reduce investment spending and inflation.

■ The steeper the money demand curve and the flatter the investment demand curve, the larger the impact of a change in the money supply on the economy.

■ The main strengths of monetary policy are **(a)** speed and flexibility and **(b)** political acceptability; its main weaknesses are **(a)** potential reduced effectiveness during recession and **(b)** the possibility that changes in velocity will offset it.

■ The Fed communicates changes in monetary policy by announcing changes it targets for the federal funds interest rate.

■ In the past two decades, the Fed has quite successfully used alternate tight and loose money policies to stabilize the economy.

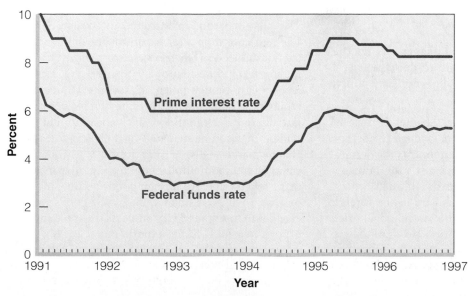

FIGURE 15-3 The prime interest rate and the Federal funds rate in the United States, 1991–1997 Changes in the prime interest rate rise and fall with changes in the Federal funds rate.

For the Fed, Life Is a Metaphor

The popular press often describes the Federal Reserve Board and its chair (Alan Greenspan, 1987–present) in colorful terms.

The Federal Reserve Board leads a very dramatic life, or so it seems when one reads journalistic accounts of its activities. It loosens or tightens reins while riding herd on a rambunctious economy, goes to the rescue of an embattled dollar, tightens spigots on credit . . . you get the picture. For the Fed, life is a metaphor.

The Fed as Mechanic The Fed sometimes must roll up its sleeves and adjust the economic machinery. The Fed spends a lot of time either tightening things, loosing things, or debating about whether to tighten or loosen.

Imagine a customer taking his car into Greenspan's Garage:

Normally calm, Skeezix Greenspan took one look at the car and started to sweat. This would be hard to fix—it was an economy car:

"What's the problem?" asked Greenspan.

"It's been running beautifully for over 6 years now," said the customer. "But recently it's been acting sluggish."

"These cars are tricky," said Greenspan.

"We can always loosen a few screws, as long as you don't mind the side effects."

"What side effects?" asked the customer.

"Nothing at first," said Greenspan. "We won't even know if the repairs have worked for at least a year. After that, either everything will be fine, or your car will accelerate wildly and go totally out of control."

"Just as long as it doesn't stall," said the customer. "I hate that."

The Fed as Warrior The Fed must fight inflation. But can it wage a protracted war? There are only seven Fed governors, including Greenspan—not a big army:

Gen. Greenspan sat in the war room plotting strategy. You never knew where the enemy would strike next—producer prices, retail sales, factory payrolls, manufacturing inventories.

Suddenly, one of his staff officers burst into the room: "Straight from the Western European front, sir—the dollar is under attack by the major industrial nations."

Greenspan whirled around toward the big campaign map. "We've got to turn back this assault!" he said.

"Yes sir." The officer turned to go.

"Hold it!" Greenspan shouted. Suddenly, his mind reeled with conflicting data. A strong dollar was good for inflation, right? Yes, but it was bad for the trade deficit. Or was it the other way around? Attack? Retreat?

Monetary Policy and the International Economy

In Chapter 12 we noted that linkages among the economies of the world complicate domestic fiscal policy. These linkages also extend to monetary policy.

Net Export Effect You saw in Chapter 12 that an expansionary U.S. fiscal policy (a budget deficit) increases the demand for money and boosts the domestic interest rate. The higher interest rate increases foreign financial investment in the United States, strengthening the demand for dollars in the foreign exchange market and boosting the international price of dollars. This dollar appreciation produces lower net exports and thus weakens the stimulus of the expansionary fiscal policy (review Figure 12-6d).

Will an easy money policy have a similar effect? The answer is no. As outlined in column 1, Table 15-4, an easy money or expansionary monetary policy does indeed produce a *net export effect*, but its direction is opposite that of an expansionary fiscal policy. An easy money policy in, say, the United States reduces the domestic interest rate. The lower interest rate discourages the inflow of financial capital to the United States. The demand for dollars in foreign exchange markets falls, causing the dollar to *depreciate* in value. It takes more dollars to buy, say, a Japanese yen or a French franc. All foreign goods become more expensive to U.S. residents, and U.S. goods become cheaper to foreigners. U.S. imports thus fall, and U.S. exports rise; so U.S. net exports increase. As a result, aggregate expenditures and equilibrium GDP expand in the United States.

Macroeconomic forces were closing in.

"Call out the Reserve!" he told the officer.

"Uh . . . we are the Reserve," the man answered.

The Fed as the Fall Guy Inflation isn't the only tough customer out there. The Fed must also withstand pressure from administration officials who are regularly described as "leaning heavily" on the Fed to ease up and relax. This always sounds vaguely threatening:

Alan Greenspan was walking down a deserted street late one night. Suddenly a couple of thugs wearing pin-stripes and wingtips cornered him in a dark alley.

"What do you want?" Greenspan asked.

"Just relax," said one.

"How can I relax?" asked Greenspan. "I'm in a dark alley talking to thugs."

"You know what we mean," said the other. "Ease up on the federal funds rate—or else."

"Or else what?" asked Greenspan.

"Don't make us spell it out. Let's just say

that if anything unfortunate happens to the gross [domestic] product, I'm holding you personally responsible."

"Yeah," added the other. "A recession could get real painful."

The Fed as Cosmic Force The Fed may be a cosmic force. After all, it does satisfy the three major criteria—power, mystery, and a New York office. Some observers even believe the Fed can control the stock market, either by action, symbolic action, anticipated action, or non-action. But saner heads realize this is ridiculous—the market has always been controlled by sunspots.

I wish we could get rid of all these romantic ideas about the Federal Reserve. If you want to talk about the Fed, keep it simple. Just say the Fed is worried about the money. This is something we all can relate to.

Source: Paul Hellman, "Greenspan and the Feds: Captains Courageous," *Wall Street Journal,* Jan. 31, 1991, p. 18. Reprinted with permission of *The Wall Street Journal* © 1990 Dow Jones & Company, Inc. All rights reserved.

Conclusion: Unlike an expansionary fiscal policy which reduces net exports, an expansionary monetary policy increases net exports. *Exchange-rate changes which occur in response to interest-rate changes strengthen domestic monetary policy.* This conclusion holds equally for a tight money policy, which we know increases the domestic interest rate. To see how this happens, follow through the analysis in column 2, Table 15-4.

Macro Stability and the Trade Balance Assume that, in addition to domestic macroeconomic stability, a widely held economic goal is that the United States should balance its exports and imports. That is, U.S. net exports should be zero. In simple terms, the United States wants to "pay its own way" in international trade by earning from its exports an amount of money sufficient to finance its imports.

Consider column 1 in Table 15-4 once again, but now suppose the United States initially has a very large balance-of-international-trade *deficit,* which means its imports substantially exceed its exports and so it is *not* paying its way in world trade. By following through the cause-effect chain in column 1, we find that an easy money policy lowers the international value of the dollar and thus U.S. exports increase and U.S. imports decline. This increase in net exports works to correct the assumed initial balance-of-trade deficit.

Conclusion: *The easy money policy which is appropriate for the alleviation of unemployment and sluggish growth is compatible with the goal of correcting a balance-of-trade deficit.* Similarly, if the initial problem was a U.S. trade surplus, a *tight* money policy would tend to resolve that surplus.

TABLE 15-4   **Monetary policy and the net export effect**

(1) Easy money policy	(2) Tight money policy
Problem: recession, slow growth ↓	*Problem:* inflation ↓
Easy money policy (lower interest rate) ↓	Tight money policy (higher interest rate) ↓
Decreased foreign demand for dollars ↓	Increased foreign demand for dollars ↓
Dollar depreciates ↓	Dollar appreciates ↓
Net exports increase (aggregate demand increases, strengthening the easy money policy)	Net exports decrease (aggregate demand decreases, strengthening the tight money policy)

Now consider column 2 in Table 15-4 and assume again that the United States has a large balance-of-trade deficit. In using a tight money policy to restrain inflation the Fed would cause net exports to decrease—U.S. exports would fall and imports would rise. This means a larger trade deficit.

Conclusion: *A tight money policy used to alleviate inflation conflicts with the goal of correcting a balance-of-trade deficit.* However, if the initial problem were a trade surplus, a tight money policy would help to resolve it.

Overall we find that an easy money policy alleviates a trade deficit and aggravates a trade surplus; a tight money policy alleviates a trade surplus and aggravates a trade deficit. The point is that certain combinations of circumstances create conflicts or trade-offs between the use of monetary policy to achieve domestic stability and the realization of a balance in the nation's international trade. **(Key Questions 6)**

THE "BIG PICTURE"

Figure 15-4 (Key Graph) on pages 326 and 327 brings together the analytical and policy aspects of macroeconomics discussed in this and the eight preceding chapters. This "big picture" shows how the many concepts and principles discussed relate to one another and how they constitute a coherent theory of the level of resource use in a market economy.

Study this diagram and you will see that the levels of output, employment, income, and prices all result from the interaction of aggregate supply and aggregate demand. In particular, note those items—shown in red—which constitute (or are strongly influenced by) public policy.

CHAPTER SUMMARY

1. Like fiscal policy, the goal of monetary policy is to assist the economy in achieving price stability, full employment, and economic growth.

2. In regard to monetary policy, the most important assets of the Federal Reserve Banks are securities and loans to commercial banks. The basic liabilities are the reserves of member banks, Treasury deposits, and Federal Reserve Notes.

3. The three instruments of monetary policy are **(a)** open-market operations, **(b)** the reserve ratio, and **(c)** the discount rate.

4. Monetary policy operates through a complex cause-effect chain: **(a)** Policy decisions affect commercial bank reserves; **(b)** changes in reserves affect the money supply; **(c)** changes in the money supply alter the interest rate;

(d) changes in the interest rate affect investment; **(e)** changes in investment affect aggregate demand; **(f)** changes in aggregate demand affect the equilibrium real GDP and the price level. Table 15-3 draws together all the basic notions relevant to the use of monetary policy.

5. The advantages of monetary policy include its flexibility and political acceptability. In the past two decades monetary policy has been used successfully both to reduce rapid inflation and to push the economy away from recession. Today, almost all economists view monetary policy as a significant stabilization tool.

6. Monetary policy has some limitations and potential problems: **(a)** Financial innovations and global considerations have made monetary policy more difficult to administer and its impact less certain. **(b)** Policy-instigated changes in the supply of money may be partially offset by changes in the velocity of money. **(c)** The impact of monetary policy will be lessened if the money demand curve is flat and the investment demand curve is steep. The investment demand curve may also shift, negating monetary policy. **(d)** Changes in interest rates resulting from monetary policy change the amount of interest income received by lenders, altering some people's spending in a way opposite to the intent of the monetary policy.

7. Recently, the Fed has communicated its changes in monetary policy via announcements concerning its targets for the Federal funds rate. When it deems it necessary, the Fed uses open-market operations to change this rate, which is the interest rate banks charge one another on overnight loans of excess reserves. Interest rates in general, including the prime interest rate, rise and fall with the Federal funds rate. The prime interest rate is the rate which banks charge to their most creditworthy loan customers.

8. The effect of an easy money policy on domestic GDP is strengthened by the increase in net exports which results from a lower domestic interest rate. Likewise, a tight money policy is strengthened by a decline in net exports. In some situations, there may be a tradeoff between the effect of monetary policy on the international value of a nation's currency (and thus on its trade balance) and the use of monetary policy to achieve domestic stability.

TERMS AND CONCEPTS

monetary policy
open-market operations

reserve ratio
discount rate

easy money policy
tight money policy

velocity of money
prime interest rate

STUDY QUESTIONS

1. Use commercial bank and Federal Reserve Bank balance sheets to demonstrate the impact of each of the following transactions on commercial bank reserves:
  a. Federal Reserve Banks purchase securities from private businesses and consumers.
  b. Commercial banks borrow from Federal Reserve Banks.
  c. The Fed reduces the reserve ratio.

2. KEY QUESTION   In the table below and on page 328 you will find simplified consolidated balance sheets for the commercial banking system and the 12 Federal Reserve Banks. Use columns 1 through 3 to indicate how the balance sheets would read after each of transactions **a** to **c** is completed. Do not cumulate your answers; that is, analyze each transaction separately, starting in each case from the figures provided. All accounts are in billions of dollars.
  a. A decline in the discount rate prompts commercial banks to borrow an additional $1 billion from the Federal Reserve Banks. Show the new balance-sheet figures in column 1 of each table.
  b. The Federal Reserve Banks sell $3 billion in securities to members of the public, who pay for the bonds with checks. Show the new balance-sheet figures in column 2 of each table.

Consolidated balance sheet: all commercial banks

	(1)	(2)	(3)
Assets:			
Reserves ....$ 33	_____	_____	_____
Securities 60	_____	_____	_____
Loans.................................. 60	_____	_____	_____
Liabilities and net worth:			
Demand deposits...................$150	_____	_____	_____
Loans from the Federal			
Reserve Banks................... 3	_____	_____	_____

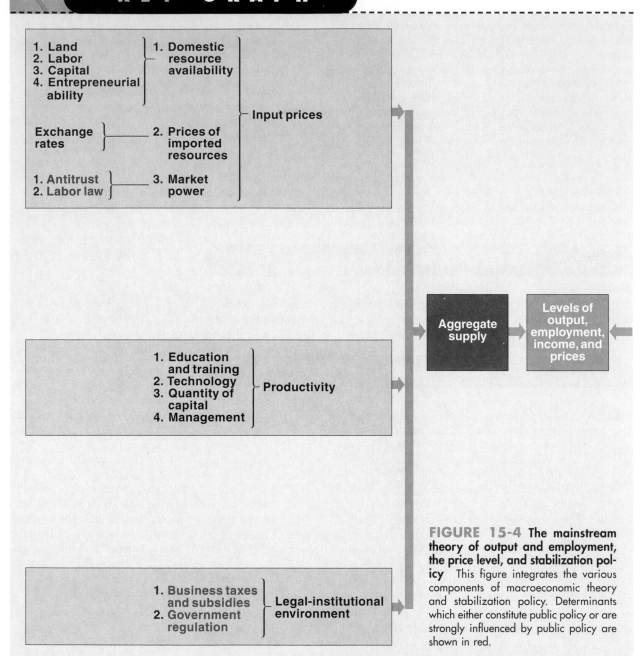

FIGURE 15-4 The mainstream theory of output and employment, the price level, and stabilization policy This figure integrates the various components of macroeconomic theory and stabilization policy. Determinants which either constitute public policy or are strongly influenced by public policy are shown in red.

QUICK QUIZ 15-4

1. All else equal, an increase in domestic resource availability will:
   a. increase input prices, reduce aggregate supply, and increase real output.
   b. raise labor productivity, reduce interest rates, and lower the international value of the dollar.
   c. increase net exports, increase investment, and reduce aggregate demand.
   d. reduce input prices, increase aggregate supply, and increase real output.

2. All else equal, an easy money policy during a recession will:
   a. lower the interest rate, increase investment, and reduce net exports.
   b. lower the interest rate, increase investment, and increase aggregate demand.
   c. increase the interest rate, increase investment, and reduce net exports.
   d. reduce productivity, aggregate supply, and real output.

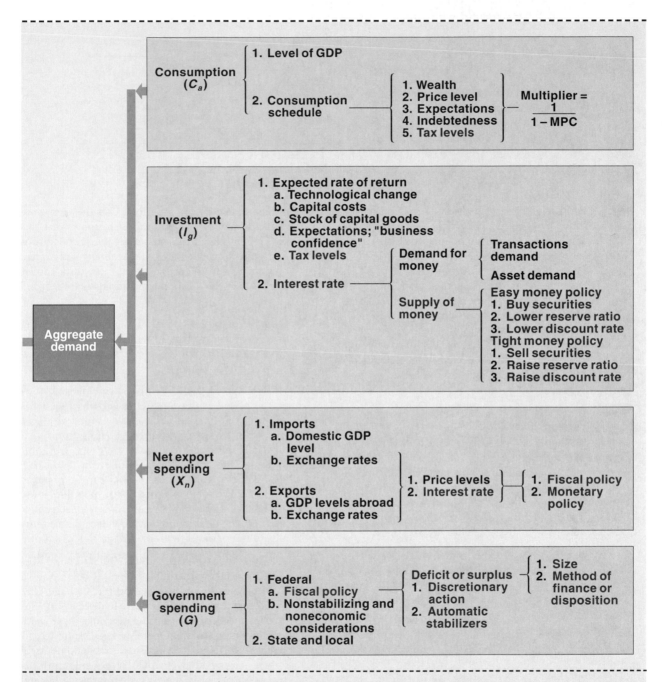

Consumption (Ca)
1. Level of GDP
2. Consumption schedule
   - 1. Wealth
   - 2. Price level
   - 3. Expectations
   - 4. Indebtedness
   - 5. Tax levels

Multiplier = $\dfrac{1}{1 - MPC}$

Investment (Ig)
1. Expected rate of return
   - a. Technological change
   - b. Capital costs
   - c. Stock of capital goods
   - d. Expectations; "business confidence"
   - e. Tax levels
2. Interest rate
   - Demand for money
     - Transactions demand
     - Asset demand
   - Supply of money
     - Easy money policy
       1. Buy securities
       2. Lower reserve ratio
       3. Lower discount rate
     - Tight money policy
       1. Sell securities
       2. Raise reserve ratio
       3. Raise discount rate

Aggregate demand

Net export spending (Xn)
1. Imports
   - a. Domestic GDP level
   - b. Exchange rates
2. Exports
   - a. GDP levels abroad
   - b. Exchange rates
   - 1. Price levels
   - 2. Interest rate
     - 1. Fiscal policy
     - 2. Monetary policy

Government spending (G)
1. Federal
   - a. Fiscal policy
   - b. Nonstabilizing and noneconomic considerations
2. State and local
   - Deficit or surplus
     1. Discretionary action
     2. Automatic stabilizers
   - 1. Size
   - 2. Method of finance or disposition

3. A personal income tax cut, combined with a reduction in corporate income and excise taxes, would:

a. increase consumption, investment, aggregate demand, and aggregate supply.

b. reduce productivity, raise input prices, and reduce aggregate supply.

c. increase government spending, reduce net exports, and increase aggregate demand.

d. increase the supply of money, reduce interest rates, increase investment, and expand real output.

4. An appreciation of the dollar would:

a. reduce the price of imported resources, lower input prices, and increase aggregate supply.

b. increase net exports and aggregate demand.

c. increase aggregate supply and aggregate demand.

d. reduce consumption, investment, net export spending, and government spending.

Answers: 1. d; 2. b; 3. a; 4. a

Consolidated balance sheet: the 12 Federal Reserve Banks

	(1)	(2)	(3)
Assets:			
Securities $60	_____	_____	_____
Loans to commercial			
banks................................ 3	_____	_____	_____
Liabilities and net worth:			
Reserves of commercial			
banks...............................$ 33	_____	_____	_____
Treasury deposits.................. 3	_____	_____	_____
Federal Reserve Notes 27	_____	_____	_____

c. The Federal Reserve Banks buy $2 billion of securities from commercial banks. Show the new balance-sheet figures in column 3 of each table.

d. Now review each of the above three transactions, asking yourself these three questions: (1) What change, if any, took place in the money supply as a direct and immediate result of each transaction? (2) What increase or decrease in the commercial banks' reserves took place in each transaction? (3) Assuming a reserve ratio of 20 percent, what change in the money-creating potential of the commercial banking system occurred as a result of each transaction?

3. KEY QUESTION Suppose you are a member of the Board of Governors of the Federal Reserve System. The economy is experiencing a sharp and prolonged inflationary trend. What changes in **(a)** the reserve ratio, **(b)** the discount rate, and **(c)** open-market operations would you recommend? Explain in each case how the change you advocate would affect commercial bank reserves, the money supply, interest rates, and aggregate demand.

4. KEY QUESTION What is the basic objective of monetary policy? State the cause-effect chain through which monetary policy is made effective. Using Figure 15-2 as a point of reference, discuss how **(a)** the shapes of the demand-for-money and investment demand curves and **(b)** the size of the MPC influence the effectiveness of monetary policy. How do feedback effects influence the effectiveness of monetary policy?

5. KEY QUESTION Distinguish between the Federal funds rate and the prime interest rate. In what way is the Federal funds rate a measure of the tightness or looseness of monetary policy? In 1994 the Fed used open-market operations to increase the Federal funds rate. What was the logic? What was the effect on the prime interest rate?

6. KEY QUESTION Suppose the Fed decides to engage in a tight money policy as a way to reduce demand-pull inflation. Use the aggregate demand–aggregate supply model to show what this policy is intended to accomplish in a closed economy. Now introduce the open economy and explain how changes in the international value of the dollar might affect the location of your aggregate demand curve.

7. (Last Word) How do each of the following metaphors apply to the Federal Reserve's role in the economy: Fed as a mechanic; Fed as a warrior; Fed as a fall guy?

8. WEB-BASED QUESTION **Principles of Monetary Policy** Each Federal Reserve District Bank has its own Web site. An index can be found at http://www.frbsf.org/system/otherdist/otherdist.html. Visit the San Francisco district bank http://www. frbsf.org/pubsindx.html to answer the following questions: How is the Fed structured to make monetary policy decisions? What are its goals? What tools does it use to implement its policies? How does monetary policy affect the U.S. economy? How does the Fed formulate strategies to reach its goals?

9. WEB-BASED QUESTION **The Federal Reserve Annual Report** The Federal Reserve Annual Report provides an extensive overview of the U.S. economy for the previous year. It discusses operations of the Board during the year; it also provides minutes of the Federal Open Market Committee, financial statements of the Board, developments in services provided by the Reserve Banks, priced-services financial statements, directories of Federal Reserve officials and advisory committees, statistical tables, and maps of the System's District and Branch boundaries. Visit the Reports to the Congress section at http://www.bog.frb.fed.us/ and retrieve the current annual report (in Adobe's PDF format only). Summarize the policy actions of the Board of Governors during the current period. In the Fed's opinion, how did the U.S. economy perform? What changes, if any, occurred on the Fed's balance sheet during this period?

4

Problems and Controversies in Macro-economics

CHAPTER SIXTEEN

Extending the Analysis of Aggregate Supply

Macroeconomic theory and stabilization policy as represented in Figure 15-4 has dominated the thinking of most economists in market-oriented industrial economies since the early 1960s. In the United States, Democratic and Republican administrations alike have accepted these precepts, at least as evidenced by policy actions. Presently, the stabilization policies of nearly all the major industrial nations can be understood through Figure 15-4.

But it would be misleading to suggest there is agreement on all aspects of macroeconomic theory and policy. In particular, there has been new, controversial thinking about aggregate supply in the short run and the long run. The result has been renewed debates on whether the economy is "self-correcting" and the desirability and effectiveness of fiscal and monetary policy.

This chapter deals with this new analysis of aggregate supply along with related topics. First, we extend the AD-AS model, distinguishing between short-run and long-run aggregate supply. Second, we apply this extended AD-AS model to demand-pull inflation, cost-push inflation, and recession, gleaning new insights on each. Next, we examine the relationships between inflation and unemployment and look at how expectations can affect the economy. Finally, we state and evaluate the tenets of so-called supply-side economics.

In Chapter 17 we use some of the ideas developed here to examine several issues and disputes about macroeconomic theory and policy. In Chapter 18 we discuss the expansion of long-run aggregate supply over time, that is, economic growth. Finally, in Chapter 19 the facts and issues relating to Federal budget deficits and the public debt are examined.

SHORT-RUN AND LONG-RUN AGGREGATE SUPPLY

Up to this point we have assumed that the aggregate supply curve is stable (does not move) when the aggregate demand curve shifts positions. This assumption greatly simplifies our analysis and is realistic for most circumstances. An increase in aggregate demand in the upsloping portion of the aggregate supply curve, for example, can be expected to increase both the price level and real output. Nevertheless, the story becomes more complicated when long periods are considered. For instance, once workers fully recognize that the price level has increased, and thus that their real wages (their nominal wages divided by the price level) have declined, they will demand and obtain higher nominal wages to restore their real wages. This increase in nominal wages, other things equal, will shift the aggregate supply curve leftward. That is, nominal wages are one of the factors which determine the location of the aggregate supply curve itself (review Figure 11-6).

To analyze longer time periods, then, we need to extend the analysis of aggregate supply to account for changes in nominal wages *which are in response to changes in the price level*. That is, we need to distinguish between short-run and long-run aggregate supply.

Definitions: Short Run and Long Run

Exactly what are the *short run* and the *long run* as they specifically relate to macroeconomics?

The Short Run For macroeconomists the short run is *a period in which nominal wages (and other input prices) remain fixed as the price level changes*. There are at least two reasons why nominal wages may remain constant for a time even though the price level has changed:

1. Workers may not immediately be aware of the extent to which inflation (or deflation) has changed their real wages, and thus they may not adjust their labor supply decisions and wage demands accordingly.

2. Many employees are hired under fixed-wage contracts. Unionized employees, for example, receive nominal wages spelled out in their collective bargaining agreements. Also, most managers and many professionals receive set salaries established in annual contracts. In these circumstances, nominal wages remain constant for the lives of the contracts, regardless of changes in the price level. The upshot of these two factors is that price-level changes do not immediately give rise to changes in nominal wages. Instead, considerable amounts of time usually pass before these adjustments occur.

The Long Run Once sufficient time has elapsed for contracts to expire and nominal wage adjustments to occur, the economy enters the long run—*a period in which nominal wages are fully responsive to changes in the price level*. With sufficient time, workers gain full information about price-level changes and thus determine how these changes have affected their real wages. For example, workers become aware that a price-level *increase* has reduced their real wages. If your *nominal* wage was $10 an hour when the price index was 100 (or, in decimals, 1.0), your *real* wage was also $10 (= $10 of nominal wage divided by 1.0). But when the price level has increased to, say, 120, your $10 real wage has declined to $8.33 (= $10/1.2). In such circumstances, you and other workers will demand and probably obtain increases in your nominal wages such that the purchasing power from an hour of work is restored. In our example, your nominal wage likely will rise from $10 to $12, returning your real wage to $10 (= $12/1.2).

Short-Run Aggregate Supply

With these definitions of short run and long run clearly in mind, we can extend Chapter 11's discussion of aggregate supply.

First, consider the **short-run aggregate supply curve** AS_1 in Figure 16-1a. (Our focus now is on the intermediate range of the AS curve of Chapter 11.) Curve AS_1 is constructed on three assumptions: (1) the initial price level is P_1, (2) nominal wages have been established on the *expectation that this specific price level will persist*, and (3) the price level is flexible both upward and downward. Observe from point a_1 that at price level P_1 the economy is operating at its full-employment output Q_f. This output is the real production forthcoming when the economy is operating at its natural rate of unemployment.

Now let's determine the short-run consequences of changes in the price level by first examining an *increase* in the price level from P_1 to P_2 in Figure 16-1a. The higher product prices associated with P_2 increase revenues to firms, and because the nominal wages they are paying are fixed, their profits rise. In response, firms collectively increase their output from Q_f to Q_2; the economy moves from a_1 to a_2 on curve AS_1. Observe that at Q_2 the economy is operating beyond its full-employment output. This is made possible by extending the work-hours of part-time and full-time workers, enticing new workers such as homemakers and retirees into the labor force, and hiring and training the structurally unemployed. Thus, the nation's unemployment rate declines below its natural rate.

How will producers respond when there is a *decrease* in the price level, say, from P_1 to P_3 in Figure

FIGURE 16-1 Short-run and long-run aggregate supply (a) In the short run, nominal wages are assumed to be fixed and based on price level P_1 and the expectation that it will continue. An increase in the price level from P_1 to P_2 increases profits and output, moving the economy from a_1 to a_2; a decrease in the price level from P_1 to P_3 reduces profits and real output, moving the economy from a_1 to a_3. The short-run aggregate supply curve therefore slopes upward. (b) In the long run, a price-level rise increases nominal wages and thus shifts the short-run aggregate supply curve leftward. Conversely, a decrease in the price level reduces nominal wages and shifts the short-run aggregate supply curve rightward. After such adjustments, the economy reaches equilibrium at points such as b_1 and c_1. Thus, the long-run aggregate supply curve is vertical.

16-1a? Firms then discover their revenues and profits have diminished or disappeared. After all, the prices they receive for their products have dropped while the nominal wages they pay workers have not. Under these circumstances, firms reduce their employment and production, and, as shown by the move from a_1 to a_3, real output falls to Q_3. The decline in real output is accompanied by increased unemployment; at output Q_3 the unemployment rate is greater than the natural rate of unemployment associated with output Q_f.

Long-Run Aggregate Supply

By definition, nominal wages in the long run are fully responsive to changes in the price level. What are the implications of this responsiveness for aggregate supply?

For the answer, look at Figure 16-1b, again assuming the economy is initially at point a_1 (P_1 and Q_f). Our previous discussion indicated that an *increase* in the price level from P_1 to P_2 will move the economy from point a_1 to a_2 along the short-run aggregate supply curve AS_1. In the long run, however, workers discover their real wages have declined *because* of

this increase in the price level. They demand and presumably obtain their previous level of real wages via hikes in their nominal wages. The short-run supply curve then shifts leftward from AS_1 to AS_2, which now reflects the higher price level P_2 *and the new expectation that* P_2, *not* P_1, *will continue.* The leftward shift in the short-run aggregate supply curve to AS_2 moves the economy from a_2 to b_1. Real output returns to its full-employment level Q_f, and the unemployment rate returns to its natural rate.

And what is the result of a decrease in the price level? *Assuming downward wage flexibility*, a decline in the price level from P_1 to P_3 in Figure 16-1b works in the opposite way from a price-level increase. The economy initially moves from point a_1 to a_3 on AS_1. Profits are squeezed or eliminated because prices have fallen and nominal wages have not. But this movement along AS_1 is the short-run response. With enough time, the lower price level P_3—which has *increased* the real wage—results in a decline in nominal wages such that the original real wage is restored. Sufficiently lower nominal wages shift the short-run aggregate supply curve rightward from AS_1 to AS_3. Real output returns to its full-employment level of Q_f at point c_1.

By tracing a line between the long-run equilibrium points b_1, a_1, and c_1, we obtain a **long-run aggregate supply curve.** Observe that it is vertical at the full-employment level of real GDP. After long-run adjustments in nominal wages, real output is Q_f, regardless of the specific price level. **(Key Question 3)**

Equilibrium in the Extended AD-AS Model

Figure 16-2 shows the long-run equilibrium in the AD-AS model, now extended to include the distinction between short-run and long-run aggregate supply. (Hereafter, we will refer to this model as the *extended AD-AS model*, with "extended" referring to inclusion of both the short-run and the long-run aggregate supply curves.) Equilibrium in the figure occurs at point *a*, where the nation's aggregate demand curve AD_1 intersects the vertical long-run aggregate supply curve AS_{LR}. Observe at point *a* that the aggregate demand curve also intersects the short-run aggregate supply curve AS_1. In long-run equilibrium, the economy's price level and real output are P_1 and Q_f.

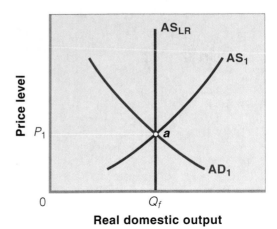

FIGURE 16-2 Equilibrium in the extended AD-AS model The equilibrium price level P_1 and level of real output Q_f occur at the intersection of the aggregate demand curve AD_1, the long-run aggregate supply curve AS_{LR}, and the short-run aggregate supply curve AS_1.

QUICK REVIEW 16-1

■ The short-run aggregate supply curve has a positive slope because nominal wages remain constant as the price level changes.

■ The long-run aggregate supply curve is vertical because nominal wages eventually change by the same amount as changes in the price level.

■ The equilibrium GDP and price level occur at the intersection of the aggregate demand curve, the long-run aggregate supply curve, and the short-run aggregate supply curve.

APPLYING THE EXTENDED AD-AS MODEL

The extended AD-AS model helps us better understand the economy and the controversies occasionally swirling around macroeconomics. We will defer discussion of most of these controversies until the next chapter. For now, our intention is simply to apply the extended AD-AS model to three situations: demand-pull inflation, cost-push inflation, and recession.

Demand-Pull Inflation in the Extended AD-AS Model

Recall that *demand-pull inflation* occurs when an increase in aggregate demand pulls up the price level. We previously depicted this inflation by shifting an aggregate demand curve rightward along a stable aggregate supply curve (see Figure 11-8b and 11-8c).

In our more complex version of aggregate supply, however, an increase in the price level will eventually produce an increase in nominal wages and thus a leftward shift of the short-run aggregate supply curve. This is shown in Figure 16-3, where we initially suppose the price level is P_1 at the intersection of aggregate demand curve AD_1, short-run supply curve AS_1, and long-run aggregate supply curve AS_{LR}. Observe that at point *a* the economy is achieving its full-employment real output Q_f.

Now consider the effects of an increase in aggregate demand as represented by the rightward shift from AD_1 to AD_2. This shift can result from any one of a number of factors, including an increase in investment spending and a rise in net exports. Whatever its cause, the increase in aggregate demand boosts the price level from P_1 to P_2 and expands real output from Q_f to Q_2 at point *b*.

So far, none of this is new to you. But now the distinction between short-run and long-run aggregate

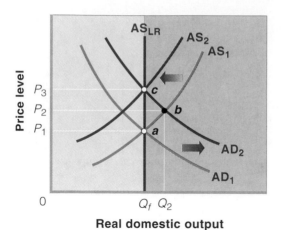

FIGURE 16-3 Demand-pull inflation in the extended AD-AS model An increase in aggregate demand from AD₁ to AD₂ drives up the price level and increases real output in the short run. But in the long run, nominal wages rise and the short-run aggregate supply curve shifts leftward, as from AS₁ to AS₂. Real output then returns to its prior level, and the price level rises even more. In this scenario, the economy moves from *a* to *b* and then eventually to *c*.

----

supply becomes important. Once workers have realized that their real wages have declined, and when their existing contracts have expired, nominal wages will rise. As they do, the short-run aggregate supply curve will ultimately shift leftward such that it intersects long-run aggregate supply at point *c*.[1] There, the economy has reestablished long-run equilibrium, with the price level and real output now P_3 and Q_f, respectively. Only at point *c* does the new aggregate demand curve AD₂ intersect both the short-run aggregate supply curve AS₂ and the long-run aggregate supply curve AS$_{LR}$.

In the short run, demand-pull inflation drives up the price level and increases real output; in the long run, only the price level rises. In the long run, the initial increase in aggregate demand has moved the economy *along* its vertical aggregate supply curve AS$_{LR}$.

----

[1]We say "ultimately" because the initial leftward shift in short-run aggregate supply will intersect the long-run aggregate supply curve AS$_{LR}$ at price level P_2 (review Figure 16-1b). But the intersection of AD₂ and this new short-run aggregate supply curve (not shown) will produce a price level above P_2. (You may want to pencil this in to make sure that you understand this point.) Again nominal wages will rise, shifting the short-run aggregate supply curve farther leftward. The process will continue until the economy moves to point *c*, where the short-run aggregate supply curve is AS₂, the price level is P_3, and real output is Q_f.

For a while, an economy can operate beyond its full-employment level of output. But the demand-pull inflation eventually causes adjustments of nominal wages which move the economy back to its full-employment output Q_f.

Cost-Push Inflation in the Extended AD-AS Model

Cost-push inflation arises from factors which increase the cost of production at each price level—that is, factors which shift the aggregate supply curve leftward—and therefore increase the price level. But in our previous analysis (Figure 11-11) we considered only short-run aggregate supply. We now want to examine cost-push inflation in its long-run context.

Analysis Look at Figure 16-4, in which we again assume the economy is initially operating at price level P_1 and output level Q_f (point *a*). Suppose that international oil producers get together and boost the price of oil by, say, 50 percent. What is the effect on the short-run aggregate supply curve of a major oil-consuming economy? The answer is that the hike in the oil price increases the per-unit production cost of producing and transporting goods and services. This

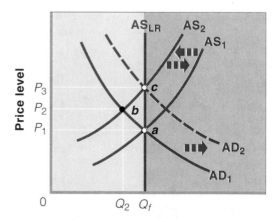

FIGURE 16-4 Cost-push inflation in the extended AD-AS model Cost-push inflation occurs when the short-run aggregate supply curve shifts leftward, as from AS₁ to AS₂. If government counters the decline in real output by increasing aggregate demand to the broken line, the price level rises even more. That is, the economy moves in steps from *a* to *b* to *c*. In contrast, if government allows a recession to occur, nominal wages eventually fall and the aggregate supply curve shifts back rightward to its original location. The economy moves from *a* to *b* and then eventually back to *a*.

----

shifts the short-run aggregate supply curve to the left, as from AS_1 to AS_2. The price level rises from P_1 to P_2, as seen by comparing points *a* and *b*. In this case, the increase in the price of a key resource—namely, oil—shifts the short-run aggregate supply curve to the left. This shift is not a *response* to a price-level increase, as it was in our previous discussions of demand-pull inflation; it is the initiating *cause* of the price-level increase.

Policy Dilemma   Cost-push inflation creates a dilemma for policymakers. Without expansionary stabilization policy, aggregate demand in Figure 16-4 remains at AD_1—the curve does not shift—and real output declines from Q_f to Q_2. Government can counter this recession and the attendant rise in unemployment by using fiscal policy and monetary policy to increase aggregate demand to AD_2. But there is a potential policy trap here: An increase in aggregate demand to AD_2 will further increase inflation by increasing the price level from P_2 to P_3 (a move from point *b* to *c*).

Also, the P_2 to P_3 increase in the price level is not likely to be the end of the story because wage earners eventually respond to their decline in real wages by seeking and presumably receiving increases in nominal wages. The higher nominal wages cause another increase in per-unit production costs, which in turn shifts the short-run aggregate supply curve to a position to the left of AS_2. This (not shown) leftward shift of the aggregate supply curve is in *response* to the higher price level P_3, which was caused by the policy-created rightward shift of aggregate demand to AD_2. The new leftward shift of short-run aggregate supply will regenerate recession. In brief, government will have to increase aggregate demand once again to restore the Q_f level of real output. But if it does so, the scenario may simply repeat itself.

Suppose government recognizes this policy trap and decides *not* to increase aggregate demand from AD_1 to AD_2 (so you can now disregard the dashed AD_2 curve). Instead, it implicitly decides to allow a cost-push-created recession to run its course. How will that happen? Widespread layoffs, plant shutdowns, and business failures eventually occur. At some point the demands for oil, labor, and other inputs fall such that oil prices and nominal wages decline. When that happens, the initial leftward shift of the short-run aggregate supply curve is undone. In time the recession will shift the short-run aggregate supply curve rightward from AS_2 to AS_1. The price level will re-

turn to P_1, and the full-employment level of output will be restored at Q_f (point *a* on the long-run aggregate supply curve AS_{LR}).

This analysis yields two generalizations:

1. If government attempts to maintain full employment when there is cost-push inflation, an inflationary spiral may occur.

2. If government takes a hands-off approach to cost-push inflation, a recession will occur. Although the recession eventually may undo the initial rise in per-unit production costs, the economy in the meantime will experience high unemployment and a loss of real output.

Recession and the Extended AD-AS Model

By far the most controversial application of the extended AD-AS model is to recession (or depression). This controversy will be looked at in some detail in Chapter 17; here we simply want to present the model and identify the key point of contention.

Suppose in Figure 16-5 that aggregate demand initially is AD_1 and that short-run and long-run aggregate supply curves are AS_1 and AS_{LR}, respectively. Therefore, as shown by point *a*, the price level is P_1

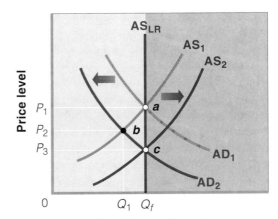

FIGURE 16-5   Recession in the extended AD-AS model
A recession occurs when aggregate demand shifts leftward, as from AD_1 to AD_2. If prices and wages are downwardly flexible, the price level falls from P_1 to P_2. This decline in the price level reduces nominal wages, which in turn eventually shift the aggregate supply curve from AS_1 to AS_2. The price level declines to P_3, and output increases back to Q_f. The economy moves from *a* to *b* and then eventually to *c*.

and output is Q_f. Now suppose that investment spending dramatically declines, reducing aggregate demand to AD_2. Real output declines from Q_f to Q_1, meaning a recession has occurred. But if we make the controversial assumption that prices and wages are flexible downward, the price level falls from P_1 to P_2. This lower price level increases *real* wages for people still working since each dollar of nominal wage has greater purchasing power. Eventually, nominal wages themselves fall to restore the previous real wage; when this happens, the short-run aggregate supply curve shifts rightward from AS_1 to AS_2. The recession ends—without expansionary fiscal or monetary policy—since real output expands from Q_1 (point *b*) back to Q_f (point *c*). The economy is again located on its long-run aggregate supply curve AS_{LR}, but now at lower price level P_3.

There is much disagreement about this theoretical scenario. The key point of dispute is how long it would take in the real world for the necessary price and wage adjustments to occur to achieve the indicated outcome. For now, suffice it to say that most economists believe that *if* such adjustments are forthcoming, they will occur only after the economy has experienced a long-lasting recession with its accompanying high unemployment and great loss of output. **(Key Question 4)**

QUICK REVIEW 16-2

■ In the short run, demand-pull inflation increases both the price level and real output; in the long run, nominal wages rise, the short-run aggregate supply curve shifts to the left, and only the price level increases.

■ Cost-push inflation creates a policy dilemma for government: If it engages in an expansionary policy to increase output, an inflationary spiral may occur; if it does nothing, a recession will occur.

■ In the short run, a decline in aggregate demand reduces real output (creates a recession); in the long run, prices and nominal wages presumably fall, the short-run aggregate supply curve shifts to the right, and real output returns to its full-employment level.

THE PHILLIPS CURVE

Cost-push inflation and the macroeconomic distinction between the short run and the long run shed light on a relationship called the **Phillips Curve,**

named after A. W. Phillips, who developed the idea in Great Britain.

The Basic Idea

To convey the concept of the Phillips Curve, let's look at the short-run aggregate supply curve in Figure 16-6 and perform a simple mental experiment. Suppose that in a specific period aggregate demand expands from AD_0 to AD_2. This shift could result from a change in any one of the determinants of aggregate demand. Businesses may decide to buy more investment goods, or government may decide to increase its expenditures. Whatever the cause of the increase in aggregate demand, in the short run the price level rises from P_0 to P_2 and real output expands from Q_0 to Q_2. We know that this increase in real output is accompanied by a decrease in the unemployment rate.

Now let's compare what would have happened if the increase in aggregate demand had been larger, say, from AD_0 to AD_3. The new equilibrium tells us that the amount of inflation and the growth of real output would both have been greater (and that the unemployment rate would have been lower). Similarly, suppose aggregate demand in our specific year had increased only modestly, from AD_0 to AD_1. Compared with our shift from AD_0 to AD_2, the amount of infla-

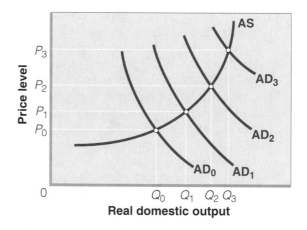

FIGURE 16-6 The effect of changes in aggregate demand on real output and the price level Comparing the effects of various possible increases in aggregate demand yields the conclusion that the larger the increase in aggregate demand, the higher the rate of inflation and the greater the increase in real output. Because real output and the unemployment rate are inversely related, we can generalize that, given short-run aggregate supply, high rates of inflation should be accompanied by low rates of unemployment.

----

tion and the growth of real output would have been smaller (and the unemployment rate higher).

The generalization from this mental experiment is this: Assuming a constant short-run aggregate supply curve, high rates of inflation are accompanied by low rates of unemployment, and low rates of inflation are accompanied by high rates of unemployment. Figure 16-7a generalizes how the expected relationship should look.

Do the facts fit the theory? Empirical work by economists in the late 1950s and 1960s verified this inverse relationship for various countries, including Great Britain and the United States. As we have noted, it came to be known as the Phillips Curve. Figure 16-7b shows the relationship between the unemployment rate and the rate of inflation in the United States for 1961–1969.

Tradeoffs

On the basis of the kind of evidence shown in Figure 16-7b, economists came to believe that a stable, predictable tradeoff existed between unemployment and inflation. Moreover, national economic policy was built on this supposed tradeoff. According to this thinking, it was impossible to achieve "full employment without inflation": Manipulation of aggregate demand through fiscal and monetary measures would simply move the economy along the Phillips Curve. An expansionary fiscal and monetary policy which boosts aggregate demand and lowers the unemployment rate would simultaneously cause a higher rate of inflation. A restrictive fiscal and monetary policy could be used to reduce the rate of inflation, but only at the cost of a higher unemployment rate and more forgone production. Society had to choose between incompatible goals of price stability and full employment; it had to decide where to *locate* on its Phillips Curve.

Stagflation: A Shifting Phillips Curve?

The stable Phillips Curve of the 1960s gave way to great instability of the curve in the 1970s and 1980s. Events during those years were clearly at odds with the notion of a stable inflation-unemployment tradeoff. Figure 16-8 enlarges Figure 16-7b by adding data for 1970 through 1997. The obvious inverse relationship of 1961–1969 has now become obscure and highly questionable.

Note in Figure 16-8 that in many years of the 1970s the economy experienced increasing inflation *and* rising unemployment—in a word, **stagflation**—a

(a) The concept

(b) Data for the 1960s

FIGURE 16-7 The Phillips Curve: concept and empirical data   (a) The Phillips Curve purports to show a stable relationship between the rate of inflation and the unemployment rate. Because this relationship is inverse, there is presumably a tradeoff between unemployment and inflation. (b) Data points for the 1960s seemed to confirm the Phillips Curve concept. (*Note:* Inflation rates are on a December-to-December basis, and unemployment rates are for all workers, including members of the armed forces.)

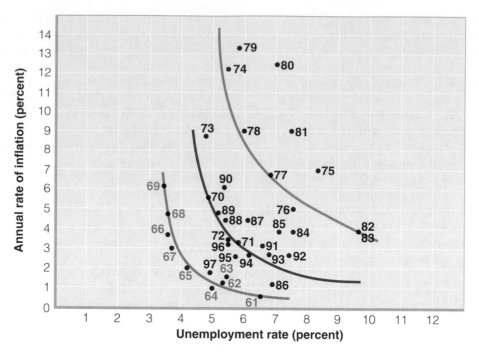

FIGURE 16-8 Inflation rates and unemployment rates, 1961–1997 Data points for 1961 to 1997 suggest no clear relationship between unemployment rates and rates of inflation. This raises questions as to the stability or existence of the Phillips Curve. Some economists think the curve shifted to the right in the 1970s and early 1980s, as shown, and then collapsed back inward during the later 1980s. (*Note:* Inflation rates are on a December-to-December basis and unemployment rates are for all workers, including members of the armed forces.)

----

term combining the words "stagnation" and "inflation." Trace, for example, the data points for 1972 to 1974 and 1977 to 1980. At best, the data in the figure suggest the Phillips Curve shifted to less desirable positions where each level of unemployment is accompanied by more inflation or where each level of inflation is accompanied by more unemployment. The downsloping curves above and to the right of the original Phillips Curve suggest such rightward shifts. At worst, the data imply *no* dependable tradeoff between unemployment and inflation.

Adverse Aggregate Supply Shocks

What caused the stagflation of the 1970s and early 1980s? One answer is that a series of adverse **aggregate supply shocks** occurred. Such shocks are rapid and significant increases in resource costs, which jolt an economy's short-run aggregate supply curve leftward. The most significant of these supply shocks was a quadrupling of oil prices by the Organization of

Petroleum Exporting Countries (OPEC). The cost of producing and distributing virtually every product and service rose rapidly. (Other factors working to increase U.S. costs during this period included agricultural shortfalls, a greatly depreciated dollar, catch-up of wages held down by earlier wage-price controls, and declining productivity.)

Leftward shifts of the short-run aggregate supply curve make a difference. Remember that we derived the inverse relationship between the rate of inflation and the unemployment rate shown in Figure 16-7a by shifting the aggregate demand curve along a *stable* short-run aggregate supply curve in Figure 16-6. But review the cost-push inflation model shown in Figure 16-4. There, a leftward shift of the short-run aggregate supply curve causes the price level to rise and the level of output to fall (unemployment to rise). This, say most economists, is what happened in two periods in the 1970s. The U.S. unemployment rate shot up from 4.8 percent in 1973 to 8.3 percent in 1975, contributing to a $42 billion decline in real GDP. In the same period, the U.S. price level rose by 21 percent. The stagflation scenario recurred in 1978, when OPEC increased oil prices by more than 100 percent. The U.S. price level increased by 26 percent over the 1978–1980 period, while unemployment increased from 6.0 to 7.5 percent.

The "Great Stagflation" of the 1970s made it clear that the Phillips Curve did not represent a stable inflation-unemployment relationship. Declines in short-run aggregate supply were at work, which explain those occasions when the inflation rate and the unemployment rate increased simultaneously. To most economists, the experience of the 1970s and early 1980s suggests that the Phillips Curve was shifting to the right and confronting the economy with higher rates of inflation and unemployment.

Stagflation's Demise

Another look at Figure 16-8 reveals a generally inward movement of the inflation-unemployment points between 1982 and 1989. By 1989 the lingering effects of the early period had subsided. One precursor to this favorable trend was the deep recession of 1981 to 1982, largely caused by a tight money policy aimed at reducing double-digit inflation. The recession upped the unemployment rate to 9.5 percent in 1982. With so many workers unemployed, those who were working accepted smaller increases in their nominal wages—or in some cases wage reductions—to preserve their jobs. Firms, in turn, restrained their price increases to try to retain their relative shares of a greatly diminished market.

Other factors were also at work. Foreign competition throughout this period held down wage and price hikes in several basic industries such as automobile and steel. Deregulation of the airline and trucking industries also resulted in wage reductions or so-called wage givebacks. A significant decline in OPEC's monopoly power produced a stunning fall in the price of oil and its derivative products, such as gasoline.

All these factors combined to reduce per-unit production costs and to shift the short-run aggregate supply curve rightward (as from AS_2 to AS_1 in Figure 16-4). Employment and output expanded and the unemployment rate fell from 9.5 percent in 1983 to 5.2 percent in 1989. Figure 16-8 reveals that the inflation-unemployment points for recent years are closer to the points associated with the Phillips Curve of the 1960s than to the points in the late 1970s and early 1980s. The points for 1996 and 1997, in fact, are

very close to points on the 1960s curve. (The low U.S. level of the so-called *misery index*, shown in Global Perspective 16-1, is also relevant to this later period.)

NATURAL-RATE HYPOTHESIS

The standard explanation for the scattering of inflation rate–unemployment points to the right of the 1960s Phillips Curve is that a series of supply shocks shifted the short-run aggregate supply curve leftward, moving the Phillips Curve rightward and upward as in Figure 16-8. The inward movement of inflation rate–unemployment points in the 1980s was caused by rightward shifts of short-run aggregate supply curves. In this view, there is still a tradeoff between

GLOBAL PERSPECTIVE 16-1

The misery index, selected nations, 1987–1997

The so-called misery index adds together a nation's unemployment rate and its inflation rate to get a measure of national economic discomfort. For example, a nation with a 5 percent rate of unemployment and 5 percent inflation rate would have a misery index number of 10, as would a nation with an 8 percent unemployment rate and 2 percent inflation.

Source: *Economic Report of the President, 1998.*

the inflation rate and the unemployment rate, but changes in short-run aggregate supply may alter the menu of inflation and unemployment choices—that is, shift the Phillips Curve itself—during abnormal periods.

A second explanation of simultaneously higher rates of unemployment and inflation, the **natural-rate hypothesis,** questions the very existence of an inverse relationship between the rate of inflation and the rate of unemployment. This view is that the economy is generally stable at its natural rate of unemployment (or full-employment rate of output). We know from Chapter 8 that the natural rate of unemployment is the rate of unemployment existing when cyclical unemployment is zero; it is the full-employment rate of unemployment.

According to the natural-rate hypothesis, the incorrect assumption of a stable Phillips Curve resulted in misguided attempts by government to push the unemployment rate below the economy's natural rate. The end result was accelerating inflation. The natural-rate hypothesis has its empirical roots in Figure 16-8, where you can argue that a vertical line located at a presumed 6 percent natural rate of unemployment for the full period represents the inflation-unemployment "relationship" better than the traditional downsloping Phillips Curve. In the natural-rate hypothesis, any rate of inflation is compatible with the economy's natural rate of unemployment.

There are two variations of this natural-rate perspective: the adaptive expectations theory and the rational expectations theory.

Adaptive Expectations Theory

The **adaptive expectations theory** assumes people form their expectations of future inflation on the basis of previous and present rates of inflation and only gradually change their expectations as experience unfolds.

In this theory, there is a short-run tradeoff between inflation and unemployment but not a long-run tradeoff. Any attempt to reduce the unemployment rate below the natural rate sets in motion forces which destabilize the Phillips Curve and shift it rightward. Thus, the adaptive expectations view distinguishes between a "short-run" and "long-run" Phillips Curve.

Short-Run Phillips Curve Consider Phillips Curve PC_1 in Figure 16-9. Suppose the economy initially is

FIGURE 16-9 The adaptive expectations theory Expansionary monetary policy and fiscal policy may temporarily boost profits, output, and employment (as from a_1 to b_1). But nominal wages will soon rise, reducing profits and thereby negating the short-run stimulus to production and employment (the economy moves from b_1 to a_2). Consequently, there is no tradeoff between the rates of inflation and unemployment in the long run; that is, the long-run Phillips Curve is vertical.

experiencing a 3 percent rate of inflation and a 6 percent natural rate of unemployment. In the adaptive expectations theory, such short-term curves as PC_1, PC_2, and PC_3 (drawn as straight lines for simplicity) exist because the actual rate of inflation is not always the same as the expected rate.

Establishing an additional point on Phillips Curve PC_1 will clarify this for you. We begin at a_1, where we assume nominal wages are set on the assumption that the 3 percent rate of inflation will continue. But suppose government mistakenly judges the full-employment unemployment rate to be 4 percent instead of 6 percent. This misjudgment might occur because the economy achieved a 4 percent rate of unemployment in some earlier, inflationary period. To achieve the targeted 4 percent rate of unemployment, government undertakes expansionary fiscal and monetary policies.

The increase in aggregate demand which results causes the rate of inflation to rise to 6 percent. With a specific level of nominal wages set on the expectation that the 3 percent rate of inflation will continue, the higher product prices raise business profits. Firms respond to these expanded profits by hiring more workers and increasing output. In the short run, the economy moves to b_1, which, in contrast to a_1, involves a lower rate of unemployment (4 percent) and higher rate of inflation (6 percent). The movement from a_1 to b_1 is consistent both with an upsloping aggregate supply curve and with our previous interpretation of the Phillips Curve. Presumably, the economy has accepted some additional inflation as the "cost" of achieving a reduced level of unemployment. But the natural-rate theory interprets the movement from a_1 to b_1 differently. In this view, it is simply a manifestation of the following principle: *When the actual rate of inflation is higher than expected, profits temporarily rise and the unemployment rate temporarily falls.*

Long-Run Vertical Phillips Curve   Point b_1 is not a stable equilibrium position in this theory. Workers will recognize their nominal wages have not increased as fast as inflation and will therefore obtain nominal wage increases to restore their lost purchasing power. But as nominal wages rise to restore the level of real wages which existed at a_1, business profits will fall to their earlier level. The reduction in profits means the original motivation to employ more workers and increase output has disappeared.

Unemployment then returns to its natural level at point a_2. Note, however, that the economy now faces a higher actual *and* expected rate of inflation—6 percent rather than 3 percent. The higher level of aggregate demand that originally moved the economy from a_1 to b_1 still exists, so the inflation it created still persists.

In view of the higher 6 percent expected rate of inflation, the short-run Phillips Curve shifts upward from PC_1 to PC_2 in Figure 16-9. An "along-the-Phillips-Curve" kind of movement from a_1 to b_1 on PC_1 is merely a short-run or transient occurrence. In the long run, after nominal wages catch up with price-level increases, unemployment returns to the natural rate at a_2, and there is a new short-run Phillips Curve PC_2 at the higher expected rate of inflation.

The process may now be repeated. Government may reason that certain extraneous events like oil price increases have frustrated its expansionary policies, and it will try again. Fiscal policy and monetary policy are then used to increase aggregate demand, and the scenario repeats. Prices rise momentarily ahead of nominal wages, profits expand, and employment and output increase (as implied by the move from a_2 to b_2). But, in time, nominal wages increase so as to restore real wages. Profits then fall to their original level, pushing employment back to the normal rate at a_3. Government's "reward" for forcing the actual rate of unemployment below the natural rate is the perverse one of a still higher (9 percent) rate of inflation.

If we conceive of a_1b_1, a_2b_2, and a_3b_3 as a series of short-run Phillips Curves, the adaptive expectations theory says that government attempts to move the economy along the short-run Phillips curve (a_1 to b_1 on PC_1) *cause* the curve to shift to a less favorable position (PC_2, then PC_3, and so on). A stable Phillips Curve with the dependable series of unemployment rate–inflation rate tradeoffs does not exist in the long run.

The vertical line through a_1, a_2, and a_3 shows the *long-run relationship* between unemployment and inflation. Any rate of inflation is consistent with the 6 percent natural rate of unemployment. So society ought to choose a low rate of inflation rather than a high one.

Disinflation   We can also employ the adaptive expectations theory to explain **disinflation**—reductions in the rate of inflation. Suppose that in Figure 16-9 the economy is at a_3, where the inflation rate is 9 percent. Next assume that a decline in aggregate demand such as that occurring in the 1981–1982 recession reduces inflation below the 9 percent expected rate, say, to 6 percent. Business profits fall because product prices are rising less rapidly than wages. The nominal wage increases, remember, were set on the assumption that the 9 percent rate of inflation would continue. In response to the profit decline, firms reduce their employment and consequently the unemployment rate rises. The economy temporarily slides downward from point a_3 to c_3 along the short-run Phillips Curve PC_3. In the natural-rate theory, *when the actual rate of inflation is lower than the expected rate, profits temporarily fall and the unemployment rate temporarily rises.*

Firms and workers eventually adjust their expectations to the new 6 percent rate of inflation, and thus newly negotiated wage increases decline. Profits are restored, employment rises, and the unemployment rate returns to its natural rate of 6 percent at a_2. Because the expected rate of inflation is now 6 percent, the short-run Phillips Curve PC_3 shifts leftward to PC_2.

If aggregate demand falls farther, the scenario will continue. Inflation declines from 6 percent to, say, 3 percent, moving the economy from a_2 to c_2 along PC_2. The lower-than-expected rate of inflation (lower prices) squeezes profits and reduces employment. But, in the long run, firms respond to the lower profits by reducing their nominal wage increases. Profits are restored and unemployment returns to its natural rate at a_1 as the short-run Phillips Curve moves from PC_2 to PC_1. Once again, the long-run Phillips Curve is vertical at the natural rate of unemployment.

Rational Expectations Theory

The adaptive expectations theory assumes that increases in nominal wages lag behind increases in the price level because the increases in the price level are not anticipated. This lag gives rise to *temporary* increases in profits which *temporarily* stimulate employment.

The **rational expectations theory** is the second version of the natural-rate hypothesis. It contends that businesses, consumers, and workers understand how government policies will affect the economy and *anticipate* the impacts in their own decision making.

Suppose, when government undertakes expansionary policies, workers anticipate that the result will be higher inflation and thus a decline in their real wages. They thus immediately incorporate this expected inflation into their nominal wage demands. If workers correctly and fully anticipate the amount of inflation and adjust their current nominal wage demands accordingly, then even the temporary increases in profit, output, and employment will *not* occur. Instead of the temporary decline in unemployment from a_1 to b_1 in Figure 16-9, the movement is directly from a_1 to a_2. Fully anticipated inflation by labor means that the price level and nominal wages rise simultaneously and by the same percent. Inflation, fully anticipated in the nominal wage demands of workers, therefore generates a vertical "Phillips Curve" through a_1, a_2, and a_3.

The policy implication is this: Fiscal and monetary policy designed to push unemployment below its natural rate will quickly (if not instantaneously) increase the rate of inflation, not reduce unemployment. Note that the adaptive and rational expectations theories are consistent with the conservative philosophy that government's attempts to do good deeds typically fail, and at a considerable cost to soci-ety. In this instance the "cost" is accelerating inflation. **(Key Question 6)**

Changing Interpretations

Interpretations of the Phillips Curve have changed dramatically over the past three decades. The original idea of a stable tradeoff between inflation and unemployment has given way to the adaptive expectations view that while there is a short-run tradeoff, there is no such tradeoff in the long run. The much more controversial rational expectations theory stresses that macroeconomic policy is completely ineffective when its outcomes are fully anticipated by workers and other participants in the economy. Not even a short-run tradeoff between inflation and unemployment exists. This conclusion is clearly contrary to the idea of the original Phillips Curve.

Which perspective is correct? Does an inverse relationship exist between the inflation rate and unemployment rate as the original Phillips Curve implies? Or is there no long-run tradeoff as the natural-rate theory contends? Perhaps the safest answer is that most economists accept the idea of a short-run tradeoff—where the short-run may last several years—while now recognizing that in the long run such a tradeoff is much less likely. Also, most economists agree that adverse aggregate supply shocks, such as those of the 1970s, can cause periods of rising unemployment rates and rising inflation, particularly when government undertakes policies to limit the rise in the unemployment rate. That is, most economists contend that the episodes of stagflation during the 1970s and early 1980s were *not* exclusively the results of misguided government stabilization policies, as some natural-rate theorists suggest.

QUICK REVIEW 16-3

■ The original Phillips Curve for the 1960s showed an apparent stable, inverse relationship between annual inflation rates and unemployment rates over a period of years.

■ Stagflation occurred from 1973 to 1975 and 1978 to 1980, producing Phillips Curve data points above and to the right of the Phillips Curve for the 1960s.

■ The central cause of the stagflation in the 1970s and early 1980s was a series of large increases in oil prices which reduced short-run aggregate supply.

■ In the natural-rate theory, the economy automatically gravitates to its natural rate of unemployment; therefore, the Phillips Curve is vertical at that rate in the long run.

SUPPLY-SIDE ECONOMICS

Our final aggregate supply topic is **supply-side economics.** "Supply-siders" contend that changes in aggregate supply must be recognized as active forces in determining the levels of both inflation and unemployment. Economic disturbances can be generated on the supply side, as well as on the demand side, of the economy. Moreover, certain government policies allegedly have reduced the growth of aggregate supply over time. By reversing these policies, say the supply-siders, the U.S. economy can achieve low levels of unemployment without producing rapid inflation.

Tax-Transfer Disincentives

Supply-side economists argue that the spectacular growth of the U.S. tax-transfer system has negatively affected incentives to work, invest, innovate, and assume entrepreneurial risks. The tax-transfer system allegedly has eroded the economy's productivity, and this decline in efficiency has slowed the expansion of long-run aggregate supply. The argument is that high taxes reduce the after-tax rewards of workers and producers, making work, innovation, investing, and risk bearing less financially attractive. According to supply-side economists, *marginal tax rates* are most relevant to decisions to undertake *additional* work and *additional* saving and investing.

Taxes and Incentives to Work   Supply-siders believe that how long and how hard individuals work depends on how much additional *after-tax* earnings they derive from work. To induce more work—to increase aggregate inputs of labor—government should reduce marginal tax rates on earned incomes. Lower marginal tax rates make work more attractive by increasing the opportunity cost of leisure. Thus, individuals choose to substitute work for leisure. This increase in productive effort can occur in many ways: by increasing the number of hours worked per day or week, by encouraging workers to postpone retirement, by inducing more people to enter the labor force, by making people willing to work harder, and by discouraging long periods of unemployment.

Transfer Disincentives   Supply-side economists also believe the existence of a wide variety of public transfer programs has eroded incentives to work. Unemployment compensation and welfare programs have made job loss less of an economic crisis for some people. The fear of being unemployed, and therefore the need to be a disciplined, productive worker, is simply less acute than it once was. Many transfer programs are structured to discourage work. Our social security program and welfare system encourage recipients *not* to be productive by imposing a "tax" in the form of a loss of transfer benefits on those who work. Only very recently have work requirements and time limits been introduced into the program providing aid to families with dependent children.

Incentives to Save and Invest   The rewards for saving and investing have also been reduced by high marginal tax rates. Assume you save $1000 at 10 percent, so you earn $100 interest per year. If your marginal tax rate is 40 percent, your after-tax-interest earnings will be $60 and the after-tax interest rate you receive is only 6 percent. While you might be willing to save (forgo current consumption) for a 10 percent return on your saving, you might prefer to consume when the return is only 6 percent.

Saving, remember, is the prerequisite of investment. Thus supply-side economists recommend lower marginal tax rates on saving. They also call for lower taxes on investment income to ensure there are ready investment outlets for the economy's enhanced pool of saving. A critical determinant of investment spending is the expected *after-tax* return of that spending.

To summarize: Lower marginal tax rates encourage saving and investing. Workers therefore find themselves equipped with more and technologically superior machinery and equipment. Labor productivity rises, and this expands aggregate supply, which in turn keeps unemployment rates and inflation low.

Laffer Curve

In the supply-side view, reductions in marginal tax rates increase the nation's aggregate supply. Moreover, according to supply-side economist Arthur Laffer, lower tax *rates* are compatible with constant or even enlarged tax *revenues*. Thus, supply-side tax cuts need not produce federal budget deficits.

This idea is based on the **Laffer Curve,** which, as shown in Figure 16-10, depicts the relationship between tax rates and tax revenues. As tax rates increase from 0 to 100 percent, tax revenues increase from zero to some maximum level (at *m*) and then decline to zero. Tax revenues decline beyond some point because higher tax rates discourage economic activity,

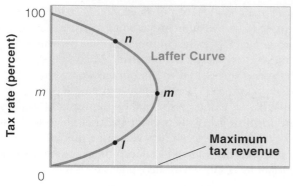

FIGURE 16-10 **The Laffer Curve** The Laffer Curve suggests that up to point *m* higher tax rates will result in larger tax revenues. But still higher tax rates will adversely affect incentives to work and produce, reducing the size of the tax base (output and income) to the extent that tax revenues will decline. It follows that if tax rates are above *m*, reductions in tax rates may produce increases in tax revenues.

---

diminishing the tax base (domestic output and income). This is easiest to see at the extreme, where tax rates are 100 percent. Tax revenues here are, in theory, reduced to zero because the 100 percent confiscatory tax rate has halted production. A 100 percent tax rate applied to a tax base of zero yields no revenue.

In the early 1980s Laffer suggested that the United States was at a point such as *n* on the curve in Figure 16-10. There, tax rates are so high that production is discouraged to the extent that tax revenues are below the maximum at *m*. If the economy is at *n*, then lower tax rates are quite compatible with constant tax revenues. Lowering tax rates moves the economy from point *n* to point *l*, and government brings in the same total amount of tax revenue as before. Laffer's reasoning is that lower tax rates stimulate incentives to work, save and invest, innovate, and accept business risks, thus triggering an expansion of real output and income. This enlarged tax base sustains tax revenues even though tax rates are lowered. Indeed, between *n* and *m* lower tax rates result in increased tax revenue.

Supply-side economists think tax rates can be lowered without producing budget deficits for two additional reasons:

1. *Less tax evasion* Tax avoidance (which is legal) and tax evasion (which is not) decline when taxes are reduced. High marginal tax rates prompt taxpayers to avoid taxes through various tax shelters, such as buying municipal bonds on which inter-

est earned is tax-free. They also encourage some taxpayers to conceal income from the Internal Revenue Service. Lower tax rates reduce the inclination to engage in tax avoidance and tax evasion.

2. *Reduced transfers* The stimulus to production and employment which a tax cut provides reduces government transfer payments. For example, having more job opportunities reduces transfer payments and decreases a budget deficit. **(Key Question 8)**

Criticisms of the Laffer Curve

The Laffer Curve and its supply-side implications have been subject to severe criticism.

Taxes, Incentives, and Time A fundamental criticism has to do with the sensitivity of economic incentives to changes in tax rates. Skeptics say there is ample empirical evidence showing that the impact of a tax cut on incentives is small, of uncertain direction, and relatively slow to emerge. For example, with respect to work incentives, studies indicate that decreases in tax rates lead some people to work more but others to work less. Those who work more are enticed by the higher after-tax pay; they substitute work for leisure because the opportunity cost of leisure has increased. Those who work less do so because the higher after-tax pay increases their ability to "buy leisure." They can meet their after-tax income goals by working fewer hours.

Inflation Most economists think that the demand-side effects of a tax cut exceed the supply-side effects. Thus, tax cuts undertaken when the economy is at or near its full-employment level of output may produce increases in aggregate demand which overwhelm any increase in aggregate supply. Demand-pull inflation is the likely result.

Position on the Curve Skeptics say the Laffer Curve is merely a logical proposition, asserting that there must be some level of tax rates between 0 and 100 percent at which tax revenues will be at their maximum. Economists of all persuasions can agree with this. But the issue of where a particular economy is located on its Laffer Curve is an empirical question. If we assume—as Laffer did in the early 1980s—that we are at point *n* in Figure 16-10, then tax cuts will increase tax revenues. But critics say that the economy's location on the Laffer Curve is undocumented and unknown. If the economy is at any point below *m* on the curve, then tax *reductions* will reduce tax revenues and create budget deficits. And, in fact, the sizable *increases* in marginal tax rates imposed by the federal government in 1993 have generated large increases in tax revenue.

Overregulation

Supply-siders also claim that government's regulatory involvement in the economy has adversely affected productivity and long-run aggregate supply. Two points should be noted here:

1. "Industrial regulation"—government regulation of specific industries such as transportation or communications—frequently provides regulated firms with a legal monopoly or cartel. Government regulation protects such firms from competition, the result being that these firms are less efficient and incur higher costs of production.

2. The "social regulation" of industry has increased substantially in the past decades. New government regulations have been imposed on industry in response to problems of pollution, product safety, worker health and safety, and equal access to job opportunities. Supply-side economists point out that social regulation has greatly increased the costs of doing business.

The overall impact of both types of regulation is that costs and prices are higher and economic growth is slower.

Reaganomics

The elements of supply-side economics just discussed provided the intellectual underpinnings of the economic policies of the Reagan administration (1981–1988). Along with a substantial reduction in government regulation, personal and corporate income tax rates were cut sharply, the latter by about 25 percent over 3 years. In 1986, the marginal tax rate on wealthy taxpayers fell from 50 to 28 percent. (Today, the top rate is 39.6 percent.)

The real world is an imperfect laboratory for judging the success of a vast socioeconomic experiment such as **Reaganomics.** For one thing, Congress did not accept all the expenditure reductions which the Reagan administration requested in its program. Even so, the Reagan years did in fact witness significant declines in inflation and interest rates, a record-long

peacetime economic expansion, and eventual attainment of full employment. These years were also characterized by a resurgence of the spirit of entrepreneurialism. Nevertheless, it is fair to say that, as such, supply-side economics largely failed to increase aggregate supply more rapidly than its historical pace. There is little evidence that this program had any significant positive impacts on saving and investment or incentive to work. The saving rate, in fact, trended downward throughout the 1980s. Productivity growth surged in 1983 and 1984, as it usually does during recovery from recession, but was disappointingly low in the rest of the 1980s. Most economists attribute the post-1982 economic recovery to the demand-side expansionary effects of the Reagan tax cuts and not to the use of tax cuts as a pro-growth, supply-side measure.

The large tax cuts, together with rising levels of government expenditures, particularly for national defense, created record-high U.S. budget deficits. The prediction of the Laffer Curve that tax cuts would enhance tax revenues beyond those associated with normal economic expansions simply did not bear fruit. The large deficits may have increased interest rates and crowded out some unknown amount of private investment. To cope with the large deficits, the Bush administration increased the top marginal tax rate from 28 to 31 percent. But huge deficits persisted, and in 1993 the Clinton administration again raised tax rates, pushing the top marginal tax rate to 39.6 percent.

In summary, the evidence casts considerable doubt on the key supply-side proposition that tax cuts can directly and significantly shift the U.S. long-run aggregate supply curve rightward.

QUICK REVIEW 16-4

■ Supply-side economists say that the U.S. tax-transfer system reduces work effort, saving and investing, innovation, and risk bearing.

■ The Laffer Curve suggests that when tax rates are higher than optimal from a revenue standpoint, reductions in tax rates can expand real output and income (the tax base) and simultaneously increase tax revenue.

■ The supply-side policies of the Reagan administration (1981–1988) did not increase aggregate supply more rapidly than otherwise would have been expected for this 8-year period.

Price and Wage Controls

If inflation is a problem for a society, why not simply outlaw inflationary price and wage increases? That is, why not enact price and wage controls?

During inflationary times, it is natural for people to look for culprits. Who exactly is causing prices and wages to rise and how can government alter their actions? Casual observation leads many to conclude that firms are the *cause* of rising prices and unions are the *cause* of rising wages. After all, firms and unions are the ones directly announcing price increases and negotiating wage increases.

If firms and unions are viewed as the causes of inflation, then one solution is to limit price and wage increases by law so that inflation would be held to, say, 2 percent annually. Such kinds of *price and wage controls* have a long history. For example, the Roman emperor Diocletian attempted them in 301. So did the Mongol, Kublai Khan, in the thirteenth century; the city leaders of Antwerp in 1584; the Continental Congress in America in 1775; U.S. president Richard Nixon in 1971; and several South American countries in the 1980s. In each case, inflation eventually won and controls lost. The reasons why are as follows:

1. Controls for Symptoms, Not Causes In most circumstances, increases in prices and wages are the *symptoms*, not the underlying *cause*, of inflation. Inflation is caused by excessive growth of the money supply, excessive investment spending, inappropriate fiscal policy, or oil price "shocks." Wage and price controls leave the root cause of inflation untreated.

2. Circumvention and Compliance Problems Wage and price controls have the force of law; therefore, government can use fines and imprisonment to coerce labor and management to obey them. Nevertheless, enforcement and compliance problems can be severe. Because the controls produce below-equilibrium prices and wages, they also produce shortages of products and workers. *Black markets*—illegal markets in which prices and wages exceed legal maximums—become common. Buyers willing to pay more than the controlled price seek out sellers willing to sell the product for more than the controlled price. Thus, price increases show up "off the books."

Businesses and workers also respond in other ways to circumvent controls. For example, firms can reduce product quality instead of raising product price. If the price of a candy bar is frozen at 60 cents, reducing its size by one-half can effectively double its price. Workers can sidestep wage controls by moving to newly created job classifications that firms set up to circumvent the wage controls. The firm, in a sense, converts *illegal* wage increases into *legal* promotions.

CHAPTER SUMMARY

1. In macroeconomics, the short run is a period in which nominal wages are fixed; they do not change in response to changes in the price level. In contrast, the long run is a period in which nominal wages are fully responsive to changes in the price level.

2. The short-run aggregate supply curve is upsloping. Because nominal wages are fixed, increases in the price level (prices received by firms) increase profits and real output. Conversely, decreases in the price level reduce profits and real output. However, the long-run aggregate supply curve is vertical. With sufficient time for adjustment, nominal wages rise and fall with the price level, moving the economy along a vertical aggregate supply curve at the economy's full-employment output.

3. In the short run, demand-pull inflation increases the price level and real output. Once nominal wages have increased, the temporary increase in real output is reversed.

4. In the short run, cost-push inflation increases the price level *and* reduces real output. Unless government expands aggregate demand, nominal wages eventually will decline under conditions of recession and the short-run aggregate supply curve will shift back to its initial location. Prices and real output will eventually return to their original levels.

5. If prices and wages are flexible downward, a decline in aggregate demand will reduce output *and* the price level. The decline in the price level will eventually reduce nom-

3. Inability to Maintain Long-Term Public Support The same public that called for wage and price controls often turns against them once it realizes their impacts. Wage and price controls interfere with accepted, well-established rights and expectations. They interfere with the right of workers to freely bargain for wages with employers through union representation. They interfere with the right of firms to freely set prices and adjust them rapidly to changing supply and demand circumstances. And the shortages they create do not fit with consumer expectations of products being available in shops and stores. As a result, the public often quickly tires of wage and price controls.

4. Allocative Inefficiency and Rationing Where effective, wage and price controls prohibit the market system from making necessary price and wage adjustments. If the demand for one product, say, retirement housing, should rise sharply (independent of inflation), its price could not rise to signal society's wish for more of this output and therefore more resources to produce it. The same problem occurs in the labor market. A large in-

crease in the demand for, say, software designers could not produce the salary increase needed to attract workers from other occupations. Nor would there be proper incentives for college students to take up this field of study.

Also, price controls strip the market mechanism of the rationing function—its ability to equate quantity demanded and quantity supplied. Which buyers are to obtain the product when there are shortages? The product can be rationed on a first-come, first-served basis or by favoritism. But both are highly arbitrary and inequitable; those first in line or those able to cultivate a friendship with the seller get as much of the product as they want, while others get none at all. Government may therefore decide to impartially ration the product to all consumers by issuing ration coupons to prospective buyers on a fair basis. But this means adding another costly government bureaucracy to that already required to police compliance with the controls.

In view of the distortions caused by price and wage controls and their overall poor results, most contemporary economists reject this approach to trying to reduce inflation.

inal wages and shift the short-run aggregate supply curve rightward. Full-employment output will thus be restored.

6. Assuming a stable upsloping aggregate supply curve, rightward shifts of the aggregate demand curve of various sizes yields the generalization that high rates of inflation are associated with low rates of unemployment, and vice versa. This inverse relationship is known as the Phillips Curve, and empirical data for the 1960s seemed to be consistent with it.

7. In the 1970s and early 1980s the Phillips Curve apparently shifted rightward, reflecting stagflation—simultaneously rising inflation rates and unemployment rates. The standard interpretation is that the stagflation mainly resulted from huge oil price increases which caused large leftward shifts in the short-run aggregate supply curve (so-called supply shocks). The Phillips Curve shifted inward

toward its original position in the 1980s. By 1989 stagflation had subsided.

8. The adaptive expectations version of the natural-rate hypothesis says that while there is a short-run tradeoff between inflation and unemployment, there is no such long-run tradeoff. Workers will adapt their expectations to new inflation realities, and when they do, the unemployment rate will return to the natural rate. The long-run Phillips Curve is therefore vertical at the natural rate, meaning that higher rates of inflation do not "buy" the economy less unemployment.

9. The rational expectations version of the natural-rate hypothesis contends that workers will anticipate the inflationary effects of monetary policy and fiscal policy and will build these expectations into their wage demands. As a result, not even a short-run Phillips Curve will exist; the economy will simply move along its vertical long-run Phillips Curve when the government undertakes expansionary policies.

10. Supply-side economists trace slow economic growth to expansion of government and, specifically, to the negative effects of the tax-transfer system on incentives. They say that excessive government regulation of business has contributed to slow growth. The Laffer Curve relates tax rates to levels of tax revenue and suggests that, under some circumstances, cuts in tax rates can expand the tax base (output and income) and increase tax revenues. Massive tax cuts undertaken by the Reagan administration failed to increase aggregate supply more rapidly than would have been expected without the cuts.

TERMS AND CONCEPTS

short-run aggregate
  supply curve
long-run aggregate
  supply curve
Phillips Curve

stagflation
aggregate supply shocks
natural-rate hypothesis
adaptive expectations
  theory

disinflation
rational expectations
  theory
supply-side economics

Laffer Curve
Reaganomics

STUDY QUESTIONS

1. Distinguish between the short run and the long run as they relate to macroeconomics.

2. Which of the following statements are true? Which are false? Explain the false statements.
   a. Short-run aggregate supply curves reflect an inverse relationship between the price level and the level of real output.
   b. The long-run aggregate supply curve assumes that nominal wages are fixed.
   c. In the long run, an increase in the price level will result in an increase in nominal wages.

3. KEY QUESTION Suppose the full-employment level of real output (Q) for a hypothetical economy is $250 and the price level (P) initially is 100. Use the short-run aggregate supply schedules below to answer the questions which follow:

AS (P_{100})		AS (P_{125})		AS (P_{75})	
P	Q	P	Q	P	Q
125	280	125	250	125	310
100	250	100	220	100	280
75	220	75	190	75	250

   a. What will be the level of real output in the *short run* if the price level unexpectedly rises from 100 to 125 because of an increase in aggregate demand? What if the price level falls unexpectedly from 100 to 75 because of a decrease in aggregate demand? Explain each situation, using numbers from the table.
   b. What will be the level of real output in the *long run* when the price level rises from 100 to 125? When it falls from 100 to 75? Explain each situation.
   c. Show the circumstances described in parts **a** and **b** on graph paper, and derive the long-run aggregate supply curve.

4. KEY QUESTION Use graphical analysis to show how each of the following would affect the economy first in the short run and then in the long run. Assume that the United States is initially operating at its full-employment level of output, that prices and wages are eventually flexible both upward and downward, and that there is no counteracting fiscal or monetary policy.
   a. Because of a war abroad, the oil supply to the United States is disrupted, sending oil prices rocketing upward.
   b. Construction spending on new homes rises dramatically, greatly increasing total U.S. investment spending.
   c. Economic recession occurs abroad, significantly reducing foreign purchases of U.S. exports.

5. Assume that a particular short-run aggregate supply curve exists for an economy and that the curve is relevant for several years. Use the AD-AS analysis to show graphically why higher rates of inflation over this period would be associated with lower rates of unemployment, and vice versa. What is this inverse relationship called?

6. KEY QUESTION Distinguish between adaptive expectations and rational expectations. Why are adaptive expectations consistent with a short-run Phillips Curve while rational expectations are not? Explain why both types of expectations result in a vertical long-run Phillips Curve.

7. Explain: "If expectations are rational and fully correct, the unemployment rate will never diverge from the natural rate."

8. KEY QUESTION What are the two broad tenets of supply-side economics? What is the Laffer Curve, and how does it relate to one of these tenets?

9. Why might one person work more, earn more, and pay more income tax when his or her tax rate is cut, while another person will work less, earn less, and pay less income tax under the same circumstance?

10. (Last Word) Relate this statement to price and wage controls: "Controlling prices to halt inflation is like breaking a thermometer to control the heat."

11. WEB-BASED QUESTION Phillips Curve—Do Real Data Confirm? The Phillips Curve purports to show a stable relationship between the rate of inflation and the unemployment rate. Plot the data points between inflation and unemployment over the past decade to the present in the following manner. For inflation data, first use the Consumer Price Index—All Urban Consumers, then the Producer Price Index—All Commodities. For unemployment data, first use Unemployment Rate—Civilian Labor Force, then use data from your population group (e.g., Unemployment Rate—Civilian Labor Force 20 Years and Over, Male). Do any of your data point plots seem to confirm the Phillips Curve concept? Retrieve unemployment data from the Bureau of Labor Statistics http://stats.bls.gov/cpshome.htm and select Most Requested Series. For inflation data, go to http://stats.bls.gov/cpihome.htm and select Most Requested Series.

12. WEB-BASED QUESTION The Laffer Curve—Does It Really Exist? The Laffer Curve suggests that beyond some point higher tax rates will result in lower tax revenues. Over the past 60 years the marginal income tax rates have varied widely, with the top rate exceeding 90 percent in the early 1940s and falling to under 30 percent in the 1980s. This would imply that personal income taxes as a percentage of gross domestic output would also vary widely. Visit the U.S. Commerce Department http://www.doc.gov/ and search for 1998 Budget Historical Table (or the latest year instead of 1998) for the document titled Tax Receipts by Source as a Percentage of GDP. At present, individual income taxes are what percentage of GDP? How has the percentage varied over the past 60 years? Does this support the Laffer Curve?

17

Disputes in Macro Theory and Policy

One of the great traditions in scholarship is the challenging of mainstream thinking. Many such challenges to the "conventional wisdom" fail; either the new theories are not logical or they do not conform to facts. At the opposite extreme, some new theories gain full support and replace the existing theories. More often, the new ideas modify the existing body of mainstream thinking, which thereafter is improved or extended. This certainly is true in economics.

As any academic discipline evolves, it draws criticism and disagreement. In this chapter we examine some of the major disputes in macro theory and policy. We initially provide historical background by contrasting classical and Keynesian macroeconomic theories. Then we turn to contemporary disagreements on three interrelated questions: (1) What causes instability in the economy? (2) Is the economy self-correcting? (3) Should government adhere to *rules* or use *discretion* in setting economic policy? Finally, we summarize the alternative perspectives discussed in this chapter and the previous chapter.

SOME HISTORY: CLASSICS AND KEYNES

Classical economics, which dominated economic thought in the 1800s, suggested that full employment is the norm in a market economy and that a *laissez-faire* ("let it be") policy by government is best. In contrast, Keynes contended in the 1930s that laissez-faire capitalism is subject to recurring recessions or depressions with widespread unemployment. In the Keynesian view, active government stabilization policy is required to avoid the waste of idle resources.

Because the classical and Keynesian views of the macroeconomic world provide great insight on modern debates, it is worthwhile to compare their basic forms through modern aggregate demand and aggregate supply analysis.

Classical View

In the classical view, the aggregate supply curve is vertical and exclusively determines the level of real output. The downsloping aggregate demand curve is stable and solely establishes the price level.

Vertical Aggregate Supply Curve In the classical perspective, the aggregate supply curve is a vertical line as shown in Figure 17-1a. This line is located at the full-employment level of real output, which in this designation is also the full-capacity real output. According to the classical economists, the economy will operate at its full-employment level of output, Q_f, because of (1) Say's law (Chapter 9) and (2) responsive, flexible prices and wages.

We stress that classical economists believed that Q_f does *not* change in response to changes in the price level. Observe that as the price level falls from P_1 to P_2 in Figure 17-1a, real output remains anchored at Q_f.

But this stability of output might seem at odds with Chapter 3's upsloping supply curves for individual products. There we found that lower prices would make production less profitable and cause producers to offer *less* output and employ *fewer* workers. The classical response to this view is that input costs would fall along with product prices to leave *real* profits and output unchanged.

Consider a one-firm economy in which the firm's owner must receive a *real* profit of $20 to produce the full-employment output of 100 units. You know from Chapter 8 that what ultimately counts is the *real* reward one receives and not the level of prices. Assume

the owner's only input (aside from personal entrepreneurial talent) is 10 units of labor hired at $8 per worker for a total wage cost of $80 (= 10 × $8). Also suppose the 100 units of output sell for $1 per unit, so total revenue is $100 (= 100 × $1). This firm's *nominal* profit is $20 (= $100 − $80), and, using the $1 price to designate the base price index of 100 percent, its *real* profit is also $20 (= $20 ÷ 1.00). Well and good; full employment is achieved. But suppose the price level declines by one-half. Would our producer still earn the $20 of real profits needed to support production of a 100-unit full-employment output?

The classical answer is "yes." Now that product price is only 50¢, total revenue will be only $50 (= 100 × 50¢). But the cost of 10 units of labor will be reduced to $40 (= 10 × $4) because the wage rate will be halved. Although *nominal* profits fall to $10 (= $50 − $40), *real* profits remain at $20. By dividing money profits of $10 by the new price index (expressed as a decimal), we obtain *real* profits of $20 (= $10 ÷ .50).

With perfectly flexible wages there would be no change in the real rewards and therefore in the production behavior of businesses. With perfect wage flexibility, a change in the price level will not cause the economy to stray from full employment.

(a) Classical theory

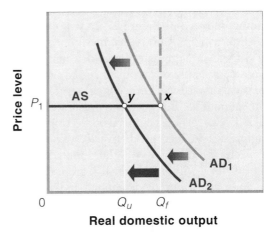

(b) Keynesian theory

FIGURE 17-1 Classical and Keynesian views of the macroeconomy (a) In classical theory, aggregate supply determines the full-employment level of real output, while aggregate demand establishes the price level. Aggregate demand normally is stable, but if it should decline, say, from AD$_1$ to AD$_2$, the price level will quickly fall from P_1 to P_2 to eliminate the temporary excess supply of *ab* and to restore full employment at *c*. (b) The Keynesian view is that aggregate demand is unstable and that prices and wages are downwardly inflexible. An AD$_1$ to AD$_2$ decline in aggregate demand has no effect on the price level. Instead, the economy moves from point *x* to *y* and real output falls to Q_u, where it can remain indefinitely.

Stable Aggregate Demand Classical economists theorize that money underlies aggregate demand. The amount of real output which can be purchased depends on (1) the quantity of money households and businesses possess and (2) the purchasing power of that money as determined by the price level. The purchasing power of the dollar refers to the real quantity of goods and services a dollar will buy. Thus, as we move down the vertical axis of Figure 17-1a, the price level is falling. This means that the purchasing power of each dollar is rising. If the price level declined by one-half, a particular quantity of money would now purchase a real output twice as large. With a fixed money supply, the price level and real output are inversely related.

And what of the *location* of the aggregate demand curve? According to the classical economists, aggregate demand will be stable as long as the nation's monetary authorities maintain a constant supply of money. With a fixed aggregate supply of output, increases in the supply of money will shift the aggregate demand curve rightward and spark demand-pull inflation. Reductions in the supply of money will shift the curve leftward and trigger deflation. The key to price-level stability, then, is to control the nation's money supply to prevent unwarranted shifts in aggregate demand.

A final observation: Even if there are declines in the money supply and therefore in aggregate demand, the economy depicted in Figure 17-1a will *not* experience unemployment. Admittedly, the immediate effect of a decline in aggregate demand from AD_1 to AD_2 is an excess supply of output since the aggregate output of goods and services exceeds aggregate spending by the amount ab. But, with the presumed downward flexibility of product and resource prices, this excess supply will reduce product prices along with workers' wages and the prices of other inputs. As a result, the price level will quickly decline from P_1 to P_2 until the amounts of output demanded and supplied are brought once again into equilibrium, this time at c. While the price level has fallen from P_1 to P_2, real output remains at the full-employment level.

Keynesian View

The core of crude, or extreme, **Keynesianism** is that product prices and wages are downwardly inflexible over very long time periods. The result is graphically represented as a horizontal aggregate supply curve. Also, aggregate demand is subject to periodic changes caused by changes in the determinants of aggregate demand.

Horizontal Aggregate Supply Curve (to Full-Employment Output) The presumed downward inflexibility of prices and wages translates to a horizontal aggregate supply curve as shown in Figure 17-1b. Here, a decline in real output from Q_f to Q_u will have no impact on the price level. Conversely, an increase in real output from Q_u to Q_f will also leave the price level unchanged. The aggregate supply curve therefore extends from zero real output rightward to point x, where real output is at its full-employment level, Q_f. Once full employment is reached, the aggregate supply curve is vertical. This is shown by the dashed line extending upward from the horizontal aggregate supply curve at x.

Unstable Aggregate Demand Keynesian economists view aggregate demand as unstable from one period to the next, even without changes in the money supply. In particular, the investment component of aggregate demand fluctuates, altering the location of the aggregate demand curve. Suppose aggregate demand in Figure 17-1b declines from AD_1 to AD_2. The sole impact is on output and employment. Real output falls from Q_f to Q_u, while the price level is unchanged at P_1. Moreover, Keynesians believe that unless there is a fortuitous offsetting increase in aggregate demand, real output may remain at Q_u, which is below the full-employment level Q_f. Active government policies to increase aggregate demand are essential to move the economy from point y to point x. Otherwise, the economy will suffer the wastes of recession and depression. **(Key Question 1)**

QUICK REVIEW 17-1

In classical macroeconomics:
- The aggregate supply curve is vertical at the full-employment level of real output.

- The aggregate demand curve is stable as long as the money supply is constant.

In Keynesian macroeconomics:
- The aggregate supply curve is horizontal up to the full-employment level of output; then it becomes vertical.

- The aggregate demand curve is unstable largely because of the volatility of investment spending; such shifts cause either recession or demand-pull inflation.

WHAT CAUSES MACRO INSTABILITY?

You are aware from previous chapters that the capitalist economies have, in fact, experienced considerable instability during this century. The United States, for example, has experienced the Great Depression, numerous recessions, and periods of inflation. Contemporary economists have different perspectives on why this instability occurs.

Mainstream View

The mainstream view is Keynesian-based. It holds that instability in the economy arises from two sources: (1) significant changes in investment spending which change aggregate demand, and, occasionally, (2) adverse aggregate supply shocks which change aggregate supply. These factors are not new to you, so let's just briefly review them here.

Changes in Investment Spending   Mainstream macroeconomics focuses on aggregate spending and its components. Recall that the basic equation underlying aggregate expenditures is

$$C_a + I_g + X_n + G = \text{GDP}$$

That is, the aggregate amount of after-tax consumption, gross investment, net exports, and government spending determines the total amount of the goods and services produced and sold. In equilibrium, $C_a + I_g + X_n + G$ (aggregate expenditures) is equal to GDP (real output). A decrease in the price level increases equilibrium GDP and thus allows us to trace out a downsloping aggregate demand curve for the economy. Any change in one of the spending components in the aggregate expenditures equation shifts the aggregate demand curve. This, in turn, changes equilibrium real output, the price level, or both.

Investment spending, in particular, is subject to wide "booms" and "busts." Significant increases in investment spending get multiplied into even greater increases in aggregate demand and thus can produce demand-pull inflation. In contrast, major declines in investment spending get multiplied into even greater decreases in aggregate demand and thus can cause recessions.

Adverse Aggregate Supply Shocks   In the mainstream view, the second source of macroeconomic instability arises on the supply side. Occasionally, such external events as wars or artificial supply restrictions boost prices of key imported resources and significantly raise per-unit production costs. The result is a sizable decline in a nation's aggregate supply, which destabilizes the economy by simultaneously causing cost-push inflation *and* recession.

Monetarist View

Classical economics has emerged in several modern forms. One is **monetarism,** which (1) focuses on the money supply, (2) holds that markets are highly competitive, and (3) says that a competitive market system gives the economy a high degree of macroeconomic stability. Like classical economics, monetarism argues that the price and wage flexibility provided by competitive markets would cause fluctuations in aggregate demand to alter product and resource prices rather than output and employment. Thus the market system would provide substantial macroeconomic stability *were it not for government interference in the economy.*

The problem, as monetarists see it, is that government has promoted downward wage inflexibility through the minimum-wage law, pro-union legislation, guaranteed prices for some farm products, pro-business monopoly legislation, and so forth. The free-market system could provide macroeconomic stability, but, despite good intentions, government interference has undermined this capability. Moreover, monetarists say that government has contributed to the economy's business cycles through its clumsy and mistaken attempts to achieve greater stability through monetary policies.

Equation of Exchange   The fundamental equation of monetarism is the **equation of exchange:**

$$MV = PQ$$

where M is the supply of money; V is the **velocity** of money, that is, *the number of times per year the average dollar is spent on final goods and services; P* is the price level or, more specifically, the average price at which each unit of physical output is sold; and Q is the physical volume of all goods and services produced.

The label "equation of exchange" is easily understood. The left side, *MV*, represents the total amount *spent* by purchasers of output, while the right side, *PQ*, represents the total amount *received* by sellers of that output. The nation's money supply (M) multiplied by the number of times it is spent each year (V) *must* equal the nation's nominal GDP ($= P \times Q$).

The dollar value of total spending has to equal the dollar value of total output.

Stable Velocity Monetarists say that velocity, V, in the equation of exchange is stable. As used here, "stable" is not synonymous with "constant." Monetarists are aware that velocity is higher today than it was several decades ago. Shorter pay periods, greater use of credit cards, and faster means of making payments enable people to hold less money and turn it over more rapidly than was possible in earlier times. These factors have enabled people to reduce their holdings of cash and checkbook money relative to the size of the nation's nominal GDP.

When monetarists say velocity is stable they mean that the factors altering velocity change gradually and predictably. Changes in velocity from one year to the next can be easily anticipated. Moreover, velocity does not change in response to changes in the money supply itself. In this view, people have a stable desire to hold money relative to holding other financial assets, holding real assets, and buying current output. The factors which determine the amount of money the public wants to hold depend mainly on the level of nominal GDP.

Example: Suppose that when the level of nominal GDP is $400 billion, the public desires $100 billion of money to purchase this output. That means V is 4 (= $400 billion of nominal GDP/$100 billion of money). If we further assume that the actual supply of money is $100 billion, the economy is in equilibrium with respect to money; the *actual* amount of money supplied equals the *desired* amount the public wants to hold.

If velocity is stable, the equation of exchange suggests there is a predictable relationship between the money supply and nominal GDP ($= PQ$). An increase in the money supply of, say, $10 billion upsets equilibrium in our example since the public finds itself holding more money or liquidity than it wants. That is, the actual amount of money held ($110 billion) exceeds the amount of holdings desired ($100 billion). The reaction of the public (households and businesses) is to restore its desired balance of money relative to other items, such as stocks and bonds, factories and equipment, houses and automobiles, and clothing and toys. But the spending of money by individual households and businesses leaves more cash in others' checkable deposits or billfolds. Those other households and firms also try to "spend down" their excess cash balances, but, overall, *the $110 billion supply of money cannot be spent down.*

Instead, the collective attempt to reduce cash balances increases aggregate demand, boosting the *nominal* GDP. Because velocity in our example is 4—that is, the typical dollar is spent four times per year—nominal GDP rises from $400 to $440 billion. At that higher nominal GDP, the money supply of $110 billion equals the amount of money desired ($440 billion/4 = $110 billion), and equilibrium is reestablished.

The $10 billion increase in the money supply thus eventually increases nominal GDP by $40 billion. Spending on goods, services, and assets expands until nominal GDP has gone up enough to restore the original 4-to-1 equilibrium relationship between nominal GDP and the money supply.

Note that the relationship GDP/M defines V. A stable relationship between nominal GDP and M means a stable V. And a change in M causes a proportionate change in nominal GDP. Thus, changes in the money supply allegedly have a predictable effect on nominal GDP ($= P \times Q$). An increase in M increases P or Q, or some combination of both; a decrease in M reduces P or Q, or some combination of both. **(Key Question 4)**

Monetary Causes of Instability *Monetarists say that inappropriate monetary policy is the single most important cause of macroeconomic instability.* An increase in the money supply directly increases aggregate demand. Under conditions of full employment, this increase in aggregate demand increases the price level. For a time, higher prices cause firms to increase their real output, and the rate of unemployment falls below its natural rate. But once nominal wages rise to reflect the higher prices and thus to restore real wages, real output moves back to its full-employment level and the unemployment rate returns to its natural rate. The inappropriate increase in the money supply leads to inflation, together with instability of real output and employment.

Conversely, a decrease in the money supply reduces aggregate demand. Real output temporarily falls, and the unemployment rate rises above its natural rate. Eventually, nominal wages fall and real output returns to its full-employment level. The inappropriate decline in the money supply leads to deflation, together with instability of real GDP and employment.

The contrast between mainstream macroeconomics and monetarism on the causes of instability thus comes into sharp focus. Mainstream economists view instability of investment as the main cause of the economy's instability. They see monetary policy as a stabilizing factor. Changes in the money supply raise or lower interest rates as needed, smooth out swings in investment, and thus reduce macroeconomic instability. In contrast, monetarists view changes in the money supply as the main cause of the instability in the economy. For example, they say that the Great Depression largely occurred because the Fed allowed the money supply to fall by nearly 40 percent in that period. According to Milton Friedman, a prominent monetarist:

> And [the money supply] fell not because there were no willing borrowers—not because the horse would not drink. It fell because the Federal Reserve System forced or permitted a sharp reduction in the [money supply], because it failed to exercise the responsibilities assigned to it in the Federal Reserve Act to provide liquidity to the banking system. The Great Contraction is tragic testimony to the power of monetary policy—not as Keynes and so many of his contemporaries believed, evidence of its impotence.[1]

Real-Business-Cycle View

A third modern view of the cause of macroeconomic instability is that business cycles are caused by *real* factors affecting aggregate supply rather than by *monetary*, or spending, factors causing fluctuations in aggregate demand. In the **real-business-cycle theory**, business fluctuations result from significant changes in technology and resource availability. Those changes affect productivity and thus the long-run growth trend of aggregate supply.

An example focusing on recession will clarify this thinking. Suppose productivity (output per worker) sharply declines because of a large increase in oil prices, which makes it prohibitively expensive to operate certain types of machinery. This decline in productivity implies a reduction in the economy's ability to produce real output. The result would be a decrease in the economy's long-run aggregate supply curve, as represented by the leftward shift from AS_{LR1} to AS_{LR2} in Figure 17-2.

As real output falls from Q_1 to Q_2, the public does not need as much money to buy the reduced volume of goods and services. So the demand for money falls. Moreover, the slowdown in business activity lessens

business borrowing from banks, reducing checkable deposits. Thus, the supply of money also falls. In this controversial scenario, changes in the supply of money respond to changes in the demand for money. The decline in the money supply then reduces aggregate demand, as from AD_1 to AD_2 in Figure 17-2. The overall outcome is a decline in real output from Q_1 to Q_2, with no change in the price level.

Conversely, a large increase in aggregate supply (not shown) caused by, say, major new innovations in the production process would shift the long-run aggregate supply curve rightward. Real output would increase, and money demand and money supply would both increase. Aggregate demand would shift rightward by an amount equal to the rightward shift of long-run aggregate supply. Real output would increase, without driving up the price level.

Conclusion: In the real-business-cycle theory, macro instability arises on the aggregate supply side of the economy, not on the aggregate demand side as mainstream economists and monetarists generally say.

FIGURE 17-2 The real-business-cycle theory   In the real-business-cycle theory, a decline in resource availability shifts the nation's long-run aggregate supply curve to the left from AS_{LR1} to AS_{LR2}. The decline in real output from Q_1 to Q_2, in turn, reduces money demand (less is needed) and money supply (fewer loans are taken out) such that aggregate demand shifts leftward from AD_1 to AD_2. The result is a recession in which the price level remains constant.

---

[1]Milton Friedman, *The Optimum Quantity of Money and Other Essays* (Chicago: Aldine, 1969), p. 97.

Coordination Failures

A fourth and final modern view of macroeconomic instability relates to so-called **coordination failures.** Such failures occur *when people do not reach a mutually beneficial equilibrium because they lack some way to jointly coordinate their actions.*

Noneconomic Example

Consider first a noneconomic example. Suppose you learn of an impending volleyball party at a nearby lake, but it looks like it might rain. If you expect others to be there, you will decide to go. If you expect that others will not attend, you will decide to stay home. There are several possible equilibrium outcomes, depending on the mix of people's expectations. Let's consider just two. If each person assumes all others will be at the party, all will go. The party and volleyball game will occur and presumably everyone will have a good time. But if each person assumes that everyone else will stay home, each person will stay home and there will be no party. When the volleyball party does *not* take place, *even though all would be better off if it did happen*, a coordination failure has occurred.

Macroeconomic Example

Now let's apply this idea to macroeconomic instability, specifically recession. Suppose individual firms and households expect other firms and consumers to cut back their investment and consumption spending. As a result, each firm and household will anticipate a reduction of aggregate demand. Firms therefore will cut back their own investment spending since they will anticipate future excess production capacity. Households will also reduce their own spending (increase their saving) because they anticipate reduced work-hours, possible layoffs, and falling income. Aggregate demand will indeed decline and the economy will experience a recession *due to a self-fulfilling prophecy.* Moreover, the economy will *stay* at a below-full-employment level of output because, once there, producers and households have no individual incentive to increase spending. If *all* producers and households would agree to simultaneously increase their investment and consumption spending, then aggregate demand would rise, and real output and real income would expand. Each producer and consumer would be better off. However, this outcome does not occur because there is no mechanism for firms and households to agree on such a joint spending increase.

In this case, the economy is stuck in an *unemployment equilibrium* because of a coordination failure. With a different set of expectations, a coordination failure might leave the economy in an *inflation equilibrium.* In this view, there are a number of such potential equilibrium positions in the economy, some good and some bad, depending on people's mix of expectations. Macroeconomic instability, then, reflects the movement of the economy from one such equilibrium position to another as expectations change.

QUICK REVIEW 17-2

■ Mainstream economists say that macroeconomic instability usually stems from swings in investment spending and, occasionally, from adverse aggregate supply shocks.

■ Monetarists view the economy through the equation of exchange $(MV = PQ)$. If velocity V is stable, changes in the money supply M directly lead to changes in nominal GDP $(= P \times Q)$. For monetarists, changes in M via inappropriate monetary policy are the single most important cause of macroeconomic instability.

■ In the real-business-cycle theory, significant changes in "real" factors such as technology, resource availability, and productivity change the economy's long-run aggregate supply, causing macroeconomic instability.

■ Macroeconomic instability can result from coordination failures—less-than-optimal equilibrium positions which occur because businesses and households lack some way to jointly coordinate their actions.

DOES THE ECONOMY "SELF-CORRECT"?

Just as there are disputes over the causes of macroeconomic instability, there are debates on whether or not the economy corrects itself when instability does occur. Also, economists disagree as to the length of time it will take for any such self-correction to happen.

New Classical View of Self-Correction

Monetarist and rational expectations economists (Chapter 16) take the view of **new classical economics,** which is that when the economy occasionally diverges from its full-employment output, internal mechanisms within the economy automatically move it back to that output. This perspective is associated with the adaptive and rational expectations theories (the natural-rate theories) discussed in Chapter 16.

Graphical Analysis

Figure 17-3a is useful for relating the new classical analysis to the issue of self-correction. Specifically, an increase in aggregate demand, say, from AD_1 to AD_2, moves the economy upward along its short-run aggregate supply curve AS_1 from a to b. The price level rises and real output increases. In the long run, however, nominal wages rise to restore real wages. Per-unit production costs then increase, and the short-run aggregate supply curve shifts leftward, eventually from AS_1 to AS_2. The economy moves from b to c and real output returns to its full-employment level, Q_1. This level of output is dictated by the economy's vertical long-run aggregate supply curve, here AS_{LR}.

Conversely, a decrease in aggregate demand from AD_1 to AD_3 in Figure 17-3b first moves the economy downward along its short-run aggregate supply curve AS_1 from point a to d. The price level *and* the level of real output fall. But in the long run, nominal wages decline such that real wages fall to their previous levels. When that happens, per-unit production costs decline and the short-run aggregate supply curve shifts to the right, eventually from AS_1 to AS_3. The economy moves back to e, where it again achieves its full-

employment level, Q_1. As in Figure 17-3a, the economy in Figure 17-3b has automatically self-corrected to its full-employment output and natural rate of unemployment.

Speed of Adjustment

There is some disagreement among new classical economists on how long it will take for self-correction to occur. Monetarists usually hold the *adaptive expectations* view that people form their expectations on present realities and only gradually change their expectations as experience unfolds. This means that the shifts in the short-run aggregate supply curves shown in Figure 17-3 may not occur for 2 or 3 years, or even longer. Other new classical economists, however, accept the *rational expectations* assumption that workers *anticipate* some future outcomes before they occur. When price-level changes are fully anticipated, adjustments of nominal wages are very quick, or even instantaneous. Let's see why.

Although several new theories incorporate rational expectations, including Keynesian ones, our interest here is the new classical version of the rational expectations theory (hereafter, RET). RET is based on two assumptions:

1. People behave rationally, gathering and intelligently processing information to form expecta-

(a) Effects of an increase in AD

(b) Effects of a decrease in AD

FIGURE 17-3 New classical view of self-correction (a) An unanticipated increase in aggregate demand from AD_1 to AD_2 first moves the economy from a to b. The economy then self-corrects to c. An anticipated increase in aggregate demand moves the economy directly from a to c. (b) An unanticipated decrease in aggregate demand from AD_1 to AD_3 moves the economy from a to d. The economy then self-corrects to e. An anticipated decrease in aggregate demand moves the economy directly from a to e. (Mainstream economists, however, say that if the price level remains at P_1, the economy will move from a to f, and even if the price level falls to P_2, the economy may remain at d because of downward wage inflexibility.)

tions about things which are economically important to them. These expectations are adjusted quickly as new developments affecting future economic outcomes occur. Where there is adequate information, people's beliefs about future economic outcomes *accurately reflect the likelihood that those outcomes will occur.* For example, if it is clear that some policy will cause inflation, people will recognize that fact and adjust their economic behavior in anticipation of inflation.

2. Like classical economists, RET economists assume that all product and resource markets are highly competitive and that prices and wages are flexible both upward and downward. RET goes further, assuming that new information is quickly (in some cases instantaneously) taken into account in the demand and supply curves of such markets. The upshot is that equilibrium prices and quantities adjust rapidly to unforeseen events, say, technological change or aggregate supply shocks. They adjust instantaneously to events with known outcomes, for example, changes in fiscal or monetary policy.

Unanticipated Price-Level Changes The implication of RET is not only that the economy is self-correcting but that self-correction occurs quickly. In this thinking, *unanticipated* changes in the price level—so called **price-level surprises**—do cause temporary changes in real output. Suppose, for example, an unanticipated increase in foreign demand for U.S. goods increases U.S. aggregate demand from AD_1 to AD_2 in Figure 17-3a. The immediate result is an unexpected increase in the price level from P_1 to P_2.

But now an interesting question arises. If wages and prices are flexible as assumed in RET, why doesn't the higher price level immediately cause nominal wages to rise, such that there is no increase in real output at all? Why does the economy temporarily move from point *a* to *b* along AS_1? In RET, firms increase output from Q_1 to Q_2 because of *misperceptions* about rising prices of their own products relative to prices of other products (and to prices of labor). They mistakenly think the higher prices of their own products have resulted from increased demand for those products relative to the demands for other products. Expecting higher profits, they increase their own production. But in fact *all* prices, including the price of labor (nominal wages), are rising because of the general increase in aggregate demand. Once firms

see that *all* prices and wages are rising, they decrease their production to previous levels.

In terms of Figure 17-3a, the increase in nominal wages shifts the short-run aggregate supply curve leftward, ultimately from AS_1 to AS_2, and the economy moves from *b* to *c*. Thus, the increase in real output caused by the *price-level surprise* corrects itself.

The same analysis applies in reverse for an *unanticipated* price-level decrease. In the economy represented by Figure 17-3b, firms misperceive that the prices for their own products are falling due to decreases in the demands for those products relative to other products. They respond to anticipated profit declines by cutting production. As a result of their collective actions, real output in the economy falls. But seeing that *all* prices and wages are dropping, firms increase their output to prior levels. The short-run aggregate supply curve in Figure 17-3b shifts rightward from AS_1 to AS_3, and the economy "self-corrects" by moving from *d* to *e*.

Fully Anticipated Price-Level Changes In RET, fully *anticipated* price-level changes do *not* change real output, even for short periods. In Figure 17-3a, again consider the increase in aggregate demand from AD_1 to AD_2. Businesses immediately recognize that the higher prices being paid for their products are part of the inflation they had anticipated. They understand that the same forces which are causing the inflation result in higher nominal wages, leaving their profits unchanged. The economy therefore moves *directly* from *a* to *c*. The price level rises as expected, and output remains at its full-employment level Q_1.

Similarly, a fully *anticipated* price-level decrease will leave real output unchanged. Firms conclude that nominal wages are declining by the same percentage amount as the declining price level, leaving profits unchanged. The economy represented by Figure 17-3b therefore moves *directly* from *a* to *e*. Deflation occurs, but the economy continues to produce its full-employment output Q_1. The anticipated decline in aggregate demand causes no change in real output.

Mainstream View of Self-Correction

Almost all economists acknowledge that new classical economists have made significant contributions to the theory of aggregate supply. In fact, mainstream economists have incorporated some aspects of RET into their own more detailed models. However, most economists strongly disagree with RET on the question of *downward* price and wage flexibility. While the stock market, foreign exchange market, and certain commodity markets experience day-to-day or minute-to-minute price changes, including price declines, this is not true in many product markets and in most labor markets. There is ample evidence, say mainstream economists, that *many prices and wages are inflexible downward for long periods*. As a result, it may take years for the economy to move from recession back to full-employment output, unless it gets help from fiscal and monetary policy.

Graphical Analysis

To understand this mainstream view, again examine Figure 17-3b. Suppose aggregate demand declines from AD_1 to AD_3 because of a significant decline in investment spending. If the price level remains at P_1, the economy will *not* move from *a* to *d* to *e*, as suggested by RET. Instead, the economy will move from *a* to *f*, as if it were moving along a *horizontal aggregate supply curve* between these two points. Real output will decline from its full-employment level, Q_1, to the recessionary level, Q_4.

But let's assume that surpluses in product markets eventually cause the price level to fall to P_4. Will this lead to the decline in nominal wages needed to shift aggregate supply from AS_1 to AS_2, as suggested by new classical economists? "Highly unlikely" say mainstream economists. Even more so than prices, nominal wages tend to be inflexible downward. If nominal wages do not decline in response to the decline in the price level, then the short-run aggregate supply curve will not shift rightward. The self-correction mechanism assumed by RET and new classical economists will break down. Instead, the economy will remain at *d*, experiencing less-than-full-employment output and a high rate of unemployment.

Downward Wage Inflexibility

In Chapter 11 we listed and discussed several reasons firms may not be able to, or may not want to, reduce nominal wages. Firms *may not be able to* cut wages because of wage contracts and the legal minimum wage. And firms *may not want* to reduce wages if they fear potential problems with morale, effort, and efficiency. Businesses also may not want to cut wages if doing so will mean losing skilled workers to other firms— workers in whom the current firms have heavy training investments.

While contracts are thought to be the main cause of wage rigidity, so-called *efficiency wages* and *insider-*

outsider relationships may also play a role. Let's explore these aspects of **new Keynesian economics.**

Efficiency Wage Theory

Recall from Chapter 11 that an **efficiency wage** is one which minimizes the firm's labor cost per unit of output. Normally, we would think that the market wage is the efficiency wage since it is the lowest wage at which a firm can obtain a particular type of labor. But where the cost of supervising workers is high, or where worker turnover is great, firms may discover that paying a wage which is higher than the market wage will lower their wage cost per unit of output. Example: Suppose a firm's workers, on average, produce 8 units of output at a $9 market wage but 10 units of output at a $10 above-market wage. The efficiency wage is $10, not the $9 market wage. At the $10 wage, the per-unit cost of output is only $1 (= $10 wage/10 units of output), compared with $1.12 (= $9 wage/8 units of output) at the $9 wage.

How can a higher wage result in greater efficiency?

1. ***Greater work effort***   The above-market wage, in effect, raises the cost to workers of losing their jobs because of poor performance. Because workers have a strong incentive to retain their relatively high-paying jobs, they are more apt to provide greater work effort. Looked at differently, workers are more reluctant to *shirk* (neglect or avoid work) because the higher wage makes job loss more costly to them. Consequently, the above-market wage can be the efficient wage; it can enhance worker productivity so much that the higher wage more than pays for itself.

2. ***Lower supervision costs***   With less worker incentive to shirk, the firm needs fewer supervisory personnel to monitor work performance. This, too, can lower the firm's overall wage cost per unit of output.

3. ***Reduced job turnover***   The above-market pay discourages workers from voluntarily leaving their jobs. The lower job turnover reduces the firm's cost of hiring and training workers. It also gives the firm a more experienced, more productive workforce.

The key implication for macroeconomic instability is that efficiency wages add to downward wage inflexibility. Firms paying efficiency wages will be reluctant to cut wages when aggregate demand declines since such cuts may encourage shirking, require more supervisory personnel, and increase turnover. In other words, wage cuts that reduce productivity and raise per-unit labor costs are self-defeating.

Insider-Outsider Relationships Other new Keynesian economists theorize that downward wage inflexibility may relate to relationships between "insiders" and "outsiders." *Insiders* are workers who retain employment even during recession. *Outsiders* are workers laid off from a particular firm and other unemployed workers who would like to work at that firm.

When recession produces layoffs and widespread unemployment, we might expect outsiders to offer to work for less than the current wage rate, in effect, bidding down wage rates. We might also expect firms to accept such wage offers to reduce their costs. But, according to the **insider-outsider theory,** outsiders may not be able to underbid existing wages because employers may view the cost of hiring them to be prohibitive. Employers might conclude that insiders would view this underbidding as undermining years of efforts to increase wages or, worse, as "stealing" jobs. Insiders therefore may refuse to cooperate with the new workers who have undercut their pay. Where teamwork is critical for production, such lack of cooperation will reduce overall productivity and thereby lower the firms' profits.

Even if firms were willing to employ outsiders at less than the present wage, these unemployed workers might not choose to work for less than the existing wage. To do so would risk harassment from the insiders whose pay they have undercut. Thus, outsiders may remain unemployed, relying on past saving, unemployment compensation, and other social programs to makes ends meet.

As in the efficiency wage theory, the insider-outsider theory implies that wages will be inflexible downward when aggregate demand declines. Self-correction may *eventually* occur, but not nearly as rapidly as the new classical economists contend. **(Key Question 7)**

QUICK REVIEW 17-3

■ New classical economists believe that the economy "self-corrects" when unanticipated events divert it from its full-employment level of real output.

■ In RET unanticipated price-level changes cause changes in real output in the short run but not in the long run.

■ According to RET, market participants immediately change their actions in response to anticipated price-level changes such that no change in real output occurs.

■ Mainstream economists believe that downward price and wage inflexibility means that the economy can get mired in recession for long periods.

■ Sources of downward wage inflexibility include contracts, efficiency wages, and insider-outsider relationships.

RULES OR DISCRETION?

The different views on the causes of instability and the speed of self-correction lead to vigorous debate on macro policy. Should government adhere to *policy rules* which prohibit it from causing instability in an economy that otherwise is stable? Or should it use *discretionary fiscal and monetary policy*, when needed, to stabilize a sometimes unstable economy?

In Support of Policy Rules

Monetarists and other new classical economists believe policy rules would reduce instability in the economy. The rules would prevent government from trying to "manage" aggregate demand. In this view, such management is misguided and thus likely to *cause* more instability than it cures.

Monetary Rule Since inappropriate monetary policy is the major source of macroeconomic instability, say monetarists, then enactment of a **monetary rule** would make sense. Such a rule would direct the Fed to expand the money supply each year at the same annual rate as the typical growth of the economy's production capacity. The Fed's sole monetary role would then be to use its tools (open-market operations, discount-rate changes, and changes in reserve requirements) to ensure that the nation's money supply grows steadily by, say, 3 to 5 percent a year. According to Milton Friedman,

> Such a rule . . . would eliminate . . . the major cause of instability in the economy—the capricious and unpredictable impact of countercyclical monetary policy. As long as the money supply grows at a constant rate each year, be it 3, 4, or 5 percent, any decline into recession will be temporary. The liquidity provided by a constantly growing money supply will cause aggregate demand to expand. Similarly, if the supply of money does not rise at a more than average rate, any

inflationary increase in spending will burn itself out for lack of fuel.[2]

Figure 17-4 helps illustrate the rationale for a monetary rule. Suppose the economy represented there is operating at its full-employment real output, Q_1. Also suppose the nation's long-run aggregate supply curve shifts rightward, as from AS_{LR1} to AS_{LR2}, each year, depicting the average annual potential increase in real output. You know from earlier chapters that these annual increases in "potential GDP" result from added resources, improved resources, and improved technology.

Monetarists argue that a monetary rule would tie increases in the money supply to the typical rightward shift of long-run aggregate supply. In view of the direct link between changes in the money supply and aggregate demand, this would ensure that the AD curve will shift rightward, as from AD_1 to AD_2, each year. As a result, real GDP would rise from Q_1 to Q_2 and the price level would remain constant at P_1. A monetary rule, then, would promote steady growth of real output along with price stability.

[2]As quoted in Lawrence S. Ritter and William L. Silber, *Money*, 5th ed. (New York: Basic Books, 1984), pp. 141–142.

FIGURE 17-4 Rationale for a monetary rule A monetary rule which fixed the annual increase in the money supply to the increase in potential GDP would shift aggregate demand rightward, as from AD_1 to AD_2, at the same pace as the shift in long-run aggregate supply, here AS_{LR1} to AS_{LR2}. Thus the economy would experience growth without inflation or deflation.

Generally, RET economists also support a monetary rule. They conclude that an easy or tight money policy will alter the rate of inflation but not real output. Suppose, for example, the Fed implements an easy money policy to reduce interest rates, expand investment spending, and boost real GDP. On the basis of past experience and economic knowledge, the public anticipates that this policy is inflationary and takes self-protective actions. Workers press for higher nominal wages; firms increase their product prices; and lenders raise their nominal interest rates on loans.

All these responses are designed to prevent inflation from having adverse effects on the real incomes of workers, businesses, and lenders. But collectively this behavior immediately raises wage and price levels. So the increase in aggregate demand brought about by the easy money policy is completely dissipated in higher prices and wages. Real output and employment do not expand.

In this view, the combination of rational expectations and instantaneous market adjustments dooms monetary policy to ineffectiveness. If monetary policy produces only inflation (or deflation), say the RET economists, then it makes sense to limit the Fed's discretion. Specifically, Congress ought to enact a monetary rule consistent with achieving zero or low inflation at all times.

Balanced Budget Monetarists and new classical economists question the effectiveness of fiscal policy. At the extreme, a few of these economists favor a constitutional amendment to require the Federal government to balance its budget annually. Others simply suggest that government be "passive" in its fiscal policy, not *intentionally* creating budget deficits or surpluses. Deficits and surpluses caused by recession or inflationary expansion will eventually correct themselves as the economy self-corrects to its full-employment output.

Monetarists particularly oppose expansionary fiscal policy. They believe that the deficit spending accompanying such a policy has a strong tendency to crowd out private investment. Suppose government runs a budget deficit by printing and selling U.S. securities, which means borrowing from the public. Through this borrowing, government competes with private businesses for funds. The added government borrowing increases the demand for money, which then raises the interest rate and crowds out a substantial amount of private investment that would otherwise have been profitable. The net effect of a

Profit Sharing: Making Wages Flexible

Are there any ways that downward wage flexibility can be increased so that declines in aggregate demand do not have such a negative effect on output and employment?

Our comparison of mainstream and new classical views on the macroeconomy suggests that if wages are inflexible downward, output and employment will decline when aggregate demand falls. Most economists recognize that labor contracts, among other considerations, make wages inflexible downward, at least in the short run. The declines in labor demand accompanying recessions therefore primarily affect real output and employment. This problem has led some economists to propose profit sharing as a way to increase the flexibility of wage rates. The idea is to make labor markets operate more like the new classical

model, with its vertical aggregate supply curve, by creating greater employment stability.

The essence of these profit-sharing proposals is to tie some portion of wages directly to the firm's profitability, making profit-sharing payments a part of workers' pay. Instead of paying workers a guaranteed wage rate of, say, $10 per hour, workers might be guaranteed $5 per hour (the base wage) and additional compensation equal to some predetermined percentage of the firm's profits (the profit-share wage). Total compensation (base wage + profit-share wage) may exceed or fall short of $10 per hour, depending on the firm's economic fortunes.

How would such a plan affect employment? Initially assume workers are receiving $10 per hour—$5 as a guaranteed wage and another $5 as profit-sharing compensation. Now suppose a recession occurs and the employer's sales and profits plummet. The $5 of profit-sharing income will fall and might decline to zero, so the actual wages paid by the firm fall from $10 to $5 an hour. With the new, depressed demand for labor, the firm would clearly choose to employ more workers under this wage system than the standard system. Hourly wages will have automatically fallen from $10 to $5.

There are a number of criticisms of such profit-sharing wage plans. The plans might jeopardize the wage uniformity and wage gains achieved by organized labor. A further criticism is that employers might respond to the low base wage by adopting production techniques which use relatively more labor and less capital. Because the amount of capital equipment per worker is critical to productivity and economic growth, this pay scheme might impair the long-run expansion of real GDP. At the pragmatic level, critics point out that wage plans linked to profits eliminate the present certainty which workers have as to whether their employers have properly fulfilled the labor contract. With profit sharing, employers might use accounting and other techniques to hide profits and therefore evade paying share wages.

Finally, there is the fundamental question of whether workers will accept more jobs and greater employment stability in exchange for a reduced hourly wage guarantee and higher variability of earnings. But it should be noted that in the past decade a growing number of union and nonunion contracts have contained profit-sharing arrangements. Although a full-blown profit-sharing economy seems improbable, limited profit sharing appears to be spreading.

---

budget deficit on aggregate demand therefore is unpredictable and, at best, modest.

If a deficit was financed through printing new money instead of borrowing, the crowding out could be avoided and the deficit would be followed by expansion of real GDP. The monetarists point out, however, that such an expansion would *not* be the result of the deficit per se but, rather, of the expansion of the money supply. Moreover, this expansion of real output would be only temporary. A boost in nominal wages would soon follow the inflation, returning real output to its previous level.

RET economists reject discretionary fiscal policy for the same reason they reject active monetary policy: they do not think it works. Business and labor will immediately adjust their behavior in anticipation of the price-level effects of a change in fiscal policy. The economy will move directly to the anticipated new price level. Like monetary policy, say the RET theorists, fiscal policy can move the economy along its vertical long-run aggregate supply curve. But because its effects on inflation are fully anticipated, fiscal policy cannot alter real GDP even in the short run. The best course of action for government is to balance its budget.

In Defense of Discretionary Stabilization Policy

Mainstream economists oppose a monetary rule and a balanced-budget requirement. They believe that monetary policy and fiscal policy are important tools for achieving and maintaining full employment, price stability, and economic growth.

Discretionary Monetary Policy In supporting discretionary monetary policy, mainstream economists argue that the rationale for a monetary rule is flawed. While there is indeed a close relationship between the money supply and nominal GDP over long periods, in shorter periods this relationship breaks down. The reason is that the velocity of money has proved to be more variable and unpredictable than monetarists contend. Arguing that velocity is variable both cyclically and over time, mainstream economists contend that a constant annual rate of increase in the money supply need not eliminate fluctuations in aggregate demand. In terms of the equation of exchange, a steady rise of M does not guarantee a steady expansion of aggregate demand because V—the rate at which money is spent—can change.

Again reconsider Figure 17-4, in which we demonstrated the monetary rule. During the period in question, optimistic business expectations might create a boom in investment spending and thus shift the aggregate demand curve to some location to the right of AD_2. (You may want to pencil in a new AD curve, labeling it AD_3.) The price level would then rise above P_1; that is, demand-pull inflation would occur. In this case, the monetary rule will not accomplish its goal of maintaining price stability. Mainstream economists say that the Fed can use a tight money policy to reduce the excessive investment spending and thereby

hold the rightward shift of aggregate demand to AD_2, thus avoiding inflation.

Similarly, suppose that investment instead declines because of pessimistic business expectations. Aggregate demand will then increase by some amount less than the increase from AD_1 to AD_2 in Figure 17-4. Again, the monetary rule fails the stability test: the price level sinks below P_1 (deflation occurs). Or if the price level is inflexible downward at P_1, the economy does not achieve its full-employment output (unemployment rises). An easy money policy can help avoid either outcome.

Mainstream economists quip that the trouble with the monetary rule is that it tells the policymaker: "Don't do something, just stand there."

Discretionary Fiscal Policy Mainstream economists support the use of fiscal policy to keep recessions from deepening or to keep mild inflation from becoming severe inflation. They recognize the possibility of crowding out but do not think it is a serious problem when business borrowing is depressed, as is usually the case in recession. Because politicians can abuse fiscal policy, most economists feel that it should be held in reserve for situations where monetary policy appears to be ineffective or working too slowly.

As indicated earlier, mainstream economists oppose requirements to balance the budget annually. Tax revenues fall sharply during recessions and rise briskly during periods of demand-pull inflation. Therefore, a law or constitutional amendment mandating an annually balanced budget would require government to *increase* tax rates and *reduce* government spending during recession and *reduce* tax rates and *increase* government spending during economic booms. The first set of actions would worsen recession, and the second set would fuel inflation. (You may want to review Figure 12-6.)

Increased Macro Stability

Finally, mainstream economists point out that, as shown in Figure 17-5, the U.S. economy has been about one-third more stable since 1946 than in earlier periods. It is not a coincidence, they say, that use of discretionary fiscal and monetary policy characterized the latter period but not the former. These policies have helped tame the business cycle. Moreover, mainstream economists point out several specific policy successes in the past two decades:

FIGURE 17-5 **American real GDP, percentage change on previous quarter (3 months), 1895–1995**   Since 1946, quarterly changes in real GDP have been about one-third less volatile than those in the 1895–1918 period and 1919–1945 period. Mainstream macroeconomists attribute at least part of this increased stability to use of fiscal and monetary policy. [*Source:* Victor Zarnowitz, *Business Cycles* (Chicago: University of Chicago Press, 1995, pp. 80–81). Truncated and updated.]

----

1. A tight money policy dropped inflation from 13.5 percent in 1980 to 3.2 percent in 1983.
2. An expansionary fiscal policy reduced the unemployment rate from 9.7 percent in 1982 to 5.5 percent in 1988.
3. An easy money policy helped the economy recover from the 1990–1991 recession.
4. Judicious tightening of monetary policy in the mid-1990s helped the economy remain on a noninflationary, full-employment growth path. **(Key Question 13)**

SUMMARY OF ALTERNATIVE VIEWS

Here and in Chapter 16 we presented the central ideas and policy implications of a number of macroeconomic theories. In Table 17-1 we summarize four of them: mainstream macroeconomics, monetarism, rational expectations theory, and supply-side economics. You will observe that we broadly defined new classical economics to include both monetarism and the rational expectations theory since both adhere to the natural-rate hypothesis that the economy tends automatically to achieve equilibrium at its full-employment output. Also note that "mainstream macroeconomics" remains based on Keynesian ideas.

These different perspectives have forced mainstream economists to rethink some of their fundamental principles. And as is true of many debates, much compromise and revision of positions have occurred. Although considerable disagreement remains, mainstream macro economists agree with monetarists that "money matters" and that excessive growth of the money supply is the major cause of long-lasting, rapid inflation. They also agree with RET proponents and theorists of coordination failures that expectations are important. If government can create expectations of price stability, full employment, and economic growth, households and firms will tend to act in ways to make that happen. Finally, mainstream economists concur with supply-side economists and real-business-cycle theorists that government needs to focus on policies to increase economic growth. In short, thanks to ongoing challenges to the conventional wisdom, macroeconomics continues to evolve.

CHAPTER SUMMARY -------------------------

1. In classical economics the aggregate supply curve is vertical and establishes the level of real output, while the aggregate demand curve is generally stable and establishes the price level. In this view the economy is highly stable.

Issue	Mainstream macroeconomics (Keynesian based)	New classical economics (natural-rate hypothesis)		Supply-side economics
		Monetarism	Rational expectations	
View of the private economy	Potentially unstable	Stable in long run at natural rate of unemployment	Stable in long run at natural rate of unemployment	May stagnate without proper work, saving, and investment incentives
Cause of the observed instability of the private economy	Investment plans unequal to saving plans (changes in AD); AS shocks	Inappropriate monetary policy	Unanticipated AD and AS shocks in the short run	Changes in AS
Appropriate macro policies	Active fiscal and monetary policy	Monetary rule	Monetary rule	Policies to increase AS
How changes in the money supply affect the economy	By changing the interest rate, which changes investment and real GDP	By directly changing AD, which changes GDP	No effect on output because price-level changes are anticipated	By influencing investment and thus AS
View of the velocity of money	Unstable	Stable	No consensus	No consensus
How fiscal policy affects the economy	Changes AD and GDP via the multiplier process	No effect unless money supply changes	No effect on output because price-level changes are anticipated	Affects GDP and price level via changes in AS
View of cost-push inflation	Possible (wage-push, AS shock)	Impossible in the long run in the absence of excessive money supply growth	Impossible in the long run in the absence of excessive money supply growth	Possible (tax-transfer disincentives, higher costs due to regulation)

2. In Keynesian economics the aggregate supply curve is horizontal at less-than-full-employment levels of real output, while the aggregate demand curve is inherently unstable. In this view the economy is highly unstable.

3. The mainstream view is that macro instability is caused by volatility of investment spending which shifts the aggregate demand curve. If aggregate demand increases too rapidly, demand-pull inflation can occur; if aggregate demand decreases, recession can occur. Occasionally, adverse supply shocks also cause instability.

4. Monetarism focuses on the equation of exchange: $MV = PQ$. Because velocity is thought to be stable, changes in M create changes in nominal GDP ($= PQ$). Monetarists believe that the most significant cause of macroeconomic instability has been inappropriate monetary policy. Too rapid increases in M cause inflation; in-

sufficient growth of M causes recession. In this view, a major cause of the Great Depression was inappropriate monetary policy which allowed the money supply to decline by nearly 40 percent.

5. Real-business-cycle theory views changes in resource availability and technology (real factors), which alter productivity, as the main causes of macroeconomic instability. In this theory, shifts in the economy's long-run aggregate supply curve change real output. In turn, money demand and money supply change, shifting the aggregate demand curve in the same direction as the initial change in long-run aggregate supply. Real output thus can change without a change in the price level.

6. A coordination failure is said to occur when people do not reach a mutually beneficial equilibrium because they lack some way to jointly coordinate their actions to achieve it. Depending on people's expectations, the economy can come to rest at a good equilibrium (noninflationary full-employment output) or bad equilibriums (less-than-full-employment output or demand-pull inflation). These bad equilibriums are coordination failures.

7. The rational expectations theory (RET) rests on two assumptions: (1) With sufficient information, people's beliefs about future economic outcomes accurately reflect the likelihood that those outcomes will occur; and (2) markets are highly competitive, meaning that prices and wages are flexible both upward and downward.

8. New classical economists (monetarists and rational expectations theorists) see the economy as automatically correcting itself when disturbed from its full-employment level of real output. In RET, unanticipated changes in aggregate demand change the price level, which in the short run leads firms to change output. But once the firms realize that all prices are changing (including nominal wages) as part of general inflation or deflation, they change their output to the previous level. Anticipated changes in aggregate demand produce only changes in the price level, not changes in real output.

9. Mainstream economists reject the new classical view that all prices and wages are flexible downward. Nominal wages, in particular, are inflexible downward because of several factors including labor contracts, efficiency wages, and insider-outsider relationships. This means that declines in aggregate demand decrease real output, not simply wages and prices.

10. Monetarist and RET economists recommend a monetary rule in which the money supply is increased at a rate equal to the long-run growth of potential GDP. They also support maintaining a "neutral" fiscal policy, as opposed to using discretionary fiscal policy to create budget deficits or budget surpluses. A few monetarists and RET economists favor a constitutional amendment that would require the Federal government to balance its budget annually.

11. Mainstream economists oppose a monetary rule and a balanced-budget requirement, vigorously defending discretionary monetary and fiscal policy. They say that theory and evidence suggest that these policies are helpful in achieving full employment, price stability, and economic growth.

TERMS AND CONCEPTS

classical economics	velocity	new classical economics	efficiency wage
Keynesianism	real-business-cycle	price-level surprises	insider-outsider theory
monetarism	theory	new Keynesian	monetary rule
equation of exchange	coordination failures	economics	

STUDY QUESTIONS

1. KEY QUESTION Use the aggregate demand–aggregate supply model to compare the "old" classical and Keynesian interpretations of **(a)** the aggregate supply curve and **(b)** the stability of the aggregate demand curve. Which of these interpretations seems most consistent with the realities of the Great Depression?

2. What is the usual cause of macroeconomic instability, according to mainstream economists? What role does the spending-income multiplier play in creating instability? How might adverse aggregate supply factors cause instability, according to mainstream economists?

3. State and explain the basic equation of monetarism. What is the major cause of macroeconomic instability, as viewed by monetarists?

4. KEY QUESTION Suppose that the money supply and the nominal GDP for a hypothetical economy are $96 billion and $336 billion, respectively. What is the velocity of money? How will households and businesses react if the central bank reduces the money supply by $20 billion? By how much will nominal GDP have to fall to restore equilibrium, according to the monetarist perspective?

5. Briefly describe the difference between a so-called real business cycle and a more traditional "spending" business cycle.

6. Andrew and Craig were walking directly toward each other in a congested store aisle. Andrew moved to his left to avoid Craig, and at the same time Craig moved to his right to avoid Andrew. They bumped into each other. What concept does this example illustrate? How does this idea relate to macroeconomic instability?

7. KEY QUESTION Use an AD-AS graph to demonstrate and explain the price-level and real-output outcome of an anticipated decline in aggregate demand, as viewed by RET economists. (Assume that the economy initially is operating at its full-employment level of output.) Then, demonstrate and explain on the same graph the outcome, as viewed by mainstream economists.

8. What is an efficiency wage? How might payment of an above-market wage reduce shirking by employees and reduce worker turnover? How might efficiency wages contribute to downward wage inflexibility, at least for a time, when aggregate demand declines?

9. How might relationships between so-called insiders and outsiders contribute to downward wage inflexibility?

10. Use the equation of exchange to explain the rationale for a monetary rule. Why does the rule run into trouble if V unexpectedly falls because of, say, a drop in investment spending by businesses?

11. Answer questions (a) and (b) on the basis of the following information for a hypothetical economy in year 1: money supply = $400 billion; long-term annual growth of potential GDP = 3 percent; velocity = 4. Assume that the banking system initially has no excess reserves and the reserve requirement is 10 percent. Also assume that velocity is constant and the economy initially is operating at its full-employment real output.
   a. What is the level of nominal GDP in year 1?
   b. Suppose the Fed adheres to a monetary rule through open-market operations. What amount of U.S. securities will it have to sell to, or buy from, banks or the public between years 1 and 2 to meet its monetary rule?

12. Explain the difference between "active" discretionary fiscal policy advocated by mainstream economists and "passive" fiscal policy advocated by new classical economists. Explain: "The problem with a balanced-budget amendment is that it would, in a sense, require active fiscal policy—but in the *wrong* direction—as the economy slides into recession."

13. KEY QUESTION Place MON, RET, or MAIN besides statements which most closely reflect monetarist, rational expectations, or mainstream views, respectively.
   a. Anticipated changes in aggregate demand affect only the price level; they have no effect on real output.

   b. Downward wage inflexibility means that declines in aggregate demand can cause long-lasting recession.
   c. Changes in the money supply M increase PQ; at first only Q rises because nominal wages are fixed, but once workers adapt their expectations to new realities, P rises and Q returns to its former level.
   d. Fiscal and monetary policy smooth out the business cycle.
   e. The Fed should increase the money supply at a fixed annual rate.

14. You have just been elected president of the United States, and the present chair of the Federal Reserve Board has resigned. You need to appoint a new person to this position, as well as a person to chair your Council of Economic Advisers. Using Table 17-1 and your knowledge of macroeconomics, identify the perspectives on macro theory and policy you would want your appointees to hold. Remember, the economic health of the entire nation—and your chances for reelection—may depend on these selections.

15. (Last Word) How would profit sharing by labor increase downward "wage" flexibility? Why is greater downward wage flexibility desirable?

16. WEB-BASED QUESTION **The Equation of Exchange—What Is the Current Velocity of Money?** The fundamental equation of monetarism is the equation of exchange: $MV = PQ = GDP$. The velocity of money, V, can be found by dividing GDP by M, the money supply. Calculate the velocity of money for the past few years. Which GDP data should be used: real or nominal GDP? Why? How stable is V during this time? Is V increasing or decreasing? Get GDP data from the NIPA Data section at the Bureau of Economic Analysis http://www.bea.doc.gov/bea/glance.htm. Money supply data can be found at the Federal Reserve http://www.bog.frb.fed.us/releases/h6/about.htm under Money Stock, Liquid Assets, and Debt Measures—Historical Data.

17. WEB-BASED QUESTION **American Real GDP—Is It Really More Stable Than Other Countries'?** Since 1946, quarterly changes in American real GDP have been less volatile than in earlier decades. How does recent U.S. GDP volitility compare to other countries? Would you expect it to be more or less stable? Why or why not? Is there a pattern (e.g., is lower volatility associated with higher GDP countries)? Would the comparison be valid if nominal GDP data was used rather than real GDP data? Visit the Quarterly Growth Rates in GDP at Constant Prices section at the OECD http://www.oecd.org/std/nahome.htm.

Economic Growth

Despite periods of macroeconomic instability, the capitalist countries have experienced impressive economic growth during this century. In the United States, real output has increased 15-fold since 1900, while population has only tripled. This means that five times more goods and services are available to the average U.S. resident than were available in 1900. Moreover, today's goods and services are of much higher quality than those of 1900. This expansion and improvement of output has created greater material abundance, lifted the standard of living, and eased the unlimited-wants–scarce-resources problem.

But the U.S. growth story is not totally upbeat. Since 1970 U.S. economic growth has slowed considerably relative to that in earlier periods and other nations. Twenty-one advanced industrial nations, not to mention many developing nations, grew more rapidly than the United States over the past three decades.

We begin our analysis of economic growth by clearly defining it. Next, we show how economic growth can be depicted within our graphical models. Then, we examine the long-term growth record of the United States, paying particular attention to the contributing factors. Since productivity is one of these factors, we examine the post-1970 slowdown of productivity growth in the United States. Next, we explore whether the United States is achieving a "new economy," which might deliver a stronger future rate of growth. Finally, we ask what government can do, if anything, to boost the rate of economic growth.

GROWTH ECONOMICS

The subset of economics called *growth economics* examines the factors which expand an economy's production capacity over time. It also analyzes public policies designed to increase economic growth.

Two Definitions

Economic growth is defined and measured in two ways:

1. An increase in real GDP occurring over some time period

2. An increase in real GDP *per capita* occurring over some time period

In measuring military potential or political preeminence, the first definition is more relevant. The second definition, however, is superior for comparing living standards. While China's GDP is $744 billion compared with Denmark's $155 billion, Denmark's GDP per capita is $29,890 compared with only $620 in China.

In either definition, economic growth is calculated as an annual percentage rate of growth. For example, if real GDP was $200 billion in some country last year and $210 billion this year, the rate of growth would be 5 percent {= [($210 − $200)/$200] × 100}.

Growth as a Goal

Growth is a widely held economic goal. The expansion of total output relative to population means rising real wages and incomes and thus higher standards of living. *An economy experiencing economic growth is better able to meet people's wants and resolve socioeconomic problems.* Rising real wages and incomes provide new opportunities to individuals and families—a vacation trip, a home computer, higher education—*without* sacrificing other opportunities and enjoyments. A growing economy can take on new programs to alleviate poverty and clean up the environment *without* impairing existing levels of consumption, investment, and public goods production.

In short, *growth lessens the burden of scarcity.* A growing economy, unlike a static economy, can consume more today while increasing its capacity to produce more in the future. By easing the burden of scarcity—by relaxing society's production constraints—economic growth allows a nation to attain economic goals more fully and to undertake new endeavors which require goods and services.

Arithmetic of Growth

Why do economists make such a big deal about small changes in the rate of growth? Because it really matters! For the United States, with a current real GDP of about $8000 billion, the difference between a 3 percent and a 4 percent rate of growth is about $80 billion of output per year. For a very poor country, a 0.5-percentage-point change in the growth rate may mean the difference between starvation and mere hunger.

When viewed over many years, an apparently small difference in the rate of growth becomes highly significant because of compounding. Suppose Alta and Zorn have identical GDPs, but Alta grows at a 4 percent yearly rate, while Zorn grows at 2 percent. Based on the rule of 70, Alta's GDP would double in about 18 years (= 70/4); Zorn's would double in 35 years (= 70/2).

Some economists argue that growth is more important to a nation's future than is economic stability. Eliminating a gap between actual GDP and potential GDP might increase the national income by, say, 3 percent on a one-time basis. In contrast, a 3 percent annual growth rate will increase the national income by more than 6 percent in 2 years, more than 9 percent in 3 years, and so on.

INGREDIENTS OF GROWTH

There are six ingredients in the growth of any economy. They can be grouped as supply, demand, and efficiency factors.

Supply Factors

Four ingredients of growth relate to the physical ability of the economy to expand. They are (1) increases in the quantity and quality of natural resources, (2) increases in the quantity and quality of human resources, (3) increases in the supply (or stock) of capital goods, and (4) improvements in technology. These **supply factors**—physical and technical agents of greater production—permit an economy to increase its real output.

Demand Factor

The fifth ingredient of economic growth is the **demand factor.** To realize its growing production potential, a nation must fully employ its expanding supplies of resources. This requires a growing level of aggregate demand.

Efficiency Factor

The sixth ingredient of economic growth is the **efficiency factor.** To reach its production potential, a nation must achieve not only full employment but also economic efficiency. The country must use its existing and added resources in the least costly way (*productive efficiency*) in producing the specific mix of goods and services that maximizes society's well-being (*allocative efficiency*). The ability to expand production, together with the full use of available resources, are *not* sufficient for achieving maximum possible growth. Also required is the efficient use of those resources.

The supply, demand, and efficiency factors in growth are related. Unemployment caused by insufficient aggregate demand (the demand factor) can retard the rate of new capital accumulation (a supply factor) and slow expenditures on research (also a supply factor). Conversely, low spending on innovation and investment (supply factors) can cause insufficient aggregate demand (the demand factor) and unemployment. Widespread inefficiency in the use of resources (the efficiency factor) may translate into higher costs of goods and services and thus lower profits. This may slow the accumulation of capital (a supply factor).

GRAPHICAL ANALYSIS

We can place the six factors underlying economic growth in proper perspective through Chapter 2's production possibilities curves and Chapter 16's extended AD-AS analysis.

Growth and Production Possibilities

Recall that a curve such as *AB* in Figure 18-1 is a production possibilities curve. It indicates the various *maximum* combinations of products the economy can produce with its fixed quantity and quality of natural, human, and capital resources and its stock of technological knowledge. An improvement in any of the supply factors will push the production possibilities curve outward, as from *AB* to *CD*.

But the demand and efficiency factors remind us the economy need not attain its maximum production potential. The curve may shift outward but leave the economy behind at some level of operation such as *a* on *AB*. Because *a* is inside the new production possibilities curve *CD*, the economy has not achieved its growth potential. This enhanced production potential will not be realized unless (1) aggregate demand increases sufficiently to sustain full employment, and (2) the additional resources are employed efficiently such that they make the maximum possible dollar contribution to output.

An increase in aggregate demand is needed to move the economy from *a* to a point on *CD*. And to realize the greatest increase in the monetary value of its output—its greatest real GDP growth—this loca-

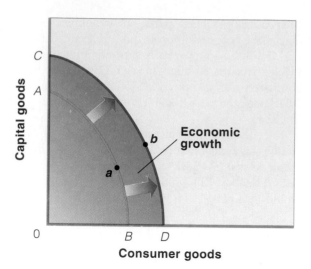

FIGURE 18-1 Economic growth and the production possibilities curve Economic growth is made possible by the four supply factors which shift the production possibilities curve outward, as from *AB* to *CD*. Economic growth is realized when the demand factor and efficiency factor move the economy from point *a* to *b*.

----

tion on *CD* must be optimal. You know from Chapter 2 that this "best allocation" is determined by expanding production of each good until its marginal benefit equals its marginal cost. Here, we assume this optimal combination of capital and consumer goods is *b*.

Example: The net increase in the labor force of the United States is roughly 1.5 million workers per year. This increment raises the production capacity of the economy. But obtaining the extra output these added workers can produce presumes they can find jobs. It also presumes these jobs are in firms and industries where their talents are fully and optimally used. Society does not want new labor-force entrants to be unemployed. Nor does it want pediatricians working as plumbers or workers producing goods which have higher marginal costs than marginal benefits. **(Key Question 2)**

Labor and Productivity Although demand and efficiency considerations are important, discussions of growth focus primarily on the supply side. Figure 18-2 provides a framework for discussing the supply factors in growth. It indicates two fundamental ways society can increase its real output and income: (1) by increasing its inputs of resources, and (2) by increasing the productivity of those inputs. Let's focus on inputs of labor. We can say that *a nation's real GDP in any year depends on the input of labor (measured in worker-*

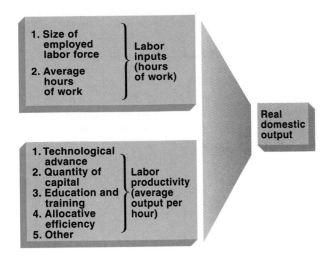

FIGURE 18-2 The supply determinants of real output
Real GDP is usefully viewed as the product of the quantity of labor inputs multiplied by labor productivity.

- -

hours) multiplied by **labor productivity** *(measured as real output per worker per hour).*

Total output = worker-hours × labor productivity

Illustration: Assume an economy has 10 workers, each working 2000 hours per year (50 weeks at 40 hours per week). The total input of worker-hours therefore is 20,000 hours. If productivity—average real output per worker-hour—is $5, then total output or real GDP will be $100,000 (= 20,000 × $5).

What determines the number of hours worked each year? And what determines labor productivity? Figure 18-2 provides some answers. The hours of labor input depend on the size of the employed labor force and the length of the average workweek. Labor-force size depends on the size of the working-age population and the **labor-force participation rate—** *the percentage of the working-age population actually in the labor force.* The average workweek is governed by legal and institutional considerations and by collective bargaining.

Productivity is determined by technological progress, the quantity of capital goods available to workers, the quality of labor itself, and the efficiency with which inputs are allocated, combined, and managed. Productivity rises when the health, training, education, and motivation of workers are improved; when workers have more and better machinery and natural resources with which to work; when production is better organized and managed; and when labor is reallocated from less efficient industries to more efficient industries.

Extended AD-AS Model

We can also view economic growth through the extended AD-AS model developed in Chapter 16.

Suppose an economy's aggregate demand curve, long-run aggregate supply curve, and short-run aggregate supply curve are AD_1 AS_{LR1}, and AS_1, as shown in Figure 18-3. The equilibrium price level

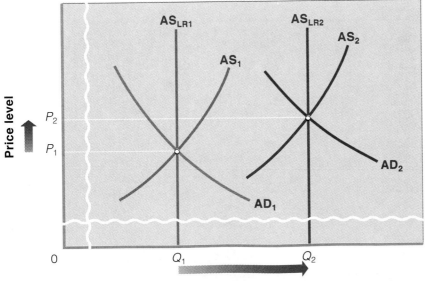

FIGURE 18-3 Economic growth in the extended AD-AS model Long-run and short-run aggregate supply have increased over time, as from AS_{LR1} to AS_{LR2} and AS_1 to AS_2. Simultaneously, aggregate demand has shifted rightward, as from AD_1 to AD_2. The outcome of these combined shifts has been economic growth, shown as the increase in real output from Q_1 to Q_2, accompanied by inflation, shown as the rise in the price level from P_1 to P_2.

- -

and level of real output are P_1 and Q_1. At price level P_1, the short-run aggregate supply is AS_1; it slopes upward because, in the short run, changes in the price level change the level of real output. However, in the long run, nominal wages change in the same direction and by the same percentage as the price level. Real output then returns to its prior level, making the long-run aggregate supply curve vertical at the economy's full-employment level of output, here Q_1. As with the location of the production possibilities curve, real supply factors—the quantity and quality of resources and technology—determine the full-employment level of real output. Price-level changes do not shift a nation's production possibilities curve; neither do they shift the nation's long-run aggregate supply curve.

Increase in Short- and Long-Run Aggregate Supply

Let's now assume that changes in the supply factors shift the long-run aggregate supply curve rightward from AS_{LR1} to AS_{LR2}. This means the production possibilities curve in Figure 18-2 has moved outward. The economy's *potential* output has increased.

Increase in Aggregate Demand

Assuming downward price and wage inflexibility, the economy can *realize* its greater production potential only through an increase in aggregate demand. In Figure 18-3, suppose that increases in consumption, investment, gov-ernment, and net export spending shift the aggregate demand curve from AD_1 to AD_2. Also suppose the economy continues to use its resources efficiently.

Economic Outcomes The increases of aggregate supply and aggregate demand in our figure have increased real output from Q_1 to Q_2 and boosted the price level from P_1 to P_2. At the higher price level P_2, the economy confronts a new short-run aggregate supply curve AS_2. The result of the dynamics described in Figure 18-3 is economic growth, accompanied by mild inflation. These outcomes are consistent with the actual secular trend of real GDP and the price level in the United States. (You can confirm this by examining items 18 and 21 on the inside covers of this book.) **(Key Question 3)**

GROWTH IN THE UNITED STATES

Table 18-1 is an overview of economic growth in the United States over past decades. Column 2 reveals strong growth as measured by increases in real GDP. Specifically, *real GDP has increased sixfold since 1940.* But the U.S. population has also increased. Nevertheless, in column 4 we find that *real GDP per capita has increased by threefold since 1940.*

TABLE 18-1   Real GDP and per capita GDP, 1929–1997

(1) Year	(2) GDP, billions of 1992 dollars	(3) Population, millions	(4) Per capita GDP, 1992 dollars (2) ÷ (3)
1929	$ 791	122	$ 6,484
1933	577	126	4,579
1940	941	132	7,129
1945	1627	140	11,621
1950	1611	152	10,599
1955	2001	166	12,054
1960	2263	181	12,503
1965	2881	194	14,851
1970	3398	205	16,576
1975	3874	214	18,103
1980	4615	228	20,241
1985	5324	239	22,276
1990	6136	250	24,544
1995	6742	263	25,635
1997	7191	268	26,832

Source: Economic Report of the President, 1998; U.S. Department of Commerce.

What has been the *rate* of U.S. growth? Observe in Global Perspective 18-1 that *real GDP* has grown at an annual rate of 3.1 percent since 1948. Not shown, *real GDP per capita* has increased nearly 2 percent annually since then. However, we must qualify these raw numbers in four ways:

1. *Improved products and services* The numbers in Table 18-1 and Global Perspective 18-1 do not fully account for improvements in products and services; they thus understate the growth of economic well-being. Purely quantitative data do not accurately compare an era of iceboxes and LPs with an era of refrigerators and CDs.

2. *Added leisure* The increases in real GDP and per capita GDP identified in Table 18-1 were accomplished despite large increases in leisure. The standard workweek, once 50 hours, is now about 40 hours. Again the raw growth numbers understate the gain in economic well-being.

3. *Environmental effects* In contrast, these measures of growth do not account for any adverse effects growth may have had on the environment and the quality of life. If growth debases the physical environment and creates a stressful work environment, the bare growth numbers will overstate the gains from growth.

4. *International comparisons* Over the past half-century, the growth record of the United States is less impressive than that of many other nations. Observe in Global Perspective 18-1 that Japan's growth rate averaged more than twice that of the United States during this period. In recent years, however, the growth rates in Japan and Germany have slowed. Also, in recent decades countries with smaller GDPs per capita have tended to grow more rapidly than countries with already high GDPs per capita.

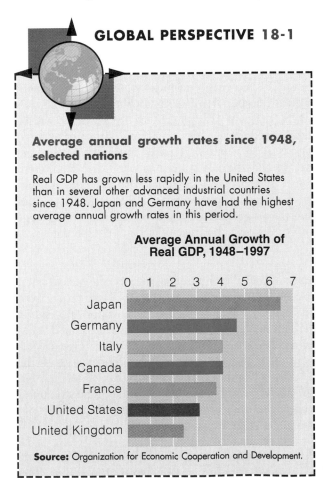

GLOBAL PERSPECTIVE 18-1

Average annual growth rates since 1948, selected nations

Real GDP has grown less rapidly in the United States than in several other advanced industrial countries since 1948. Japan and Germany have had the highest average annual growth rates in this period.

Average Annual Growth of Real GDP, 1948–1997

	0 1 2 3 4 5 6 7
Japan	
Germany	
Italy	
Canada	
France	
United States	
United Kingdom	

Source: Organization for Economic Cooperation and Development.

QUICK REVIEW 18-1

■ Economic growth can be measured as **(a)** an increase in real GDP over time or **(b)** an increase in real GDP per capita over time.

■ Graphically, economic growth is shown as **(a)** an outward shift of a nation's production possibilities curve (accompanied by movement from some point on the old curve to a point on the new curve), or **(b)** combined rightward shifts of the long-run aggregate supply curve, the short-run aggregate supply curve, and the aggregate demand curve.

■ Growth of real GDP in the United States has averaged slightly more than 3 percent annually since World War II.

ACCOUNTING FOR GROWTH

Table 18-2 provides estimates of the relative importance of the factors contributing to U.S. economic growth. The categories and data are based on the work of Edward Denison, who estimated what percentage of annual U.S. growth between 1929 and 1982 was accounted for by each factor listed in the table. We have projected Denison's estimates to the present, making only slight adjustments to his numbers on the basis of post-1982 trends.

Inputs versus Productivity

The most evident conclusion from Table 18-2 is that productivity growth has been the most important force underlying the growth of U.S. real output and

TABLE 18-2   The sources of growth in U.S. real national income, 1929–1997

Sources of growth	Percentage of total growth
1. Increase in quantity of labor	33
2. Increase in labor productivity	67
3. Technological advance	28
4. Quantity of capital	20
5. Education and training	12
6. Economies of scale	8
7. Improved resource allocation	8
8. Legal-human environment and other	−9
	100

Source: Edward F. Denison, *Trends in American Economic Growth, 1929–1982* (Washington: Brookings Institution, 1985), p. 30; *Economic Report of the President,* various years; authors' estimates.

income. Increases in the quantity of labor (item 1) account for only about one-third of the increase in real output since 1929; two-thirds is attributable to rising labor productivity (item 2).

Quantity of Labor

The U.S. population and labor force have both expanded significantly. Since 1929 total population grew from 122 to 268 million and the labor force increased from 49 to 136 million workers. Reductions in the length of the workweek reduced the growth of labor inputs before World War II, but the workweek has declined little since then. Falling birthrates in the past 30 years have slowed the growth of the native population, but increased immigration has partly offset this slowdown. Of most significance, however, has been a surge of participation of women in the labor force. Largely because of this trend, the U.S. labor force has grown by about 2 million workers per year during the past 25 years.

Technological Advance

Technological advance (item 3 in Table 18-2) is a critical engine of growth, accounting for 28 percent of the increase in real output since 1929.

Technological advance includes not merely new production techniques but also new managerial methods and new forms of business organization. Generally, it is linked with *the discovery of new knowledge*, which permits firms to combine a specific amount of resources in new ways to achieve a greater output.

Technological advance and capital formation (investment) are closely related; technological advance often, but not always, requires investment in new machinery and equipment. The purchase of new computers not only means more computers but quicker, more powerful computers embodying new technology. In contrast, modern crop-rotation practices and contour plowing are ideas which contribute to expanded output, although they do not necessarily use new kinds of, or increased amounts of, capital equipment.

Technological advance has been both rapid and profound. Gas and diesel engines, conveyor belts, and assembly lines are significant developments of the past. More recently, technology has produced automation and the push-button factory. Bigger, faster, and more fuel-efficient commercial aircraft, integrated microcircuits, computers, xerography, containerized shipping, and the Internet—not to mention biotechnology, lasers, and superconductivity—are technological achievements which were in the realm of fantasy only a generation or two ago.

Quantity of Capital

Some 20 percent—one-fifth—of the annual growth of real output since 1929 is attributable to increases in the quantity of capital (item 4). A worker will be more productive when equipped with more capital goods. And a nation acquires more capital through saving and the investment in plant and equipment which saving makes possible. A recent estimate suggests that total output will increase by about one-fourth of a percentage point for each extra percentage of GDP invested in machinery and equipment.

The critical consideration for labor productivity is the amount of capital goods *per worker*. The aggregate stock of capital might expand in a specific period, but if the labor force also increases rapidly, labor productivity may not rise because each worker will not necessarily be better-equipped. This happened in the United States in the 1970s and 1980s when the labor force surged, contributing to a slowing of U.S. productivity growth.

The quantity of capital per worker, however, has greatly increased in the United States. The amount of capital equipment (machinery and buildings) per worker is currently about $90,000.

Two addenda:

1. The United States has been saving and investing a smaller percentage of its GDP in recent years than have most other industrially advanced nations. This helps explain the lower growth rate in the United States. Lower levels of investment as a percentage of GDP are associated with lower growth rates of real GDP per capita (review Global Perspective 2-1).

2. Investment is not only private but also public. Some observers contend that U.S. **infrastructure**—highways and bridges, public transit systems, wastewater treatment facilities, municipal water systems, airports, and so on—faces growing problems of deterioration, technological obsolescence, and insufficient capacity to serve future growth.

Also, public capital (infrastructure) and private capital are complementary. Investments in new highways promote private investment in new factories and retail establishments along their routes. Industrial parks which are developed by local governments in turn attract manufacturing firms. Some economists view the slowdown in the development of U.S. infrastructure as a significant source of reduced private investment.

Education and Training

Ben Franklin once said: "He that hath a trade hath an estate." He meant that education and training improve a worker's productivity and result in higher earnings. Like investment in physical capital, investment in human capital is an important means of increasing labor productivity. As shown in Table 18-2, an estimated 12 percent of the growth of U.S. real output since 1929 is attributable to such improvements in the quality of labor (item 5).

Perhaps the simplest measure of labor quality is the level of educational attainment. Figure 18-4 reflects educational gains in the past several decades. Currently 82 percent of the U.S. population, aged 25 or more, has at least a high school education; 22 percent has a college education or more. It is clear from Figure 18-4 that education has become accessible to more people in the United States.

But there are concerns about the quality of U.S. education. Scores on standardized college admissions tests have declined relative to scores of a few decades ago. Furthermore, U.S. students in science and mathematics do not do as well as students in many other industrialized nations (see Global Perspective 18-2). Japanese children have a longer school day and attend school 240 days per year compared with 180 in the United States. Also, we have been producing fewer

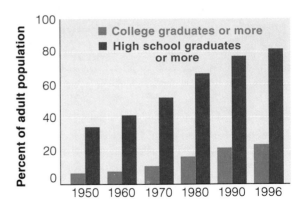

FIGURE 18-4 Changes in the educational attainment of the U.S. adult population The percentage of the U.S. adult population, aged 25 or more, completing high school and college has been rising in recent decades (*Source: Statistical Abstract of the United States, 1997, p. 159.*)

engineers and scientists, a problem which may trace back to inadequate training in math and science in elementary and high schools. And it is argued that on-the-job training (apprenticeship programs) in Japan and Germany—nations with high rates of productivity growth—are more available and superior to those in the United States.

Resource Allocation and Scale Economies

Table 18-2 also tells us that U.S. labor productivity has increased because of economies of scale (item 6) and improved resource allocation (item 7).

Economies of Scale Economies of scale are production advantages deriving from increased market and firm size. A large corporation often can select more efficient production techniques than can a small-scale firm. A large manufacturer of autos can use elaborate assembly lines with computerization and robotics, while smaller producers must settle for less advanced technologies. Markets have increased in scope over time and firms have increased in size, allowing more efficient production methods to be used. Accordingly, U.S. labor productivity has increased and economic growth has occurred.

Improved Resource Allocation Improved resource allocation means that workers over time have reallocated themselves from low-productivity em-

GLOBAL PERSPECTIVE 18-2

Average test scores of 13-year-olds in math and science, top 10 countries and the United States

The test performance of U.S. 13-year-olds did not rank favorably with that of 13-year-olds in several other nations in the Third International Math and Science Study (1997).

Mathematics

Rank		Score
1	Singapore	643
2	South Korea	607
3	Japan	605
4	Hong Kong	588
5	Belgium	565
6	Czech Republic	564
7	Slovakia	547
8	Switzerland	545
9	Netherlands	541
10	Slovenia	541
28	United States	500

Science

Rank		Score
1	Singapore	607
2	Czech Republic	574
3	Japan	571
4	South Korea	565
5	Bulgaria	565
6	Netherlands	560
7	Slovenia	560
8	Austria	558
9	Hungary	554
10	England	552
17	United States	534

ployment to high-productivity employment. Historically, much labor has shifted from agriculture, where labor productivity is low, to manufacturing, where it is quite high. More recently, labor has shifted away from some manufacturing industries to even higher-productivity industries such as computer software, business consulting, and pharmaceuticals. As a result of such shifts, the average productivity of U.S. workers in the aggregate has increased.

Also, labor market discrimination has historically denied women and minorities access to high-productivity jobs. The decline of such discrimination over time has shifted these groups from low-productivity jobs to higher-productivity jobs, increasing overall labor productivity and raising real GDP.

Tariffs, import quotas, and other barriers to international trade often keep resources in relatively unproductive employments. The long-run movement toward liberalized international trade has therefore improved the allocation of resources and expanded real output in the United States.

Detriments to Growth

Some developments *detract* from the growth of real output and income. The entry for the legal and human environment (item 8) in Table 18-2 aggregates these detriments to productivity growth. Since 1929 there have been several changes in the regulation of industry, environmental pollution, and worker health and safety which have negatively affected growth. The expansion of government regulation in such areas as pollution control, worker health and safety, and access for the disabled has diverted investment spending away from growth-increasing capital goods and toward expenditures for cleaner air and water, greater worker protection, and improved access for disabled workers and consumers.

A firm required to spend $1 million on a new scrubber to meet government standards for air pollution or to make its stores accessible to the disabled will not have that $1 million to spend on machinery and equipment which would expand real output. The diversion of resources to deal with dishonesty and crime, the effects of work stoppages because of labor disputes, and the impact of bad weather on agricultural output are also factors which impede economic growth.

It should be noted that while worker safety, clean air and water, equal access for the disabled, and the overall quality of life may come at the expense of economic growth, the reverse is also true. Economic growth does not automatically enhance society's welfare. Growth of real output may involve opportunity costs of other things (a clean environment, a fair society) we value more highly. *Productivity measures output per hour of work*, not *overall well-being per hour of work*. Increases in real GDP are not necessarily matched with equal increases in well-being. Thus, society may rationally decide to "trade off" some economic growth to achieve other desirable ends. **(Key Question 5)**

Other Contributing Factors

There are other difficult-to-quantify characteristics which affect an economy's growth rate. For example, large and varied supplies of natural resources in the United States have been an important contributor to its economic growth. The United States enjoys an abundance of fertile soil, desirable climatic and weather conditions, large quantities of most mineral resources, and generous sources of power. With the possible exceptions of Russia and Canada, the United States has a larger variety and greater quantity of natural resources than any other nation.

While an abundant natural resource base is helpful to growth, a meager resource base does not doom a nation to slow growth. Although Japan's natural resources are severely constrained, its post-World War II growth has been remarkable. In contrast, some of the lower-income countries of Africa and South America have substantial amounts of natural resources but have grown slowly.

There are additional unmeasurable factors affecting a nation's growth rate. In particular, the overall social-cultural-political environment of the United States generally has promoted economic growth. Several factors contribute to this favorable environment:

1. Unlike the case in many other nations, there are virtually no social or moral taboos on production and material progress in the United States. The nation's social philosophy has embraced material advance as an attainable and desirable economic goal. The inventor, the innovator, and the business executive are accorded high degrees of prestige and respect in U.S. society.

2. Americans have traditionally possessed positive attitudes toward work and risk taking; the United States has benefited from a willing labor force and an ample supply of entrepreneurs.

3. The market system has many personal and corporate incentives encouraging growth; the U.S. economy rewards actions which increase output.

4. The U.S. economy is founded on a stable political system characterized by democratic principles, internal order, the right of property ownership, the legal status of enterprise, and the enforcement of contracts. Recent studies show that politically open societies grow much more rapidly on average than those where freedom is limited.

Although difficult to quantify, these "other characteristics" have provided an excellent foundation for U.S. economic growth and stability.

Macroeconomic Instability and Growth

The information in Table 18-2 reflects the actual growth experience of the United States, not the growth which would have occurred if the economy had achieved its potential output year after year. Without macroeconomic instability, the annual growth rate in the United States would have been about 0.2 to 0.3 percentage point higher than the 2.9 percent rate actually occurring since 1929.

The Great Depression of the 1930s, in particular, was a serious blow to the long-run growth record of the United States. Between 1929 and 1933 real output (measured in 1992 prices) declined from $791 billion to $577 billion. In 1938, U.S. real GDP was at about the same level as in 1929. More recently, the back-to-back recessions of 1980 to 1982 cost the economy more than $600 billion in lost real output.

But that is only part of the picture. Recession and unemployment can have harmful "carryover" effects on the growth rate in subsequent years of full employment through negative effects on other growth factors. Recession and unemployment may depress investment and capital accumulation. Moreover, firms may cut back on research and development efforts during recession, so technological advance diminishes; union resistance to technological change may stiffen; skills of idle workers deteriorate; and so forth. While it is difficult to quantify the effect of these considerations on the growth rate, they undoubtedly are important.

QUICK REVIEW 18-2

■ Improvements in labor productivity account for about two-thirds of increases in U.S. real GDP; the use of more labor inputs accounts for the remaining one-third.

■ Improved technology, more capital, greater education and training, and better resource allocation have been the main contributors to U.S. economic growth.

■ The average annual growth rate in the United States has been diminished by periods of depression and recession.

THE PRODUCTIVITY SLOWDOWN

In the 1970s—and to a lesser degree in the 1980s and early 1990s—the United States experienced a much-publicized productivity slowdown. This has led to concern among some Americans that the nation is in relative economic decline. Table 18-3 portrays the course of U.S. labor productivity in the post-World War II period. Observe in column 2 that for about two decades following World War II (1948–1966) labor productivity increased at a vigorous average annual rate of 3.2 percent, only to decline sharply in the 1966–1973 period. This was followed by a dismal performance in the years 1973 to 1981 and a modest resurgence of productivity growth since 1981. Although labor productivity growth has been slowing worldwide, U.S. productivity growth has been slower than that in most other major industrialized nations. The United States still enjoys the highest absolute level of output per worker, but its productivity advantage is diminishing.

Significance

The U.S. productivity slowdown has many implications.

Standard of Living Productivity growth is the basic source of improvements in real wage rates and the standard of living. Over long periods, real income per worker-hour can increase only at the same rate as real output per worker-hour. More output per hour means more real income to distribute for each hour worked. The simplest case is of Robinson Crusoe on his deserted island. The number of fish he can catch or coconuts he can pick per hour *is* his real income or wage per hour.

TABLE 18-3 Growth of labor productivity and real per capita GDP, 1948–1997

(1) Period	(2) Annual productivity growth rate, %	(3) Annual real per capita GDP growth rate, %
1948–1966	3.2	2.2
1966–1973	2.0	2.0
1973–1981	0.7	1.1
1981–1990	1.3	1.8
1990–1997	1.2	1.3

Source: *Economic Report of the President, 1988,* p. 67. End points of calculations are cyclical peaks, except for 1997. Updated.

We observe in column 3 in Table 18-3 that the broadest measure of living standards—the growth of real per capita GDP—followed the path of labor productivity. Living levels thus measured grew by only 1.1 percent per year during the severe 1973–1981 productivity stagnation compared with 2.2 percent in the 1948–1966 postwar decades.

The slowdown in productivity is also reflected in Figure 18-5, which tracks the median real income of U.S. families since 1947. Median family income increased substantially in real terms from 1947 to 1973. But it fell during the 1980s and is not a whole lot higher today than it was in 1973.

Inflation Productivity increases offset increases in nominal wage rates, partly or fully lessening cost-push inflationary pressures. Other things equal, a decline in the rate of productivity growth contributes to rising unit labor costs and a higher rate of inflation. Many economists believe that productivity stagnation contributed to the unusually high inflation rates of the 1970s.

World Markets Other things equal, the slow rate of productivity growth in the United States compared with its major international trading partners increases relative prices of U.S. goods in world markets. The result is a decline in U.S. competitiveness and a loss of international markets for U.S. producers.

Causes of the Slowdown

There is no consensus among experts as to why U.S. productivity growth has slowed and fallen behind the

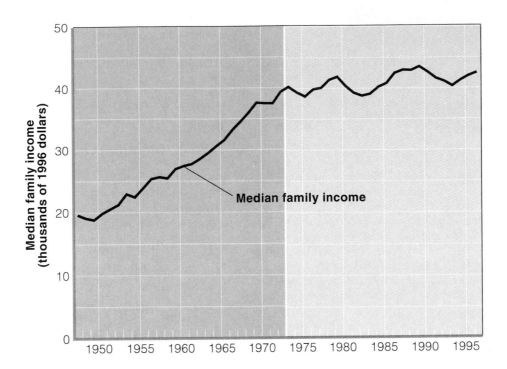

FIGURE 18-5 Median income of U.S. families, 1947–1996 After World War II the median real income of U.S. families grew rapidly until the early 1970s. Since 1973 real family income has stagnated. (*Source:* Bureau of the Census.)

----

rates of Japan and western Europe. Because so many factors affect productivity, there may be no simple explanation. Nevertheless, let's survey some of the possible causes.

Labor Quality One possibility is that slower improvements in labor quality may have dampened productivity growth. Three factors may have been at work.

1. Decline in Experience Level The experience level of the labor force may have declined. The large number of baby-boom workers who entered the labor force had little experience and training and were therefore less productive. The labor-force participation of women increased significantly over the past two decades. But many were married women with little or no prior labor-force experience who therefore had low productivity.

2. Less Able Workers The declining test scores of students on standardized examinations during the past few decades may indicate a decline in worker ca-

pabilities. If so, this decline may have contributed to the productivity slowdown.

3. Slowing of Rise in Educational Attainment The historical rise in the average level of educational attainment of the labor force has been slowing in recent years. The median number of years of school completed by the adult population was 12.1 in 1970 and increased to only 12.8 by 1996.

Technological Progress Technological advance—usually reflected in improvements in the quality of capital goods and the efficiency with which inputs are combined—may also have faltered. Technological progress is fueled by expenditures for formal research and development (R&D) programs. In the United States, R&D spending declined as a percentage of GDP from a peak of 3 percent in the mid-1960s to about 1 percent by the late 1970s, before rising again in the 1980s.

However, some economists discount the R&D decline in explaining the productivity slowdown. They say R&D *spending* alone tells us little about R&D *ac-*

Is Growth Desirable?

Economists usually take for granted that growth is desirable. Is It?

The Antigrowth View Critics of growth say industrialization and growth result in pollution, global warming, ozone depletion, and other environmental problems. These adverse spillover costs occur because inputs in the production process reenter the environment as some form of waste. The more rapid our growth and the higher our standard of living, the more waste the environment must absorb—or attempt to absorb. In an already wealthy society, further growth usually means satisfying increasingly trivial wants at the cost of mounting threats to our ecological system.

Critics of growth also argue there is little compelling evidence that economic growth has solved sociological problems such as poverty, homelessness, and discrimination. Consider poverty. In the antigrowth view, American poverty is a problem of distribution, not production. The requisite for solving the problem is commitment and political courage to redistribute wealth and income, not further increases in output.

Antigrowth sentiment also says that while growth may permit us to "make a better living," it does not give us "the good life." We may be producing more and enjoying it less. Growth means assembly-line jobs, worker burnout, and alienated employees who have little or no control over decisions affecting their lives. The changing technology at the core of growth poses new anxieties and new sources of insecurity for workers. Both high-level and low-level workers face the prospect of having their hard-earned skills and experience rendered obsolete by an onrushing technology. High-growth economies are high-stress economies, which may impair our physical and mental health.

In Defense of Growth The primary defense of growth is that it is the path to greater material abundance and rising living standards. Rising output and incomes allow us to buy:

> more education, recreation, and travel, more medical care, closer communications, more skilled personal and professional services, and better-designed as well as more numerous products. It also means more art, music, and poetry, theater, and drama. It can even mean more time and resources devoted to spiritual growth and human development.*

Growth also enables us to improve the nation's infrastructure, enhance the care of the sick and elderly, provide greater access for the disabled, and provide more police

complishments. There is clear evidence of continuing technological advance during the past two decades.

Investment Other things equal, the greater the percentage of a nation's GDP devoted to investment goods, the larger its productivity gains. A worker using a bulldozer can move more earth per hour than the same worker using a hand shovel. An engineer using a computer can complete a design task more rapidly than is possible with pencil and paper.

The United States has been investing a smaller percentage of its GDP than it did in earlier periods. Several factors may have contributed to the weak growth of investment:

1. Low Saving Rate The United States has had a low saving rate which, coupled with strong private and public demands for credit, has resulted in high real interest rates relative to historical standards. High real interest rates discourage investment spending.

2. Import Competition Growing import competition may have made some U.S. producers reluctant to invest in new capital equipment. They may have shifted more investment overseas toward nations with low-wage workers.

3. Regulation The expansion of government regulations in the areas of pollution control, worker health and safety, and access for the disabled diverted some investment spending away from output-increasing capital goods. This investment spending surely increased total utility to society but did not directly increase output itself. The composition of investment may have shifted toward uses which do not increase productivity.

4. Reduced Infrastructure Spending Reduced spending on the economy's infrastructure may have slowed productivity growth. We have noted that these public capital goods are complementary to private and fire protection. Economic growth may be the only realistic way to reduce poverty, since there is little political support for greater redistribution of income. The way to improve the economic position of the poor is to increase household incomes through higher productivity and economic growth. Also, a no-growth policy among industrial nations might severely limit growth in poor nations. Foreign investment and development assistance in these nations would fall, keeping the world's poor in poverty longer.

Economic growth has not made labor more unpleasant or hazardous, as critics suggest. New machinery is usually less taxing and less dangerous than the machinery it replaces. Air-conditioned workplaces are more pleasant than steamy workshops. Furthermore, why would an end to economic growth reduce materialism or alienation? The loudest protests against materialism are heard in those nations and groups who now enjoy the highest levels of material abundance! The high standard of living which growth provides has increased our leisure and given us more time for reflection and self-fulfillment.

Does growth threaten the environment? The connection between growth and environment is tenuous, say growth proponents. Increases in economic growth need not mean increases in pollution. Pollution is not so much a by-product of growth as it is a "problem of the commons." Much of the environment—streams, lakes, oceans, and the air—is treated as "common property," with no restrictions on its use. The commons have become our dumping grounds; we have overused and debased them. Environmental pollution is a case of spillover or external costs, and correcting this problem involves regulatory legislation or specific taxes ("effluent charges") to remedy misuse of the environment.

There *are* serious pollution problems. But limiting growth is the wrong solution. Growth has allowed economies to reduce pollution, be more sensitive to environmental considerations, set aside wilderness, and clean up hazardous waste, while still enabling rising household incomes.

*Alice M. Rivlin, *Reviving the American Dream* (Washington: Brookings Institution, 1992), p. 36.

---

capital goods. Data show that between 1950 and 1970 the public capital stock of infrastructure grew at a 4.1 percent annual rate and labor productivity growth was 2.0 percent per year. During 1971 to 1985, however, the yearly increase in the infrastructure fell to 1.6 percent and the annual productivity increase dropped to 0.8 percent. A slowing of spending on public investment goods may have contributed to diminishing private investments and to declines in productivity growth.

Energy Prices Perhaps the prime suspect in the productivity slowdown was the large increases in oil prices occurring from 1973 to 1975 and 1978 to 1980. Productivity growth diminished sharply after the quadrupling of oil prices between 1973 and 1975. Also, the impact of rocketing energy prices was worldwide, as was the productivity slowdown.

The *direct* impact of higher oil prices was an increase in the cost of operating capital equipment, which in effect raised the "price" of capital relative to labor. Producers were therefore more inclined to use less-productive labor-intensive techniques.

The *indirect* macroeconomic effects of rising energy prices may have had even more to do with reducing productivity growth. The two episodes of soaring energy prices produced stagflation—simultaneous inflation and rising unemployment. Government's restrictive macroeconomic policies to control inflation worsened and prolonged the periods of recession and slow economic growth. Recessions diminish productivity—output per worker—since output normally declines more rapidly than employment. The long periods of underuse of production capacity in many industries probably contributed to the productivity slowdown.

Dismal Growth of Service Productivity Finally, it is important to note that the slowdown in U.S. productivity growth has been greater in the service sector than in the manufacturing (goods-producing) sector. Since 1973 productivity in manufacturing has increased by about 2.75 percent annually compared with 3.4 percent between 1960 and 1972. But productivity in the service sector has increased by only 0.7 percent annually since 1973, compared with 2.7 percent between 1960 and 1972. This slow growth of service-sector productivity has been a drag on the overall productivity rate.

There are several possible reasons for the slower productivity growth in services:

1. It may be more difficult for service companies to increase their productivity by substituting capital for workers. How do you substitute machinery for a barber, dentist, cook, day-care worker, or retail clerk?

2. The competitive pressures to increase productivity may be weaker in services. Customers may be more loyal to service providers than to brands of manufactured products. Moreover, the U.S. service sector has been relatively immune from stiff foreign competition.

3. As they become wealthier, consumers usually demand higher-quality services, which often require more, not fewer, service workers. Service firms may need to employ more retail clerks, security personnel, pizza deliverers, maintenance workers, or stock market analysts to stay competitive.

Some economists contend that the slow growth of productivity in services is at least partly illusory. Unlike the case in manufacturing, there are no "product quantities" to count in determining service productivity. Many increases in productivity show up as improvements in services, and such improvements are not always reflected in higher product prices (and thus greater output). Because present measurement methods do not adequately "pick up" increases in service productivity, say some economists, the overall increase of U.S. productivity growth is greatly understated.

A "NEW ECONOMY"?

Since 1981 there has been a modest improvement in productivity growth. Observe in Table 18-3 that the 0.7 percent annual productivity growth for 1973 to 1981 improved to a 1.3 percent annual increase between 1981 and 1990. The recession of 1990 to 1991 halted this upward trend, but productivity growth

eventually picked up during the recovery and averaged 1.2 percent over the 1990–1997 period. In 1996 productivity growth was 2.0 percent; in 1997 it was 1.9 percent. In 1997 real GDP grew by a healthy 3.4 percent. Moreover, the unemployment rate and inflation rates were both low (4.9 percent and 2.3 percent, respectively), with no signs of rising inflation.

Is the United States experiencing a resurgence of productivity growth? Is it, as a few economists claim, establishing a "new economy," based on innovations in computers and communications, coupled with global capitalism? Can it now grow at a 3 to 4 percent annual rate, rather than the previous 2 to 2.5 percent annual rate, without igniting inflation?

Indeed, many of the factors which were depressing productivity growth have eased or been reversed. Energy prices are stable, and the stagflation problem has been overcome. Research and development spending has generally increased as a percentage of GDP. Innovations in computers, telecommunications, genetic engineering, and medicine are providing a stimulus to productivity. Also, real interest rates are now low, promoting purchases of new plant and equipment. Downsizing of workforces has boosted productivity in many firms. Wages of college graduates have risen relative to wages of high school graduates, and this wage premium is attracting more students to universities. The inexperienced baby boomers who flooded labor markets in previous decades are now more mature, more experienced, and thus more productive workers. International markets are opening up, expanding U.S. exports. Meanwhile, global competition is spreading, holding down the U.S. rate of inflation.

Nevertheless, whether these factors will produce a long period of high U.S. productivity and real GDP growth remains to be seen; 1 or 2 years does not constitute a trend. The current higher rates of productivity and real GDP growth *are* consistent with that possibility. Unfortunately, they are also consistent with the possibility that the United States is simply experiencing a rapid short-run economic expansion fueled by high levels of investment and consumption spending. Such "booms" raise productivity by increasing real output faster than employment (labor inputs), but they are unsustainable over longer periods. History tells us that demand-pull inflation, restrictive government stabilization policy, and economic recession often follow short-run surges in productivity and GDP growth. Hence, only time will tell whether the very recent increases in productivity are permanent or transitory. The jury is still out on the notion of a "new economy." **(Key Question 8)**

GROWTH POLICIES

If we accept the view that economic growth is desirable and sustainable, then a question arises as to what public policies might stimulate growth. Several policies either are in use or have been suggested. They fit within two broad categories: demand-side policies and supply-side policies.

Demand-Side Policies

Low growth is often the consequence of inadequate aggregate demand and the GDP gap to which it gives rise. The purpose of demand-side policies is to eliminate or reduce the severity of recessions through discretionary fiscal and monetary policies. The idea is to use these tools to ensure that aggregate demand increases at an appropriate, noninflationary pace. Adequate aggregate demand not only keeps present resources fully employed, it also creates an incentive for firms to expand their operations.

In particular, monetary policy which provides low real interest rates helps promote high levels of investment spending. This spending not only sustains full employment of existing resources but also expands capital resources and thus the economy's production capacity. Government can achieve low real interest rates through a combination of a relatively easy money policy and a fiscal policy which eliminates budget deficits. Recall that the government borrowing required for financing large budget deficits drives up real interest rates, particularly when the economy is near or at full employment.

Supply-Side Policies

These policies emphasize factors which directly increase the potential output of the economy over time. Regarding Figure 18-3, the goal is to shift the economy's long-run aggregate supply curve rightward. Policies fitting this category include *education and training policies* designed to increase the nation's stock of human capital. Recent examples are (1) programs which provide retraining for workers who lose jobs because of international trade, and (2) tuition tax credits designed to increase college enrollment.

Other programs fitting the supply-side category include *tax policies* designed to increase saving, investment, and R&D. An example is tax deductions for those who save money in a special retirement account. Some economists favor a national consumption tax as a full or partial replacement for the personal income tax. The idea is to make consumption more expensive and thereby encourage saving. Similarly, some economists propose eliminating the corporate income tax or allowing more generous tax credits for investment and research spending. Such spending often "pays off" in rightward shifts of the nation's long-run aggregate supply curve.

Government might also promote growth via other pro-growth initiatives. Specifically, it might redirect some of its current expenditures away from transfer payments and toward expansion of public infrastructure and funding of research, basic education, and skill training. It might promote growth by further deregulating industries where sufficient competition exists to ensure improved efficiency. And it might negotiate further international trade agreements, which increase specialization, boost output, and expand trade.

While the litany of potential growth-enhancing policies is long and involved, most economists agree that it is not easy to increase a nation's growth rate through public policy. Nevertheless, they also agree there is ample international evidence to suggest that government policies *can make a difference;* they can affect an economy's long-term growth rate for better or worse.

QUICK REVIEW 18-3

■ Economists have cited the following reasons for the U.S. slowdown in productivity over the past 25 years: **(a)** declines in labor quality, **(b)** a slowing of technological progress, **(c)** decreasing investment spending as a percentage of GDP, **(d)** high energy prices during the 1970s and early 1980s, and **(e)** lagging growth of service productivity.

■ Some observers see the recent upsurge in productivity as evidence of a "new economy" that can achieve higher rates of GDP growth than those in the past two decades. This new economy is based on innovation in computers and communications coupled with the globalization of capitalism.

■ Skeptics of the new-economy view say that it is far too early to tell whether the recent upsurge of productivity growth is transient or permanent.

CHAPTER SUMMARY

1. Economic growth may be defined as either **(a)** an expanding real output or **(b)** an expanding per capita real output. Growth lessens the burden of scarcity and provides increases in real output which can be used to resolve socioeconomic problems.

2. The supply factors in economic growth are **(a)** the quantity and quality of a nation's natural resources, **(b)** the quantity and quality of its human resources, **(c)** its stock of capital facilities, and **(d)** its technology. Two other factors—a sufficient level of aggregate demand and economic efficiency—are essential for the economy to realize its growth potential.

3. Economic growth is shown graphically as an outward shift of a nation's production possibilities curve or as a rightward shift of its aggregate supply curve.

4. The post-World War II growth rate of real GDP for the United States has been slightly more than 3 percent annually; real GDP per capita has grown at about a 2 percent annual rate.

5. U.S. real GDP has grown, partly because of increased inputs of labor and primarily because of increases in the productivity of labor. Technological progress, increases in the quantity of capital per worker, improvements in the quality of labor, economies of scale, and an improved allocation of labor are among the more important factors which increase labor productivity.

6. The rate of productivity growth declined sharply in the 1970s, causing a slowdown in the rise of U.S. living standards and contributing to inflation. Although productivity growth has increased somewhat in the 1980s and 1990s, it remains substantially below the rates attained in the two decades after World War II.

7. Suspected causes of the decline in productivity growth include decreases in labor quality, slowing of technological progress, declining investment spending as a percentage of GDP, higher energy prices, and dismal growth in service productivity.

8. Many of the trends that are thought to have slowed productivity growth in the 1970s and 1980s have slowed or reversed themselves. Also, the U.S. economy has recently had a surge of innovation in computers and communications. This technological progress, coupled with the opening of global markets, has led a few economists to speak of a "new economy" characterized by high growth of productivity and real GDP.

9. Skeptics of the new-economy notion urge a wait-and-see approach. They point out that surges in productivity and real GDP growth are common during vigorous economic expansions but are not necessarily permanent.

10. Government can promote economic growth through demand-side policies (fiscal policy, monetary policy) which ensure that present production capacity is fully used and that the capital stock enlarges. It can also promote growth through supply-side policies (education and training policies, tax policies, and other pro-growth initiatives) which directly increase the economy's potential output over time.

TERMS AND CONCEPTS

economic growth
supply factors
demand factor

efficiency factor
labor productivity

labor-force participation
rate

infrastructure

STUDY QUESTIONS

1. Why is economic growth important? Explain why the difference between a 2.5 percent and a 3.0 percent annual growth rate might be of great significance over many years.

2. KEY QUESTION What are the major causes of economic growth? "There are both a demand side

and a supply side to economic growth." Explain. Illustrate the operation of both sets of factors in terms of the production possibilities curve.

3. KEY QUESTION Suppose an economy's real GDP is $30,000 in year 1 and $31,200 in year 2. What is the growth rate of its real GDP? Assume that population was 100 in year 1 and 102 in year 2. What is the growth rate of GDP per capita? Between 1959 and 1996 the U.S. price level rose by about 285 percent while its real output increased by about 212 percent. Use the aggregate demand-aggregate supply model to show these outcomes graphically.

4. Briefly describe the growth record of the United States. Compare the rates of growth in real GDP and real GDP per capita, explaining any differences. How does the U.S. growth rate compare to the rates of Japan and Germany since World War II? To what extent might growth rates understate or overstate economic well-being?

5. KEY QUESTION To what extent have increases in U.S. real GDP been the result of more labor inputs? Of increasing labor productivity? Discuss the factors which contribute to productivity growth in order of their quantitative importance.

6. Using examples, explain how changes in the allocation of labor can affect labor productivity.

7. How do you explain the close correlation between changes in the rate of productivity growth and changes in real wage rates? Discuss the relationship between productivity growth and inflation.

8. KEY QUESTION Account for the slowdown in the U.S. rate of productivity growth. What are the consequences of this slowdown? "Most of the factors which contributed to poor productivity growth in the 1970s are now behind us and are unlikely to recur in the near future." Do you agree?

9. "If we want economic growth in a free society, we may have to accept a measure of instability." Evaluate. The philosopher Alfred North Whitehead once remarked that "the art of progress is to preserve order amid change and to preserve change amid order." What did he mean? Is this contention relevant for economic growth? What implications might this have for public policy? Explain.

10. True or false? If false, explain why.
  a. Technological advance, which thus far has played only a small role in U.S. economic growth, is destined to play a more important role in the future.
  b. Nations lacking political freedom on average have faster growth rates than democratic nations.
  c. Many public capital goods are complementary to private capital goods.
  d. The rate of productivity growth in the manufacturing sector severely lags such advances in the service sector.

11. Suppose you are the chair of the Council of Economic Advisers and have been asked to prepare a set of proposals for increasing the productivity of U.S. workers as a way to raise the rate of economic growth. What would you put on your list? What impediments do you see in accomplishing your policies?

12. Evaluate: "Major innovations in computer and communication technologies in the United States, together with the globalization of markets, is creating a 'new economy' capable of achieving much faster rates of productivity and real GDP growth than those in the 1970s and 1980s."

13. Productivity often rises during economic expansions and falls during economic recessions. Can you think of reasons why? Briefly explain. (Hint: Remember that the level of productivity involves both levels of output and levels of labor input.)

14. (Last Word) Do you think economic growth is desirable? Explain your position on this issue.

15. WEB-BASED QUESTION **Current GDP Growth Rates and Per Capita Incomes—Is There a Relationship?** The OECD (Organization for Economic Cooperation and Development) http://www.oecd.org/std/nahome.htm provides both quarterly growth rates of real gross domestic product (GDP) for OECD member countries and an annual comparison of levels of GDP per capita based on exchange rates and purchasing power parities (PPPs). Which countries have the highest and lowest current GDP growth rates? Which have the highest and lowest per capita incomes? Does there seem to be a relationship? In your comparison, does it matter if you use per capita income based on exchange rates or PPPs? Which is more reliable?

16. WEB-BASED QUESTION **Increased Productivity Through Technology—Find Examples of Innovations in Computers and Communications** Recent innovations in computers and communications technologies are increasing productivity. Lucent Technologies (formerly Bell Labs) http://www.lucent.com/ideas2/ideas.html provides a timeline of innovations over the past 70 years. During this period, which increased the fastest: technological "home runs" (e.g., the transitor in 1947) or technological "singles" (e.g., free space optical switching in 1990)? Which innovation do you think has increased productivity the most? What are some current innovations which could increase productivity and in what way?

CHAPTER NINETEEN

Budget Deficits and the Public Debt

The United States has amassed $5.4 trillion of public debt. How large is $5.4 trillion? We can put it into perspective this way: "One *million* seconds have ticked by in the past 12 days. One *billion* seconds took more than 31 years to elapse. One *trillion* seconds ago, it was around 30,000 BC—the Ice Age—and much of America was buried by glaciers."[1] So a debt of $5.4 trillion is a huge amount! It took more than 200 years for the public debt to reach $1 trillion. Then in only 15 years—1982 to 1997—it reached the $5.4 trillion mark. These are stunning numbers. Should we be concerned about them?

In this chapter we examine the Federal budget deficits and the rising public debt resulting from these deficits. We first present relevant definitions and then compare different budget philosophies. Next, we explore the quantitative dimensions of the public debt. How large is the debt relative to American GDP? We then consider the alleged "problems" associated with the public debt, explaining why some are bogus while others are real. Next, we look at the budget deficits during the past two decades and explain why these deficits may have negatively affected U.S. investment and international trade. Finally, we examine recent laws and proposals to eliminate budget deficits and point out that the budget deficit is quickly nearing zero.

DEFICITS AND DEBT: DEFINITIONS

A *budget deficit* is the amount by which government expenditures exceed its revenues in a particular year. For example, in 1997 the Federal government spent $1601 billion while its revenues were $1579 billion, resulting in a $22 billion deficit.

The national or **public debt** is the total accumulation of the Federal government's total deficits and surpluses which have occurred

through time. At the end of 1997 the public debt was about $5.4 trillion.

The term "public debt" as ordinarily used does *not* include the entire public sector; in particular, state and local finance is omitted. While the Federal government has been incurring large deficits, state and local governments in the aggregate have been realizing

---

[1]Marcia Stepanek, "The National Debt: Red Ink Rising," *Seattle Post-Intelligencer* (Hearst Newspapers), Apr. 13, 1994, p. 1.

surpluses. For example, in 1997 all state and local governments combined had a budgetary surplus in excess of $105 billion.[2]

BUDGET PHILOSOPHIES

Is it good or bad to incur deficits and let the public debt grow? Should the budget be balanced annually, if necessary by constitutional amendment? You saw in Chapter 12 that countercyclical fiscal policy should move the Federal budget toward a deficit during recession and toward a surplus during inflation. This means discretionary fiscal policy is unlikely to result in a balanced budget in any particular year. Is this a matter of concern?

Let's approach this question by examining the economic implications of several contrasting budget philosophies.

Annually Balanced Budget

Until the Great Depression of the 1930s, the **annually balanced budget** was viewed as the desirable goal of public finance. On examination, however, it becomes clear that an annually balanced budget is not compatible with government fiscal activity as a countercyclical, stabilizing force. Worse yet, an annually balanced budget intensifies the business cycle.

Illustration: Suppose the economy encounters an onset of unemployment and falling incomes. As Figure 12-3 shows, in such circumstances tax receipts automatically decline. To balance its budget, government must either (1) increase tax rates, (2) reduce government expenditures, or (3) do both. All these policies are contractionary; each further dampens, rather than expands, aggregate demand.

Similarly, an annually balanced budget will intensify inflation. Again, Figure 12-3 tells us that as nominal incomes rise during the course of inflation, tax collections automatically increase. To avoid the impending surplus, government must either (1) cut tax rates, (2) increase government expenditures, or (3) do both. But any of these policies adds to inflationary pressures.

An annually balanced budget is not economically neutral; the pursuit of such a policy is pro-cyclical, not coun-

tercyclical. Despite this problem, there is considerable support for a constitutional amendment requiring an annually balanced budget.

More recently, some economists have advocated an annually balanced budget not because of a fear of deficits and a mounting public debt but because they feel an annually balanced budget is essential in constraining an undesirable expansion of the public sector. Budget deficits, they argue, are a manifestation of political irresponsibility. Deficits allow politicians to give the public the benefits of government programs while *currently* avoiding raising taxes to pay for them.

These economists believe government has a tendency to grow larger than it should because there is less popular opposition to this growth when it is financed by deficits rather than taxes. Wasteful governmental expenditures are likely to creep into the Federal budget when deficit financing is readily available. Some conservative economists and politicians want a constitutional amendment to force a balanced budget to slow government growth. They view deficits as a symptom of a more fundamental problem—government encroachment on the private sector.

Cyclically Balanced Budget

The idea of a **cyclically balanced budget** is that government exerts a countercyclical influence and at the same time balances its budget. However, the budget would not be balanced annually—there is nothing sacred about 12 months as an accounting period—but, rather, over the course of the business cycle.

The rationale is simple, plausible, and appealing. To offset recession, government should lower taxes and increase spending, purposely incurring a deficit. During the ensuing inflationary upswing, taxes would be raised and government spending slashed. The resulting surplus could be used to retire the Federal debt incurred in financing the recession. Government fiscal operations would therefore exert a positive countercyclical force, and the government could still balance its budget—not annually, but over a period of years.

The problem with this budget philosophy is that the upswings and downswings of the business cycle may not be of equal magnitude and duration. The goal of stabilization may therefore conflict with balancing the budget over the cycle. A long and severe slump followed by a modest and short period of prosperity would mean a large deficit during the slump, little or no surplus during prosperity, and a cyclical deficit in the budget.

---

[2]This figure includes the states' pension funds. Exclusion of these funds greatly reduces the size of this collective surplus.

Functional Finance

With **functional finance,** a balanced budget—annually or cyclically—is secondary. The primary purpose of Federal finance is to provide for noninflationary full employment—to balance the economy, not the budget. If this objective causes either persistent surpluses or a large and growing public debt, so be it. In this philosophy, the problems of government deficits or surpluses are minor compared with the undesirable alternatives of prolonged recession or persistent inflation. The Federal budget is first and foremost an instrument for achieving and maintaining macroeconomic stability. How best to finance government spending—through taxation or borrowing—depends on existing economic conditions. Government should not hesitate to incur any deficits and surpluses required to achieve macroeconomic stability and growth.

To those who express concern about the large Federal debt which might result from the pursuit of functional finance, advocates of this budget philosophy offer three arguments:

1. The U.S. tax system is such that tax revenues automatically increase as the economy expands. Assuming constant government expenditures, a deficit successful in increasing GDP will be partially self-liquidating.
2. Because of its taxing powers and the ability to create money, the government has a remarkable capacity to finance deficits.
3. A large Federal debt is less burdensome than most people think. **(Key Question 1)**

THE PUBLIC DEBT: FACTS AND FIGURES

Because modern fiscal policy endorses unbalanced budgets to stabilize the economy, its application may lead to a growing public debt. Let's consider the public debt—its causes, characteristics, and size—and its burdens and benefits.

The public debt, as column 2 in Table 19-1 shows, has grown considerably in nominal terms since 1929. (Not shown, it has also increased rapidly in real terms.) As we have noted, the public debt is the accumulation of all past deficits, minus surpluses, of the Federal budget.

TABLE 19-1   Quantitative significance of the public debt: the public debt and interest payments in relation to GDP, select years, 1929–1997

(1) Year	(2) Public debt, billions*	(3) Gross domestic product, billions*	(4) Interest payments, billions*	(5) Public debt as percentage of GDP, (2) ÷ (3)	(6) Interest payments as percentage of GDP, (4) ÷ (3)	(7) Per capita public debt*
1929	$ 16.9	$ 103.8	$ 0.7	16%	0.7%	$ 134
1940	50.7	100.2	0.9	51	0.9	384
1946	271.0	222.6	4.1	122	1.8	1917
1950	256.9	294.6	4.8	87	1.6	1667
1955	274.4	415.1	4.9	66	1.2	1654
1960	290.5	526.6	6.9	55	1.3	1610
1965	322.3	719.1	8.6	45	1.2	1659
1970	380.9	1035.6	14.4	37	1.4	1858
1975	541.9	1630.6	23.2	33	1.4	2507
1980	909.1	2784.2	52.5	33	1.9	3992
1985	1817.5	4180.7	129.5	43	3.1	7622
1990	3206.6	5743.8	184.2	56	3.2	12,829
1995	4921.0	7265.4	232.2	68	3.2	18,708
1997	5369.7	8083.4	244.0	66	3.0	20,044

*In current dollars

Source: Economic Report of the President, 1998; U.S. Department of Commerce.

Causes

Why has the U.S. public debt increased historically? What has caused the nation to incur these large and persistent deficits? The answer is fourfold: wars, recessions, tax cuts, and lack of political will.

Wars Some of the public debt has resulted from the deficit financing of wars. The public debt increased substantially during World War I and grew more than fivefold during World War II.

Consider World War II and the options it posed. The task was to reallocate a substantial portion of the economy's resources from civilian to war goods production. Government expenditures for armaments and military personnel soared. There were three financing options: increase taxes, print the needed money, or use deficit financing. Government feared that tax financing would require tax rates so high they would diminish incentives to work. The national interest required attracting more people into the labor force and encouraging those already participating to work longer hours. Very high tax rates were felt to interfere with these goals. Printing and spending additional money would be inflationary. Thus, much of World War II was financed by selling bonds to the public, thereby draining off spendable income and freeing resources from civilian production so they would be available for defense industries.

Recessions Another cause of the public debt is recessions and, more specifically, the built-in stability characterizing the U.S. fiscal system. In periods when the national income declines, tax collections automatically fall and deficits arise. Thus the public debt rose during the Great Depression of the 1930s and, more recently, during the recessions of 1974 to 1975, 1980 to 1982, and 1990 to 1991.

Tax Cuts A third consideration has accounted for much of the large deficits since 1981. The Economic Recovery Tax Act of 1981 provided for substantial cuts in both individual and corporate income taxes. The Reagan administration and Congress did *not* make offsetting reductions in government outlays. Therefore, a *structural deficit* was built into the Federal budget in the sense that the budget would not balance even if the economy were operating at full employment. Unfortunately, the economy was not at full employment during the early 1980s. The 1981 tax cuts combined with the severe 1980–1982 recessions to generate rapidly rising annual deficits which were $128 billion in 1982 and accelerated to $221 billion by 1986. Although annual budget deficits declined between 1986 and 1989, they remained historically high even though the economy reached full employment. Due partly to the earlier tax-rate cuts, tax revenues were not high enough to cover rising Federal spending. Annual deficits, and thus the public debt, again rose between 1991 and 1993 as the economy experienced recession and the Federal government incurred massive expenses in bailing out failed savings and loan associations.

Lack of Political Will Without being too cynical, we might also assert that deficits and a growing public debt are the result of lack of political will and determination. Spending often gains votes; tax increases precipitate political disfavor. While opposition to deficits is expressed by politicians and their constituencies, *specific* proposals to cut spending programs or raise taxes typically encounter more opposition than support.

Particularly difficult to cut are **entitlement programs,** the subject of this chapter's Last Word. These programs, such as social security, Medicaid (health care for the poor), Medicare (health care for those on social security), and veterans' benefits, "entitle" or guarantee particular levels of transfer payments to all who fit the programs' criteria. Total spending on these programs automatically rises along with the number of qualifying individuals and has rocketed in recent years, contributing to budget deficits and the rising public debt. Cutting these benefits produces severe political opposition. For example, older Americans may favor smaller budget deficits as long as funds for social security and Medicare are not reduced.

Similarly, new taxes or tax increases to reduce budget deficits may be acceptable in the abstract but are far less popular when specific tax changes are proposed. The popular view of taxation seems to be "Don't tax me, don't tax thee, tax the person behind the tree." But there are not enough taxpayers "behind the tree" to raise the amounts of new revenue needed to close the budget deficit.

The Clinton administration's struggle to pass a deficit-reduction package in 1993 is an example of political difficulties of reducing spending and increasing taxes. The specific package of spending cuts and tax increases passed the Senate by only a single vote, even though nearly all senators agreed that deficit reduction was a worthy goal. (With the package in place, the annual deficit shrank from $255 billion in 1993 to $22 billion in 1997. Based on present economic projections, the Federal budget will achieve a surplus in 1999).

Quantitative Aspects

In 1997 the U.S. debt reached $5400 billion—or 5.4 trillion. That amount is more than twice what the debt was just 10 years earlier. But *we must not fear large, seemingly incomprehensible numbers*. You will see why when we put the size of the U.S. public debt into better perspective.

Debt and GDP   A bald statement of the absolute size of the debt ignores that the wealth and productive ability of the U.S. economy is also vast. A wealthy nation can incur and carry a large public debt more easily than a poor nation, which is why it is more meaningful to measure the public debt *in relation to* the economy's GDP, as shown in column 5 in Table 19-1. Instead of the 20-fold increase in the debt between 1950 and 1997 shown in column 2, observe that the relative size of the debt was considerably less in 1997 than in 1950. However, our data *do* show that the relative size of the debt has doubled since 1980. Also, column 7 indicates that, on a per capita basis, the nominal debt has increased more or less steadily through time.

International Comparisons   As shown in Global Perspective 19-1, public debts of many other industrial nations are greater than those in the United States as a percentage of GDP. On this basis, for example, public debt in 1997 was larger in Italy, Canada, Japan, Sweden, and Germany than in the United States.

Interest Charges   Many economists conclude that the primary burden of the debt is the annual interest charge accruing as a result. The absolute size of these interest payments is shown in column 4 in Table 19-1. Interest payments have increased sharply beginning in the 1970s. This reflects not only increases in the debt but also periods of very high interest rates. Interest on the debt is now the fourth-largest item of expenditures in the Federal budget (see Figure 5-7). Interest charges as a percentage of the GDP are shown in column 6 in Table 19-1. Interest payments as a proportion of GDP have increased significantly in recent years. This ratio reflects the level of taxation (the

average tax rate) required to service the public debt. In 1997 the Federal government had to collect taxes equal to 3.0 percent of GDP to pay interest on its debt.

Ownership   Figure 19-1 shows that slightly less than two-thirds of the total public debt is held outside the Federal government by state and local governments, banks and other financial institutions, and private parties. The remaining debt is held by Federal agencies and the Federal Reserve. Foreign individuals and institutions hold about 23 percent of the total debt. This statistic is significant because, as you will see shortly, there are different implications of internally and externally held debt.

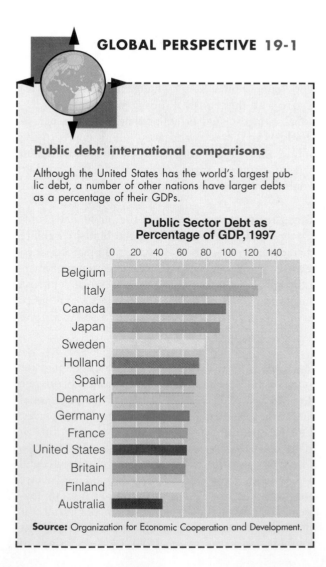

GLOBAL PERSPECTIVE 19-1

Public debt: international comparisons

Although the United States has the world's largest public debt, a number of other nations have larger debts as a percentage of their GDPs.

Public Sector Debt as Percentage of GDP, 1997

Source: Organization for Economic Cooperation and Development.

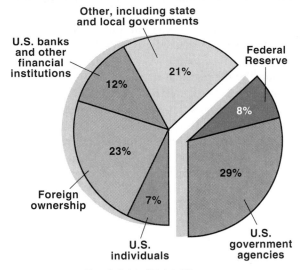

Debt held outside the Federal government and Federal Reserve (63%)

Debt held by the Federal government and Federal Reserve (37%)

Other, including state and local governments

U.S. banks and other financial institutions

Federal Reserve

21%

12%

8%

23%

29%

7%

Foreign ownership

U.S. individuals

U.S. government agencies

Total debt: $5.4 trillion

FIGURE 19-1 Ownership of the public debt Less than two-thirds of the public debt is held outside the Federal government; more than one-third is held internally by Federal agencies and the Federal Reserve System. Twenty-three percent of the public debt is foreign-owned.

Accounting and Inflation

The data on budget deficits and public debt may not be as straightforward as they appear. Governmental accounting procedures may not reflect government's actual financial position. Private firms have a separate *capital budget* because, in contrast to current expenses on labor and raw materials, expenditures for capital equipment represent tangible money-making assets. In calculating its budget deficit, the Federal government treats expenditures for highways, harbors, and public buildings the same as it does welfare payments. But, in fact, the former outlays are investments in physical assets. Federal budget deficits in the 1980s and 1990s would have been smaller had the Federal government employed a capital budget which included depreciation costs.

Also, inflation works to benefit debtors. A rising price level reduces the real value or purchasing power of the dollars paid back by borrowers. Taking this "inflationary tax" into account further reduces the sizes of budget deficits and public debt.

The point is there are different ways of measuring the public debt and government's overall financial po-

sition. Some of these alternative measures differ greatly from the data presented in Table 19-1.

ECONOMIC IMPLICATIONS: FALSE ISSUES

How does the public debt and its growth affect the economy? Can a rising public debt bankrupt the nation? Does the debt place a burden on our children and grandchildren?

Fortunately, these are false or bogus issues. The debt is not about to bankrupt the government or the nation. Nor, except under certain specific circumstances explored later, does the debt place a burden on future generations.

Going Bankrupt?

Can a large public debt bankrupt the Federal government, leaving it unable to meet its financial obligations? No, for the following three reasons.

1. Refinancing There is no reason why the public debt needs to be reduced, much less eliminated. As portions of the debt come due each month, government does not cut expenditures or raise taxes to provide funds to *retire* the maturing bonds. Rather, the government *refinances* the debt; it sells new bonds and uses the proceeds to pay off holders of the maturing bonds.

2. Taxation Government has the constitutional authority to levy and collect taxes. A tax increase is a government option for gaining sufficient revenue to pay interest and principal on the public debt. Financially distressed private households and corporations *cannot* raise revenue via taxes; governments *can*. Private households and corporations *can* go bankrupt; the Federal government *cannot*.

3. Creating Money Bankruptcy is also difficult to imagine because the Federal government (via the "Fed") can print money to pay both the principal and the interest on the debt. A government bond obligates the government to redeem that bond for some specific amount of money on its maturity date. Government can use the proceeds from the sale of other bonds *or* it can borrow newly created money from the Fed to retire the maturing bonds. The creation of new money to pay interest on debt or to retire debt *may* be inflationary. But it is difficult to conceive of governmental bankruptcy when government has the power to create new money by running the printing presses.

Shifting Burdens

Does the public debt impose a burden on future generations? Recall that per capita public debt in 1997 was $20,044. Did each child born in 1997 enter the world to be handed a $20,044 bill from Uncle Sam? Not really!

We first must ask to whom the United States owes the public debt. The answer is that it owes a substantial portion of it to itself. About 77 percent of U.S. government bonds are owned and held by citizens and institutions—banks, businesses, insurance companies, governmental agencies, and trust funds—within the United States. Thus *the public debt is also a public credit.* While the public debt is a liability to Americans (as taxpayers), *most* of the same debt is simultaneously an asset to Americans (as holders of Treasury bills, Treasury notes, Treasury bonds, and U.S. savings bonds).

To retire the public debt would call for a gigantic transfer payment from Americans to Americans. Taxpayers would pay higher taxes, and government would pay out those tax revenues to the same taxpaying individuals in the aggregate in redeeming the U.S. securities they hold. Although a redistribution of income would result from this huge financial transfer, it need not entail any immediate decline in the economy's aggregate wealth or standard of living. Repayment of an internally held public debt entails no leakage of purchasing power from the economy as

a whole. New babies who on the average inherit the $20,044-per-person public debt obligation are also bequeathed that same amount of government securities.

We noted earlier that the public debt increased sharply during World War II. Was some of the economic burden of World War II shifted to future generations by the decision to finance military purchases through the sale of government bonds? No. Recalling the production possibilities curve, we realize that the economic cost of World War II was the civilian goods society had to forgo in shifting scarce resources to war goods production. Regardless of whether society financed this reallocation through higher taxes or borrowing, the real economic burden of the war would have been the same. The burden of the war was borne almost entirely by those who lived during the war; they were the ones who did without a multitude of consumer goods to permit the United States to arm itself and its allies.

Also, wartime production may slow the growth of a nation's stock of capital as resources are shifted from production of capital goods to production of war goods. As a result, future generations inherit a smaller stock of capital goods. This occurred in the United States during World War II. But, again, this shifting of costs is independent of how a war is financed.

QUICK REVIEW 19-2

■ There is no danger of the Federal government's going bankrupt because it need only refinance (not retire) the public debt and can raise revenues, if needed, through higher taxes or printing money.

■ Usually, the public debt is not a means of shifting economic burdens to future generations.

IMPLICATIONS AND ISSUES

We must be careful not to leave the impression that the public debt is of no concern to economists. The large debt *does* pose some real potential problems, although economists attach varying importance to them.

Income Distribution

The distribution of government security ownership is uneven. Some people own much more than their $20,044 per capita share of government securities; others, less or none at all. Although our knowledge of the ownership of the public debt by income class is limited, we presume that ownership is concentrated among wealthier groups. Because the tax system is only mildly progressive, payment of interest on the public debt probably increases income inequality. Income is transferred from people who, on average, have lower incomes to the higher-income bondholders. If greater income equality is one of our social goals, then this redistributive effect is clearly undesirable.

Incentives

Table 19-1 indicates that the present public debt necessitates annual interest payments of $244 billion. With no increase in the size of the debt, this annual interest charge must be paid out of tax revenues. These added taxes may dampen incentives to bear risk, to innovate, to invest, and to work. In this indirect way, a large public debt can impair economic growth. As noted earlier, the ratio of interest payments to GDP indicates the level of taxation needed to pay interest on the debt. Thus, many economists are concerned that this ratio is roughly twice as high as it was two decades earlier (column 6, Table 19-1).

External Debt

External debt—U.S. debt held by citizens and institutions of foreign countries—*is a burden.* This part of the public debt is *not* "owed to ourselves," and in real terms the payment of interest and principal requires transferring some of U.S. real output to other nations. Foreign ownership of the public debt is higher today than in earlier periods. In 1960 only 5 percent of the debt was foreign-owned; today foreign ownership is 23 percent. The assertion that "we owe the debt to ourselves" and the implication that the debt should thus be of little concern is less accurate than it was four decades ago. **(Key Question 3)**

Curb on Fiscal Policy

A large and growing public debt makes it politically difficult to use fiscal policy during a recession. For example, in 1991 and 1992 the Fed substantially reduced interest rates to stimulate a sluggish economy. But this easy money policy was slow to expand output and reduce unemployment. Had the public debt not been at a historic high and increasing due to the aforementioned structural deficit, it would have been politically feasible to reduce taxes or increase govern-

ment spending to generate the stimulus of a deficit. But the growing "debt problem" ruled out this stimulus on political grounds. In general, a large and growing public debt creates political impediments to the use of antirecessionary fiscal policy.

Crowding Out and the Stock of Capital

There is a potentially more serious problem. One way the public debt can transfer a real economic burden to future generations is by causing future generations to inherit a smaller stock of capital goods: a smaller "national factory." This possibility involves the *crowding-out effect*, the idea that deficit financing will increase interest rates and reduce private investment spending. If this happens, future generations would inherit an economy with a smaller production capacity and, other things equal, the standard of living would be lower than otherwise.

Suppose the economy is operating at its full-employment level of output and the Federal budget is initially in balance. Then assume that for some reason government increases its spending. The impact of this increase in government spending will fall on those living when it occurs. Think of a nation's production possibilities curve with "government goods" on one axis and "private goods" on the other. In a full-employment economy an increase in government spending will move the economy *along* the curve toward the government goods axis, meaning fewer private goods.

But private goods may be consumer or investment goods. If the increased government goods are provided at the expense of *consumer goods*, then the present generation bears the entire burden as a lower current standard of living. The current investment level is *not* affected, and therefore neither is the size of the national factory inherited by future generations. But if the increase in government goods means a reduction in production of *capital goods*, then the present generation's level of consumption (standard of living) will be unimpaired. But in the future our children and grandchildren will inherit a smaller stock of capital goods and will have lower income levels than otherwise.

Two Scenarios Let's sketch the two scenarios yielding these different results.

First Scenario Suppose the presumed increase in government spending is financed by an increase in taxation, say, personal income taxes. We know that most income is consumed. Therefore, consumer spending falls by almost as much as the increase in taxes. Here, the burden of the increase in government spending falls primarily on today's generation; it has fewer consumer goods.

Second Scenario   Assume the increase in government spending is financed by increasing the public debt, meaning government enters the money market and competes with private borrowers for funds. With the supply of money fixed, this increase in money demand will increase the interest rate—the "price" paid for the use of money.

In Figure 19-2 the curve I_{d1} reproduces the investment demand curve in Figure 9-5. (Ignore curve I_{d2} for now.) The investment demand curve is downsloping, indicating investment spending varies inversely with the interest rate. Here, government deficit financing drives up the interest rate, reducing private investment. If government borrowing in-

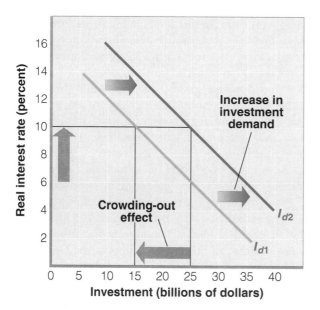

FIGURE 19-2 The investment demand curve and the crowding-out effect   The crowding-out effect suggests that with a fixed investment demand curve (I_{d1}), an increase in the interest rate caused by a government deficit will reduce private investment spending and decrease the size of the "national factory" inherited by future generations. In this case an increase in the interest rate from 6 to 10 percent crowds out $10 billion of private investment. However, if the economy is initially in a recession, the government deficit may improve profit expectations of businesses and shift the investment demand curve rightward as from I_{d1} to I_{d2}. This shift may offset the crowding-out effect wholly or in part.

creases the interest rate from 6 to 10 percent, investment spending would fall from $25 to $15 billion. That is, $10 billion of private investment would be crowded out.

Conclusion: An assumed increase in public goods production is more likely to come at the expense of private investment goods when financed by deficits. In comparison with the tax-financing scenario, the future generation inherits a smaller national factory and therefore has a lower standard of living with deficit financing.

Two Qualifications   But there are two loose ends to our discussion which might mitigate or even eliminate the size of the economic burden shifted to future generations.

1. Public Investment   Our discussion has neglected the character of the increase in government spending. Just as private goods may involve consumption or investment, so it is with public goods. If the increase in government spending consists of consumption-type outlays—purchases of recreational equipment for prisons or provision of limousines for government officials—then our second scenario's conclusion that the debt increase has shifted a burden to future generations is correct. But what if the government spending is investment-type outlays, for example, for construction of highways, harbors, and flood-control projects? Similarly, what if they are "human capital" investments in education, job training, and health?

Like private expenditures on machinery and equipment, **public investments** increase the economy's future production capacity. The capital stock of future generations need not be diminished; rather, its composition is changed so there is more public capital and less private capital.

2. Unemployment   The other qualification relates to our assumption that the initial increase in government expenditures occurs when the economy is at full employment. Again the production possibilities curve reminds us that *if* the economy is at less than full employment or, graphically, at a point inside the production possibilities curve, then an increase in government expenditures can move the economy *to* the curve without any sacrifice of either current consumption or private capital accumulation. If unemployment exists initially, deficit spending by government need *not* mean a burden for future generations in the form of a smaller national factory.

Look at Figure 19-2 again. If deficit financing increases the interest rate from 6 to 10 percent, a crowding-out effect of $10 billion will occur. But suppose the increase in government spending stimulates a recession economy via the multiplier effect, improving profit expectations and shifting private investment demand rightward to I_{d2}. Then, investment spending remains at $25 billion despite the higher 10 percent interest rate. Of course, the increase in investment demand might be smaller or larger than that in Figure 19-2. In the former case, the crowding-out effect would not be fully offset; in the latter, it would be more than offset. The point? An increase in investment demand may counter the crowding-out effect. **(Key Question 7)**

RECENT FEDERAL DEFICITS

Federal deficits and the growing public debt have been in the economic spotlight in the last two decades.

Large Size

As Figure 19-3 makes clear, the absolute size of annual Federal deficits increased enormously in the 1980s and 1990s. The average annual deficit for the 1970s was approximately $35 billion. In the 1980s annual deficits averaged five times that amount. Consequently, the public debt tripled during the same time (Table 19-1).

The Federal deficit jumped to $269 billion in 1991 and $290 billion in 1992, mainly because of the 1990–1991 recession and a weak recovery, which slowed the inflow of tax revenues. Government's expensive bailout of the savings and loan associations also contributed to the huge deficits in these years. The deficits then began to fall in 1993 and 1994 as the economy's expansion quickened and the Clinton administration's efforts to reduce the deficit took hold. By 1997 the deficit had dropped to $22 billion.

Understatement? The most recent annual budget deficits shown in Figure 19-3 may be understated. Over the past few years government has raised more money from social security taxes than it has paid out as benefits to current retirees. The purpose of this surplus is to prepare for the future time when "baby boomers" retire. Some economists argue that these revenues should be excluded when calculating present deficits because they represent future government obligations on a dollar-for-dollar basis. In this view

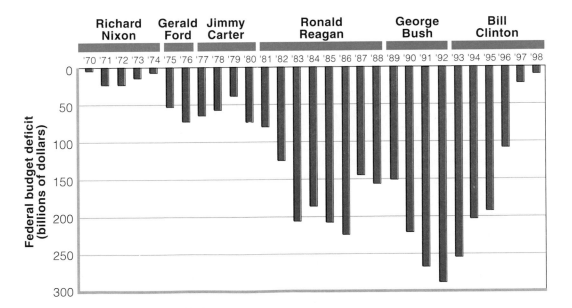

FIGURE 19-3 Annual Federal budget deficits, fiscal years 1970–1998 (in billions of dollars) Compared with the 1970s, annual budget deficits (here in nominal terms) ballooned in the 1980s and 1990s. (*Source: Economic Report of the President, 1998.* Fiscal years are 12-month periods ending September 30 of each year, rather than December 31 as in calendar years. The amount for 1998 is an estimate.)

the social security surplus should not be considered as an offset to *current* government spending. When we exclude the social security surplus from the deficit figures, recent budget deficits rise by $60 to $80 billion annually.

Rising Interest Costs   Column 4 in Table 19-1 indicates that interest payments on the public debt have increased about 17-fold since 1970. Interest payments were $244 billion in 1997, an amount greater than the entire deficit in many previous years! Because interest payments are part of government expenditures, the debt feeds on itself through interest charges. Interest payments on the debt are the only component of government spending which Congress cannot cut. The spiraling of such payments therefore complicates the problem of controlling government spending and the size of future deficits.

Inappropriate Policy   Some large U.S. annual deficits have occurred in an economy operating at or near full employment. Historically, deficits—particularly sizable ones—have been associated with wartime finance and recessions. While the 1980–1982 and 1990–1991 recessions contributed to huge deficits, it is clear that a major part of the deficits reflect the 1981 tax cuts and rising government spending. In terms of Figure 12-3, the 1981 tax cuts shifted the tax line downward. Meanwhile, mainly due to increased entitlement spending, the government spending line shifted upward. Thus, even at a full-employment level of output (GDP$_2$) sizable structural deficits remained.

Large deficits during times of economic prosperity raise the concern of fueling demand-pull inflation. To counteract potentially rising prices, the Federal Reserve is forced to employ a tighter monetary policy. Along with the strong demand for money in the private sector, the tight money policy raises real interest rates and reduces investment spending. The greatest potential for budget deficits to produce a crowding-out effect occurs when the economy is at or near full employment.

Balance-of-Trade Problems   Large budget deficits make it difficult for the nation to achieve a balance in its international trade. As you will see, large annual budget deficits promote imports and stifle exports. Also, budget deficits are thought to be a main cause of two related phenomena: (1) the nation's status as the "world's leading debtor nation" and (2) the so-called selling of the United States to foreign investors.

BUDGET DEFICITS AND TRADE DEFICITS

Many economists see cause-effect between Federal budget deficits and balance-of-trade deficits. Figure 19-4 is a guide to understanding their thinking.

Higher Interest Rates

Beginning with boxes 1 and 2, we note again that in financing its deficits, government must enter the money market to compete with the private sector for funds. We know this drives up real interest rates. High real interest rates have two important effects. First, as shown in box 3, they discourage private investment spending; this is the crowding-out effect. When the economy is close to full employment, the crowding-out effect is likely to be large. Therefore, although willing to admit that the short-run impact of deficits is expansionary, some economists express concern that the long-run effect of structural deficits is to retard the economy's growth rate. They envision deficits being used to finance entitlement programs and consumption-type government goods at the expense of investment in modernized factories and equipment. Deficits, it is contended, push the economy onto a slower long-run growth path.

Dollar Appreciation

The second effect, shown by box 4, is that high real interest rates on both U.S. government and private securities make financial investment in the United States more attractive for foreigners. While the resulting inflow of foreign funds helps finance both the deficit and private investment, box 5 reminds us that this inflow represents an increase in the U.S. external debt. Paying interest on and retiring debts to the rest of the world means a reduction in future real output available to the U.S. domestic economy.

Box 6 indicates that, to purchase high-yielding U.S. securities, foreigners must first buy U.S. dollars with their own currencies. This increases the worldwide demand for dollars and increases the international price or exchange value of the dollar. To illustrate: Suppose that before the United States incurred large deficits, the dollar ($) and the French franc (F) exchanged in the market at a rate of $1 = F10. But now the financing of large U.S. deficits increases real interest rates in the United States, increasing the demand for dollars with which to buy U.S. securities.

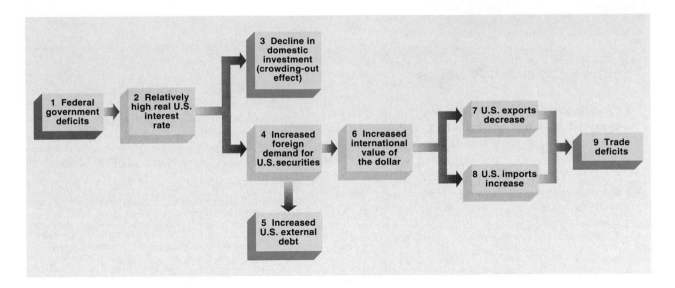

FIGURE 19-4 Budget deficits and trade deficits   Large U.S. budget deficits can have a variety of effects. They can raise domestic interest rates, resulting in both a crowding out of private investment and an increase in the demand for U.S. securities. The latter increases the U.S. external debt and the demand for dollars. The strong demand for dollars causes the dollar to appreciate, making U.S. exports more expensive to foreigners and imports less costly to Americans. As U.S. exports fall and imports rise, a trade deficit arises.

Suppose this raises the price of the dollar to, say, $1 = F11.

Trade Deficits

This appreciation of the dollar will eventually depress U.S. exports (box 7) and increase U.S. imports (box 8), leading to an "unfavorable" balance of trade. Let's see how this comes about. We know that exchange rates link the price levels of the world's nations. When the value of the dollar increases—when dollars become more expensive to foreigners—all U.S. goods become more expensive to foreign buyers.

In our example the increase in the value of the dollar from $1 = F10 to $1 = F11 increases prices of all U.S. goods by 10 percent to the French. The U.S. product that formerly cost 10 francs now costs 11 francs. The French will react to this by buying fewer U.S. goods; U.S. exports will fall. Conversely, at the higher exchange rate Americans get 11 rather than 10 francs for a dollar, so French goods are cheaper to people in the United States. They therefore buy more French goods; U.S. imports rise. Bringing these together, U.S. net exports (exports *minus* imports) fall and a trade deficit emerges (box 9).

Related Effects

There are three complications here.

1. The inflow of foreign funds does augment domestic funds and helps keep U.S. real interest rates from rising as much as they would otherwise. The inflow of foreign funds to the United States diminishes the size of the crowding-out effect. In contrast, domestic saving and investment will be smaller in foreign nations transferring funds to the United States.

2. Deficit-caused high real interest rates in the United States impose an increased burden on heavily indebted developing countries such as Mexico and Brazil. Their dollar-denominated debts to U.S. banks, in effect, go up since the dollar appreciation that results means they need a greater amount of their own currencies to pay interest and principal on their debts. Also, any refinancing of their debts with U.S. banks means higher real interest rates.

3. A trade deficit means a nation is not exporting enough to pay for its imports. The difference can be paid for either by borrowing from abroad or by selling assets. The United States has been doing both. It has become the world's leading debtor nation and has sold off assets such as factories, shopping centers, and

"The Entitlements Problem"

Spending on programs which "entitle" people to specified transfer payments is rising rapidly, absorbing a greater part of total government spending

The accompanying figure divides Federal spending into three components and shows spending trends as a percentage of GDP.

1. *Interest spending* consists of Federal interest payments on the public debt. Since 1980 interest payments have increased from 1.9 to 3.0 percent of GDP, mainly because of the enormous growth of the public debt.
2. *Discretionary spending* involves programs controlled by annual appropriations bills. Congress can decide how much it wants to spend on these programs each year; it has full "discretion" over the amounts spent. This component of Federal expenditures includes spending on defense, transportation, law enforcement, and government operations. Observe that discretionary spending shrank from 13.5 percent of GDP in 1962 to about 7 percent in 1998.
3. *Mandatory spending*—or "entitlement spending"—comprises benefits paid out in programs such as so-

cial security, Medicare, Medicaid, veterans' compensation and pensions, agricultural subsidies, aid to families with dependent children, Supplementary Security Income, and food stamps. This spending is mandated by past legislation which directs Congress to pay out specified benefits to all eligible recipients. Entitlement spending grows when Congress adds new transfer programs or raises benefit levels in existing programs. It also expands when more people become eligible for

Components of Federal spending as a percentage of gross domestic product, 1962–2004

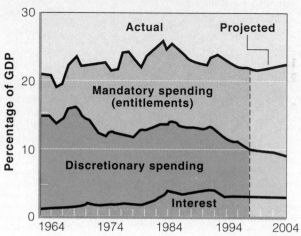

farms to foreign investors. To repay these debts and repurchase these assets, the United States would have to export more in the future than it imports. That is, it would have to consume and invest less than it produces. **(Key Question 8)**

■ Federal budget deficits are linked to U.S. trade deficits as follows: Budget deficits increase domestic interest rates; the dollar appreciates; U.S. exports fall, and U.S. imports rise; and a trade deficit emerges.

QUICK REVIEW 19-3

■ The borrowing and interest payments associated with the public debt **(a)** increase income inequality, **(b)** require higher taxes which dampen incentives, **(c)** curb the use of antirecessionary fiscal policy, and **(d)** impede the growth of the nation's capital stock through crowding out of private investment.

■ The Federal deficits of the past two decades have caused great concern because of **(a)** their enormous size, **(b)** the possibility of their understatement, **(c)** the rising total interest costs associated with them, and **(d)** their inappropriateness in the years when the economy was near, or at, full employment.

Policy Responses

Concern about large budget deficits and an expanding public debt has spawned several major policy responses.

Deficit-Reduction Legislation By 1992 it became clear that previous legislative efforts to reduce the budget deficit—including an increase in the top marginal tax rate on personal income from 28 to 31 percent—would still leave annual budget deficits of $175 to $225 billion. Spurred by the Clinton administration, in 1993 Congress passed the Deficit the benefits. Entitlement spending doubled between 1962 and 1998, rising from 6 to 13 percent of GDP.

It is clear from the diagram that rapidly rising Federal entitlements and interest payments are squeezing discretionary spending. Entitlements and interest are projected to consume *all* Federal tax revenues by 2015, leaving the Federal government with no money for education, children's programs, highways, national defense, or anything else.

Solutions proposed to avoid this startling scenario include:

1. Increasing tax rates
2. Eliminating some entitlement programs
3. Reducing benefit levels in some or all entitlement programs
4. Denying wealthier citizens social security and Medicare benefits
5. Reducing health care benefits under Medicare
6. Fully taxing entitlement benefits as if they were ordinary income

None of these possibilities is politically popular. *About half of all U.S. families receive benefits from one or more of the 11 largest entitlement programs.* A mid-1990s poll found that 61 percent of the public favored cutting government entitlement programs to curb the deficit. But when asked if they favored cuts in programs such as social security, Medicare, and farm subsidies, 66 percent said "no."

Social security and Medicare are the largest Federal entitlement programs. Social security is currently sound, collecting more revenues from 124 million workers than it pays to 44 million beneficiaries. But this self-financing will end in 2029 because of growing social security payments to the massive baby-boom generation. Spending for Medicare—the fastest growing entitlement program—will rise even more when the baby boomers retire.

Policymakers have begun to confront this issue. For example, Congress recently ended the entitlement aspect of the aid to families with dependent children program. There is little doubt the question of what to do about entitlements will continue to be the subject of intense discussion over the next several years.

Reduction Act, designed to increase tax revenues by $250 billion over the following 5 years and to reduce Federal spending by the same amount.

Specifically, this legislation (1) increased the top marginal tax rate on personal income from 31 to 39.6 percent, (2) raised the corporate income tax from 34 to 35 percent, and (3) added 4.3 cents per gallon to the Federal excise tax on gasoline. The largest spending "cut" resulted from holding all *discretionary spending*—the spending not mandated by law—to 1993 nominal levels. Normally, this spending would have increased at least as fast as inflation. Aided by strong economic growth, the Deficit Reduction Act reduced the deficit to $22 billion by 1997.

In 1996 Congress and the president agreed to a tax and spending package which included selected tax reductions but also increased some tax rates and reduced several types of government spending. Under this law, the deficit is designed to fall to zero by 2002, if the economy avoids recession. Recent estimates indicate that budget balance may occur as early as 1998. This outcome would be historic; not since 1969 has the Federal government balanced its budget.

Line-Item Veto In 1995 Congress gave the president the authority to veto individual spending items (called *line items*) in legislation passed by Congress. A typical appropriations bill merges hundreds of programs and projects into a single piece of legislation. The **line-item veto** will allow the president to cull from such legislation those projects whose benefits go to relatively few in a particular state, at a far greater expense to the nation's taxpayers. As a hypothetical example, the president could veto a specific provision to spend, say, $30 million for a monument in Chicago in honor of a local politician. Thus, the line-item veto—and perhaps even the threat of its use—might reduce government spending and help the Federal government balance its budget.

In 1996 President Clinton used the line-item veto for the first time. This use has enabled critics to challenge the constitutionality of the line-item veto in the courts, and the outcome of that challenge is still pending. Critics say that the line-item veto gives too much power to the president—power that the Constitution allegedly reserves for Congress. They also point out that this power could be abused for political purposes. For example, the president could veto a home-state project of a political "enemy" in Congress, leaving untouched a home-state project of a political "friend."

Proposed Constitutional Amendment   The most extreme proposal is that a constitutional amendment should be passed which mandates that Congress balance the budget each year. Proponents of this proposed **balanced-budget amendment** assume that future Congresses will find it difficult to act "responsibly" because government spending enhances and tax increases diminish a politician's popular support. Political rhetoric and recent deficit reductions aside, Federal deficits allegedly will continue to occur until a constitutional amendment requires an annually balanced budget.

Thus far, the proposed amendment has not passed Congress. Critics have successfully pointed out that a strict requirement to balance the budget annually would force government to increase tax rates or reduce government spending during recession. As previously noted, such actions would worsen a recession (review Figure 12-6).

Positive Role of Debt

Having completed this survey of imagined and real problems of deficits and the public debt, we conclude our discussion on a more positive note. Debt, both public and private, plays a positive role in a prosperous and growing economy. As national income increases, saving also rises. For the economy to continue to grow, this saving must be obtained and spent. The process by which saving is transferred to spenders is *debt creation*. Ideally, consumers and firms borrow and spend this growing saving. And, in fact, this usually is the case; the total private debt in the United States is about $11 trillion.

But, at times, consumers and firms are unwilling to borrow and thereby increase private debt sufficiently fast to absorb the growing volume of saving. When that happens, it is appropriate for government to expand its debt in order to absorb the remainder. Otherwise, the economy might falter from full employment and not realize its growth potential.

CHAPTER SUMMARY

1. A budget deficit is the excess of government expenditures over its receipts; the public debt is the total accumulation of its deficits and surpluses over time.

2. Budget philosophies include the annually balanced budget, the cyclically balanced budget, and functional finance. The basic problem with an annually balanced budget is that it is pro-cyclical rather than countercyclical. Similarly, it may be difficult to balance the budget over the course of the business cycle if upswings and downswings are not of roughly comparable magnitude. Functional finance is the view that the primary purpose of Federal finance is to stabilize the economy, and problems associated with consequent deficits or surpluses are of secondary importance.

3. Historically, growth of the public debt has been caused by the deficit financing of wars and by recessions. The large structural deficits of the 1980s and most of the 1990s primarily resulted from tax-rate reductions, accompanied by increases in entitlement spending.

4. The U.S. public debt (1997) is $5.4 trillion, or $20,044 per person. The public holds about two-thirds of this debt, while the other one-third is held by government agencies and the Federal Reserve System. In the 1980s and early 1990s, the public debt and its associated interest expense increased sharply as percentages of GDP. Only very recently have these percentages declined.

5. The contention that a large public debt may bankrupt the government is false because **(a)** the debt need only be refinanced rather than refunded and **(b)** the Federal government has the power to levy taxes and create money.

6. The crowding-out effect aside, the public debt is not a vehicle for shifting economic burdens to future generations.

7. More substantive problems associated with public debt include the following: **(a)** Payment of interest on the debt may increase income inequality. **(b)** Interest payments on the debt require higher taxes, which may impair incentives. **(c)** A large and growing public debt creates political impediments to the use of antirecessionary fiscal policy. **(d)** Paying interest or principal on the portion of the debt held by foreigners means a transfer of real output abroad. **(e)** Government borrowing to refinance or pay interest on the debt may increase interest rates and crowd out private investment spending.

8. The large Federal budget deficits of the 1980s and early 1990s increased real interest rates in the United States, and this then **(a)** crowded out private investment and **(b)** increased the foreign demand for U.S. securities. Increased demand for U.S. securities in turn caused the dollar to appreciate, reducing U.S. exports and increasing U.S. imports. Thus the large budget deficits contributed to U.S. trade deficits.

9. The large deficits and expanding public debt of the 1980s and early 1990s produced several policy responses. Legislation in 1993 cut expenditures and raised tax rates on personal income, corporate profit, and gasoline. In 1996, Congress gave the president the authority to veto specific spending items ("line items") from larger spending bills. Also in 1996, Congress passed a tax-spending package projected to reduce the budget deficit to zero by 2002 or earlier. The large deficits also created a call for a constitutional amendment which would require the Federal government to balance its budget annually.

TERMS AND CONCEPTS

public debt
annually balanced budget
cyclically balanced
 budget

functional finance
entitlement programs
external debt
public investments

line-item veto
balanced-budget
 amendment

STUDY QUESTIONS

1. KEY QUESTION Assess the potential for using fiscal policy as a stabilization tool under **(a)** an annually balanced budget, **(b)** a cyclically balanced budget, and **(c)** functional finance.

2. What have been the major sources of the public debt historically? Why were deficits so large in the 1980s? Why did the deficit rise sharply in 1991 and 1992?

3. KEY QUESTION Discuss the two ways of measuring the size of the public debt. How does an internally held public debt differ from an externally held public debt? What would be the effects of retiring an internally held public debt? An externally held public debt? Distinguish between refinancing and retiring the debt.

4. Explain or evaluate each of the following statements:
    a. A public debt is like a debt of the left hand to the right hand.
    b. The least likely problem arising from a large public debt is that the Federal government will go bankrupt.
    c. The basic cause of the growing Federal debt is a lack of political courage.

    d. The social security reserves are not being reserved. They are being spent, masking the real deficit.

5. Is the crowding-out effect likely to be larger during recession or when the economy is near or at full employment? Explain.

6. Some economists argue that the quantitative importance of the public debt can best be measured by interest payments on the debt as a percentage of the GDP. Explain why.

7. KEY QUESTION Is the $5.4 trillion public debt a burden to future generations? If so, in what sense? Why might deficit financing be more likely to reduce the future size of the U.S. "national factory" than would financing government expenditures through taxes?

8. KEY QUESTION Trace the cause-and-effect chain through which large deficits might affect domestic real interest rates, domestic investment, the international value of the dollar, and U.S. international trade. Comment: "There is too little recognition that the deterioration of the United States' position in world trade is more the result of our own policies than the harm wrought by foreigners."

9. Explain how a significant decline in the nation's budget deficit would be expected to affect **(a)** the size of the U.S. trade deficit, **(b)** the total debt Americans owe to foreigners, and **(c)** foreign purchases of U.S. assets such as factories and farms.

10. What major legislative actions has Congress taken since 1993 to reduce the size of the Federal deficit? Why has this process been so politically painful to Congress? Have the actions succeeded?

11. Do you favor a constitutional amendment which would require the Federal government to balance its budget each year? Why or why not? Relate your answer to the "rules versus discretion debate" discussed in Chapter 17.

12. Explain: "Congressional knowledge that the president *has* the line-item veto, more than such vetoes themselves, may reign in some government spending."

13. (Last Word) What does the term "entitlement programs" mean? Cite several examples of such programs. Why have entitlement programs grown so rapidly? What are the implications for future generations if this growth continues?

14. WEB-BASED QUESTION The Debt—To the Penny Go to the Web site of the Department of Treasury–Bureau of the Public Debt http://www.publicdebt.treas.gov/opd/opdpenny.htm and find the amount of the public debt, to the penny, as of the latest date. How does it compare to the debt of 10 years ago? What has been the trend over the past 12 months? For general information, visit http://www.publicdebt.treas.gov/opd/opd.htm.

15. WEB-BASED QUESTION Frequently Asked Questions About the Public Debt Visit the U.S. Treasury's Public Debt Frequently Asked Questions (FAQ) site http://www.publicdebt.treas.gov/opd/opdfaq.htm and answer the following questions. Why does the public debt sometimes go down? Why does the public debt change only once a day? As of today, who owns the public debt?

5

PART FIVE

Microeconomics of Product Markets

20

Demand and Supply: Elasticities and Applications

Scarce resources. Unlimited wants. That is what economics is about. Because of its unlimited wants, society desires to use all its available resources fully and efficiently. The full employment of all available resources and the long-run expansion of output are the focus of *macroeconomics*. Efficiently using employed resources is the subject of *microeconomics*, to which we now turn.

We have seen that mixed economies rely heavily on the self-interested behavior of market participants to allocate resources efficiently. Our goal now is to examine this behavior—and the resulting price, output, and efficiency outcomes—in much greater depth than in earlier chapters.

In this chapter we extend Chapter 3's discussion of demand and supply. (If your recollection of supply and demand is hazy, review Chapter 3's Quick Reviews, Key Graph, and Chapter Summary). Specifically, we now introduce and discuss the concept of *price* elasticity, a measure of consumers' and producers' responses to price changes. We then extend the elasticity concept by explaining the ideas of *cross* and *income* elasticity of demand. Finally, we apply our more detailed supply and demand analysis to markets in which government sets maximum or minimum prices.

PRICE ELASTICITY OF DEMAND

The law of demand tells us that consumers will respond to a decline in a product's price by buying more of that product. But how much more of it will they purchase? That amount can vary considerably by product and over different price ranges for the same product.

The responsiveness, or sensitivity, of consumers to a change in the price of a product is measured by the product's **price elasticity of demand.** Demand for some products is such that consumers are highly responsive to price changes; modest price changes lead to very large changes in the quantity purchased, for example, restaurant meals. The demand for such products is said to be *relatively elastic* or simply *elastic.* For other products, consumers are quite unresponsive to price changes; substantial price changes result only in small changes in the amount purchased, for example, salt. For such products, demand is *relatively inelastic* or simply *inelastic.*

The Price Elasticity Coefficient and Formula

Economists measure the degree of price elasticity or inelasticity of demand with the coefficient E_d, defined as

$$E_d = \frac{\text{percentage change in quantity demanded of product X}}{\text{percentage change in price of product X}}$$

These *percentage* changes are calculated by dividing the change in price by the original price and the consequent change in quantity demanded by the original quantity demanded. Thus, our definition can be restated as the formula:

$$E_d = \frac{\text{change in quantity demanded of X}}{\text{original quantity demanded of X}} \div \frac{\text{change in price of X}}{\text{original price of X}}$$

Use of Percentages   Why use percentages rather than absolute amounts in measuring consumer responsiveness? There are two reasons.

1 Choice of Units   If we use absolute changes, our impression of buyer responsiveness will be arbitrarily affected by the choice of units. To illustrate: If the price of product X falls from $3 to $2 and consumers increase their purchases from 60 to 100 pounds, it may appear that consumers are quite sensitive to price changes and therefore that demand is elastic. After all, a price change of 1 unit has caused a change in the amount demanded of 40 units. But by changing the monetary unit from dollars to pennies (why not?), we find that a price change of 100 units causes a quantity change of 40 units, giving the impression of inelasticity. Using percentage changes avoids this problem. This particular price decline is 33 percent whether measured in terms of dollars ($1/$3) or pennies (100¢/300¢).

2 Comparing Products   By using percentages, we can correctly compare consumer responsiveness to changes in the prices of *different* products. It makes little sense to compare the effects on quantity demanded of (1) a $1 increase in the price of a $10,000 auto with (2) a $1 increase in the price of a $1 can of cola. Here the price of the auto is rising by .01 percent while the price of the cola is up by 100 percent! If we increased the price of both products by 1 percent—$100 for the car and 1¢ for the cola—we could obtain a more sensible comparison of consumer sensitivity to the price changes.

Elimination of Minus Sign   We know from the downsloping demand curve that price and quantity demanded are inversely related. Thus, the price elasticity coefficient of demand E_d will always be a *negative* number. As an example, if price declines, then quantity demanded will increase. This means that the numerator in our formula will be positive and the denominator negative, yielding a negative E_d. For an increase in price, the numerator will be negative but the denominator positive, again yielding a negative E_d.

Economists usually ignore the minus sign and simply present the *absolute value* of the elasticity coefficient to avoid an ambiguity which might otherwise arise. It can be confusing to say that an E_d of -4 is greater than one of -2. This possible confusion is avoided when we say an E_d of 4 reveals greater elasticity than one of 2. In what follows we thus ignore the minus sign in the coefficient of price elasticity of demand and show only the absolute value. Incidentally, the ambiguity does not arise with supply because price and quantity supplied are positively related.

Interpretations of E_d

We can interpret the coefficient of price elasticity of demand as follows.

Elastic Demand   Demand is said to be **elastic** if a specific percentage change in price results in a larger percentage change in quantity demanded. Then E_d will be greater than 1. Example: If a 2 percent decline in price results in a 4 percent increase in quantity demanded, then demand is elastic and

$$E_d = \frac{.04}{.02} = 2$$

Inelastic Demand   If a specific percentage change in price is accompanied by a smaller percentage change in quantity demanded, demand is said to be **inelastic**. Then E_d will be less than 1. Example: If a 3 percent decline in price leads to only a 1 percent increase in quantity demanded, demand is inelastic and

$$E_d = \frac{.01}{.03} = .33$$

Unit Elasticity   The case separating elastic and inelastic demands occurs where a percentage change in price and the accompanying percentage change in quantity demanded are equal. Example: A 1 percent drop in price causes a 1 percent increase in quantity demanded. This special case is termed **unit elasticity** because E_d is exactly 1, or unity. In this example,

$$E_d = \frac{.01}{.01} = 1$$

Extreme Cases When we say demand is "inelastic," we do not mean that consumers are *completely* unresponsive to a price change. In that extreme situation, where a price change results in no change whatsoever in the quantity demanded, economists say that demand is **perfectly inelastic.** Examples include an acute diabetic's demand for insulin or an addict's demand for heroin. A line parallel to the vertical axis, such as D_1 in Figure 20-1a, shows perfectly inelastic demand graphically.

Conversely, when we say demand is "elastic," we do not mean that consumers are completely responsive to a price change. In that extreme situation, where a small price reduction would cause buyers to increase their purchases from zero to all they could obtain,

economists say demand is **perfectly elastic.** A line parallel to the horizontal axis, such as D_2 in Figure 20-1b, shows perfectly elastic demand. You will see in Chapter 23 that such a demand applies to a firm, say, a raspberry grower, selling its product in a purely competitive market.

Refinement: Midpoint Formula

The hypothetical demand data in Table 20-1 are useful for explaining an annoying problem that arises in computing the price elasticity coefficient: To calculate E_d for, say, the $5–$4 price range, which price-quantity combination should we use as a point of reference? We have two choices—the $5–4-unit combination and the $4–5-unit combination—and our choice will influence the outcome.

For the $5–4-unit reference point, the price change is from $5 to $4, so the percentage decrease in price is 20 percent; the quantity change is from 4 to 5 units, so the percentage increase in quantity is 25 percent. Substituting in the formula, we get E_d = 25/20, or 1.25, indicating that demand is somewhat elastic.

But for the $4–5-unit reference point, the price change is from $4 to $5, making the percentage increase in price 25 percent; the quantity change is from 5 to 4 units, or a 20 percent decline in quantity. The elasticity coefficient is therefore 20/25, or 0.80, meaning demand is slightly inelastic. Which is it? Is demand elastic or inelastic?

A solution to this problem is to use *averages* of the two prices and two quantities as the reference point. For the same $5–$4 price range, the price reference is $4.50, and the quantity reference 4.5 units. The percentage change in price is now $1/$4.50, or about 22 percent, and the percentage change in quantity is 1/4.50, or also about 22 percent, providing an E_d of 1. This solution estimates elasticity at the midpoint of the relevant price range. We now can restate the formula for E_d as

$$E_d = \frac{\text{change in quantity}}{\text{sum of quantities/2}} \div \frac{\text{change in price}}{\text{sum of prices/2}}$$

Substituting data for the $5–$4 price range, we get

$$E_d = \frac{1}{9/2} \div \frac{1}{9/2} = 1$$

This indicates that *at* the $4.50–4.5-unit midpoint the price elasticity of demand is unity. Here a 1 percent price change would result in a 1 percent change in quantity demanded.

(a) Perfectly inelastic demand

(b) Perfectly elastic demand

FIGURE 20-1 Perfectly inelastic and elastic demand
Demand curve D_1 in (a) represents *perfectly inelastic* demand. A price increase will result in no change in quantity demanded. Demand curve D_2 in (b) represents *perfectly elastic* demand. A price increase will cause quantity demanded to decline from an infinite amount to zero.

TABLE 20-1   Price elasticity of demand as measured by the elasticity coefficient and the total-revenue test

(1) Total quantity demanded per week (units)	(2) Price per unit	(3) Elasticity coefficient, E_d	(4) Total revenue (1) × (2)	(5) Total-revenue test
1	$8		$ 8	
2	7	5.00	14	Elastic
3	6	2.60	18	Elastic
4	5	1.57	20	Elastic
5	4	1.00	20	Unit elastic
6	3	0.64	18	Inelastic
7	2	0.38	14	Inelastic
8	1	0.20	8	Inelastic

Assignment: Verify the elasticity coefficients for the $1–$2 and $7–$8 price ranges in Table 20-1. The interpretation of E_d for the $1–$2 range is that a 1 percent change in price will change quantity demanded by 0.20 percent. For the $7–$8 range a 1 percent change in price will change quantity demanded by 5 percent.

Graphical Analysis

Demand curve D in Figure 20-2a was plotted using the data in columns 1 and 2, Table 20-1. The curve illustrates two important ideas.

1. Elasticity Varies with Price Range
Elasticity typically varies over the different price ranges of the same demand schedule or curve. For all straight-line and most other demand curves, demand is more elastic toward the upper left (the $5–$8 price range of D) than toward the lower right (the $4–$1 price range of D).

This is the consequence of arithmetic properties of the elasticity measure. Specifically, in the upper left segment of the demand curve, the percentage change in quantity is large because the original reference quantity is small. Similarly, the percentage change in price is small in that segment because the original reference price is large. The relatively large percentage change in quantity divided by the relatively small change in price yields a large E_d—an elastic demand.

The reverse holds true for the lower right segment of the demand curve. Here the percentage change in quantity is small because the original reference quantity is large; similarly, the percentage change

in price is large because the original reference price is small. The relatively small percentage change in quantity divided by the relatively large percentage change in price results in a low E_d—an inelastic demand.

2. Slope Does Not Measure Elasticity
The graphical appearance of a demand curve—its slope—is *not* a sound basis for judging elasticity. The catch is that the slope—the flatness or steepness—of a demand curve is computed from *absolute* changes in price and quantity, while elasticity involves *relative* or *percentage* changes in price and quantity.

The demand curve in Figure 20-2a is linear, which by definition means the slope is constant throughout. But we have demonstrated that such a curve is elastic in its high-price ($8–$5) range and inelastic in its low-price ($4–$1) range. **(Key Question 2)**

QUICK REVIEW 20-1

■ Price elasticity of demand measures the sensitivity of consumers to changes in the price of a product.

■ The price elasticity of demand coefficient E_d is the ratio of the percentage change in quantity demanded to the percentage change in price. The averages of the prices and quantities are used as references in calculating the percentage changes.

■ When E_d is greater than 1, demand is elastic; when E_d is less than 1, it is inelastic; when E_d is equal to 1, demand is of unit elasticity.

■ Demand is typically elastic in the high-price (low-quantity) range of the demand curve and inelastic in the low-price (high-quantity) range of the curve.

(a) Demand curve

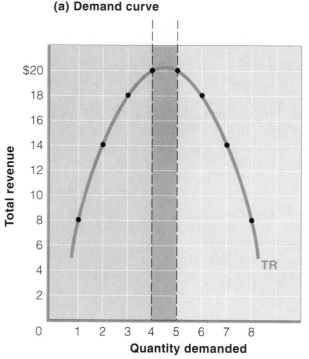

(b) Total-revenue curve

FIGURE 20-2 Relation between price elasticity of demand and total revenue   Demand curve *D* in (a) is based on Table 20-1 and marked to show that, typically, demand is elastic at higher price ranges and inelastic at lower price ranges. The total-revenue curve TR in (b) is derived from demand curve *D*. When price falls and TR increases, demand is elastic; when price falls and TR is unchanged, demand is unit-elastic; and when price falls and TR declines, demand is inelastic.

- -

The Total-Revenue Test

Total revenue (TR) is the total amount the seller receives from the sale of a product; it is calculated by multiplying the product price (*P*) by the quantity demanded and sold (*Q*). In equation form:

$$TR = P \times Q$$

Total revenue and the price elasticity of demand are related. Indeed, perhaps the easiest way to infer whether demand is elastic or inelastic is to employ the **total-revenue test,** where we observe what happens to total revenue when product price changes.

Elastic Demand   If demand is *elastic*, a *decrease* in price will *increase* total revenue. Even though a lesser price is received per unit, enough additional units are sold to more than make up for the lower price. For an example, look at demand curve *D* in Figure 20-2a, specifically the elastic-demand region at the upper left. (Disregard Figure 20-2b for the moment.) At point *a* on the curve, price is $8 and quantity demanded is 1 unit. So total revenue, or price times quantity, is $8. Geometrically, total revenue is area $0P_8aQ_1$, found by multiplying one side of the rectangle ($0P_8$) by the other ($0Q_1$).

If the price declines to $7 (point *b*), the quantity demanded becomes 2 units, and total revenue is $14 (= 2×7 units), or area $0P_7bQ_2$. As a result of the price decline from $8 to $7, total revenue has increased from $8 to $14. This increase has occurred because the *loss* in revenue from the lower price per unit (area P_7P_8ac) is *less* than the *gain* in revenue from the larger quantity demanded (area Q_1cbQ_2) accompanying the lower price. Specifically, the $1 price reduction applies to the original 1 unit (Q_1), for a loss of $1. But the lower price increases quantity demanded by 1 unit (Q_1 to Q_2), with a resulting gain in revenue of $7. Thus, there is a *net increase* in total revenue of $6 (= $7 − $1).

The reasoning is reversible: If demand is elastic, a price *increase* will *reduce* total revenue. If we shift from *b* to *a* on the demand curve, the gain in total revenue caused by the higher unit price (area P_7P_8ac) is *less* than the *loss* in revenue from the drop in sales (area Q_1cbQ_2). Combining these results tells us that *demand is elastic if a price change causes total revenue to change in the opposite direction.*

Inelastic Demand   If demand in inelastic, a price decrease will reduce total revenue. The modest increase in sales will not offset the decline in revenue per unit, and the net result is that total revenue declines. To see this, look toward the lower right of demand curve D in Figure 20-2a, specifically the inelastic-demand region. At point f on the curve, price is $2 and quantity demanded is 7 units. So total revenue is $14, or area $0P_2fQ_7$. If the price drops to $1 (point h), quantity demanded increases to 8 units. Total revenue becomes $8, which is clearly less than $14; area $0P_1hQ_8$ is less than area $0P_2fQ_7$. Total revenue has declined because the loss of revenue from the lower unit price (area P_1P_2fg) is larger than the gain in revenue from the accompanying increase in sales (area Q_7ghQ_8). The $1 decline in price applies to 7 units, with a consequent revenue loss of $7. The sales increase accompanying this lower price is 1 unit, which results in a revenue gain of $1. The overall result is a net decrease in total revenue of $6 (= $1 − $7).

Again our analysis is reversible: If demand is inelastic, a price *increase* will *increase* total revenue. Together, these results tell us that *demand is inelastic if a price change causes total revenue to change in the same direction.*

Unit Elasticity In the special case of *unit elasticity*, an increase or decrease in price leaves total revenue unchanged. The loss in revenue from a lower unit price is exactly offset by the gain in revenue from the accompanying increase in sales. Conversely, the gain in revenue from a higher unit price is exactly offset by the revenue loss associated with the accompanying decline in the amount demanded.

In Figure 20-2a we find that at the $5 price 4 units will be sold, yielding total revenue of $20. At $4 a total of 5 units will be sold, again resulting in $20 of total revenue. The $1 price reduction causes the loss of $4 in revenue on the 4 units that could have been sold for $5 each. This is exactly offset by a $4 revenue gain which results from the sale of 1 more unit at the lower $4 price.

Price Elasticity and the Total-Revenue Curve

In Figure 20-2b we graphed the total revenue corresponding to each price-quantity combination indicated in columns 1 and 4 in Table 20-1 and demand curve D in Figure 20-2a. The price–quantity demanded combination represented by point a on the demand curve yields total revenue of $8 (= $8 × 1 unit). In Figure 20-2b, we graphed this $8 amount vertically at 1 unit of quantity demanded. Similarly, the price–quantity-demanded combination repre-

sented by point b in the upper panel yields total revenue of $14 (= $7 × 2 units). This amount is graphed vertically at 2 units of quantity demanded in the lower panel. The ultimate result of such graphing is total-revenue curve TR, which initially slopes upward, reaches a maximum, and then turns downward.

Comparison of curves D and TR brings the relationship between elasticity and total revenue into sharp focus. Lowering the price in the elastic range of demand—say, from $8 to $5—increases total revenue. Conversely, increasing the price in that range reduces total revenue. In both cases, price and total revenue change in opposite directions, confirming that demand is elastic.

The $5–$4 price range of demand curve D is characterized by unit elasticity. When price either decreases from $5 to $4 or increases from $4 to $5, total revenue remains $20. In both cases, price has changed and total revenue has remained constant, confirming that demand is unit-elastic when we consider these particular price changes.

In the inelastic range of demand curve D, lowering the price—say, from $4 to $1—decreases total revenue, as shown in Figure 20-2b. Raising the price boosts total revenue. In both cases, price and total revenue move in the same direction, confirming that demand is inelastic.

So here again is the total-revenue test: Note what happens to total revenue when the price of a product changes. If total revenue changes in the *opposite* direction from price, demand is elastic. If total revenue changes in the *same* direction as price, demand is inelastic. If total revenue *does not change* when price changes, demand is unit-elastic.

Table 20-2 summarizes the characteristics of price elasticity of demand, and you should study it carefully. **(Key Questions 4 and 5)**

Determinants of Price Elasticity of Demand

We cannot say just what will determine the price elasticity of demand in each individual situation. However, the following generalizations are often helpful.

Substitutability Generally, the larger the number of substitute goods that are available, the greater the elasticity of demand. We will find later that in a purely competitive market, where by definition there are many perfect substitutes for the product of any specific seller, the demand curve seen by that single seller

TABLE 20-2   **Price elasticity of demand: a summary**

Absolute value of elasticity coefficient	Demand is:	Description	Impact on total revenue of a:	
			Price increase	Price decrease
Greater than 1 $(E_d > 1)$	Elastic or relatively elastic	Quantity demanded changes by a larger percentage than does price	Total revenue decreases	Total revenue increases
Equal to 1 $(E_d = 1)$	Unit or unitary elastic	Quantity demanded changes by the same percentage as does price	Total revenue is unchanged	Total revenue is unchanged
Less than 1 $(E_d < 1)$	Inelastic or relatively inelastic	Quantity demanded changes by a smaller percentage than does price	Total revenue increases	Total revenue decreases

is perfectly elastic. If one competitive seller of carrots or potatoes raises its price, buyers will turn to the readily available perfect substitutes provided by its many rivals. Similarly, we would expect the lowering of world trade barriers to increase the elasticity of demand for most products by making more substitutes available. With unimpeded trade Hondas, Toyotas, Nissans, Mazdas, Volkswagens, and other foreign cars become effective substitutes for domestic autos. At the other extreme, we saw earlier that the diabetic's demand for insulin and the addict's demand for heroin are highly inelastic—there are no close substitutes.

The elasticity of demand for a product depends on how narrowly the product is defined. Demand for Quaker State motor oil is more elastic than is the overall demand for motor oil. Many other brands are readily substitutable for Quaker State's oil, but there are few, if any, good substitutes for motor oil.

Proportion of Income   Other things equal, the higher the price of a good relative to people's incomes and hence to their budgets, the greater the good's price elasticity of demand. A 10 percent increase in the price of relatively low-priced pencils or chewing gum amounts to a few pennies, and quantity demanded will probably decline only slightly. Thus, price elasticity for such low-priced items tends to be low. But a 10 percent increase in the price of relatively high-priced automobiles or housing means additional expenditures of perhaps $2000 or $10,000, respectively. These price increases are significant fractions of the annual incomes and budgets of most families, and quantities demanded will likely diminish significantly. Price elasticity for such items tends to be high, meaning demand will be elastic.

Luxuries versus Necessities   The demand for "necessities" tends to be price-inelastic; that for "luxuries," price-elastic. Bread and electricity are generally regarded as necessities; it is difficult to get along without them. A price increase will not significantly reduce the amount of bread consumed or the amounts of lighting and power used in a household. (Note the very low price elasticity coefficient of these goods in Table 20-3.) An extreme case: A person does not decline an operation for acute appendicitis because the physician's fee has just gone up.

On the other hand, Caribbean cruises and emeralds are luxuries, which, by definition, can be forgone. If the price of cruises or emeralds rises, an individual need not buy them and will suffer no great hardship without them.

What about the demand for a common product like salt? It is highly inelastic on three counts: There

TABLE 20-3   Selected price elasticities of demand*

Product or service	Coefficient of price elasticity of demand, E_d	Product or service	Coefficient of price elasticity of demand, E_d
Housing	.01	Gasoline	.60
Electricity (household)	.13	Milk	.63
Bread	.15	Household appliances	.63
Major league baseball tickets	.23	Movies	.87
Telephone service	.26	Beer	.90
Sugar	.30	Shoes	.91
Medical care	.31	Motor vehicles	1.14
Eggs	.32	Beef	1.27
Legal services	.37	China, glassware, tableware	1.54
Automobile repair	.40	Restaurant meals	2.27
Clothing	.49	Lamb and mutton	2.65

*Compiled from numerous studies and sources reporting price elasticity of demand.

are few good substitutes available; salt is a negligible item in the family budget; and it is a "necessity" rather than a luxury.

Time Generally, product demand is more elastic the longer the time period under consideration. Many consumers are creatures of habit. When the price of a product rises, it takes time to find and experiment with other products to see if they are acceptable. Consumers may not immediately reduce their purchases very much when the price of beef rises by 10 percent, but in time they may shift to chicken or fish, for which they will "develop a taste."

Another consideration is product durability. Studies show that "short-run" demand for gasoline is more inelastic ($E_d = 0.2$) than is "long-run" demand ($E_d = 0.7$). In the long run, large, gas-guzzling automobiles wear out and, with rising gasoline prices, are replaced by smaller, more fuel-efficient cars.

Table 20-3 shows estimated price elasticity coefficients for a number of products. You should be able to explain each coefficient with the elasticity determinants just discussed. **(Key Question 6)**

QUICK REVIEW 20-2

■ When the price of a good changes, total revenue will change in the opposite direction if demand for the good

is price-elastic, in the same direction if demand is price-inelastic, and not at all if demand is unit-elastic.

■ Price elasticity of demand is greater **(a)** the larger the number of substitutes available; **(b)** the higher the price of a product relative to one's budget; **(c)** the greater the extent to which the product is a luxury; and **(d)** the longer the time period involved.

Applications of Price Elasticity of Demand

The concept of price elasticity of demand has great practical significance, as seen in the following examples.

Bumper Crops The demand for most farm products is highly inelastic; E_d is perhaps 0.20 or 0.25. As a result, increases in the output of farm products arising from a good growing season or from increased productivity tend to depress both the prices of farm products and the total revenues (incomes) of farmers. For farmers as a group, the inelastic nature of the demand for their products means a bumper crop may be undesirable. For policy makers it means higher total farm income requires that farm output be restricted.

Automation The impact of technological advances on employment depends in part on the elasticity of demand for the product or service that is involved. Suppose a firm installs new labor-saving machinery that replaces 500 of its workers, who are then laid off. Assume too that part of the cost reduction from this technological advance is passed on to consumers as reduced product prices. The effect of the price reduction on the firm's sales will depend on the price elasticity of demand for the product. If demand is elastic, sales might increase so much that some of, all of, or even more than the 500 displaced workers will have to be rehired. If demand is inelastic, the price reduction will result in only a small increase in sales, and few, if any, displaced workers will be rehired.

Airline Deregulation Deregulating the airlines in the late 1970s initially increased the profits of many carriers. The reason was that deregulation increased price competition among the airlines, lowering airfares. Lower fares, coupled with an elastic demand for air travel, increased revenues. Because the additional costs associated with flying full, as opposed to partially empty, aircraft are minimal, revenues increased more than costs and profits were enhanced. This profitability was not to last, for three reasons: The entry of competitors on profitable routes drove down profits; rising fuel prices increased operating costs; and persistent "fare wars" further cut profits.

Excise Taxes Government pays attention to elasticity of demand when selecting goods and services on which to levy excise taxes. If a $1 tax is levied on a product and 10,000 units are sold, tax revenue will be $10,000. If government now raises the tax to $1.50 and the consequent higher price reduces sales to 5000 because of an elastic demand, tax revenue will *decline* to $7500. A higher tax on a product with an elastic demand will bring in less tax revenue. Therefore, legislatures seek out products having inelastic demands—liquor, gasoline, and cigarettes—when levying excises. In fact, the Federal government increased taxes on these three categories of goods in 1991 in its effort to reduce the budget deficit.

But government's record is not impeccable in this regard. In 1991 Congress imposed a 10 percent excise tax on yachts costing more than $100,000. Believing the demand for yachts was inelastic, Congress felt the impact on sales would be small and therefore anticipated that the tax would raise $1.5 billion over 5 years. But demand turned out to be more elastic than lawmakers thought. Many boat owners responded by keeping their old boats longer, and some prospective first-

time buyers abandoned their plans to buy pleasure boats. In southern Florida sales dropped by nearly 90 percent, since many prospective buyers avoided the tax by buying their craft in the Bahamas. Government revenue from the tax was also reduced by the 1990–1991 recession, which shifted the demand curve for most durable goods, yachts included, to the left. In 1991 the 10 percent tax raised only $30 million in revenue.

The tax, coupled with the recession, had a devastating effect on boat manufacturers. In the first year of the tax a third of all United States yacht-building companies halted production, and more than 20,000 workers lost their jobs. In 1993 Congress repealed the tax.

Drugs and Street Crime The belief that addicts' demand for crack cocaine and heroin is highly inelastic poses some awkward tradeoffs in law enforcement. The approach typically used to reduce drug addiction is restricting supply, that is, making the drugs less readily available by intercepting their shipment into the United States.

But what will happen if this policy is successful? In view of the highly inelastic demand for cocaine and heroin, the street price to addicts will rise sharply while the amounts purchased will decrease only slightly. From the drug dealers' perspective this means greatly increased revenues and profits. From the addicts' viewpoint it means greater total expenditures on these drugs. Because much of the income which addicts spend on drugs comes from shoplifting, burglary, prostitution, and muggings, these crimes will increase as addicts increase their total expenditures for drugs. Here, the effort of law-enforcement authorities to control the spread of drug addiction may increase the amount of crime committed by addicts.

In recent years proposals to legalize drugs have been widely debated. Proponents contend that drugs should be treated like alcohol; they should be made legal for adults and regulated for purity and potency. The current war on drugs, it is argued, has been unsuccessful and the associated costs—including enlarged police forces, the construction of more prisons, an overburdened court system, and untold human costs—have increased markedly. Legalization would allegedly reduce drug trafficking greatly by taking the profit out of it. Crack cocaine and heroin, for example, are cheap to produce and could be sold at low prices in legal markets. Because the demand of addicts is highly inelastic, the amounts consumed at the lower prices would increase only modestly. Addicts' total expenditures for cocaine and heroin would decline and so would the street crime which finances these expenditures.

Opponents of legalization say that the overall demand for cocaine and heroin is much more elastic than proponents of legalization think. In addition to the inelastic demand of addicts, there is another market segment whose demand is relatively elastic. This segment consists of the occasional users or "dabblers," who use hard drugs when their prices are low but abstain or substitute, say, alcohol when their prices are high. Thus, the lower prices associated with legalization of these drugs would increase consumption by dabblers. Also, removal of the legal prohibitions against using drugs might make drug use more socially acceptable, shifting the demand curve for cocaine and heroin to the right.

Many economists predict that the legalization of cocaine and heroin would reduce their street prices by 60 percent. According to a recent study, price declines of that size would increase the number of occasional users of heroin by 54 percent and the number of occasional users of cocaine by 33 percent. The total quantity of heroin demanded would rise by an estimated 100 percent; the quantity of cocaine demanded, by 50 percent.[1] Moreover, many existing and new dabblers might in time become addicts. The overall result, say the opponents of legalization, would be higher social costs associated with drug use, possibly including an *increase* in street crime.

Minimum Wage   The Federal minimum wage prohibits employers from paying covered workers less than $5.15 per hour. Critics say that such a minimum wage, if it is above the equilibrium market wage, moves employers upward along their downsloping labor demand curves toward lower quantities of labor demanded. In this way it causes unemployment, particularly among teenage workers. On the other hand, workers who remain employed at the minimum wage receive higher incomes than otherwise. The amount of income lost by the newly unemployed and the amount of income gained by those who keep their jobs depend on the elasticity of demand for teenage labor. Research suggests the demand for teenage labor is quite inelastic, with E_d possibly as low as 0.15 or 0.25. If correct, this means income gains associated

with the minimum wage exceed income losses. The "unemployment argument" made by critics of the minimum wage would be stronger if the demand for teenage workers were elastic.

PRICE ELASTICITY OF SUPPLY

The concept of price elasticity also applies to supply. If producers are relatively responsive to price changes, supply is elastic. If they are relatively insensitive to price changes, supply is inelastic.

We measure the degree of price elasticity or inelasticity of supply with the coefficient E_s, defined almost like E_d except that we substitute "percentage change in quantity *supplied*" for "percentage change in quantity *demanded*":

$$E_s = \frac{\text{percentage change in quantity supplied of product X}}{\text{percentage change in price of product X}}$$

For reasons explained earlier, the averages, or midpoints, of the before and after quantities supplied and prices are used as reference points for the percentage changes. Suppose the price of a good increases from $4 to $6, increasing the quantity supplied from 10 units to 14 units. The percentage change in price would be 2/5, or 40 percent, and the percentage change in quantity would be 4/12, or 33 percent:

$$E_s = \frac{.33}{.40} = .83$$

In this case, supply is inelastic, since the price elasticity coefficient is less than 1. If E_s is greater than 1, supply is elastic. If it is equal to 1, supply is unit-elastic. Also, E_s is never negative; price and quantity supplied are *directly* related. Thus, there are no minus signs to drop, as was necessary with elasticity of demand.

The main determinant of **price elasticity of supply** is the amount of time available to producers for responding to a change in product price. A firm's response to, say, an increase in the price of Christmas trees depends on its ability to shift resources from the production of other products (whose prices we assume remain constant) to the production of trees. And shifting resources takes time: the longer the time, the greater the resource "shiftability." Thus, we c⌐ expect a greater response—and therefore greate⌐ ticity of supply—the longer a firm has to price change.

---

[1]Henry Saffer and Frank Chaloupka, "The Demand for Illegal Drugs," National Bureau of Economic Research, Working Paper 5238.

In analyzing the impact of time on elasticity, economists distinguish among the immediate market period, the short run, and the long run.

Supply Elasticity: The Market Period

The **market period** is the time immediately after a change in market price during which producers cannot respond with a change in quantity supplied. Suppose the owner of a small truck farm brings an entire season's output of tomatoes—one truckload—to market. The supply curve for these tomatoes is perfectly inelastic (vertical); the farmer will sell the truckload whether the price is high or low. Why? Because the farmer can offer only one truckload of tomatoes even if the price of tomatoes is much higher than anticipated. He or she might like to offer more tomatoes, but tomatoes cannot be produced overnight. Another full growing season is needed to respond to a higher-than-expected price by producing more than one truckload. Similarly, because the product is perishable, the farmer cannot withhold it from the market. If the price is lower than anticipated, he or she will still sell the entire truckload.

The farmer's costs of production, incidentally, will not enter into this decision to sell. Though the price of tomatoes may fall far short of production costs, the farmer will nevertheless sell out to avoid a total loss through spoilage. During the market period, our

farmer's supply of tomatoes is fixed: only one truckload is offered no matter how high or low the price.

Figure 20-3a shows the farmer's vertical supply curve in the market period. Supply is perfectly inelastic because the farmer does not have time to respond to a change in demand, say from D_1 to D_2. The resulting price increase from P_0 to P_m simply determines which buyers get the fixed quantity supplied; it elicits no increase in output.

However, not all supply curves need be perfectly inelastic immediately after a price change. If the product is not perishable and the price rises, producers may choose to increase quantity supplied by drawing down their inventories of unsold, stored goods. This will cause the market supply curve to have some positive slope. For our tomato farmer, the market period may be a full growing season; for producers of goods which can be inexpensively stored, there may be no market period at all.

Supply Elasticity: The Short Run

In the **short run,** the plant capacity of individual producers and the industry is presumed fixed. But firms *do* have time to use their fixed plants more or less intensively. Thus, in the short run, our truck farmer's plant—made up of land and farm machinery—is fixed. But he does have time in the short run to cultivate tomatoes more intensively by applying more labor and more fertilizer and pesticides to the crop. The re-

(a) Immediate market period

(b) Short run

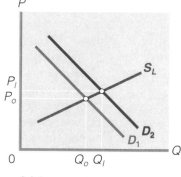
(c) Long run

FIGURE 20-3 Time and the elasticity of supply   The greater the amount of time producers have to adjust to a change in demand, here from D_1 to D_2, the greater will be their output response. In the immediate market period (a) there is insufficient time to change output, and so supply is perfectly inelastic. In the short run (b) plant capacity is fixed, but output can be altered by changing the intensity of its use; supply is therefore more elastic. In the long run (c) all desired adjustments, including changes in plant capacity, can be made, and supply becomes still more elastic.

sult is a somewhat greater output in response to a presumed increase in demand; this greater output is reflected in a more elastic supply of tomatoes, as shown by S_s in Figure 20-3b. Note now that the increase in demand from D_1 to D_2 is met by an increase in quantity (from Q_0 to Q_s), so there is a smaller price adjustment (from P_0 to P_s) than in the market period. The equilibrium price is therefore lower in the short-run than in the market period.

Supply Elasticity: The Long Run

The **long run** is a time period sufficiently long so that firms can make all desired resource adjustments; individual firms can expand (or contract) their plant capacities, and new firms can enter (or existing firms can leave) the industry. In the "tomato industry" our truck farmer can acquire additional land and buy more machinery and equipment. Furthermore, more farmers may be attracted to tomato production by the increased demand and higher price. These adjustments mean an even greater supply response, that is, the even more elastic supply curve S_L. In Figure 20-3c, the result is a smaller price rise (P_0 to P_l) and a larger output increase (Q_0 to Q_l) in response to the increase in demand from D_1 to D_2. **(Key Question 10)**

There is no total-revenue test for elasticity of supply. Supply shows a positive or direct relationship between price and amount supplied; the supply curve is upsloping. Regardless of the degree of elasticity or inelasticity, price and total revenue always move together.

CROSS AND INCOME ELASTICITY OF DEMAND

The price elasticities measure the responsiveness of the quantity of a product demanded or supplied when its price changes. It is also useful to know how the consumption of a good is affected by a change in the price of a *related product* or by a change in *income*.

Cross Elasticity of Demand

Suppose Coca-Cola is considering a reduction in the price of its Sprite brand. Not only will it want to know something about the price elasticity of demand for Sprite (will the price cut increase or decrease total revenue?), but it will also be interested in knowing if the increased sales of Sprite will come at the expense of Coke itself. How sensitive is the quantity demanded of one product (Coke) to a change in the price of a second product (Sprite)? To what extent will the lower price and increased sales of Sprite reduce the sales of Coke?

Or suppose government is trying to assess whether a proposed merger between two large firms will substantially reduce competition and therefore should be blocked. One question it needs to answer is this: Are the two firms' products highly substitutable for one another, or are they largely unrelated to one another? If the former, then competition might be reduced; if the latter, there is probably no cause for concern.

The concept of **cross elasticity of demand** sheds light on such questions from firms and government. It does so by measuring how sensitive consumer purchases of *one* product (say, X) are to a change in the price of some *other* product (say, Y). We calculate the coefficient of cross elasticity of demand E_{xy} just as we do the coefficient of simple price elasticity, except that we relate the percentage change in the consumption of X to the percentage change in the price of Y:

$$E_{xy} = \frac{\text{percentage change in quantity demanded of product X}}{\text{percentage change in price of product Y}}$$

This cross elasticity concept allows us to quantify and more fully understand substitute and complementary goods, introduced in Chapter 3.

Substitute Goods If cross elasticity of demand is positive—that is, the quantity demanded of X moves in the same direction as a change in the price of Y—then X and Y are *substitute goods*. An example is Kodak film (X) and Fuji film (Y). An increase in the price of Kodak film causes consumers to buy more Fuji film. The larger the positive cross elasticity coefficient, the greater the substitutability between the two products.

Complementary Goods When cross elasticity is negative, we know that X and Y "go together"; an increase in the price of one decreases the demand for the other. So the two are *complementary goods*. For example, an increase in the price of cameras will decrease the amount of film purchased. The larger the negative cross elasticity coefficient, the greater the complementarity between the two goods.

Independent Goods A zero or near-zero cross elasticity suggests that the two products are unrelated or *independent goods*. An example is walnuts and film: We would not expect a change in the price of walnuts to have any effect on purchases of film.

Income Elasticity of Demand

Income elasticity of demand measures the degree to which consumers respond to a change in their *incomes* by buying more or less of a particular good. The coefficient of income elasticity of demand E_i is determined with the formula

$$E_i = \frac{\text{percentage change in quantity demanded}}{\text{percentage change in income}}$$

Normal Goods For most goods the income elasticity coefficient E_i is *positive*, meaning that more of them is demanded as incomes increase. Such goods are called *normal* or *superior goods*, which we first described in Chapter 3. But the value of E_i varies greatly among normal goods. For example, the income elasticity of demand for automobiles is about +3.00, while income elasticity for most farm products is only about +0.20.

Inferior Goods A negative income elasticity coefficient designates an *inferior good*. Retreaded tires, cabbage, long-distance bus tickets, used clothing, and muscatel wine are likely candidates. Consumers *decrease* their purchases of such products as incomes *increase*.

Insights Income elasticity of demand coefficients provide insights about the economy. Here are two examples:

1. Income elasticity helps explain the relative expansion and contraction of industries in the United States. On average, total income in the economy has grown 2 to 3 percent annually. As income has expanded, industries producing products for which demand is quite income-elastic have expanded their outputs. Thus automobiles ($E_i = +3$), housing ($E_i = +1.5$), books ($E_i = +1.4$), and restaurant meals ($E_i = +1.4$) have all experienced strong growth of output. Meanwhile, industries producing products for which income elasticity is low or negative have tended to grow less rapidly or to decline. For example, agriculture ($E_i = +0.20$) has grown far more slowly than has the economy's total output.

2. Some estimates of the coefficient of the income elasticity of demand for U.S. health care are about +1, indicating that spending on health care rises proportionately with incomes. This coefficient tells policy makers that the inordinate rise in health care spending in the United States over the past two or three decades is caused by factors other then just income growth. **(Key Questions 12 and 13)**

Table 20-4 is a convenient synopsis of the cross and income elasticity concepts.

TABLE 20-4   Cross and income elasticities of demand

Value of coefficient	Description	Type of good(s)
Cross elasticity: Positive $(E_{wz} > 0)$	Quantity demanded of W changes in same direction as change in price of Z	Substitutes
Negative $(E_{xy} < 0)$	Quantity demanded of X changes in opposite direction from change in price of Y	Complements
Income elasticity: Positive $(E_i > 0)$	Quantity demanded of the product changes in same direction as change in income	Normal or superior
Negative $(E_i < 0)$	Quantity demanded of the product changes in opposite direction from change in income	Inferior

APPLICATIONS: GOVERNMENT-CONTROLLED PRICES

Supply and demand analysis and the elasticity concept are applied repeatedly in the remainder of this book. To show you the usefulness of these ideas, we use them here to examine some of the implications of prices that are in some way controlled by government.

On occasion the general public and government conclude that supply and demand result in prices either unfairly high to buyers or unfairly low to sellers. In such instances government may intervene by legally limiting how high or low the price may go.

Price Ceilings and Shortages

A **price ceiling** is the maximum legal price a seller may charge for a product or service. A price at or below the ceiling is legal; a price above it is not. The rationale for establishing price ceilings (or *ceiling prices*) on specific products is that they purportedly enable consumers to obtain some "essential" good or service that consumers could not afford at the equilibrium price. Rent controls and usury laws (which specify maximum interest rates that may be charged to borrowers) are examples. Also, government has at times imposed price ceilings either on all products or on a very wide range of products—so-called price controls—in its attempts to restrain inflation. Price controls were invoked during World War II, during the Korean conflict, and in the 1970s.

World War II Price Controls   Let's turn back the clock to World War II and analyze the effects of a price ceiling on butter. The booming wartime prosperity of the early 1940s was shifting demand for butter to the right so that the equilibrium or market price P_0 reached, say, $1.20 per pound as in Figure 20-4. The rapidly rising price of butter was contributing to inflation and excluding from the butter market those families whose money incomes were not keeping up with the soaring cost of living. To help stop inflation and to keep butter on the tables of the poor, government imposed a ceiling price P_c of, say, $0.90 per pound. To be effective, a price ceiling must be *below* the equilibrium price. Clearly, a ceiling price of, say, $1.50 would have no immediate effect on the butter market.

What are the effects of this $0.90 ceiling price? The rationing ability of the free market is rendered ineffective. At the ceiling price there is a lasting short-age of butter. The quantity of butter demanded at P_c is Q_d and the quantity supplied is only Q_s; a persistent excess demand or shortage in the amount $Q_d - Q_s$ occurs. The actual size of such a shortage varies directly with the price elasticities of supply and demand. The greater these elasticities, the greater the shortage.

The important point is that the price ceiling P_c prevents the usual market adjustment in which competition among buyers bids up price, inducing more production and rationing some buyers out of the market. This process would continue until the shortage disappears at the equilibrium price and quantity, P_0 and Q_0.

By preventing these market adjustments from occurring, a price ceiling poses problems born of the market disequilibrium.

Rationing Problem   How is the available supply Q_s to be apportioned among buyers who want the greater amount Q_d? Should supply be distributed on a first-come, first-served basis, that is, to those willing and able to stand in line the longest? Or should grocers distribute the product on the basis of favoritism? An unregulated shortage does not lead to an equitable distribution of the product. Instead, government must establish some formal system for rationing it to consumers. This was done during World War II by issuing ration coupons, which authorized bearers to purchase butter. The rationing system entailed first the printing of coupons for Q_s pounds of butter and then their equitable distribution among consumers so that

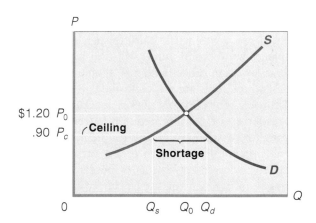

FIGURE 20-4 A price ceiling results in a persistent shortage   A price ceiling—a maximum legal price—such as P_c results in a persistent product shortage, here equal to the horizontal distance between Q_d and Q_s.

the wealthy family of four and the poor family of four both received the same number of coupons.

Black Markets But ration coupons do not prevent a second problem from arising. Specifically, the demand curve in Figure 20-4 tells us there are many buyers willing to pay more than the ceiling price P_c. And, of course, it is more profitable for grocers to sell at prices above the ceiling. Thus, despite the sizable enforcement bureaucracy which accompanied World War II price controls, illegal *black markets*—markets where products were bought and sold at prices above the legal limits—flourished for many goods. Counterfeiting of ration coupons was also a problem.

Rent Controls About 200 cities in the United States, including New York City, Boston, and San Francisco, have at one time or another had rent controls: maximum rents established by law. Such laws are well-intended. Their goals are to protect low-income families from escalating rents caused by perceived housing shortages and to make housing more affordable to the poor.

What are the actual economic effects? On the demand side, it is true that below-equilibrium rents mean that more families are willing to consume rental housing; the quantity of rental housing demanded increases at the lower price. The problem occurs on the supply side. Price controls make it less attractive for landlords to offer housing on the rental market. In the short run owners may sell their rental units or convert them to condominiums. In the long run low rents make it unprofitable for owners to repair or renovate their rental units. (Rent controls are one cause of the many abandoned apartment buildings found in larger cities.) Also, potential new investors in housing such as insurance companies and pension funds will find it more profitable to invest in office buildings, shopping malls, or motels, where rents are not controlled.

In brief, rent controls distort market signals so that resources are misallocated: too few resources are allocated to rental housing, and too many to alternative uses. Ironically, although rent controls are often legislated to lessen the effects of perceived housing shortages, in fact, controls are a primary cause of such shortages.

Credit Card Interest Ceilings In recent decades several bills have been introduced in Congress to impose a nationwide interest-rate ceiling on credit card accounts. Several states now have such laws. The usual rationale for interest-rate ceilings is that the banks

and retail stores issuing such cards are presumably "gouging" users and, in particular, lower-income users by charging interest rates that average about 16 or 17 percent.

What might be the responses to the legal imposition of below-equilibrium interest rates on credit cards? The lower interest income associated with a legal interest ceiling would require card issuers to reduce their costs or enhance their revenues:

1. Card issuers might tighten credit standards to reduce losses due to nonpayment and collection costs. In particular, low-income people and young people who have not yet established their creditworthiness would find it more difficult to obtain credit cards.

2. The annual fee charged to cardholders might be increased, as might the fee charged to merchants for processing credit card sales. Similarly, card users might be charged a fee for every transaction.

3. Card users now have a postpurchase "grace period" during which credit provided is interest-free. This period might be shortened or eliminated.

4. Certain "enhancements" which accompany some credit cards (for example, extended warranties on products bought with a card) might be eliminated.

5. Finally, retail stores which issue their own cards might increase their merchandise prices to help offset the decline of interest income. This would mean that customers who pay cash would in effect be subsidizing customers who use credit cards.

Rock Concerts Below-equilibrium pricing should not be associated solely with government policies. Rock superstars (or "alternative" or "country and western" superstars) sometimes price their concert tickets below the market-clearing price. Tickets are usually rationed on a first-come, first-served basis and ticket "scalping" is common. Why should these stars want to subsidize their fans—at least those fortunate enough to obtain tickets—with below-equilibrium prices? Why not set ticket prices at a higher, market-clearing level and realize more income from a tour?

The answer is that long lines of fans waiting hours or days for bargain-priced tickets catch the attention of the press, as does an occasional attempt by ticketless fans to "crash" a sold-out concert. The millions of dollars' worth of free publicity that results undoubtedly stimulates cassette and CD sales from which much of any musician's income is derived. Thus the "gift" of below-equilibrium ticket prices from a rock star to fans also benefits the star. And the gift imposes costs upon fans—the opportunity cost of time spent waiting in line to buy tickets.

Incidentally, many people regard the ticket scalping often associated with musical or athletic events as a form of extortion, where the extortionist's (seller's) gain is the victim's (buyer's) loss. But the fact that scalping is a voluntary transaction suggests that both seller and buyer gain; otherwise, the exchange would not occur. Such exchanges redistribute assets (tickets) from those who value them less to those who value them more.

Price Floors and Surpluses

Price floors are minimum prices fixed by government. A price at or above the price floor is legal; a price below it is not. Price floors above equilibrium prices have generally been invoked when society has felt that the free functioning of the market system has not provided a sufficient income for certain groups of resource suppliers or producers.

The minimum wage and supported prices for agricultural products are two types of government price floors. Here we examine an example of the latter.

Suppose the equilibrium price for corn is $2 per bushel and, because of this low price, many farmers have extremely low incomes. Government decides to help out by establishing a legal price floor or *price support* of $3 per bushel.

What will be the effects? At any price above the equilibrium price, quantity supplied will exceed quantity demanded; that is, there will be a persistent excess supply or *surplus* of the product. Farmers will be willing to produce and offer for sale more than private buyers are willing to purchase at the price floor. The size of this surplus will vary directly with the elasticity of demand and supply. The greater the elasticity of demand and supply, the greater the resulting surplus. As we saw with a price ceiling, the rationing ability of the free market is disrupted by an imposed legal price.

Figure 20-5 illustrates the effect of a price floor. Let S and D be the supply and demand curves for corn. Equilibrium price and quantity are P_0 and Q_0, respectively. If government imposes a price floor of P_f, farmers will produce Q_s but private buyers will purchase only Q_d. The surplus is the excess of Q_s over Q_d.

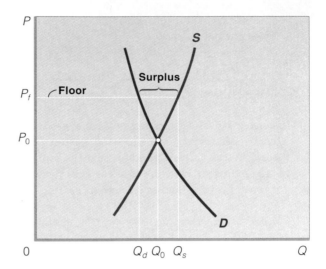

FIGURE 20-5 A price floor results in a persistent surplus A price floor—a minimum legal price—such as P_f results in a persistent product surplus, here equal to the horizontal distance between Q_s and Q_d.

Government may cope with the surplus resulting from a price floor in two ways:

1. It can restrict supply (for example, by instituting acreage allotments by which farmers agree to take a certain amount of land out of production) or increase demand (for example, by researching new uses for the product involved). These actions may reduce the difference between the equilibrium price and the price floor and thereby reduce the size of the resulting surplus.

2. If these efforts are not wholly successful, then government must purchase the surplus output (thereby subsidizing farmers) and store or otherwise dispose of it.

Controversial Tradeoffs

In a free market, the forces of supply and demand bring the supply decisions of producers and demand decisions of buyers into accord. But price ceilings and floors interfere with this outcome. Government must step in and provide a rationing system to handle product shortages stemming from price ceilings and devise ways to eliminate product surpluses arising from price floors. Legal maximum and minimum prices thus entail controversial tradeoffs. The alleged benefits of price ceilings and floors to consumers and producers, respectively, must be balanced against the costs associated with the consequent shortages and surpluses.

Market Forces and the Value of Education

Recent growth in the earnings of college-educated workers relative to less educated workers in the United States reflects the fact that the supply of highly educated workers has not kept pace with a rapidly growing demand for their skills.

Comparisons of the average (median) real incomes of college and high school graduates show that the gap between the two—called the "college premium"—has risen sharply since 1980. In other words, the value of education has been increasing. This widening income disparity can be understood in terms of the changing demand and supply for the services of college- and high school–educated workers.

The vertical axis of the accompanying graph gives the ratio of the median income of college graduates to the median income of high school graduates (a measure of the college premium). A ratio of 1.5 would indicate that college graduates earn 50 percent more than high school graduates. The horizontal axis indicates the percentage of young people (aged 25 to 34) with 4 years or more of college. The vertical (perfectly inelastic) supply curves S reflect the fact that the quantity of college graduates does not respond quickly to a change in the income ratio. For example, if the ratio rises today, it will take 4 or 5 years for the additional college enrollees to earn their degrees and enter the labor market. The downsloping demand curves D indicate that as the college premium decreases, employers will choose to hire more college-trained workers.

The 1967 data show an earnings ratio of nearly 1.5, indicating that in that year college graduates earned almost 50 percent more than high school graduates. But by 1995 this gap had risen to over 80 percent. Explanation: Despite the increase in the supply of college graduates

---

Furthermore, our discussion of price controls, rent controls, and interest-rate ceilings on credit cards shows that government interference with the market can have unintended, undesirable side effects. Price controls, for example, create illegal black markets. Rent controls may discourage housing construction and repair. And instead of protecting low-income families from higher interest charges, interest-rate ceilings may simply deny credit to those families.

QUICK REVIEW 20-3

■ Price elasticity of supply measures the sensitivity of suppliers to changes in the price of a product. The price elasticity of supply coefficient E_s is the ratio of the percentage change in quantity supplied to the percentage change in price. The elasticity of supply varies directly with the amount of time producers have to respond to the price change.

■ The cross elasticity of demand coefficient E_{xy} is computed as the percentage change in the quantity demanded of product X divided by the percentage change in the price of product Y. If the cross elasticity coefficient is positive, the two products are substitutes; if negative, they are complements.

■ The income elasticity coefficient E_i is computed as the percentage change in quantity demanded divided by the percentage change in income. A positive coefficient indicates a normal or superior good. The coefficient is negative for an inferior good.

■ Government-controlled prices—ceilings and floors—stifle the rationing function of prices and cause unintended side effects.

(from about $16\frac{1}{2}$ to about 25 percent of the 25-to-34 age group), demand increased by a relatively greater amount.

Why? It appears that technological advance since about 1980 has been increasingly "skill-biased." Innovation has raised the productivity of (and therefore the demand for) more educated workers to a greater degree than that of less educated workers. Computerization of the workplace alone may explain one-third to two-thirds of the increased returns to education. Greater use of high-tech capital goods in manufacturing is also relevant.

The demand side of the market has also been affected by the lowering of world trade barriers. Lower barriers have increased the demand for the high-tech products that U.S. firms export and for the more educated workers producing them. Conversely, freer trade has expanded domestic demand for low-cost imports made by less skilled workers abroad. Such imports have effectively increased the competition faced by less educated workers in the United States, stifling their earnings growth. A rise in the number of low-skilled immigrants to the United States in the 1980s and 1990s has also slowed the earnings growth of less educated workers.

Why didn't the supply of college graduates increase more than shown in the graph and thereby keep the college premium from rising? Why didn't increases in the earnings gap in the 1980s induce more people to enter and eventually graduate from college? Other factors—in particular, the rising real costs of a college education—have restricted growth in the supply of college graduates. In the 1980s the cost of college rose by two times the rate

of inflation in public colleges and by three times the inflation rate in private schools. At the same time, government grants and loans to students fell behind the inflation rate.

Some implications: First, an individual's economic well-being is now more closely tied to her or his educational attainment than in the past. Second, wage differences between more and less educated workers have been growing and contribute to greater income inequality in the economy as a whole. Third, the prosperity of any city, state, or region depends increasingly upon its commitment to education.

Source: Based on Erica L. Groshen and Colin Drozdowski, "The Recent Rise in the Value of Education: Market Forces at Work," *Economic Commentary* (Federal Reserve Bank of Cleveland, August 15, 1992). Updated.

CHAPTER SUMMARY

1. Price elasticity of demand measures consumer response to price changes. If consumers are relatively sensitive to price changes, demand is elastic. If they are relatively unresponsive to price changes, demand is inelastic.

2. The price elasticity coefficient measures the degree of elasticity or inelasticity of demand. The coefficient is found by the formula

$$E_d = \frac{\text{percentage change in quantity demanded of X}}{\text{percentage change in price of X}}$$

Economists use the averages of prices and quantities under consideration as reference points in determining percentage changes in price and quantity. If E_d is greater than 1, demand is elastic. If E_d is less than 1, demand is inelastic. Unit elasticity is the special case in which E_d equals 1.

3. Perfectly inelastic demand is graphed as a line parallel to the vertical axis; perfectly elastic demand is shown by a line above and parallel to the horizontal axis.

4. Elasticity varies at different price ranges on a demand curve, tending to be elastic in the upper left segment and inelastic in the lower right segment. Elasticity cannot be judged by the steepness or flatness of a demand curve.

5. If total revenue changes in the opposite direction from prices, demand is elastic. If price and total revenue change in the same direction, demand is inelastic. Where demand is of unit elasticity, a change in price leaves total revenue unchanged.

6. The number of available substitutes, the size of an item's price relative to one's budget, whether the product is a luxury or necessity, and time are all determinants of elasticity of demand.

7. The elasticity concept also applies to supply. The coefficient of price elasticity of supply is found by the formula

$$E_s = \frac{\text{percentage change in quantity supplied of X}}{\text{percentage change in price of X}}$$

Elasticity of supply depends on the ease of shiftability of resources between alternative uses. This shiftability in turn varies directly with the time producers have to adjust to a particular price change.

8. Cross elasticity of demand indicates how sensitive the purchase of one product is to changes in the price of another product. The coefficient of cross elasticity of demand is found by the formula

$$E_{xy} = \frac{\text{percentage change in quantity demanded of X}}{\text{percentage change in price of Y}}$$

Positive cross elasticity of demand identifies substitute goods; negative cross elasticity identifies complementary goods.

9. Income elasticity of demand indicates the responsiveness of consumer purchases to a change in income. The coefficient of income elasticity of demand is found by the formula

$$E_i = \frac{\text{percentage change in quantity demanded of X}}{\text{percentage change in income}}$$

The coefficient is positive for normal goods and negative for inferior goods.

10. Legally fixed prices stifle the rationing function of equilibrium prices. Effective price ceilings result in persistent product shortages, and if an equitable distribution of the product is sought, government must ration the product to consumers. Price floors lead to product surpluses; government must purchase these surpluses *or* eliminate them by imposing restrictions on production or by increasing private demand.

TERMS AND CONCEPTS

price elasticity of demand	perfectly inelastic demand	price elasticity of supply	income elasticity of demand
elastic demand	perfectly elastic demand	market period	price ceiling
inelastic demand	total revenue	short run	price floor
unit elasticity	total-revenue test	long run	
		cross elasticity of demand	

STUDY QUESTIONS

1. Review questions 1, 4, and 8 at the end of Chapter 3.

2. KEY QUESTION Graph the accompanying demand data and then use the midpoint formula for E_d to determine price elasticity of demand for each of the four possible $1 price changes. What can you conclude about the relationship between the slope of a curve and its elasticity? Explain in a nontechnical way why demand is elastic in the northwest segment of the demand curve and inelastic in the southeast segment.

Product price	Quantity demanded
$5	1
4	2
3	3
2	4
1	5

3. Draw two linear demand curves parallel to one another. Demonstrate that for any specific price change demand is more elastic on the curve closer to the origin.

4. KEY QUESTION Calculate total-revenue data from the demand schedule in question 2. Graph total revenue below your demand curve. Generalize about the relationship between price elasticity and total revenue.

5. KEY QUESTION How would the following changes in price affect total revenue—that is, would total revenue increase, decline, or remain unchanged?
a. Price falls and demand is inelastic.
b. Price rises and demand is elastic.
c. Price rises and supply is elastic.
d. Price rises and supply is inelastic.
e. Price rises and demand is inelastic.

f. Price falls and demand is elastic.

g. Price falls and demand is of unit elasticity.

6. KEY QUESTION What are the major determinants of price elasticity of demand? Use these determinants in judging whether demand for each of the following products is elastic or inelastic: **(a)** oranges; **(b)** cigarettes; **(c)** Winston cigarettes; **(d)** gasoline; **(e)** butter; **(f)** salt; **(g)** automobiles; **(h)** football games; **(i)** diamond bracelets; **(j)** this textbook.

7. What effect would a rule stating that university students must live in university dormitories have on the price elasticity of demand for dormitory space? What impact might this in turn have on room rates?

8. "If the demand for farm products is highly price inelastic, a bumper crop may reduce farm incomes." Evaluate and illustrate graphically.

9. You are chairperson of a state tax commission responsible for establishing a program to raise new revenue through excise taxes. Would elasticity of demand be important to you in determining those products on which the taxes should be levied? Explain.

10. KEY QUESTION In May 1990 Vincent van Gogh's painting *Portrait of Dr. Gachet* sold at auction for $82.5 million. Portray this sale in a demand and supply diagram and comment on the elasticity of supply.

11. In the 1950s the local Boy Scout troop in Jackson, Wyoming, decided to gather and sell at auction elk antlers shed by thousands of elk wintering in the area. Buyers were mainly local artisans who used the antlers to make belt buckles, buttons, and tie clasps. Price per pound was 6¢ and the troop took in $500 annually. In the 1970s a fad developed in Asia which involved grinding antlers into powder to sprinkle on food for purported aphrodisiac benefits. In 1979 the price per pound of elk antlers in the Jackson auction was $6 per pound and the Boy Scouts earned $51,000! Show graphically and explain these dramatic increases in price and total revenue. Assuming no shift in the supply curve of elk antlers, use the midpoint formula to calculate the coefficient for the elasticity of supply.

12. KEY QUESTION Suppose the cross elasticity of demand for products A and B is +3.6 and for products C and D is −5.4. What can you conclude about how products A and B are related? Products C and D?

13. KEY QUESTION The income elasticities of demand for movies, dental services, and clothing have been estimated to be +3.4, +1.0, and +0.5, respectively. Interpret these coefficients. What does it mean if an income elasticity coefficient is negative?

14. Why is it desirable for price ceilings to be accompanied by government rationing? And for price floors to be accompanied by surplus-purchasing, output-restricting, or demand-increasing programs? Show graphically why price ceilings entail shortages and price floors result in surpluses. What effect, if any, do elasticity of demand and supply have on the size of these shortages and surpluses? Explain.

15. (Last Word) What has happened to the earnings gap between college-educated and high school-educated workers in recent years? Use demand- and supply-side factors to explain this change.

16. WEB-BASED QUESTION K mart—Determinants of Demand Elasticities and "Blue Light Specials" Generally, the elasticity of demand for a product will be greater **(a)** the larger the number of substitutes, **(b)** the greater the proportion of income an item takes, and **(c)** the more the item is a nonnecessity. K mart http://www.kmart.com/ posts a weekly sales circular on selected merchandise. K mart must conclude that demand for these Blue Light Specials is elastic: The decrease in price will increase total revenue. Check out this week's specials and, for each item, score 1 point for meeting the criterion of each determinant above. How many specials score a 3? Do any score 0? Why would K mart include any item which scored less than a 3?

17. WEB-BASED QUESTION New York Apartments—The Impact of Price Ceilings In New York City rent control was enacted during World War II and then maintained by New York City. In 1997, there were approximately 71,000 rent-controlled apartments in New York City. Visit Tenant Net http://www.tenant.net/ and NYC Rent Guidelines Board http://www.nycrgb.com/ and find out the difference between "rent control" and "rent stabilization" in New York City. Are both price ceilings? What has been the impact of such controls? Are rent controls increasing or decreasing?

21

Consumer Behavior and Utility Maximization

You have probably seen the T-shirts that say "I'd rather be shopping," or "Shop 'till you drop." We do seem to be a nation of shoppers. In 1997, people in the United States spent about $5.2 trillion on goods and services. This spending amounted to about 93 percent of U.S. after-tax income. Consumption per person was $19,410 in that year.

One concern of microeconomics is explaining consumer spending. If you were to compare the shopping carts of almost any two consumers, you would observe striking differences. Why does Paula have potatoes, parsnips, pomegranates, and Pepsi in her cart while Sam has sugar, saltines, soap, Spam, and 7-Up in his? Why didn't Paula also buy pork and pimentos? Why didn't Sam have soup and spaghetti on his grocery list? In this chapter, you will see how individual consumers allocate their money incomes among the various goods and services available to them. Why does a consumer buy a certain bundle of goods rather than any of the other possible bundles? As we examine these issues, you will also strengthen your understanding of the law of demand.

TWO EXPLANATIONS OF THE LAW OF DEMAND

The law of demand is based on common sense. A high price discourages consumers from buying; a low price encourages them to buy. We now explore two complementary explanations of the downsloping nature of the demand curve that will back up our everyday observations. (A third explanation, based on indifference curves, is more advanced and is summarized in the appendix to this chapter.)

Income and Substitution Effects

Our first explanation of the downward slope of the demand curve—introduced in Chapter 3—involves the income and substitution effects:

1. Income Effect The *income effect* is the impact a change in the price of a product has on a consumer's real income and consequently on the quantity demanded of that good. If the price of a product—say, steak—declines, the real income or purchasing power of anyone buying that product increases. The increase in real income will be reflected in increased purchases of many normal goods, including steak. For example, with a constant money income of $20 per week you can buy 10 pounds of steak at $2 per pound. But if the price of steak falls to $1 per pound and you buy 10 pounds, $10 per week is freed to buy more of both steak and other commodities. A decline in the price of steak increases the consumer's real income, enabling him or her to purchase more steak. This is called the **income effect.**

2. Substitution Effect

The *substitution effect* is the impact a change in a product's price has on its relative expensiveness, and consequently on the quantity demanded. When the price of a product falls, that product becomes cheaper relative to all other products. Consumers will substitute the cheaper product for other products which are now relatively more expensive. In our example, as the price of steak falls—prices of other products being unchanged—steak becomes more attractive to the buyer. At $1 per pound it is a "better buy" than at $2. The lower price will induce the consumer to substitute steak for some of the now relatively less attractive items in the budget—perhaps pork, chicken, veal, fish, or other foods. Because a lower price increases the relative attractiveness of a product, the consumer buys more of it. This is the **substitution effect**.

The income and substitution effects combine to make a consumer able and willing to buy more of a specific good at a lower price than at a higher price.

Law of Diminishing Marginal Utility

A second explanation of the downsloping demand curve is that, although consumer wants in general may be insatiable, wants for specific commodities can be fulfilled. In a specific span of time over which buyers' tastes are unchanged, consumers can get as much of a particular good or service as they want. The more of that product consumers obtain, the less they want more units of the same product.

This can be readily seen for durable goods. A consumer's want for an automobile, when he or she has none, may be very strong. But the desire for a second car is less intense; for a third or fourth, very weak. Even the wealthiest families rarely have more than a half-dozen cars, although their incomes would allow them to purchase a whole fleet of vehicles.

Terminology Economists theorize that specific consumer wants can be fulfilled with succeeding units of a commodity but that each unit provides less utility than the previous unit. Recall that a product has utility if it can satisfy a want: **utility** *is want-satisfying power.* The utility of a good or service is the satisfaction or pleasure one gets from consuming it. Three characteristics of this concept must be emphasized.

1. "Utility" and "usefulness" are not synonymous. Paintings by Picasso may be useless functionally and yet offer great utility to art connoisseurs.

2. Implied in the first characteristic is the fact that utility is subjective. The utility of a specific product will vary widely from person to person. A bottle of inexpensive muscatel wine may yield substantial utility to the Skid Row alcoholic but zero or negative utility to the local MADD president. Eyeglasses have great utility to someone who is extremely far- or near-sighted, but no utility to a person with 20-20 vision.

3. Because utility is subjective, it is difficult to quantify. But for purposes of illustration, we assume that people can measure satisfaction with units called *utils* (units of utility). For example, a particular consumer may get 100 utils of satisfaction from an ice cream cone, 10 utils of satisfaction from a candy bar, and 1 util of satisfaction from a single stick of gum. These mythical units of satisfaction are convenient for quantifying consumer behavior.

Total Utility and Marginal Utility We must carefully distinguish between total utility and marginal utility. **Total utility** is the total amount of satisfaction or pleasure a person derives from consuming some specific quantity—say, 10 units—of a good or service. **Marginal utility** is the *extra* satisfaction a consumer realizes from an additional unit of that product—say, from the eleventh unit. Alternatively, we can say marginal utility is the *change* in total utility resulting from the consumption of one more unit of a product.

Figure 21-1 and the accompanying table reveal the relation between total utility and marginal utility. The curves are drawn from the data in the table. Column 2 shows the total utility associated with each level of hamburger consumption; column 3, the marginal utility—the change in total utility—resulting from the consumption of each successive hamburger. Starting at the origin in Figure 21-1a, we observe that each of the first 5 units increases total utility (TU), but by a diminishing amount. Total utility reaches a

(1)	(2)	(3)
Hamburgers consumed per meal	Total utility, utils	Marginal utility, utils
0	0	
1	10	10
2	18	8
3	24	6
4	28	4
5	30	2
6	30	0
7	28	-2

(a) Total utility

(b) Marginal utility

FIGURE 21-1 Total and marginal utility Curves TU and MU are graphed from the data in the table. (a) As more of a product is consumed, total utility increases at a diminishing rate, reaches a maximum, and then declines. (b) Marginal utility, by definition, reflects the changes in total utility. Thus marginal utility diminishes with increased consumption, becomes zero when total utility is at a maximum, and is negative when total utility declines. As shown by the shaded rectangles in (a) and (b), marginal utility is the change in total utility associated with each added hamburger. Or, alternatively, each new level of total utility is found by adding marginal utility to the previous level of total utility.

maximum at the sixth unit and then declines. Hence, in Figure 21-1b we find that marginal utility (MU) remains positive but diminishes through the first 5 units (because total utility increases at a declining rate). Marginal utility is zero for the sixth unit (be- cause that unit doesn't change total utility). Marginal utility then becomes negative with the seventh unit and beyond (because total utility is falling). Figure 21-1b and table column 3 tell us that each successive hamburger yields less extra utility—fewer utils—than the previous one as the consumer's want for hamburgers comes closer and closer to fulfillment.[1] The principle that marginal utility declines as the consumer acquires additional units of a specific product is known as the **law of diminishing marginal utility. (Key Question 2)**

Relation to Demand and Elasticity How does this law explain why the demand curve for a specific product is downsloping? If successive units of a good yield smaller and smaller amounts of marginal, or extra, utility, then the consumer will buy additional units of a product only if its price falls. The consumer for whom Figure 21-1 is relevant may buy two hamburgers at a price of $1 each. But because he or she obtains less marginal utility from additional hamburgers, the consumer will choose *not* to buy more at this price. The consumer would rather spend additional dollars on products that provide more (or equal) utility, not less utility. Therefore, additional hamburgers with less utility are not worth buying unless the price declines.

(When marginal utility becomes negative, McDonald's or Burger King would have to pay *you* to consume another hamburger!) Thus, diminishing marginal utility supports the notion that price must decrease for quantity demanded to increase—that is, that the demand curve slopes downward.

The amount by which marginal utility declines as more units of a product are consumed helps determine that product's price elasticity of demand. Other things equal, if marginal utility falls sharply as successive units of a product are consumed, demand is inelastic. A particular decline in price will elicit only a relatively small increase in quantity demanded, since the MU of extra units drops off so rapidly. Conversely, modest declines in marginal utility as consumption increases imply an elastic demand. A particular decline in price will entice consumers to buy considerably more units of the product, since the MU of additional units declines so slowly.

---

[1] Technical footnote: For a time the marginal utility of successive units of a product may increase. A second glass of lemonade on a hot day may yield more extra satisfaction than the first. But beyond some point we can expect the marginal utility of additional glasses to decline. Also, note in Figure 21-1b that marginal utility is graphed at half-units. For example, we graph the marginal utility of 4 utils at $3\frac{1}{2}$ units because the 4 utils refers neither to the third nor the fourth unit per se but to the *addition* of the fourth unit.

QUICK REVIEW 21-1

■ The law of demand can be explained in terms of the income effect (a decline in price raises the consumer's purchasing power) and the substitution effect (a product whose price falls is substituted for other products).

■ Utility is the benefit or satisfaction a person receives from consuming a good or service.

> ■ The law of diminishing marginal utility indicates that gains in satisfaction become smaller as successive units of a specific product are consumed.
>
> ■ Diminishing marginal utility provides another rationale for the law of demand, as well as one for differing price elasticities.

THEORY OF CONSUMER BEHAVIOR

In addition to explaining the law of demand, the idea of diminishing marginal utility explains how consumers allocate their money incomes among the many goods and services available for purchase.

Consumer Choice and Budget Restraint

The typical consumer's situation has four dimensions:

1. *Rational behavior*   The consumer is a rational person, trying to use his or her money income to derive the greatest amount of satisfaction, or utility, from it. Consumers want to get "the most for their money" or, technically, to maximize their total utility.

2. *Preferences*   Each consumer has clear-cut preferences for certain goods and services available in the market. We assume buyers also have a good idea of how much marginal utility they will get from successive units of the various products they might purchase.

3. *Budget restraint*   At any point in time the consumer has a fixed, limited amount of money income. Each consumer supplies a finite amount of human and property resources to businesses or government. Therefore, he or she earns only limited income payments. Thus, all consumers face a *budget restraint*, even those who earn millions of dollars each year. Of course, this income limitation is more severe for typical consumers with average incomes than for those with extraordinarily high incomes.

4. *Prices*   Goods and services are scarce in relation to the demand for them or, stated differently, producing them involves opportunity costs. Thus every good and service carries a price tag. We assume that the product prices are not affected by the amounts of specific goods which the individual consumer buys. Each consumer's purchase is such a small part of total demand that it alone does not affect a product's price.

If a consumer has limited dollars and the products he or she wants have price tags on them, the consumer can purchase only a limited amount of goods. The consumer cannot buy everything wanted when each purchase exhausts a portion of a fixed money income. It is precisely this point that brings the economic fact of scarcity home to the individual consumer.

The consumer must therefore compromise; he or she must choose among alternative goods to obtain, with limited money income, the most satisfying mix of goods and services. Different individuals will choose different mixes of goods. And, as is shown in Global Perspective 21-1, mixes of goods will vary among nations.

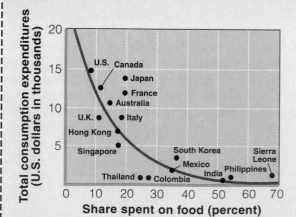

GLOBAL PERSPECTIVE 21-1

Shares of household budgets spent on food, selected nations

Consumer spending patterns differ not only among individuals but among nations. One striking feature is that, although households in rich countries spend larger absolute amounts on food than those in poor countries, households in poor nations spend a much larger proportion of their budgets on food.

Source: Judith Jones Putnam and Jane E. Allhouse, *Food Consumption, Prices, and Expenditures, 1970–92* (U.S. Department of Agriculture, 1993, *Economic Research Service Statistical Bulletin* 867).

Utility-Maximizing Rule

Of all the different combinations of goods and services a consumer can obtain within his or her budget, which specific combination will yield the maximum utility or satisfaction? To maximize satisfaction *the consumer should allocate his or her money income so that the last dollar spent on each product yields the same amount of extra (marginal) utility.* We call this the **utility-maximizing rule.** When the consumer has "balanced his or her margins" using this rule, there is no incentive to alter the expenditure pattern. The consumer is in *equilibrium* and would be worse off—total utility would decline—if there was any alteration in the bundle of goods purchased, providing there is no change in taste, income, products, or prices.

Numerical Example

An illustration will help explain the utility-maximizing rule. For simplicity our discussion is limited to two products, but the analysis applies as well if there are more. Suppose consumer Holly is trying to decide which combination of two products, A and B, she should purchase with her fixed daily income of $10. Holly's preferences for products A and B and their prices are the basic data determining the combination which will maximize her satisfaction. Table 21-1 summarizes those data, with column 2a showing the

TABLE 21-1 **The utility-maximizing combination of products A and B obtainable with an income of $10***

(1) Unit of product	(2) Product A: price = $1		(3) Product B: price = $2	
	(a) Marginal utility, utils	(b) Marginal utility per dollar (MU/price)	(a) Marginal utility, utils	(b) Marginal utility per dollar (MU/price)
First	10	10	24	12
Second	8	**8**	20	10
Third	7	7	18	9
Fourth	6	6	16	**8**
Fifth	5	5	12	6
Sixth	4	4	6	3
Seventh	3	3	4	2

*It is assumed in this table that the amount of marginal utility received from additional units of each of the two products is independent of the quantity of the other product. For example, the marginal utility schedule for product A is independent of the amount of B obtained by the consumer.

amount of marginal utility she will derive from each successive unit of A and column 3a showing the same thing for product B. Both columns reflect the law of diminishing marginal utility, which is assumed to begin with the second units of each product purchased.

Marginal Utility per Dollar Before applying the utility-maximizing rule to these data, we must put the marginal utility information in columns 2a and 3a on a per-dollar-spent basis. A consumer's choices are influenced not only by the extra utility which successive units of product A will yield but also by how many dollars (and therefore how many units of alternative good B) she must give up to obtain those added units of A.

The rational consumer must compare the extra utility from each product with its added cost (that is, its price). Suppose you prefer a pizza whose marginal utility is, say, 36 utils to a movie whose marginal utility is 24 utils. But if the pizza's price is $12 and the movie costs only $6, you would choose the movie rather than the pizza! Why? Because the marginal utility per dollar spent would be 4 utils for the movie (= 24 utils ÷ $6) compared to only 3 utils for the pizza (= 36 utils ÷ $12). You could buy two movies for $12 and, assuming the marginal utility of the second movie is, say, 16 utils, your total utility would be 40 utils. Clearly, 40 units of satisfaction from two movies is superior to 36 utils from the same $12 expenditure on one pizza. *To make the amounts of extra utility derived from differently priced goods comparable, marginal utilities must be put on a per-dollar-spent basis.* This is done in columns 2b and 3b by dividing the marginal utility data of columns 2a and 3a by the prices of A and B—$1 and $2, respectively.

Decision-Making Process Now we have Holly's preferences—on a unit and a per-dollar basis—and the price tags of A and B before us. With $10 to spend, in what order should Holly allocate her dollars on units of A and B to achieve the highest degree of utility within the $10 limit imposed by her income? And what specific combination of A and B will she have obtained at the time she exhausts her $10?

Concentrating on columns 2b and 3b in Table 21-1, we find that Holly should first spend $2 on the first unit of B, because its marginal utility per dollar of 12 utils is higher than A's 10 utils. But now Holly finds herself indifferent about whether she should buy a second unit of B or the first unit of A because the marginal utility per dollar of both is 10 utils. So she buys both of them. Holly now has 1 unit of A and 2 units of B. Also, the last dollar she spent on each good yielded the same marginal utility per dollar (10 utils). But this combination of A and B does not represent the maximum amount of utility which Holly can obtain. It cost her only $5 [= (1 × $1) + (2 × $2)], so she has $5 remaining, which she can spend to achieve a still higher level of total utility.

Examining columns 2b and 3b again, we find that Holly should spend the next $2 on a third unit of B because marginal utility per dollar for the third unit of B is 9 compared with 8 for the second unit of A. But now, with 1 unit of A and 3 units of B, we find she is again indifferent between a second unit of A and a fourth unit of B; both provide 8 utils per dollar. So Holly purchases 1 more unit of each. Now the last dollar spent on each product provides the same marginal utility per dollar (8 utils), and Holly's money income of $10 is exhausted. *The utility-maximizing combination of goods attainable by Holly is 2 units of A and 4 of B.* By summing marginal utility information from columns 2a and 3a we find that Holly is realizing 18 (= 10 + 8) utils of satisfaction from the 2 units of A and 78 (= 24 + 20 + 18 + 16) utils of satisfaction from the 4 units of B. Her $10, optimally spent, yields 96 (= 18 + 78) utils of satisfaction.

Table 21-2 summarizes our step-by-step process for maximizing Holly's utility, and it merits careful study. Note that we have implicitly assumed that Holly spends her entire income; she neither borrows nor saves. However, saving can be regarded as a utility-yielding good and incorporated into our analysis. It is treated that way in question 4 at the end of this chapter. **(Key Question 4)**

Inferior Options   Other combinations of A and B can be obtained with $10. But none will yield as great a total utility as does 2 units of A and 4 of B. As an example, 4 units of A and 3 of B can be obtained for $10. However, this combination yields only 93 utils, clearly inferior to the 96 utils provided by 2 of A and 4 of B. Furthermore, there are other combinations of A and B (such as 4 of A and 5 of B *or* 1 of A and 2 of B) where the marginal utility of the last dollar spent is the same for both A and B. But all such combinations are either unobtainable with Holly's limited money income (as 4 of A and 5 of B) or fail to exhaust her money income (as 1 of A and 2 of B) and therefore do not yield the maximum utility attainable.

Problem: Suppose Holly's money income is $14 rather than $10. What now is the utility-maximizing combination of A and B? Are A and B normal or inferior goods?

Algebraic Restatement

Our allocation rule says that a consumer will maximize her satisfaction when she allocates her money income so that the last dollar spent on product A, the last on product B, and so forth, yield equal amounts of additional, or marginal, utility. The marginal utility per dollar spent on A is indicated by MU of product A divided by the price of A (column 2b in Table 21-1) and the marginal utility per dollar spent on

TABLE 21-2   Sequence of purchases to achieve consumer equilibrium, given the data in Table 21-1

Choice number	Potential choices	Marginal utility per dollar	Purchase decision	Income remaining
1	First unit of A First unit of B	10 12	First unit of B for $2	$8 = $10 − $2
2	First unit of A Second unit of B	10 10	First unit of A for $1 and second unit of B for $2	$5 = $8 − $3
3	Second unit of A Third unit of B	8 9	Third unit of B for $2	$3 = $5 − $2
4	Second unit of A Fourth unit of B	8 8	Second unit of A for $1 and fourth unit of B for $2	$0 = $3 − $3

B by MU of product B divided by the price of B (column 3b in Table 21-1). Our utility-maximizing rule merely requires that these ratios be equal. Algebraically,

$$\frac{\text{MU of product A}}{\text{Price of A}} = \frac{\text{MU of product B}}{\text{price of B}}$$

and, of course, the consumer *must* exhaust her available income. Table 21-1 shows us that the combination of 2 units of A and 4 of B fulfills these conditions in that

$$\frac{8 \text{ utils}}{\$1} = \frac{16 \text{ utils}}{\$2}$$

and the consumer's $10 income is spent.

If the equation is not fulfilled, then some reallocation of the consumer's expenditures between A and B (from the low to the high marginal-utility-per-dollar product) will increase the consumer's total utility. For example, if the consumer spent $10 on 4 of A and 3 of B, we would find that

$$\frac{\text{MU of A: 6 utils}}{\text{Price of A: \$1}} < \frac{\text{MU of B: 18 utils}}{\text{price of B: \$2}}$$

Here the last dollar spent on A provides only 6 utils of satisfaction, and the last dollar spent on B provides 9 (= 18 ÷ $2). Hence, the consumer can increase total satisfaction by purchasing more of B and less of A. As dollars are reallocated from A to B, the marginal utility per dollar of A will increase while the marginal utility per dollar of B will decrease. At some new combination of A and B—specifically, 2 of A and 4 of B—the two will be equal and consumer equilibrium will be achieved.

UTILITY MAXIMIZATION AND THE DEMAND CURVE

Once you understand the utility-maximizing rule, you can easily see why the demand curve is downsloping. Recall that the basic determinants of an individual's demand for a specific product are (1) preferences or tastes, (2) money income, and (3) the prices of other goods. The utility data in Table 21-1 reflect our consumer's preferences. We continue to suppose that her money income is $10. And, concentrating on the construction of a simple demand curve for product B, we assume that the price of A, representing "other goods," is still $1.

Deriving the Demand Schedule and Curve

We can derive a single consumer's demand schedule for product B by considering alternative prices at which B might be sold and then determining the quantity the consumer will purchase. We have already determined one such price-quantity combination in the utility-maximizing example: Given tastes, income, and prices of other goods, our rational consumer will purchase 4 units of B at $2.

Now let's assume the price of B falls to $1. The marginal-utility-per-dollar data of column 3b in Table 21-1 will double because the price of B has been halved; the new data for column 3b are in fact identical to those in column 3a. But the purchase of 2 units of A and 4 of B is no longer an equilibrium combination. By applying the same reasoning we used in the initial utility-maximizing example, we now find that Holly's utility-maximizing combination is 4 units of A and 6 units of B. As summarized in the table in Figure 21-2, Holly will purchase 6 units of B when the price of B is $1. Using the data in this table, we can sketch the downsloping demand curve D_B shown in Figure 21-2. This exercise, then, clearly links the utility-maximizing behavior of a consumer and that person's demand curve for a particular product.

Income and Substitution Effects Revisited At the beginning of this chapter we indicated that the law of demand can be understood in terms of the substitution and income effects. Our analysis does not let us sort out these two effects quantitatively. However, we can see through utility maximization how each is involved in the increased purchase of product B when the price of B falls.

To see the *substitution effect*, recall that before the price of B declined, Holly was in equilibrium when purchasing 2 units of A and 4 units of B in that $MU_A(8)/P_A(\$1) = MU_B(16)/P_B(\$2)$. But after B's price falls from $2 to $1, we have $MU_A(8)/P_A(\$1) < MU_B(16)/P_B(\$1)$; more simply stated, the last dollar spent on B now yields more utility (16 utils) than does the last dollar spent on A (8 utils). This indicates that a switching of purchases from A to B is needed to restore equilibrium; that is, a *substitution* of now cheaper B for A will occur when the price of B drops.

What about the *income effect*? The assumed decline in the price of B from $2 to $1 increases Holly's

Price per unit of B

Quantity demanded of B

Price per unit of B	Quantity demanded
$2	4
1	6

FIGURE 21-2 Deriving an individual demand curve
At a price of $2 for B, the consumer represented by the data in the table maximizes utility by purchasing 4 units of product B. The decline in the price of B to $1 upsets the consumer's initial utility-maximizing equilibrium. The person restores equilibrium by purchasing 6 rather than 4 units of B. Thus, a simple price-quantity schedule emerges, which locates two points on a downsloping demand curve.

- -

real income. Before the price decline, Holly was in equilibrium when buying 2 of A and 4 of B. But at the lower $1 price for B, Holly would have to spend only $6 rather than $10 on this same combination of goods. She has $4 left over to spend on more of A, more of B, or more of both. In short, the price decline of B has caused Holly's *real* income to increase so that she can now obtain larger amounts of A and B with the same $10 of *money* income. The portion of the increase in her purchases of B due to this increase in *real* income is the income effect. **(Key Question 5)**

APPLICATIONS AND EXTENSIONS

Many real-world phenomena can be explained by applying the theory of consumer behavior.

The Compact Disc Takeover

Compact discs made their debut in the United States in 1983. The CD revolutionized the retail music industry, pushing the vinyl long-playing record to virtual extinction. In 1983 fewer than 1 million CDs were sold in the United States as compared with almost 210 million LP discs. But by 1997 over 500 million CDs were sold, while the sales of LPs plummeted to less than 2 million. Two events caused this swift turnabout:

1. *Preference changes* The quality of CDs prompted a massive shift of consumer preferences from LPs to CDs. CDs are played with a laser beam, not a phonograph needle, and therefore are virtually impervious to the scratches and wear which plague LPs. CDs also provide a wider range of sound and greater brilliance of tone. They can also hold much more music than LPs. All these features make CDs preferable to LPs for most consumers.

2. *Decreases in the prices of CD players* While prices of CDs themselves have not fallen significantly, prices of CD players have. Costing $1000 or more a decade ago, most players currently sell for under $200. While CDs and LPs are substitute goods, CD players and CDs are complementary goods. The lower prices for players has increased the demand for CDs.

In short, a technologically based change in consumer tastes coupled with a sharp drop in the prices of CD players has revolutionized the retail music market.

The Diamond-Water Paradox

Before economists understood the distinction between total utility and marginal utility, they were puzzled by the fact that some "essential" goods had much lower prices than other "unimportant" goods. Why would water, essential to life, be priced below diamonds, which have much less usefulness? The paradox is resolved when we first acknowledge that water is in great supply relative to demand and thus has a very low price per gallon. Diamonds, in contrast, are rare and are costly to mine, cut, and polish. Because their supply is small relative to demand, their price is very high per caret.

Further, the *marginal* utility of the last unit of water consumed is very low. The reason follows from our utility-maximizing rule. Consumers (and producers) respond to the very low price of water by using a great deal of it—for generating electricity, irrigating crops, drinking, heating buildings, watering lawns, and so on. Consumption is expanded until marginal utility, which declines as more water is consumed, equals this low price. In contrast, relatively few diamonds are purchased because of their prohibitively high price, meaning that their marginal utility remains high. In equilibrium:

$$\frac{\text{MU of water (low)}}{\text{Price of water (low)}} = \frac{\text{MU of diamonds (high)}}{\text{price of diamonds (high)}}$$

Although the *marginal* utility of the last unit of water consumed is low and the marginal utility of the last diamond purchased is high, the *total* utility of water is very high and the *total* utility of diamonds quite low. The total utility derived from the consumption of water is so large because of the enormous amounts of water consumed. Total utility is the sum of the marginal utilities of *all* the gallons of water consumed, including the trillions of gallons which have far higher marginal utilities than the last unit consumed. In contrast, the total utility derived from diamonds is low since their high price means that relatively few of them are bought. Thus the water-diamond "paradox" is solved: Water has much more total utility (roughly, usefulness) than diamonds even though the price of diamonds greatly exceeds the price of water. These relative prices relate to marginal utility, not total utility.

The Value of Time

The theory of consumer behavior has been generalized to account for the economic value of *time*. Both consumption and production activities take time.

Time is a valuable economic commodity; by working—by using an hour in productive activity—a person may earn $6, $10, $50, or more, depending on her or his education and skills. By using that hour for leisure or in consumption activities, the individual incurs the opportunity cost of forgone income; she or he sacrifices the $6, $10, or $50 which could have been earned by working.

Imagine a consumer who is considering buying a round of golf, on the one hand, and a concert, on the other. The market price of the golf game is $15 and that of the concert is $20. But the golf game takes more time than the concert. Suppose this consumer will spend 4 hours on the golf course but only 2 hours at the concert. If her time is worth $7 per hour—as evidenced by the $7 wage rate she can obtain by working—then the "full price" of the golf game is $43 (the $15 market price *plus* $28 worth of time). Similarly, the full price of the concert is $34 (the $20 market price *plus* $14 worth of time). We find that, contrary to what market prices alone indicate, the full price of the concert is really *less* than the full price of the golf game.

If we now assume that the marginal utilities derived from successive golf games and concerts are identical, traditional theory would indicate that our consumer should consume more golf games than concerts because the market price of the former ($15) is lower than that of the latter ($20). But when time is taken into account, the situation is reversed and golf games ($43) are more expensive than concerts ($34). Hence, it is rational in this case for this person to consume more concerts than golf games.

By accounting for time, we can explain certain observable phenomena which traditional theory does not. It may be rational for the unskilled worker or retiree whose time has little market value to ride a bus from Peoria to Pittsburgh. But the corporate executive, whose time is very valuable, will find it cheaper to fly, even though bus fare is only a fraction of plane fare. It is sensible for the retiree, living on a modest social security check and having ample time, to spend many hours shopping for bargains. It is equally intelligent for the highly paid physician, working 55 hours per week, to patronize the hospital cafeteria and to buy a new television set over the phone.

People in other nations feel affluent Americans are "wasteful" of food and other material goods but "overly economical" in the use of time. Americans who visit developing countries find that time is used casually or "squandered," while material goods are very highly prized and carefully used. These

The Inefficiency of Christmas Gift-Giving

The theory of consumer behavior assumes that individual consumers know their preferences better than anyone else. This raises a question as to whether gift-giving—consumer choices rendered by someone other than the ultimate consumer—is inefficient.

A recent study by Yale's Joel Waldfogel* suggests that Christmas gift-giving is inefficient to the extent that between one-tenth and one-third of the value of Christmas gifts is lost because they do not match their recipients' tastes. Professor Waldfogel surveyed two groups of his students, asking them to compare the estimated price of each Christmas gift with what they would be willing to pay for it. For example, Aunt Flo may have paid $13 for the Barry Manilow CD she gave you, but you would pay only $6.50 for it. Thus, a $6.50, or 50 percent, value loss is involved.

In one of the surveys, students estimated that while family and friends paid an average of $438 for a recipient's total gifts, the recipient would be willing to pay only $313 for the same gifts, reflecting a value loss of $125. Conclusion: Christmas gift-giving destroyed more than one-quarter of the gift value.

Two other questions were explored. First, does the value loss vary with the social distance between giver and recipient? Second, which givers are most likely to give cash?

On the first question it was found that noncash gifts from more distant relatives such as grandparents, aunts, and uncles entail greater value loss than gifts received from friends, siblings, parents, and "significant others." Furthermore, gifts from grandparents, aunts, and uncles are much more likely to be exchanged. The most probable reason is that more distant relatives are less likely to be aware of the recipient's consumption preferences.

The answer to the second question entails an offsetting consideration. Many grandparents, aunts, and uncles apparently realize they are uninformed about the receiver's tastes and therefore are more likely to give cash. The survey found that 42 percent of grandparents gave cash, while only about 10 percent of parents and no significant others did so. Cash gifts, of course, can be spent by the recipient as he or she wishes and therefore entail no efficiency loss.

Noting that holiday gift-giving nationwide was estimated to be $38 billion in 1992, Professor Waldfogel calculated an aggregate efficiency loss of between $4 and $13 billion.

_____

*Joel Waldfogel, "The Deadweight Loss of Christmas," *American Economic Review*, December 1993, pp. 1328–1336.

differences are not a paradox or a case of radically different temperaments. The differences are primarily a rational reflection that the high productivity of labor in an industrially advanced society gives time a high market value, whereas the opposite is true in a low-income developing country.

Medical Care Purchases

The way we pay for certain goods and services affects their prices at the time we buy them and significantly alters the amount purchased. Let's go back to Table 21-1. Suppose the $1 price for A is its "true" unit value or opportunity cost. But now, for some reason, its price is only, say, $.20. A rational consumer clearly would buy more units at $.20 than at the $1 price.

That is what happens with medical care. People in the United States who have health insurance pay a fixed premium once a month that covers, say, 80 percent of all incurred health care costs. This means that when they actually need health care, its price to them will be only 20 percent of the actual market price. How would you act in such a situation? When ill, you would likely purchase a great deal more medical services than if you were confronted with the full price. As a result, financing health care through insurance is an important factor in explaining today's high expenditures on health care and the historical growth of such spending as a percentage of domestic output.

Similar reasoning applies to purchases of buffet meals. If you buy a meal at an all-you-can-eat buffet, you will tend to eat more than if you purchased it item by item. Why not eat that second dessert—marginal utility is positive and its "price" is zero!

Transfers and Gifts

Government provides to eligible households both *cash transfers* (social security and public assistance) and in-kind or *noncash transfers* which specify particular purchases (food stamps and subsidies for housing and medical care). Most economists believe noncash transfers are less efficient than cash transfers because the specified uses (food, housing, medical care) may not match the recipient's preferences. Stated differently, consumers know their own preferences better than the government does.

Look back at Table 21-1. Suppose Holly has zero earned income but is given the choice of a $2 cash transfer or a noncash transfer of 2 units of A. Because 2 units of A can be bought with $2, these two transfers are of equal monetary value. But by spending the $2 *cash* transfer on the first unit of B, Holly could obtain 24 utils. The *noncash* transfer of the first 2 units of A would yield only 18 (= 10 + 8) units of utility. Conclusions: The noncash transfer is less efficient—it yields less utility—than the cash transfer.

As this chapter's Last Word demonstrates, the same reasoning applies to private gifts. Research suggests that noncash gifts to others entail a substantial loss of efficiency or utility. Of course, there may be perceived *benefits* of providing noncash gifts which offset this efficiency loss.

CHAPTER SUMMARY

1. The law of demand can be explained in terms of the income and substitution effects or the law of diminishing marginal utility.

2. The income effect implies that a decline in the price of a product increases the consumer's real income and enables the consumer to buy more of that product with a fixed money income. The substitution effect implies that a lower price makes a product relatively more attractive and therefore increases the consumer's willingness to substitute it for other products.

3. The law of diminishing marginal utility states that beyond some quantity, additional units of a specific good will yield declining amounts of extra satisfaction to a consumer.

4. We assume the typical consumer is rational and acts on the basis of well-defined preferences. Because income is limited and goods have prices, the consumer cannot purchase all the goods and services he or she might want. The consumer therefore selects that attainable combination of goods which maximizes his or her utility or satisfaction.

5. A consumer's utility is maximized when income is allocated so that the last dollar spent on each product purchased yields the same amount of extra satisfaction. Algebraically, the utility-maximizing rule is fulfilled when

$$\frac{\text{MU of product A}}{\text{Price of A}} = \frac{\text{MU of product B}}{\text{price of B}}$$

and the consumer's total income is spent.

6. The utility-maximizing rule and the demand curve are logically consistent. Because marginal utility declines, a lower price is needed to induce the consumer to buy more of a particular product.

TERMS AND CONCEPTS

income effect	total utility	law of diminishing	utility-maximizing rule
substitution effect	marginal utility	marginal utility	
utility			

STUDY QUESTIONS

1. Explain the law of demand through the income and substitution effects, using a price increase as a point of departure for your discussion. Explain the law of demand in terms of diminishing marginal utility.

2. KEY QUESTION Complete the following table and answer the questions below.

Units consumed	Total utility	Marginal utility
0	0	
1	10	10
2	—	8
3	25	—
4	30	—
5	—	3
6	34	—

a. At which rate is total utility increasing: a constant rate, a decreasing rate, or an increasing rate? How do you know?

b. "A rational consumer will purchase only 1 unit of the product represented by these data, since that amount maximizes marginal utility." Do you agree? Explain why or why not.

c. "It is possible that a rational consumer will not purchase any units of the product represented by these data." Do you agree? Explain why or why not.

3. Mrs. Wilson buys loaves of bread and quarts of milk each week at prices of $1 and 80 cents, respectively. At present she is buying these two products in amounts such that the marginal utilities from the last units purchased of the two products are 80 and 70 utils, respectively. Is she buying the utility-maximizing combination of bread and milk? If not, how should she reallocate her expenditures between the two goods?

4. KEY QUESTION Columns 1 through 4 in the table at the top of the next page show the marginal utility, measured in utils, which Ricardo would get by purchasing various amounts of products A, B, C, and D. Column 5 shows the marginal utility Ricardo gets from saving. Assume that the prices of A, B, C, and D are $18, $6, $4, and $24, respectively, and that Ricardo has a money income of $106.

a. What quantities of A, B, C, and D will Ricardo purchase in maximizing his utility?

b. How many dollars will Ricardo choose to save?

c. Check your answers by substituting them into the algebraic statement of the utility-maximizing rule.

5. KEY QUESTION You are choosing between two goods, X and Y, and your marginal utility from each is as shown below. If your income is $9 and the prices of X and Y are $2 and $1, respectively, what quantities of each will you purchase to maximize utility? What total utility will you realize? Assume that, other things remaining unchanged, the price of X falls to $1. What quantities of X and Y will you now purchase? Using the two prices and quantities for X, derive a demand schedule for X.

Units of X	MU_x	Units of Y	MU_y
1	10	1	8
2	8	2	7
3	6	3	6
4	4	4	5
5	3	5	4
6	2	6	3

6. How can time be incorporated into the theory of consumer behavior? Foreigners frequently point out that Americans are very wasteful of food and other material goods and very conscious of, and overly economical in, their use of time. Can you explain this observation?

7. Explain:
a. "Before economic growth, there were too few goods; after growth, there is too little time."
b. "It is irrational for an individual to take the time to be completely rational in economic decision making."

8. In the last decade or so there has been a dramatic expansion of small retail convenience stores (such as Kwik Shops, 7-Elevens, Gas 'N Shops), although their prices are generally much higher than those in the large supermarkets. Can you explain their success?

9. "Nothing is more useful than water: but it will purchase scarce any thing; scarce any thing can be had in exchange for it. A diamond, on the contrary, has scarce any value in use; but a very great quantity of goods may frequently be had in exchange for it."[2] Explain.

---
[2]Adam Smith, *The Wealth of Nations* (New York: Modern Library, Inc., originally published in 1776), p. 28.

Column 1		Column 2		Column 3		Column 4		Column 5	
Units of A	MU	Units of B	MU	Units of C	MU	Units of D	MU	Number of dollars saved	MU
1	72	1	24	1	15	1	36	1	5
2	54	2	15	2	12	2	30	2	4
3	45	3	12	3	8	3	24	3	3
4	36	4	9	4	7	4	18	4	2
5	27	5	7	5	5	5	13	5	1
6	18	6	5	6	4	6	7	6	$\frac{1}{2}$
7	15	7	2	7	$3\frac{1}{2}$	7	4	7	$\frac{1}{4}$
8	12	8	1	8	3	8	2	8	$\frac{1}{8}$

10. Many apartment complex owners are installing water meters for each individual apartment and billing the occupants according to the amount of water they use. This is in contrast to the former procedure of having a central meter for the entire complex and dividing up the water expense as part of the rent. Where individual meters have been installed, water usage has declined 10 to 40 percent. Explain this drop, referring to price and marginal utility.

11. **Advanced analysis:** Let $MU_A = z = 10 - x$ and $MU_B = z = 21 - 2y$, where z is marginal utility per dollar measured in utils, x is the amount spent on product A, and y is the amount spent on B. Assume the consumer has $10 to spend on A and B; that is, $x + y = 10$. How is the $10 best allocated between A and B? How much utility will the marginal dollar yield?

12. **(Last Word)** Explain why private and public gift-giving might entail economic inefficiency. Distinguish between cash and noncash gifts in your answer.

13. **WEB-BASED QUESTION** The ESPN Sportszone—To Fee or Not to Fee The ESPN Sportszone http://espn.sportszone.com/ is a major sports information site. Most of the content is free, but ESPN has a Premium Membership available for a monthly or an annual fee. Similar, but fee-free, sports content can be found at USA Today Sports http://www.usatoday.com/, CNN/Sports Illustrated http://www. cnnsi.com/, and CBS Sports Line http://cbs.sportsline.com/. Since ESPN has put a price tag on some of its sports content, it implies that the utility of a premium membership cannot be found at a no-fee site and is therefore worth the price. Is this the case? Use the utility maximization rule to justify your subscription or nonsubscription to the Premium Membership.

14. **WEB-BASED QUESTION** Visit Wal-Mart Online—Here's $500, Go Spend It Assume that you and several classmates each receive a $500 credit voucher (good for today only) from Wal-Mart Online. Go to http://www.wal-mart.com/ and select $500 worth of merchandise, using Add to Cart to keep a running total, and use Review Cart to print your final selection. Compare your list with your classmates' lists. What explains the differences? How many of your items were on sale? Would you have purchased these items if you had received $500 *in cash*?

Indifference Curve Analysis

A more advanced explanation of consumer behavior and equilibrium is based on (1) budget lines and (2) indifference curves.

The Budget Line: What Is Attainable

A **budget line** *is a schedule or curve that shows various combinations of two products a consumer can purchase with a specific money income.* If the price of product A is $1.50 and the price of B is $1.00, then a consumer could purchase all the combinations of A and B shown in Table 1 with $12 of money income. At one extreme the consumer might spend all of his or her income on 8 units of A and have nothing left to spend on B. Or, by giving up 2 units of A and thereby "freeing" $3, the consumer could have 6 units of A and 3 of B. And so on to the other extreme, at which the consumer

could buy 12 units of B at $1.00 each, spending his or her entire money income on B with nothing left to spend on A.

Figure 1 shows the same budget line graphically. Note that the graph is not restricted to whole units of A and B as is the table. Every point on the graph represents a possible combination of A and B, including fractional quantities. The slope of the graphed budget line measures the ratio of the price of B to the

TABLE 1 The budget line: whole-unit combinations of A and B attainable with an income of $12

Units of A (price = $1.50)	Units of B (price = $1.00)	Total expenditure
8	0	$12 (= $12 + $0)
6	3	$12 (= $9 + $3)
4	6	$12 (= $6 + $6)
2	9	$12 (= $3 + $9)
0	12	$12 (= $0 + $12)

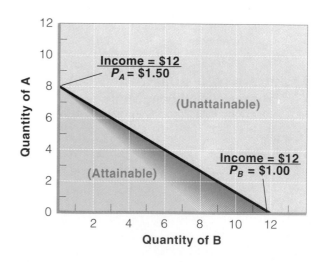

FIGURE 1 A consumer's budget line The budget line shows all the combinations of any two products which can be purchased, given the prices of the products and the consumer's money income.

price of A; more precisely, the absolute value of the slope is $P_B/P_A = \$1.00/\$1.50 = 2/3$. This is the mathematical way of saying that the consumer must forgo 2 units of A (measured on the vertical axis) to buy 3 units of B (measured on the horizontal axis). In moving down the budget or price line, 2 of A (at $1.50 each) must be given up to obtain 3 more of B (at $1.00 each). This yields a slope of $\frac{2}{3}$.

There are two other characteristics of the budget line you should know about:

1. **Income changes** The location of the budget line varies with money income. An *increase* in money income shifts the budget line to the *right*; a *decrease* in money income moves it to the *left*. To verify this, recalculate Table 1 assuming money income is (*a*) $24 and (*b*) $6 and plot the new budget lines in Figure 1.

2. **Price changes** A change in product prices also shifts the budget line. A decline in the prices of both products—the equivalent of a real income increase—shifts the curve to the right. (You can verify this by recalculating Table 1 and replotting Figure 1 assuming that $P_A = \$.75$ and $P_B = \$.50$.) Conversely, an increase in the prices of A and B shifts the curve to the left. (Assume $P_A = \$3$ and $P_B = \$2$ and rework Table 1 and Figure 1 to substantiate this statement.)

Note what happens if P_B changes while P_A and money income remain constant. In particular, if P_B drops, say, from $1.00 to $.50, the lower end of the budget line fans outward to the right. Conversely, if P_B increases, say, from $1.00 to $1.50, the lower end of the line fans inward to the left. In both instances the line remains "anchored" at 8 units on the vertical axis because P_A has not changed.

Indifference Curves: What Is Preferred

Budget lines reflect "objective" market data, specifically income and prices. The budget line reveals combinations of products A and B which can be purchased, given current money income and prices.

Indifference curves, on the other hand, reflect "subjective" information about consumer preferences for A and B. An **indifference curve** *shows all combinations of two products A and B which will yield the same total satisfaction or total utility to a consumer.* Table 2 and Figure 2 present a hypothetical indifference curve for products A and B. The consumer's subjective preferences are such that he or she will realize the same to-

TABLE 2 **An indifference schedule (whole units)**

Combination	Units of A	Units of B
j	12	2
k	6	4
l	4	6
m	3	8

tal utility from each combination of A and B shown in the table or on the curve. Hence, the consumer will be *indifferent* as to which combination is actually obtained.

Several characteristics of indifference curves are important.

They Are Downsloping An indifference curve slopes downward because more of one product means less of the other, if total utility is to remain unchanged. Suppose the consumer moves from one combination of A and B to another, say, from *j* to *k* in Figure 2. In so doing, the consumer obtains more of product B, increasing his or her total utility. But because total utility is the same everywhere on the curve, the consumer must give up some of the other product, A, to reduce total utility by a precisely offsetting amount. Thus "more of B" necessitates "less of A," and the

FIGURE 2 A consumer's indifference curve Every point on indifference curve *I* represents some combination of products A and B, and all those combinations are equally satisfactory to the consumer. That is, each combination of A and B on the curve yields the same total utility.

quantities of A and B are inversely related. A curve which reflects inversely related variables is downsloping.

They Are Convex from the Origin

As viewed from the origin, a downsloping curve can be *concave (bowed outward)* or *convex (bowed inward)*. A concave curve has an increasing (steeper) slope as one moves down the curve, while a convex curve has a diminishing (flatter) slope as one moves down it. Note in Figure 2 that *the indifference curve is convex as viewed from the origin.* Its slope diminishes or becomes flatter as we move from *j* to *k* to *l*, and so on down the curve. Technically, the slope of the indifference curve at each point measures the **marginal rate of substitution** (MRS) of the combination represented by that point. The slope or MRS shows the rate at which the consumer who possesses that combination will substitute one good for the other (say, B for A) to remain equally satisfied. The diminishing slope of the indifference curve means the willingness to substitute B for A diminishes as one moves down the curve.

The rationale for this convexity, that is, for a diminishing MRS, is that a consumer's subjective willingness to substitute B for A (or A for B) will depend on the amounts of B and A he or she has to begin with. Consider Table 2 and Figure 2 again, beginning at point *j*. Here, in relative terms, the consumer has a substantial amount of A and very little of B. Within this combination, a unit of B is very valuable (that is, its marginal utility is high), while a unit of A is less valuable (its marginal utility is low). The consumer will then be willing to give up a substantial amount of A to get, say, 2 more units of B. In this case, the consumer is willing to forgo 6 units of A to get 2 more units of B; the MRS is $\frac{6}{2}$, or 3.

But at point *k* the consumer has less A and more B. Here A is somewhat more valuable, and B less valuable, "at the margin." In a move from point *k* to point *l*, the consumer is willing to give up only 2 units of A to get 2 more units of B, so the MRS is only $\frac{2}{2}$, or 1. Having still less of A and more of B at point *l*, the consumer is willing to give up only 1 unit of A in return for 2 more units of B and the MRS falls to $\frac{1}{2}$.

In general, as the amount of B *increases*, the marginal utility of additional units of B *decreases*. Similarly, as the quantity of A *decreases*, its marginal utility *increases*. In Figure 2 we see that in moving down the curve, the consumer will be willing to give up smaller and smaller amounts of A to offset acquiring each additional unit of B. The result is a curve with a dimin-

ishing slope, a curve which is convex viewed from the origin. The MRS declines as one moves southeast along the indifference curve.

The Indifference Map

The single indifference curve of Figure 2 reflects some constant (but unspecified) level of total utility or satisfaction. It is possible and useful to sketch a whole series of indifference curves or an **indifference map** as shown in Figure 3. Each curve reflects a different level of total utility. Specifically, each curve to the *right* of our original curve (labeled I_3 in Figure 3) reflects combinations of A and B which yield *more* utility than I_3. Each curve to the *left* of I_3 reflects *less* total utility than I_3. *As we move out from the origin, each successive indifference curve represents a higher level of utility.* To demonstrate this fact, draw a line in a northeasterly direction from the origin; note that its points of intersection with successive curves entail larger amounts of *both* A and B and therefore higher levels of total utility.

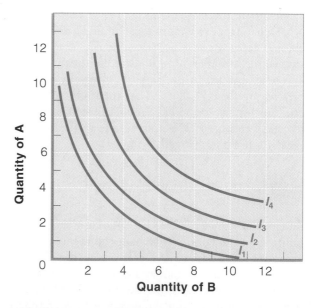

FIGURE 3 An indifference map An indifference map is a set of indifference curves. Curves farther from the origin indicate higher levels of total utility. Thus any combination of products A and B represented by a point on I_4 has greater total utility than any combination of A and B represented by a point on I_3, I_2, and I_1.

Equilibrium at Tangency

Since the axes in Figures 1 and 3 are identical, we can superimpose a consumer's budget line on his or her indifference map, as shown in Figure 4. By definition, the budget line indicates all combinations of A and B the consumer can attain with his or her money income, given the prices of A and B. Of these attainable combinations, the consumer will most prefer that combination which yields the greatest satisfaction or utility. Specifically, *the utility-maximizing combination will be the one lying on the highest attainable indifference curve.* That utility-maximizing combination is called the consumer's **equilibrium position.**

In Figure 4 the consumer's utility-maximizing or equilibrium combination of A and B is at point X, where the budget line is *tangent* to I_3. Why not point Y? Because Y is on a lower indifference curve, I_2. By moving "down" the budget line—by shifting dollars from purchases of A to purchases of B—the consumer can attain an indifference curve farther from the origin and thereby increase total utility from the same income. Why not point Z? Same reason: Point Z is on a lower indifference curve, I_1. By moving "up" the

budget line—by reallocating dollars from B to A—the consumer can get on higher indifference curve I_3 and increase total utility.

How about point W on indifference curve I_4? While it is true that W would yield a greater total utility than X, point W is beyond (outside) the budget line and hence *not* attainable by the consumer. Point X represents the optimal *attainable* combination of products A and B. At this point we note that, by definition of tangency, the slope of the highest attainable indifference curve equals the slope of the budget line. Because the slope of the indifference curve reflects the MRS and the slope of the budget line is P_B/P_A, the optimal or equilibrium position is the point where

$$\text{MRS} = \frac{P_B}{P_A}$$

Appendix Key Question 3 is recommended at this time.

The Measurement of Utility

There is an important difference between the marginal utility theory of consumer demand and the indifference curve theory. The marginal utility theory assumes that utility is *numerically* measurable. The consumer is assumed to be able to say *how much* extra utility he or she derives from each extra unit of A or B. The consumer needs that information to realize the utility-maximizing (equilibrium) position, as indicated by

$$\frac{\text{Marginal utility of A}}{\text{Price of A}} = \frac{\text{marginal utility of B}}{\text{price of B}}$$

The indifference curve approach poses a less stringent requirement for the consumer. He or she need only specify whether a particular combination of A and B yields more, less, or the same amount of utility than some other combination of A and B. The consumer need only say, for example, that 6 of A and 7 of B yield more (or less) satisfaction than 4 of A and 9 of B. Indifference curve theory does *not* require that the consumer specify *how much* more (or less) satisfaction will be realized.

When the equilibrium situations in the two theories are compared, we find that in the indifference curve analysis the MRS equals P_B/P_A at equilibrium; however, in the marginal utility approach the ratio of marginal utilities equals P_B/P_A. We therefore deduce

FIGURE 4 The consumer's equilibrium position The consumer's equilibrium position is represented by point X, where the black budget line is tangent to indifference curve I_3. The consumer buys 4 units of A at $1.50 per unit and 6 of B at $1.00 per unit with a $12 money income. Points Z and Y represent attainable combinations of A and B but yield less total utility, as is evidenced by the fact that they are on lower indifference curves. Point W would entail more utility than X, but it requires a greater income than the $12 represented by the budget line.

that at equilibrium the MRS is equivalent in the marginal utility approach to the ratio of the marginal utilities of the last purchased units of the two products.[3]

The Derivation of the Demand Curve

We noted earlier that with a fixed price for A, an increase in the price of B will cause the bottom of the budget line to fan inward to the left. This fact can be used to derive a demand curve for product B. In Figure 5a we reproduce the part of Figure 4 that shows our initial consumer equilibrium at point X. The budget line determining this equilibrium position assumes that money income is $12 and that $P_A = \$1.50$ and $P_B = \$1.00$. Let's examine what happens to the equilibrium position if we increase P_B to $1.50, holding money income and the price of A constant.

The result is shown in Figure 5a. The budget line fans to the left, yielding a new equilibrium point X' where it is tangent to lower indifference curve I_2. At X' the consumer buys 3 units of B and 5 of A compared with 4 of A and 6 of B at X. Our interest is in B, and we now have sufficient information to locate two points on the demand curve for product B. We know that at equilibrium point X the price of B is $1.00 and 6 units are purchased; at equilibrium point X' the price of B is $1.50 and 3 units are purchased.

These data are shown graphically in Figure 5b as points on the consumer's demand curve for B. Note that the horizontal axes of Figure 5a and b are identical; both measure the quantity demanded of B. We can therefore drop vertical reference lines from Figure 5a down to the horizontal axis of Figure 5b. On the vertical axis of Figure 5b we locate the two chosen prices of B. Knowing that these prices yield the relevant quantities demanded, we locate two points on the demand curve for B. By simple manipulation of the price of B in an indifference curve–budget line context, we have obtained a downsloping demand curve for B. We have thus again derived the law of demand assuming "other things equal" since only the price of B was changed (the price of A and the consumer's income and tastes remained constant). But, in this case, we have derived the demand curve without

resorting to the questionable assumption that consumers can measure utility in units called "utils." In this indifference curve approach, consumers simply compare combinations of products A and B and determine which combination they prefer, given their incomes and the prices of the two products.

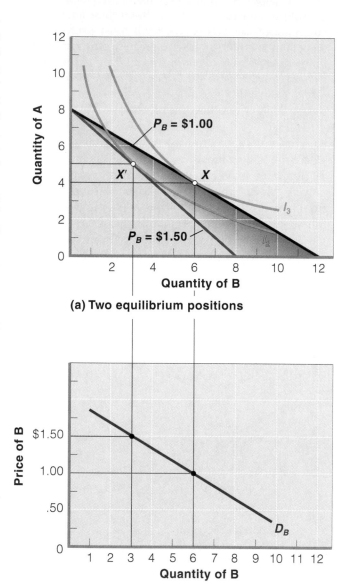

(a) Two equilibrium positions

(b) The demand curve for product B

FIGURE 5 Deriving the demand curve (a) When the price of B is increased from $1.00 to $1.50, the equilibrium position moves from X to X', decreasing the quantity of B demanded from 6 to 3 units. (b) The demand curve for B is determined by plotting the $1.00–6-unit and the $1.50–3-unit price-quantity combinations for B.

---

[3]Technical footnote: If we begin with the utility-maximizing rule, $MU_A/P_A = MU_B/P_B$, and then multiply through by P_B and divide through by MU_A, we obtain $P_B/P_A = MU_B/MU_A$. In indifference curve analysis we know that at the equilibrium position MRS = P_B/P_A. Hence, at equilibrium MRS also equals MU_B/MU_A.

APPENDIX SUMMARY

1. The indifference curve approach to consumer behavior is based on the consumer's budget line and indifference curves.

2. The budget line shows all combinations of two products which the consumer can purchase, given his or her money income and product prices.

3. A change in product prices or money income moves the budget line.

4. An indifference curve shows all combinations of two products which will yield the same total utility to a consumer. Indifference curves are downsloping and convex from the origin.

5. An indifference map consists of a number of indifference curves; the farther from the origin, the higher the total utility associated with a curve.

6. The consumer is in equilibrium (utility is maximized) at that point on the budget line which lies on the highest attainable indifference curve. At that point the budget line and indifference curve are tangent.

7. Changing the price of one product shifts the budget line and determines a new equilibrium point. A downsloping demand curve can be determined by plotting the price-quantity combinations associated with two or more equilibrium points.

APPENDIX TERMS AND CONCEPTS

budget line
indifference curve

marginal rate of
substitution

indifference map
equilibrium position

APPENDIX STUDY QUESTIONS

1. What information is embodied in a budget line? What shifts occur in the budget line when money income **(a)** increases and **(b)** decreases? What shifts occur in the budget line when the price of the product shown on the vertical axis **(a)** increases and **(b)** decreases?

2. What information is contained in an indifference curve? Why are such curves **(a)** downsloping and **(b)** convex from the origin? Why does total utility increase as the consumer moves to indifference curves farther from the origin? Why can't indifference curves intersect?

3. **APPENDIX KEY QUESTION** Using Figure 4, explain why the point of tangency of the budget line with an indifference curve is the consumer's equilibrium position. Explain why any point where the budget line intersects an indifference curve is not equilibrium. Explain: "The consumer is in equilibrium where MRS = P_B/P_A."

4. Assume that the data in the accompanying table give an indifference curve for Mr. Chen. Graph this curve, putting A on the vertical axis and B on the horizontal axis. Assuming that the prices of A and B are $1.50 and $1.00, respectively, and that Chen has $24 to spend, add his budget line to your graph. What combination of A and B will Chen purchase? Does your answer meet the MRS = P_B/P_A rule for equilibrium?

Units of A	Units of B
16	6
12	8
8	12
4	24

5. Explain graphically how indifference analysis can be used to derive a demand curve.

6. **Advanced analysis:** Demonstrate mathematically that the equilibrium condition MRS = P_B/P_A is the equivalent of the utility-maximizing rule $MU_A/P_A = MU_B/P_B$.

The Costs of Production

In the previous chapter we looked at the behavior of *consumers* and how that behavior relates to product demand. Now we turn to the behavior of *producers,* asking how it relates to product supply. As we observed in Chapter 3, the basic factor underlying the ability and willingness of firms to supply a product is the cost of making that product. Production requires using economic resources which, because of their relative scarcity, bear price tags. The amount of a product a firm is willing to supply depends on:

- The prices (costs) and productivity of the resources essential to its production
- The price the product will bring in the market

In this chapter we consider the general nature of *production costs*. Then, in the next several chapters, we bring product demand, product prices, and revenue back into the picture, explaining how firms compare revenues and costs in setting their profit-maximizing levels of output. Our ultimate purpose is to show how these decisions relate to economic efficiency.

ECONOMIC COSTS

Costs exist because resources are scarce and have alternative uses. When we use a bundle of resources to produce some particular good, all alternative production opportunities relating to those specific resources are forgone. Production costs in economics arise from forgoing the opportunity to produce other goods or services. The **economic cost,** or **opportunity cost,** of any resource used in producing a good is measured as its value or worth in its best alternative use.

This view of costs is that stressed in the production possibilities analysis in Chapter 2. The opportunity cost of producing more pizzas is the industrial robots which must be forgone. Similarly, steel used for constructing office buildings is not available for manufacturing automobiles or refrigerators. Paper used for economics textbooks is not available for encyclopedias or romance novels. And if an assembly line worker can assemble either personal computers or washing machines, then the cost to society of employing this worker in a personal-computer plant is the contribution the worker would otherwise have made in producing washing machines.

Explicit and Implicit Costs

Let's now consider costs from the firm's viewpoint. Keeping in mind the notion of opportunity costs, we can say that *economic costs are those payments a firm must make, or incomes it must provide, to resource suppliers to attract the resources away from alternative production opportunities.* These payments or incomes may be either explicit or implicit.

The monetary payments—the "out-of-pocket" or cash expenditures a firm makes to "outsiders" who supply labor services, materials, fuel, transportation services, and the like—are called **explicit costs.** Explicit costs are money payments to nonowners of the firm for the resources they supply.

But, in addition, a firm may use certain resources the firm itself owns. Our concept of opportunity costs tells us that, regardless of whether a resource is owned by an enterprise or hired, there is a cost involved in using that resource in a specific employment. The costs of such self-owned, self-employed resources are called **implicit costs.** To the firm, implicit costs are the money payments the self-employed resources could have earned in their best alternative use.

Example: Suppose you are earning $20,000 a year as a sales representative for a compact disc manufacturer. You decide to open a store to sell CDs at the retail level. You invest $20,000 of savings which has been earning you $1000 per year. Also, you decide your new firm will occupy a small store which you own and have been renting out for $5000 per year. One clerk is hired to help you in the store.

After a year's operations you total up your accounts and find the following:

Total sales revenue		$120,000
Cost of CDs	$40,000	
Clerk's salary	20,000	
Utilities	5,000	
Total (explicit) costs		65,000
Accounting profit		55,000

But this accounting profit does not accurately reveal the economic status of your venture because it ignores implicit costs. What is significant here is the total amount of resources used (as opposed to dollars expended) in your enterprise. By providing your own financial capital, building, and labor, you incur im-

plicit costs (forgone incomes) of $1000 in interest, $5000 in rent, and $20,000 in wages. Also, let's suppose that your entrepreneurial talent is worth $5000 annually in other business endeavors of similar scope. Then:

Accounting profit		$55,000
Forgone interest	$ 1,000	
Forgone rent	5,000	
Forgone wages	20,000	
Forgone entrepreneurial income	5,000	
Total implicit costs		31,000
Economic profit		24,000

Normal Profit as a Cost

The $5000 implicit cost of your entrepreneurial talent in the above example is called a **normal profit.** As is true of the forgone rent and forgone wages, the payment you could otherwise receive for performing entrepreneurial functions is indeed an implicit cost. If you did not realize at least this minimum, or normal, payment for your effort, you could withdraw from this line of production and shift to a more attractive business endeavor.

The economist includes as costs of production all the costs—explicit and implicit, including a normal profit—required to attract and retain resources in a specific line of production.

Economic, or Pure, Profit

Obviously, then, economists and accountants use the term "profit" differently. *Accounting profit is the firm's total revenue less its explicit costs.* But economists define profit in another way. **Economic profit** *is total revenue less all costs (explicit and implicit, the latter including a normal profit to the entrepreneur).* Therefore, when an economist says a particular firm is earning only enough revenue to cover its costs, this means all explicit and implicit costs are being met and the entrepreneur is receiving a payment just large enough to retain his or her talents in the present line of production.

If a firm's total revenue *exceeds* all its economic costs, any residual goes to the entrepreneur. This residual is called an *economic, or pure, profit.* In short:

$$\text{Economic profit} = \text{total revenue} - \text{opportunity costs of all inputs}$$

In our example, the economic profit is $24,000 (= $120,000 of revenue minus $96,000 of explicit and implicit costs). An economic profit is not a cost, because by definition it is a return in excess of the normal profit required to retain the entrepreneur in this particular line of production. Even if the economic profit is zero, the entrepreneur is still covering all explicit and implicit costs, including a normal profit. In our example, as long as accounting profit is $31,000 or more (so that economic profit is zero or more), you will be earning the $5000 normal profit and will continue to operate your CD store.

Figure 22-1 shows the relationship among various cost and profit concepts. To test yourself, you might want to enter cost data from our example in the appropriate blocks. **(Key Question 2)**

Short Run and Long Run

When the demand for a firm's product changes, the firm's profitability may depend on how quickly it can adjust the amounts of the various resources it employs. The quantities employed of many resources—most labor, raw materials, fuel, and power—can be varied easily and quickly. Capital resources, however, require more time for adjustment. The capacity of a manufacturing plant, that is, the size of the factory building and the amount of machinery and equipment in it, can be varied only over a considerable period of time. In some heavy industries it may take several years to alter plant capacity. Because of these differences in adjustment time, economists find it useful to distinguish between the *short run* and the *long run*.

Short Run: Fixed Plant The **short run** is a period too brief for a firm to alter its plant capacity, yet long enough to permit a change in the degree to which the fixed plant is used. The firm's plant capacity is fixed in the short run. However, the firm can vary its output by applying larger or smaller amounts of labor, materials, and other resources to that plant. Existing plant capacity can be used more or less intensively in the short run.

Long Run: Variable Plant From the viewpoint of an existing firm, the **long run** is a period long enough for that firm to adjust the quantities of *all* the resources it employs, including plant capacity. From the industry's viewpoint, the long run also encompasses enough time for existing firms to dissolve and leave the industry or for new firms to be created and enter the industry. *While the short run is a "fixed-plant" period, the long run is a "variable-plant" period.*

Illustrations If Boeing hires 100 extra workers for one of its commercial airline plants or adds an entire shift of workers, we are speaking of the short run. If it adds a new production facility and installs more equipment, we are referring to the long run. The first situation is a *short-run adjustment*; the second is a *long-run adjustment*.

Note that the short run and the long run are *conceptual* periods rather than calendar time periods. In light-manufacturing industries, changes in plant capacity may be accomplished almost overnight. A small T-shirt firm can increase its plant capacity in days by ordering and installing a couple of new cutting tables and several extra sewing machines. But for heavy industry the long run is a different story. Exxon may require several years to construct a new oil refinery.

FIGURE 22-1 **Economic and accounting profits** Economic profit is equal to total revenue less opportunity costs. Opportunity costs are the sum of explicit and implicit costs and include a normal profit to the entrepreneur. Accounting profit is equal to total revenue less accounting (explicit) costs.

QUICK REVIEW 22-1

■ Explicit costs are money payments a firm makes to outside suppliers of resources; implicit costs are the opportunity costs associated with a firm's use of resources it owns.

■ Normal profit is the implicit cost of entrepreneurship. Economic profit is total revenue less all explicit and implicit costs, including normal profit.

■ In the short run a firm's plant capacity is fixed; in the long run a firm can vary its plant size and firms can enter or leave the industry.

SHORT-RUN PRODUCTION RELATIONSHIPS

A firm's costs of producing a specific output depend not only on the *prices* of needed resources but also on the *quantities* of resources (inputs) needed to produce that output. These quantities are determined by technological aspects of production, specifically, relationships between inputs and output. Before examining these relationships, we need to define three terms:

1. *Total product* (TP) is the total quantity, or total output, of a particular good produced.
2. *Marginal product* (MP) is the extra output or added product associated with adding a unit of a variable resource, in this case labor, in the production process. Thus,

$$\text{Marginal product} = \frac{\text{change in total product}}{\text{change in labor input}}$$

3. *Average product* (AP), also called labor productivity, is output per unit of labor input:

$$\text{Average product} = \frac{\text{total product}}{\text{units of labor}}$$

In the short run, a firm can combine a variable resource (labor) with its fixed resource (plant) to produce output. For a time, it can increase its output by adding units of labor to its fixed plant. But by how much will output rise when it adds this labor? Why do we say, "for a time"?

Law of Diminishing Returns

The answers are provided in general terms by the **law of diminishing returns,** also called the *law of diminishing marginal product* and the *law of variable proportions.* This law assumes that technology is fixed, meaning that the techniques of production do not change. It states that *as successive units of a variable resource (say, labor) are added to a fixed resource (say, capital or land), beyond some point the extra, or marginal, product attributable to each additional unit of the variable resource will decline.* If additional workers are applied to a constant amount of capital equipment, output will eventually rise by smaller and smaller amounts as more workers are employed.

Rationale Suppose a farmer has a fixed amount of land—80 acres—planted in corn. If the farmer does not cultivate the cornfields (clear the weeds) at all, the yield will be 40 bushels per acre. If the land is cultivated once, output may rise to 50 bushels per acre. A second cultivation may increase output to 57 bushels per acre, a third to 61, and a fourth to 63. Succeeding cultivations would add less and less to the land's yield. If this were not so, the world's needs for corn could be fulfilled by extremely intense cultivation of this single 80-acre plot of land. Indeed, if diminishing returns did not occur, the world could be fed out of a flowerpot.

The law of diminishing returns also holds true in nonagricultural industries. Assume a wood shop is manufacturing wooden furniture frames. It has a specific amount of equipment—lathes, planers, saws, sanders. If this firm hired just one or two workers, total output and productivity (output per worker) would be very low. These workers would perform many different jobs, and the advantages of specialization would not be realized. Time would be lost in switching from one job to another, and machines would stand idle much of the time. In short, the plant would be understaffed, and production inefficient because there was too much capital relative to labor.

These difficulties would disappear if more workers were added. Equipment would be more fully used, and workers could now specialize on a single job. Time would no longer be lost from job switching. Thus as more workers were added to the initially understaffed plant, the marginal product of each succeeding worker would rise, as the operation became more efficient.

But this cannot go on indefinitely. If still more workers were added, problems of overcrowding would arise. Workers would have to wait in line to use the machinery, so now *workers* would be underused. Total output would increase at a diminishing rate because, with the fixed plant size, each worker would have less capital equipment to work with as more and more labor was hired. The marginal product of additional workers would decline because the plant was more intensively staffed; there would be more labor in proportion to the fixed amount of capital. Eventually, adding still more workers would cause so much congestion in the plant that marginal product would become negative—total product would decline. In the extreme, the continuous addition of labor would use up all the standing room, and total product would fall to zero.

Note that the law of diminishing returns assumes all units of variable inputs—workers in this case—are of equal quality. Each successive worker is presumed to have the same innate ability, motor coordination, education, training, and work experience. Marginal product ultimately diminishes not because successive workers are qualitatively inferior but because more workers are being used relative to the amount of plant and equipment available.

Tabular Example

Table 22-1 is a numerical illustration of the law of diminishing returns. Column 2 shows the total product, or total output, resulting from combining each level of variable input, labor, in column 1 with a fixed amount of capital.

Column 3 shows the marginal product, the change in total product associated with each additional unit of labor. Note that with no labor input, total product is zero; a plant with no workers in it will produce no output. The first 3 units of labor reflect increasing marginal returns, their marginal products being 10, 15, and 20 units, respectively. But beginning with the fourth unit of labor, marginal product diminishes continuously, actually becoming zero with the seventh unit of labor and negative with the eighth.

Average product or output per labor unit is shown in column 4. It is calculated by dividing total product (column 2) by the number of labor units needed to produce it (column 1). At 5 units of labor, for example, AP is 14 (= 70/5).

Graphical Portrayal

Figure 22-2 (Key Graph) shows the diminishing returns data in Table 22-1 graphically and further clarifies the relationships between total, marginal, and average products. (Marginal product in Figure 22-2b is plotted halfway between the units of labor since it applies to the *addition* of each labor unit.)

Note first in Figure 22-2a that total product, TP, goes through three phases: it rises initially at an increasing rate; then it increases, but at a diminishing rate; finally, after reaching a maximum, it declines.

Geometrically, marginal product—shown by the MP curve in Figure 22-2b—is the slope of the total product curve. Marginal product measures the change in total product associated with each succeeding unit of labor. Thus, the three phases of total product are also reflected in marginal product. Where total product is increasing at an increasing rate, marginal product is necessarily rising. Here, extra units of labor are adding larger and larger amounts to total product. Similarly, where total product is increasing but at a decreasing rate, marginal product is positive but falling. Each additional unit of labor adds less to total product than did the previous unit. When total product is at a maximum, marginal product is zero. When total product declines, marginal product becomes negative.

Average product, AP (Figure 22-2b), displays the same tendencies as marginal product. It increases, reaches a maximum, and then decreases as more and more units of labor are added to the fixed plant. But note the relationship between marginal product and average product: Where marginal product exceeds average product, average product rises. And where marginal product is less than average product, average product declines. It follows that marginal product intersects average product where average product is at a maximum.

TABLE 22-1 Total, marginal, and average product: The law of diminishing returns

(1) Units of the variable resource (labor)	(2) Total product (TP)	(3) Marginal product (MP), change in (2)/ change in (1)		(4) Average product (AP), (2)/(1)
0	0			—
1	10	10	Increasing marginal returns	10.00
2	25	15		12.50
3	45	20		15.00
4	60	15	Diminishing marginal returns	15.00
5	70	10		14.00
6	75	5		12.50
7	75	0	Negative marginal returns	10.71
8	70	−5		8.75

(a) Total product

(b) Marginal and average product

FIGURE 22-2 **The law of diminishing returns** (a) As a variable resource (labor) is added to fixed amounts of other resources (land or capital), the resulting total product will eventually increase by diminishing amounts, reach a maximum, and then decline. (b) Marginal product is the change in total product associated with each new unit of labor. Average product is simply output per labor unit. Note that marginal product intersects average product at the maximum average product.

QUICK QUIZ 22-2

1. **Which of the following is an assumption underlying these figures?**
   a. Firms first hire "better" workers and then hire "poorer" workers.
   b. Capital and labor are both variable, but labor increases more rapidly than capital.
   c. Consumers will buy all the output (total product) produced.
   d. Workers are of equal quality.

2. **Marginal product is:**
   a. the change in total product divided by the change in the quantity of labor.
   b. total product divided by the quantity of labor.
   c. always positive.
   d. unrelated to total product.

3. **Marginal product in graph (b) is zero when:**
   a. average product in graph (b) stops rising.

   b. the slope of the marginal-product curve in graph (b) is zero.
   c. total product in graph (a) begins to rise at a diminishing rate.
   d. the slope of the total-product curve in graph (a) is zero.

4. **Average product in graph (b):**
   a. rises when it is less than marginal product.
   b. is the change in total product divided by the change in the quantity of labor.
   c. can never exceed marginal product.
   d. falls whenever total product in graph (a) rises at a diminishing rate.

Answers: 1. d; 2. a; 3. d; 4. a

This relationship is a mathematical necessity. If you add to a total a number which is greater than the current average of that total, the average must rise. And if you add to a total a number which is less than the current average of that total, the average must fall. You raise your average examination grade only when your score on an additional (marginal) examination is greater than the average of all your past scores. You lower your average when your grade on an additional exam is below your current average. In our production example, when the amount an extra worker adds to total product exceeds the average product of all workers already employed, average product will rise. Conversely, when an extra worker adds to total product an amount which is less than the present average product, then average product will decrease.

The law of diminishing returns is embodied in the shapes of all three curves. But, as our definition of the law of diminishing returns indicates, economists are most concerned with its effects on marginal product. The regions of increasing, diminishing, and negative marginal product (returns) are shown in Figure 22-2b. **(Key Question 4)**

SHORT-RUN PRODUCTION COSTS

Production information such as that provided in Table 22-1 and Figure 22-2a and b must be coupled with resource prices to determine the total and per-unit costs of producing various levels of output. We know that in the short run some resources, those associated with the firm's plant, are fixed. Others are variable. This means that in the short run costs can be classified as either fixed or variable.

Fixed, Variable, and Total Cost

Fixed Costs Fixed costs *are those costs which in total do not vary with changes in output.* Fixed costs are associated with the very existence of a firm's plant and therefore must be paid even if its output is zero. Such costs as interest on a firm's debts, rental payments, a portion of depreciation on equipment and buildings, and insurance premiums are generally fixed costs. In column 2 in Table 22-2 we assume that the firm's total fixed cost is $100. By definition, this fixed cost is incurred at all levels of output, including zero. Fixed costs cannot be avoided in the short run.

Variable Costs Variable costs *are those costs that change with the level of output.* They include payments for materials, fuel, power, transportation services, most labor, and similar variable resources. In column 3 of Table 22-2 we find that the total of variable costs changes directly with output. But note that *the increases in variable cost associated with succeeding 1-unit increases in output are not equal.* As production begins, variable cost will for a time increase by a *decreasing* amount; this is true through the fourth unit of output in Table 22-2. Beyond the fourth unit, however, variable cost rises by *increasing* amounts for succeeding units of output.

The reason for this lies in the shape of the marginal product curve. At first, as in Figure 22-2b, we have increasing marginal product, so smaller and smaller increases in the amounts of variable resources are needed to produce successive units of output. Hence the variable cost of successive units of output decreases. But when marginal product begins to decline as diminishing returns are encountered, larger and larger additional amounts of variable resources are needed to produce successive units of output. Total variable cost therefore increases by increasing amounts.

Total Cost Total cost is the *sum of fixed cost and variable cost at each level of output.* It is shown in column 4 in Table 22-2. At zero units of output, total cost is equal to the firm's fixed cost. Then for each unit of production—1 through 10—total cost varies by the same amounts as does variable cost.

Figure 22-3 shows graphically the fixed-, variable-, and total-cost data in Table 22-2. Note that total variable cost is measured vertically from the horizontal axis and total cost is added vertically to total variable cost to obtain points on the total-cost curve.

The distinction between fixed and variable costs is significant to the business manager. Variable costs can be controlled or altered in the short run by changing production levels. Fixed costs are beyond the business executive's present control; they are incurred in the short run and must be paid regardless of output level.

Per-Unit, or Average, Costs

Producers are certainly interested in their total costs, but they are equally concerned with *per-unit*, or *average*, costs. In particular, average-cost data are more meaningful for making comparisons with product price, which is always stated on a per-unit basis.

TABLE 22-2 Total-, average-, and marginal-cost schedules for an individual firm in the short run

	Total-cost data			Average-cost data			Marginal cost
(1) Total product (Q)	(2) Total fixed cost (TFC)	(3) Total variable cost (TVC)	(4) Total cost (TC) $TC = TFC + TVC$	(5) Average fixed cost (AFC) $AFC = \dfrac{TFC}{Q}$	(6) Average variable cost (AVC) $AVC = \dfrac{TVC}{Q}$	(7) Average total cost (ATC) $ATC = \dfrac{TC}{Q}$	(8) Marginal cost (MC) $MC = \dfrac{\text{change in TC}}{\text{change in Q}}$
0	$100	$ 0	$ 100				
1	100	90	190	$100.00	$90.00	$190.00	$ 90
2	100	170	270	50.00	85.00	135.00	80
3	100	240	340	33.33	80.00	113.33	70
4	100	300	400	25.00	75.00	100.00	60
5	100	370	470	20.00	74.00	94.00	70
6	100	450	550	16.67	75.00	91.67	80
7	100	540	640	14.29	77.14	91.43	90
8	100	650	750	12.50	81.25	93.75	110
9	100	780	880	11.11	86.67	97.78	130
10	100	930	1030	10.00	93.00	103.00	150

Average fixed cost, average variable cost, and average total cost are shown in columns 5 to 7, Table 22-2.

AFC **Average fixed cost** (AFC) for any output level is found by dividing total fixed cost (TFC) by that output (Q). That is,

$$AFC = \frac{TFC}{Q}$$

Because the total fixed cost is, by definition, the same regardless of output, AFC must decline as output increases. As output rises, the total fixed cost is spread over a larger and larger output. When output is just 1 unit in Table 22-2, TFC and AFC are the same at $100. But at 2 units of output, the total fixed cost of $100 becomes $50 of AFC or fixed cost per unit; then it becomes $33.33 per unit as $100 is spread over 3 units, and $25 per unit when spread over 4 units. This process is sometimes referred to as "spreading the overhead." Figure 22-4 shows that AFC graphs as a continuously declining curve as total output is increased.

AVC **Average variable cost** (AVC) for any output level is calculated by dividing total variable cost (TVC) by that output (Q):

$$AVC = \frac{TVC}{Q}$$

As output is increased by adding variable resources, AVC declines initially, reaches a minimum, and then increases again. A graph of AVC is a U-shaped or saucer-shaped curve, as shown in Figure 22-4.

Because total variable cost reflects the law of diminishing returns, so must AVC, which is derived from total variable cost. Due to initially increasing marginal returns, it takes fewer and fewer additional variable resources to produce each of the first 4 units of output. As a result, variable cost per unit declines. AVC hits a minimum with the fifth unit of output, and beyond this point AVC rises as diminishing returns require more and more variable resources to produce each additional unit of output.

In simpler terms, at very low levels of output production is relatively inefficient and costly. Because the firm's fixed plant is understaffed, average variable cost is relatively high. As output expands, however, greater specialization and better use of the firm's capital equipment yield more efficiency, and variable cost per unit of output declines. As still more variable resources are added, a point is reached where diminishing returns are incurred. The firm's capital equipment is now staffed more intensively, and therefore each added

FIGURE 22-3 **Total cost is the sum of fixed cost and variable cost** Total variable cost (TVC) changes with output. Total fixed cost (TFC) is independent of the level of output. The total cost (TC) at any output is the vertical sum of the fixed cost and variable cost at that output.

----

input unit does not increase output by as much as preceding inputs. This means AVC eventually increases.

You can verify the U or saucer shape of the AVC curve by returning to Table 22-1. Assume the price of labor is $10 per unit. By dividing average product (output per labor unit) into $10 (price per labor unit), we determine the labor cost per unit of output. Because we have assumed labor to be the only variable input, the labor cost per unit of output is the variable cost per unit of output or AVC. When average product is initially low, AVC is high. As workers are added, average product rises and AVC falls. When average product is at its maximum, AVC is at its minimum. Then, as still more workers are added and average product declines, AVC rises. The "hump" of the average-product curve is reflected in the saucer or U shape of the AVC curve. As you will soon see, the two are mirror images of each other.

ATC Average total cost (ATC) for any output level is found by dividing total cost (TC) by that output (Q) or by adding AFC and AVC at that output:

$$\text{ATC} = \frac{\text{TC}}{Q} = \text{AFC} + \text{AVC}$$

Graphically ATC can be found by adding vertically the AFC and AVC curves, as in Figure 22-4. Thus the vertical distance between the ATC and AVC curves measures AFC at any level of output.

Marginal Cost

One final and very crucial cost concept remains—marginal cost. **Marginal cost** (MC) *is the extra, or additional, cost of producing 1 more unit of output.* MC can be determined for each added unit of output by noting the *change* in total cost which that unit's production entails:

$$\text{MC} = \frac{\text{change in TC}}{\text{change in } Q}$$

Calculations In column 4, Table 22-2, production of the first unit of output increases total cost from $100 to $190. Therefore, the additional, or marginal, cost of that first unit is $90 (column 8). The marginal cost of the second unit is $80 (= $270 − $190); the MC of the third is $70 (= $340 − $270); and so forth. The MC for each of the 10 units of output is shown in column 8.

MC can also be calculated from the total-variable-cost column because the only difference between to-

FIGURE 22-4 **The average-cost curves** AFC falls as a given amount of fixed costs is apportioned over a larger and larger output. AVC initially falls because of increasing marginal returns but then rises because of diminishing marginal returns. Average total cost (ATC) is the vertical sum of average variable cost (AVC) and average fixed cost (AFC).

----

tal cost and total variable cost is the constant amount of fixed costs ($100). Thus, the *change* in total cost and the *change* in total variable cost associated with each additional unit of output are always the same.

Marginal Decisions

Marginal costs are costs the firm can directly and immediately control. Specifically, MC designates all the cost incurred in producing the last unit of output. Thus, it also designates the cost that can be "saved" by not producing that last unit. Average-cost figures do *not* provide this information. For example, suppose the firm is undecided whether to produce 3 or 4 units of output. At 4 units Table 22-2 indicates that ATC is $100. But the firm does not increase its total costs by $100 by producing the fourth unit, nor does it save $100 by not producing that unit. Rather, the change in costs involved here is only $60, as the MC column in Table 22-2 reveals.

A firm's decisions as to what output level to produce are typically marginal decisions, that is, decisions to produce a few more or a few less units. Marginal cost is the change in costs when 1 more or 1 less unit of output is produced. When coupled with marginal revenue (which we will find in Chapter 23 indicates the change in revenue from 1 more or 1 less unit of output), marginal cost allows a firm to determine if it is profitable to expand or contract its production. The analysis in the next three chapters centers on these marginal calculations.

Graphical Portrayal

Marginal cost is shown graphically in **Figure 22-5 (Key Graph).** Marginal cost at first declines sharply, reaches a minimum, and then rises rather abruptly. This reflects the fact that variable costs, and therefore total cost, increase first by decreasing amounts and then by increasing amounts (see columns 3 and 4, Table 22-2).

MC and Marginal Product

The marginal-cost curve's shape is a consequence of the law of diminishing returns. The relationship between marginal product and marginal cost can be seen by looking back to Table 22-1. If all units of a variable resource (here labor) are hired at the same price, the marginal cost of each extra unit of output will *fall* as long as the marginal product of each additional worker is *rising*. This is so because marginal cost is the (constant) cost of an extra worker divided by his or her marginal product. Therefore, in Table 22-1, suppose each worker can be hired for $10. Because the first worker's

marginal product is 10 output units and hiring this worker increases the firm's costs by $10, the marginal cost of each of these 10 extra units of output is $1 (= $10 ÷ 10 units). The second worker also increases costs by $10, but the marginal product is 15, so the marginal cost of each of these 15 extra units of output is $.67 (= $10 ÷ 15 units). Similarly, the MC of each of the 20 extra units of output contributed by the third worker is $.50 (= $10 ÷ 20 units). In general, as long as marginal product is rising, marginal cost will fall.

But as diminishing returns set in—in this case, with the fourth worker—marginal cost will begin to rise. Thus, for the fourth worker, marginal cost is $.67 (= $10 ÷ 15 units); for the fifth worker, MC is $1.00 ($10 ÷ 10 units); for the sixth, MC is $2.00 (= $10 ÷ 5 units), and so on. *If the price (cost) of the variable resource remains constant, increasing marginal returns will be reflected in a declining marginal cost, and diminishing marginal returns in a rising marginal cost.* The MC curve is a mirror reflection of the marginal-product curve. As you can see in Figure 22-6, when marginal product is rising, marginal cost is necessarily falling. When marginal product is at its maximum, marginal cost is at its minimum. And when marginal product is falling, marginal cost is rising.

Relation of MC to AVC and ATC

Figure 22-5 shows that the marginal-cost curve MC intersects both the AVC and ATC curves at their minimum points. As noted earlier, this marginal-average relationship is a mathematical necessity, which a simple illustration will reveal. Suppose a professional baseball pitcher has allowed his opponents an average of 3 runs per game in the first three games he has pitched. Now, whether his average falls or rises as a result of pitching a fourth (marginal) game will depend on whether the additional runs he allows in that extra game are fewer or more than his current 3-run average. If he allows fewer than 3 runs—for example, 1—in the fourth game, his total runs will rise from 9 to 10, and his average will fall from 3 to $2\frac{1}{2}$ (= 10 ÷ 4). Conversely, if he allows more than 3 runs—say, 7—in the fourth game, his total will increase from 9 to 16 and his average will rise from 3 to 4 (= 16 ÷ 4).

So it is with costs. When the amount (the marginal cost) added to total cost is less than the current average total cost, ATC will fall. Conversely, when the marginal cost exceeds ATC, ATC will rise. This

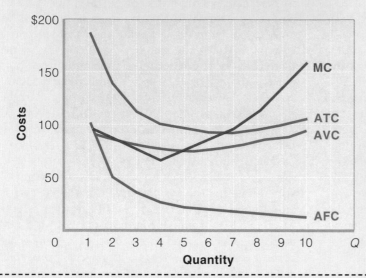

FIGURE 22-5 The relationship of the marginal-cost curve to the average-total-cost and average-variable-cost curves The marginal-cost (MC) curve cuts through the average-total-cost (ATC) curve and the average-variable-cost (AVC) curve at their minimum points. When MC is below average total cost, ATC falls; when MC is above average total cost, ATC rises. Similarly, when MC is below average variable cost, AVC falls; when MC is above average variable cost, AVC rises.

QUICK QUIZ 22-5

1. The marginal-cost curve first declines and then increases because of:
  a. increasing, then diminishing, marginal utility.
  b. the decline in the gap between ATC and AVC as output expands.
  c. increasing, then diminishing, marginal returns.
  d. constant marginal revenue.

2. The vertical distance between ATC and AVC measures:
  a. marginal cost.
  b. total fixed cost.
  c. average fixed cost.
  d. economic profit per unit.

3. ATC is:
  a. AVC − AFC.
  b. MC + AVC.
  c. AFC + AVC.
  d. (AFC + AVC) × Q.

4. When the marginal-cost curve lies:
  a. above the ATC curve, ATC rises.
  b. above the AVC curve, ATC rises.
  c. below the AVC curve, total fixed cost increases.
  d. below the ATC curve, total fixed cost falls.

Answers: 1. c; 2. c; 3. c; 4. a.

---

means in Figure 22-5 that as long as MC lies below ATC, ATC will fall, and whenever MC is above ATC, ATC will rise. Therefore, at the point of intersection where MC equals ATC, ATC has just ceased to fall but has not yet begun to rise. This, by definition, is the minimum point on the ATC curve. *The marginal-cost curve intersects the average-total-cost curve at the ATC curve's minimum point.*

Marginal cost can be defined as the addition either to total cost *or* to total variable cost resulting from 1 more unit of output; thus this same rationale explains why the MC curve also crosses the AVC curve at the AVC curve's minimum point. No such relationship exists between the MC curve and the average-fixed-cost curve, because the two are not related; marginal cost includes only those costs that change with output, and fixed costs by definition are those that are independent of output. **(Key Question 7)**

Shifting the Cost Curves

Changes in either resource prices or technology will cause cost curves to shift. If fixed costs rose—say, to $200 rather than the $100 we assumed in Table 22-2—then the AFC curve in Figure 22-5 would be shifted upward. The ATC curve would also move upward because AFC is a component of ATC. But the positions of the AVC and MC curves would be unal-

FIGURE 22-6 The relationship between productivity curves and cost curves The marginal-cost (MC) curve and average-variable-cost (AVC) curve in (b) are mirror images of the marginal-product (MP) and average-product (AP) curves in (a). Assuming that labor is the only variable input and that its price (the wage rate) is constant, then when MP is rising, MC is falling and when MP is falling, MC is rising. Under the same assumptions, when AP is rising, AVC is falling and when AP is falling, AVC is rising.

----

tered because their locations are based on the prices of variable rather than fixed resources. However, if the price (wage) of labor or some other variable input rose, the AVC, ATC, and MC curves would all shift upward, but the position of AFC would remain unchanged. Reductions in the prices of fixed or variable resources would entail cost curve shifts exactly opposite those just described.

If a more efficient technology were discovered, then the productivity of all inputs would increase. The cost figures in Table 22-2 would all be lower. To illustrate, if labor is the only variable input, wages are $10 per hour, and average product is 10 units, then AVC would be $1. But if a technological improvement increases the average product of labor to 20

units, then AVC will decline to $.50. More generally, an upward shift in the productivity curves shown in Figure 22-6a means a downward shift in the cost curves portrayed in Figure 22-6b. (See Global Perspective 22-1.)

QUICK REVIEW 22-2

■ The law of diminishing returns indicates that, beyond some point, output will increase by diminishing amounts as more units of a variable resource (labor) are added to a fixed resource (capital).

■ In the short run the total cost of any level of output is the sum of fixed and variable costs (TC = TFC + TVC).

■ Average fixed, average variable, and average total costs are fixed, variable, and total costs per unit of output; marginal cost is the extra cost of producing 1 more unit of output.

■ Average fixed cost declines continuously as output increases; average-variable-cost and average-total-cost curves are U-shaped, reflecting increasing and then diminishing returns; the marginal-cost curve falls but then rises, intersecting both the average-variable- and the average-total-cost curves at their minimum points.

LONG-RUN PRODUCTION COSTS

In the long run an industry and the individual firms it comprises can undertake all desired resource adjustments. The firm can alter its plant capacity; it can build a larger plant or revert to a smaller plant than assumed in Table 22-2. The industry can also change its plant size; the long run allows sufficient time for new firms to enter or existing firms to leave an industry. We will discuss the impact of the entry and exodus of firms to and from an industry in the next chapter; here we are concerned only with changes in plant capacity made by a single firm. We will couch our analysis in terms of average total cost (ATC), making no distinction between fixed and variable costs because all resources, and therefore all costs, are variable in the long run.

Firm Size and Costs

Suppose a single-plant manufacturer begins on a small scale and, as the result of successful operations, expands to successively larger plant sizes with larger

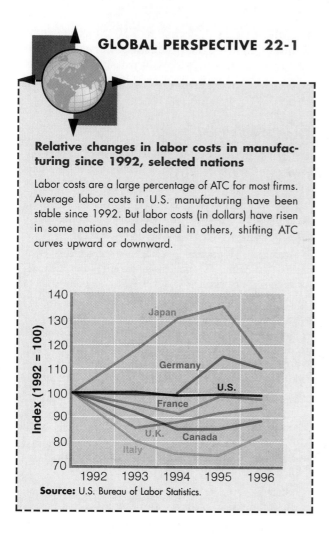
output capacities. What happens to average total cost as this occurs? For a time successively larger plants will lower average total cost. However, eventually the building of a still larger plant may cause ATC to rise.

Figure 22-7 illustrates this situation for five possible plant sizes. ATC-1 is the short-run average-total-cost curve for the smallest of the five plants, and ATC-5 that for the largest. Constructing larger plants will lower the minimum average total costs through plant size 3. But then larger plants will mean higher minimum average total costs.

The Long-Run Cost Curve

The vertical lines perpendicular to the output axis in Figure 22-7 indicate those outputs at which the firm should change plant size to realize the lowest attainable average total costs of production. These are the

outputs at which the per-unit costs for a larger plant drop below those for the current, smaller plant. For all outputs up to 20 units, the lowest average total costs are attainable with plant size 1. However, if the firm's volume of sales expands to some level greater than 20 units but less than 30, it can achieve lower per-unit costs by constructing a larger plant—plant size 2. Although *total* cost will be higher at the greater levels of production, the cost *per unit* of output will be less. For any output between 30 and 50 units, plant size 3 will yield the lowest average total costs. From 50 to 60 units of output, plant size 4 must be built to achieve the lowest unit costs. Lowest average total costs for any output over 60 units require construction of the still larger plant size 5.

Tracing these adjustments, we find that the long-run ATC curve for the enterprise is made up of segments of the short-run ATC curves for the various plant sizes which can be constructed. *The long-run ATC curve shows the least average total cost at which any output can be produced after the firm has had time to make all appropriate adjustments in its plant size.* In Figure 22-7 the dark green, bumpy curve is the firm's long-run ATC curve or, as it is often called, the firm's *planning curve.*

In most lines of production the choice of plant sizes is much wider than in our illustration. In many industries the number of possible plant sizes is virtually unlimited, and in time quite small changes in the volume of output will lead to changes in plant size. Graphically, this implies an unlimited number of short-run ATC curves, one for each output level, as suggested by **Figure 22-8 (Key Graph).** Then, rather than being comprised of *segments* of short-run ATC curves as in Figure 22-7, the long-run ATC curve is made up of all the *points of tangency* of the unlimited number of short-run ATC curves from which the long-run ATC curve is derived. Therefore, the planning curve is smooth rather than bumpy. Each point on it tells us the minimum ATC of producing the corresponding level of output.

Economies and Diseconomies of Scale

We have assumed that for a time larger and larger plant sizes will lead to lower unit costs but that beyond some point successively larger plants will mean higher average total costs. That is, we have assumed the long-run ATC curve is U-shaped. But why should this be? Note, first, that the law of diminishing re-

FIGURE 22-7 **The long-run average-total-cost curve: five possible plant sizes** The long-run average-total-cost curve is made up of segments of the short-run cost curves (ATC-1, ATC-2, etc.) of the various-size plants from which the firm might choose. Each point on the bumpy planning curve shows the least unit cost attainable for any output when the firm has had time to make all desired changes in its plant size.

----

turns does *not* apply in the long run. That's because diminishing returns presumes one resource is fixed in supply while the long run means all resources are variable. Also, our discussion assumes resource prices are constant. We can explain the U-shaped long-run average-total-cost curve in terms of economies and diseconomies of large-scale production.

Economies of Scale **Economies of scale,** meaning economies of mass production, explain the downsloping part of the long-run ATC curve, as indicated in Figure 22-9a, b, and c. As plant size increases, a number of factors will for a time lead to lower average costs of production.

1. *Labor specialization* Increased specialization in the use of labor becomes more possible as a plant increases in size. Hiring more workers means jobs can be divided and subdivided. Each worker may now have just one task to perform instead of five or six. Workers can work full time on those particular tasks for which they have special skills. In a small plant, skilled machinists may spend half their time performing unskilled tasks, leading to higher production costs.

Further, by working at fewer tasks, workers become proficient at those tasks. The jack-of-all-trades doing five or six jobs will not likely be efficient in any of them. Concentrating on one task, the same worker may become highly efficient.

Finally, greater labor specialization eliminates the loss of time which accompanies each shift of a worker from one task to another.

2. *Managerial specialization* Large-scale production also means better use of, and greater specialization in, management. A supervisor who can handle 20 workers is underused in a small plant which employs only 10 people. The production staff could be doubled with no increase in supervisory costs.

Small firms cannot use management specialists to best advantage. In a small plant a sales specialist may have to divide his or her time between several executive functions, for example, marketing, personnel, and finance. A larger scale of operations means the marketing expert can supervise marketing full time, while appropriate specialists perform other managerial functions. Greater efficiency and lower unit costs are the net result.

3. *Efficient capital* Small firms often cannot afford the most efficient equipment. In many lines of production this machinery is available only in very large and extremely expensive units.

FIGURE 22-8 **The long-run average-total-cost curve: unlimited number of plant sizes** If the number of possible plant sizes is very large, the long-run average-total-cost curve approximates a smooth curve. Economies of scale, followed by diseconomies of scale, cause the curve to be U-shaped.

QUICK QUIZ 22-8

1. **The unlabeled tinted curves in this figure illustrate the:**
   a. long-run average-total-cost curves of various firms constituting the industry.
   b. short-run average-total-cost curves of various firms constituting the industry.
   c. short-run average-total-cost curves of various plant sizes available to a particular firm.
   d. short-run marginal-cost curves of various plant sizes available to a particular firm.

2. **The unlabeled tinted curves in this figure derive their shapes from:**
   a. decreasing, then increasing, short-run returns.
   b. increasing, then decreasing, short-run returns.
   c. economies, then diseconomies, of scale.
   d. diseconomies, then economies, of scale.

3. **The long-run ATC curve in this figure derives its shape from:**
   a. decreasing, then increasing, short-run returns.
   b. increasing, then decreasing, short-run returns.
   c. economies, then diseconomies, of scale.
   d. diseconomies, then economies, of scale.

4. **The long-run ATC curve is often called the firm's:**
   a. planning curve.
   b. capital-expansion path.
   c. total-product curve.
   d. production possibilities curve.

Answers: 1. c; 2. b; 3. c; 4. a

Furthermore, effective use of this equipment demands a high volume of production, and that again requires large-scale producers.

In the automobile industry the most efficient fabrication method employs robotics and elaborate assembly line equipment. Effective use of this equipment demands an annual output of perhaps 200,000 to 400,000 automobiles. Only very large-scale producers can afford to purchase and use this equipment efficiently. The small-scale producer is faced with a dilemma. To fabricate automobiles using other equipment is inefficient and therefore more costly per unit. The alternative of purchasing the efficient equipment and underusing it at low levels of output is also inefficient and costly.

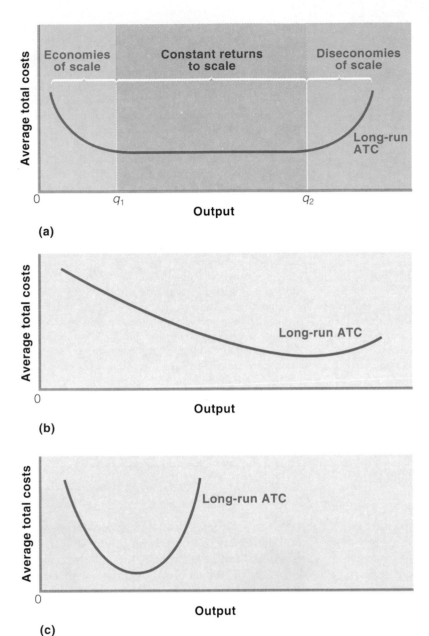

(a)

(b)

(c)

FIGURE 22-9 **Various possible long-run average-total-cost curves** In (a), economies of scale are rather rapidly obtained as plant size rises, and diseconomies of scale are not encountered until a considerably large scale of output has been achieved. Thus, long-run average total cost is constant over a wide range of output. In (b), economies of scale are extensive, and diseconomies of scale occur only at very large outputs. Average total cost therefore declines over a broad range of output. In (c), economies of scale are exhausted quickly, followed immediately by diseconomies of scale. Minimum ATC thus occurs at a relatively low output.

4. *Other factors* Many products entail design and development costs, as well as other "start-up" costs, which must be incurred irrespective of projected sales. These costs decline per unit as output is increased. Similarly, advertising costs decline per auto, per computer, per stereo system, and per box of detergent as more units are produced and sold.

All these factors contribute to lower average total costs for the producer able to expand its scale of operations. Where economies of scale are possible, an increase in *all* resources of, say, 10 percent will cause a more-than-proportionate increase in output of, say, 20 percent. The result will be a decline in ATC.

In many American manufacturing industries economies of scale have been of great significance. Firms which have expanded their scale of operations to obtain economies of mass production have survived and flourished. Those unable to expand became relatively high-cost producers, doomed to a struggle to survive.

Irrelevancy of Sunk Costs

Sunk costs should be disregarded in decision making.

There is an old saying: Don't cry over spilt milk. The message is that once you have spilled a glass of milk, there is nothing you can do to recover it, so you should forget about it and "move on from there." This saying has great relevance to what economists call *sunk costs*. Such costs are like sunken ships on the ocean floor: Once these costs are incurred, they cannot be recovered.

Let's gain an understanding of this idea by initially applying it to consumers and then to businesses. Suppose you bought an expensive ticket to an upcoming football game, but the morning of the game you wake up with a bad case of the flu. Feeling miserable, you step outside to find that the wind chill is about −10 degrees. You absolutely do *not* want to go to the game, but you remind yourself that you paid a steep price for the ticket. You call several people to try to sell the ticket, but you soon discover that no one is interested in it, even at a discounted price. You conclude that everyone who wants a ticket has one.

Should you go to the game? Economic analysis says that you should *not* take actions for which marginal cost exceeds marginal benefit. And, in this situation, *the price you paid for the ticket* is irrelevant to the decision. Both marginal or *additional* cost and marginal or *additional* benefit are forward looking. If the marginal cost of going to the game is greater than the marginal benefit, the best decision is to go back to bed. This decision should be the same whether you paid $2, $20, or $200 for the game ticket because the price that you pay for something does not affect its marginal benefit. Once the ticket has been purchased and cannot be resold, its cost is irrelevant to the decision to attend the game. Since "you absolutely do not want to go," clearly the marginal cost exceeds the marginal benefit of the game.

Here is a helpful second consumer example. Suppose a family is on vacation and stops at a roadside stand to buy some apples. The kids get back into the car and bite into their apples, immediately pronouncing them "totally mushy" and unworthy of another bite. Both parents agree that the apples are "terrible," but the father continues to eat his, because, as he says, "we paid a premium price for them." One of the older children replies, "Dad, that is irrelevant." Although not stated very diplomatically, the child, of course, is exactly right. In making a new decision, you should ignore all costs that are not affected by the decision. The prior bad decision (in retrospect) to buy

Diseconomies of Scale In time the expansion of a firm *may* lead to diseconomies and therefore higher average total costs.

The main factor causing **diseconomies of scale** is the difficulty of efficiently controlling and coordinating a firm's operations as it becomes a large-scale producer. In a small plant a single key executive may make all the basic decisions for the plant's operation. Because of the firm's small size, the executive is close to the production line, understands the firm's operations, and can digest information and make efficient decisions.

This neat picture changes as a firm grows. There are now many management levels between the executive suite and the assembly line; top management is far removed from the actual production operations of the plant. One person cannot assemble, digest, and understand all the information essential to decision making on a large scale. Authority must be delegated to many vice-presidents, second vice-presidents, and so forth. This expansion of the management hierar-

chy leads to problems of communication and cooperation, bureaucratic red tape, and the possibility that decisions will not be coordinated. Similarly, decision making may be slowed down to the point that decisions fail to quickly reflect changes in consumer tastes or technology. The result is impaired efficiency and rising average total costs.

Also, in massive production facilities workers may feel alienated from their employers and care little about working efficiently. Opportunities to shirk—to avoid work in favor of on-the-job leisure—may be greater in large plants than in small ones. Countering worker alienation and shirking may require additional worker supervision, which increases costs.

Where diseconomies of scale are operative, an increase in all inputs of, say, 10 percent will cause a less-than-proportionate increase in output of, say, 5 percent. As a consequence, ATC will increase. Diseconomies of scale are illustrated by the rising portion of the long-run cost curves in Figure 22-9.

the apples should not dictate a second decision for which marginal benefit is less than marginal cost.

Now let's apply the idea of sunk costs to firms. Some of a firm's costs are not only fixed (recurring, but unrelated to the level of output), but sunk (unrecoverable). For example, a nonrefundable annual lease payment for the use of a store cannot be recouped once it has been paid. A firm's decision about whether to move from the store to a more profitable location does not depend on the amount of time remaining on the lease. If moving means greater profit, it makes sense to move whether there are 300 days, 30 days, or 3 days left on the lease.

Or, as another example, suppose a firm spends $1 million on R&D to bring out a new product, only to discover that the product sells very poorly. Should the firm continue to produce the product at a loss even when there is no realistic hope for future success? Obviously, it should not. In making this decision, the firm realizes that the amount it has spent in developing the product is irrelevant; it should stop production of the product and cut its losses. In fact, many firms have dropped products after spending millions of dollars on their development. Examples are the quick decision by Coca-Cola to drop its New Coke and the eventual decision by McDonald's to drop its McLean Burger.

Consider a final real-world example. For decades, Boeing and McDonnell Douglas were keen rivals in the worldwide sale of commercial airplanes. Each company spent billions of dollars on R&D and marketing in an attempt to gain competitive advantages over each other. Then, in 1996 they suddenly merged. Many observers wondered how two fierce rivals who had spent such huge amounts to compete could suddenly forget the past and agree to merge. But these past efforts and expenditures were irrelevant to the decision; they were sunk costs. The forward-looking decision led both companies to conclude, each for their own reasons, that the marginal benefit of a merger would outweigh the marginal cost.

In short, if a cost has been incurred and cannot be partly or fully recouped by some other choice, a rational consumer or firm should ignore it. Sunk costs are irrelevant. Or, as the saying goes, Don't cry over spilt milk.

Constant Returns to Scale   In some industries there may exist a rather wide range of output between the output at which economies of scale end and the output at which diseconomies of scale begin. That is, there may be a range of **constant returns to scale** over which long-run average cost does not change. The q_1q_2 output range of Figure 22-9a is an example. Here a given percentage increase in *all* inputs of, say, 10 percent will cause a proportionate 10 percent increase in output. Thus, in this range ATC is constant.

Applications and Illustrations

The business world contains many examples relating to economies and diseconomies of scale. Here are just a few.

Textbooks   Next semester when you buy texts at your bookstore, compare the prices of introductory or basic texts with the prices of more specialized, advanced books. You may be surprised that the price of a two-semester principles of economics text is not much more, and perhaps less, than that of a one-semester advanced text. This is true even if the principles text is 200 pages longer and has a multicolor format, while the advanced book is in mundane black and white. Economies of scale are at work here. Both introductory and advanced texts entail design, editing, and typesetting costs which are about the same per page whether 5000 copies (of the advanced text) or 100,000 copies (of the introductory text) are printed. With introductory books these costs are spread over many more units of output, meaning lower unit costs and a comparatively low price per book.

Stealth Bombers   The notion of economies of scale has been invoked in debates over the national defense budget. When the Pentagon was proposing a fleet of 132 B-2 Stealth bombers, the estimated cost per plane was $580 million. But a proposed cut to 75 bombers by the Secretary of Defense caused the cost per plane to surge to over $800 million. The per-plane cost increase was due to the loss of scale economies associated with the smaller order. Much of the cost of designing and developing the plane is the same regardless of the number of units produced. This cost is significantly less per plane as more planes are manufactured.

A "Monster Machine" We pointed out that the use of the most technologically efficient equipment—and thus achievement of economies of scale—often demands a high volume of output. Specific example: In 1996 Verson (an American firm located in Chicago) introduced a 49-foot-tall metal stamping machine that is the size of a house and weighs as much as 12 locomotives. This $30 million machine, which cuts and sculpts raw sheets of steel into automobile hoods and fenders, enables automakers to make new parts in just 5 *minutes* compared with 8 *hours* for older stamping presses. A single so-called monster machine is designed to make 5 million auto parts a year. A firm desiring to achieve the cost saving delivered by this machine must have sufficient auto production to use all these parts.

General Motors Monster machines aside, executives of General Motors, the world's largest auto producer, are well aware of the realities of diseconomies of scale. In a classic statement relating to diseconomies of scale, a former GM president commented thus on GM's Chevrolet division:

> Chevrolet is such a big monster that you twist its tail and nothing happens at the other end for months and months. It is so gigantic that there isn't any way to really run it. You just sort of try to keep track of it.[1]

Experts on the auto industry have concluded that GM's large size is a liability; the company is one-third larger than Ford, more than three times larger than Chrysler, and larger than Toyota and Nissan combined. Compared with these domestic and foreign competitors, GM has a substantial cost disadvantage and a declining long-term market share. Despite billions of dollars of investment in modern equipment, GM still has the lowest productivity and the highest

cost-per-car in the industry.[2] To try to reduce scale diseconomies, GM has taken several actions. It has established joint ventures (combined projects) with smaller foreign rivals such as Toyota to reduce its production costs. It has created Saturn, a separate, stand-alone auto manufacturing company. It has given each of its five automotive divisions (Chevrolet, Buick, Pontiac, Oldsmobile, and Cadillac) greater autonomy with respect to styling, engineering, and marketing decisions to reduce the layers of managerial approval required in decision making. Finally, GM has reorganized into a small-car group and a midsize and luxury group to try to cut costs and bring new cars to the market faster. Whether these actions can overcome GM's diseconomies of scale remains to be seen.

Minimum Efficient Scale and Industry Structure

Economies and diseconomies of scale are an important determinant of an industry's structure. Here it is helpful to introduce the concept of **minimum efficient scale** (MES), which is the lowest level of output at which a firm can minimize long-run average costs. In Figure 22-9a this occurs at q_1 units of output. Because of the extended range of constant returns to scale, firms producing substantially greater outputs could also realize the minimum attainable average costs. Specifically, firms would be equally efficient within the q_1 to q_2 range. We would therefore not be surprised to find an industry with such cost conditions to be populated by firms of quite different sizes. The apparel, food processing, furniture, wood products, and small-appliance industries provide approximate examples. With an extended range of constant returns to scale, relatively large and relatively small firms could coexist in an industry and be equally successful.

Compare this with Figure 22-9b, where economies of scale occur over a wide range of output and diseconomies of scale appear only at very high levels of output. This pattern of declining long-run average total cost occurs over an extended range of output, as is the case in the automobile, aluminum, steel, and other heavy industries. Given consumer demand, ef-

---

[1] As quoted in Walter Adams (ed.), *The Structure of American Industry*, 8th ed. (New York: Macmillan, 1990), p. 115.

[2] Walter Adams and James W. Brock (eds.), *The Structure of American Industry*, 9th ed. (Englewoods Cliffs, NJ: Prentice-Hall, 1995), pp. 76–77, and F. M. Scherer, *Industry Structure, Strategy, and Public Policy* (New York: HarperCollins, 1996), pp. 324–325.

ficient production will be achieved with a few large-scale producers. Small firms cannot realize the minimum efficient scale and will not be able to compete. In the extreme, economies of scale might extend beyond the market's size, resulting in what is termed **natural monopoly**, a market situation in which average total cost is minimized when only one firm produces the particular good or service.

Where economies of scale are few and diseconomies come into play quickly, the minimum efficient size occurs at a low level of output, as shown in Figure 22-9c. In such industries a particular level of consumer demand will support a large number of relatively small producers. Many retail trades and some types of farming fall into this category. So do certain types of light manufacturing, such as the baking, clothing, and shoe industries. Fairly small firms are as efficient as, or more efficient than, large-scale producers in such industries.

Our point here is that the shape of the long-run average-total-cost curve is determined by technology and resulting economies and diseconomies of scale. The shape of the long-run ATC curve, in turn, can be significant in determining whether an industry is pop-

ulated by a relatively large number of small firms or dominated by a few large producers, or is somewhere between the two.

But we must be cautious because industry structure does not depend on cost conditions alone. Government policies, the geographic size of markets, managerial ability, and other factors must be considered in explaining the structure of a particular industry. **(Key Question 10)**

QUICK REVIEW 22-3

■ Most firms have U-shaped long-run average-total-cost curves, reflecting economies and then diseconomies of scale.

■ Economies of scale are the consequence of greater specialization of labor and management, more efficient capital equipment, and the spreading of start-up costs among more units of output.

■ Diseconomies of scale are caused by problems of coordination and communication which arise in large firms.

■ Minimum efficient scale is the lowest level of output at which a firm's long-run average total cost is at a minimum.

CHAPTER SUMMARY

1. Economic costs include all payments which must be received by resource owners to ensure a continued supply of needed resources to a particular line of production. This includes explicit costs, which flow to resources owned and supplied by others, and implicit costs, which are payments for the use of self-owned and self-employed resources. One implicit cost is a normal profit to the entrepreneur. Economic profit occurs when total revenue exceeds total cost (= explicit costs + implicit costs, including a normal profit).

2. In the short run a firm's plant capacity is fixed. The firm can use its plant more or less intensively by adding or subtracting units of variable resources, but the firm does not have sufficient time in the short run to alter plant size.

3. The law of diminishing returns describes what happens to output as a fixed plant is used more intensively. As successive units of a variable resource such as labor are added to a fixed plant, beyond some point the marginal product associated with each additional worker declines.

4. Because some resources are variable and others fixed, costs can be classified as variable or fixed in the short run. Fixed costs are independent of the level of output; variable costs vary with output. The total cost of any output is the sum of fixed and variable costs at that output.

5. Average fixed, average variable, and average total costs are fixed, variable, and total costs per unit of output. Average fixed cost declines continuously as output increases because a fixed sum is being spread over a larger and larger number of units of production. A graph of average variable cost is U-shaped, reflecting the law of diminishing returns. Average total cost is the sum of average fixed and average variable costs; its graph is also U-shaped.

6. Marginal cost is the extra, or additional, cost of producing 1 more unit of output. It is the amount by which total cost and total variable cost change when 1 more or 1 less unit of output is produced. Graphically, the marginal-cost curve intersects the ATC and AVC curves at their minimum points.

7. Lower resource prices shift cost curves downward, as does technological progress. Higher input prices shift cost curves upward.

8. The long run is a period of time sufficiently long for a firm to vary the amounts of all resources used, including plant size. In the long run all costs are variable. The long-run ATC, or planning, curve is composed of segments of the short-run ATC curves, and it represents the various plant sizes a firm can construct in the long run.

9. The long-run ATC curve is generally U-shaped. Economies of scale are first encountered as a small firm ex-

pands. Greater specialization in the use of labor and management, the ability to use the most efficient equipment, and the spreading of start-up costs among more units of output all contribute to economies of scale. As the firm continues to grow, it will encounter diseconomies of scale stemming from the managerial complexities which accompany large-scale production. The output ranges over which economies and diseconomies of scale occur in an industry are often an important determinant of the structure of that industry.

TERMS AND CONCEPTS

economic (opportunity)
    cost
explicit costs
implicit costs
normal profit
economic profit

short run
long run
total product
marginal product
average product
law of diminishing returns

fixed costs
variable costs
total cost
average fixed cost
average variable cost
average total cost

marginal cost
economies of scale
diseconomies of scale
constant returns to scale
minimum efficient scale
natural monopoly

STUDY QUESTIONS

1. Distinguish between explicit and implicit costs, giving examples of each. What are some explicit and implicit costs of attending college? Why does the economist classify normal profit as a cost? Is economic profit a cost of production?

2. KEY QUESTION Gomez runs a small pottery firm. He hires one helper at $12,000 per year, pays annual rent of $5000 for his shop, and spends $20,000 per year on materials. Gomez has $40,000 of his own funds invested in equipment (pottery wheels, kilns, and so forth) which could earn him $4000 per year if alternatively invested. Gomez has been offered $15,000 per year to work as a potter for a competitor. He estimates his entrepreneurial talents are worth $3000 per year. Total annual revenue from pottery sales is $72,000. Calculate the accounting profit and economic profit for Gomez's pottery.

3. Which of the following are short-run and which are long-run adjustments? **(a)** Wendy's builds a new restaurant. **(b)** Acme Steel Corporation hires 200 more workers. **(c)** A farmer increases the amount of fertilizer used on his corn crop. **(d)** An Alcoa aluminum plant adds a third shift of workers.

4. KEY QUESTION Complete the following table by calculating marginal product and average product from the data given.

Inputs of labor	Total product	Marginal product	Average product
0	0		
1	15	———	
2	34	———	———
3	51	———	———
4	65	———	———
5	74	———	———
6	80	———	———
7	83	———	———
8	82	———	———

Plot the total, marginal, and average products and explain in detail the relationship between each pair of curves. Explain why marginal product first rises, then declines, and ultimately becomes negative. What bearing does the law of diminishing returns have on short-run costs? Be specific. "When marginal product is rising, marginal cost is falling. And when marginal product is diminishing, marginal cost is rising." Illustrate and explain graphically.

5. Why can the distinction between fixed and variable costs be made in the short run? Classify the following as fixed or variable costs: advertising expenditures, fuel, interest on company-issued bonds, shipping charges, payments for raw materials, real estate taxes, executive salaries, insurance premiums, wage payments, depreciation and obsolescence charges, sales taxes, and rental payments on leased office machinery. "There are no fixed costs in the long run; all costs are variable." Explain.

6. List several fixed and variable costs associated with owning and operating an automobile. Suppose you are considering whether to drive your car or fly 1000 miles to Florida for spring break. Which costs—fixed, variable, or both—would you take into account in making your decision? Would any implicit costs be relevant? Explain.

7. KEY QUESTION A firm has $60 fixed costs and variable costs as indicated in the table below. Complete the table; check your calculations by referring to question 4 at the end of Chapter 23.
　a. Graph total fixed cost, total variable cost, and total cost. Explain how the law of diminishing returns influences the shapes of the variable-cost and total-cost curves.
　b. Graph AFC, AVC, ATC, and MC. Explain the derivation and shape of each of these four curves and their relationships to one another. Specifically, explain in nontechnical terms why the MC curve intersects both the AVC and ATC curves at their minimum points.
　c. Explain how the location of each curve graphed in question 7b would be altered if (1) total fixed cost had been $100 rather than $60, and (2) total variable cost had been $10 less at each level of output.

8. Indicate how each of the following would shift the **(a)** marginal-cost curve, **(b)** average-variable-cost

curve, **(c)** average-fixed-cost curve, and **(d)** average-total-cost curve of a manufacturing firm. In each case specify the direction of the shift.
　(1) A reduction in business property taxes
　(2) An increase in the nominal wages of production workers
　(3) A decrease in the price of electricity
　(4) An increase in insurance rates on plant and equipment
　(5) An increase in transportation costs

9. Suppose a firm has only three possible plant size options, represented by the ATC curves shown in the accompanying figure. What plant size will the firm choose in producing **(a)** 50, **(b)** 130, **(c)** 160, and **(d)** 250 units of output? Draw the firm's long-run average-cost curve on the diagram and describe this curve.

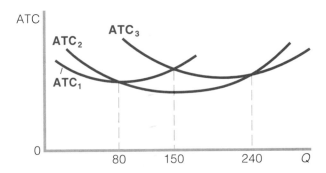

10. KEY QUESTION Use the concepts of economies and diseconomies of scale to explain the shape of a firm's long-run ATC curve. What is the concept of minimum efficient scale? What bearing can the shape of the long-run ATC curve have on the structure of an industry?

Total product	Total fixed cost	Total variable cost	Total cost	Average fixed cost	Average variable cost	Average total cost	Marginal cost
0	$_____	$ 0	$_____	$_____	$_____	$_____	$_____
1	_____	45	_____	_____	_____	_____	_____
2	_____	85	_____	_____	_____	_____	_____
3	_____	120	_____	_____	_____	_____	_____
4	_____	150	_____	_____	_____	_____	_____
5	_____	185	_____	_____	_____	_____	_____
6	_____	225	_____	_____	_____	_____	_____
7	_____	270	_____	_____	_____	_____	_____
8	_____	325	_____	_____	_____	_____	_____
9	_____	390	_____	_____	_____	_____	_____
10	_____	465	_____	_____	_____	_____	_____

11. (**Last Word**) What is a sunk cost? Why are such costs irrelevant in making decisions about future actions?

12. **WEB-BASED QUESTION** Economies/Diseconomies of Scale—Internal versus External Search Yahoo http://www.yahoo.com/ (select Options, then choose "An exact phrase match" for "diseconomies of scale" or "economies of scale") and answer the following: What is the difference between internal and external economies or diseconomies of scale? What are the factors which cause *internal* diseconomies of scale? What are the factors which cause *external* economies and diseconomies of scale? Would these internal/external factors affect small and large firms the same way?

13. **WEB-BASED QUESTION** Corporate Annual Reports—Identify Fixed and Variable Costs Every year, major corporations publish their annual reports, which show how well they performed financially during the past year. Part of the annual report is the income statement, which shows revenues, costs, and profit. Use one of the major search engines—http:/www.yahoo.com, http://www.infoseek.com, http:/www.aol.com/netfind/, http://www.excite.com, or http:// www.lycos.com—to locate the company of your choice. Review the company's income statement in its annual report and classify the nonrevenue items as either fixed or variable costs. Are all costs clearly identifiable as either fixed or variable? What item would be considered accounting profit? Would economic profit be higher or lower than this accounting profit? Explain. Note: Most annual reports on the Web are in Acrobat PDF file formats. Download the free PDF reader at http://www.adobe.com/prodindex/acrobat/readstep.htm.

23

Pure Competition

Chapters 20 to 22 provided the basic tools of analysis for understanding how product price and output are determined. But a firm's decisions concerning price and production will depend greatly on the character of the industry in which it is operating. There is no "average" or "typical" industry. At one extreme is a single producer that dominates the market; at the other extreme are industries in which thousands of firms each supply a minute fraction of total output. And between these extremes lies an unlimited variety of market structures.

We cannot possibly hope to examine each industry individually. Therefore, in the next three chapters we will focus on several basic *models* of market structures. Together, these models will help you understand, in a general way, how price and output are determined in the many product markets in our economy. They will also help you assess the extent of efficiency or inefficiency in those markets.

FOUR MARKET MODELS

Economists group the many industries into four distinct market structures: pure competition, pure monopoly, monopolistic competition, and oligopoly. These four market models differ as to the number of firms in the industry, whether those firms produce a standardized product or try to differentiate their products from those of other firms, and how easy or difficult it is for firms to enter the industry.

The main characteristics of the four models are summarized in Table 23-1. Briefly, we can describe them as follows:

1. *Pure competition* involves a very large number of firms producing a standardized product (one identical to that of other producers, such as corn or cucumbers). New firms can enter the industry very easily.

2. *Pure monopoly* is a market structure in which one firm is the sole seller of a product or service (a local electric company). Entry of additional firms is blocked so that the one firm *is* the industry. Because the monopolist produces a unique product, it makes no effort to differentiate its product.

3. *Monopolistic competition* is characterized by a relatively large number of sellers producing differentiated products (clothing, furniture, books). There is much *nonprice competition*, a selling strategy in which one firm tries to distinguish its product or service from all competing products on

TABLE 23-1 Characteristics of the four basic market models

Characteristic	Market model			
	Pure competition	Monopolistic competition	Oligopoly	Pure monopoly
Number of firms	A very large number	Many	Few	One
Type of product	Standardized	Differentiated	Standardized or differentiated	Unique; no close substitutes
Control over price	None	Some, but within rather narrow limits	Limited by mutual interdependence; considerable with collusion	Considerable
Conditions of entry	Very easy, no obstacles	Relatively easy	Significant obstacles	Blocked
Nonprice competition	None	Considerable emphasis on advertising, brand names, trademarks	Typically a great deal, particularly with product differentiation	Mostly public relations advertising
Examples	Agriculture	Retail trade, dresses, shoes	Steel, automobiles, farm implements, many household appliances	Local utilities

the basis of attributes like design and workmanship (an approach called *product differentiation*). Entry to these monopolistically competitive industries is quite easy.

4. *Oligopoly* involves only a few sellers; this "fewness" means that each firm is affected by the decisions of rivals and must take those decisions into account in determining its own price and output.

These descriptions and the characteristics outlined in Table 23-1 will come into sharper focus as we examine each model in detail. In discussing these four market models, we will occasionally distinguish the characteristics of a purely competitive market from those of the other basic market structures—pure monopoly, monopolistic competition, and oligopoly. To facilitate such comparisons we will employ the generic term **imperfect competition** to designate all those market structures which deviate from the purely competitive model.

PURE COMPETITION: CHARACTERISTICS AND OCCURRENCE

Let's expand our description of pure competition—the subject of this chapter:

1. *Very large numbers* A basic feature of a purely competitive market is the presence of a large number of independently acting sellers, often offering their products in large national or international markets. Markets for farm commodities, the stock market, and the foreign exchange market are illustrative.

2. *Standardized product* Purely competitive firms produce a standardized or homogenous product. If the price is the same, consumers will be indifferent about which seller to buy the product from. Buyers view the products of firms B, C, D, and E as perfect substitutes for firm A's product. Because purely competitive firms sell standardized products, they make no attempt to differentiate their

products and do not engage in other forms of nonprice competition.

3. **"Price takers"** In a purely competitive market *individual firms* exert no significant control over product price. This characteristic follows from the preceding two. Under pure competition each firm produces such a small fraction of total output that increasing or decreasing its output will not perceptibly influence total supply or, therefore, product price.

Assume there are 10,000 competing firms, each currently producing 100 units of output. Total supply is therefore 1,000,000. Now suppose one of these firms cuts its output to 50 units. This reduces the total quantity supplied from 1,000,000 to 999,950—not nearly enough of a change to affect product price noticeably. In short, the individual competitive producer is a **price taker:** the competitive firm cannot change market price but can only adjust to it.

That means the individual competitive producer is at the mercy of the market; product price is a given fact over which the producer exerts no influence. The firm gets the same price per unit for a large output as it does for a small output. To ask a price higher than the going market price would be futile. Consumers will not buy from firm A at $2.05 when its 9999 competitors are selling an identical product, and therefore a perfect substitute, at $2 per unit. Conversely, because firm A can sell as much as it chooses at $2 per unit, there is no reason for it to charge a lower price, say, $1.95, for to do so would shrink its profit.

4. **Free entry and exit** New firms can freely enter and existing firms can freely leave purely competitive industries. No significant obstacles—legal, technological, financial, or other—prohibit new firms from forming and selling their output in any competitive market.

Relevance of Pure Competition

Although pure competition is somewhat rare in practice, this market model is highly relevant for several reasons:

1. A few industries more closely approximate pure competition than any other market structure. In particular, much can be learned about markets for agricultural produce (wheat, rice), foreign exchange (pesos, yen), and seafood (salmon, lobsters) by understanding the pure competition model.

2. Pure competition provides the simplest context in which to apply the revenue and cost concepts developed in previous chapters. Pure competition is a clear and meaningful starting point for any discussion of price and output determination.

3. The operation of a purely competitive economy gives us a standard, or norm, against which the efficiency of the real-world economy can be compared and evaluated.

Pure competition is thus a market model which will help us observe and evaluate what goes on in the real world.

DEMAND AS SEEN BY A PURELY COMPETITIVE SELLER

In developing a tabular and graphical model of pure competition, let's first examine demand from a competitive seller's viewpoint and see how it affects revenue. Because each purely competitive firm offers a negligible fraction of total supply, it cannot influence the market price established by the forces of supply and demand. The purely competitive firm does not have a pricing strategy—it cannot *choose* the price for its product. Rather, it must accept the price predetermined by the market. The competitive seller is a *price taker,* not a *price maker.*

Perfectly Elastic Demand

Stated technically, the demand curve of the individual competitive firm is *perfectly elastic.* Columns 1 and 2 in Table 23-2 show perfectly elastic demand where the market price is assumed to be $131. The firm cannot obtain a higher price by restricting its output; nor does it have to lower price to increase its sales volume.

We are *not* saying that *market* demand is perfectly elastic in a competitive market. Instead, it graphs as a downsloping curve, as a glance ahead at Figure 23-7b reveals. In fact, the total-demand curves for most agricultural products are quite *in*elastic, even though agriculture is the most competitive industry in the U.S. economy. However, the demand schedule faced by the *individual firm* in a purely competitive industry is perfectly elastic.

The distinction comes about in this way: An entire industry—all firms producing a particular product—can affect price by changing industry output. For example, all firms, acting independently but simultaneously, can increase price by restricting supply.

TABLE 23-2 The demand and revenue schedules for a purely competitive firm

Firm's demand schedule		Firm's revenue data	
(1) Product price, P (average revenue)	(2) Quantity demanded, Q	(3) Total revenue, TR (1) × (2)	(4) Marginal revenue, MR
$131	0	$ 0	
131	1	131	$131
131	2	262	131
131	3	393	131
131	4	524	131
131	5	655	131
131	6	786	131
131	7	917	131
131	8	1048	131
131	9	1179	131
131	10	1310	131

But not so for the individual firm. If a single producer increases or decreases output, and the outputs of all other competing firms are constant, the effect on total supply and market price is negligible. Demand as seen by the single firm is therefore perfectly elastic, that is, horizontal, as in Figures 23-1 and 23-7a. This is the fallacy of composition at work. What is true for the industry or group of firms (a downsloping, less than perfectly elastic demand curve) is *not* true for the individual, purely competitive firm (a perfectly elastic demand curve).

Average, Total, and Marginal Revenue

The firm's demand schedule is simultaneously a revenue schedule. What appears in column 1, Table 23-2 as price per unit to the purchaser is also revenue per unit, or **average revenue,** to the seller. To say that all buyers must pay $131 per unit is to say that the revenue per unit, or average revenue, received by the seller is $131. Price and average revenue are the same thing seen from different points of view.

The **total revenue** for each sales level can be determined by multiplying price by the corresponding quantity the firm can sell. Multiply column 1 by column 2, and the result is column 3. In this case, total revenue increases by a constant amount, $131, for each additional unit of sales. Each unit sold adds exactly its constant price to total revenue.

When a firm is pondering a change in its output, it will consider how its revenue will *change* as a result of that change in output. What will be the additional revenue from selling another unit of output? **Marginal revenue** is the change in total revenue, that is, the extra revenue, which results from selling 1 more unit of

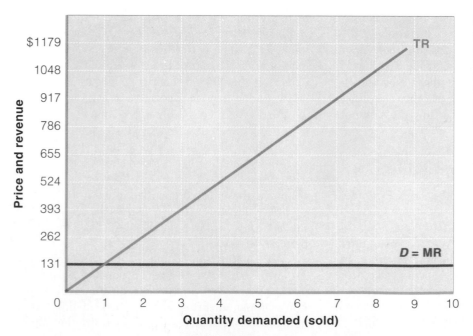

FIGURE 23-1 Demand, marginal revenue, and total revenue of a purely competitive firm Because a purely competitive firm can sell additional units of output at the market price, its marginal-revenue curve (MR) coincides with its perfectly elastic demand curve (*D*). The firm's total-revenue curve (TR) is a straight upsloping line.

output. In column 3, Table 23-2, total revenue is zero when zero units are sold. The first unit of output sold increases total revenue from zero to $131. Marginal revenue—the increase in total revenue from the sale of the first unit of output—is therefore $131. The second unit sold increases total revenue from $131 to $262, so marginal revenue is again $131. Note in column 4 that marginal revenue is a constant $131, because total revenue increases by a constant amount with every extra unit sold.

Under purely competitive conditions, product price is constant to the individual firm. Added units of output therefore can be sold without lowering product price. Each additional unit of sales contributes exactly its price ($131) to total revenue, and marginal revenue ($131) is precisely this addition to total revenue. So marginal revenue *equals* price in pure competition; it is constant because additional units can be sold at the constant price. **(Key Question 3)**

Graphical Portrayal

The purely competitive firm's demand curve and total-revenue and marginal-revenue curves are shown in Figure 23-1. The demand curve (*D*) is horizontal, indicating perfect elasticity. The marginal-revenue curve (MR) coincides with the demand curve because the product price (and hence MR) is constant. Total revenue (TR) is a line that slopes upward to the right. Its slope is constant—it is a straight line—because each extra unit of sales increases TR by the same $131.

> ### QUICK REVIEW 23-1
>
> ■ In a purely competitive industry a large number of firms produce a standardized product and there are no significant barriers to entry.
>
> ■ The demand seen by a competitive firm is perfectly elastic—horizontal on a graph—at the market price.
>
> ■ Marginal revenue and average revenue for a competitive firm coincide with the firm's demand curve; total revenue rises by the product price for each additional unit sold.

PROFIT-MAXIMIZATION IN THE SHORT RUN

Because the purely competitive firm is a price taker, it can maximize its economic profit (or minimize its loss) only by adjusting its *output*. And, in the short run, the firm has a fixed plant. Thus it can adjust its output only through changes in the amount of variable resources (materials, labor) it uses. The economic profit it seeks by adjusting its variable resources is the difference between *total revenue* and *total cost*. That fact gives us our direction. We will combine the revenue data of the previous section and the cost data of Chapter 22 to determine the profit-maximizing output of the competitive firm.

There are two ways to determine the level of output at which a competitive firm will realize maximum profit or loss. One way is to compare total revenue and total cost; the other is to compare marginal revenue and marginal cost. Both approaches apply not only to a purely competitive firm but also to firms operating in any of the other three basic market structures. To make sure you understand these approaches, we will apply both of them to output determination under pure competition. But since we want to emphasize the marginal approach, we will limit our graphical application of the total-revenue approach to a situation where the firm maximizes profits. We will then use the marginal approach to examine three cases: profit maximization, loss minimization, and shutdown.

Total-Revenue–Total-Cost Approach: Profit-Maximization Case

Confronted with the market price of its product, the competitive producer is faced with three related questions: (1) Should we produce? (2) If so, in what amount? (3) What profit (or loss) will we realize?

Let's demonstrate how a pure competitor answers these questions, given particular cost data and a specific market price. The cost data we will use are already familiar to you. They are the fixed-cost, variable-cost, and total-cost data in Table 22-2, repeated in columns 1 to 4, Table 23-3. Assuming that the market price is $131, we can obtain the total revenue for each output level by multiplying output (total product) by price. These data are presented in column 5. Then in column 6 the profit or loss at each output level is found by subtracting total cost, TC (column 4), from total revenue, TR (column 5). Now we have all the data needed to answer the three questions.

Should the firm produce? Definitely. It can realize a profit by doing so. How much should it produce? Nine units, because column 6 tells us this is the output at which total economic profit will be at a

TABLE 23-3   The profit-maximizing output for a purely competitive firm: total-revenue-total-cost approach (price $131)

| | | | | Price: **$131** | |
(1) Total product (output), Q	(2) Total fixed cost, TFC	(3) Total variable cost, TVC	(4) Total cost, TC	(5) Total revenue, TR	(6) Profit (+) or loss (−)
0	$100	$ 0	$ 100	$ 0	$−100
1	100	90	190	131	− 59
2	100	170	270	262	− 8
3	100	240	340	393	+ 53
4	100	300	400	524	+124
5	100	370	470	655	+185
6	100	450	550	786	+236
7	100	540	640	917	+277
8	100	650	750	1048	+298
9	100	780	**880**	**1179**	**+299**
10	100	930	1030	1310	+280

maximum. What will be the size of that profit? It will be $299, the difference between total revenue ($1179) and total cost ($880).

Figure 23-2a compares total revenue and total cost graphically for this *profit-maximizing case.* Total revenue is a straight line because under pure competition each additional unit adds the same amount—its price—to total revenue (Table 23-2). Total cost increases with output; more production requires more resources. But the rate of increase in total cost varies with the relative efficiency of the firm. Specifically, the cost data reflect Chapter 22's law of diminishing marginal returns. From zero to 4 units of output, total cost increases at a decreasing rate as the firm uses its fixed resources more efficiently. With additional output, total cost begins to rise by ever-increasing amounts because of the diminishing returns accompanying more intensive use of the plant.

Where the two curves in Figure 23-2a intersect (at roughly 2 units of output), total revenue and total cost are equal. All costs (including a normal profit) are covered by revenues, but there is no economic profit. For this reason economists call this output a **break-even point:** an output at which a firm makes only a *normal profit.* If we extended the data beyond 10 units of output, another break-even point would occur where total cost would catch up with total revenue somewhere between 13 and 14 units of output in Figure 23-2a. Any output within the two break-even

points identified in the figure will produce an economic profit. The firm achieves maximum profit where the vertical distance between the total-revenue and total-cost curves is greatest. For our particular data, this is at 9 units of output, where maximum profit is $299.

The profit-maximizing output is easily seen in Figure 23-2b, where we have graphed total profit for each level of output. Where the total-revenue and total-cost curves intersect in Figure 23-2a, economic profit is zero, as shown by the total-profit line in Figure 23-2b. Where the vertical distance between TR and TC is greatest in the upper graph, economic profit is at its peak ($299), as shown in the lower graph. This firm will choose to produce 9 units, since that output maximizes its profit.

Marginal-Revenue–Marginal-Cost Approach

There is another way a firm can decide how much to produce—one that fits perfectly with Chapter 1's discussion of the economic perspective. In this approach, the firm compares the amounts that each *additional* unit of output would add to total revenue and to total cost. In other words, the firm compares the *marginal revenue* (MR) and *marginal cost* (MC) of each successive unit of output. Any unit whose marginal revenue exceeds its marginal cost should be produced

(a) Profit-maximizing case

(b) Total economic profit

FIGURE 23-2 Total-revenue–total-cost approach to profit maximization for a purely competitive firm (a) The firm's profit is maximized at that output (9 units) where total revenue, TR, exceeds total cost, TC, by the maximum amount. (b) The vertical distance between TR and TC in (a) is plotted as a total-economic-profit curve. Maximum economic profit is $299 at 9 units of output.

----

because the firm would gain more in revenue from selling that unit than it would add to costs by producing it. Conversely, if the marginal cost of a unit of output exceeds its marginal revenue, the firm should not produce that unit because producing it would reduce profit (or increase loss). Production of that unit would add more to costs than to revenue; such a unit would not "pay its way."

MR = MC Rule In the initial stages of production, where output is relatively low, marginal revenue will usually (but not always) exceed marginal cost. It is

therefore profitable to produce through this range of output. But at later stages of production, where output is relatively high, rising marginal costs will exceed marginal revenue. Obviously, a profit-maximizing firm will want to avoid output levels in this range. Separating these two production ranges is a unique point at which marginal revenue equals marginal cost. This point is the key to the output-determining rule: *In the short run, the firm will maximize profit or minimize loss by producing that output at which marginal revenue equals marginal cost.* We call this profit-maximizing guide the **MR = MC rule.** For most sets of MR and MC data, MR and MC will be precisely equal at a fractional level of output. In such instances the firm should produce the last complete unit of output whose MR exceeds its MC.

Three Characteristics
There are three features of the MR = MC rule that you should know:

1. The rule assumes the firm will choose to produce rather than shut down. Shortly, we will note that marginal revenue must equal or exceed average variable cost or the firm will prefer to shut down rather than produce the MR = MC output.

2. The rule is an accurate guide to profit maximization for all firms—purely competitive, monopolistic, monopolistically competitive, or oligopolistic. The rule is *not* limited to the special case of pure competition.

3. The rule can be restated in a slightly different form when applied to a purely competitive firm. We have noted that the purely competitive firm can sell as much or as little as it chooses at the market price but cannot manipulate the price itself. In technical terms the demand, or sales, schedule faced by a competitive seller is perfectly elastic at the going market price. The result is that product price and marginal revenue are equal; that is, each extra unit sold adds precisely its price to total revenue, as shown in Table 23-2 and Figure 23-1. Thus, under pure competition—and *only* under pure competition—we may substitute price for marginal revenue in the rule, so that it

reads as follows: *To maximize profit or minimize loss, the competitive firm should produce at that point where price equals marginal cost* (P = MC).

Now let's apply the MR = MC or, because we are considering pure competition, the *P* = *MC* rule, first using the same price as in our total-revenue–total-cost approach to profit maximization. Then, by considering other prices, we can demonstrate two additional cases: loss minimization and shut down. *It is crucial that you understand the MR = MC analysis which follows; it is used not only in the remainder of this chapter but in the two chapters which follow.*

Profit-Maximizing Case
The first five columns in Table 23-4 reproduce the AFC, AVC, ATC, and MC data derived for our product in Table 22-2. It is the marginal-cost data of column 5 which we will compare with price (equals marginal revenue) for each unit of output. Suppose first that the market price, and therefore marginal revenue, is $131, as shown in column 6.

What is the profit-maximizing output? Every unit of output up to and including the ninth unit represents a greater marginal revenue than marginal cost of output. Each of the first 9 units therefore adds to the firm's profit and should be produced. The tenth unit, however, should not be produced. It would add more to cost ($150) than to revenue ($131).

Profit Calculations
The economic profit realized by producing 9 units can be calculated from the average-total-cost data. Multiplying price ($131) by

TABLE 23-4 The profit-maximizing output for a purely competitive firm: marginal-revenue–marginal-cost approach (price = **$131**)

(1) Total product (output)	(2) Average fixed cost, AFC	(3) Average variable cost, AVC	(4) Average total cost, ATC	(5) Marginal cost, MC	(6) Price = marginal revenue, MR	(7) Total economic profit (+) or loss (−)
0						$−100
1	$100.00	$90.00	$190.00	$ 90	$131	− 59
2	50.00	85.00	135.00	80	131	− 8
3	33.33	80.00	113.33	70	131	+ 53
4	25.00	75.00	100.00	60	131	+124
5	20.00	74.00	94.00	70	131	+185
6	16.67	75.00	91.67	80	131	+236
7	14.29	77.14	91.43	90	131	+277
8	12.50	81.25	93.75	110	131	+298
9	**11.11**	**86.67**	**97.78**	**130**	**131**	**+299**
10	10.00	93.00	103.00	150	131	+280

FIGURE 23-3 The short-run profit-maximizing position of a purely competitive firm The MR = MC output allows the purely competitive firm to maximize profits or minimize losses. In this case MR (= *P* in pure competition) and MC are equal at an output *Q* of 9 units. There *P* exceeds the average total cost *A* = $97.78, so the firm realizes an economic profit of *P* − *A* per unit. The total economic profit is represented by the gray rectangle and is 9 × (*P* − *A*).

---

output (9), we find that total revenue is $1179. Multiplying average total cost ($97.78) by output (9) gives us total cost of $880.[1] The difference of $299 (= $1179 − $880) is the economic profit.

Another way to calculate the economic profit is to determine the profit *per unit* by subtracting the average total cost ($97.78) from the product price ($131)

and multiplying the difference (a per-unit profit of $33.22) by output (9). Take some time now to verify the figures in column 7 in Table 23-4. You will find that any output other than that adhering to the MR = MC rule will mean either losses or profits below $299.

Graphical Portrayal Figure 23-3 (Key Graph) shows price (= MR) and marginal cost graphically. They are equal at the profit-maximizing output of 9 units. There the per-unit economic profit is *P* − *A*, where *P* is the market price and *A* is the average total cost for an output of 9 units. The total economic profit is 9 × (*P* − *A*), shown by the gray rectangular area.

---

[1]Most of the unit-cost data are rounded figures. Therefore, economic profits calculated from them will typically vary by a few cents from the profits determined in the total-revenue—total-cost approach. We here ignore the few-cents differentials to make our answers consistent with the results of the total-revenue—total-cost approach.

Note that the firm wants to maximize its total profit, not its per-unit profit. Per-unit profit is greatest at 7 units of output, where price exceeds average total cost by $39.57 (= $131 − $91.43). But by producing only 7 units, the firm would be forgoing the production of 2 additional units of output which would clearly contribute to total profit. The firm is happy to accept lower per-unit profits for additional units of output because they nonetheless add to total profit.

Loss-Minimizing Case

Now let's assume that the market price is $81 rather than $131. Should the firm still produce? If so, how much? And what will be the resulting profit or loss? The answers, respectively, are "Yes," "Six units," and "A loss of $64."

The first five columns in Table 23-5 are the same as those in Table 23-4. Column 6 shows the new price (equal to MR), $81. Comparing columns 5 and 6, we find that the first unit of output adds $90 to total cost but only $81 to total revenue. One might conclude: "Don't produce—close down!" But this would be hasty. Remember that in the very early stages of production, marginal product is low, making marginal cost unusually high. The price–marginal-cost relationship improves with increased production. For the next 5 units—units 2 through 6—price exceeds marginal cost. Each of these 5 units adds more to revenue than to cost. Column 7 shows that each of these units decreases the total loss. They more than compensate for the "loss" taken on the first unit. Beyond 6 units, however, MC exceeds MR (= P). The firm should therefore produce 6 units. In general, the profit-seeking producer should always compare marginal revenue (or price under pure competition) with the *rising* portion of the marginal-cost schedule or curve.

Loss Determination Will production be profitable? No, because at 6 units of output the average total cost of $91.67 exceeds the price of $81 by $10.67 per unit. If we multiply that by the 6 units of output, we find the firm's total loss is $64. Alternatively, comparing the total revenue of $486 (= 6 × $81) with the total cost of $550 (= 6 × $91.67), we see again that the firm's loss is $64.

Then why produce? Because this loss is less than the firm's $100 of fixed costs—the $100 loss the firm would incur in the short run by closing down. The firm receives enough revenue per unit ($81) to cover its average variable costs of $75 and also provide $6 per unit, or a total of $36, to apply against fixed costs. Therefore, the firm's loss is only $64 (= $100 − $36), rather than $100.

Graphical Portrayal This loss-minimizing case is shown graphically in Figure 23-4. Wherever price P exceeds average variable cost AVC, the firm can pay part, but not all, of its fixed costs by producing. The loss is minimized by producing the output at which MC = MR (here, 6 units). At that output, each unit contributes P − V to covering fixed cost, where V is the AVC at 6 units of output. The per-unit loss is A − P = $10.67, and the total loss is 6 × (A − P), or $64, as shown by the white area.

Shutdown Case Suppose now that the market yields a price of only $71. Should the firm produce?

FIGURE 23-4 The short-run loss-minimizing position of a purely competitive firm If price P exceeds the minimum AVC (here $74 at Q = 5) but is less than ATC, the MR = MC output (here 6 units) will permit the firm to minimize its losses. In this instance the loss is A − P per unit, where A is the average total cost at 6 units of output. The total loss is shown by the white area and is equal to 6 × (A − P).

TABLE 23-5 The loss-minimizing outputs for a purely competitive firm: marginal-revenue–marginal-cost approach (prices = $81 and $71)

(1) Total product (output)	(2) Average fixed cost, AFC	(3) Average variable cost, AVC	(4) Average total cost, ATC	(5) Marginal cost, MC	(6) **$81** price = marginal revenue, MR	(7) Profit (+) or loss (−), **$81** price	(8) **$71** price = marginal revenue, MR	(9) Profit (+) or loss (−), **$71** price
0						$−100		**$−100**
1	$100.00	$90.00	$190.00	$ 90	$81	−109	$71	−119
2	50.00	85.00	135.00	80	81	−108	71	−128
3	33.33	80.00	113.33	70	81	− 97	71	−127
4	25.00	75.00	100.00	60	81	− 76	71	−116
5	20.00	74.00	94.00	70	81	− 65	71	−115
6	**16.67**	**75.00**	**91.67**	**80**	**81**	**− 64**	71	−124
7	14.29	77.14	91.43	90	81	− 73	71	−143
8	12.50	81.25	93.75	110	81	−102	71	−182
9	11.11	86.67	97.78	130	81	−151	71	−241
10	10.00	93.00	103.00	150	81	−220	71	−320

No, because at every output the firm's average variable cost is greater than the price (compare columns 3 and 8 in Table 23-5). The smallest loss it can incur by producing is greater than the $100 fixed cost it will lose by shutting down (as shown by column 9). The best action is to shut down.

This shutdown situation can be seen in Figure 23-5. Price comes closest to covering average variable costs at the MR (= P) = MC output of 5 units. But even here, price or revenue per unit would fall short of average variable cost by $3 (= $74 − $71). By producing at the MR (= P) = MC output, the firm would lose its $100 worth of fixed cost *plus* $15

($3 of variable cost on each of the 5 units), for a total loss of $115. This compares unfavorably with the $100 fixed-cost loss the firm would incur by shutting down and producing no output. Hence, it will pay the firm to shut down rather than produce at a $71 price—or at any price less than the minimum average variable cost of $74.

The shutdown case obligates us to modify our MR (= P) = MC rule. *A competitive firm will maximize profit or minimize loss in the short run by producing that output at which MR (= P) = MC, provided that market price exceeds minimum average variable cost.*

FIGURE 23-5 The short-run shutdown position of a purely competitive firm If price P falls below the minimum AVC (here $74 at Q = 5), the competitive firm will minimize its losses in the short run by shutting down. There is no level of output at which the firm can produce and realize a loss smaller than its total fixed cost.

MARGINAL COST AND SHORT-RUN SUPPLY

You will recognize that in the preceding section we simply selected three different prices and asked what quantity the profit-seeking competitive firm, faced with certain costs, would choose to offer in the market at each of these prices. This information—product prices and corresponding quantities supplied—constitutes the supply schedule for the competitive firm.

Table 23-6 summarizes the supply schedule data for those three prices ($131, $81, and $71) and four others. This table confirms the direct relationship between product price and quantity supplied that we identified in Chapter 3. Note first that the firm will not produce at price $61 or $71 because both are less than the $74 minimum AVC. Then note that quantity supplied increases as price increases. Observe finally that economic profit is higher at higher prices.

Generalized Depiction

Figure 23-6 (Key Graph) generalizes the MR = MC rule and the relationship between short-run production costs and the firm's supply behavior. The ATC, AVC, and MC curves are shown, along with several marginal-revenue lines drawn at possible market prices. Let's observe quantity supplied at each of these prices:

1. Price P_1 is below the firm's minimum average variable cost, so at this price the firm won't operate at all. Quantity supplied will be zero, as it will be at all other prices below P_2.
2. Price P_2 is just equal to the minimum average variable cost. The firm will supply Q_2 units of output (where $MR_2 = MC$) and just cover its to-

tal variable cost. Its loss will equal its total fixed cost. (Actually, the firm would be indifferent as to shutting down or supplying Q_2 units of output, but we assume it produces.)

3. At price P_3 the firm will supply Q_3 units of output to minimize its short-run losses. At any other price between P_2 and P_4 the firm will minimize its losses by producing and supplying the quantity at which MR (= P) = MC.
4. The firm will just break even at price P_4. There it will supply Q_4 units of output (where MR_4 = MC), earning a normal profit but not an economic profit. Total revenue will just cover total cost, including a normal profit, because the revenue per unit ($MR_4 = P_4$) and the total cost per unit (ATC) are the same.
5. At price P_5 the firm will realize an economic profit by producing and supplying Q_5 units of output. In fact, at any price above P_4 the firm will obtain economic profit by producing to the point where MR (= P) = MC.

Note that each of the MR (= P) = MC intersection points labeled b,c,d and e in Figure 23-6 indicates a possible product price (on the vertical axis) and the corresponding quantity which the firm would supply at that price (on the horizontal axis). Thus, points such as these are on the upsloping supply curve of the competitive firm. Note too that quantity supplied would be zero at any price below the minimum average variable cost (AVC). *We can conclude that the portion of the firm's marginal-cost curve lying above its average-variable-cost curve is its* **short-run supply curve.** In Figure 23-6, the solid segment of the marginal cost curve MC *is* this firm's short-run supply curve. It tells us the amount of output the firm will supply at each price in a series of prices.

Diminishing Returns, Production Costs, and Product Supply

We have now identified the links between *the law of diminishing returns* (Chapter 22), *production costs,* and *product supply* in the short run. Because of the law of diminishing returns, marginal cost eventually rises as more units of output are produced. And because marginal cost rises with output, a purely competitive firm must get successively higher prices to entice it to produce additional units of output.

Viewed alternatively, higher product prices and marginal revenue encourage a purely competitive firm to expand output. As its output increases, its marginal

TABLE 23-6   The supply schedule of a competitive firm confronted with the cost data in Table 23-4

Price	Quantity supplied	Maximum profit (+) or minimum loss (−)
$151	10	$+480
131	9	+299
111	8	+138
91	7	− 3
81	6	− 64
71	0	−100
61	0	−100

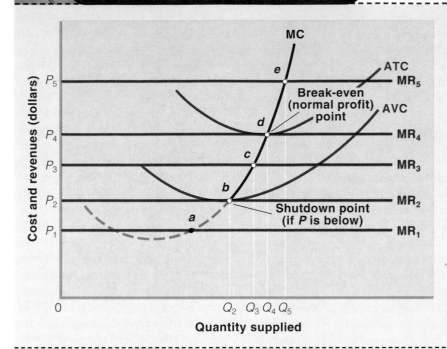

FIGURE 23-6 **The $P = MC$ rule and the competitive firm's short-run supply curve** Application of the $P = MC$ rule, as modified by the shutdown case, reveals that the (solid) segment of the firm's MC curve which lies above AVC is the firm's short-run supply curve. More specifically, at price P_1, $P = MC$ at point a, but the firm will produce no output because P_1 is less than minimum AVC. At price P_2 the firm will operate at point b, where it produces Q_2 units and incurs a loss equal to its total fixed cost. At P_3 it operates at point c, where output is Q_3 and loss is less than total fixed cost. With the price of P_4, the firm operates at point d; in this case the firm earns a normal profit because at output Q_4 price equals ATC. At price P_5 the firm operates at point e and maximizes its economic profit by producing Q_5 units.

QUICK QUIZ 23-6

1. **Which of the following might increase product price from P_3 to P_5?**
   a. An improvement of production technology
   b. A decline in the price of a substitute good
   c. An increase in the price of a complementary good
   d. Rising incomes if the product is a normal good

2. **An increase of price from P_3 to P_5 would:**
   a. shift this firm's MC curve to the right.
   b. mean that MR_5 exceeds MC at Q_3 units, inducing the firm to expand output to Q_5.
   c. decrease this firm's average variable costs.
   d. enable this firm to obtain a normal, but not an economic, profit.

3. **At P_4:**
   a. this firm has no economic profit.
   b. this firm will earn only a normal profit and thus will shut down.
   c. MR_4 will be less than MC at the profit-maximizing output.
   d. the profit-maximizing output will be Q_5.

4. **Suppose P_4 is $10, P_5 is $15, Q_4 is 8 units, and Q_5 is 10 units. This firm's:**
   a. supply curve is elastic over the Q_4–Q_5 range of output.
   b. supply curve is inelastic over the Q_4–Q_5 range of output.
   c. total revenue will decline if price goes up from P_4 to P_5.
   d. marginal-cost curve will shift downward if price falls from P_5 to P_4.

Answers: 1. d; 2. b; 3. a; 4. b.

cost of output rises as a result of the law of diminishing returns. At some now greater output, this higher MC equals the new product price and MR. Profit once again is maximized, but now at a greater total amount. Quantity supplied has increased in direct response to an increase in product price and the desire to maximize profit.

Supply Curve Shifts

In Chapter 22 we saw that changes in such factors as the prices of variable inputs or in technology will shift the marginal-cost or short-run supply curve to a new location. All else equal, for example, a wage increase would shift the supply curve in Figure 23-6 upward as viewed from the horizontal axis (leftward as viewed from the vertical axis), constituting a decrease in supply. Similarly, technological progress which increases the productivity of labor would shift the marginal-cost or supply curve downward as viewed from the horizontal axis (rightward as viewed from the vertical axis). This represents an increase in supply.

Firm and Industry: Equilibrium Price

In the preceding section we developed the competitive firm's short-run supply curve by applying the MR ($= P$) $=$ MC rule. We now determine which of the various possible prices will actually be the market equilibrium price.

From Chapter 3 we know that in a purely competitive market, equilibrium price is determined by *total*, or market, supply and total demand. To derive total supply, the supply schedules or curves of the individual competitive sellers must be summed. Columns 1 and 3 in Table 23-7 repeat the supply schedule for the individual competitive firm, as derived in Table 23-6. We now assume that there are 1000 competitive firms in this industry, all having the same total and unit costs as the single firm we discussed. This lets us calculate the market supply schedule (columns 2 and 3) by multiplying the quantity-supplied figures of the single firm (column 1) by 1000.

Market Price and Profits To determine the equilibrium price and output, these total-supply data must be compared with total-demand data. Let's assume total demand is as shown in columns 3 and 4 in Table 23-7. By comparing the total quantity supplied and total quantity demanded at the seven possible prices, we determine that the equilibrium price is $111 and the equilibrium quantity 8000 units for the industry— 8 units for each of the 1000 identical firms.

Will these conditions of market supply and demand make this a prosperous or an unprosperous industry? Multiplying produce price ($111) by output (8 units), we find the total revenue of each firm is $888. The total cost is $750, found by looking at column 4 in Table 23-3. The $138 difference is the economic profit of each firm. For the industry, total economic profit is $138,000. This, then, is a prosperous industry.

Another way of calculating economic profit is to determine per-unit profit by subtracting average total cost ($93.75) from product price ($111) and multiplying the difference (per-unit profit of $17.25) by the firm's equilibrium level of output (8). Again we obtain an economic profit of $138 per firm and $138,000 for the industry.

Graphical Portrayal Figure 23-7 shows this analysis graphically. The individual supply curves of each of the 1000 identical firms—one of which is shown as $s =$ MC in Figure 23-7a—are summed horizontally to get the total-supply curve $S = \Sigma$MC of Figure 23-7b. With total-demand curve D, it yields the equilibrium price $111 and equilibrium quantity (for the industry) 8000 units. This equilibrium price is given and unalterable to the individual firm; that is, each firm's demand curve is perfectly elastic at the equilibrium price, as indicated by d in Figure 23-7a. Because the individual firm is a "price taker," the marginal-revenue curve coincides with the firm's demand curve d. This $111 price exceeds the average total cost at the firm's equilibrium MR = MC output of 8 units, so the firm earns an economic profit represented by the gray area in Figure 23-7a.

Assuming no changes in costs or market demand, these diagrams reveal a genuine equilibrium in the short run. There are no shortages or surpluses in the market to cause price or total quantity to change. Nor can any of the firms in the industry increase its profit by altering its output. Note, too, that higher unit and marginal costs, on the one hand, or weaker market demand, on the other, could change the situation so that Figure 23-7a resembles Figure 23-4 or Figure 23-5. You are urged to sketch, in Figure 23-7a and b,

TABLE 23-7 Firm and market supply and market demand

(1) Quantity supplied, single firm	(2) Total quantity supplied, 1000 firms	(3) Product price	(4) Total quantity demanded
10	10,000	$151	4,000
9	9,000	131	6,000
8	*8,000*	*111*	*8,000*
7	7,000	91	9,000
6	6,000	81	11,000
0	0	71	13,000
0	0	61	16,000

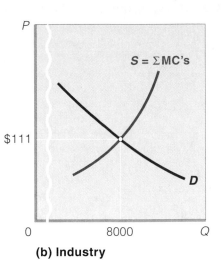

(a) Single firm   **(b) Industry**

FIGURE 23-7 Short-run competitive equilibrium for (a) a firm and (b) the industry The horizontal sum of the 1000 firms' individual supply curves (s) determines the industry supply curve (S). Given industry demand (D), the short-run equilibrium price and output for the industry are $111 and 8000 units. Taking the equilibrium price as given, the individual firm establishes its profit-maximizing output at 8 units and, in this case, realizes the economic profit represented by the gray area.

----

how higher costs or decreased demand could produce short-run losses.

Firm versus Industry Figure 23-7 underscores a point made earlier: Product price is a given fact to the *individual* competitive firm, but the supply plans of all competitive producers *as a group* are a basic determinant of product price. If we recall the fallacy of composition, we find there is no inconsistency here. Though one firm, supplying a negligible fraction of total supply, cannot affect price, the sum of the supply curves of all the firms in the industry constitutes the industry supply curve, and this curve does have an important bearing on price. **(Key Question 4)**

QUICK REVIEW 23-2

■ Profit is maximized, or loss minimized, at that output at which marginal revenue (or price in pure competition) equals marginal cost.

■ If the market price is below the minimum average variable cost, the firm will minimize its losses by shutting down.

■ The segment of the firm's marginal-cost curve which lies above the average-variable-cost curve is its short-run supply curve.

■ Table 23-8 summarizes the MR = MC approach to determining the competitive firm's profit-maximizing output. It also shows the equivalent analysis in terms of total revenue and total cost.

■ Under competition, equilibrium price is a given to the individual firm and simultaneously is the result of the production (supply) decisions of all firms as a group.

PROFIT MAXIMIZATION IN THE LONG RUN

In the short run there are a specific number of firms in an industry, each with a fixed, unalterable plant. True, firms may shut down in the sense that they can produce zero units of output in the short run, but they do not have sufficient time to liquidate their assets and go out of business. By contrast, in the long run firms already in an industry have sufficient time either to expand or to contract their plant capacities. More important, the number of firms in the industry may either increase or decrease as new firms enter or existing firms leave. We now examine how these long-run adjustments modify our conclusions concerning short-run output and price determination.

Assumptions

We make three simplifying assumptions, none of which affects our conclusions:

1. *Entry and exit only* The only long-run adjustment is the entry or exit of firms. Moreover, we ignore all short-run adjustments to concentrate on the effects of the long-run adjustments.

2. *Identical costs* All firms in the industry have identical cost curves. This assumption lets us discuss an "average," or "representative," firm knowing that all other firms in the industry are similarly affected by any long-run adjustments which occur.

3. *Constant-cost industry* The industry under discussion is a constant-cost industry. This means that the entry and exit of firms does *not* affect re-

TABLE 23-8   Output determination in pure competition in the short run

Question	Answer
Should this firm produce?	Yes, if price is equal to, or greater than, minimum average variable cost. This means that the firm is profitable or that its losses are less than its fixed cost.
What quantity should this firm produce?	Produce where MR (= P) = MC; there, profit is maximized (TR exceeds TC by a maximum amount) or loss is minimized.
Will production result in economic profit?	Yes, if price exceeds average total cost (TR will exceed TC). No, if average total cost exceeds price (TC will exceed TR).

source prices or, therefore, the locations of the average-total-cost curves of individual firms.

Goal

The basic conclusion we seek to explain is this: *After all long-run adjustments are completed, product price will be exactly equal to, and production will occur at, each firm's minimum average total cost.*

This conclusion follows from two basic facts: (1) Firms seek profits and shun losses, and (2) under pure competition, firms are free to enter and leave industries. If market price initially exceeds average total costs, the resulting economic profits will attract new firms to the industry. But this industry expansion will increase supply until price is brought back down to equality with minimum average total cost. Conversely,

if price is initially less than average total cost, resulting losses will cause firms to leave the industry. As they leave, total supply will decline, bringing the price back up to equality with minimum average total cost.

Long-Run Equilibrium

Consider the average firm in a purely competitive industry that is initially in long-run equilibrium. This firm is represented in Figure 23-8a, where MR = MC and price and minimum average total cost are equal at $50. Economic profit here is zero; the industry is in equilibrium or "at rest" because there is no tendency for firms to enter or to leave. The existing firms are earning normal profits, which, recall, are included in their cost curves. The $50 market price is determined in Figure 23-8b by market or industry demand

(a) Single firm

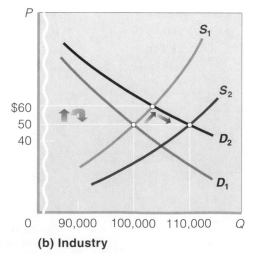

(b) Industry

FIGURE 23-8 Temporary profits and the reestablishment of long-run equilibrium in (a) a representative firm and (b) the industry A favorable shift in demand (D_1 to D_2) will upset the original industry equilibrium and produce economic profits. But those profits will cause new firms to enter the industry, increasing supply (S_1 to S_2) and lowering product price until economic profits are once again zero.

D_1 and supply S_1. (S_1 is a short-run supply curve; we will develop the long-run industry supply curve in our discussion.)

As shown on the quantity axes of the two graphs, equilibrium output in the industry is 100,000 while equilibrium output for the single firm is 100. If all firms in the industry are identical, there must be 1000 firms ($= 100,000/100$).

Entry Eliminates Economic Profits Let's upset the long-run equilibrium in Figure 23-8 and see what happens. Suppose a change in consumer tastes increases product demand from D_1 to D_2. Price will rise to $60, as determined at the intersection of D_2 and S_1, and the firm's marginal-revenue curve will shift upward to $60. This $60 price exceeds the firm's average total cost of $50 at output 100, creating an economic profit of $10 per unit. This economic profit will lure new firms into the industry. Some entrants will be newly created firms; others will shift from less prosperous industries.

As firms enter, the market supply of the product increases, pushing the product price below $60. Economic profits persist, and entry continues until short-run supply increases to S_2. Market price falls to $50, as does marginal revenue for the firm. Price and minimum average total cost are again equal at $50. The economic profits caused by the boost in demand have been eliminated, and as a result, the previous incentive for more firms to enter the industry has disappeared. Long-run equilibrium has been restored.

Exit Eliminates Losses Now let's consider a shift in the opposite direction. We begin in Figure 23-9a

with curves S_1 and D_1 setting the same initial long-run equilibrium situation as in our previous analysis, including the $50 price.

Suppose consumer demand declines from D_1 to D_3. This forces the market price and marginal revenued down to $40, making production unprofitable at the minimum ATC of $50. In time the resulting losses will induce firms to leave the industry. Their owners will seek a normal profit elsewhere rather than accept the below-normal profits (loss) now confronting them. And as capital equipment wears out, some firms will simply go out of business. As this exodus of firms proceeds, however, industry supply decreases, pushing the price up from $40 toward $50. Losses continue and more firms leave the industry until the supply curve shifts to S_3. Once this happens, price is again $50, just equal to the minimum average total cost. Losses have been eliminated and long-run equilibrium is restored.

Observe in Figure 23-9a and b that total quantity supplied is now 90,000 units and each firm is producing 100 units. The industry is populated by only 900 firms rather than the original 1000; losses have forced 100 firms out of the industry.

You may have noted that we have sidestepped the question of which firms will leave the industry when losses occur by assuming all firms have identical cost curves. In the "real world" entrepreneurial talents differ. Even if resource prices and technology are the same for all firms, inferior entrepreneurs tend to incur higher costs and therefore are the first to leave an industry when demand declines. Similarly, firms with less productive labor forces will be higher-cost producers and likely candidates to quit an industry when demand decreases.

(a) Single firm

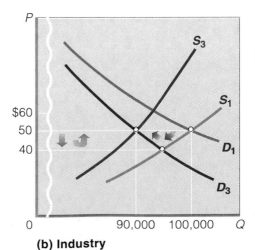

(b) Industry

FIGURE 23-9 Temporary losses and the reestablishment of long-run equilibrium in (a) a representative firm and (b) the industry An unfavorable shift in demand (D_1 to D_3) will upset the original industry equilibrium and produce losses. But those losses will cause firms to leave the industry, decreasing supply (S_1 to S_3) and increasing product price until all losses have disappeared.

We have now reached an intermediate goal: Our analysis verifies that competition, reflected in the entry and exit of firms, eliminates economic profits or losses by adjusting price to equal minimum long-run average total cost. In addition, this competition forces firms to select output levels at which average total cost is minimized.

Long-Run Supply for a Constant-Cost Industry

Although our analysis has dealt with the long run, we have noted that the market supply curves in Figures 23-8b and 23-9b are short-run curves. What then is the character of the **long-run supply curve** of a competitive industry? The analysis points us toward an answer. The crucial factor here is the effect, if any, that changes in the number of firms in the industry will have on costs of the individual firms in the industry.

Constant-Cost Industry   In our analysis of long-run competitive equilibrium we assumed the industry under discussion was a **constant-cost industry.** This means that industry expansion or contraction will not affect resource prices and therefore production costs. Graphically, it means the entry or exit of firms does not shift the long-run ATC curves of individual firms. This is the case when the industry's demand for resources is small in relation to the total demand for those resources. Then the industry can expand or contract without significantly affecting resource prices and costs.

Perfectly Elastic Long-Run Supply   What does the long-run supply curve of a constant-cost industry look like? The answer is contained in our previous analysis. There we saw that the entry and exit of firms changes industry output but always brings the product price back to its original level, where it is just equal to the constant minimum ATC. Specifically, we discovered that the industry would supply 90,000, 100,000, or 110,000 units of output, all at a price of $50 per unit. In other words, the long-run supply of a constant-cost industry is perfectly elastic.

This is demonstrated graphically in Figure 23-10, which uses data from Figures 23-8 and 23-9. Suppose industry demand is originally D_1, industry output is Q_1 (100,000 units), and product price is P_1 ($50). This situation, from Figure 23-8, is one of long-run equilibrium. We saw that when demand increases to D_2,

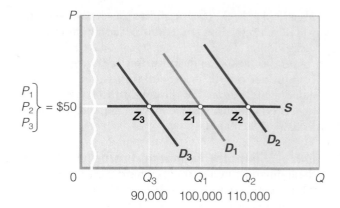

FIGURE 23-10 **The long-run supply curve for a constant-cost industry is horizontal**   Because the entry or exodus of firms does not affect resource prices or, therefore, unit costs, an increase in demand (D_1 to D_2) causes an expansion in industry output (Q_1 to Q_2) but no alteration in price ($50). Similarly, a decrease in demand (D_1 to D_3) causes a contraction of output (Q_1 to Q_3) but no change in price. This means that the long-run industry supply curve (S) is horizontal through points Z_1, Z_2 and Z_3.

upsetting this equilibrium, the resulting economic profits attract new firms. Because this is a constant-cost industry, entry continues and industry output expands until the price is driven back down to the level of the unchanged minimum ATC. This is at price P_2 ($50) and output Q_2 (110,000).

From Figure 23-9, we saw that a decline in market demand from D_1 to D_3 causes an exit of firms and ultimately restores equilibrium at price P_3 ($50) and output Q_3 (90,000 units). The points Z_1, Z_2, and Z_3 in Figure 23-10 represent these three price-quantity combinations. A line or curve connecting all such points shows the various price-quantity combinations that firms would produce if they had enough time to make all desired adjustments to changes in demand. This line or curve is the industry's long-run supply curve. In a constant-cost industry this curve (straight line) is horizontal, as in Figure 23-10, thus representing perfectly elastic supply.

Long-Run Supply for an Increasing-Cost Industry

Constant-cost industries are a special case. Most industries are **increasing-cost industries,** in which firms' ATC curves shift upward as the industry expands and downward as the industry contracts.

Usually, the entry of new firms will increase resource prices, particularly so in industries using specialized resources whose supplies are not readily increased in response to an increase in resource demand. Higher resource prices result in higher long-run average total costs for all firms in the industry. These higher costs cause upward shifts in each firm's long-run ATC curve.

Thus, when an increase in product demand results in economic profits and attracts new firms to an increasing-cost industry, a two-way squeeze works to eliminate those profits. As before, the entry of new firms increases market supply and lowers the market price. But now the entire ATC curve shifts upward. The overall result is a higher-than-original equilibrium price. The industry produces a larger output *at a higher product price* because the industry expansion has increased resource prices and the minimum average total cost. We know that, in the long run, the product price must cover ATC.

Since greater output will be supplied at a higher price, the long-run industry supply curve is upsloping. Instead of supplying either 90,000, 100,000, or 110,000 units at the same price of $50, an increasing-cost industry might supply 90,000 units at $45, 100,000 units at $50, and 110,000 units at $55. A higher price is required to induce more production because costs per unit of output increase as production rises.

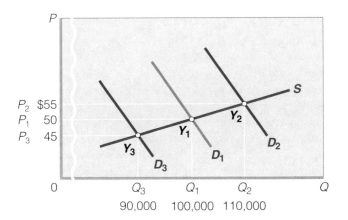

FIGURE 23-11 The long-run supply curve for an increasing-cost industry is upsloping In an increasing-cost industry the entry of new firms in response to an increase in demand (D_3 to D_1 to D_2) will bid up resource prices and thereby increase unit costs. As a result, an increased industry output (Q_3 to Q_1 to Q_2) will be forthcoming only at higher prices ($55 > $50 > $45). The long-run industry supply curve (S) therefore slopes upward through points Y_3, Y_1, and, Y_2.

We show this in Figure 23-11. Original market demand is D_1 and industry price and output are P_1 ($50) and Q_1 (100,000 units), respectively, at equilibrium point Y_1. An increase in demand to D_2 upsets this equilibrium and leads to economic profits. New firms enter the industry, increasing both market supply and production costs of individual firms. A new price is established at point Y_2, where P_2 is $55 and Q_2 is 110,000 units.

Conversely, a decline in demand from D_1 to D_3 makes production unprofitable and causes firms to leave the industry. The resulting decline in resource prices reduces the minimum average total cost of production for firms which stay. A new equilibrium price is established at some level below the original price, say, at point Y_3, where P_3 is $45 and Q_3 is 90,000 units. Connecting these three equilibrium positions, we derive the upsloping long-run supply curve S in Figure 23-11.

Long-Run Supply for a Decreasing-Cost Industry

In industries known as **decreasing-cost industries,** firms may experience lower costs as the industry expands. Classic example: As more mines are established in a particular locality, each firm's costs of pumping out water seepage decline because with more mines pumping, seepage into each is less. Moreover, with only a few mines in an area, industry output might be so small that only relatively primitive and therefore costly transportation facilities are available. But as the number of firms and their output expand, a railroad might build a spur into the area and thereby significantly reduce transportation costs.

We urge you to rework the analysis underlying Figure 23-11 to show that the long-run supply curve of a decreasing-cost industry is *downsloping.* **(Key Question 6)**

PURE COMPETITION AND EFFICIENCY

Our final goal in this chapter is to relate pure competition to efficiency. Whether a purely competitive industry is a constant-cost industry or an increasing-cost industry, the final long-run equilibrium positions of all firms have the same basic characteristics relating to economic efficiency. As shown in **Figure 23-12 (Key Graph),** price (and marginal revenue) will

FIGURE 23-12 The long-run equilibrium position of a competitive firm: *P* = MC = minimum ATC The equality of price and minimum average total cost indicates that the firm is using the most efficient known technology and is charging the lowest price *P* and producing the greatest output *Q* consistent with its costs. The equality of price and marginal cost indicates that resources are being allocated in accordance with consumer preferences.

settle where it is equal to minimum average total cost: *P* (and MR) = minimum ATC. Moreover, since the marginal-cost curve intersects the average-total-cost curve at its minimum point, marginal cost and average total cost are equal: MC = minimum ATC. Thus in long-run equilibrium there is a multiple equality: *P* (and MR) = MC = minimum ATC.

This triple equality tells us that although a competitive firm may realize economic profit or loss in the short run, it will earn only a normal profit by producing in accordance with the MR (= *P*) = MC rule in the long run. Also, this triple equality suggests certain conclusions of great social significance concerning the efficiency of a purely competitive economy.

Economists agree that, subject to certain qualifications discussed shortly, a purely competitive economy leads to an efficient use of society's scarce resources. *A competitive market economy uses the limited amounts of resources available to society in a way which maximizes the satisfaction of consumers.* As we discussed in Chapter 2, efficient use of limited resources requires both productive efficiency and allocative efficiency.

Productive efficiency requires that goods be produced in the least costly way. **Allocative efficiency** requires that resources be apportioned among firms and industries so as to yield the mix of products and services which is most wanted by society (consumers). Allocative efficiency has been realized when it is impossible to alter the composition of total output and achieve a net gain for society. Let's look at how productive and allocative efficiency would be achieved under purely competitive conditions.

Productive Efficiency: *P* = Minimum ATC

In the long run, pure competition forces firms to produce at the minimum average total cost of production and to charge a price which is just consistent with that cost, a highly favorable situation from the consumer's point of view. It means that firms must use the best-available (least-cost) production methods and combinations of inputs or they will not survive. Stated differently, it means the minimum amount of resources will be used to produce any particular output.

For an example, in the final equilibrium position shown in Figure 23-9a, each firm in the industry is producing 100 units of output by using $5000 (equal to average total cost of $50 times 100 units) worth of resources. If one firm produced that same output at a total cost of, say, $7000, its resources would be used inefficiently. Society would be faced with a net loss of $2000 worth of alternative products. But this cannot happen in pure competition; this firm would incur a loss of $2000, requiring it either to reduce its costs or quit its business.

Note, too, that consumers benefit from productive efficiency by paying the lowest product price possible under the prevailing technology and cost conditions.

Allocative Efficiency: *P* = MC

Productive efficiency alone does not ensure the efficient allocation of resources. Productive efficiency must be used to provide society with the "right goods"—the goods consumers want most. Before we can show that the competitive market system does just that, we must discuss the social meaning of product prices. There are two critical elements here:

1. The money price of any product—say, product X—is society's measure of the relative worth of an additional unit of that good. In other words, the price of a product reflects the *marginal benefit* derived from the good.

2. Similarly, recalling the idea of opportunity cost, we see that the marginal cost of product X measures the value, or relative worth, of the other goods which the resources used in producing an extra unit of X could otherwise have produced. In short, the *marginal cost* of producing a unit of X measures society's sacrifice of goods that could have been produced instead of X.

To understand why *P* = MC defines allocative efficiency, let's first look at situations where this is not the case.

Underallocation: *P* > MC In pure competition, a firm will realize the maximum possible profit only by producing where price equals marginal cost (Figure 23-12). Producing less of X, so that MR (and thus *P*) exceeds MC, yields less than maximum profit. It also entails an *underallocation* of resources to this product from society's standpoint. The fact that price still exceeds marginal cost indicates that society values additional units of X more highly than the alternative products the appropriate resources could otherwise produce.

To illustrate, if the price or marginal benefit of a shirt is $20 and its marginal cost is $16, producing an additional shirt will cause a net increase in total well-being of $4. Society will gain a shirt valued at $20, while the alternative products sacrificed by allocating more resources to shirts would be valued at only $16. Whenever society can gain something valued at $20 by giving up something valued at $16, the initial allocation of resources must have been inefficient.

Overallocation: *P* < MC For similar reasons, the production of X should not go beyond the output at which price equals marginal cost. To produce where MR (and thus *P*) is less than MC would yield less than the maximum profit for the producer and entail an *overallocation* of resources to X from the standpoint of society. Producing X where its marginal cost exceeds its price or marginal benefit means than X is being produced by sacrificing alternative goods while society values more highly than added units of X.

For example, if the price of a shirt is $20 and its marginal cost is $26, then the production of one less shirt would result in a net increase in society's total well-being of $6. Society would lose a shirt valued at $20, but reallocating the freed resources to their best alternative uses would increase the output of some other good valued at $26. Whenever society is able to give up something of lesser value in return for something of greater value, the original allocation of resources must have been inefficient.

Efficient Allocation Our conclusion must be that in pure competition, when profit-motivated firms produce each good or service to the point where price (marginal benefit) and marginal cost are equal, society's resources are being allocated efficiently. Each item is being produced to the point at which the value

Pure Competition and Consumer Surplus

Pure competition provides consumers with the largest utility surplus that is consistent with keeping the product in production.

In almost all markets, consumers collectively obtain more utility (total satisfaction) from their purchases than the amount of their expenditures (product price × quantity). This surplus of utility arises because some consumers are willing to pay more than the equilibrium price but need not do so.

Consider the market for oranges depicted in the accompanying figure. The demand curve D tells us that some consumers of oranges are willing to pay more than the $4 equilibrium price per bag. For example, assume Bob is willing to pay $9; Barb, $8; Bill, $7; Bart, $6; and Brent, $5. Betty, in contrast, is *un*willing to pay one penny more than the $4 equilibrium price.

There are many other consumers besides Bob, Barb, Bill, Bart, and Brent in this market who are willing to pay prices above $4. Only Betty pays exactly the price she is willing to pay; the others receive some amount of utility beyond their expenditures. The difference between that util-

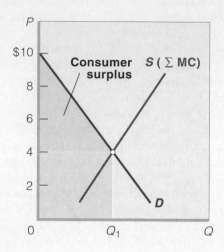

of the last unit is equal to the value of the alternative goods sacrificed by its production. To alter the production of product X would reduce consumer satisfaction. To produce X beyond the $P = MC$ point would sacrifice alternative goods whose value to society exceeds that of the extra units of X. To produce X short of the $P = MC$ point would sacrifice units of X which society values more than the alternative goods its resources can produce.

Dynamic Adjustments A further attribute of purely competitive markets is their ability to restore efficiency when disrupted by changes in the economy. A change in consumer tastes, resource supplies, or technology will automatically set in motion the appropriate realignments of resources. We have already explained what happens when a change in consumer tastes increases the demand for product X. First, its price will increase so that, at its present output, the price of X will exceed its marginal cost. At this point efficiency will be lost, but the higher price will create economic profits in industry X and stimulate its expansion. The profitability of X will permit the industry to bid resources away from now less pressing uses. Expansion of this industry will end only when the price of X and its marginal cost are

equal, that is, when allocative efficiency has been restored.

Similarly, a change in the supply of a particular resource or in a production technique will upset an existing price-marginal-cost equality by either raising or lowering marginal cost. The resulting inequality will cause business executives, in either pursuing profit or avoiding loss, to reallocate resources until price once again equals marginal cost. In so doing, they will correct any inefficiency in the allocation of resources which the original change may have temporarily imposed on the economy.

"Invisible Hand" Revisited A final point: The highly efficient allocation of resources which a purely competitive economy promotes comes about because businesses and resource suppliers freely seek to further their own self-interests. The "invisible hand" (Chapter 4) is at work in a competitive market system. The competitive system not only maximizes profits for individual producers but simultaneously results in a pattern of resource allocation which maximizes consumer satisfaction. The invisible hand thus organizes the *private interests* of producers in a way that is fully in accord with *society's interest* in using scarce resources efficiently. **(Key Question 7)**

ity value (measured by the vertical height of the points on the demand curve) and the $4 price is called *consumer surplus*. When we add together each buyer's utility surplus, we obtain the consumer surplus for all the consumers in the market. To get the Q_1 bags of oranges, consumers collectively are *willing to pay* the sum of the amounts represented by the blue-green triangle and gray rectangle. However, they only *have to pay* the amount represented by the gray rectangle. The blue-green triangle thus represents consumer surplus.

A glance at the figure shows that the amount of consumer surplus—the size of the blue-green triangle—would be less if the sellers could charge some price above $4. As just one example, at a price of $8, only a very small triangle of consumer surplus would exist. But purely competitive firms cannot charge $8 because they are price takers. Any firm that charged a price above $4 would immediately lose all its business to the other firms.

Moreover, we know that in pure competition the equilibrium price equals the marginal cost of the Q_1 bags of oranges. And, since we are assuming that entry and exit have resulted in this price being equal to lowest average total cost, each seller is earning only a normal profit. By

definition, this profit is just sufficient to continue production of oranges.

The principle that emerges is this: By establishing the lowest price consistent with continued production, pure competition yields the largest sustainable amount of consumer surplus.

QUICK REVIEW 23-3

■ In the long run, the entry of firms into an industry will compete away any economic profits and the exit of firms will eliminate losses so that price and minimum average total cost are equal.

■ The long-run supply curves of constant-, or increasing-, and decreasing-cost industries are horizontal, upsloping, and downsloping, respectively.

■ In purely competitive markets both productive efficiency (price equals minimum average total cost) and allocative efficiency (price equals marginal cost) are achieved in the long run.

Qualifications

Our conclusion that a purely competitive market system results in both productive and allocative efficiency must be qualified in several respects.

Market Failure: Spillovers and Public Goods

In the market system, each producer will assume only those costs which it *must* pay. In some lines of production there are significant costs producers can and do avoid, usually by polluting the environment. Recall from Chapter 5 that these avoided costs accrue to so-

ciety and are aptly called *spillover* or *external costs*. On the other hand, when individuals consume certain goods and services, such as education and measles vaccinations, widespread benefits accrue to society as a whole. These satisfactions are called *spillover* or *external benefits*.

The profit-seeking activities of pure competitors will bring about an allocation of resources which is efficient from society's point of view only if (1) marginal cost embodies *all* the costs which production entails and (2) product price accurately reflects *all* the benefits which society gets from a good. Only then will competitive production at the MR (= P) = MC point balance the *total* sacrifices and satisfactions of society and result in an efficient allocation of resources. If price and marginal cost are not accurate indexes of sacrifices and satisfactions—if sizable spillover costs and benefits exist—production at the MR (= P) = MC point will *not* signify an efficient allocation of resources.

Remember, too, the point of the lighthouse example in Chapter 5: The market system does not provide for social or public goods, that is, for goods to which the exclusion principle does *not* apply. Despite its other virtues, the competitive price system ignores an important class of goods and services—national defense, flood control, public parks, and so forth—which can and do yield satisfaction to consumers but which cannot be priced and sold through the market system.

Economies of Scale In developing the pure competition model, we assumed that all producers were operating at their optimal size. But in certain lines of production, existing technology may be such that a firm must be a large-scale producer to realize the lowest per-unit costs of production. Given consumer demand, this suggests that in some industries a relatively small number of large-scale producers are needed if production is to be carried out efficiently. If the large number of small-scale producers needed for pure competition populated those industries, then major efficiencies would be lost.

Technological Advance Some economists believe that a purely competitive economy would not foster a very rapid rate of technological progress. The incentive for research and development may be weak under pure competition since profit, even that resulting from a technological improvement, is at best only

temporary because of ease of entry. Also, the small size of the typical competitive firm and the fact that it tends to "break even" in the long run make it difficult for producers to finance substantial research and development programs. Thus, pure competition may not motivate the development of new production techniques or lead to improvements in existing products or the creation of new ones. We will return to the question of technological progress after our discussion of the other market structures.

Range of Consumer Choice A purely competitive economy might not provide a sufficient range of product choice for consumers. Pure competition means product standardization, whereas other market structures—for example, monopolistic competition and, frequently, oligopoly—promote a wide range of types, styles, and quality levels of products. This product variety widens the range of free choice available to consumers and simultaneously allows them to more completely fulfill their preferences.

CHAPTER SUMMARY

1. Economists group industries into four models based on their market structures: (**a**) pure competition, (**b**) pure monopoly, (**c**) monopolistic competition, and (**d**) oligopoly.

2. A purely competitive industry consists of a large number of independent firms producing a standardized product. Pure competition assumes that firms and resources are mobile among different industries.

3. No single firm can influence market price in a competitive industry; the firm's demand curve is perfectly elastic and price therefore equals marginal revenue.

4. Short-run profit maximization by a competitive firm can be analyzed by comparing total revenue and total cost or applying marginal analysis. A firm maximizes its short-run profit by producing that output at which total revenue exceeds total cost by the greatest amount.

5. Provided price exceeds minimum average variable cost, a competitive firm maximizes profit or minimizes loss in the short run by producing that output at which price or marginal revenue equals marginal cost. If price is less than average variable cost, the firm minimizes its loss by shutting down. If price is greater than average variable cost but less than average total cost, the firm minimizes its loss by producing the $P = MC$ output. If price also exceeds average to-

tal cost, the firm maximizes its economic profit at the $P = MC$ output.

6. Applying that MR $(= P) = $ MC rule at various possible market prices leads to the conclusion that the segment of the firm's short-run marginal-cost curve lying above its average-variable-cost curve is its short-run supply curve.

7. In the long run, the market price of a product will equal the minimum average total cost of production. At a greater price, economic profits would cause firms to enter the competitive industry until those profits had been competed away. At a lesser price, losses would force the exit of firms from the industry until the product price rose to equal average total cost.

8. The long-run supply curve is horizontal for a constant-cost industry, upsloping for an increasing-cost industry, and downsloping for a decreasing-cost industry.

9. The long-run equality of price and minimum average total cost means that competitive firms will use the most efficient known technology and charge the lowest price consistent with their production costs.

10. The long-run equality of price and marginal cost implies that resources will be allocated in accordance with consumer tastes. The competitive price system will reallocate resources in response to a change in consumer tastes, technology, or resource supplies to maintain allocative efficiency over time.

11. Economists recognize four possible deterrents to allocative efficiency in a competitive economy. (**a**) In allocating resources, the competitive model does not allow for spillover costs and benefits of for the production of public goods. (**b**) A purely competitive industry may preclude the large-scale production needed for individual firms to achieve economies of scale and therefore obtain the lowest possible per-unit production costs. (**c**) Pure competition may not motivate the development of new and improved production techniques and new and improved products. (**d**) The product standardization associated with pure competition limits product variations which provide consumers with a wide range of choice.

TERMS AND CONCEPTS

- -

pure competition	price taker	MR = MC rule	decreasing-cost industry
pure monopoly	average revenue	short-run supply curve	productive efficiency
monopolistic competition	total revenue	long-run supply curve	allocative efficiency
oligopoly	marginal revenue	constant-cost industry	
imperfect competition	break-even point	increasing-cost industry	

STUDY QUESTIONS

- -

1. Briefly indicate the basic characteristics of pure competition, pure monopoly, monopolistic competition, and oligopoly. Under which of these market classifications does each of the following most accurately fit? (**a**) a supermarket in your home town; (**b**) the steel industry; (**c**) a Kansas wheat farm; (**d**) the commercial bank in which you or your family has an account; (**e**) the automobile industry. In each case justify your classification.

2. Strictly speaking, pure competition has never existed and probably never will. Then why study it?

3. **KEY QUESTION** Use the following demand schedule to determine total and marginal revenue for each possible level of sales:

Product price	Quantity demanded	Total revenue	Marginal revenue
$2	0	$_____	$_____
2	1	_____	_____
2	2	_____	_____
2	3	_____	_____
2	4	_____	_____
2	5	_____	_____

   a. What can you conclude about the structure of the industry in which this firm is operating? Explain.

   b. Graph the demand, total-revenue, and marginal-revenue curves for this firm.

   c. Why do the demand and marginal-revenue curves coincide?

   d. "Marginal revenue is the change in total revenue associated with additional units of output." Explain verbally and graphically, using the data in the table.

4. **KEY QUESTION** Assume the following unit-cost data are for a purely competitive producer:

Total product	Average fixed cost	Average variable cost	Average total cost	Marginal cost
0				$45
1	$60.00	$45.00	$105.00	40
2	30.00	42.50	72.50	35
3	20.00	40.00	60.00	30
4	15.00	37.50	52.50	35
5	12.00	37.00	49.00	40
6	10.00	37.50	47.50	45
7	8.57	38.57	47.14	55
8	7.50	40.63	48.13	65
9	6.67	43.33	50.00	75
10	6.00	46.50	52.50	

   a. At a product price of $32, will this firm produce in the short run? Why or why not? If it does produce, what will be the profit-maximizing or loss-minimizing output? Explain. What economic profit or loss will the firm realize per unit of output?

b. Answer the questions of 4a assuming product price is $41.

c. Answer the questions of 4a assuming product price is $56.

d. In the table below, complete the short-run supply schedule for the firm (columns 1 and 2) and indicate the profit or loss incurred at each output (column 3).

(1) Price	(2) Quantity supplied, single firm	(3) Profit (+) or loss (−)	(4) Quantity supplied, 1500 firms
$26	_____	$_____	_____
32	_____	_____	_____
38	_____	_____	_____
41	_____	_____	_____
46	_____	_____	_____
56	_____	_____	_____
66	_____	_____	_____

e. Explain: "That segment of a competitive firm's marginal-cost curve which lies above its average-variable-cost curve constitutes the short-run supply curve for the firm." Illustrate graphically.

f. Now assume that are 1500 identical firms in this competitive industry; that is, there are 1500 firms, each of which has the cost data shown in the table. Complete the industry supply schedule (column 4).

g. Suppose the market demand data for the product are as follows:

Price	Total quantity demanded
$26	17,000
32	15,000
38	13,500
41	12,000
46	10,500
56	9,500
66	8,000

What will be the equilibrium price? What will be the equilibrium output for the industry? For each firm? What will profit or loss be per unit? Per firm? Will this industry expand or contract in the long run?

5. Why is the equality of marginal revenue and marginal cost essential for profit maximization in all market structures? Explain why price can be substituted for marginal revenue in the MR = MC rule when an industry is purely competitive.

6. **KEY QUESTION** Using diagrams for both the industry and a representative firm, illustrate competitive long-run equilibrium. Assuming constant costs, employ these diagrams to show how (a) an increase and (b) a decrease in market demand will upset this long-run equilibrium. Trace graphically and describe verbally the adjustment processes by which long-run equilibrium is restored. Now rework your analysis for increasing- and decreasing-cost industries and compare the three long-run supply curves.

7. **KEY QUESTION** In long-run equilibrium, $P =$ minimum ATC = MC. Of what significance for economic efficiency is the equality of P and minimum ATC? The equality of P and MC? Distinguish between productive efficiency and allocative efficiency in your answer.

8. **(Last Word)** Suppose that improved technology causes the supply curve for oranges to shift rightward in the market discussed in this Last Word (see the figure there). Assuming no change in the location of the demand curve, what will happen to consumer surplus? Explain why.

9. **WEB-BASED QUESTION** Pure Competition—Locate Some Real-World Examples Pure competition is rare in practice. However, Yahoo http://www.yahoo.com/Business/Companies includes a collection of firms in various industries. Find three industries which have the characteristics of pure competition: very large number of firms, standardized products, price taker, and free entry and exit. Hint: Start by looking at the number of firms in each industry link. In Explosives there are fewer than 10 companies, while Internet Services lists more than 30,000 firms.

10. **WEB-BASED QUESTION** Agricultural Commodities—Examples of Purely Competitive Markets In a purely competitive market, individual firms produce homogeneous products and exert no significant control over product price. The U.S. Department of Agriculture Market News reports http://www.ams.usda.gov/marketnews.htm provides up-to-the-minute information on commodity prices, demand, movement, volume, and quality. Select one commodity (e.g., grains: U.S. 1 Hard Red Winter Wheat) and compare its price in several states. Then compare prices to a similar product (e.g., U.S. Soft Red Wheat). Are there differences? Which of the six commodity categories best exemplifies a purely competitive market?

24

Pure Monopoly

We now jump from pure competition to pure monopoly, which is at the opposite end of the spectrum of industry structures listed previously in Table 23-1. You deal with monopolies—sole sellers of products and services—more often than you might think. When you mail a letter, you are using the services of the United States Postal Service, a government-sponsored monopoly. Similarly, when you make a local telephone call, turn on your lights, or subscribe to cable TV, you are patronizing a monopoly.

We begin by defining what we mean by "pure monopoly," and then we discuss some of the conditions which allow a monopoly to arise and persist. Then we get to the core of the chapter: the determination of product price and output quantity for a monopolistic firm. We also ask whether monopoly can achieve the productive and allocative efficiency associated with pure competition and, if not, whether government policies can improve the pricing and output practices of a pure monopolist.

PURE MONOPOLY: INTRODUCTION

Pure monopoly exists when *a single firm is the sole producer of a product for which there are no close substitutes.* Let's first examine the characteristics of pure monopoly and then provide some examples.

Characteristics

1. *Single seller* A pure, or absolute, monopoly is a one-firm industry. A single firm is the only producer of a specific product or the sole supplier of a service; the firm and the industry are synonymous.

2. *No close substitutes* The monopolist's product is unique in that there are no good, or close, substitutes. From the buyer's viewpoint, there are no reasonable alternatives. The consumer who does not buy the product from the monopolist has no alternative but to do without it.

3. *"Price maker"* The individual firm operating under pure competition exercises no influence over product price; it is a "price taker." This is so because it contributes only a negligible portion of total

supply. In contrast, the pure monopolist is a *price maker;* the firm exercises considerable control over price because it is responsible for, and therefore controls, the total quantity supplied. Confronted with the usual downsloping demand curve for its product, the monopolist can change product price by changing the quantity of the product supplied. The monopolist will use this power whenever there is an advantage to doing so.

4. *Blocked entry* A pure monopolist has no immediate competitors because there are barriers which keep potential competitors from entering the industry. These barriers may be economic, technological, legal, or of some other type. But under conditions of pure monopoly, entry is totally blocked.

5. *Nonprice competition* Since there are no close substitutes for a monopolist's product, the monopolist need not differentiate or advertise it. Yet, depending on the type of product or service offered, some monopolists do advertise. For example, a pure monopolist selling a luxury good, say, diamonds, might advertise heavily to increase demand for diamonds. The result might be that more people buy diamonds rather than take vacations. Local public utilities, on the other hand, normally see no point in large expenditures for advertising: people wanting water, gas, electric power, or local telephone service already know the one firm from which they must buy each of these necessities.

Examples of Monopoly

In most cities government-owned or -regulated public utilities—gas and electric companies, the water company, the cable TV company, and the telephone company—are all monopolies or virtually so. There are no close substitutes for services provided by these public utilities. Of course, there is almost always *some* competition. Candles or kerosene lights are imperfect substitutes for electricity; telegrams, letters, and courier services can be substituted for the telephone. But such substitutes are typically either costly, less convenient, or unappealing.

The classic example of a private, unregulated monopoly is the De Beers diamond syndicate, which effectively controls 70 percent of the world's diamond supply (see this chapter's Last Word). But in the United States, major manufacturing monopolies are rare and usually short-lived; eventually competitors emerge to destroy the single-producer status:

> . . . monopoly in the sense of a single seller is virtually nonexistent in nationwide U.S. manufacturing industries of appreciable size. The rate at which near-monopolies have faded appears to have exceeded the rate of new appearance by a substantial margin. In 1962 Gillette made 70 percent of domestic razor blade sales, but its position was eroded, first by the appearance of Wilkinson's stainless steel blades and then by Bic's aggressive marketing of disposable razors. Eastman Kodak's 90 percent share of amateur film sales and 65 percent share of all film sales, including instant photo packs, was sharply challenged in the 1980s by import competition from Fuji. General Motors' share of diesel locomotive sales probably remains near 75 percent. . . . Xerox's 75 to 80 percent share of electrostatic copier revenues declined with the erosion of its patent position during the 1970s. . . . During much of the 1960s and 1970s, Boeing controlled roughly two-thirds of noncommunist world jet airliner placements. With the rise of Europe's Airbus Consortium, Boeing's share declined to 50 percent in the late 1980s.[1]

Professional sports teams are, in a sense, monopolies because they are the sole suppliers of specific services in large geographic areas. With a few exceptions, each large American city is served by a single major-league team in each sport. If you want to see a live major-league baseball game in St. Louis or Seattle, you must patronize the Cardinals or the Mariners, respectively.

Other geographic monopolies exist. A small town may be served by only one airline or railroad. The local bank, movie, or bookstore may approximate a monopoly in a small, isolated community.

Importance of Monopoly and Its Study

You should understand the workings of pure monopoly for two reasons.

1. A significant amount of economic activity—perhaps 5 or 6 percent of domestic output—is carried out under conditions approaching pure monopoly.

2. A study of pure monopoly will help you understand the more common market structures of mo-

---

[1]F. M. Scherer and David Ross, *Industrial Market Structure and Economic Performance*, 3d ed. (Chicago: Rand McNally College Publishing, 1990), p. 82.

nopolistic competition and oligopoly, discussed in Chapter 25. These two market structures combine, in differing degrees, characteristics of pure competition and pure monopoly.

BARRIERS TO ENTRY

The factors that prohibit firms from entering an industry are called **barriers to entry.** In pure monopoly, strong barriers to entry effectively block all potential competition. Barriers that are a bit weaker may permit the existence of oligopoly, a market dominated by a few firms. Still weaker barriers allow the fairly large number of competing firms which characterize monopolistic competition. And the absence of entry barriers permits the very large number of firms, which is the basis of pure competition. Hence, barriers to entry are pertinent not only to the extreme case of pure monopoly but also to many other markets in which there is some degree of monopoly-like conditions and behavior.

Economies of Scale

Modern technology in some industries is such that efficient, low-cost production can be achieved only if producers are extremely large both absolutely and in relation to the market. Where economies of scale are very significant, a firm's long-run average-cost schedule will decline over a wide range of output. Given market demand, the achieving of low unit costs and therefore low unit prices for consumers depends on the existence of a few large firms or, in the extreme case, only one firm.

Figure 24-1 indicates the presence of economies of scale—declining average total cost—throughout a wide range of outputs. If total consumer demand is within that output range, then demand can be satisfied at least cost when there is a single producer—a monopoly. Note, for example, that a monopolist can produce 200 units at a per-unit cost of $10 and a total cost of $2000. If there are two firms in the industry and each produces 100 units, the unit cost is $15 and total cost rises to $3000 (= 200 units × $15). A still more competitive situation with four firms each producing 50 units would boost unit and total cost to $20 and $4000, respectively. Conclusion: When ATC is declining, only a single producer, a monopolist, can produce any particular output at minimum total cost.

If a pure monopoly exists in such an industry, economies of scale will be an entry barrier and will protect the monopolist from competition. New firms attempting to enter the industry as small-scale producers cannot realize the cost economies of the monopolist and therefore obtain the profits necessary for survival or growth. A new firm might try to start out big, that is, to enter the industry as a large-scale producer so as to achieve the necessary economies of scale. But the massive plant facilities would necessitate huge amounts of financing, which a new and untried enterprise would find difficult to secure. The financial obstacles and risks to "starting big" are so great in most cases that they are prohibitive. This explains why efforts to enter such industries as automobiles, commercial aircraft, and basic steel are very rare.

In the extreme circumstance, in which the market demand curve cuts the long-run ATC curve where average total costs are still declining, the single firm is called a *natural monopoly*. Our discussion implies that

FIGURE 24-1 Economies of scale: the natural monopoly case A declining average-total-cost curve over a wide range of output quantities indicates extensive economies of scale. A single monopoly firm can produce, say, 200 units of output at lower cost ($10 each) than could two or more firms whose combined output is 200 units.

----

a natural monopolist's lower unit cost allows it to charge a lower price than if the industry were more competitive. But this won't happen. As you will see, a pure monopolist may set its price far above ATC and obtain substantial economic profit. Then the lowest-unit-cost advantage of a natural monopolist may accrue to the monopolist as profit and not to consumers in the form of lower prices. For this reason government typically regulates natural monopolies, specifying the price they may charge.

Most of the so-called public utilities—electric and gas companies, bus firms, local water and telephone companies—are regulated natural monopolies. It would be wasteful if a community had several firms supplying water or electricity when a single firm can do so at least cost. Technology is such in these industries that extensive capital expenditures on generators, pumping and purification equipment, water mains, and transmission lines are required. Duplicating this equipment would waste society's scarce resources.

So single producers are given exclusive distribution rights—so-called franchises—by government. But in return for the sole right to supply electricity, water, or bus transportation to a particular geographic area, government reserves the right to regulate prices and services to prevent abuses of the monopoly power it has granted.

Legal Barriers to Entry: Patents and Licenses

We have just noted that government frequently allows and regulates natural monopolies. Government also creates legal entry barriers by awarding patents and licenses.

Patents A *patent* is the exclusive right of an inventor to use, or allow another to use, her or his invention. Patents and patent laws aim to protect the inventor from rivals who would use the invention without having shared in the effort and expense of its development. At the same time, patents provide the inventor with a monopoly position for the life of the patent. Historically, patents have extended for 17 years in the United States. But in the 1995 GATT agreement (Chapter 6), the world's nations agreed on a uniform patent length of 20 years from the time of application.

Patents figured prominently in the growth of modern-day industrial giants such as NCR Corporation (formerly National Cash Register), General Motors, Xerox, Polaroid, General Electric,

and Du Pont. The United Shoe Machinery Company is a notable example of a firm that abused patents to achieve monopoly power. United Shoe became the exclusive supplier of certain essential shoemaking machines through its control of patents for those machines. The firm leased, but did not sell, its machines. It extended its monopoly power to other types of shoemaking machinery by requiring all lessees of its patented machines to sign a "tying agreement" in which shoe manufacturers also agreed to lease all other shoemaking machinery from United Shoe. This allowed United Shoe to monopolize the market until antitrust action was taken by the government in 1955.

Research and development (R&D) is what leads to patentable inventions and products. Firms which gain monopoly power through their own research or by purchasing the patents of others can use patents to strengthen their market position. The profit from one patent can finance the research required to develop new patentable products. In the pharmaceutical industry, patents on prescription drugs have produced large monopoly profits which have helped finance the discovery of new patentable medicines. Monopoly power achieved through patents may well be self-sustaining.

Licenses Entry into an industry or occupation may be limited by government and the limit enforced through *licensing*. At the national level the Federal Communications Commission licenses only so many radio and television stations in each geographic area. In many large cities you need a municipal license to drive a taxicab. The consequent restriction of the supply of cabs creates economic profit for cab owners and drivers. New cabs cannot enter the industry to drive down prices and profit. In a few instances government might "license" itself to provide some product and thereby create a public monopoly. For example, in some states liquor is sold only through state-owned retail outlets. Similarly, many states have "licensed" themselves to run lotteries.

Ownership or Control of Essential Resources

Private property can be used by a monopolist as an obstacle to potential rivals. A firm owning or controlling a resource essential to the production process can prohibit the creation of rival firms. The Aluminum Company of America allegedly maintained its monopoly position in the aluminum industry for many years through its control of developed sources of bauxite, the ore from which aluminum is refined. At one time the International Nickel Company of Canada (now called Inco) controlled 90 percent of the world's known nickel reserves. As this chapter's Last Word details, most of the world's known diamond mines are owned or effectively controlled by the De Beers Company of South Africa. Similarly, it is very difficult for new professional sports leagues to evolve when existing leagues have contracts with the best players and leases on the major stadiums and arenas.

Pricing and Other Strategic Barriers

Even if a firm is not protected from entry by, say, extensive economies of scale or ownership of essential resources, entry may effectively be blocked by the way the monopolist responds to attempts by rivals to enter the industry. Confronted with a new entrant, the monopolist may "create an entry barrier" by slashing its price, greatly increasing its advertising, or taking other strategic actions to make it difficult for the entrant to succeed. Example: Before its breakup in 1980, AT&T allegedly undertook several entry-deterring actions, including significant price cutting, to maintain its monopoly in the long-distance telephone industry.

The very *threat* of price cuts and other retaliatory actions by the monopolist may dissuade firms from attempting to enter a monopolized industry. Monopolists have been known to purposely create excess production capacity to warn potential entrants that they can quickly lower price and expand output if a new firm tries to enter. Example: In the 1970s and 1980s Du Pont allegedly deliberately built excess capacity in the titanium dioxide industry to deter the entry of rivals.

Two Implications

Our discussion of barriers to entry suggests two noteworthy points about monopoly.

Rarity Barriers to entry are seldom complete—meaning pure monopoly is relatively rare. Although research and technological advance may strengthen the market position of a firm, technology may also undermine existing monopoly power. Over time the creation of new technologies can destroy existing monopoly positions. The development of courier delivery systems, fax machines, and electronic mail has eroded the monopoly power of the postal service. Cable television monopolies are now challenged by satellite TV and by new technologies that permit the transmission of audio and visual signals through telephone lines.

Similarly, existing patent advantages may be circumvented by the development of new and distinct, yet substitutable, products. New sources of major resources may be found and competition from foreign firms may emerge (see Global Perspective 24-1). It is probably only a modest overstatement to say that monopoly in the sense of a one-firm industry persists over time only with the sanction or aid of government, as with the postal service's monopoly on the delivery of first-class mail.

GLOBAL PERSPECTIVE 24-1

Competition from foreign multinational corporations

The market power of firms in the United States is diminished by competition from foreign corporations operating within the United States. The table shows the top 10 foreign multinational manufacturing corporations ranked by sales from U.S. operations. Foreign multinationals produced an estimated 20 percent of U.S. manufacturing output in 1993, up from 4 percent in 1977. They employ over 12 percent of the U.S. industrial labor force.

Corporation	Sales (billions of dollars)
Royal Dutch Shell (Netherlands)	
British Petroleum (U.K.)	
Sony (Japan)	
Hanson PLC (U.K.)	
Unilever (Netherlands)	
Nestlé (Switzerland)	
Petroleos de Venezuela (Venezuela)	
Mastushita Electric Ind. (Japan)	
Hoechst AG (Germany)	
Aramco Oil (Saudi Arabia)	

Source: *Wall Street Journal*, Dec. 2, 1994. Data from the Wharton School, University of Pennsylvania.

Desirability   Monopolies may be desirable or undesirable from the standpoint of economic efficiency. Where economies of scale are available, market demand may be such that monopoly can yield efficient low-cost production. But, for reasons we discuss later, to benefit fully from the lower costs, society may need to limit the prices the monopolists charge.

On the other hand, where ownership of resources, patents, licensing, and entry-deterring actions are sources of monopoly, the result may be inefficient and undesirable.

MONOPOLY DEMAND

We begin our analysis of the price and output decisions of a pure monopolist by making three assumptions:

1. Our monopolist's status is secured by patents, economies of scale, or resource ownership.
2. The firm is *not* regulated by any unit of government.
3. The firm is a *single-price* monopolist; it charges the same price for all units of output.

The crucial difference between a pure monopolist and a purely competitive seller lies on the demand side of the market. Recall from Chapter 23 that the purely competitive seller faces perfectly elastic de-

mand at the price determined by market supply and demand. The competitive firm is a price taker which can sell as much or as little as it wants at the going market price. Each additional unit sold will add a constant amount—its price—to the firm's total revenue. That means marginal revenue for the competitive seller is constant and equal to product price. (Refer to Table 23-2 and Figure 23-1 for price, marginal-revenue, and total-revenue relationships for the purely competitive firm.)

The monopolist's demand curve—indeed, the demand curve of any imperfectly competitive seller—is very different. Because the pure monopolist *is* the industry, its demand curve *is* the market demand curve. And because market demand is not perfectly elastic, its demand curve is downsloping. Columns 1 and 2 in Table 24-1 illustrate this concept; note that quantity demanded increases as price decreases.

Recall that in Chapter 23 we drew separate demand curves for the purely competitive industry and for a single firm in the industry. But only a single demand curve is needed in pure monopoly because the firm and the industry are one and the same. Part of the demand data in Table 24-1 is graphed as demand curve D in Figure 24-2.

The downsloping demand curve has three implications you must understand in order to understand the monopoly model.

TABLE 24-1   Revenue and cost data of a pure monopolist

Revenue data				Cost data			
(1) Quantity of output	(2) Price (average revenue)	(3) Total revenue (1) × (2)	(4) Marginal revenue	(5) Average total cost	(6) Total cost (1) × (5)	(7) Marginal cost	(8) Profit (+) or loss (−)
0	$172	$ 0			$ 100		$−100
1	162	162	$162	$190.00	190	$ 90	− 28
2	152	304	142	135.00	270	80	+ 34
3	142	426	122	113.33	340	70	+ 86
4	132	528	102	100.00	400	60	+128
5	**122**	**610**	**82**	**94.00**	**470**	**70**	**+140**
6	112	672	62	91.67	550	80	+122
7	102	714	42	91.43	640	90	+ 74
8	92	736	22	93.75	750	110	− 14
9	82	738	2	97.78	880	130	−142
10	72	720	−18	103.00	1030	150	−310

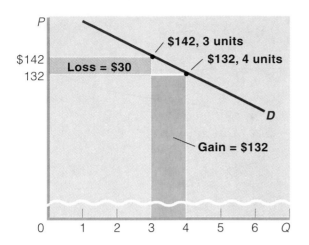

FIGURE 24-2 Price and marginal revenue in pure monopoly A pure monopolist—or any other imperfect competitor with a downsloping demand curve such as D—must set a lower price to sell more output. Here, by charging $132 rather than $142, the monopolist sells an extra unit (the fourth unit) and gains $132 from that sale. But from this gain must be subtracted $30, which reflects the $10 less the monopolist charged for each of the first 3 units. Thus, the marginal revenue of the fourth unit is $102 (= $132 − $30), considerably less than its $132 price.

Marginal Revenue Is Less Than Price

The downsloping demand curve faced by a pure monopolist means it can increase sales only by charging a lower price. *Because the monopolist must set a lower price to obtain greater sales, marginal revenue is less than price (average revenue) for every level of output except the first.* The reason is that the lower price applies not only to the extra output sold but also to all prior units of output. These prior units could have been sold at a higher price if the extra output had not been produced and sold. Each additional unit of output sold increases total revenue by an amount equal to its own price *less* the sum of the price cuts which apply to all prior units of output.

Figure 24-2 confirms this point. There, we have highlighted two price-quantity combinations from the monopolist's demand curve. The monopolist can sell 1 more unit at $132 than it can at $142 and thereby obtain $132 of extra revenue. But to sell this fourth unit for $132, the monopolist must also sell the first 3 units at $132 rather than $142. This $10 reduction in revenue on 3 units results in a $30 revenue loss. The *net* difference in total revenue from selling a fourth unit is $102, the $132 gain minus the $30 loss.

This net gain of $102—the *marginal revenue* of the fourth unit—is obviously less than the $132 *price* of the fourth unit.

Column 4 in Table 24-1 shows that marginal revenue is always less than the corresponding product price in column 2, except for the first unit of output. Because marginal revenue is the change in total revenue associated with each additional unit of output, the declining amounts of marginal revenue in column 4 mean that total revenue increases at a diminishing rate (as shown in column 3).

The relationship between the monopolist's marginal-revenue curve and total-revenue curve is shown in Figure 24-3. For this figure the demand and revenue data of columns 1 through 4 in Table 24-1 were extended assuming that successive $10 price cuts will each elicit 1 additional unit of sales. That is, 11 units can be sold at a price of $62, 12 at $52, and so on.

Note that the monopolist's MR curve lies below the demand curve, indicating that marginal revenue is *less than* price at every output quantity but the very first unit. Observe also the special relationship between total revenue and marginal revenue. Because marginal revenue is the change in total revenue, marginal revenue is positive while total revenue is increasing. When total revenue reaches its maximum, marginal revenue is zero. When total revenue is diminishing, marginal revenue is negative.

The Monopolist Is a "Price Maker"

In all imperfectly competitive markets with downsloping demand curves—that is, in pure monopoly, oligopoly, and monopolistic competition—firms can to one degree or another influence total supply through their own output decisions. In changing market supply, they can also affect product price. Rather than being price takers, as are pure competitors, firms with downsloping demand curves are "price makers."

This is most evident in pure monopoly, where one firm controls total output. The monopolist faces a downsloping demand curve in which each output is associated with some unique price. Thus, in deciding on what volume of output to produce, the monopolist is also indirectly determining the price it will charge. Through control of output, it can "make the price." From columns 1 and 2 in Table 24-1 we find that the monopolist can charge a price of $72 if it produces and offers for sale 10 units, a price of $82 if it produces and offers for sale 9 units, and so forth.

(a) Demand and marginal-revenue curves

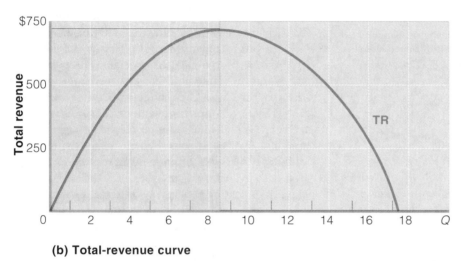

(b) Total-revenue curve

FIGURE 24-3 Demand, marginal revenue, and total revenue for an imperfectly competitive firm (a) Because it must lower price on all units sold to increase its sales, an imperfectly competitive firm's marginal-revenue curve (MR) lies below its downsloping demand curve (D). The elastic and inelastic regions of demand are highlighted. (b) Total revenue (TR) increases at a decreasing rate, reaches a maximum, and then declines. Note that in the elastic region, TR is increasing and hence MR is positive. When TR reaches its maximum, MR is zero. In the inelastic region of demand, TR is declining, so MR is negative.

The Monopolist Prices in the Elastic Region of Demand

The total-revenue test for price elasticity of demand is the basis for our third implication. Recall from Chapter 20 that the total-revenue test reveals that when demand is elastic, a decline in price will increase total revenue. Similarly, when demand is inelastic, a decline in price will reduce total revenue. Beginning at the top of demand curve *D* in Figure 24-3a, observe that as the price declines from $172 to approximately $82, total revenue increases (and marginal revenue therefore is positive). This means that demand is elastic in this price range. Conversely, for price declines below $82, total revenue decreases

(marginal revenue is negative), which indicates that demand is inelastic there.

The implication is that a monopolist will never choose a price-quantity combination where price declines cause total revenue to decrease (marginal revenue to be negative). *The profit-maximizing monopolist will always want to avoid the inelastic segment of its demand curve in favor of some price-quantity combination in the elastic region.* Here's why: To get into the inelastic region, the monopolist must lower the price and increase output. In the inelastic region a lower price means less total revenue. And increased output always means increased total cost. Less total revenue and higher total cost yield diminished profit. **(Key Question 4)**

OUTPUT AND PRICE DETERMINATION

At what specific price-quantity combination will a profit-maximizing monopolist choose to operate? To answer this question, we must add production costs to our analysis.

Cost Data

On the cost side, we will assume that although the firm is a monopolist in the product market, it hires resources competitively and employs the same technology as our competitive firm in the preceding chapter. This lets us use the cost data we developed in Chapter 22 and applied in Chapter 23, so we can compare the price-output decisions of a pure monopoly with those of a pure competitor. Columns 5 through 7 in Table 24-1 restate the pertinent cost data in Table 22-2.

MR = MC Rule

A monopolist seeking to maximize total profit will employ the same rationale as a profit-seeking firm in a competitive industry. It will produce another unit of output as long as that unit adds more to total revenue than it adds to total cost. The firm will increase output up to that output at which marginal revenue equals marginal cost (MR = MC).

A comparison of columns 4 and 7 in Table 24-1 indicates that the profit-maximizing output is 5 units; the fifth unit is the last unit of output whose marginal revenue exceeds its marginal cost. What price will the

monopolist charge? The demand schedule shown as columns 1 and 2 in Table 24-1 indicates that there is only one price at which 5 units can be sold: $122.

This analysis is shown in **Figure 24-4 (Key Graph),** where the demand, marginal-revenue, average-total-cost, and marginal-cost data in Table 24-1 have been graphed. The profit-maximizing output occurs where MR = MC. We see that the marginal-revenue (MR) and marginal-cost (MC) curves intersect—that is, MR = MC—at 5 units of output, which we call Q_m. What price will the monopolist charge? This price is found by extending a vertical line from Q_m up to the demand curve D. The unique price P_m at which Q_m units can be sold is the price corresponding to 5 units on demand curve D. In this case, the profit-maximizing price is $122.

Columns 2 and 5 in Table 24-1 indicate that, at 5 units of output, the product price ($122) exceeds the average total cost ($94). An economic profit of $28 per unit is therefore earned; the total economic profit is then $140 (= 5 units × $28). In Figure 24-4, per-unit profit is $P_m - A$ where A is the average total cost of producing Q_m units. Total economic profit is found by multiplying this per-unit profit by the profit-maximizing output Q_m.

The profit-maximizing output can also be determined by comparing total revenue and total cost at each possible level of production and choosing the output with the greatest positive difference. You should use columns 3 and 6 in Table 24-1 to verify our conclusion that 5 units is the profit-maximizing output. Accurately graphing total revenue and total cost against output will also show the greatest difference (the maximum profit) at 5 units of output. Table 24-2 is a step-by-step summary of the process for determining the profit-maximizing output, the profit-maximizing price, and economic profit in pure monopoly. **(Key Question 5)**

No Monopoly Supply Curve

Recall that MR equals P in pure competition and that the supply curve of a purely competitive firm is determined by applying the MR (= P) = MC profit-maximizing rule. At any specific market-determined price the purely competitive seller will maximize profit by supplying the quantity at which MC is equal to that price. When the market price increases or decreases, the competitive firm produces more or less output. Each market price is thus associated with a specific output, and all such price-output pairs define the

FIGURE 24-4 The profit-maximizing position of a pure monopolist The pure monopolist maximizes profit by producing the MR = MC output, here $Q_m = 5$ units. Then, as seen from the demand curve, it will charge price $P_m = \$122$. Average total cost will be $A = \$94$, meaning that per-unit profit is $P_m - A$ and total profit is $5 \times (P_m - A)$. Total economic profit is thus represented by the gray rectangle.

QUICK QUIZ 24-4

1. The MR curve lies below the demand curve in this figure because the:
a. demand curve is linear (a straight line).
b. demand curve is highly inelastic throughout its full length.
c. demand curve is highly elastic throughout its full length.
d. gain in revenue from an extra unit of output is less than the price charged for that unit of output.

2. The area labeled "Economic profit" can be found by multiplying the difference between *P* and ATC by quantity. It also can be found by:
a. dividing profit per unit by quantity.
b. subtracting total cost from total revenue.
c. multiplying the coefficient of demand elasticity by quantity.
d. multiplying the difference between *P* and MC by quantity.

3. This pure monopolist:
a. charges the highest price it can get.
b. earns only a normal profit in the long run.
c. restricts output to create an insurmountable entry barrier.
d. restricts output to increase its price and total economic profit.

4. At this monopolist's profit-maximizing output:
a. price equals marginal revenue.
b. price equals marginal cost.
c. price exceeds marginal cost.
d. profit per unit is maximized.

Answers: 1. d; 2. b; 3. d; 4. c

---

supply curve. This supply curve turns out to be that portion of the firm's MC curve which lies above the average-variable-cost curve (Figure 23-6 shows it).

At first glance we would suspect that the pure monopolist's marginal-cost curve would also be its supply curve. But this is *not* the case. *The pure monopolist has no supply curve.* The reason is that there is no unique relationship between price and quantity supplied for a monopolist. Like the competitive firm, the

monopolist equates marginal revenue and marginal cost to determine output, but for the monopolist marginal revenue is less than price. Because the monopolist does not equate marginal cost to price, it is possible for different demand conditions to bring about different prices for the same output. To convince yourself of this, refer to Figure 24-4 and pencil in a new, steeper marginal-revenue curve that intersects the marginal-cost curve at the same point as does the

TABLE 24-2 Steps for graphically determining the profit-maximizing output, the profit-maximizing price, and economic profit (if any) in pure monopoly

Step 1. Determine the profit-maximizing output by finding where MR = MC.

Step 2. Determine the profit-maximizing price by extending a vertical line upward from the output determined in step 1 to the pure monopolist's demand curve.

Step 3. Determine the pure monopolist's economic profit using one of two methods.

Method 1. Find profit per unit by subtracting the average total cost of the profit-maximizing output from the profit-maximizing price. Then multiply the difference by the profit-maximizing output to determine economic profit (if any).

Method 2. Find total cost by multiplying the average total cost of the profit-maximizing output by that output. Find total revenue by multiplying the profit-maximizing output by the profit-maximizing price. Then subtract total cost from total revenue to determine economic profit (if any).

present marginal-revenue curve. Then draw in a new demand curve that roughly corresponds with your new marginal-revenue curve. With the new curves, the same MR = MC output of 5 units now corresponds with a higher profit-maximizing price. Conclusion: There is no single, unique price associated with each output level Q_m, and so there is no supply curve for the pure monopolist.

Misconceptions Concerning Monopoly Pricing

Our analysis explodes two fallacies concerning monopoly behavior.

Not Highest Price Because a monopolist can manipulate output and price, people often believe it "will charge the highest price it can get." This is incorrect. There are many prices above P_m in Figure 24-4, but the monopolist shuns them because they yield a smaller-than-maximum total profit. The monopolist seeks maximum total profit, not maximum price. Some high prices that could be charged would reduce sales and total revenue too severely to offset any decrease in total cost.

Total, Not Unit, Profit The monopolist seeks maximum *total* profit, not maximum *unit* profit. In Figure 24-4 a careful comparison of the vertical distance between average total cost and price at various possible outputs indicates that per-unit profit is greater at a point slightly to the left of the profit-maximizing

output Q_m. This is seen in Table 24-1, where unit profit at 4 units of output is $32 (= $132 − $100) compared with $28 (= $122 − $94) at the profit-maximizing output of 5 units. Here the monopolist accepts a lower-than-maximum per-unit profit because additional sales more than compensate for the lower unit profit. A profit-seeking monopolist would rather sell 5 units at a profit of $28 per unit (for a total profit of $140) than 4 units at a profit of $32 per unit (for a total profit of only $128).

Possibility of Monopolist Losses

The likelihood of economic profit is greater for a pure monopolist than for a pure competitor. In the long run the latter is destined to have only a normal profit, whereas barriers to entry mean that any economic profit realized by the monopolist can persist. In pure monopoly there are no entrants to increase supply, drive down price, and eliminate economic profit.

But pure monopoly does not guarantee profit. The monopolist is not immune from changes in tastes which reduce the demand for its product. Nor is it immune from upward-shifting cost curves due to escalating resource prices. If the demand and cost situation faced by the monopolist is far less favorable than that in Figure 24-4, the monopolist will incur losses in the short run. Despite its dominance in the market, the monopoly in Figure 24-5 suffers a loss, as shown, because of weak demand and relatively high costs. Yet it continues to operate for the time being because its total loss is less than its fixed cost. More precisely, at

FIGURE 24-5 The loss-minimizing position of a pure monopolist If demand D is weak and costs are high, the pure monopolist may be unable to make a profit. Because P_m exceeds V, the average variable cost at the MR = MC output Q_m, the monopolist will minimize losses in the short run by producing at that output. The loss per unit is $A - P_m$, and the total loss is indicated by the pink rectangle.

output Q_m the monopolist's price P_m exceeds its average variable cost V. Its loss per unit is $A - P_m$, and the total loss is shown by the pink rectangle.

Like the pure competitor, the monopolist will not persistently operate at a loss. Faced with continuing losses, in the long run the firm's owners will move their resources to alternative industries offering better profit opportunities. Thus we can expect the monopolist to realize a normal profit or better in the long run.

ECONOMIC EFFECTS OF MONOPOLY

Let's now evaluate pure monopoly from the standpoint of society as a whole. Our reference for this evaluation will be the long-run efficiency outcome in a purely competitive market, identified by the triple equality $P = MC = $ minimum ATC.

Price, Output, and Efficiency

Figure 24-6 graphically contrasts the price, output, and efficiency outcomes of pure monopoly and a purely competitive *industry*. Starting with Figure 24-6a, we are reminded that the purely competitive industry's market supply curve S is the horizontal sum of the marginal-cost curves of all the firms in the industry. Let's suppose there are 1000 such firms. Comparing their combined supply curves S with market demand D, we get the purely competitive price and output of P_c and Q_c.

(a) Purely competitive industry

(b) Pure monopoly

FIGURE 24-6 Inefficiency of pure monopoly relative to a purely competitive industry (a) In a purely competitive industry, entry and exit of firms ensures that price (P_c) equals marginal cost (MC) and that the minimum average-total-cost output (Q_c) is produced. Both productive efficiency ($P = $ minimum ATC) and allocative efficiency ($P = $ MC) are obtained. (b) In pure monopoly, the MR curve lies below the demand curve. The monopolist maximizes profit at output Q_m, where MR = MC, and charges price P_m. Thus, output is lower (Q_m rather than Q_c) and price is higher (P_m rather than P_c) than they would be in a purely competitive industry. Monopoly is inefficient, since output is less than that required to achieve minimum ATC (here at Q_c) and because price exceeds MC.

Recall that this price-output combination results in both productive efficiency and allocative efficiency. *Productive efficiency* is realized because free entry and exit forces firms to operate where average total cost is at a minimum. The sum of the minimum-ATC outputs of the 1000 pure competitors is the industry output, here, Q_c. Product price is at the lowest level consistent with minimum average total cost. The *allocative efficiency* of pure competition results because production occurs up to that output at which price (the measure of a product's value or marginal benefit to society) equals marginal cost (the worth of the alternative products forgone by society in producing any given commodity). In short: $P = \text{MC} = \text{minimum ATC}$.

Now let's suppose this industry becomes a pure monopoly (Figure 24-6b) as a result of one firm buying out all its competitors. We also assume that no changes in costs or market demand result from this dramatic change in the industry structure. What were formerly 1000 competing firms are now a single pure monopolist consisting of 1000 noncompeting branches.

The competitive market supply curve S has become the marginal-cost curve (MC) of the monopolist, the summation of the MC curves of its many branch plants. (Since the monopolist does not have a supply curve, as such, we have removed the S label). The important change, however, is on the demand side. From the viewpoint of each of the 1000 individual competitive firms, demand was perfectly elastic, and marginal revenue was therefore equal to price. Each firm equated MR (= price) and MC in maximizing profits. But market demand and individual demand are the same to the pure monopolist. The firm *is* the industry, and thus the monopolist sees the downsloping demand curve D shown in Figure 24-6b.

This means that marginal revenue is less than price, that graphically the MR curve lies below demand curve D. In using the MR = MC rule, the monopolist selects output Q_m and price P_m. A comparison of both graphs in Figure 24-6 reveals that the monopolist finds it profitable to sell a smaller output at a higher price than do the competitive producers. Monopoly yields neither productive nor allocative efficiency. The monopolist's output is less than Q_c, the output at which average total cost is lowest. And price is higher than the competitive price P_c, which in long-run equilibrium pure competition equals minimum average total cost. Thus the monopoly price *exceeds* minimum average total cost. Also, at the monopolist's Q_m output, product price is considerably higher than marginal cost, which means that society values additional units of this monopolized product more highly than it values the alternative products the resources could otherwise produce. So the monopolist's profit-maximizing output results in an underallocation of resources. The monopolist finds it profitable to restrict output and therefore employ fewer resources than are justified from society's standpoint. Hence the monopolist does not achieve allocative efficiency.

In monopoly, then, $P > \text{MC}$ and $P > \text{minimum ATC}$.

Income Distribution

In general, monopoly contributes to inequality in income distribution. By virtue of their market power, monopolists charge a higher price than would a purely competitive firm with the same costs; monopolists in effect can levy a "private tax" on consumers and obtain substantial economic profits. These monopolistic profits are not widely distributed because corporate stock ownership is largely concentrated in the hands of upper-income groups. The owners of monopolistic enterprises thus tend to be enriched at the expense of the rest of society.

Exception: If the buyers of a monopoly product are wealthier than the owners of the monopoly, the monopoly may *reduce* income inequality. But, in general, this is not the case, and we thus conclude that monopoly contributes to income inequality.

Cost Complications

Our evaluation of pure monopoly has led us to conclude that, *given identical costs*, a pure monopolist will charge a higher price, produce a smaller output, and allocate economic resources less efficiently than a purely competitive industry. These inferior results are rooted in the entry barriers characterizing monopoly.

Now we must recognize that costs may *not* be the same for purely competitive and monopolistic producers. The unit cost incurred by a monopolist may be either larger or smaller than that incurred by a purely competitive firm. There are four reasons why costs may differ: (1) economies of scale, (2) a factor called "X-inefficiency," (3) the need for monopoly-preserving expenditures, and (4) the "very long-run" perspective, which allows for technological advance.

Economies of Scale Once Again
Where there are extensive economies of scale, market demand may not be sufficient to support a large number of com-

peting firms, each producing at minimum efficient scale. In such cases, an industry of one or two firms would have a lower average total cost than would the same industry made up of numerous competitive firms. At the extreme, only a single firm—a natural monopoly—might be able to achieve the lowest long-run average total cost.

Most economists, however, conclude that natural monopoly is rare. And, in the more usual cases of monopoly, it's unlikely that cost reduction arising from monopoly is sufficient to offset the inefficiencies caused by the monopolist's reduced output and higher price. That is, the possibility of some cost reduction from size does not change our general conclusion that, compared with more competitive industries, monopolies yield inferior overall efficiency results.

X-Inefficiency

All the average-total-cost curves used in this book are based on the assumption that the firm uses the most efficient existing technology. In other words, it uses the technology that permits it to achieve the lowest average total cost of whatever level of output it chooses to produce. **X-inefficiency** occurs *when a firm's actual cost of producing any output is greater than the lowest possible cost of producing it.* In Figure 24-7 X-inefficiency is represented by operation at points X and X' above the lowest-cost ATC curve. At these points, per-unit costs are ATC_x (as opposed to ATC_1) for output Q_1 and $ATC_{x'}$ (as opposed to ATC_2) for output Q_2. Any point above the average-total-cost-curve in Figure 24-7 is possible but reflects inefficiency or "bad management" by the firm.

Why is X-inefficiency allowed to occur if it reduces profits? The answer is that managers may have goals—firm growth, an easier work life, avoidance of business risk, giving jobs to incompetent friends and relatives—which conflict with cost minimization. Or X-inefficiency may arise because a firm's workers are poorly motivated or ineffectively supervised. Or a firm may simply become lethargic and inert, relying on rules of thumb in decision making as opposed to relevant calculations of costs and revenues.

For our purposes the relevant question is whether monopolistic firms tend more to X-inefficiency than competitive producers. Presumably they do. Firms in competitive industries are continually under pressure from rivals, forcing them to be internally efficient to survive. But monopolists are sheltered from such competitive forces by entry barriers, and this lack of pressure leads to X-inefficiency.

There is no indisputable evidence of X-inefficiency, but what we have suggests than X-inefficiency

increases as the amount of competition decreases. A reasonable estimate is that X-inefficiency may be 10 percent or more of costs for monopolists but only 5 percent for an "average" oligopolistic industry in which the four largest firms produce 60 percent of total output.[2] In the words of one authority: "The evidence is fragmentary, but it points in the same direction. X-inefficiency exists, and it is more apt to be reduced when competitive pressures are strong than when firms enjoy insulated market positions."[3]

Rent-Seeking Expenditures

Rent-seeking behavior is any activity designed to transfer income or wealth to a particular firm or resource supplier at someone else's, or even society's, expense. We have seen that a monopolist can earn an economic profit even in the long run. Therefore, it is no surprise that a firm may go to great expense to acquire or maintain a monopoly granted by government through legislation or an exclusive license. Such rent-seeking expenditures add nothing to the firm's output, but they clearly increase its costs. They imply that monopoly involves higher costs and less efficiency than suggested in Figure 24-6b.

Technological Advance

In the very long run, firms can reduce their costs through discovery and implementation of new technology. If monopolists are more likely than competitive producers to develop more efficient production techniques over time, then the inefficiency of monopoly might be overstated. Since research and development (R&D) is the topic of Chapter 26, we will provide only a brief assessment here.

The general view of economists is that a pure monopolist will not be technologically progressive. Although its economic profit provides ample means to finance research and development, it has little incentive to implement new techniques (or products). The absence of competitors means there is no external pressure for technological advance in a monopolized market. Because of its sheltered market position, the pure monopolist can afford to be inefficient and lethargic; there simply is no penalty for being so.

One caveat: Research and technological advance may be one of the monopolist's barriers to entry. Thus, the monopolist may continue to seek technological ad-

---

[2]William G. Shepherd, *The Economics of Industrial Organization*, 4th ed. (Englewood Cliffs, NJ: Prentice-Hall, 1997), p. 107. For a rather extensive review of case study evidence of X-inefficiency, see Scherer and Ross, *op. cit.*, pp. 668–672.

[3]Scherer and Ross, *op. cit.*, p. 672.

FIGURE 24-7 **X-inefficiency** The average-total-cost curve (ATC) is assumed to reflect the minimum cost of producing each particular unit of output. Any point above this "lowest-cost" ATC curve, such as X or X', implies X-inefficiency: operation at greater than lowest cost for a particular level of output.

----

vance or fall prey to new rivals. In this case technological advance is essential to the maintenance of monopoly. But it is then potential *competition*, not the monopoly market structure, which is driving the technological advance. In theory, there is no such competition in the pure monopoly model; entry is completely blocked.

Policy Options

Our overall conclusion is that pure monopoly is economically inefficient. What then should society do about monopoly when it arises in the real world? Three general policy options are available:

1. If the monopoly creates substantial economic inefficiency and appears to be long-lasting, government can file charges against the monopoly under the antitrust laws, seeking to break up the monopoly into several competing firms. (Antitrust action is the subject of Chapter 32.)

2. If the monopoly is a natural monopoly, society can allow it to continue but directly regulate its prices and operations. (We discuss this option later in this chapter and in Chapter 32.)

3. If the monopoly appears to be relatively short-lived, say, because of emerging new technology, society can simply choose to ignore it. (The potential for real-world monopoly to collapse in the very long run is discussed in Chapter 26.)

QUICK REVIEW 24-2

■ The monopolist maximizes profit (or minimizes loss) at the output where MR = MC and charges the price which corresponds to this output on its demand curve.

■ The monopolist has no supply curve since any of several prices can be associated with a specific quantity of output supplied.

■ Assuming identical costs, a monopolist will be less efficient than a purely competitive industry because the monopolist produces less output and charges a higher price.

■ The inefficiencies of monopoly may be offset or lessened by economies of scale and, less likely, technological progress, but intensified by the presence of X-inefficiency and rent-seeking expenditures.

PRICE DISCRIMINATION

We have assumed in this chapter that the monopolist charges a single price to all buyers. But under certain conditions the monopolist can increase its profit by charging different prices to different buyers. In so doing, the monopolist is engaging in **price discrimination,** *the practice of selling a specific product at more than one price when the price differences are not justified by cost differences.*

Conditions

The opportunity to engage in price discrimination is not readily available to all sellers. Price discrimination is possible when three conditions are realized:

1. *Monopoly power* The seller must be a monopolist or, at least, possess some degree of monopoly power, that is, some ability to control output and price.

2. *Market segregation* The seller must be able to segregate buyers into distinct classes, each of which has a different willingness or ability to pay for the product. This separation of buyers is usually based on different elasticities of demand, as the illustrations below will make clear.

3. *No resale* The original purchaser cannot resell the product or service. If buyers in the low-price segment of the market could easily resell in the high-price segment, the monopolist's price discrimination strategy would create competition in the high-price segment. This competition would reduce the price in the high-price segment and undermine the monopolist's price discrimination policy. This condition suggests that service industries such as the transportation industry or legal and medical services, where resale is impossible, are candidates for price discrimination.

Examples

Price discrimination is widely practiced in the U.S. economy:

1. The sales representative who must communicate important information to corporate headquarters has a highly inelastic demand for long-distance telephone service and pays the high daytime rate. The college student "reporting in" to the folks at home has an elastic demand and can wait to take advantage of lower evening or weekend rates.

2. Electric utilities frequently segment their markets by end uses, such as lighting and heating. The absence of reasonable lighting substitutes means the demand for electricity for illumination is inelastic and the price per kilowatt-hour for this use is high. But the availability of natural gas and petroleum for heating makes the demand for electricity less inelastic for this purpose and the price charged is lower.

3. Movie theaters and golf courses vary their charges on the basis of time (higher rates in the evening and on weekends when demand is strong) and age (ability to pay).

4. Railroads vary the rate charged per ton-mile of freight according to the market value of the product being shipped. The shipper of 10 tons of television sets or costume jewelry is charged more than the shipper of 10 tons of gravel or coal.

5. Airlines charge high fares to traveling executives, whose demand for travel is inelastic, and offer lower fares such as "family rates" and "14-day advanced purchase fares" to attract vacationers and others whose demands are more elastic.

6. The issuance of discount coupons, redeemable at purchase, is a form of price discrimination. It permits firms to give price discounts to their most price-sensitive customers—those with elastic demand. Less price-sensitive consumers—those with less elastic demand—are not as likely to undertake the clipping and redeeming of coupons. The firm thus makes a larger profit than if it had used a single-price, no-coupon strategy.

7. In international trade, price discrimination is often called "dumping." A South Korean electronics manufacturer, for example, might sell a particular TV set for $100 less in the United States than in South Korea. In the United States, this seller faces an elastic demand because several substitute brands are available. But in South Korea, where the manufacturer dominates the market, consumers have fewer choices and thus demand is less elastic.

Consequences of Price Discrimination

As you will see shortly, a monopolist can increase its profit by practicing price discrimination. At the same time, perfect price discrimination results in greater output than that occurring with a single monopoly price.

More Profit The simplest way to understand why price discrimination can yield additional profit is to look again at our monopolist's downsloping demand curve in Figure 24-4. There we saw that the profit-maximizing single price is $P_m = \$122$. However, the segment of the demand curve lying above the gray economic profit area tells us some buyers are willing to pay *more than* $122 rather than forgo the product.

If the monopolist can identify and segregate these buyers and charge the maximum price each would pay, total revenue—and hence profit—would increase. In columns 1 and 2 in Table 24-1 we note that buyers of the first 4 units of output would be willing to pay $162, $152, $142, and $132, respectively, for those units. If the seller could practice perfect price discrimination by charging the maximum price for each unit, total revenue would increase from $610 (= $122 × 5) to $710 (= $122 + $132 + $142 + $152 + $162) and profit would increase from $140 (= $610 − $470) to $240 (= $710 − $470).

More Production Other things equal, the discriminating monopolist will choose to produce a larger output than the nondiscriminating monopolist. Recall that when the nondiscriminating monopolist lowers its price to sell additional output, the lower price applies not only to the additional output but also to *all prior* units of output. As a result, marginal revenue is less than price and, graphically, the marginal-revenue curve lies below the demand curve. The fact that marginal revenue is less than price acts as a disincentive to increased production.

But when a perfectly discriminating monopolist lowers price, the reduced price applies *only* to the additional unit sold and *not* to prior units. Hence, price and marginal revenue are equal for each unit of output. For the perfectly discriminating monopolist the marginal-revenue curve coincides with the demand curve, so the disincentive to increased production is removed.

Table 24-1 shows that, because marginal revenue now equals price, the discriminating monopolist finds it profitable to produce 7, rather than 5, units of output. The additional revenue from the sixth and seventh units is $214 (= $112 + $102). Thus total revenue for 7 units is $924 (= $710 + $214). Total cost for 7 units is $640, so profit is $284.

Ironically, although price discrimination increases the monopolist's profit compared with that of a nondiscriminating monopolist, it also results in greater output and thus less allocative inefficiency. In

our example, the output level of 7 units matches the output which would occur in pure competition. That is, allocative efficiency ($P = MC$) is achieved.

Graphical Portrayal Figure 24-8 shows the effects of price discrimination. Figure 24-8a merely restates Figure 24-4 in a generalized form to show the position of a nondiscriminating monopolist as a benchmark. The nondiscriminating monopolist produces output Q_1 (where MR = MC) and charges a price of P_1. Total revenue is area $0bce$ and economic profit is area $abcd$.

The monopolist in Figure 24-8b engages in perfect price discrimination, charging each buyer the highest price he or she is willing to pay. Starting at the very first unit, each additional unit is sold for the price indicated by the corresponding point on the demand curve. This monopolist's demand and marginal-revenue curves coincide because it does *not* cut price on preceding units to sell more output. Thus, the most profitable output is Q_2 (where MR = MC), which is greater than Q_1. Total revenue is area $0fgk$ and total cost is area $0hjk$. The discriminating monopolist's economic profit of $hfgj$ is clearly larger than the single-price monopolist's profit of $abcd$.

The impact of discrimination on consumers is mixed. Those buying each unit out to Q_1 will pay more than the nondiscriminatory price of P_1. But

(a) Single-price monopolist

(b) Perfectly discriminating monopolist

FIGURE 24-8 Single-price versus perfectly discriminating monopoly pricing (a) The single-price monopolist produces output Q_1 at which MR = MC, charges price P_1 for all units, incurs an average total cost of A_1, and realizes an economic profit represented by area $abcd$. (b) The perfectly discriminating monopolist has MR = D and, as a result, produces output Q_2 (where MR = MC). It then charges the maximum price for each unit of output, incurs average total cost A_2, and realizes an economic profit represented by area $hfgj$.

those additional consumers brought into the market by discrimination will pay less than P_1. Specifically, they will pay the various prices shown on segment cg of the $D = MR$ curve.

Overall, then, as compared with uniform pricing, perfect price discrimination results in greater profit, greater output, and higher prices for many consumers but lower prices for those purchasing the extra output. **(Key Question 6)**

REGULATED MONOPOLY

Monopolies that are natural monopolies normally are subject to regulation. The public utilities (local telephone companies, natural gas and local electricity suppliers) are all natural monopolies, and the prices they charge are determined by a Federal, state, or local regulatory commission.

Figure 24-9 shows the demand faced by, and long-run costs of, a natural monopoly. Because of extensive economies of scale, the demand curve cuts the long-run average-total-cost curve at a point where it is still falling. It would be inefficient to have several firms in such an industry. Each would produce a much smaller output, operating well to the left on the average-total-cost curve, so that its per-unit cost would be substantially higher. Attaining the lowest per-unit cost in such a situation requires a single producer.

We know by application of the $MR = MC$ rule that Q_m and P_m are the profit-maximizing output and

FIGURE 24-9 Regulated monopoly The socially optimal price P_r, found where D and MC intersect, will result in an efficient allocation of resources but may entail losses to the monopoly. The fair-return price P_f will allow the monopolist to break even but will not fully correct the underallocation of resources.

price which an unregulated monopolist would choose. Because price exceeds average total cost at output Q_m, the monopolist enjoys a substantial economic profit. Furthermore, price exceeds marginal cost, indicating an underallocation of resources to this product or service. Can government regulation bring about better results from society's point of view?

Socially Optimal Price: $P = MC$

If the objective of a regulatory commission is to achieve allocative efficiency, it should attempt to establish a legal (ceiling) price for the monopolist that is equal to *marginal cost*. Remembering that each point on the market demand curve designates a price-quantity combination, and noting that the marginal-cost curve cuts the demand curve only at point r, we see that P_r is the only price on the demand curve equal to marginal cost. The maximum or ceiling price effectively causes the monopolist's demand curve to become horizontal (indicating perfectly elastic demand) from zero out to point r, where the regulated price ceases to be effective. Also, out to point r we have $MR = P_r$.

Confronted with the legal price P_r, the monopolist will maximize profit or minimize loss by producing Q_r units of output, because it is at this output that $MR (= P_r) = MC$. By making it illegal to charge more than P_r per unit, the regulatory agency has removed the monopolist's incentive to restrict output to Q_m to obtain a higher price and greater profit.

In short, by imposing the legal price P_r and letting the monopolist choose its profit-maximizing or loss-minimizing output, the allocative forces of pure competition can be simulated. Production takes place where $P_r = MC$, and this equality indicates an efficient allocation of resources to this product or service. The price which achieves allocative efficiency is called the **socially optimal price.**

Fair-Return Price: $P = ATC$

But the socially optimal price P_r may pose a problem of losses for the regulated firm. The price which equals marginal cost may be so low that average total costs are not covered, as is the case in Figure 24-9. The result is losses. The reason lies in the basic character of public utilities. Because they are required to meet the heaviest "peak" demands (both daily and seasonally) for their product or service, they have substantial excess production capacity when demand is relatively "normal." Their high level of investment in produc-

De Beers' Diamonds: Are Monopolies Forever?

De Beers Consolidated Mines of South Africa is one of the world's strongest and most enduring monopolies, having dominated the diamond market for over 60 years.

De Beers produces about 50 percent of all rough-cut diamonds in the world and buys for resale a large portion of the diamonds produced by other mines worldwide. As a result, it markets about 70 percent of the world's diamonds to a select group of diamond cutters and dealers.

Monopoly Behavior De Beers' behavior and results are well represented by the unregulated monopoly model in Figure 24-4. It sells only that quantity of diamonds which will yield an "appropriate" (monopoly) price. This price bears little relationship to production costs, and profits have been enormous. In "good" years profits are 60 percent of total revenues and rates of return on equity (ownership) capital are 30 percent or more.

When demand falls, De Beers restricts sales to maintain price. The excess of production over sales is then reflected in growing diamond stockpiles held by De Beers. It also attempts to bolster demand through advertising ("diamonds are forever"). When demand is strong, it increases sales by reducing its diamond inventories.

De Beers controls the production of mines it does not own in several ways. First, it tries to convince independent producers that "single-channel" or monopoly marketing through De Beers is in their best interests in that it maximizes profit. Second, mines which circumvent De Beers are likely to find that the market is suddenly flooded from

De Beers' stockpiles with the particular kind of diamonds that the "rogue" mine produces. The resulting price decline and loss of profit are likely to bring the mine into the De Beers fold. Finally, De Beers will simply purchase and stockpile diamonds produced by independent mines so their added supply will not "spoil" the market.

Threats and Problems But even such an enduring monopoly as De Beers faces threats and problems. New diamond discoveries have resulted in a growing leakage of diamonds into world markets outside De Beers' control. For example, wildcat prospecting and trading in Angola has forced De Beers to spend as much as $500 million per year to keep such diamonds off the market. The recent diamond supplies discovered in Canada's northwest territories pose a future threat. Similarly, although Russia is part of the De Beers' monopoly, this cash-strapped country has been selling about $300 million in diamonds per year directly into the world markets. When new Siberian mines are brought into production, the additional output will pose a further threat to De Beers. Russia's estimated $4 to $8 billion stockpile of diamonds constitutes another potential future source of uncontrolled supply.

Of more immediate concern to De Beers, Australian diamond producer Argyle has opted to withdraw from the De Beers' monopoly. Its annual production of mostly low-grade industrial diamonds accounts for about 6 percent of the global $6 billion diamond market.

De Beers' diamond inventories now exceed $5 billion, an amount greater than its annual sales. Observers wonder whether De Beers' capacity to absorb future unregulated production will reach a breaking point. They also speculate that Argyle will team up with Canadian producers to directly market the diamonds mined in the northwest territories. This one-two punch may cause the De Beers' monopoly to unravel. Although diamonds may be forever, the De Beers' monopoly may soon be history.

---

tion facilities and economies of scale mean that their average total cost is likely to be greater than their marginal cost over a very wide range of outputs. In particular, as in Figure 24-9, average total cost is likely to be greater than the price P_r at the intersection of the demand curve and marginal-cost curve. Therefore, imposing the socially optimal price P_r on the regu-

lated monopolist would mean short-run losses and long-run bankruptcy for the utility.

What to do? One option is to provide a public subsidy to cover the loss which marginal-cost pricing would entail. Another possibility is to condone price discrimination and hope that the additional revenue gained will permit the firm to cover costs.

In practice, regulatory commissions have pursued a third option: They modify the objective of allocative efficiency and $P = MC$ pricing. Most regulatory agencies in the United States establish a **fair-return price.** They do so because, as the courts have seen it, a socially optimal price leading to losses and bankruptcy would deprive the monopoly's owners of their private property without "due process of law." The Supreme Court has held that regulatory agencies must permit a "fair return" to utility owners.

Remembering that total cost includes a normal or "fair" profit, we see in Figure 24-9 that a fair-return price should be on the average-total-cost curve. Because the demand curve cuts average total cost only at point f, clearly P_f is the only price on the demand curve which permits a fair return. The corresponding output at regulated price P_f will be Q_f. Total revenue of $0afb$ will equal the utility's total cost of the same amount, and the firm will realize a normal profit.

Dilemma of Regulation

Comparing results of the socially optimal price ($P = MC$) and the fair-return price ($P = ATC$) suggests a policy dilemma, sometimes termed the **dilemma of regulation.** When its price is set to achieve the most efficient allocation of resources ($P = MC$), the regulated monopoly is likely to suffer losses. Survival of the firm would presumably depend on permanent public subsidies out of tax revenues. On the other hand, although a fair-return price ($P = ATC$) allows

the monopolist to cover costs, it only partially resolves the underallocation of resources that the unregulated monopoly price would foster. That is, the fair-return price would increase output only from Q_m to Q_f in Figure 24-9, while the socially optimal output is Q_r. Despite this dilemma, regulation can improve on the results of monopoly from the social point of view. Price regulation (even at the fair-return price) can simultaneously reduce price, increase output, and reduce the economic profits of monopolies. **(Key Question 11)**

QUICK REVIEW 24-3

■ Price discrimination occurs when a firm sells a product at different prices which are not based on cost differences.

■ The conditions necessary for price discrimination are (a) monopoly power, (b) the ability to segregate buyers on the basis of demand elasticities, and (c) the inability of buyers to resell the product.

■ Compared with single pricing by a monopolist, perfect price discrimination results in greater profit and greater output. Many consumers pay higher prices, but other buyers pay prices below the single price.

■ Monopoly price can be reduced and output increased through government regulation.

■ The socially optimal price ($P = MC$) achieves allocative efficiency but may result in losses; the fair-return price ($P = ATC$) yields a normal profit but falls short of allocative efficiency.

CHAPTER SUMMARY

1. A pure monopolist is the sole producer of a commodity for which there are no close substitutes.

2. Barriers to entry, in the form of (a) economies of scale, (b) patent ownership and research, (c) ownership or control of essential resources, and (d) pricing and other strategic behavior, help explain the existence of pure monopoly and other imperfectly competitive market structures.

3. The pure monopolist's market situation differs from a competitive firm's in that the monopolist's demand curve is downsloping, causing the marginal-revenue curve to lie below the demand curve. Like the competitive seller, the pure monopolist will maximize profit by equating marginal revenue and marginal cost. Barriers to entry may permit a monopolist to acquire economic profit even in the long run. However, (a) the monopolist does not charge "the highest price it can get"; (b) the price that yields maximum total

profit to the monopolist rarely coincides with the price that yields maximum unit profit; (c) high costs and a weak demand may prevent the monopolist from realizing any profit at all; and (d) the monopolist avoids the inelastic region of its demand curve.

4. With the same costs, the pure monopolist will find it profitable to restrict output and charge a higher price than would sellers in a purely competitive industry. This restriction of output causes resources to be misallocated, as is evidenced by the fact that price exceeds marginal cost in monopolized markets.

5. In general, monopoly increases income inequality.

6. The costs monopolists and competitive producers face may not be the same. On the one hand, economies of scale may make lower unit costs available to monopolists but not to competitors. Also, pure monopoly may be more likely than pure competition to reduce costs via technological advance because of the monopolist's ability to realize economic profit, which can be used to finance research. On the other hand, X-inefficiency—the failure to produce with the least costly combination of inputs—is more common to monopolists than to competitive firms. Also, monopolists may make costly expenditures to maintain monopoly privileges that are conferred by government. Finally, the blocked entry of rival firms weakens the monopolist's *incentive* to be technologically progressive.

7. A monopolist can increase its profit by practicing price discrimination, provided **(a)** it can segregate buyers on the basis of elasticities of demand and **(b)** its product or service cannot be readily transferred between the segregated markets. Other things equal, the perfectly discriminating monopolist will produce a larger output than the nondiscriminating monopolist.

8. Price regulation can be invoked to eliminate wholly or partially the tendency of monopolists to underallocate resources and to earn economic profits. The socially optimal price is determined where the demand and marginal-cost curves intersect; the fair-return price is determined where the demand and average-total-cost curves intersect.

TERMS AND CONCEPTS

pure monopoly	X-inefficiency	price discrimination	fair-return price
barriers to entry	rent-seeking behavior	socially optimal price	dilemma of regulation

STUDY QUESTIONS

1. "No firm is completely sheltered from rivals; all firms compete for consumer dollars. If that is so, then pure monopoly does not exist." Do you agree? Explain. How might you use Chapter 20's concept of cross elasticity of demand to judge whether monopoly exists?

2. Discuss the major barriers to entry into an industry. Explain how each barrier can foster monopoly or oligopoly. Which barriers, if any, do you feel give rise to monopoly that is socially justifiable?

3. How does the demand curve faced by a purely monopolistic seller differ from that confronting a purely competitive firm? Why does it differ? Of what significance is the difference? Why is the pure monopolist's demand curve not perfectly inelastic?

4. KEY QUESTION Use the demand schedule that follows to calculate total revenue and marginal revenue at each quantity. Plot the demand, total-revenue, and marginal-revenue curves and carefully explain the relationships between them. Explain why the marginal revenue of the fourth unit of output is $3.50, even though its price is $5.00. Use Chapter 20's total-revenue test for price elasticity to designate the elastic and inelastic segments of your graphed demand curve. What generalization can you make as to the relationship between marginal revenue and elasticity of demand? Suppose the marginal cost of successive units of output were zero. What output would the profit-seeking firm produce? Finally, use your analysis to explain why a monopolist would never produce in the inelastic region of demand.

Price (P)	Quantity demanded (Q)	Price (P)	Quantity demanded (Q)
$7.00	0	$4.50	5
6.50	1	4.00	6
6.00	2	3.50	7
5.50	3	3.00	8
5.00	4	2.50	9

5. KEY QUESTION Suppose a pure monopolist is faced with the demand schedule shown below and the same cost data as the competitive producer discussed in question 4 at the end of Chapter 23. Calculate the missing total- and marginal-revenue amounts, and determine the profit-maximizing price and output for this monopolist. What is the monopolist's profit? Verify your answer graphically and by comparing total revenue and total cost.

Price	Quantity demanded	Total revenue	Marginal revenue
$115	0	$_____	$_____
100	1	_____	_____
83	2	_____	_____
71	3	_____	_____
63	4	_____	_____
55	5	_____	_____
48	6	_____	_____
42	7	_____	_____
37	8	_____	_____
33	9	_____	_____
29	10	_____	_____

6. KEY QUESTION If the firm described in question 5 could engage in perfect price discrimination, what would be the level of output? Of profits? Draw a diagram showing the relevant demand, marginal-revenue, average-total-cost, and marginal-cost curves and the equilibrium price and output for a nondiscriminating monopolist. Use the same diagram to show the equilibrium position of a monopolist able to practice perfect price discrimination. Compare equilibrium outputs, total revenues, economic profits, and consumer prices in the two cases. Comment on the economic desirability of price discrimination.

7. Assume a pure monopolist and a purely competitive firm have the same unit costs. Contrast the two with respect to **(a)** price, **(b)** output, **(c)** profits, **(d)** allocation of resources, and **(e)** impact on the distribution of income. Since both monopolists and competitive firms follow the MC = MR rule in maximizing profits, how do you account for the different results? Why might the costs of a purely competitive firm and a monopolist be different? What are the implications of such a cost difference?

8. Critically evaluate and explain:

   a. "Because they can control product price, monopolists are always assured of profitable production by simply charging the highest price consumers will pay."

   b. "The pure monopolist seeks that output which will yield the greatest per-unit profit."

   c. "An excess of price over marginal cost is the market's way of signaling the need for more production of a good."

   d. "The more profitable a firm, the greater its monopoly power."

   e. "The monopolist has a pricing policy; the competitive producer does not."

   f. "With respect to resource allocation, the interests of the seller and of society coincide in a purely competitive market but conflict in a monopolized market."

   g. "In a sense the monopolist makes a profit for not producing; the monopolist produces profit more than it does goods."

9. Assume a monopolistic publisher has agreed to pay an author 15 percent of the total revenue from the sales of a text. Will the author and the publisher want to charge the same price for the text? Explain.

10. Explain verbally and graphically how price (rate) regulation may improve the performance of monopolies. In your answer distinguish between **(a)** socially optimal (marginal-cost) pricing and **(b)** fair-return (average-total-cost) pricing. What is the "dilemma of regulation"?

11. KEY QUESTION It has been proposed that natural monopolists should be allowed to determine their profit-maximizing outputs and prices and then government should tax their profits away and distribute them to consumers in proportion to their purchases from the monopoly. Is this proposal as socially desirable as requiring monopolists to equate price with marginal cost or average total cost?

12. (Last Word) Explain how De Beers has an almost complete monopoly of the world diamond market although it only produces one-half of world output. What are the threats to its market power?

13. WEB-BASED QUESTION **Microsoft—Is It a Monopoly?** Microsoft is often accused of having a monopoly in the personal computer software industry. However, like most firms, Microsoft is a multiproduct company. Go to Computer Shopper's Netbuyer http://www.netbuyer.com/ and search for companies which compete with Microsoft in marketing the following software: operating systems, applications suites (word processing, spreadsheet, and database software bundled together), and Internet/Online software (Web browsers and Web design packages). Does Microsoft have a monopoly in any of these areas? Is there a correlation between the maturity of the software area (operating systems are more mature than browsers) and the number of competitors?

14. WEB-BASED QUESTION **Duke Energy—How Does a Monopoly Advertise?** Duke Energy Corporation is a global energy company with more than $20 billion in assets. Many of its units are regulated public utilities and are good examples of natural monopolies. What is their advertising message at http://www.duke-energy.com/? How does it differ from a nonmonopoly? Can you find any examples of Duke Energy units using advertising to actually decrease the demand for their products or services? Why might they do this?

Monopolistic Competition and Oligopoly

Pure competition and pure monopoly are the exceptions, not the rule, in the U.S. economy. Most market structures fall somewhere between these two extremes. Two examples are:

- If you want to go out to eat, you have an amazing variety of choices. You can get a meal at a fast-food place such as McDonald's, Subway, or Taco Bell. Or you can go to a restaurant with a fuller menu and with table service, say, Applebee's, Chili's, or Denny's. For a special meal you can choose an Italian, French, or Japanese fine-food restaurant where your bill may be $20 or more per person. Each of these establishments serves food and beverages, but all have different menus and prices. Competition among them is based not only on price but also on product quality, location, service, and advertising.

- Do you plan to buy a new car once you graduate from college and land a good job? Although you will have many choices of brands and models, most likely you will buy your new car from one of a handful of auto producers—General Motors, Ford, Honda, Chrysler, or Toyota. In many of our manufacturing, mining, and wholesaling industries there are only a few dominant firms, not the thousands of producers presumed in pure competition or the single producer characterizing monopoly.

In this chapter we examine two market structures that more closely approximate "real-world" markets: *monopolistic competition* and *oligopoly*. You will see that monopolistic competition suggests a considerable amount of competition mixed with a small dose of monopoly power, as in our restaurant example. Oligopoly, in contrast, implies a blend of greater monopoly power and less competition; there are only a few firms in an oligopolistic industry, and entry is difficult, as suggested by the automobile illustration.

Our discussion proceeds as follows: First, we define monopolistic competition, detail its characteristics, and examine its occurrence. Then, we evaluate the price, output, and efficiency outcomes of monopolistic competition. Next, we turn to oligopoly, surveying the possible courses of price, output, and advertising behavior that oligopolistic industries might follow. Finally, we assess whether oligopoly is an efficient or inefficient market structure.

MONOPOLISTIC COMPETITION: CHARACTERISTICS AND OCCURRENCE

The defining characteristics of **monopolistic competition** are (1) a relatively large number of sellers; (2) differentiated products (often accompanied by heavy advertising); and (3) easy entry to, and exit from, the industry. The first and third characteristics provide the "competitive" aspect of monopolistic competition; the second characteristic contributes the "monopolistic" aspect.

Relatively Large Number of Sellers

Monopolistic competition does not require hundreds or thousands of firms, as does pure competition, but only a fairly large number, say, 25, 35, 60, or 70 firms in each industry. Several characteristics of monopolistic competition follow from the presence of these relatively large number of firms.

1. **Small market share**   Each firm has a comparatively small percentage of the total market, so each has limited control over market price.
2. **No collusion**   The presence of a relatively large number of firms ensures that *collusion*—action by a group of firms to restrict output and set prices—is very unlikely.
3. **Independent action**   With numerous firms in an industry, there is no feeling of interdependence among them; each firm can determine its own pricing policy without considering the possible reactions of rival firms. Firm X may realize a 10 or 15 percent increase in sales by cutting its price, but the effect on competitors' sales will be spread so thinly over the 20, 40, or 60 other firms that it will be nearly imperceptible. And if rivals cannot feel the impact of firm X's actions, they will have no reason to react to those actions.

Differentiated Products

In contrast to pure competition, monopolistic competition has the fundamental feature of **product differentiation.** Purely competitive firms produce a standardized or homogeneous product; monopolistically competitive producers turn out variations of a particular product. That is, monopolistic competitors provide products slightly different from competing products with regard to product attributes, services to customers, location and accessibility, or other qualities, real or imagined.

Let's examine these aspects of product differentiation in more detail.

Product Attributes   Product differentiation may take the form of physical or qualitative differences in the products themselves. Real differences in functional features, materials, design, and workmanship are vital aspects of product differentiation. Personal computers, for example, differ in terms of storage capacity, speed, graphic displays, and user-friendliness. There are scores of competing principles of economics texts that differ in content, organization, presentation and readability, pedagogical aids, and graphics and design. Most cities have a variety of retail stores selling men's and women's clothing varying greatly in styling, materials, and quality of work. Similarly, one fast-food hamburger chain may feature its curly fries, while a competitor stresses its traditional fries.

Credit cards may seem like homogeneous "products," differing only in annual fees and interest-rate charges. Not so. Some provide rebates on purchases; others offer free airline travel miles; and still others offer extended warranties on products purchased on credit.

Service   Service and the conditions surrounding the sale of a product are forms of product differentiation. One grocery store may stress the helpfulness of its clerks who bag your groceries and carry them to your car. A warehouse competitor may leave bagging and carrying to its customers but feature lower prices. One-day cleaning may be preferred to cleaning of equal quality that takes 3 days. The prestige appeal of a store, the courteousness and helpfulness of clerks, the firm's reputation for servicing or exchanging its products, and credit availability are all service aspects of product differentiation.

Location   Products may also be differentiated through location and accessibility. Small minigroceries or convenience stores successfully compete with large supermarkets, even though they have a more limited range of products and charge higher prices. They compete on the basis of location—being close to customers and on busy streets—and by being open 24 hours a day. A gas station's proximity to an interstate highway gives it a locational advantage that may allow it to sell gasoline at a higher price than gas stations farther from the interstate.

Brand Names and Packaging   Product differentiation may also be created through the use of brand names and trademarks, packaging, and celebrity connections. Most aspirin tablets are very much alike, but many headache sufferers feel that one brand—Bayer, or Anacin, or Bufferin—is superior and worth a higher price than a generic substitute. A celebrity's name associated with jeans, perfume, or athletic equipment may enhance those products in the minds of buyers. Many consumers prefer toothpaste in a pump container to the same toothpaste in a conventional tube. Environment-friendly "green" packaging or "natural spring" bottled water is used to attract additional customers.

Some Control over Price

One implication of product differentiation is that, despite the relatively large number of firms, monopolistically competitive producers do have some control over the prices of their products. If consumers prefer the products of specific sellers, then *within limits* they will pay more to satisfy their preferences. Sellers and buyers are not linked randomly, as in a purely competitive market. But the monopolistic competitor's control over price is very limited since there are numerous potential substitutes for its product.

Easy Entry and Exit

Entry into monopolistically competitive industries is relatively easy. Because monopolistic competitors are typically small firms, both absolutely and relatively, economies of scale are few and capital requirements are low. On the other hand, compared with pure competition, financial barriers may result from the need to develop a product different from rivals' products and the obligation to advertise it. Some existing firms may hold patents on their products and copyrights on their brand names and trademarks, increasing the difficulty and cost of successfully imitating them.

Exit from monopolistically competitive industries is also relatively easy. Nothing prevents an unprofitable monopolistic competitor from holding a going-out-of-business sale and permanently shutting down.

Nonprice Competition and Advertising

The expense and effort involved in product differentiation would be wasted if consumers were not made aware of product differences. Thus, monopolistic competitors advertise their products, often heavily. The goal of product differentiation and advertising—so-called **nonprice competition**—is to make price

less of a factor in consumer purchases, and product differences a greater factor. If successful, the firm's demand curve will shift to the right and become less elastic.

Monopolistically Competitive Industries

Table 25-1 lists manufacturing industries approximating monopolistic competition. (We will explain the data in the last column later in this chapter.) In addition, retail establishments in metropolitan areas are generally monopolistically competitive; grocery stores, gasoline stations, barbershops, dry cleaners, clothing stores, and restaurants operate under monopolistically competitive conditions.

MONOPOLISTIC COMPETITION: PRICE AND OUTPUT DETERMINATION

We now analyze the price and output decisions of a monopolistically competitive firm. We assume initially that each firm in the industry is producing a specific differentiated product and engaging in a particular amount of advertising. Later we'll see how changes in the product and the amount of advertising modify our conclusions.

The Firm's Demand Curve

Our explanation is couched in terms of **Figure 25-1 (Key Graph)**. The basic feature of this diagram is the elasticity of demand, as shown by the individual firm's demand curve. *The demand curve faced by a monopolistically competitive seller is highly, but not perfectly, elastic.* This feature distinguishes monopolistic competition from our analysis of pure monopoly and pure competition. The monopolistic competitor's demand is more elastic than the demand faced by a pure monopolist because the monopolistically competitive seller has many competitors producing close substitute goods. The pure monopolist has no rivals at all. Yet, for two reasons, the monopolistically competitive seller's demand is not perfectly elastic like the purely competitive producer's. First, the monopolistically competitive firm has fewer rivals; second, the products of monopolistic competitors are differentiated, so they are not perfect substitutes.

The degree of price elasticity of demand the monopolistically competitive firm sees will depend on

TABLE 25-1   Percentage of output produced by firms in selected low-concentration U.S. manufacturing industries

(1) Industry	(2) Percentage of industry output* produced by the four largest firms	(3) Herfin- dahl index	(1) Industry	(2) Percentage of industry output* produced by the four largest firms	(3) Herfin- dahl index
Manufactured ice	24	264	Textile bags	17	164
Plastic pipe	23	268	Bolts, nuts,		
Book publishing	23	251	and rivets	17	134
Paperboard boxes	23	237	Jewelry	16	95
Curtains and			Typesetting	16	106
draperies	22	184	Asphalt paving	15	103
Textile machinery	21	197	Sawmills	14	78
Leather goods	21	196	Women's dresses	11	61
Lighting fixtures	21	191	Sheet metal work	9	34
Wood furniture	20	167	Wood pallets	6	14
Wooden kitchen					
cabinets	19	156			

*As measured by value of shipments. Data are for 1992.
Source: Bureau of Census, Census of Manufacturers, 1992.

the exact number of rivals and the degree of product differentiation. The larger the number of rivals and the weaker the product differentiation, the greater the elasticity of each seller's demand; that is, the closer monopolistic competition will be to pure competition.

The Short Run: Profit or Loss

The monopolistically competitive firm maximizes its profit or minimizes its loss in the short run just as do the other firms we have discussed: by producing the output at which marginal revenue equals marginal cost (MR = MC). In Figure 25-1a the firm produces output Q_1, where MR = MC. As shown by demand curve D_1, it then can charge price P_1. Here, it realizes an economic profit shown by the gray area $[= (P_1 - A_1) \times Q_1]$.

But with less favorable demand or costs, the firm may incur a loss in the short run. This possibility is shown in Figure 25-1b, where the firm's best strategy is to minimize its loss. It does this by producing output Q_2 (where MR = MC) and, as determined by demand curve D_2, charging price P_2. Because price P_2 is less than average total cost A_2, the firm incurs the loss shown by the pink area $[= (A_2 - P_2) \times Q_2]$.

The Long Run: Only a Normal Profit

In the long run, firms will enter a profitable monopolistically competitive industry and leave an unprofitable one. As a result, in the long run a monopolistically competitive firm will earn only a normal profit or, in other words, only break even.

Profits: Firms Enter   In the case of short-run profit (Figure 25-1a), economic profits attract new rivals because entry to the industry is easy. As new firms enter, the demand curve faced by the typical firm will shift to the left (fall). Why? Because each firm has a smaller share of total demand and now faces a larger number of close-substitute products. This decline in the firm's demand reduces its economic profit. When entry of new firms has caused the demand curve to fall to the degree that it is tangent to the average-total-cost curve at the profit-maximizing output, the firm is just making a normal profit. This situation is shown in Figure 25-1c, where demand is D_3 and the firm's long-run equilibrium output is Q_3. As Figure 25-1c clearly indicates, any greater or lesser output will entail an average total cost that exceeds product price P_3, meaning losses for the firm. At the tangency point between the demand curve and ATC, there are

(a) Short-run profits

(b) Short-run losses

(c) Long-run equilibrium

FIGURE 25-1 A monopolistically competitive firm: short run and long run The monopolistic competitor maximizes profit or minimizes loss by producing the output at which MR = MC. The economic profit shown in (a) will induce new firms to enter, eventually eliminating economic profit. The loss shown in (b) will cause an exit of firms until normal profit is restored. After such entry and exit, the price will settle in (c) to where it just equals average total cost at the MR = MC output. At this price P_3 and output Q_3, the monopolistic competitor earns only a normal profit and the industry is in long-run equilibrium.

QUICK QUIZ 25-1

1. Price exceeds MC in:
   a. graph (a) only.
   b. graph (b) only.
   c. graphs (a) and (b) only.
   d. graphs (a), (b), and (c).

2. Price exceeds ATC in:
   a. graph (a) only.
   b. graph (b) only.
   c. graphs (a) and (b) only.
   d. graphs (a), (b), and (c).

3. The firm represented by Figure 25-1c is:
   a. making a normal profit.
   b. incurring a loss, once opportunity costs are considered.

   c. producing at the same level of output as a purely competitive firm.
   d. producing a standardized product.

4. Which of the following pairs are both "competitionlike elements" in monopolistic competition?
   a. Price exceeds MR; standardized product.
   b. Entry is relatively easy; only a normal profit in the long run.
   c. Price equals MC at the profit-maximizing output; economic profits are likely in the long run.
   d. The firms' demand curve is downsloping; differentiated products.

Answers: 1. d; 2. a; 3. a; 4. b

no more economic profits, and thus no incentive for additional firms to enter.

Losses: Firms Leave   When the industry suffers short-run losses, as in Figure 25-1b, some firms will exit in the long run. Faced with fewer substitute products and blessed with an expanded share of total demand, surviving firms will see their demand curves shift to the right (rise), as to D_3, and their losses disappear and give way to normal profits (Figure 25-1c). (For simplicity we have assumed constant costs; shifts in the cost curves as firms enter or leave would complicate our discussion slightly but would not alter the conclusions.)

Complications   The representative firm in the monopolistic competition model earns only a *normal* profit in the long run. This outcome may not always occur, however, in the real world of small firms. Two complications are noteworthy:

1. Some firms may achieve product differentiation to an extent that other firms cannot duplicate, even over time. A hotel in a major city may have the best location relative to business and tourist activities. Or a firm may hold a patent giving it a slight but more or less permanent advantage over imitators. Such firms may have sufficient monopoly power to realize a sliver of economic profits even in the long run.

2. Entry to some monopolistically competitive industries is not as free in reality as it is in theory. Because of product differentiation, there are likely to be greater financial barriers to entry than there would be if the product were standardized. This suggests some monopoly power, with small economic profits continuing even in the long run.

With all things considered, however, the long-run normal profit equilibrium of Figure 25-1c is a reasonable portrayal of reality.

MONOPOLISTIC COMPETITION AND ECONOMIC EFFICIENCY

From our evaluation of competitive pricing in Chapter 23, we know that economic efficiency requires the triple equality $P = MC = $ minimum ATC. The equality of price and minimum average total cost yields *productive efficiency*. The good is produced in the least costly way, and the price is just sufficient to cover

average total cost, including a normal profit. The equality of price and marginal cost yields *allocative efficiency*. The right amount of output is being produced, and thus the right amount of society's scarce resources is being devoted to this specific use.

How efficient is monopolistic competition, as measured with this triple equality?

Neither Productive nor Allocative Efficiency

In monopolistic competition, neither productive nor allocative efficiency occurs in long-run equilibrium. Figure 25-2, which includes an enlargement of part of Figure 25-1c, shows this fact. First note that the profit-maximizing price P_3 slightly exceeds the lowest average total cost, A_4. Therefore, in producing the profit-maximizing output Q_3, the firm's average total cost is slightly higher than optimal from society's perspective—productive efficiency is not achieved. Also note that the profit-maximizing price P_3 exceeds marginal cost (here M_3), which means the monopolistic element in monopolistic competition causes a small underallocation of resources. Society values each unit of output between Q_3 and Q_4 more highly than the goods it would have to forgo to produce these units. Thus, to a modest extent, monopolistic competition also fails the allocative-efficiency test. Consumers pay a higher-than-competitive price and obtain a less-than-optimal output. Indeed, monopolistic competitors *must* charge a higher-than-competitive price in the long run to achieve a normal profit.

Excess Capacity

In monopolistic competition, the output gap Q_4 to Q_3 in Figure 25-2 identifies **excess capacity:** *plant and equipment that are underused because firms are producing less than the minimum-ATC output.* If each monopolistic competitor could profitably produce at the minimum-ATC output, fewer firms could produce the same total output, and the product could be sold at a lower price. Monopolistically competitive industries thus tend to be overcrowded with firms, each operating below its optimal capacity, that is, without achieving productive efficiency. This situation is typified by many kinds of retail establishments. An example is the numerous small motels, many operating with excess capacity, that are found in most cities. **(Key Question 2)**

FIGURE 25-2 The inefficiency of monopolistic competition   In long-run equilibrium a monopolistic competitor achieves neither productive nor allocative efficiency. Productive efficiency is not realized because production occurs where the average total cost A_3 exceeds the minimum average total cost A_4. Allocative efficiency is not realized because the product price P_3 exceeds the marginal cost M_3. The result is an underallocation of resources and excess productive capacity of $Q_4 - Q_3$.

MONOPOLISTIC COMPETITION: NONPRICE COMPETITION

The situation portrayed in Figures 25-1c and 25-2 is not very satisfying to monopolistic competitors since it foretells only a normal profit. These producers would like to improve on that long-run situation.

How can they do this? It can be accomplished through nonprice competition in the form of product differentiation and advertising. Each firm has a product distinguishable in some way from those of the other producers. Developing or improving it can presumably further differentiate the product. And advertising can be used to emphasize real product differences and help create perceived differences. So the profit-realizing firm of Figure 25-1a need not stand by and watch new competitors eliminate its profit by imitating its product, matching its customer service, and copying its advertising. Rather, the firm can attempt to sustain its profit and stay ahead of competitors through further product differentiation and better advertising. In this way it might prevent the long-run outcome of Figure 25-1c from becoming re-

ality. True, product differentiation and advertising will add to the firm's costs, but they can also increase the demand for its product. If demand increases by more than enough to compensate for the added costs, the firm will have improved its profit position. As Figure 25-2 suggests, the firm has little or no prospect of increasing profit by price cutting. So why not practice nonprice competition?

The likelihood that easy entry promotes product variety and product improvement is to some observers a positive feature of monopolistic competition—one that offsets, at least partly, its inefficiency. In fact, product differentiation is at the center of a tradeoff between consumer choice and productive efficiency. The stronger the product differentiation, the greater the excess capacity and, hence, the greater the productive *inefficiency. But the greater the product differentiation, the more likely the variety of diverse consumer tastes will be fully satisfied. The greater the excess capacity problem, the wider the range of consumer choice.

There are two considerations here: (1) product differentiation at a point in time, and (2) product development over a period of time.

Product Differentiation

If a product is differentiated, then at any time the consumer will be offered a wide range of types, styles, brands, and quality gradations of that product. Compared with pure competition, this suggests possible advantages to the consumer. The range of choice is widened, and variations in consumer taste are more fully met by producers.

But skeptics warn that product differentiation may reach the point where the consumer becomes confused and rational choice becomes time-consuming and difficult. Variety may add spice to the consumer's life, but only up to a point. Worse, some observers fear that the consumer, faced with a myriad of similar products, may judge product quality by price; the consumer may irrationally assume that price is always a measure of product quality.

Product Development

Product development is the process that, over time, leads to product changes and thus to most product differentiation. Its purpose usually is to develop a more useful or otherwise improved product. Product development may cause still more product development in two ways. First, a successful product improvement by one firm obligates rivals to imitate or improve on that firm's temporary market advantage or suffer losses. Second, profit realized from a successful product improvement can finance *further* improvements.

Again, there are critics. They say that many product changes are more apparent than real, that they are superficial changes which do *not* improve the product's durability, efficiency, or usefulness. A more exotic container or bright packaging is frequently the extent of "product development." It is argued, too, that particularly with durable and semidurable consumer goods, development may follow a pattern of "planned obsolescence," with firms improving a product only by the amount necessary to make the average consumer dissatisfied with last year's model.

Monopolistic Competition and Economic Analysis

The ability to engage in nonprice competition makes the market situation of a monopolistically competitive firm more complex than Figure 25-1 indicates. That figure assumes a *given* (unchanging) product and *given* level of advertising expenditures. But we know that,

in practice, product attributes and advertising are not fixed. The monopolistically competitive firm juggles three factors—price, product, and advertising—in seeking maximum profit. It must determine what variety of product, selling at what price, and supplemented by what level of advertising activity will result in the greatest profit. This complex situation is not easily expressed in a simple, meaningful economic model. At best, we can say that each possible combination of price, product, and advertising poses a different demand and cost (production cost plus advertising cost) situation for the firm, and one of them will yield the maximum profit.

In practice, this optimal combination cannot be readily forecast but must be found by trial and error. Even then, in some instances certain limitations may be imposed by the actions of rivals: A firm may not be free to eliminate its advertising for fear its share of the market will decline sharply, benefiting rivals that do advertise. Similarly, patents held by rivals may rule out certain desirable product improvements.

QUICK REVIEW 25-1

■ Monopolistic competition involves a relatively large number of firms operating noncollusively and producing differentiated products with easy entry and exit.

■ In the short run, a monopolistic competitor will maximize profit or minimize loss by producing that output at which marginal revenue equals marginal cost.

■ In the long run, easy entry and exit of firms cause monopolistic competitors to earn only a normal profit.

■ A monopolistic competitor's long-run equilibrium output is such that price exceeds the minimum average total cost (implying that consumers do not get the product at the lowest price attainable) and price exceeds marginal cost (indicating that resources are underallocated to the product).

OLIGOPOLY: CHARACTERISTICS AND OCCURRENCE

In terms of competitiveness, the spectrum of market structures moves from pure competition, to monopolistic competition, to oligopoly, to pure monopoly (review Table 23-1). We now direct our attention to **oligopoly,** *a market dominated by a few large producers of a homogeneous or differentiated product.* Because of their "fewness," oligopolists have considerable control over their prices, but each must consider the possible reaction of rivals to its own pricing, output, and advertising decisions.

A Few Large Producers

What does "a few large producers" mean? This term is necessarily vague because the market model of oligopoly covers much ground, ranging between pure monopoly, on the one hand, and monopolistic competition, on the other. Thus oligopoly encompasses the U.S. aluminum industry, in which three huge firms dominate an entire national market, and the situation in which four or five much smaller auto parts stores may enjoy roughly equal shares of the market in a medium-sized town. Generally, when you hear a term such as "Big Three," "Big Four," or "Big Six," you can be sure it refers to an oligopolistic industry.

Homogeneous or Differentiated Products

An oligopoly may be either a **homogeneous oligopoly** or a **differentiated oligopoly,** depending on whether the firms in the oligopoly produce standardized or differentiated products. Many industrial products (steel, zinc, copper, aluminum, lead, cement, industrial alcohol) are virtually standardized products that are produced in oligopolies. Alternatively, many consumer goods industries (automobiles, tires, household appliances, electronics equipment, breakfast cereals, cigarettes, and many sporting goods) are differentiated oligopolies. These differentiated oligopolies typically engage in considerable nonprice competition, supported by heavy advertising.

Control over Price, but Mutual Interdependence

Because firms are few in oligopolistic industries, each firm is a "price maker"; like the monopolist, it can *set* its price and output levels to maximize its profit. But unlike the monopolist, which has no rivals, the oligopolist must consider how its rivals will react to any change in its price, output, product characteristics, or advertising. Oligopoly is thus characterized by **mutual interdependence:** *a situation in which each firm's profit depends not on its own price and sales strategies but on those of its rivals.* Example: In deciding whether to increase the price of its baseball gloves, Rawlings will try to predict the response of the other major producers, such as Wilson. Second example: In deciding

on its advertising strategy, Burger King will take into consideration how McDonald's might react.

Entry Barriers

The same barriers to entry that create pure monopoly are relevant in explaining the existence of oligopoly. Economies of scale are important entry barriers in a number of oligopolistic industries such as the aircraft, rubber, and cement industries. In these industries, three or four firms can each have sufficient sales to achieve economies of scale, but new firms would have such a small market share that they could not do so. They would then be high-cost producers, and they could not survive. A closely related barrier is the large expenditure for capital—the cost of obtaining necessary plant and equipment—required to enter certain industries. The jet engine, automobile, and petroleum-refining industries, for example, are all characterized by very high capital requirements.

The ownership and control of raw materials explain the oligopoly that exists in many mining industries, including gold, silver, and copper. In the electronics, chemicals, photographic equipment, office machine, and pharmaceutical industries, patents have served as entry barriers. Also, oligopolists have been known to deter entry of potential new competitors through preemptive and retaliatory pricing and advertising strategies. In the 1980s, for example, a major attempt to enter the soft-drink industry by a new producer (King Cola) allegedly was thwarted by price discounts and heavy advertising by Coca-Cola and Pepsi.

Mergers

Some oligopolies have emerged mainly through *internal* growth of the dominant firms (examples: breakfast cereals, chewing gum, candy bars). But for other industries the route to oligopoly has been *external*, specifically via mergers (examples: steel, in its early history, and, more recently, airlines, banking, and entertainment). The merging, or combining, of two or more formerly competing firms may substantially increase their market share, enabling the new and larger producer to achieve greater economies of scale.

Another motive underlying the "urge to merge" is monopoly power. A larger firm may have greater ability to control market supply and thus the price of its product. Also, since it is a larger buyer of inputs, it may be able to demand and obtain lower prices (costs) on its production inputs.

Measures of Industry Concentration

Several means are used to measure the degree to which oligopolistic industries are concentrated in the "hands" of their largest firms. We will discuss the most-often-used measures here: concentration ratios and the Herfindahl index.

Concentration Ratio   A **concentration ratio** gives the percentage of an industry's total sales which is obtained by its largest firms. Column 2 in Table 25-2 lists the *four-firm concentration ratio*—the percentage of total industry sales accounted for by the four largest firms—for a number of oligopolistic industries. For example, the four largest U.S. producers of breakfast cereals manufacture 85 percent of all breakfast cereals produced in the United States.

When the largest four firms in an industry control 40 percent or more of the market (as in Table 25-2), that industry is considered oligopolistic. Using this benchmark, about one-half of all U.S. manufacturing industries are oligopolies.

Although concentration ratios provide useful insights into the competitiveness or monopoly power of various industries, they have three shortcomings, discussed below.

Localized Markets   Concentration ratios pertain to a nation as a whole, while the relevant markets for some products are actually highly localized because of high transportation costs. For example, the four-firm concentration ratio for ready-mix concrete is only 6 percent, suggesting a highly competitive industry. But the sheer bulk of this product limits the relevant market to a specific town or metropolitan area, and in such localized markets we often find oligopolistic suppliers. At the local level, some aspects of the retail trade, particularly in small- and medium-sized towns, are characterized by oligopoly.

Interindustry Competition   Definitions of industries are somewhat arbitrary, and we must be aware of **interindustry competition,** that is, competition between two products associated with different indus-

TABLE 25-2   Percentage of output produced by firms in selected high-concentration U.S. manufacturing industries

(1) Industry	(2) Percentage of industry output* produced by the four largest firms	(3) Herfindahl index	(1) Industry	(2) Percentage of industry output* produced by the four largest firms	(3) Herfindahl index
Primary copper	98	2827	Aircraft	79	2711
Cigarettes	93	ND†	Photo equipment and supplies	78	2408
Beer	90	ND	Gypsum products	75	2078
Electric light bulbs	86	2702	Men's slacks	75	2338
Breakfast cereals	85	2253	Tires and inner tubes	70	1743
Motor vehicles	84	2676	Roasted coffee	66	1501
Greeting cards	84	2922	Motorcycles and bicycles	65	1419
Glass containers	84	2162	Soap and detergents	63	1584
Small-arms ammunition	84	ND	Lawn and garden equipment	62	1085
Household refrigerators and freezers	82	1891			
Flat glass	81	1988			
Turbines and generators	79	2549			

*As measured by value of shipments. Data are for 1992.
†ND = not disclosed.
Source: Bureau of Census, Census of Manufacturers, 1992.

tries. Table 25-2's high concentration ratio for the copper industry understates the competition in that industry because aluminum competes with copper in many applications, for example, in the market for electrical transmission lines. Similarly, steel and aluminum are in intense competition for use in some components of automobiles, for instance, exterior body panels and engines.

World Trade The data in Table 25-2 are for products produced in the United States only and may overstate concentration because they do not account for the **import competition** of foreign suppliers. The motorcycle and bicycle industry is a good example. Although Table 25-2 shows that four U.S. firms produce 65 percent of the domestic output of these goods, it ignores the fact that a very large portion of the motorcycles and bicycles bought in the United States are imports. Many of the world's largest corporations are foreign (Global Perspective 25-1), and many of these firms do business in the United States.

Herfindahl Index The shortcomings listed above actually apply to many measures of concentration, but one shortcoming can be eliminated: Suppose that in some industry, say, industry X, one firm produces all the market output. In a second industry, say, industry Y, there are four firms and each has 25 percent of the market. The concentration ratio is 100 percent for both these industries. But industry X is a pure monopoly, while industry Y is an oligopoly that may be facing significant economic rivalry. Most economists would concur that monopoly power (or market power) is substantially greater in industry X than in industry Y, a fact disguised by their identical 100 percent concentration ratios.

The **Herfindahl index** addresses this problem. This index is *the sum of the squared percentage market shares of all firms in the industry*. In equation form:

$$\text{Herfindahl index} = (\%S_1)^2 + (\%S_2)^2 + (\%S_3)^2 + \cdots + (\%S_n)^2$$

where $\%S_1$ is the percentage market share of firm 1, $\%S_2$ is the percentage market share of firm 2, and so on for each firm in the industry. By squaring the percentage market shares of all firms in the industry, the Herfindahl index gives much greater weight to larger, and thus more powerful, firms than to smaller ones. In the case of the single-firm industry X, the index would be at its maximum of 100^2 (100 percent squared), or 10,000, indicating an industry with com-

GLOBAL PERSPECTIVE 25-1

Geographical distribution of the world's 500 largest companies by sales, 1995

Although the United States is home to more large firms than any other single nation, 347 of the world's largest 500 companies are located abroad. Many of the foreign producers sell products in the United States, creating import competition for U.S. firms.

Number of Companies

0   32   64   96   128   160

United States
Japan
France
Germany
United Kingdom
Switzerland
South Korea
Italy
All Others

Source: *Statistical Abstract of the United States, 1996,* p. 844.

plete monopoly power. For our supposed four-firm industry Y, the index would be $25^2 + 25^2 + 25^2 + 25^2$, or 2500, indicating much less market power. (For a purely competitive industry, the index would approach zero since each firm's market share—$\%S$ in the equation—is extremely small.)

To generalize, the larger the Herfindahl index, the greater the market power within an industry. Note in Table 25-2 that the four-firm concentration ratios for the glass-container industry and the greeting-card industry are both 84 percent. But the Herfindahl index of 2922 for the greeting-card industry suggests greater market power than the 2162 index for the glass-container industry. Also, contrast the *much* larger Herfindahl indexes in Table 25-2 with those for the low-concentration industries in Table 25-1. **(Key Question 7)**

OLIGOPOLY BEHAVIOR: A GAME THEORY OVERVIEW

Oligopoly pricing behavior has the characteristics of a game of strategy such as poker, chess, or bridge. The best way to play such a game depends on the way opponents play. Players (and oligopolists) must pattern their actions according to the actions and expected reactions of rivals. The science of strategy is called *game theory*, and we will use a simple **game theory model** to analyze the pricing behavior of oligopolists. We assume a *duopoly*, or two-firm oligopoly, producing athletic shoes. Each of the two firms—let's call them RareAir and Uptown—has a choice of two pricing strategies: price high or price low. The profit each firm earns will depend on the strategy it chooses and the strategy its rival chooses.

There are four possible combinations of strategies for the two firms, and a lettered cell in Figure 25-3 represents each. For example, cell C represents a low-price strategy for Uptown along with a high-price strategy for RareAir. Figure 25-3 is called a *payoff matrix* because each cell shows the payoff (profit) to each firm that would result from each combination of strategies. Cell C shows that if Uptown adopts a low-price strategy and RareAir a high-price strategy, then Uptown will earn $15 million (green portion) and RareAir will earn $6 million (gold portion).

Mutual Interdependence Revisited

The data in Figure 25-3 are hypothetical, but their relationships are typical of real situations. Recall that oligopolistic firms can increase their profits, and affect rivals' profits, by changing their pricing strategies. Each firm's profit depends on its own pricing strategy and that of its rivals. This mutual interdependence of oligopolists is the most obvious point demonstrated by Figure 25-3. If Uptown adopts a high-price strategy, its profit will be $12 million *provided* RareAir also employs a high-price strategy (cell A). But if RareAir uses a low-price strategy against Uptown's high-price strategy (cell B), RareAir will increase its market share and boost its profit from $12 to $15 million. RareAir's higher profit will come at the expense of Uptown, whose profit will fall from $12 to $6 million. Uptown's high-price strategy is a good strategy only if RareAir also employs a high-price strategy.

FIGURE 25-3 **Profit payoff (in millions) for a two-firm oligopoly** Each firm has two possible pricing strategies. RareAir's strategies are shown in the top margin, and Uptown's in the left margin. Each lettered cell of this four-cell payoff matrix represents one combination of a RareAir strategy and an Uptown strategy and shows the profit that combination would earn for each firm.

Collusive Tendencies

A second point of Figure 25-3 is that oligopolists often can benefit from **collusion**, meaning cooperation among rivals. To see the benefits of collusion, first suppose that both firms in Figure 25-3 are acting *independently* and following high-price strategies. Each realizes a $12 million profit (cell A).

Note that either RareAir or Uptown could increase its profit by switching to a low-price strategy (cell B or C). The low-price firm would increase its profit to $15 million, and the high-price firm's profit would fall to $6 million. The high-price firm would be better off if it, too, adopted a low-price policy. Doing so would increase its profit from $6 million to $8 million (cell D). The upshot is that all this independent strategy shifting would have the effect of reducing both firms' profits from $12 million (cell A) to $8 million (cell D).

In real situations, too, independent action by oligopolists may lead to mutual "competitive" low-price strategies: Independent oligopolists compete with respect to price, which leads to lower prices *and* lower profits. This is clearly beneficial to consumers but not to the oligopolists whose profits decrease.

How could oligopolists avoid the low-profit outcome of cell D? The answer is that they could collude, rather than establish prices competitively or independently. In our example, the two firms could agree to establish and maintain a high-price policy. Each firm thus will increase its profit from $8 million (cell D) to $12 million (cell A).

Incentive to Cheat

The payoff matrix also explains why an oligopolist might be strongly tempted to cheat on a collusive agreement. Suppose Uptown and RareAir agree to maintain high-price policies, with each earning $12 million in profit (cell A). Both are tempted to cheat on this collusive pricing agreement because either firm can increase its profit to $15 million by lowering its price. If Uptown secretly cheats on the agreement by charging low prices, the payoff moves from cell A to cell C. Uptown's profit rises to $15 million, and RareAir's falls to $6 million. If RareAir cheats, the payoff moves from cell A to cell B and RareAir gets the $15 million. **(Key Question 8)**

QUICK REVIEW 25-2

■ An oligopolistic industry is made up of relatively few firms producing either homogeneous or differentiated products; these firms are mutually interdependent.

■ Barriers to entry such as scale economies, control of patents or strategic resources, or the ability to engage in retaliatory pricing characterize oligopolies. Oligopolies can result from internal growth of firms, mergers, or both.

■ The four-firm concentration ratio shows the percentage of an industry's sales accounted for by its four largest firms; the Herfindahl index measures the degree of market power in an industry by summing the squares of the percentage market shares held by the individual firms in the industry.

■ Game theory reveals that **(a)** oligopolies are mutually interdependent in their pricing policies; **(b)** collusion enhances oligopoly profits; and **(c)** there is a temptation for oligopolists to cheat on a collusive agreement.

THREE OLIGOPOLY MODELS

To gain further insights into oligopolistic pricing and output behavior, we will examine three distinct pricing models: (1) the kinked demand curve, (2) collusive pricing, and (3) price leadership.

Why not a single model as in our discussions of the other market structures? There is no standard portrait of oligopoly for two reasons:

1. *Diversity of oligopolies*   Oligopoly encompasses a greater range and diversity of market situations than other market structures. It includes the *tight oligopoly*, in which two or three firms dominate an entire market, and the *loose oligopoly*, in which six or seven firms share, say, 70 or 80 percent of a market while a "competitive fringe" of firms shares the remainder. It includes both differentiated and standardized products. It includes cases in which firms act in collusion and those in which they act independently. It embodies situations in which barriers to entry are very strong and those in which they are not quite so strong. In short, the diversity of oligopoly does not allow us to explain all oligopolistic behaviors with a single market model.

2. *Complications of interdependence*   The mutual interdependence of oligopolistic firms complicates matters significantly. Because firms cannot predict the reactions of their rivals with certainty, they cannot estimate their own demand and marginal-revenue data. Without such data, firms cannot determine their profit-maximizing price and output, even in theory, as you will see.

Despite these analytical difficulties, two interrelated characteristics of oligopolistic pricing have been observed. First, if the macroeconomy is generally stable, oligopolistic prices are typically inflexible (or "rigid" or "sticky"). Prices change less frequently under oligopoly than under pure competition, monopolistic competition and, in some instances, pure monopoly. Second, when oligopolistic prices do change, firms are likely to change their prices together; this suggests there is a tendency to act in concert, or collusively, in setting and changing prices (as we discussed in the preceding section). The diversity of oligopolies and the presence of mutual interdependence are reflected in the models that follow.

Kinked-Demand Theory: Noncollusive Oligopoly

Imagine an oligopolistic industry made up of three firms, A, B, and C, each having about one-third of the total market for a differentiated product. Assume the firms are "independent," meaning they do *not* engage in collusive price practices. Suppose, too, that the going price for firm A's product is P_0 and its current sales are Q_0, as shown in **Figure 25-4a (Key Graph).**

FIGURE 25-4 The kinked demand curve (a) The slope of a noncollusive oligopolist's demand and marginal-revenue curves depends on whether its rivals match (straight lines D_1 and MR_1) or ignore (straight lines D_2 and MR_2) any price changes which it may initiate from the current price P_0. (b) In all likelihood an oligopolist's rivals will ignore a price increase but follow a price cut. This causes the oligopolist's demand curve to be kinked (D_2eD_1) and the marginal-revenue curve to have a vertical break, or gap (fg). Because any shift in marginal costs between MC_1 and MC_2 will cut the vertical (dashed) segment of the marginal-revenue curve, no change in either price P_0 or output Q_0 will result from such a shift.

QUICK QUIZ 25-4

1. **Suppose Q_0 in this figure represents annual sales of 5 million units for this firm. The other two firms in this three-firm industry sell 3 million and 2 million units, respectively. The Herfindahl index for this industry is:**
   a. 100 percent.
   b. 400.
   c. 10.
   d. 3800.

2. **The D_2e segment of the demand curve D_2eD_1 in graph (b) implies that:**
   a. this firm's total revenue will fall if it increases its price above P_0.
   b. other firms will match a price increase above P_0.
   c. the firm's relevant marginal-revenue curve will be MR_1 for price increases above P_0.

   d. the product in this industry is necessarily standardized.

3. **By matching a price cut, this firm's rivals can:**
   a. increase their market shares.
   b. increase their marginal revenues.
   c. maintain their market shares.
   d. lower their total costs.

4. **A shift of the marginal-cost curve from MC_2 to MC_1 in graph (b) would:**
   a. increase the "going price" above P_0.
   b. leave price at P_0, but reduce this firm's total profit.
   c. leave price at P_0, but reduce this firm's total revenue.
   d. make this firm's demand curve more elastic.

Answers: 1. d; 2. a; 3. c; 4. b

Now the question is, "What does the firm's demand curve look like?" Mutual interdependence *and* the uncertainty about rivals' reactions make this question difficult to answer. The location and shape of an oligopolist's demand curve depend on how the firm's rivals will react to a price change introduced by A. There are two plausible assumptions about the reactions of A's rivals:

1. *Match price changes* One possibility is that firms B and C will exactly match any price change initiated by A. In this case, A's demand and marginal-revenue curves will look like the straight lines labeled D_1 and MR$_1$ in Figure 25-4a. Why are they so steep? Reason: If A cuts its price, its sales will increase only modestly because its two rivals will also cut their prices to prevent A from gaining an advantage over them. The small increase in sales which A (and its two rivals) will realize is at the expense of other industries; A will gain no sales from B and C. If A raises its price, its sales will fall only modestly because B and C will match its price increase. The industry will lose sales to other industries, but A will lose no customers to B and C.

2. *Ignore price changes* The other possibility is that firms B and C will ignore any price change by A. In this case, the demand and marginal-revenue curves faced by A will resemble the straight lines D_2 and MR$_2$ in Figure 25-4a. Demand in this case is considerably more elastic than under the previous assumption. The reasons are clear: If A lowers its price and its rivals do not, A will gain sales significantly at the expense of its two rivals because it will be underselling them. Conversely, if A raises its price and its rivals do not, A will lose many customers to B and C, which will be underselling it. Because of product differentiation, however, A's sales will not fall to zero when it raises its price; some of A's customers will pay the higher price because they have strong preferences for A's product.

A Combined Strategy
Now, which is the most logical assumption for A to make about how its rivals will react to any price change it might initiate? The answer is "some of each." Common sense and observation of oligopolistic industries suggest that price declines below P_0 will be matched as a firm's rivals act to prevent the price cutter from taking their customers. But price increases above P_0 will be ignored because rivals of the price-increasing firm stand to gain the business lost by the price booster. In other words, the dark blue left-hand segment of the "rivals ignore" demand curve D_2 seems relevant for price increases, and the dark blue right-hand segment of the "rivals follow" demand curve D_1 seems relevant for price cuts. It is logical, then, or at least a reasonable assumption, that the noncollusive oligopolist faces the **"kinked"** **demand curve** D_2eD_1, as shown in Figure 25-4b. Demand is highly elastic above the going price P_0 but much less elastic or even inelastic below that price.

Note also that if it is correct to suppose that rivals will follow a price cut but ignore an increase, the marginal-revenue curve of the oligopolist will also have an odd shape. It, too, will be made up of two segments—the brown left-hand part of marginal-revenue curve MR$_2$ in Figure 25-4a and the brown right-hand part of marginal-revenue curve MR$_1$. Because of the sharp difference in elasticity of demand above and below the going price, there is a gap, or what we can treat as a vertical segment, in the marginal-revenue curve. This gap is shown by the dashed segment in the combined marginal-revenue curve MR$_2$*fg*MR$_1$ in Figure 25-4b.

Price Inflexibility This analysis goes far to explain why prices are generally stable in noncollusive oligopolistic industries.

On the Demand Side The kinked demand curve gives each oligopolist reason to believe that any change in price will be for the worse. If it raises its price, many of its customers will desert it. If it lowers its price, its sales at best will increase very modestly since rivals will match the lower price. Even if a price cut increases the oligopolist's total revenue somewhat, its costs may well increase by a greater amount. And if its demand is inelastic to the right of Q_0, as it may well be, then the firm's profit will surely fall. A price decrease in the inelastic region lowers the firm's total revenue, and the production of a larger output increases its total cost.

On the Cost Side The broken marginal-revenue curve suggests that even if an oligopolist's costs change substantially, the firm may have no reason to change its price. In particular, all positions of the marginal-cost curve between MC$_1$ and MC$_2$ in Figure 25-4b will result in the firm's deciding on exactly the same price and output. For all those positions, MR equals MC at output Q_0; at that output, price P_0 will be charged.

Criticisms The kinked-demand analysis has two shortcomings. First, *it does not explain how the going price gets to be at* P_0 *in Figure 25-4 in the first place.* It only helps explain why oligopolists tend to stick with an existing price. The kinked demand curve explains price inflexibility but not price itself.

Second, when the macroeconomy is unstable, oligopoly prices are not as rigid as the kinked-demand theory implies. During inflationary periods, many oligopolists have raised their prices often and substantially. And during downturns (recessions) in the macroeconomy, some oligopolists have cut prices. In some instances these price reductions have set off a **price war:** *successive and continuous rounds of price cuts by rivals as they attempt to maintain their market shares.* **(Key Question 9)**

Cartels and Other Collusion

Our game theory model suggests that oligopoly is conducive to collusion. We can say that *collusion occurs whenever firms in an industry reach an agreement to fix prices, divide up the market, or otherwise restrict competition among themselves.* The disadvantages and uncertainties of noncollusive, kinked-demand oligopoly are obvious. There is always the danger of a price war breaking out—especially during a general business recession. Then each firm finds itself with unsold goods and excess capacity and can reduce per-unit costs by increasing market share. Then, too, a new firm may surmount entry barriers and initiate aggressive price cutting to gain a foothold in the market. In addition, the kinked demand curve's tendency toward rigid prices may adversely affect profits if general inflationary pressures increase costs. However, by controlling price through collusion, oligopolists may be able to reduce uncertainty, increase profits, and perhaps even prohibit the entry of new rivals.

Price and Output   Assume once again that there are three oligopolistic firms—A, B, and C—producing, in this instance, homogeneous products. All three firms have identical cost curves. Each firm's demand curve is indeterminate unless we know how its rivals will react to any price change. Therefore, we suppose each firm assumes its two rivals will match either a price cut or a price increase. In other words, each firm has a demand curve like the straight line D_1 in Figure 25-4a. And since they have identical cost data, and the same demand and thus marginal-revenue data, we can say that Figure 25-5 represents the position of each of our three oligopolistic firms.

What price and output combination should, say, A choose? If A were a pure monopolist, the answer would be clear: Establish output at Q_0, where marginal revenue equals marginal cost, charge the corresponding price P_0, and enjoy the maximum profit attainable. However, firm A *does* have two rivals selling identical products, and if A's assumption that its rivals will match its price of P_0 proves to be incorrect, the consequences could be disastrous for A. Specifically, if B and C actually charge prices below P_0 then A's demand curve D

FIGURE 25-5 Collusion and the tendency toward joint-profit maximization   If oligopolistic firms face identical or highly similar demand and cost conditions, they may collude to limit their joint output and to set a single, common price. Thus each firm acts as if it were a pure monopolist, setting output at Q_0 and charging price P_0. This price and output combination maximizes each oligopolist's profit (gray area) and thus their combined or joint profit.

will shift sharply to the left as its potential customers turn to its rivals, which are now selling the same product at a lower price. Of course, firm A can retaliate by cutting its price too, but this will move all three firms down their demand curves, lowering their profits. It may even drive them to a point where average total cost exceeds price and losses are incurred.

So the question becomes, "Will B and C want to charge a price below P_0?" Under our assumptions, and recognizing that A has little choice except to match any price they may set below P_0, the answer is "no." Faced with the same demand and cost circumstances, B and C will find it in their interest to produce Q_0 and charge P_0. This is a curious situation; each firm finds it most profitable to charge the same price, P_0, but only if its rivals actually do so! How can the three firms ensure the price P_0 and quantity Q_0 solution in which each is keenly interested? How can they avoid the less profitable outcomes associated with either higher or lower prices?

The answer is evident: Collusion—get together, talk it over, and agree to charge the same price, P_0. In addition to reducing the possibility of price wars, this will give each firm the maximum profit. And for society, the result will be the same as would occur if the industry were a pure monopoly composed of three identical plants.

Overt Collusion: The OPEC Cartel Collusion may assume a variety of forms. The most comprehensive form is the **cartel,** *a group of producers which typically develops a formal written agreement as to how much each member will produce and charge.* Output must be controlled—the market must be divided up—to maintain the agreed-upon price. The collusion is *overt,* or open to be seen.

The most spectacularly successful international cartel of recent decades has been the Organization of Petroleum Exporting Countries (OPEC). Comprising 13 oil-producing nations, OPEC was extremely effective in the 1970s in restricting the oil supply and raising prices. The cartel was able to raise world oil prices from $2.50 to $11.00 per barrel within a 6-month period in 1973–1974. By early 1980, price hikes had brought the per-barrel price into the $32 to $34 range. The result was enormous profits for cartel members, a substantial stimulus to worldwide inflation, and serious international trade deficits for oil importers.

OPEC was highly effective in the 1970s for several reasons. First, it dominated the world market for oil. If a nation imported oil, it was almost obligated to do business with OPEC. Second, world demand for oil was strong and expanding in the 1970s. Finally, the short-run demand for oil was highly inelastic because the economies of oil-importing nations such as the United States were locked into low-gas-mileage automobiles and energy-intensive housing and capital equipment. This inelasticity meant that a small restriction of output by OPEC would result in a relatively large price increase. As shown in Figure 25-6, between 1973 and 1980 OPEC was able to achieve an enormous increase in oil price by reducing output only very modestly. With inelastic demand, higher prices meant greatly increased total revenues to OPEC members. The accompanying smaller output meant lower total costs. The combination of increased total revenues and lower total costs resulted in greatly expanded profits. (We discuss the serious weakening of the OPEC cartel later in this chapter.)

Covert Collusion: The Electrical Equipment Conspiracy Cartels are illegal in the United States, and hence what collusion there is has been *covert* or secret. In 1960 an extensive price-fixing and market-sharing scheme involving heavy electrical equipment such as transformers, turbines, circuit breakers, and switch gear was uncovered. Such participants as General Electric, Westinghouse, and Allis-Chalmers had developed elaborate covert schemes to rig prices and divide the market. Consider switch gear equipment:

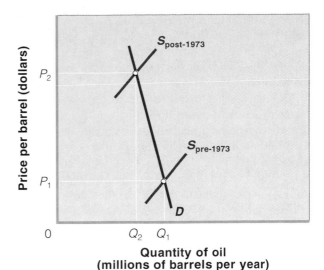

FIGURE 25-6 The OPEC cartel and the world oil market Because of the inelasticity of the demand for oil (as evidenced by D), in the 1970s the OPEC oil cartel was able to obtain a dramatic increase in the price of oil (P_1 to P_2) by means of only a very modest decline in production and sales (Q_1 to Q_2).

At . . . periodic meetings, a scheme or formula for quoting nearly identical prices to electric utility companies, private industrial corporations and contractors was used by defendant corporations, designated by their representatives as a "phase of the moon" or "light of the moon" formula. Through cyclic rotating positioning inherent in the formula one defendant corporation would quote the low price, others would quote intermediate prices and another would quote the high price; these positions would be periodically rotated among the defendant corporations. . . . This formula was designed to permit each defendant corporation to know the exact price it and every other defendant corporation would quote on each prospective sale.

At these periodic meetings, a cumulative list of sealed bid business secured by all of the defendant corporations was also circulated and the representatives present would compare the relative standing of each corporation according to its agreed upon percentage of the total sales pursuant to sealed bids. The representatives present would then discuss particular future bid invitations and designate which defendant corporation should submit the lowest bid therefor, the amount of such bid, and the amounts of the bid to be submitted by others.[1]

---

[1]Jules Backman, *The Economics of the Electrical Equipment Industry* (New York: New York University Press, 1962), pp. 135–138, abridged. Reprinted by permission.

Overall, 29 manufacturers and 46 company officials were indicted in this "great electrical conspiracy," which violated U.S. antitrust laws. Substantial fines, jail penalties, and lawsuits by victimized buyers were the final outcome.

In many other instances collusion is even more subtle. **Tacit understandings** (historically called *gentlemen's agreements*) are frequently made at cocktail parties, on golf courses, by phone calls, or at trade association meetings. In such agreements, competing firms reach a verbal understanding on product price, leaving market shares to be decided by nonprice competition. Although these agreements, too, violate antitrust laws—and can result in severe personal and corporate penalties—the elusive character of tacit understandings makes them more difficult to detect.

Other Examples
Additional illustrations of covert collusion are not difficult to find. In 1993 the Borden, Pet, and Dean food companies, among others, either pleaded guilty or were convicted of rigging bids on the prices of milk products sold to schools and military bases. By phone or at luncheons, company executives agreed in advance on which firm would submit the low bid for each school district or military base. In 1996 American agribusiness Archer Daniels Midland and three Japanese and South Korean firms were found to have conspired to fix the worldwide price and sales volume of a livestock feed additive. Executives for the firms secretly met in Hong Kong, Paris, Mexico City, Vancouver, and Zurich to discuss their plans.

Obstacles to Collusion
Normally, cartels and similar collusive arrangements are difficult to establish and maintain. Let's briefly consider several important barriers to collusion.

Demand and Cost Differences
When oligopolists face different costs and demand curves, it is difficult to agree on a price. This is particularly the case in industries where products are differentiated and change frequently. Even with highly standardized products, firms usually have somewhat different market shares and operate with differing degrees of productive efficiency. Thus it is unlikely that even homogeneous oligopolists would have the same demand and cost curves.

In either case, differences in costs and demand mean that the profit-maximizing price will differ among firms; no single price will be readily acceptable to all, as we assumed was true in Figure 25-5. Price

collusion will therefore depend on compromises and concessions. These are not always easy to obtain and hence act as an obstacle to collusion.

Number of Firms
Other things equal, the larger the number of firms, the more difficult it is to achieve a cartel or other form of price collusion. Agreement on price by three or four producers which control an entire market may be relatively easy to accomplish. But such agreement is more difficult to secure where there are, say, 10 firms, each with roughly 10 percent of the market, or where the Big Three have 70 percent of the market while a competitive fringe of 8 or 10 smaller firms battles for the remainder.

Cheating
As is clear from the game theory model, there is a temptation for collusive oligopolists to engage in secret price cutting to increase sales and profit. The difficulty with such cheating is that buyers paying a high price may become aware of the lower-priced sales and demand similar treatment. Or buyers receiving a price concession (decrease) from one producer may use the concession as a wedge to get even larger price concessions from that producer's rival. Buyers' attempts to play producers against one another may precipitate price wars among the producers. Although they are potentially profitable, secret price concessions threaten collusive oligopolies over time. Collusion is more likely to be successful when cheating is easy to detect and punish. In those circumstances, the conspirators are less likely to cheat on the price agreement.

Recession
Long-lasting recession is usually an enemy of collusion because slumping markets increase average total cost. In technical terms, as the oligopolists' demand and marginal-revenue curves shift to the left in Figure 25-5 due to a recession, each firm moves leftward and upward to a higher operating point on its average-total-cost curve. Firms find they have substantial excess production capacity, sales are down, unit costs are up, and so profits are being squeezed. Under these conditions, businesses may feel they can avoid serious profit reductions (or even losses) by cutting price and thus gaining sales at the expense of rivals.

Potential Entry
The greater prices and profits that result from collusion may attract new entrants, including foreign firms. This would increase market supply and reduce prices and profits. Therefore, successful collusion requires that colluding oligopolists block the entry of new producers.

Legal Obstacles: Antitrust Law United States antitrust laws prohibit cartels and the kind of price-fixing collusion we have been discussing. So less obvious means of price control have evolved in the United States.

OPEC in Disarray The highly successful OPEC oil cartel of the 1970s fell into disarray in the 1980s. The reasons for OPEC's decline relate closely to the obstacles to collusion just examined.

New Suppliers The dramatic surge of oil prices in the 1970s stimulated the search for new oil reserves, and soon non-OPEC nations, which OPEC could not block from entering world markets, became part of the world oil industry. Great Britain, Norway, Mexico, and Russia have all become major oil suppliers. As a result, OPEC's share of world oil production has declined.

Declining Demand On the demand side, oil conservation, worldwide recession in the early 1980s, and expanded use of alternative energy sources (such as coal, natural gas, and nuclear power) all reduced the demand for oil. The combination of greater production by non-OPEC nations and decline in world demand generated an "oil glut" and seriously impaired OPEC's ability to control world oil prices.

Cheating OPEC has had a serious cheating problem stemming from the relatively large number of members (13) and the diversity of their economic circumstances. Saudi Arabia is the dominant cartel member; it has the largest oil reserves and is probably the lowest-cost producer. Saudi Arabia has favored a "moderate" pricing policy because it has feared that very high oil prices would hasten the development of more alternative energy sources (such as solar power and synthetic fuels) and increase the attractiveness of existing substitutes such as coal and natural gas. These developments would greatly reduce the value of its vast oil reserves. Saudi Arabia also has a small population and a very high per capita domestic output. But other OPEC members (for example, Nigeria and Venezuela) are relatively poor, have large populations, and are burdened with large external debts. Still others (Iran, Iraq, and Libya) have had large military commitments. All these members have immediate needs for cash. Thus, there has been substantial cheating whereby some members have exceeded assigned production quotas and have sold oil at prices below those agreed to by the cartel. Result: Although

OPEC's official oil price reached $34 per barrel in 1979, it is currently only about $19 per barrel.

Price Leadership Model

Price leadership is a type of implicit understanding by which oligopolists can coordinate prices without engaging in outright collusion. Formal agreements and secret meetings are not involved. Rather, a practice evolves whereby the "dominant firm"—usually the largest or most efficient in the industry—initiates price changes and all other firms more or less automatically follow that lead. Many industries, including farm machinery, cement, copper, newsprint, glass containers, steel, beer, fertilizer, cigarettes, and tin, are practicing, or have in the recent past practiced, price leadership.

Leadership Tactics An examination of price leadership in a variety of industries suggests that the price leader is likely to observe the following tactics.

Infrequent Changes Because price changes always carry some risk that rivals will not follow the lead, price adjustments are made infrequently. The price leader does not respond to minuscule day-to-day changes in costs and demand. Price is changed only when cost and demand conditions have been altered significantly and on an industrywide basis as the result of, for example, industrywide wage increases, an increase in excise taxes, or an increase in the price of some basic input such as energy. In the automobile industry, price adjustments traditionally have been made when new models are introduced each fall.

Communications The price leader often communicates impending price adjustments to the industry through speeches by major executives, trade publication interviews, and so forth. By publicizing "the need to raise prices," the price leader can seek agreement among its competitors regarding the actual increase.

Limit Pricing The price leader does not necessarily choose the price that maximizes short-run profits for the industry because the industry may want to discourage new firms from entering. If the cost advantages (economies of scale) of existing firms are a major barrier to entry, this barrier could be surmounted by new entrants if product price were set high enough by the existing firms: New firms that are relatively inefficient because of their small size might survive and grow if the industry's price were very high. So, to discourage new competitors and maintain the current oligopolistic structure of the industry, price may be kept below the short-run profit-maximizing level. The strategy of establishing a price which prevents the entry of new firms is called *limit pricing*.

Breakdowns in Price Leadership: Price Wars

Price leadership in oligopoly occasionally breaks down, at least temporarily, and sometimes results in a price war. A recent disruption of price leadership occurred in the breakfast cereal industry, in which Kellogg traditionally had been the price leader. General Mills countered Kellogg's leadership in 1995 by reducing the prices of its cereals by 11 percent. In 1996 Post responded with a 20 percent price cut, which Kellogg then followed. Not to be outdone, Post reduced its prices by another 11 percent.

Most price wars eventually run their course. When all firms recognize that low prices are severely reducing their profits, they again cede price leadership to one of the industry's leading firms. That firm begins to increase prices, and the other firms willingly follow.

QUICK REVIEW 25-3

■ In the kinked-demand theory of oligopoly, price is relatively inflexible because a firm contemplating a price change assumes that rivals will follow a price cut and ignore a price increase.

■ Cartels agree on production limits and set a common price to maximize the joint profit of their members as if each were a unit of a single pure monopoly.

■ Collusion among oligopolists is difficult because of (a) demand and cost differences among sellers, (b) the complexity of output coordination among producers, (c) the potential for cheating, (d) a tendency for agreements to break down during recessions, (e) the potential entry of new firms, and (f) antitrust laws.

■ Price leadership involves an informal understanding among oligopolists to match any price change initiated by a designated firm (often the industry's dominant firm).

OLIGOPOLY AND ADVERTISING

We noted that oligopolists would rather not compete via price and may become involved in price collusion. Nonetheless, each firm's share of the total market is typically determined through product development and advertising. This emphasis has its roots in two facts:

1. Product development and advertising campaigns are less easily duplicated than price cuts. Price cuts can be quickly and easily matched by a firm's rivals to cancel any potential gain in sales from that strategy. Product improvements and successful advertising, however, can produce more permanent gains in market share. They cannot be duplicated as quickly and completely as price reductions.

2. Oligopolists have sufficient financial resources to engage in product development and advertising. For most oligopolists, the economic profits earned in the past can help finance current advertising and product development.

Product development (or, more broadly, "research and development") is the subject of the next chapter, so we will confine our present discussion to advertising. In recent years, U.S. advertising has exceeded $170 billion annually, and worldwide advertising, $380 billion. Both monopolistic competitors and differentiated oligopolists engage in advertising. Table 25-3 lists the 10 leading U.S. advertisers in a recent year.

Advertising can affect prices, competition, and efficiency both positively and negatively, depending on the circumstances. While our focus here is on advertising by oligopolists, the analysis is equally applicable to advertising by monopolistic competitors.

Positive Effects of Advertising

Consumers need information about product characteristics and prices to make rational (efficient) decisions. Advertising can be a low-cost means of providing that information. Suppose you are in the market

---

TABLE 25-3   **The 10 largest U.S. advertisers, 1995**

Company	Advertising spending, (millions of dollars)
Procter & Gamble Co.	$2777
Philip Morris Cos.	2577
General Motors Corp.	2047
Time Warner	1307
Walt Disney Co.	1296
Sears, Roebuck & Co.	1226
Chrysler Corp.	1222
PepsiCo	1197
Johnson & Johnson	1173
Ford Motor Co.	1149

Source: Advertising Age.

for a high-quality camera and there is no newspaper or magazine advertising of this product. To make a rational choice, you may have to spend several days visiting stores to determine the prices and features of various brands. This search entails both direct costs (gasoline, parking fees) and indirect costs (the value of your time). Advertising reduces your *search time* and minimizes these costs.

By providing information about the various competing goods that are available, advertising diminishes monopoly power. In fact, advertising is frequently associated with the introduction of new products designed to compete with existing brands. Could Toyota and Honda have so strongly challenged U.S. auto producers without advertising? Could Federal Express have sliced market share away from UPS and the U.S. Postal Service without advertising? How about upstart Mentadent toothpaste, which recently has gained market share from long-time leaders Crest and Colgate?

Viewed this way, advertising is an efficiency-enhancing activity. It is a relatively inexpensive means of providing useful information to consumers and thus lowering their search costs. By enhancing competition, advertising results in greater economic efficiency. By facilitating the introduction of new products, advertising speeds up technological progress. And by increasing output, advertising can reduce long-run average total cost by enabling firms to obtain economies of scale.

Potential Negative Effects of Advertising

Not all the effects of advertising are positive. Much advertising is designed to manipulate or persuade consumers, that is, to alter their preferences in favor of the advertiser's product. A television commercial indicating that a popular personality drinks a particular brand of soft drink—and therefore that you should too—conveys little or no information to consumers about price or quality. In addition, advertising is sometimes based on misleading and extravagant claims that confuse consumers rather than enlighten them. Indeed, in some cases advertising may well persuade consumers to pay high prices for much-acclaimed but inferior products, forgoing better but unadvertised products selling at lower prices. Example: *Consumer Reports* recently found that heavily advertised premium motor oils and fancy additives provide no better engine performance and longevity than do cheaper brands.

Firms often establish substantial brand-name loyalty and thus monopoly power via their advertising (see Global Perspective 25-2). As a consequence, they are able to increase their sales, expand their market shares, and enjoy greater profits. Larger profit permits still more advertising and further enlargement of a firm's market share and profit. In time, consumers may lose the advantages of competitive markets and face the disadvantages of monopolized markets. Moreover, potential new entrants to the industry need to incur large advertising costs to establish their products in the marketplace; thus, advertising costs may be a barrier to entry.

Advertising can also be self-canceling. The advertising campaign of one fast-food hamburger chain may be offset by equally costly campaigns waged by rivals, so each firm's demand is actually unchanged. Few, if any, extra burgers will be purchased, and each firm's market share will stay the same. But because of

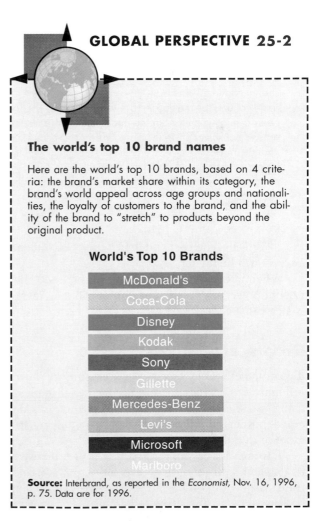

GLOBAL PERSPECTIVE 25-2

The world's top 10 brand names

Here are the world's top 10 brands, based on 4 criteria: the brand's market share within its category, the brand's world appeal across age groups and nationalities, the loyalty of customers to the brand, and the ability of the brand to "stretch" to products beyond the original product.

World's Top 10 Brands

McDonald's
Coca-Cola
Disney
Kodak
Sony
Gillette
Mercedes-Benz
Levi's
Microsoft
Marlboro

Source: Interbrand, as reported in the *Economist*, Nov. 16, 1996, p. 75. Data are for 1996.

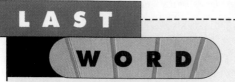

The Beer Industry: Oligopoly Brewing?

The beer industry was once populated by hundreds of firms and an even larger number of brands. But this industry has increasingly become concentrated and is now an oligopoly.

The brewing industry has undergone profound changes since World War II, and those changes have increased the degree of concentration in the industry. In 1947 more than 400 independent brewing companies existed in the United States. By 1967 there were 124, and by 1980 only 33 survived. While the five largest brewers sold only 19 percent of the nation's beer in 1947, the Big Five brewers currently sell 93 percent of the nation's domestically produced beer. The Big Two—Anheuser-Busch (at 45 percent) and Miller (at 22 percent)—produce 67 percent.

Changes on the demand side of the market have contributed to the "shakeout" of small brewers from the industry. First, in the 1970s consumer tastes shifted from the stronger-flavored beers of the small brewers to the light, dry products of the larger brewers. Second, there has been a relative shift from the consumption of beer in taverns to consumption in the home. The significance of this change is that taverns were usually supplied with kegs from local brewers to avoid the relatively high cost of shipping kegs. But the acceptance of aluminum cans for home consumption made it possible for large, distant brewers to compete with the local brewers because the former could now ship their products by truck or rail without breakage.

Developments on the supply side of the market have been even more profound. Technological advances speeded up the bottling and canning lines so that, for example, the number of cans of beer filled and closed per line per minute increased from 900 to 1500 between 1965 and the late 1970s. Currently the most modern canning lines can close 2000 cans per minute. Large plants are also able to reduce labor costs through the automating of brewing and warehousing. Furthermore, plant construction costs per barrel are about one-third less for a 4.5-million-barrel plant than for a 1.5-million-barrel plant. As a consequence of these and other economies, it is estimated that unit production costs decline sharply up to the point at which a plant produces 1.25 million barrels per year. Average costs continue to decline, but less significantly, up to the 4.5-million-barrel capacity, at which all scale economies seem to be exhausted. Evidence of the importance of scale economies is reflected in statistics which show that over time there has been a steady decline in breweries producing less than 2 million barrels per year. Because the construction of a modern 4-million-barrel-capacity brewery costs about $250 million, economies of scale may now constitute a significant barrier to entry.

"Blindfold" taste tests confirm that most mass-produced American beers taste alike. Thus great emphasis has been placed on advertising. And here the large firms which sell nationally (Anheuser-Busch, Miller) enjoy cost advantages over regional producers (Grain Belt, Pearl) because national television advertising is less costly per viewer than local spot TV advertising.

---

the advertising, the cost and hence the price of hamburgers will be higher.

When advertising either leads to increased monopoly power or is self-canceling, economic inefficiency results.

Graphical Analysis

Two of the efficiency aspects of advertising are shown in Figure 25-7, which focuses on the idea that advertising usually has two effects. First, it increases demand, output, and sales; and second, it adds an extra expense to the firm.

Through successful advertising, a firm increases its demand, permitting it to expand output and sales from, say, Q_1 to Q_2. Despite the fact that advertising outlays will shift the firm's long-run ATC curve upward, per-unit cost declines from A_1 to A_2 as the firm moves from point a to point b. Greater productive efficiency from economies of scale more than offsets the increase in per-unit cost from advertising. Assuming no increase in monopoly power, consumers therefore get the product at a lower price with advertising than they would without.

But what if the advertising efforts of all firms are self-canceling? Then output may stay at Q_1 while the long-run ATC curve shifts upward. Instead of moving the firm from a to b, self-canceling advertising moves it from a to c. In this case, per-unit cost rises to A_3, and the consumer pays a higher price because of advertising.

As this analysis indicates, no *general* conclusion can be reached as to the impact of advertising on price, competition, and efficiency. There are possibilities for positive and negative outcomes, and the net impact

Although mergers have occurred, they have not been a fundamental cause of increased concentration in the brewing industry. Rather, mergers have been largely the result of failing smaller breweries (such as Heileman) selling out. Dominant firms have expanded by creating new brands—Lite, Keystone, Milwaukee's Best, and Genuine Draft, for example—rather than acquiring them. This has sustained product differentiation, despite the declining number of major brewers.

The rise of the Miller Brewing Comapny from the seventh- to the second-largest producer in the 1970s was due in large measure to advertising and product differentiation. When Miller was acquired by the Philip Morris Company in 1970, the new management made two big changes. First, Miller High Life beer was "repositioned" into that segment of the market where potential sales were the greatest. Sold previously as the "champagne of beers," High Life had appealed heavily to upper-income consumers and women who drank beer only occasionally. Miller's new television ads featured young blue-collar workers who were inclined to be greater beer consumers. Second, Miller then developed its low-calorie Lite beer, which was extensively promoted with Philip Morris advertising dollars. Lite proved to be the most popular new product in the history of the beer industry.

Currently, the beer industry does not appear to engage in economically undesirable behavior, although Anheuser-Busch clearly acts as the price leader. There has been no evidence of overt collusion, and current excess productive capacity prompts the large brewers to compete for market shares. The fact that historically there has been considerable turnover in the ranking of the largest firms is further evidence of competition. Miller, ranked eighth in 1968, rose to number two in 1977 and has maintained that position. In comparison, Schlitz and Pabst were the second- and third-largest brewers in the mid-1970s but now are "also rans." Moreover, in an ironic twist, history is reversing itself slightly with the advent of small local or regional microbreweries. These brewers of specialty beers charge super-premium prices, but nevertheless have whittled into the sales of the major brewers. Anheuser-Busch and Miller have taken notice, responding with specialty brands of their own (Redwolf, Elk Mountain, Crossroads, Red Dog, Icehouse) and bought stakes in microbrewers Redhook Ale and Celis.

Source: Based on Kenneth G. Elzinga, "Beer," in Walter Adams and James Brock (eds.), *The Structure of American Industry,* 9th ed. (Englewood Cliffs, NJ: Prentice-Hall, 1995), pp. 119–151; and Douglas F. Greer, "Beer: Causes of Structural Change," in Larry Duetsch (ed.), *Industry Studies* (Englewood Cliffs, NJ: Prentice-Hall, 1993). Updated.

may well vary by industry and by particular situation. **(Key Question 11)**

OLIGOPOLY AND EFFICIENCY

Is oligopoly, then, an efficient market structure from society's standpoint? How do the, price and output decisions of the oligopolist measure up to the triple equality $P = MC =$ minimum ATC occurring in pure competition?

Productive and Allocative Efficiency

Many economists believe that the outcome of some oligopolistic markets is approximately that shown in Figure 25-5. This view is bolstered by evidence that many oligopolists sustain sizable economic profits year after year. In that case, the oligopolist's production occurs where price exceeds marginal cost and average total cost. Moreover, production is below the output at which average total cost is minimized. In this view, neither productive efficiency ($P =$ minimum ATC) nor allocative efficiency ($P = MC$) is likely to occur under oligopoly.

A few observers assert that oligopoly is actually less desirable than pure monopoly because pure monopoly in the United States is usually regulated by government to guard against abuses of monopoly power. Informal collusion among oligopolists may yield price and output results similar to those under pure monopoly yet give the outward appearance of competition involving independent firms.

FIGURE 25-7 The possible effects of advertising on a firm's output and average total cost In some cases, advertising may expand the firm's production from, say, point *a* to *b* and lower average total cost from A_1 to A_2 through economies of scale. But in other instances, it may be self-canceling, increase average total cost, and leave output largely unchanged. If so, the firm may move from, say, *a* to *c*, experiencing an increase in average total cost from A_1 to A_3.

Qualifications

We should note, however, three qualifications to this view:

1. *Increased foreign competition* In the past decade, foreign competition has increased rivalry in a number of oligopolistic industries—steel, automobiles, photographic film, electric shavers, outboard motors, and copy machines, for example. This has helped break down such cozy arrangements as price leadership and stimulate more competitive pricing.

2. *Limit pricing* Recall that some oligopolists may purposely keep prices below the short-run profit-maximizing level to bolster entry barriers. In essence, consumers and society may get some of the benefits of competition—prices closer to marginal cost and minimum average total cost—even without the competition that free entry would provide.

3. *Technological advance* Over time, oligopolistic industries may foster more rapid product development and greater improvement of production techniques than would be possible if they were purely competitive. Oligopolists have large economic profits from which they can fund expensive research and development (R&D). Moreover, the existence of barriers to entry may give the oligopolist some assurance that it will reap the rewards of successful R&D. Thus, short-run economic inefficiencies of oligopolists may be partly or wholly offset by oligopolists' contributions to better products, lower prices, and lower costs over time. We will have more to say about these more dynamic aspects of rivalry in Chapter 26.

CHAPTER SUMMARY

1. The distinguishing features of monopolistic competition are **(a)** there are enough firms in the industry so that each has only limited control over price, mutual interdependence is absent, and collusion is nearly impossible; **(b)** products are characterized by real or perceived differences so that economic rivalry entails both price and nonprice competition; and **(c)** entry to the industry is relatively easy. Many aspects of retailing, and some manufacturing industries where economies of scale are few, approximate monopolistic competition.

2. Monopolistically competitive firms may earn economic profits or incur losses in the short run. The easy entry and exit of firms results in only normal profits in the long run.

3. The long-run equilibrium position of the monopolistically competitive producer is less socially desirable than that of the pure competitor. Under monopolistic competition, price exceeds marginal cost, suggesting an underallocation of resources to the product, and price exceeds minimum average total cost, indicating that consumers do not get the product at the lowest price which cost conditions might allow.

4. Nonprice competition provides a means by which monopolistically competitive firms can offset the long-run tendency for economic profit to fall to zero. Through product differentiation and advertising, a firm may strive to increase the demand for its product more than enough to cover the added cost of such nonprice competition.

5. In practice, the monopolistic competitor seeks that specific combination of price, product, and advertising which will maximize profit.

6. Oligopolistic industries are characterized by the presence of few firms, each having a significant fraction of the market. Firms thus situated are mutually interdependent: the behavior of any one firm directly affects, and is affected by, the actions of rivals. Products may be virtually uniform or significantly differentiated. Various barriers to entry, including economies of scale, underlie and maintain oligopoly.

7. Concentration ratios help measure oligopoly (monopoly) power. By giving more weight to larger firms, the Herfindahl index is designed to measure market dominance in an industry.

8. Game theory **(a)** shows the mutual interdependence of oligopolists' pricing policies; **(b)** reveals the tendency of oligopolists to collude; and **(c)** explains the temptation of oligopolists to cheat on collusive arrangements.

9. Noncollusive oligopolists may face a kinked demand curve. This curve and the accompanying marginal-revenue curve help explain the price rigidity that often characterizes oligopolies; they do not, however, explain how the actual prices of products were first established.

10. The uncertainties inherent in oligopoly promote collusion. Collusive oligopolists such as cartels maximize joint profits—that is, they behave like pure monopolists. Demand and cost differences, a "large" number of firms, cheating through secret price concessions, recessions, and the antitrust laws are all obstacles to collusive oligopoly.

11. Price leadership is an informal means of collusion whereby one firm, usually the largest or most efficient, initiates price changes and other firms in the industry follow.

12. Market shares in oligopolistic industries are usually determined on the basis of product development and advertising. Oligopolists emphasize nonprice competition because **(a)** advertising and product variations are less easy for rivals to match and **(b)** oligopolists frequently have ample resources to finance nonprice competition.

13. Advertising can affect prices, competition, and efficiency either positively or negatively. Positive: It can provide consumers with low-cost information about competing products, help introduce new competing products into concentrated industries, and generally reduce monopoly power and its attendant inefficiencies. Negative: It can promote monopoly power via persuasion and the creation of entry barriers. Moreover, it can be self-canceling when engaged in by rivals; then it boosts costs and increases economic inefficiency while accomplishing little else.

14. Neither productive nor allocative efficiency is realized in oligopolistic markets, but oligopoly may be superior to pure competition in promoting research and development and technological progress.

TERMS AND CONCEPTS

monopolistic competition	homogeneous oligopoly	import competition	price war
product differentiation	differentiated oligopoly	Herfindahl index	cartel
nonprice competition	mutual interdependence	game theory model	tacit understandings
excess capacity	concentration ratio	collusion	price leadership
oligopoly	interindustry competition	kinked demand curve	

STUDY QUESTIONS

1. How does monopolistic competition differ from pure competition in its basic characteristics? From pure monopoly? Explain fully what product differentiation may involve. Explain how the entry of firms into its industry affects the demand curve facing a monopolistic competitor and how that, in turn, affects its economic profit.

2. **KEY QUESTION** Compare the elasticity of the monopolistic competitor's demand with that of a pure competitor and a pure monopolist. Assuming identical long-run costs, compare graphically the prices and outputs that would result in the long run under pure competition and monopolistic competition. Contrast the two market structures in terms of productive and allocative efficiency. Explain: "Monopolistically competitive industries are characterized by too many firms, each of which produces too little."

3. "Monopolistic competition is monopolistic up to the point at which consumers become willing to buy close-substitute products and competitive beyond that point." Explain.

4. "Competition in quality and service may be just as effective as price competition in giving buyers more for their money." Do you agree? Why? Explain why monopolistically competitive firms frequently prefer nonprice competition to price competition.

5. Critically evaluate and explain:
  a. "In monopolistically competitive industries economic profits are competed away in the long run; hence, there is no valid reason to criticize the performance and efficiency of such industries."
  b. "In the long run, monopolistic competition leads to a monopolistic price but not to monopolistic profits."

6. Why do oligopolies exist? List five or six oligopolists whose products you own or regularly purchase. What distinguishes oligopoly from monopolistic competition?

7. **KEY QUESTION** Answer the following questions, which relate to measures of concentration:
  a. What is the meaning of a four-firm concentration ratio of 60 percent? 90 percent? What are the shortcomings of concentration ratios as measures of monopoly power?
  b. Suppose that the five firms in industry A have annual sales of 30, 30, 20, 10, and 10 percent of total industry sales. For the five firms in industry B the figures are 60, 25, 5, 5, and 5 percent. Calculate the Herfindahl index for each industry and compare their likely competitiveness.

8. **KEY QUESTION** Explain the general meaning of the following profit payoff matrix for oligopolists C and D. All profit figures are in thousands.

C's possible prices

	$40	$35
D's possible prices $40	$57 / $60	$59 / $55
$35	$50 / $69	$55 / $58

  a. Use the payoff matrix to explain the mutual interdependence which characterizes oligopolistic industries.

  b. Assuming no collusion between C and D, what is the likely pricing outcome?
  c. In view of your answer to 8b, explain why price collusion is mutually profitable. Why might there be a temptation to cheat on the collusive agreement?

9. **KEY QUESTION** What assumptions about a rival's response to price changes underlie the kinked demand curve for oligopolists? Why is there a gap in the oligopolist's marginal-revenue curve? How does the kinked demand curve explain price rigidity in oligopoly? What are the shortcomings of the kinked-demand model?

10. Why might price collusion occur in oligopolistic industries? Assess the economic desirability of collusive pricing. What are the main obstacles to collusion? Discuss the weakening of OPEC in the 1980s in terms of these obstacles.

11. **KEY QUESTION** Advertising can have two effects: It can increase a firm's output, and it can shift a firm's average-total-cost curve upward. Explain how the relative sizes of these two effects may affect consumers.

12. **(Last Word)** What demand and supply factors have altered the beer industry from monopolistic competition to oligopoly?

13. **WEB-BASED QUESTION** **Bookselling on the Internet—How Do Sellers Differentiate Identical Books?** An upstart company called Amazon http://www.amazon.com introduced bookselling to the Web. Amazon's success enticed a long-time bookseller, Barnes and Noble http://www.barnesandnoble.com/ to go online with a major Web site. Search both sites for Viktor Frankl's *Man's Search for Meaning* (paperback). Find the price delivered to your address. Is one cheaper? Identify the nonprice competition which would lead you to order from one company rather than the other.

14. **WEB-BASED QUESTION** **Grocery Stores—Can You Buy Spuds Online?** Grocery stores are now using the Web for advertising and sales promotion. Examples can be found at Yahoo http://www.yahoo.com/Business and Economy/Companies/Food/Retail/Grocers/. How are the large national and regional grocery chains using the Web for advertising and sales promotion? Several small companies have set up virtual grocery stores. Consumers put together a shopping list over the Internet and select a payment method, and then the groceries are delivered to their door. Are any of the large chains doing this? Is there anything preventing them from doing this?

26

Technology, R&D, and Efficiency

- "Just do it!" In 1968 two entrepreneurs in Oregon developed a lightweight sport shoe and formed a new company called Nike, incorporating a "swoosh" logo (designed by a graduate student for $35). Today, Nike employs 14,200 workers and sells $5.9 billion worth of athletic shoes, hiking boots, and sports apparel annually.
- "Intel inside." Intel? In 1967 neither this company nor its product existed. Today it is the world's largest producer of microprocessors for personal computers, with 40,500 employees and more than $16 billion of annual sales.
- When Wal-Mart arrives, "look for falling prices." Much like Clint Eastwood, Wal-Mart has burst into town, setting up huge retail stores and sending competitors scurrying for cover, or worse. Expanding from a single store in 1962 to 1990 stores today, Wal-Mart employs 648,500 full- and part-time workers and has greater annual revenues than Procter & Gamble, IBM, or AT&T.
- Build a restaurant around a particular theme, such as "rock and roll"; then sell clothing with your logo on it: Hard Rock Café. A novel idea? Ask Planet Hollywood, Harley Davidson Café, and other imitators.

These brief descriptions involve elements of **technological advance,** broadly defined as *new and better goods and services and new and better ways of producing or distributing them.* For economists, technological advance involves the very long run. Recall that in our four market models (pure competition, monopolistic competition, oligopoly, and pure monopoly), the *short run* is a period in which technology and plant and equipment are fixed. Also recall that in the *long run,* technology is constant but firms can change their plant sizes and are free to enter or exit industries. In contrast, the **very long run** is *a period in which technology can change and in which firms can introduce entirely new products.*

In this chapter we first define several terms relating to technological advance and then examine how it is motivated and implemented. One way to implement technological advance is through research and development (R&D), so we explain how a firm determines its optimal amount of R&D spending and how innovation can expand profit by enhancing revenue or reducing cost. Then we discuss the extent and implications of the possible imitation problem facing innovators. Finally, we assess whether particular market structures are conducive to technological advance and how technological advance, in turn, relates to economic efficiency.

TECHNOLOGICAL ADVANCE: INVENTION, INNOVATION, AND DIFFUSION

In Chapter 2 we saw that technological advance shifts an economy's production possibilities curve outward, enabling the economy to obtain more goods and services. Technological advance is a three-step process of invention, innovation, and diffusion. Let's see what these steps entail.

Invention

The most basic element of technological advance is **invention:** *the first discovery of a product or process through the use of imagination, ingenious thinking, and experimentation and the first proof that it will work.* While invention is a process, the result of the process, unfortunately, is also called an invention. The first prototype (basic working model) of the telephone, the automobile, the television set, the microchip—each of these is an invention. Invention is usually based on scientific knowledge and is the product of individuals, either working on their own or as members of corporate R&D staffs. Later on you will see how governments encourage invention by providing the originator with a **patent,** *an exclusive right to sell any new and useful process, machine, or product for a set period of time.* In 1996 four leading high-technology firms—IBM, Canon, Motorola, and NEC—*each* secured more than 1000 new U.S. patents. Such patents now have a worldwide uniform duration of 20 years from the time of application.

Innovation

Innovation, a second element of technological change, draws directly on invention. While invention is "first discovery and proof of workability," **innovation** is *the first successful commercial introduction of a new product, the first use of a new method, or the creation of a new form of business enterprise.* Innovation is of two broad types: **product innovation,** which involves new and improved products or services; and **process innovation,** which involves new and improved production or distribution methods.

Unlike inventions, innovations, as such, cannot be patented. Nevertheless, innovation is a major factor in competition since it sometimes enables a firm to "leapfrog" competitors by making their products or processes obsolete. For example, personal computers coupled with software for word processing unceremoniously pushed some typewriter manufacturers into relative obscurity. More recently, innovations in hardware retailing (large warehouse stores such as Home Depot) have threatened the very existence of smaller, more traditional hardware stores.

But innovation need not destroy existing firms. Aware that new products and processes can threaten their survival, existing firms have a powerful incentive to engage continuously in R&D of their own. Innovative new products and processes often enable these firms to maintain or increase their profit. The introduction of aluminum cans by Reynolds, disposable contact lenses by Johnson & Johnson, and scientific calculators by Hewlett-Packard are good examples. Thus, innovation can either diminish or strengthen existing market power.

Diffusion

The spread of an innovation through imitation or copying is known as **diffusion.** To take advantage of new profit opportunities or slow the erosion of their profit, new and existing firms emulate the successful innovations of others. Years ago McDonald's successfully introduced the fast-food hamburger; Burger King, Wendy's, and other firms soon copied that idea. Alamo greatly increased its auto rentals by offering renters unlimited mileage, but Hertz, Avis, Budget, and others eventually followed. More recently, new restaurant chains such as Boston Market and Kenny Rogers Roasters have popularized oven-roasted chicken. KFC, the chicken-market leader, has responded by adding this menu item, too. Chrysler Corporation profitably introduced a luxury version of its Jeep Grand Cherokee; other manufacturers including Ford, Acura, and Mercedes have countered with luxury sport-utility vehicles of their own. In each of these cases, innovation has led eventually to widespread imitation—that is, diffusion.

R&D Expenditures

As it relates to *businesses,* the term "research and development" is used loosely to include direct efforts toward invention, innovation, and diffusion. However, *government* also engages in R&D, particularly that related to national defense. In 1995 *total* U.S. R&D expenditures (business *plus* government) were $179 billion. This amount was about 2.5 percent of U.S. GDP and is a reasonable measure of the emphasis an economy puts on technological advance. As shown in Global Perspective 26-1, this is a high percentage relative to that in several other nations.

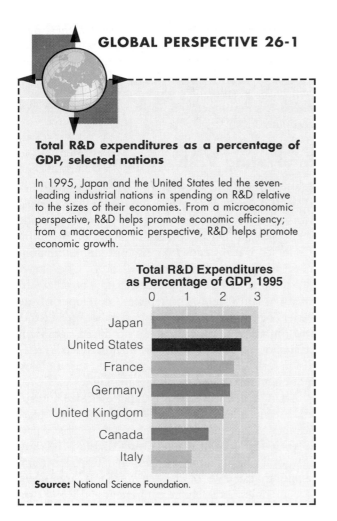

Total R&D expenditures as a percentage of GDP, selected nations

In 1995, Japan and the United States led the seven-leading industrial nations in spending on R&D relative to the sizes of their economies. From a microeconomic perspective, R&D helps promote economic efficiency; from a macroeconomic perspective, R&D helps promote economic growth.

Total R&D Expenditures as Percentage of GDP, 1995

Source: National Science Foundation.

American *businesses* spent $132 billion on R&D in 1995. Figure 26-1 shows how these R&D expenditures were divided by type of activity. Observe that U.S. firms collectively channeled 74 percent of their R&D expenditures to "development" (innovation and imitation, the route to diffusion). They used another 21 percent for applied research, roughly equivalent to pursuing invention. For reasons we will address later, only 5 percent of business R&D expenditures went for basic research—the search for general scientific principles. Of course, different industries, and different firms within industries, vary greatly in the amounts of emphasis they place on these three processes.

Modern View of Technological Advance

For decades most economists envisioned technological advance as being *external* to the economy—a ran-

dom *outside* force to which the economy adjusted. From time to time fortuitous advances in scientific and technological knowledge occurred, paving the way for major new products (automobiles, airplanes) and new production processes (assembly lines). Firms and industries, each at its own pace, then incorporated the new technology into products or processes, to enhance or maintain their profit. After making the appropriate adjustments, industries settled back into new long-run equilibrium positions. Although technological advance has been vitally important to the economy, economists thought it was rooted in the independent advance of science, an element largely external to the market system.

Most contemporary economists have a different view. They see capitalism itself as the driving force of technological advance. In this view, invention, innovation, and diffusion occur in response to incentives within the economy, meaning that technological advance is *internal* to capitalism. Specifically, technological advance arises from intense rivalry among individuals and firms which motivates them to seek and exploit new profit opportunities or to expand existing opportunities. This rivalry occurs both among existing firms and between them and new firms. Moreover,

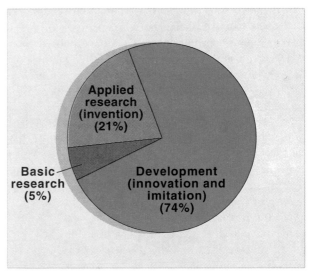

FIGURE 26-1 The composition of business R&D outlays in the United States, 1995 Firms channel the bulk of their R&D spending to innovation and imitation because both have direct commercial value; less to applied research, that is, invention; and a relatively small amount to basic scientific research. (*Source:* National Science Foundation. Data are for 1995.)

many advances in "pure" scientific knowledge are also motivated, at least in part, by the prospect of commercial applicability and eventual profit. In the modern view, entrepreneurs and other innovators are at the heart of technological advance.

ROLE OF ENTREPRENEURS AND OTHER INNOVATORS

It will be helpful to distinguish between "entrepreneurs" and "other innovators:"

1. *Entrepreneurs*   Recall that the entrepreneur is an initiator, innovator, and risk bearer—the catalyst who combines land, labor, and capital resources in new and unique ways to produce new goods and services. Historically, a single individual carried out the entrepreneurial role—an Andrew Carnegie in steel, a Henry Ford in automobiles, or a Levi Strauss in blue jeans. Such substantial advances as air conditioning, power steering, the ballpoint pen, cellophane, the jet engine, insulin, xerography, the helicopter, and the refining of petroleum all have an individualistic heritage. But in today's more technologically complex economy, entrepreneurship is just as likely to be carried out by *entrepreneurial teams.* Such collaborative teams may include only two or three people working "as their own bosses" on some new product idea or may consist of larger groups of entrepreneurs who have pooled their resources.

2. *Other innovators*   This designation includes the other key people involved in the pursuit of innovation, but unlike entrepreneurs, other innovators do not bear personal financial risk. These people include key executives, scientists, and other salaried employees engaged in commercial R&D activities. (They are sometimes referred to as *intrapreneurs* since they provide the spirit of entrepreneurship *within* existing firms.)

Forming Start-Ups

Quite often, entrepreneurs form small new companies called **start-ups:** *firms focused on creating and introducing a particular new product or employing a specific new production or distribution technique.* Two people, working out of their garages, founded one such start-up in the mid-1970s. Neither of their employers—Hewlett-Packard and Atari, the developer of Pong (the first video game)—was interested in their proto-

type personal computer. So they founded their own company: Apple Computers. More recent examples of successful start-ups are Amgen, a biotechnology firm specializing in new medical treatments; Starbucks, a seller of gourmet coffee; and Iomega, which has developed innovative storage devices for computers.

Innovating Within Existing Firms

Innovators are also found within *existing* corporations, large and small. While such innovators are salaried workers, many firms have pay systems which provide them with substantial bonuses or shares of the profit. Examples of firms known for their skillful internal innovators are the 3M Corporation, the U.S. developer of Scotch tape, Post-it Note Pads, and Thinsulate insulation, and Canon, the Japanese developer of the "laser engine" for personal copiers and printers. R&D work in major corporations has produced significant technological improvements in such products as television sets, telephones, home appliances, automobiles, automobile tires, and sporting equipment.

Many large firms are aware that excessive bureaucracy can stifle creative thinking and technological advance. A few such firms have actually separated part of their R&D and manufacturing divisions to form new, more flexible, innovative firms. Two recent and significant examples of such "spinoff firms" are Lucent Technologies, a telephone equipment and R&D firm created by AT&T, and Imation, a new high-technology firm spun off by 3M Corporation.

Anticipating the Future

In 1949 a writer for *Popular Mechanics* magazine boldly predicted that "computers in the future may weigh no more than 1.5 tons." Today's notebook computers weigh less than 5 *pounds.* It is difficult to anticipate the future, but that is what innovators try to do. Those with strong anticipatory ability and determination have a knack for introducing new and improved products or services at just the right time. The rewards are both nonmonetary and monetary. Product innovation and development are creative endeavors, with attendant intangible rewards of personal satisfaction. Also, many people simply enjoy participating in the competitive "contest." But arguably of greatest importance, the "winners" can reap large monetary rewards in the form of economic profits, stock appreciation, or large bonuses. Extreme example: Paul Allen and Bill Gates, who founded Microsoft in 1975, had net worths in 1997 of $40 billion and $17 billion, respectively, mainly in the form of Microsoft stock.

Past successes often give entrepreneurs and innovative firms access to *more* resources for further innovation—further actions which anticipate consumer wants. They may or may not again succeed, but in general, the market entrusts the production of goods and services to businesses which have consistently succeeded in filling consumer wants. And the market does not care whether these "winning" entrepreneurs and innovative firms are American, Brazilian, Japanese, German, or Swiss. Entrepreneurship and innovation are global in scope.

Exploiting University and Government Scientific Research

In Figure 26-1 we saw that only 5 percent of business R&D spending in the United States is for basic scientific research. This percentage is so small because scientific principles, as such, cannot be patented, nor do they usually have immediate commercial uses. Yet new scientific knowledge is highly important to technological advance. For that reason, entrepreneurs actively study the scientific output of university and government laboratories to find discoveries with commercial applicability.

In fact, government and university labs have been fertile grounds for many technological breakthroughs, including hybrid seed corn, nuclear energy, satellite communications, the computer "mouse," genetic engineering, and the Internet. Entire new high-tech industries—computers and biotechnology, for example—have sprung up close to major research universities and government laboratories. And nations with strong scientific communities tend to have the most technologically progressive firms and industries.

Also, firms increasingly help fund university research which relates to their products. As shown in Figure 26-2, business-funded R&D at universities has grown rapidly. Today, the separation between university scientists and innovators is narrowing; scientists increasingly realize their work may have commercial value and are teaming with innovators to share in the potential profit. A few firms, of course, *do* find it profitable to conduct basic scientific research on their own. New scientific knowledge can give them a major head-start in creating an invention or new product. This is particularly true in the pharmaceutical industry, where it is not uncommon for firms to parlay new scientific knowledge from their corporate labs into new, patentable drugs.

QUICK REVIEW 26-1

■ Broadly defined, technological advance means new or improved products and services and new or improved production and distribution processes.

■ Invention is the *discovery* of a new product or method; innovation is the *successful commercial application* of some invention; and diffusion is the *widespread imitation* of the innovation.

■ Many economists view technological advance as mainly a response to profit opportunities arising within a capitalist economy.

■ Technological advance is fostered by entrepreneurs and other innovators and is supported by the scientific research of universities and government-sponsored laboratories.

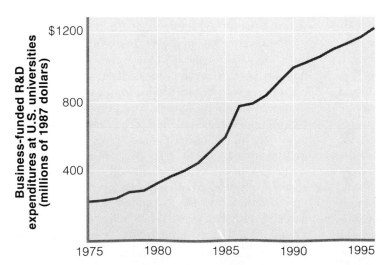

FIGURE 26-2 Growth of business-funded R&D expenditures at U.S. universities, 1975–1996 Although the total amounts are still relatively small, firms have greatly expanded their funding of R&D at U.S. universities over the past two decades. (*Source:* National Science Foundation)

A FIRM'S OPTIMAL AMOUNT OF R&D

How does a firm decide on its optimal amount of research and development? This amount will depend on the firm's perception of the marginal benefit and marginal cost of R&D activity. The decision rule here flows from basic economics: *To earn the greatest profit, expand a particular activity until its marginal benefit (MB) equals its marginal cost (MC).* A firm which sees the marginal benefit of a particular R&D activity, say, innovation, as exceeding the marginal cost should expand that activity. In contrast, an activity whose marginal benefit is less than its marginal cost should be cut back. But the R&D spending decision is complex since it involves a present sacrifice for a future expected gain. While the cost of R&D is immediate, the expected benefits occur at some future time and are highly uncertain. So estimating these benefits is often more art then science. Nevertheless, the MB = MC framework remains relevant for analyzing R&D decisions and provides direction to our discussion.

Interest-Rate Cost of Funds

Firms have several means available for obtaining the funds needed to finance their R&D activities:

1. **Bank loans** Some firms may be able to obtain a loan from a bank or other financial institution. Then the cost of using the funds is the interest paid to the lender. The marginal cost is the cost per extra dollar borrowed, which is simply the market interest rate for borrowed funds.

2. **Bonds** Established, profitable firms may be able to borrow funds for R&D by issuing bonds and selling them in the bond market. In this case, the cost is the interest paid to the lenders—the bondholders. Again the marginal cost of using the funds is the interest rate. (We discussed bonds in Chapter 5's Last Word).

3. **Retained earnings** A larger, more established firm may be able to draw on its own corporate saving to finance R&D. Typically, such a firm retains part of its profit rather than paying it all out as dividends to its corporate owners. Some of the undistributed corporate profit, called *retained earnings*, can be used to finance R&D activity. The marginal cost is the rate at which these funds could have earned interest as deposits in a financial institution.

4. **Venture capital** A smaller start-up firm might be able to attract venture capital to finance its R&D projects. **Venture capital** is financial capital—that, is *money*—not real capital. It consists of *that part of household saving used to finance high-risk business ventures in exchange for shares of the profit if the ventures succeed.* The marginal cost of venture capital is the share of expected profit which the firm will have to pay to those who provided the money. This can be stated as a percentage of the venture capital, so it has the basic nature of an interest rate.

5. **Personal savings** Finally, individual entrepreneurs might draw on their own savings to finance the R&D for a new venture. The marginal cost of the financing is again the forgone interest rate.

Thus, whatever the source of the R&D funds, we can state the marginal cost of these funds as an interest rate *i*. For simplicity, let's assume this interest rate is the same no matter how much financing is required. Further, we suppose that a certain firm called MedTech must pay an interest rate of 8 percent, the least expensive funding available to it. Then a graph of the marginal cost of each funding amount for this firm is a horizontal line at the 8 percent interest rate, as shown in Figure 26-3. Such a graph is called an **interest-rate cost-of-funds curve.** This one tells us that MedTech can borrow $10, $10,000, $10,000,000 or more at the 8 percent interest rate. The table accompanying the graph contains the data used to construct the graph and tells us much the same thing.

With these data in hand, MedTech wants to determine how much R&D to finance in the coming year.

Expected Rate of Return

A firm's marginal benefit from R&D is its expected profit (or return) from the last (marginal) dollar spent on R&D. That is, the R&D is expected to result in a new product or production method which will increase revenue, reduce production costs, or both (in ways we will soon discuss). This return is expected, *not* certain—there is risk in R&D decisions. Let's suppose that after considering such risks, MedTech anticipates that an R&D expenditure of $1 million will result in a new product which will yield a one-time added profit of $1.2 million a year later. The expected rate of return *r* on the $1 million R&D expenditure (after $1 million is repaid) is 20 percent (= $200,000/$1,000,000). This is the marginal benefit of the first

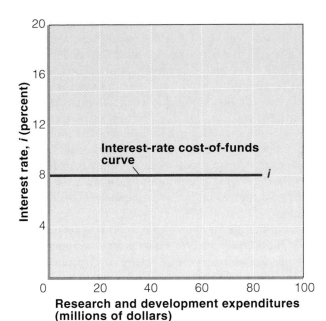

FIGURE 26-3 **The interest-rate cost-of-funds schedule and curve**   As it relates to R&D, a firm's interest-rate cost-of-funds schedule (the table) and curve (the graph) show the interest rate the firm must pay to obtain any particular amount of funds to finance R&D. Curve *i* indicates the firm can finance as little or as much R&D as it wants at a constant 8 percent rate of interest.

R&D, millions	Interest-rate cost of funds, %
$10	8
20	8
30	8
40	8
50	8
60	8
70	8
80	8

- -

$1 million of R&D. (Stretching the return over several years complicates the computation of *r*, but it does not alter the basic analysis.)

MedTech can use this same method to estimate the expected rates of return for R&D expenditures of $2 million, $3 million, $4 million, and so on. Suppose those marginal rates of return are the ones indicated in the table in Figure 26-4, where they are also graphed as the **expected-rate-of-return curve**. This curve shows the expected rate of return—the mar-

ginal benefit—of each dollar of expenditure on R&D. The curve slopes downward because of diminishing returns to R&D expenditures. A firm will direct its initial R&D expenditures to the highest expected-rate-of-return activities and then use additional funding for activities with successively lower expected rates of return. That is, as R&D spending is increased, it is used to finance R&D activities with lower and lower expected rates of return.

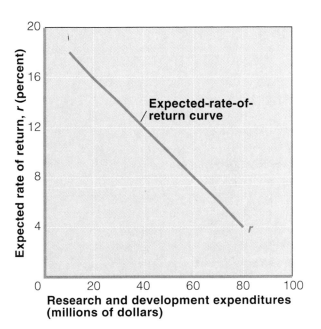

R&D, millions	Expected rate of return, %
$10	18
20	16
30	14
40	12
50	10
60	8
70	6
80	4

FIGURE 26-4 **The expected-rate-of-return schedule and curve**   As it relates to R&D, a firm's expected-rate-of-return schedule (the table) and curve (the graph) show its expected gain in profit, as a percentage of R&D spending, for each level of R&D spending. Curve *r* slopes downward because the firm assesses its potential R&D projects in descending order of expected rates of return.

- -

Optimal R&D Expenditures

Figure 26-5 combines the interest-rate-cost-of-funds curve (Figure 26-3) and the expected-rate-of-return curve (Figure 26-4). The curves intersect at MedTech's **optimal amount of R&D,** which is $60 million. This amount can also be determined from the table as the amount of funding for which the expected rate of return and the interest cost of borrowing are equal

Expected rate of return, %	R&D, millions	Interest-rate cost of funds, %
18	$10	8
16	20	8
14	30	8
12	40	8
10	50	8
8	**60**	**8**
6	70	8
4	80	8

FIGURE 26-5 A firm's optimal level of R&D expenditures The firm's optimal level of R&D expenditures ($60 million) occurs where its expected rate of return equals the interest-rate cost of funds, as shown in both the table and the graph. At $60 million of R&D spending, the firm has taken advantage of all R&D opportunities for which the expected rate of return, r, exceeds or equals the 8 percent interest cost of borrowing, i.

(here, 8 percent). Both the curve and the table tell us that at $60 million of R&D expenditures, the marginal benefit and marginal cost of the last dollar spent on R&D are equal. This firm should undertake all R&D expenditures up to $60 million, since these outlays yield a higher marginal benefit or expected rate of return, r, than the 8 percent marginal cost or interest-rate cost of borrowing, i. But it should not undertake R&D expenditures beyond $60 million; for these outlays, r (marginal benefit) is less than i (marginal cost). Only at $60 million do we have $r = i$, telling us that MedTech will spend $60 million on R&D.

Our analysis reinforces two important points:

1. **Optimal versus affordable R&D**   From previous discussions we know there can be too much, as well as too little, of a "good thing." So it is with R&D and technological advance. Figure 26-5 shows that R&D expenditures make sense to a firm only as long as the expected return from the outlay equals or exceeds the cost of obtaining the funds needed to finance it. Many R&D expenditures may be affordable but not worthwhile, because their marginal benefit is less than their marginal cost.

2. **Expected, *not* guaranteed, returns**   The outcomes from R&D are *expected,* not guaranteed. With 20-20 hindsight, a firm can always look back and decide whether a particular expenditure for R&D was worthwhile. But this assessment is irrelevant to the original decision. At the time of the decision, the expenditure was thought to be worthwhile, based on existing information and expectations. Some R&D decisions may be more like an informed gamble rather than the typical business decision. Invention and innovation, in particular, carry with them a great deal of risk. For every successful outcome, there are scores of costly disappointments. **(Key Questions 4 and 5)**

INCREASED PROFIT VIA INNOVATION

In discussing how a firm determines its optimal amount of R&D spending, we sidestepped the question of how technological change can increase a firm's profit. Although the answer may seem obvious—by increasing revenue or reducing production cost—there are insights to be gained by exploring these two potential outcomes in some detail.

Increased Revenue via Product Innovation

Firms have profitably introduced hundreds of new products in the past two or three decades. Examples include rollerblades, laser pointers, cordless drills, laser printers, "snake" lights, camcorders, fiber-optic cable, compact discs, projection TVs, and microwave popcorn. Other new products are gourmet coffee, cellular phones, notebook computers, telephone pagers, automobile air bags, mountain bikes, new artificial sweeteners, "breathable" waterproof fabrics, and snowboards. All these reflect technological advance in the form of *product innovation.*

It will be useful to see how such new products gain consumer acceptance. As you know from Chapter 21, to maximize their satisfaction, consumers purchase products having the highest marginal utility per dollar. They determine which products to buy in view of their limited money incomes by comparing the ratios of MU/price for the various goods. They first select the unit of the good with the highest MU/price ratio, then the one with the next highest, and so on, until their income is used up.

The first five columns of Table 26-1 repeat some of the information in Table 21-1. Before the introduction of new product C, the consumer maximized total utility from $10 of income by buying 2 units of A at $1 per unit and 4 units of B at $2 per unit. The total $10 budget was thus expended, with $2 spent on A and $8 on B. As shown in columns 2b and 3b, the marginal utility per dollar spent on the last unit of each product was 8 (= 8/$1 = 16/$2). The total utility, derived from columns 2a and 3a, was 96 utils (= 10 + 8 from the first 2 units of A *plus* 24 + 20 + 18 + 16 from the first 4 units of B). (If you are uncertain about this outcome, please review the discussion of Table 21-1).

Now suppose an innovative firm offers new product C (columns 4a and 4b in Table 26-1), priced at $4 per unit. Note that the first unit of C has a *higher* marginal utility per dollar (13) than any unit of A and B and that the second unit of C and the first unit of B have equal MU/price ratios of 12. To maximize satisfaction, the consumer now buys 2 units of C at $4 per unit, 1 unit of B at $2 per unit, and zero units of A. Our consumer has spent the entire $10 of income ($8 on C and $2 on B), and the MU/price ratios of the last units of B and C are equal at 12. But as determined via columns 3a and 4a, the consumer's total utility is now 124 utils (= 24 from the first unit of B *plus* 52 + 48 from the first 2 units of C). Total utility has increased by 30 utils (= 124 utils − 96 utils)—and that is why product C was purchased. *Consumers will buy a new product only if it increases the total utility they obtain from their limited incomes.*

From the innovating firm's perspective, these "dollar votes" represent new product demand which yields increased revenue. When per-unit revenue exceeds per-unit cost, the product innovation creates per-unit profit. Total profit rises by the per-unit profit multiplied by the number of units sold. As a percentage of the

TABLE 26-1 Utility maximization with the introduction of a new product (income = $10)

(1) Unit of product	(2) Product A: price = $1		(3) Product B: price = $2		(4) New product C: price = $4	
	(a) Marginal utility, utils	(b) Marginal utility per dollar (MU/price)	(a) Marginal utility, utils	(b) Marginal utility per dollar (MU/price)	(a) Marginal utility, utils	(b) Marginal utility per dollar (MU/price)
First	10	10	24	*12*	52	13
Second	8	*8*	20	10	48	*12*
Third	7	7	18	9	44	11
Fourth	6	6	16	*8*	36	9
Fifth	5	5	12	6	32	8

*It is assumed in this table that the amount of marginal utility received from additional units of each of the three products is independent of the quantity purchased of the other products. For example, the marginal-utility schedule for product C is independent of the amount of A and B purchased by the consumer.

original R&D expenditure, the rise in total profit is the return on that R&D expenditure. It was the basis for the expected-rate-of-return curve r in Figure 26-4.

Three other points:

1. *Importance of price* Consumer acceptance of a new product depends on both its marginal utility *and* its price. You should confirm that the consumer represented in Table 26-1 would buy zero units of new product C if its price were $8 rather than $4. To be successful, a new product must not only deliver utility to consumers but do so at an acceptable price.

2. *Unsuccessful new products* For every successful new product, there are hundreds of others which do not succeed; the *expected* return that motivates product innovation is not always realized. Examples of colossal product flops are Ford's Edsel automobile, 3-D movies, quadraphonic stereo, New Coke by Coca-Cola, Kodak disc cameras, and McDonald's McLean burger. In each of these cases, millions of dollars of R&D and promotion expense ultimately resulted in loss, not profit.

3. *Product improvements* Most product innovation consists of incremental improvements to existing products rather than radical inventions. Examples: more fuel-efficient automobile engines, new styles of pizza, lighter-weight shafts for golf clubs, more flavorful bubble-gum, "rock shocks" for mountain bikes, and clothing made of wrinkle-free fabrics. **(Key Question 6)**

Reduced Cost via Process Innovation

The introduction of better methods of producing products—*process innovation*—is also a path toward enhanced profit and a positive return on R&D expenditures. Suppose a firm introduces a new and better production process, say, assembling its product by teams rather than by a standard assembly line. Alternatively, suppose this firm replaces old equipment with more productive equipment embodying technological advance. In either case, the innovation yields an upward shift in the firm's total-product curve from TP_1 to TP_2 in Figure 26-6a. Now more units of output can be produced *at each level of resource usage*. Note from the figure, for example, that this firm can now produce 2500 units of output, rather than 2000 units, when using 1000 units of labor. So its average product has increased from 2 (= 2000 units of

(a) Upward shift of the total-product curve

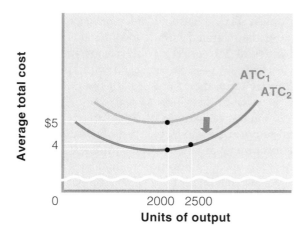

(b) Downward shift of the average-total-cost curve

FIGURE 26-6 Process innovation, total product, and average total cost (a) Process innovation shifts a firm's total-product curve upward from TP_1 to TP_2, meaning that the firm can produce more output at each level of labor input. As shown, with 1000 units of labor it can produce 2500 rather than 2000 units of output. (b) The upward shift in the total-product curve results in a downward shift in the firm's average-total-cost curve, from ATC_1 to ATC_2. This means the firm can produce any particular unit of output at a lower average total cost than it could previously. For example, the original 2000 units can be produced at less than $4 per unit, versus $5 per unit originally. Or 2500 units can now be produced at $4 per unit.

- -

output ÷ 1000 units of labor) to 2.5 (= 2500 units of output ÷ 1000 units of labor).

The result is a downward shift in the firm's average-total-cost curve, from ATC_1 to ATC_2 in Figure

26-6b. To understand why, let's assume this firm pays $1000 for the use of its capital and $9 for each unit of labor. Since it uses 1000 units of labor, its labor cost is $9000 (= $9 × 1000); its capital cost is $1000; and thus its total cost is $10,000. When its output increases from 2000 to 2500 units due to the process innovation, its total cost remains $10,000; however, its average total cost declines from $5 (= $10,000/2000) to $4 (= $10,000/2500). Alternatively, the firm could produce the original 2000 units of output with fewer units of labor at an even lower average total cost.

This reduction in average total cost enhances the firm's profit. As a percentage of the R&D expenditure which fostered it, this extra profit is the expected return r, the basis for the rate-of-return-curve in Figure 26-4. In this case, the expected rate of return arose from the prospect of lower production costs through process innovation.

Approximate example: Computer-based inventory control systems, such as those pioneered by Wal-Mart, enabled innovators to reduce the number of people keeping track of inventories and placing reorders of sold goods. They have also enabled firms to keep goods arriving "just in time," reducing the cost of storing inventories. The consequence? Significant increases in sales per worker, declines in average total cost, and increased profit. **(Key Question 8)**

IMITATION AND R&D INCENTIVES

Our analysis of product and process innovation explains how technological advance can enhance a firm's profit, but it also hints at a potential **imitation problem:** a firm's rivals may be able to imitate its new product or process, greatly reducing the originator's profit from its R&D effort. As just one example, in the 1980s U.S. auto firms took apart Japanese Honda Accords, piece by piece, to discover the secrets of their high quality. This *reverse engineering*—which ironically was perfected earlier by the Japanese—helped the U.S. firms incorporate innovative features into their own cars. This type of imitation is perfectly legitimate and fully anticipated; it is often the main path to widespread diffusion of an innovation.

In fact, a dominant firm which is making large profits from its existing products may let smaller firms in the industry incur the high costs of product innovation while it closely monitors their successes and failures. The dominant firm then moves quickly to imitate any successful new product; its goal is to become the *second* firm to embrace the innovation. In using this so-called **fast-second strategy,** the dominant firm counts on its own product-improvement abilities, marketing prowess, or economies of scale to prevail.

Examples abound: Royal Crown introduced the first diet cola, but Diet Coke and Diet Pepsi dominate diet-cola sales today. Meister-Brau introduced the first low-calorie beer, but Miller popularized the product with its Miller Lite. Gillette moved quickly with its own stainless-steel razor blade only after a smaller firm, Wilkinson, introduced this product innovation.

Benefits of Being First

Imitation and the fast-second strategy raise an important question: What incentive is there for *any* firm to bear the expenses and risks of innovation if competitors can imitate its new or improved products? Why not let others bear the costs and risks of product development and then just imitate the successful innovations? Although we have seen that this may be a plausible strategy in some situations, there are several protections for, and potential advantages to, taking the lead.

Patents Some technological breakthroughs, specifically inventions, can be patented. Then they cannot be legally imitated for two decades. The purpose of patents is, in fact, to reduce imitation and its negative effect on the incentive for engaging in R&D. Example: Polaroid's patent of its instant camera enabled it to earn high economic profits for many years. When Kodak "cloned" the camera, Polaroid won a patent-infringement lawsuit against its rival. Kodak not only had to stop producing its version of the camera but also had to buy back the Kodak instant cameras it had sold and pay millions of dollars of damages to Polaroid.

There are hundreds of other examples of long-run profits based on U.S. patents; they involve things from weed trimmers and pop-top cans to vise-grip tools and fishing lures. As shown in Global Perspective 26-2, such patents are secured not only by U.S. citizens and firms but by citizens and firms of foreign nations.

Copyrights and Trademarks *Copyrights* protect publishers of books, computer software, movies, videos, and musical compositions from having their works copied. *Trademarks* give the original innovators of products the exclusive right to use a particular product name ("M&Ms," "Barbie Doll,"

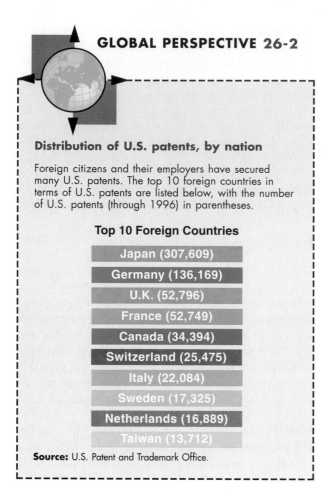

"Wheaties"). By reducing the problem of direct copying, these legal protections increase the incentive for product innovation. They have been strengthened worldwide through recent international trade agreements.

Brand-Name Recognition   Along with trademark protection, brand-name recognition may give the original innovator a major marketing advantage for years or even decades. Consumers often identify a new product with the firm first introducing and popularizing it in the mass market. Examples: *Levi's* blue jeans, *Kleenex* soft tissues, Johnson and Johnson's *Band-Aids*, Sony's *Walkman*, and Kellogg's *Corn Flakes*.

Trade Secrets and Learning by Doing   Some innovations involve *trade secrets*, without which competitors cannot imitate the product or process. Example: Coca-Cola has successfully kept its formula for Coke a secret from potential rivals. Many other firms have perfected special production techniques known only to them. In a related advantage, a firm's head-start with a new product often allows it to achieve substantial cost reductions through *learning by doing*. The innovator's lower cost may enable it to continue to profit even after imitators have entered the market.

Time Lags   Time lags between innovation and diffusion often permit innovating firms to realize a substantial economic profit. It takes time for an imitator to gain knowledge of the properties of a new innovation. And once it has that knowledge, the imitator must design a substitute product, gear up a factory for its production, and conduct a marketing campaign. Various entry barriers—large financial requirements, economies of scale, and price cutting—may extend the time lag between innovation and imitation. In practice, it may take years or even decades before rival firms can successfully imitate a profitable new product and cut into the market share of the innovator. In the meantime, the innovator continues to profit.

Profitable Buyouts   A final advantage of being first arises from the potential of a *buyout*—an outright purchase—of the innovating firm by a larger firm. Here, the innovative entrepreneurs take their rewards immediately, as cash or as shares in the buying firm, rather than waiting for perhaps uncertain long-run profits from their own production and marketing efforts.

Two examples: Once the popularity of cellular communications became evident, AT&T simply bought out McCaw Communications, an early leader in this new technology. When Minnetonka's Softsoap became a huge success, it sold its product to Colgate-Palmolive. Such buyouts are legal under current antitrust laws as long as they do not substantially lessen competition in the affected industry. For this to be the case, there must be other strong competitors in the market. That was not true, for example, when Microsoft tried to buy out Intuit (maker of Quicken, the best-selling financial software). That buyout was disallowed because Intuit and Microsoft were the two main suppliers of financial software for personal computers.

In short, even with the imitation problem, there are significant protections and advantages which enable most innovating firms to profit from their R&D efforts. The continuing high levels of R&D spending by firms year after year imply this fact. As shown in

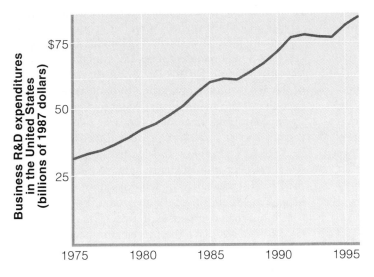

FIGURE 26-7 The growth of business R&D expenditures in the United States, 1975–1996 R&D expenditures by firms are substantial and growing, suggesting that R&D continues to pay off for firms, even in the face of possible imitation. (*Source:* National Science Foundation.)

Figure 26-7, business R&D spending in the United States not only remains substantial but has grown over the past quarter-century. The high levels of spending simply would not continue if imitation consistently and severely depressed actual rates of return on R&D expenditures.

QUICK REVIEW 26-2

■ A firm's optimal R&D expenditure is that amount at which the expected rate of return (marginal benefit) from the R&D expenditure just equals the interest-rate cost of borrowing (marginal cost) required to finance it.

■ Product innovation can entice consumers to substitute a new product for existing products to increase their total utility, thereby increasing the innovating firm's revenue and profit.

■ Process innovation can lower a firm's production costs and increase its profit by increasing total product and decreasing average total cost.

■ A firm faces reduced profitability from R&D if competitors can successfully imitate its new product or process. Nevertheless, there are significant potential protections and benefits to being first, including patents, copyrights, and trademarks; brand-name recognition, trade secrets, and cost reductions from learning by doing; and major time lags between innovation and imitation.

ROLE OF MARKET STRUCTURE

In view of our discussion of market structures in the last three chapters, it is logical to ask whether there is some particular market structure or firm size that is best suited to technological progress. Is a highly competitive industry in the traditional sense of pure competition preferable to an industry comprising only two or three large firms? Or is some intermediate structure best?

Market Structure and Technological Advance

As a first step toward answering these questions, let's survey our four market models, evaluating their strengths and shortcomings in regard to technological advance.

Pure Competition The willingness and ability of purely competitive firms to undertake R&D is debatable. On the positive side, strong competition provides a reason for these firms to innovate; competitive firms tend to be less complacent than monopolists. If a pure competitor does not seize the initiative, one or more rivals may introduce a new product or cost-reducing production technique which could drive it from the market. As a matter of short-term profit and long-term survival, pure competitors are under continual pressure to improve products and lower costs through innovation. Also, where there are many competing firms, there is a reduced chance that an idea for improving a product or process will be overlooked by a single firm.

On the negative side, the expected rate of return on R&D may be low or even negative for a pure competitor. Because of easy entry, its profit rewards from innovation may quickly be competed away by existing or entering firms which also produce the new product or adopt the new technology. Also, the small size of competitive firms and the fact that they earn only a normal profit in the long run leads to serious questions as to whether such producers can finance substantial R&D programs. Observers have noted that the high rate of technological advance in the purely competitive agricultural industry, for example, has come not from the R&D of individual farmers but from government-sponsored research and oligopolistic firms' development of fertilizers, hybrid seed, and farm implements.

Monopolistic Competition   Like pure competitors, monopolistic competitors cannot afford to be complacent. But unlike pure competitors, which sell standardized products, monopolistic competitors have a strong profit incentive to engage in product development. This incentive to differentiate products from those of competitors stems from the fact that sufficiently novel products may create monopoly power and thus economic profit. There are many examples of innovative firms (McDonald's, Blockbuster Video) which started out as monopolistic competitors in localized markets but soon gained considerable national market power, with the attendant economic profit.

For the typical firm, however, the shortcomings of monopolistic competition in relation to technological advance are the same as those of pure competition. Most monopolistic competitors remain small, which limits their ability to secure inexpensive financing for R&D. In addition, monopolistic competitors find it very difficult to extract large profits from technological advances. Any economic profits from innovation are usually temporary, because entry to monopolistically competitive industries is relatively easy. In the long run, new entrants with similar goods reduce the demand for the innovator's product, leaving the innovator with only a normal profit. Monopolistic competitors therefore usually have relatively low expected rates of return on R&D expenditures.

Oligopoly   Many of the characteristics of oligopoly are conducive to technological advance. First, the large size of oligopolists enables them to finance the often very expensive R&D costs associated with major product or process innovation. In particular, the typical oligopolist realizes ongoing economic profits, a part of which is retained. This undistributed profit serves as a major source of readily available, relatively low-cost funding for R&D. Moreover, the existence of barriers to entry gives the oligopolist some assurance that it can maintain any economic profit it gains from innovation. Then, too, the large sales volume of the oligopolist allows it to spread the cost of specialized R&D equipment and teams of specialized researchers over a great many units of output. Finally, the broad scope of R&D activity within oligopolistic firms helps them offset the inevitable R&D "misses" with more than compensating R&D "hits." Thus, oligopolists clearly have the means and incentive to innovate.

But there is also a negative side to R&D in oligopoly. In many instances, the oligopolist's incentive to innovate may be far less than we have implied above because oligopoly tends to breed complacency. An oligopolist may reason that it makes little sense to introduce costly new technology and produce new products when it currently is earning a sizable economic profit without them. The oligopolist wants to maximize its profit by exploiting fully all its capital assets. Why rush to develop a new product (say, batteries for electric automobiles) when that product's success will render obsolete much of the firm's current equipment designed to produce its existing product (say, gasoline engines)? It is not difficult to cite oligopolistic industries in which the largest firms' interest in R&D has been quite modest. Examples: the steel, cigarette, and aluminum industries.

Pure Monopoly   In general, the pure monopolist has little incentive to engage in R&D; its high profit is maintained by entry barriers which, in theory, are complete. The only incentive for the monopolist to engage in R&D is defensive—to reduce the risk of being blindsided by some new product or production process which destroys its monopoly. If such a product is out there to be discovered, the monopolist may have an incentive to find it. By so doing, it can either exploit the new product or process for continued monopoly profit or suppress the product until it has extracted the maximum profit from its present capital assets. But, in general, economists agree that pure monopoly is the market structure *least* conducive to innovation.

Inverted-U Theory

Analysis like this has led some experts on technological progress to postulate a so-called **inverted-U theory** of the relationship between market structure and technological advance. This theory is illustrated in Figure 26-8, which relates R&D spending as a percentage of a firm's sales (vertical axis) with the industry's four-firm concentration ratio (horizontal axis). The "inverted-U" shape of the curve suggests that R&D effort is at best weak in both very low concentration industries (pure competition) *and* very high concentration industries (pure monopoly). Starting from the lowest concentrations, R&D spending as a percentage of sales rises with concentration until a concentration ratio of 50 percent or so is reached, meaning that the four largest firms account for about one-half the total industry output. Beyond that, relative R&D spending decreases as concentration rises.

The logic of the inverted-U theory follows from our discussion. Firms in industries with very low concentration ratios are mainly competitive firms. They are small, which makes it difficult for them to finance R&D. Moreover, entry to these industries is easy, making it difficult to sustain economic profit from innovations which are not supported by patents. As a result, firms in these industries spend little on R&D relative to their sales. At the other end (far right) of the curve, where concentration is exceptionally high, monopoly profit is already high and innovation will not add much more profit. Furthermore, innovation typically requires costly retooling of very large factories, which will cut into whatever additional profit is realized. As a result, the expected rate of return from R&D is quite low, as are expenditures for R&D relative to sales. Finally, the lack of rivals makes the monopolist quite complacent about R&D.

The optimal industry structure for R&D is one in which expected returns on R&D spending are high and funds to finance it are readily available and inexpensive. From our discussion, these factors seem to occur in industries where a few firms are absolutely and relatively large but where the concentration ratio is not so high as to prohibit vigorous competition by smaller rivals. Rivalry among the larger oligopolistic firms and competition between the larger and smaller firms then provide a strong incentive for R&D. The inverted-U theory, as represented by Figure 26-8, also points toward this "loose" oligopoly as the optimal structure for R&D spending.

Market Structure and Technological Advance: The Evidence

Dozens of actual industry studies have tried to pin down the relationship between market structure and technological advance. Because these studies involved different industries, time periods, and methodologies, they are not easily compared and summarized. Nevertheless, the overall evidence provides general support for the inverted-U theory.[1] Other things

---

[1]Douglas F. Greer, *Industrial Organization and Public Policy*, 3d ed. (New York: Macmillan, 1992), pp. 680–687.

FIGURE 26-8 The inverted-U theory of R&D expenditures The inverted-U theory suggests that R&D expenditures as a percentage of sales rise with industry concentration until the four-firm concentration ratio reaches about 50 percent. Further increases in industry concentration are associated with lower relative R&D expenditures.

On the Path to the Personal Computer and Internet

Technological advance is clearly evident in the development of the modern personal computer and the emergence of the Internet. Here is a brief history of these events.

1945 Grace Murray Hopper finds a dead moth between relay contacts in the experimental Mark II computer at Harvard University. Whenever the computer subsequently malfunctions, workers set out to "debug" the device.

1946 ENIAC is revealed. It is a precursor to the modern-day computer that relies on 18,000 vacuum tubes and fills 3000 cubic feet of space.

1947 AT&T scientists invent the "transfer resistance device," later known as the transistor. It replaces the less reliable vacuum tubes in computers.

1961 Bob Noyce (who later founded Intel Corporation) and Jack Kilby invent the first integrated circuit, which miniaturizes electronic circuitry onto a single silicon chip.

1964 IBM introduces the System/360 computer. Configured as a system, it takes up nearly the same space as two tennis courts.

1965 Digital Equipment Corporation unveils its PDP-8, the first relatively small-sized computer (a "minicomputer").

1969 A networking system called ARPANET is born; it is the beginning of the Internet.

1971 Intel introduces its 4004 processor (a "microprocessor"). The $200 chip is the size of a thumbnail and has as much computing capability as the earlier ENIAC.

1975 Xerox markets Alto, the first personal computer (a "microcomputer"). Bill Gates and Paul Allen found Microsoft. MITS Corporation's Altair 8800 arrives on the scene. It contains the Intel's 8080 microprocessor that Intel developed a year earlier to control traffic lights.

1977 Apple II, Commodore's PET, and Tandy Radio Shack TRS-80 go on sale, setting the stage for the personal computer revolution.

1981 IBM enters the market with its personal computer powered by the Intel 8800 chip and operated by the Microsoft Disc Operating System (MS-DOS). Osborne Computer markets the Osborne 1, the first self-contained microcomputer, but within 2 years the firm declares bankruptcy. Logitech commercializes the "X-Y Position Indicator for a Display System," invented earlier by Douglas Engelbart in a government-funded research lab. Someone dubs it a "computer mouse" because it appears to have a tail.

1982 Compaq Computer "clones" the IBM machines; others do the same. Eventually Compaq becomes the leading seller of personal computers.

1984 Apple introduces its Macintosh computer, with its "user-friendly" icons, attached mouse, and preloaded software. College student Michael Dell founds Dell Computers,

---

equal, the optimal market structure for technological advance seems to be an industry in which there is a mix of large oligopolistic firms (a 40 to 60 percent concentration ratio), with several highly innovative smaller firms.

But our "other things equal" qualification is quite important here. The technical nature of a particular industry may well be a more important determinant of R&D than its structure. While some concentrated industries (electronics, aircraft, and petroleum) devote large quantities of resources to R&D and are very innovative, others (cigarettes, aluminum, gypsum products) are not. *The level of R&D spending within an industry seems to result as much from an industry's scientific character and "technological opportunities" as from its market structure.* There simply may be more opportunities to innovate in the computer and pharmaceutical industries than in the brick-making and coal-mining industries.

Conclusion: The inverted-U curve shown in Figure 26-8 is a useful depiction of the general relationship between R&D spending and market structure, *other things equal.*

TECHNOLOGICAL ADVANCE AND EFFICIENCY

Technological advance plays an important role in enhancing economic efficiency. New and better processes and products enable society to produce more output, as well as a higher-valued mix of output.

which builds personal computers and sells them through mail order. IBM, Sears Roebuck, and CBS team up to launch Prodigy Services, the first on-line computer business.

1985 Microsoft releases its Windows graphical interface operating system that improves upon MS-DOS. Ted Waitt starts a mail-order personal computer business (Gateway 2000) out of his South Dakota barn.

1990 Microsoft introduces Windows 3.0 which, like Macintosh, features windows, icons, and pull-down menus. Apple sues Microsoft for copyright infringement.

1991 The World Wide Web (an Internet system) is invented.

1993 Intel introduces its first of several Pentium chips, which greatly speed up computing. The courts reject Apple's claim that Microsoft violated its copyrights on its Macintosh operating system.

1994 Marc Andreessen starts up Netscape Communications and markets Netscape Navigator, which quickly becomes the leading software browser for the emerging Internet. David Filo and Jerry Yang develop Yahoo, a system for locating material stored on the Internet.

1995 Microsoft releases Windows 95 operating system, and it becomes the dominant operating system of personal computers (90 percent market share). Microsoft is now well established as the world's leading software producer. Sun Microsystems introduces Java, an Internet programming language.

1996 Playing catch-up with Netscape, Microsoft develops Microsoft Internet Explorer and gives it away free. More than 40 million personal computers are manufactured worldwide during this year alone.

1997 Oracle Computers introduces a relatively inexpensive "network" computer that bypasses Windows and goes directly to the Internet. *Forbes* magazine reports that among the top-50 wealthiest Americans are several people associated with the personal computer business: Gates ($40 billion), Allen ($17 billion), Lawrence Ellison (Oracle; database and spreadsheet software, $9 billion), Gordon Moore (Intel; $9 billion), Steven Ballmer (Microsoft; $8 billion), Dell ($6 billion), William Hewlett (Hewlett-Packard; $4 billion), and Waitt ($3 billion). More than one out of four U.S. households have a personal computer, and the use of the Internet explodes. Employment in the U.S. software industry tops 2 million.

Source: Based partly on Diedtra Henderson, "Moore's Law Still Reigns," *Seattle Times,* Nov. 24, 1996. Augmented and updated.

Productive Efficiency

Technological advance as embodied in *process* innovation improves *productive efficiency* by increasing the productivity of inputs (as indicated in Figure 26-6a) and by reducing average total costs (as in Figure 26-6b). This means that society can produce any particular good or service using fewer of its scarce resources, thereby freeing the unneeded resources to produce other desired goods and services. Alternatively, process innovation means that society can produce a greater quantity of any particular good using the same number of resources as it used previously. Viewed either way, process innovation enhances productive efficiency: it reduces society's per-unit cost of whatever mix of goods and services it chooses. It thus is an important means of shifting an economy's production possibilities curve rightward.

Allocative Efficiency

Technological advance as embodied in *product* (or service) innovation enhances *allocative efficiency* by giving society a more preferred mix of goods and services. Recall from our previous discussion that consumers buy a new product rather than an old product only when purchasing the new one increases the utility obtained from their limited incomes. Obviously, then, the new product—and the new mix of products which it implies—creates a higher level of total utility for society.

In terms of markets, the demand for the new product rises and the demand for the old product declines. The high economic profit of the new product attracts resources away from less valued uses and to the production of the new product. In theory, such shifting of resources continues until the price of the new product equals its marginal cost.

There is a caveat here, however. Innovation (product or process) can create monopoly power through patents or through the many advantages of being first. When new monopoly power results from innovation, society may lose *part* of the improved efficiency it otherwise would have gained from the innovation. The reason is that the profit-maximizing monopolist restricts output to keep its product price above marginal cost. Possible example: Microsoft has used its early innovation in computer software (its DOS operating system) to achieve a commanding presence in some parts of the software industry. It has built its monopoly power partly on a strategy of continual, identifiable product upgrades, from MS-DOS to Windows to Windows 95, with new versions in between. These product improvements are often announced well in advance and contain more and more features of competing software. Moreover, Microsoft has extended some of its monopoly power to related software products (Word, PowerPoint). So although society has greatly benefited from the surge of product improvements flowing from Microsoft, another result has been rising entry barriers in the software industry. Also, Microsoft continues to have economic profit far above the long-run normal profit associated with allocative efficiency.

On the other hand, innovation can reduce or even disintegrate existing monopoly power by providing competition where there was none. Economic efficiency is enhanced when this results, because the new competition helps push prices down closer to marginal cost and minimum average total cost. Innovation that leads to greater competition within an industry reduces the inefficiency associated with reduced output restriction and monopoly prices. In the Microsoft example, the new technology of the Internet has, at least temporarily, reduced Microsoft's dominance in some emerging areas of the software industry. Specifically, firms such as Sun Microsystems and Netscape have pioneered new software relating to the Internet (Java programming language, Netscape Navigator browser), leaving Microsoft working hard to catch up. Thus far, there are no signs that

Microsoft's monopoly power has resulted in complacency toward innovation; currently it spends $2 billion per year on research.

Creative Destruction

At the extreme, innovation may generate **creative destruction,** where the *creation* of new products and production methods simultaneously *destroys* the monopoly market positions of firms committed to existing products and old ways of doing business. As stated many years ago by Joseph Schumpeter, who championed this view:

> In capitalist reality . . . it is . . . competition from the new commodity, the new technology, the new source of supply, the new type of business organization—competition which commands a decisive cost or quality advantage and which strikes not at the margins of profits of the existing firms but at their foundation and their very lives. This kind of competition is . . . so . . . important that it becomes a matter of comparative indifference whether competition in the ordinary sense functions more or less promptly; the powerful lever that in the [very] long run expands output and brings down prices is in any case made of other stuff.[2]

There are many examples of creative destruction: In the 1800s wagons, ships, and barges were the only means of transporting freight until the railroads broke up their monopoly; the dominant market position of the railroads was, in turn, undermined by trucks, and later, by airplanes. Movies brought new competition to live theater, at one time the "only show in town," but were later challenged by television. Vinyl long-playing records supplanted acetate 78-rpm phonograph records; cassettes then challenged LP records, and now compact discs have undermined cassettes. Aluminum cans and plastic bottles have displaced glass bottles in many uses. Cable television has assaulted the networks, and now satellite dishes threaten cable. Fax machines, overnight delivery services, and e-mail have challenged the postal service. Mass discounters such as Wal-Mart and Toys "Я" Us have gained market share at the expense of Sears and Montgomery Ward.

According to Schumpeter, any monopolist that no longer delivers superior performance will *automatically* be displaced by a new innovator. But many con-

---

[2]Joseph A. Schumpeter, *Capitalism, Socialism, and Democracy,* 3d ed. (New York: Harper & Row, 1950), pp. 84–85.

temporary economists think this notion reflects more wishful thinking than fact. In this view, the idea that creative destruction is automatic

> . . . neglects the ability of powerful established firms to erect private storm shelters—or lobby government to build public storm shelters for them—in order to shield themselves from the Schumpeterian gales of creative destruction. It ignores the difference between the legal freedom of entry and the economic reality deterring the entry of potential newcomers into concentrated industries.[3]

That is, some dominant firms may be able to use such strategies as selective price cutting, buyouts, and

---

[3]Walter Adams and James Brock, *The Structure of American Industry*, 9th ed. (Englewood Cliffs, NJ: Prentice-Hall, 1995), p. 310.

massive advertising to block competition from even the most innovative new firms and existing rivals. Moreover, dominant firms have been known to collude to fix prices and to persuade government to give them tax breaks, subsidies, and tariff protection which strengthen their market power.

In short, while innovation in general enhances economic efficiency, in some cases it can lead to entrenched monopoly power. Further innovation may eventually destroy this monopoly power, but the process of creative destruction is neither automatic nor inevitable. On the other hand, our discussion has made it clear that rapid technological change, innovation, and efficiency are not *necessarily* inconsistent with monopoly power.

CHAPTER SUMMARY

1. Technological advance consists of new and improved goods and services and new and improved production or distribution processes. In economists' models, technological advance occurs only in the *very long run*.

2. *Invention* is the first discovery of a product or process through the use of imagination, ingenious thinking, and experimentation. *Innovation* is the first successful commercial introduction of a new product, the first use of a new method, or the creation of a new form of business enterprise. *Diffusion* is the spread of an earlier innovation among competing firms. Firms channel a majority of their R&D expenditures to innovation and imitation, rather than to basic scientific research and invention.

3. Historically, most economists viewed technological advance as a random, *external* force to which the economy adjusted. Many contemporary economists see technological advance as an *internal* element of capitalism, occurring in response to profit incentives within the economy.

4. Entrepreneurs and other innovators attempt to anticipate the future, thus playing central roles in technological advance by initiating changes in products and processes. Entrepreneurs often form start-ups which focus on creating and introducing new products. In other cases, innovators are located in the R&D labs of major corporations. Entrepreneurs and innovative firms often rely heavily on the basic research done by university and government scientists.

5. A firm's optimal amount of R&D spending occurs where its expected return (marginal benefit) from the R&D equals its interest-rate cost of funds (marginal cost) to finance the R&D. Entrepreneurs and firms use several sources to finance R&D, including **(a)** bank loans, **(b)** bonds, **(c)** venture capital (funds loaned in return for a share of the profits if the business succeeds), **(d)** undistributed corporate profits (retained earnings), and **(e)** personal savings.

6. *Product innovation*, the introduction of new products, succeeds when it provides consumers with higher marginal utility per dollar spent than do existing products. The new product enables consumers to obtain greater total utility from a given income. From the firm's perspective, product innovation increases revenue and, net of production cost, yields a positive rate of return on the R&D spending that produced it.

7. *Process innovation* can lower a firm's production costs by improving its internal production techniques. This increases the firm's total product, lowering its average total cost and increasing its profit. This added profit provides a positive rate of return on the R&D spending that produced the process innovation.

8. Imitation poses a potential problem for innovators since it threatens their returns on R&D expenditures. Some dominant firms use a fast-second strategy, letting smaller firms initiate new products and then quickly imitating the successes. Nevertheless, there are significant protections and potential benefits for firms which take the lead with R&D and innovation, including **(a)** patent protection, **(b)** copyrights and trademarks, **(c)** lasting brand-name recognition, **(d)** benefits from trade secrets and learning by doing, **(e)** high economic profits during the time lag between a product's introduction and its imitation, and **(f)** the possibility of lucrative buyout offers from larger firms.

9. Each of the four basic market structures has potential strengths and weaknesses regarding the likelihood of R&D and innovation. The *inverted-U theory* holds that a firm's R&D spending as a percentage of its sales rises with its industry four-firm concentration ratio, reaches a peak at a 50 percent concentration ratio, and then declines as concentration increases further. Empirical evidence is not clear-cut but lends general support to this theory. For any specific industry, however, the technological opportunities that are available may count more than market structure in determining R&D spending and innovation.

10. In general, technological advance enhances both productive and allocative efficiency. But in some situations patents and the advantages of being first with an innovation can increase monopoly power. While in some cases *creative destruction* eventually destroys monopoly, most economists doubt that this process is either automatic or inevitable.

TERMS AND CONCEPTS

technological advance	product innovation	interest-rate cost-of-	imitation problem
very long run	process innovation	funds curve	fast-second strategy
invention	diffusion	expected-rate-of-return	inverted-U theory of
patent	start-ups	curve	R&D
innovation	venture capital	optimal amount of R&D	creative destruction

STUDY QUESTIONS

1. What is meant by technological advance, as broadly defined? How does technological advance enter into the definition of the very long run? Which of the following are examples of technological advance, and which are not: an improved production process; entry of a firm into a profitable purely competitive industry; the imitation of a new production process by another firm; an increase in a firm's advertising expenditures?

2. Listed below are several possible actions by firms. Write INV beside those that reflect invention, INN beside those that reflect innovation, and DIF beside those that reflect diffusion.
   a. An auto manufacturer adds "heated seats" as a standard feature in its luxury cars to keep pace with a rival firm whose luxury cars already have this feature.
   b. A television production company pioneers the first music video channel.

   c. A firm develops and patents a working model of a self-erasing whiteboard for classrooms.
   d. A maker of light bulbs becomes the first firm to produce and market lighting fixtures using halogen lamps.
   e. A rival toy maker introduces a new Jenny doll to compete with Mattel's Barbie doll.

3. Contrast the older and modern views of technological advance as they relate to the economy. What is the role of entrepreneurs and other innovators in technological advance? How does research by universities and government affect innovators and technological advance? Why do you think some university researchers are increasingly becoming more like entrepreneurs and less like "pure scientists"?

4. **KEY QUESTION** Suppose a firm expects that a $20 million expenditure on R&D will result in a new product which will increase its revenue by a total of $30 million 1 year from now. The firm also estimates that the production cost of the new product will be $29 million.

  a. What is the expected rate of return on this R&D expenditure?

  b. Suppose the firm can get a bank loan at 6 percent interest to finance its $20 million R&D project. Will the firm undertake the project? Explain why or why not.

  c. Now suppose the interest-rate cost of borrowing, in effect, falls to 4 percent because the firm decides to use its own retained earnings to finance the R&D. Will this lower interest rate change the firm's R&D decision? Explain.

5. KEY QUESTION Answer the lettered questions below on the basis of the information in this table:

Amount of R&D, millions	Expected rate of return on R&D, %
$10	16
20	14
30	12
40	10
50	8
60	6

  a. If the interest-rate cost of funds is 8 percent, what will be the optimal amount of R&D spending for this firm?

  b. Explain why $20 million of R&D spending will *not* be optimal.

  c. Why won't $60 million be optimal either?

6. KEY QUESTION Refer to Table 26-1 and suppose the price of new product C is $2 instead of $4. How does this affect the optimal combination of products A, B, and C for the person represented by the data? Explain: "The success of a new product depends not only on its marginal utility but also on its price."

7. Learning how to use software takes time. So once customers have learned to use a particular software package, it is easier to sell them software upgrades than to convince them to switch to new software. What implications does this have for expected rates of return on R&D spending for software firms developing upgrades versus those developing imitative products?.

8. KEY QUESTION Answer the following questions on the basis of this information for a single firm: total cost of capital = $1000; price paid for labor = $12 per labor unit; price paid for raw materials = $4 per raw-material unit.

  a. Suppose the firm can produce 5000 units of output by combining its fixed capital with 100 units of labor and 450 units of raw materials. What are the total cost and average total cost of producing the 5000 units of output?

  b. Now assume the firm improves its production process so that it can produce 6000 units of output by combining its fixed capital with 100 units of labor and 450 units of raw materials. What are the total cost and average cost of producing the 6000 units of output?

  c. In view of your answers to 8a and 8b, explain how process innovation can improve economic efficiency.

9. Why might a firm making a large economic profit from its existing product employ a fast-second strategy in relationship to new or improved products? What risks does it run in pursuing this strategy? What incentive does a firm have to engage in R&D when rivals can imitate its new product?

10. Do you think the overall level of R&D would increase or decrease over the next 20 to 30 years if the lengths of new patents were extended from 20 years to, say, "forever"? What if the duration were reduced from 20 years to, say, 3 years?

11. Make a case that neither pure competition nor pure monopoly is very conducive to a great deal of R&D spending and innovation. Why is oligopoly more favorable to R&D spending and innovation than either pure competition or pure monopoly? What is the inverse-U theory and how does it relate to your answers to these questions?

12. Evaluate: "Society does not need laws outlawing monopolization and monopoly. Inevitably, monopoly causes its own self-destruction, since its high profit is the lure for other firms or entrepreneurs to develop substitute products."

13. (**Last Word**) Identify a specific example of each of the following in this Last Word: (**a**) entrepreneurship, (**b**) invention, (**c**) innovation, and (**d**) diffusion.

14. WEB-BASED QUESTION The National Science Foundation R&D Statistics—Is the Government Helping? The Division of Science Resource Studies http://www.nsf.gov/sbe/srs/stats.htm provides information on the nation's science, engineering, and technology sectors. Review the current report *(in PDF format)* titled Gross Domestic Product and R&D (Federally funded, Nonfederal, and Total): Comparative Measures of Growth in the National Patterns of Research and Development Resources sector. Determine if the following R&D figures are increasing or decreasing: (a) R&D expenditures in constant dollars, (b) Federal support for R&D in constant dollars, (c) nonfederal support for R&D in constant dollars, (d) R&D as a percentage of GDP, (e) Federal support of R&D as a percentage of GDP, and (f) nonfederal support of R&D as a percentage of GDP. What are the technological implications of these figures for the United States? Has the Federal government been an engine of R&D growth? For fun, visit the NSF student site http://www.nsf.gov/home/students/start.htm.

15. **WEB-BASED QUESTION**   **NASA—What Are the Commercial Spinoffs?** NASA (National Aeronautics and Space Administration) maintains that its research and development over the past three decades has had a favorable impact on individuals, firms, and industries. Visit NASA's Technology Transfer Office http://www.sti.nasa.gov/tto to determine if there have been significant commercial benefits from secondary use of NASA technology. Are there any that have been inconsequential? How does the NASA Commercial Technology Network http://nctn.hq.nasa.gov/ move technology from the lab to the marketplace?

6

PART SIX

Microeconomics of Resource Markets

27

The Demand for Resources

In the preceding chapters we explored the pricing and output of goods and services under four product market structures: pure competition, monopolistic competition, oligopoly, and pure monopoly. Although firms operating under these four market structures differ greatly, they have something in common: In producing their products, they need productive resources. A purely competitive cucumber farmer needs land, tractors, fertilizers, and pickers. A monopolistically competitive restaurant buys kitchen equipment and hires cooks and waiters. An oligopolistic auto producer buys machinery and hires executives, accountants, engineers, and assembly-line workers. A local telephone monopolist leases land, buys telephone poles and wire, and hires operators and billing clerks.

We now turn from the pricing and production of goods and services to the pricing and employment of *resources*. Land, labor, capital, and entrepreneurial resources indirectly or directly are owned and supplied by households. In terms of the circular flow model (Chapters 2, 5, and 6), we shift attention from the bottom loop of the diagram (where firms supply products which households demand) to the top loop (where households supply resources which businesses demand).

In this chapter we examine the factors underlying the *demand* for all economic resources. We will at times couch our discussion in terms of labor, but the principles developed also apply to land, capital, and entrepreneurial ability. In Chapter 28 we will combine resource (labor) demand with labor *supply* to analyze wage rates. Then in Chapter 29 resource demand and resource supply will be used to analyze the prices of, and returns to, the other productive resources.

SIGNIFICANCE AND COMPLEXITY OF RESOURCE PRICING

There are several reasons to study resource pricing:
1. *Money-income determination* The elemental fact about resource prices is that they are a major factor in determining

households' money incomes. The expenditures firms make in acquiring economic resources flow as wage, rent, interest, and profit incomes to those households which supply these human and property resources.

2. *Resource allocation* Just as product prices ration finished goods and services to consumers, so do resource prices allo-

cate resources among industries and firms. In a dynamic economy, where technology and tastes change often, the efficient allocation of resources over time calls for continuing shifts in resources among alternative uses. The role of resource pricing in producing those shifts is particularly significant.

3. *Cost minimization* To the firm, resource prices are costs; to realize maximum profit, it must produce the profit-maximizing output with the most efficient (least costly) combination of resources. Given technology, resource prices play the major role in determining the quantities of land, labor, capital, and entrepreneurial ability which will be combined in producing each good or service (see Table 4-1).

4. *Policy issues* There are many ethical questions and public policy issues surrounding the resource market. What degree of income inequality is acceptable? Should government levy a special tax on "excess" pay of corporate executives? Is it desirable for government to establish a legal minimum wage? Does it make sense for government to provide subsidies to farmers? The facts, ethics, and debates relating to income distribution are based on resource pricing.

Economists generally agree on the basic principles of resource pricing. Yet they disagree on how these principles vary when they are applied to particular resource markets. Economists agree, for example, that the pricing and employment of economic resources are supply-and-demand-based; however, they also recognize that in particular markets, resource supply and demand may assume unique dimensions. Further complications result when supply and demand are altered or even replaced by the policies and practices of government, business firms, or labor unions.

MARGINAL PRODUCTIVITY THEORY OF RESOURCE DEMAND

To keep things simple, let's initially assume that a firm hires a certain resource in a purely competitive resource market and sells its output in a purely competitive product market. The simplicity of this situation is twofold: In a competitive product market the firm is a "price taker" and can dispose of as little or as much output as it chooses at the market price. The firm is selling such a negligible fraction of total out-

put that it exerts no influence on product price. Similarly, in the competitive resource market, the firm is a "wage taker," hiring such a small fraction of the total supply of the resource that it cannot affect the resource price.

Resource Demand as a Derived Demand

The demand for resources is a **derived demand;** it is derived from the products which those resources help produce. Resources usually do not directly satisfy customer wants but do so indirectly by producing goods and services. No one wants to consume an acre of land, a John Deere tractor, or the labor services of a farmer, but households do want to consume the food and fiber products these resources help produce. Similarly, the demand for automobiles generates a demand for automobile workers and the demands for such services as income tax preparation, haircuts, and child care create derived demands for accountants, barbers, and child-care workers. Global Perspective 27-1 shows emphatically that the global demand for labor is derived.

Marginal Revenue Product (MRP)

The derived nature of resource demand means that the strength of the demand for any resource will depend on (1) the productivity of the resource in helping to create a good, and (2) the market value or price of the good it is producing. A resource which is highly productive in turning out a highly valued commodity will be in great demand. On the other hand, demand will be very weak for a relatively unproductive resource which is capable only of producing a good that few households demand. And there will be *no* demand for a resource which is phenomenally efficient in producing something *no one* wants to buy.

Productivity The roles of productivity and product price in determining resource demand are clearly seen in Table 27-1. Here we assume a firm adds one variable resource—labor—to its fixed plant. Columns 1 and 2 give the number of units of the resource applied to production and the resulting total product (output). Column 3 provides the **marginal product** (MP), or additional output, due to each additional resource unit. Columns 1 through 3 remind us that the law of diminishing returns applies here, causing the marginal product of labor to fall beyond some point. For simplicity, we assume these diminishing marginal re-

GLOBAL PERSPECTIVE 27-1

Labor demand and allocation: developing countries, industrially advanced countries, and the United States.

The idea of derived demand implies that the composition of a country's product-market demand will determine the allocation of its labor force among agricultural products, industrial goods, and services. Because poor nations must spend most of their incomes for food and fiber, the bulk of their labor is allocated to agriculture. The much richer industrially advanced economies allocate most of their labor to industrial products and services.

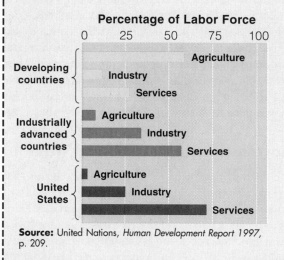

Percentage of Labor Force

Source: United Nations, *Human Development Report 1997,* p. 209.

turns—these declines in marginal product—begin with the first worker hired.

Product Price   But the derived demand for a resource also depends on the price of the commodity it produces. Column 4 in Table 27-1 adds this price information. Product price is constant, in this case at $2, because we are supposing a competitive product market. The firm is a price taker and will sell units of output only at this market price.

Multiplying column 2 by column 4 gives us the total-revenue data of column 5. These are the amounts of revenue the firm realizes from the various levels of resource usage. From these total-revenue data we can compute **marginal revenue product** (MRP)—*the change in total revenue resulting from the use of each additional unit of a resource* (labor, in this case). In equation form,

$$\text{Marginal revenue product} = \frac{\text{change in total revenue}}{\text{change in resource quantity}}$$

The MRPs are listed in column 6 in Table 27-1.

Rule for Employing Resources: MRP = MRC

The MRP schedule—columns 1 and 6—is the firm's demand schedule for labor. To explain why, we must first discuss the rule which guides a profit-seeking firm in hiring any resource: *To maximize profit, a firm should hire additional units of a specific resource as long as each*

TABLE 27-1   The demand for labor: pure competition in the sale of the product

(1) Units of resource	(2) Total product (output)	(3) Marginal product, MP	(4) Product price	(5) Total revenue, or (2)×(4)	(6) Marginal revenue product, MRP
0	0		$2	$ 0	
		7			$14
1	7		2	14	
		6			12
2	13		2	26	
		5			10
3	18		2	36	
		4			8
4	22		2	44	
		3			6
5	25		2	50	
		2			4
6	27		2	54	
		1			2
7	28		2	56	

successive unit adds more to the firm's total revenue than it adds to total cost.

Economists have special terms designating what each additional unit of labor or other variable resource adds to total cost and what it adds to total revenue. We already saw that MRP measures how much each successive unit of a resource adds to total revenue. The amount which each additional unit of a resource adds to the firm's total (resource) cost is called its **marginal resource cost** (MRC).

In equation form,

$$\begin{array}{l}\text{Marginal} \\ \text{resource} \\ \text{cost}\end{array} = \frac{\text{change in total (resource) cost}}{\text{change in resource quantity}}$$

Thus we can restate our rule for hiring resources as follows: *It will be profitable for a firm to hire additional units of a resource up to the point at which that resource's MRP is equal to its MRC.* If the number of workers a firm is currently hiring is such that the MRP of the last worker exceeds his or her MRC, the firm can profit by hiring more workers. But if the number being hired is such that the MRC of the last worker exceeds the MRP, the firm is hiring workers who are not "paying their way," and it can increase its profit by discharging some workers. You may have recognized that this **MRP = MRC rule** is similar to the MR = MC profit-maximizing rule employed throughout our discussion of price and output determination. The rationale of the two rules is the same, but the point of reference is now *inputs* of a resource, rather than *outputs* of a product.

MRP as Resource Demand Schedule

In a purely competitive labor market the wage rate is established by market supply and market demand. Because each firm hires such a small fraction of market supply, it cannot influence the market wage rate; it is a wage taker, not a wage maker. This means that for each additional unit of labor hired, total resource cost increases by exactly the same amount—the market wage rate. Or put another way, the MRC of labor exactly equals the constant market wage rate. Thus, resource "price" (the market wage rate) and resource "cost" (marginal resource cost) are equal for a firm hiring a resource in a competitive labor market. Then the MRP = MRC rule tells us that in pure competition, the firm will hire workers to the point at which the market *wage rate* (its MRC) is equal to its MRP.

In terms of the data in columns 1 and 6 in Table 27-1, if the market wage rate is, say, $13.95, the firm will hire only one worker. This is so because the first worker adds $14 to total revenue and slightly less— $13.95—to total cost. In other words, because MRP exceeds MRC for the first worker, it is profitable to hire that worker. For each successive worker, however, MRC (= $13.95) exceeds MRP (= $12 or less), indicating that it will not be profitable to hire any of those workers. If the wage rate is $11.95, by the same reasoning we discover that it will pay the firm to hire both the first and second workers. Similarly, if the wage rate is $9.95, three will be hired. If $7.95, four. If $5.95, five. And so forth. Hence *the MRP schedule constitutes the firm's demand for labor, because each point on this schedule (or curve) indicates the number of workers the firm would hire at each possible wage rate.* The D = MRP curve for the data in Table 27-1 is shown in Figure 27-1.

The logic here should be familiar to you: In Chapter 23 we applied the price-equals-marginal-cost (P = MC) rule for the profit-maximizing output to discover that the portion of the purely competitive firm's short-run marginal-cost curve lying above the AVC curve is the short-run *product supply* curve. Here, we are applying the MRP = MRC (= resource price) rule for the profit-maximizing input to discover that the purely competitive firm's MRP curve is its *resource demand* curve.

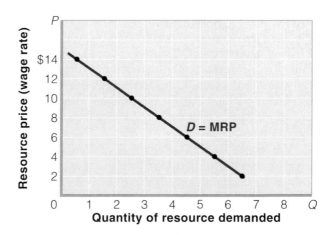

FIGURE 27-1 The purely competitive seller's demand for a resource   The MRP curve *is* the resource demand curve; each of its points relates a particular resource price (= MRP when profit is maximized) with a corresponding quantity of the resource demanded. Under pure competition, product price is constant; therefore, the downward slope of the D = MRP curve is due solely to the decline in the resource's marginal product (law of diminishing marginal returns).

TABLE 27-2   The demand for labor: imperfect competition in the sale of the product

(1) Units of resource	(2) Total product (output)	(3) Marginal product, MP	(4) Product price	(5) Total revenue, or (2) × (4)	(6) Marginal revenue product, MRP
0	0		$2.80	$ 0	
		7			$18.20
1	7		2.60	18.20	
		6			13.00
2	13		2.40	31.20	
		5			8.40
3	18		2.20	39.60	
		4			4.40
4	22		2.00	44.00	
		3			2.25
5	25		1.85	46.25	
		2			1.00
6	27		1.75	47.25	
		1			−1.05
7	28		1.65	46.20	

Resource Demand Under Imperfect Product Market Competition

Our analysis of labor demand becomes more complex when the firm is selling its product in an imperfectly competitive market, one in which the firm is a price maker. Pure monopoly, oligopoly, and monopolistic competition in the product market all mean that the firm's product demand curve is downsloping; the firm must set a lower price to increase its sales.

The productivity data in Table 27-1 are retained in columns 1 to 3 in Table 27-2. But here we show in column 4 that product price must be lowered to sell the marginal product of each successive worker. The MRP of the purely competitive seller of Table 27-1 falls for one reason: marginal product diminishes. But the MRP of the imperfectly competitive seller of Table 27-2 falls for two reasons: marginal product diminishes *and* product price falls as output increases.

We emphasize that the lower price accompanying each increase in output (total product) applies not only to the marginal product of each successive worker but also *to all prior output units that otherwise could have been sold at a higher price*. Note that the second worker's marginal product is 6 units. These 6 units can be sold for $2.40 each, or, as a group, for $14.40. But this is *not* the MRP of the second worker. To sell these 6 units, the firm must take a 20-cent price cut on the 7 units produced by the first worker—units which otherwise could have been sold for $2.60 each. Thus, the MRP of the second worker is only $13.00 [= $14.40 − (7 × 20 cents)], as shown.

Similarly, the third worker adds 5 units to total product, and these units are worth $2.20 each, or $11.00 total. But to sell these 5 units the firm must take a 20-cent price cut on the 13 units produced by the first two workers. So the third worker's MRP is only $8.40 [= $11.00 − (13 × 20 cents)]. The other figures in column 6 are derived similarly.

The result is that the MRP curve—the resource demand curve—of the imperfectly competitive producer is less elastic than that of the purely competitive producer. At a wage rate or MRC of $11.95, both the purely competitive and the imperfectly competitive seller will hire two workers. But at $9.95 the competitive firm will hire three, and the imperfectly competitive firm only two. And at $7.95 the purely competitive firm will employ four employees, and the imperfect competitor only three. This difference in resource demand elasticity can be seen by graphing the MRP data in Table 27-2 and comparing the graph with Figure 27-1, as is done in Figure 27-2.[1]

It is not surprising that the imperfectly competitive producer is less responsive to resource price cuts than the purely competitive producer. The imperfect competitor's relative reluctance to employ more resources, and produce more output, when resource prices fall reflects the imperfect competitor's tendency

---

[1]Note that the points in Figures 27-1 and 27-2 are plotted halfway between succeeding numbers of resource units because MRP is associated with the *addition* of 1 *more* unit. Thus, in Figure 27-2, for example, the MRP of the second unit ($13.00) is plotted not at 1 or 2, but rather at $1\frac{1}{2}$. This "smoothing" allows us to sketch a continuously downsloping curve rather than one which moves downward in discrete steps as each new unit of labor is hired.

FIGURE 27-2 The imperfectly competitive seller's demand curve for a resource An imperfectly competitive seller's resource demand curve D (solid) slopes downward because both marginal product *and* product price fall as resource employment and output rise. This downward slope is greater than that for a purely competitive seller (dashed resource demand curve) because the pure competitor can sell the added output at a constant price.

to restrict output in the product market. Other things equal, the imperfectly competitive seller produces less of a product than a purely competitive seller. In producing this smaller output, it demands fewer resources.

But one important qualification exists. We noted in Chapter 25 that the market structure of oligopoly *might* lead to technological progress and greater production, more employment, and lower prices in the very long run than would a purely competitive market. The resource demand curve in these cases would lie farther to the right than it would if output were restricted due to monopoly power. **(Key Question 2)**

Market Demand for a Resource

We have now explained the individual firm's demand curve for a resource. Recall that the total, or market, demand curve for a *product* is found by summing horizontally the demand curves of all individual buyers in the market. The market demand curve for a particular *resource* is derived in essentially the same way—by summing the individual demand or MRP curves for all firms hiring that resource.

DETERMINANTS OF RESOURCE DEMAND

What will alter the demand for a resource, that is, shift the resource demand curve? The fact that resource demand is derived from *product demand* and depends on *resource productivity* suggests two "resource demand shifters." Also, our analysis of how changes in the prices of other *products* can shift a product's demand curve (Chapter 3) suggests another factor: changes in the prices of other *resources*.

Changes in Product Demand

Other things equal, a change in the demand for a product will change the demand for the resource used to make the product. More precisely, *a change in the demand for a product that uses a particular resource will change the demand for the resource in the same direction.*

Let's see how this works. The first thing to recall is that a change in the demand for a product will change its price. In Table 27-1, let's assume an increase in product demand occurs which boosts product price from $2 to $3. You should calculate the new resource demand schedule (columns 1 and 6) which would result, and plot it in Figure 27-1 to verify that the new resource demand curve lies to the right of the old demand curve. Similarly, a decline in the product demand (and price) will shift the resource demand curve to the left. This effect—resource demand changing along with product demand—demonstrates that resource demand is derived from product demand.

Changes in Productivity

Other things equal, a change in the productivity of a resource will change the demand for the resource in the same direction. If we doubled the MP data of column 3 in Table 27-1, the MRP data of column 6 would also double, indicating an increase (rightward shift) in the resource demand curve.

The productivity of any resource can be altered in several ways:

1. *Quantities of other resources* The marginal productivity of any resource will vary with the quantities of the other resources used with it. The greater the amount of capital and land resources used with, say, labor, the greater will be labor's marginal productivity and, thus, labor demand.

2. *Technological progress* Technological improvements which increase the *quality* of other resources, say, capital, have the same effect. The better the quality of capital, the greater the productivity of labor used with it. Dockworkers employed with a specific amount of real capital in the form of unloading cranes are more productive than dockworkers with the same amount of real capital embodied in older conveyor-belt systems.

3. *Quality of the variable resource* Improvements in the quality of the variable resource itself, say, labor, will increase its marginal productivity and therefore its demand. In effect, there will be a new demand curve for a different, more skilled, kind of labor.

All these considerations help explain why the average level of (real) wages is higher in industrially advanced nations (United States, Germany, Japan, France, and so forth) than in developing nations (India, Ethiopia, Angola, Cambodia, and so on). Workers in industrially advanced nations are generally healthier, more educated, and better trained than are workers in developing countries. Also, in most industries they work with a larger and more efficient stock of capital goods and more abundant natural resources. This creates a strong demand for labor. On the supply side of the market, labor is *relatively* scarce compared with that in most developing nations. A strong demand and a relatively scarce supply of labor result in high wage rates in nations like the United States, Japan, and Germany.

Changes in the Prices of Other Resources

Just as changes in the prices of other products will change the demand for a specific product, changes in the prices of other resources will change the demand for a specific resource. Also recall that the effect of a change in the price of product X on the demand for product Y depends on whether X and Y are substitute or complementary goods *in consumption*. Similarly, the effect of a change in the price of resource A on the demand for resource B depends on their substitutability or their complementarity *in production*.

Substitute Resources Suppose the technology in a certain production process is such that labor and capital are substitutable. A firm can produce some specific amount of output using a relatively small amount of labor and a relatively large amount of capital, or vice versa. Now assume the price of machinery (capital) falls. The effect on the demand for labor will be the net result of two opposed effects: the substitution effect and the output effect.

1. *Substitution effect* The decline in the price of machinery prompts the firm to substitute machinery for labor. This allows the firm to produce its output at lower cost. So, at the fixed wage rate, smaller quantities of labor are now employed. This **substitution effect** decreases the demand for labor. More generally, the substitution effect indicates that a firm will purchase more of an input whose relative price has declined and, conversely, use less of an input whose relative price has increased.

2. *Output effect* Because the price of machinery has fallen, the costs of producing various outputs must also decline. With lower costs, the firm finds it profitable to produce and sell a greater output. The greater output increases the demand for all resources, including labor. So this **output effect** increases the demand for labor. More generally, the output effect means that the firm will purchase more of one particular input when the price of the other input falls and less of that particular input when the price of the other input rises.

3. *Net effect* The substitution and output effects are both present when the price of an input changes, but they work in opposite directions. For a decline in the price of capital, the substitution effect decreases the demand for labor and the output effect increases it. The net change in labor demand depends on the relative sizes of the two effects. (This is analogous to a boat drifting on the ocean, being pushed in one direction by the tide and in the opposite direction by the wind. The actual course of the boat will depend on which of the two effects is strongest.)

In terms of resource demand, *if the substitution effect outweighs the output effect, a change in the price of a resource changes the demand for a substitute resource in the same direction. If the output effect exceeds the substitution effect, a change in the price of a resource changes the demand for a substitute resource in the opposite direction.*

Complementary Resources   Recall from Chapter 3 that certain products, such as cameras and film or computers and software, are complementary goods; they "go together" and are jointly demanded. Resources may also be complementary; an increase in the quantity of one of them used in the production process requires an increase in the amount used of the other as well, and vice versa. Suppose a small manufacturer of metal products uses punch presses as its basic piece of capital equipment. Each press is designed to be operated by one worker; the machine is not automated—it will not run itself—and a second worker would have nothing to do.

Now assume technological advance in the production of these presses substantially reduces their price.

There can be no substitution effect because labor and capital must be used in *fixed proportions*, one person for one machine. Capital cannot be substituted for labor. But there *is* an output effect. Other things equal, the reduction in the price of capital goods means lower production costs. It will therefore be profitable to produce a larger output. In doing so, the firm will use both more capital and more labor. When labor and capital are complementary, a decline in the price of capital increases the demand for labor through the output effect. Conversely, when there is an increase in the price of capital, the output effect reduces the demand for labor. *A change in the price of a resource will cause the demand for a complementary resource to change in the opposite direction.*

We have cast our analysis of substitute resources and complementary resources mainly in terms of a decline in the price of capital. In Table 27-3 we summarize the effects of an increase in the price of capital on the demand for labor. You should study this table carefully.

Now that we have discussed the full list of the determinants of labor demand, let's again review their effects. Stated in terms of the labor resource, the demand for labor will *increase* (the labor demand curve will shift *rightward*) when:

1. The demand for (and therefore the price of) the product produced by that labor *increases.*

TABLE 27-3   **The effect of an increase in the price of capital on the demand for labor, D_L**

(1) Relationship of inputs	(2) Increase in the price of capital		
	(a) Substitution effect	(b) Output effect	(c) Combined effect
Substitutes in production	Labor substituted for capital	Production costs up, output down, and less of both capital and labor used	D_L increases if the substitution effect exceeds the output effect; D_L decreases if the output effect exceeds the substitution effect
Complements in production	No substitution of labor for capital	Production costs up, output down, and less of both capital and labor used	D_L decreases

2. The productivity (MP) of labor *increases*.
3. The price of a substitute input *decreases*, provided the output effect exceeds the substitution effect.
4. The price of a substitute input *increases*, provided the substitution effect exceeds the output effect.
5. The price of a complementary input *decreases*.

Be sure that you can "reverse" these effects to explain a *decrease* in labor demand.

Real-World Applications

The determinants of labor demand have much significance, as seen by the following examples.

Restaurant Workers In the past decade, the demand for fast-food and other restaurant workers has increased significantly; in 1997 about 1.5 million more people worked in these establishments than in 1987. One reason is that more and more women are working outside the home, causing families to substitute restaurant meals for home-prepared meals. Also, incomes have increased, and with this increase has come greater demand for restaurant meals. Both factors have resulted in increases in the derived demand for restaurant workers.

Computer-Related Workers In the last decade or so there has been a remarkable drop in the average price of personal computers and an equally impressive rise in the computing power of the typical personal computer. These developments have increased the demand for some kinds of labor and decreased it for other kinds.

Demand for software designers and computer-assembly workers has rocketed. So, too, has the demand for salesclerks in computer stores. But the effect on the demand for office workers has been mixed. In some offices, computers and labor (keyboard personnel) are complementary inputs. There, the decline in computer prices has reduced production costs, increased the number of computers purchased, and increased the demand for computer operators. In other offices the decline in computer prices has caused computers to be substituted for labor, reducing the demand for labor and allowing these offices to use fewer workers to produce their goods and services.

Defense Personnel The end of the Cold War, and the resulting reductions in U.S. defense spending, has reduced labor demand by the U.S. military and by firms supplying military equipment. Military jobs de-clined by nearly 1 million workers between 1993 and 1998. Also, the demand for labor in industries producing military aircraft, missiles, tanks, and other military hardware has declined, reducing civilian employment in defense-related industries by about 1 million between 1993 and 1998.

Contingent Workers One of the biggest labor market changes of recent years has been that many employers have reduced the size of their full-time "core" work forces and simultaneously increased their use of contingent workers (part-time, temporary, and subcontracted). Why has the demand for contingent workers increased? First, increasingly expensive fringe benefits such as health insurance, pension plans, paid vacations, and sick leave are typically not provided for contingent workers, making their employment less costly. Second, contingent workers give firms more flexibility in responding to changing economic conditions. As product demand changes, firms can readily increase or decrease the sizes of their work forces by employing more or fewer contingent workers. This flexibility allows firms to compete more effectively, especially in international markets.

Table 27-4 provides additional illustrations of the determinants of labor demand.

ELASTICITY OF RESOURCE DEMAND

The demand changes we have just discussed are shifts in the location of a resource demand curve. These changes in demand must be distinguished from a change in the *quantity* of a resource demanded. The latter is not a shift of the demand curve. Rather, it is a movement from one point to another on a fixed resource demand curve because of a change in the price of the specific resource under consideration. Example: In Figure 27-1 we note that an increase in the wage rate from $5 to $7 will reduce the quantity of labor demanded from 5 to 4 units. This is a change in the quantity of labor demanded.

The sensitivity of producers to changes in resource prices is measured by the **elasticity of resource demand.** In coefficient form,

$$E_{rd} = \frac{\text{percentage change in resource quantity}}{\text{percentage change in resource price}}$$

When E_{rd} is greater than 1, resource demand is elastic; when E_{rd} is less than 1, resource demand is in-

TABLE 27-4 Determinants of labor demand: factors which shift the labor demand curve

Determinant	Examples
Change in product demand	Gambling increases in popularity, increasing the demand for workers at casinos. Consumers decrease their demand for leather coats, decreasing the demand for tanners.
Change in productivity	An increase in the skill levels of glassblowers increases the demand for their services. Computer-assisted graphic design increases the productivity of, and demand for, graphic artists.
Change in the price of another resource	An increase in the price of electricity increases the cost of producing aluminum and reduces the demand for aluminum workers. The price of security equipment used by businesses to protect against illegal entry falls, decreasing the demand for night guards. The price of telephone switching equipment decreases, greatly reducing the cost of telephone service, which in turn increases the demand for telemarketers.

elastic; and when E_{rd} equals 1, resource demand is unit-elastic. What determines the elasticity of resource demand? There are several factors at work.

Rate of MP Decline A purely technical consideration is the rate at which the marginal product of the particular resource declines. If the marginal product of one resource declines slowly as it is added to a fixed amount of other resources, the demand (MRP) curve for that resource declines slowly and tends to be highly elastic. A small decline in the price of such a resource will yield a relatively large increase in the amount demanded. Conversely, if the marginal product of the resource declines sharply as more of it is added, the resource demand curve also declines rapidly. This means that a relatively large decline in the wage rate will be accompanied by a modest increase in the amount of labor hired; labor demand is inelastic.

Ease of Resource Substitutability The degree to which resources are substitutable is also a determinant of elasticity. *The larger the number of good substitute resources available, the greater the elasticity of demand for a particular resource.* If a furniture manufacturer finds that five or six different types of wood are equally satisfactory in making coffee tables, a rise in the price of any one type of wood may cause a sharp drop in the amount demanded as the producer substitutes other woods. At the other extreme, there may be no

reasonable substitutes; bauxite is absolutely essential in the production of aluminum ingots. Thus, the demand for bauxite by aluminum producers is inelastic.

Time can play a role in the input substitution process. For example, a firm's truck drivers may obtain a substantial wage increase with little or no immediate decline in employment. But over time, as the firm's trucks wear out and are replaced, that wage increase may motivate the company to purchase larger trucks and in that way deliver the same total output with fewer drivers. As a second example, new commercial aircraft have been specifically designed to require only two cockpit personnel rather than the customary three, again indicating some substitutability between labor and capital if there is enough time.

Elasticity of Product Demand The elasticity of demand for any resource depends on the elasticity of demand for the product it helps produce. *The greater the elasticity of product demand, the greater the elasticity of resource demand.* The derived nature of resource demand leads us to expect this relationship. A small rise in the price of a product with great elasticity of demand will sharply reduce output, bringing about a relatively large decline in the amounts of various resources demanded. This means that the demand for the resource is elastic.

Remember that the resource demand curve of Figure 27-1 is more elastic than the resource demand curve shown in Figure 27-2. The difference arises because in Figure 27-1 we assume a perfectly elastic product demand curve, while Figure 27-2 is based on a downsloping or less than perfectly elastic product demand curve.

Ratio of Resource Cost to Total Cost *The larger the proportion of total production costs accounted for by a resource, the greater the elasticity of demand for that resource.* In the extreme, if labor cost is the only production cost, then a 20 percent increase in wage rates will shift all the firm's cost curves upward by 20 percent. If product demand is elastic, this substantial increase in costs will cause a relatively large decline in sales and a sharp decline in the amount of labor demanded. So labor demand is highly elastic. But if labor cost is only 50 percent of production cost, then a 20 percent increase in wage rates will increase costs by only 10 percent. With the same elasticity of product demand, this will cause a relatively small decline in sales and therefore in the amount of labor demanded. In this case the demand for labor is much less elastic. **(Key Question 3)**

QUICK REVIEW 27-2

■ A resource demand curve will shift because of changes in product demand, changes in the productivity of the resource, and changes in the prices of other inputs.

■ If resources A and B are substitutable, a decline in the price of A will decrease the demand for B provided the substitution effect exceeds the output effect. But if the output effect exceeds the substitution effect, the demand for B will increase.

■ If resources C and D are complements, a decline in the price of C will increase the demand for D.

■ Elasticity of resource demand measures the extent to which producers change the quantity of a resource they hire when its price changes.

■ The elasticity of resource demand will be less the more rapid the decline in marginal product, the smaller the number of substitutes, the smaller the elasticity of product demand, and the smaller the proportion of total cost accounted for by the resource.

OPTIMAL COMBINATION OF RESOURCES

Thus far we have considered one variable input, usually labor. But in the long run firms can vary the amounts of all the resources they use. That's why we need to consider what combination of resources a firm will choose when *all* its inputs are variable. While our analysis is based on two resources, it can be extended to any number of inputs.

We will consider two interrelated questions:

1. What combination of resources will minimize costs at a specific level of output?

2. What combination of resources will maximize profit?

The Least-Cost Rule

A firm is producing a specific output with the **least-cost combination of resources** *when the last dollar spent on each resource yields the same marginal product.* That is, the cost of any output is minimized when the ratios of marginal product to price of the last units of resources used are the same for each resource. In competitive resource markets, recall, marginal resource cost is the market resource price; the firm can hire as many or as few units of the resource as it wants at that price. Then, with just two resources, labor and capital, a competitive firm minimizes its total cost of a specific output when

$$\frac{\text{Marginal product of labor (MP}_L)}{\text{Price of labor (P}_L)} = \frac{\text{marginal product of capital (MP}_C)}{\text{price of capital (P}_C)} \quad (1)$$

Throughout, we will refer to the marginal products of labor and capital as MP_L and MP_C, respectively. The price of labor will be symbolized by P_L and the price of capital by P_C.

A concrete example shows why fulfilling the condition in equation (1) means least-cost production. Suppose the prices of capital and labor are both $1 per unit but capital and labor are currently employed in such amounts that the marginal product of labor is 10 and the marginal product of capital is 5. Our equation immediately tells us this is *not* the least costly combination of resources:

$$\frac{MP_L = 10}{P_L = \$1} > \frac{MP_C = 5}{P_C = \$1}$$

Suppose the firm spends $1 less on capital and shifts that dollar to labor. It loses 5 units of output produced by the last dollar's worth of capital, but it gains 10 units of output from the extra dollar's worth of labor. Net output increases by 5 (= 10 − 5) units for the same total cost. More such shifting of dollars from capital to labor will push the firm *down* along its MP curve for labor and *up* along its MP curve for capital, increasing output and moving the firm toward a position of equilibrium where equation (1) is fulfilled. At that equilibrium position, the MP per dollar for the last unit of both labor and capital might be, for example, 7. And the firm will be producing a greater output for the same (original) cost.

Whenever the same total resource cost can result in a greater total output, the cost per unit—and therefore the total cost of any specific level of output—can be reduced. Being able to produce a *larger* output with a *specific* total cost is the same as being able to produce a *specific* output with a *smaller* total cost. If the firm in our example buys $1 less of capital, its output will fall by 5 units. If it spends only $.50 of that dollar on labor, the firm will increase its output by a compensating 5 units ($= \frac{1}{2}$ of the MP per dollar). Then the firm will realize the same total output at a $.50 lower total cost.

The cost of producing any specific output can be reduced as long as equation (1) does not hold. But when dollars have been shifted among capital and labor to the point where equation (1) holds, no additional changes in the use of capital and labor will reduce costs further. The firm is now producing that output using the least-cost combination of capital and labor.

All the long-run cost curves developed in Chapter 22 and used thereafter assume that the least-cost combination of inputs has been realized at each level of output. Any firm that combines resources in violation of the least-cost rule would have a higher-than-necessary average total cost at each level of output. That is, it would incur *X-inefficiency*, as discussed in Figure 24-7.

The producer's least-cost rule is analogous to the consumer's utility-maximizing rule in Chapter 21. In achieving the utility-maximizing combination of goods, the consumer considers both his or her preferences as reflected in diminishing-marginal-utility data *and* the prices of the various products. Similarly, in achieving the cost-minimizing combination of resources, the producer considers both the marginal product data and the price (costs) of the various resources.

The Profit-Maximizing Rule

Minimizing cost is not sufficient for maximizing profit. A firm can produce any level of output in the least costly way by applying equation (1). But there is only *one* unique level of output which maximizes profit. Our earlier analysis of product markets showed that this profit-maximizing output occurs where marginal revenue equals marginal cost (MR = MC). Near the beginning of this chapter we determined that we could write this profit-maximizing condition as MRP = MRC as it relates to resource inputs.

In a purely competitive resource market the marginal resource cost (MRC) is exactly equal to the resource price P. Thus, for any competitive resource market, we have as our profit-maximizing equation

MRP (resource) = P (resource)

This condition must hold for every variable resource, and in the long run all resources are variable. In competitive markets, a firm will therefore achieve its **profit-maximizing combination of resources** when each resource is employed to the point at which its marginal revenue product equals its price. For two resources, labor and capital, we need both

$$P_L = \text{MRP}_L \qquad \text{and} \qquad P_C = \text{MRP}_C$$

We can combine these conditions by dividing both sides of each equation by their respective prices and equating the results to get

$$\frac{\text{MRP}_L}{P_L} = \frac{\text{MRP}_C}{P_C} = 1 \qquad (2)$$

Note in equation (2) that it is not sufficient that the MRPs of the two resources be *proportionate* to their prices; the MRPs must be *equal* to their prices and the ratios therefore equal to 1. For example, if $\text{MRP}_L = \$15$, $P_L = \$5$, $\text{MRP}_C = \$9$, and $P_C = \$3$, the firm is underemploying both capital and labor even though the ratios of MRP to resource price are identical for both resources. The firm can expand its profit by hiring additional amounts of both capital and labor until it moves down their downsloping MRP curves to the points at which $\text{MRP}_L = \$5$ and $\text{MRP}_C = \$3$. The ratios will then be 5/5 and 3/3 and equal to 1.

The profit-maximizing position in equation (2) includes the cost-minimizing condition of equation (1). That is, if a firm is maximizing profit according to equation (2), then it must be using the least-cost combination of inputs to do so. However, the converse is not true: a firm operating at least cost according to equation (1) may not be operating at the output that maximizes its profit.

Numerical Illustration

A numerical illustration will help you understand the least-cost and profit-maximizing rules. In columns 2, 3, 2′, and 3′ in Table 27-5 we show the total products and marginal products for various amounts of labor

TABLE 27-5 Data for finding the least-cost and profit-maximizing combination of labor and capital*

Labor (price = $8)					Capital (price = $12)				
(1) Quantity	(2) Total product (output)	(3) Marginal product	(4) Total revenue	(5) Marginal revenue product	(1′) Quantity	(2′) Total product (output)	(3′) Marginal product	(4′) Total revenue	(5′) Marginal revenue product
0	0		$ 0		0	0		$ 0	
		12		$24			13		$26
1	12		24		1	13		26	
		10		20			9		18
2	22		44		2	22		44	
		6		12			6		*12*
3	28		56		**3**	28		56	
		5		10			4		8
4	33		66		4	32		64	
		4		**8**			3		6
5	37		74		5	35		70	
		3		6			2		4
6	40		80		6	37		74	
		2		4			1		2
7	42		84		7	38		76	

*To simplify, it is assumed in this table that the productivity of each resource is independent of the quantity of the other. For example, the total and marginal product of labor is assumed not to vary with the quantity of capital employed.

and capital that are assumed to be the only inputs needed in producing some product, say, key chains. Both inputs are subject to diminishing returns.

We also assume that labor and capital are supplied in competitive resource markets at $8 and $12, respectively, and that key chains sell competitively at $2 per unit. For both labor and capital we can determine the total revenue associated with each input level by multiplying total product by the $2 product price. These data are shown in columns 4 and 4′. They allow us to calculate the marginal revenue product of each successive input of labor and capital as shown in columns 5 and 5′, respectively.

Producing at Least Cost What is the least-cost combination of labor and capital to use in producing, say, 50 units of output? The answer, which we can obtain by trial and error, is 3 units of labor and 2 units of capital. Columns 2 and 2′ indicate that this combination of labor and capital does, indeed, result in the required 50 (= 28 + 22) units of output. Now, note from columns 3 and 3′ that hiring 3 units of labor gives us $MP_L/P_L = 6/8 = 3/4$ and hiring 2 units of capital gives us $MP_C/P_C = 9/12 = 3/4$, so equation (1) is fulfilled. How can we verify that costs are actually minimized? First, we see that the total cost of employing 3 units of labor and 2 of capital is $48 [= (3 × $8) + (2 × $12)].

Other combinations of labor and capital will also yield 50 units of output, but at a higher cost than $48. For example, 5 units of labor and 1 unit of capital will produce 50 (= 37 + 13) units, but total cost is higher, at $52 [= (5 × $8) + (1 × $12)]. This comes as no surprise because 5 units of labor and 1 unit of capital violate the least-cost rule—$MP_L/P_L = 4/8 < MP_C/P_C = 13/12$. Only that combination (3 units of labor and 2 units of capital) which minimizes total cost will satisfy equation (1). All other combinations capable of producing 50 units of output violate the cost-minimizing rule, and therefore cost more than $48.

Maximizing Profit Will 50 units of output maximize the firm's profit? No, because the profit-maximizing terms of equation (2) are not satisfied when the firm employs 3 units of labor and 2 of capital. To maximize profit, each input should be employed until its price equals its marginal revenue product. But for 3 units of labor, labor's MRP in column 5 is $12 while its price is only $8. This means the firm could increase its profit by hiring more labor. Similarly, for 2 units of capital, we see in column 5′ that capital's MRP is $18 and its price is only $12. This indicates that more capital should also be employed. By producing only 50 units of output (even though they are produced at least cost), labor and capital are being used in less-than-profit-maximizing amounts. The firm needs to expand its employment of labor and capital, thereby increasing its output.

Table 27-5 shows that the MRPs of labor and capital are equal to their prices, so that equation (2) is fulfilled, when the firm is employing 5 units of labor and

Input Substitution: The Case of ATMs

Banks are using more automatic teller machines (ATMs) and employing fewer human tellers.

From this chapter you know that a firm achieves its least-cost combination of inputs when the last dollar it spends on each input makes the same contribution to total output. This raises an interesting real-world question: What happens when technological advance makes available a new, highly productive capital good for which MP/P is greater than for other inputs, say a particular type of labor? The answer is that the least-cost mix of resources abruptly changes and the firm responds accordingly. If the new capital is a substitute for labor (rather than a complement), the firm replaces the particular type of labor with the new capital. *That is exactly what is happening in the banking industry, in which ATMs are replacing human bank tellers.*

ATMs made their debut about 25 years ago when Diebold, a U.S. firm, introduced the product. Today, Diebold and NCR (also a U.S. firm) dominate global sales, with the Japanese firm Fujitsu being a distant third. The number of ATMs and their usage have exploded, and currently there are more than 150,000 ATMs in the United States. In 1975, about 10 *million* ATM transactions worth $1 billion occurred in the United States. In contrast, since 1995 there have been more than 10 *billion* U.S. ATM transactions worth $650 billion each year. Since 1992 alone, banks have added more than 150,000 *new* ATMs around the globe.

ATMs are highly productive: A single machine can handle hundreds of transactions daily, thousands weekly, and millions over the course of several years. ATMs can handle not only cash withdrawals, they also accept deposits and facilitate switches of funds between various accounts. Although ATMs are expensive for banks to buy and install, they are available 24 hours a day, and their cost-per transaction is one-fourth the cost for human tellers. They rarely get "held up," and they do not quit their jobs (turnover among human tellers is nearly 50 percent per year). Moreover, ATMs are highly convenient; unlike human tellers, they are located not only at banks but also at busy street corners, workplaces, universities, and shopping malls. The same bankcard that allows you to withdraw cash from your local ATM also allows you to withdraw pounds from an ATM in London, yen from an ATM in Tokyo, and even rubles from an ATM in Moscow. (All this, of course, assumes that you have money in your checking account.)

In the terminology of this chapter, the more productive, lower priced ATMs have reduced the demand for a substitute in production—human tellers. Between 1990 and 1995, 40,000 human tellers lost their jobs, and half the remaining tellers could lose their jobs by the end of the next decade. Where will they go? Most will eventually move to other occupations. Although the lives of individual tellers are disrupted, society clearly wins. Society gets cheaper, more convenient banking services *and* more of the other goods that these "freed-up" labor resources help produce.

Source: Based partly on Ben Craig, "Where Have All the Tellers Gone?," *Economic Commentary* (Federal Reserve Bank of Cleveland), Apr. 15, 1997; and statistics provided by the American Bankers Association.

---

3 units of capital. This is therefore the profit-maximizing combination of inputs.[2] The firm's total cost will be $76, made up of $40 (= 5 × $8) of labor and

$36 (= 3 × $12) of capital. Total revenue will be $130, found either by multiplying the total output of 65 (= 37 + 28) by the $2 product price or by summing the total revenues attributable to labor ($74) and to capital ($56). The difference between total revenue and total cost in this instance is $54 (= $130 − $76). You should experiment with other combinations of labor and capital to demonstrate that they yield an economic profit of less than $54.

---

[2]Because we are dealing with discrete (nonfractional) units of the two outputs here, the use of 4 units of labor and 2 units of capital is equally profitable. The fifth unit of labor's MRP and its price (cost) are equal at $8, so that the fifth labor unit neither adds to nor subtracts from the firm's profit; similarly, the third unit of capital has no effect on profit.

Note that the profit-maximizing combination of 5 units of labor and 3 units of capital is also a least-cost combination for this particular level of output. Using these resource amounts satisfies the least-cost requirement of equation (1) in that $MP_L/P_L = 4/8 = 1/2$ and $MP_C/P_C = 6/12 = 1/2$. **(Key Questions 4 and 5)**

MARGINAL PRODUCTIVITY THEORY OF INCOME DISTRIBUTION

Our discussion of resource pricing is the cornerstone of the controversial view that fairness and economic justice are one of the outcomes of a competitive capitalist economy. Table 27-5 tells us, in effect, that labor receives an income payment (wage) equal to the marginal contribution it makes to the firm's output and thus its revenue. Bluntly stated, labor is paid what it is economically worth. So, too, are the owners of the other resources. In this **marginal productivity theory of income distribution,** labor and other resources are paid according to their contributions to society's output. Therefore, if you are willing to accept the ethical proposition "To each according to what he or she creates," rewards based on marginal revenue product seem to provide a fair and equitable distribution of society's income.

This all sounds fair, but there are serious criticisms of this theory of income distribution:

1. *Inequality* Critics argue that the distribution of income resulting from payment according to marginal productivity may be highly unequal because productive resources are very unequally distributed in the first place. Aside from their differences in genetic endowments, individuals encounter substantially different opportunities to enhance their productivity through education and training. Some people may not be able to participate in production at all because of mental or physical disabilities, and they would obtain *no* income under a system of distribution based solely on marginal productivity. Ownership of property resources is also highly unequal. Many landlords and capitalists obtain their property by inheritance rather than through their own productive effort. Hence, income from inherited property resources conflicts with the "To each according to what he or she creates" idea. This reasoning calls for government policies that modify the income distributions made strictly according to marginal productivity.

2. *Market imperfections* The marginal productivity theory rests on the assumptions of competitive markets. Yet labor markets, for example, are riddled with imperfections, as you will see in Chapter 28. Some employers exert pricing power in hiring workers. And some workers, through labor unions, professional associations, and occupational licensing laws, wield monopoly power in selling their services. Even the process of collective bargaining over wages suggests a power struggle over the division of income. In this struggle market forces—and income shares based on marginal productivity—may get pushed into the background. In addition, discrimination in the labor market can distort earnings patterns. In short, because of real-world market imperfections, wage rates and other resource prices frequently are *not* based solely on contributions to output.

CHAPTER SUMMARY

1. Resource prices are a determinant of money incomes, and they simultaneously ration resources to various industries and firms.

2. The demand for any resource is derived from the product it helps produce. That means the demand for a resource will depend on its productivity and the market value (price) of the good it is producing.

3. Marginal revenue product is the extra revenue a firm obtains when it employs 1 more unit of a resource. The marginal revenue product curve for any resource is the demand curve for that resource. This follows because the firm equates resource price and MRP in determining its profit-maximizing level of resource employment. Thus each point on the MRP curve indicates how many resource units the firm will hire at a specific resource price.

4. The firm's demand curve for a resource slopes downward because the marginal product of additional units declines in accordance with the law of diminishing returns. When a firm is selling in an imperfectly competitive market, the resource demand curve falls for a second reason: Product price must be reduced for the firm to sell a larger output. The market demand curve for a resource can be derived by summing horizontally the demand curves of all firms hiring that resource.

5. The demand curve for a resource will shift as the result of (a) a change in the demand for, and therefore the price of, the product the resource is producing; (b) changes in the productivity of the resource; and (c) changes in the prices of other resources.

6. If resources A and B are substitutable for each other, a decline in the price of A will decrease the demand for B provided the substitution effect is greater than the output effect. But if the output effect exceeds the substitution effect, a decline in the price of A will increase the demand for B.

7. If resources C and D are complementary or jointly demanded, there is only an output effect; a change in the price of C will change the demand for D in the opposite direction.

8. The elasticity of demand for a resource measures the responsiveness of producers to a change in the resource's price. The coefficient of the elasticity of resource demand is

$$E_{rd} = \frac{\text{percentage change in resource quantity}}{\text{percentage change in resource price}}$$

When E_{rd} is greater than 1, resource demand is elastic; when E_{rd} is less than 1, resource demand is inelastic; and when E_{rd} equals 1, resource demand is unit-elastic.

9. The elasticity of demand for a resource will be greater (a) the more slowly the marginal product of the resource declines, (b) the larger the number of good substitute resources available, (c) the greater the elasticity of demand for the product, and (d) the larger the proportion of total production costs attributable to the resource.

10. Any specific level of output will be produced with the least costly combination of variable resources when the marginal product per dollar's worth of each input is the same, that is, when

$$\frac{\text{MP of labor}}{\text{Price of labor}} = \frac{\text{MP of capital}}{\text{price of capital}}$$

11. A firm is employing the profit-maximizing combination of resources when each resource is used to the point where its marginal revenue product equals its price. In terms of labor and capital, this occurs when the MRP of labor equals the price of labor and the MRP of capital equals the price of capital, that is, when

$$\frac{\text{MRP of labor}}{\text{Price of labor}} = \frac{\text{MRP of capital}}{\text{price of capital}} = 1$$

12. The marginal productivity theory of income distribution holds that all resources are paid what they are economically worth: their marginal contribution to output. Critics assert that such an income distribution is too unequal and that real-world market imperfections result in pay above and below marginal contributions to output.

TERMS AND CONCEPTS

derived demand
marginal product
marginal revenue product
marginal resource cost
MRP = MRC rule

substitution effect
output effect
elasticity of resource demand

least-cost combination of resources
profit-maximizing combination of resources

marginal productivity theory of income distribution

STUDY QUESTIONS

1. What is the significance of resource pricing? Explain how the factors determining resource demand differ from those underlying product demand. Explain the meaning and significance of the fact that the demand for a resource is a derived demand. Why do resource demand curves slope downward?

2. **KEY QUESTION** Complete the following labor demand table for a firm which is hiring labor competitively and selling its product in a competitive market.

Units of labor	Total product	Marginal product	Product price	Total revenue	Marginal revenue product
0	0		$2	$____	$____
1	17	____	2	____	____
2	31	____	2	____	____
3	43	____	2	____	____
4	53	____	2	____	____
5	60	____	2	____	____
6	65	____	2	____	____

a. How many workers will the firm hire if the market wage rate is $27.95? $19.95? Explain why the firm will not hire a larger or smaller number of units of labor at each of these wage rates.

b. Show in schedule form and graphically the labor demand curve of this firm.

c. Now redetermine the firm's demand curve for labor, assuming that it is selling in an imperfectly competitive market and that, although it can sell 17 units at $2.20 per unit, it must lower product price by 5 cents to sell the marginal product of each successive labor unit. Compare this demand curve with that derived in question 2b. Which curve is more elastic? Explain.

3. **KEY QUESTION** What factors determine the elasticity of resource demand? What effect will each of the following have on the elasticity or the location of the demand for resource C, which is being used to produce commodity X? Where there is any uncertainty as to the outcome, specify the causes of that uncertainty.

a. An increase in the demand for product X
b. An increase in the price of substitute resource D
c. An increase in the number of resources substitutable for C in producing X
d. A technological improvement in the capital equipment with which resource C is combined
e. A decline in the price of complementary resource E
f. A decline in the elasticity of demand for product X due to a decline in the competitiveness of the product market

4. **KEY QUESTION** Suppose the productivity of capital and labor are as shown at the top of the next column. The output of these resources sells in a purely competitive market for $1 per unit. Both capital and labor are hired under purely competitive conditions at $3 and $1, respectively.

a. What is the least-cost combination of labor and capital the firm should employ in producing 80 units of output? Explain.

b. What is the profit-maximizing combination of labor/capital the firm should use? Explain. What is the resulting level of output? What is the economic profit? Is this the least costly way of producing the profit-maximizing output?

5. **KEY QUESTION** In each of the following four cases MRP_L and MRP_C refer to the marginal revenue products of labor and capital, respectively, and P_L and P_C refer to their prices. Indicate in each case whether the conditions are consistent with maximum profits for the firm. If not, state which resource(s) should be used in larger amounts and which resource(s) should be used in smaller amounts.

a. $MRP_L = \$8$; $P_L = \$4$; $MRP_C = \$8$; $P_C = \$4$
b. $MRP_L = \$10$; $P_L = \$12$; $MRP_C = \$14$; $P_C = \$9$
c. $MRP_L = \$6$; $P_L = \$6$; $MRP_C = \$12$; $P_C = \$12$
d. $MRP_L = \$22$; $P_L = \$26$; $MRP_C = \$16$; $P_C = \$19$

6. **(Last Word)** Explain the economics of the substitution of ATMs for human tellers. Some banks are beginning to assess transaction fees when customers use human tellers rather than ATMs. What are these banks trying to accomplish?

7. **WEB-BASED QUESTION** Textile Workers and Computer Workers—Sunrise or Sunset Occupations? The demand for resources is a derived demand, derived from the products or services which resources help produce. Search the Bureau of Labor Statistics http://stats.bls.gov/search/search.asp using the keyword "textiles" for the current Occupational Outlook for textile, apparel, and furnishings occupations. Next, search using "computer" for the Occupational Outlook for computer scientists and systems analysts and for computer and peripheral equipment operators. What is the job outlook for the three occupations? Why do they differ? Do both computer occupations have the same job outlook?

8. **WEB-BASED QUESTION** Military Pay—Does the MRP = MRC Rule Apply? A profit maximizing firm will hire workers up to a point where MRP = MRC (the wage rate). Since the Army is not a profit maximizing firm, what is the MRP for Army personnel? Does the MRP = MRC rule apply? If not, how are military pay rates determined? Assume you are to graduate this semester with an Army ROTC commission as a 2nd Lieutenant. What would be your basic monthly salary? Check the Defense Finance and Accounting Service http://www.dfas.mil/money/milpay/index.htm for an O1 (officer 1), < 2 (under 2 years of service). Compare that to what is being offered for a graduate with your degree and experience at http://www.yahoo.com/Business_and_Economy/Employment/Careers/ under Salary Information. Is the Army competitive? Based on these figures, did you make the right decision to Go Army?

Units of capital	MP of capital	Units of labor	MP of labor
0		0	
1	24	1	11
2	21	2	9
3	18	3	8
4	15	4	7
5	9	5	6
6	6	6	4
7	3	7	1
8	1	8	$\frac{1}{2}$

28

Wage Determination

The most important price you will encounter in your lifetime will likely be your hourly wage rate. Together with your annual hours of work, this price will be critical in determining your economic well-being. The following facts and questions may therefore be of interest to you:

- *Fact:* Real wages have increased historically in the United States but have stagnated during the past two decades. *Question:* What forces account for these trends?
- *Fact:* More than 125 million of us go to work each day in the United States. We work at an amazing variety of jobs, for thousands of different firms. *Question:* How do employers determine what wage to pay and how many workers to employ?
- *Fact:* Union workers generally receive higher wages than nonunion workers in the same occupation. *Question:* How do unions obtain this wage advantage?
- *Fact:* The average salary for major league baseball players in 1997 was $1,383,578, compared with about $40,000 for teachers. *Question:* What causes differences in wages and earnings?
- *Fact:* Most people are paid a certain hourly wage rate or an annual salary. But others are paid by the number of units of output produced or receive commissions and royalties. *Question:* What is the rationale for such varied compensation schemes?

Having explored the major factors underlying resource demand, we now bring resource supply into our analysis. The supply of labor, land, capital, and entrepreneurial ability—interacting with the demand for these resources—explains how wages, rents, interest, and profits are determined. We discuss wages first because of their importance as a basic source of income for most households: nearly three-fourths of the national income arises as wages and salaries.

More specifically, our first goal is to understand how the general level of wage rates comes about in the United States. Then we develop several models that help explain how wage rates are determined in particular labor markets. Next, we look at the effects of unions on wages and discuss the economic impacts of the minimum-wage law. Finally, we examine the reasons for the great differences in wages among different jobs, and then we explore some compensation schemes that link pay to worker performance.

LABOR, WAGES, AND EARNINGS

Economists use the term "labor" broadly to apply to (1) workers in the popular sense of the term, that is, blue- and white-collar workers of all varieties; (2) professional people such as lawyers, physicians, dentists, and teachers; and (3) owners of small businesses, including barbers, plumbers, television repairers, and a host of retailers, who provide labor in operating their own businesses.

Wages, and *wage rates,* are the price paid for labor. Wages may take the form of weekly or monthly salaries, bonuses, royalties, or commissions, but unless otherwise noted, we will use "wage" to mean the wage rate per unit of time—per hour, per day, and so forth. This will remind us that a wage rate is a price paid per unit of labor services. It will also let us distinguish between the *wage rate* and labor *earnings,* the latter being determined by multiplying the number of hours worked per week, per month, or per year by the hourly wage or wage rate.

We will also distinguish between nominal wages and real wages. A **nominal wage** is the amount of *money* received per hour, per day, and so on. A **real wage** is the quantity of *goods and services* a person can obtain with nominal wages; real wages are the "purchasing power" of nominal wages.

Your real wage depends on your nominal wage and the prices of the goods and services you purchase. Suppose you receive an 8 percent increase in your nominal wage during a certain year but in that same year the price level increases by 5 percent. Then your real wage has increased by only 3 percent (= 8 percent *minus* 5 percent). Unless otherwise indicated, we will assume that the level of product prices is constant so that our discussions involve only real wages.

GENERAL LEVEL OF WAGES

Wages differ among nations, regions, occupations, and individuals. Wage rates are much higher in the United States than in China or India. They are slightly higher in the north and east of the United States than in the south. Plumbers are paid less than NFL punters. And physician Adam may earn twice as much as physician Bennett for the same number of hours of work. Wage rates also differ by gender, race, and ethnic background.

The general level of wages, like the general level of prices, is a composite concept which includes a wide range of different wage rates. It includes the wages of bakers, barbers, baseball players, and brain surgeons, but it is not the wage of any real person. Nevertheless, such an average wage is useful for comparing international and interregional wages.

International wage comparisons are admittedly complex because wages are paid in different currencies and productivity varies from country to country. But data such as those in Global Perspective 28-1 suggest that the general level of real wages in the United States is relatively high—although not the highest globally.

The simplest explanation for high real wages in the United States and other industrially advanced

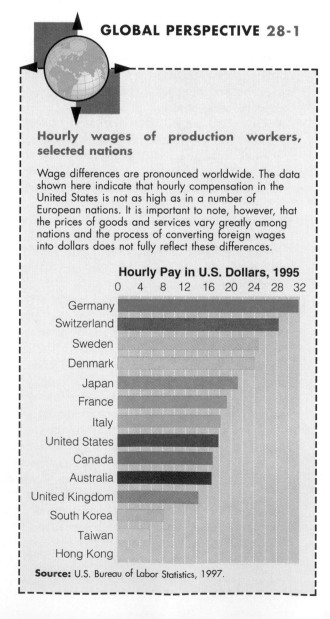

GLOBAL PERSPECTIVE 28-1

Hourly wages of production workers, selected nations

Wage differences are pronounced worldwide. The data shown here indicate that hourly compensation in the United States is not as high as in a number of European nations. It is important to note, however, that the prices of goods and services vary greatly among nations and the process of converting foreign wages into dollars does not fully reflect these differences.

Hourly Pay in U.S. Dollars, 1995

	0	4	8	12	16	20	24	28	32
Germany									
Switzerland									
Sweden									
Denmark									
Japan									
France									
Italy									
United States									
Canada									
Australia									
United Kingdom									
South Korea									
Taiwan									
Hong Kong									

Source: U.S. Bureau of Labor Statistics, 1997.

economies (referred to hereafter as *advanced economies*) is that the demand for labor in these nations is quite large relative to the supply of labor.

Role of Productivity

We know that the demand for labor, or for any other resource, depends on productivity. In general, the greater the productivity of labor, the greater the demand for it. And if the total supply of labor is fixed, then the stronger the labor demand, the higher the average level of real wages. The demand for labor in the United States and the other major advanced economies has been strong because it is highly productive. There are several reasons for this high productivity:

1. *Plentiful capital* Workers in the advanced economies have access to large amounts of capital equipment in the production process. A recent estimate indicates that the total physical capital (machinery and buildings) available per worker in the United States is about $90,000.

2. *Access to abundant natural resources* In advanced economies, natural resources tend to be abundant in relation to the size of the labor force. These resources either are available domestically or are imported from abroad. The United States, for example, is richly endowed with arable land, mineral resources, and sources of energy for industry. The fact that U.S. workers have large amounts of high-quality natural resources to work with is perhaps most evident in agriculture, where, historically, the growth of productivity has been highly impressive.

3. *Advanced technology* The level of technological progress is generally high in advanced economies. Workers in these economies not only use *more* capital equipment but also use *technologically superior* equipment, compared with the vast majority of workers worldwide. Similarly, work methods in the advanced economies are steadily being improved through scientific study and research.

4. *Labor quality* The health, vigor, education, and training of workers in advanced economies are generally superior to those in developing nations. This means that, even with the same quantity and quality of natural and capital resources, workers in advanced economies tend to be more efficient than many of their foreign counterparts.

5. *Intangible factors* Less tangible factors also may underlie the high productivity in some of the advanced economies. In the United States, for example, such factors include (*a*) the efficiency and flexibility of American management; (*b*) a business, social, and political environment which emphasizes production and productivity; and (*c*) the vast size of the domestic market, which provides the opportunity for firms to realize mass-production economies.

Real Wages and Productivity

The dependence of real hourly wages on the productivity level is implied by Figure 28-1, which shows the close long-run relationship between output per labor-hour and real hourly wages in the United States. Because real income and real output are two ways of viewing the same thing, *real income (earnings) per worker can increase only at about the*

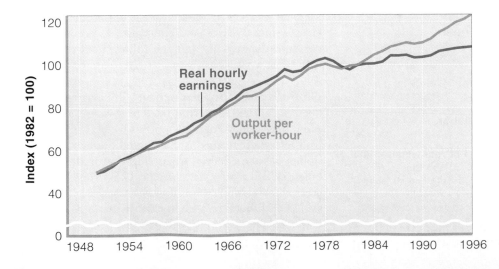

FIGURE 28-1 Output per hour and real average earnings in the United States Over a long period of years there has been a close relationship between output per worker-hour and real hourly earnings. (*Source:* Bureau of Labor Statistics)

same rate as output per worker. When workers produce more real output per hour, more real income is available to distribute to them for each hour worked. The simplest example is Robinson Crusoe alone on an island: The number of coconuts he can pick per hour *is exactly* his real wage per hour. Then, too, Crusoe is his own entrepreneur. Since no one supplies him with property resources (land, capital), he receives as "income" *all* the coconuts he picks in an hour.

In the real world, however, suppliers of land, capital, and entrepreneurial talent also share in the income from production. Real wages therefore need not rise in lockstep with productivity increases over short spans of time. Nevertheless, our generalization holds true: Over very long periods, productivity and real wages travel similar upward paths.

Secular Growth of Real Wages

Basic supply and demand analysis helps explain the long-term trend of real wage growth in the United States. The nation's labor force has grown significantly over the decades, increasing the supply of labor. But, as a result of the productivity-increasing factors discussed previously, labor demand has increased *more rapidly* than labor supply. Several such increases in labor supply and labor demand are shown in Figure 28-2. The result has been a long-run, or *secular*, increase in wage rates and employment.

FIGURE 28-2 The secular trend of real wages in the United States The productivity of U.S. labor has increased substantially over the long run, causing the demand for labor *D* to shift rightward (increase) more rapidly than increases in the supply of labor *S*. The result has been increases in real wages.

Recent Stagnation of Real Wage Growth

Figure 28-2 might mislead you to think that real wages rise at a continuous, steady rate. But hourly wages rise more rapidly in some periods than in others. Of particular importance, real hourly wages in the United States have been relatively stagnant in the 1980s and 1990s. Why so?

Slower Productivity Growth The first reason for the recent stagnation of real wage growth is that productivity has grown less rapidly in the past two decades than previously. This productivity slowdown is thought to have resulted from a combination of these factors:

1. A diminished rate of capital accumulation
2. An overburdened infrastructure—that is, a failure to expand highways, bridges, transit systems, school systems, and airports to keep pace with population growth
3. The rapid expansion of employment and output in service industries, where productivity gains tend to be low
4. The deterioration of labor-force skills due to a declining quality of education
5. A surge in the size of the work force, associated with large numbers of "baby boomers," immigrants, and married women
6. Management strategies that stress short-term profitability at the expense of R&D and to the detriment of innovative labor-relations programs that might increase productivity

Downward Wage Pressure But there is more to the recent stagnation of real wage growth than slower productivity growth. As indicated in Figure 28-1, real wage increases have not *kept pace* with productivity increases since 1982 or so. Economists do not fully understand the reasons, but the following two factors may be at work.

Globalization of Production Today, much production can be transferred from high-wage advanced economies to developing countries where workers are paid less. As it relates to the United States, this possibility has the effect of expanding greatly the supply of less skilled workers available to U.S. firms. This increased labor supply pulls down the real wages of less skilled U.S. workers, who in essence compete for jobs with workers in lower-wage nations. If U.S. workers do not compete, they may lose their jobs when production is relocated to those nations. In fact, the real wages of less skilled U.S. workers has declined in the past two decades. This decline served as a drag on the growth of real wages, helping to explain why the average level of real wages did not keep pace with productivity growth.

Statistical Illusion? Many economists claim that much of the alleged stagnation of real wages is a "statistical illusion." Average hourly earnings include only wage and salary compensation, not fringe benefits such as medical insurance and contributions for social insurance. Because these fringe benefits have been increasing faster than wages and salaries, average hourly earnings understate compensation growth.

Also, critics say that current measures of inflation used in the United States overstate by about 1 percentage point per year the actual rises in prices faced by workers in the past two decades. (This overstatement arises for several technical reasons: shifts in spending away from products whose prices have risen; failure to account for rapid price declines on new products; quality improvements not reflected in prices; and expansion of discount pricing and shopping.) If overstatement of inflation has occurred, then nominal wage increases have been overly adjusted downward in calculating real wage increases. In this view, real wages plus fringe benefits have in fact grown at about the same rate as productivity, rather than at the slower rate indicated by the hourly real wage line in Figure 28-1.[1]

A PURELY COMPETITIVE LABOR MARKET

We now turn from the general level of wages to specific wage rates. What determines the wage rate paid for some specific type of labor? Demand and supply analysis again is revealing. Let's begin by examining labor demand and labor supply in a **purely competitive labor market.** In this type of market:

1. Many firms compete with one another in hiring a specific type of labor.

2. Numerous qualified workers with identical skills independently supply this type of labor.

3. "Wage-taker" behavior pertains to both individual firms and individual workers; neither can exert any control over the market wage rate.

Market Demand for Labor

Suppose many—say, 200—firms demand a particular type of semiskilled or skilled labor. These firms need not be in the same industry; industries are defined in terms of the products they produce and not the resources they employ. Thus, firms producing wood-frame furniture, wood windows and doors, and wood cabinets will all demand carpenters. The total, or market, labor demand curve for the labor service in question is found by summing horizontally the labor demand curves (the marginal revenue product curves) of the individual firms, as suggested in **Figure 28-3 (Key Graph).** The horizontal summing of the 200 labor demand curves like *d* in Figure 28-3a yields the market labor demand curve *D* in Figure 28-3b.

Market Supply of Labor

On the supply side of the labor market, we assume there is no union; workers compete individually for available jobs. The supply curve for each type of labor slopes upward, indicating that employers as a group must pay higher wage rates to obtain more workers. This is so because firms must bid these workers away from other industries, occupations, and localities. Within limits, workers have alternative job opportunities; that is, they may work in other industries in the same locality, or they may work in their present occupations in different cities or states, or they may work in other occupations. Firms wanting to hire these workers must pay higher wage rates to attract more of them away from the alternative job opportunities. Similarly, higher wages are necessary to induce individuals who are not currently in the labor force—those doing household activities or enjoying leisure—to seek employment. Assuming that wages are constant in other labor markets, higher wages in a particular labor market entice more workers to offer their labor services in that market. In Figure 28-3b, this fact is confirmed by the upsloping market supply of labor curve *S*.

Labor Market Equilibrium

The equilibrium wage rate and level of employment for this type of labor are determined by the intersec-

---

[1]For a particularly succinct and readable presentation of this view, see "Trends in Real Wage Growth," *Chicago Fed Letter* (Federal Reserve Bank of Chicago), March 1997.

FIGURE 28-3 The supply of, and demand for, labor in (a) a single competitive firm and (b) a purely competitive labor market In a purely competitive labor market (b) the equilibrium wage rate W_c and number of workers Q_c are determined by labor supply S and labor demand D. Because this market wage rate is given to the individual firm (a) hiring in this market, its labor supply curve $s = MRC$ is perfectly elastic. Its labor demand curve is its MRP curve (here labeled *mrp*). The firm maximizes its profit by hiring workers up to where $MRP = MRC$. Area $0abc$ represents both the firm's total revenue and its total cost. The green area is its total wage cost; the lavender area is nonlabor costs, that is, its payments to the suppliers of land, capital, and entrepreneurship.

QUICK QUIZ 28-3

1. The supply of labor curve S slopes upward in graph (b) because:
   a. the law of diminishing marginal utility applies.
   b. the law of diminishing returns applies.
   c. workers can afford to "buy" more leisure when their wage rates rise.
   d. higher wages are needed to attract workers away from other labor markets, household activities, and leisure.

2. This firm's labor demand curve d in graph (a) slopes downward because:
   a. the law of diminishing marginal utility applies.
   b. the law of diminishing returns applies.
   c. the firm must lower its price to sell additional units of its product.
   d. the firm is a competitive employer, not a monopsonist.

3. In employing 5 workers, the firm represented in graph (a):
   a. has a total wage cost of $6000.
   b. is adhering to the general principle of undertaking all actions for which the marginal benefit exceeds the marginal cost.
   c. uses less labor than would be ideal from society's perspective.
   d. experiences increasing marginal returns.

4. A rightward shift of the labor supply curve in graph (b) would shift curve:
   a. $d = mrp$ leftward in graph (a).
   b. $d = mrp$ rightward in graph (a).
   c. $s = MRC$ upward in graph (a).
   d. $s = MRC$ downward in graph (a).

Answers: 1. d; 2. b; 3. b; 4. d

---

tion of the market labor demand and supply curves. In Figure 28-3b the equilibrium wage rate is W_c ($6), and the number of workers hired is Q_c (1000). To the individual firm the market wage rate W_c is given. Each of the many firms employs such a small fraction of the total available supply of this type of labor that none

can influence the wage rate. The supply of this labor is perfectly elastic to the individual firm, as shown by horizontal line s in Figure 28-3a.

Each individual firm will find it profitable to hire this type of labor up to the point at which marginal revenue product is equal to marginal resource cost.

TABLE 28-1 The supply of labor: pure competition in the hire of labor

(1) Units of labor	(2) Wage rate	(3) Total labor cost (wage bill)	(4) Marginal resource (labor) cost
0	$6	$ 0	
1	6	6	$6
2	6	12	6
3	6	18	6
4	6	24	6
5	6	30	6
6	6	36	6

This is merely an application of the MRP = MRC rule developed in Chapter 27. (In fact, the demand curve in Figure 28-3a is based on Table 27-1.)

As Table 28-1 indicates, when a resource's price is given to the individual competitive firm, the marginal cost of that resource (MRC) is constant and equal to the resource price. In particular here, MRC *is constant and equal to the wage rate.* Each additional worker hired adds precisely his or her own wage rate ($6 in this case) to the firm's total resource cost. So the firm in a purely competitive labor market maximizes its profit by hiring workers to the point at which its wage rate equals MRP. In Figure 28-3a this "typical" firm will hire q_c (5) workers, paying each of them the market wage rate W_c ($6).

A firm's total revenue from employing a particular number of labor units can be found by summing their MRPs. For example, if a firm employs 3 labor units with marginal revenue products of $7, $6, and $5, respectively, then the firm's total revenue is $18 (= $7 + $6 + $5). In Figure 28-3a, where we are not restricted to whole units of labor, total revenue is represented by area 0*abc* under the MRP curve to the left of q_c. And what area represents the firm's total cost, including a normal profit? Answer: For q_c units, the same area—0*abc*. The green rectangle represents the firm's total wage cost ($0q_c \times 0W_c$). The lavender triangle (total revenue minus total wage cost) represents the firm's nonlabor costs—its payments to land, capital, and entrepreneurship. Thus, total cost (wages plus other income payments) equals total revenue. Again we are reminded that a purely competitive firm breaks even, earning only a normal profit. **(Key Questions 3 and 4)**

MONOPSONY MODEL

In the purely competitive labor market of the previous section, each employer hires too small an amount of labor to influence the wage rate. Each firm can hire as little or as much labor as it needs, but only at the market wage rate, as reflected in its horizontal labor supply curve. The situation is quite different in **monopsony,** a market in which an employer of resources has monopolistic buying (hiring) power. Labor market monopsony has the following characteristics:

1. There is only a single buyer of a particular kind of labor.

2. This type of labor is relatively immobile, either geographically or because workers would have to acquire new skills.

3. The firm is a "wage maker" in that the wage rate it must pay varies directly with the number of workers it employs.

In its pure form, the monopsonistic power of an employer is virtually complete because there is only one major employer in a labor market. For example, the economies of some towns and cities depend almost entirely on one major firm. A silver-mining concern may be the basic source of employment in a remote Idaho or Colorado town. A New England textile mill, a Wisconsin paper mill, or a farm-belt food processor may provide most of the employment in its locale. Maytag (maker of appliances) is the dominant employer in Newton, Iowa.

In other cases *oligopsony* may prevail; three or four firms may each hire a large portion of the supply of labor in a particular market. Our study of oligopoly correctly suggests there is a stronger tendency for oligopsonists to act in concert—much like a single monopsonist—in hiring labor.

Upsloping Labor Supply to Firm

When a firm hires most of the available supply of a particular type of labor, its decision to employ more or fewer workers affects the wage rate paid to that labor. Specifically, *if a firm is large in relation to the labor market, it will have to pay a higher wage rate to obtain more labor.* For simplicity, suppose there is only one employer of a particular type of labor in a certain geographic area. In this extreme case, the labor supply curve to that firm and the total supply curve for the labor market are identical. This supply curve is upsloping, indicating that the firm must pay a higher wage rate to attract more workers. The supply curve,

S in Figure 28-4, is also the average-cost-of-labor curve for the firm; each point on it indicates the wage rate (cost) per worker which must be paid to attract the corresponding number of workers.

MRC Higher than the Wage Rate

When a monopsonist pays a higher wage to attract an additional worker, it must pay that higher wage to all the workers it currently employs at a lower wage. If not, labor morale will deteriorate, and the employer will be plagued with labor unrest because of wage-rate differences existing for the same job. Paying a uniform wage to all workers means that the cost of an extra worker—the marginal resource (labor) cost (MRC)—is the sum of that worker's wage rate and the amount necessary to bring the wage rate of all current workers up to the new wage level.

Table 28-2 illustrates this point. One worker can be hired at a wage rate of $6. But hiring a second worker forces the firm to pay a higher wage rate of $7. The marginal resource (labor) cost of the second worker is $8—the $7 paid to the second worker plus a $1 raise for the first worker. From another viewpoint, total labor cost is now $14 (= 2 × $7), up from $6. So the MRC of the second worker is $8 (= $14 − $6), not just the $7 wage rate paid to the second worker. Similarly, the marginal labor cost of

TABLE 28-2   The supply of labor: monopsony in the hire of labor

(1) Units of labor	(2) Wage rate	(3) Total labor cost (wage bill)	(4) Marginal resource (labor) cost
0	$ 5	$ 0	
1	6	6	$ 6
2	7	14	8
3	8	24	10
4	9	36	12
5	10	50	14
6	11	66	16

the third worker is $10—the $8 which must be paid to attract this worker from alternative employment plus $1 raises, from $7 to $8, for the first two workers.

The important point is that *to the monopsonist, marginal resource (labor) cost exceeds the wage rate.* Graphically, the MRC curve lies above the average-cost-of-labor curve, or labor supply curve *S*, as is clearly shown in Figure 28-4.

Equilibrium Wage and Employment

How much labor will the monopsonist hire and what wage rate will it pay? To maximize profit, it will employ the quantity of labor Q_m in Figure 28-4 because at that quantity MRC and MRP are equal (point *b*).[2]

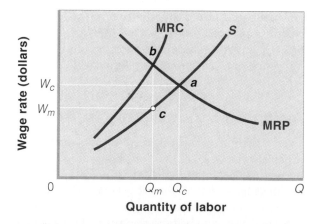

FIGURE 28-4 The wage rate and level of employment in a monopsonistic labor market In a monopsonistic labor market the employer's marginal resource (labor) cost curve (MRC) lies above the labor supply curve *S*. Equating MRC with MRP at point *b*, the monopsonist will hire Q_m workers (compared with Q_c under competition) and pay wage rate W_m (compared with the competitive wage W_c).

------

[2] The fact that MRC exceeds resource price when resources are hired or purchased under imperfectly competitive (monopsonistic) conditions calls for adjustments in Chapter 27's least-cost and profit-maximizing rules for hiring resources. [See equations (1) and (2) in the "Optimal Combination of Resources" section of Chapter 27.] Specifically, we must substitute MRC for resource price in the denominators of our two equations. That is, with imperfect competition in the hiring of both labor and capital, equation (1) becomes

$$\frac{MP_L}{MRC_L} = \frac{MP_C}{MRC_C} \tag{1'}$$

and equation (2) is restated as

$$\frac{MRP_L}{MRC_L} = \frac{MRP_C}{MRC_C} = 1 \tag{2'}$$

In fact, equations (1) and (2) can be regarded as special cases of (1') and (2') in which firms happen to be hiring under purely competitive conditions and resource price is therefore equal to, and can be substituted for, marginal resource cost.

The monopsonist next determines how much it must pay to attract these Q_m workers. From the supply curve S, specifically point c, it sees that it must pay wage rate W_m. Clearly, it need not pay a wage equal to MRP; it can attract exactly the number of workers it wants (Q_m) with wage rate W_m. That is what it will pay.

Contrast these results with those which a competitive labor market would yield. With competition in the hire of labor, the level of employment would be greater (at Q_c) and the wage rate would be higher (at W_c). *Other things equal, the monopsonist maximizes its profit by hiring a smaller number of workers and thereby paying a less-than-competitive wage rate.*[3] Society gets a smaller output, and workers get a wage rate that is less by bc than their marginal revenue product. Just as a monopolistic seller finds it profitable to restrict product output to realize an above-competitive price for its goods, so the monopsonistic employer of resources finds it profitable to restrict employment to depress wage rates and therefore costs, that is, to realize below-competitive wage rates.[4]

Examples

Monopsonistic labor market outcomes are not common in the U.S. economy. There are typically many potential employers for most workers, particularly when these workers are occupationally and geographically mobile. Also, unions tend to counteract monopsony power in labor markets. Nevertheless, economists have found evidence of monopsony in such diverse labor markets as those for nurses, professional athletes, public school teachers, newspaper employees, and some building trades workers.

In the case of nurses the major employers in most locales are a relatively small number of hospitals. Further, the highly specialized skills of nurses are not readily transferable to other occupations. It has been found in accordance with the monopsony model that,

other things equal, the smaller the number of hospitals in a town or city (that is, the greater the degree of monopsony), the lower the beginning salaries of nurses.

Although *potential* employers for professional athletes are quite numerous, those employers historically have used ingenious devices to limit competition in the hire of labor. The National Football League, the National Basketball Association, and the American and National Baseball Leagues have established rules which tie a player to one team and prevent him from selling his talents to the highest bidder on the open (competitive) market. In particular, through the new-player draft, the team which selects or "drafts" a player has the exclusive right to bargain a contract with that player. Further, the so-called reserve clause in each player's contract gives his team the exclusive right to purchase his services for the next season. Recently, new agreements that provide "free agency" to certain experienced players have made the labor markets for professional athletes more competitive, but collusive monopsony persists.

Empirical studies have shown that prior to 1976 baseball players (despite very high salaries) were paid substantially less than their estimated MRPs, which is, of course, consistent with Figure 28-4. However, since 1976, players have been allowed to become "free agents"—that is, to sell their services to any interested team—after their sixth season of play. A comparison of the salaries of current free agents with their estimated MRPs indicates that competition among teams for free agents has brought their salaries and MRPs into close accord, as our competitive model suggests. **(Key Question 6)**

---

[3]This is analogous to the monopolist's restricting output as it sets product price and output on the basis of marginal revenue, not product demand. In this instance, resource price is set on the basis of marginal labor (resource) cost, not resource supply.

[4]Will a monopsonistic employer also be a monopolistic seller in the product market? Perhaps, but not necessarily. The New England textile mill may be a monopsonistic employer yet face severe domestic and foreign competition in selling its product. In other cases—for example, the automobile and steel industries—firms have both monopsonistic and monopolistic (oligopolistic) power.

QUICK REVIEW 28-1

■ Real wages have increased historically in the United States because labor demand has increased relative to labor supply.

■ Over the long term, real wages per worker have increased at approximately the same rate as worker productivity.

■ The competitive employer is a "wage taker" and employs workers at the point where the wage rate (= MRC) equals MRP.

■ The labor supply curve to a monopsonist is upsloping, causing MRC to exceed the wage rate for each worker. Other things equal, the monopsonist, hiring where MRC = MRP, will employ fewer workers and pay a lower wage rate than would a purely competitive employer.

THREE UNION MODELS

Thus far, we have assumed that workers compete with each other in selling their labor services. In some labor markets, though, workers sell their labor services collectively through unions. To view the economic impact of unions in the simplest context, let's first suppose a union is formed in an otherwise competitive labor market. That is, a union is now bargaining with a relatively large number of employers. It seeks many goals, the most important of which is to raise wage rates. This objective can be persued in several ways.

Demand-Enhancement Model

From the union's viewpoint, the most desirable technique for raising wage rates is to increase the demand for labor. As shown in Figure 28-5, an increase in the demand for labor will result in both higher wage rates *and* more jobs. The relative sizes of these increases will depend on the elasticity of labor supply.

A union might increase labor demand by altering one or more of the determinants of labor demand. Specifically, a union can attempt to increase the demand for the product or service it is producing, enhance labor productivity, or alter the prices of other inputs.

Increase Product Demand   Unions may attempt to increase the demand for the products they help

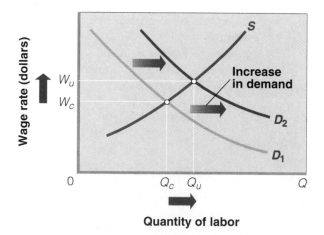

FIGURE 28-5 Unions and the demand for labor
When unions can increase the demand for labor, say, from D_1 to D_2, higher wage rates (W_c to W_u) and more jobs (Q_c to Q_u) can be realized.

produce—and thus increase the derived demand for their own labor services—by advertising, political lobbying, or requiring redundant labor.

Union television ads urging consumers to "buy the union label" are relevant. Historically, the International Ladies Garment Workers Union (ILGWU) has joined with its employers to finance advertising campaigns to bolster demand for products. Also, the Communications Workers of America (CWA) helped finance a $2 million "Call or Buy Union" campaign to convince telephone users to choose the long-distance services and equipment of AT&T and Western Union Corporation, which together provided almost 100,000 CWA jobs.

On the political front we see construction unions lobbying for new highway or urban renewal projects. Teachers' unions and associations push for increased public spending on education. Unions connected with the aerospace industry lobby to increase military and space exploration spending. And some unions have vigorously supported their employers in seeking protective tariffs or import quotas designed to exclude competing foreign products. Both the steelworkers and the automobile workers have sought such forms of protection. They recognize that a decline in the supply of imported cars through tariffs or negotiated international agreements will increase import prices, thus increasing the demand for highly substitutable domestically made autos. This will boost the derived demand for U.S. autoworkers.

Some unions have sought to expand the demand for labor by forcing make-work, or "featherbedding," rules on employers. Before contrary court rulings, the Railway Brotherhoods forced railroads to hire train crews of a certain minimum size; diesel engines had to have a fireman even though there was no steam engine fueled by fire.

Increase Productivity   Many decisions affecting labor productivity—for example, decisions concerning the quantity and quality of real capital used by workers—are made unilaterally by management. However, there is a growing interest in establishing joint labor-management committees designed to increase labor productivity.

Change Prices of Other Inputs   Unions can enhance the demand for their labor by increasing the prices of substitute resources. For example, unions—whose workers are generally paid significantly more than the minimum wage—strongly support increases in the minimum wage. One alleged reason for this backing is that unions want to increase the price of substitutable low-wage, nonunion labor. A higher minimum wage for nonunion workers will deter employers from substituting them for union workers, bolstering the demand for union workers.

Similarly, unions can increase the demand for their labor by supporting public actions which *reduce* the price of a complementary resource. Unions in industries using large amounts of energy might actively oppose rate increases proposed by electric or natural gas utilities. Where labor and energy are complementary, an energy price increase might reduce the demand for labor through Chapter 27's output effect.

Unions recognize that their ability to influence the demand for labor is very limited. As many of our illustrations imply, unions frequently must try to *prevent declines* in labor demand rather than *cause increases*. Hence, it is not surprising that union efforts to increase wage rates have concentrated on the supply side of the labor market.

Exclusive or Craft Union Model

Unions can boost wage rates by reducing the supply of labor. Historically, organized labor has favored policies restricting the supply of labor to the U.S. economy as a whole to raise the general level of wages. Labor unions have supported legislation which has (1) restricted immigration, (2) reduced child labor, (3) encouraged compulsory retirement, and (4) enforced a shorter workweek.

More relevant to our discussion, specific types of workers have adopted, through unions, techniques designed to restrict their numbers. This is especially true of *craft unions*—unions which comprise workers of a given skill, such as carpenters or bricklayers or plumbers. These unions have frequently forced employers to agree to hire only union workers, giving the union virtually complete control of the supply of labor. Then, by following restrictive membership policies—long apprenticeships, very high initiation fees, limits on new memberships—the unions have caused an artificial restriction of the labor supply. As indicated in Figure 28-6, this results in higher wage rates. This approach to achieving wage increases is called **exclusive unionism.** Higher wages result from excluding workers from the union and therefore from the supply of labor.

Occupational licensing is another means of restricting the supply of specific kinds of labor. Here a

FIGURE 28-6 Exclusive or craft unionism By reducing the supply of labor (say, from S_1 to S_2) through the use of restrictive membership policies, exclusive unions achieve higher wage rates (W_c to W_u). However, restriction of the labor supply also reduces the number of workers employed (Q_c to Q_u).

group of workers in an occupation will pressure state or municipal governments to pass a law which provides that, say, barbers (or physicians, plumbers, cosmetologists, egg graders, pest controllers) can practice their trade only if they meet certain specified requirements. These requirements might include level of education, amount of work experience, the passing of an examination, and personal characteristics ("the practitioner must be of good moral character"). The licensing board administering the law is typically dominated by members of the licensed occupation. The result is self-regulation which often leads to policies that serve only to restrict entry to the occupation.

The purpose of licensing is supposedly to protect consumers from incompetent practitioners, and this is a worthy goal. But by restricting the number of qualified workers, it also results in above-competitive wages and earnings for those in the occupation (Figure 28-6). Moreover, licensing requirements often include a residency requirement which inhibits the interstate movement of qualified workers. Some 600 occupations are now licensed in the United States.

Inclusive or Industrial Union Model

Most unions, however, do not attempt to limit their membership. On the contrary, they seek to organize all available workers. This is characteristic of the so-called *industrial unions*—unions, such as the automobile workers and steelworkers, which seek all unskilled, semiskilled, and skilled workers in an industry as members. A union can afford to be exclusive when its members are skilled craftspersons for whom there are few substitute workers. But a union composed of unskilled and semiskilled workers would be hurting itself by limiting its membership; doing so would result in numerous highly substitutable *nonunion* workers who would be available for employment.

If an industrial union includes virtually all available workers in its membership, firms will be under great pressure to agree to union wage demands. By going on strike, the union could deprive those firms of their entire labor supply.

This **inclusive unionism** is illustrated in Figure 28-7. Initially, the competitive equilibrium wage rate is W_c and the level of employment is Q_c. Now suppose an industrial union is formed and it imposes a higher, above-equilibrium wage rate of, say, W_u. This wage rate W_u creates a pefectly elastic labor supply over the range *ae* in Figure 28-7. If employers hire any number of workers in this range, the union-imposed wage rate is effective and must be paid or the union will supply no labor at all—the firms will be faced with a strike. If the employers decide it is better to pay this higher wage rate than to suffer a strike, they will cut back on employment from Q_c to Q_u.

FIGURE 28-7 Inclusive or industrial unionism By organizing virtually all available workers to control the supply of labor, inclusive industrial unions may impose a wage rate, such as W_u, which is above the competitive wage rate W_c. The effect is to change the labor supply curve from S to aeS. At wage rate W_u, employers will cut employment from Q_c to Q_u.

By agreeing to the union's W_u wage demand, individual employers become wage takers. Because labor supply is perfectly elastic over range *ae*, the marginal resource (labor) cost is equal to the wage rate W_u over this range. The Q_u level of employment results from employers' equating this MRC (now equal to the *wage rate*) with MRP according to our profit-maximizing rule.

Note from point *e* on labor supply curve S that Q_e workers desire employment at wage W_u. But as indicated by point *b* on labor demand curve D, only Q_u workers are hired. The result is a surplus of labor in the amount $Q_e - Q_u$ (also shown by distance *eb*). Without the union—that is, in a purely competitive labor market—this surplus of unemployed workers would result in lower wages. Specifically, the wage rate would fall to the equilibrium level W_c, where the quantity of labor supplied equals the quantity of labor demanded (each Q_c). But this doesn't happen because workers are acting collectively through their union. Workers cannot individually offer to work for less than W_u; nor can employers contractually pay less than that wage rate.

Wage Increases and Unemployment

Have unions been successful in raising the wages of their members? Evidence suggests that union members on the average achieve a 10 to 15 percent wage advantage over nonunion workers.

As Figures 28-6 and 28-7 suggest, the wage-raising actions of both exclusive and inclusive unionism reduce employment. A union's success in achieving above-equilibrium wage rates is thus tempered by an accompanying decline in the number of workers employed. This unemployment effect acts as a restraining influence on union wage demands. A union cannot expect to maintain solidarity within its ranks if it seeks a wage rate so high that joblessness will result for, say, 20 or 30 percent of its members.

The unemployment effect of union wage increases might be reduced in two ways:

1. *Growth* The normal growth of the economy increases the demand for most kinds of labor through time. This continual rightward shift of the labor demand curves in Figures 28-6 and 28-7 could offset, or more than offset, the unemployment effects associated with the indicated wage increases. Then union wage increases would tend to decrease the *rate of growth* of job opportunities but not the firm's total employment.

2. *Elasticity* The size of the unemployment effect will depend on the elasticity of demand for labor. The more inelastic the demand, the smaller the amount of unemployment accompanying a given wage-rate increase. And if unions have sufficient bargaining strength, they *may* obtain provisions in their collective bargaining agreements which reduce the substitutability of other inputs for labor and thereby reduce the elasticity of demand for union labor. For example, a union may force employers to accept rules blocking the introduction of new machinery and equipment. Or the union may bargain successfully for severance or layoff pay, which increases the cost to the firm of substituting capital for labor when wage rates are increased. Similarly, the union might gain a contract provision prohibiting the firm from subcontracting production to nonunion (lower-wage) firms or relocating work to low-wage workers overseas, thereby restricting the substitution of cheaper labor for union workers.

For these and other reasons the unemployment restraint on union wage demands may be less pressing than our exclusive and inclusive union models suggest.

BILATERAL MONOPOLY MODEL

Suppose a strong industrial union is formed in a labor market which is monopsonistic rather than competitive. In other words, we combine the monopsony model with the inclusive unionism model. The result is **bilateral monopoly.** The union is a monopolistic "seller" of labor which controls labor supply and can influence wage rates, but it faces a monopsonistic employer (or combination of oligopsonistic employers) of labor which can also affect wages by altering its employment. This is not an extreme or special case. In such industries as steel, automobile, meatpacking, and farm machinery, "big labor"—one huge industrial union—bargains with "big business"—a few industrial giants.

Indeterminate Outcome of Bilateral Monopoly

This situation is shown in Figure 28-8, which superimposes Figure 28-7 on 28-4. The monopsonistic employer will seek the below-competitive-equilib-

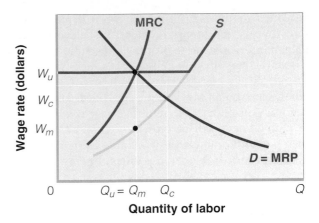

FIGURE 28-8 Bilateral monopoly in the labor market
A monopsonist seeks to hire Q_m workers (where MRC = MRP) and pay wage rate W_m corresponding to Q_m labor on labor supply curve S. The inclusive union it faces seeks the above-equilibrium wage rate W_u. The actual outcome cannot be predicted by economic theory.

rium wage rate W_m, and the union presumably will press for some above-competitive-equilibrium wage rate such as W_u. Which will result? We cannot say with certainty. The outcome is "logically indeterminate" since economic theory does not explain what will happen at the collective bargaining table. We can expect the wage outcome to lie somewhere between W_m and W_u. Beyond that, about all we can say is that the party with the most bargaining power and the most effective bargaining strategy will probably get a wage closer to the one it seeks.

Desirability of Bilateral Monopoly

The wage and employment outcomes in this situation might be more socially desirable than the term "bilateral monopoly" would imply. The monopoly on one side of the market *might* in effect cancel out the monopoly on the other side, yielding competitive or near-competitive results. If either the union or management prevailed in this market—that is, if the actual wage rate were determined at either W_u or W_m— employment would be restricted to Q_m (where MRP = MRC), which is below the competitive level.

But now suppose the monopoly power of the union roughly offsets the monopsony power of management, and a bargained wage rate of W_c, which is the competitive wage, is agreed upon. Once management accepts this wage rate, its incentive to restrict employment disappears; no longer can it depress wage rates by restricting employment. Instead, management hires at the most profitable resource quantity, where the bargained wage rate W_c (which is now the firm's MRC) is equal to the MRP. It hires Q_c workers. Thus, with monopoly on both sides of the labor market, it is possible that the resulting wage rate and level of employment will be closer to competitive levels than would be the case if monopoly existed on only one side of the market. **(Key Question 7)**

QUICK REVIEW 28-2

■ In the demand-enhancement union model, a union increases the wage rate by increasing labor demand through actions which increase product demand, raise labor productivity, or alter the prices of related inputs.

■ In the exclusive (craft) union model, a union increases wage rates by artificially restricting labor supply, say, through long apprenticeships or occupational licensing.

■ In the inclusive (industrial) union model, a union raises the wage rate by gaining control over a firm's labor supply and threatening to withhold labor via a strike unless a negotiated wage is obtained.

■ Bilateral monopoly occurs in a labor market where a monopsonist bargains with an inclusive, or industrial, union. Wage and employment outcomes are determined by collective bargaining in this situation.

THE MINIMUM-WAGE CONTROVERSY

Since the passage of the Fair Labor Standards Act in 1938, the United States has had a Federal **minimum wage.** The minimum wage has ranged from about 40 to 50 percent of the average wage paid to manufacturing workers and is currently $5.15 per hour. Roughly 90 percent of all nonsupervisory workers are covered by the minimum-wage law. Our analysis of union efforts to increase wages raises the question of how effective a minimum wage is as an antipoverty device.

Case Against the Minimum Wage

Critics, reasoning in terms of Figure 28-7, contend that an above-equilibrium minimum wage (say, W_u) will simply push employers back up their labor demand curves, causing them to hire fewer workers.

The higher labor costs may even force some firms out of business. And some of the poor, low-wage workers whom the minimum wage was designed to help will find themselves out of work! Critics say a worker who is unemployed at a minimum wage of $5.15 per hour is clearly worse off than he or she would be if employed at a market wage rate of, say, $4.50 per hour.

A second criticism of the minimum wage is that it is "poorly targeted" as an antipoverty device. It is designed to provide a "living wage" which will allow less-skilled workers to earn enough for them and their families to escape poverty. However, critics point out that the primary impact of the minimum wage is on teenage workers, many of whom are members of relatively affluent families.

Case for the Minimum Wage

Advocates say critics analyze the impact of the minimum wage in an unrealistic context. Figure 28-7, advocates claim, assumes a competitive and static market. But in a more real, monopsonistic labor market (Figure 28-8), the minimum wage can increase wage rates without causing unemployment. Indeed, a higher minimum wage may even produce more jobs by eliminating the monopsonistic employer's motive for restricting employment.

Also, an effective minimum wage may increase labor productivity; that would shift the labor demand curve to the right and offset any unemployment which the minimum wage might cause.

But how might a minimum wage increase productivity? First, a minimum wage may have a *shock effect* on employers. Firms using low-wage workers may be using those workers inefficiently; the higher wage rates imposed by the minimum wage would presumably shock these firms into using labor more efficiently, and so the productivity of labor would increase. Second, some argue that higher wages would increase the real incomes and therefore the health, vigor, and motivation of workers, making them more productive.

Evidence and Conclusions

Which view is correct? The consensus of the many research studies of the minimum wage is that it does cause some unemployment, particularly among teenage (16- to 19-year-old) workers. It is estimated that a 10 percent increase in the minimum wage will reduce teenage employment by 1 to 3 percent. Young adults (age 20 to 24) are also adversely affected; a 10 percent increase in the minimum wage will reduce employment for this group by 1 percent or less. Blacks and women, who are overrepresented in low-wage occupations, tend to suffer larger declines in employment than white males. Nevertheless, those who remain employed receive higher incomes and may escape poverty. The overall antipoverty effect of the minimum wage is thus an ambivalent one. Those who lose their jobs fall deeper into poverty; those who remain employed may escape poverty.

WAGE DIFFERENTIALS

Why do some corporate executives and professional athletes get paid $5,000,000 or more per year while laundry workers and retail clerks receive $14,000 or $15,000 per year? Why does an entertainer from San Diego dressed as a chicken earn $250,000 a year while someone frying chickens at KFC earns $12,000? Although these wage differences are obviously some of the most extreme, **wage differentials** are common, as Table 28-3 shows. Our objective now is to provide some insight as to why these differentials exist.

Once again the forces of supply and demand provide a general answer. If the supply of a particular type of labor is great in relation to the demand for it,

TABLE 28-3 **Hourly wages in selected occupations, 1996**

Occupation	Median hourly wage
Physicians	$60.01
Law professors	45.02
Petroleum engineers	34.90
Aircraft pilots	34.02
Financial managers	23.34
Fire inspectors	18.44
Construction workers	17.65
Social workers	13.08
Locksmiths	11.17
Medical secretaries	10.22
Teacher aides	7.40
Recreation workers	7.29
Retail salespersons	6.92
Fast-food cooks	5.48

Source: U.S. Department of Labor, *Occupational Employment Statistics Survey,* December 1997.

the resulting wage rate will be low. But if demand is great and the supply relatively small, the wage will be high. Although it is a good starting point, this supply and demand explanation is not particularly revealing. To discover *why* supply and demand conditions differ in various labor markets, we must probe the factors underlying the supply of and demand for particular types of labor.

If (1) all workers were homogeneous, (2) all jobs were equally attractive to workers, and (3) labor markets were perfectly competitive, all workers would receive precisely the same wage rate. This is not a startling statement. It suggests that in an economy having one type of labor and in effect one type of job, competition would result in a single wage rate for all workers. The statement is important only because it suggests reasons why wage rates do differ in practice: (1) Workers are not homogeneous. They differ in abilities and in education and training and, as a result, fit into a number of distinct occupational groups. (2) Jobs vary in attractiveness; the nonmonetary aspects of various jobs are not the same. (3) Labor markets do not work perfectly.

Noncompeting Groups

Workers are not homogeneous; they differ in their mental and physical capacities *and* in their education and training. At any time the labor force is made up of many **noncompeting groups** of workers, each representing several occupations for which the members of the group qualify. Workers from one group do not qualify for occupations of another group.

Ability Few workers have the ability to be brain surgeons, concert violinists, research chemists, entertainers, or professional athletes. The result is that supplies of these particular types of labor are very small in relation to the demand for them, and consequently their wages are high. These and similar groups do not compete with one another or with other skilled or semiskilled workers. The violinist does not compete with the surgeon, nor does the surgeon compete with either the violinist or the professional athlete.

The concept of noncompeting groups is flexible; it can be applied to various subgroups and even to specific individuals in a particular group. Some especially skilled surgeons can command higher fees than their run-of-the-mill colleagues who perform the same operations. Shaquille O'Neal, Hakeem Olajuwon, Michael Jordan, and a few others demand and get salaries many times more than the average professional basketball player. A handful of top corporate executives earn 10 to 20 times as much as the average chief executive officer (CEO). In each of these cases, less talented colleagues are only imperfect substitutes.

Education and Training Noncompeting groups—and therefore wage differentials—also exist because of differing amounts of investment in human capital. A **human capital investment** *is an expenditure on education or training which improves the skills and therefore the productivity of workers.* Like expenditures on machinery and equipment, expenditures on education or training which increase a worker's productivity can be regarded as investments. In both cases, current costs are incurred with the intention that these costs will lead to a greater *future* flow of earnings.

Figure 28-9 indicates, first, that individuals with greater investments in education do achieve higher

incomes during their careers. A second point is that the earnings of more educated workers rise more rapidly than those of less educated workers. The primary reason is that employers provide more on-the-job training to the more educated workers, boosting their productivity and therefore their earnings.

Although education yields higher incomes, it also has costs. A college education involves not only direct costs (tuition, fees, books) but also indirect or opportunity costs (forgone earnings). Does the higher pay received by more educated workers compensate for these costs? The answer is "yes." Rates of return are estimated to be 10 to 13 percent for investments in secondary education and 8 to 12 percent for college education. One generally accepted estimate is that each year of schooling raises a worker's wage by about 8 percent. Also, in recent years the pay gap between college graduates and high school graduates has increased sharply. Since 1980 the college–high school pay gap has risen from 37 to 66 percent for women and from 34 to 60 percent for men.

Compensating Differences

If the workers in a particular noncompeting group are equally capable of performing several different jobs, you might expect the wage rates to be identical for all these jobs. Not so. A group of high school graduates may be equally capable of becoming salesclerks or unskilled construction workers. But these jobs pay different wages. In virtually all locales, construction laborers receive higher wages than salesclerks.

This difference results from differences in the *nonmonetary aspects* of the two jobs. The construction job involves dirty hands, a sore back, the hazard of accidents, and irregular employment, both seasonally and cyclically. The retail sales job means clean clothing, pleasant air-conditioned surroundings, and little fear of injury or layoff. Other things equal, it is easy to see why workers would rather pick up a credit card than a shovel. So construction firms must pay higher wages than retailers to compensate for the unattractive nonmonetary aspects of construction jobs. These wage differentials are called **compensating differences** because they must be paid to compensate for nonmonetary differences in various jobs.

Market Imperfections

The notions of noncompeting groups and differences in nonmonetary aspects of jobs explain many of the

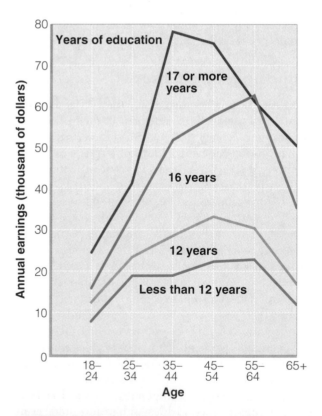

FIGURE 28-9 Education levels and individual annual earnings Annual earnings by age are higher for workers with more education than less. Investment in education yields a return in the form of earnings differences enjoyed through one's work life. (*Source:* U.S. Bureau of the Census. Data for males in 1995.)

wage differentials in the economy. Other persistent differentials result from several types of market imperfections which impede workers from moving from their current jobs to take higher-paying jobs.

Lack of Job Information Workers may simply not be aware of job opportunities and wage rates in other geographic areas and in other jobs for which they qualify. Consequently, the flow of qualified labor from lower-paying to higher-paying jobs—and thus the adjustments in labor supply—may not be sufficient to equalize wages within occupations.

Geographic Immobility Workers take root geographically. Many are reluctant to move to new places; to leave friends, relatives, and associates; to force their children to change schools; to sell their houses; and to incur the costs and inconveniences of adjusting to a new job and a new community. As Adam Smith noted over two centuries ago, "A [person] is of all sorts of luggage the most difficult to be transported." The reluctance or inability of workers to move enables geographic wage differentials within the same occupation to persist.

Unions and Government Restraints Wage differentials may be reinforced by artificial restrictions on mobility imposed by unions and government. We have noted that craft unions find it to their advantage to restrict membership. After all, if carpenters and bricklayers become too plentiful, the wages they can command will decline. Thus the low-paid nonunion carpenter of Brush, Colorado, may be willing to move to Chicago in the pursuit of higher wages. But her chances for successfully doing so are slim. She may be unable to get a union card, and no card means no job. Similarly, an optometrist or lawyer qualified to practice in one state may not meet licensing requirements of other states, so his or her ability to move geographically is limited. Other artificial barriers involve pension plans, health insurance benefits, and seniority rights which might be jeopardized by leaving current employment for another job.

Discrimination Despite legislation to the contrary, discrimination often results in women and minority workers being paid less than white men doing virtually identical work. Also, women and minorities may be crowded into certain low-paying occupations, driving down wages there and raising them elsewhere. If discrimination keeps qualified women and minorities

from taking these higher-paying jobs, then differences in pay among these occupations can persist.

A final point: Typically, all three considerations—noncompeting groups, nonmonetary differences, and market imperfections—come into play in explaining actual wage differentials. For example, the differential between the wages of a physician and a construction worker is largely explainable on the basis of noncompeting groups. Physicians fall into a noncompeting group where, because of mental and financial requisites to entry, the supply of labor is small in relation to demand and wages are therefore high. In construction work, where mental and financial prerequisites are much less significant, the supply of labor is great in relation to demand and wages are low when compared with those of physicians. However, were it not for the unpleasantness of the construction worker's job and the fact that his craft union pursues restrictive membership policies, the differential would probably be even greater than it is.

PAY FOR PERFORMANCE

The models of wage determination presented in this chapter presume that worker pay is always a standard amount for each hour's work, for example, $15 per hour. But pay schemes are often more complex than that in composition and in purpose. For example, many workers receive annual salaries rather than hourly pay. Many workers also receive fringe benefits: health insurance, life insurance, paid vacation, paid sick-leave days, pension contributions, and so on. Finally, some pay plans are designed to elicit a desired level of performance from workers. This last aspect of pay requires further elaboration.

The Principal-Agent Problem Revisited

In Chapter 4 we identified the *principal-agent problem* as it relates to possible differences in the interests of corporate stockholders (principals) and the executives (agents) they hire. This problem extends to all workers. Firms hire workers because they are needed to help produce the goods and services which the firms sell for a profit. Workers are the firms' *agents;* they are hired to advance the interest (profit) of the firms. The *principals* are the firms; they hire agents to advance their goals. Firms and workers have a common self-

Of African-Style Hairbraiders and Stodgy Economists

Newspaper columnist Michelle Malkin finds a connection between textbook economics and real-world barriers to occupational entry.

What do African-style hairbraiders and stodgy economists have in common? More than you ever might have imagined.

According to economics professors, stringent licensing requirements that are passed under the guise of protecting the "public interest" often simply benefit special interests by erecting barriers to entry into the marketplace.

Economists make their case with painstaking analytical rigor in obscure academic journals. But some of the most convincing teachers of this basic lesson in law and economics don't wear tweed and don't need textbook formulas to prove the point. In urban neighborhoods and inner-city storefronts from Washington state to Washington, D.C., African-style hairbraiders are battling the effects of restrictive business regulations.

And they're winning.

Take Taalib-Din Uqdah, owner of Cornrows, Co. in the District of Columbia. Uqdah's tough course in the politics of regulation began four years ago when city inspectors demanded that he obtain an occupational license

in cosmetology to run his hair-braiding business. The license required a year of training in everything from manicures to eyebrow arching at a cost of thousands of dollars—but none of the classes covered hairbraiding techniques and other African styles.

"I don't have any problem with government wanting to protect public health and safety," Uqdah explained to me last week. "But the city's code required me to go to an expensive cosmetology school for a year and learn chemical techniques and practices that have nothing to do with what we do. Complying would have killed my company—and pushed many other law-abiding minority business owners underground."

Uqdah is blunt when asked why the city would crack down on hairbraiders: "We're new, we're popular, we're a threat. Licensing is a way for old-line cosmetologists to squash a growing cottage industry of people who are skilled in a cultural art form that's foreign to them."

Uqdah and his wife successfully challenged the city's outdated cosmetology code with legal help from the nonprofit Institute for Justice based in D.C. As a result, the D.C. government deregulated the cosmetology industry and allowed hairbraiders to obtain a separate operating license with sensible training requirements.

To spread the word, Uqdah founded the American Hairbraiders and Natural Hair Care Association. One member in Memphis, Tenn., pushed successfully for creation of a "natural hair styling" license that requires one-third the hours of instruction required of cosmetologists. And in San Diego this month, the association and the Institute for Justice moved forward with a federal civil-rights

interest: they both want the firm to survive and thrive. That will ensure profit for the firm and continued employment and wage income for the workers.

But the interests of the firm and of workers are not *identical*. A principal-agent problem arises when those interests diverge. Workers may seek to increase their utility by shirking on the job, that is, by providing less than agreed-upon worker effort or by taking unauthorized work breaks. Workers may improve their well-being by increasing their leisure, during paid work hours, without forfeiting income. The night security guard in a warehouse may leave work early or spend time reading a novel rather than making the assigned rounds. A salaried manager may spend much time out of the office, visiting with friends, rather than attending to company business.

Firms (principals) have a profit incentive to reduce or eliminate shirking. One option is to monitor

workers, but monitoring is difficult and costly. Hiring another worker to supervise or monitor our security guard might double the cost of having a secure warehouse. Another way of resolving a principal-agent problem is through some sort of **incentive pay plan** which ties worker compensation (pay) more closely to worker output or performance. Such incentive pay schemes include piece rates, commissions and royalties, bonuses and profit sharing, and efficiency wages.

Piece Rates Piece rates are pay or compensation paid in proportion to the number of units of output a worker produces. If a principal pays fruit pickers by the bushel or typists by the page, it need not be concerned with shirking or monitoring costs.

Commissions or Royalties Unlike piece rates which link pay to units of output, commissions and suit against the state cosmetology board on behalf of African-American studies professor and hairbraider JoAnne Cornwell.

Cornwell, who has been braiding hair since she was a young girl, sees this as a fight not only for the "economic liberty rights of hairbraiders," but for many other working poor immigrants and minorities struggling to enter the workforce. A victory looks promising. Two weeks ago, federal court judge Rudi Brewster rejected a motion to dismiss the lawsuit. Observing that only 4 percent of the required curriculum actually relates to health and safety—the state's supposed "compelling interest" in regulating hairbraiding—Brewster concluded that the rules place "an almost insurmountable barrier in front of anyone who seeks to practice African hair styling," the effect of which "is to force African hair stylists out of business in favor of mainstream hair stylists and barbers."

. . .

Economist Milton Friedman wrote in *Capitalism and Freedom*, "In practice, the considerations taken into account in determining who shall get a license often involve matters that, so far as a layman can see, have no relation whatsoever to professional competence."

Shari Hamilton, owner of Sista's United of Styles in Seattle, says it better. "They don't teach you nothing about nothing. I think it's more of a money and power thing." Hamilton wishes she could have used some of the money she "spent on useless training to hire a few more employees instead." Straight up.

Critics of welfare reform complain there aren't enough jobs to absorb new entrants into the marketplace. But Uqdah of the American Hairbraiders and Natural Hair Care Association has a message for politicians from President Clinton on down: "Open your eyes! I alone could put 3,000 people to work if we got rid of all the insane barriers and rules that keep people from earning an honest living."

The message is easy to discount when delivered by ivory-tower intellectuals—but impossible to ignore when sounded by small-business owners fighting for their livelihoods, off the chalkboards, out of the theoretical realm, in living color.

Source: Michelle Malkin, "Braiders' Protest Breathes Life into Textbook Economics," *Seattle Times*, May 20, 1997, p. 4. Abridged and printed by permission of the *Seattle Times*.

royalties tie pay to the value of sales. Employees who sell products or services—including real estate agents, insurance agents, stockbrokers, retail salespersons—commonly receive *commissions* that are computed as a percentage of the monetary value of their sales. Recording artists and authors are paid *royalties*, computed as a certain percentage of sales revenues from their works (and we thank you). These types of pay align the financial interests of the salespeople or creative artists with the profit interest of the firms.

Bonuses and Profit Sharing

Bonuses are payments beyond one's annual salary that are based on some factor such as the performance of the individual worker, a group of workers, or the overall firm. A professional baseball player may receive bonuses for a high batting average, the number of home runs hit, or the number of runs batted in. A business manager may receive a bonus based on the profitability of her or his unit. Profit-sharing plans allocate a percentage of a firm's profit to its employees. Such plans, for example, have in recent years resulted in large annual payments to many U.S. autoworkers.

Global Perspective 28-2 compares the extent of participation of workers in profit-sharing plans in various nations.

Efficiency Wages

The notion of *efficiency wages* suggests employers might get greater effort from their workers by paying them relatively high, above-equilibrium wage rates. Glance back at Figure 28-3, which shows a competitive labor market where the equilibrium wage rate is $6. What if an employer decides to pay an above-equilibrium wage of $7 per hour? Rather than put the firm at a cost disadvantage compared with rival firms paying only $6, the higher wage *might*

Participation in profit-sharing plans, selected nations

The percentage of workers participating in profit-sharing plans varies substantially across countries.

Percentage of Workers Participating in Profit-Sharing Plans, 1995

France
Canada
United States
Germany
United Kingdom

Source: Organization for Economic Cooperation and Development.

---

improve worker effort and productivity so unit labor costs actually fall. For example, if each worker produces 10 units of output per hour at the $7 wage rate compared with only 6 units at the $6 wage rate, unit labor costs will be only $.70 (= $7 ÷ 10) for the high-wage firm as opposed to $1.00 (= $6 ÷ 6) for firms paying the equilibrium wage.

An above-equilibrium wage can enhance worker efficiency in several ways. The higher wage permits the firm to attract higher-quality workers. Worker morale should be higher. Turnover should be lower, resulting in a more experienced work force, greater worker productivity, and lower recruitment and training costs. Because the opportunity cost of losing a higher-wage job is greater, workers are more likely to put forth their best efforts with less supervision and monitoring. In fact, efficiency wage payments have proved effective for many employers.

Addenda: Negative Side Effects

Pay for performance can help overcome the principal-agent problem and enhance worker productivity. But such plans require careful design since they some-

times have negative side effects. Here are just a few examples:

1. The rapid production pace that piece rates elicit may result in poor product quality. It may also compromise the safety of workers. These outcomes can be costly to the firm over the long run.

2. Commissions may cause some salespeople to engage in questionable or even fraudulent sales practices, such as making exaggerated claims about products or recommending unneeded repairs. These practices can hurt the employer by leading to private lawsuits or government legal action.

3. Bonuses based on personal performance may disrupt the close cooperation needed for maximum team production. A professional basketball player who receives a bonus for points scored may be reluctant to pass the ball to teammates.

4. Since profit sharing is usually tied to the performance of the entire firm, less energetic workers can "free-ride" by obtaining their profit share on the basis of others' hard work.

5. There may be a downside to the reduced turnover resulting from above-market wages: Firms paying efficiency wages have fewer opportunities to hire *new* workers, yet this so-called new blood sometimes energizes a workplace.

QUICK REVIEW 28-3

■ Proponents of the minimum wage argue it is needed to assist the working poor and counter monopsony where it might exist; critics say it is poorly targeted and reduces employment.

■ Wage differentials are attributable in general to the forces of supply and demand, influenced by differences in workers' skills and nonmonetary differences in jobs. But several labor market imperfections also play a role.

■ As it applies to labor, the principal-agent problem is one of workers pursuing their own interests to the detriment of the employer's profit objective.

■ Pay-for-performance plans (piece rates, commissions, royalties, bonuses, profit sharing, and efficiency wages) are designed to improve worker productivity by overcoming the principal-agent problem

CHAPTER SUMMARY

1. The term "labor" encompasses all people who work for pay. The wage rate is the price paid per unit of time for labor. Labor earnings comprise total pay and are found by multiplying the number of hours worked by the hourly wage rate. The nominal wage rate is the amount of money received per unit of time; the real wage rate is the purchasing power of the nominal wage.

2. The long-run growth of real hourly earnings—the average real wage—roughly matches that of productivity, with both increasing over the long run. But real wage growth has stagnated since 1982, due to **(a)** a slowdown in productivity growth and **(b)** real wage growth which has not kept pace with productivity growth.

3. Global comparisons suggest that real wages in the United States are relatively high, but not the highest, internationally. High real wages in the advanced industrial countries stem largely from high labor productivity.

4. Specific wage rates depend on the structure of the particular labor market. In a competitive labor market the equilibrium wage rate and level of employment are determined at the intersection of the labor supply curve and labor demand curve. For the individual firm, the market wage rate establishes a horizontal labor supply curve, meaning that the wage rate equals the firm's constant marginal resource cost. The firm hires workers to the point where its MRP equals this MRC.

5. Under monopsony the marginal resource cost curve lies above the resource supply curve because the monopsonist must bid up the wage rate to hire extra workers and must pay that higher wage rate to *all* workers. The monopsonist hires fewer workers than are hired under competi-

tive conditions, pays less-than-competitive wage rates (has lower labor costs), and thus obtains greater profit.

6. A union may raise competitive wage rates by **(a)** increasing the derived demand for labor, **(b)** restricting the supply of labor through exclusive unionism, or **(c)** directly enforcing an above-equilibrium wage rate through inclusive unionism.

7. In many industries the labor market takes the form of bilateral monopoly, in which a strong union "sells" labor to a monopsonistic employer. The wage rate outcome of this labor market model depends on union and employer bargaining power.

8. On average, unionized workers realize wage rates 10 to 15 percent higher than comparable nonunion workers.

9. Economists disagree about the desirability of the minimum wage as an antipoverty mechanism. While it causes unemployment for some low-income workers, it raises the incomes of others who retain their jobs.

10. Wage differentials are largely explainable in terms of **(a)** noncompeting groups arising from differences in the capacities and education of different groups of workers; **(b)** compensating wage differences, that is, wage differences which must be paid to offset nonmonetary differences in jobs; and **(c)** market imperfections in the form of lack of job information, geographical immobility, union and government restraints, and discrimination.

11. The principal-agent problem arises when workers provide less-than-expected effort. Firms may combat this by monitoring workers or by creating incentive pay schemes which link worker compensation to effort.

TERMS AND CONCEPTS

nominal wage
real wage
purely competitive labor
  market

monopsony
exclusive unionism
occupational licensing
inclusive unionism

bilateral monopoly
minimum wage
wage differentials
noncompeting groups

human capital investment
compensating differences
incentive pay plan

STUDY QUESTIONS

1. Explain why the general level of wages is high in the United States and other industrially advanced countries. What is the most important single factor underlying the long-run increase in average real wage rates in the United States?

2. What factors might explain the stagnation of real wages in the United States in the past two decades?

3. **KEY QUESTION** Describe wage determination in a labor market in which workers are unorganized and many firms actively compete for the services of labor. Show this situation graphically, using W_1 to indicate the equilibrium wage rate and Q_1 to show the number of workers hired by the firm as a group. Show the labor supply curve of the individual firm and compare it with that of the total market. Why the differences? In the diagram representing the firm, identify total revenue, total wage cost, and revenue available for the payment of nonlabor resources.

4. KEY QUESTION Complete the following labor supply table for a firm hiring labor competitively:

Units of labor	Wage rate	Total labor cost (wage bill)	Marginal resource (labor) cost
0	$14	$_____	
1	14	_____	$_____
2	14	_____	_____
3	14	_____	_____
4	14	_____	_____
5	14	_____	_____
6	14	_____	_____

a. Show graphically the labor supply and marginal resource (labor) cost curves for this firm. Explain the relationship of these curves to one another.

b. Plot the labor demand data of question 2 in Chapter 27 on the graph used in *a*. What is the equilibrium wage rate and level of employment? Explain.

5. Suppose the formerly competing firms in question 3 form an employers' association which hires labor as a monopsonist would. Describe verbally the effect on wage rates and employment. Adjust the graph you drew for question 3, showing the monopsonistic wage rate and employment level as W_2 and Q_2, respectively. Using this monopsony model, explain why hospital administrators sometimes complain about a "shortage" of nurses. How might such a "shortage" be corrected?

6. KEY QUESTION Assume a firm is a monopsonist which can hire its first worker for $6 but must increase the wage rate by $3 to attract each successive worker. Draw the firm's labor supply and marginal labor cost curves and explain their relationships to one another. On the same graph, plot the labor demand data of question 2 in Chapter 27. What are the equilibrium wage rate and level of employment? Why do these differ from your answer to question 4?

7. KEY QUESTION Assume a monopsonistic employer is paying a wage rate of W_m and hiring Q_m workers, as indicated in Figure 28-8. Now suppose an industrial union is formed and it forces the employer to accept a wage rate of W_c. Explain verbally and graphically why in this instance the higher wage

rate will be accompanied by an increase in the number of workers hired.

8. On average, do union workers receive higher wages than comparable nonunion workers?

9. "Many of the lowest-paid people in society—for example, short-order cooks—also have relatively poor working conditions. Hence, the notion of compensating wage differentials is disproved." Do you agree? Explain.

10. What is meant by investment in human capital? Use this concept to explain **(a)** wage differentials, and **(b)** the long-run rise of real wage rates in the United States.

11. What is the principal-agent problem? Have you ever worked in a setting where this problem has arisen? If so, do you think increased monitoring would have eliminated the problem? Why don't firms simply hire more supervisors to eliminate shirking?

12. (Last Word) Do you think that African-style hairbraiders should be allowed to braid hair without a cosmetology license? If so, do you think that you would have the same view if you were a licensed cosmetologist?

13. WEB-BASED QUESTION Real Wages and Productivity—Are Workers' Paychecks Keeping Up? The long-run growth of real wages is correlated with labor productivity. Check the Bureau of Labor Statistics http://stats.bls.gov/gov/lprhome.htm for current labor productivity and cost data. Go to Durable manufacturing sector: Productivity, hourly compensation, and unit labor costs, seasonally adjusted, and compare the indexes for Output per hour of all persons, Compensation per hour, and Real compensation per hour. Compared to the base year, rank the indexes. What should be the ranking according to economic theory? Is compensation (both actual and real) per hour keeping up with output per hour? Are workers' paychecks keeping up?

14. WEB-BASED QUESTION Top Sports Salaries in Football, Basketball, and Baseball—Is There Equality? In poll after poll, professional football has been called the country's most popular sport. It commands billions from TV contracts. Yet the top football salaries pale in comparison with the mega contracts players in other professional sports sign. Use the major sports sites http://espn.sportszone.com/, http://www.cnnsi.com/, and http://cbs.sportsline.com/ to identify the top yearly salary in the National Football League, the National Basketball Association, and the Major Baseball Leagues. Which league has the highest salaried player? Speculate as to why. What is the difference between productivity on the field and the productivity of business revenue which the game generates?

CHAPTER TWENTY-NINE

Rent, Interest, and Profit

We began the previous chapter with some facts and questions about wages. We do the same here for three other sources of income: rent, interest, and profit.

- *Fact:* In urban areas such as Tokyo or Hong Kong, an acre of land may sell for more than $85 million. An acre of desert may cost $700,000 along the Las Vegas casino strip, while an acre of land in the middle of the Nevada desert can be purchased for as little as $50. *Question:* How do land prices and rents get established?
- *Fact:* If you put money in a 3-month certificate of deposit (CD) in early 1991, you probably received an interest rate of 7 percent. One year later that CD paid only 3.7 percent interest. In early 1998 the interest rate on this type of CD was 4.3 percent. *Question:* What factors determine interest rates and cause those rates to change?
- *Fact:* The news media continually document the annual profit and loss performance of firms and industries. In 1995, Allstate Insurance's profit was up 293 percent from the year earlier, Dow Chemical had a 122 percent profit increase, and Intel's profit increased by 56 percent. Meanwhile, Mead Paper's profit declined by 51 percent, Kellogg's profit was down 31 percent, and PepsiCo's profit was down 10 percent. All these firms were profitable, but a few major firms (Boston Market, Apple Computer) suffered losses in 1995. *Questions:* What are the sources of profits and losses? What functions do they serve? What causes profits and losses of individual firms to change over time?

Our emphasis in Chapter 28 was on labor markets; wages account for about three-fourths of national income in the United States. In this chapter we focus on rent, interest, and profit, which compose the remaining one-fourth of national income.

ECONOMIC RENT

To most people "rent" means the money one must pay for a two-bedroom apartment or a dormitory room. To the business executive "rent" is a payment made for the use of a factory building, machine, or warehouse facility. These common definitions of rent can be confusing and ambiguous. Dormitory room rent, for example, may include other payments as well—interest on money the university borrowed to finance the dormitory, wages for custodial services, utility payments, and so on.

Economists use "rent" in a narrower sense. **Economic rent** *is the price paid for the use of land and other natural resources that are completely fixed in total supply.* The unique supply conditions of land and other natural resources—their fixed overall supply—make rental payments distinguishable from wage, interest, and profit payments.

Let's examine this idea and some of its implications through supply and demand analysis. We first assume that all land is of the same grade or quality; each arable (tillable) acre of land is as productive as every other acre. Suppose, too, that all land has a single use: producing corn. And also assume that land is rented in a competitive market in which many corn farmers are demanding land and many landowners are offering land in the market.

In Figure 29-1, curve S represents the supply of arable farmland available in the economy as a whole, and D_2 the demand of farmers for use of that land. As with all economic resources, this demand is derived from the demand for the product being produced. The demand curve for land is downsloping because of diminishing returns and because, for farmers as a group, product price must be reduced to sell additional units of output.

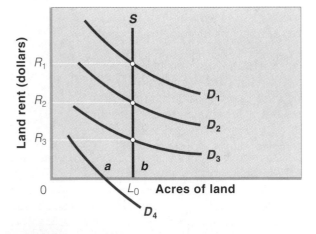

FIGURE 29-1 **The determination of land rent** Because the supply S of land (and other natural resources) is perfectly inelastic, demand is the sole active determinant of land rent. An increase in demand from D_2 to D_1 or a decrease in demand from D_2 to D_3 will cause a considerable change in rent: from R_2 to R_1 in the first instance and from R_2 to R_3 in the second. But the amount of land supplied will remain at L_0. If demand is very weak (D_4) relative to supply, land will be a "free good," commanding no rent.

Perfectly Inelastic Supply

The unique feature of our analysis is on the supply side. For all practical purposes the supply of land is perfectly inelastic, as reflected in supply curve S. Land has no production cost; it is a "free and nonreproducible gift of nature." The economy has only so much land, and that is that. Of course, within limits any parcel of land can be made more usable by clearing, drainage, and irrigation. But these are capital improvements and not changes in the amount of land itself. Also, these increases in the usability of land affect only a small fraction of the total amount of land and do not change the basic fact that land and other natural resources are virtually fixed in supply.

Changes in Demand

Because the supply of land is fixed, demand is the only active determinant of land rent; supply is passive. And what determines the demand for land? The factors discussed in Chapter 27: the price of the product grown on the land, the productivity of land (which depends in part on the quantity and quality of the resources with which land is combined), and the prices of the other resources which are combined with land.

If the demand for land in Figure 29-1 should increase from D_2 to D_1, land rent would increase from R_2 to R_1. On the other hand, if the demand for land declined from D_2 to D_3, land rent would fall from R_2 to R_3. But, in either case, the amount of land supplied would remain the same at L_0. Changes in economic rent can have no effect on the amount of land available since the supply of land cannot be augmented. If the demand for land were only D_4, land rent would be zero. Land would be a *free good*—one whose demand is so weak relative to supply that there is an excess supply of it even if the market price is zero. In Figure 29-1, this excess supply is shown as distance $b - a$ at rent of zero. This situation was approximated in the free-land era of U.S. history.

Figure 29-1 helps explain the high Japanese land prices noted at the start of this chapter. Japan's population is 120 million, roughly one-half that of the United States. Japan's land area, however, is only about 4 percent of that of the United States. Additionally, habitable land in Japan is roughly 1/60th that of the United States. Knowing land is in such short supply, we can see why 1 square meter of land in central Tokyo was priced at about $250,000 in 1997.

Land Rent: A Surplus Payment

The perfectly inelastic supply of land must be contrasted with the relatively elastic supply of capital, such as apartment buildings, machinery, and warehouses. In the long run, capital is *not* fixed in total supply. A higher price gives entrepreneurs the incentive to construct and offer larger quantities of these property resources. Conversely, a decline in price induces suppliers to allow existing facilities to depreciate and not be replaced. The supply curves of these nonland resources are upsloping, meaning the prices paid to such resources provide an **incentive function.** A high price provides an incentive to offer more of the resource; a low price, an incentive to offer less.

Not so with land. Rent serves no incentive function because the total supply of land is fixed. Whether rent is $10,000, $500, $1, or $0 per acre, the same amount of land is available to society for use in production, which is why economists consider rent a *surplus payment* not necessary to ensure that land is available to the economy as a whole.

A Single Tax on Land

If land is a free gift of nature, costs nothing to produce, and would be available even without rental payments, why should rent be paid to those who by historical accident, by inheritance, or by crook happen to be landowners? Socialists have long argued that all land rents are unearned incomes. They argue land should be nationalized—owned by the state—so that any payments for its use can be used by the government to further the well-being of the entire population rather than being used by a landowning minority.

Henry George's Proposal In the United States, criticism of rental payments has taken the form of a **single-tax movement,** which gained much support in the late nineteenth century. Spearheaded by Henry George's provocative book *Progress and Poverty* (1879), this reform movement maintained that economic rent could be taxed away without impairing the available supply of land or, therefore, the productive potential of the economy as a whole.

George observed that as population grew and the geographic frontier closed, landowners enjoyed larger and larger rents from their landholdings. These increasing rents were the result of a growing demand for a resource whose supply was perfectly inelastic. Some landlords were receiving fabulously high incomes not through their productive effort but solely from holding advantageously located land. George stated that these increases in land rent belonged to the economy; he held that land rents should be heavily taxed and the revenue spent for public uses.

George held that there was no reason to tax away, say, only 50 percent of the landowner's unearned rental income. Why not take 70 or 90 or 99 percent? In seeking popular support for his ideas on land taxation, George proposed that taxes on rental income be the *only* tax levied by government.

George's case for taxing land was based not only on equity or fairness but also on efficiency. That is, a tax on land is efficient because, unlike virtually every other tax, it does not alter the use of the resource. A tax on wages reduces after-tax wages and can weaken incentives to work; an individual who decides to work for a $6 before-tax wage may decide to quit and go on welfare when an income tax reduces the wage to an after-tax $4.50. Similarly, a property tax on buildings lowers returns to investors in such property and might cause some to look for other investments. But no such reallocations of resources occur when land is taxed. The most profitable use of land before it is taxed remains the most profitable use after a tax is imposed. Of course, a landlord could withdraw land from production when a tax is imposed, but this would mean no rental income at all. Some rental income, no matter how small, is better than none.

Criticisms Critics of the single tax on land say:

1. Current levels of government spending are such that a land tax alone would not bring in enough revenue; it cannot be considered realistically as a *single* tax.

2. Most income payments involve two or more elements of interest, rent, wages, and profits. Land is typically improved in some way, and economic rent cannot be readily disentangled from payments for such improvements. In practice, it would be difficult to determine how much of any specific income payment is actually economic rent.

3. So-called unearned income accrues to many people other than landowners, especially with a growing economy. For example, consider the *capital gains* income received by someone who, some 20 or 25 years ago, chanced to purchase (or inherit) stock in a firm which has experienced rapid growth. How is this income more "earned" than the rental income of the landowner?

4. Historically, a piece of land is likely to have changed ownership many times. Former owners may have been the beneficiaries of past increases in the value of the land (and in land rent). It is hardly fair to place a heavy tax on current owners who paid the competitive market price for the land.

Productivity Differences and Rent Differences

Thus far we have assumed all units of land are of the same grade. This is plainly not so. Different pieces of land vary greatly in productivity, depending on soil fertility and such climatic factors as rainfall and temperature. These factors explain, for example, why Iowa soil is excellently suited to corn production, the plains of Colorado are much less well suited, and the desert of Arizona is incapable of corn production. Such productivity differences are reflected in resource demand and prices. Competitive bidding by farmers will establish a high rent for the very productive Iowa land; less productive Colorado land will command a much lower rent; and Arizona desert land perhaps will command no rent at all.

Location may be equally important in explaining differences in land rent. Other things equal, renters will pay more for a unit of land which is strategically located with respect to materials, labor, and customers than for a unit of land whose location is remote from these things. Examples: the enormously high land rents in large metropolitan areas and at the bases of major alpine ski areas.

The rent differentials arising from quality differences in land can be seen by viewing Figure 29-1 from a slightly different perspective. Suppose, as before, that only corn can be produced on four grades of land, each of which is available in the fixed amount L_0. When combined with identical amounts of labor, capital, and entrepreneurial talent, the productivity or, more specifically, the marginal revenue product of each of the four grades of land is reflected in demand curves D_1, D_2, D_3, and D_4. Grade 1 land is the most productive, as shown by D_1, while grade 4 is the least productive, as shown by D_4. The resulting economic rents for grades 1, 2, and 3 land will be R_1, R_2, and R_3, respectively; the rent differential will mirror the differences in productivity of the three grades of land. Grade 4 land is so poor in quality that, given its supply S, farmers won't pay to use it. It will be a free good because it is not sufficiently scarce in relation to the demand for it to command a price and a rent.

Alternative Uses of Land

We have also supposed that land has only one use. Actually, we know that land normally has alternative uses. An acre of Iowa farmland may be useful in raising not only corn but also wheat, oats, barley, and cattle; or it may be used for a house, highway, or factory site. This tells us that a particular use of land involves an opportunity cost—the forgone production from the next best use of the resource. Where there are alternative uses, individual firms must pay rent to cover these opportunity costs if they are to secure the use of land for their particular purposes. To individual firms rent is a cost of production, just like wages and interest.

Recall that, as viewed by society, economic rent is *not* a cost. Society would have the same amount of land with or without the payment of economic rent. From society's perspective economic rent is a surplus payment above that needed for society to gain the use of a resource. But individual firms *do* need to pay rent to attract land resources away from alternative uses; for firms, rental payments are a *cost*. **(Key Question 2)**

QUICK REVIEW 29-1

■ Economic rent is the price paid for resources such as land whose supply is perfectly inelastic.

■ Land rent is a surplus payment because land would be available to society even if this rent were not paid.

■ The surplus nature of land rent was the basis for Henry George's single-tax movement.

■ Differential rents allocate land among alternative uses.

INTEREST

Interest is the price paid for the use of money. It is, in essence, the amount of money which must be paid for the use of $1 for 1 year.

1. *Interest is stated as a percentage.* Interest is paid in kind; that is, money (interest) is paid for the loan of money. For that reason, interest is typically stated as a percentage of the amount of money borrowed rather than as a dollar amount. It is less clumsy to say that interest is "12 percent annually" than to say that interest is "$120 per year per $1000." Also, stating interest as a percentage makes it easier to compare interest paid on loans of different amounts. By expressing interest as a percentage, we can immediately compare an interest payment of, say, $432 per year per $2880 with one of $1800 per year per $12,000. Both interest payments are 15 percent per year, which is not obvious from the actual dollar figures. This interest of 15 percent per year is referred to as a 15 percent interest rate.

2. *Money is not a resource.*   Money is *not* an economic resource. As coins, paper currency, or checking accounts, money is not productive; it cannot produce goods and services. However, businesses "buy" the use of money because it can be used to acquire capital goods—factories, machinery, warehouses, and so on. These facilities clearly do contribute to production. Thus, in "hiring" the use of money capital, business executives are often indirectly buying the use of real capital goods.

Loanable Funds Theory of Interest

In *macroeconomics* the interest rate is viewed through the lens of the economy's total supply of and demand for money. But since our present focus is microeconomics, it will be useful to consider a more micro-based theory of interest here. Specifically, the **loanable funds theory of interest** explains the interest rate not in terms of the total supply of and demand for *money* but, rather, in terms of the supply of and demand for *funds available for lending (and borrowing)*. As shown in Figure 29-2, the equilibrium interest rate (here, 8 percent) is the rate at which the quantities of loanable funds supplied and demanded are equal.

Let's first consider the loanable funds theory in a simplified form. Specifically, assume households or consumers are the sole suppliers of loanable funds and businesses are the only demanders. Also suppose that lending occurs directly between households and businesses; there are no intermediate financial institutions.

Supply of Loanable Funds   The supply of loanable funds is represented as curve *S* in Figure 29-2. Its upward slope indicates that households will make available a larger quantity of funds at high interest rates than at low interest rates. Most people prefer to use their incomes to purchase pleasurable goods and services *today*, rather than delay purchases to sometime in the *future*. For people to delay consumption— that is, to increase their saving—they must be "bribed" or compensated by an interest payment. The larger

FIGURE 29-2 The market for loanable funds   The up-sloping supply curve *S* for loanable funds reflects the idea that at higher interest rates, households will defer more of their present consumption (save more) making more funds available for lending. The downsloping demand curve *D* for loanable funds indicates that businesses will borrow more at lower interest rates than at higher interest rates. At the equilibrium interest rate (here, 8 percent) the quantities of loanable funds lent and borrowed are equal (here, F_0 each).

the amount of this payment, the greater the deferral of household consumption and thus the greater the amount of money made available for loans.

There is disagreement among economists as to how much the quantity of loanable funds made available by suppliers changes in response to changes in the interest rate. Most economists view saving as being relatively insensitive to changes in the interest rate. The supply curve of loanable funds may therefore be more inelastic than implied by *S* in Figure 29-2.

Demand for Loanable Funds   Businesses borrow loanable funds primarily to add to their stocks of capital goods—new plants or warehouses, machinery, and equipment. Suppose a firm wants to buy a machine which will increase output and sales such that its total revenue will rise by $110 for the year. Also assume the machine costs $100 and has a useful life of just 1 year. Comparing the $10 earned beyond the cost of the machine with the $100 cost, we find that the *expected rate of return* on this investment is 10 percent (= $10/$100) for the 1 year.

To determine whether the investment is profitable and should be made, the firm must compare the interest rate—the price of loanable funds—with the 10 percent expected rate of return. If funds can be borrowed at some rate less than the rate of return, say, at 8 percent, as in Figure 29-2, then the investment is profitable and should be undertaken. But if funds are available only at an interest rate above the 10 percent rate of return, say, at 14 percent, this investment is unprofitable and should not be made.

Why is the demand for loanable funds downsloping, as in Figure 29-2? At higher interest rates fewer investment projects will be profitable to businesses and hence a smaller quantity of loanable funds will be demanded. At lower interest rates, more investment projects will be profitable and therefore more loanable funds will be demanded. Indeed, we have just seen in our example that it is profitable to purchase the $100 machine if funds can be borrowed at 8 percent but not if the firm must borrow at 14 percent.

Extending the Model

We now make this simple model more realistic in several ways.

Financial Institutions Households rarely lend their savings directly to the businesses which are borrowing funds for investment. Instead, households place their savings in banks (and other financial institutions). The banks pay interest to savers to attract loanable funds and in turn lend these funds to businesses. Businesses borrow the funds from the banks, paying them interest for the use of the money. Financial institutions profit by charging borrowers higher interest rates than the interest rates they pay savers. Both these interest rates, however, are based on the supply of and demand for loanable funds.

Changes in Supply Anything which causes households to be more thrifty will prompt them to save more at each interest rate, shifting the supply curve rightward. For example, if interest earned on savings were suddenly exempted from taxation, we would expect the supply of loanable funds to increase and the equilibrium interest rate to decrease.

Conversely, a decline in thriftiness would shift the supply-of-loanable-funds curve leftward and increase the equilibrium interest rate. Illustration: If government expanded social insurance to more fully cover the costs of hospitalization and retirement, the incentives of households to save might diminish.

Changes in Demand On the demand side, anything which increases the rates of return on potential investments will increase the demand for loanable funds. Let's return to our earlier example, where a firm would receive additional revenue of $110 by purchasing a $100 machine and, therefore, would realize a 10 percent return on investment. What factors might increase or decrease the rate of return? Suppose a technological advance raises the productivity of the machine so that it increases the firm's total revenue by $120 rather than $110. The rate of return is now 20 percent, not 10 percent. Before the technological advance the firm would have demanded zero loanable funds at, say, an interest rate of 14 percent. But now it will demand $100 of loanable funds at that interest rate, meaning the demand curve for loanable funds has been shifted to the right.

Similarly, an increase in consumer demand for the firm's product will increase the price of its product. So even though the productivity of the machine is unchanged, its potential revenue will rise from $110 to perhaps $120, increasing its rate of return from 10 to 20 percent. Again the firm will be willing to borrow more than previously at our presumed 8 or 14 percent interest rate, implying that the demand curve for loanable funds has shifted rightward. This shift in demand increases the equilibrium interest rate.

Conversely, a decline in productivity or in the price of the firm's product would shift the demand curve for loanable funds leftward, reducing the equilibrium interest rate.

Other Participants We must recognize there are more participants on both the demand and supply sides of the loanable funds market. For example, while households are suppliers of loanable funds, many are also demanders of those funds. Households borrow to finance expensive purchases such as housing, automobiles, furniture, and household appliances. Governments are also on the demand side of the loanable funds market when they borrow to finance budgetary deficits. Similarly, businesses which have revenues in excess of their current expenditures may offer some of those revenues in the market for loanable funds. Thus, like households, businesses operate on both the supply and demand sides of the market.

Finally, if you have studied macroeconomics, you will recall that banks and other financial institutions not only gather and make available the savings of households but also *create* funds through the lending process. This bank creation of money is another source of loanable funds. **(Key Question 4)**

Range of Interest Rates

Although economists often speak in terms of a single interest rate, there are in reality a number of interest rates. Table 29-1 lists several interest rates often referred to in the media. These rates range from 5 to 16 percent. Why the differences?

1. *Risk*   Loans to different borrowers for different purposes carry varying degrees of risk. The greater the chance that the borrower will not repay the loan, the more interest the lender will charge to compensate for this risk.

2. *Maturity*   The time length or *maturity* of a loan also affects the interest rate. Other things equal, longer-term loans command higher interest rates than shorter-term loans. The long-term lender suffers the inconvenience and possible financial sacrifice of forgoing alternative uses for his or her money for a greater period of time.

3. *Loan size*   If there are two loans of equal maturity and risk, the interest rate on the smaller of the two loans usually will be higher. The costs of issuing a large loan and a small loan are about the same in dollars, but the cost is greater as a percentage of the smaller loan.

4. *Taxability*   Interest on certain state and municipal bonds is exempt from Federal income taxation. Because lenders are interested in their after-tax rate of interest, borrowing by states and local governments can attract lenders even though these borrowers pay low interest rates. Consider a high-income lender who pays a 39.6 percent Federal income tax on marginal income. He or she may prefer a 6 percent interest rate on a tax-exempt municipal bond to an 8 percent taxable interest rate on a corporate bond.

5. *Market imperfections*   Market imperfections also explain some interest-rate differentials. The small-town bank which monopolizes local lending may charge high interest rates on consumer loans because households find it inconvenient and costly to "shop around" at banks in somewhat distant cities. The large corporation, on the other hand, can survey a number of rival lenders to float a new bond issue and secure the lowest obtainable rate.

Pure Rate of Interest

Economists talk of "the" interest rate to simplify the cluster of rates (Table 29-1). When they do so, they usually have in mind the **pure rate of interest.** The

TABLE 29-1   Selected interest rates, October 1997

Type of interest rate	Annual percentage
30-year Treasury bond rate (interest rate on Federal government security used to finance the public debt)	6.33%
90-day Treasury Bill rate (interest rate on Federal government security used to finance the public debt)	4.95
Prime interest rate (interest rate charged by banks to their best corporate customers)	8.50
30-year mortgage rate (fixed-interest rate on loans for houses)	7.29
4-year automobile loan rate (interest rate for new autos by automobile finance companies)	7.27
Tax-exempt state and municipal bond rate (interest rate paid on a low-risk bond issued by a state or local government)	5.38
Federal funds rate (interest rate on overnight loans between banks)	5.50
Consumer credit card rate (interest rate charged for credit card purchases)	15.75

Source: Federal Reserve data.

pure rate is best approximated by the interest paid on long-term, virtually riskless securities such as long-term bonds of the U.S. government (30-year Treasury bonds). This interest payment can be thought of as being made solely for the use of money over an extended time period, because risk and administrative costs are negligible and the interest rate on these bonds is not distorted by market imperfections. In fall 1997 the pure rate of interest in the United States was 6.3 percent.

Role of the Interest Rate

The interest rate is a critical price; it affects both the *level* and the *composition* of investment goods production, as well as the *amount* of R&D spending.

Interest and Total Output A lower equilibrium interest rate encourages more borrowing by businesses for investment. Total spending in the economy therefore rises, and if the economy has unused resources, so does total output. Conversely, a higher equilibrium interest rate discourages business borrowing for investment, reducing investment and total spending. Such a decrease in spending may be desirable if an economy is experiencing inflation.

Government often manipulates the interest rate to try to expand investment and output, on the one hand, or reduce investment and inflation, on the other. If you have studied macroeconomics, you know that government affects the interest rate by changing the supply of money. Increases in the money supply increase the supply of loanable funds, causing the equilibrium interest rate to fall. This boosts investment spending and expands the economy. In contrast, decreases in the money supply decrease the supply of loanable funds, boosting the equilibrium interest rate. As a result, investment is constrained and so is the economy.

Interest and the Allocation of Capital Prices are rationing devices. The interest rate is no exception; it rations the available supply of loanable funds to investment projects whose rate of return or expected profitability is sufficiently high to allow payment of the going interest rate.

If, say, the computer industry expects to earn a return of 12 percent on the money it invests in physical capital and it can secure the required funds at an interest rate of 8 percent, it can borrow and expand its physical capital. If the expected rate of return on additional capital in the steel industry is only 6 percent, that industry will find it unprofitable to expand its capital at 8 percent interest. The interest rate allocates money, and ultimately physical capital, to those industries in which it will be most productive and therefore most profitable. Such an allocation of capital goods is in the interest of society as a whole.

But the interest rate does not perfectly ration capital to its most productive uses. Large oligopolistic borrowers are in a better position than competitive borrowers to pass interest costs on to consumers because they are able to change prices by controlling output. Also, the size and prestige of large industrial concerns may help them obtain funds on more favorable terms than can less-well-known firms with superior profit expectations.

Interest and the Level and Composition of R&D Spending Recall from Chapter 26 that like the investment decision, the decision on how much to spend on R&D depends on the cost of borrowing funds in relationship to the expected rate of return. Other things equal, the *lower* the interest rate—that is, the less the cost of borrowing funds for R&D—the greater the amount of R&D spending which is profitable. The *higher* the interest rate, the less the amount of R&D spending.

Also, the interest rate allocates R&D funds to those firms and industries for which the expected rate of return on R&D is the greatest. Ace Microcircuits may have an expected rate of return of 16 percent on an R&D project, while Glow Paints has a 2 percent expected rate of return on its project. With the interest rate at 8 percent, loanable funds will flow to Ace, not to Glow. Society will benefit by having R&D spending allocated to projects with sufficiently high expected rates of return to justify using scarce resources for R&D rather than for other purposes.

Nominal and Real Interest Rates This discussion of the role of the interest rate in the investment and R&D decisions assumes no inflation. If inflation occurs, we must distinguish between nominal and real *interest rates*, just like we needed to distinguish between nominal and real *wages* in the previous chapter. The **nominal interest rate** is the rate of interest expressed in dollars of current value. The **real interest rate** is the rate of interest expressed in purchasing power—dollars of inflation-adjusted value. (For a comparison of *nominal* interest rates on bank loans in selected countries, see Global Perspective 29-1.)

An example will clarify this distinction. Suppose the nominal interest rate and rate of inflation are both 10 percent. If you borrow $100, you must pay back $110 a year from now. However, because of 10 percent inflation, each of these 110 dollars will be worth 10 percent less. Thus, the real value or purchasing power of your $110 at the end of the year is only $100. In inflation-adjusted dollars you are borrowing $100 and at year's end paying back $100. While the nominal interest rate is 10 percent, the real interest rate is zero. We determine this by subtracting the 10 percent inflation rate from the 10 percent nominal interest rate.

It is the real interest rate, not the nominal rate, which affects investment and R&D decisions. **(Key Question 6)**

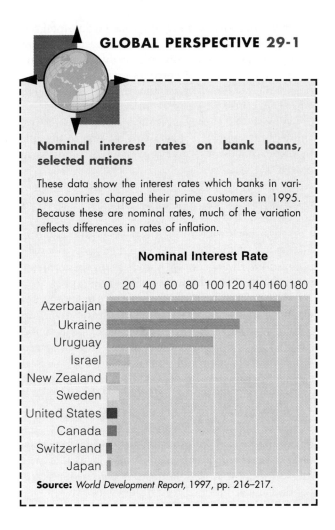

Nominal interest rates on bank loans, selected nations

These data show the interest rates which banks in various countries charged their prime customers in 1995. Because these are nominal rates, much of the variation reflects differences in rates of inflation.

Nominal Interest Rate

Source: *World Development Report,* 1997, pp. 216–217.

Application: Usury Laws

A number of states have passed **usury laws,** which specify a maximum interest rate at which loans can be made. The purpose is to hold down the interest cost of borrowing, particularly for low-income borrowers. ("Usury" simply means exorbitant interest.)

We can assess the impact of such legislation with the help of Figure 29-2. The equilibrium interest rate there is 8 percent, but suppose a usury law specifies that lenders cannot charge more than 6 percent. The effects are as follows:

1. *Nonmarket rationing* At 6 percent the quantity of loanable funds demanded exceeds the quantity supplied: there is a shortage of loanable funds. The market interest rate no longer can ration the available loanable funds to borrowers, so lenders (banks) have to do the rationing. We can expect

them to make loans only to the most creditworthy borrowers (mainly wealthy, high-income people), which defeats the goal of the usury law. Low-income, riskier borrowers are excluded from the market and may be forced to turn to loan sharks who charge illegally high interest rates.

2. *Gainers and losers* Creditworthy borrowers gain from usury laws because they pay below-market interest rates. Lenders (ultimately bank shareholders) are losers, receiving 6 percent rather than 8 percent on each dollar loaned.

3. *Inefficiency* We just discussed how the equilibrium interest rate allocates money to the investments and R&D projects whose expected rate of return is greatest. Under usury laws, funds are much less likely to be allocated by banks to the most productive projects. Suppose Wilson has a project so promising she would pay 8 percent for funds to finance it. Chen has a less promising investment, and he would be willing to pay only 6 percent for financing. If the market rationed funds, Wilson's highly productive project would receive funds and Chen's would not. This allocation of funds is in the interest of both Wilson and society. But with a 6 percent usury rate, there is a 50-50 chance that Chen will be funded and Wilson will not. Legal maximum interest rates may ration funds to less-productive investments or R&D projects.

ECONOMIC PROFIT

As with rent, economists define profit narrowly. To accountants, "profit" is what remains of a firm's total revenue after it has paid individuals and other firms for the materials, capital, and labor they have supplied to the firm. To the economist, this definition overstates profit. The difficulty is that the accountant's view of profit considers only **explicit costs:** payments made by the firm to outsiders. It ignores **implicit costs:** the monetary income the firm sacrifices when it uses resources that it owns, rather than supplying those resources to the market. The economist considers implicit costs to be opportunity costs, and hence to be real costs which must be accounted for in determining profit. **Economic,** or **pure, profit** is what remains after all costs—both explicit and implicit costs, the latter including a normal profit—have been subtracted from a firm's total revenue. Economic profit may be either positive or negative (a loss).

For example, suppose a certain person owns her own bagel shop, including the land, building, and equipment, and also provides her own labor. As economists see it, she grossly overstates the economic profit if she merely subtracts from her total revenue her payments to outsiders for, say, baking ingredients, electricity, and insurance. She has not yet subtracted the cost of the resources *she* has contributed. Those costs are the rent, interest, and wage payments she could have received by making her land, labor, and capital resources available for alternative uses. They are her implicit costs, and they must be taken into account in determining her economic profit. She certainly would have to pay these costs if outsiders supplied these resources to her bagel shop.

Role of the Entrepreneur

The economist views profit as the return to a very special type of human resource: entrepreneurial ability. We know from previous chapters that the entrepreneur (1) combines resources to produce a good or service, (2) makes basic, nonroutine policy decisions for the firm, (3) introduces innovations in the form of new products or production processes, and (4) bears the economic risks associated with all these functions.

Part of the entrepreneur's return is a **normal profit.** This is the minimum payment necessary to retain the entrepreneur in the current line of production. We saw in Chapter 22 that normal profit is a cost—the cost of using entrepreneurial ability for a particular purpose. We saw also that a firm's total revenue may exceed its total cost; the excess revenue above all costs is its economic profit. This residual profit also goes to the entrepreneur. The entrepreneur is the *residual claimant:* the resource that receives what is left after all costs are paid.

Why should there be residual profit? We next examine three possible reasons, two relating to the risks involved in business and one based on monopoly power.

Sources of Economic Profit

Let's first construct an artificial economic environment where economic profit would be zero. Then, by noting how the real world differs from this environment, we will see where economic profit arises.

We begin with a purely competitive economy, and we make it also a static economy. A **static economy** is one in which the basic forces—such as resource supplies, technological knowledge, and consumer tastes—are constant and unchanging. As a result, all cost and supply data on the one hand, and all demand and revenue data on the other, are also constant.

Given the nature of these data, the economic future is *perfectly foreseeable;* there is *no uncertainty.* The outcome of any price or production policy can be *accurately predicted.* Furthermore, no product or production process is ever improved. Under pure competition any economic profit or loss which might have existed in an industry will disappear with the entry or exit of firms in the long run. All costs, explicit and implicit, are just covered in the long run, so there is no economic profit in our static economy.

The notion of zero economic profit in a static competitive economy suggests that profit is linked to the dynamic nature of real-world capitalism and its accompanying uncertainty. Moreover, it indicates that economic profit may arise from a source other than the directing, innovating, and risk-bearing functions of the entrepreneur. That source is the presence of some amount of monopoly power.

Risk and Profit In a real, dynamic economy the future is not predictable; it is uncertain. This means the entrepreneur must assume risks. Economic profit can be thought of in part as a reward for assuming these risks.

In linking economic profit with uncertainty and risk bearing, we must distinguish between risks which are insurable and those which are not. Some types of risks—fire, floods, theft, and accidents to employees—are measurable; that is, their frequency of occurrence can be estimated accurately. Firms can avoid losses due to **insurable risks** by paying an annual fee (an insurance premium) to an insurance company. The entrepreneur need not bear such risks.

However, the entrepreneur must bear the **uninsurable risks** of business, and it is those risks which are a potential source of economic profit. The uninsurable risks are mainly the uncontrollable and unpredictable changes in the demand and supply conditions facing the firm (and hence its revenues and costs). Uninsurable risks may stem from three general sources:

1. *Changes in the general economic environment* A downturn in business (a recession), for example, can lead to greatly reduced demand, sales, and revenues, and thus to business losses. A prosperous firm can suffer these losses through no fault of its own.

2. *Changes in the structure of the economy* Consumer tastes, technology, and resource availability and prices change constantly in the real world, bringing changes in production costs and revenues. For example, an airline earning economic profit one year may find its profit plunging the next due to a significant increase in the price of jet fuel.

3. *Changes in government policy* A newly instituted regulation, the removal of a tariff, or a change in national defense policy may significantly alter the cost and revenue data of the affected industry and firms.

Regardless of how such revenue and cost changes may come about, they are risks which the firm and entrepreneur must take to be in business. *Economic profit in a real, dynamic economy may be compensation for taking those risks.*

Innovations and Profit The uncertainties we just discussed are external to the firm, meaning they are beyond the control of the individual firm or industry. One other dynamic feature of capitalism—innovation—occurs at the initiative of the entrepreneur. Business firms deliberately introduce new methods of production to affect their costs favorably and new products to affect their revenues favorably. The entrepreneur purposely undertakes to upset existing cost and revenue data in a way which hopefully will be profitable.

But again, uncertainty enters the picture. Despite exhaustive market surveys, new products or modifications of existing products may be economic failures. Similarly, of the many new novels, textbooks, movies, and music albums appearing every year, only a handful garner large profits. Nor is it known with certainty whether new production machinery will actually yield projected cost economies. Thus, innovations undertaken by entrepreneurs entail uncertainty and the possibility of losses, not just the potential for increased profit. *Economic profit in an innovative economy may be compensation for dealing with the uncertainty of innovation.*

Monopoly and Profit Thus far, we have linked economic profit with the uncertainties surrounding (1) the dynamic environment to which enterprises are exposed, and (2) the dynamic business processes they initiate themselves. *The existence of monopoly in some form is a final source of economic profit.* Because a monopolist can restrict output and deter entry, it may persistently enjoy above-competitive prices and economic profit if demand is strong relative to cost.

Economic uncertainty and monopoly are closely intertwined as sources of economic profit. A firm with some monopoly power can reduce business risk, or at least manipulate it enough to reduce its adverse effects, and thus increase and prolong economic profit. Furthermore, a firm can use innovation as a source of monopoly power and a means of sustaining itself and its economic profit.

An important distinction between profit stemming from uncertainty and that from monopoly has to do with the social desirability of these two sources of profit. Bearing business risk and undertaking innovation in an uncertain economic environment are socially desirable functions. Obtaining monopoly profit is not so socially desirable. This profit typically is founded on reduced output, above-competitive prices, and economic inefficiency. **(Key Question 8)**

Functions of Profit

Economic profit is the main energizer of the capitalistic economy. It influences both the level of economic output and the allocation of resources among alternative uses.

Profit and Total Output It is the expectation of economic profit which induces firms to innovate. Their innovation stimulates new investment, increas-

Determining the Price of Credit

A variety of lending practices can cause the effective interest rate to be quite different from what it appears to be.

Borrowing and lending—receiving and granting credit—are a way of life. Individuals receive credit when they negotiate a mortgage loan and when they use their credit cards. Individuals make loans when they open a savings account in a commercial bank or buy a government bond.

It is sometimes difficult to determine exactly how much interest we pay and receive when we borrow and lend. Let's suppose that you borrow $10,000 which you agree to repay plus $1000 of interest at the end of 1 year. In this instance, the interest rate is 10 percent per year. To determine the interest rate i, we compare the interest paid with the amount borrowed:

$$i = \frac{\$1000}{\$10,000} = 10\%$$

But in some cases a lender, say, a bank, will *discount* the interest payment at the time the loan is made. Thus, in-

stead of giving the borrower $10,000, the bank discounts the $1000 interest payment in advance, giving the borrower only $9000. This increases the interest rate:

$$i = \frac{\$1000}{\$9000} = 11\%$$

While the absolute amount of interest paid is the same, in this second case the borrower has only $9000 available for the year.

An even more subtle point is that, to simplify their calculations, many financial institutions assume a 360-day year (twelve 30-day months). This means the borrower has the use of the lender's funds for 5 days less than the normal year. This use of a "short year" also increases the actual interest rate paid by the borrower.

The interest rate paid can change dramatically if a loan is repaid in installments. Suppose a bank lends you $10,000 and charges interest in the amount of $1000 to be paid at the end of the year. But the loan contract requires that you repay the $10,000 loan in 12 equal monthly installments. In effect, then, the average amount of the loan outstanding during the year is only $5000. Therefore:

$$i = \frac{\$1000}{\$5000} = 20\%$$

---

ing total output and employment. Thus, through innovation, it is the pursuit of profit which underlies economic growth.

Profit and Resource Allocation Profit is also effective in allocating resources among alternative lines of production. Entrepreneurs seek profit and shun losses. The occurrence of economic profit in an industry is a signal that society wants that particular industry to expand. It attracts resources from industries which are not profitable. But profit rewards are more than an inducement for an industry to expand; they also attract the financing which firms in that industry need for expansion. In contrast, losses penalize businesses which fail to adjust their productive efforts to the goods and services most preferred by customers. They signal society's desire for the afflicted industries to contract.

Profits and losses do not, however, result in an allocation of resources which is perfectly attuned to consumer preferences. The presence of monopoly, for example, impedes the shiftability of firms and resources from industry to industry in response to economic profit.

QUICK REVIEW 29-3

■ Pure or economic profit is what remains after all explicit and implicit costs (including a normal profit) are subtracted from a firm's total revenue.

■ Economic profit has three sources: the bearing of uninsurable risk, the uncertainty of innovation, and monopoly power.

■ Profit and profit expectations affect the levels of investment, total spending, and domestic output; profit and loss also allocate resources among alternative uses.

INCOME SHARES

Our discussion in this and the previous chapter would not be complete without a brief reexamination of how U.S. national income is distributed among wages, rent, interest, and profit.

Look back at Figure 5-1. Although the income categories shown in that chart do not neatly fit the economic definitions of wages, rent, interest, and profits, they do provide insights about income

Here interest is paid on the total amount of the loan ($10,000) rather than on the outstanding balance (which averages $5000 for the year), making for a much higher interest rate.

Another factor that influences the effective interest rate is whether or not interest is *compounded*. Suppose you deposit $10,000 in a savings account which pays a 10 percent interest rate compounded semiannually. In other words, interest is paid on your "loan" to the bank twice a year. At the end of the first 6 months, $500 of interest (10 percent of $10,000 for half a year) is added to your account. At the end of the year, interest is calculated on $10,500 so that the second interest payment is $525 (10 percent of $10,500 for half a year). Thus:

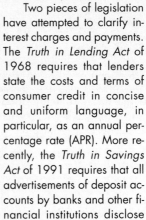

$$i = \frac{\$1025}{\$10,000} = 10.25\%$$

This means that a bank advertising a 10 percent interest rate compounded semiannually is actually paying more interest to its customers than a competitor paying a simple (noncompounded) interest rate of 10.20 percent.

Two pieces of legislation have attempted to clarify interest charges and payments. The *Truth in Lending Act* of 1968 requires that lenders state the costs and terms of consumer credit in concise and uniform language, in particular, as an annual percentage rate (APR). More recently, the *Truth in Savings Act* of 1991 requires that all advertisements of deposit accounts by banks and other financial institutions disclose all fees connected with such accounts, their interest rate, and the annual percentage return on each account. Nevertheless, some check cashing firms that lend money to people in return for postdated personal checks have been found to receive interest equivalent to 261 to 913 percent a year. "Let the borrower (or depositor) beware" remains a fitting motto in the world of credit.

shares in the United States. Note the dominant role of the labor resource and thus labor income in the U.S. economy. Even with labor income defined narrowly as "wages and salaries," labor receives about 71 percent of national income. But some economists contend that proprietors' income is largely composed of implicit wages and salaries and therefore should be added to the "wages and salaries" category to determine labor income. When we use this broad definition, *labor's share* rises to nearly 80 percent of national income, a percentage which has been remarkably stable in the United States since 1900. That leaves about 20 percent for capitalists in the form of rent, interest, and profit—a relatively small share considering we call the U.S. economy a capitalist system.

CHAPTER SUMMARY

1. Economic rent is the price paid for the use of land and other natural resources whose total supplies are fixed.

2. Rent is a surplus payment which is socially unnecessary since land would be available to the economy even without rental payments. The idea of land rent as a surplus payment gave rise to the single-tax movement of the late 1800s.

3. Differences in land rent result from differences in the fertility and climatic features of the land and differences in location.

4. Although land rent is a surplus payment rather than a cost to the economy as a whole, to individual firms and industries, rental payments are correctly regarded as costs. These payments must be made to gain the use of land, which has alternative uses.

5. Interest is the price paid for the use of money. In the loanable funds theory, the equilibrium interest rate is determined by the demand for and supply of loanable funds. Other things equal, changes in the supply of loanable funds cause the equilibrium interest rate to move in the opposite direction from the change in supply; changes in the demand for loanable funds cause the equilibrium interest rate to move in the same direction as the change in demand.

6. Interest rates vary in size because loans differ as to risk, maturity, amount, and taxability; market imperfections cause additional variations. The *pure rate of interest* is the interest rate on long-term, virtually riskless, 30-year U.S. Treasury bonds.

7. The equilibrium interest rate influences the level of investment and helps ration financial and physical capital to specific firms and industries. Similarly, this rate influences the size and composition of R&D spending. The *real interest rate*, not the nominal rate, is critical to investment and R&D decisions.

8. Although designed to make funds available to low-income borrowers, usury laws tend to allocate credit to high-income persons, subsidize high-income borrowers at the expense of lenders, and lessen the efficiency with which loanable funds are allocated.

9. Economic, or pure, profit is the difference between a firm's total revenue and the sum of its explicit and implicit costs, the latter including a normal profit. Profit accrues to entrepreneurs for assuming the uninsurable risks associated with organizing and directing economic resources and for innovating. Profit also results from monopoly power.

10. Profit expectations influence innovating and investment activities and therefore the economy's levels of employment and economic growth. The basic function of profits and losses, however, is to induce that allocation of resources most in accord with the tastes of consumers.

11. The largest share of national income—about 71 percent—goes to labor, a share narrowly defined as "wages and salaries." When labor's share is more broadly defined to include "proprietors' income," it rises to about 80 percent of national income. So-defined, labor's share has been remarkably stable since 1900.

TERMS AND CONCEPTS

economic rent
incentive function
single-tax movement
loanable funds theory of
  interest

pure rate of interest
nominal interest rate
real interest rate
usury laws

explicit costs
implicit costs
economic or pure profit
normal profit

static economy
insurable risks
uninsurable risks

STUDY QUESTIONS

1. How does the economist's use of the term "rent" differ from everyday usage? Explain: "Though rent need not be paid by society to make land available, rental payments are very useful in guiding land into the most productive uses."

2. KEY QUESTION Explain why economic rent is a surplus payment when viewed by the economy as a whole but a cost of production from the standpoint of individual firms and industries. Explain: "Rent performs no 'incentive function' in the economy."

3. If money is not an economic resource, why is interest paid and received for its use? What considerations account for interest rates differing greatly on various types of loans? Use these considerations to explain the relative sizes of the interest rates on the following:
a. A 10-year $1000 government bond
b. A $20 pawnshop loan

c. A 30-year mortgage loan on a $97,000 house
d. A 24-month $12,000 commercial bank loan to finance an automobile
e. A 60-day $100 loan from a personal finance company

4. KEY QUESTION Why is the supply of loanable funds upsloping? Why is the demand for loanable funds downsloping? Explain the equilibrium interest rate. List some factors which might cause it to change.

5. What are the major economic functions of the interest rate? How might the fact that many businesses finance their investment activities internally affect the efficiency with which the interest rate performs its functions?

6. KEY QUESTION Distinguish between nominal and real interest rates. Which is more relevant in making investment and R&D decisions? If the nominal interest rate is 12 percent and the inflation rate is 8 percent, what is the real rate of interest?

7. Historically, usury laws which put below-equilibrium ceilings on interest rates have been used by some states to make credit available to poor people who could not otherwise afford to borrow. Critics contend that it is poor people who are most likely to be hurt by such laws. Which view is correct?

8. KEY QUESTION   How do the concepts of accounting profit and economic profit differ? Why is economic profit smaller than accounting profit? What are the three basic sources of economic profit? Classify each of the following according to those sources:
   a. A firm's profit from developing and patenting a ballpoint pen containing a permanent ink cartridge
   b. A restaurant's profit which results from construction of a new highway past its door
   c. The profit received by a firm due to an unanticipated change in consumer tastes

9. Why is the distinction between insurable and uninsurable risks significant for the theory of profit? Carefully evaluate: "All economic profit can be traced to either uncertainty or the desire to avoid it." What are the major functions of economic profit?

10. Explain the absence of economic profit in a purely competitive, static economy. Realizing that the major function of profit is to allocate resources according to consumer preferences, describe the allocation of resources in such an economy.

11. What is the rent, interest, and profit share of national income if proprietors' income is included within the labor (wage) share? Has the capitalists' share (proprietors' income included as wages) increased, decreased, or stayed about the same since 1900?

12. (Last Word) Assume you borrow $5000 and pay back the $5000 plus $250 in interest at the end of the year. Assuming no inflation, what is the real interest rate? What would the interest rate be if the $250 of interest had been discounted at the time the loan was made? What would the interest rate be if you were required to repay the loan in 12 equal monthly installments?

13. WEB-BASED QUESTION   What's the Real Interest Today? The real interest rate is the nominal rate less the rate of inflation. Assume the Consumer Price Index (CPI) is a proxy for the inflation rate and 1-year Treasury Bill rates represent the nominal interest rate. Find the current CPI (percent changes in CPI for Urban Consumers, unadjusted 12-month ended current month) at http://stats.bls.gov/news.release/cpi.nws.htm, and then subtract it from the current 1-year U.S. Treasury Bill rate http://www.bog.frb.fed.us/releases/h15/update/. Repeat the process for the 3-month Treasury Bills and the CPI rate of change for the past 3 months (compounded annually). Is there a difference between the 3-month and the 12-month real interest rates? If so, why is there a difference?

14. WEB-BASED QUESTION   Corporate Profits— What Industry Makes the Most? The occurrence of economic profit in an industry is a signal that society wants that particular industry to expand. The Bureau of Economic Analysis has profit data for various industries in the United States. Go to http://www.bea.doc.gov/briefrm/tables/ebr7.htm. Based on current figures, which industry has the largest profits: **(a)** financial or nonfinancial; **(b)** manufacturing, transportation, wholesale trade, or retail trade; **(c)** durable goods or nondurable goods? During the past year, which sectors had the largest and smallest percentage increases? Which sectors are experiencing negative profits (i.e., losses)? What explains the profit differences?

7

Microeconomics of Government

30

Government and Market Failure: Public Goods, Externalities, and Information Problems

The economic activities of government affect your well-being every day. If you attend a public college or university, taxpayers subsidize your education. When you receive a check from your part-time or summer job, you see deductions for income and social security taxes. The beef in your Big Mac has been examined by government inspectors to prevent contamination and ensure quality. Laws requiring seat belts, motorcycle helmets, and the sprinkler system in your dormitory are all government mandates. If you are a woman, a member of a minority group, or a person with a disability, legislation has been designed to reduce discrimination and enhance your education and employment opportunities.

In this chapter and in Chapter 31 we examine the microeconomics of government. We begin by returning to the topic of *market failure* introduced in Chapter 5. In particular, marginal analysis permits us to provide a fuller discussion of public goods and externalities. Our discussion of externalities in turn facilitates an extensive discussion of pollution and pollution policies. Finally, we examine information failures in the private sector to determine their implications for government participation in the economy.

In Chapter 31 our discussion of the microeconomics of government continues with an analysis of potential government inefficiencies—so-called *government failure*—and the economics of taxation. Then in Part 8 we look at several microeconomic problems in which government has traditionally played some role.

PUBLIC GOODS: EXTENDING THE ANALYSIS

Recall from Chapter 5 that a private good is divisible; it comes in units small enough to be afforded by individual buyers. It is also subject to the exclusion principle: people unwilling or unable to pay for the product are barred from obtaining its benefits. Because of these characteristics, the demand for a private good gets expressed in the marketplace, and profit-seeking suppliers satisfy this demand. In contrast, a public good is indivisible and does *not* fit the exclusion principle; once the good is provided, the producer cannot bar nonpayers from obtaining the benefits. Consequently, the demand for the good gets understated in the marketplace, and firms thus lack a profit incentive to offer it for sale. If it is to exist, government will have to provide it. Two very simple examples will help clarify these ideas.

The market demand for a private good is the horizontal summation of the demand curves representing all individual buyers (review Table 3-2 and Figure 3-2). Suppose there are just two people in society who enjoy hot dogs, which cost $.80 each to produce. If Adams wants to buy 3 hot dogs at $1 each and Benson wants to buy 2 hot dogs at that same price, the market demand curve will reflect that 5 hot dogs are demanded at a $1 price. A seller charging $1 for each hot dog can gain $5 of revenue and earn $1 of profit ($5 of total revenue minus $4 of cost).

It is different with public goods. Suppose an enterprising sculptor creates a permanent piece of art costing $600 and places it in the town square. Also suppose that Adams gets $300 of enjoyment from the art and Benson gets $400. Sensing this enjoyment—and hoping to make a profit—the sculptor approaches Adams for a donation equal to his satisfaction. Adams falsely says that, unfortunately, he doesn't much like the art. The artist then tries Benson, hoping to get $400 or so. Same deal: Benson professes not to like the art either. Adams and Benson have become *free riders*. Although feeling a bit guilty, both reason that it makes no sense to pay for something when you can receive the benefits without paying for them. The artist is a quick learner; he vows not to try anything like *that* again.

Generalization: Because of the free-rider problem, the *market* demand for a public good is nonexistent or significantly understated. *Where a producer cannot exclude nonpayers from receiving the benefits from a good, it is difficult, if not impossible, for the producer to profitably offer the good for sale.* Government will have to provide it.

Demand for Public Goods

If consumers need not reveal their true demand for a public good in the marketplace, then how can the optimal amount of that good be determined? The answer is that government has to try to estimate the demand for a public good through surveys or public votes. Suppose Adams and Benson are the only two people in the society, and their marginal willingness to pay for a public good, this time national defense, is as shown in columns 1 and 2 and columns 1 and 3 in Table 30-1. Economists might have discovered these schedules through a survey asking hypothetical questions about how much each citizen is willing to pay for various types and amounts of public goods rather than go without them.

Notice that the schedules in Table 30-1 are price-quantity schedules, implying that they are demand schedules. Rather than depicting demand in the usual way—the quantity of a product someone is willing to buy at each possible price—these schedules show the price someone is willing to pay for the marginal unit of each possible quantity. That is, Adams is willing to pay $4 for the first unit of the public good, $3 for the second, $2 for the third, and so on.

Suppose government produces 1 unit of this public good. Because the exclusion principle does not apply, Adams' consumption of the good does not preclude Benson from also consuming it, and vice versa. So both consume the good, and neither volunteers to pay for it. But from Table 30-1 we can find the amount

TABLE 30-1 Demand for a public good, two individuals

(1) Quantity	(2) Adams' willingness to pay (price)		(3) Benson's willingness to pay (price)		(4) Collective willingness to pay (price)
1	$4	+	$5	=	$9
2	3	+	4	=	7
3	2	+	3	=	5
4	1	+	2	=	3
5	0	+	1	=	1

these two people would be willing to pay, together, rather than do without this 1 unit of the good. Columns 1 and 2 show that Adams would be willing to pay $4 for the first unit of the public good; columns 1 and 3 show that Benson would be willing to pay $5 for it. So the two people are jointly willing to pay $9 (= $4 + $5) for this unit.

For the second unit of the public good, the collective price they are willing to pay is $7 (= $3 from Adams plus $4 from Benson); for the third unit they will pay $5 (= $2 plus $3); and so on. By finding the collective willingness to pay for each additional unit (column 4), we can construct a collective demand schedule (willingness-to-pay schedule) for the public good. Here we are *not* adding the *quantities demanded at each possible price*, as when we determine the market demand for a private good. Instead, we are adding *the prices that people are willing to pay for the last unit of the public good at each possible quantity demanded.*

Figure 30-1 shows the same adding procedure graphically, using the data from Table 30-1. Note that we sum Adams' and Benson's willingness-to-pay curves vertically to derive the collective willingness-to-pay curve (demand curve). The height of the collective demand curve D_c at 2 units of output, for example, is $7—the sum of the amounts that Adams and Benson are each willing to pay for the second unit (= $3 + $4). Likewise, the height of the collective demand curve at 4 units of the public good is $3 (= $1 + $2).

What does it mean in Figure 30-1a that, for example, Adams is willing to pay $3 for the second unit of the public good? It means that Adams expects to receive $3 of extra benefit or utility from that unit. And we know from the law of diminishing marginal utility that successive units of any good yield less and less added benefit. This is also true for public goods, explaining the downward slope of Adams' willingness-to-pay curve, as well as Benson's curve, and the collective demand curve. These curves, in essence, are marginal-*benefit* curves. **(Key Question 1)**

Supply of Public Goods

The supply curve for any good, private or public, is its marginal-*cost* curve. Marginal cost rises as more of a good is produced. The reason is the law of diminishing returns, which applies whether a society is making missiles (a public good) or mufflers (a private good). In the short run, government has fixed re-

(c) Collective demand and supply

(b) Benson

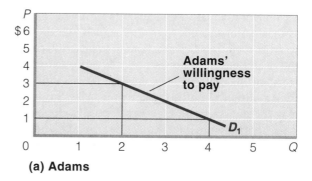

(a) Adams

FIGURE 30-1 The optimal amount of a public good
The collective demand curve for a public good, as shown by D_c in (c), is found by summing vertically the individual willingness-to-pay curves D_1 in (a) and D_2 in (b) of Adams and Benson, the only two people in the economy. The supply curve of a public good in (c) slopes upward and to the right, reflecting rising marginal costs. The optimal amount of the public good is 3 units, determined by the intersection of D_c and S. At that output, marginal benefit (reflected in the collective demand curve D_c) equals marginal cost (reflected in the supply curve S).

sources (public capital) with which to "produce" public goods such as national defense. As it adds more units of a variable resource (labor) to these fixed resources, marginal product eventually rises at a diminishing rate. That means marginal cost rises, explaining why curve S in Figure 30-1c slopes upward.

Optimal Quantity of a Public Good

We can now determine the optimal quantity of the public good. The collective demand curve D_c in Figure 30-1c measures society's marginal benefit of each unit of this particular good. The supply curve S in that figure measures society's marginal cost of each unit. The optimal quantity of this public good occurs where marginal benefit equals marginal cost, or where the two curves intersect. In Figure 30-1c we see that the optimal quantity of the public good is 3 units—at the intersection of supply and demand. There the collective willingness to pay for the last (third) unit—the marginal benefit—just matches that unit's marginal cost ($5 = $5). As we saw in Chapter 2, equating marginal benefit and marginal cost allocates society's resources most efficiently. **(Key Question 2)**

Benefit-Cost Analysis

The above example suggests a practical means, called **benefit-cost analysis,** for deciding whether to provide a particular public good and how much of it to provide. Like our example, it involves a comparison of marginal benefits and marginal costs.

Concept Suppose government is contemplating a flood-control project. Because the economy's resources are limited, any decision to use more resources in the public sector will mean fewer resources for the private sector. There will be both a benefit and a cost. The benefit is the extra satisfaction resulting from the output of more public goods; the cost is the loss of satisfaction resulting from the accompanying decline in the production of private goods. Should the needed resources be shifted from the private to the public sector? The answer is "yes" if the benefit from the extra public goods exceeds the cost resulting from having fewer private goods. The answer is "no" if the cost of the forgone private goods is greater than the benefit associated with the extra public goods.

But benefit-cost analysis can indicate more than whether a public program is worth doing. It can also help government decide on the extent to which a project should be pursued. Real economic questions cannot usually be answered simply by "yes" or "no" but, rather, are matters of "how much" or "how little."

Illustration There is no doubt that a flood-control project is a public good since the exclusion principle is not readily applicable. Should government undertake a flood-control project in a particular river valley? If so, what is the proper size or scope for the project?

Table 30-2 lists a series of increasingly ambitious and increasingly costly flood-control plans for the

TABLE 30-2 Benefit-cost analysis for a flood-control project

(1) Plan	(2) Total annual cost of project	(3) Marginal cost	(4) Total annual benefit (reduction in damage)	(5) Marginal benefit	(6) Net benefit or (4) − (2)
Without protection	$ 0		$ 0		$ 0
		$ 3,000		$ 6,000	
A: Levees	3,000		6,000		3,000
		7,000		10,000	
B: Small reservoir	10,000		16,000		6,000
		8,000		**9,000**	
C: Medium reservoir	**18,000**		**25,000**		**7,000**
		12,000		7,000	
D: Large reservoir	30,000		32,000		2,000

Source: Adopted from Otto Eckstein, *Public Finance,* 3d ed. (Englewood Cliffs, NJ: Prentice-Hall, 1973), p. 23. Used with permission.

valley. The extent to which government should undertake flood control depends on the costs and benefits. The costs are largely the costs of constructing and maintaining levees and reservoirs; the benefits are reduced flood damage.

The table shows that total annual benefit (column 4) exceeds total annual cost (column 2) for each plan, indicating that a flood-control project on this river is economically justifiable. We can see this directly in column 6, where total annual costs (column 2) are subtracted from total annual benefits (column 4).

But the question of optimal size or scope for this project remains. Comparing the additional, or marginal, cost and the additional, or marginal, benefit relating to each plan determines the answer. The guideline is essentially the one we just established: Increase an activity or project or output as long as the marginal benefit (column 5) exceeds the marginal cost (column 3). Stop the activity at, or as close as possible to, the point at which the marginal benefit equals the marginal cost.

In this case plan C—the medium-size reservoir—is the best plan. Plans A and B are too modest; in both cases the marginal benefit exceeds the marginal cost. Plan D's marginal cost ($12,000) exceeds the marginal benefit ($7000) and therefore cannot be justified; it overallocates resources to the project. Plan C is closest to the optimum since its marginal benefit still exceeds marginal cost but approaches the MB = MC ideal.

This **marginal benefit = marginal cost rule** actually tells us which plan provides the maximum excess of total benefits over total costs—in other words, the plan which yields the maximum net benefit to society. You can confirm directly in column 6 that the maximum net benefit (of $7000) is associated with plan C.

Benefit-cost analysis shatters the myth that "economy in government" and "reduced government spending" are synonymous. "Economy" is concerned with using scarce resources efficiently. If the cost of a proposed government program exceeds its benefits, then the proposed public program should not be undertaken. But if the benefits exceed the cost, then it would be uneconomical or "wasteful" not to spend on that government program. Economy in government does *not* mean minimization of public spending. It means allocating resources between the private and public sectors to achieve maximum net benefit. **(Key Question 3)**

> ### QUICK REVIEW 30-1
>
> ■ The demand (marginal-benefit) curve for a public good is found by vertically adding the prices all members of the society are willing to pay for the last unit of output at various output levels.
>
> ■ The socially optimal amount of a public good is the amount at which the marginal benefit and marginal cost of the good are equal.
>
> ■ Benefit-cost analysis is the method of evaluating alternative projects or sizes of projects by comparing marginal benefits and marginal cost and applying the MB = MC rule.

EXTERNALITIES REVISITED

We return now to Chapter 5's discussion of government policies designed to correct the market failures we call externalities, or spillovers. Recall that a spillover is a cost or benefit accruing to an individual or group—a third party—which is external to a market transaction. An example of a spillover cost or *negative externality* is the cost of breathing polluted air; an example of a spillover benefit or *positive externality* is the benefit of having everyone else inoculated against some disease. When there are spillover costs, an overproduction of the related product occurs and there is an overallocation of resources to this product. Conversely, underproduction and underallocation of resources result when spillover benefits are present. We can demonstrate both graphically.

Spillover Costs

Figure 30-2a illustrates how spillover costs affect the allocation of resources. When spillover costs occur—when producers shift some of their costs onto the community—producers' marginal costs are lower than otherwise. So their supply curves do not include or "capture" all the costs legitimately associated with production of their goods. Thus a polluting producer's supply curve—S in Figure 30-2a—understates the total cost of production: the producer's supply curve lies to the right of (or below) the full-cost supply curve S_t, which would include the spillover cost. Through polluting and thus transferring cost to society, the firm enjoys lower production costs and has the supply curve S.

The outcome is shown in Figure 30-2a, where equilibrium output Q_e is *larger* than the optimal out-

(a) Spillover costs

(b) Spillover benefits

FIGURE 30-2 Spillover costs and spillover benefits (a) With spillover costs borne by society, the producers' supply curve S is to the right of (below) the full-cost curve S_t. Consequently, the equilibrium output Q_e is greater than the optimal output Q_o. (b) When spillover benefits accrue to society, the market demand curve D is to the left of (below) the full-benefit demand curve D_t. As a result, the equilibrium output Q_e is less than the optimal output Q_o.

put Q_o. This means that resources are overallocated to the production of this commodity; too many units of it are produced.

Spillover Benefits

Figure 30-2b shows the impact of spillover benefits on resource allocation. When spillover benefits occur, the market demand curve D lies to the left of (or below) the full-benefits demand curve. That is, D does not include the spillover benefits of the product, whereas D_t does. Consider inoculations against a communicable disease. Watson and Weinberg benefit when they get vaccinated, but so do their associates Alvarez and Anderson, who are less likely to contract the disease from them. The market demand curve reflects only the direct, private benefits to Watson and Weinberg. It does not reflect the spillover benefits—the positive externalities—to Alvarez and Anderson, which are included in D_t.

The outcome is that the equilibrium output Q_e is less than the optimal output Q_o. The market fails to produce enough vaccinations; resources are underallocated to this product.

Economists have explored several approaches to the problems of spillover costs and benefits. We will look first at situations where government intervention is not needed and then at some government solutions.

Individual Bargaining: Coase Theorem

In the **Coase theorem,** conceived by Ronald Coase, government is not needed to remedy spillover costs

or benefits where (1) property ownership is clearly defined, (2) the number of people involved is small, and (3) bargaining costs are negligible. Under these circumstances government should confine its role to encouraging bargaining between affected individuals or groups. Property rights place a price tag on an externality, creating opportunity costs for all parties. Because the economic self-interests of the parties are at stake, bargaining will enable them to find a mutually acceptable solution to the externality problem.

Example Suppose the owner of a large parcel of forestland is considering a plan to clear-cut (totally level) thousands of acres of mature fir trees. The complication is that the forest surrounds a lake with a popular resort on its shore. The resort is on land owned by the resort. The unspoiled beauty of the general area attracts vacationers from all over the nation to the resort, and the resort owner is against the clear-cutting. Should state or local government intervene to allow or prevent the tree cutting?

According to the Coase theorem, the forest owner and the resort owner can resolve this situation without government intervention. As long as *one* of the parties to the dispute has property rights to what is at issue, an incentive will exist for *both* parties to negotiate a solution acceptable to each. In our example, the owner of the timberland holds the property rights to the land to be logged and thus has the right to clear-cut it. The owner of the resort therefore has an economic incentive to negotiate with the forest owner to reduce the logging impact. Excessive logging of the forest surrounding the resort will reduce tourism and revenues to the resort owner.

But what is the economic incentive to the forest owner to negotiate with the resort owner? The answer draws directly on the idea of opportunity cost. One cost incurred in logging the forest is the forgone payment which the forest owner could obtain from the resort owner for agreeing *not* to clear-cut the fir trees. The resort owner might be willing to make a lump-sum or annual payment to the owner of the forest to avoid or minimize the spillover cost. Or perhaps the resort owner will be willing to buy the forested land to prevent the logging. As viewed by the forest owner, a payment for not clear-cutting or a purchase price above the market value of the land is an *opportunity cost* of logging the land.

It is likely that both parties would regard a negotiated agreement as better than clear-cutting the firs.

Limitations   Unfortunately, many externalities involve large numbers of affected parties, high bargaining costs, and community property such as air and water. In these situations private bargaining cannot be used as a remedy. As an example, the acid-rain problem in the United States and Canada affects millions of people in both nations. The vast number of affected parties could not independently negotiate an agreement to remedy this problem. Instead, we must rely on the two governments to represent the millions of affected parties and find an acceptable solution.

Nevertheless, the Coase theorem reminds us that in many situations bargaining can be useful in remedying spillover costs and spillover benefits.

Liability Rules and Lawsuits

Although private negotiation may not be a realistic solution to many externality problems, clearly established property rights may help in another way. Government has established a framework of laws which define private property and protect it from damage done by other parties. These laws—and the damage recovery system to which they give rise—permit those suffering spillover costs to sue for compensation.

Suppose the Ajax Degreaser Company regularly dumps leaky barrels containing solvents into a nearby canyon owned by Bar Q ranch. Bar Q eventually discovers this dump site and, after tracing the drums to Ajax, immediately contacts its lawyer. Soon after, Bar Q sues Ajax. Not only will Ajax have to pay for the cleanup; it may also have to pay Bar Q additional damages for ruining its property.

Clearly defined property rights and government liability laws thus help remedy some externality problems. They do so directly by forcing the perpetrator of the harmful externality to pay damages to those injured. They do so indirectly by discouraging firms and individuals from generating spillover costs, for fear of being sued. It is not surprising, then, that many spillovers do *not* involve private property but rather property held in common by society. It is the *public* bodies of water, the *public* lands, and the *public* air, where ownership is less clear, which often bear the brunt of spillovers.

Caveat: Like private negotiations, private lawsuits to resolve externalities have their own limitations. Large legal fees and major time delays in the court system are commonplace. Also, the uncertainty associated with the court outcome reduces the effectiveness of this approach. Will the court accept your claim that your emphysema has resulted from the smoke emitted by the factory next door, or will it conclude that your ailment is unrelated to the plant's pollution? Can you prove that a specific firm in the area is the source of the contamination of your well? What happens to Bar Q's suit if Ajax Degreaser goes out of business during the litigation?

Government Intervention

Government intervention may be needed to achieve economic efficiency when externalities affect large numbers of people or when community interests are at stake. Direct controls and taxes can be used to counter spillover costs; government may provide subsidies or public goods to deal with spillover benefits.

Direct Controls   The direct way to reduce spillover costs due to a certain activity is to pass legislation placing limits on that activity. Such direct controls force the offending firms to incur the actual costs associated with the offending activity. To date, this approach has dominated public policy in the United States. Clean-air legislation limits the amounts of nitrogen oxide, particulates, and other substances factories can emit into the air. Clean-water legislation limits the amount of heavy metals, detergents, and other pollutants firms can discharge into rivers and bays. Toxic-waste laws dictate special procedures and dump sites for disposing of contaminated soil and solvents. Violations of these laws mean fines and, in some cases, imprisonment.

Direct controls raise the marginal cost of production, since the firms must operate and maintain pollution-control equipment. The supply curve S in Figure 30-3b, which does not reflect the spillover costs, shifts leftward (upward) to the full-cost supply curve, S_t. Product price increases, equilibrium output falls from Q_e to Q_o, and the initial overallocation of resources shown in Figure 30-3a is corrected.

Specific Taxes A second policy approach to spillover costs is to levy taxes or charges specifically on the related good. For example, the government has placed a manufacturing excise tax on chlorofluorocarbons (CFCs) which deplete the stratospheric ozone layer protecting the earth from excessive solar ultraviolet radiation. (CFCs are used widely as a coolant in refrigeration, a blowing agent for foam, and a solvent in the electronics industry.) Facing such an excise tax, manufacturers must decide whether to pay the tax or expend additional funds to purchase or develop substitute products. In either case, the tax raises the marginal cost of producing CFCs, shifting the private supply curve for this product leftward (or upward).

In Figure 30-3b, a tax equal to T per unit increases the firm's marginal cost, shifting the supply curve from S to S_t. The equilibrium price increases, and the equilibrium output declines from Q_e to the economically efficient level Q_o. The initial overallocation of resources is eliminated.

Subsidies and Government Provision Where spillover benefits are large and diffuse, as in our earlier example of inoculations, government has three options for correcting the underallocation of resources:

1. **Subsidies to buyers** Figure 30-4a again shows the supply-demand situation for spillover benefits. Government could correct the underallocation of resources—say, to inoculations—by subsidizing consumers of the product. It could give each new mother in the United States a discount coupon to be used to obtain a series of inoculations for her child. The coupon would reduce the "price" to the mother by, say, 50 percent. As shown in Figure 30-4b, this program would shift the demand curve for inoculations from the too low D to D_t. The number of inoculations would rise from Q_e to the economically optimal Q_o, eliminating the underallocation of resources shown in Figure 30-4a.

2. **Subsidies to producers** A subsidy to producers is a specific tax in reverse; taxes impose an extra cost on producers, while subsidies reduce producers' costs. As shown in Figure 30-4c, a subsidy of U per inoculation to physicians and medical clinics would reduce their marginal costs and shift their supply curve rightward from S_t to S_t'. The output of inoculations would increase from Q_e to the optimal level Q_o, correcting the underallocation of resources shown in Figure 30-4a.

3. **Government provision** Finally, where spillover benefits are extremely large, government may decide to provide the product as a public good. The U.S. government largely eradicated the crippling disease polio by administering free vaccines to all children. India ended smallpox by paying people in rural areas to come to public clinics to have their children vaccinated. **(Key Question 4)**

(a) Spillover costs

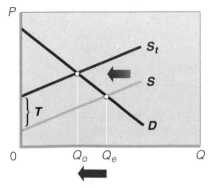

(b) Correcting the overallocation of resources via direct controls or via a tax

FIGURE 30-3 Correcting for spillover costs (negative externalities) (a) Spillover costs result in an overallocation of resources. (b) This overallocation can be corrected in two ways: (1) use of direct controls, which would shift the supply curve from S to S_t and reduce output from Q_e to Q_o; or (2) imposition of a specific tax T, which would also shift the supply curve from S to S_t, eliminating the overallocation of resources.

(a) Spillover benefits

(b) Correcting the underallocation of resources via a subsidy to consumers

(c) Correcting the underallocation of resources via a subsidy to producers

FIGURE 30-4 Correcting for spillover benefits (positive externalities) (a) Spillover benefits result in an underallocation of resources. (b) This underallocation can be corrected by a subsidy to consumers, which shifts market demand from D to D_t and increases output from Q_e to Q_o. (c) Alternatively, the underallocation can be eliminated by providing producers with a subsidy of U, which shifts their supply curve from S_t to S'_t, raising output from Q_e to Q_o.

A Market for Externality Rights

One novel policy approach to spillover costs involves only limited government action. The idea is that government would create a **market for externality rights.** We confine our discussion to pollution, although this approach might also be used with other externalities.

The air, rivers, lakes, oceans, and public lands, such as parks and streets, are all objects for pollution because the *rights* to use these resources are held "in common" by society. No private individual or institution has an incentive to maintain the purity or quality of these resources because no one has the right to realize a monetary return from doing so.

We maintain the property we own—we paint and repair our homes periodically—in part because we will gain the value of these improvements at the time of resale. But as long as "rights" to air, water, and certain land resources are commonly held and these resources are freely available, there is no incentive to maintain them or use them carefully. As a result, these natural resources are "overconsumed" and thereby polluted. But would they be overconsumed and polluted if there were a cost to pollute them—and a market for the right to pollute?

Operation of the Market
In this approach, an appropriate pollution-control agency determines the amount of pollutants which can be discharged into the water or air of a specific region annually while maintaining the water or air quality at some acceptable level. The agency may determine that 500 tons of pollutants can be discharged into Metropolitan Lake and "recycled" by nature each year. Then 500 pollution rights, each entitling the owner to dump 1 ton of pollutants into the lake in 1 year, are made available for sale to producers each year. The supply of these pollution rights is fixed and therefore perfectly inelastic, as shown in Figure 30-5.

The demand for pollution rights—D_{1999} in the figure—takes the same downsloping form as the demand for any other input. At higher prices there is less pollution, as polluters either stop polluting or pollute less by acquiring pollution-abatement equipment. An equilibrium market price for pollution rights, here $100, will be determined at which the environment-preserving quantity of pollution rights is rationed to polluters. Figure 30-5 shows that without this market—that is, if the use of the lake as a dump site for pollutants were free—750 tons of pollutants would be discharged into the lake; it would be "overconsumed," or polluted, in the amount of 250 tons.

Over time, as human and business populations expand, demand will increase, as from D_{1999} to D_{2009}. *Without* a market for pollution rights, pollution in 2009 would be 1000 tons, 500 tons beyond what can

FIGURE 30-5 **A market for pollution rights** The supply of pollution rights *S* is set by government, which determines that a specific body of water can safely recycle 500 tons of waste. In 1999, the demand for pollution rights is *D*₁₉₉₉ and the 1-ton price is $100. The quantity of pollution is 500 tons, not the 750 tons it would have been without the pollution rights. Over time, the demand for pollution rights increases to *D*₂₀₀₉ and the 1-ton price rises to $200. But the amount of pollution stays at 500 tons, rather than rising to 1000 tons.

---

be assimilated by nature. *With* the market for pollution rights, the price would rise from $100 to $200 and the amount of pollutants would remain at 500 tons—the amount which the lake can recycle.

Advantages This scheme has several advantages over direct controls. Most important, it reduces society's costs by allowing pollution rights to be bought and sold. Suppose it costs Acme Pulp Mill $20 a year to reduce a specific noxious discharge by 1 ton while it costs Zemo Chemicals $8000 a year to accomplish the same 1-ton reduction. Also assume that Zemo wants to expand production, but doing so will increase its pollution discharge by 1 ton.

Without a market for pollution rights, Zemo would have to use $8000 of society's scarce resources to keep the 1-ton pollution discharge from occurring. But with a market for pollution rights, Zemo has a better option: it buys 1 ton of pollution rights for the $100 price shown in Figure 30-5. Acme is willing to sell Zemo 1 ton of pollution rights for $100 because that amount is more than Acme's $20 cost of reducing its pollution by 1 ton. Zemo increases its discharge by 1 ton; Acme reduces its discharge by 1 ton. Zemo benefits (by $8000 − $100), Acme benefits (by $100 − $20), and society benefits (by $8000 − $20).

Rather than using $8000 of its scarce resources to hold the discharge at the specified level, society uses $20 of these resources.

Market-based plans have other advantages. Potential polluters have a monetary incentive not to pollute: they must pay for the rights to pollute. Conservation groups can fight pollution by buying up and withholding pollution rights, reducing actual pollution below governmentally determined standards. As the demand for pollution rights increases over time, the growing revenue from the sale of a fixed quantity of pollution rights could be devoted to environmental improvement. At the same time, the rising price of pollution rights should stimulate the search for improved pollution-control techniques.

Administrative and political problems have kept government from replacing direct controls—uniform emission limits—with a full-scale market for pollution rights. But, as we will soon discuss, such markets *have* emerged for air pollution rights. Also, a system of pollution rights, or "tradeable emission allowances," was established as part of a plan to reduce the sulfur dioxide emitted by coal-burning public utilities. These firms are the major source of acid rain.

Table 30-3 reviews the methods for correcting externalities, and we urge you to study it.

Society's Optimal Amount of Externality Reduction

Negative externalities such as pollution reduce the utility of those affected, rather than increase it. These spillovers are not economic goods but "economic bads." If something is bad, shouldn't society eliminate it? Why should society allow firms or municipalities to discharge *any* impure waste into public waterways or emit *any* pollution into our air?

Reducing a negative externality has a "price." Society must decide how much of a reduction it wants to "buy." Totally eliminating pollution might not be desirable, even if it were technologically feasible. Because of the law of diminishing returns, cleaning up the last 10 percent of pollutants from an industrial smokestack normally is far more costly than cleaning up the previous 10 percent. Eliminating that 10 percent is likely more costly than cleaning up the prior 10 percent, and so on.

The marginal cost (MC) to the firm and hence to society—the opportunity cost of the extra resources used—rises as more and more pollution is reduced. At some point MC may rise so high that it exceeds society's marginal benefit (MB) of further pollution abate-

TABLE 30-3   Methods for dealing with externalities

Problem	Resource allocation outcome	Ways to correct
Spillover costs (negative externalities)	Overallocation of resources	1. Individual bargaining 2. Liability rules and lawsuits 3. Tax on producers 4. Direct controls 5. Market for externality rights
Spillover benefits (positive externalities)	Underallocation of resources	1. Individual bargaining 2. Subsidy to consumers 3. Subsidy to producers 4. Government provision

ment (reduction). Additional actions to reduce pollution will therefore lower society's well-being; total cost will rise more than total benefit.

MC, MB, and Equilibrium Quantity

Figure 30-6 shows both the rising marginal-cost curve, MC, for pollution reduction and the downsloping marginal-benefit curve, MB, for this outcome. MB slopes downward because of the law of diminishing marginal utility: The more pollution reduction society accomplishes, the lower the utility (and benefit) of the next unit of pollution reduction.

The **optimal reduction of an externality** occurs where society's marginal benefit and marginal cost of reducing that externality are equal (MB = MC). In Figure 30-6 this optimal amount of pollution abatement is Q_1 units. When MB exceeds MC, additional abatement moves society toward economic efficiency; the added benefit of cleaner air or water exceeds the benefit of any alternative use of the required resources. When MC exceeds MB, additional abatement reduces economic efficiency; there would be greater benefits from using resources in some other way than to further reduce pollution.

In reality, it is difficult to measure the marginal costs and benefits of pollution control. Nevertheless, Figure 30-6 is useful in demonstrating that some pollution may be economically efficient. This is so not because pollution is desirable but because beyond some level of control, further abatement may reduce our net well-being.

Shifts in Locations of Curves

The locations of the marginal-cost and marginal-benefit curves in

Figure 30-6 are not forever fixed; they can, and probably do, shift over time. For example, suppose the technology of pollution-control equipment improves noticeably. We would expect the cost of pollution abatement to fall, society's MC curve to shift rightward, and the optimal level of abatement to rise. As another example, suppose society wants cleaner air

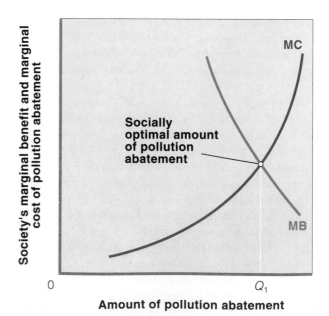

FIGURE 30-6 Society's optimal amount of pollution abatement The optimal amount of externality reduction—in this case, pollution abatement—occurs at Q_1, where society's marginal cost MC and marginal benefit MB of reducing the spillover are equal.

and water because of new information about the adverse health effects of pollution. The MB curve in Figure 30-6 would shift rightward, and the optimal level of pollution control would increase beyond Q_1. You can test your understanding of these statements by drawing the new MC and MB curves in Figure 30-6. **(Key Question 7)**

QUICK REVIEW 30-2

■ Policies for coping with the overallocation of resources caused by spillover costs are **(a)** private bargaining, **(b)** liability rules and lawsuits, **(c)** direct controls, **(d)** specific taxes, and **(e)** markets for externality rights.

■ Policies for correcting the underallocation of resources associated with spillover benefits are **(a)** private bargaining, **(b)** subsidies to producers, **(c)** subsidies to consumers, and **(d)** government provision.

■ The optimal amount of negative-externality reduction occurs where society's marginal cost and marginal benefit of reducing the externality are equal.

A CLOSER LOOK AT POLLUTION

Pollution, the most acute external cost facing industrial society, provides a relevant real-life illustration of several of the concepts just discussed.

Dimensions of the Problem

There are many dimensions to the pollution problem. The United States alone has identified 25,000 major industrial sources of air pollution, which contribute to lung cancer, emphysema, pneumonia, and other respiratory diseases. Municipal and industrial sewers severely pollute many of the nation's rivers, lakes, and bays. Solid-waste disposal has become an acute problem for many cities as the most readily available dump sites have been filled and everyone says "not in my backyard" to new dumps or incinerators. The U.S. government has identified hundreds of toxic-waste disposal sites across the country. Oil spills continue to occur, creating various degrees of environmental damage.

Global aspects of environmental pollution are equally disturbing. Russia, along with the former communist region of eastern Europe (Poland, eastern Germany, and so on) are so polluted that it will take decades to clean them up. Some scientists contend that the concentrations of industry, people, structures, and concrete which constitute cities are creating air and heat pollution sufficient to cause potential global warming through the so-called *greenhouse effect*.

Causes: The Law of Conservation of Matter and Energy

The root of the pollution problem can be envisioned through the **law of conservation of matter and energy.** This law holds that matter can be transformed to other matter or into energy but can never vanish. All inputs (fuels, raw materials, water, and so forth) used in the economy's production processes will ultimately result in an equivalent amount of waste. For example, unless it is continuously recycled, the cotton found in a T-shirt ultimately will be abandoned in a closet, buried in a dump, or burned in an incinerator. Even if it is burned, it will not truly vanish; instead, it will be transformed into heat, smoke, and ash.

Fortunately, the ecological system has a self-generating capacity which allows it, within limits, to absorb or recycle such waste. But the volume of waste now tends to outrun this absorptive capacity.

Why has this happened? Why do the United States and most other nations have pollution problems? There are many reasons, but four stand out.

Population Growth   One reason is population growth and the accompanying greater density of population. An ecological system which can accommodate 50 to 100 million people may begin to break down under the pressure of 200 or 300 million.

Rising Per Capita Consumption   As economies grow, each person consumes and disposes of more output. Unfortunately, a rising GDP (gross domestic product) means a rising "GDG" ("gross domestic garbage"). In the United States, for example, a higher standard of living permits people to own more than 200 million motor vehicles. But autos and trucks pollute the air and give rise to the problem of disposing of some 12 or 13 million junked vehicles annually. Additionally, about 200 million tires hit U.S. scrap heaps each year.

But we must not overgeneralize. Although solid waste increases with GDP, this is not so for all pollutants. Because expanded national income enables countries to "buy" cleaner air and water through pollution-control measures, airborne concentrations of smoke (fine particles), heavier particles, and sulfur dioxide on average tend to decline when GDP grows beyond a threshold level of about $5000 per capita. Nevertheless, there is no doubt that industrialization itself—and the resulting increase in GDP—has brought with it serious pollution problems.

Technological Change

Some kinds of technological change have contributed to pollution. The development and widespread use of "throwaway" containers made of virtually indestructible aluminum or plastics have added to the solid-waste problem. Some detergent soap products have been highly resistant to decomposition or recycling. Nuclear energy has brought with it nuclear-waste products which must be stored and monitored for centuries.

The "Tragedy of the Commons" and Incentives

The so-called tragedy of the commons is the tendency for society to overuse and thus abuse *common resources* to which no one holds property rights. A common pasture in which anyone can graze cattle will quickly be overgrazed, since each rancher has an incentive to graze as many cattle as possible. Similarly, commonly owned resources such as rivers, lakes, oceans, and the air get used beyond their capacities to absorb pollution. Profit-seeking manufacturers will choose the least-cost combination of inputs and bear only unavoidable costs. If they can dump waste chemicals into rivers and lakes rather than pay for proper disposal, businesses might well be inclined to do so. Firms will discharge smoke into the air if they can, rather than purchase expensive abatement facilities. Even governments—Federal, state, and local—often discharge inadequately treated waste into rivers, lakes, or oceans because it is cheap and convenient to do so. Many individuals avoid the costs of proper refuse pickup and disposal by burning their garbage or dumping it in the woods.

The problem is mainly one of incentives. There is no incentive to incur internal costs associated with reducing or eliminating pollution when these costs can be transferred externally to the commons—to society at large. The fallacy of composition also comes into play. Each person and firm reasons that their individual contribution to pollution is so small that it is of little or no overall consequence. But their actions, multiplied by hundreds, thousands, or millions, overwhelm the absorptive capacity of the common resources. Society ends up with a pollution problem.

Antipollution Policy in the United States

The United States and other nations have addressed their pollution problems through a complex maze of laws, regulations, taxes, pollution rights, and government-financed cleanup activity. Much of the complexity of antipollution policy comes from the sheer number of pollution sources and the thousands of substances which are emitted into the air, discharged into the water, or placed in garbage dumps. To stay focused, we will confine our discussion to the United States and look only at selected facets of American antipollution policy.

The Superfund Law

Before the **Superfund law of 1980,** companies disposed of their chemical waste by storing it next to their plants, flushing it into nearby waterways, or paying to have it hauled away for disposal. Once this mostly toxic waste was removed from their premises, those who produced it had no further responsibility. Many of the individuals and firms hauling the waste improperly stored it in leaky drums or dumped it into private and public landfills.

The Superfund law established direct controls, specific taxes, and stringent regulations for toxic waste. It asserted Federal control over contaminated dump sites and assigned liability for the improperly dumped waste to the firms producing, transporting, and dumping it. The law imposed a tax on manufacturers of toxic chemicals, with revenues flowing into a "Superfund," to be used by the Environmental Protection Agency (EPA) to help finance the cleanup of 1250 toxic dump sites. Once the decontamination work is under way, the Federal government can sue the allegedly responsible parties in an attempt to recover all or part of the cleanup expense.

How has the Superfund concept worked? On the plus side, the tax on chemical producers has raised billions of dollars, and some of the nation's most toxic-waste sites have been cleaned up. On the negative side, the Superfund became a political "public works" project. Politicians fought among themselves to get their own state or local dump sites on the cleanup list and to establish the highest priority for cleanup efforts in their own locales. Decontamination of a toxic-waste site not only eliminates health hazards; it brings Federal money and jobs to the area. Also, litigation has drained billions of dollars from the cleanup fund, as firms have fought government suits, have sued one another to determine liability, and have sued their own insurance companies for payment.

After 17 years, less than one-third of the original 1250 toxic-waste sites have been decontaminated, although work on many more sites is in progress.

Clean Air Act of 1990 Direct controls in the form of *uniform emisson standards*—limits on allowable pollution—have historically dominated American air pollution policy. The **Clean Air Act of 1990** has continued this tradition. Specifically, the law (1) forces factories and businesses to install "maximum achievable control technology" to reduce emissions of 189 toxic chemicals by 90 pecent by the year 2000; (2) required a 30 to 60 percent reduction in tailpipe emissions from automobiles by 1998; (3) mandates a 50 percent reduction in the use of CFCs, which deplete the ozone layer; and (4) forces coal-burning utilities to cut their emissions of sulfur dioxide by about 50 percent to reduce the acid-rain destruction of lakes and forests.

Trading of Pollution Rights But the Clean Air Act has also established a limited market for pollution rights, similar to that shown in Figure 30-5, by allowing utilities to trade *emission credits* provided by government. Utilities can obtain credits by reducing sulfur dioxide emissions by more than the specified amount. They can then sell their emission credits to other utilities which find it less costly to buy the credits than install additional pollution-control equipment.

This buying and selling of sulfur dioxide emission credits complements earlier air pollution policies which also permitted the exchange of pollution rights. The EPA now allows firms to exchange pollution rights internally and externally.

Polluters are allowed to transfer air pollution internally between individual sources within their plants. That is, as long as it meets the overall pollution standard assigned to it, a firm may increase one source of pollution by offsetting it with reduced pollution from another part of its operations.

The EPA also permits external trading of pollution rights. It has set targets for reducing air pollution in regions where the minimum standards are not being met. Previously, new pollution sources could not enter these regions unless existing polluters went out of business. In the last 15 years, the EPA has allowed firms which reduce their pollution below set standards to sell their pollution rights to other firms. A new firm desiring to locate in the Los Angeles area,

for example, might be able to buy rights to emit 20 tons of nitrous oxide annually from an existing firm which has reduced its emissions below its allowable limit. The price of emission rights depends on their supply and demand.

A growing market for such rights has emerged, greatly expanded by the acid-rain provisions of the Clean Air Act.

Progress Against Air Pollution According to the EPA, clean-air laws and antipollution efforts by businesses and local governments have reduced major air pollutants by almost 30 percent over the past 25 years, despite an almost doubling in the size of the economy. Lead concentration fell by nearly 80 percent from 1986 to 1995, mainly because of the phase-out of leaded gasoline. In that same period, concentrations of both sulfur dioxide (the major source of acid rain) and carbon monoxide declined by nearly 40 percent. Since 1987, nitrogen dioxide has declined by 14 percent; smog has decreased by 6 percent; and particulates (dust, soot, and dirt) have dropped 22 percent.

Solid-Waste Disposal and Recycling

Nowhere is the law of conservation of matter and energy more apparent than in solid-waste disposal (Global Perspective 30-1). The 165 million tons of garbage which accumulate annually in U.S. landfills (trash dumps) have become a growing externality problem. Landfills in the northeast, in particular, are either completely full or rapidly filling up. Garbage from there and elsewhere is now being transported hundreds of miles across state lines to dumps in other states.

On the receiving end, people in rural areas near newly expanding dumps are understandably upset about the increased truck traffic on their highways and growing mounds of smelly garbage in local dumps. Also, some landfills are producing serious water-supply pollution.

The high opportunity cost of urban and suburban land and the negative externalities created by dumps make landfills increasingly expensive. An alternative policy is to incinerate garbage in plants which produce electricity. But people object to having garbage incinerators—a source of truck traffic and air pollution—close to their homes. Is there a better solution to the growing problem of solid waste?

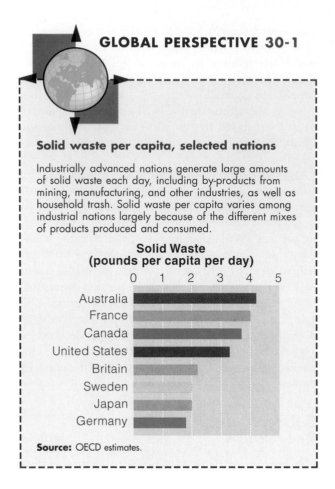

Source: OECD estimates.

GLOBAL PERSPECTIVE 30-1

Solid waste per capita, selected nations

Industrially advanced nations generate large amounts of solid waste each day, including by-products from mining, manufacturing, and other industries, as well as household trash. Solid waste per capita varies among industrial nations largely because of the different mixes of products produced and consumed.

**Solid Waste
(pounds per capita per day)**

Australia
France
Canada
United States
Britain
Sweden
Japan
Germany

Although garbage dumps and incinerators remain the primary garbage disposal methods, recycling is receiving increased attention. According to the EPA, 90 percent of lead-acid batteries, 63 percent of aluminum cans, 45 percent of corrugated boxes, 30 percent of newspapers, 21 percent of plastic soft-drink bottles, and 25 percent of glass bottles are now being recycled.

Market for Recyclable Inputs

We can examine the incentives for recycling using Figure 30-7a, which shows the demand and supply curves for some recyclable product, say, glass.

The demand for recyclable glass derives from manufacturers which use recycled glass as a resource in producing new glass. This demand curve slopes downward, telling us that manufacturers will increase their purchases of recyclable glass as its price falls.

The location of the demand curve in Figure 30-7a depends partly on the demand for the products for which the recycled glass is used. The greater the demand for these products, the greater the demand for the recyclable input. The location of the curve also depends on the technology and thus the cost of using original raw materials rather than recycled glass in the production process. The more costly it is to use original materials relative to recycled glass, the farther to the right will be the demand curve for recyclable glass.

The supply curve for recyclable glass slopes upward in the typical fashion because higher prices increase the incentive for households to recycle. The location of the supply curve depends on such factors as the attitudes of households toward recycling and the cost to them of alternative disposal.

The equilibrium price P_1 and quantity Q_1 in Figure 30-7a are determined at the intersection of the supply and demand curves. At price P_1 the market clears; there is neither a shortage nor a surplus of recyclable glass.

Policy Suppose government wants to encourage recycling as an alternative to land dumps or incineration. It could do this in one of two ways.

Demand Incentives Government could increase recycling by increasing the demand for recycled inputs. If the demand curve in Figure 30-7b shifts from D_1 rightward to D_2, the equilibrium price and quantity of recycled glass will increase to P_2 and Q_2; more recycling will occur. A policy which might increase demand would be to place specific taxes on the inputs which are substitutable for recycled glass in the production process. Such taxes would encourage firms to use more of the untaxed recycled glass and less of the taxed inputs. Or government could shift its purchases toward goods produced with recycled inputs and require that its contractors do the same. Example: In 1993 the Federal government announced a new policy requiring 20 percent or more recycled content in every piece of writing and copying paper purchased by Federal agencies.

Also, environmental awareness by the public can contribute to rightward shifts of the demand curve for recycled resources. Many large firms which produce waste-intensive goods have concluded that it is in their interest to support recycling, for fear of a consumer backlash against their products. Examples: Procter & Gamble (disposable diapers) and McDonald's (packaging of fast foods) have undertaken multimillion-dollar campaigns to use recycled plastic and paper.

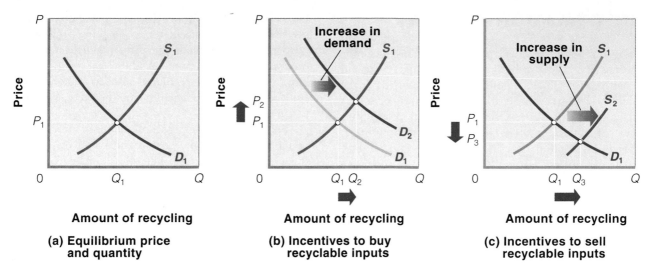

FIGURE 30-7 **The economics of recycling** (a) The equilibrium price and amount of materials recycled are determined by supply S_1 and demand D_1. (b) Policies that increase the incentives for producers to buy recyclable inputs shift the demand curve rightward, say, to D_2, and raise both the equilibrium price and the amount of recycling. (c) Policies that encourage households to recycle shift the supply curve rightward, say, to S_2, and expand the equilibrium amount of recycling. These policies, however, also reduce the equilibrium price of the recycled inputs.

Supply Incentives As shown in Figure 30-7c, government can also increase recycling by shifting the supply curve rightward, as from S_1 to S_2. The equilibrium price would fall from P_1 to P_3, but the equilibrium quantity—in this case recyclable glass—would rise from Q_1 to Q_3. That is, more recycling would occur. Many local governments have implemented specific policies which fit within this framework. For example, they encourage recycling by providing curbside pickup of recyclable goods such as glass, aluminum cans, and newspapers at a lower monthly fee than that for pickup of other garbage.

In a few cases, supply incentives for recyclables have been so effective that the price of a recycled item has fallen to zero. You can envision this outcome by shifting the supply curve in Figure 30-7c farther rightward. Some cities now are *paying* users of recycled inputs such as mixed paper to truck them away from the recycling center, meaning that these items have a negative price. If the cost of paying firms to take away recyclable products is lower than the cost of alternative methods, even such paid-for recycling will promote economic efficiency. However, if it is more costly to recycle trash than to bury or incinerate it, even when externalities are considered, such recycling will *reduce* efficiency rather than increase it. Again we are re-minded that there can be either too little *or* too much of a good thing.

Government's task is to find the optimal amount of recycling compared with the alternative disposal of garbage. It can do this by estimating and comparing the marginal benefit and marginal cost of recycling. And, incidentally, consumers as a group can reduce the accumulation of garbage by buying products which have minimal packaging.

QUICK REVIEW 30-3

■ The ultimate reason for pollution is the law of conservation of matter and energy, which holds that matter can be transformed into other matter or into energy but cannot vanish.

■ Society's pollution problem has largely resulted from increasing population, rising per capita consumption, certain changes in technology, and the so-called tragedy of the commons.

■ The Superfund law of 1980 set up the financing of, and procedure for, cleaning up toxic-waste sites; the Clean Air Act of 1990 established tougher air pollution standards and broadened the market for pollution rights.

■ Government can encourage recycling through demand and supply incentives; its task is to determine the optimal amount of recycling.

INFORMATION FAILURES

Thus far we have added new detail and insights concerning two types of market failure: public goods and externalities. There is another, more subtle, market failure. This one results when either buyers or sellers have incomplete or inaccurate information and their cost of obtaining better information is prohibitive. Technically stated, this market failure occurs because of **asymmetric information**—unequal knowledge possessed by the parties to a market transaction. Buyers and sellers do not have identical information about price, quality, or some other aspect of the good or service.

Sufficient market information normally is available to ensure that goods and services are produced and purchased efficiently. But in some cases, inadequate information makes it difficult to distinguish trustworthy from untrustworthy sellers or trustworthy from untrustworthy buyers. In these markets, society's scarce resources may not be used efficiently, implying that government should intervene by increasing the information available to the market participants. Under rarer circumstances government may itself supply a good for which information problems have prohibited efficient production.

Inadequate Information Involving Sellers

Inadequate information about sellers and their products can cause market failure in the form of underallocation of resources. Examining the markets for gasoline and for the services of surgeons will show us how this comes about.

Example: Gasoline Market
Assume an absurd situation: Suppose there is no system of weights and measures established by law, no government inspection of gasoline pumps, and no law against false advertising. Each gas station can use whatever measure it chooses; it can define a gallon of gas as it pleases. A station can advertise that its gas is 87 octane when in fact it is only 75. It can rig its pumps to indicate it is providing more gas than the amount being delivered.

Obviously, the consumer's cost of obtaining reliable information under these conditions is exceptionally high, if not prohibitive. Each consumer would have to buy samples of gas from various gas stations, have them tested for octane level, and pour gas samples into a measuring device to see how each station

has calibrated its pump. Also, the consumer would need to use a hand calculator to check that the pump is correctly multiplying the price per gallon by the number of gallons pumped. And these activities would have to be repeated regularly, since a station owner could alter the product quality and the accuracy of the pump at will.

Because of the high costs of obtaining information about the seller, many customers would opt out of this chaotic market. One tankful of a 50 percent solution of gasoline and water would be enough to discourage most motorists from further driving. More realistically, the conditions in this market would encourage consumers to vote for political candidates who promise to provide a governmental solution. The oil companies and honest gasoline stations would not object to this government intervention. They would realize that accurate information, by enabling this market to work, would expand their total sales and profit.

Government has in fact intervened in the market for gasoline and other markets with similar potential information difficulties. It has established a system of weights and measures, employed inspectors to check the accuracy of gasoline pumps, and passed laws against fraudulent claims and misleading advertising. There can be no doubt that these government activities have produced net benefits for society.

Example: Licensing of Surgeons
Suppose now that anyone can hang out a shingle and claim to be a surgeon, much as anyone can become a house painter. The market would eventually sort out the true surgeons from those who are "learning by doing" or are fly-by-night operators who move into and out of an area. As people died from unsuccessful surgery, lawsuits for malpractice eventually would eliminate the medical imposters. People needing surgery for themselves or their loved ones could obtain information from newspaper reports or from people who have undergone similar operations.

But this process of obtaining information for those needing surgery would take considerable time and would impose unacceptably high human and economic costs. There is a fundamental difference between getting an amateurish paint job on one's house and being on the receiving end of heart surgery by a bogus physician. The marginal cost of obtaining information about sellers in the surgery market would be excessively high. The risk of proceeding without good information would result in much less surgery than desirable—an underallocation of resources to surgery.

Government has remedied this market failure through a system of qualifying tests and licensing. The licensing provides consumers with inexpensive information about a service they only infrequently buy. Government has taken a similar role in several other areas of the economy. For example, it approves new medicines, regulates the securities industry, and requires warnings on containers of potentially hazardous substances. It also requires warning labels on cigarette packages and disseminates information about communicable diseases. And it issues warnings about unsafe toys and inspects restaurants for health-related violations.

Inadequate Information Involving Buyers

Just as inadequate information involving sellers can keep markets from achieving economic efficiency, so can inadequate information relating to buyers. The buyers may be consumers buying products or firms buying resources.

Moral Hazard Problem   Private markets may underallocate resources to a particular good or service for which there is a severe **moral hazard problem.** *The moral hazard problem is the tendency of one party to a contract to alter her or his behavior after the contract is signed in ways which could be costly to the other party.*

To understand this problem, suppose a firm offers an insurance policy which pays a set amount of money per month to people who suffer divorces. The attraction of this insurance is that it pools the economic risk of divorce among thousands of people and, in particular, protects spouses and children from the economic hardship which divorce often brings. Unfortunately, the moral hazard problem reduces the likelihood that insurance companies can profitably provide this type of insurance.

After taking out this insurance, some people will alter their behavior in ways which impose heavy costs on the insurer. For example, married couples would have less of an incentive to get along and to iron out marital difficulties. At the extreme, some people might be motivated to obtain a divorce, collect the insurance, and then live together. The insurance could promote *more* divorces, the very outcome it protects against. The moral hazard problem would force the insurer to charge such high premiums for this insur-

ance that few policies would be bought. If the insurer could identify in advance those people most prone to alter their behavior, the firm could exclude them from buying it. But the firm's marginal cost of getting this information is too high compared with the marginal benefit. Thus, this market fails.

Divorce insurance is not available in the marketplace. But society recognizes the benefits of insuring against the hardships of divorce. It has corrected for this underallocation of "hardship insurance" through child-support laws which dictate payments—when the economic circumstances warrant—to the spouse who retains the children. Alimony laws also play a role.

Since, unlike private firms, government does not have to earn a profit when supplying services, it provides "divorce insurance" of sorts through the Aid to Families with Dependent Children (AFDC) program. If a divorce leaves a spouse with children destitute, the family is eligible for AFDC payments. Government intervention does not eliminate the moral hazard problem; instead, it offsets the problem's adverse effects.

The moral hazard problem has numerous applications. Several are used here to reinforce your understanding of the basic principle:

1. Drivers may be less cautious because they have car insurance.
2. Medical malpractice insurance may increase the amount of malpractice.
3. Guaranteed contracts for professional athletes may reduce the quality of their performances.
4. Unemployment compensation insurance may lead some workers to shirk.
5. Government insurance on bank deposits may encourage banks to make risky loans.

Adverse Selection Problem   Another information problem resulting from inadequate information involving buyers is the **adverse selection problem.** *The adverse selection problem arises when information known by the first party to a contract is not known by the second and, as a result, the second party incurs major costs.* Unlike the moral hazard problem, which arises *after* a person signs a contract, the adverse selection problem arises *at the time* a person signs a contract.

In insurance, the adverse selection problem is that people most likely to need insurance payouts are those who will buy insurance. For example, those in poorest health will seek to buy the most generous health insurance policies. Or, at the extreme, a person plan-

Used Cars: The Market for "Lemons"

Asymmetric product information could result in markets in which sellers offer only defective goods.

A new car loses much of its market value as the buyer drives it off the dealer's sales lot. Physical depreciation cannot explain this large loss of value since the same new car can sit on the dealer's lot for weeks, or even months, and retain its value.

One explanation of this paradox rests on the idea of asymmetric information about *used* cars.* Auto owners have much more knowledge about the mechanical condition of their vehicles than do potential buyers of used cars. At the time of the purchase, individual buyers of used cars find it difficult to distinguish between so-called lemons—defective cars—and vehicles of the same make and model that operate perfectly. Therefore, a single price emerges for used cars of the same year, make, and model whether they are lemons or high-quality vehicles. This price roughly reflects the average quality of the vehicles, influenced by the proportion of lemons to high-quality cars. The higher the proportion of lemons, lower are the prices of used cars.

An adverse selection problem now becomes evident. Owners of lemons have an incentive to sell their cars to unsuspecting buyers, while owners of high-quality autos will wish to keep their cars. Therefore, most used cars on the market will be of lower quality than the same car models which are *not* for sale. As people become aware of

*The classic article on this topic is George A. Akerlof's "The Market for 'Lemons': Qualitative Uncertainty and the Market Mechanism," *Quarterly Journal of Economics*, August 1970, pp. 488–500.

this, the demand for used cars will decline and prices of used cars will fall. These lower prices will further reduce the incentive of owners of high-quality used cars to offer them for sale. At the extreme, only lemons will appear on the market; *poor-quality products will drive out high-quality products.* This suggests a solution to our paradox. Once a buyer drives a new car away from the dealership, the auto's value becomes the value set in the used-car lemons market. This is true even though the probability is high that the new car is of high quality.

The instantaneous loss of new-car value would be even greater were it not for several factors. Because new-car warranties are transferable to used-car buyers, purchasers of low-mileage late-model cars are protected against costly repairs. Thus, the demand for these vehicles rises. Also, prospective buyers can distinguish good cars from lemons by hiring mechanics to perform inspections. Moreover, sellers can signal potential buyers that their cars are not lemons through ads such as "Must sell, transferred abroad" or "Divorce forces sale." Of course, the buyer must determine the truth of these claims. Also, auto rental companies routinely sell high-quality, late-model cars, increasing the ratio of good used cars to lemons.

Government also plays a role in solving the market failure evident in the lemons market. Many states have "lemon laws" which force auto dealers to take back defective new cars. Dealers cannot offer these lemons for sale in the used-car market until completing all needed repairs. Also, some states require dealers to either offer warranties on used cars or state that a car is offered "as is." The latter designation clues the buyer that the car may be defective.

In brief, both private and governmental actions reduce the lemons problem. Nevertheless, the principle is applicable to a wide variety of used products such as autos, computers, and cameras, which are complex and occasionally defective. Buying any of these used products remains a somewhat risky transaction.

---

ning to hire an arsonist to "torch" his failing business has an incentive to buy fire insurance.

Our hypothetical divorce insurance sheds further light on the adverse selection problem. If the insur-

ance firm sets the premiums on the basis of the average divorce rate, many married couples who are about to obtain a divorce will buy insurance. An insurance premium based on average probabilities will make a great insurance buy for those about to get divorced. Meanwhile, those in highly stable marriages will not buy it.

The adverse selection problem thus tends to eliminate the pooling of low and high risks, which is the basis for profitable insurance. Insurance rates then must be so high that few people would want to (or be able to) buy this insurance.

Where private firms underprovide insurance because of information problems, government often establishes some type of social insurance. Government can require everyone in a particular group to take the insurance and thereby can overcome the adverse selection problem. Example: Although the social security system in the United States is partly an insurance and partly a welfare program, in its broadest sense it is insurance against poverty during old age. The social security insurance program requires nearly universal participation: People who are most likely to need the minimum benefits that social security provides are automatically participants in the program. So, too, are those not likely to need the benefits. There is, then, no adverse selection problem.

Workplace Safety   The labor market also provides an example of how inadequate information about buyers (employers) can produce market failures.

For several reasons employers have an economic incentive to provide safe workplaces. A safe workplace reduces the amount of disruption of the production process created by job accidents and lowers the costs of recruiting, screening, training, and retaining new workers. It also reduces a firm's worker compensation insurance premiums (legally required insurance against job injuries).

But a safe workplace is expensive: Safe equipment, protective gear, and slower paces of work all entail costs. The firm will decide how much safety to provide by comparing its marginal cost and marginal benefit of providing a safer workplace. Will this amount of job safety achieve economic efficiency, as well as maximize the firm's profit?

The answer is "yes" if the labor and product markets are competitive and workers are fully aware of the job risks at various places of employment. With full information, workers will avoid employers having unsafe workplaces. The supply of labor to these establishments will be greatly restricted, forcing them to boost their wages to attract a work force. The higher wages will then give these em-

ployers an incentive to provide increased workplace safety; safer workplaces will reduce wage expenses. Only firms which find it very costly to provide safer workplaces will choose to pay high compensating wage differentials rather than reduce workplace hazards.

But a serious problem arises when workers *do not know* that particular occupations or workplaces are unsafe. Because information involving the buyer— that is, about the employer and the workplace—is inadequate, the firm *may not* need to pay a wage premium to attract its work force. Its incentive to remove safety hazards therefore will be diminished, and its profit-maximizing level of workplace safety will be less than economically desirable. In brief, the labor market will fail because of asymmetric information— in this case, sellers (workers) having less information than buyers (employers).

Government has several options for remedying this information problem:

1. It can directly provide information to workers about the injury experience of various employers, much like it publishes the on-time performance of the various airlines.

2. It can require that firms provide information to workers about known workplace hazards.

3. It can establish standards of workplace safety and enforce them through inspection and penalties.

The Federal government has mainly employed the "standards and enforcement" approach to improve workplace safety, but some critics contend that an "information" strategy might be less costly and more effective. **(Key Question 13)**

Qualification

People have found many ingenious ways to overcome information difficulties without government intervention. For example, many firms offer product warranties to overcome the lack of information about themselves and their products. Franchising also helps overcome this problem. When you visit McDonald's or Marriot, you know precisely what you are going to get, as opposed to stopping at Bob's Hamburger Shop or the Bates Motel.

Also, some private firms and organizations specialize in providing information to buyers and sellers. *Consumer Reports* and the *Mobil Travel Guide* provide product information; labor unions collect and disseminate information about job safety; and credit bureaus provide information to insurance companies.

Brokers, bonding agencies, and intermediaries also provide information to clients.

However, economists agree that the private sector cannot remedy all information problems. In some situations, government intervention is desirable to promote an efficient allocation of society's scarce resources.

QUICK REVIEW 30-4

■ Asymmetric information is a source of potential market failure, causing society's scarce resources to be allocated inefficiently.

■ Inadequate information about sellers and their products may lead to an underallocation of resources to those products.

■ The moral hazard problem is the tendency of one party to a contract to alter its behavior in ways that are costly to the other party; for example, a person who buys insurance may willingly incur added risk.

■ The adverse selection problem arises when one party to a contract has less information than the other party and incurs a cost because of that asymmetrical information. For example, an insurance company offering "no-medical-exam-required" life insurance policies may attract customers who have life-threatening diseases.

CHAPTER SUMMARY

- -

1. Graphically, the collective demand curve for a particular public good can be found by summing *vertically* each of the individual demand curves for that good. The demand curve resulting from this process indicates the collective willingness to pay for the last unit of any given amount of the public good.

2. The optimal quantity of a public good occurs where the combined willingness to pay for the last unit—the marginal benefit of the good—equals the good's marginal cost.

3. Benefit-cost analysis can provide guidance as to the economic desirability and most efficient scope of public goods output.

4. Spillovers or externalities cause the equilibrium output of certain goods to vary from the optimal output. Spillover costs (negative externalities) result in an overallocation of resources which can be corrected by legislation or specific taxes. Spillover benefits (positive externalities) are accompanied by an underallocation of resources which can be corrected by subsidies to consumers, subsidies to producers, or government provision.

5. According to the Coase theorem, private bargaining is capable of solving potential externality problems where **(a)** the property rights are clearly defined, **(b)** the number of people involved is small, and **(c)** bargaining costs are negligible.

6. Clearly established property rights and liability rules permit some spillover costs to be prevented or remedied through private lawsuits. Lawsuits, however, can be costly, time-consuming, and uncertain as to their results.

7. Direct controls and specific taxes can improve resource allocation in situations where negative externalities affect many people and community resources. Both direct

controls (e.g., smokestack emission standards) and specific taxes (e.g., taxes on firms producing toxic chemicals) increase production costs and hence product price. As product price rises, the externality is reduced since less of the output is bought and sold.

8. Markets for pollution rights, where people can buy and sell the right to discharge a fixed amount of pollution, put a price on pollution and encourage firms to reduce or eliminate it.

9. The socially optimal amount of externality abatement occurs where society's marginal cost and marginal benefit of reducing the externality are equal. This optimal amount of pollution abatement is likely to be less than a 100 percent reduction. Changes in technology or changes in society's attitudes about pollution can affect the optimal amount of pollution abatement.

10. The law of conservation of matter and energy is at the heart of the pollution problem. Matter can be transformed into other matter or into energy but does not disappear. If not recycled, all production will ultimately end up as waste. More immediate causes of pollution are a growing population, rising per-person consumption, some new technologies, and the tendency to overuse and abuse resources owned in common.

11. The Superfund law of 1980 places a tax on producers of chemicals and uses the proceeds to clean up toxic-waste dumps. The Clean Air Act of 1990 seeks to **(a)** reduce toxic air pollution, **(b)** hasten smog reduction in urban areas, **(c)** limit the use of substances which are depleting the earth's ozone layer, and **(d)** reduce acid rain by cutting emissions of sulfur dioxide. Under the law, utilities are able to buy and sell emission credits for sulfur dioxide.

12. Recycling is a recent response to the growing garbage disposal problem. The equilibrium price and quantity of recyclable inputs depend on their demand and supply. Government can encourage recycling through either demand or supply incentives.

13. Asymmetric information between sellers and buyers can cause markets to fail. The moral hazard problem occurs when people alter their behavior after they sign a contract, imposing costs on the other party. The adverse selection problem occurs when one party to a contract takes advantage of the other party's inadequate information, resulting in an unanticipated loss to the latter party.

TERMS AND CONCEPTS

benefit-cost analysis

marginal benefit = marginal cost rule

Coase theorem

market for externality rights

optimal reduction of an externality

law of conservation of matter and energy

Superfund law of 1980

Clean Air Act of 1990

asymmetric information

moral hazard problem

adverse selection problem

STUDY QUESTIONS

1. KEY QUESTION Based on the following three individual demand schedules for a particular good, and assuming these three people are the only ones in the society, determine **(a)** the market demand schedule on the assumption that the good is a private good, and **(b)** the collective demand schedule on the assumption that the good is a public good. Explain the differences, if any, in your schedules.

Individual 1		Individual 2		Individual 3	
P	Q_d	P	Q_d	P	Q_d
$8	0	$8	1	$8	0
7	0	7	2	7	0
6	0	6	3	6	1
5	1	5	4	5	2
4	2	4	5	4	3
3	3	3	6	3	4
2	4	2	7	2	5
1	5	1	8	1	6

2. KEY QUESTION Use your demand schedule for a public good, determined in question 1, and the following supply schedule to ascertain the optimal quantity of this public good. Why is this the optimal quantity?

P	Q_s
$19	10
16	8
13	6
10	4
7	2
4	1

3. KEY QUESTION The following table shows the total costs and total benefits in billions for four different antipollution programs of increasing scope. Which program should be undertaken? Why?

Program	Total cost	Total benefit
A	$ 3	$ 7
B	7	12
C	12	16
D	18	19

4. KEY QUESTION Why are spillover costs and spillover benefits also called negative and positive externalities? Show graphically how a tax can correct for a spillover cost and a subsidy to producers can correct for a spillover benefit. How does a subsidy to consumers differ from a subsidy to producers in correcting for a spillover benefit?

5. An apple grower's orchard provides nectar to a neighbor's bees, while the beekeeper's bees help the apple grower by pollinating the apple blossoms. Use Figure 30-2b to explain why this situation might lead to an underallocation of resources to apple growing and to beekeeping. How might this underallocation get resolved via the means suggested by the Coase theorem?

6. Explain: "Without a market for pollution rights, dumping pollutants into the air or water is costless; in the presence of the right to buy and sell pollution rights, dumping pollution creates an opportunity cost for the polluter." What is the significance of this opportunity cost to the search for better technology to reduce pollution?

7. KEY QUESTION Explain the following statement, using the MB curve in Figure 30-6 to illustrate: "The optimal amount of pollution abatement for some substances, say, water from storm drains, is very low; the optimal amount of abatement for other substances, say, cyanide poison, is close to 100 percent."

8. Relate the law of conservation of matter and energy to **(a)** the air pollution problem and **(b)** the solid-waste disposal problem. What is the "tragedy of the commons," as it relates to pollution?

9. What is the Superfund? How is it financed and for what purpose is it used? Are there any Superfund sites in your area? If so, determine the current status of the cleanup efforts.

10. Which aspects of the Clean Air Act of 1990 reflect the direct-control approach to pollution? Which part of this law incorporates a market for pollution rights?

11. Explain why there may be insufficient recycling of products when the externalities associated with land-fills and garbage incinerators are not considered. What demand and supply incentives might government provide to promote more recycling? Explain how there could be too much recycling in some situations.

12. Why is it in the interest of new home buyers *and* builders of new homes to have government building codes and building inspectors?

13. KEY QUESTION Place an M beside those items in the following list which describe a moral hazard problem and an A beside those which describe an adverse selection problem.
   a. A person with a terminal illness buys several life insurance policies through the mail.
   b. A person drives carelessly because he or she has automobile insurance.

   c. A person who intends to "torch" his warehouse takes out a large fire insurance policy.
   d. A professional athlete who has a guaranteed contract fails to stay in shape during the off-season.
   e. A woman anticipating having a large family takes a job with a firm which offers exceptional child-care benefits.

14. (Last Word) Explain how the prices of used cars are affected by **(a)** asymmetric information and **(b)** adverse selection.

15. WEB-BASED QUESTION **Clean Water and Government Intervention** Government can use direct controls in the form of legislation to reduce negative externalities such as water pollution. The Office of Water http://www.epa.gov/ow/ is responsible for implementing the Clean Water Act and Safe Drinking Water Act. What is the Clean Water Act, and how does the Office of Water enforce it? In 1972 only a third of the nation's waters were safe for fishing and swimming, wetlands losses were estimated at about 460,000 acres annually, and sewage-treatment plants served only 85 million people. Has the Clean Water Act and the Office of Water been successful in improving these numbers?

16. WEB-BASED QUESTION **Information Failures—AMA's Physician Quality Program** Information failures occur when either buyers or sellers have incomplete or inaccurate information and their cost of obtaining better information is prohibitive. Physicians have passed qualifying tests and are licensed by the government, yet there still is concern about physician quality. The American Medical Association http://www.ama-assn.org/ developed the American Medical Accreditation Program (AMAP) as a way to establish and maintain the high quality of physician care. How is AMAP different from the existing requirements physicians must meet to practice medicine? Is AMAP accreditation a substitute for or equivalent to Board Certification?

CHAPTER THIRTY-ONE

Public Choice Theory and Taxation

31

Why are so many people disenchanted with—even distrustful of—government? One reason is the apparent failure of costly government programs to resolve socio-economic ills. For example, despite billions of dollars spent on the problem, wide-spread poverty in the United States remains. The U.S. farm programs were designed to save the family farm; instead, they have subsidized large corporate farms, which, in turn, have driven family farms out of business. While per-pupil spending has shot upward in U.S. public education, the academic performance of U.S. students on stan-dardized tests compares unfavorably with that of students in many other nations.

There are charges that government agencies have become bogged down in pa-perwork; that the public bureaucracy produces trivial regulations and great dupli-cation of effort; that obsolete programs persist; that various agencies work at cross purposes; and so on.

Just as there are failures in the private sector's market system, the above sug-gests there are also deficiencies within the public sector. In this chapter we exam-ine some of those shortcomings. We begin with two topics from **public choice the-ory**—the economic analysis of government decision making. First, we examine the problem society has in revealing its true preferences through majority voting; then we discuss so-called *government failure*—the idea that certain characteristics of the public sector keep it from promoting an efficient allocation of resources. Next we shift to **public finance**—the study of public expenditures and revenues. There, we examine taxes and tax incidence to see how taxes are apportioned in the United States, analyze inefficiencies arising through taxation, and discuss two proposed types of tax reforms.

The chapter ends with a very brief discussion of conservative and liberal stances on government and economic freedom.

REVEALING PREFERENCES THROUGH MAJORITY VOTING

Which public goods should government pro-duce and in what amounts? In what circum-stances and through what methods should gov-ernment intervene to correct for externalities? How should the tax burden of financing gov-ernment be apportioned?

Decisions like these are made collectively in the United States through a democratic process relying heavily on majority voting. Candidates for office offer alternative policy packages, and citizens elect people whom they think will make the best decisions on their collective behalf. Voters "retire" officials who do not adequately represent their collective wishes and elect persons they think do. Also, citizens periodically have opportunities at the state and local levels to vote directly on public expenditures or new legislation.

This democratic process generally works well at revealing society's true preferences, but it has shortcomings. Just as the market sometimes fails to allocate resources efficiently, the system of voting sometimes produces inefficiencies and inconsistencies.

Inefficient Voting Outcomes

Providing a public good which has a total benefit greater than its total cost will add to society's well-being. Unfortunately, majority voting does not always produce such an economically efficient outcome. Voters may defeat a proposal to provide a public good even though it may yield total benefits exceeding its total cost. Conversely, it is possible that majority voting could result in the provision of a public good costing more than the benefits it yields.

Illustration: Inefficient "No" Vote Suppose government can provide a public good, say, national defense, at a total expense of $900. Also, assume there are only three individuals—Adams, Benson, and

Conrad—in the society and they will share the $900 tax expense equally, each paying $300 of tax if the proposed good is provided. Suppose, as illustrated in Figure 31-1a, that Adams is willing to pay $700 to have this good; Benson, $250; and Conrad, $200.

What will be the result if a majority vote determines whether or not this good will be provided? Although people do not always vote strictly according to their own economic interest, it is likely Benson and Conrad will vote "no" because they will incur tax expenses of $300 each while gaining benefits of only $250 and $200, respectively. Adams will vote "yes." So the majority vote will defeat the proposal even though the total benefit of $1150 (= $700 for Adams + $250 for Benson + $200 for Conrad) exceeds the total cost of $900. Resources should be devoted to this good, but they will not be.

Illustration: Inefficient "Yes" Vote We can also construct an example in which the majority favors a public good even though its total cost exceeds its total benefit. Figure 31-1b shows the details. Again, Adams, Benson, and Conrad will equally share the $900 cost of the public good; they will each be taxed $300. But now Adams is only willing to pay $100 for the public good, rather than forgo it. Meanwhile, Benson and Conrad are willing to pay $350 each. They will vote for the public good; Adams will vote against it. The majority vote will provide a public good costing $900 which produces total benefits of only $800 (= $100 for Adams + $350 for

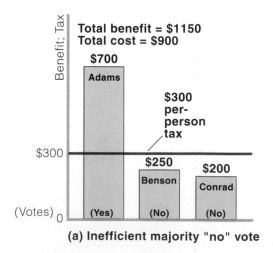
(a) Inefficient majority "no" vote

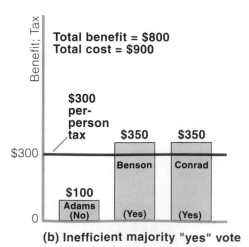
(b) Inefficient majority "yes" vote

FIGURE 31-1 Inefficient voting outcomes Majority voting can produce inefficient decisions. (a) Majority voting leads to rejection of a public good which would entail a greater total benefit than total cost. (b) Majority voting results in acceptance of a public good having a higher total cost than total benefit.

Benson + $350 for Conrad). Society's resources will be inefficiently allocated to this public good.

Conclusion The point of our examples is that an inefficiency may occur as either an overproduction or an underproduction of a specific public good, and therefore as an overallocation or underallocation of resources for that particular use. In Chapter 30 we saw that government can improve economic efficiency by providing public goods which the market system will not make available. Now we have extended that analysis to reveal that government might fail to provide some public goods whose production is economically justifiable while providing other goods that are not economically warranted.

In our examples, each person has only a single vote, no matter how much he or she might gain or lose from a public good. In the first example (inefficient "no" vote), Adams would be willing to purchase a vote from either Benson or Conrad if buying votes were legal. That way Adams could be assured of obtaining the national defense he so highly values. But buying votes is illegal, so many people with strong preferences for certain public goods may have to go without them.

When individual consumers have a strong preference for a specific *private good*, they usually can find it in the marketplace even though it may be unpopular with the majority of consumers. A consumer can buy beef tongue, liver, and squid in some supermarkets, although it is doubtful that these products would be available if majority voting stocked the shelves. But a person cannot easily "buy" a *public good* such as national defense once the majority has decided against it.

On the other hand, a consumer in the marketplace can decide *not* to buy a particular product, even a popular one. But although you may not want national defense, you must "buy" it through your tax payments when it is favored by the majority.

Conclusion: *Because it fails to incorporate the strength of the preferences of the individual voter, majority voting may produce economically inefficient outcomes.*

Interest Groups and Logrolling There are avenues for resolving the just-mentioned inefficiencies associated with majority voting. Two examples follow.

Interest Groups Those who have a strong preference for a public good may band together into interest groups and use advertisements, mailings, and direct persuasion to convince others of the merits of

that public good. Adams might try to persuade Benson and Conrad that it is in their best interest to vote for national defense—that national defense is much more valuable to them than their $250 and $200 valuations. Such appeals are common in democratic politics.

Political Logrolling Logrolling—the trading of votes to secure favorable outcomes—can also turn an inefficient outcome into an efficient one. In our first example (Figure 31-1a), perhaps Benson has a strong preference for a different public good, say, a new road, which Adams and Conrad do not think is worth the tax expense. That would provide an opportunity for Adams and Benson to trade votes to ensure provision of both national defense and the new road. That is, Adams and Benson would each vote "yes" on both measures. Adams would get the national defense and Benson would get the road. Without the logrolling, both public goods would have been rejected. Moreover, the logrolling will add to society's well-being if, as was true for national defense, the road creates a greater overall benefit than cost.

But logrolling need not increase economic efficiency. Even if national defense and the road each cost more than the total benefit it produces, both might still be provided because of the vote trading. Adams and Benson might still engage in logrolling if each expects to secure a sufficient net gain from her or his favored public good, even though the gains would come at the clear expense of Conrad.

Logrolling can either increase or diminish economic efficiency, depending on the circumstances.

Paradox of Voting

Another difficulty with majority voting is the **paradox of voting,** *a situation in which society may not be able to rank its preferences consistently through paired-choice majority voting.*

Preferences Consider Table 31-1, in which we again assume a community of three voters: Adams, Benson, and Conrad. Suppose the community has three alternative public goods from which to choose: national defense, a road, and a weather warning system. We expect that each member of the community prefers the three alternatives in a certain order. For example, one person might prefer national defense to a road, and a road to a weather warning system. We can attempt to determine the preferences of the community through paired-choice majority voting. Specifically, a vote can be held between any two

TABLE 31-1   Paradox of voting

Public Good	Preferences		
	Adams	Benson	Conrad
National defense	1st choice	3d choice	2d choice
Road	2d choice	1st choice	3d choice
Weather warning system	3d choice	2d choice	1st choice

Election	Voting outcomes: winner
1. National defense vs. road	National defense (preferred by Adams and Conrad)
2. Road vs. weather warning system	Road (preferred by Adams and Benson)
3. National defense vs. weather warning system	Weather warning system (preferred by Benson and Conrad)

of the public goods, and the winner of that vote can then be matched against the third public good in another vote.

The three goods and the assumed individual preferences of the three voters are listed in the top part of Table 31-1. The data indicate that Adams prefers national defense to the road and the road to the weather warning system. This implies also that Adams prefers national defense to the weather warning system. Benson values the road more than the weather warning system and the warning system more than national defense. Conrad's order of preference is weather warning system, national defense, and road.

Voting Outcomes The lower part of Table 31-1 shows the outcomes of three hypothetical elections decided through majority vote. In the first, national defense wins against the road because a majority of voters (Adams and Conrad) prefer national defense to the road. In the second election, to see whether this community wants a road or a weather warning system, a majority of voters (Adams and Benson) prefer the road.

We have determined that the majority of people in this community prefer national defense to a road *and* prefer a road to a weather warning system. It seems logical to conclude that the community prefers national defense to a weather warning system. But it does not!

To demonstrate this conclusion, we hold a direct election between national defense and the weather warning system. Row (3) shows that a majority of voters (Benson and Conrad) prefer the weather warning system to national defense. As listed in Table 31-1, then, the three paired-choice majority votes imply that this community is irrational: it seems to prefer national defense to a road *and* a road to a weather warning system, but would rather have a weather warning system than national defense.

The problem is not irrational community preferences but rather a flawed procedure for determining those preferences. We see that the outcome from paired-choice majority voting may depend on the order in which the votes are taken up. Under some circumstances majority voting fails to make *consistent* choices which reflect the community's underlying preferences. As a consequence, government may find it difficult to provide the "correct" public goods by acting in accordance with majority voting. Important note: This critique is *not* to suggest there is some better procedure. Majority voting is much more likely to reflect community preferences than decisions by, say, dictators or groups of self-appointed leaders. (**Key Question 2**)

Median-Voter Model

One final aspect of majority voting reveals insights into real-world phenomena. The **median-voter model** suggests that *under majority rule the median voter will in a sense determine the outcomes of elections.* The median voter is the person holding the middle position on an issue: half the other voters have stronger preferences for a public good, amount of taxation, or degree of government regulation, and half have weaker—or negative—preferences. The extreme voters on each side of an issue prefer the median choice rather than the other extreme position, so the median voter's choice predominates.

Example Suppose a society composed of Adams, Benson, and Conrad has reached agreement that as a society it needs a weather warning system. Each independently is to submit a total dollar amount he or she thinks should be spent on the warning system, assuming each will be taxed one-third of that amount. An election will determine the size of the system. Because each person can be expected to vote for his or her own proposal, no majority will occur if all the proposals are placed on the ballot at the same time. Thus, the group decides on a paired-choice vote: they will first vote between two of the proposals and then match the winner of that vote against the remaining proposal.

The three proposals are as follows: Adams desires a $400 system; Benson wants an $800 system; Conrad opts for a $300 system. Which proposal will win? The median-voter model suggests it will be the $400 proposal submitted by the median voter, Adams. Half the other voters favor a more costly system; half favor a less costly system. To understand why the $400 system will be the outcome, let's conduct the two elections.

First, suppose that the $400 proposal is matched against the $800 proposal. Adams naturally votes for her $400 proposal, and Benson votes for his own $800 proposal. Conrad—who proposed a $300 expenditure for the warning system—votes for the $400 proposal because it is closer to his own. So Adams' $400 proposal is selected by a 2-to-1 majority vote.

Next, we match the $400 proposal against the $300 proposal. Again the $400 proposal wins, because it gets a vote from Adams and one from Benson, who proposed the $800 expenditure and for that reason prefers a $400 expenditure to a $300 one. Adams—the median voter in this case—in a sense is the person who has decided the level of expenditure on a weather warning system for this society.

Real-World Applicability Although our illustration is a simple one, this idea explains much. We *do* note a tendency for public choices to match most closely the median view. Political candidates, for example, take one set of positions to win the nomination of their political parties; in so doing, they tend to appeal to the median voter *within their party* to get the nomination. They then shift their views more closely to the political center when they square off against opponents from the opposite political party. In effect, they redirect their appeal toward the median voter *within the total population.* They also try to label their opponents as being too liberal, or too conservative, and out of touch with "mainstream America." And they conduct polls and adjust their positions on issues accordingly.

Implications The median-voter model has two important implications:

1. Many people will be dissatisfied by the extent of government involvement in the economy. The size of government will largely be determined by the median preference, leaving many people desiring a much larger, or a much smaller, public sector. In the marketplace you can buy zero zucchinis, 2 zucchinis, or 200 zucchinis, depending on how much you enjoy them. In the public sector you get the number of Stealth bombers and interstate highways the median voter prefers.

2. Some people may "vote with their feet" by moving into political jurisdictions where the median voter's preferences are closer to their own. Someone may move from the city to a suburb where the level of government services, and therefore taxes, is lower. Or they may move into an area known for its excellent, but expensive, school system.

For these reasons, and because our personal preferences for government activity are not static, the median preference shifts over time. Also, information about people's preferences is imperfect, leaving much room for politicians to misjudge the true median position. **(Key Question 3)**

PUBLIC SECTOR FAILURE

We have seen that the economic results of the marketplace are not always satisfactory and that government actions can help. Economists agree that government has a legitimate function in dealing with instances of *market failure.* They advocate the use of benefit-cost analysis to make efficient decisions, including adjustments for widespread spillover costs and benefits, provision of public goods and services, appropriate market information, and so on.

But as implied in our discussion of voting problems, the economic functions of government are not always performed effectively and efficiently. In fact, there may be inherent shortcomings within the public sector which keep it from promoting economic efficiency. These shortcomings may result in so-called **public sector failure**—inefficient operation of the public sector in an economic sense. Let's consider some sources of government inefficiency.

Special Interests and Rent Seeking

Casual reflection suggests there may be a significant gap between "sound economics" and "good politics."

Sound economics calls for the public sector to pursue various programs as long as marginal benefits exceed marginal costs. Good politics, however, suggests that politicians support programs and policies which will maximize their chance of getting elected and staying in office. This gap may result in government promoting the goals of groups of voters which have special interests to the detriment of the larger public. In the process, economic inefficiency can result.

Special-Interest Effect   Efficient public decision making is often impaired by the **special-interest effect.** This is any outcome of the political process whereby *a small number of people obtain a government program or policy which gives them large gains at the expense of a much greater number of persons who individually suffer small losses.*

The small group of potential beneficiaries are well informed and highly vocal on the issue in question; they press politicians for approval. The large numbers facing very small individual losses are generally uninformed on this issue. Politicians feel they will lose the support of the small special-interest group which backs the issue if they legislate against it but will *not* lose the support of the large group of uninformed voters, who will likely evaluate them on other issues in which these voters have a stronger interest.

The special-interest effect is also evident in so-called *pork-barrel politics,* which involves securing a government project yielding benefits mainly to a single political district and its political representative. In this case, the special-interest group comprises local constituents, while the larger group consists of relatively uninformed taxpayers scattered across a much larger geographic area. Politicians clearly have a strong incentive to secure public goods ("pork") for local constituents. These goods win political favor; they are highly valued by constituents and paid for mainly by the much larger group of relatively uninformed taxpayers.

Finally, a politician's inclination to support the smaller group of special beneficiaries is enhanced because special-interest groups are often quite willing to help finance the campaigns of "right-minded" politicians and politicians who "bring home the pork." The result is that politicians may support special-interest programs and projects which are not justifiable on economic grounds.

Rent-Seeking Behavior   The appeal to government for special benefits at taxpayers' or someone else's expense is called **rent seeking.** To economists, "rent" is a payment beyond that necessary to keep a resource supplied in its current use. Corporations, trade associations, labor unions, and professional organizations employ vast resources to secure favorable government policies which result in rent—higher profit or income than would occur under competitive market conditions. Government is *able* to dispense such rent directly or indirectly through laws, rules, hiring, and purchases. Elected officials are *willing* to provide such rent because they want to be responsive to key constituents, who in turn help them remain in office.

Here are some examples of "rent-providing" legislation or policies: tariffs on foreign products which limit competition and raise prices to consumers; tax breaks which benefit specific corporations; public works projects which create union jobs but cost more than the benefits they yield; occupational licensing which goes beyond what is needed to protect consumers; and large subsidies to farmers by taxpayers. None of these is justified by economic efficiency.

Clear Benefits, Hidden Costs

Some critics say vote-seeking politicians will not objectively weigh all costs and benefits of various programs, as economic rationality demands, in deciding which to support and which to reject. Because political officeholders must seek voter support every few years, they favor programs with immediate and clear-cut benefits and with vague or deferred costs. Conversely, politicians will reject programs with immediate and easily identifiable costs but with long-term, less measurable benefits.

Such biases can lead politicians to reject economically justifiable programs and to accept programs which are economically irrational. Example: A proposal to construct and expand mass-transit systems in large metropolitan areas may be economically rational on the basis of benefit-cost analysis. But if (1) the program is to be financed by immediate increases in highly visible income or sales taxes and (2) benefits will occur years from now when the project is completed, then the vote-seeking politician may oppose the program.

Assume, on the other hand, that a program of Federal aid to municipal police forces is not justifiable on the basis of benefit-cost analysis. But if the cost is deferred through deficit financing, the program's modest benefits may seem so large that it gains approval.

Limited and Bundled Choice

Some public choice theorists say the political process forces citizens and their elected representatives to be less selective in choosing public goods and services than they are in choosing private goods and services.

In the marketplace, the citizen as a consumer can exactly satisfy personal preferences by buying certain goods and not buying others. However, in the public sector the citizen as a voter is confronted with, say, only two or three candidates for an office, each representing a different "bundle" of programs (public goods and services). None of these bundles of public goods is likely to exactly fit the preferences of any particular voter. Yet the voter must choose one of them. The candidate who comes closest to voter Smith's preference may endorse national health insurance, increases in social security benefits, subsidies to tobacco farmers, and tariffs on imported goods. Smith will likely vote for this candidate even though Smith may oppose tobacco subsidies.

In other words, the voter must take the bad with the good. In the public sector, people are forced to "buy" goods and services they do not want. It is as if, in going to a sporting-goods store, you were forced to buy an unwanted pool cue to get a wanted pair of running shoes. This is a situation where resources are not being used efficiently to best satisfy consumer wants. In this sense, the provision of public goods and services is inherently inefficient.

Congress is confronted with a similar limited-choice, bundled-goods problem. Appropriations legislation combines hundreds, even thousands, of spending items into a single bill. Many of these spending items may be completely unrelated to the main purpose of the legislation. Yet congressional representatives must vote the entire package—yea or nay. Unlike consumers in the marketplace, they cannot be selective. **(Key Question 4)**

Bureaucracy and Inefficiency

Some economists contend that public agencies are generally less efficient than private businesses. The reason is *not* that lazy and incompetent workers somehow end up in the public sector, while ambitious and capable people gravitate to the private sector. Rather, it is that the market system creates incentives and pressures for internal efficiency which are absent in the public sector. Private enterprises have a clear goal—profit. Whether a private firm is in a competitive or monopolistic market, efficient management means lower costs and enlarged profit. The increased profit not only benefits the firm's owners but enhances the promotion prospects of managers. Moreover, part of the managers' pay may be tied to profit via profit-sharing plans and bonuses. There is no similar identifiable gain to government agencies and their managers—no counterpart to profit—which creates a strong incentive to achieve efficiency.

The market system imposes a very obvious test of performance on private firms: the test of profit and loss. An efficient firm is profitable and therefore successful; it survives, prospers, and grows. An inefficient firm is unprofitable and unsuccessful; it declines and in time goes bankrupt and ceases to exist. But there is no similar, clear-cut test that assesses the efficiency or inefficiency of public agencies. How can anyone determine whether a public hydroelectricity provider, a state university, a local fire department, the Department of Agriculture, or the Bureau of Indian Affairs is operating efficiently?

Cynics even argue that a public agency which uses its resources inefficiently is likely to survive and grow! In the private sector, inefficiency and monetary loss lead to the abandonment of certain activities or products or even firms. But government, they say, does not like to abandon activities in which it has failed. Some suggest that the typical response of government to a program's failure is to double its budget and staff. This means public sector inefficiency just continues on a larger scale.

Furthermore, economists assert that government employees, together with the special-interest groups they serve, often gain sufficient political clout to block attempts to pare down or eliminate their agencies. Politicians attempting to reduce the size of the huge Federal bureaucracies such as those relating to agriculture, education, health and welfare, and national defense will incur sizable political risk, since bureaucrats and special-interest groups will team up to defeat them.

Finally, critics point out that there is a tendency for government bureaucracy to justify continued employment by looking for and eventually finding new problems to solve. Perhaps it is not surprising that social "problems," as defined by government, tend to persist or even expand.

The Last Word at the end of this chapter highlights several recent media-reported examples of the special-interest effect, the problem of limited and bundled choices, and problems of government bureaucracy. You might want to read through these examples now, relating each to the discussion we just completed.

Imperfect Institutions

It is possible to argue that these criticisms of public sector efficiency are exaggerated and cynical. Perhaps so. Nevertheless, they do tend to shatter the concept of a benevolent government which responds with precision and efficiency to the wants of its citizens. The market system of the private sector is far from perfectly efficient. Government's economic function is mainly to correct the market system's shortcomings. But the public sector is also subject to deficiencies in fulfilling its economic function. "The relevant comparison is not between perfect markets and imperfect governments, nor between faulty markets and all-knowing, rational, benevolent governments, but between inevitably imperfect institutions."[1]

Because the market system and public agencies are both imperfect, it can sometimes be difficult to determine whether a particular activity can be performed with greater success in the private sector or the public sector. It is easy to reach agreement on opposite extremes: national defense must lie with the public sector, while wheat production can best be accomplished by the private sector. But what about health insurance? Parks and recreation areas? Fire protection? Garbage collection? Housing? Education? It is very hard to assess every good or service and to say absolutely that it should be assigned to either the public sector or the private sector. Evidence: All the goods and services just mentioned are provided in part by both private enterprises and public agencies.

QUICK REVIEW 31-1

■ Majority voting can produce voting outcomes which are inefficient; projects having greater total benefits than total costs can be defeated and projects having greater total costs than total benefits can be approved.

■ The paradox of voting occurs where voting by majority rule does not provide a consistent ranking of society's preferences for public goods and services.

■ The median-voter model suggests that under majority rule the voter having the middle preference will determine the outcome of an election.

■ Public sector failure allegedly occurs because of rent seeking, pressure by special-interest groups, shortsighted political behavior, limited and bundled choices, and bureaucratic inefficiency.

---

[1]Otto Eckstein, *Public Finance*, 3d ed. (Englewood Cliffs, NJ: Prentice-Hall, 1973), p. 17.

APPORTIONING THE TAX BURDEN

We now turn from the difficulties of making collective decisions about public goods to the difficulties of deciding how those goods should be financed.

The characteristics of public goods make it difficult to measure precisely how their benefits are apportioned among individuals and institutions. We cannot accurately determine how much citizen Mildred Moore benefits from military installations, a network of highways, a public school system, the national weather bureau, and local police and fire protection.

The situation is different in regard to paying for those benefits. Studies do reveal with reasonable clarity how the overall tax burden is apportioned. (By "tax burden" we mean the total cost of taxes imposed on society.) This apportionment question affects each of us. The overall level of taxes is important, but the average citizen is much more concerned with his or her part of the overall tax burden.

Benefits Received versus Ability to Pay

There are two basic philosophies on how the economy's tax burden should be apportioned.

Benefits-Received Principle The **benefits-received principle** of taxation asserts that households and businesses should purchase the goods and services of government in the same way they buy other commodities. Those who benefit most from government-supplied goods or services should pay the taxes necessary to finance them. A few public goods are now financed on this basis. Money collected as gasoline taxes is typically used to finance highway construction and repairs. Thus, people who benefit from good roads pay the cost of those roads. Difficulties immediately arise, however, when we consider widespread application of the benefits-received principle.

1. How will government determine the benefits individual households and businesses receive from national defense, education, and police and fire protection? Recall that public goods provide widespread spillover benefits and that the exclusion principle does not apply. Even in the seemingly straightforward case of highway financing it is difficult to measure benefits. Individual car owners benefit in different degrees from good

roads. But others also benefit. For example, businesses benefit because good roads bring customers to them.

2. The benefits-received principle cannot logically be applied to income redistribution programs. It would be absurd and self-defeating to ask poor families to pay the taxes needed to finance their welfare payments. It would be ridiculous to think of taxing only unemployed workers to finance the unemployment compensation payments they receive.

Ability-to-Pay Principle The **ability-to-pay principle** of taxation asserts that the tax burden should be apportioned according to taxpayers' income and wealth. In the United States this means that individuals and businesses with larger incomes should pay more taxes—both absolutely and relatively—than those with smaller incomes.

What is the rationale of ability-to-pay taxation? Proponents argue that each additional dollar of income received by a household yields a smaller amount of satisfaction or marginal utility when it is spent. Because consumers act rationally, the first dollars of income received in any period of time will be spent on high-urgency goods yielding the greatest marginal utility. Successive dollars of income will go for less urgently needed goods and finally for trivial goods and services. This means a dollar taken through taxes from a poor person who has few dollars represents a greater utility sacrifice than a dollar taken by taxes from the rich person who has many dollars. To balance the sacrifices which taxes impose on income receivers, taxes should be apportioned according to the amount of income a taxpayer receives.

This argument is appealing, but application problems crop up here too. Although we might agree that the household earning $100,000 per year has a greater ability to pay taxes than a household receiving $10,000, we don't know exactly *how much more* ability to pay the first family has. Should the wealthier family pay the *same percentage* of its larger income—and hence a larger absolute amount—as taxes? Or should the richer family be made to pay a *larger fraction* of this income as taxes? And how much larger should that fraction be?

There is no scientific way of measuring someone's ability to pay taxes—and that's the main problem. In practice, the solution hinges on guesswork, the tax views of the political party in power, expediency, and how urgently the government needs revenue.

Progressive, Proportional, and Regressive Taxes

Any discussion of taxation leads ultimately to the question of tax rates. Recall from Chapter 5 that an *average tax rate* is the total tax paid divided by some base against which the tax is compared.

Definitions Taxes are classified as progressive, proportional, or regressive, depending on the relationship between tax rates and taxpayer *incomes*. We focus on incomes because all taxes—whether on income or on a product or a building or parcel of land—are ultimately paid out of someone's income.

1. A tax is **progressive** if its average rate *increases* as income increases. Such a tax claims not only a larger absolute (dollar) amount but also a larger percentage of income as income increases.

2. A tax is **regressive** if its average rate *declines* as income increases. Such a tax takes a smaller proportion of income as income increases. A regressive tax may or may not take a larger absolute amount of income as income increases.

3. A tax is **proportional** if its average rate *remains the same* regardless of the size of income.

We can illustrate these ideas with the personal income tax. Suppose tax rates are such that a household pays 10 percent of its income in taxes regardless of the size of its income. This is a proportional income tax.

Now suppose the rate structure is such that a household with an annual taxable income of less than $10,000 pays 5 percent in income taxes; a household with an income of $10,000 to $20,000 pays 10 percent; one with a $20,000 to $30,000 income pays 15 percent; and so forth. This is a *progressive* income tax.

Finally, suppose the rate declines as taxable income rises: you pay 15 percent if you earn less than $10,000; 10 percent if you earn $10,000 to $20,000; 5 percent if you earn $20,000 to $30,000; and so forth. This is a *regressive* income tax.

In general, progressive taxes are those which fall most heavily on the rich; regressive taxes are those which fall most heavily on the poor. **(Key Question 7)**

Applications Let's examine the progressivity, or regressivity, of several taxes.

Personal Income Tax We noted in Chapter 5 that the Federal *personal income tax* is progressive, with marginal tax rates—those assessed on *additional* income—ranging from 15 to 39.6 percent. Rules that allow individuals to deduct from income interest on home mortgages and property taxes, and that exempt interest on state and local bonds from taxation, tend to make the tax less progressive than these marginal rates suggest. Nevertheless, average tax rates rise with income.

Sales Taxes At first thought, a *general sales tax* with, say, a 3 percent rate would seem to be proportional. But in fact it is regressive with respect to income. A larger portion of a poor person's income is exposed to the tax than is the case for a rich person; the rich pay no tax on the part of income which is saved, whereas the poor are unable to save. Example: "Poor" Smith has an income of $15,000 and spends it all. "Rich" Jones has an income of $300,000 but spends only $200,000. Assuming a 3 percent sales tax applies to all expenditures of each individual, we find that Smith pays $450 (3 percent of $15,000) in sales taxes and Jones pays $6000 (3 percent of $200,000). But Smith pays $450/$15,000 or 3 percent of income as sales taxes, while Jones pays $6000/$300,000 or 2 percent of income. The general sales tax therefore is regressive.

Corporate Income Tax The Federal *corporate income tax* is essentially a proportional tax with a flat 35 percent tax rate. But this assumes that corporation owners (shareholders) bear the tax. Some tax experts argue that at least part of the tax is passed through to consumers in the form of higher product prices. To the extent that this occurs, the tax is like a sales tax and thus regressive.

Payroll Taxes Payroll (social security) taxes are regressive because they apply to only a fixed amount of income. For example, in 1998, payroll tax rates were 7.65 percent, but only of the first $68,400 of a person's wage income. Someone earning exactly $68,400 would pay $5232.60 or 7.65 percent of his or her wage income; someone with twice that income, or $136,800, would also pay $5232.60—only 3.825 percent of his or her wage income. Thus payroll taxes are also regressive.

Moreover, payroll taxes are not collected on non-wage income (like interest, dividends, or rents). This makes them even more regressive. If our individual with the $136,800 wage income also received $63,200 in nonwage income, then the payroll tax would be only 2.62 percent (= $5232.60/$200,000) of his or her total income.

Property Taxes Most economists conclude that *property taxes* on buildings are regressive for the same reasons as are sales taxes. First, property owners add the tax to the rents which tenants are charged. Second, property taxes, as a percentage of income, are higher for poor families than for rich families because the poor must spend a larger proportion of their incomes for housing. This alleged regressivity of property taxes may be increased by differences in property-tax rates from locality to locality. In general, property-tax rates are higher in poorer areas, to make up for lower property values.

TAX INCIDENCE AND EFFICIENCY LOSS

Determining whether a particular tax is progressive, proportional, or regressive is complicated because taxes are not always paid by those on whom they are levied. We therefore need to locate as best we can the final resting place of a tax, or the **tax incidence.** The tools of elasticity of supply and demand will help. We will focus on a hypothetical excise tax on wine levied on producers. Do the producers really pay this tax, or do they shift it to wine consumers?

Elasticity and Tax Incidence

In Figure 31-2, *S* and *D* represent the pretax market for a certain domestic wine; the no-tax equilibrium price and quantity are $4 per bottle and 15 million bottles. If government levies an excise tax of $1 per bottle at the winery, who actually pays it?

Division of Burden Since government places the tax on the sellers (suppliers), the tax can be viewed as an addition to the marginal cost of the product. Now sellers must get $1 more for each bottle to receive the same per-unit profit they were getting before the tax. While sellers are willing to offer, for example, 5 million bottles of untaxed wine at $2 per bottle, they must now receive $3 per bottle—$2 plus the $1 tax—to offer the same 5 million bottles. The tax shifts the supply curve upward (leftward) as shown in Figure 31-2, where S_t is the "after-tax" supply curve.

The after-tax equilibrium price is $4.50 per bottle, whereas the before-tax price was $4. So, in this case, half the $1 tax is paid by consumers as a higher price; the other half must be paid by producers in the form of a lower after-tax per-unit revenue. That is, af-

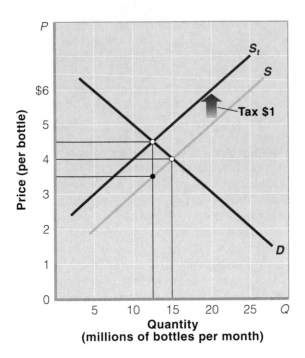

FIGURE 31-2 The incidence of an excise tax An excise tax of a specified amount, here $1 per unit, shifts the supply curve upward by the amount of the tax per unit: the vertical distance between S and S_t. This results in a higher price (here $4.50) to consumers and lower after-tax price (here $3.50) to producers. Thus, consumers and producers share the burden of the tax in some proportion (here equally at $.50 per unit).

----

ter remitting the $1 tax per unit to government, producers receive $3.50, or 50 cents less than the $4 before-tax price. In this instance, consumers and producers share the burden of this tax equally; producers shift half the tax to consumers in the form of a higher price and bear the other half themselves.

Note also that the equilibrium quantity decreases as a result of the tax levy and the higher price it imposes on consumers. In Figure 31-2, that decline in quantity is from 15 million bottles to 12.5 million bottles per month.

Elasticities If the elasticities of demand and supply were different from those shown in Figure 31-2, the incidence of tax would also be different. Two generalizations are relevant.

1. *With a specific supply, the more inelastic the demand for the product, the larger the portion of the tax shifted to consumers.* To verify this, sketch graphically the extreme cases where demand is perfectly elastic and perfectly inelastic. In the first case, the incidence of the tax is entirely on sellers; in the second, the tax is shifted entirely to consumers.

Figure 31-3 contrasts the more usual cases where demand is either relatively elastic or relatively inelastic in the relevant price range. With elastic demand (Figure 31-3a), a small portion of the tax $(P_e - P_1)$ is shifted to consumers and most of the tax $(P_1 - P_a)$ is borne by the producers. With inelastic demand (Figure 31-3b), most of the tax $(P_i - P_1)$ is shifted to consumers and only a small amount $(P_1 - P_b)$ is paid by producers. In both graphs the per-unit tax is represented by the *vertical* distance between S_t and S.

Note also that the decline in equilibrium quantity $(Q_1 - Q_2)$ is smaller when demand is more inelastic. This is the basis of our previous applications of the elasticity concept: Revenue-seeking legislatures place heavy excise taxes on liquor, cigarettes, automobile tires, telephone service, and other products whose demands are thought to be inelastic. Since demand for these

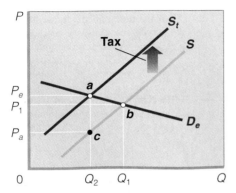

(a) Tax incidence and elastic demand

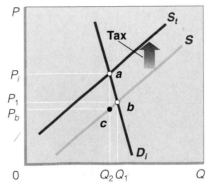

(b) Tax incidence and inelastic demand

FIGURE 31-3 Demand elasticity and the incidence of an excise tax (a) If demand is elastic in the relevant price range, price rises modestly (P_1 to P_e) when an excise tax is levied. Hence, the producer bears most of the tax burden. (b) If demand is inelastic, the price to the buyer increases substantially (P_1 to P_i) and most of the tax is shifted to consumers.

----

products is relatively inelastic, the tax does not reduce sales much, so the tax revenue stays high.

2. *With a specific demand, the more inelastic the supply, the larger the portion of the tax borne by producers.* When supply is elastic (Figure 31-4a), most of the tax $(P_e - P_1)$ is shifted to consumers and only a small portion $(P_1 - P_a)$ is borne by sellers. But where supply is inelastic (Figure 31-4b), the reverse is true: The major portion of the tax $(P_1 - P_b)$ falls on sellers, and a relatively small amount $(P_i - P_1)$ is shifted to buyers. The equilibrium quantity also declines less with an inelastic supply than it does with an elastic supply.

Gold is an example of a product with an inelastic supply and therefore one where the burden of an excise tax would mainly fall on producers. On the other hand, because the supply of baseballs is elastic, producers would pass on to consumers much of an excise tax on baseballs.

Efficiency Loss of a Tax

We just observed that an excise tax levied on producers typically is borne partly by producers and partly by consumers. Let's now look more closely at the overall economic effect of the excise tax. We will use Figure 31-5, which is identical to Figure 31-2 but contains additional detail needed for our discussion.

Tax Revenues In our example, a $1 excise tax on wine increases the market price from $4 to $4.50 per bottle and reduces the equilibrium quantity from 15 million bottles to 12.5 million. Government tax revenue is $12.5 million (=$1 × 12.5 million bottles), an amount shown as the rectangle *efac* in Figure 31-5. The elasticities of supply and demand in this case are

such that consumers and producers each pay half this total amount, or $6.25 million apiece (= $.50 × 12.5 million bottles). Government uses this $12.5 million of tax revenue to provide public goods and services. So this transfer of dollars from consumers and producers to government involves no loss of well-being to society.

Efficiency Loss The $1 tax on wine does more than require consumers and producers to pay $12.5 million of taxes; *it also reduces the equilibrium amount of wine produced and consumed by 2.5 million bottles.* The fact that 2.5 million more bottles of wine were demanded and supplied before the tax means those 2.5 million bottles provided benefits in excess of their production costs. We can see this from the following analysis.

Segment *ab* of demand curve *D* in Figure 31-5 indicates the willingness to pay—the marginal benefit—associated with each of the 2.5 million bottles consumed before (but not after) the tax. Segment *cb* of supply curve *S* reflects the marginal cost of each of the bottles of wine. For all but the very last one of these 2.5 million bottles, the marginal benefit (shown by a point on *ab*) exceeds the marginal cost (shown by a point on *cb*). Not producing all 2.5 million bottles reduces well-being by an amount indicated by the triangle *abc*. The area of this triangle represents the **efficiency loss of the tax** (also called the *deadweight loss of the tax*). *This loss is society's sacrifice of net benefit because the tax reduces production and consumption of the product below their levels of economic efficiency where marginal benefit and marginal cost are equal.*

Role of Elasticities Most taxes create some degree of efficiency loss; how much depends on the supply and demand elasticities. Glancing back at Figure 31-3,

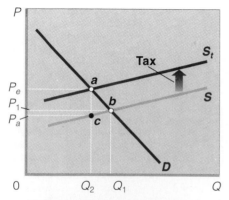

(a) Tax incidence and elastic supply

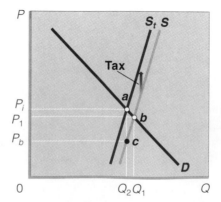

(b) Tax incidence and inelastic supply

FIGURE 31-4 Supply elasticity and the incidence of an excise tax (a) With elastic supply, an excise tax results in a large price increase (P_1 to P_e) and the tax is therefore paid mainly by consumers. (b) If supply is inelastic, the price rise is small (P_1 to P_i) and sellers bear most of the tax.

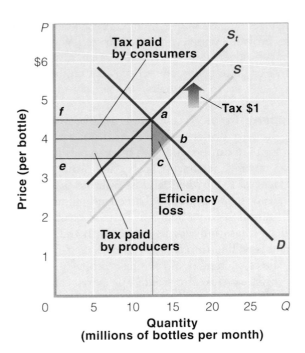

FIGURE 31-5 Efficiency loss of a tax The levy of a $1 tax per bottle of wine increases the price per bottle from $4 to $4.50 and reduces the equilibrium quantity from 15 million to 12.5 million. Tax revenue to government is $12.5 million (area *efac*). The efficiency loss of the tax arises from the 2.5 million decline in output; the amount of this loss is shown as triangle *abc*.

----

we see that the efficiency loss area *abc* is greater in Figure 31-3a, where demand is relatively elastic, than in Figure 31-3b, where demand is relatively inelastic. Similarly, area *abc* is greater in Figure 31-4a than in Figure 31-4b, indicating a larger efficiency loss where supply is more elastic. *Other things equal, the greater the elasticities of supply and demand, the greater the efficiency loss of a particular tax.*

Two taxes yielding equal revenues do not necessarily impose equal costs on society. Government must keep this fact in mind in designing a tax system to finance beneficial public goods and services. In general, it should minimize the efficiency loss of the tax system in raising any specific dollar amount of tax revenue.

Qualifications We must acknowledge, however, that there may be other tax goals just as important, or even more important, than minimizing efficiency losses from taxes. Here are two examples:

1. *Redistributive goals* Government may wish to impose progressive taxes as a way to redistribute

income. The 10 percent excise tax the Federal government placed on selected luxuries in 1990 was an example. Because the demand for luxuries is elastic, substantial efficiency losses from this tax were to be expected. However, Congress apparently concluded that the benefits from the redistribution effects of the tax would exceed the efficiency losses.

In 1993 Congress repealed the luxury taxes on personal airplanes and yachts, mainly because the taxes had reduced quantity demanded so much that widespread layoffs of workers were occurring in these industries. But the 10 percent tax on automobiles priced above $30,000 remained.

2. *Reducing negative externalities* Government may have intended the $1 tax on wine in Figure 31-5 to reduce consumption of wine by 2.5 million bottles. It may have concluded that consumption of alcoholic beverages produces certain negative externalities. Therefore, it might have levied this tax to shift the market supply curve so as to reduce the amount of resources allocated to wine (as in Figure 30-3b). **(Key Question 9)**

Probable Incidence of U.S. Taxes

Let's now look at the probable incidence of each of the major sources of tax revenue in the United States.

Personal Income Tax The incidence of the personal income tax generally is on the individual because there is a little chance for shifting it. But there might be exceptions. Individuals and groups who can control the price of their labor services may be able to shift a part of the tax. Doctors, dentists, lawyers, and other professional people who can readily increase their fees may do so because of the tax. Unions might regard personal income taxes as part of the cost of living and, as a result, bargain for higher wages when tax rates increase. If they are successful, they may shift part of the tax from workers to employers, who, by increasing prices, shift the wage increase to the public. Generally, however, the individual on whom the tax is initially levied bears the burden of the personal income tax. The same ordinarily holds true for payroll and inheritance taxes.

Corporate Income Tax The incidence of the corporate income tax is much less certain. The traditional view is that a firm currently charging the profit-maximizing price and producing the profit-maximizing output will have no reason to change price or output when a tax on corporate income (profit) is imposed. The price and output combination yielding the greatest profit before the tax will still yield the greatest profit after a fixed percentage of the firm's profit is taken away in the form of an income tax. In this view, the company's stockholders (owners) must bear the burden of the tax in the form of lower dividends or a smaller amount of retained earnings.

However, economists recognize that where a small number of firms control a market, producers may be able to shift part of their corporate income tax to consumers through higher prices and to resource suppliers through lower prices and wages. That is, some firms may be able to use their monopoly power as sellers and monopsony power as buyers to reduce the actual amount of the tax paid by their corporate stockholders.

There simply is no consensus among experts on the overall incidence of the corporate income tax. The tax burden may well be shared by stockholders, customers, and resource suppliers.

Sales and Excise Taxes Recall that a sales tax is a general excise tax levied on a full range of consumer goods and services, whereas a specific excise tax is one levied only on a particular product. Sales and excise taxes are the "hidden taxes" of our economy. They are hidden because they are often partly or largely shifted by sellers to consumers through higher product prices. There may be some difference in the shiftability of sales taxes and excise taxes, however. Because a sales tax covers a much wider range of products than an excise tax, there is little chance for consumers to resist the price boosts which sales taxes entail. They cannot reallocate their expenditures to untaxed, lower-priced products. Therefore, sales taxes tend to be shifted in their entirety to consumers.

Excise taxes, however, fall on a select list of goods. Therefore, the possibility of consumers turning to substitute goods and services is greater. An excise tax on theater tickets which does not apply to other types of entertainment might be difficult to pass on to consumers via price increases. Why? The answer is provided in Figure 31-3a, where demand is elastic. A price boost to cover the excise tax on theater tickets might cause consumers to substitute alternative types of entertainment. The higher price would reduce sales so much that a seller would be better off to bear all, or a large portion of, the excise tax.

With other products, modest price increases to cover taxes may have smaller effects on sales. The ex-

cise taxes on gasoline, cigarettes, and alcoholic beverages provide examples. Here there are few good substitute products to which consumers can turn as prices rise. For these goods, the seller is better able to shift the excise tax to consumers.

Property Taxes Many property taxes are borne by the property owner because there is no other party to whom they can be shifted. This is typically true for taxes on land, personal property, and owner-occupied residences. Even when land is sold, the property tax is not likely to be shifted. The buyer will understand that future taxes will have to be paid on it, and this expected taxation will be reflected in the price the buyer is willing to offer for the land.

Taxes on rented and business property are a different story. Taxes on rented property can be, and usually are, shifted wholly or in part from the owner to the tenant by the process of boosting the rent. Business property taxes are treated as a business cost and are taken into account in establishing product price; hence such taxes are ordinarily shifted to the firm's customers.

Table 31-2 summarizes this discussion of the shifting and incidence of taxes.

The U.S. Tax Structure

Is the overall U.S. tax structure—Federal, state, and local taxes combined—progressive, proportional, or regressive? This question is difficult to answer because estimates of the distribution of the total tax burden depend on the assumptions we make regarding tax incidence. The extent to which the various taxes are shifted and who bears the ultimate burden are subject to dispute. We have already noted, for example, that there is no consensus among experts as to who actually pays the corporate income tax.

But the majority view of experts can be summarized as follows:

1. *The Federal tax system is progressive.* In 1995, the average tax rates for the bottom 50 percent of all Federal income-tax payers was only 4.4 percent. It was 17.5 percent for the top 25 percent of taxpayers, 20.8 percent for the top 10 percent of taxpayers, and 28.5 percent for the top 1 percent of taxpayers.

The top 10 percent of all taxpayers paid 60.5 percent of the total Federal income tax collected. (Because wealthy Americans earn a disproportionately high amount of the total income, they

TABLE 31-2   The probable incidence of taxes

Type of tax	Probable incidence
Personal income tax	The household or individual on which it is levied.
Corporate income tax	Some economists conclude the firm on which it is levied bears the tax; others conclude the tax is shifted, wholly or in part, to consumers and resource suppliers.
Sales tax	Consumers who buy the taxed products.
Specific excise taxes	Consumers, producers, or both, depending on elasticities of demand and supply.
Property taxes	Owners in the case of land and owner-occupied residences; tenants in the case of rented property; consumers in the case of business property.

pay a disproportionately high amount of the total tax. This would be true even for a proportional tax system.)

Partly offsetting some of this progressivity, however, is the effect of the Federal payroll (social security) tax. If all income were subject to the social security tax, the tax would be proportional. But, as we saw, the payroll tax applies only to income from work and then only to a set maximum amount ($68,400 in 1998). Thus this tax is regressive; tax payments are a higher percentage of income for low- and middle-income people than for high-income people.

2. *The state and local tax structures are largely regressive.*   As a percentage of income, property taxes and sales taxes fall as income rises. Also, state income taxes are generally less progressive than the Federal income tax.

3. *The overall U.S. tax system is slightly progressive.*   This means the tax system alone only slightly redistributes income from the wealthy to the poor. Caution: While the U.S. tax system does not substantially alter the distribution of income, the system of transfer payments *does* considerably reduce income inequality. Transfer payments to the poorest fifth of U.S. households almost quadruple their collective incomes. The *tax-transfer system* redistributes income by much more than does the tax system alone.

TAX REFORM

In recent years, two major concerns have led to calls for reform of the Federal tax code: (1) low rates of saving, investment, and economic growth; and (2) tremendous tax complexity. Consequently, two general tax proposals have attracted considerable interest.

The Value-Added Tax

Higher saving rates enable a nation to produce and purchase more capital goods, which we know from Chapter 2, increase economic growth. But production possibilities analysis reminds us that, with full employment, more capital goods require offsetting cuts in consumption. Some economists contend that the required increases in investment and reductions in consumption can be attained through a structural overhaul of our tax system.

One proposal is to substantially reduce or replace personal and corporate income taxes with a tax on consumption. One such tax is the **value-added tax (VAT),** which is like a retail sales tax except that it applies only to the *difference* between the value of a firm's sales and the value of its purchases from other firms. For example, Intel would pay the VAT—say, 7 percent—on the difference between the value of the microchips it produces and sells and the value of the materials used to make the chips. Compaq, IBM, and other firms which buy the chips and other components to make personal computers would subtract the value of these materials from the value of their sales of personal computers. They would then pay the 7 percent tax on that difference—on the value they added.

Economists reason that since the VAT would apply to all firms, sellers could shift their VATs to buyers in the form of higher prices without loss of sales to other firms. Final consumers, who cannot shift the tax, would end up paying the full VAT as 7 percent higher prices. So a VAT would amount to a national sales tax on consumer goods. Most European nations—for example, Great Britain, Germany, and Sweden—currently use VATs as a source of revenue. This is reflected in Global Perspective 31-1.

The point to note is that a VAT penalizes consumption. It is possible to avoid paying a VAT by saving rather than consuming. And we know that saving (refraining from consumption) will release resources from consumer goods production and make them available for producing capital goods. Reducing or eliminating personal and corporate income taxes and installing a VAT will allegedly alter the composition of U.S. domestic output away from consumption and toward investment, with the result being greater economic growth.

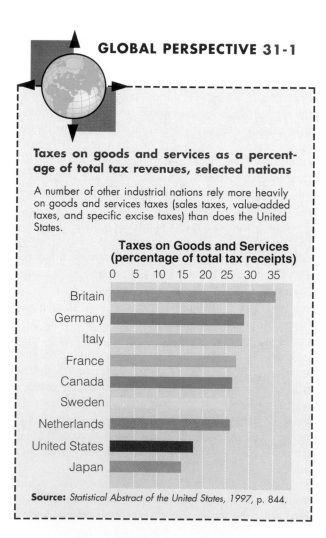

GLOBAL PERSPECTIVE 31-1

Taxes on goods and services as a percentage of total tax revenues, selected nations

A number of other industrial nations rely more heavily on goods and services taxes (sales taxes, value-added taxes, and specific excise taxes) than does the United States.

**Taxes on Goods and Services
(percentage of total tax receipts)**

Britain
Germany
Italy
France
Canada
Sweden
Netherlands
United States
Japan

Source: *Statistical Abstract of the United States, 1997*, p. 844.

The Flat Tax

Economists generally agree that the current Federal tax code is much too complicated to achieve economic efficiency. The tremendous complexity of the personal income tax, in particular, requires that society devote large amounts of its scarce resources to keeping records and calculating the amount of tax owed. Thus, some economists advocate integrating the personal income tax and corporate income tax, using a single, flat tax rate, say, 20 percent, which would apply to households and businesses. Such a **flat tax**, say proponents, would simplify the tax system and, like a VAT, promote saving, investment, and economic growth.

In the simplest flat tax plan, the taxpayer would fill out a form no larger than a postcard. The taxpayer would first determine total wage and salary income and then subtract a large personal allowance for each family member. The tax owed would be 20 percent of this taxable income. Businesses would also fill out a simple tax form. Each firm would determine its taxable income by subtracting allowable costs from gross revenues and would then pay 20 percent of that amount as tax.

Proponents of the flat tax say it would result in a simple, efficient tax system. It would free up numerous valuable resources—thousands of tax accountants, tax lawyers, tax preparers, IRS personnel, and the like—who no longer would be demanded. Society could then shift these resources to other uses, meeting a variety of unmet wants. And because the flat tax would tax neither interest nor capital gains from saving, people presumably would save more and consume less. Moreover, the lower overall tax rate on businesses' profit allegedly would promote greater investment and more rapid economic growth.

Criticisms of the VAT and the Flat Tax

Critics of the VAT and the flat tax contend that either tax reform would reduce the progressivity of Federal taxation and thus increase after-tax income inequality. A VAT is essentially a national sales tax and, as such, is regressive. And under the flat tax, while the poorest families would pay no income tax, middle-class families would pay more, and the very wealthy, much less. Thus, say critics, both tax reforms would undermine government's efforts to redistribute income.

Also, many individuals and firms would be hurt during the transition to the new tax system, as might the economy itself. Numerous businesses relating to the present tax system would be decimated, including those involving tax preparation services, tax preparation software, tax-advice books, and so on. More subtle consequences might also occur: House values might fall, since mortgage interest payments and property taxes would no longer be deductible; and charitable contributions might dry up because that deduction, too, would be eliminated. Under a VAT, the general price level would jump upward, automatically boosting social security benefits, which are tied to the general level of prices. This would increase Federal expenditures. Workers with cost-of-living adjustment (COLA) clauses would get automatic pay increases; other workers would not.

THE ISSUE OF FREEDOM

We end our discussion of government decision making by considering a question having an elusive answer: What is the relationship between individual freedom and the size and power of government? We make no attempt here to answer this question; we merely outline two opposing views.

The Conservative Position

Many conservative economists feel that, in addition to the economic costs of an expanding public sector, there is also a cost in the form of diminished individual freedom. Here's why.

First, there is the "power corrupts" argument. "Freedom is a rare and delicate plant . . . history confirms that the great threat to freedom is the concentration of power . . . by concentrating power in political hands, [government] is . . . a threat to freedom."[2]

Second, we can be selective in the market system of the private sector, using our income to buy precisely what we choose and rejecting unwanted commodities. But, as noted previously, in the public sector—even assuming a high level of political democracy—conformity and coercion are inherent. If the majority decides in favor of certain governmental actions—to build a reservoir, to establish a system of national health insurance, to provide a guaranteed annual income—the minority must conform. The "use

of political channels, while inevitable, tends to strain the social cohesion essential for a stable society."[3] Because decisions can be rendered selectively by individuals through markets, the need for conformity and coercion is lessened and the "strain" is reduced when decisions are made in the marketplace. The scope of government should be strictly limited.

Finally, centralization of the power and activities of government into bigger government eliminates at least one check on government:

> If government is to exercise power, better in the county than in the state, better in the state than in Washington. If I do not like what my local community does, be it in sewage disposal, or zoning, or schools, I can move to another local community, and though few may take this step, the mere possibility acts as a check. If I do not like what my state does, I can move to another. If I do not like what Washington imposes, I have few alternatives in this world of jealous nations.[4]

The Liberal Position

But liberal economists are skeptical of the conservative position. They say the conservative view is based on the **fallacy of limited decisions.** That is, conservatives implicitly assume that during any particular period there is a limited, or fixed, number of decisions to be made in the operation of the economy. If government makes more of these decisions in performing its functions, the private sector of the economy will necessarily have fewer decisions left to make "freely." This is considered fallacious reasoning. By sponsoring the production of public goods, government is *extending* the range of free choice by permitting society to enjoy goods and services which would not be available without governmental provision.

We can argue that it is largely through the economic functions of government that we have freed ourselves in some measure from ignorance, unemployment, poverty, disease, crime, discrimination, and other ills. In providing most public goods, government does not typically undertake production itself but, rather, purchases these goods through private enterprise. When government decides to build an interstate highway, private concerns are given the responsibility of making many specific decisions and choices in connection with carrying out this decision.

---

[2]Milton Friedman, *Capitalism and Freedom* (Chicago: University of Chicago Press, 1962), p. 2.

[3]Ibid., p. 23.
[4]Ibid., p. 3.

"Public Sector Failure" in the News

The media continually report instances of the special-interest effect, limited and bundled choices, and government bureaucractic inefficiency.

Examples:

- An agricultural aid package to Russia required that 75 percent of the goods be shipped by high-cost U.S. flag vessels. The donation of $121 million of food thus cost U.S. taxpayers an extra $45 million, which was in effect a subsidy to the American shipping industry. (Associated Press)

- Tacked onto the 1994 Defense Appropriations bill were many items of nondefense spending, including **(a)** $20 million for breast cancer research, **(b)** $6 million for the World Cup soccer tournament, **(c)** $3.7 million to renovate a pier in New London, Connecticut, **(d)** $2.5 million for an exhibit at the Queens Hall of Science in New York, **(e)** $2.3 million for cell-adhesion research at an unidentified non-profit institution, **(f)** $2 million for the 1996 Olympic Games in Atlanta, and **(g)** $5 million for a redevelopment project in Waterbury, Connecticut. (*Boston Globe*)

- In 1997 the Federal government built a two-hole restroom facility costing $333,000 in a national recreation area in Pennsylvania. The toilets are $13,000 composting models that will not work in the winter. (Knight-Ridder Newspapers)

- Among the deals offered for votes for the North American Free Trade Agreement were **(a)** a $10 million Trade Center in Texas named after a representative from Texas; **(b)** a $10 million bridge over railroad tracks in Houston; **(c)** a requirement that manhole covers bear the clear imprint of the countries where they were made, to satisfy lawmakers from 21 states where "Made in America" manhole covers are produced; and **(d)** a delay in a move to increase grazing fees on western rangeland. (Knight-Ridder Newspapers)

- Appropriation bills for 1998 included provisions such as **(a)** prohibiting the use of any funds to demolish any bridge built between Jersey City, NJ, and Ellis Island; **(b)** restricting funds for testing in connection with growth or production in a foreign country of any farm commodity that would compete with commodities grown in the United States; **(c)** directing the Coast Guard to buy twice as many coastal patrol boats from the Bollinger Machine Shop and Shipyard in Louisiana as were requested by the Coast Guard—at a cost of $68.1 million for 15 boats; and **(d)** prohibiting the closing or relocating of the FDA's Division of Drug Analysis in St. Louis. (Senator McCain's Internet "Pork" home page).

- A standard, regulation Federal ashtray has 10 pages of specifications. The testing procedures include putting the ashtray on a maple plank, 44.5 millimeters thick, and using a hammer to hit the ashtray with a steel punch point ground to a 60 percent angle. "The specimen should break into a small number of irregularly shaped pieces, not greater in number than 35." To be counted as regulation shards, they must be "6.4 millimeters or more, on any three of its adjacent edges." (*Newsweek*)

- It took 23 Federal employees to approve the purchase of laptop computers bought for $3500 each. These computers were priced at $1500 each at the local retail computer store. (*Newsweek*)

A leading U.S. economist has summarized the liberal view in these words:

> Traffic lights coerce me and limit my freedom. Yet in the midst of a traffic jam on the unopen road, was I really "free" before there were lights? And has the algebraic total of freedom, for me or the representative motorist or the group as a whole, been increased or decreased by the introduction of well-engineered stop lights? Stop lights, you know, are also go lights.... When we introduce the traffic light, we have, although the arch individualist may not like the new order, by cooperation and coercion created . . . greater freedom.[5]

[5]Paul A. Samuelson, "Personal Freedoms and Economic Freedoms in the Mixed Economy," in Earl F. Cheit (ed.), *The Business Establishment* (New York: John Wiley & Sons, 1964), p. 219.

CHAPTER SUMMARY

1. Majority voting creates a possibility of **(a)** an underallocation or overallocation of resources to a particular public good and **(b)** inconsistent voting outcomes. The median-voter model predicts that, under majority rule, the person holding the middle position on an issue will determine the outcome of an election involving that issue.

2. Public choice theorists cite reasons why government might be inefficient in providing public goods and services. **(a)** There are strong reasons for politicians to support special-interest legislation. **(b)** Politicians may be biased in favor of programs with immediate and clear-cut benefits and difficult-to-identify costs *and* against programs with immediate and easily identified costs and vague or deferred benefits. **(c)** Citizens as voters and congressional representatives face limited and bundled choices as to public goods and services, whereas consumers in the private sector can be highly selective in their choices. **(d)** Government bureaucracies have less incentive to operate efficiently than do private businesses.

3. The benefits-received principle of taxation states that those who receive the benefits of goods and services provided by government should pay the taxes required to finance them. The ability-to-pay principle states that those who have greater income should be taxed more, absolutely and relatively, than those who have less income.

4. The Federal personal income tax is progressive. The corporate income tax is roughly proportional. General sales, excise, payroll, and property taxes are regressive.

5. Excise taxes affect supply and therefore equilibrium price and quantity. The more inelastic the demand for a product, the greater the portion of an excise tax shifted to consumers. The greater the inelasticity of supply, the larger the portion of the tax borne by the seller.

6. Taxation involves the loss of some output whose marginal benefit exceeds its marginal cost. The more elastic the supply and demand curves, the greater this efficiency loss resulting from a particular tax.

7. Sales taxes normally are shifted to consumers; personal income taxes are not shifted. Specific excise taxes may or may not be shifted to consumers, depending on the elasticities of demand and supply. There is disagreement as to whether corporate income taxes are shifted. Property taxes on owner-occupied property are borne by the owner; those on rental property are borne by tenants.

8. The Federal tax structure is progressive; the state-local tax structure, regressive; and the overall tax structure, slightly progressive.

9. Proponents of a value-added tax—a tax similar to a national sales tax—contend that it should replace some or all of personal and corporate income taxes. A VAT supposedly would reduce consumption, spur saving and investment, and thus boost economic growth. Proponents of a flat tax—a single-rate personal and corporate income tax—say that it would greatly simplify the U.S. tax system. And like the VAT, it would promote saving, investment, and economic growth, because income from saving is untaxed. Critics say that the VAT would reduce the progressivity of the Federal tax system, weakening the redistribution effect of the overall tax system.

10. Conservatives believe that individual freedom necessarily shrinks as government grows in size or power; liberals believe it does not.

TERMS AND CONCEPTS

public choice theory	public sector failure	ability-to-pay principle	efficiency loss of a tax
public finance	special-interest effect	progressive tax	value-added tax (VAT)
logrolling	rent seeking	regressive tax	flat tax
paradox of voting	benefits-received	proportional tax	fallacy of limited
median-voter model	principle	tax incidence	decisions

STUDY QUESTIONS

1. Explain how affirmative and negative majority votes can sometimes lead to inefficient allocations of resources to public goods. Is this problem likely to be greater under a benefits-received or an ability-to-pay tax system? Use the information in Figure 31-1a and b to show how society might be better off if Adams were allowed to buy votes.

2. KEY QUESTION Explain the paradox of voting through reference to the accompanying table, which shows the ranking of three public goods by voters Larry, Curley, and Moe:

Public good	Rankings		
	Larry	Curley	Moe
Courthouse	2d choice	1st choice	3d choice
School	3d choice	2d choice	1st choice
Park	1st choice	3d choice	2d choice

3. KEY QUESTION Suppose there are only five people in a society and each favors one of the five flood-control options in Table 30-2 (include no protection as one of the options). Explain which of these flood-control options will be selected using a majority paired-choice vote. Will this option be the optimal size of the project from an economic perspective?

4. KEY QUESTION How does the problem of limited and bundled choice in the public sector relate to economic efficiency? Why are public bureaucracies alleged to be less efficient than private enterprises?

5. Explain: "Politicians would make more rational economic decisions if they weren't running for reelection every few years." Do you favor term limits for elected officials?

6. Distinguish between the benefits-received and the ability-to-pay principles of taxation. Which philosophy is more evident in our present tax structure? Justify your answer. To which principle of taxation do you subscribe? Why?

7. KEY QUESTION Suppose a tax is such that an individual with an income of $10,000 pays $2000 of tax, a person with an income of $20,000 pays $3000 of tax, a person with an income of $30,000 pays $4000 of tax, and so forth. What is each person's average tax rate? Is this tax regressive, proportional, or progressive?

8. What is meant by a progressive tax? A regressive tax? A proportional tax? Comment on the progressivity or regressivity of each of the following taxes, indicating in each case where you think the tax incidence lies: **(a)** the Federal personal income tax, **(b)** a 3 percent state general sales tax, **(c)** a Federal excise tax on automobile tires, **(d)** a municipal property tax on real estate, **(e)** the Federal corporate income tax.

9. KEY QUESTION What is the incidence of an excise tax when demand is highly inelastic? Elastic? What effect does the elasticity of supply have on the incidence of an excise tax? What is the efficiency loss of a tax, and how does it relate to elasticity of demand and supply?

10. Advanced analysis: Suppose the equation for the demand curve for some product X is $P = 8 - .6Q$ and the supply curve is $P = 2 + .4Q$. What are the equilibrium price and quantity? Now suppose an excise tax is imposed on X such that the new supply equation is $P = 4 + .4Q$. How much tax revenue will this excise tax yield the government? Graph the curves and label the area of the graph which represents the tax collection "TC" and the area which represents the efficiency loss of the tax "EL." Briefly explain why area EL is the efficiency loss of the tax but TC is not.

11. (Last Word) How do the concepts of "pork-barrel" politics and "logrolling" relate to the items listed in the Last Word?

12. WEB-BASED QUESTION Bureaucracy and Inefficiency—The Post Office versus UPS Some economists contend that public agencies generally are less efficient than private businesses. The United States Parcel Service (UPS) http://www.ups.com/ competes directly with the U.S. Postal Service http://www.usps.gov/ for delivery of express mail and packages. Assume you need to send an express letter and a package from your address to either New York City or Los Angeles. Based on their interactive rate and options calculators, which service is more competitive as to price and delivery? Does a lower rate with greater delivery options mean greater efficiency? Why or why not?

13. WEB-BASED QUESTION Progressive Tax Rates and the Marriage Penalty The Internal Revenue Service (IRS) http://www.irs.ustreas.gov/prod/ind_info/tax_tables/index.html provides current tax tables online. Assume Mr. Brown and Ms. Smith are single and dating, and both earn $25,000 taxable income per year. How much in total taxes does the IRS receive from this couple? If Brown and Smith marry and file jointly, what will be their total tax bill? If Mr. Brown-Smith quits his job to be a househusband and Ms. Brown-Smith receives a promotion and salary increase to $50,000, what taxes will the couple pay if they file as Married—Filing Separately? The taxable income in all three cases is equal to $50,000, but the taxes paid differ substantially. Is the tax rate more progressive for dual-income married couples than for dual-income dating couples? Which situation results in the most taxes paid? Is this fair?

8

PART EIGHT

Microeconomic Issues and Policies

CHAPTER THIRTY-TWO

Antitrust Policy and Regulation

Here are several Trivial Pursuit-type questions for you:

- What do baby formula, citric acid, and catfish have in common? Answer: Each has been the object of recent government lawsuits based on **antitrust policy:** laws and government actions designed to promote competition.

- How are electricity, natural gas, and local phone calls related? (This question is easier.) All are produced by so-called *public utilities* and are subject to **industrial regulation:** government regulation of prices (or rates) within selected industries.

- What do workplace safety standards, air bags, affirmative action, access for the disabled, antipollution laws, and auto fuel standards have in common? All are the objects of **social regulation:** government regulation of the conditions under which goods are produced, the physical characteristics of goods, and the impact of goods' production and consumption on society.

- And what do government subsidies to promote fuel-efficient automobiles, develop flat-glass monitor screens, and enhance U.S. exports have in common? All are components of **industrial policy:** government policies to promote selected industries, products, or technologies.

Antitrust policy, industrial regulation, social regulation, and industrial policy are government interventions which relate to the structure, conduct, and performance of industry. This chapter examines the purposes and effects of these interventions but first defines and clarifies the debate over industrial concentration.

DEFINITION OF INDUSTRIAL CONCENTRATION

In Chapter 24 we developed and applied a strict definition of monopoly. A *pure monopoly*, we said, is a one-firm industry—a situation whereby a unique product is being produced entirely by a single firm and entry to the industry is totally blocked.

In this chapter we will use the term "industrial concentration" to include pure monopoly and markets in which there is much potential monopoly power. **Industrial concentration** exists *whenever a single firm or a small number of firms control the major portion of* *the output of an industry.* One, two, or three firms dominate the industry, potentially resulting in higher-than-competitive prices and profits. This definition, which is closer to how the general public understands the "monopoly problem," includes many industries we previously designated as oligopolies.

"Industrial concentration" in this chapter thus refers to industries in which firms are large in absolute terms *and* in relation to the total market. Examples are the electrical equipment industry, where General Electric and Westinghouse are large by any standard and dominate the market; the automobile industry, where General Motors, Ford, and Chrysler are dominant; the chemical industry, led by DuPont, Dow Chemical, and Union Carbide; the aluminum industry, where three firms—Alcoa, Alumax, and Reynolds—reign supreme; and the cigarette industry, where Philip Morris and RJR Nabisco command the lion's share of the market.

INDUSTRIAL CONCENTRATION: BENEFICIAL OR HARMFUL?

Does industrial concentration help or hinder the working of our economy? There are contrasting arguments for and against industrial concentration.

The Case Against Industrial Concentration

We stated the case against monopoly and oligopoly in previous chapters. Here we simply review and extend those arguments.

Inefficient Resource Allocation Monopolists and oligopolists find it possible and profitable to produce less output and charge higher prices than they could if their industries were competitive. With pure competition, production occurs where $P = MC$. This equality represents an efficient allocation of resources because price P measures the marginal benefit to society of an extra unit of output, while marginal cost MC reflects the cost of an extra unit. When $P = MC$, society cannot gain by producing 1 more or 1 less unit of the product. In contrast, a monopolist maximizes profit by equating marginal revenue (not price) with marginal cost. At this $MR = MC$ point, price exceeds marginal cost, meaning that society would obtain more benefit than it would incur cost by producing extra units. There is an underallocation of resources

to the monopolized product, and thus the economic well-being of society is less than it would be with pure competition.

Unnecessary for Economies of Scale and Technological Progress Critics say industrial concentration normally is not needed to achieve either economies of scale or technological progress. In most industries, they contend, less than 5 percent of the market is necessary for achieving minimum average total cost; industrial concentration is *not* a prerequisite for productive efficiency.

Furthermore, most technological efficiency is attained, not in a firm, but in each individual plant. You can correctly argue that productive efficiency requires, say, a large-scale integrated auto-manufacturing plant. But it would be perfectly consistent to argue that there is no technological justification for a huge firm such as General Motors, which is composed of many geographically separate production plants, none of which increases the other's efficiency. In this view, many existing firms have become far larger than necessary for achieving full economies of scale.

Nor does technological progress require huge firms with substantial monopoly power. Large firms with great market power are not necessarily the ones which create new products and better methods of production. Instead, the sheltered positions of such firms may promote lethargy; there is no competition to spur innovation. Furthermore, monopolists and oligopolists may resist or suppress technological advances which cause sudden obsolescence of their existing machinery and equipment.

Income Inequality Industrial concentration is criticized as a contributor to income inequality. Because of entry barriers, monopolists and oligopolists can charge a price above average total cost and consistently obtain economic profits. These profits go to corporate stockholders and executives who are generally among the upper-income groups.

Political Dangers Because economic power and political clout go hand in hand, it is argued that giant corporations exert undue influence over government. This is reflected in legislation and government policies which are less suited to the public interest than to the preservation and growth of large firms. Large corporations allegedly have exerted political power to become primary beneficiaries of defense contracts, tax loopholes, patent policy, tariff and quota protection, and other subsidies and privileges. (Recall our discussion of rent-seeking activities in Chapter 31.)

Defenses of Industrial Concentration

Industrial concentration, however, *does* have significant defenses.

Superior Products One defense is that monopolists and oligopolists have gained their market dominance by offering superior products. Large firms cannot *coerce* consumers to buy, say, Colgate or Crest toothpaste, soft drinks from Coca-Cola and Pepsi, greeting cards from Hallmark, ketchup from Heinz, or soup from Campbell. Consumers have collectively decided that these products are more desirable than those offered by other producers. Monopoly profits and large market shares have been "earned," according to this view.

Underestimated Competition Another defense of industrial concentration rests on the assertion that economists often view competition too narrowly. While there may be only a few firms producing a specific product, those firms may face **interindustry competition.** That is, large firms may have competition from other industries producing different but highly substitutable products. There may be only a handful of firms responsible for the nation's output of aluminum. But aluminum faces competition from steel, copper, wood, plastics, and a host of other products, depending on the specific market.

  Foreign competition must also be taken into account. While General Motors (GM), Ford, and Chrysler dominate domestic automobile production, strong import competition affects all their pricing and output decisions. While there are only a few U.S. aluminum producers, they still face stiff competition from foreign producers.

  Furthermore, the large profit which would result from the full use of a monopolist's market power would attract potential competitors to the industry. This **potential competition** moderates the price and output decisions of firms now possessing market power. These firms wish to deter entry, and one way to do that is to keep prices low.

Economies of Scale Where economies of scale are extensive, only producers which are large both absolutely and in relation to the market can obtain low unit costs and therefore sell their output to consumers at low prices. The traditional antimonopoly contention that industrial concentration means less output, higher prices, and an inefficient allocation of resources assumes that cost economies would be equally available to firms whether the industry's structure were highly competitive or quite monopolistic. This is frequently not so; minimum average total cost may require such high levels of output that competition *in the sense of a large number of firms* is inefficient. Society is clearly better off with say, 3 firms producing 1 million units of X at a per-unit cost of $50 and charging $70 per unit than with 1000 firms producing X at a per-unit cost of $100 and charging $100 per unit. In this situation, the fact that the 3 firms are obtaining large economic profits is irrelevant; consumers and society benefit from the industrial concentration.

Technological Progress In direct rebuttal to the critics, defenders of industrial concentration assert that large oligopolistic industries tend to be technologically progressive because they have both the financial resources *and* the incentive to undertake technological research. The financial resources derive from retained earnings, while the strong incentive for R&D results from entry barriers which allow oligopolists to sustain high returns from these efforts.

QUICK REVIEW 32-1

■ Industrial concentration exists where a single firm or a small number of firms control the major portion of an industry's output.

■ The case against industrial concentration is that it creates allocative inefficiency, impedes technological progress, promotes income inequality, and poses political dangers.

■ Those who defend industrial concentration say it results from superior performance and economies of scale; is countered by interindustry, foreign, and potential competition; and provides both the wherewithal and the incentives for technological progress.

THE ANTITRUST LAWS

The sharp conflict of opinion over the merits of industrial concentration is reflected in U.S. antitrust policy, which has been neither clear-cut nor consistent.

Historical Background

The U.S. economy is steeped in the philosophy of competitive markets, free from government intervention. However, just after the Civil War the public began to distrust big business. Improved transportation facilities, mechanized production methods, and sophisticated corporate structures helped widen local markets into national markets and led to the development of "trusts"—monopolies—in the 1870s and 1880s. Specifically, trusts developed in the petroleum, meatpacking, railroad, sugar, lead, coal, whiskey, and tobacco industries, among others.

Firms used questionable tactics to monopolize these industries and exerted the resulting market power against all doing business with their trusts. Farmers and owners of small businesses were particularly vulnerable to the power of large corporate monopolies and were among the first to oppose them. Consumers and labor unions were not far behind in their opposition.

In these monopolized industries, market forces no longer provided adequate control to ensure socially tolerable behavior. In response, opponents adopted two means of control as substitutes for, or supplements to, market forces:

1. *Regulatory agencies* In the few markets where the nature of the product precludes effective working of the market—where there is "natural monopoly"—the United States has established public regulatory agencies to control economic behavior.
2. *Antitrust laws* In most other markets, where economic conditions have not made monopoly essential, social control has taken the form of antitrust (antimonopoly) legislation designed to inhibit or prevent the growth of monopoly.

Four particular pieces of Federal legislation, as refined and extended by various amendments, constitute the basic law of the land with respect to corporate size and concentration.

Sherman Act of 1890

The public resentment of trusts which developed in the 1870s and 1880s culminated in the **Sherman Act** in 1890. This cornerstone of antitrust legislation is surprisingly brief and, at first glance, directly to the point. The core of the act resides in two provisions. In Section 1:

> Every contract, combination in the form of a trust or otherwise, or conspiracy, in restraint of trade or commerce among the several states, or with foreign nations is hereby declared to be illegal.

In Section 2:

> Every person who shall monopolize, or attempt to monopolize, or combine or conspire with any person or persons, to monopolize any part of the trade or commerce among the several states, or with foreign nations, shall be deemed guilty of a misdemeanor.

This act made monopoly and "restraints of trade"—for example, collusive price fixing or the dividing up of markets among competitors—criminal offenses against the Federal government. Either the Department of Justice or parties injured by monopoly or anticompetitive behavior could file suits under the Sherman Act. Firms found in violation of the act could be ordered dissolved by the courts, or *injunctions* could be issued to prohibit practices deemed unlawful under the act. Fines and imprisonment were also possible punishments for violators. Further, parties injured by illegal combinations and conspiracies could sue for *treble damages*—triple the amount of monetary injury done them. The Sherman Act seemed to provide a sound foundation for positive government action against business monopolies.

However, early court interpretations raised serious questions about the effectiveness of the Sherman Act, and it became clear that a more explicit statement of the government's antitrust sentiments was needed. The business community itself sought a clearer statement of what was legal and illegal.

Clayton Act of 1914

The needed elaboration of the Sherman Act came in 1914, in the form of the **Clayton Act.** Four sections of the act, in particular, were designed to strengthen and make explicit the intent of the Sherman Act:

1. Section 2 *outlaws price discrimination* when such discrimination is not justified on the basis of cost differences and when it reduces competition.
2. Section 3 *forbids* **"tying" contracts,** whereby a producer would sell a desired product only on condition that the buyer acquire other products from the same producer.
3. Section 7 *prohibits acquisition of stocks* of competing corporations when the outcome would be less competition.

4. Section 8 *prohibits formation of* **interlocking directorates**—situations where a director of one firm is also a board member of a competing firm—in large corporations where the effect would be to reduce competition.

There was little in the Clayton Act which was not already implied by the Sherman Act. The Clayton Act simply attempted to sharpen and clarify the general provisions of the Sherman Act. Also, the Clayton Act sought to outlaw the techniques by which monopoly might develop and, in this sense, was a preventive measure. The Sherman Act, by contrast, was aimed more at punishing existing monopolies.

Federal Trade Commission Act of 1914

The **Federal Trade Commission Act** created the five-member Federal Trade Commission (FTC), which has joint responsibility with the U.S. Justice Department for enforcing the antitrust laws. The FTC was given the power to investigate unfair competitive practices on its own initiative or at the request of injured firms. The commission could hold public hearings on such complaints and, if necessary, issue **cease-and-desist orders** in cases where "unfair methods of competition in commerce" were discovered.

The **Wheeler-Lea Act** of 1938 gave the FTC the additional responsibility of policing "deceptive acts or practices in commerce." As a result, the FTC tries to protect the public against false or misleading advertising and the misrepresentation of products.

The Federal Trade Commission Act, as it was modified by the Wheeler-Lea Act, thus (1) established the FTC as an independent antitrust agency, and (2) broadened the range of business behavior defined as unlawful.

Celler-Kefauver Act of 1950

This act amended Section 7 of the Clayton Act, which, you may recall, prohibits a firm from merging with a competing firm (and thereby lessening competition) by acquiring its *stock*. Firms could evade Section 7 by instead acquiring the *physical assets* (plant and equipment) of competing firms. The **Celler-Kefauver Act** removed this loophole by prohibiting one firm from obtaining the physical assets of another firm when the effect would be less competition. Thus, Section 7 of the Clayton Act now prohibits anticompetitive mergers regardless of how they are undertaken. **(Key Question 2)**

ANTITRUST POLICY: ISSUES AND IMPACTS

The effectiveness of any law depends on how the courts interpret it and the vigor of government enforcement. The courts have been inconsistent in interpreting antitrust laws. At times, they have applied them vigorously, adhering closely to the spirit and objectives of the laws. In other cases, their interpretations have rendered certain laws nearly powerless. The Federal government has also varied considerably in its willingness to apply the antitrust acts. Administrations holding a laissez-faire philosophy about industrial concentration have sometimes weakened the laws by ignoring them or by cutting the budgets of enforcement agencies.

Issues of Interpretation

Differences in judicial interpretations have led to vastly different applications of the antitrust laws. Two questions, in particular, have arisen: (1) Should the focus of antitrust policy be on monopoly behavior or on monopoly structure? (2) How broadly should markets be defined in antitrust cases?

Monopoly Behavior versus Monopoly Structure A comparison of two landmark Supreme Court decisions reveals two distinct interpretations of Section 2 of the Sherman Act as it relates to monopoly behavior and structure.

In the 1920 **U.S. Steel case** the courts applied the **rule of reason,** saying that not every monopoly is illegal. Only monopolies which "unreasonably" restrain trade—so-called bad trusts—are subject to antitrust action. The Supreme Court held in this case that size alone was not an offense; although U.S. Steel clearly *possessed* monopoly power, it was innocent of "monopolizing" because it had not resorted to illegal acts against competitors in obtaining that power nor had it unreasonably used its monopoly power.

In the **Alcoa case** of 1945 the courts did a brief turnabout. The Supreme Court held that, even though a firm's behavior might be legal, the mere possession of monopoly power (Alcoa held 90 percent of the aluminum ingot market) violated the antitrust laws.

These two cases point to a controversy in antitrust policy. Should an industry be judged by its *behavior* (as in the U.S. Steel case) or by its *structure* (as in the Alcoa case)?

"Structuralists" say an industry which is highly concentrated will behave like a monopolist. The economic performance of such industries will be undesirable. These industries are therefore legitimate targets for antitrust action.

"Behavioralists" assert that the relationship between structure and performance is tenuous and unclear. They feel a concentrated industry may be technologically progressive and have a good record of providing products of increasing quality at reasonable prices. If the industry has served society well and engaged in no anticompetitive practices, it should not be accused of antitrust violation simply because it is highly concentrated. "Why use antitrust laws to penalize efficient, well-managed firms?", they ask.

Since the Alcoa decision in 1945, the courts have returned to the rule of reason. Many economists and antitrust enforcers have also rejected the strict structuralist view. For example, in 1982 the government dropped its 13-year-long monopolization case against IBM on the grounds that IBM had not unreasonably restrained trade. More recently, the government has made no attempt to break up Intel's monopoly in the sale of microprocessors for personal computers.

The Relevant Market   Courts often decide about the existence of market power on the basis of the share of the market held by the dominant firm. If the market is defined broadly to *include* a wide range of somewhat similar products, the firm's market share will appear small. If the market is defined narrowly to *exclude* those products, the market share will seem large. The Supreme Court's task is to determine how broadly to define relevant markets, and it has not always been consistent.

In the Alcoa case, the Court used a narrow definition of the relevant market: the aluminum ingot market. But in the **DuPont cellophane case** of 1956 the Court defined the market very broadly. The government contended that DuPont, along with a licensee, controlled 100 percent of the cellophane market. But the Court accepted DuPont's contention that the relevant market included all "flexible packaging materials"—waxed paper, aluminum foil, and so forth, in addition to cellophane. Despite DuPont's monopoly in the "cellophane market," it controlled only 20 percent of the market for "flexible wrapping materials."

The Court ruled that this did not constitute a monopoly.

Issues of Enforcement: Tradeoffs Among Goals

Promoting competition is only one of society's goals. Strict enforcement of antitrust laws occasionally may conflict with some other goal. Here are three examples:

1. Balance of Trade   Large U.S. trade deficits have led government to seek ways to increase exports. Antitrust actions which, say, undo a merger between two chemical suppliers, break up a dominant aircraft manufacturer, or dissolve an emerging software monopolist might weaken the targeted firms, reducing their competitiveness and sales abroad. Consequently, U.S. exports might decline and the nation's trade deficit worsen. Should government strictly enforce antitrust laws, even when significant amounts of U.S. exports are potentially at stake? Or should the antitrust goal of efficiency be superseded by the goal of balancing exports and imports?

2. Defense Cutbacks   Recent cutbacks in defense spending have reduced government purchases of military equipment, placing some major defense suppliers in financial jeopardy. Should government allow defense firms to merge to bolster sagging profits and thus reduce the number of worker layoffs which otherwise might occur? Or should government block such mergers as violations of Section 7 of the Clayton Act and, instead, allow the market to sort matters out, perhaps through bankruptcies? In 1994 the Defense Department and antitrust regulators reached an informal agreement, easing the way for consolidation of the defense industry via mergers. Several large mergers quickly followed.

3. Emerging New Technologies   Occasionally, new technologies combine to create new products and services. A current example is the meshing of computers and communications technologies to create the "information superhighway," a generic name for the worldwide network linking computers, telephones, television sets, and other communications devices. This interactive network is improving the communications capabilities of households, businesses, and governments across the globe. It also allows them to access unprecedented amounts of information and directly buy and sell goods and services. The emergence of this new technology has set off a spate of "megamergers" involving entertainment companies, telecommunication companies, computer manufacturers, and software producers.

Should government strictly enforce the Clayton Act to block some of these mergers, specifically those which increase industrial concentration and threaten to reduce competition? Or should government temporarily suspend antitrust rules to encourage the major restructuring of industries and speed the expansion of this new technology? Hastening the progress of the information superhighway may also increase U.S. exports of "electronic services" and decrease the U.S. trade deficit.

Each of these enforcement tradeoffs, by itself, triggers controversy. Some argue that gains from an antitrust policy must be weighed against the effects of the policy on conflicting objectives. Others contend that selective enforcement of antitrust laws dangerously interferes with the market process. Obviously, different policymakers and different administrations may view these considerations and tradeoffs differently.

Effectiveness of Antitrust Laws

Have the antitrust laws been effective? Although this question is difficult to answer, we can gain some in-

sight by observing how the laws have been applied to existing market structures, mergers, price fixing, and tying contracts.

Existing Market Structures The government generally has been lenient in applying antitrust laws to market structures which have already developed or to firms which have grown "naturally." Generally, a firm will be sued only if it has more than 60 percent of the relevant market and there is evidence suggesting that it used abusive conduct to achieve or maintain its market dominance. The most significant recent "victory" against an existing market structure was the 1982 out-of-court settlement between the government and AT&T. That firm was charged in 1974 with violating the Sherman Act by engaging in anticompetitive actions designed to maintain its domestic telephone monopoly. As part of the settlement, AT&T agreed to divest itself of its 22 regional telephone operating companies. Since 1982, however, the Federal government has not filed a significant antitrust suit to break up an existing market structure.

Mergers The treatment of *mergers*, or combinations of existing firms, varies with the type of merger and its effect on industry concentration.

Merger Types There are three basic types of mergers, as shown in Figure 32-1. This diagram shows

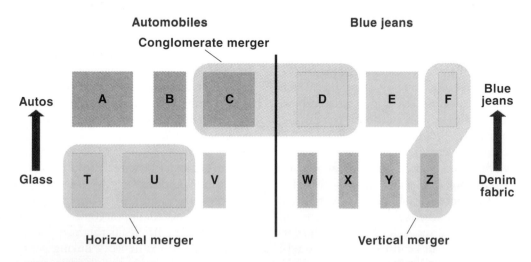

FIGURE 32-1 Types of mergers Horizontal mergers (T + U) bring together firms selling the same product in the same geographical market; vertical mergers (F + Z) connect firms having a buyer-seller relationship; and conglomerate mergers (C + D) join firms in different industries or firms operating in different geographical areas.

two stages of production—the input stage and the output, or final-product, stage—for two distinct final-goods industries: autos and blue jeans. Each rectangle (A, B, C, . . . X, Y, X) represents a particular firm.

A **horizontal merger** is *a merger between two competitors selling similar products in the same geographical market.* In Figure 32-1 this type of merger is shown as a combination of glass producers T and U. Possible examples of horizontal mergers would be United Airlines merging with Delta Airlines or Wendy's merging with Burger King. Actual examples of such mergers include Chase Manhattan's 1996 merger with Chemical Bank and Boeing's 1997 merger with McDonnell Douglas.

A **vertical merger** is *a merger between firms at different stages of the production process.* In Figure 32-1, the merger between firm Z, a producer of denim fabric, and firm F, a producer of blue jeans, is a vertical merger. Vertical mergers involve firms having buyer-seller relationships. Actual examples of such mergers are PepsiCo's mergers with Pizza Hut, Taco Bell, and Kentucky Fried Chicken. PepsiCo supplies soft drinks to each of these fast-food outlets. (In 1997, PepsiCo spun off these entities into a separate company called Tricon Global Restaurants.)

A **conglomerate merger** is officially defined as *any merger which is not horizontal or vertical; in general, it is the combination of firms in different industries or firms operating in different geographical areas.* Conglomerate mergers can extend the line of products sold, extend the territory in which products are sold, or combine totally unrelated companies. In Figure 32-1, the merger between firm C, an auto manufacturer, and firm D, a blue jeans producer, is a conglomerate merger. Real-world examples of conglomerate mergers include the merger of cigarette manufacturer Philip Morris and beer maker Miller Brewing and the merger between Walt Disney Company (movies) and the American Broadcasting Company (television).

Merger Guidelines: The Herfindahl Index

The Federal government has established merger guidelines based on the Herfindahl index. Recall from Chapter 25 that this measure of concentration is the sum of the squared percentage market shares of the firms within an industry. An industry of only four firms, each with a 25 percent market share, has a Herfindahl index of 2500 $(= 25^2 + 25^2 + 25^2 + 25^2)$. In pure competition, where each firm's market share is minute, the index approaches $0 (= 0^2 + 0^2 + \cdots + 0^2)$. In pure monopoly, the index for that one firm is 10,000 $(= 100^2)$.

The U.S. government uses Section 7 of the Clayton Act to block *horizontal mergers* which will substantially lessen competition. It is likely to challenge a horizontal merger if the postmerger Herfindahl index would be high (above 1800) and the merger has substantially increased the index (added 200 or more points). However, other factors such as cost savings, the degree of foreign competition, and the ease of entry of new firms are also considered. Furthermore, horizontal mergers are usually allowed if one of the merging firms is suffering major and continuing losses. (This is one reason Boeing was allowed to acquire McDonnell Douglas in 1996: MD was losing money in producing its commercial airplanes.)

Within the past decade, the Federal government has undone several proposed horizontal mergers. For example, it blocked the merger between Microsoft and Intuit, two competing producers of financial software, and the merger of Staples and Office Depot, two major office-supply retailers.

Most *vertical mergers* escape antitrust prosecution because they do not substantially lessen competition in either of the two markets. (In Figure 32-1 neither the Herfindahl index in the industry producing denim fabric nor the index in the blue jeans industry changes when firms Z and F merge vertically.) However, a vertical merger between large firms in highly concentrated industries may be challenged. In a classic 1949 case, it was shown that DuPont had acquired a controlling interest in General Motors (GM). GM was found to be purchasing from DuPont about two-thirds of its paint and almost one-half of the fabrics it used in auto manufacturing. The impact of DuPont's control of GM effectively prevented other paint and fabric manufacturers from selling to GM. The Court ordered DuPont to sell its GM stock and sever the tie between the two firms.

Conglomerate mergers are generally permitted. If an auto manufacturer acquires a blue jeans producer, no antitrust action is likely since neither firm has increased its own market share as a result. That means the Herfindahl index remains unchanged in each industry. **(Key Question 5)**

Price Fixing Price fixing is treated strictly. Evidence of price fixing, even by small firms, will bring antitrust action, as will other collusive activities such as scheming to rig bids on government contracts or dividing up sales in a market. In antitrust law, these activities are known as **per se violations;** they are "in and of themselves" illegal, and therefore *not* subject to the rule of reason. To gain a conviction, the government or other party making the charge need only show that there was a conspiracy to fix prices, rig bids, or divide up markets, not that the conspiracy succeeded or caused serious damage to other parties.

Price-fixing investigations and court actions are common. Recent examples include:

1. The three largest makers of baby formula have agreed to pay $50 million to settle several lawsuits charging that they fixed the price of baby formula for more than a decade.
2. Archer Daniels Midland (ADM) and other agribusinesses have admitted fixing the prices of an additive to livestock feed, a sweetener made from corn, and citrus acid.
3. Miles Inc. and Bayer's Dial Corporation were found to have fixed the price of S.O.S and Brillo soap pads.
4. ConAgra and Hormel agreed to pay more than $21 million to settle their roles in a nationwide price-fixing case involving catfish.
5. Reebok agreed to pay nearly $10 million in damages to settle a lawsuit in which it was accused of fixing the minimum price retailers could charge for its footwear.

Tying Contracts The Federal government also has strictly enforced the Clayton Act's prohibition of *tying contracts*. For example, it has successfully stopped movie distributors from forcing theaters to "buy" the projection rights to a full package of films as a condition of showing a blockbuster movie. More recently, it has taken action against Microsoft for "bundling" its Internet Explorer (IE) browser with its Windows 95 operating software. According to the government, Microsoft has illegally required computer manufacturers wanting to include Windows on their machines to also include IE (rather than Netscape's Navigator).

What then can we conclude about the overall effectiveness of antitrust laws? Antitrust policy has *not* been very effective in restricting the rise of, or in breaking up, monopolies or oligopolies resulting from internal expansions of firms. In contrast, antitrust policy *has* been effective in blocking blatantly anticompetitive mergers and in identifying and prosecuting price fixing and tying contracts. Most economists conclude that, overall, U.S. antitrust policy has been moderately effective in achieving its goal of promoting competition and efficiency.

QUICK REVIEW 32-2

■ The Sherman Act of 1890 outlaws restraints of trade and monopolization; the Clayton Act of 1914 as amended by the Celler-Kefauver Act of 1950 outlaws price discrimination, tying contracts, anticompetitive mergers, and interlocking directorates.

■ The Federal Trade Commission Act of 1914 as bolstered by the Wheeler-Lea Act of 1938 created the Federal Trade Commission (FTC) and gave it authority to investigate unfair methods of competition and deceptive acts or practices in commerce.

■ "Structuralists" say highly concentrated industries will behave like monopolists; "behaviorists" hold that the relationship between industry structure and firm behavior is uncertain.

■ Enforcement of antitrust laws may be moderated when other government goals might be affected.

■ Presently, government treats existing industrial concentration leniently; blocks most horizontal mergers between large, profitable firms in concentrated industries; and vigorously prosecutes price fixing and tying contracts engaged in by firms of all sizes.

NATURAL MONOPOLIES AND THEIR REGULATION

Antitrust policy assumes society will benefit if monopoly is prevented from evolving or is dissolved where it already exists. We now return to a special situation in which there is an economic reason for an industry to be organized monopolistically.

Natural Monopoly

A **natural monopoly** exists when economies of scale are so extensive that a single firm can supply the entire market at lower unit cost than could a number of competing firms. Such conditions exist for the *public utilities*, such as electricity, water, gas, and local telephone service (discussed in Chapter 24). In these cases, large-scale operations are necessary if low unit costs, and a low price, are to be obtained. Where there is natural monopoly, competition is uneconomical. If the market were divided among many producers, economies of scale would not be achieved, unit costs would be high, and high prices would be necessary to cover those costs.

There are two possible alternatives for promoting socially acceptable behavior on the part of a natural monopoly. One is public ownership, and the other is public regulation.

Public ownership or some approximation of it has been established in a few instances: the Postal Service, the Tennessee Valley Authority, and Amtrak at the national level; mass transit, water supply systems, and garbage collection at the local level.

But *public regulation*, or what economists call *industrial regulation*, has been the preferred option in the United States. In this type of regulation, government commissions regulate the prices (or rates) charged by natural monopolists. Because of deregulation over the past two decades, such control is on the wane. Table 32-1 lists the two remaining major Federal regulatory commissions and their jurisdictions. It also notes that all 50 states still have commissions which regulate the intrastate activities and "utility rates" of natural monopolies.

The intent of legislation that regulates a natural monopoly is embodied in the **public interest theory of regulation.** This theory says that such an industry should be regulated for the benefit of the public so that consumers may be assured quality service at reasonable rates. If competition is inappropriate or impractical, monopoly should be established but *regulated* to avoid possible abuses of uncontrolled monopoly power. Regulation should guarantee that *consumers* benefit from the economies of scale—the lower per-unit costs—which natural monopolists are able to achieve. In practice, regulators seek to establish rates which will cover production costs and yield a "fair" or "reasonable" return to the enterprise. The goal is to set price equal to average total cost, as de-

TABLE 32-1 The main regulatory commissions providing industrial regulation

Commission (year established)	Jurisdiction
Federal Energy Regulatory Commission (1930)*	Electricity, gas, gas pipelines, oil pipelines, water-power sites
Federal Communications Commission (1934)	Telephones, television, cable television, radio, telegraph, CB radios, ham operators, etc.
State public utility commissions (50 states)	Electricity, gas, telephones

*Originally called the Federal Power Commission; renamed in 1977.

scribed in the "Regulated Monopoly" section of Chapter 24.

Problems

There is considerable disagreement on the effectiveness of regulation. Let's examine three criticisms.

Costs and Inefficiency An unregulated firm has great incentive to reduce its production costs because doing so will increase profit. A regulated firm, however, is confined to a normal profit or a "fair return" on the value of its assets. If a regulated firm lowers its operating costs, the rising profit will lead the regulatory commission to require that the firm lower its rates so only a normal profit is earned. The regulated firm therefore has little or no incentive to reduce such costs. Worse yet, higher costs do not result in lower profits. Because the regulatory commissions must allow the public utility a fair return, higher production costs simply get passed through to consumers in the form of higher rates. A regulated firm may reason that it might as well have high salaries for its workers, nice working conditions for management, and the like since the "return" is the same whether costs are minimized or not. So although natural monopoly reduces cost through economies of scale, industrial regulation fosters considerable X-inefficiency.

There is still another potential for inefficiency. Since the regulated firm receives a certain rate of return on the value of its assets (real capital), the firm may make uneconomical substitutions of capital for labor. This, too, would contribute to X-inefficiency.

Commission Deficiencies Some critics say that regulatory commissions function inadequately because they and their staffs are often populated by people who were once in the industries they are now supposed to control. Therefore, regulation may not be in the public interest but, rather, may protect and nurture the comfortable position of the natural monopolist. Regulation allegedly becomes a way to guarantee profits and protect the regulated industry from new competition that technological change might create.

Regulation of Competitive Industries Perhaps the most severe criticism of industrial regulation is that it has sometimes been applied to industries which are not natural monopolies and which, without regulation, would be quite competitive. Specifically, regulation has been used in industries such as trucking and airlines, where economies of scale are not great and entry barriers are relatively weak. In such instances regulation itself, by limiting entry, may create the monopoly. The result is higher prices and less output than without regulation. Contrary to the public interest theory of regulation, the beneficiaries of regulation are then the regulated firms and their employees. The losers are the public and potential competitors barred from entering the industry.

Example: Regulation of the railroads by the Interstate Commerce Commission (ICC) was justified in the late 1800s and early 1900s. But by the 1930s the nation had developed a network of highways and the trucking industry had seriously undermined the monopoly power of the railroads. At that time it would have been desirable to dismantle the ICC and let railroads and truckers, along with barges and airlines, compete with one another. Instead, the regulatory net of the ICC was cast wider in the 1930s to include interstate truckers. The ICC remained in place until its elimination in 1996. **(Key Question 10)**

Legal Cartel Theory

The regulation of potentially competitive industries has produced the **legal cartel theory of regulation.** In place of socially minded officials *forcing* regulation on natural monopolies to protect consumers, this view sees practical politicians as supplying the "service" of regulation to firms which *want* to be regulated. Regulation is desired by these firms because it yields a legal cartel which can be highly profitable to regulated firms. Specifically, the regulatory commission performs such functions as dividing up the market (for example, prior to airline deregulation, the Civil Aeronautics Board assigned routes to specific airlines) and restricting potential competition by enlarging the cartel (for example, adding the trucking industry to the ICC's domain). While private cartels are unstable and often break down, the special attraction of a government-sponsored cartel under the guise of regulation is that it endures. The legal cartel theory of regulation suggests that regulation results from rent-seeking activities.

Proponents of the legal cartel theory of regulation note that the Interstate Commerce Commission was welcomed by the railroads and that the trucking and airline industries both supported the extension of ICC regulation to their industries, arguing that unregulated competition was severe and destructive.

Occupational licensing is a labor market application of the legal cartel theory. Certain occupational groups—barbers, interior designers, dietitians—demand licensing because it protects the public from charlatans and quacks. But the real reason may be to limit occupational entry so that practitioners may receive monopoly incomes.

DEREGULATION

The legal cartel theory, evidence of inefficiency in regulated industries, and the contention that government was regulating potentially competitive industries all contributed to a wave of deregulation beginning in the 1970s. Since then Congress has passed legislation which has deregulated in varying degrees the airline, trucking, banking, railroad, natural gas, and television broadcasting industries. Deregulation has also occurred in the telecommunications industry, where antitrust authorities dismantled the *regulated monopoly* known as the Bell System (AT&T). The deregulation in the 1970s and 1980s comprised one of the most extensive experiments in economic policy in the past 50 years.

Controversy

Deregulation was controversial, and the nature of the dispute was predictable. Basing their arguments on the legal cartel theory, proponents of deregulation contended it would lower prices, increase output, and eliminate bureaucratic inefficiencies. Some critics of deregulation, embracing the public interest theory, argued deregulation would result in gradual monopolization of some of the deregulated industries by one or two firms. They predicted higher prices, diminished output, and deteriorating service. Other critics were concerned that deregulation would lead to excessive competition and industry instability and that vital services (for example, transportation) would be withdrawn from smaller communities. Still others stressed that as increased competition reduced each firm's revenues, firms would lower their safety standards to reduce costs and remain profitable.

Deregulation Outcomes

While there are still some critics, most economists say that deregulation has clearly benefited consumers and the economy. According to recent studies, deregulation of formerly regulated industries is now contributing about $50 billion annually to society's well being through lower prices, lower costs, and increased output.[1] The majority of these gains are accruing in three industries: airlines, railroads, and trucking. Airfares (adjusted for inflation) have declined by about one-third, and airline safety has continued to improve. Trucking and railroad freight rates (again, adjusted for inflation) have dropped by about one-half. Significant efficiency gains have occurred in long-distance telecommunications, and there have been smaller efficiency gains in cable television, stock brokerage services, and the natural gas industry. Moreover, deregulation has unleashed a wave of technological advances which have resulted in such new and improved products and services as fax machines, cellular phones, fiber-optic cable, and microwave systems in communications.

QUICK REVIEW 32-3

■ Natural monopoly occurs where economies of scale are so extensive that only a single firm can produce the product at minimum average total cost.

■ The public interest theory of regulation says that government must regulate natural monopolies to prevent abuses arising from monopoly power.

■ The legal cartel theory of regulation suggest that some firms seek government regulation to reduce price competition and ensure stable profits.

■ Deregulation initiated by government in the past three decades has yielded large annual efficiency gains for society.

SOCIAL REGULATION

The industrial regulation of the previous sections focuses on the regulation of prices (or rates) in natural monopolies. But in the early 1960s a new type of regulation began to evolve and grow. This *social regulation* is concerned with the conditions under which goods and services are produced, the impact of production on society, and the physical qualities of the goods themselves.

---

[1]Clifford Winston, "Economic Deregulation: Days of Reckoning for Microeconomists," *Journal of Economic Literature*, September 1993, p. 1284; and Robert Crandall and Jerry Ellig, "Economic Deregulation and Consumer Choice," Center for Market Processes, Fairfax, Virginia.

The Federal government carries out most social regulation, although states also play a role. The main Federal regulatory commissions engaged in social regulation are listed in Table 32-2.

Distinguishing Features

Social regulation differs from industrial regulation in several ways:

1. Social regulation applies to far more firms than industrial regulation. Social regulation is often applied "across the board" to all industries and directly affects more producers than industrial regulation. For instance, while the rate regulation of the Federal Energy Regulatory Commission (FERC) applies to a relatively small number of firms, Occupational Safety and Health Administration (OSHA) rules and regulations apply to firms in all industries.

2. Social regulation intrudes into the day-to-day production process to a greater extent than industrial regulation. While industrial regulation focuses on rates, costs, and profits, social regulation often dictates the design of products, the conditions of employment, and the nature of the production process. As examples, the Consumer Product Safety Commission (CPSC) regulates the design of potentially unsafe products, and the

TABLE 32-2   **The main Federal regulatory commissions providing social regulation**

Commission (year established)	Jurisdiction
Food and Drug Administration (1906)	Safety and effectiveness of food, drugs, and cosmetics
Equal Employment Opportunity Commission (1964)	Hiring, promotion, and discharge of workers
Occupational Safety and Health Administration (1971)	Industrial health and safety
Environmental Protection Agency (1972)	Air, water, and noise pollution
Consumer Product Safety Commission (1972)	Safety of consumer products

Environmental Protection Agency (EPA) regulates the amount of pollution allowed as production occurs.

3. Social regulation has expanded rapidly during the same period in which industrial regulation has waned. Between 1970 and 1980, the U.S. government created 20 new social regulatory agencies. More recently, Congress has established new social regulations to be enforced by existing regulatory agencies. For instance, the Equal Employment Opportunity Commission, which is responsible for enforcing laws against workplace discrimination on the basis of race, gender, age, or religion, has been given the added duty of enforcing the Americans with Disabilities Act of 1990. Under this social regulation, firms must provide reasonable accommodations for qualified workers and job applicants with disabilities. Also, sellers must provide reasonable access for customers with disabilities.

The names of the regulatory agencies in Table 32-2 suggest the reasons for their creation and growth: Much of our society had achieved a fairly affluent standard of living by the 1960s and attention shifted to improvement in the quality of life. This focus called for safer and better products, less pollution, improved working conditions, and greater equality of economic opportunity.

Overregulation?

While economists agree on the need for social regulation, they disagree on whether or not the current level of such regulation is optimal. Recall that *no* activity should be expanded to such an extent that its marginal cost exceeds its marginal benefit. Critics of social regulation contend that this is precisely what has happened in the United States. In this view, society would achieve net benefits by cutting back on social regulation. In contrast, defenders of social regulation argue that it has achieved notable successes and, overall, has greatly enhanced society's well-being. They say that cutbacks are unwarranted.

Let's look at the costs and criticisms of social regulation and then examine some counterarguments.

Costs The costs of social regulation are *administrative costs*, such as salaries paid to employees of the commissions, office expenses, and the like, and *compliance costs*, the costs incurred by businesses and state and local governments in meeting the requirements.

In 1997, 126,000 employees worked for Federal regulatory agencies involved in social regulation.[2] That year the administrative costs of social regulation were about $17 billion, and compliance costs were roughly $340 billion. Therefore, the total cost of social regulation in 1997 reached roughly $357 billion.

Criticisms Critics of social regulation argue that the U.S. economy is now subject to overregulation.

Uneconomical Goals First, critics say that many social regulation laws are poorly written, so that regulatory objectives and standards are difficult to understand. As a result, regulators pursue goals well beyond the original intent of the legislation. Businesses complain that regulators often press for additional increments of improvement, unmindful of costs. For example, once certain pollution has been reduced by, say, 60 percent, a requirement to reduce it by an added 5 percent may cost much more than did the first 60 percent reduction. The marginal cost of that last 5 percent reduction, critics argue, may far exceed the marginal benefit.

Inadequate Information Decisions must often be made and rules formed on the basis of inadequate information. For example, CPSC officials may make decisions about certain cancer-causing ingredients in products on the basis of limited laboratory experiments with animals. Or government agencies may establish costly pollution standards to attack the global-warming problem without knowing for certain whether pollution is the main cause of the problem. These efforts, say critics, tend to overregulate business.

Unintended Side Effects Critics argue that social regulations produce many unintended and costly side effects. For example, the Federal gas mileage standard for automobiles has been blamed for an estimated 2000 to 3900 traffic deaths a year because auto manufacturers have reduced the weight of vehicles to meet the higher miles-per-gallon standards. Other things equal, drivers of lighter cars have a higher fatality rate than drivers of heavier vehicles.

Overzealous Personnel Opponents of social regulation say the regulatory agencies may attract

---

[2]Data in this paragraph provided by the Center for the Study of American Business, Washington University.

overzealous workers who are hostile toward the market system and "believe" too fervently in regulation. For example, the EPA staff allegedly sees all pollution as bad and all polluters as "bad guys." They have been accused of avoiding the challenge of trying to identify the optimal amount of pollution, based on a careful analysis of marginal costs and marginal benefits.

The critics also assert there is a tendency for the personnel involved with social regulation to find ever more problems in need of social regulation. As a result, continued employment and expanding bureaucracies are ensured (recall the theory of public choice from Chapter 31).

Economic Implications of Overregulation
If overregulation exists—and that is subject to debate—what are its consequences?

Higher Prices   Social regulation increases product prices in two ways. It does this directly because compliance costs normally get passed on to consumers, and it does so indirectly by reducing labor productivity. Resources invested in antipollution equipment, for example, are not available for investment in new machinery designed to increase output per worker. Where the wage rate is fixed, a drop in labor productivity increases the marginal and average total costs of production. In effect, the supply curve for the product shifts leftward, causing its price to rise.

Slower Innovation   Social regulation may have a negative impact on the rate of innovation. Technological advance may be stifled by, say, the fear that a new plant will not meet EPA guidelines or that a new medicine will require years of testing before being approved by the Food and Drug Administration (FDA).

Reduced Competition   Social regulation may have an anticompetitive effect since it usually places a relatively greater burden on small firms than on large ones. The costs of complying with social regulation are, in effect, fixed costs. Because smaller firms produce less output over which to distribute these costs, their compliance costs per unit of output put them at a competitive disadvantage with their larger rivals. Social regulation is more likely to force smaller firms out of business, thus contributing to the increased concentration of industry.

In Support of Social Regulation   Supporters of social regulation strongly defend it. They point out that the problems which social regulation confront are serious and substantial. Nearly 8000 workers die annually in job-related accidents. Air pollution continues to cloud major U.S. cities, imposing large costs in terms of reduced property values and increased health care expense. Numerous children and adults die each year in accidents involving poorly designed products or tainted food. Discrimination against blacks and other minorities, women, persons with disabilities, and older workers reduces their earnings and imposes heavy costs on society.

The proponents of social regulation correctly point out that a high "price" for something does not necessarily mean that it should not be purchased. They say the relevant economic test should be not whether costs of social regulation are high or low but, rather, whether the benefits of social regulation *exceed* the costs. After years of neglect, they further assert, society cannot expect to cleanse the environment, enhance the safety of the workplace, and promote economic opportunity for all without substantial costs. So statements about the huge costs of social regulation are irrelevant, say defenders, since the benefits are even greater. These benefits are often underestimated by the public since they are more difficult to measure than costs and often become apparent only after some time has passed.

Proponents of social regulation point to its many specific benefits. Here are just a few examples: It is estimated that highway fatalities would be 40 percent greater annually without auto safety features mandated through regulation. Compliance with child safety-belt laws has significantly reduced the auto fatality rate for small children. The national air quality standards set by law have been reached in nearly all parts of the nation for sulfur dioxide, nitrogen dioxide, and lead. Affirmative action regulations have increased the labor demand for blacks and females. The use of childproof lids has resulted in a 90 percent decline in child deaths caused by accidental swallowing of poisonous substances.

Defenders say these and many other benefits are well worth the costs of social regulation. The costs are simply the "price" we must pay to create a hospitable, sustainable, and just society. **(Key Question 12)**

QUICK REVIEW 32-4

■ Social regulation is concerned with conditions under which goods and services are produced, the effects of production on society, and physical characteristics of goods themselves.

■ Critics of social regulation say uneconomical policy goals, inadequate information, unintended side effects, and overzealous personnel create overregulation and regulatory costs which exceed regulatory benefits.

■ Defenders of social regulation point to the benefits arising from policies which keep dangerous products from the marketplace, reduce workplace injuries and deaths, contribute to clean air and water, and reduce employment discrimination.

INDUSTRIAL POLICY

In recent years industrial policy has joined antitrust activities, industrial regulation, and social regulation as a distinct form of government involvement with business. *Industrial policy consists of governmental actions to promote the economic vitality of specific firms or industries.* The other forms of government involvement alter the structure or restrict the conduct of private firms, generally reducing their revenues or increasing their costs. Industrial policy *promotes* the interests of selected firms and industries, usually adding to their profitability.

Antecedents

Governmental promotion of industries has a long, controversial history. In the 1600s and 1700s European governments practiced an economic policy known as mercantilism. At the heart of mercantilism was the belief that a nation's wealth consisted of its precious metals. Because merchants received inflows of gold in return for their exports, governments established elaborate policies to promote exports and reduce imports. Such policies included tariffs on imports of finished goods, free importation of resources, and the granting of monopoly trading privileges to selected companies (such as the East India Company and the Hudson Bay Company). Governments also regulated production techniques to ensure the quality of exports and, in general, subsidized production in their exporting industries.

The history of the United States is also full of examples of industrial policy. In the 1800s government granted free land to railroads to promote their westward expansion. This expansion hastened economic development, increased productivity, and raised national output and employment. Government has heav-

ily subsidized U.S. agriculture over the decades, boosting profits in that industry. And government's spending on national defense has built up a military armament industry which is a major world exporter.

Recent Emphasis

In the past decade or so there has been concern that the United States is losing its industrial superiority. U.S. domestic markets have been flooded with foreign steel, automobiles, motorcycles, cameras, watches, sporting goods, and electronic equipment. Some believe these imports imply that the United States is losing global competitiveness.

Noting Japanese export success, many union and business leaders and politicians—but very few economists—feel the United States needs a strong industrial policy to maintain its industrial strength. They argue that government should take a more active and direct role in determining the structure and composition of U.S. industry. Government, they say, should use low-interest loans, loan guarantees, favorable tax treatment, research and development subsidies, antitrust immunity, and even protection against foreign goods to accelerate the development of high-tech industries and to revitalize basic core manufacturing industries such as steel. Presumably, as a result, the U.S. economy will enjoy a higher average level of productivity and be more competitive in world markets.

Although the Federal government does not have a full industrial policy, several of its programs are consistent with this idea.

1. *Auto industry* The surge of Japanese auto imports during the 1970s and 1980s placed tremendous financial pressure on U.S. auto producers. The Federal government responded with a series of actions to promote the domestic auto industry. In 1979 it "bailed out" the failing Chrysler Corporation by guaranteeing repayment of $1.5 billion of private loans to Chrysler to keep it afloat. In the mid-1980s the U.S. negotiated "voluntary" limits on the number of automobiles Japan exported to the United States. More recently, the Federal government has initiated and heavily subsidized a research and development program with GM, Ford, and Chrysler; its goal is to design and produce a revolutionary fuel-efficient gasoline engine.

2. *Synfuel program* In response to the "oil crisis" of the mid-1970s, the U.S. government established a program of subsidies to firms developing

alternative fuels. Much money went into developing synthetic fuels such as oil squeezed from oil shale and natural gas converted from coal. Overall, this effort was a dismal failure: It cost the government $1.3 billion and was shut down in 1991. However, the government still provides a $600 million annual subsidy to the ethanol industry, which develops fuel from corn.

3. *Export-import bank* This Federal "bank" offers credit insurance, which protects U.S. exporters against loan defaults by foreign customers who buy U.S. exports through loans from the sellers or the sellers' banks. The subsidies directly benefit U.S. exporters who sell goods on credit; in effect, they reduce the total price (product price plus loan interest) to the foreign buyer.

4. *Sematech* In 1987 government and industry set up a consortium called Sematech, which exempts semiconductor-chip producers from antitrust regulations while they join together to engage in research and share production techniques. The purpose was to help U.S. firms compete with Japanese firms. It is generally agreed that this effort has accomplished its intended goal.

5. *Flat-glass technology* In 1994 the Clinton administration announced a $1 billion plan to help U.S. industry compete against Japan in producing flat-glass computer screens. At the time, the U.S. share of this market was only 3 percent, with Japanese and South Korean firms accounting for the remainder. Because these screens have many high-tech military applications, the administration justified this massive subsidy on a national defense basis. But it was clear that the subsidy had as much to do with industrial policy as with military needs.

Controversy

Advocates of industrial policy—or what some now label "technology policy"—point out that several leading U.S. products were developed with direct government support, particularly through national defense spending. Commercial aircraft, the supercomputer, the PC mouse, and the Internet are examples. They argue that well-targeted government industrial policy enhances private-sector entrepreneurial forces and, ultimately, expands economic growth. By subsidizing R&D efforts, industrial policy purportedly reduces the risk of exploring and applying new technologies. In this view, these technologies often spur complementary products and entire new industries, boosting a nation's productivity, standard of living, and international competitiveness.

Proponents of industrial policy cite Japan's Ministry of International Trade and Industry (MITI) as a model. Since World War II, Japan has achieved rapid economic growth because it has been highly successful in penetrating world markets. During this time, MITI has had a much-publicized industrial policy. Yet the role of industrial policy in Japan's industrial success is not at all clear. Subsidies to some of Japan's industries have surely succeeded (in particular, the semiconductor, machine tool, steel, and shipbuilding industries). In others, Japan's industrial policy has failed (in the aluminum-smelting, petrochemical, and high-definition-television industries). Still other Japanese industries (autos, electronics, and motorcycles) have developed successfully without government support.

Critics of industrial policy point out that Japan's MITI has made major errors in judgment. Two examples: It tried to block Honda from entering its auto industry; Honda now is one of Japan's most successful and innovative auto manufacturers. MITI pushed Japanese industry to develop an analog version of high-definition television. But U.S. producers, with minimal government support, have implemented a far superior digital technology. Japan, in essence, spent $8.3 billion for naught, mainly because MITI decided on analog.

European industrial policy has also had mixed results. Europe's subsidizing of Airbus Industries, a manufacturer of commercial aircraft, was successful, but its subsidization of a supersonic transport aircraft was an economic failure.

"Short-circuiting" the market mechanism by promoting selected technologies and industries sounds appealing, but critics question any government's ability to identify the technologies and industries which will be winners and losers. The question is who can better determine where R&D and investment funds ought to be channeled. Critics say that private investors, who invest their *own* funds, have a greater incentive to obtain accurate information about technologies and industries than bureaucrats investing *taxpayers'* funds.

They also argue that government might be tempted to use investment funds to buy the political support of subsidized industries. If that were to happen, the economic goals of enhanced industrial efficiency and increased exports might become secondary

Deregulation of the Airlines

Perhaps the most publicized case of deregulation began with the Airline Deregulation Act of 1978. Previously, the Civil Aeronautics Board (CAB) controlled airline fares, allocated interstate routes, and controlled entry to the industry. Deregulation freed airlines to set their own rates and select their own routes, and it allowed newcomers to compete. Has airline deregulation succeeded?

Although the airline industry was deregulated two decades ago, it is still adjusting to deregulation. Nevertheless, some of the effects have become clear.

Fares Deregulation has exerted downward pressure on fares, with overall fares rising less rapidly than the general price level. Discount air tickets, in particular, have increased in availability and declined in price.

Today, fares generally are about one-third lower in real terms than before deregulation. Of course, fare reductions have not been uniform in all markets, and some fares have decreased more than others.

Deregulation has produced lower fares for two reasons. First, competition among air carriers has driven down prices. Before regulation, ticket prices greatly exceeded the average total cost (ATC) of passenger service. Competition has reduced fares and economic profits;

prices are closer to ATC. Second, competition has pressured firms to reduce costs. The industry's "hub-and-spoke" route system—analogous to a bicycle wheel—has reduced costs by allowing airlines to use smaller planes on the spoke routes and wide-bodied craft between the major hub airports. Wide-body aircraft cost less to operate per seat mile than smaller aircraft.

Also, the entry of nonunionized airlines has forced the major carriers to negotiate wage reductions with their unions. Some airlines have established two-tier wage systems, paying new workers less than current employees. Union work rules have been made more flexible to increase worker productivity and reduce wage costs. Airlines are increasingly leasing work such as airline maintenance to lower-cost outside companies.

Service and Safety While some major airlines have withdrawn service to and from smaller cities, commuter airlines usually fill the resulting void. The hub-and-spoke system has increased flight frequencies at most airports. It has also reduced the amount of airline switching required of passengers. Measures of service quality such as "complaints per 10,000 passengers" are sharply lower today than in the era of regulation.

On the negative side, the hub-system's added stopovers have increased average travel time between cities. Also, by increasing the volume of traffic, deregulation has contributed to greater airport congestion, resulting in more frequent and longer flight delays.

There is mixed evidence as to whether deregulation has reduced the safety of air transportation. The greater volume of air traffic has resulted in higher reported in-

to the political goal of collecting campaign contributions and getting reelected. In addition, the expansion of industrial policy might lead to "lemon socialism": government support or ownership of declining industries' dying companies and inefficient technologies. **(Key Question 14)**

1. The case against industrial concentration contends that it **(a)** causes a misallocation of resources; **(b)** retards the rate of technological advance; **(c)** promotes income inequality; and **(d)** creates undo political influence by large firms.

2. The defense of industrial concentration maintains **(a)** firms have obtained their large market shares by offering superior products; **(b)** interindustry and foreign competition, along with potential competition from new industry entrants, make U.S. industries more competitive stances of near-collisions in midair. But the accident and fatal accident rates of airlines are much lower today than before deregulation. Furthermore, deregulation has prevented an estimated 800 deaths annually on the nation's highways, because lower fares have enticed people to substitute air travel for more dangerous automobile travel.

Industry Structure Airline deregulation initially induced the entry of many new carriers. But in the past several years the industry has gone through a "shakeout" in which some firms have failed and others have merged with stronger competitors. Today, American, United, and Delta account for about 60 percent of domestic air service.

Growing concentration in the airlines industry is of some concern. Some think consolidation of the industry eventually may be detrimental to the very goals of deregulation itself. Studies show that fares at airports dominated by one or two airlines are as much as 25 percent higher than at airports where competition is greater. Moreover, entry of new carriers into the industry is more difficult than many economists predicted. The lack of airport capacity—at least in the short term—means that airline markets are far from being perfectly competitive. A firm wishing to enter a particular market because existing carriers are earning economic profits cannot do so if long-term leases allow existing carriers to control the airport boarding gates.

Airline tactics also make successful entry difficult. Airline reservation systems developed by the major carriers often give their own flights priority listings on the computers used by travel agents. Frequent-flyer programs—discounts based on accumulated flight mileage—encourage passengers to use dominant existing carriers rather than new entrants. Also, price matching by existing carriers makes it difficult for new entrants to lure customers through lower ticket prices.

Conclusion Although it is too soon for a definitive assessment of airline deregulation, most economists see a positive outcome to date. Although lasting entry has proved difficult, there are some success stories. In particular, Southwest Airlines has expanded its direct-flight, low-fare approach far beyond its original geographical domain. The Federal government has estimated that airline deregulation produced a $100 billion net benefit to society in the 1980s alone. Today, airline deregulation is yielding society net benefits of about $20 billion annually.

---

than generally believed; **(c)** some degree of monopoly may be essential to realize economies of scale; and **(d)** monopolies and oligopolies are technologically progressive.

3. The cornerstone of antitrust policy consists of the Sherman Act of 1890 and the Clayton Act of 1914. The Sherman Act specifies that "every contract, combination . . . or conspiracy in the restraint of interstate trade . . . is . . . illegal" and that any person who monopolizes or attempts to monopolize interstate trade is guilty of a misdemeanor.

4. The Clayton Act was designed to bolster and make more explicit the provisions of the Sherman Act. It declared that price discrimination, tying contracts, intercorporate stockholding, and interlocking directorates are illegal when their effect is the lessening of competition.

5. The Federal Trade Commission Act of 1914 created the Federal Trade Commission to investigate antitrust violations and to prevent the use of "unfair methods of competition." Empowered to issue cease-and-desist orders, the commission also serves as a watchdog agency for the false and deceptive representation of products.

6. The Celler-Kefauver Act of 1950 prohibits one firm from acquiring the assets of another firm when the result is a lessening of competition.

7. Issues in applying antitrust laws include **(a)** determining whether an industry should be judged by its structure or its behavior; **(b)** defining the scope and size of the dominant firm's market; and **(c)** balancing the gains from antitrust against other desirable goals such as balancing exports and imports, consolidating the defense industry, and encouraging new technologies.

8. Antitrust officials are more likely to challenge price fixing, tying contracts, and horizontal mergers than they are to break up existing market structures.

9. The objective of industrial regulation is to protect the public from the market power of natural monopolies by regulating prices and quality of service. Critics contend that industrial regulation can lead to inefficiency and rising costs and that in many instances it constitutes a legal cartel for the regulated firms. Legislation passed in the late 1970s and the 1980s has brought about varying degrees of deregulation in the airline, trucking, banking, railroad, and television broadcasting industries. Studies indicate that deregulation is producing sizable annual gains to society through lower prices, lower costs, and increased output.

10. Social regulation is concerned with product safety, working conditions, and the effects of production on society. Critics contend that businesses are overregulated to the point where costs exceed benefits, while defenders dispute that contention.

11. Industrial policy consists of government actions promoting the economic vitality of specific industries or firms. Proponents of industrial policy see it as a way to strengthen the industrial sector, speed development of new technologies, increase productivity, and increase international competitiveness. Critics charge that industrial policy may substitute the whims of politicians and bureaucrats for the hard scrutiny of entrepreneurs and business executives in allocating society's resources.

TERMS AND CONCEPTS

antitrust policy	Sherman Act	Celler-Kefauver Act	per se violations
industrial regulation	Clayton Act	U.S. Steel case	natural monopoly
social regulation	tying contracts	rule of reason	public interest theory of
industrial policy	interlocking directorates	Alcoa case	regulation
industrial concentration	Federal Trade	DuPont cellophane case	legal cartel theory of
interindustry competition	Commission Act	horizontal merger	regulation
foreign competition	cease-and-desist order	vertical merger	
potential competition	Wheeler-Lea Act	conglomerate merger	

STUDY QUESTIONS

1. Suppose you are president of General Motors or Ford. Discuss critically the case *against* industrial concentration. Now suppose you are a representative for a consumer organization, attempting to convince a congressional committee that industrial concentration is a significant factor contributing to high prices. Critically evaluate the case *for* industrial concentration.

2. KEY QUESTION   Describe the major provisions of the Sherman and Clayton acts. Who is responsible for enforcing these laws?

3. Briefly indicate the basic issue involved in the U.S. Steel, Alcoa, and DuPont cellophane cases. What issues in antitrust enforcement are implicit in these cases?

4. Explain how strict enforcement of the antitrust laws might conflict with **(a)** promoting exports to achieve a balance of trade, **(b)** easing the burdens of cutbacks in the defense industry, and **(c)** encouraging new technologies. Do you see any dangers of using selective antitrust enforcement as part of an industrial policy?

5. KEY QUESTION   How would you expect antitrust authorities to react to **(a)** a proposed merger of Ford and Chrysler; **(b)** evidence of secret meetings by contractors to rig bids for highway construction projects; **(c)** a proposed merger of a large shoe manufacturer and a chain of retail shoe stores; and **(d)** a proposed merger of a small life insurance company and a regional candy manufacturer.

6. Suppose a proposed merger of firms will simultaneously lessen competition and reduce unit costs through economics of scale. Do you think such a merger should be allowed?

7. In the 1980s PepsiCo Inc., which then had 28 percent of the soft-drink market, proposed to acquire the Seven-Up Company. Shortly thereafter the Coca-Cola Company, with 39 percent of the market, indicated it wished to acquire the Dr. Pepper Company. Seven-Up and Dr. Pepper each controlled about 7 percent of the market. In your judgment, was the government's decision to block these mergers appropriate?

8. "The antitrust laws serve to penalize efficiently managed firms." Do you agree? Why or why not?

9. "The social desirability of any particular firm should be judged not on the basis of the structure of the industry in which it finds itself but, rather, on the basis of the market performance and behavior of that firm." Analyze critically.

10. KEY QUESTION What types of industries, if any, should be subjected to industrial regulation? What specific problems does industrial regulation entail? Why might an inefficient combination of capital and labor be employed by a regulated natural monopoly?

11. In view of the problems in regulating natural monopolies, compare socially optimal (marginal-cost) pricing and fair-return pricing by referring again to Figure 24-9. Assuming a government subsidy might be used to cover any loss resulting from marginal-cost pricing, which pricing policy would you favor? Why? What problems might this subsidy entail?

12. KEY QUESTION How does social regulation differ from industrial regulation? What types of benefits and costs are associated with social regulation?

13. Here are research estimates of the average cost per life saved of three specific social regulations: 1967 automobile steering-column protection rule, $100,000 per life saved; 1979 FDA ban on DES (a suspected carcinogen) in cattle feed, $132 million per life saved; the EPA's proposed restrictions on disposal of dioxins and solvents on land, $3.5 billion per

life saved.[3] Based on this information, do you favor each of these social regulations? If not, why not? Discuss: "Implicit within the setting of safety standards for products is the valuation of human life."

14. KEY QUESTION What is industrial policy, and how does it differ from antitrust policy, industrial regulation, and social regulation? Why might businesses look more favorably on industrial policy than on these other policies? Cite an example of industrial policy. What are the pros and cons of industrial policy?

15. (Last Word) What is meant by saying that the airline industry has been deregulated? What have been the impacts of deregulation on fares, service and safety, and industry structure? Some say, "The jury is still out on airline deregulation." Speculate on what they may mean.

16. WEB-BASED QUESTION Industrial Policy Example—Japan's Ministry of International Trade and Industry The United States does not have a comprehensive industrial policy. The most extensive industrial policy among developed countries is carried out by Japan's Ministry of International Trade and Industry (MITI) http://www.miti.go.jp/index-e.html. What is the structure of MITI, and how does MITI carry out its industrial policy? What are the Current Topics which relate to an industrial policy? MITI's current emphasis is "economic structural reform." What does this mean? What industries have been chosen as "new and growth fields"?

17. WEB-BASED QUESTION Enforcement of Antitrust Laws—Who Is Responsible? The antitrust laws http://www.law.cornell.edu/uscode/15/ch1.html are enforced by both the Federal Trade Commission's Bureau of Competition http://www.ftc.gov/ftc/antitrust.htm and the Antitrust Division of the Department of Justice http://www.usdoj.gov/atr/index.html. How do these agencies prevent duplication of effort? What are their current antitrust activities? Are any of the activities of major significance? Do other antitrust organizations http://www.usdoj.gov/atr/otheratr.htm view antitrust activities differently?

---

[3]*Economic Report of the President, 1987* (Washington: 1987), p. 183.

Agriculture: Economics and Policy

In the United States, agriculture is economically important for a number of reasons:

- Agriculture is one of the nation's largest industries. Consumers spend about 15 percent of their after-tax income on food and other farm products. Gross farm income was about $240 billion in 1997, and about 2 percent of the labor force is employed in agriculture.

- Agriculture is an industry which, in the absence of government farm programs, is a real-world example of Chapter 23's pure-competition model. The industry consists of many firms selling virtually standardized products and can be understood by applying the demand and supply tools of competitive markets.

- Farm products provide evidence of the intended and unintended effects of government policies which interfere with the forces of supply and demand.

- Agriculture reflects the increasing globalization of markets. In recent decades the economic ups and downs of U.S. agriculture have been closely tied to its ability to gain access to world markets. Currently, U.S. farmers produce 49 percent of the world's soybeans, 40 percent of all corn, and 25 percent of the world's beef.

- Farm policies are excellent illustrations of Chapter 31's special-interest effect and rent-seeking behavior.

    In this chapter we examine the problems within agriculture which have resulted in government intervention, the forms that intervention has taken and some of its results, and recent major changes in farm policy.

ECONOMICS OF AGRICULTURE

Over the years, farmers have faced severely fluctuating prices and periodically low incomes. There are actually two separate problems: the **short-run farm problem** of year-to-year fluctuations of farm prices and incomes, and the **long-run farm problem** of agriculture's being a declining industry.

Short-Run Problem: Price and Income Instability

The short-run farm problem is the result of (1) an inelastic demand for agricultural products, combined with (2) fluctuations in farm output and (3) shifts of the demand curve for farm products.

Inelastic Demand for Agricultural Products

In most developed societies, the price elasticity of demand for agricultural products is low. For farm products in the aggregate, the elasticity coefficient is between .20 and .25. These figures suggest that the prices of agricultural products would have to fall by 40 to 50 percent for consumers to increase their purchases by a mere 10 percent. Consumers apparently put a low value on additional farm output compared with alternative goods.

Why is this so? Recall that the basic determinant of elasticity of demand is substitutability. When the price of a product falls, the consumer tends to substitute *that* product for other products whose prices presumably have not fallen. But in relatively wealthy societies this "substitution effect" is very modest for food. People do not switch from three meals a day to, say, five or six meals a day in response to a decline in the relative prices of farm products. An individual's capacity to substitute food for other products is subject to very real biological constraints.

The inelasticity of agricultural demand can also be understood in terms of diminishing marginal utility. In a wealthy society, the population is generally well fed and well clothed; it is relatively saturated with the food and fiber of agriculture. Therefore, additional farm output involves rapidly diminishing marginal utility. Thus it takes very large price cuts to induce small increases in consumption.

Fluctuations in Output

Farm output tends to fluctuate from year to year, mainly because farmers have limited control over their output. Floods, droughts, unexpected frost, insect damage, and similar disasters can mean poor crops, while an excellent growing season may mean bumper crops. Natural phenomena are beyond the control of farmers, yet they exert an important influence on output.

In addition to these natural phenomena, it is the highly competitive nature of agriculture which makes it difficult for farmers to form huge combinations to control production. If the thousands of widely scattered and independent producers happen to plant an unusually large or an abnormally small portion of their land one year, an extra-large or very small farm output will result even if the growing season is normal.

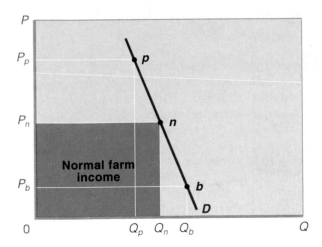

FIGURE 33-1 The effect of output changes on farm prices and income Because of the inelasticity of demand for farm products, a relatively small change in output (from Q_n to Q_p or Q_b) will cause a relatively large change in farm prices (from P_n to P_p or P_b). Farm income will change from the green area to $0P_ppQ_p$ or $0P_bbQ_b$).

Curve D in Figure 33-1 depicts the inelastic demand for agricultural products. Combining this demand with the instability of farm production, we can see why farm prices and incomes are unstable. Even if the market demand for agriculture products remains fixed at D, its price inelasticity will magnify small output changes into relatively large changes in farm prices and income. For example, assume that a "normal" crop of Q_n results in a "normal" price of P_n and a "normal" farm income represented by the green rectangle. A bumper crop or a poor crop will cause large deviations from these normal prices and incomes because of the inelasticity of demand.

If a good growing season occurs, the resulting bumper crop of Q_b will reduce farm income to that of area $0P_bbQ_b$. When demand is inelastic, an increase in the quantity sold will be accompanied by a *more-than-proportionate* decline in price. The net result is that total revenue, that is, total farm income, will decline disproportionately.

Similarly, a poor crop caused by, say, drought will boost total farm income to that represented by area $0P_ppQ_p$. A decline in output will cause a *more-than-proportionate* increase in price and in income when demand is inelastic. Ironically, for farmers as a group, a poor crop may be a blessing, and a bumper crop a hardship. Conclusion: *With a stable market demand for farm products, the inelasticity of that demand will turn relatively small changes in output into relatively larger changes in farm prices and income.*

Fluctuations in Domestic Demand The third factor in the short-run instability of farm income has to do with shifts in the demand curve for agricultural products. Suppose that somehow agricultural output is stabilized at the "normal" level of Q_n in Figure 33-2. Now, because of the inelasticity of the demand for farm products, short-run changes in the demand for these products—prompted perhaps by cyclical changes in the nation's total income—will cause markedly different prices and incomes to be associated with this fixed level of output.

A slight drop in demand from D_1 to D_2 will reduce farm income from area $0P_1aQ_n$ to $0P_2bQ_n$. That is, a relatively small decline in demand gives farmers a drastically reduced money reward for the same amount of farm output. Conversely, a slight increase in demand—as from D_2 to D_1—will bring an equally sharp increase in farm income for the same volume of output. Again, large price and income changes occur because demand is inelastic.

It is tempting to argue that the sharp declines in farm prices which accompany a decrease in demand will cause many farmers to close down in the short run, reducing total output and alleviating the price and income declines. But farm production is relatively insensitive to price changes because farmers' fixed costs are high compared with their variable costs. Interest, rent, tax, and mortgage payments on land, buildings, and equipment are the major costs faced by the farmer. These are fixed charges. Furthermore, the labor supply of farmers and their families can also be regarded as a fixed cost. As long as they stay on their farms, farmers cannot reduce their costs by firing themselves. Their variable costs are the costs of the small amounts of extra help they may employ, as well as expenditures for seed, fertilizer, and fuel. As a result of their high proportion of fixed costs, farmers are usually better off working their land than they are sitting idle and attempting to pay their fixed costs out of pocket.

Unstable Foreign Demand The dependence of U.S. agriculture on world markets is another source of demand volatility and hence of income instability. The incomes of U.S. farmers are sensitive to changes in weather and crop production *in other countries:* Better crops there mean less foreign demand for U.S. farm products. Similarly, cyclical fluctuations in incomes in Europe or Japan, for example, can shift the demand for U.S. farm products. So can changes in foreign economic policies. If the nations of western Europe decide to provide their farmers with greater protection from foreign (U.S.) competition, U.S. farmers will have less access to those markets and export demand will fall.

International politics can also add to demand instability. Changing political relations between the United States and the Soviet Union boosted U.S. grain sales in the early 1970s but reduced them at the end of that decade. Changes in the international value of the dollar can be critical. Depreciation of the dollar in the 1970s increased the demand for U.S. farm products (which became cheaper to foreigners), while appreciation of the dollar decreased foreign demand for U.S. farm products in the early 1980s.

To summarize: The increasing relative importance of exports has increased the short-run instability of the demand for U.S. farm products. Farm exports are affected not only by weather, income fluctuations, and economic policies abroad but also by international politics and changes in the international value of the dollar. **(Key Question 1)**

Figure 33-3 shows the Department of Agriculture's (USDA's) index of inflation-adjusted prices received

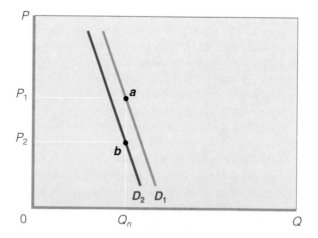

FIGURE 33-2 The effect of demand shifts on farm prices and income Because of the highly inelastic demand for agricultural products, a small shift in demand (from D_1 to D_2) will cause drastically different levels of farm prices (P_1 to P_2) and farm income (area $0P_1aQ_n$ to area $0P_2bQ_n$) to be associated with a fixed level of production Q_n.

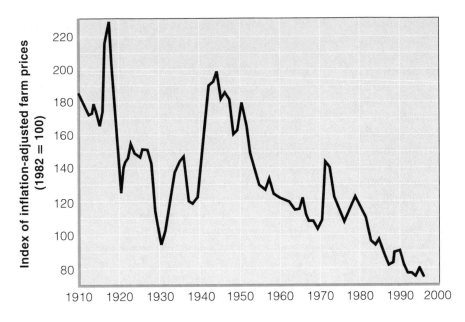

FIGURE 33-3 Index of inflation-adjusted prices received by
farmers The course of farm prices
during the twentieth century reflects
both volatility and decline. All the individual crop and livestock prices that
make up this index show a similar long-
term decline, and most reflect even
greater short-run volatility.

----

by farmers for crops and livestock during most of the
twentieth century. The short-run problem of price
volatility is clearly evident. So too is the long-run
problem of declining farm prices.

Long-Run Problem: A Declining Industry

Two other characteristics of agricultural markets explain why agriculture has been a declining industry:

1. Over time the supply of farm products has increased rapidly because of technological progress.

2. The demand for farm products has increased
slowly because it is inelastic with respect to income.

Technology and Supply Increases A rapid rate
of technological advance, particularly since World
War I, has significantly increased the supply of agricultural products. This technological progress has
many roots: the electrification and mechanization of
farms, improved techniques of land management and
soil conservation, irrigation, development of hybrid
crops, availability of improved fertilizers and insecticides, and improvements in breeding and care of livestock. The amount of capital used per worker increased 15 times between 1930 and 1980, permitting
a fivefold increase in the amount of land cultivated
per farmer. The simplest measure of these advances is
the increasing number of people a single farmer's out-

put will support. In 1820 each farmworker produced
enough food and fiber to support 4 persons; by 1947,
about 13. By 1997 each farmer produced enough to
support 110 people. Unquestionably, physical productivity in agriculture has risen spectacularly; since
World War II, it has advanced *twice* as fast as that in
the nonfarm economy.

Most technological advances in agriculture have
not been initiated by farmers but rather are the result
of government-sponsored programs of research and
education and the work of farm machinery producers.
Land-grant colleges, experiment stations, county
agents of the Agricultural Extension Service, educational pamphlets issued by the USDA, and the research departments of farm machinery, pesticide, and
fertilizer producers are the primary sources of technological advance in U.S. agriculture.

Lagging Demand Increases in demand for agricultural products have failed to keep pace with technologically caused increases in their supply. The reason lies in the two major determinants of agricultural
demand: income and population.

Income-Inelastic Demand In developing countries, consumers must devote most of their meager incomes to agricultural products—food and clothing—
to sustain themselves. But as income expands beyond
subsistence and the problem of hunger diminishes,
consumers increase their outlays on food at ever-

declining rates. Once consumers' stomachs are filled, they turn to the amenities of life which manufacturing and services, not agriculture, provide. Economic growth in the United States has boosted average per capita income far beyond the level of subsistence. As a result, *increases in the incomes of U.S. consumers lead to less-than-proportionate increases in spending on farm products.*

In economic terms, the demand for farm products is *income-inelastic*; it is quite insensitive to increases in income. Estimates indicate that a 10 percent increase in real per capita after-tax income means at most an increase of only 2 percent in consumption of farm products. Certain farm products—for example, cabbages and lard—may be inferior goods. As income increases, purchases of these products may actually *decrease.*

Population Growth Once a minimum income level is reached, each individual consumer's intake of food and fiber becomes relatively fixed. Thus subsequent increases in demand depend on growth in the number of consumers. In most advanced nations, the demand for farm products increases at a rate roughly equal to the rate of population growth, and this is the case in the United States. However, U.S. population growth has not been rapid. Therefore, the increase in

U.S. demand for farm products has not kept pace with the rapid growth of farm output.

Graphical Portrayal The combination of an inelastic and slowly increasing demand for agricultural products with a rapidly increasing supply puts strong downward pressure on farm prices and income. This is illustrated in Figure 33-4, where a large increase in agricultural supply is shown with a very modest increase in demand. Because of the inelastic demand, these shifts result in a sharp decline in farm prices, accompanied by a relatively small increase in output. Farm income therefore declines. On the graph, we see that farm income before the increases in demand and supply (measured by rectangle $0P_1aQ_1$) exceeds farm income after these increases ($0P_2bQ_2$). *Because of an inelastic demand for farm products, an increase in supply of such products relative to demand creates a persistent downward pressure on farm income.*

Consequences The actual consequences over time have been those predicted by the pure-competition model. Because of the demand and supply conditions just outlined, many small, high-cost farms which cannot benefit from scale economies or productivity gains cannot operate profitably. In the long run, financial losses in agriculture have triggered a massive exit to other sectors of the economy, as shown by Table 33-1.

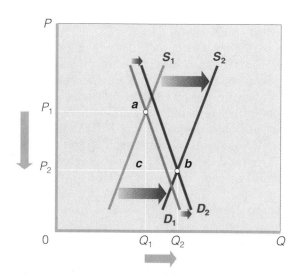

FIGURE 33-4 A graphical depiction of the long-run farm problem In the long run, increases in the demand for farm products (from D_1 to D_2) have not kept pace with the increases in supply (from S_1 to S_2) that technological advances have permitted. Because agricultural demand is inelastic, these shifts have tended to depress farm prices (from P_1 to P_2) and reduce farm income (from $0P_1aQ_1$ to $0P_2bQ_2$) while increasing output only modestly (from Q_1 to Q_2).

TABLE 33-1   The U.S. farm population, select years, 1910–1996

Year	Farm population		Number of farms, thousands
	In millions of people	As percentage of total population	
1910	32.1	35	6366
1920	31.9	30	6454
1930	30.5	25	6295
1940	30.5	23	6102
1950	23.0	15	5388
1960	15.6	9	3962
1970	9.7	5	2954
1980	7.2	3	2440
1990	4.6	2	2146
1996	4.2*	2	2063

*Authors' estimate.
Source: Statistical Abstract of the United States; Economic Report of the President.

GLOBAL PERSPECTIVE 33-1

Percentage of labor force in agriculture, selected nations

Rich nations devote a much smaller percentage of their labor forces to agriculture than do poor nations. Because their workforces are so heavily committed to producing the food and fiber needed for their populations, poor nations have relatively less labor available to produce housing, schools, autos, and the other goods and services which contribute to a high standard of living.

Percentage of Labor Force in Agriculture

Nation	0 — 25 — 50 — 75 — 100
Ethiopia	
Mozambique	
China	
India	
Brazil	
Japan	
France	
Germany	
United States	

Source: *World Development Report, 1997. Latest data.*

They have also caused a major consolidation of smaller farms into larger ones. A person farming, say, 240 acres of corn three decades ago is today likely to be farming two or three times that number of acres. Huge corporate firms called *agribusinesses* have emerged in some parts of farming such as potatoes, beef, fruits, vegetables, and poultry.

As a consequence of outmigration and consolidation, net farm income per farm household has increased relative to nonfarm income. Currently, average incomes of farm households and nonfarm households are very similar. **(Key Question 3)**

(As Global Perspective 33-1 shows, poor nations have much higher percentages of their labor forces in agriculture than do the United States and other industrialized nations.)

QUICK REVIEW 33-1

■ Agricultural prices and income are volatile in the short run because an inelastic demand translates small changes in farm output and demand into relatively larger changes in prices and income.

■ Technological progress has generated large increases in supplies of farm products over time.

■ Increases in demand for farm products have been modest in the United States because demand is inelastic with respect to income and because population growth has been modest.

■ The combination of large increases in supply and small increases in demand has made U.S. agriculture a declining industry.

ECONOMICS OF FARM POLICY

Government has subsidized U.S. agriculture since the 1930s. The "farm program" includes (1) support for farm prices, income, and output; (2) soil and water conservation; (3) agricultural research; (4) farm credit; (5) crop insurance; and (6) subsidized sale of farm products in world markets. However, the typical farmer and the average politician both have viewed the farm program primarily as one to prop up prices and income, and it is this "price-support" aspect of farm policy which we will explore.

This topic is particularly timely because in 1996 Congress passed historic legislation which ended 60 years of price supports for several, but not all, farm products. To understand the impact of this legislation, you need to know about the purposes and outcomes of farm subsidies. Between 1990 and 1996, U.S. farmers received an average of $5.5 billion of such subsidies each year. (As indicated in Global Perspective 33-2, farm subsidies are common globally.)

Rationale for Farm Subsidies

A variety of arguments have been made over the years to justify farm subsidies:

1. Although their products are needed, many farmers are comparatively poor; they should therefore receive higher prices and incomes through public help.

2. Farming—and particularly the "family farm"—is a fundamental U.S. institution and should be nurtured as a way of life.

3. Farmers are subject to extraordinary hazards—floods, droughts, and insects—which other indus-

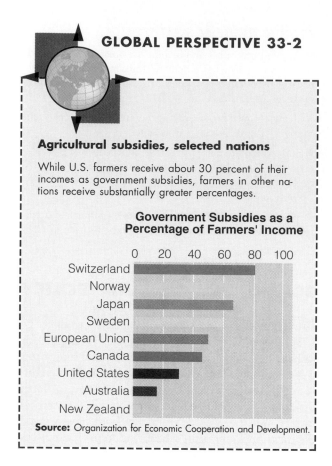

Source: Organization for Economic Cooperation and Development.

tries do not face. For the most part, farmers cannot fully insure themselves against these disasters.

4. While farmers face purely competitive markets for their outputs, they buy inputs of fertilizer, farm machinery, and gasoline from industries which have considerable market power. While these industries have an ability to control their prices, farmers are at the "mercy of the market" in selling their output. The supporters of subsidies argue that agriculture warrants public aid in order to offset the disadvantageous terms of trade which result.

Background: The Parity Concept

The *Agricultural Adjustment Act of 1993* established the **parity concept** as a cornerstone of agricultural policy. The rationale of the parity concept can be stated in both real and nominal terms. In real terms, parity says that year after year for a fixed output of farm products, a farmer should be able to acquire a specific total amount of other goods and services. A

particular real output should always result in the same real income: "If a farmer could take a bushel of corn to town in 1912 and sell it for enough money to buy a shirt, he should be able to sell a bushel of corn today and buy a shirt." In nominal terms, *the parity concept suggests that the relationship between the prices received by farmers for their output and the prices they must pay for goods and services should remain constant*. The parity concept implies that if the price of shirts tripled over some time period, then the price of corn should have tripled too. Such a situation is said to represent 100 percent of parity.

Figure 33-5 indicates why farmers would benefit from having the prices of their products based on 100 percent of parity. It shows the prices paid and received by farmers from 1910 to 1996 relative to prices in the 1910–1914 base period. By 1996 prices paid had increased almost 14-fold, while prices received had increased only 7 times compared with the base period.

The **parity ratio** graphed in Figure 33-5 is the ratio of prices received to prices paid, expressed in percent. That is:

$$\text{Parity ratio} = \frac{\text{prices received by farmers}}{\text{prices paid by farmers}}$$

In 1996 the parity ratio was 47 percent, indicating that prices received in 1996 could buy only about half as much as prices received in the 1910–1914 period. A farm policy calling for 100 percent of parity would require substantially higher prices for farm products.

Economics of Price Supports

The concept of parity provides the rationale for government price floors on farm products. In agriculture these minimum prices are called **price supports.** You saw that, in the long run, the market prices received by farmers have not kept up with the prices paid by them. One way to achieve parity, or some percentage thereof, is to have government establish above-equilibrium price supports for farm products.

Many different price-support programs have been tried, but they all tend to have similar effects, some of which are subtle and negative. Suppose in Figure 33-6 that the equilibrium price is P_e and the price support is P_s. Then the major effects are as follows.

Surplus Output The most obvious result is a product surplus. Consumers are willing to purchase only

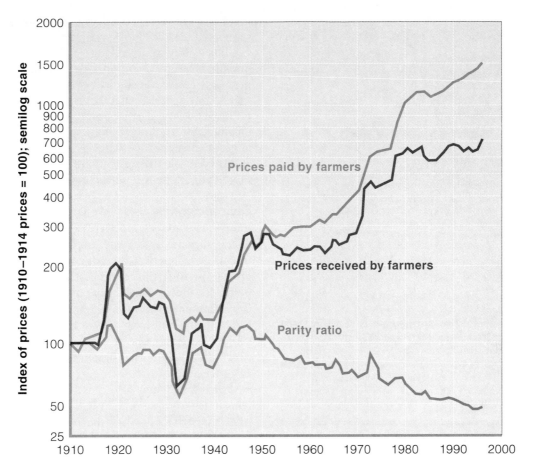

FIGURE 33-5 **Prices paid and received by farmers, 1910–1996** In the past six decades the prices paid by farmers have increased ahead of prices received. As a result, the parity ratio—the ratio of prices received to prices paid—has been less than 100 percent.

Q_c units at the supported price, while farmers supply Q_s units. What about the unpurchased surplus $(Q_s - Q_c)$ which results? The government must buy it to make the above-equilibrium price support effective. As you will see, this surplus output means there is an overallocation of resources to agriculture.

Gain to Farmers Farmers benefit from price supports. In Figure 33-6, gross farm revenue rises from the free-market level represented by area $0P_ebQ_e$ to the larger, supported level of area $0P_saQ_s$.

Loss to Consumers Consumers lose; they pay a higher price (P_s rather than P_e) and consume less (Q_c rather than Q_e) of the product. In some instances differences between the market price and the supported price can be substantial. For example, the U.S.-

supported price of a pound of sugar is double the world market price; a quart of fluid milk is estimated to cost consumers twice as much as it would without government programs. Also, the burden of higher food prices falls disproportionately on the poor because they spend a larger part of their incomes on food.

Resource Overallocation Society loses because price supports create economic inefficiency by encouraging an overallocation of resources to agriculture. A price floor (P_s) attracts more resources to the agricultural sector than would the free-market price (P_e). In terms of Chapter 23's pure-competition model, the market supply curve in Figure 33-6 represents the marginal costs of all farmers producing this product at the various output levels. An efficient allocation of

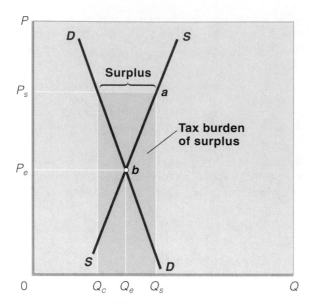

FIGURE 33-6 Effective price supports result in farm surpluses The market demand D and supply S of a farm product yield equilibrium price P_e and quantity Q_e. An above-equilibrium price support P_s results in consumption of quantity Q_c, production of quantity Q_s, and a surplus of quantity $Q_s - Q_c$. The green rectangle represents a transfer of money from taxpayers to farmers.

- -

resources occurs where the market price P_e is equal to marginal cost, and that is at point b. The output Q_e reflects that efficient allocation of resources. In contrast, the output Q_s associated with the price support P_s represents an overallocation of resources; for all units of output between Q_e and Q_s, marginal costs (on curve S) exceed the prices people are willing to pay for these units (on curve D). Simply stated, the marginal cost of the extra production exceeds its marginal benefit to society. Society incurs an "efficiency loss."

Other Social Losses Society at large loses in three other ways.

First, taxpayers pay higher taxes to finance the government's purchase of the surplus. This added tax burden is equal to the surplus output $Q_s - Q_c$ multiplied by its price P_s—as shown by the shaded area in Figure 33-6. Recall, too, that the mere collection of taxes imposes an efficiency loss (Figure 31-5). Also, the cost of storing surplus farm output adds to this tax burden.

Second, government's intervention in agriculture entails administrative costs. Thousands of govern-

ment workers are needed to administer U.S. price supports and other farm programs.

Third, the "rent-seeking" activity involved—the pursuit of political support to maintain price supports—is costly and socially wasteful. Farm groups spend considerable sums to sustain political support for price floors and other programs that enhance farm incomes. Illustration: In the United States the third-largest contributor to campaign funds—after doctors and lawyers—is the sugar industry, which contributes more than all labor unions combined.

Environmental Costs We know from Figure 33-6 that price supports motivate additional production. Although some of this extra output may require additional land, much of the added output comes from greater use of fertilizer and pesticides. Unfortunately, pesticides and fertilizers may pollute the environment (for example, groundwater) and create residues in food which pose health risks to farmworkers and consumers. Research shows a positive relationship between the level of price-support subsidies and the use of agrichemicals.

Farm policy may also cause environmental problems in less obvious ways. First, farmers benefit from price supports only when they use their land consistently for a specific crop such as corn or wheat. This creates a disincentive to practice crop rotation, which is a nonchemical technique for controlling pests. Farm policy thus encourages the substitution of chemical for nonchemical pest control.

Second, we know from the concept of derived demand that an increase in the price of a product will increase the demand for relevant inputs. In particular, price supports for farm products increase the demand for land. And the land which farmers bring into farm production is often environmentally sensitive "marginal" land such as steeply sloped, highly erodable land or wetlands which provide wildlife habitat. Similarly, price supports result in the use of more water for irrigation, and the resulting runoff may contribute to soil erosion.

International Costs The costs of farm price supports go beyond those indicated by Figure 33-6. Price supports generate economic distortions which cross national boundaries. For example, price supports make the U.S. agricultural market attractive to foreign producers. But inflows of foreign agricultural products would increase supplies in the United States, aggravating the problem of U.S. surpluses. To prevent this from happening, the United States is likely to impose import barriers in the form of tariffs or quotas. These barriers often restrict the output of more efficient foreign producers, while simultaneously encouraging more output from less efficient U.S. producers. The result is a less efficient use of world agricultural resources. This chapter's Last Word suggests that this is indeed the case for sugar.

Similarly, as the United States and other industrially advanced countries with similar agricultural programs dump surplus farm products on world markets, the prices of such products are depressed. Developing countries—heavily dependent on world commodity markets for their incomes—are hurt because their export earnings are reduced. Thus, U.S. subsidies for rice production have imposed significant costs on Thailand, a major rice exporter. Similarly, U.S. cotton programs have adversely affected Egypt, Mexico, and other cotton-exporting nations. **(Key Question 8)**

Reduction of Surpluses

Figure 33-6 suggests that programs designed to reduce market supply (shift S leftward) or increase market demand (shift D rightward) would help boost the market price toward the supported price P_s. Further, such programs would reduce or eliminate farm surpluses. The U.S. government has tried both supply *and* demand approaches to reduce surpluses.

Restricting Supply   Until recently, public policy focused mainly on restricting farm output. In particular, **acreage allotment programs** accompanied price supports. In return for guaranteed prices for their crops, farmers had to agree to limit the number of acres they planted with that crop. The USDA first set the price support and then estimated the amount of the product consumers would buy at the supported price. That amount was then translated into the total number of planted acres necessary to provide it. The total acreage was apportioned among states, counties, and ultimately individual farmers.

These supply-restricting programs were only partially successful. They did not eliminate surpluses, mainly because acreage reduction did not result in a proportionate decline in production. Farmers retired their worst land and kept their best land in production. They also cultivated their tilled acres more intensively. Superior seed, more and better fertilizer and insecticides, and more labor were used to enhance output per acre. And nonparticipating farmers

expanded their planted acreage in anticipation of overall higher prices. No doubt, however, farm surpluses and their associated costs to taxpayers would have been greater without acreage allotment.

Bolstering Demand   Government has tried several ways to increase demand for U.S. agricultural products.

New Uses   Both government and private industry have spent large sums on research to create new uses for agricultural goods. The production of "gasohol"—a blend of gasoline and alcohol made from grain—is one such attempt to create demand for farm output. Another example is the use of soybeans to replace wax in producing crayons. Most experts conclude that such endeavors have been only modestly successful.

Domestic and Foreign Demand   Government has initiated a variety of programs to increase domestic consumption of farm products. For example, the *food stamp program* is designed to bolster low-income families' demand for food. Similarly, the *Food for Peace program* has permitted developing countries to buy U.S. surplus farm products with their own currencies, rather than with dollars. The Federal government spends millions of dollars each year to advertise and promote global sales of U.S. farm products. Furthermore, in international trade negotiations, U.S. negotiators have pressed hard to persuade foreign nations to reduce protective tariffs and other barriers to the importing of farm products. The government's supply-restricting and demand-increasing efforts helped reduce the amount of surplus production, but they were not successful in eliminating surpluses.

QUICK REVIEW 33-2

■ The parity concept suggests that farmers should obtain a constant ratio of the prices they receive for their farm products and the prices they pay for goods and services in general.

■ Price supports are government-imposed price floors (minimum prices) on selected farm products.

■ Price supports cause surplus production, which government must buy and store; raise farm income; increase food prices to consumers; and cause an overallocation of resources to agriculture.

■ Domestic price supports encourage nations to erect trade barriers against imported farm products and to dump surplus farm products on world markets.

CRITICISM, POLITICS, AND REFORM

Sixty years of experience with government price-support programs suggested that these programs were not working well. There was a growing feeling among economists and political leaders that the goals and techniques of farm policy needed to be reexamined and revised. In 1996, Congress ended the price-support programs for several farm commodities.

Criticisms

Here are some of the key criticisms of agricultural subsidies which led to the recent reform:

Symptoms, Not Causes The subsidy strategy in agriculture is designed to treat symptoms of the farm problem, not its causes. The root cause of the problem is a misallocation of resources between agriculture and the rest of the economy. Historically, the problem has been one of too many farmers. The effect or symptom of this misallocation is relatively low incomes in agriculture. For the most part, public policy was oriented toward supporting farm prices and incomes rather than toward fixing the resource allocation problem, which is the fundamental cause of relatively low farm income.

Further, price and income supports have kept people in agriculture who otherwise would have moved to nonfarm occupations. That is, the price and income orientation of the farm program has slowed the reallocation of resources necessary to resolve the long-run farm problem.

Misguided Subsidies Price supports and subsidy programs most benefit farmers who need them least. If the goal of farm policy is to raise low farm incomes, it follows that any program of Federal aid should be aimed at farmers with the lowest incomes. But the poor, small-output farmer does not produce and sell enough in the market to get much aid from price supports. It is the large corporate farm which reaps the benefits by virtue of its sizable output.

In 1996, for example, the 6 percent of all farms with sales of $250,000 or more received 46 percent of all direct government subsidies. The poorest 61 percent of all farmers—those who earned less than $20,000 from farming in 1996—received about 4 percent of all direct-subsidy payments. If public policy must be designed to supplement farm incomes, a strong case can be made for having its benefits vary

inversely, rather than directly, with individual farm income. Furthermore, an income-support program might better be geared to *people* than *products*. Most economists say that, on equity grounds, direct income subsidies to poor farmers are highly preferable to indirect price-support subsidies which go primarily to large and prosperous farmers.

A related point concerns land values. The price and income benefits which farm programs provide tend to increase the value of farmland. By making crops more valuable, price supports make the land itself more valuable. Sometimes this is helpful to farmers, but often it is not. Farmers rent about 50 percent of their farmland, mostly from well-to-do nonfarm landlords. Thus, price supports become a subsidy to people *not* actively engaged in farming.

Policy Contradictions Because farm policy has many objectives, it often leads to contradictions. Subsidized research is aimed at increasing farm productivity and increasing the supply of farm products, while acreage allotment programs require that farmers take land out of production to reduce supply. Price supports for crops mean increased feed costs for ranchers and high consumer prices for animal products. Tobacco farmers are subsidized at a time when serious health problems are associated with tobacco consumption. The U.S. sugar program raises sugar prices for domestic growers by imposing import quotas which conflict with free-trade policies. Conservation programs call for setting aside land for wildlife habitat, while price supports provide incentives to bring such acreage into production.

The Politics of Farm Policy

In view of these criticisms and inconsistencies, we might ask why the United States has continued its price-support program for so many decades. Why has it taken so long for government to restore free markets for some farm products? Why do price-support programs for such commodities as sugar, peanuts, and tobacco continue?

Public Choice Theory Revisited We can respond to these questions largely in terms of Chapter 31's public choice theory. Recall that *rent-seeking behavior* occurs when a group (a labor union, firms in a specific industry, or farmers producing a particular crop) uses political means to transfer income or wealth to itself at the expense of another group or of society as a whole. The *special-interest effect* involves a program or policy from which a small group receives large benefits at the expense of a much larger group whose members individually suffer small losses. Both rent-seeking behavior and the special-interest effect help explain the politics of farm subsidies.

Suppose a specific group of farmers, say, peanut or sugar growers, organize and establish a well-financed political action committee (PAC). The PAC's job is to promote government programs which will transfer income to the group (this is rent-seeking behavior). The PAC vigorously lobbies U.S. senators and representatives to enact or continue price supports and import quotas for peanuts or sugar. The PAC does this in part by making political contributions to sympathetic legislators. Although peanut production is heavily concentrated in a few states such as Georgia, Alabama, and Texas, the peanut PAC will also make contributions to legislators from other states in order to gain support.

But how can a small interest group, again peanut or sugar growers, successfully lobby to increase its own income at the expense of society as a whole? Because, even though the total cost of the group's programs might be considerable, the cost imposed on *each individual* taxpayer is small (this is the special-interest effect). Citizen-taxpayers are likely uninformed about and indifferent to these programs since they have little at stake. Unless you grow sugar beets or peanuts, you probably have no idea how much these programs cost you as an individual taxpayer and consumer and therefore do not object when your legislator votes for, say, a sugar program. Thus, there is little or no counterlobbying to negate the PAC's efforts.

Political *logrolling*, the trading of votes on policies and programs, also works to perpetuate certain programs: Senator Foghorn agrees to vote for a program which benefits Senator Moribund's constituents, and Moribund returns the favor. Example: Many members of Congress who represent low-income urban areas vote in favor of farm subsidies. In return, representatives of agricultural areas support such programs as food stamps, which provide subsidized food for the poor. The result is a rural-urban coalition through which representatives from both areas provide benefits for their constituents and enhance their reelection chances. Such coalitions help explain why farm subsidies persist and why the food stamp program has, until recently, been expanded over the years.

Large agribusinesses which supply inputs to agriculture also lend political support to farm subsidies because subsidies increase the amounts of agrichemi-

cals and farm machinery which farmers are able to buy. And, needless to say, most of the 100,000 or so government employees whose jobs depend on farm programs are highly supportive.

Public choice theory also tells us that politicians are more likely to favor programs having hidden costs. As you have seen, this is often true of farm programs. The discussion of Figure 33-6 showed that price supports involve not simply a transfer of money from taxpayer to farmer but costs which are hidden as higher food prices, storage costs for surplus output, costs of administering farm programs, and costs associated with both domestic and international misallocations of resources. While the direct cost of the peanut program to taxpayers is only about $4 million a year, the price increase provided by the program carries a hidden subsidy (cost) of $190 million per year. Because the cost of the peanut program is largely indirect and hidden, the program is much more acceptable to politicians and the public than it would be if all costs were explicit.

Changing Politics   In spite of rent seeking, special interests, and logrolling, a combination of factors has led to a change in the politics of farm subsidies, for several reasons.

Declining Political Support   As the farm population has declined, agriculture's political power has also diminished. The farm population was about 25 percent of the general population in the 1930s, when many U.S. farm programs were established; now it is less than 2 percent. Urban congressional representatives are now a 9 to 1 majority over their rural colleagues. More and more legislators are critically examining farm programs for their effect on consumers' grocery bills as well as on farm incomes. Also, more farmers themselves resent the intrusion of the Federal government into their farming decisions. Many rural-state congressional members now support free-market agriculture.

Budget Deficits   Continued pressure to balance the Federal budget has brought farm subsidies under increased political scrutiny.

Program Excesses   The excesses of farm programs have been increasingly publicized, thereby weakening the special-interest effect. In one year in the late 1980s, for instance, a large California cotton grower received $12 million in subsidy payments; the

The Sugar Program: A Sweet Deal

The sugar program is a sweet deal for domestic sugar producers, but it imposes heavy costs on domestic consumers and foreign producers.

The continuing U.S. program of price supports for sugar has significant effects, both domestic and international.

1. Domestic Costs Price supports for some 15,000 U.S. sugar producers have maintained domestic sugar prices at about double the world price. The estimated aggregate cost to domestic consumers is about $1.5 billion per year. Furthermore, the effect of artificially high sugar prices is regressive because poor households spend a larger percentage of their income on food than do high-income households. On the other hand, each sugar grower receives from subsidies alone an amount estimated to be twice the nation's average family income. In one recent year, a single farm received an estimated $30 million in benefits! Many sugar producers obtain more than $1 million each in benefits.

2. Import Quotas As a consequence of high U.S. domestic price supports, foreign sugar producers have a strong incentive to sell their output in the United States. But an influx of lower-priced foreign sugar into the U.S. domestic market would undermine U.S. price supports. Hence, the government has imposed import quotas on foreign sugar. As the difference between U.S.-supported prices and world prices has increased, the import quotas have become more restrictive, with the result that imported sugar accounts for a declining proportion of our consumption of sweeteners. About 30 percent of the sugar consumed in the United States was imported in 1975; currently only 3 or 4 percent is imported. Domestic policy regarding the U.S. sugar industry largely dictates the nation's international trade policy with respect to sugar.

3. Developing Countries The loss of the U.S. market has had a number of harmful effects on developing sugar-exporting countries such as the Philippines, Brazil, and several Central American countries.

First, exclusion from the U.S. market has significantly reduced their export revenues—by an amount estimated to be as much as $7 billion per year. The decline in export revenues is important because many of the sugar-producing countries depend on such revenues to pay interest and principal on large debts owed to the United States and other industrially advanced nations.

Second, barred by quotas from sale in the U.S. market, the sugar produced by the developing countries has

crown prince of Liechtenstein received a subsidy in excess of $2 million as a partner in a Texas rice farm; and 112 dairy farmers received $1 million each under a program designed to reduce the size of dairy herds. The Gallo Winery received $5 million to promote its products in world markets, and Sunkist Growers got almost $10 million to promote citrus.

World Trade Considerations The new, more critical attitude toward farm subsidies has also resulted from the U.S. lead in attempting to reduce barriers to world trade in agricultural products. The 15 nations of the European Union (EU) and many other nations support agricultural prices. To maintain high domestic prices, these nations restrict imports of foreign farm products. They do this by imposing tariffs (excise taxes) and quotas (specific limits on imports of foreign goods). They then try to rid themselves of domestic surpluses by subsidizing their exports into world markets.

The effects on the United States are that (1) trade barriers hinder U.S. farmers from selling to EU nations, and (2) subsidized exports from these other nations depress world prices for agricultural products, making world markets less attractive to U.S. farmers.

Perhaps most importantly, farm programs such as those in the EU and the United States distort both world agricultural trade and the international allocation of agricultural resources. Encouraged by artificially high prices, farmers in industrially advanced nations produce more farm output than they would otherwise. The resulting surpluses flow into world markets where they depress prices. This means farmers in countries with no farm programs—often developing countries—face artificially low prices for their exports, and this signals them to produce less. Overall, the result is a shift in production away from what would occur on the basis of comparative advantage. As an example, price supports cause U.S. agricultural resources to be used for sugar production, although been added to world markets, where the increased supply has depressed the world price of sugar.

Third, domestic price supports have caused U.S. sugar production to expand to the extent that the United States may soon change from a sugar-importing to a sugar-exporting nation. That is, the U.S. sugar program may soon be a source of new competition for the sugar producers of the developing countries. Sugar price supports in the European Union have already turned that group of nations into sugar exporters.

4. Global Resource Misallocation Both domestically and globally, the sugar price-support programs of the United States and other industrially advanced economies have distorted the worldwide allocation of agricultural resources. Price supports have caused a shift of resources to sugar production by less efficient U.S. producers, and U.S. import quotas and consequent low world sugar prices have caused more efficient foreign producers

to restrict their production. Thus high-cost producers are producing more sugar and low-cost producers are producing less, resulting in the inefficient use of the world's agricultural resources.

5. Substitutes and Jobs The artificially high price of sugar, coupled with nutritional concerns, has shifted demand toward corn-based and artificial sweeteners. Sugar's share of the U.S. market for sweeteners has declined by one-half since 1970. One estimate suggests that the artificial sweetener industry makes almost as much from the sugar program ($1 billion per year) as do sugar growers themselves.

Also, in the past decade an estimated 7000 jobs have been lost because of refinery closings resulting from the decline of sugar imports. Domestic candy manufacturers ponder the relocation of plants and jobs abroad, where sugar prices are lower.

sugar can be produced at perhaps half the cost in the Caribbean countries and Australia.

Recognizing these distortions, in 1994 the world's trading nations agreed to reduce farm price-support programs by 20 percent by the year 2000 and reduce tariffs and quotas on imported farm products by 15 percent. The United States made such a strong case against price supports in these discussions that its stance undoubtedly altered the domestic debate on whether supports should be continued within the country.

Recent Reform: Freedom to Farm

In 1996 Congress radically revamped 60 years of U.S. farm policy by passing what has been dubbed the **Freedom to Farm Act.** This law immediately ended price supports and acreage allotments for wheat, corn, barley, oats, sorghum, rye, cotton, and rice. Farmers can now respond to changing crop prices by planting

as much or as little of these crops as they choose. Moreover, they can freely switch to alternative crops. If the world demand for, say, cotton rises, U.S. farmers can now switch production from peanuts to cotton to take advantage of cotton's higher price. If the market price of corn falls, farmers can plant less corn and more sorghum. Markets, not government programs, are beginning to determine what products farmers grow, where they are grown, and the total outputs.

To ease the transition away from farm subsidies, farmers will receive guaranteed, but declining, annual "transition payments" through 2002. These payments, which will total nearly $37 billion, are *not* based on crop prices or farmers' incomes. Instead, they are based on the past subsidies farmers received as part of the price-support program. For example, a wheat farmer will receive annual, but declining, cash payments for 7 years regardless of the price of wheat or the amount of wheat he or she grows. The purpose is to assist farmers during the transition, while freeing them to grow crops based on market profitability, rather than on what qualifies for a Federal farm subsidy.

While it is far too soon to assess the results of this reform, economists expect it to increase the overall agricultural output in the United States. They also predict the reform will increase the variability of agricultural prices and farm income from year to year. For example, when the price of corn is high, farmers who have planted corn will earn high incomes. But others will then plant corn, and the increased output of corn at the end of the next growing season will increase its supply, lower its price, and reduce the income of corn farmers. To protect themselves against the greater volatility of prices and income, farmers can be expected to use more tools to manage risk. For instance, they may diversify their plantings, sell crops for a set price per bushel in advance of their harvest, and consolidate into larger corporate farms. A sizable part of the Federal agricultural bureaucracy will no longer be needed since paperwork will decline and government will not have to monitor acreage allotments.

One result *has* already become clear: the law has greatly increased flexibility for farmers. Example: In 1997 many Kansas farmers were hit by a severe hailstorm which destroyed half their wheat crop. They responded by plowing up the failed crop and replanting with sorghum. That would not have happened under the price-support system since such replanting would have eliminated their wheat subsidies. More generally, farmers across the country have begun experimenting with different crops than they had grown in the past. The recent policy reform in agriculture has made this an exciting, somewhat risky time for U.S. farmers.

QUICK REVIEW 33-3

■ Farm policy in the United States has been heavily criticized for delaying the shift of resources away from farming, directing most subsidies to wealthier farmers, and being fraught with policy contradictions.

■ The persistence of price supports can largely be explained in terms of rent-seeking behavior, the special-interest effect, political logrolling, and other aspects of public choice theory.

■ Recently, the politics of farm subsidies has changed due to the declining political clout of farmers, the need to address Federal budget deficits, the widespread publication of program excesses, and world trade considerations.

■ The Freedom to Farm Act of 1996 eliminated price supports and acreage allotments for many of the nation's crops, while continuing direct subsidies to farmers for 7 years.

CHAPTER SUMMARY

1. In the short run, the highly inelastic nature of agricultural demand translates small changes in output and small shifts in domestic or foreign demand into large changes in prices and income.

2. Over the long run, rapid technological advance, together with a highly inelastic and relatively slow-growing demand for agricultural output, has caused agriculture to be a declining industry.

3. Historically, farm policy has been centered on price and based on the parity concept, which suggests that the relationship between prices received and paid by farmers should be constant over time.

4. The use of price floors or price supports has a number of economic effects: **(a)** Surplus production occurs; **(b)** the incomes of farmers are increased; **(c)** consumers pay higher prices for farm products; **(d)** an overallocation of resources to agriculture occurs; **(e)** society pays higher taxes to finance the purchase and storage of surplus output; **(f)** pollution increases because of the greater use of agrichemicals and vulnerable land; and **(g)** other nations bear the costs associated with import barriers and depressed world agricultural prices.

5. Government has pursued with limited success programs to reduce agricultural supply and increase agricultural demand as a method of reducing the surpluses associated with price supports.

6. Economists have criticized farm policy for **(a)** confusing symptoms (low farm incomes) with causes (excess capacity), **(b)** providing the largest subsidies to high-income farmers, and **(c)** creating contradictions among specific farm programs.

7. The persistence of agricultural subsidies can be explained in terms of public choice theory and, in particular, in terms of rent-seeking behavior, the special-interest effect, and political logrolling.

8. Political backing for price supports and acreage allotments has eroded for several reasons: **(a)** The number of farmers, and thus their political clout, has declined dramatically relative to the number of urban consumers of farm products; **(b)** farm subsidies have received close scrutiny due to efforts to eliminate the Federal budget deficit; **(c)** the media have highlighted how wealthy farmers and profitable agribusinesses benefit disproportionately from farm subsidies and efforts to promote farm exports; and **(d)** successful efforts by the United States to get other nations to reduce their farm subsidies have altered the domestic debate on the desirability of its own subsidies.

9. The Freedom to Farm Act of 1996 ended price supports and acreage allotments for wheat, corn, barley, oats, sorghum, rye, cotton, and rice. Government will pay farmers declining transition payments through the year 2002, but these payments will no longer depend on crop prices or the crop that is produced. The idea is to create a market-driven agricultural economy, rather than one managed by the Federal government.

TERMS AND CONCEPTS

short-run farm problem
long-run farm problem
parity concept

parity ratio
price supports

acreage allotment
  programs

Freedom to Farm Act

STUDY QUESTIONS

1. KEY QUESTION Carefully evaluate: "The supply and demand for agricultural products are such that small changes in agricultural supply result in drastic changes in prices. However, large changes in farm prices have modest effects on agricultural output." (Hint: A brief review of the distinction between supply and quantity supplied may be helpful.) Do exports increase or reduce the instability of demand for farm products? Explain.

2. What relationship, if any, can you detect between the fact that the farmer's fixed costs of production are large and the fact that the supply of most agricultural products is generally inelastic? Be specific in your answer.

3. KEY QUESTION Explain how each of the following contributes to the farm problem: **(a)** the inelasticity of demand for farm products, **(b)** the rapid technological progress in farming, **(c)** the modest long-run growth in demand for farm commodities, and **(d)** the competitiveness of agriculture.

4. The key to efficient resource allocation is shifting resources from low-productivity to high-productivity uses. In view of the high and expanding physical productivity of agricultural resources, explain why many economists want to divert additional resources from farming to achieve allocative efficiency.

5. Explain and evaluate: "Industry complains of the higher taxes it must pay to finance subsidies to agriculture. Yet the trend of agricultural prices has been downward while industrial prices have been moving upward, suggesting that on balance agriculture is actually subsidizing industry."

6. "Because consumers as a whole must ultimately pay the total incomes received by farmers, it makes no real difference whether the income is paid through free farm markets or through price supports supplemented by subsidies financed out of tax revenue." Do you agree?

7. If in a specific year the indexes of prices received and paid by farmers were 120 and 165 respectively, what would the parity ratio be? Explain the meaning of this ratio.

8. KEY QUESTION Explain the economic effects of price supports. Explicitly include environmental and global impacts in your answer. On what grounds do economists contend that price supports cause a misallocation of resources?

9. Use supply and demand curves to depict equilibrium price and output in a competitive market for some farm product. Then show how an above-equilibrium price floor (price support) would cause a surplus in this market. Demonstrate in your graph how government could reduce the surplus through a policy which **(a)** changes supply or **(b)** changes demand. Identify each of the following actual government policies as primarily affecting the supply of or the demand for a particular farm product: acreage allotments, food stamp program, Food for Peace program, a government buyout of dairy herds, export promotion.

10. Do you agree with each of the following statements? Explain why or why not.
   a. The problem with U.S. agriculture is that there are too many farmers. This is not the fault of farmers but the fault of government programs.
   b. The Federal government ought to buy up U.S. farm surpluses and give them away to developing nations.
   c. All industries would like government price supports if they could get them; agriculture got price supports *only* because of its strong political clout.

11. What are the effects of farm subsidies such as those of the United States and the European Union on **(a)** domestic agricultural prices, **(b)** world agricultural prices, and **(c)** the international allocation of agricultural resources?

12. Use public choice theory to explain the persistence of farm subsidies in the face of major criticisms of these subsidies. If the special-interest effect is so strong, then what factors made it possible in 1996 for government to end price supports and acreage allotments for several crops?

13. What is the major intent of the Freedom to Farm Act of 1996? Do you agree with this purpose? Why or why not?

14. (Last Word) Who benefits and who loses from the U.S. sugar subsidy program?

15. WEB-BASED QUESTION Agriculture Parity Ratios—Crop Farmers and Livestock Farmers The United States Department of Agriculture http://www.usda.gov/nass/aggraphs/agprices.htm provides detailed color charts of current data for agricultural prices paid by farmers and received by farmers. Based on the most recent graphs, which type of farmers have been doing better: crop farmers or livestock farmers?

16. WEB-BASED QUESTION The NAFTA Sugar Provisions In general, the North American Free Trade Agreement liberalized trade in agricultural commodities between Mexico and the United States. In the case of trade in sugar, however, the transition period to free trade will occur over 15 years. Based on the concerns of the domestic U.S. sugar industry, several unique provisions were negotiated with respect to trade in sugar. What are these provisions, and how do they differ from those between the United States and other sugar-producing countries? See http://www.fas.usda.gov/itp/sugar-import.html and http://www.fas.usda.gov/itp/imp-exp-require.html.

CHAPTER THIRTY-FOUR

Income Inequality and Poverty

34

It is easy to find evidence which suggests wide income disparity in the United States. In 1997 movie producer Steven Spielberg earned $283 million, comedian Jerry Seinfeld received $66 million, and magician David Copperfield made $45 million. Several major league baseball players earned more than $5 million each. In contrast, the president of the United States was paid $200,000 that year, and the typical schoolteacher received $40,000. A full-time minimum-wage worker at a fast-food restaurant earned $10,300. An unemployed welfare recipient with two children received cash welfare payments of about $5000.

The Census Bureau reports that about 36 million people in the United States—more than 13 percent of the population—live in poverty. Estimates indicate that about 500,000 are homeless. At present the richest fifth of the population receives 47 percent of total income, while the poorest fifth receives only about 4 percent.

The question of how income should be distributed is controversial. Should the national income and wealth in the United States be more equally distributed than it is now? Or, in the language of Chapter 4, is society making the proper responses to the "for whom" question? In discussing this issue, we begin by surveying basic facts about the distribution of income in the United States. After considering the major causes of income inequality, we examine the debate over income inequality and the tradeoff between equality and efficiency. Next, we look at poverty in the United States, and finally, we consider public policy regarding income redistribution and welfare.

FACTS ABOUT INCOME INEQUALITY

How equally—or unequally—is income distributed in the United States? How wide is the gulf between rich and poor? Has income inequality increased or lessened over time? We can answer these questions by examining some data.

Personal Income Distribution

The average income in the United States is among the highest in the world; for all families it was $56,674 in 1996. But this average tells us nothing about income equality or inequality. We must also examine how income is distributed around the average. In Table 34-1 we see that 10 percent of all families have an-

TABLE 34-1 The distribution of personal income by families, 1996

(1) Personal income class	(2) Percentage of all families in this class
Under $10,000	7.6
$10,000–$14,999	6.1
$15,000–$24,999	13.5
$25,000–$34,999	13.5
$35,000–$49,999	17.7
$50,000–$74,999	21.3
$75,000–$99,999	10.0
$100,000 and over	10.3
	100.0

Source: Bureau of the Census.

nual incomes of $100,000 or more, while 1 family in 7 has an annual income of less than $15,000. The data in the table suggest *considerable* **income inequality** in the United States.

Trends in Income Inequality

Over a period of years economic growth has raised incomes in the United States: In *absolute* dollar amounts, the entire distribution of income has been moving upward. But has this changed the *relative* distribution of income? Incomes can move up in absolute terms, and the degree of inequality may or may not be affected. Table 34-2 shows the relative distribution of income over time. It divides the total number of in-

come receivers into five numerically equal groups or *quintiles* and shows the percentage of total personal (before-tax) income obtained by each in selected years. Let's use the data in Table 34-2 to see how the income distribution has changed over three periods: 1929 to 1947, 1947 to 1969, and 1969 to 1996.

1929–1947 Period Comparison of the income distribution data for 1929 and 1947 suggests a significant reduction in income inequality between these years. The percentage of personal income going to the top quintile declined, and the percentages received by the other four quintiles increased. Many of the forces at work during World War II contributed to this decline in inequality. Wartime prosperity eliminated the many low incomes caused by the severe unemployment of the 1930s, reduced wage and salary differentials, boosted depressed farm incomes through sharp increases in farm prices, temporarily diminished discrimination in employment, and was accompanied by a decline in property incomes as a share of the national income.

1947–1969 Period Many of the forces contributing to greater equality during World War II became less effective after the war. Between 1947 and 1969, the income distribution continued its trend toward less inequality, but at a far slower pace. The income share of the lowest income group rose by .6 of a percentage point between 1947 and 1969, while that of the wealthiest quintile fell by 2.4 percentage points.

1969–1996 Period The distribution of income by quintiles has become more unequal since 1969. In 1996 the lowest 20 percent of families received only

TABLE 34-2 Percentage of total before-tax income received by each one-fifth, and by the top 5 percent, of families, select years

Quintile	1929	1935–1936	1947	1955	1969	1985	1996
Lowest 20 percent	} 12.5	4.1	5.0	4.8	5.6	4.8	4.2
Second 20 percent		9.2	11.8	12.2	12.4	10.9	10.0
Third 20 percent	13.8	14.1	17.0	17.7	17.7	16.9	15.8
Fourth 20 percent	19.3	20.9	23.1	23.7	23.7	24.3	23.1
Highest 20 percent	54.4	51.7	43.0	41.6	40.6	43.1	46.8
Total	100.0	100.0	100.0	100.0	100.0	100.0	100.0
Top 5 percent	30.0	25.6	17.2	16.8	15.6	16.1	20.3

Source: Bureau of the Census.

4.2 percent of total before-tax income, compared with 5.6 percent in 1969. Meanwhile, the income share received by the highest 20 percent rose from 40.6 to 46.8 percent.

Global Perspective 34-1 compares income inequality in the United States (here by individuals, not families) with that in several other nations. Income inequality tends to be highest in developing nations.

Causes of Growing Inequality

Growing U.S. income inequality in the past three decades has attracted the attention of many scholars, who have suggested three major interrelated explanations:

1. *Greater demand for highly skilled workers* Perhaps the most significant contributor to growing income inequality has been an increasing demand for workers who are highly skilled and well educated. Many firms have restructured their production methods in ways which require more highly skilled, better-educated workers. Also, several industries requiring highly skilled workers have recently emerged or expanded greatly, such as computer software development, business consulting, biotechnology, health care, and advanced communications systems. Because highly skilled workers remain relatively scarce, their wages have been bid up, so the wage differences between them and less skilled workers have increased. Since 1980 the wage difference between college graduates and high school graduates has risen from 37 to 66 percent for women and from 34 to 60 percent for men. One study found that workers who use computers earn 10 to 15 percent more than similar workers who do not.

2. *Demographic changes* The entrance of large numbers of less experienced and less skilled "baby boomers" into the labor force in the 1970s and 1980s may have contributed to greater income inequality. Because younger workers tend to earn less income than older workers, their growing numbers contribute to income inequality. There has also been a growing tendency for men and women with high earnings potential to marry each other, thus increasing family income among the highest-income quintiles. Finally, the number of families headed by single or divorced women has increased greatly. This has increased income inequality because many such families lack a second wage earner, and women tend to receive low wage earnings or, in some cases, no wage earnings at all.

3. *International trade, immigration, decline in unionism* Other factors are also at work. More *international competition* from imports in the 1970s and 1980s reduced the demand for and employment of less skilled (but highly paid) workers in such industries as automobile and steel. The decline in such jobs reduced the average wage for less skilled workers. It also swelled the ranks of workers in already low-paying industries, placing further downward pressure on wages in those industries. Similarly, the transfer of jobs to lower-wage workers in developing countries has exerted downward wage pressure on less skilled workers in the United States. Also, an upsurge in *immigration* of unskilled workers has increased the number of low-income families in the United States. Finally, the decline in *unionism* in the United States undoubtedly has contributed to

GLOBAL PERSPECTIVE 34-1

Percentage of total income received by top one-fifth of income receivers, selected nations

The share of income going to the highest 20 percent of income receivers varies among nations. Frequently, income is less equally shared in poor nations than in rich ones.

Percentage of Total Income Earned by Top Fifth of Income Receivers

Source: *World Development Report, 1997, pp. 222–223.*

wage inequality since unions tend to equalize pay within firms and industries.

Two cautions: First, when we note growing income inequality, we are *not* saying that the "rich are getting richer and the poor are getting poorer" in terms of absolute income. Both the rich and the poor are getting richer. Rather, what has happened is that, while incomes grew in all quintiles, growth was fastest in the top quintile. Second, increased income inequality is *not* solely a U.S. phenomenon. The recent move toward greater inequality has also occurred in several other industrially advanced nations.

The Lorenz Curve

The degree of inequality in income distribution can be shown with a **Lorenz curve.** In Figure 34-1, we plot the cumulative percentage of families on the horizontal axis and the percentage of income they obtain on the vertical axis. The diagonal line 0e represents a *perfectly equal distribution of income* because each of its points indicates that a particular percentage of families receive that same percentage of income. In other words, points representing 20 percent of all families

receiving 20 percent of total income, 40 percent receiving 40 percent, 60 percent receiving 60 percent, and so on, all lie on the diagonal line.

By plotting the 1996 quintile data from Table 34-2, we obtain the Lorenz curve for that year to help us visualize the actual distribution of income. Observe from point *a* that the bottom 20 percent of all families received 4.2 percent of the income; the bottom 40 percent received 14.2 percent (= 4.2 + 10.0), as shown by point *b*; and so forth. The orange area between the diagonal line and the Lorenz curve, determined by the extent to which the Lorenz curve sags away from the diagonal, indicates the degree of income inequality. If the actual income distribution were perfectly equal, the Lorenz curve and the diagonal would coincide and the orange area would disappear.

At the opposite extreme is a situation of complete inequality, where all families but one have zero income. In this case the Lorenz curve would coincide with the horizontal axis from 0 to point *f* (at 0 percent of income), then move immediately up from *f* to point *e* along the vertical axis (indicating that a single family has 100 percent of the income). The entire area below the diagonal line—area 0*ef*—would indicate this extreme degree of inequality.

Economists use the Lorenz curve to contrast the distribution of income at different points in time. If we also plotted Table 34-2's data for 1947 and 1969 as Lorenz curves in Figure 34-1, we would find that the curve shifted toward the diagonal between 1947 and 1969 and then shifted back away from the diagonal between 1969 and 1996.

In addition, Lorenz curves can be plotted to contrast the income distributions of different racial groups, of different countries, and before and after taxes and transfers are taken into account. **(Key Question 2)**

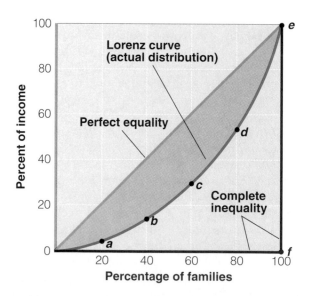

FIGURE 34-1 The Lorenz curve The Lorenz curve is a graph of the percentage of total income obtained by cumulative percentages of families. It is a convenient means of visualizing the degree of income inequality. Specifically, the area between the diagonal (the line of perfect equality) and the Lorenz curve represents the degree of inequality in the U.S. distribution of total income.

INCOME MOBILITY: THE TIME DIMENSION

There is a major limitation of the income data we have used thus far: The income accounting period of 1 year is too short to be very meaningful. Because the Census Bureau data portray the distribution of income in only a single year, they may conceal a more equal distribution over a few years, a decade, or even a lifetime. If Brad earns $1000 in year 1 and $100,000 in year 2, while Jenny earns $100,000 in year 1 and only $1000 in year 2, do we have income inequality? The answer depends on the period of measurement.

Annual data would reveal great income inequality, but there is complete equality over the 2-year period.

This is important because there is evidence to suggest considerable "churning around" in the distribution of income over time. In fact, for most income receivers, income starts at a relatively low level, reaches a peak during middle age, and then declines. A glance back at Figure 28-9 reveals this general pattern. It follows that if all people receive exactly the same stream of income over their lifetimes, considerable income inequality would still exist in any specific year because of age differences. In any single year, the young and old would receive low incomes while the middle-aged received high incomes.

If we change from a "snapshot" view of income distribution in a single year to a "time exposure" portraying incomes over much longer periods, we find considerable movement of income receivers among income classes. This correctly suggests that income is more equally distributed over a 5-, 10-, 20-year period than in a single year. Such movement of individuals or families from one income quintile to another over time is called **income mobility.**

A recent Dallas Federal Reserve Bank study traced the movement of individuals from their quintile locations in 1975 to their quintile locations in 1991 and found that 95 percent of the people in the lowest income quintile in 1975 had moved to a higher quintile by 1991. Almost 30 percent of the lowest quintile jumped to the richest quintile during that period. Undoubtedly this group included many people who were in college in 1975 but who graduated and became, say, high-income doctors, lawyers, and accountants by 1991. Nearly two-thirds of the people in the middle quintile changed to another quintile between 1975 and 1991. For the richest quintile in 1975, about 37 percent had fallen to a lower quintile by 1991.

In short, there is significant individual and family income mobility over time; for many people, "low income" and "high income" are not permanent conditions. Also, the longer the time period considered, the more equal the distribution of income.

EFFECT OF GOVERNMENT REDISTRIBUTION

The income data in Tables 34-1 and 34-2 include wages, salaries, dividends, and interest. They also include all *cash* transfer payments such as social security, unemployment compensation benefits, and welfare

payments to families with dependent children. The data are *before-tax* data and therefore do not take into account the effects of personal income and payroll (social security) taxes which are levied directly on income receivers. Nor do they include in-kind or **noncash transfers,** which provide specific goods or services rather than cash. Noncash transfers include such things as Medicare, Medicaid, housing subsidies, subsidized school lunches, and food stamps. These transfers are "incomelike" since they enable the "purchase" of goods and services.

One function of government is to redistribute income. Figure 34-2 and its table[1] reveal that *government significantly redistributes income from higher- to lower-income households through its taxes and transfers.* This is shown by the fact that the U.S. distribution of household income *before* taxes and transfers are taken into account (green Lorenz curve) is substantially less equal than the distribution *after* taxes and transfers (orange Lorenz curve). Without government redistribution, the lowest 20 percent of households in 1996 would have received only 1.2 percent of total income. With redistribution, they received 4.9 percent, or about 300 percent more.

Which contributes more to redistribution, government taxes or transfers? The answer is transfers. Because the U.S. tax system is only modestly progressive, after-tax data would reveal only about 20 percent less inequality. Roughly 80 percent of the reduction in income inequality is attributable to transfer payments, which account for more than 75 percent of the income of the lowest quintile. Together with growth of job opportunities, transfer payments have been the most important means of alleviating poverty in the United States.

CAUSES OF INCOME INEQUALITY

There are several causes of income inequality in the United States. In general, we note that the market system is an impersonal mechanism. It has no conscience or ethical standards concerning what is an

---

[1]The "before" data in this table differ from the data in Table 34-2 because the latter include cash transfers. Also, the data in Table 34-2 are for families (a group of two persons or more related by birth, marriage, or adoption and residing together), whereas the data in Figure 34-2 are for all households (one or more persons occupying a housing unit). Finally, the data in Figure 34-2 are based on a broader concept of income than the data in Table 34-2.

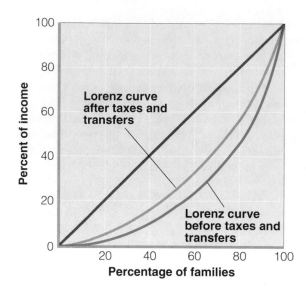

Percentage of total income received, 1996		
Quintile	(1) Before taxes and transfers	(2) After taxes and transfers
Lowest 20 percent	1.2	4.9
Second 20 percent	8.4	10.8
Third 20 percent	15.7	16.2
Fourth 20 percent	24.6	23.2
Highest 20 percent	50.1	45.0

Source: Bureau of the Census. The data include all money income from private sources, including realized capital gains and employer-provided health insurance. The "after taxes and transfers" data include the value of noncash transfers as well as cash transfers.

FIGURE 34-2 The impact of taxes and transfers on U.S. income inequality The distribution of personal income is significantly more equal after taxes and transfers are taken into account than before. Transfers account for most of the lessening of inequality and provide most of the income received by the lowest quintile of families.

"equitable" or "just" distribution of income. The basic environment of the capitalist economy is permissive of a high degree of income inequality since it rewards individuals on the basis of their contributions to society's output.

More specifically, the factors contributing to income inequality include those discussed below.

Ability Differences

People have different mental, physical, and aesthetic talents. Some people have inherited the exceptional mental qualities essential to such high-paying fields as medicine, corporate leadership, and law. Some people are blessed with the physical capacity and coordination to become highly paid professional athletes. A few have the talent to become great artists or musicians or have the beauty to become top fashion models. Others have very weak mental endowments and work in low-paying occupations or are incapable of earning income at all. Most people's intelligence and skills fall somewhere in between.

Education and Training

Native ability, alone, rarely produces high income; people must develop and refine their capabilities through education and training. Individuals differ significantly in the amounts of education and training they obtain and thus in their capacities to earn income. These differences may be a matter of choice: Chin enters the labor force after graduating from high school, while Rodriguez takes a job after earning a college degree. On the other hand, the differences may be involuntary: Chin and her parents may simply be unable to finance a college education.

People also get varying degrees of on-the-job training, which also contributes to income inequality. Some workers learn valuable new skills each year on the job and therefore experience significant income growth over time; others get little or no on-the-job training and earn no more at age 50 than at age 30. Moreover, firms tend to select for advanced on-the-job training those workers who have the most formal education. This added training magnifies the education-based income differences between less educated and more educated individuals.

Discrimination

Simple supply and demand analysis suggests how discrimination—in this case, labor market discrimination—generates income inequality. Suppose that discrimination restricts racial and ethnic minorities (or women) to low-paying occupations. This means that the supplies of labor will be great relative to demand in these occupations; wages and incomes will be low. Conversely, discrimination means that whites (or men) do not face as much competition in the occupations in which they are predominant. Thus, labor supply is artificially limited relative to demand in these occupations, with the result that wages and incomes are high.

Tastes and Risks

Incomes also differ because of differences in tastes for market work relative to nonmarket activities as well as differences in tastes for types of work. People who choose to stay home with children, work part-time, or retire early have less income than people who make the opposite choices. Those willing to take arduous, unpleasant jobs—for example, underground mining or heavy construction—or to work long hours with great intensity will tend to earn more. Individuals also differ in their willingness to assume risk. We refer here not only to the auto race driver or the professional boxer but to the entrepreneur who assumes risk. Although many entrepreneurs fail, those who develop successful new products or services often realize very substantial incomes.

Unequal Distribution of Wealth

Income is a *flow*; it represents a stream of wage and salary earnings, along with rent, interest, and profits, as depicted in Chapter 2's circular flow diagram. In contrast, wealth is a *stock*, reflecting at a particular moment the financial and real assets an individual has accumulated over time. A retired person may have very little income, yet a home, mutual fund shares, and a pension plan can add up to considerable wealth. A new college graduate may be earning a substantial income as an accountant, middle manager, or engineer but has yet to accumulate significant wealth.

The ownership of wealth in the United States is very unequal. A recent Federal Reserve study showed than in 1992 the top 20 percent of all households owned 81 percent of total net assets. The bottom 20 percent had no net assets at all; the bottom 40 percent had less than 2 percent of total net assets. This inequality of wealth leads to inequality in rent, interest, and dividends, which in turn contributes to income inequality. Those who own more machinery,

real estate, farmland, stocks and bonds, and savings accounts obviously receive greater income from that ownership than people with less or no such wealth.

Market Power

The ability to "rig the market" on one's own behalf is one factor which contributes to income inequality. For example, certain unions and professional groups have adopted policies limiting the supplies of their services, thereby boosting the incomes of those "on the inside." Also, legislation which requires occupational licensing for, say, hunting guides, barbers, or beauticians can exert market power favoring the licensed groups. In product markets, "rigging the market" means gaining or enhancing monopoly power, which means greater profit and thus greater income to the firms' owners.

Luck, Connections, and Misfortune

Other forces also play roles in producing income inequality. Luck and "being in the right place at the right time" have caused individuals to stumble into fortunes. Discovering oil on a ranch, owning land along a proposed freeway interchange, and hiring the right press agent have accounted for some high incomes. Personal contacts and political connections are other potential routes to attaining high income.

In contrast, economic misfortunes such as prolonged illness, serious accident, death of the family breadwinner, or unemployment may plunge a family into the low range of income. The burden of such misfortune is borne very unevenly by the population and thus contributes to income inequality. **(Key Question 5)**

QUICK REVIEW 34-1

■ Income inequality in the United States has increased in the last decade; currently the top fifth of all families receive 47 percent of before-tax income, and the bottom fifth receives 4 percent.

■ The Lorenz curve depicts income inequality graphically by comparing percentages of total families and percentages of total income.

■ The distribution of income is less unequal over longer time periods.

■ Government taxes and transfers significantly reduce income inequality by redistributing income from higher-income groups to lower-income groups; the bulk of this redistribution is from transfer payments.

■ Differences in ability, education and training, tastes for market work versus nonmarket activities, property ownership, and market power—along with discrimination and luck—help explain income inequality.

EQUALITY VERSUS EFFICIENCY

The critical policy issue concerning income inequality is how much is necessary and justified. While there is no general agreement on the amount, we can learn much by exploring the cases for and against greater equality.

The Case for Equality: Maximizing Total Utility

The basic argument for an equal distribution of income is that income equality maximizes total consumer satisfaction (utility). The rationale for this argument is shown in

Figure 34-3, in which we assume that the money incomes of two individuals, Anderson and Brooks, are subject to diminishing marginal utility. In any time period, income receivers spend the first dollars received on products they value most—products whose marginal utility is high. As their most pressing wants become satisfied, consumers then spend additional dollars of income on less important, lower-marginal-utility goods. The identical diminishing-*marginal-utility-from-income curves* (MU_A and MU_B in the figure) reflect the assumption that Anderson and Brooks have the same capacity to derive utility from income.

Now suppose there is $10,000 worth of income (output) to be distributed between Anderson and Brooks. According to proponents of income equality, the optimal distribution is an equal distribution, which causes the marginal utility of the last dollar spent to be the same for both persons. We can prove this by demonstrating that if the income distribution is initially unequal, then distributing income more equally can increase the combined utility of the two individuals.

Suppose the $10,000 of income initially is distributed unequally, with Anderson getting $2500 and

(a) Anderson's marginal utility from income

(b) Brooks' marginal utility from income

FIGURE 34-3 The utility-maximizing distribution of income With identical marginal-utility-of-income curves MU_A and MU_B, Anderson and Brooks will maximize their combined utility when any amount of income (say, $10,000) is equally distributed. If income is unequally distributed (say, $2500 to Anderson and $7500 to Brooks), the marginal utility derived from the last dollar will be greater for Anderson than for Brooks, and a redistribution toward equality will result in a net increase in total utility. The utility gained by equalizing income at $5000 each, shown by area G in panel (a), exceeds the utility lost, indicated by area L in (b).

Brooks $7500. The marginal utility, *a*, from the last dollar received by Anderson is high, and the marginal utility, *b*, from Brooks' last dollar of income is low. If a single dollar of income is shifted from Brooks to Anderson—that is, toward greater equality—then Anderson's utility increases by *a* and Brooks' utility decreases by *b*. The combined utility then increases by *a* minus *b* (Anderson's large gain minus Brooks' small loss). The transfer of another dollar from Brooks to Anderson again increases their combined utility, this time by a slightly smaller amount. Continued transfer of dollars from Brooks to Anderson increases their combined utility until the income is evenly distributed and both receive $5000. At that time their marginal utilities from the last dollar of income are equal (at *a'* and *b'*), and any further income redistribution beyond the $2500 already transferred would begin to create inequality and decrease their combined utility.

The area under the MU curve, and to the left of the individual's particular level of income, represents the total utility of that income. Therefore, as a result of the transfer of the $2500, Anderson has gained utility represented by the gray area G, and Brooks has lost utility represented by the pink area L. Area G is obviously greater than area L, so income equality yields greater combined total utility than income inequality.

The Case for Inequality: Incentives and Efficiency

Although the logic of the argument for equality is sound, critics attack its fundamental assumption that there is some fixed amount of income to be distributed. Critics of income equality argue that *the way in which income is distributed is an important determinant of the amount of income which is produced and is available for distribution.*

Suppose once again in Figure 34-3 that Anderson earns $2500 and Brooks earns $7500. In moving toward equality, society (government) must *tax* away some of Brooks' income and *transfer* it to Anderson. This tax and transfer process diminishes the income rewards of high-income Brooks and raises the income rewards of low-income Anderson; in so doing, it reduces the incentives of both to *earn* high incomes. Why should high-income Brooks work hard, save and invest, or undertake entrepreneurial risks when the rewards from such activities will be reduced by taxation? And why should low-income Anderson be motivated to increase his income through market activi-

ties when government stands ready to transfer income to him? Taxes are a reduction in the rewards from increased productive effort; redistribution through transfers is a reward for diminished effort.

In the extreme, imagine a situation in which government levies a 100 percent tax on income and distributes the tax revenue equally to its citizenry. Why would anyone work hard? Why would anyone work at all? Why would anyone assume business risk? Or why would anyone save (forgo current consumption) to invest? The economic incentives to "get ahead" will have been removed, greatly reducing society's total production and income. In other words, the way the income pie is distributed affects the size of that pie. The basic argument for income inequality is that inequality is essential to maintain incentives to produce output and income—to get the pie baked year after year.

The Equality-Efficiency Tradeoff

The essence of this income equality-inequality debate is that there is a fundamental **tradeoff between equality and efficiency:**

> The contrasts among American families in living standards and in material wealth reflect a system of rewards and penalties that is intended to encourage effort and channel it into socially productive activity. To the extent that the system succeeds, it generates an efficient economy. But that pursuit of efficiency necessarily creates inequalities. And hence society faces a tradeoff between equality and efficiency.[2]

The problem for a society which is inclined toward equality is to redistribute income in a way which minimizes the adverse effects on economic efficiency. Consider this *leaky-bucket analogy:* Assume society agrees to shift income from the rich to the poor. But the money must be carried from affluent to indigent in a leaky bucket. The leak represents an efficiency loss—the loss of output and income—caused by the harmful effects of the redistribution on incentives to work, to save and invest, and to accept entrepreneurial risk. The leak also reflects the fact that resources must be diverted to the bureaucracies which administer the redistribution system.

How much leakage will society accept and still agree to the redistribution? If cutting the income pie into more equal slices shrinks the pie, what amount of

---

[2]Arthur M. Okun, *Equality and Efficiency: The Big Tradeoff* (Washington: Brookings Institution, 1975), p. 1.

shrinkage will society tolerate? Is a loss of 1 cent on each redistributed dollar acceptable? 5 cents? 25 cents? 50 cents? This is the basic question in any debate over the ideal size of a nation's income-maintenance programs.

Studies suggest that the loss from the leaky redistribution bucket may be quite high:

> [Economists] Edgar Browning and William Johnson . . . concluded that the upper-income groups bearing the costs of the taxes would sacrifice $350 for every $100 that the poor gained—a net efficiency loss of $250. In Arthur Okun's terms, the leaks in the redistribution bucket are enormous—starting out with a bucket of $350 raised from the nonpoor, $250 is lost on the way to delivering it to the poor. For several reasons, critics of this study have found the estimate to be substantially too high. However, even if cut in half, this loss would be troublesome. Would our society be willing to accept a loss of economic efficiency of $125—or even $100—in order to equalize the distribution of income by transferring $100 to the poor? The answer is by no means clear.[3]

THE ECONOMICS OF POVERTY

The larger issue of income distribution contains the more specific issue of very low income, or "poverty."

---

[3]Robert H. Haveman, "New Policy for the New Poverty," *Challenge*, September–October 1988, p. 32.

Our discussion now turns to the extent of poverty in the United States, the characteristics of the poor, and the programs designed to lessen poverty.

Definition of Poverty

Poverty is a condition in which a person or family does not have the *means* to satisfy *basic needs* for food, clothing, shelter, and transportation. The means include currently earned income, transfer payments, past savings, and property owned. The basic needs have many determinants, including family size and the health and ages of its members.

The Federal government has established a minimum income level below which a person or family is "in poverty." In 1996 an unattached individual receiving less than $7995 per year was living in poverty. For a family of 4, the poverty line was $16,036; for a family of 6, it was $21,389. Applying these definitions to income data in the United States, we find that 13.7 percent of the population—about 36 million people—lives in poverty.

Incidence of Poverty

Unfortunately for purposes of public policy, the poor are heterogeneous: They can be found in all parts of the nation; they are whites and nonwhites, rural and urban, young and old. But as Figure 34-4 indicates, poverty is far from randomly distributed. For example, the **poverty rate** (the percentage of the

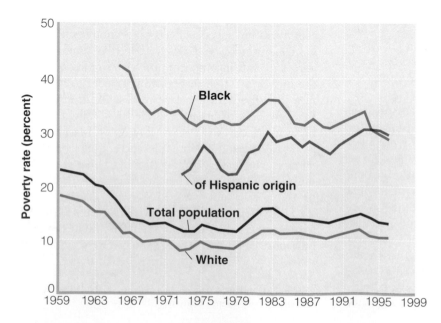

FIGURE 34-4 **Poverty rates: for total population and by race and ethnicity, 1959–1996** Over the 1959–1996 period, poverty rates for blacks and Hispanics were much higher than the rate for the total population, while the rate for whites was below that for the total population. Although the national poverty rate declined sharply in the 1959–1969 period, it stabilized in the 1970s only to increase significantly in the early 1980s. Recently, it has again declined.

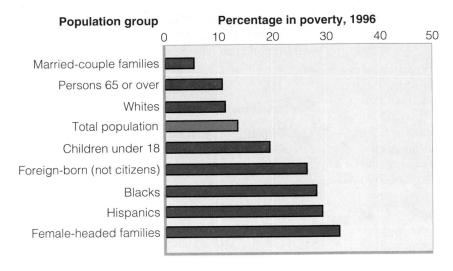

Population group   **Percentage in poverty, 1996**

Married-couple families
Persons 65 or over
Whites
Total population
Children under 18
Foreign-born (not citizens)
Blacks
Hispanics
Female-headed families

FIGURE 34-5 **The distribution of poverty among selected population groups, 1996**   Poverty is disproportionately borne by minorities, children, foreign-born residents who are not citizens, and families headed by women. People who are employed full-time, have a college degree, or are married tend to have low poverty rates.

population living in poverty) is above the national average for blacks, as is the rate for Hispanics, while the rate for whites is below the average. In 1996, the poverty rates for blacks and Hispanics were 28.4 and 29.4 percent, respectively; the rate for whites was 11.2 percent.

Figure 34-5 shows that the incidence of poverty is extremely high among female-headed families, foreign-born people who are not citizens, and children under 18 years of age. Marriage is associated with a low poverty rate, and thanks to a generous social security system, the incidence of poverty among the elderly is less than that for the population as a whole.

The high poverty rate for children is especially disturbing because poverty tends to breed poverty. Poor children are at greater risk for a range of long-term problems, including poor health and inadequate education, crime, drug use, and teenage pregnancy. Many of today's impoverished children will reach adulthood unhealthy and illiterate and be unable to earn above-poverty incomes.

Although in general there is considerable movement out of poverty, poverty is much more long-lasting among some groups. In particular, black and Hispanic families, families headed by women, persons with little education and few labor market skills, and people who are dysfunctional because of drug use, alcoholism, or mental illness are more likely than others to remain in poverty.

Poverty Trends

As Figure 34-4 shows, the total poverty rate fell significantly between 1959 and 1969, stabilized between 11 and 13 percent over the next decade, and then increased in the early 1980s. In 1993 the rate was 15.1 percent, the highest since 1983. Since 1993 the rate has again turned downward.

The "Invisible" Poor

The facts and figures on the extent and character of poverty may be difficult to accept. After all, the United States is an affluent society. The troubling statistics on poverty fit with our everyday observations of abundance mainly because much U.S. poverty is hidden; it is largely invisible.

There are three reasons for this invisibility. First, research has shown that as many as one-half of those in poverty are poor for only one or two years before successfully climbing out of poverty. Many of those people are not visible as permanently downtrodden and needy. Second the "permanently poor" are increasingly isolated geographically. Poverty persists in depressed areas of large cities and is not readily visible from the freeway. Similarly, rural poverty and the chronically depressed areas of Appalachia, the deep south, and the southwest are also off the beaten paths. Third, and perhaps most important, the poor are politically invisible. In general, they do not belong to advocacy organizations such as business groups (Chamber of Commerce), workers groups (unions and professional groups), or groups of senior citizens (American Association of Retired People). They do not have newsletters and political lobbyists, and they do not propose legislation and endorse candidates. They have very little direct voice in U.S. politics and are therefore easy to ignore.

THE INCOME-MAINTENANCE SYSTEM

The reduction of poverty is a widely accepted goal of public policy and a number of income-maintenance programs have been devised to reduce it, the most important of which are listed in Table 34-3. Despite recent attempts to slow the upward trend in spending on such programs, they still involve enormous expenditures and large numbers of beneficiaries. Total spending for income maintenance has expanded from about 4 percent of domestic production in 1940 to more than 14 percent today.

The U.S. income-maintenance system consists of two kinds of programs: (1) social insurance and (2) public assistance or "welfare." Both are known as **entitlement programs** because all eligible are assured (entitled to) the benefits currently set forth in the programs.

Social Insurance Programs

Social insurance programs partially replace earnings which are lost due to retirement, disability, and temporary unemployment, and they provide health insurance for the elderly. The main social insurance programs are "social security" (technically Old Age, Survivors, and Disability Health Insurance, or OASDHI), unemployment compensation, and Medicare. Benefits are viewed as earned rights and do

TABLE 34-3 Characteristics of major income-maintenance programs

Program	Basis of eligibility	Source of funds	Form of aid	Expenditures,* billions	Beneficiaries, millions
Social Insurance Programs					
Old Age, Survivors, and Disability Health Insurance (OASDHI)	Age, disability, or death of parent or spouse; individual earnings	Federal payroll taxes on employers and employees	Cash	$333	43
Medicare	Age or disability	Federal payroll tax on employers and employees	Subsidized health insurance	191	38
Unemployment compensation	Unemployment	State and Federal payroll taxes on employers	Cash	20	8
Public Assistance Programs					
Supplemental Security Income (SSI)	Age or disability; income	Federal revenues	Cash	27	7
Aid to Families with Dependent Children (AFDC)	Certain families with children; income	Federal-state-local revenues	Cash and services	23	14
Food Stamps	Income	Federal revenues	Vouchers	22	26
Medicaid	Persons eligible for AFDC or SSI and medically indigent	Federal-state-local revenues	Subsidized medical services	120	35

*Expenditures by Federal, state, and local governments; excludes administrative expenses.
Source: Statistical Abstract of the United States, 1997. Latest data.

not carry the stigma of public charity. These programs are financed primarily out of Federal payroll taxes. In these programs the entire population shares the risk of an individual's losing income because of retirement, unemployment, disability, or illness. Workers (and employers) pay a part of wages into a government fund while they are working, and then they are *entitled* to benefits when they retire or when the specified misfortunes occur.

OASDHI and Medicare
OASDHI is a gigantic social insurance program financed by compulsory payroll taxes levied on both employers and employees. Generically known as *social security*, the program replaces earnings lost because of a worker's retirement, disability, or death. Workers may retire at age 65 and receive full benefits or at age 62 with reduced benefits. When a worker dies, benefits accrue to his or her survivors. Special provisions provide benefits for disabled workers. Currently, social security covers over 90 percent of the workforce; some 43 million people receive OASDHI benefits averaging about $720 per month. These benefits are financed with a payroll tax of 15.3 percent, with both the worker and the employer paying 7.65 percent on the first $68,400 of each worker's wage income. Self-employed workers pay a tax of 15.3 percent.

Medicare was added to OASDHI in 1965. It provides hospital insurance for the elderly and disabled and is financed out of the payroll tax. This 2.9 percent tax, however, is paid on *all* work income. Medicare also makes available a low-cost voluntary insurance program which helps pay doctor fees.

Unemployment Compensation
All 50 states sponsor unemployment insurance programs. **Unemployment compensation** is financed by a modest payroll tax, paid by employers, which varies by state and by the size of the firm's payroll. Any insured worker who becomes unemployed can, after a short waiting period (usually 1 week), become eligible for benefit payments. Almost all wage and salary workers are covered by the program. The size of payments and the number of weeks they may be received vary considerably from state to state. Generally, benefits approximate 35 percent of a worker's wages up to a certain maximum payment. Benefits averaged $197 weekly in 1995. The number of beneficiaries and the level of total disbursements vary with economic conditions.

Public Assistance Programs

Public assistance programs (welfare) provide benefits for those who are unable to earn income because of permanent handicaps or have no or very low income and also have dependent children. These programs are financed out of general tax revenues and are regarded as public charity. They include "means tests" which require individuals and families to demonstrate low incomes to qualify for aid. The Federal government finances about two-thirds of the welfare program expenditures.

Many needy persons who do not qualify for social insurance programs are assisted through the Federal government's **Supplemental Security Income (SSI)** program. The purpose of SSI is to establish a uniform, nationwide minimum income for the aged, blind, and disabled who are unable to work and do not qualify for OASDHI aid. Over half the states provide additional income supplements to the aged, blind, and disabled.

The **Aid to Families with Dependent Children (AFDC)** program is state-administered but partly financed with Federal grants. The program provides aid to families in which dependent children do not have the financial support of a parent, usually the father, because of death, disability, divorce, or desertion.

The **food stamp program** is designed to provide all low-income Americans with a "nutritionally adequate diet." Under the program, eligible households receive monthly allotments of coupons which are redeemable for food. The amount of food stamps received varies inversely with a family's earned income.

Medicaid helps finance the medical expenses of individuals participating in the SSI and the AFDC programs.

There are also a variety of welfare programs not listed in Table 34-3. Most provide help in the form of noncash transfers. Head Start provides education, nutrition, and social services to economically disadvantaged 3- and 4-year-olds. Housing assistance in the form of rent subsidies and funds for construction is available to low-income families. The Job Training Partnership Act finances education and training for the poor, and Pell grants provide assistance to needy undergraduate students. Of special interest is the **earned-income tax credit (EITC),** which is a tax credit for low-income working families with children. Established in 1975, the credit reduces the taxes such families owe or provides them with a cash payment if the credit exceeds their tax liability.

WELFARE: GOALS AND CONFLICTS

An ideal public assistance (welfare) program should simultaneously achieve three goals. First, the plan should be effective in getting individuals and families out of poverty. Second, it should provide adequate incentives for able-bodied, nonretired people to work. Third, the plan's cost should be "reasonable." Unfortunately, these three goals conflict, causing tradeoffs and necessitating compromises. To understand this, consider the three hypothetical welfare plans shown in Table 34-4.

Common Features

Let's first examine the two common elements in each of the three plans (and in real-world public assistance plans). First, there is a *minimum annual income* which government will provide if the family has no earned income. Second, each plan has a *benefit-reduction rate*, which is the rate at which benefits are reduced or "lost" as a result of earned income.

Consider plan 1. The minimum annual income provided by government is $8000, and the benefit-reduction rate is 50 percent. If a family earns no income, it will receive cash transfer payments totaling $8000. If it earns $4000, it will lose $2000 ($4000 of earnings *times* the 50 percent benefit-reduction rate) of transfer payments; its total income will then be $10,000 (= $4000 of earnings *plus* $6000 of transfer payments). If $8000 is earned, transfer payments will fall to $4000, and so on. Note that at an income of $16,000, transfer payments are zero. The level of earned income at which the transfer payments disappear is called the *break-even income*.

We might criticize plan 1 on the grounds that a 50 percent benefit-reduction rate is too high and therefore does not provide sufficient incentives to work. As earned income increases, the loss of transfer payments constitutes a "tax" on earnings. Some people may choose not to work when they lose 50 cents of each extra dollar earned. Thus in plan 2 the $8000 minimum income is retained, but the benefit-reduction rate is reduced to 25 percent. But note that the break-even level of income increases to $32,000, so

TABLE 34-4 Tradeoffs among goals: three public assistance plans

Plan 1 ($8000 minimum income and 50% benefit-reduction rate)			Plan 2 ($8000 minimum income and 25% benefit-reduction rate)			Plan 3 ($12,000 minimum income and 50% benefit-reduction rate)		
Earned income	Transfer payment	Total income	Earned income	Transfer payment	Total income	Earned income	Transfer payment	Total income
$ 0	$8000	$ 8,000	$ 0	$8000	$ 8,000	$ 0	$12,000	$12,000
4,000	6000	10,000	8,000	6000	14,000	8,000	8,000	16,000
8,000	4000	12,000	16,000	4000	20,000	16,000	4,000	20,000
12,000	2000	14,000	24,000	2000	26,000	24,000*	0	24,000
16,000*	0	16,000	32,000*	0	32,000			

*Indicates break-even income. Determined by dividing the minimum income by the benefit-reduction rate.

many more families would now qualify for transfer payments. Furthermore, a family with any earned income under $32,000 will receive a larger total transfer payment. For both reasons, a reduction of the benefit-loss rate to enhance work incentives will raise the cost of the income-maintenance plan.

After examining plans 1 and 2, we might argue that the $8000 minimum annual income is too low—it does not get families out of poverty. Plan 3 raises the minimum income to $12,000 and retains the 50 percent benefit-reduction rate of plan 1. While plan 3 does a better job of raising the incomes of the poor, it too yields a higher break-even income than plan 1 and therefore will be more costly. Also, if the $12,000 income guarantee of plan 3 were coupled with plan 2's 25 percent benefit-reduction rate to strengthen work incentives, the break-even income level would shoot up to $48,000 and add even more to the costs of the public assistance program.

Conflicts Among Goals

Our discussion points clearly to the conflicting goals of eliminating poverty, maintaining work incentives, and holding down program costs.

Plan 1, with a low minimum income and a high benefit-reduction rate, keeps cost down. But the low minimum income means that this plan is not very effective in eliminating poverty, and the high benefit-reduction rate weakens work incentives.

In comparison, plan 2 has a lower benefit-reduction rate and therefore stronger work incentives. But it is more costly because it sets a higher break-even income and therefore pays benefits to more families.

Compared with plan 1, plan 3 has a higher minimum income and is more effective in eliminating poverty. While work incentives are the same as those in plan 1, the higher guaranteed income in plan 3 makes the plan more costly. **(Key Question 11)**

WELFARE: CRITICISM AND REFORM

The tradeoffs just discussed shed light on recent reform of the welfare system. This reform resulted from a growing sense that welfare spending was not ending poverty. While the number of people receiving welfare benefits under the AFDC program increased substantially in the 1980s and early 1990s, the number of people in poverty went up, instead of down.

Criticisms Leading to Reform

The welfare system has been subject to many criticisms in recent years:

1. *Administrative inefficiency* Critics charge that the haphazard growth of welfare has created a clumsy and inefficient system characterized by red tape and dependence on a huge administrative bureaucracy which absorbs valuable funds that could be going to the poor.

2. *Serious inequities* Because states can set their own benefit levels, AFDC payments vary. A family living in California might receive welfare benefits two times as great as they would if they lived in Mississippi. Moreover, control of the system is fragmented, so some low-income families fall between the cracks while other families collect benefits to which they are not entitled.

3. *Lack of work incentives* The welfare system reduces incentives to work. Critics point out that the income provided in the AFDC program means that welfare recipients can afford to "buy more leisure" (work fewer hours). And because benefit-loss rates in most states are 67 percent, the opportunity cost of leisure is much less than it would be without the system. For a minimum-wage worker, an hour of leisure "costs" $5.15—the income sacrificed. But for someone receiving welfare, the cost of an hour of leisure is only $1.70 because $3.45 of the $5.15 hourly wage is replaced with a welfare payment.

   When the loss of program benefits and the effect of income and payroll taxes on earnings are taken into account, an individual or family participating in several welfare programs may be financially worse off by working. In effect, the marginal tax rate on earned income exceeds 100 percent. Small wonder that a minimum-wage job may be unattractive to a welfare mother who will lose both AFDC benefits and (after a year) Medicaid health care coverage and must, in addition, pay for child care while she works.

4. *Dependency* Critics say that long-term welfare payments create "a culture of poverty" which is actually detrimental to individuals and families because it creates dependency on the government, robbing family members of motivation and dignity.

5. *Divisiveness* Welfare programs foster social divisiveness between people working and people receiving welfare. For example, working mothers with small children may wonder why poor moth-

The Future of Social Security

Unless something is done, the U.S. social security system will be bankrupt in 32 years.

Over the past six decades, the Federal government has greatly expanded the social security retirement program, which has grown from less than one-half of 1 percent of U.S. GDP in 1950 to more than 4 percent of GDP today. By 2020, social security will transfer more than 6 percent of GDP from workers to beneficiaries.

The current system is mainly a "pay-as-you go" plan, meaning that nearly all the current revenues from the 15.3 percent social security tax are paid out to current beneficiaries. In anticipation of the large benefits owed to the baby boomers when they retire, however, in the past decade the Social Security Administration has been placing an excess of current revenues over payouts in a trust fund. But the accumulation of money in the trust fund is not nearly large enough to pay the benefits promised future retirees; in fact, the fund will be totally exhausted by 2030. One reason is that law restricts investment of the funds to safe, but low-interest yield, U.S. Treasury securities. A more fundamental reason is that the number of workers per beneficiary has declined from 5:1 in 1960 to 3:1 today. Declining birthrates and rising life expectancy are expected to reduce this ratio below 2:1 by 2070. In the future, fewer people will be paying social security taxes and more people will be receiving social security benefits for more years.

Along with the deteriorating program finances, two other factors motivate calls for social security reform. First, while present retirees are in effect earning a high rate of return on their social security contributions, the average worker born after 1930 can expect a very low rate of return (perhaps as low as 1 to 4 percent). Second, the nation's savings rate has fallen, and many economists attribute a substantial part of this decline to the growth of social security benefits. Guaranteed retirement benefits reduce the incentive for individuals to save for their old age, and such saving is required to finance the expansion of capital goods needed for economic growth.

A Federal advisory panel on social security recently identified three general options for reforming the retirement system.

1. **The *Maintain Benefits* Plan** This plan increases social security revenues to allow the current program to continue. The proposal would increase the payroll tax by 1.6 percentage points in 2045. Up to 40 percent of the social security trust fund would be invested in corporate stocks. The Federal government would own the stock investments, and an appointed panel would oversee the direction of these investments. Social security benefits would be paid partly from social security tax revenues and partly from the returns on the stock investments in the trust fund.

ers receiving AFDC should not also work for their money.

6. ***High program costs*** Finally, critics of the welfare system point to its enormous costs. In 1996 the United States spent about $140 billion on public assistance programs. This amount was greater than the *national* income of such countries as Greece, Norway, Saudi Arabia, and Chile.

Welfare Reform

These criticisms have led to many piecemeal reforms of the public assistance programs. For instance, several states began experimenting with *workfare plans* which altered AFDC payments by providing work, training, and education to help welfare recipients move from public assistance to employment. In these programs, people shifting from welfare to work received child-care and transportation subsidies. In addition, the earnings of absentee (nonsupportive) parents—whether married or unmarried—could be taken directly from their paychecks to help support their children. Finally, states began to provide Medicaid coverage for 1 year to families who left welfare rolls for employment. (The purpose was to reduce the costs of switching from welfare to work and to lessen the incentives to stay on welfare.)

Some states went further: They (1) required welfare recipients to do community work in return for their welfare checks and (2) set 2- to 5-year time limits on each family's welfare benefits. Wisconsin adopted a "pay-after-performance" principle, paying welfare checks only after the recipients met monthly community-service requirements. Several of the states initiating reform experienced remarkable declines in their welfare rolls. For example, the number of families receiving welfare in Wisconsin fell from 9500 in 1985 to 4500 in 1997. While much of this decline re-

2. **The *Individual Accounts* Plan** In this second proposal, the Federal government would immediately increase the payroll tax by 1.6 percentage points and allocate the new revenues to individual accounts. Government would own the accumulations in the individual accounts, but individuals could direct their investment to a restricted list of broad stock or bond funds. When they retire, recipients would convert these individual account balances to annuities, which are securities that pay monthly payments for life. This annuity income would then supplement the monthly benefits from the pay-as-you go system. To ensure solvency of the system, this plan would accelerate the already legislated increase in the age of eligibility for retirement benefits.

3. **The *Personal Security Accounts* Plan.** This plan would shift 5 percentage points of the current payroll tax to individual accounts which individuals, not the government, would own and maintain. Individuals could invest these funds in bank certificates of deposits or in approved stock and bond funds. A flat monthly benefit equivalent to $410 in 1996 would supplement the accumulations in the private accounts. The Federal government would phase in this partial privatization of social security over time, so those individuals now receiving or about to receive social security benefits would continue to receive the current benefits.

These three plans clearly do not exhaust the possible reforms since the variations on each plan are endless. Reaching consensus on social security reform will be very difficult because every U.S. citizen has a direct economic stake in the outcome. Nevertheless, it is clear that social security faces long-run trouble and that, sooner or later, some type of reform of the system will be absolutely critical.

Source: Based on Harvey Rosenblum, "Why Social Security Should Be Privatized," *Southwest Economy* (Federal Reserve Bank of Dallas, May/June 1997), pp. 6–11; Susan Miller, "The Market to the Rescue? The Promise—and the Price—of the New Social Security Investment Proposals," *Current Issues in Economics and Finance* (Federal Reserve Bank of New York, August 1997), pp. 1–6; and C. Alan Garner, "Social Security Privatization: Balancing Efficiency and Fairness," *Economic Review* (Federal Reserve Bank of Kansas City, Third quarter 1997), pp. 21–33.

---

sulted from a highly favorable job market, welfare reform was also a major contributing factor.

Because of the criticisms of welfare and the general success of the state plans, in 1996 Congress passed the **Personal Responsibility Act,** which was designed "to end welfare as we know it." Specifically, it eliminated the Federal government's six-decade-old guarantee of cash assistance for poor families. Instead, each state now receives a lump sum of Federal money to operate its own welfare and work programs. These lump-sum payments will save the Federal government about $55 billion over the first 6 years of the new law.

In its key provisions, the new Federal welfare law sets a lifetime limit of 5 years on receiving AFDC benefits and requires able-bodied adults to work after receiving assistance for 2 years. Able-bodied recipients age 18 to 50 with no dependents are ineligible for food stamps unless they are engaged in work or state work programs. The law has tightened the definition of "disabled children" in regard to SSI assistance for low-income families. Finally, future legal immigrants who have not become citizens will be ineligible for public assistance during their first 5 years in the United States.

Supporters of the law believe that it can play a key role in helping to end a "culture of welfare" in which dropping out of school, having a child, and going on welfare have allegedly become a normal way of life for part of the welfare population. They cite large recent declines in the welfare rolls as evidence of the law's effectiveness. Critics say the law places blame for poverty on its victims and not on the larger social and economic forces which actually cause it. They point out that nearly two-thirds of people receiving AFDC are children, not adults, and that the law penalizes these children for their parents' inability or unwillingness to find and retain employment. Critics also say that the test of the new law will come if the economy experiences recession and widespread unemployment. Those who have left welfare to take jobs in the recent strong labor market will surge back to welfare as they are laid off. To maintain their work requirements, states will have to expand their very expensive "public employment" programs. Critics say that such programs will prove to be far more costly to taxpayers than simply transferring income to those in need.

CHAPTER SUMMARY

1. The distribution of income in the United States reflects considerable inequality. The top 20 percent of families earn 47 percent of total income, while the bottom 20 percent earn only 4 percent.

2. The Lorenz curve shows the percentage of total income received by each percentage of families. The extent of the gap between the Lorenz curve and a line of total equality illustrates the degree of income inequality.

3. Census data show that income inequality lessened significantly between 1929 and the end of World War II but has increased since 1969. The major cause of recent increases in income inequality is a rising demand for highly skilled workers, which has greatly boosted their earnings.

4. Recognizing that the positions of individual families in the distribution of income change over time *and* incorporating the effects of noncash transfers and taxes would reveal less income inequality than do standard census data. Government transfers (cash and noncash) greatly lessen the degree of income inequality; taxes also reduce inequality, but not nearly as much as transfers.

5. Causes of income inequality include differences in abilities, education and training, and job tastes, along with discrimination, inequality in the distribution of wealth, and an unequal distribution of market power.

6. The basic argument for income equality is that it maximizes consumer satisfaction (total utility) from a particular level of total income. The main argument for income inequality is that it provides the incentives to work, invest, and assume risk; it is necessary for the production of output, which, in turn, creates income that is then available for distribution.

7. Current statistics reveal that 13.7 percent of the U.S. population lives in poverty. Poverty rates are particularly high for female-headed families, young children, blacks, and Hispanics.

8. The present income-maintenance program in the United States is composed of social insurance programs (OASDHI, Medicare, and unemployment compensation) and public assistance programs (SSI, AFDC, food stamps, and Medicaid).

9. Public assistance programs (welfare) are difficult to design because their goals of reducing poverty, maintaining work incentives, and holding down program costs are often in direct conflict with one another.

10. Before recent reforms, welfare programs were heavily criticized as administratively inefficient, fraught with inequities, detrimental to work incentives, and fostering dependence. Critics also asserted that the welfare system caused family breakups, out-of-marriage births, and social divisiveness. Finally, detractors were concerned about the enormous annual cost of the system.

11. The Personal Responsibility Act of 1996 shifted responsibility for welfare from the Federal government to the states. Among its provisions are work requirements on those receiving welfare and a 5-year lifelong limit on welfare benefits.

TERMS AND CONCEPTS

income inequality
Lorenz curve
income mobility
noncash transfers
tradeoff between equality and efficiency
poverty rate

entitlement programs
social insurance programs
OASDHI
Medicare
unemployment compensation

public assistance programs
Supplemental Security Income (SSI)
Aid to Families with Dependent Children (AFDC)

food stamp program
Medicaid
earned-income tax credit (EITC)
Personal Responsibility Act

STUDY QUESTIONS

1. Using quintiles, briefly summarize the degree of income inequality in the United States. What criticisms have been made of standard Census Bureau data on income inequality? How and to what extent does government contribute to income equality?

2. **KEY QUESTION** Assume Al, Beth, Carol, David, and Ed receive incomes of $500, $250, $125, $75, and $50 respectively. Construct and interpret a Lorenz curve for this five-person economy. What percentage of total income is received by the richest quintile and by the poorest quintile?

3. What factors have contributed to increased income inequality in the past decade or so?

4. Why is the lifetime distribution of income more equal than the distribution in any specific year?

5. **KEY QUESTION** Briefly discuss the major causes of income inequality. With respect to income inequality, is there any difference between inheriting property and inheriting a high IQ? Explain.

6. Use the "leaky-bucket analogy" to discuss the equality-efficiency tradeoff. Do you think the Personal Responsibility Act of 1996 will reduce the leak? Explain.

7. Should a nation's income be distributed to its members according to their contributions to the production of that total income or according to the members' needs? Should society attempt to equalize income *or* economic opportunities? Are the issues of "equity" and "equality" in the distribution of income synonymous? To what degree, if any, is income inequality equitable?

8. Analyze in detail: "There need be no tradeoff between equality and efficiency. An 'efficient' economy which yields an income distribution which many regard as unfair may cause those with meager incomes to become discouraged and stop trying. Hence, efficiency may be undermined. A fairer distribution of rewards may generate a higher average productive effort on the part of the population, thereby enhancing efficiency. If people think they are playing a fair economic game and this belief causes them to try harder, an economy with an equitable income distribution may be efficient as well."[4]

[4]Paraphrased from Andrew Schotter, *Free Market Economics* (New York: St. Martin's Press, 1985), pp. 30–31.

9. Comment on or explain:
  a. To endow everyone with equal income will make for very unequal enjoyment and satisfaction.
  b. Equality is a "superior good"; the richer we become, the more of it we can afford.
  c. The mob goes in search of bread, and the means it employs is generally to wreck the bakeries.
  d. Under our welfare system we have foolishly clung to the notion that employment and receipt of assistance must be mutually exclusive.
  e. Some freedoms may be more important in the long run than freedom from want on the part of every individual.
  f. Capitalism and democracy are really a most improbable mixture. Maybe that is why they need each other—to put some rationality into equality and some humanity into efficiency.
  g. The incentives created by the attempt to bring about a more equal distribution of income are in conflict with the incentives needed to generate increased income.

10. What are the essential differences between social insurance and public assistance programs? What are the criticisms of the present income-maintenance system in the United States?

11. **KEY QUESTION** The table shown below contains three hypothetical public assistance plans.

Plan 1

Earned income	Transfer payment	Total income
$ 0	$4000	$4000
2000	3000	5000
4000	2000	6000
6000	1000	7000

Plan 2

Earned income	Transfer payment	Total income
$ 0	$4000	$ 4,000
4,000	3000	7,000
8,000	2000	10,000
12,000	1000	13,000

Plan 3

Earned income	Transfer payment	Total income
$ 0	$8000	$ 8,000
4,000	6000	10,000
8,000	4000	12,000
12,000	2000	14,000

a. Determine the minimum income, the benefit-reduction rate, and the break-even income for each plan.

b. Which plan is the most costly? The least costly? Which plan is the most effective in reducing poverty? The least effective? Which plan contains the strongest disincentive to work? The weakest disincentive to work?

c. Use your answers in part (b) to explain the following statement: "The dilemma of public assistance is that you cannot bring families up to the poverty level and simultaneously preserve work incentives (without work requirements) and minimize program costs."

12. What major criticisms of the U.S. welfare system led to its reform in 1996 (via the Personal Responsibility Act of 1996)? How does this reform try to address these criticisms? Do you agree with the general tenor of the reform and with its emphasis on work requirements and time limits on benefits?

13. (Last Word) Why is there so much concern about the future of social security in the United States? Which, if any, of the general remedies discussed in the Last Word do you support? Explain.

14. WEB-BASED QUESTION How Much Family Income Does It Take to Be in the Top 5 Percent? The U.S. Census Bureau provides information on the historical distribution of family income via http://www.census.gov/hhes/histinc/f01.html. What is the lower limit of family income for the top 5 percent of families in the most recent year listed? Do the historical data in the table suggest that the poor are getting poorer and the rich are getting richer in *absolute* terms? Use http://www.census.gov/hhes/histinc/f02.html to determine whether the *relative* income share of the top 5 percent of families has increased in the past decade.

15. WEB-BASED QUESTION Is Poverty on the Rise? The U.S. Census Bureau http://www.census.gov/hhes/poverty.html also compiles information about poverty in the United States. Use that site to answer the following questions: (a) Is the number of people living below the official government poverty level higher or lower than in the previous year reported? Compared to a decade earlier? (b) Is the poverty rate (in percent) higher or lower than the previous year for the general population, children under 18, blacks, Asians, Pacific Islanders, and whites? (c) How many states had increases in the poverty rate compared to the previous year?

35

The Economics of Health Care

Rarely can you read a newspaper or look at television news without encountering a story about the high costs of health care in the United States, seriously ailing people with no health insurance, or government health insurance programs draining Federal and state budgets. News stories also document disputes between employers and workers over sharing the cost of health insurance or cite instances of insurance companies dictating the medical care which doctors can provide. We even learn of companies breaking promises to provide health insurance to retirees, and lawsuits challenging such actions. Moreover, difficult ethical questions concerning "extreme care" for the acutely or terminally ill have arisen.

The U.S. health care system is only one of several possible systems, each with different mixes of private sector and public sector participation. Reform or overhaul of the health care system continues to be debated in Congress. In this chapter we look at the U.S. system, identify key health care issues, and discuss actual and proposed reforms.

THE HEALTH CARE INDUSTRY

The boundaries of the health care industry are not definite, so the industry is difficult to define. But, in general, the health care industry includes services provided in hospitals, nursing homes, laboratories, and physicians' and dentists' offices. It also includes prescription and nonprescription drugs, artificial limbs, and eyeglasses. Note, however, that many goods and services which may affect health are not included, for example, low-fat foods, vitamins, and health club services.

Health care is one of the largest U.S. industries, employing about 9 million people, including over 600,000 physicians. There are more than 6000 hospitals containing more than 1 million beds. Americans make more than 680 million visits to office-based physicians each year.

TWIN PROBLEMS: COSTS AND ACCESS

There are two highly publicized problems with the U.S. health care system:

1. The cost of health care is high and has increased rapidly. Higher health care prices combined with an increase in the quantity of services provided has resulted in rising health care costs. (The spending on health care involves "prices" and "quantities" and is often loosely referred to as "health care costs.")

2. Many Americans have limited or no access to health care. The efforts to reform health care have focused on controlling costs and making it accessible to everyone. These two goals are related since high and rising prices make health care services unaffordable to a significant portion of the U.S. population. In fact, a dual system of health care may be evolving in the United States. Those with insurance or other financial means receive the world's best medical treatment, but many people do not seek out even the most basic treatment because of their inability to pay.

HIGH AND RISING HEALTH CARE COSTS

Let's look at several aspects of health care costs and health care spending in the United States.

Health Care Spending

Health care spending in the United States is high and rising in absolute terms, as a percentage of domestic output, and on a per capita basis.

Total Spending on Health Care Figure 35-1a is an overview of the major types of U.S. health care spending. It shows that 36 cents of each health care dollar is spent on hospitals, while physicians and other health care services (dental, vision, and home care) account for 20 and 25 cents, respectively.

Figure 35-1b shows the sources of funds for health care spending. Its key message is that three-fourths of health care spending is financed by insurance. Public insurance (Medicaid, Medicare, and insurance for veterans, current military personnel, and government employees) is the source of 46 cents of each dollar spent. Private insurance accounts for 31 cents, meaning that public and private insurance combined provide 77 cents of each dollar expended. The remaining 23 cents comes directly out of the health care consumer's pocket. It is paid mainly as insurance **deductibles** (that is, the insured pays the first $250 or $500 of each year's health care costs before the insurer begins paying) or **copayments** (that is, the

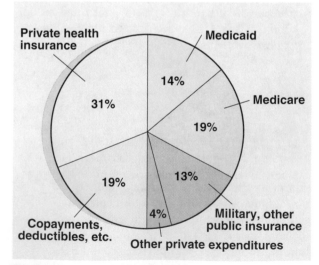

(a) **Health care expenditures**

(b) **Sources of funds**

FIGURE 35-1 Health care expenditures and finance (a) Most health care expenditures are for hospitals and physicians' services. (b) Public and private insurance pays for roughly three-fourths of health care. (*Source: Health Care Financing Administration.* Data are for 1995.)

insured pays, say, 20 percent of all health care costs and the insurance company pays 80 percent).

Recall that *Medicare* is a nationwide Federal health care program available to social security beneficiaries and persons with disabilities. One part is a *hospital insurance* program which, after a deductible of $760 (in 1997), covers all reasonable costs for the first 60 days of inpatient care per "benefit period" and lesser amounts (on a cost-sharing basis) for additional days. Coverage is also provided for posthospital nursing services, home health care, and hospice care for the terminally ill. The second part of Medicare, a *medical insurance* program (for physicians' services, laboratory and other diagnostic tests, and outpatient hospital services) is voluntary but is heavily subsidized by government. The $43.80 monthly premiums (in 1997) which participants pay cover about one-fourth of the cost of the benefits provided.

Medicaid provides payment for medical benefits to certain low-income people, including the elderly, blind, persons with disabilities, children, and adults with dependent children. Those who qualify for Aid to Families with Dependent Children (AFDC) or the Supplementary Security Income (SSI) program are automatically eligible for Medicaid. Nevertheless, Medicaid covers less than half of those living in poverty. The cost of Medicaid is shared by the Federal government and the states. On average, the states fund 43 percent and the Federal government 57 percent of each Medicaid dollar spent.

Overall, about 23 percent of each dollar spent on health care is financed by direct out-of-pocket payments by individuals. The fact that most U.S. health care is paid for by third parties—private insurance companies or government—is an important contributor to rising health care costs.

Percentage of Domestic Output

Figure 35-2 shows how health care spending has been increasing as a percentage of total domestic output. Health care spending absorbed 6.1 percent of domestic output in 1965 but rose to 13.6 percent by 1995. Congressional Budget Office projections indicate that if current trends and government policies continue, health care spending could amount to 16 percent of domestic output by the year 2000.

Per Capita Spending: International Comparisons

Global Perspective 35-1 reveals that among 24 of the most industrialized nations, per capita health care spending is highest in the United States. It seems rea-

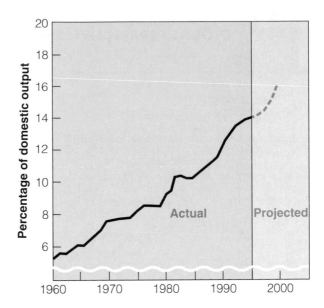

FIGURE 35-2 U.S. health care expenditures as a percentage of total domestic output U.S. health care spending as a percentage of domestic output has greatly increased since 1960 and is projected to rise still further.

sonable to assume that health care spending varies directly with output and incomes; the figure shows that health care expenditures per person rise approximately in proportion with per capita income. But the United States is clearly "off the trend line." The high per capita output does not fully explain the nation's very high level of health care spending per capita.

Quality of Care: Are We Healthier?

It is difficult to compare health care quality among countries. Yet there is general agreement that medical care (though not health) in the United States is probably *the* best in the world. Average life expectancy in the United States has increased by 5 years since 1960, and U.S. physicians and hospitals employ the most advanced medical equipment and technologies. Furthermore, more than half the world's medical research funding is done in the United States. As a result, the incidence of disease has been declining and the quality of treatment improving. Polio has been virtually eliminated, ulcers are now successfully treated without surgery, angioplasty and coronary bypass surgery greatly benefit those with heart disease, sophisticated body scanners are increasingly available

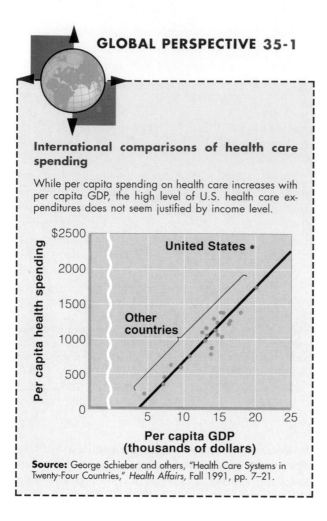

GLOBAL PERSPECTIVE 35-1

International comparisons of health care spending

While per capita spending on health care increases with per capita GDP, the high level of U.S. health care expenditures does not seem justified by income level.

Source: George Schieber and others, "Health Care Systems in Twenty-Four Countries," *Health Affairs*, Fall 1991, pp. 7–21.

Economic Implications of Rising Costs

When the price of health care is rising, the cost of health insurance is rising along with it. And, of course, increases in health care costs are the major reason for rising health care *spending*. But there are other effects of rising health care costs as well.

Reduced Access to Care   Because of rising health care costs, fewer employers offer health insurance to their workers. The number of uninsured is large and growing. We will consider this issue in detail momentarily.

Labor Market Effects   Surging health care costs have two main effects on labor markets:

1. *Slower wage growth*   Gains in workers' total compensation (wage *plus* fringe benefits, including health insurance paid for by employers) generally match gains in productivity. When health care costs (and thus insurance prices) rise more rapidly than productivity, firms wishing to maintain the existing level of health care benefits for their workers must reduce the growth of the wage portion of the total compensation package. Thus, in the long run, workers bear the burden of rising health care costs in the form of slower-growing wages.

2. *Use of part-time and temporary workers*   The high cost of employer-provided health insurance has led some employers to restructure their workforces: Full-time workers with health insurance benefits are employed in smaller numbers, and uninsured part-time or temporary workers in greater numbers. Similarly, a large, prosperous employer with a generous health care plan might reduce its health insurance expense by discharging its insured lower-wage workers—janitors, gardeners, and cafeteria staff—replacing them with outside independent contractors who offer no health insurance.

Impact on Government Budgets   The budgetary problems of Federal, state, and local governments are worsened by spiraling and often unpredictable health care expenditures. In the past two decades, spending for health care through Medicare and Medicaid has been by far the fastest-growing segment of the Federal budget. Higher taxes or reductions in other budget components such as national defense, education,

diagnostic tools, and organ transplants and prosthetic joint replacements are more and more common.

That is the good news. But there is other news as well. Despite new screening and treatment technologies, the breast cancer mortality rate has shown little change. Tuberculosis—a virtually forgotten disease—has reappeared. The AIDS epidemic has claimed over 380,000 American lives. More generally, some experts contend that high levels of health care spending do *not* result in significantly better health and well-being. Although U.S. health care expenditures are the highest in the world—absolutely, as a proportion of domestic output, and on a per capita basis—the United States ranks eighth in world life expectancy, eleventh in maternal mortality, and twenty-second in infant mortality. The U.S. Office of Technology Assessment concludes that "the U.S. ranks low internationally on most health indicators."

environmental programs, and scientific research must cover these increasing expenditures. States, most of which are required by law to balance their budgets each year, are also finding it difficult to cover their share of the Medicaid bill; most have been forced to raise their tax rates and search for new sources of revenue. Many states have had to reduce spending on nonhealth programs such as infrastructure maintenance, welfare, and education. In fact, the financial difficulties some state universities face are partly a reflection of increasing state Medicaid spending. Local governments face similar budget strains in trying to finance public health services, hospitals, and clinics.

The Basic Problem

Increased spending on computers or houses would be a sign of prosperity, not a cause for alarm. So what is different about health care spending? The difference is that the increased spending on health care may be inefficient. We will see that this possibility arises from the way health care is financed, the asymmetry of information between consumers and providers, and the interaction of health care insurance with technological progress in the industry.

The production of health care requires scarce resources such as capital in the form of hospitals and diagnostic equipment and the highly skilled labor of physicians, technicians, and nurses. It may be that the total production and consumption of health care in the United States is so large that health care, at the margin, is worth less than the alternative goods and services these resources could otherwise have produced. In other words, the United States may be consuming health care beyond the point at which the marginal benefits from health care equal the marginal costs of producing it. If there is an overallocation of resources to health care, society incurs a real economic loss. Resources used excessively in health care could be used more productively to build new factories, support research and development, construct new bridges and roads, support education, improve the environment, or provide more consumer goods.

LIMITED ACCESS

The other health care problem is limited access. Even though there may be an overallocation of resources to health care, not all Americans can obtain the health care they need. In 1996 almost 42 million Americans,

or about 16 percent of the population, had no health insurance for the entire year. As health care costs (and therefore health care insurance premiums) continue to rise, the number of uninsured will grow.

Who are the medically uninsured? As incomes rise, so does the probability of being insured. So it is no surprise that the uninsured are concentrated among the poor. Medicaid is designed to provide health care for the poor who are on welfare. But many poor people work at low- or minimum-wage jobs without health care benefits, earning "too much" to qualify for Medicaid yet not enough to afford private health insurance. About 50 percent of the uninsured have a family head who works full-time. Many single-parent families, black Americans, and Hispanics are uninsured simply because they are more likely to be poor.

Curiously, those with excellent health and those with the poorest health also tend to be uninsured. Many young people with excellent health simply choose not to buy health insurance. The chronically ill find it very difficult and too costly to obtain insurance because of the likelihood they will incur substantial future health care costs. Because private health insurance is most frequently obtained through an employer, the unemployed are also likely to lack insurance.

Workers for smaller firms are also less likely to have health insurance. The main reason is that administrative expenses for a small firm may be 30 to 40 percent of insurance premiums, as opposed to only 10 percent for a large firm. Furthermore, corporations can deduct health insurance premiums from income for tax purposes, thereby realizing substantial tax savings. Small unincorporated businesses do not receive this full tax break.

Low-wage workers are also less likely to be insured. Earlier we noted that in the long run the increasing expense of health care insurance is passed on by employers to workers as lower wages. This option is not available to employers paying the minimum wage. Thus as health care insurance premiums increase, employers cut or eliminate this benefit from the compensation package for their minimum- and low-wage workers. As a result, these workers are typically uninsured.

Although many of the uninsured forgo health care, some do not. A few are able to pay for it out of pocket. Others may wait until their illness reaches a critical stage and then go to a hospital for admittance or to be treated in the emergency room. These methods of treatment are inappropriate and unnecessarily costly.

It is estimated that hospitals provide more than $10 billion of uncompensated ("free") health care per year. Hospitals then attempt to shift these costs to those who have insurance or who can pay out of pocket. **(Key Question 2)**

QUICK REVIEW 35-1

■ Health care spending in the United States has been increasing absolutely, as a percentage of domestic output, and per capita.

■ Rising health care costs have caused **(a)** more people to find health insurance unaffordable; **(b)** adverse labor market effects, including slower real wage growth and increased use of part-time and temporary workers; and **(c)** restriction of nonhealth spending by governments.

■ The basic problem with rising health care spending is that it may reflect an overallocation of resources to the health care industry.

■ Approximately one-sixth of all Americans have no health insurance and, hence, no (or limited) access to health care.

WHY THE RAPID RISE IN COSTS?

Simplifying somewhat, the rising prices and costs of health care services are the result of demand increasing much more quickly than supply. We will examine the reasons for this in some detail. But first we need to highlight certain characteristics of the health care market.

Peculiarities of the Health Care Market

We know that purely competitive markets achieve both allocative and productive efficiency—the most desired products are produced in the least costly way. We also found that many imperfectly competitive markets—perhaps aided by regulation or the threat of antitrust action—provide outcomes generally accepted as efficient. What then are the special features of the health care market which have contributed to rising prices and thus escalating costs to buyers?

1. *Ethical and equity considerations* When buying and selling decisions involve the quality of human life—indeed, life or death—ethical questions inevitably intervene. While we might not consider it immoral or unfair if a person cannot buy a Lincoln Town Car or a personal computer, society does regard it as unjust for people to be denied access to basic health care. In general, society regards health care as an "entitlement" or a "right" and is reluctant to ration it solely by price and income.

2. *Asymmetric information* Health care buyers typically have little or no understanding of complex diagnostic and treatment procedures, while health care sellers of those procedures—the physicians—possess detailed information. This creates the unusual situation in which the doctor (supplier) as the agent of the patient (consumer) tells the patient what health care services he or she should consume. We will say more about this shortly.

3. *Spillover benefits* The medical care market often generates external or spillover benefits—benefits to third parties. For example, an immunization against polio, smallpox, or measles benefits the immediate purchaser. But it also benefits society because it reduces the risk that other members of society will be infected with a highly contagious disease. Similarly, a healthy labor force is more productive, contributing to the general prosperity and well-being of society.

4. *Third-party payments: insurance* Because about three-fourths of all health care expenses are paid through public or private insurance, health care consumers directly pay much lower out-of-pocket "prices" than they would otherwise. These lower prices are a distortion which results in "excess" consumption of health care services.

The Increasing Demand for Health Care

With these four features in mind, let's consider some factors which have increased the demand for health care over time.

Rising Incomes: The Role of Elasticities
Health care is a normal good and therefore increases in domestic income have resulted in increases in the demand for health care. While there is some disagreement as to the exact *income* elasticity of demand for health care, several studies for industrially advanced countries suggest that the income elasticity coefficient is about $+1.0$. This means that per capita health care spending rises approximately in proportion to increases in per capita income (see Global Perspective

35-1). For example, a 3 percent increase in incomes will generate a 3 percent increase in health care expenditures.

Estimates of the *price* elasticity of demand for health care suggest it is quite inelastic, with this coefficient being as low as 0.2. This means that the quantity of health care consumed declines relatively little as price increases. For example, a 10 percent increase in price would reduce quantity demanded by only 2 percent. An important consequence is that total health care spending will increase as the price of health care rises.

The relative insensitivity of health care spending to price changes results from four factors. First, people consider health care a necessity, not a luxury. There are few, if any, good substitutes for medical care in treating injuries and infections and alleviating various ailments. Second, medical treatment is often provided in an emergency situation in which price considerations are secondary or irrelevant. Third, most consumers prefer a long-term relationship with their doctors and therefore do not "shop around" when health care prices rise. Fourth, most patients have insurance and are therefore not directly affected by the price of health care. If insured patients pay only, for example, 20 percent of their health care expenses, they are less concerned with price increases or price differences between hospitals and between doctors than they would be if they paid 100 percent themselves. **(Key Question 7)**

An Aging Population

The U.S. population is aging. People 65 years of age and older constituted approximately 9 percent of the population in 1960 but almost 13 percent by 1997. Projections for the year 2030 indicate 20 percent of the population will be 65 or over.

This aging of the population affects the demand for health care because older people encounter more frequent and more prolonged spells of illness. Specifically, those 65 and older consume about three and one-half times as much health care as those between 19 and 64. In turn, people over 84 consume almost two and one-half times as much health care as those in the 65 to 69 age group. Health care expenditures are often extraordinarily high in the last year of one's life.

Looking ahead, in 2011 the baby boomers—the 76 million people born between 1946 and 1964—will begin turning 65. We can expect this to create a substantial surge in the demand for health care.

Unhealthy Lifestyles

Substance abuse helps drive up health care costs. The abuse of alcohol, tobacco, and illicit drugs damages health and is therefore an important component of the demand for health care services. Alcohol is a major cause of injury-producing traffic accidents and liver disease. An estimated 25 to 40 percent of all general-hospital patients are there because of complications relating to alcoholism. Tobacco use markedly increases the probability of cancer, heart disease, bronchitis, and emphysema. Illicit drugs are a major contributor to violent crime, health problems in infants, and the spread of AIDS. In addition, illicit drug users make more than 370,000 costly visits to hospital emergency rooms each year.[1]

Other unhealthy behaviors also contribute to high health care costs. A 1996 Transportation Department study found that auto crash victims who did not buckle up incurred about $5000 more of health care expenses than buckled-up victims. Failure to wear seat belts contributed an additional $68 million of health care expense in just the seven states studied.

The Role of Doctors

Physicians may increase health care demand several ways.

Supplier-Induced Demand

We mentioned previously that doctors, the *suppliers* of medical services, have much more information about those services than consumers, who are the *demanders*. While a patient might be well informed about hamburgers or more complex products such as computers, he or she is not likely to be well informed about diagnostic tests such as magnetic resonance imaging or medical procedures such as joint replacements. Because of this *asymmetric information*—that is, imbalance of information—the supplier, not the demander, decides the types and amounts of health care to be consumed. This situation creates a possibility of "supplier-induced demand."

This becomes especially relevant when doctors are paid on a **fee-for-service** basis, that is, paid separately for each service they perform. In light of the asymmetric information and fee-for-service arrangement, doctors have an opportunity and incentive to oversuggest health care services (just as an auto repair shop has an opportunity and incentive to recommend replacement of parts which are worn but still working).

---

[1] *Substance Abuse: The Nation's Number One Health Problem*, prepared by the Institute of Health Policy, Brandeis University, for the Robert Wood Johnson Foundation, Princeton, NJ, 1993.

More surgery is performed in the United States, where many doctors are paid a fee for each operation, than in foreign countries, where doctors are often paid annual salaries unrelated to the number of operations they perform. Furthermore, a recent study concludes that doctors who own x-ray or ultrasound machines do 4 to $4\frac{1}{2}$ times as many tests as doctors who refer their patients to radiologists. More generally, studies suggest that up to one-third of common medical tests and procedures are either inappropriate or of questionable value.

This control of consumption decisions by the seller has another result: It eliminates much of the power buyers might have in controlling the growth of health care prices and spending.

Defensive Medicine   "Become a doctor and support a lawyer," says a bumper sticker. The number of medical malpractice lawsuits is high. Today, every patient represents not only a need for medical care but also a possible malpractice suit. As a result, physicians tend to practice *defensive medicine*. That is, they recommend more tests and procedures than warranted medically or economically, to protect themselves against malpractice suits.

Medical Ethics   Medical ethics may drive up the demand for health care in two ways: First, doctors are ethically committed to use "best-practice" techniques in serving their patients. This often means the use of costly medical procedures which may be of only marginal benefit to patients.

Second, public values seem to support the medical ethic that human life should be sustained as long as possible. This makes it difficult to confront the notion that health care is provided with scarce resources and therefore must be rationed like any other good. Can society afford to provide $5000-per-day intensive care to a comatose patient unlikely to be restored to reasonable health? Prevailing public priorities seem to indicate that such care should be provided, and this again increases the demand for health care.

Role of Health Insurance

We noted in Figure 35-1 that three-fourths of health care spending is done not by health care consumers through direct out-of-pocket payments but by private health insurance companies or government through Medicare and Medicaid.

Individuals and families are faced with potentially devastating monetary losses from a variety of hazards. Your house might burn down; you may be in an auto accident; or you may suffer a serious illness. An insurance program is a means of protection against the huge monetary losses which can result from such hazards. A number of people agree to pay certain amounts (premiums) periodically in return for the guarantee that they will be compensated if they should incur a particular misfortune. Insurance is a means by which one pays a relatively small known cost for protection against an uncertain and much larger cost. While health insurance is in this way highly beneficial, we must also recognize that it contributes to rising costs and overconsumption of health care.

The Moral Hazard Problem   The *moral hazard problem* is the tendency of one party to an agreement to alter her or his behavior in a way which is costly to the other party. Health care insurance can change behavior in two ways. First, some insured people might be less careful about their health, taking fewer steps to prevent accident or illness. Second, insured individuals have greater incentives to use health care more intensively than they would if they did not have insurance. Let's consider both aspects of moral hazard.

Less Prevention   Health insurance may increase the demand for health care by encouraging behaviors which require more health care. Although most people with health care insurance are probably as careful about their health as those without insurance, some might be more inclined to smoke, avoid exercise, and eat unhealthy foods, knowing they have insurance. Similarly, some individuals may take up ski jumping or rodeo bull-riding if they have insurance covering the costs of orthopedic surgeons. And if their insurance covers rehabilitation programs, some people might be more inclined to experiment with alcohol or drugs.

Overconsumption   Insured people go to doctors more often and request more diagnostic tests and more complex treatments than they would if they were uninsured because, with health insurance, the price or opportunity cost of consuming health care is minimal. For example, many individuals with private insurance pay a fixed premium for coverage, and beyond that, aside from a modest deductible, their health care is "free." This differs from most markets in which the price to the consumer reflects the full opportunity cost of each unit of the good or service. In all markets, price provides a direct economic incentive to restrict use of the product. The minimal direct price to the insured consumer of health care, in contrast, creates an incentive to overuse the health care system. Of course, the penalty for overuse will ultimately show up in higher insurance premiums, but these will be shared by all policyholders. The cost increase for the individual health consumer will be relatively small.

Also, the availability of insurance removes the consumer's *budget restraint* when he or she decides to consume health care. Recall from Chapter 21 that budget restraints limit the purchases of most products. But insured patients face minimal or no out-of-pocket expenditures at the time they purchase health care. Affordability is not the issue, and the result is that health care is overconsumed.

Government Tax Subsidy Federal tax policy toward employer-financed health insurance works as a **tax subsidy** which strengthens the demand for health care services. Specifically, employees do not pay Federal income or payroll tax (social security) on the value of the health insurance they receive as an employee benefit. Employees thus request and receive more of their total compensation as *nontaxed* health care benefits and less in *taxed* wages and salaries.

The government rationale for this tax treatment is that positive spillover benefits are associated with having a healthy, productive workforce. So it is appropriate to encourage health insurance for workers. The tax break *does* enable more of the population to have health insurance, but it also contributes to greater consumption of health care. Combined with other factors, the tax break results in an overconsumption of health care.

To illustrate: If the marginal tax rate is, say, 28 percent, $1 worth of health insurance is equivalent to 72 cents in after-tax pay. Because the worker can get more insurance for $1 than for 72 cents, the exclusion of health insurance from taxation increases purchases of health insurance, thus increasing the demand for health care. In essence, the 28 cent difference acts as a government subsidy to health care. One recent estimate suggests that this subsidy costs the Federal government $65 billion per year in forgone tax revenue and boosts private health insurance spending by about one-third. Actual health care spending may be 10 to 20 percent higher than otherwise because of the subsidy.

Graphical Portrayal A simple demand and supply model illustrates the effect of health insurance on the health care market. Figure 35-3a depicts a competitive market for health care services; curve D shows the demand for health care services if all consumers were *uninsured*, and S represents the supply of health care. At market price P_u the equilibrium quantity of health care is Q_u.

Recall from our theory of competitive markets that output Q_u results in allocative efficiency, which means there is no better alternative use for the resources allocated to producing that level of health care. To see what we mean by "no better use," we must realize that:

1. As we move down along demand curve D, each succeeding point indicates, via the price it represents, the marginal benefit which consumers receive from that unit.

2. The supply curve is the producers' marginal-cost curve. As we move up along the supply curve, each succeeding point indicates the marginal cost of that unit of health care.

(a) Without health insurance

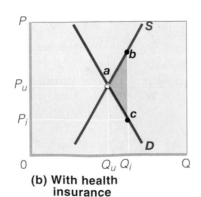

(b) With health insurance

FIGURE 35-3 Insurance and the overallocation of resources to health care (a) Without health insurance, the optimal amount of health care consumed is Q_u, where the marginal benefit and marginal cost of health care are equal. (b) The availability of private and public insurance reduces the direct price of health care from P_u to P_i, resulting in its overconsumption (Q_i rather than Q_u) and an overallocation of resources to the health care industry. Area *abc* represents the efficiency loss from this overallocation.

3. For each unit produced up to the equilibrium quantity Q_u, marginal benefit exceeds marginal cost (because points on D are above those on S). At Q_u marginal benefit equals marginal cost, designating allocative efficiency. No matter what else those resources could have produced, the greatest net benefit to society is obtained by using those resources to produce Q_u units of health care.

But allocative efficiency occurs only when we pay in full for a product, as is assumed in Figure 35-3a. What happens when we introduce health insurance which covers, say, one-half of all health care costs? In Figure 35-3b, with health insurance paying half the price, the consumer in effect is confronted with price $P_i (= \frac{1}{2}P_u)$. The health care consumer reacts by purchasing Q_i units rather than just Q_u. This is economically inefficient because between Q_u and Q_i each unit's marginal cost to society (on curve S) exceeds its marginal benefit (on curve D). Each unit of health care between Q_u and Q_i reflects an overallocation of resources to health care. The total efficiency loss is represented by area abc. Because health insurance typically covers 80, not just 50, percent of health care costs, the efficiency loss in Figure 35-3b understates the actual efficiency loss to society. On the other hand, this loss may not be as large as the 80 percent figure would imply because of the positive spillovers associated with health care.[2]

Figure 35-3b implies there is a tradeoff between efficiency and equity. Standards of fairness or equity in the United States lead people to believe all citizens should have access to basic health care, which is why government created social insurance in the form of Medicare and Medicaid. Also, it helps explain the Federal tax subsidy to private health insurance. Again, this makes health care more accessible. The problem, as Figure 35-3b shows, is that the greater the availability of insurance (and thus the more equitable society makes access to health care), the greater the overallocation of resources to the health care industry. This overallocation would be even greater if health care were provided completely "free" under a program of national health insurance. Consumers would purchase health care as long as the marginal benefit to themselves as individuals was positive, regardless of the true cost to society. **(Key Question 10)**

---

[2]Technical footnote: There is no shortage at price P_i in Figure 35-3b. Insurance reduces the direct cost of health care to the insured, so the supply curve in effect shifts rightward (not shown) and intersects demand at point c.

Supply Factors in Rising Health Care Prices

Supply factors have also played a role in rising health care prices. Specifically, the supply of health care services has increased, but more slowly than demand. A combination of factors has produced this relatively slow growth of supply.

Physician Supply The supply of physicians in the United States has increased over the years; in 1975 there were 169 physicians per 100,000 people; by 1995 there were 243. But this increase in supply has not kept up with the increase in the demand for physicians' services. As a result, physicians' fees and incomes have increased more rapidly than average prices and incomes for the economy as a whole.

Conventional wisdom has been that physician groups—for example, the American Medical Association—have purposely kept admissions to medical schools, and therefore the supply of doctors, artificially low. But there is more to the story than that. A rapidly rising cost of medical education seems to be the main cause of the relatively slow growth of doctor supply. Medical training requires 4 years of college, 4 years of medical school, an internship, and perhaps 3 or 4 years of training in a medical specialty. The opportunity cost of this education has increased because the salaries of similarly capable people have soared in other professions. The direct expenses have also increased, largely due to the increasingly sophisticated levels of medical care and therefore of medical training.

High and rising education and training costs have necessitated high and rising doctors' fees to ensure an adequate return on this sort of investment in human capital. Physicians' incomes are indeed high, averaging $180,000 in 1996, but so too are the costs of obtaining the skills necessary to become a physician. Recent data show that while doctors have high rates of return on their educational expenses, these returns are below those for lawyers and holders of masters of business administration degrees.

Slow Productivity Growth Productivity growth in an industry tends to reduce costs and increase supply. In the health care industry, such productivity growth has been modest. One reason is that health care is a service, and it is generally more difficult to increase productivity for services than for goods. How, for example, would you significantly increase the productivity of nursing-home employees?

Also, competition for patients among many providers of health care has not been sufficiently brisk to force them to look for ways to reduce cost by increasing productivity. When buying most goods, customers typically shop around for the lowest price. This shopping requires that sellers keep their prices low and look to productivity increases to maintain or expand their profits. But patients rarely shop for the lowest prices when seeking medical care. A patient may feel uncomfortable being operated on by a physician who charges the lowest price. In addition, if insurance pays for the surgery, there is no reason to consider price at all. The point is that unusual features of the market for health care limit competitive pricing and thus reduce incentives to achieve cost saving via productivity advance.

Changes in Medical Technology Some technological advances in medicine have decreased costs. For example, the development of vaccines for polio, smallpox, and measles have greatly reduced health care expenditures for the treatment of those diseases.

But many medical technologies developed since World War II have greatly increased the cost of medical care either by increasing prices or extending procedures to a greater number of people. For example, because they give more accurate information, advanced body scanners costing up to $2500 per scan are often used in place of x-rays that cost less than $100 each. Fearful of becoming technologically obsolete, hospitals want to offer the latest equipment and procedures. These newer, more expensive treatments are surely more effective than older ones. But doctors and hospital administrators both realize that the high cost of such equipment means it must be used extensively.

As another example, organ transplants are extremely costly. Before the development of this technology, a person with a serious liver malfunction died. Now a liver transplant can cost $200,000 or more, with subsequent medical attention costing $10,000 to $20,000 per year for the patient's entire life.

The historical willingness of private and public insurance to pay for new treatments without regard to price and number of patients has contributed to the incentive to develop and use new technologies. Insurers, in effect, have encouraged research into and development of health care technologies, regardless of their cost. Recently, when insurance companies resisted paying for new expensive treatments such as bone marrow transplants, public outcries led them to change their minds. So expanding insurance coverage leads to new, often more expensive medical technologies, and these technologies, in turn, lead to a demand for a wider definition of what should be covered by insurance. Example: After expensive magnetic resonance imaging (MRI) scans were developed, doctors and their patients demanded that such scans be covered under Medicare. After the government agreed to such coverage in 1985, sales of MRI machines rose very dramatically.

Relative Importance

According to most analysts, the demand and supply factors we have discussed vary significantly in their impact on escalating health care costs. Rising income does not alone explain the rocketing increase in health care spending as a percentage of total domestic output (income). As we noted, the income elasticity of demand for health care is estimated to be +1.0, meaning that increased income brings with it only proportionate increases in health care spending. Furthermore, government studies estimate that the aging population accounts for only about 5 percent of the current increase in per capita health care spending.

Most experts attribute the relative rise in health care spending to (1) advances in medical technology, combined with (2) the medical ethic of providing the best treatment available, (3) private and public health insurance, and (4) fee-for-service physicians' payments by health insurance firms. Through technological progress, great strides have been made in the diagnosis, treatment, and prevention of illness. But the third-party (insurance) payment system provides little incentive to limit the development or use of such technologies because it has no mechanism to force an equating of marginal costs and marginal benefits. And the "best treatment available" ethic, together with the fee-for-service payment system, ensures that any new technology with a positive marginal benefit will get used and be billed for, regardless of the marginal cost to society.

QUICK REVIEW 35-2

■ Characteristics of the health care market are **(a)** the widespread view of health care as a "right," **(b)** asymmetric information between consumers and suppliers, **(c)** the presence of spillover benefits, and **(d)** payment mostly by insurance.

■ The demand for health care has increased for many reasons, including rising incomes, an aging population, unhealthy lifestyles, the role of doctors as advisers to patients, the practice of defensive medicine, and a fee-for-service payment system via health insurance.

■ The supply of health care has grown slowly primarily because of **(a)** relatively slow productivity growth in the health care industry, **(b)** rising costs of medical education and training, and **(c)** greater use of very high cost health care technologies.

HEALTH CARE SYSTEM REFORM

What, if anything, can be done to increase access to the health care system? And how might health care costs be contained? Reform of the health care system to achieve these two goals will be difficult. First, there is a tradeoff between the two objectives: Greater access to the system will mean rising costs. Second, health care reform is complex because expectations (for example, access to the "best" medical care), tradition (the "right" to choose one's doctor), and the goals of self-interest groups (private insurers, drug companies, physicians, and hospitals) all come into play.

This latter point is especially significant. No rearrangement of costs and benefits in an industry which accounts for almost one-seventh of total U.S. spending will be accepted passively by the numerous affected interest groups. Physicians, hospitals, health insurers, and drug companies seek to prevent price controls on their services and products. Older people—represented by the American Association of Retired Persons—want government to pay a larger portion of long-term (nursing home) health care. Health insurance companies hope their business will not be curtailed by reforms. Labor unions advocate a generous basic-benefits package and oppose taxation of employer-financed health insurance. Psychiatrists, physical therapists, acupuncturists, and chiropractors want their services included in any new proposal. Trial lawyers want existing malpractice laws left alone. Small businesses strongly oppose any law requiring *all* companies to provide health insurance for their employees. The liquor and tobacco industries do not want additional "sin" taxes levied on them to help finance any reform proposal.

Universal Access

How can health care—or, more specifically, health care insurance—be made available to all U.S. citizens? Let's briefly consider three proposals.

"Play or Pay" Because much of the nation's health insurance is paid by employers, one way is to expand that coverage using a **play-or-pay** approach. *All* employers would be required to either provide a basic health insurance program for their workers and their dependents ("play") or pay a special payroll tax to finance health insurance for uninsured workers ("pay"). People not insured because they are not in the labor force would be covered by some form of publicly sponsored health care plan.

Such proposals, however, would likely lead to lower real wages. Also, unemployment might increase in firms currently paying wages at or near the minimum wage.

Tax Credits and Vouchers Another approach, using tax credits and vouchers, would help the poor pay for health insurance. A tax credit would be provided for low-income individuals and families—perhaps $1500 for a single person and $4000 for a family of four—to be used for purchasing health insurance. The size of the tax credit would diminish as the recipient's income rises. Those whose incomes are so low as to be exempt from the income tax would be issued a voucher for purchasing health insurance. This proposal is essentially a tax subsidy designed to make insurance more affordable to low-income people.

National Health Insurance (NHI) The most far-reaching and controversial proposal is to establish a system of **national health insurance** along the lines of the present Canadian system. The Federal government would provide a basic package of health care to every citizen at no direct charge or at a low cost-sharing level. The system would be financed out of tax revenues rather than insurance premiums.

NHI is *not* the same as socialized medicine. Under NHI the government would not own health care facilities such as hospitals, clinics, and nursing homes. Nor would health care practitioners—doctors, nurses, and technicians—be government employees. Under NHI government would simply sponsor and finance basic health care for all citizens. Although the role of private health insurers would be reduced under NHI, they could provide health insurance for any medical procedures not covered in the basic NHI health care package.

Arguments for NHI

1. It is the simplest and most direct way of providing universal access to health care.

2. It allows patients to choose their own physicians.

3. It would reduce administrative costs. The present system, it is argued, is administratively chaotic and expensive because hundreds of private health care insurers are involved, each with its own procedures and claim forms. Administration costs in the Canadian system are less than 5 percent of total health care costs compared with almost 17 percent in the United States.

4. It separates health care availability from employment and therefore would eliminate the use of part-time and temporary workers as a way to avoid providing health care insurance.

5. It would allow government to use its single-insurer market power to contain costs. Government could apply its buying power to mandate fees for various medical procedures and thus control physicians' and hospital costs. Hospitals would operate on budgets set by the government.

Arguments Against NHI

1. Government-determined price ceilings on physicians' services are not likely to control costs. Doctors can protect their incomes from fixed fees by manipulating the amount of care they provide a patient. Suppose the maximum fee for an office visit is $30. Doctors might spread a given number of diagnostic tests over three or four office visits, although the tests could be done in one visit. Or a doctor might require an office visit to explain test results instead of phoning the patient. Similar arguments apply to government regulation of hospital charges.

2. In the Canadian system patients often have long waits for certain diagnostic procedures and surgeries. This is the result of the Canadian government's effort to control expenditures by restricting hospitals' capital spending. To illustrate, there are only one-fifth as many magnetic resonance imaging machines (MRIs) per million population in Canada as in the United States. This results in a waiting list for use of MRIs in Canada. NHI might strongly conflict with U.S. expectations of medical care "on demand."

3. The Federal government has a very poor record of containing costs. Despite its considerable buying power, the Department of Defense, for example, has a long history of cost overruns and mismanagement. And, as you have seen, spending has spiraled upward under the government's Medicare and Medicaid programs. Also recall

(Figure 35-3b) that insurance is a critical factor in the overconsumption of health care. Under NHI a completely "free" basic health care package would prompt consumers to "purchase" health care as long as marginal benefits were positive, regardless of the true cost to society.

4. Subtle and perhaps undesirable redistributional effects would result under NHI. Under private health insurance, a particular health care insurance package costs the same regardless of the insured's income. This makes the cost of insurance resemble a regressive tax since low-income workers pay a larger percentage of their income for the insurance than do high-income insurees. If NHI were financed out of personal income tax revenues, this financing would be progressive. Under NHI those with low incomes would receive health insurance and pay little or none of the cost. While some might view this as desirable, others believe that income redistribution in the United States has been overdone and that further redistribution through NHI would be unfair. Depending on the type of tax and its size, employers and workers in industries such as automobile and steel might receive windfalls in the form of higher profits and wages when their health insurance programs were replaced by NHI. Employers and workers in small retail establishments and fast-food restaurants, where health insurance is typically absent, might not realize such gains.

Cost Containment: Altering Incentives

Can the United States control the growth of health care costs, prices, and spending by reducing incentives to overconsume health care?

Deductibles and Copayments Insurance companies have reacted to rising health care costs by imposing sizable *deductibles* and *copayments* on those they insure. Instead of covering all of an insuree's medical costs, a policy might now specify that the insuree pay the first $250 or $500 of each year's health care costs (the deductible) and 15 or 20 percent of all additional costs (the copayment). The deductible and copayment are intended to alleviate the overuse problem by creating a direct payment and therefore an opportunity cost to the health care consumer. The deductible has the added advantage of reducing the administra-

A Market for Human Organs?

A market might eliminate the present shortage of human organs for transplant. But there are many serious objections to turning human body parts into commodities for purchase and sale.

Advances in medical technology make it possible for surgeons to replace some human body parts with donated "used parts," much like a backyard mechanic might replace a worn out alternator in an automobile with one from a junked vehicle. It has become increasingly commonplace in medicine to transplant kidneys, lungs, livers, eye corneas, pancreases, and hearts from deceased individuals to those whose organs have failed or are failing. But surgeons and many of their patients face a growing problem: There are shortages of donated organs available for transplant. Not everyone who needs a transplant can get one.

Why Shortages?   Seldom, if ever, do we hear of shortages of used auto parts such as alternators, batteries, transmissions, or water pumps. What is different about organs for transplant? One difference is that there is a market for used auto parts but not for human organs. To understand this situation, observe the demand curve D_1 and supply curve S_1 in the accompanying figure. The downward slope of the demand curve tells us that if there were a market for human organs, the quantity of organs demanded would be greater at lower prices than at higher prices. Perfectly inelastic supply curve S_1 represents the

fixed quantity of human organs now donated via consent before death. Because the price of these donated organs is in effect zero, quantity demanded Q_3 exceeds quantity supplied Q_1. The shortage of $Q_3 - Q_1$ is rationed through a waiting list of those in medical need of transplants. Many people die while still on the waiting list.

Use of a Market   A market for human organs would increase the incentive to donate organs. Such a market might work like this: An individual might specify in a legal document that he or she is willing to sell one or more usable human organs upon death. The person could specify where

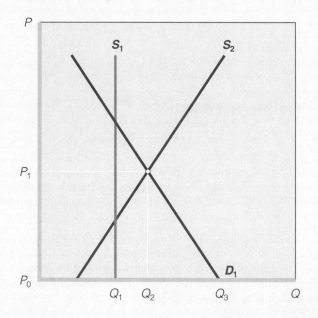

tive costs of insurance companies in processing many small claims.

Managed Care   *Managed-care organizations* (or systems) are those in which medical services are controlled or coordinated by insurance companies or health care organizations to reduce health care expenditures. In 1996 about three-fifths of all U.S. workers received health care through such "managed care." These organizations are of two main types:

1. *Preferred provider organizations (PPOs)*   Some insurance companies have set up **preferred**

provider organizations, which require hospitals and physicians to provide discounted prices for their services as a condition for being included in the insurance plan. The policyholder receives a list of participating hospitals and doctors and is given, say, 80 to 100 percent reimbursement of health care costs when treated by PPO physicians and hospitals. The insurance company reimburses only 60 to 70 percent if a patient chooses a doctor or hospital outside the PPO. In return for being included as a PPO provider, doctors and hospitals agree to rates set by the insurance company the money from the sale would go, for example, to family, a church, an educational institution, or a charity. Firms would then emerge to purchase organs and resell them where needed for profit. Under such a system, the supply curve of usable organs would take on the normal upward slope of typical supply curves. The higher the expected price of an organ, the greater the number of people willing to have their organs sold at death. Suppose that the supply curve is S_2 in the figure. At the equilibrium price P_1, the number of organs made available for transplant (Q_2) would equal the number purchased for transplant (also Q_2). In this generalized case, the shortage of organs would be eliminated and, of particular importance, the number of organs available for transplanting would rise from Q_1 to Q_2. This means more lives would be saved and enhanced than is the case under the present donor system.

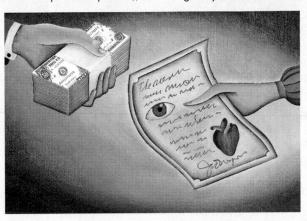

Objections In view of this positive outcome, why is there no such market for human organs? There are several reasons. The first is a *moral objection:* Many people feel that turning human organs into commodities commercializes human beings and diminishes the special nature of human life. Critics say there is something unseemly about selling and buying body organs as if they were bushels of wheat or ounces of gold. (There is, however, a market for blood!) Moreover, critics note that the market would ration the available organs (as represented by Q_2 in the figure) to people who either can afford them (at P_1) or have health insurance for transplants.

Another reason is based on an *analytical critique:* The elasticity of the supply of human organs may not be as great as shown. Although a market price would most likely increase the number of potential organ "donors," it may not greatly increase the actual number of usable organs available for transplants. The full $Q_1 Q_2$ increase in organs shown in the figure thus may not occur. That quantity response is determined both by the number of people providing consent *and* the untimely death rate of those individuals. Critics point out that this death rate does not increase along with market price.

Finally, a *health-cost concern* suggests that a market for body organs would greatly increase the cost of health care. Rather than obtaining freely donated (although "too few") body organs, patients or their insurance companies would have to pay market prices for them, further increasing the cost of medical care. Moreover, as transplant procedures are further perfected, the demand for transplants is expected to greatly increase. Rapid increases in demand relative to supply would boost the prices of human organs and thus further contribute to the problem of escalating health care costs.

for each service. Because these fees are less than those usually charged, PPOs reduce health insurance premiums and health care expenditures.

2. *Health maintenance organizations (HMOs)* Many Americans now receive their medical care from **health maintenance organizations,** which provide health care services to a specific group of enrollees in exchange for a set annual fee per enrollee. HMOs employ their own physicians and contract for specialized services with outside providers and hospitals. They then contract with firms or government units to provide medical care for their workers, who thereby become HMO members.

Because HMOs have fixed annual revenue, they can lose money if they provide "too much" care. So they have an incentive to hold down costs. They also have an incentive to provide preventive care in order to reduce the far larger expense of corrective care.

Both PPOs and HMOs are managed-care organizations because medical use and spending are "managed" by close monitoring of physicians' and hospitals' behavior; the purpose is to eliminate unnecessary diagnostic tests and remedial treatments. Doctors in managed-care organizations might not order a CAT scan or an ultrasound test or suggest surgery because their work is monitored and because they may have a fixed budget. In contrast, an independent fee-for-service physician may face little or no control and have a financial incentive to order the test or do the surgery. Doctors and hospitals in a managed-care organization often share in an "incentive pool" of funds when they meet their cost-control goals.

The advantages of managed-care plans are that they provide health care at lower prices than traditional insurance and emphasize preventive medicine. The disadvantages are that the patient usually is restricted to physicians employed by or under contract with the managed-care plan. Also, patients sometimes must wait to get certain tests and procedures done, particularly under HMOs. Finally, critics are concerned that the focus on reducing costs could go too far; it might result in denial of highly expensive, but effective, treatment and thus produce inferior medical care.

Medicare and DRG In 1983 the Federal government altered the way it makes payments for hospital services received by Medicare patients. Rather than automatically paying all costs related to a patient's treatment and length of hospital stay, Medicare submitted payments based on a **diagnosis-related-group (DRG) system.** Under DRG a hospital receives a fixed payment for treating each patient; that payment is an amount associated with the one of several hundred carefully detailed diagnostic categories which best characterize the patient's condition and needs.

DRG-system payments obviously give hospitals the incentive to restrict the amount of resources used in treating patients. It is no surprise that under DRG the length of hospital stays has fallen sharply and more patients are treated on an outpatient basis. Critics, however, argue that this is evidence of diminished quality of medical care.

Status Report on Health Care Reform

In October 1993 the Clinton administration proposed to Congress a major health care reform. A primary feature of this Health Security Act (HSA) was *universal insurance coverage* for a standard package of health care benefits, to be realized through *employer mandates* which would have obligated all employers to provide

health insurance for their workers. The unemployed and those not in the labor force were to obtain insurance through *regional health alliances* established by each state as either a government agency or a non-profit organization.

But HSA was heavily criticized for its complexity and because it would create new, costly government bureaucracies. It also was criticized on the grounds that the employer mandates were a costly intrusion on the private sector. After extended and often rancorous debate, Congress rejected the Clinton plan.

Since HSA's defeat, Congress has sought to make more modest changes in the nation's health care system. One such reform occurred in 1996 when Congress passed the Health Insurance Portability and Accountability Act. This law ensures that workers with a group health plan can continue to buy health insurance when they change their jobs or become self-employed, even if they have major health problems. It also prohibits group insurance plans from dropping coverage of a sick employee or of a business which has a sick employee.

The 1996 legislation introduced, on a trial basis, *medical saving accounts (MSAs)* for small businesses, the self-employed, and the uninsured. Consumers can make tax-deductible contributions into these accounts, which include a catastrophic health insurance plan for large medical expenses. Earnings on the funds in the account are tax-free, and the money in the account can be used to pay routine medical expenses. Unused funds continue to grow from year to year. Withdrawals for non-medical purposes are permitted but taxed as income.

MSAs are highly controversial. On the positive side, they encourage people to stay healthy and use funds in their medical account sparingly. This could decrease health care spending. But critics say that such accounts pull the healthiest and wealthiest people away from the general health insurance market, potentially raising premiums for others.

The importance of health care issues ensures their continued attention. New reform, however, is likely to be piecemeal, not massive. Meanwhile, the health care system is changing on its own. In particular, the growth of managed-care organizations (PPOs and HMOs) has transformed the medical care industry into one dominated by large insurance and health care firms rather than by individual health care providers (physicians, for example). The full impact of this trend on health care costs and health care quality remains to be determined.

CHAPTER SUMMARY

1. The U.S. health care industry comprises 9 million workers, including more than 600,000 physicians and more than 6000 hospitals.

2. Health care spending has been rising absolutely, as a percentage of GDP, and on a per capita basis.

3. Rising health care costs and prices have **(a)** reduced access to the health care system, **(b)** contributed to slower real wage growth and expanded the employment of part-time and temporary workers, and **(c)** caused governments to restrict spending on nonhealth programs and to raise taxes.

4. The core of the health care problem is an alleged overallocation of resources to the health care industry.

5. About 42 million Americans—about one-sixth of the population—do not have health insurance. The uninsured are concentrated among the poor, the chronically ill, the unemployed, the young, those employed by small firms, and low-wage workers.

6. Special characteristics of the health care market include **(a)** the belief that health care is a "right," **(b)** an imbalance of information between consumers and suppliers, **(c)** the presence of spillover benefits, and **(d)** the payment of most health care expenses by private or public insurance.

7. While rising incomes, an aging population, and substance abuse have all contributed to an increasing demand for health care, the role of doctors is also significant. Because of asymmetric information, physicians influence the demand for their own services. The fee-for-service payment system, combined with defensive medicine to protect against malpractice suits, also increases demand for health care.

8. The moral hazard problem arising from health insurance takes two forms: **(a)** People may be less careful of their health, and **(b)** there is an incentive to overconsume health care.

9. The exemption of employer-paid health insurance from the Federal income tax subsidizes health care.

10. Slow productivity growth in the health care industry and, more important, cost-increasing advances in health care technology have restricted the expansion of the supply of medical care and boosted prices.

11. Reforms designed to increase access to the health care system include **(a)** "play-or-pay" proposals designed to increase employer-sponsored health insurance, **(b)** tax credits and vouchers to help low-income families afford health care, and **(c)** national health insurance.

12. Insurance companies have introduced deductibles and copayments in an attempt to contain health care prices and spending.

13. Managed-care organizations attempt to control their enrolled members' use of health care as a way of containing health care costs. In a preferred provider organization (PPO), a group of health providers agrees to provide services to a defined group of patients at an agreed-upon rate for each service. In a health maintenance organization (HMO), groups of workers prepay for health services at an agreed-upon annual rate. The HMO then provides services to the group, using its own physicians or physicians and hospitals under contract.

14. The Health Insurance Portability and Accountability Act of 1996 **(a)** ensures paid access to continuing health insurance to workers who change jobs or become self-employed, even if they have medical problems; **(b)** prohibits insurance firms from dropping coverage of workers or businesses which have high medical bills; and **(c)** establishes, on a trial basis, medical savings accounts.

TERMS AND CONCEPTS

deductibles	"play or pay"	health maintenance	diagnosis-related-group
copayments	national health insurance	organizations	system
fee for service	preferred provider		
tax subsidy	organizations		

STUDY QUESTIONS

1. Why would increased spending on, say, household appliances or television sets in a particular economy be regarded as economically desirable? Why, then, is there so much concern about rising expenditures on health care?

2. KEY QUESTION What are the "twin problems" of the health care industry as viewed by society? How are they related?

3. Briefly describe the main features of Medicare and Medicaid, indicating how each is financed.

4. What are the implications of rapidly rising health care prices and spending for **(a)** the growth of real wage rates and **(b)** government budgets? Explain.

5. Who are the main groups without health insurance?

6. List the special characteristics of the U.S. health care market, and specify how each affects health care problems.

7. KEY QUESTION What are the estimated income and price elasticities of demand for health care? How does each relate to rising health care costs?

8. Briefly discuss the demand and supply factors which contribute to rising health costs. Specify how **(a)** asymmetric information, **(b)** fee-for-service payments, **(c)** defensive medicine, and **(d)** medical ethics might cause health care costs to rise.

9. "Health care expenditures have been rising principally because of the technological transformation of medical care." Do you agree? Explain.

10. KEY QUESTION Using the concepts in Chapter 21's discussion of consumer behavior, explain how health care insurance results in an overallocation of resources to the health care industry. Use a demand and supply diagram to specify the resulting efficiency loss.

11. How is the moral hazard problem relevant to the health care market?

12. What is the rationale for exempting a firm's contribution to its workers' health insurance from taxation as worker income? What is the impact of this exemption on allocative efficiency in the health care industry?

13. Comment on or explain:

a. Providing health insurance to achieve equity goals creates a tradeoff with the efficient allocation of resources to the health care industry.

b. Improved health habits are desirable but would not necessarily reduce health care costs. For example, the deaths of many smokers are from sudden and lethal heart attacks and are therefore medically inexpensive.

c. If government were to require employer-sponsored health insurance for all workers, the likely result would be an increase in the unemployment of low-wage workers.

14. Briefly describe **(a)** "play or pay," **(b)** tax credits and vouchers, and **(c)** national health insurance as means of increasing access to health care. What are the major criticisms of national health insurance?

15. What are **(a)** preferred provider organizations and **(b)** health maintenance organizations? In your answer, explain how each is designed to alleviate the overconsumption of health care.

16. How successful have been government attempts to reform health care over the past decade?

17. (Last Word) Do you favor the establishment of a market for "donated" human organs? Why or why not?

18. WEB-BASED QUESTION Hospital Charges— What Is the Average Cost of a Visit to a Hospital Near You? The cost of health care is high and has increased rapidly. Visit the American Hospital Directory http://www.ahd.com/ and search for two hospitals near you. Compare their average charges and average length of stay. Which type of treatment averages the most, which the least? Are the figures for each hospital similar? Does this imply competition? Today could you afford an average heart operation at a hospital near you?

19. WEB-BASED QUESTION Medicare and AARP—What Is Their Opinion? The American Association of Retired Persons (AARP) is a national organization for people 50 and older. Visit the AARP Advocacy Center for Medicare http://www.aarp.org/monthly/medicare/home.htm and answer the following questions: What are the short- and long-run issues or problems with Medicare? Why is Medicare spending growing? How will we pay for Medicare when the baby boomers start to retire about 2011? Will you be able to receive Medicare when you retire? Do you sense any bias in AARP's Medicare position? Other viewpoints can be found at http://www.aarp.org/monthly/medicare3/viewhd.htm.

CHAPTER THIRTY-SIX

Labor Market Issues: Unionism, Discrimination, Immigration

36

In this chapter we examine three labor market issues: unionism, discrimination, and immigration. (Since these three topics are largely unrelated, instructors may choose to assign one or all of them, depending on time and preference.)

- The first part of the chapter looks at labor unions. We first see who belongs to unions, examine collective bargaining, and discuss the reasons for unionism's recent decline. Then we assess the effect of unions on wages, efficiency, and productivity.
- With regard to labor market discrimination, we discuss the types and costs of discrimination, economic theories of discrimination, and current antidiscrimination policies.
- The last part of the chapter examines immigration: the inflow of people (workers) to the United States from abroad. Here we focus on the size of both legal and illegal immigration and its economic effects.

UNIONISM IN AMERICA

About 17 million U.S. workers—16 percent of employed wage and salary workers—now belong to unions. (Global Perspective 36-1 compares this percentage with that of several other nations.) About 14 million of the 17 million U.S. union members belong to one of the many unions loosely and voluntarily affiliated with the **American Federation of Labor and Congress of Industrial Organizations** (AFL-CIO). Examples of AFL-CIO unions are the Teamsters, United Autoworkers, Communications Workers, and Carpenters. Another 3 million union workers belong to **independent unions** which are not affiliated

with the AFL-CIO. These include the National Education Association, the Nurses' Union, and the United Mine Workers.

Business Unionism

In the United States, unions generally have adhered to a philosophy of **business unionism**: unionism which is concerned with the practical short-run economic objectives of higher pay, shorter hours, and improved working conditions. They have not sponsored long-run idealistic schemes aimed at significantly modifying or overthrowing the capitalistic system. Nor have union members organized into a distinct political party, such as the "labor

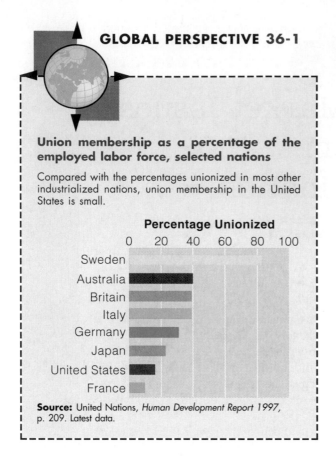

GLOBAL PERSPECTIVE 36-1

Union membership as a percentage of the employed labor force, selected nations

Compared with the percentages unionized in most other industrialized nations, union membership in the United States is small.

Percentage Unionized

Sweden
Australia
Britain
Italy
Germany
Japan
United States
France

Source: United Nations, *Human Development Report 1997*, p. 209. Latest data.

parties" of several European nations. Unionism's political philosophy has been to reward its friends and

punish its enemies at the polls, regardless of political party.

Union Membership

The likelihood that any particular worker will be a union member depends mainly on the industry in which the person works and the person's occupation. As shown in Figure 36-1a, the *rate of unionization* (percentage of workers unionized) is high in government, transportation, construction, manufacturing, and mining. The rate of unionization is very low in agriculture; finance, insurance, and real estate; wholesale and retail trade; and services. Figure 36-1b shows that unionism also varies greatly by occupation. Protective service workers, transportation workers, machine operators, and craft workers have high rates of unionization; sales workers and managers have very low rates.

Because disproportionately more men than women work in the industries and occupations with high unionization rates, men are more likely to be union members than women. Specifically, 19 percent of male wage and salary workers belong to unions compared with 13 percent of women. For the same reason, blacks have higher unionization rates than whites: 21 percent compared with 15 percent. Unionism in the United States is largely an urban phenomenon. Six heavily urbanized, heavily industrialized states—New York, California, Pennsylvania,

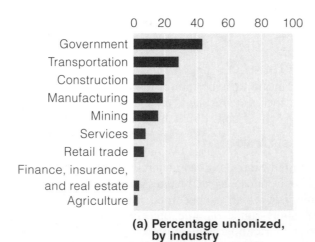

(a) Percentage unionized, by industry

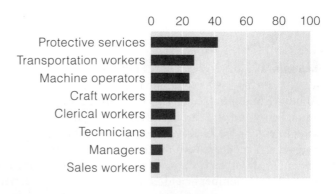

(b) Percentage unionized, by occupation

FIGURE 36-1 **Union membership as a percentage of employed wage and salary workers, selected industries and occupations, 1996** In percentage terms, union membership varies greatly by (a) industry and (b) occupation. (*Source: Employment and Earnings*, January 1997, p. 213.)

Illinois, Ohio, and Michigan—account for approximately half of all union members.

The Decline of Unionism

Since the mid-1950s, union membership has not kept pace with the growth of the labor force. While 25 percent of employed wage and salary workers belonged to unions in the mid-1950s, currently only about 16 percent are union members. In recent years, even the absolute number of union members has declined significantly. More than 22 million workers were unionized in 1980 but only about 17 million in 1997.

What explains the decline in unionization, relatively and absolutely?

Structural Changes The **structural-change hypothesis** says that changes unfavorable to expansion of union membership have occurred in both the economy and the labor force.

Employment patterns have shifted away from traditionally unionized industries. More specifically, U.S. domestic employment has moved away from manufactured goods (where unions have been strong) and toward services (where unions have been weak). Also, consumer demand in some cases has shifted toward foreign manufactured goods and away from goods produced by union labor in the United States. Increased foreign competition in several highly unionized manufacturing industries such as automobile and steel has reduced unionized workforces and, therefore, union membership.

Another factor in the decline in unionism is that an unusually high proportion of the increase in employment in recent years has been concentrated among women, youths, and part-time workers. These groups are allegedly difficult to organize into unions because they are less strongly attached to the labor force. Furthermore, the long-term trend of industry's shifting from the northeast and midwest, where unionism is "a way of life," to "hard-to-organize" areas of the south and southwest has reduced the growth of union membership.

An ironic possibility is that the relative decline of unionism may in part reflect the success unions have had in gaining a sizable wage advantage over nonunion workers in the United States. Confronted with high union wages, employers may have substituted machinery for workers, subcontracted more work to nonunion suppliers, opened nonunion plants in less industrialized areas, or shifted production of components to low-wage nations. All these actions reduce the employment of union workers and thus the level of union membership.

The success of unions in raising wages may have also raised prices of union-produced goods relative to the prices of goods produced by nonunion workers. If so, we would expect output and employment in lower-cost nonunion firms and industries to increase at the expense of output and employment in higher-cost union firms and industries.

Managerial Opposition Another view of unionism's decline is that intensified managerial opposition to unions has deterred union growth. In this **managerial-opposition hypothesis,** it is argued that the wage advantage union workers enjoy causes union firms to be less profitable than nonunion firms. The managements of nonunionized and unionized firms have therefore undertaken policies to oppose or dissuade unionization. One aggressive managerial strategy has been to employ labor-management consultants who specialize in mounting aggressive antiunion drives to dissuade workers from unionizing, or, alternatively, to persuade union workers to decertify (officially vote out) their union. Also, confronted with strikes by union workers, management has increasingly hired permanent strikebreakers to take the place of striking workers. These nonunion workers later vote to eliminate the union. A conciliatory strategy by management has been to improve working conditions and personnel policies. When management treats workers with dignity and respect, workers feel less need to join unions.

COLLECTIVE BARGAINING

Despite the decline of unionism, **collective bargaining**—the negotiation of labor contracts—remains an important feature of labor-management relations. The goal of collective bargaining is to establish a "work agreement" between the firm and the union.

The Work Agreement

Collective bargaining agreements (contracts) assume many forms. Some contracts are brief, taking up only 2 or 3 pages; others are lengthy and highly detailed, requiring 200 or 300 pages of print. Some agreements involve only a local union and a single plant; others set wages, hours, and working conditions for entire industries.

Typically, however, collective bargaining agreements cover several topics.

Union Status and Managerial Prerogatives

As for *union status*, the closed shop affords the union the greatest security. In a **closed shop,** a worker must be (or become) a member of the union before being hired. Under Federal labor law, such shops are illegal in industries other than transportation and construction. In contrast, a **union shop** permits the employer to hire nonunion workers but provides that these workers must join the union within a specified period, say, 30 days, or relinquish their jobs. An **agency shop** requires nonunion workers to pay union dues or donate an equivalent amount to charity. Union and agency shops are legal, except in the 20 states which expressly prohibit them through so-called **right-to-work laws.** In the **open shop,** an employer may hire union or nonunion workers. Those who are nonunion are not obligated to join the union or pay union dues; they may continue on their jobs indefinitely as nonunion workers. Nevertheless, the wage, hours, and working conditions set forth in the work agreement apply to the nonunion workers as well as the union workers.

The management side of the union-status issue is *managerial prerogatives.* Most work agreements contain clauses outlining certain decisions reserved solely for management. These prerogatives usually cover such matters as size and location of plants, products to be manufactured, types of equipment and materials to be used in production and in production scheduling.

Wages and Hours

The focal point of any bargaining agreement is wages and hours. Both labor and management press for the advantage in wage bargaining. The arguments which unions use most frequently in demanding (and by the firm in resisting) wage boosts are (1) "what others are getting," (2) the employer's ability to pay, based on its profitability, (3) increases in the cost of living, and (4) increases in labor productivity. In some cases, unions achieve success in tying wages to the cost of living through *cost-of-living adjustment* (COLA) clauses.

Hours of work, voluntary versus mandatory overtime, holiday and vacation provisions, profit sharing, and fringe benefits—health plans and pension benefits—are other contract issues which must be addressed in the bargaining process.

Seniority and Job Protection

The uncertainty of employment in a market economy, along with the fear of antiunion discrimination on the part of employers, has made workers and their unions "job conscious." The explicit and detailed provisions covering job opportunities which most agreements contain reflect this concern. Unions stress seniority (length of service) as the basis for worker promotion and for layoff and recall. They want the worker with the longest continuous service to have the first chance at relevant promotions, be the last one laid off, and be the first one recalled from layoff.

In recent years, unions have become increasingly sensitive to losing jobs to nonunion subcontractors and to overseas workers. Unions sometimes seek limits on the firm's ability to subcontract out work or to relocate production facilities overseas.

Grievance Procedures

Even the most detailed and comprehensive work agreement cannot spell out all the specific issues and problems which might occur during its life. For example, suppose that Nelson gets reassigned to a less pleasant job. Was this reassignment for legitimate business reasons or, as Nelson suspects, because of a personality conflict with a particular manager? Labor contracts contain *grievance procedures* to resolve such matters.

The Bargaining Process

The date for the beginning of collective bargaining on a new contract is usually set in the existing contract and is usually 60 days before the current one expires. The union normally takes the initiative, presenting its *demands* in the form of specific wage, fringe-benefit, and other adjustments to the present union-management contract. The firm counters with an *offer* relating to these and other contract provisions. It is not unusual for the original union demand and the first offer by the firm to be far apart, not only because of the parties' conflicting interests but also because the parties know they are obligated by law to bargain in good faith. The initial "large demand–low offer situation" leaves plenty of room for compromise during the negotiations.

The negotiating then begins in earnest on items in dispute. Hanging over the negotiations is the *deadline,* which occurs the moment the present contract expires. At that time there is a possibility of a **strike**—a "work stoppage" by the union—if it thinks its demands are not satisfactorily met. But there is also the possibility that at that time the firm may engage in a **lockout,** in which it forbids the workers to return to work until a new contract is signed. In this setting of uncertainty prior to the deadline, both parties feel pressure to find mutually acceptable terms.

Although bluster and bickering often occur in collective bargaining, labor and management display a remarkable capacity for compromise and agreement. Typically they reach a compromise solution which is written into a new contract. Nevertheless, strikes and lockouts occasionally *do* occur. When they happen, workers lose income and firms lose profit. To stem their losses, both parties look for and usually eventually find ways to settle the labor dispute and get the workers back to work.

Bargaining, strikes, and lockouts occur within a framework of Federal labor law, specifically the **National Labor Relations Act** (NLRA). This act was first passed as the Wagner Act of 1935 and later amended by the Taft-Hartley Act of 1947 and the Landrum-Griffin Act of 1959. The act sets forth the dos and don'ts of union and management labor practices. For example, while union members can picket in front of a firm's business, they cannot block access to the business by customers, coworkers, or strikebreakers hired by the firm. As a second example, firms cannot refuse to meet and talk with the union's designated representatives.

Either unions or management can file charges of unfair labor practices under the labor law. The **National Labor Relations Board** (NLRB) has the authority to investigate these charges and to issue cease-and-desist orders in the event of violation. (The board also conducts worker elections to decide which specific union, if any, a group of workers might want to have represent them.)

QUICK REVIEW 36-1

■ About 14 million of the 17 million union workers in the United States are members of the AFL-CIO, with the rest belonging to independent unions.

■ The rate of unionization varies greatly by industry and occupation.

■ The decline of unionism in recent decades has been attributed to **(a)** changes in the structures of the economy and the labor force, and **(b)** growing managerial opposition to unions.

■ Collective bargaining determines the terms of work agreements, which typically cover **(a)** union status and

managerial prerogatives, **(b)** wages, hours, and working conditions, **(c)** control over job opportunities, and **(d)** grievance procedures.

ECONOMIC EFFECTS OF UNIONS

What effects do unions have on the economy? Do unions raise wages? Do they increase or diminish economic efficiency?

The Union Wage Advantage

The three union models in Chapter 28 (see Figures 28-5, 28-6, and 28-7 and the accompanying discussions) all imply that unions are capable of raising wages. Has unionization really done so?

Empirical research overwhelmingly suggests that unions do raise the wages of their members relative to those of comparable nonunion workers, although the size of the union wage advantage varies according to occupation, industry, race, and gender. The consensus estimate is that the overall union wage advantage is about 10 to 15 percent. On the other hand, unions have had little impact on the *average* level of real wages received by U.S. workers taken as a whole.

These two conclusions (higher union pay, no overall impact) may seem inconsistent, but they are not. The higher union wages apply to only a relatively small part of the labor force. Moreover, these wages may come at the expense of lower wages for some nonunion workers. As you will see (in Figure 36-2), higher wages in unionized labor markets may cause employers to hire fewer workers. The workers who are left unemployed may seek employment in nonunion labor markets. The resulting increase in the supply of labor in the nonunion labor markets reduces wage rates there. The net result may be no change in the average level of wages.

The long-run relationship between productivity and the average level of real wages shown previously in Figure 28-1 suggests that unions have little power to raise the average real wage over long periods of time. But Figure 28-1 is an average relationship; it is therefore compatible with the idea that certain groups of (union) workers get higher relative wages while other (nonunion) workers simultaneously get lower real wages.

Efficiency and Productivity

Do labor unions increase or decrease efficiency and productivity? There is much disagreement on this question, but we can consider some of the ways unions might affect efficiency, both negatively and positively.

Negative View

There are three ways unions might exert a negative impact on productivity and efficiency.

Losses via Featherbedding and Work Rules

Some unions undoubtedly have diminished efficiency by engaging in "make-work" or "featherbedding" practices and resisting the introduction of output-increasing machinery and equipment. These productivity-reducing practices often appear in periods of technological change. Historical examples: For many years the Brotherhood of Locomotive Firemen and Engineers retained a fireman on train crews, even though his function was eliminated by the shift from steam engines to diesel engines. Similarly, union painters resisted the use of spray guns and even limited the width of paintbrushes used on union jobs.

More generally, unions might reduce efficiency by establishing work rules and practices that impede putting the most productive workers in particular jobs. Under seniority rules, for example, workers may be promoted for their employment tenure rather than for their ability to perform the available job with the greatest efficiency. Also, unions might restrict the kinds of tasks workers may perform. Contract provisions may prohibit sheet-metal workers or bricklayers from doing the simple carpentry work often associated with their jobs. Observance of such rules means, in this instance, that firms must hire unneeded and underused carpenters. Finally, critics of unions contend that union contracts often chip away at managerial prerogatives to establish work schedules, determine production targets, introduce new technology, and make other decisions contributing to productive efficiency.

Losses via Strikes

A second way unions may adversely affect efficiency is through strikes. If union and management reach an impasse in their negotiations, a strike will result and the firm's production will cease for the strike's duration. The firm will forgo sales and profit; workers will sacrifice income; and the economy may lose output.

Statistics on U.S. strike activity suggests that strikes are rare and the associated aggregate economic losses are less than might be expected. In 1996, 411 major collective bargaining agreements (those covering 1000 or more employees) were negotiated. Strikes occurred in only 37 of these instances. Furthermore, many strikes last only a few days. The amount of work time lost each year because of strikes is the equivalent of 4 hours per U.S. worker per year, which is less than 5 minutes per worker per week.

However, the economic costs associated with strikes may be greater or less than is suggested by the amount of work time lost. The costs may be *greater* if strikes disrupt production in nonstruck firms which either provide inputs to or buy goods and services from the struck firm. Example: An extended strike in the auto industry might reduce output and cause layoffs in firms producing, say, glass, tires, paints, and fabrics used in producing cars. It may also reduce sales and cause layoffs in auto dealerships.

On the other hand, the costs of strikes may be *less* than is implied by the work time lost by strikers if nonstruck firms increase their output to offset the loss of production by struck firms. While the output of General Motors declines when its workers strike, auto buyers may shift their demand to Ford, Honda, or Chrysler, which will respond by increasing their employment and output. Thus, although GM and its employees are hurt by a strike, society as a whole may experience little or no decline in employment, real output, and income.

Losses via Labor Misallocation

A more subtle way in which unions might adversely affect efficiency is through the union wage advantage itself. Figure 36-2 shows (for simplicity) identical labor demand curves for a unionized sector and a nonunionized sector of the market for some particular kind of labor. We assume there is pure competition in both the product market and all resource markets.

If there were no union in either sector initially, the wage rate which would result from the competitive hiring of labor would be W_n, while N_1 workers would be hired in each sector. Now suppose workers form a union in sector 1 and succeed in increasing the wage rate from W_n to W_u. As a consequence, N_1N_2 workers lose their jobs in the union sector. Assume that they all move to nonunion sector 2, where they are employed. This increase in labor supply (not shown) in the nonunion sector increases the quantity of labor supplied there from N_1 to N_3, reducing the wage rate from W_n to W_s.

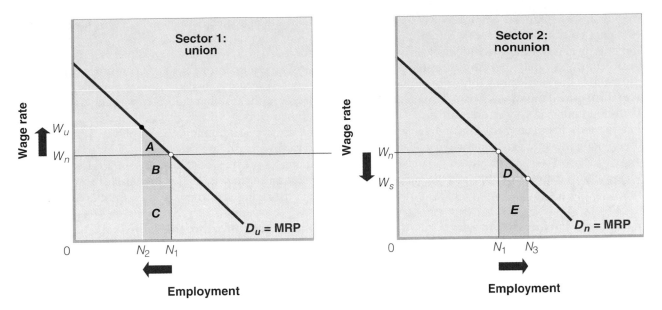

FIGURE 36-2 The effects of the union wage advantage on the allocation of labor   The higher wage W_u that the union receives in sector 1 causes the displacement of $N_1 N_2$ workers. The reemployment of these workers in sector 2 increases employment from N_1 to N_3 and reduces the wage rate there from W_n to W_s. The associated loss of output in the union sector is area $A + B + C$, while the gain in the nonunion sector is only $D + E$. The net loss of output is area B. This loss of output suggests that the union wage advantage has resulted in a misallocation of labor and a decline in economic efficiency.

Recall that the labor demand curves reflect the marginal revenue products (MRPs) of workers or, in other words, the contribution each additional worker makes to domestic output. This means that the area $A + B + C$ in the union sector represents the sum of the MRPs—the total contribution to domestic output—of the workers displaced by the wage increase achieved by the union. The reemployment of these workers in nonunion sector 2 results in an increase in domestic output indicated by the area $D + E$. Because the area $A + B + C$ exceeds area $D + E$, there is a net loss of domestic output. More precisely, because $A = D$ and $C = E$, the net loss attributable to the union wage advantage is represented by area B. Since the same amount of employed labor is now producing a smaller output, labor is being misallocated and inefficiently used.

From a slightly different perspective, after the shift of $N_1 N_2$ workers from the union sector to the nonunion sector has occurred, workers will be paid a wage rate equal to their MRPs in both sectors. But the workers who shifted sectors will be working at lower-MRP jobs after the shift. An economy always

obtains a larger domestic output when labor is reallocated from a low-MRP use to a high-MRP use. But here the opposite occurred. And assuming the union can maintain the W_u wage rate in its sector, a reallocation of labor from sector 2 to sector 1 will *never* occur.

Attempts to estimate the output loss associated with union wage gains, however, suggest the loss is small: perhaps 0.2 to 0.4 percent (or one-fifth of 1 percent to two-fifths of 1 percent) of domestic product. In 1997 this cost would be about $16 to $32 billion, or $60 to $120 per person. **(Key Question 4)**

Positive View   Other economists take the position that, on balance, unions make a positive contribution to efficiency and productivity.

Longer-Run Positive Impacts: The Shock Effect   A wage increase won by a union may have a *shock effect* on affected firms, causing them in the long run to substitute capital for labor and in the very long run to implement productivity-increasing technologies. When faced with higher production costs due to the union wage increase, employers will be motivated to reduce costs by using more machinery and by seeking improved production techniques which use less of both labor and capital per unit of output. In fact, if the product market is reasonably competitive, a unionized firm with labor costs 10 to 15 percent higher than nonunionized competitors will not survive over long periods unless productivity can be raised. Hence, union wage pressure may generate managerial actions which increase worker productivity and justify the higher union wages. If so, the overall economy benefits.

Reduced Worker Turnover Unions may also contribute to raising productivity within firms through reduced worker turnover and improved worker security. A union functions as a **collective voice** for its members by taking their side in resolving disputes and bettering working conditions.

If a group of workers are dissatisfied with their conditions of employment, they can respond in either of two ways: through the "exit mechanism" or through the "voice mechanism." With the **exit mechanism,** workers leave their present jobs in search of better ones as a way of reacting to undesirable employers and working conditions; it relies on the labor market. The use of this mechanism obviously increases *worker turnover*, which is the rate at which workers quit jobs and must be replaced.

The **voice mechanism** involves communication by workers with the employer to improve working conditions and resolve worker grievances. It might be risky for individual workers to express their dissatisfaction to employers because employers may retaliate by firing them as "troublemakers." But a union can provide workers with a collective voice to communicate problems and grievances to management and to press for satisfactory resolutions.

Unions may help reduce worker turnover in two ways:

1. Unions provide the voice mechanism as a substitute for the exit mechanism. They use communication to correct job dissatisfactions which otherwise would be "resolved" by workers through the exit mechanism of changing jobs.
2. The union wage advantage is a deterrent to job change. Higher wages make unionized firms more attractive places to work.

Compared with the rates at nonunion firms, the *quit rate* (resignation rate) for union workers is 31 to 65 percent lower, depending on the industry. A lower quit rate increases efficiency because it gives a firm a more experienced, and thus a more productive, workforce. Also, having fewer resignations reduces the firm's recruitment, screening, and hiring costs. Finally, reduced turnover makes employers more willing to invest in the training (and therefore the productivity) of their workers. If a worker quits or "exits" at the end of, say, a year's training, the employer will get no return from providing that training. But lower turnover increases the likelihood that the employer will receive a return on the training it provides, thereby increasing its willingness to upgrade its workforce.

Increased Informal Training Much productivity-increasing training is transmitted informally. Workers who are more skilled may share their experience with less skilled workers on the job, during lunch, or during coffee breaks. However, a more skilled senior worker may want to conceal his or her knowledge from less skilled junior workers, who might become competitors for the skilled worker's job. Because of union insistence on the use of seniority in such matters as promotion and layoff, worker security is enhanced and this problem is overcome. With this security, senior workers are more willing to pass on their job knowledge and skills to new or subordinate workers. This informal training enhances the quality and productivity of the firm's workforce.

Mixed Research Findings Many studies have tried to measure the effect of unionization on productivity, but their results are inconclusive. For every study which finds a positive union effect on productivity, another study using different methodology or data concludes there is a negative effect. At present there simply is no generally accepted conclusion regarding the overall impact of unions on productivity.

QUICK REVIEW 36-2

■ Union wages average about 10 to 15 percent higher than comparable nonunion wages.

■ Union work rules, strikes, and the misallocation of labor associated with the union wage advantage are ways by which unions may reduce efficiency.

■ Unions may enhance productivity by causing a shock effect, by reducing worker turnover, and by providing the worker security that is a prerequisite to informal on-the-job training.

LABOR MARKET DISCRIMINATION

Broadly defined, **labor market discrimination** occurs when equivalent labor resources are paid or treated differently even though their productive contributions are equal. Table 36-1 shows various economic disparities by race, ethnicity, and gender. These statistical differences result from a combination of nondiscriminatory and discriminatory factors. For example, studies indicate that about one-half the differences in *earnings* between men and women and whites and blacks can be explained by such nondiscriminatory factors as differences in education, age, training,

industry and occupation, union membership, location, work experience, continuity of work, and health. (Of course, some of these factors may be influenced by discrimination.) The other half is an *unexplained difference*, the bulk of which economists attribute to discrimination.

In labor market discrimination, certain groups of people are accorded inferior treatment with respect to hiring, occupational access, education and training, promotion, wage rates, or working conditions even though they have the same abilities, education and training, and experience as the more preferred groups. People who practice discrimination are said to exhibit a *prejudice* or *bias* against the targets of their discrimination.

TABLE 36-1 Selected economic disparities by gender, race, and ethnicity, 1996

Selected measures	Blacks	Hispanics	Whites
Earnings and income			
Median weekly earnings:			
Men	$412	$356	$508
Women	$362	$316	$428
Median income of families	$26,522	$26,179	$44,756
Percent of families in poverty	26.1	26.4	8.6
Labor-force participation and employment			
Labor-force participation rate:			
Men	68.7	79.6	75.8
Women	60.4	53.4	59.1
Unemployment rate:			
Men	11.1	7.9	4.7
Women	10.0	10.2	4.7
Education			
Percent of population with at least 4 years of high school:			
Men	74.3	53.0	82.7
Women	74.2	53.3	82.8
Percent of population with at least 4 years of college:			
Men	12.4	10.3	26.9
Women	14.6	8.3	21.8
Occupational distribution (percent of group's total employment)			
Managerial and professional occupations:			
Men and women	20.0	14.2	29.8
Service occupations:			
Men and women	21.9	20.1	12.5

Source: Statistical Abstract of the United States, 1997; Economic Report of the President, 1997; Employment and Earnings, January 1997.

Types of Discrimination

Labor market discrimination can take several forms:
1. **Wage discrimination** occurs when women or members of minorities are paid less than white males for doing the same work. This kind of discrimination is declining because of its explicitness and the fact that it clearly violates Federal law. But wage discrimination can be subtle and difficult to detect. For example, women and minorities sometimes find that their job classifications carry lower pay than job classifications held by white males, even though they are performing essentially the same tasks.
2. **Employment discrimination** takes place when women or minority workers receive inferior treatment in hiring, promotions, assignments, temporary layoffs, and permanent discharges. This type of discrimination also encompasses sexual and racial harassment—demeaning treatment in the workplace by coworkers or administrators.
3. **Occupational discrimination** occurs when women or minority workers are arbitrarily restricted or prohibited from entering the more desirable, higher-paying occupations. Businesswomen have found it difficult to break through the "glass ceiling" which keeps them from moving up to executive ranks. Blacks and Hispanics in executive and sales positions are relatively few. In addition, skilled and unionized work such as electrical work, bricklaying, and plumbing do not have high minority representation.
4. **Human capital discrimination** occurs when women or members of minorities do not have the same access to productivity-enhancing investments in education and training as white males. Example: The lower average educational attainment (Table 36-1) of blacks and Hispanics has reduced their opportunities in the labor market.

Costs of Discrimination

Discrimination imposes costs on those who are discriminated against. The groups which discriminate get the good jobs and the better pay that are withheld from the targets of their discrimination. But discrimination does more than simply transfer benefits from women, blacks, and Hispanics to men and whites. Where it exists, discrimination actually *diminishes* the economy's output and income; like any other artificial barrier to free competition, it decreases economic efficiency and reduces production. By arbitrarily blocking certain qualified groups of people from high-productivity (and thus high-wage) jobs, discrimination prevents them from making their maximum contribution to the society's output, income, and well-being.

The effects of discrimination can be depicted as a point inside the economy's production possibilities curve, such as point D in Figure 36-3. At such a point, the economy obtains some combination of capital and consumption goods—here, $K_d + C_d$—which is less desirable than combinations represented by points such as X, Y, or Z on the curve. By preventing the economy from achieving productive efficiency, discrimination reduces the nation's real output and income. Very rough estimates suggest the U.S. economy would gain $325 billion per year by eliminating racial and ethnic discrimination and $180 billion per year by ending gender discrimination.

FIGURE 36-3 Discrimination and production possibilities Discrimination represents a failure to achieve productive efficiency. The cost of discrimination to society is the sacrificed output associated with a point such as D inside the nation's production possibilities curve, compared with points such as X, Y, and Z on the curve.

ECONOMIC ANALYSIS OF DISCRIMINATION

Prejudice reflects complex, multifaceted, and deeply ingrained beliefs and attitudes. Thus, economics can contribute some insights into discrimination but no detailed explanations. With this caution in mind, let's look deeper at the economics of discrimination.

Taste-for-Discrimination Model

The **taste-for-discrimination model** examines prejudice by using the emotion-free language of demand theory. It views discrimination as resulting from a preference or *taste* for which the discriminator is willing to pay. The model assumes that, for whatever reason, prejudiced people experience a subjective or psychic cost—a *disutility*—whenever they must interact with those they are biased against. Consequently, they are willing to pay a certain "price" to avoid interactions with the nonpreferred group. The size of this price depends directly on the degree of prejudice.

The taste-for-discrimination model is general since it can be applied to race, gender, age, and religion. But our discussion focuses on *employer discrimination*, in which employers discriminate against nonpreferred workers. For concreteness, we will look at a white employer discriminating against black workers.

Discrimination Coefficient
A prejudiced white employer behaves as if employing black workers adds a cost. The amount of this cost—this disutility—is reflected in a **discrimination coefficient,** d, measured in monetary units. Because the employer is not prejudiced against whites, the cost of employing a white worker is the white wage rate, W_w. However, the employer's perceived "cost" of employing a black worker is the black worker's wage rate, W_b, *plus* the cost d involved in the employer's prejudice, or $W_b + d$.

The prejudiced white employer will have no preference between black and white workers when the total cost per worker is the same, that is, when $W_w = W_b + d$. Suppose the market wage rate for whites is $10 and the monetary value of the disutility the employer attaches to hiring blacks is $2 (that is, $d = 2). This employer will be indifferent between hiring blacks and whites only when the black wage rate is $8 since at this wage the perceived cost of hiring either a white or a black worker is $10:

$10 white wage = $8 black wage
             + $2 discrimination coefficient

It follows that our prejudiced white employer will hire blacks only if their wage rate is sufficiently below that of whites. By "sufficiently" we mean at least the amount of the discrimination coefficient.

The greater a white employer's taste for discrimination as reflected in the value of d, the larger the difference between white wages and the lower wages at which blacks will be hired. A "color-blind" employer whose d is $0 will hire equally productive blacks and whites impartially if their wages are the same. A blatantly prejudiced white employer whose d is infinity will refuse to hire blacks, even if the black wage were zero.

Most prejudiced white employers will not refuse to hire blacks under all conditions. They will, in fact, *prefer* to hire blacks if the actual white-black wage difference in the market exceeds the value of d. In our example, if whites can be hired at $10 and equally productive blacks at only $7.50, the biased white employer will hire blacks. That employer is willing to pay a wage difference of up to $2 per hour for whites to satisfy his or her bias, but no more. At the $2.50 actual difference, the employer will hire blacks.

Conversely, if whites can be hired at $10 and blacks at $8.50, whites will be hired. Again, the biased employer is willing to pay a wage difference of up to $2 for whites; a $1.50 actual difference means that hiring whites is a "bargain" for this employer.

Prejudice and the Market Black-White Wage Ratio
For a particular supply of black workers, the *actual* black-white wage ratio—the ratio determined in the labor market—will depend on the collective prejudice of white employers. To see why, consider Figure 36-4, which shows a labor market for *black* workers. Initially, suppose the relevant labor demand curve is D_1, so the equilibrium *black* wage is $8 and the equilibrium level of black employment is 16 million. If we assume that the *white* wage (not shown) is $10, then the initial black-white wage ratio is .80 (= $8/$10).

Now assume that prejudice against black workers increases—that is, the collective d of white employers rises. An increase in d means an increase in the perceived cost of black labor at each black wage rate, and that reduces the demand for black labor, say, from D_1 to D_2. The black wage rate falls from $8 to $6 in the market, and the level of black employment declines from 16 million to 12 million. *The increase in white employer prejudice reduces the black wage rate and thus the actual black-white wage ratio.* If the white wage rate remains at $10, the new black-white ratio is .6 (= $6/$10).

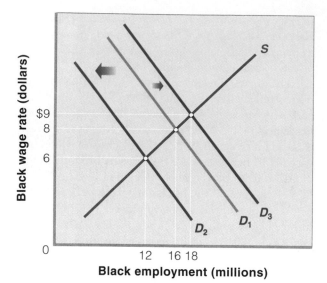

FIGURE 36-4 The black wage and employment level in the taste-for-discrimination model An increase in prejudice by white employers as reflected in higher discrimination coefficients would decrease the demand for black workers, here from D_1 to D_2, and reduce the black wage rate and level of black employment. Not shown, this drop in the black wage rate would lower the black-white wage ratio. In contrast, if prejudice were reduced such that discrimination coefficients of employers declined, the demand for black labor would increase, as from D_1 to D_3, boosting the black wage rate and level of employment. The higher black wage rate would increase the black-white wage ratio.

- -

Conversely, suppose social attitudes change such that white employers become less biased and their discrimination coefficient as a group declines. This decreases the perceived cost of black labor at each black wage rate, so the demand for black labor increases, as from D_1 to D_3. In this case, the black wage rate rises to $9, and employment of black workers increases to 18 million. *The decrease in white employer prejudice increases the black wage rate and thus the actual black-white wage ratio.* If the white wage remains at $10, the new black-white wage ratio is .9 (= $9/$10).

Competition and Discrimination The taste-for-discrimination model suggests that competition will reduce discrimination in the very long run, as follows: The actual black-white wage difference for equally productive workers—say, $2—allows nondiscriminators to hire blacks for less than whites. Firms which hire black workers will therefore have lower actual wage costs per unit of output and lower average total costs than will the firms which discriminate. These lower costs will allow nondiscriminators to under-

price discriminating competitors, eventually driving them out of the market.

But critics of this implication of the taste-for-discrimination model note that progress in eliminating racial discrimination has been modest. Discrimination based on race has persisted in the United States and other market economies decade after decade. To explain why, economists have proposed alternative models. **(Key Question 7)**

Statistical Discrimination

A second theory of discrimination centers on the concept of **statistical discrimination,** in which *people are judged on the basis of the average characteristics of the group to which they belong, rather than on their own personal characteristics or productivity.* The uniqueness of this theory is that discriminatory outcomes are possible even where there is no prejudice.

Basic Idea Suppose you are given a complex, but solvable, mathematical problem and told you will get $1 million in cash if you can find a student on campus to solve it. The catch is that you have only 15 minutes, are restricted to the campus area, and must approach students one at a time. Who among the thousands of students—all strangers—would you approach first? Obviously, you would like to select a mathematics, physics, or engineering major. Would you select a man or a woman? A white, black, Hispanic, or Asian student? If gender or race plays *any* role in your selection, you have engaged in statistical discrimination.

Labor Market Example How does statistical discrimination work in labor markets? Employers with job openings want to hire the most productive workers available. Their personnel departments collect information concerning each job applicant, including age, education, and prior work experience. They may supplement this information with preemployment tests, whose results they feel are helpful indicators of potential job performance. But it is very expensive to collect detailed information about a job applicant, and it is difficult to predict job performance from limited data. Consequently, some employers looking for inexpensive information may consider average characteristics of women and minorities in determining whom to hire. In thus practicing statistical discrimination, employers are not satisfying some taste for discrimination but, rather, are using gender, race, or ethnic background as a very crude indicator of production-related attributes of workers which are not easily discernible.

Example: Suppose an employer who plans to invest heavily in training a worker knows that on average women are less likely to be career-oriented than men, more likely to quit work to care for young children, and more likely to refuse geographical transfers. Thus, on average, the return on the employer's investment will be less for a woman than for a man. All else equal, when choosing between two job applicants, one a woman and the other a man, this employer will likely hire the man.

Note what is happening here. Average characteristics for a *group* are being applied to *individual* members of that group. The employer is falsely assuming that *each and every* woman worker has the same employment tendencies as the *average* woman. This stereotyping means that numerous women who are career-oriented, plan to work when they have families, and are flexible as to geographical transfers will be discriminated against.

Profitable, Undesirable, but Not Malicious

The firm practicing statistical discrimination is not being malicious in its hiring behavior (although it may be violating antidiscrimination laws). The decisions it makes will be rational and profitable because *on average* its hiring decisions will likely be correct. Nevertheless, many people suffer because of statistical discrimination since it blocks the economic betterment of capable people. And since it is profitable, statistical discrimination can persist.

Occupational Segregation: The Crowding Model

The practice of **occupational segregation**—*the crowding of women, blacks, and certain ethnic groups into less desirable, lower-paying occupations*—is still apparent in the U.S. economy. Statistics indicate that women are disproportionately concentrated in a limited number of occupations such as teaching, nursing, and secretarial and clerical jobs. Blacks and Hispanics are crowded into low-paying jobs such as those of laundry workers, cleaners and household aides, hospital orderlies, agricultural workers, and other manual laborers.

Let's look at a model of occupational segregation, using women and men as an example.

The Model   The character and income consequences of occupational discrimination are revealed through a labor supply and demand model. We make the following assumptions:

1. The labor force is equally divided between men and women workers. Let's say there are 6 million male and 6 million female workers.
2. The economy comprises three occupations, X, Y, and Z, with identical labor demand curves as shown in Figure 36-5.
3. Men and women have the same labor force characteristics; each of the three occupations could be filled equally by men or women.

Effects of Crowding   Suppose that, as a consequence of discrimination, the 6 million women are

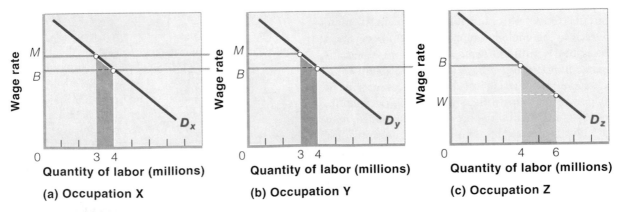

FIGURE 36-5 The economics of occupational segregation   By crowding women into one occupation, men enjoy high wage rates of *M* in occupations X and Y, while women receive low wages of *W* in occupation Z. The elimination of discrimination will equalize wage rates at *B* and result in a net increase in the nation's output.

excluded from occupations X and Y and crowded into occupation Z, where they earn wage *W.* Men distribute themselves equally among occupations X and Y, meaning that 3 million male workers are in each occupation and have a common wage of *M.* (If we assume there are no barriers to mobility between X and Y, any initially different distribution of males between X and Y would result in a wage differential between the two occupations. This would prompt labor shifts from the low- to the high-wage occupation until an equal distribution occurred.)

Because women are crowded into occupation Z, their wage rate *W* is much lower than *M.* Because of the discrimination, this is an equilibrium situation. The occupational barrier means women *cannot* reallocate themselves to occupations X and Y in pursuit of a higher wage.

The result is a loss of output for society. To see this, recall again that labor demand reflects labor's marginal revenue product, which is labor's contribution to domestic output. Thus, the gray areas for occupations X and Y in Figure 36-5 show the *decrease* in domestic output—the market value of the marginal output—caused by subtracting 1 million women from each of these occupations. Similarly, the orange area for occupation Z shows the *increase* in domestic output caused by moving 2 million women into occupation Z. Although society gains the added output represented by the orange area in occupation Z, it loses the output represented by the sum of the two gray areas in occupations X and Y. This output loss exceeds the output gain, producing a net output loss for society.

Eliminating Occupational Segregation Now assume that through legislation or sweeping changes in social attitudes, discrimination disappears. Women, attracted by higher wage rates, shift from occupation Z to X and Y; 1 million women move into X and another 1 million move into Y, leaving 4 million workers in Z and eliminating occupational segregation. At that point 4 million workers are in each occupation, and wage rates in all three occupations are equal, here at *B.* This wage equality eliminates the incentive for further reallocations of labor.

The new, nondiscriminatory equilibrium clearly benefits women, who now receive higher wages; it hurts men, who now receive lower wages. But women were initially harmed and men benefited through discrimination; thus, removing discrimination corrects that situation.

Society also gains. The elimination of occupational segregation reverses the net output loss just discussed.

Adding 1 million women to each of occupations X and Y in Figure 36-5 *increases* domestic output by the sum of the two gray areas. The *decrease* in domestic output caused by losing 2 million women from occupation Z is shown by the orange area. The sum of the two increases in domestic output in X and Y exceeds the decrease in domestic output in Z. Women workers move from occupation Z, where their contribution to domestic output (their MRP) is low, to occupations X and Y, where their contribution to domestic output is high. Thus society gains a more efficient allocation of resources when discrimination, an occupational barrier, is removed. (In terms of Figure 36-3, society moves from a point inside its production possibilities curve to a point closer to, or on, the curve.)

Example: The easing of occupational barriers has led to a surge of women gaining advanced degrees in some high-paying professions. In recent years, for instance, the percentage of law degrees and medical degrees awarded to women has exceeded 40 percent, compared with less than 10 percent in 1970. **(Key Question 9)**

QUICK REVIEW 36-3

■ Discrimination reduces domestic output and occurs when workers who have the same abilities, education, training, and experience as other workers receive inferior treatment with respect to hiring, occupational access, promotion, or wages.

■ Nondiscriminatory factors explain about one-half of the gender and racial earnings gaps; most of the remaining one-half is thought to reflect discrimination.

■ The taste-for-discrimination model sees discrimination as representing a preference or "taste" for which the discriminator is willing to pay.

■ The theory of statistical discrimination says that employers often wrongly judge *individuals* on the basis of average *group* characteristics rather than on personal characteristics, thus harming those discriminated against.

■ The crowding model of discrimination suggests that when women and minorities are systematically excluded from high-paying occupations and crowded into low-paying ones, their wages and society's domestic output are reduced.

ANTIDISCRIMINATION POLICIES AND ISSUES

Government might attack the problems of discrimination in several ways. One indirect policy is to promote a strong, growing economy. An expanding demand for products increases the demand for all workers. When the economy is at or near full employment, prejudiced employers must pay higher and higher wages to entice preferred workers away from other employers. Many, and perhaps most, such employers will likely decide that their taste for discrimination is not worth the cost. Tight labor markets also help overcome stereotyping. Once they obtain good jobs in tight labor markets, women and minorities have an opportunity to show they can do the work as well as white males.

A second indirect antidiscrimination policy is to improve the education and training opportunities of women and minorities. As an example, upgrading the quantity and quality of schooling received by blacks and Hispanics will make them more competitive with whites for higher-paying positions.

The third way of reducing discrimination is through direct governmental intervention. As summarized in Table 36-2, the U.S. government has outlawed certain practices in hiring, promotion, and compensation and has required that government contractors take affirmative action to ensure that women and minorities are hired at least up to their proportions of the labor force.

The Affirmative Action Controversy

Let's consider the last item in Table 36-2. **Affirmative action** consists of special efforts by employers to increase employment and promotion opportunities for groups which have suffered past discrimination and continue to experience discrimination. To say that affirmative action has stirred controversy is to make an understatement. There are strong arguments for and against this approach to remedying discrimination.

In Support of Affirmative Action   Those who support affirmative action say that historically women and minorities have been forced to carry the extra burden of discrimination in their attempt to achieve economic success. Thus, they find themselves far behind white males, who have been preferred workers. Merely removing the discrimination burden does nothing to close the present socioeconomic gap. Something more than equal opportunity—preferential treatment—is necessary to counter the inherent bias in favor of white men if women and minorities are to catch up.

Supporters of affirmative action argue that job discrimination is so pervasive that it will persist for decades if society is content to accept only marginal antidiscriminatory changes in employment practices. Moreover, such changes are hampered by the fact that white males have achieved seniority which protects them from layoffs and places the burden of unemployment disproportionately on women and minorities. And women and minorities have been discriminated against in acquiring human capital—the education and job training needed to compete on

TABLE 36-2   Major antidiscrimination laws and policies in the United States

Equal Pay Act of 1963   Makes it illegal to pay men and women different wage rates if they "do equal work on jobs, the performance of which requires equal skill, effort, and responsibility, and which are performed under similar working conditions."

Title VII of the Civil Rights Act of 1964   Makes it unlawful for any employer "to refuse to hire or to discharge any individual, or otherwise to discriminate against any individual with respect to compensation, terms, conditions, or privileges of employment, because of such individual's race, color, religion, sex, or national origin."

Affirmative action requirement   Presidential executive orders issued in 1965 and 1968 outlaw discriminatory practices of businesses and other institutions holding government contracts. The 1968 order also states that the "contractor will take *affirmative action* to ensure that applicants are employed, and that employees are treated during employment, without regard to their race, color, religion, sex, or national origin." This affirmative action was to apply to employment, upgrading, demotion, and transfer; recruitment and recruitment advertising; layoff and termination; rates of pay and other forms of compensation; and selection for training, including apprenticeships.

equal terms with white males. Discrimination has supposedly become so highly institutionalized that extraordinary countermeasures are required.

Those who accept this line of reasoning endorse affirmative action and other forms of preferential treatment as appropriate means for hastening the elimination of discrimination. In this view, affirmative action is not only a path toward social equity but also a good national strategy for enhancing efficiency and economic growth since it brings formerly excluded groups directly into the productive economic mainstream.

Opposing View Those against affirmative action claim that preferential treatment frequently has forced employers to hire less qualified women and minority workers and therefore has *impaired* economic efficiency. Critics also say that quotas and preferential treatment are a form of **reverse discrimination.** Preferential treatment and discrimination, they say, are simply two views of the same thing: To show preference for A is to discriminate against B.

Some opponents of affirmative action go further, contending that policies that give preferential treatment to disadvantaged groups have actually worked to these groups' long-term detriment. Such policies, say critics, have placed many persons in positions where their skill deficiencies become evident to their employers and coworkers. This has two effects, both negative: First, majority workers who have been passed over for jobs or promotions resent the groups who are given special treatment. Second, the highly qualified women and minority members of the workforce, who have no need of preferential treatment, mistakenly get stereotyped by others as "affirmative action hires." In this view, continuing racial tension not only reflects the long legacy of discrimination but also the more recent ill-conceived policies designed to end it.

Recent Developments

Affirmative action recently has come under harsh legal and political attack. A series of important Supreme Court decisions in 1986 and 1987 upheld the constitutionality of affirmative action programs, but more recent decisions have undermined some specific programs. For example, in 1989 the Court declared illegal a program by the city of Richmond, Virginia, designed to provide a specified proportion of the city's construction work to minority-owned firms; the Court

argued that the program constituted reverse discrimination. Similarly, another 1989 ruling permitted white Birmingham, Alabama, firefighters to challenge an existing affirmative action program on grounds that the program denied them promotions in favor of less qualified blacks. The Birmingham ruling has triggered a number of reverse-discrimination lawsuits throughout the country. Other Court rulings have made it necessary for minorities to prove that job discrimination exists in a *particular* firm, not just in the overall industry or economy.

In mid-1995 the Court ruled that race-based preferences in Federal programs could be allowed *only* if the programs are "narrowly tailored" to remedy identifiable past discrimination in a particular firm or government entity. A Federal circuit court of appeals ruled later that year that public universities in Texas, Mississippi, and Louisiana may not justify affirmative action programs on the basis of the benefits of racial diversity. Later that year, the Supreme Court let this ruling stand.

On the political scene, in 1996 Congress debated legislation restricting affirmative action, and the Clinton administration halted several Federal minority programs designed to give preference in Federal contracting to minorities. And in late 1996 Californians voted in favor of a state constitutional amendment ending all state programs which give gender or racial preferences in government hiring and contracting, as well as in public education.

QUICK REVIEW 36-4

■ The Equal Pay Act of 1963 and Title VII of the Civil Rights Act of 1964 outlaw wage and employment discrimination based on race, color, religion, gender, and national origin.

■ Affirmative action programs are designed to overcome past and present discrimination by giving preferences to women and minorities; they are highly controversial and recently have come under attack by those who feel they reflect reverse discrimination.

IMMIGRATION

Immigration has long been a focus of controversy. Should more or fewer people be allowed to migrate to the United States? How should the problem of illegal entrants be handled?

Number of Immigrants

The annual flows of **legal immigrants,** those with permission to reside in the United States, were roughly 250,000 in the 1950s, 320,000 in the 1960s, and 500,000 to 600,000 during the 1970s and 1980s. Immigration has averaged about 850,000 per year in the 1990s. About one-third of recent annual population growth in the United States is the result of immigration. (Global Perspective 36-2 shows where U.S. legal immigrants arrived from in 1995.)

Such data are imperfect, however, because they do not include **illegal immigrants,** those who arrive without permission. The Census Bureau estimates that the net inflow of illegal immigrants (illegal aliens) is now about 100,000 per year, most coming from Mexico, the Caribbean, and Latin America.

Economics of Immigration

We can use Figure 36-6 to gain some insight into the economic effects of immigration. In Figure 36-6a, D_u is the demand for labor in the United States; in Figure 36-6b, D_m is the demand for labor in Mexico. The demand for labor is greater in the United States, presumably because the nation has more capital and more advanced technologies that enhance the productivity of labor. (Recall from Chapter 27 that the labor demand curve is based on the marginal-revenue-productivity of labor.) Conversely, we assume that machinery and equipment are scarce in Mexico and technology is less sophisticated; hence, labor demand

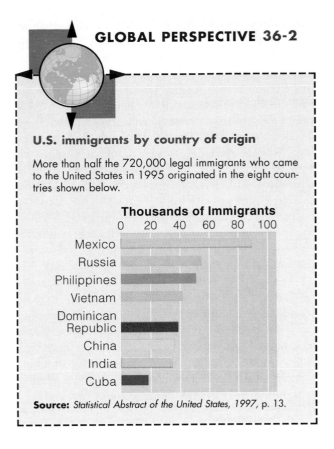

GLOBAL PERSPECTIVE 36-2

U.S. immigrants by country of origin

More than half the 720,000 legal immigrants who came to the United States in 1995 originated in the eight countries shown below.

Thousands of Immigrants

Source: *Statistical Abstract of the United States, 1997,* p. 13.

there is weak. We also assume that the before-migration labor forces of the United States and Mexico are c and C, respectively, and that both countries are at full employment.

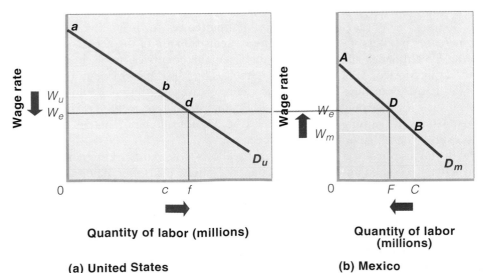

(a) United States

(b) Mexico

FIGURE 36-6 The simple economics of immigration The migration of labor to high-income United States (a) from low-income Mexico (b) increases U.S. domestic output, reduces the average level of U.S. wages, and increases U.S. business income while having the opposite effects in Mexico. The U.S. domestic output gain of *cbdf* exceeds Mexico's domestic output loss of *FDBC;* thus the migration yields a net increase in world output.

Wage Rates and World Output If we further assume that migration (1) has no cost, (2) occurs solely in response to wage differentials, and (3) is unimpeded by law in either country, then workers will migrate from Mexico to the United States until wage rates in the two countries are equal at W_e. At that point, CF (equals cf) workers will have migrated from Mexico to the United States. Although the U.S. wage level will fall from W_u to W_e, domestic output (the sum of the marginal revenue products of the entire workforce) will increase from $0abc$ to $0adf$. In Mexico, the wage rate will rise from W_m to W_e, but domestic output will decline there from $0ABC$ to $0ADF$. Because the gain in domestic output $cbdf$ in the United States exceeds the output loss $FDBC$ in Mexico, the world's output has increased.

We can conclude that the elimination of barriers to the international flow of labor tends to increase worldwide economic efficiency. The world gains because the freedom to migrate enables people to move to countries where they can make larger contributions to world production. Migration involves an efficiency gain. It enables the world to produce a larger real output with a particular amount of resources.

Income Shares Our model also suggests that this flow of immigrants will enhance business income (or capitalist income) in the United States and reduce it in Mexico. We just noted that before-immigration domestic output in the United States is represented by area $0abc$. The total wage bill is $0W_ubc$—the wage rate multiplied by the number of workers. The remaining triangular area W_uab represents business income before immigration. The same reasoning applies to Mexico, where W_mAB is before-immigration business income.

Unimpeded immigration increases business income from W_uab to W_ead in the United States and reduces it from W_mAB to W_eAD in Mexico. U.S. businesses benefit from immigration; Mexican businesses are hurt by emigration. This is what we would expect intuitively; the United States is gaining "cheap" labor, and Mexico is losing "cheap" labor. This conclusion is consistent with the historical fact that U.S. employers have often actively recruited immigrants.

Complications and Modifications

Our model includes some simplifying assumptions and overlooks a relevant factor. Let's now relax some of the more critical assumptions and introduce the omitted factor to see how our conclusions are affected.

Costs of Migration We assumed that international movement of workers is without personal cost, but obviously it is not. There are both the explicit, out-of-pocket costs of physically moving a worker and his or her possessions and the implicit opportunity cost of lost income while the worker is moving and becoming established in the new country. Still more subtle costs are involved in adapting to a new culture, language, climate, and so forth. All such *costs* must be estimated by the potential immigrant and weighed against the expected *benefits* of higher wages in the new country. A person who estimates that benefits exceed costs will migrate; a person who sees costs as exceeding benefits will stay put.

In terms of Figure 36-6, the reality of migration costs means that the flow of labor from Mexico to the United States will not continue until wages are equalized. Wages will remain somewhat higher in the United States than in Mexico; the wage difference will not cause further migration because it does not cover migration costs. Thus, the world production gain from migration will be reduced since wages will not equalize.

Remittances and Backflows Most migration is permanent; workers who acquire skills in the receiving country tend not to return home. However, some migrants view their moves as temporary. They move to a more developed country, accumulate some wealth or education through hard work and frugality, and return home to establish their own enterprises. During their period in the new country, migrants frequently make sizable remittances to their families at home. This causes a redistribution of the net gain from migration between the countries involved. In Figure 36-6, remittances by Mexican workers in the United States to their relatives in Mexico would cause the gain in U.S. domestic output to be less than shown and the loss to Mexican domestic output to also be less than shown.

Actual backflows—the return of migrants to their home country—might also alter gains and losses through time. For example, if some Mexican workers who migrated to the United States acquired substantial labor market or managerial skills and then returned home, their enhanced human capital might make a substantial contribution to economic development in Mexico.

Full Employment versus Unemployment Our model assumes full employment in the sending and receiving countries. Mexican workers presumably leave low-paying jobs to take (more or less immediately) higher-paying jobs in the United States. However, in many cases the factor that "pushes" immigrants from their homelands is not low wages but chronic unemployment and underemployment. Many developing countries are overpopulated and have surplus labor; workers are either unemployed or so grossly underemployed that their marginal revenue product is zero.

If we allow for this possibility, then Mexico actually gains (not loses) by having such workers emigrate. The unemployed workers are making no contribution to Mexico's domestic output and must be sustained by transfers from the rest of the labor force. The remaining Mexican labor force will be better off by the amount of the transfers after the unemployed workers have migrated to the United States. Conversely, if the Mexican immigrant workers are unable to find jobs in the United States and are sustained through transfers from employed U.S. workers, then the after-tax income of working Americans will decline.

Fiscal Impacts What effects do immigrants have on tax revenues and government spending in the receiving country? Are immigrants contributors to output, or do they go on welfare and become a drain on the national treasury?

Prior to the 1970s, the belief was that the immigrant population was less likely to receive public assistance than the native population. Migrants were typically young, single men with significant education and job training. Thus they were readily employable and were net contributors. Illegal immigrants avoided the welfare system for fear of detection and deportation.

But since the 1970s the situation has reversed, and immigrants now use the welfare system proportionately more than natives. The main factor in the turnabout is the changing mix of immigrants, which today includes relatively fewer skilled workers and more unskilled workers. In fact, critics of the U.S. welfare system say it is drawing unskilled (and often illegal) workers to the United States from some of the world's poorest nations. Indeed, immigrants now make up more than 10 percent of Supplemental Security Income (SSI) rolls, compared with only 3.3 percent a decade earlier. As a result of this trend, the 1996 welfare reform (Personal Responsibility Act) denied welfare benefits to new immigrants for their first 5 years in the United States. **(Key Question 12)**

Immigration: Two Views

As we noted, the traditional perception of immigration is that it consists of young, ambitious workers seeking opportunity in the United States. They are destined for success because of the courage and determination they exhibit in leaving their cultural roots to improve their lives. These energetic workers increase the *supply* of goods and services with their labor and simultaneously increase the *demand* for goods and services with their incomes and spending. In short, immigration is an engine of economic progress.

The counterview is that immigration is a socioeconomic drag on the receiving country. Immigrants compete with domestic workers for scarce jobs, pull down the average level of real wages, and burden the U.S. welfare system.

Both these views are far to simplistic. Immigration can either benefit or harm the receiving nation depending on the number of immigrants; their education, skills, and work ethic; and the rate at which they can be absorbed into the economy without disruption. From a strictly economic perspective, nations seeking to maximize net benefits from immigration should expand immigration until its marginal benefits equal its marginal costs. The MB = MC conceptual framework explicitly recognizes there can be too few immigrants, just as there can be too many. Moreover, it recognizes that from a strictly *economic* standpoint, not all immigrants are alike. The immigration of, say, a highly educated scientist has a different impact on the economy than does the immigration of a long-term welfare recipient.

QUICK REVIEW 36-5

■ All else equal, immigration reduces wages, increases domestic output, and increases business income in the receiving nation; it has the opposite effects in the sending nation.

■ Assessing the impacts of immigration is complicated by factors such as unemployment, backflows and remittances, and fiscal impacts.

Orchestrating Impartiality

Have "blind" musical auditions, in which "screens" are used to hide the identity of candidates, affected the success of women in obtaining positions in major symphony orchestras?

There have long been allegations of discrimination against women in the hiring process in some occupations. But such discrimination is usually difficult to demonstrate. Economists Claudia Goldin and Cecilia Rouse* spotted a unique opportunity for testing such discrimination as it relates to major symphony orchestras. In the past, orchestras relied on their musical directors to extend invitations to candidates, audition them, and handpick new members. Concerned with the potential for bias, in the 1970s and 1980s orchestras altered the process in two ways. First, orchestra members were included as judges, and, second, orchestras began open competitions using "blind" auditions with a physical "screen" (usually a room divider) to conceal the identity of the candidates. (These blind auditions, however, did *not* extend to the final competition in most orchestras.) Did the change in procedures increase the probability of women being hired?

To answer this question, Goldin and Rouse gained access to orchestral management files to examine auditions for eight major orchestras. These records contained the names of all candidates and identified those who advanced to the next round, including the ultimate winner of the competition. The researchers then looked for women in the sample who had "competed" in auditions both before and after the introduction of the blind screening.

There was a strong suspicion of bias against women in hiring musicians for the nation's finest orchestras. These positions are highly desirous, not only because they are prestigious but also because they offer high pay (often more than $75,000 annually). In 1970 only 5 percent of the members of the top five orchestras in the United States were women, and many music directors publicly suggested that women players, in general, have less musical talent.

The change to screens provided direct evidence of past discrimination. The screens increased by 50 percent the probability that a woman would be advanced from the preliminary rounds. The screens also greatly increased the likelihood that a woman would be selected in the final round. Without the screens about 10 percent of all hires were women, but with the screens about 35 percent were women. Today, about 25 percent of the membership of top symphony orchestras are women, in contrast to 5 percent in 1970. The screens explain from 25 to 45 percent of the increases in the proportion of women in the orchestras studied.

Was the past discrimination in hiring an example of *statistical discrimination* based on, say, a presumption of greater turnover by women or more leaves for medical (including maternity) or other reasons? To answer that question, Goldin and Rouse examined information on turnover and leaves of orchestra members for the period 1960–1996. They found that neither differed by gender, so leaves and turnover should *not* have influenced hiring decisions.

Instead, the discrimination in hiring seemed to reflect a *taste for discrimination* by musical directors. Male musical directors apparently had a positive discrimination coefficient *d*. At the fixed (union-determined) wage, they simply preferred male musicians, at women's expense.

*Claudia Goldin and Cecilia Rouse, "Orchestrating Impartiality: The Impact of 'Blind' Auditions on Female Musicians," National Bureau of Economic Research, Working Paper 5903, January 1997.

CHAPTER SUMMARY

1. Presently there are about 17 million union workers in the United States, with most belonging to the loose federation called the AFL-CIO. Unionism has declined relatively in the United States since the mid-1950s. Some economists attribute this decline to changes in the composition of domestic output and in the demographic structure of the labor force. Others contend that employers, recognizing that unions reduce profitability, have more aggressively sought to dissuade workers from being union members.

2. Labor and management "live together" under the terms of collective bargaining agreements. These work agreements cover **(a)** union status and managerial prerogative; **(b)** wages, hours, and working conditions; **(c)** seniority and job control; and **(d)** a grievance procedure.

3. There is disagreement about whether unions increase or decrease efficiency and productivity. The negative view cites **(a)** inefficiencies associated with featherbedding and union-imposed work rules, **(b)** loss of output through strikes, and **(c)** the misallocation of labor caused by the union wage advantage. The positive view holds that **(a)** through the shock effect, union wage pressure spurs technological advance and mechanization of the production process; **(b)** as collective-voice institutions, unions contribute to rising productivity by reducing labor turnover; and **(c)** the enhanced security of union workers increases their willingness to teach their skills to less experienced workers.

4. Discrimination relating to the labor market occurs when women or minorities having the same abilities, education, training, and experience as men or white workers are given inferior treatment with respect to hiring, occupational choice, education and training, promotion, and wage rates. Forms of discrimination are wage discrimination, employment discrimination, occupational discrimination, and human capital discrimination. Discrimination redistributes national income and, by creating inefficiencies, diminishes its size.

5. In the taste-for-discrimination model, some white employers have a preference for discrimination, measured by a discrimination coefficient *d*. Prejudiced white employers will hire black workers only if their wages are at least *d* dollars below those of whites. The model indicates that declines in the discrimination coefficients of white employers will increase the demand for black workers, raising the black wage rate and the ratio of black to white wages. It also suggests that competition may eliminate discrimination in the long run.

6. Statistical discrimination occurs when employers base employment decisions about *individuals* on the average characteristics of *groups* of workers. This can lead to discrimination against individuals even in the absence of prejudice.

7. The crowding model of occupational segregation indicates how white males gain higher earnings at the expense of women and minorities who are confined to a limited number of occupations. The model shows that discrimination also causes a net loss of domestic output.

8. Government antidiscrimination legislation and policies that involve direct governmental intervention include the Equal Pay Act of 1963, Title VII of the Civil Rights Act of 1964, and executive orders applicable to Federal contractors. The executive orders include the requirement that these firms enact affirmative action programs to benefit women and certain minority groups.

9. Those who support affirmative action say it is needed to help women and minorities compensate for decades of discrimination. Opponents say affirmative action causes economic inefficiency and reverse discrimination. Recent Supreme Court decisions have limited the use of affirmative action programs to situations where past discrimination is clearly identifiable.

10. Supply and demand analysis suggests that the movement of migrants from a poor to a rich country **(a)** increases domestic output in the rich country, **(b)** reduces the average wage in the rich country, and **(c)** increases business income in the rich country. The opposite effects occur in the poor country, but the world as a whole realizes a larger total output.

11. The outcomes of immigration predicted by simple supply and demand analysis become more complicated upon consideration of **(a)** the costs of moving, **(b)** the possibility of remittances and backflows, **(c)** the level of unemployment in each country, and **(d)** the fiscal impacts on the taxpayers of each country.

TERMS AND CONCEPTS

American Federation of
   Labor and Congress of
   Industrial
   Organizations
independent unions
business unionism
structural-change
   hypothesis
managerial-opposition
   hypothesis
collective bargaining
closed shop

union shop
agency shop
right-to-work laws
open shop
strike
lockout
National Labor Relations
   Act
National Labor Relations
   Board
collective voice
exit mechanism

voice mechanism
labor market
   discrimination
wage discrimination
employment
   discrimination
occupational
   discrimination
human-capital
   discrimination
taste-for-discrimination
   model

discrimination coefficient
statistical discrimination
occupational
   segregation
affirmative action
reverse discrimination
legal immigrants
illegal immigrants

STUDY QUESTIONS

1. Other things equal, who is more likely to be a union member: Stephen, who works as a salesperson at a furniture store, or Susan, who works as a machinist for an aircraft manufacturer? Explain.

2. Contrast the structural-change and managerial-opposition hypotheses as they relate to the decline in unionism. In your opinion, which view is more convincing?

3. Suppose that you are president of a newly established local union about to bargain with an employer for the first time. List the basic areas you want covered in the work agreement. Why might you begin with a larger wage demand than you actually are willing to accept?

4. KEY QUESTION What is the estimated size of the union wage advantage? How might this advantage diminish the efficiency with which labor resources are allocated?

5. Explain the logic of each of the following statements:
   a. By constraining the decisions of management, unions reduce efficiency and productivity growth.
   b. As collective-voice institutions, unions increase productivity by reducing worker turnover, inducing managerial efficiency, and enhancing worker security.

6. Explain how discrimination reduces domestic output and income. Demonstrate this loss using production possibilities analysis.

7. KEY QUESTION The labor demand and supply data in the table below relate to a single occupation.

Use them to answer the questions that follow. Base your answers on the taste-for-discrimination model.

Quantity of Hispanic labor demanded, thousands	Hispanic wage rate	Quantity of Hispanic labor supplied, thousands
24	$16	52
30	14	44
36	12	36
42	10	28
48	8	20

a. Plot the labor demand and supply curves for Hispanic workers in this occupation.
b. What are the equilibrium Hispanic wage rate and quantity of Hispanic employment?
c. Suppose the white wage rate in this occupation is $16. What is the Hispanic-to-white wage ratio?
d. Suppose a particular employer has a discrimination coefficient d of $5 per hour. Will that employer hire Hispanic or white workers at the Hispanic-white wage ratio indicated in part **(c)**? Explain.
e. Suppose employers as a group become less prejudiced against Hispanics and demand 14 more units of Hispanic labor at each Hispanic wage rate in the table. What are the new equilibrium Hispanic wage rate and level of Hispanic employment? Does the Hispanic-white wage ratio rise or fall? Explain.
f. Suppose Hispanics as a group increase their labor services in this occupation, collectively offering 14 more units of labor at each Hispanic wage

rate. Disregarding the changes indicated in part **(e)**, what are the new equilibrium Hispanic wage rate and level of Hispanic employment? Does the Hispanic-white wage ratio rise, or does it fall?

8. Males under the age of 25 must pay far higher auto insurance premiums than females in this age group. How does this fact relate to statistical discrimination? Statistical discrimination implies that discrimination can persist indefinitely, while the taste-for-discrimination model suggests that competition might reduce discrimination in the long run. Explain the difference.

9. KEY QUESTION Use a demand and supply model to explain the impact of occupational segregation or "crowding" on the relative wage rates and earnings of men and women. Who gains and who loses from the *elimination* of occupational segregation? Is there a net gain or net loss to society? Explain.

10. "Current affirmative action programs are based on the belief that to overcome discrimination, we must practice discrimination. That perverse logic has created a system that undermines the fundamental values it was intended to protect." Do you agree? Why or why not?

11. Suppose Ann and Becky are applicants to your university and that they have *identical* admission qualifications (SAT scores, high school GPA, etc.). Ann is black, growing up in a public housing development; Becky is white, growing up in a wealthy suburb. You can admit only one of the two. Which person would you admit and why? Now suppose that *Ann* is white and *Becky* is black, *all else equal*. Does this change your selection? Why or why not?

12. KEY QUESTION Use graphical analysis to show the gains and losses resulting from the migration of population from a low-income country to a high-income country. Explain how your conclusions are affected by **(a)** unemployment, **(b)** remittances to the home country, **(c)** backflows of migrants to their home country, and **(d)** the personal characteristics of

the migrants. If the migrants are highly skilled workers, is there any justification for the sending country to levy a "brain drain" tax on emigrants?

13. If a person favors the free movement of labor within the United States, is it then inconsistent to also favor restrictions on the international movement of labor? Why or why not?

14. Evaluate: "If the United States deported, say, 1 million illegal immigrants, the number of unemployed workers in the United States would decline by 1 million."

15. (Last Word) What two types of discrimination are represented by the discrimination evidenced in this chapter's Last Word?

16. WEB-BASED QUESTION Unions—The AFL-CIO The AFL-CIO http://www.aflcio.org/ states that its mission is to "improve the lives of working families and to bring economic justice to the workplace and social justice to the nation." What unions are affiliated with the AFL-CIO? What current labor issues concern the AFL-CIO? Are they macroeconomic or microeconomic issues? How is the AFL-CIO trying to appeal to working women? What is the union doing about repetitive strain injuries? Why has the AFL-CIO set up an "Executive Pay Watch" http://aflcio.paywatch.org/ceopay/?

17. WEB-BASED QUESTION Discrimination—and the NAACP and NOW Both the National Association for the Advancement of Colored People (NAACP) http://www.naacp.org/ and the National Organization for Women (NOW) http://www.now.org/ fight political, educational, social, and economic discrimination. Compare and contrast each organization with respect to reasons for their formation and their changing objectives over the decades. Are there any similarities between them with regard to their policy focuses? What proportion of the policy issues are economic? Which organization has had the greatest economic impact on the American economy?

9

International Economics and the World Economy

37

International Trade

The WTO, trade deficits, dumping. Exchange rates, the EU, the G-7 nations. The IMF, official reserves, currency interventions. Capital flight, brain drains, the ruble. This is the language of international economics, and people across the globe are speaking it in newspapers, corporate offices, retail outlets, and union halls.

This chapter builds on Chapter 6, providing deeper analysis of international trade and protectionism. We begin by reviewing key facts about world trade, and then we look more closely at how international specialization based on comparative advantage can mutually benefit the participating nations. After using supply and demand analysis to examine equilibrium prices and quantities of imports and exports, we examine the economic impact of trade barriers such as tariffs and import quotas and evaluate the arguments for protectionism. Finally, we discuss the costs of protectionism and look at continuing controversies in international trade.

Subsequent chapters discuss other international topics. Chapter 38 examines exchange rates and the balance of payments; Chapter 39 looks at the special problems of developing economies, and Chapter 40 focuses on two economies—Russia and China—which are making transitions from central planning to capitalism.

FACTS OF INTERNATIONAL TRADE

In Chapter 6 we developed a number of facts about international trade. Let's briefly review those facts and add a few others.

1. Exports of goods and services make up about 12 percent of total U.S. output. This percentage is far lower than in many other nations. Examples: Netherlands, 56 percent; Canada, 38 percent; New Zealand, 30 percent; the United Kingdom, 30 percent.

2. The United States leads the world in the volume of exports and imports. Currently, it provides about one-eighth of the world's exports, down from one-third in 1947. Germany, Japan, Britain, and France follow in the list of top five merchandise exporters by volume.

3. Since 1965, U.S. exports and imports have increased in volume and more than doubled as a percentage of GDP.

4. In 1996 the United States had a $191 billion trade deficit—meaning that imports of goods exceeded exports of goods by

this amount. But in that year U.S. exports of services exceeded its imports of services by $80 billion. Thus, the combined goods and services deficit was $111 billion.

5. The U.S.'s principal commodity exports are computers, chemicals, semiconductors, consumer durables, and aircraft. Its main imports are petroleum, automobiles, computers, and clothing.

6. Like other advanced industrial nations, the United States imports some of the same categories of goods that it exports. Examples: automobiles, computers, chemicals, semiconductors, and telecommunications equipment.

7. The bulk of U.S. export and import trade is with other industrially advanced nations, specifically Canada, nations of western Europe, and Japan.

8. Improved transportation and communications technologies, declines in tariffs, and peaceful relations among major industrial nations have all helped expand world trade since World War II.

9. Although trade is still dominated by the United States, Japan, and western European nations (Global Perspective 37-1), several new "players" have greatly increased their roles. Collectively, Hong Kong, Singapore, South Korea, and Taiwan have expanded their share of world trade from 3 percent in 1972 to nearly 10 percent today. China has emerged as a new international trader, and the collapse of communism has led eastern European nations and Russia to look globally for new trade partners.

10. International trade (and finance) link economies. Through trade, changes in economic conditions in one spot on the globe can quickly affect other places. Example: In early 1998, economists scaled back forecasts for economic growth in the United States and Europe because of economic problems in the southeast Asian countries of Japan, South Korea, Indonesia, Malaysia, and the Philippines. Reduced purchases of U.S. and European imports mean lower U.S. and European exports and thus slower U.S. and European output growth.

11. International trade is often at the center of international policy. Examples: the North American Free Trade Agreement (NAFTA), the conclusion of negotiations on the General Agreement on Tariffs and Trade (GATT), and U.S.-Japan negotiations on reducing U.S. deficits with Japan.

Global Perspective 37-1

Shares of world exports, selected nations

The United States has the largest share of world exports, followed closely by Germany and Japan. The seven largest export nations account for nearly 50 percent of world exports.

Percentage Share of World Exports, 1997

Source: Organization for Economic Cooperation and Development.

With these facts in mind, let's now look closer at the economics of international trade.

THE ECONOMIC BASIS FOR TRADE

In Chapter 6 we found that international trade allows nations to specialize, increase the productivity of their resources, and obtain more goods and services. Sovereign nations, like individuals and regions of a nation, can gain by specializing in products they can produce with greatest relative efficiency and by trading for goods they cannot produce as efficiently. This rationale for trade is correct, but a more detailed understanding is needed. The more complete answer to the question "Why do nations trade?" hinges on two facts:

1. The distribution of economic resources—natural, human, and capital goods—among nations is uneven; nations vary in their endowments of economic resources.

2. Efficient production of various goods requires different technologies or combinations of resources.

The character and interaction of these two facts can be readily illustrated. Japan, for example, has a large, well-educated labor force; skilled labor is abundant and therefore inexpensive. Japan can produce efficiently (at low cost) a variety of goods whose design and production require much skilled labor: Cameras, transistor radios, and video recorders are examples of such **labor-intensive goods.**

In contrast, Australia has vast amounts of land compared with its human and capital resources and can inexpensively produce goods requiring much land; it produces such **land-intensive goods** as wheat, wool, and meat. Brazil has the soil, tropical climate, rainfall, and lots of unskilled labor needed for efficient, low-cost production of coffee.

Industrially advanced economies with relatively large amounts of capital can produce inexpensively those goods whose production requires much capital. Automobiles, agricultural equipment, machinery, and chemicals are such **capital-intensive goods.**

The distribution of both resources and technology among nations, however, is not forever fixed. When the distribution changes, the relative efficiency with which nations produce goods also changes. For example, in the past few decades South Korea has upgraded the quality of its labor force and has greatly expanded its stock of capital. Although South Korea was primarily an exporter of agricultural products and raw materials a half-century ago, it now exports large

quantities of manufactured goods. Similarly, the new technologies which gave us synthetic fibers and synthetic rubber drastically altered the resource mix needed to produce these goods and changed the relative efficiency of nations in manufacturing them.

As national economies evolve, the size and quality of their labor forces may change, the volume and composition of their capital stocks may shift, new technologies will develop, and even the quality of land and quantity of natural resources may be altered. As these changes occur, the relative efficiency with which a nation can produce specific goods will also change.

COMPARATIVE ADVANTAGE: GRAPHICAL ANALYSIS

Implicit in what we just discussed is the principle of comparative advantage, described in Chapter 6. Let's again look at that idea, now using graphical analysis.

Two Isolated Nations

Suppose the world economy is composed of just two nations: the United States and Brazil. Each nation can produce both wheat and coffee, but at differing levels of economic efficiency. Suppose U.S. and Brazilian domestic production possibilities curves for coffee and wheat are as shown in Figure 37-1a and b. Two characteristics of these production possibilities curves should be noted:

(a) United States

(b) Brazil

FIGURE 37-1 Production possibilities for the United States and Brazil The two production possibilities curves show the combinations of coffee and wheat which (a) the United States and (b) Brazil can produce domestically. The curves for both countries are straight lines because we are assuming constant opportunity costs. The different cost ratios, 1 coffee ≡ 1 wheat for the United States, and 2 coffee ≡ 1 wheat for Brazil, are reflected in the different slopes of the two lines.

1. *Constant costs* The "curves" are drawn as straight lines, in contrast to the concave-from-the-origin production possibilities frontiers introduced in Chapter 2. This means that the law of increasing opportunity costs has been replaced with the assumption of constant costs. This simplifies our discussion but does not impair the validity of our analysis and conclusions. We later will consider the effects of the more realistic increasing costs.

2. *Different costs* The production possibilities curves of the United States and Brazil are different, reflecting different resource mixes and differing levels of technological progress. Specifically, the curves tell us that the opportunity costs of producing wheat and coffee differ between the two nations.

United States In Figure 37-1a, with full employment, the United States will operate on its production possibilities curve. On that curve, it can increase its output of wheat 30 tons by forgoing 30 tons of coffee output. This means that the slope of the production possibilities curve is -1 (= -30 coffee/$+30$ wheat), implying that 1 ton of coffee must be sacrificed for each extra 1 ton of wheat. In the United States the domestic exchange ratio or **cost ratio** for the two products is 1 ton of coffee for 1 ton wheat, or $1C \equiv 1W$. The United States can "exchange" a ton of coffee for a ton of wheat. Our constant-cost assumption means that this exchange or opportunity cost equation prevails for all possible moves from one point to another along the U.S. production possibilities curve.

Brazil Brazil's production possibilities curve in Figure 37-1b represents a different full-employment opportunity cost ratio. In Brazil, 20 tons of coffee must be given up to get 10 tons of wheat. The slope of the production possibilities curve is -2 (= -20 coffee/$+10$ wheat). This means that in Brazil the cost ratio for the two goods is 2 tons of coffee for 1 ton of wheat, or $2C \equiv 1W$.

Self-Sufficiency Output Mix If the United States and Brazil are isolated and are to be self-sufficient, then each country must choose some output mix on its production possibilities curve. Assume point *A* in Figure 37-1a is the optimal output mix in the United States; that is, the combination of 18 tons of wheat and 12 tons of coffee equates the marginal benefit and marginal cost of both goods. Suppose Brazil's optimal product mix is 8 tons of wheat and 4 tons of coffee, indicated by point *B* in Figure 37-1b. These choices are also reflected in column 1, Table 37-1.

Specializing According to Comparative Advantage

With these different cost ratios, determining the products in which the United States and Brazil should specialize is as follows: The **principle of comparative advantage** says that *total output will be greatest when each good is produced by that nation which has the lowest domestic opportunity cost for that good.* In our two-nation illustration, the United States has the lower domestic opportunity cost for wheat; the United States need only forgo 1 ton of coffee to produce 1 ton of wheat,

TABLE 37-1 International specialization according to comparative advantage and the gains from trade
(in tons)

Country	(1) Outputs before specialization	(2) Outputs after specialization	(3) Amounts exported (−) and imported (+)	(4) Outputs available after trade	(5) = (4) − (1) Gains from specialization and trade
United States	18 wheat 12 coffee	30 wheat 0 coffee	−10 wheat +15 coffee	20 wheat 15 coffee	2 wheat 3 coffee
Brazil	8 wheat 4 coffee	0 wheat 20 coffee	+10 wheat −15 coffee	10 wheat 5 coffee	2 wheat 1 coffee

whereas Brazil must forgo 2 tons of coffee for 1 ton of wheat. *The United States has a comparative (cost) advantage in wheat and should specialize in wheat production.* The "world" (the United States and Brazil) clearly is *not* economizing in the use of its resources if a specific product (wheat) is produced by a high-cost producer (Brazil) when it could have been produced by a low-cost producer (the United States). To have Brazil produce wheat would mean that the world economy would have to give up more coffee than is necessary to obtain a ton of wheat.

Brazil has the lower domestic opportunity cost for coffee; it must sacrifice only $\frac{1}{2}$ ton of wheat in producing 1 ton of coffee, while the United States must forgo 1 ton of wheat in producing a ton of coffee. *Brazil has a comparative advantage in coffee and should specialize in coffee production.* Again, the world would *not* be employing its resources economically if coffee were produced by a high-cost producer (the United States) rather than a low-cost producer (Brazil). If the United States produced coffee, the world would be giving up more wheat than necessary to obtain each ton of coffee. *Economizing—using fixed quantities of scarce resources to obtain the greatest total output—requires that any particular good be produced by that nation having the lowest domestic opportunity cost, or the comparative advantage for that good.* The United States should produce wheat and Brazil, coffee.

In column 2 of Table 37-1 we verify that specialized production in accordance with the principle of comparative advantage allows the world to get more output from its fixed amount of resources. By specializing completely in wheat, the United States can produce 30 tons of wheat and no coffee. Brazil, by specializing completely in coffee, can produce 20 tons of coffee and no wheat. The world ends up with more wheat—30 tons compared with 26 (= 18 + 8)—*and* more coffee—20 tons compared with 16 (= 12 + 4)—than when there is self-sufficiency or unspecialized production.

Terms of Trade

But consumers of each nation want *both* wheat and coffee. They can have both if the two nations trade or exchange the two products. But what will be the **terms of trade?** That is, at what exchange ratio will the United States and Brazil trade wheat and coffee?

Because $1W \equiv 1C$ in the United States, the United States must get *more than* 1 ton of coffee for each ton of wheat exported or it will not benefit from export-

ing wheat in exchange for Brazilian coffee. The United States must get a better "price" (more coffee) for its wheat in the world market than it can get domestically, or there is no gain from trade and it will not occur.

Similarly, because $1W \equiv 2C$ in Brazil, Brazil must get 1 ton of wheat by exporting some amount *less than* 2 tons of coffee. Brazil must be able to pay a lower "price" for wheat in the world market than it must pay domestically, or it will not want to trade. The international exchange ratio or *terms of trade* must lie somewhere between

$1W \equiv 1C$ (United States' cost conditions)

and

$1W \equiv 2C$ (Brazil's cost conditions)

But where between these limits will the world exchange ratio fall? The United States will prefer a rate close to $1W \equiv 2C$, say, $1W \equiv 1\frac{3}{4}C$. The United States wants to get much coffee for each ton of wheat it exports. Similarly, Brazil wants a rate near $1W \equiv 1C$, say, $1W \equiv 1\frac{1}{4}C$. Brazil wants to export as little coffee as possible for each ton of wheat it receives in exchange. The exchange ratio or terms of trade determines how the gains from international specialization and trade are divided between the two nations.

The final exchange ratio depends on world supply and demand for the two products. If overall world demand for coffee is weak relative to its supply and the demand for wheat is strong relative to its supply, the price of coffee will be lower and the price of wheat higher. The exchange ratio will settle nearer the $1W \equiv 2C$ figure the United States prefers. Under the opposite world supply and demand conditions, the ratio will settle nearer the $1W \equiv 1C$ level favorable to Brazil. (We discuss equilibrium world prices later in this chapter.)

Gains from Trade

Suppose the international terms of trade are $1W \equiv 1\frac{1}{2}C$. The possibility of trading on these terms permits each nation to supplement its domestic production possibilities line with a **trading possibilities line.** This can be seen in **Figure 37-2 (Key Graph).** Just as a production possibilities curve shows the amounts of these products a full-employment economy can obtain by shifting resources from one to the other, a trading possibilities line shows the amounts of two products a nation can obtain by specializing in one product and trading for the other. The trading

(a) United States

(b) Brazil

FIGURE 37-2 Trading possibility lines and the gains from trade   As a result of specialization and trade, the United States and Brazil both can have higher levels of output than those attainable on their domestic production possibilities curves. (a) The United States can move from point A on its domestic production possibilities curve to, say, A' on its trading possibilities line. (b) Brazil can move from B to B'.

QUICK QUIZ 37-2

1. The production possiblities curves in graphs (a) and (b) imply:
  a. increasing domestic opportunity costs.
  b. decreasing domestic opportunity costs.
  c. constant domestic opportunity costs.
  d. first decreasing, then increasing, domestic opportunity costs.

2. Before specialization, the domestic opportunity cost of producing 1 unit of wheat is:
  a. 1 unit of coffee in both the United States and Brazil.
  b. 1 unit of coffee in the United States and 2 units of coffee in Brazil.
  c. 2 units of coffee in the United States and 1 unit of coffee in Brazil.
  d. 1 unit of coffee in the United States and 1/2 unit of coffee in Brazil.

3. After specialization and trade, the world output of wheat and coffee is:
  a. 20 tons of wheat and 20 tons of coffee.
  b. 45 tons of wheat and 15 tons of coffee.
  c. 30 tons of wheat and 20 tons of coffee.
  d. 10 tons of wheat and 30 tons of coffee.

4. After specialization and international trade:
  a. the United States can obtain units of coffee at less cost than before trade.
  b. Brazil can obtain more than 20 tons of coffee, if it so chooses.
  c. the United States no longer has a comparative advantage in producing wheat.
  d. Brazil can benefit by prohibiting coffee imports from the United States.

Answers: 1. c; 2. b; 3. c; 4. a

possibilities lines in Figure 37-2 are drawn on the assumption that both nations specialize based on comparative advantage—the United States specializes completely in wheat (at point W in Figure 37-2a) and Brazil completely in coffee (at point c in Figure 37-2b).

Improved Options   Now, the United States is not constrained by its domestic production possibilities line, which requires it to give up 1 ton of wheat for every ton of coffee it wants as it moves up its domestic production possibilities line from, say, point W. Instead, the United States, through trade with Brazil, can get $1\frac{1}{2}$ tons of coffee for every ton of wheat it exports to Brazil, so long as Brazil has coffee to export. Trading possibilities line WC' thus represents the $1W \equiv 1\frac{1}{2}C$ trading ratio.

Similarly, Brazil, starting at, say, point c, no longer has to move down its domestic production possibilities curve, giving up 2 tons of coffee for each ton of wheat it wants. It can now export just $1\frac{1}{2}$ tons of coffee for each ton of wheat it wants by moving down its trading possibilities line cw'.

Specialization and trade create a new exchange ratio between wheat and coffee, reflected in each nation's trading possibilities line. This exchange ratio is superior for both nations to the unspecialized self-sufficiency exchange ratio embodied in their production possibilities curves. By specializing in wheat and trading for Brazil's coffee, the United States can obtain *more than* 1 ton of coffee for 1 ton of wheat. By specializing in coffee and trading for U.S. wheat, Brazil can get 1 ton of wheat for *less than* 2 tons of coffee.

Added Output   By specializing based on comparative advantage and trading for those goods produced in the other nation with greater domestic efficiency, the United States and Brazil can realize combinations of wheat and coffee beyond their production possibilities boundaries. *Specialization according to comparative advantage results in a more efficient allocation of world resources, and larger outputs of both products are therefore available to both nations.*

Suppose that at the $1W \equiv 1\frac{1}{2}C$ terms of trade, the United States exports 10 tons of wheat to Brazil and in return Brazil exports 15 tons of coffee to the United States. How do the new quantities of wheat and coffee available to the two nations compare with the optimal product mixes that existed before specialization and trade? Point A in Figure 37-2a reminds us that the United States chose 18 tons of wheat and 12 tons of coffee originally. But, by producing 30 tons of

wheat and no coffee, and by trading 10 tons of wheat for 15 tons of coffee, the United States can obtain 20 tons of wheat and 15 tons of coffee. This new, superior combination of wheat and coffee is indicated by point A' in Figure 37-2a. Compared with the nontrading figures of 18 tons of wheat and 12 tons of coffee, the United States' **gains from trade** are 2 tons of wheat and 3 tons of coffee.

Similarly, recall that Brazil's optimal product mix was 4 tons of coffee and 8 tons of wheat (point B) before specialization and trade. Now, by specializing in coffee and trading—producing 20 tons of coffee and no wheat and exporting 15 tons of its coffee in exchange for 10 tons of American wheat—Brazil can have 5 tons of coffee and 10 tons of wheat. This new position is indicated by point B' in Figure 37-2b. Brazil's gains from trade are 1 ton of coffee and 2 tons of wheat.

As a result of specialization and trade, both countries have more of both products. Table 37-1 summarizes the transactions and outcomes. You should study it very carefully.

The fact that points A' and B' are economic positions superior to A and B is extremely important. Recall from Chapter 2 that a nation can expand its production possibilities boundary by (1) expanding the quantity and improving the quality of its resources or (2) realizing technological progress. We have now explained another way—international trade—for a nation to circumvent the output constraint imposed by its production possibilities curve. The effects of international specialization and trade are the equivalent of having more and better resources or discovering improved production techniques.

Trade with Increasing Costs

To explain the basic principles underlying international trade, we simplified our analysis in several ways. For example, we limited discussion to two products and two nations. But multiproduct/multinational analysis yields the same conclusions. We also assumed constant opportunity costs (linear) production possibilities curves, which is a more substantive simplification. Let's consider the effect of allowing increasing opportunity costs (concave-from-the-origin production possibilities curves) to enter the picture.

Suppose that the United States and Brazil initially are at positions on their concave production possibilities curves where their domestic cost ratios are $1W \equiv 1C$ and $1W \equiv 2C$, as they were in our constant-cost analysis. As before, comparative advantage indicates that the United States should specialize in wheat and Brazil in coffee. But now, as the United States begins to expand wheat production, its $1W \equiv 1C$ cost ratio will *fall*; it will have to sacrifice *more than* 1 ton of coffee to get 1 additional ton of wheat. Resources are no longer perfectly shiftable between alternative uses, as the constant-cost assumption implied. Resources less and less suitable to wheat production must be allocated to the U.S. wheat industry in expanding wheat output, and this means increasing costs—the sacrifice of larger and larger amounts of coffee for each additional ton of wheat.

Similarly, Brazil, starting from its $1W \equiv 2C$ cost ratio position, expands coffee production. But as it does, it will find that its $1W \equiv 2C$ cost ratio begins to *rise*. Sacrificing a ton of wheat will free resources which are only capable of producing something *less than* 2 tons of coffee because these transferred resources are less suitable to coffee production.

As the U.S. cost ratio falls from $1W \equiv 1C$ and the Brazilian ratio rises from $1W \equiv 2C$, a point will be reached where the cost ratios are equal in the two nations, perhaps at $1W \equiv 1\frac{3}{4}C$. At this point the underlying basis for further specialization and trade—differing cost ratios—has disappeared, and further specialization is therefore uneconomical. And most importantly, this point of equal cost ratios may be reached while the United States is still producing some coffee along with its wheat and Brazil is producing some wheat along with its coffee. *The primary effect of increasing opportunity costs is to make specialization less than complete.* For this reason we often find domestically produced products competing directly against identical or similar imported products within a particular economy. **(Key Question 4)**

The Case for Free Trade

The case for free trade reduces to one potent argument: *Through free trade based on the principle of comparative advantage, the world economy can achieve a more efficient allocation of resources and a higher level of material well-being than without free trade.* The resource mixes and technological knowledge of the world's nations are all somewhat different. Therefore, each nation can produce particular commodities at different real costs. Each nation should produce goods for which its domestic opportunity costs are lower than the domestic opportunity costs of other nations and exchange these goods for products for which its do-

mestic opportunity costs are high relative to those of other nations. If each nation does this, the world can realize the advantages of geographic and human specialization. The world—and each free-trading nation—can obtain a larger real income from the fixed supplies of resources available to it. Protection—barriers to free trade—lessens or eliminates gains from specialization. If nations cannot freely trade, they must shift resources from efficient (low-cost) to inefficient (high-cost) uses to satisfy their diverse wants.

One side benefit of free trade is that it promotes competition and deters monopoly. The increased competition from foreign firms forces domestic firms to find and use the lowest-cost production techniques. It also compels them to be innovative with respect to both product quality and production methods, thereby contributing to economic growth. And free trade gives consumers a wider range of product choices. The reasons to favor free trade are the same reasons which endorse competition.

A second side-benefit of free trade is that it links national interest and breaks down national animosities. Confronted with political disagreements, trading partners tend to negotiate rather than make war.

QUICK REVIEW 37-1

■ International trade is increasingly important to the United States and other nations of the world; the percentage of total output traded has increased since World War II.

■ International trade enables nations to specialize, enhance the productivity of their resources, and obtain a greater output.

■ Comparative advantage means total world output will be greatest when each good is produced by that nation having the lowest domestic opportunity cost.

■ Specialization is less than complete among nations because opportunity costs normally rise as any particular nation produces more of a particular good.

SUPPLY AND DEMAND ANALYSIS OF EXPORTS AND IMPORTS

Supply and demand analysis helps us see how equilibrium prices and quantities of exports and imports are determined. The amount of a good or service a nation will export or import depends on differences between the equilibrium world price and the domestic price. The equilibrium **world price** is determined by interaction of *world* supply and demand; it is the price at which the quantities supplied and demanded are equal globally. The equilibrium **domestic price** is determined by *domestic* supply and demand; it is the price which would prevail in a closed economy—one having no international trade. It is the price at which domestic quantity supplied and demanded are equal.

Because of comparative advantages and disadvantages, no-trade domestic prices *may* or *may not* equal world equilibrium prices. When economies are opened for international trade, differences between world and domestic prices motivate exports or imports. To see how, let's now look at the international effects of such price differences in a simple two-nation world.

Supply and Demand in the United States

Suppose the world consists of just the United States and Canada, each producing aluminum. There are no trade barriers such as tariffs and quotas. Also, to keep things simple, let's ignore international transportation costs.

Figure 37-3a shows the domestic supply curve S_d and domestic demand curve D_d for aluminum in the United States. The intersection of S_d and D_d determines the equilibrium domestic price of $1 per pound and the equilibrium domestic quantity of 100 million pounds. Domestic suppliers produce 100 million pounds and sell them all at $1, meaning that there are no domestic surpluses or shortages of aluminum.

But what if the U.S. economy is opened to trade and the *world price* of aluminum is above or below this $1 domestic price?

United States Export Supply If the world aluminum price exceeds $1, U.S. firms will produce more than 100 million pounds and export the excess domestic output to the rest of the world (Canada). First, consider a world price of $1.25. We see from the supply curve S_d that U.S. aluminum firms will produce 125 million pounds of aluminum at that price. The demand curve D_d tells us the United States will purchase only 75 million pounds at $1.25. A domestic surplus of 50 million pounds of aluminum will result. U.S. producers will export these 50 million pounds at the $1.25 world price.

What if the world price is $1.50? The supply curve shows that U.S. firms will produce 150 million pounds of aluminum, while the demand curve tells us that U.S. consumers will buy only 50 million pounds. The domestic surplus of 100 million pounds will be exported.

Toward the top of Figure 37-3b we plot the domestic surpluses—the U.S. exports—occurring at world prices above the $1 domestic equilibrium price. When the world and domestic prices are equal (= $1), the quantity of exports supplied is zero (point *a*). There is *no* surplus of domestic output to export. But when the world price is $1.25, U.S. firms export 50 million pounds of surplus aluminum (point *b*). At a $1.50 world price, the domestic surplus of 100 million pounds is exported (point *c*).

The U.S. **export supply curve,** found by connecting points *a*, *b*, and *c*, shows the amount of aluminum U.S. producers will export at each world price above $1. This curve *slopes upward*, indicating a direct or positive relationship between the world price and the amount of U.S. exports. *As world prices rise relative to domestic prices, U.S. exports increase.*

United States Import Demand If the world price is below the domestic $1 price, the United States will end up importing aluminum. Consider a $.75 world price. The supply curve in Figure 37-3a reveals that at that price U.S. firms will produce only 75 million pounds of aluminum. But the demand curve shows that the United States wants to buy 125 million pounds at that price. The result is a domestic shortage of 50 million pounds. To satisfy this shortage, 50 million pounds of aluminum will be imported into the United States.

At an even lower $.50 world price, U.S. producers will supply only 50 million pounds. Because U.S. consumers want to buy 150 million pounds at that price, there is a domestic shortage of 100 million pounds. Imports will flow to the United States to make up the difference. That is, at a $.50 world price U.S. firms will supply 50 million pounds and foreign firms will supply 100 million pounds.

In Figure 37-3b we plot the U.S. **import demand curve** from these data. This *downsloping curve* shows the amounts of aluminum which will be imported at world prices below the $1 U.S. domestic price. The relationship between world prices and imported amounts is inverse or negative. At a world price of $1, domestic output will satisfy U.S. demand; imports will

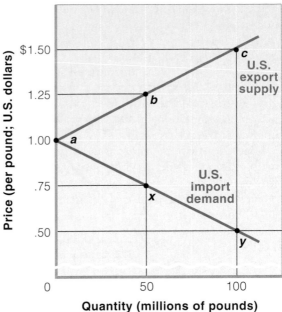

FIGURE 37-3 **United States' export supply and import demand** (a) Domestic supply S_d and demand D_d set the domestic equilibrium price of aluminum at $1 per pound. At world prices above $1 there are domestic surpluses of aluminum. At prices below $1 there are domestic shortages. (b) Surpluses are exported (top curve), and shortages are met by importing aluminum (lower curve). The export supply curve shows the direct relationship between world prices and U.S. exports; the import supply curve portrays the inverse relationship between world prices and U.S. imports.

----

be zero (point *a*). But at $.75 the United States will import 50 million pounds of aluminum (point *x*); at $.50, they will import 100 million pounds (point *y*). Connecting points *a*, *x*, and *y* yields the *downsloping* U.S. import demand curve. *It reveals that as world prices fall relative to U.S. domestic prices, U.S. imports increase.*

Supply and Demand in Canada

We repeat our analysis in Figure 37-4, this time for Canada. (We have converted Canadian dollar prices to U.S. dollar prices via the exchange rate.) Note that the domestic supply curve S_d and demand curve D_d for aluminum in Canada yield a domestic price of $.75, which is $.25 lower than the $1 U.S. domestic price.

The analysis proceeds exactly as for the United States. If the world price is $.75, Canadians will neither export nor import aluminum (which gives us

point *q* in Figure 37-4b). At world prices above $.75, Canadian firms will produce more aluminum than Canadian consumers will buy. The surplus will be exported. At a $1 world price, Figure 37-4a tells us that Canada will have and export a domestic surplus of 50 million pounds (yielding point *r*). At $1.25, it will have and export a domestic surplus of 100 million pounds (point *s*). Connecting these points yields the upsloping Canadian *export supply curve*, which reflects the domestic surpluses (and hence exports) occurring when the world price exceeds the $.75 Canadian domestic price.

Domestic shortages occur in Canada at world prices below $.75. At a $.50 world price, Figure 37-4a shows that Canadian consumers want to buy 125 million pounds of aluminum but Canadian firms will produce only 75 million pounds. The shortage will bring 50 million pounds of imports to Canada (point *t* in Figure 37-4b). The Canadian *import demand curve*

FIGURE 37-4 **Canadian export supply and import demand**   (a) At world prices above the $.75 domestic price, production in Canada exceeds domestic consumption. At world prices below $.75, domestic shortages occur. (b) Surpluses result in exports, and shortages result in imports. The Canadian export supply curve and import demand curve depict the relationships between world prices and exports or imports.

----

in that figure shows Canadian imports which will occur at all world aluminum prices below the $.75 Canadian domestic price.

Equilibrium World Price, Exports, and Imports

We now have the tools to determine the equilibrium world price of aluminum and the equilibrium world levels of exports and imports. Figure 37-5 combines the U.S. export supply curve and import demand curve in Figure 37-3b and the Canadian export supply curve and import demand curve in Figure 37-4b. The two U.S. curves proceed rightward from the $1 U.S. domestic price; the two Canadian curves proceed rightward from the $.75 Canadian domestic price. *International equilibrium occurs in this two-nation model where one nation's import demand curve intersects another nation's export supply curve.* In this case the U.S. import demand curve intersects Canada's export supply curve at *e*. There, the world price of aluminum is

$.88. The Canadian export supply curve indicates that Canada will export 25 million pounds of aluminum at this price. Also at this price the United States will import 25 million pounds from Canada, indicated by the U.S. import demand curve. The $.88 world price equates the quantity of imports demanded and the quantity of exports supplied (25 million pounds). Thus there will be world trade of 25 million pounds of aluminum at $.88 per pound.

Note that after trade, the single $.88 world price will prevail in both Canada and the United States. *Only one price for a standardized commodity can persist in a highly competitive world market.* With trade, all consumers can buy a pound of aluminum for $.88, and all producers can sell it for that price. This world price means that Canadians will pay more for aluminum with trade ($.88) than without it ($.75). The increased Canadian output caused by trade raises Canadian per-unit production costs and therefore raises the price of aluminum in Canada. The United States, however, pays less for aluminum with trade ($.88) than without

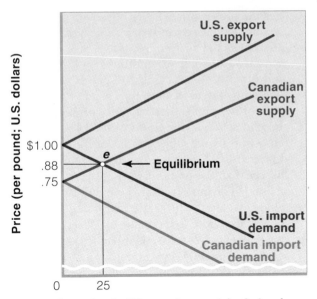

FIGURE 37-5 Equilibrium world price and quantity of exports and imports In a two-nation world, the equilibrium world price (= $.88) is determined by the intersection of one nation's export supply curve and the other nation's import demand curve. This intersection also decides the equilibrium volume of exports and imports. Here, Canada exports 25 million pounds of aluminum to the United States.

---

it ($1). The U.S. gain comes from Canada's comparative cost advantage in producing aluminum.

Why would Canada willingly send 50 million pounds of its aluminum output to the United States for U.S. consumption? After all, producing this output uses up scarce Canadian resources and drives up the price of aluminum for Canadians. Canadians are willing to export aluminum to the United States because Canadians gain the means—the U.S. dollars—to import other goods, say, computer software, from the United States. Canadian exports enable Canadians to acquire imports that have greater value to Canadians than the exported aluminum. Canadian exports to the United States finance Canadian imports from the United States. **(Key Question 6)**

TRADE BARRIERS

No matter how compelling the case for free trade, barriers to free trade *do* exist. Let's examine Chapter 6's list of trade impediments more closely.

1. **Tariffs** are excise taxes on imported goods; they may be imposed to obtain revenue or to protect domestic firms.

A **revenue tariff** is usually applied to a product not produced domestically, for example, tin, coffee, or bananas in the case of the United States. Rates on revenue tariffs are modest; their purpose is to provide the Federal government with revenues.

A **protective tariff** is designed to shield domestic producers from foreign competition. Although protective tariffs are usually not high enough to stop the importation of foreign goods, they put foreign producers at a competitive disadvantage in selling in domestic markets.

2. An **import quota** specifies the maximum amount of a commodity which may be imported in any period. Import quotas can more effectively retard international commerce than tariffs. A product might be imported in large quantities despite high tariffs; low import quotas completely prohibit imports once quotas are filled.

3. A **nontariff barrier** (NTB) is a licensing requirement, unreasonable standards pertaining to product quality and safety, or unnecessary bureaucratic red tape which is used to restrict imports. Japan and the European countries frequently require their domestic importers of foreign goods to obtain licenses. By restricting the issuance of licenses, imports can be restricted. Great Britain uses this barrier to bar importation of coal.

4. A **voluntary export restriction** (VER) is a trade barrier by which foreign firms "voluntarily" limit the amount of their exports to a particular country. VERs, which have the effect of import quotas, are agreed to by exporters in the hope of avoiding more stringent trade barriers. Japanese auto manufacturers agreed to a VER on exports to the United States under the threat of higher U.S. tariffs or the imposition of low import quotas.

Later in this chapter we will consider the specific arguments and appeals which are made to justify protection.

Economic Impact of Tariffs

Once again we turn to supply and demand analysis—now to examine the economic effects of protective tariffs. Curves D_d and S_d in Figure 37-6 show

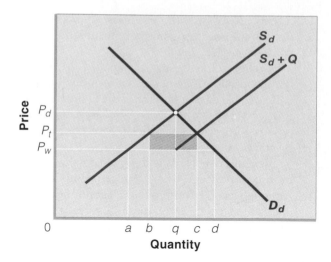

FIGURE 37-6 The economic effects of a protective tariff or an import quota A tariff that increases the price of a good from P_w to P_t will reduce domestic consumption from d to c. Domestic producers will be able to sell more output (b rather than a) at a higher price (P_t rather than P_w). Foreign exporters are injured because they sell less output (bc rather than ad). The orange area indicates the amount of tariff paid by domestic consumers. An import quota of bc units has the same effect as the tariff, with one exception: The amount represented by the orange area will go to foreign producers rather than to the domestic government.

- -

domestic demand and supply for a product in which a nation, say, the United States, has a comparative *dis*advantage, for example, video cassette recorders (VCRs). (Disregard curve $S_d + Q$ for now.) Without world trade, the domestic price and output would be P_d and q, respectively.

Assume now that the domestic economy is opened to world trade and that the Japanese, who have a comparative advantage in VCRs, begin to sell their recorders in the United States. We assume that with free trade the domestic price cannot differ from the world price, which here is P_w. At P_w domestic consumption is d and domestic production is a. The horizontal distance between the domestic supply and demand curves at P_w represents imports of ad. Thus far, our analysis is similar to the analysis of world prices in Figure 37-3.

Direct Effects Suppose now that the United States imposes a tariff on each imported VCR. The tariff raises the price of imported VCRs from P_w to P_t and has four effects:

1. *Decline in consumption* Consumption of video recorders in the United States declines from d to

c as the higher price moves buyers up and to the left along their demand curve. The tariff prompts consumers to buy fewer recorders; they reallocate a portion of their expenditures to less desired substitute products. U.S. consumers are clearly injured by the tariff since they pay $P_w P_t$ more for each of the c units they buy at price P_t.

2. *Increased domestic production* U.S. producers—who are *not* subject to the tariff—receive the higher price P_t per unit. Because this new price is higher than the pretariff world price P_w, the domestic VCR industry moves up and to the right along its supply curve S_d, increasing domestic output from a to b. Domestic producers thus enjoy both a higher price and expanded sales, which explains why domestic producers lobby for protective tariffs. But from a social point of view, the greater domestic production from a to b means the tariff permits domestic producers of recorders to bid resources away from other, more efficient, U.S. industries.

3. *Decline in imports* Japanese producers are hurt. Although the sales price of each recorder is higher by $P_w P_t$, that amount accrues to the U.S. government, not to Japanese producers. The after-tariff world price, and thus the per-unit revenue to Japanese producers, remains at P_w, while the volume of U.S. imports (Japanese exports) falls from ad to bc.

4. *Tariff revenue* The orange rectangle represents the amount of revenue which the tariff yields. Total revenue from the tariff is determined by multiplying the tariff, $P_w P_t$ per unit, by the number of recorders imported, bc. This tariff revenue is a transfer of income from consumers to government and does *not* represent any net change in the nation's economic well-being. The result is that government gains this portion of what consumers lose by paying more for VCRs.

Indirect Effect Tariffs have a subtle effect beyond what our supply and demand diagram can show. Because Japan sells fewer VCRs in the United States, it earns fewer dollars and so must buy fewer U.S. exports. U.S. export industries—industries in which the United States has a comparative advantage—must then cut production and release resources. These are highly efficient industries, as we know from their comparative advantage and ability to sell goods in world markets.

Tariffs directly promote the expansion of inefficient industries which do not have a comparative advantage; they

also indirectly cause the contraction of relatively efficient industries which do have a comparative advantage. This means tariffs cause resources to be shifted in the wrong direction—and that is not surprising. We know that specialization and world trade lead to more efficient use of world resources and greater world output. But protective tariffs reduce world trade. Therefore, tariffs also reduce efficiency and the world's real output.

Economic Impact of Quotas

We noted previously that an import quota is a legal limit placed on the amount of some product which can be imported each year. Quotas have the same economic impact as a tariff, with one big difference: While tariffs generate revenue for the domestic government, a quota transfers that revenue to foreign producers.

Suppose in Figure 37-6 that, instead of imposing a tariff, the United States prohibits any Japanese imports of VCRs in excess of bc units. In other words, an import quota of bc recorders is imposed on Japan. We deliberately chose the size of this quota to be the same amount as imports would be under a P_wP_t tariff so that we are comparing "equivalent" situations. As a consequence of the quota, the supply of recorders is $S_d + Q$ in the United States. This supply consists of the domestic supply plus the fixed amount bc ($= Q$) which importers will provide at each domestic price. The supply curve $S_d + Q$ does not extend below price P_w because Japanese producers would not export recorders to the United States at any price *below* P_w; instead they would sell them to other countries at the world market price of P_w.

Most of the economic results are the same as with a tariff. VCR prices are higher (P_t instead of P_w) because imports have been reduced from ad to bc. Domestic consumption of VCRs is down from d to c. U.S. producers enjoy both a higher price (P_t rather than P_w) and increased sales (b rather than a).

The difference is that the price increase of P_wP_t paid by U.S. consumers on imports of bc—the orange area—no longer goes to the United States Treasury as tariff (tax) revenue but flows to those Japanese firms which have acquired the rights to sell VCRs in the United States. For consumers in the United States, a tariff produces a better economic outcome than a quota, other things being the same. A tariff generates government revenue which can be used to cut other taxes or to finance public goods and services which benefit the United States. In contrast, the higher price created by quotas results in additional revenue for foreign producers. **(Key Question 7)**

THE CASE FOR PROTECTION: A CRITICAL REVIEW

Despite the logic of specialization and trade, there are still protectionists in some union halls, corporate boardrooms, and the halls of Congress. What arguments do protectionists make to justify trade barriers? How valid are these arguments?

Military Self-Sufficiency Argument

The argument here is not economic but political-military: Protective tariffs are needed to preserve or strengthen industries which produce the materials essential for national defense. In an uncertain world, the political-military objectives (self-sufficiency) sometimes must take precedence over economic goals (efficiency in the use of world resources.)

Unfortunately, it is difficult to measure and compare the benefit of increased national security against the cost of economic inefficiency when protective tariffs are imposed. The economist can only point out that there are economic costs when a nation levies tariffs to increase military self-sufficiency.

All people in the United States would agree that it is not a good idea to import missile guidance systems from Iraq, yet the self-sufficiency argument is open to serious abuse. Nearly every industry can claim that it makes direct or indirect contributions to national security and hence deserves protection from imports.

Are there not better ways than tariffs to provide needed strength in strategic industries? When it is achieved through tariffs, this self-sufficiency increases the domestic prices of the products of the protected industry. Thus only those consumers who buy the industry's products shoulder the cost of greater military security. A direct subsidy to strategic industries, financed out of general tax revenues, would distribute these costs more equitably.

Increased Domestic Employment Argument

Arguing for a tariff to "save U.S. jobs" becomes fashionable as an economy encounters a recession. In an economy which engages in international trade, exports involve spending on domestic output and imports reflect spending to obtain part of another nation's output. So, in this argument, reducing imports will divert spending on another nation's output to spending on domestic output. Thus domestic output and employment will rise. But this argument has several shortcomings:

1. *Job creation from imports*   While imports may eliminate some U.S. jobs, they create others. Imports may have eliminated the jobs of some U.S. steel and textile workers in recent years, but other workers have gained jobs unloading ships and selling imported cars and imported electronic equipment. Import restrictions alter the composition of employment, but they may have little or no effect on the volume of employment.

2. *Fallacy of composition*   All nations cannot simultaneously succeed in restricting imports while maintaining their exports; what is true for *one* nation is not true for *all* nations. The exports of one nation must be the imports of another nation. To the extent that one country is able to expand its economy through an excess of exports over imports, the resulting excess of imports over exports worsens another economy's unemployment problem. It is no wonder that tariffs and import quotas meant to achieve domestic full employment are called "beggar my neighbor" policies: They achieve short-run domestic goals by making trading partners poorer.

3. *Possibility of retaliation*   Nations adversely affected by tariffs and quotas are likely to retaliate, causing a "trade-barrier war" which will choke off trade and make all nations worse off. The *Smoot-Hawley Tariff Act of 1930*, which imposed the highest tariffs ever enacted in the United States, backfired miserably. Rather than increasing U.S. output, this tariff act only led to retaliatory restrictions by affected nations. This trade war caused a further contraction of international trade and lowered the income and employment levels of all nations. As stated by a U.S. international trade expert:

A trade war in which countries restrict each other's exports in pursuit of some illusory advantage is not much like a real war. On the one hand, nobody gets killed. On the other, unlike real wars, it is almost impossible for anyone to win, since the main losers when a country imposes barriers to trade are not foreign exporters but domestic residents. In effect, a trade war is a conflict in which each country uses most of its ammunition to shoot itself in the foot.[1]

4. *Long-run feedbacks*   In the long run, forcing an excess of exports over imports cannot exceed in raising domestic employment. It is through U.S. imports that foreign nations earn dollars for buying U.S. exports. In the long run a nation must import to export. The long-run impact of tariffs is not to increase domestic employment but at best to reallocate workers away from export industries and to protected domestic industries. This shift implies a less efficient allocation of resources.

Diversification for Stability Argument

Highly specialized economies such as Saudi Arabia's (based on oil) and Cuba's (based on sugar) are very dependent on international markets for their incomes. In these economies, wars, international political developments, recessions abroad, and random fluctuations in world supply and demand for one or two particular goods can cause deep declines in export revenues and therefore in domestic income. Tariff and quota protection are allegedly needed in such nations to enable greater industrial diversification. That way, these economies will not be so dependent on exporting one or two products to obtain the other goods they need. Such goods will be available domestically, thereby providing greater domestic stability.

There is some truth in this diversification for stability argument. There are also two serious shortcomings:

1. The argument has little or no relevance to the United States and other advanced economies.

2. The economic costs of diversification may be great; for example, one-crop economies may be highly inefficient at manufacturing.

Infant Industry Argument

The infant industry argument contends that protective tariffs are needed to allow new domestic industries to establish themselves. Temporarily shielding young domestic firms from the severe competition of more mature and more efficient foreign firms will give infant industries a chance to develop and become efficient producers.

This argument for protection rests on an alleged exception to the case for free trade. The exception is that young industries have not had, and if they face mature foreign competition will never have, the chance to make the long-run adjustments needed for larger

[1]Paul Krugman, *Peddling Prosperity* (New York: W. W. Norton, 1994), p. 287.

scale and greater efficiency in production. In this view, tariff protection for such infant industries will correct a misallocation of world resources perpetuated by historically different levels of economic development between domestic and foreign industries.

Counterarguments   There are some logical problems with this infant industry argument:

1. In the developing nations it is difficult to determine which industries are the infants that are capable of achieving economic maturity and therefore deserving protection.

2. Protective tariffs may persist even after industrial maturity has been realized.

3. Most economists feel that if infant industries are to be subsidized, there are better means than tariffs for doing it. Direct subsidies, for example, have the advantage of making explicit which industries are being aided and to what degree.

Strategic Trade Policy   In recent years the infant industry argument has taken a modified form in advanced economies. Now proponents contend that government should use trade barriers to reduce the risk of investing in product development by domestic firms, particularly where advanced technology is involved. Firms protected from foreign competition can grow more rapidly and achieve greater economies of scale than unprotected foreign competitors. The protected firms can eventually dominate world markets because of their lower costs. Supposedly, dominance of world markets will enable the domestic firms to return high profits to the home nation. These profits will exceed the domestic sacrifices caused by trade barriers. Also, advances in high-technology industries are deemed beneficial because the advances achieved in one domestic industry often can be transferred to other domestic industries.

Japan and South Korea, in particular, have been accused of using this form of **strategic trade policy.** The problem with this strategy and therefore this argument for tariffs is that the nations put at a disadvantage by strategic trade policies tend to retaliate with tariffs of their own. The outcome may be higher tariffs worldwide, reductions of world trade, and the loss of potential gains from technological advances.

Protection Against Dumping Argument

This argument contends that tariffs are needed to protect domestic firms from "dumping" by foreign producers. **Dumping** is the selling of excess goods in a foreign market at a price below cost. Economists cite two plausible reasons for this behavior:

1. Firms may use dumping abroad to drive out domestic competitors there, thus obtaining monopoly power and monopoly prices and profits for the importing firm. The long-term economic profits resulting from this strategy may more than offset the earlier losses that accompany the below-cost sales.

2. Dumping may be a form of *price discrimination*, which is charging different prices to different customers even though costs are the same. The foreign seller may find it can maximize its profit by charging a high price in its monopolized domestic market while unloading its surplus output at a lower price in the United States. The surplus output may be needed so the firm can obtain the overall per-unit cost saving associated with large-scale production. The higher profit in the home market more than makes up for the losses incurred on sales abroad.

Because dumping is a legitimate concern, many nations prohibit it. For example, where dumping is shown to injure U.S. firms, the Federal government imposes tariffs called "antidumping duties" on the specific goods. But there are relatively few documented cases of dumping each year, and those few cases do *not* justify widespread, permanent tariffs.

In fact, foreign producers argue that the United States uses dumping allegations and antidumping duties to restrict legitimate trade. Some foreign firms clearly can produce certain goods at substantially less per-unit cost than U.S. competitors. So, what may seem to be dumping actually is comparative advantage at work. If antidumping laws are abused, they can increase the price of imports and restrict competition in the U.S. market. This reduced competition can allow U.S. firms to raise prices at consumers' expense. And even where true dumping does occur, U.S. consumers gain from the lower-priced product, at least in the short run, much as they gain from a price war among U.S. producers.

Cheap Foreign Labor Argument

The cheap foreign labor argument says that domestic firms and workers must be shielded from the ruinous competition of countries where wages are low. If protection is not provided, cheap imports will flood U.S. markets and the prices of U.S. goods—along with the wages of U.S. workers—will be pulled down. That is, the domestic living standards in the United States will be reduced.

This argument can be rebutted at several levels. The logic of the argument suggests that it is *not* mutually beneficial for rich and poor persons to trade with one another. However, that is not the case. A low-income farm worker may pick lettuce or tomatoes for a rich landowner, and both may benefit from the transaction. And U.S. consumers gain when they buy a Taiwanese-made pocket radio for $12 as opposed to a similar U.S.-made radio selling for $20.

Also, recall that gains from trade are based on comparative advantage, not on absolute advantage. Looking back at Figure 37-1, suppose the United States and Brazil have labor forces of exactly the same size. Noting the positions of the production possibilities curves, we observe that U.S. labor can produce more of *either* good. Thus, it is more productive. Because of this greater productivity, we can expect wages and living standards to be higher for U.S. labor. Brazil's less productive labor will receive lower wages.

The cheap foreign labor argument suggests that, to maintain our standard of living, the United States should not trade with low-wage Brazil. Suppose it does not. Will wages and living standards rise in the United States as a result? No. To obtain coffee the United States will have to reallocate a portion of its labor from its efficient wheat industry to its inefficient coffee industry. As a result, the average productivity of U.S. labor will fall, as will real wages and living standards. The labor forces of *both* countries will have diminished standards of living because without specialization and trade they will have less output available to them. Compare column 4 with column 1 in Table 37-1 or points A' and B' with A and B in Figure 37-2 to confirm this point.

A Summing Up

These many arguments for protection are not weighty. Under proper conditions, the infant-industry argument stands as a valid exception, justifiable on economic grounds. And on political-military grounds, the self-sufficiency argument can be used to validate some protection. But both arguments are open to severe overuse, and both neglect other ways of promoting industrial development and military self-sufficiency. Most other arguments are emotional appeals—half-truths and fallacies. These arguments

see only the immediate and direct consequences of protective tariffs. They ignore the fact that in the long run a nation must import to export.

There is also compelling historical evidence suggesting that free trade has led to prosperity and growth and that protectionism has had the opposite effects. Here are several examples:

1. The U.S. Constitution forbids individual states from levying tariffs, and that makes the United States a huge free-trade area. Economic historians cite this as a positive factor in the economic development of the United States.

2. Great Britain's shift toward freer international trade in the mid-nineteenth century was instrumental in its industrialization and growth at that time.

3. The creation of the Common Market in Europe after World War II eliminated tariffs among member nations. Economists agree that creation of this free-trade area, now the European Union, was a major ingredient in western European prosperity.

4. The trend toward tariff reduction since the mid-1930s stimulated post-World War II expansion of the world economy.

5. The high tariffs imposed by the Smoot-Hawley Act of 1930 and the retaliation which it engendered worsened the Great Depression of the 1930s.

6. Studies of developing countries strongly suggest that those which have relied on import restrictions to protect their domestic industries have had slow growth compared to those pursuing more open economic policies (see Global Perspective 37-2).

QUICK REVIEW 37-2

■ A nation will export a particular product if the world price exceeds the domestic price; it will import the product if the world price is less than the domestic price.

■ In a two-country model, equilibrium world prices and equilibrium quantities of exports and imports occur where one nation's export supply curve intersects the other nation's import demand curve.

■ Trade barriers include tariffs, import quotas, nontariff barriers, and voluntary export restrictions.

■ A tariff on a product increases price, reduces consumption, increases domestic production, reduces imports, and generates tariff revenue for government; an import quota does the same, except a quota generates revenue for

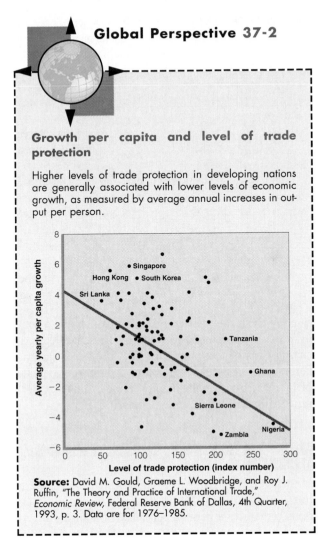

Global Perspective 37-2

Growth per capita and level of trade protection

Higher levels of trade protection in developing nations are generally associated with lower levels of economic growth, as measured by average annual increases in output per person.

Source: David M. Gould, Graeme L. Woodbridge, and Roy J. Ruffin, "The Theory and Practice of International Trade," *Economic Review,* Federal Reserve Bank of Dallas, 4th Quarter, 1993, p. 3. Data are for 1976–1985.

foreign producers rather than for the government imposing the quota.

■ Most arguments for trade protection are special-interest pleas which, if followed, would create gains for protected industries and their workers at the expense of greater losses for the economy.

COSTS OF PROTECTION

In spite of the weakness of most arguments for trade protection, the United States and most other countries continue to impose some protective measures. (These tariffs and quotas, however, are falling under terms of the recent world trade agreements.) How costly are trade protections to the United States?

Cost to Society

Figure 37-6 shows that tariffs and quotas impose costs on domestic consumers but provide gains to domestic producers, and in the case of tariffs, revenue to the Federal government. The consumer cost of trade restrictions can be calculated by determining the effect they have on the prices of protected goods. Protection raises the price of a product in three ways:

1. The price of the imported product goes up.
2. The higher price of imports causes some consumers to shift their purchases to higher-priced domestically produced goods.
3. The prices of domestically produced goods rise because import competition has declined.

Recent studies indicate that costs to consumers of protected products substantially exceed gains to producers and government.[2] There is a sizable net cost or efficiency loss to society from trade protection. Most recently the United States International Trade Commission (USITC)—the agency which hears unfair trade complaints—estimated that U.S. trade barriers resulted in a net cost to the United States of more than $15 billion annually in the mid-1990s.

Furthermore, net losses from trade barriers are greater than the losses reported in most studies. Tariffs and quotas produce many costly, difficult-to-quantify secondary effects. For example, import restraints on steel in the 1980s drove up the price of steel to all U.S. buyers of steel, including the U.S. automobile industry. Therefore, U.S. automakers had higher costs than otherwise and were less competitive in world markets.

Finally, industries employ large amounts of economic resources to influence Congress to pass and retain protectionist laws. Because these rent-seeking efforts divert resources away from more socially desirable purposes, trade restrictions also impose that cost on society.

Conclusion: The gains which U.S. trade barriers create for protected industries and their workers come at the expense of much greater losses for the entire economy. The result is economic inefficiency.

Column 1 in Table 37-2 lists the U.S. industries with the highest net costs due to trade protection; column 2 lists those net costs. Column 3 shows the

[2]United States International Trade Commision, *The Economic Effects of Significant U.S. Import Restraints: First Biannual Investigation,* December, 1995; Gary C. Hufbauer and Kimberly A. Elliot, *Measuring the Costs of Protectionism in the United States* (Washington: Institute for International Economics, 1994), pp. 8–9.

TABLE 37-2 The net costs of trade protection, eight industries

(1) Industry	(2) Annual loss to economy from barriers	(3) Net employment loss if barrier removed	(4) Annual cost per job saved
Textile and apparel	$ 10.04 billion	55,000	$ 182,545
Maritime transport	2.79 billion	2,450	1,138,775
Dairy	1.01 billion	2,083	484,878
Motor vehicles	710.00 million	3,400	208,824
Sugar	661.00 million	1,694	390,200
Meat	185.00 million	100	1,850,000
Steel mills	162.00 million	1,265	128,063
Nonrubber footwear	147.00 million	1,316	111,702

Source: Compiled from United States International Trade Commission data released in December 1995. Data are for 1993.

number of U.S. jobs which would be lost if the trade barriers were eliminated. Column 4 reveals how much the trade barriers cost per U.S. job they save (column 2 divided by column 3). Two items stand out in the table:

1. Trade restrictions in the textile and apparel industries are especially costly to the United States. The Federal government has imposed import quotas on more than 3000 kinds of textile products. [These quotas eventually will be replaced with tariffs under the terms of the General Agreement on Tariffs and Trade (Chapter 6).]

2. The cost of saving jobs through trade protection is enormous. Because annual wages per job in these industries are only a fraction of the amounts in column 4, protectionism to save jobs is hardly a bargain. Moreover, it is clear from historical experience that eliminating trade barriers does not cause a *net* loss of jobs in the United States; it simply redistributes employment, and it may even increase it.

Impact on Income Distribution

Also, import restrictions affect low-income families proportionately more than high-income families. Because tariffs and quotas act much like sales or excise taxes, these trade restrictions are highly regressive. That is, the "overcharge" associated with trade protection falls *as a percentage of income* as income increases. For example, a family with an annual income of $10,000 may pay an overcharge of $100 per year be-

cause of the trade restrictions on apparel, while a family with an income of $100,000 may pay a $500 overcharge. As a percentage of income, the lower-income family pays 1 percent (= $100 of overcharge/$10,000 of income); the higher-income family, only 0.5 percent ($500/$100,000). **(Key Question 11)**

U.S. INTERNATIONAL TRADE POLICY

In the past decade U.S. international trade policy has been a mixture of generalized trade liberalization, aggressive export promotion, and bilateral negotiations on specific trade disputes.

Generalized Trade Liberalization

In Chapter 6 we discussed two recent regional and global agreements to reduce trade barriers.

North American Free Trade Agreement This accord, which took effect in 1994, eliminates tariffs and other trade barriers among Canada, Mexico, and the United States over a 15-year period. When fully implemented, the North American Free Trade Agreement (NAFTA) will constitute the largest geographical free-trade zone in the world.

General Agreement on Tariffs and Trade In 1994 more than 120 of the world's nations successfully completed negotiation of the Uruguay Round of the General Agreement on Tariffs and Trade (GATT). GATT provisions to be implemented between 1995 and 2005 include:

1. Reduction of tariffs worldwide

2. Liberalization of rules which have impeded trade in services

3. Reduction of agricultural subsidies which have distorted the global pattern of trade in agricultural goods

4. New protections for intellectual property (copyrights, patents, trademarks)

5. Phasing out quotas on textiles and apparel, replacing them with gradually declining tariffs

6. Establishment of the **World Trade Organization** to oversee the provisions of the agreement and to resolve any disputes under the new rules

When completed in 2005, GATT will boost the world's GDP by an estimated $6 trillion, or 8 percent.

Aggressive Export Promotion

The Federal government recently began aggressively promoting U.S. exports in a number of ways. Undoubtedly, the reason is that such exports generally support high-paying jobs and increases in exports are needed to end U.S. trade deficits. Perhaps, too, the popular myth that the global marketplace is a battleground for economic supremacy played a role. But trade is not like war, or like a World Cup match, in which one nation wins and the other loses. Every nation is both seller *and* buyer in the world market. Gains from trade come from the increased consumable output shared by the trading countries. Exports are *not* the end goal of international trade; they simply enable a country to pay for imports—goods which would cost the nation more to produce at home.

Here are five recent examples of export promotion policy at work:

1. Direct government advocacy of export interests of U.S. producers. High U.S. government officials have hawked U.S. goods throughout the world. Example: President Clinton and other administration officials directly lobbied King Fahd of Saudi Arabia to buy commercial aircraft from America's Boeing rather than from Europe's Airbus.

2. Relaxation of **export controls.** In the past, national security and foreign policy objectives restricted the exporting of certain high-technology products such as computers and advanced communications equipment. Many of these controls have now been ended.

3. Increased government funding of America's Export-Import Bank. This government-funded "bank" provides interest-rate subsidies to foreign firms which buy U.S. exports on credit. The result is a lower total price (product price + interest on loan) and therefore increased exports.

4. Renewed emphasis on *industrial policy* designed to aid exporting firms or industries. This involves the payment of government subsidies to specific high-technology industries for the development of products which bolster exports. The government payments are actually **export subsidies** which reduce development or production costs. Thus the payments tend to lower the price of exported goods and increase their sales in world markets.

Example: In 1994 the Clinton administration initiated a $1 billion plan to help industry compete with Japan in developing advanced flat-panel computer screens. The administration justified this massive subsidy as necessary for national defense. But this action had as much to do with competing with Japan in a burgeoning world export market as with ensuring national defense.

5. Threats or actual uses of *retaliatory tariffs* to force other nations to reduce their trade barriers with the United States. Such retaliation has resulted in negotiations which have given some U.S. firms freer access to foreign markets. Since 1989 the United States has used retaliatory tariffs to address specific trade issues with Japan, Brazil, India, South Korea, Taiwan, France, and other nations. For example, in 1992 the United States tripled the import duty on French white wine to spur France to reduce its barriers against U.S. soybean exports.

Bilateral Negotiations

Bilateral trade negotiations, discussions between two countries rather than among many, are another facet of U.S. international trade policy. Such negotiations have occurred directly between the United States and China, Japan, South Korea, and Canada. Usually these negotiations have focused on specific trade restrictions or on alleged dumping of specific goods. But negotiations with China and Japan have dealt with broader trade issues.

Continuing Renewal of China's Most-Favored-Nation Status (MFN) The United States continues to renew (annually) China's **most-favored-**

Petition of the Candlemakers, 1845

French economist Frédéric Bastiat (1801–1850) devastated the proponents of protectionism by satirically extending their reasoning to its logical and absurd conclusions.

Petition of the Manufacturers of Candles, Waxlights, Lamps, Candlesticks, Street Lamps, Snuffers, Extinguishers, and of the Producers of Oil Tallow, Rosin, Alcohol, and, Generally, of Everything Connected with Lighting.

TO MESSIEURS THE MEMBERS OF THE CHAMBER OF DEPUTIES.

Gentlemen—You are on the right road. You reject abstract theories, and have little consideration for cheapness and plenty. Your chief care is the interest of the producer. You desire to emancipate him from external competition, and reserve the *national market* for *national industry*.

We are about to offer you an admirable opportunity of applying your—what shall we call it? your theory? No; nothing is more deceptive than theory; your doctrine? your system? your principle? but you dislike doctrines, you abhor systems, and as for principles, you deny that there are any in social economy: we shall say, then, your practice, your practice without theory and without principle.

We are suffering from the intolerable competition of a foreign rival, placed, it would seem, in a condition so far superior to ours for the production of light, that he absolutely *inundates* our *national market* with it at a price fabulously reduced. The moment he shows himself, our trade leaves us—all consumers apply to him; and a branch of native industry, having countless ramifications, is all at once rendered completely stagnant. This rival . . . is no other than the Sun.

What we pray for is, that it may please you to pass a law ordering the shutting up of all windows, skylights, dormerwindows, outside and inside shutters, curtains, blinds, bull's-eyes; in a word, of all openings, holes, chinks, clefts, and fissures, by or through which the light of the sun has been in use to enter houses, to the prejudice of the meritorious manufacturers with which we flatter ourselves we have accommodated our country,—a country which, in gratitude, ought not to abandon us now to a strife so unequal.

If you shut up as much as possible all access to natural light, and create a demand for artificial light, which of our French manufacturers will not be encouraged by it?

If more tallow is consumed, then there must be more oxen and sheep; and, consequently, we shall behold the multiplication of artificial meadows, meat, wool, hides, and, above all, manure, which is the basis and foundation of all agricultural wealth.

The same remark applies to navigation. Thousands of vessels will proceed to the whale fishery; and, in a short time, we shall possess a navy capable of maintaining the honor of France, and gratifying the patriotic aspirations of your petitioners, the undersigned candlemakers and others.

Only have the goodness to reflect, Gentlemen, and you will be convinced that there is, perhaps, no Frenchman, from the wealthy coalmaster to the humblest vender of lucifer matches, whose lot will not be ameliorated by the success of this our petition.

Source: Frédéric Bastiat, *Economic Sophisms* (Edinburgh: Oliver and Boyd, Tweeddale Court, 1873), pp. 49–53, abridged.

---

nation status, first conferred in 1980. The MFN status applies to most U.S. trading partners and means that imports from China face the lowest U.S. tariffs. Also, this status means that any reductions in tariffs which the United States negotiates with other nations will also apply to Chinese imports to the United States. These low U.S. tariffs are important to China because the United States buys about $60 billion worth of such Chinese-made goods as toys, shoes, and clothes each year.

Renewal of MFN status for China is controversial for two reasons. First, China has had a poor record on "human rights"; its government has been dictatorial and repressive. Some critics of China's MFN status see it as supporting the current government in China. Second, the United States has a $44 billion trade deficit with China. Removal of MFN status, say these critics, would send notice to China that it needs to increase its access to U.S. goods.

Thus far, U.S. presidents and Congress have concluded that the benefits of renewing MFN status for China outweigh the costs. Proponents of MFN status have successfully argued that U.S. international trade with China is consistent with the U.S. goal of improved Chinese human rights. International trade opens China to the outside world and exposes it to the personal and social benefits of economic freedom. Greater freedom in one sphere may whet the appetite for freedom in other spheres. Also, international trade expands the political influence of leaders in China's business sector. These business leaders are more reform-minded than the older political leadership and, in general, lack commitment to communist ideology—an ideology which supports dictatorship and political repression.

Despite the renewal of China's MFN status, trade relations between the United States and China remain fragile. Example: In 1995 the United States temporarily invoked high tariffs against selected Chinese imports in retaliation for China's unwillingness to crack down on massive, unauthorized reproduction and sale of U.S.-made software, videos, and recordings. Although the situation was resolved with a negotiated agreement, trade discussions between China and the United States continue over issues such as China's trade barriers and its desire to join the World Trade Organization.

Negotiations with Japan Much recent U.S. bilateral negotiation has centered on the United States' annual $50 billion trade deficit with Japan. Specific goods for which there are large deficits are automobiles and parts, computers and office machines, elec-

trical machinery and appliances, television sets and radios, and photo and optical gear.

The United States and Japan have held numerous, sometimes testy, negotiations on this deficit problem. The initial U.S. position was that Japan needed to set numerical targets for increasing imports from the United States. The Japanese retorted that it vehemently opposed "managed trade" of this sort. The trade balance between two nations should be determined by market forces, say the Japanese. U.S. negotiators counter that the deficit is not totally a "market" deficit. Japan's widespread system of nontariff trade barriers impedes the working of the global market, contributing heavily to Japan's trade surplus. Also, the Japanese system of *keiretsu*—large groups of interlocked Japanese firms which buy and sell exclusively from one another—denies U.S. firms access to Japanese markets. U.S. negotiators have pointed out that even products such as cellular phones, which U.S. firms produce in high quality and at low cost, have not made inroads in Japan. And while U.S. firms hold about 45 percent of the global market for large-scale construction projects, their share in Japan is less than 1 percent.

The Japanese have pointed out that the average Japanese spends more on U.S. imports than the average person in the United States spends on Japanese imports. (The U.S. trade deficit results from the far greater number of U.S. citizens.) Japan also points to its large annual *deficit* in *services* (as opposed to goods) with the United States. No one in the United States views that U.S. *surplus* as a problem, say the Japanese.

While new trade agreements between the United States and Japan have been reached, the two nations will not end their trade imbalance soon. Elimination of *all* tariffs and nontariff trade barriers in Japan would increase U.S. exports to Japan by only an estimated $9 billion to $18 billion annually, while the current deficit is $50 billion.

CHAPTER SUMMARY

1. The United States is the world's largest international trader in terms of volume. Since 1965 U.S. exports and imports have more than doubled as a percentage of GDP. Other major trading nations are Germany, Japan, the western European nations, and the newly industrialized Asian tigers (Hong Kong, Singapore, South Korea, and Taiwan).

2. World trade is based on two considerations: the uneven distribution of economic resources among nations

and the fact that efficient production of various goods requires particular techniques or combinations of resources.

3. Mutually advantageous specialization and trade are possible between any two nations if they have different domestic opportunity-cost ratios for any two products. By specializing based on comparative advantage, nations can obtain larger real incomes with fixed amounts of resources. The terms of trade determine how this increase in world output is shared by the trading nations. Increasing (rather than constant) opportunity costs limit specialization and trade.

4. A nation's export supply curve shows the quantities of a product it will export at world prices which exceed the domestic price—the price in a closed, no-international-trade economy. Its import demand curve reveals the quantities of a product it will import at world prices below the domestic price. In a two-nation model, the equilibrium world price and the equilibrium quantities of exports and imports occur where one nation's export supply curve intersects the other nation's import demand curve.

5. Trade barriers take the form of protective tariffs, quotas, nontariff barriers, and "voluntary" export restrictions. Supply and demand analysis reveals that protective tariffs and quotas increase the prices and reduce the quantities demanded of affected goods. Sales by foreign exporters diminish; domestic producers, however, gain higher prices and enlarged sales. Tariffs and quotas promote a less efficient allocation of domestic and world resources.

6. The strongest arguments for protection are the infant-industry and military self-sufficiency arguments. Most other arguments for protection are half-truths, emotional appeals, or fallacies which emphasize the immediate effects of trade barriers while ignoring long-run consequences. Numerous historical examples suggest that free trade promotes economic growth; protectionism does not.

7. Protectionism costs U.S. consumers substantial amounts annually. The cost to consumers for each job saved is far greater than the average salary paid. Consumer losses from trade restrictions greatly exceed producer and government gains, creating an efficiency loss to society.

8. Recent U.S. international trade policy entails: **(a)** general liberalization of trade through NAFTA and GATT; **(b)** aggressive export promotion by government, and **(c)** bilateral negotiations over specific trade disputes, including the problem of the large U.S. trade deficits with Japan and China.

TERMS AND CONCEPTS

labor-intensive goods
land-intensive goods
capital-intensive goods
cost ratio
principle of comparative
  advantage
terms of trade

trading possibilities line
gains from trade
world price
domestic price
export supply curve
import demand curve
tariffs

revenue tariff
protective tariff
import quota
nontariff barrier
voluntary export
  restriction
strategic trade policy

dumping
World Trade
  Organization
export controls
export subsidies
most-favored-nation
  status

STUDY QUESTIONS

1. Quantitatively, how important is international trade to the United States relative to other nations?

2. Distinguish among land-, labor-, and capital-intensive commodities, citing one nontextbook example of each. What role do these distinctions play in explaining international trade?

3. Suppose nation A can produce 80 units of X by using all its resources to produce X and 60 units of Y by devoting all its resources to Y. Comparable figures for nation B are 60 units of X and 60 units of Y. Assuming constant costs, in which product should each nation specialize? Why? What are the limits of the terms of trade?

4. KEY QUESTION Here are hypothetical production possibilities tables for New Zealand and Spain.

New Zealand's production possibilities table
(millions of bushels)

| Product | Production alternatives | | | |
	A	B	C	D
Apples	0	20	40	60
Plums	15	10	5	0

Spain's production possibilities table (millions of bushels)

Product	Production alternatives			
	R	S	T	U
Apples	0	20	40	60
Plums	60	40	20	0

Plot the production possibilities data for each of the two countries separately. Referring to your graphs, determine:

a. Each country's cost ratio of producing plums and apples.

b. Which nation should specialize in which product.

c. The trading possibilities lines for each nation if the actual terms of trade are 1 plum for 2 apples. (Plot these lines on your graph.)

d. Suppose the optimum product mixes before specialization and trade were alternative B in New Zealand and alternative S in Spain. What are the gains from specialization and trade?

5. "The United States can produce X more efficiently than can Great Britain. Yet we import X from Great Britain." Explain.

6. KEY QUESTION Refer to Figure 3-5. Assume the graph depicts the United States' domestic market for corn. How many bushels of corn, if any, will the United States export or import at a world price of $1, $2, $3, $4, and $5? Use this information to construct the U.S. export supply curve and import demand curve for corn. Suppose the only other corn-producing nation is France, where the domestic price is $4. Which country will export corn; which will import it?

7. KEY QUESTION Draw a domestic supply and demand diagram for a product in which the United States does not have a comparative advantage. What impact do foreign imports have on domestic price and quantity? On your diagram show a protective tariff which eliminates approximately one-fourth the assumed imports. What are the price-quantity effects of this tariff on **(a)** domestic consumers, **(b)** domestic producers, and **(c)** foreign exporters? How would the effects of a quota which creates the same amount of imports differ?

8. "The most valid arguments for tariff protection are also the most easily abused." What are these particular arguments? Why are they susceptible to abuse? Evaluate the use of artificial trade barriers, such as tariffs and import quotas, as a means of achieving and maintaining full employment.

9. Evaluate the following statements:

a. Protective tariffs limit both the imports and the exports of the nation levying tariffs.

b. The extensive application of protective tariffs destroys the ability of the international market system to allocate resources efficiently.

c. Unemployment can often be reduced through tariff protection, but by the same token inefficiency typically increases.

d. Foreign firms which "dump" their products onto the U.S. market are in effect giving gifts to the country's citizens.

e. In view of the rapidity with which technological advance is dispersed around the world, free trade will inevitably yield structural maladjustments, unemployment, and balance of payments problems for industrially advanced nations.

f. Free trade can improve the composition and efficiency of domestic output. Only the Volkswagen forced Detroit to make a compact car, and only foreign success with the oxygen process forced American steel firms to modernize.

g. In the long run foreign trade is neutral with respect to total employment.

10. Between 1981–1985 the Japanese agreed to a voluntary export restriction which reduced U.S. imports of Japanese automobiles by about 10 percent. What would you expect the short-run effects of these restrictions to be on the U.S. and Japanese automobile industries? If this restriction were permanent, what would be its long-run effects in the two nations on **(a)** the allocation of resources, **(b)** the volume of employment, **(c)** the price level, and **(d)** the standard of living?

11. KEY QUESTION What are the costs and the benefits of protectionist policies? Which are larger?

12. What are NAFTA and GATT, and how do they relate to international trade? What policies has the U.S. government recently used to promote U.S. exports? What factors make it difficult for U.S. firms to sell their goods in Japan? What actions do you think the United States should take to reduce U.S. trade deficits with Japan and China?

13. (Last Word) What point is Bastiat trying to make with his petition of the candlemakers?

14. WEB-BASED QUESTION **Multilateral Trade Liberalization—GATT and WTO** GATT (General Agreement on Tariffs and Trade) was founded in 1947 to reduce world trade barriers on a multilateral basis. GATT partners have to grant one another the lowest tariffs they grant any of the other nations which have most-favored-nation status. GATT was subsumed by the World Trade Organization (WTO) http://www.wto.org/ on Jan. 1, 1995. Review how the WTO is trying to reduce trade barriers in two disparate industries: information technology and textiles; visit http://www.wto.org/wto/goods/goods.htm. What types of trade barriers are present in each industry? What timetable has been set for barrier reductions? Why is it more difficult to negotiate trade barrier reductions in textiles rather than information technology?

15. WEB-BASED QUESTION   The Economic Basis for Trade—Japan and the United States   The United States and Japan are major traders with each other. Both nations are industrially advanced and

ranked 1 and 2, respectively, in gross domestic product. A comparison of their economic fundamentals can be found at JETRO (Japan External Trade Organization) http://www.jetro.go.jp/FACTS/UA-HANDBOOK/1.html. JETRO is a nonprofit, Japanese-government-related organization whose main activity is trade-related public relations. At http://www.jetro.go.jp/FACTS/UA-HANDBOOK/index.html, look at the statistics on United States and Japan. Can the principle of comparative advantage be applied to actual United States-Japan trade? How can two industrially advanced nations export capital-intensive goods to each other? Does this violate the principle of comparative advantage?

38

Exchange Rates, The Balance of Payments, and Trade Deficits

If you take a U.S. dollar to the bank and ask to exchange it for U.S. currency, you will get a puzzled look. If you persist, you may get a dollar's worth of change: One U.S. dollar can buy exactly one U.S. dollar. But on January 8, 1998, for example, one U.S. dollar could buy 210,035 Turkish lira, 1.58 Australian dollars, .62 British pounds, 1.43 Canadian dollars, 6.09 French francs, 1.82 German marks, 132.72 Japanese yen, or 8.03 Swedish krona. What explains this seemingly haphazard array of exchange rates?

In Chapter 37 we examined comparative advantage as the underlying economic basis of world trade and discussed the effects of barriers to free trade. Here we first introduce the monetary or financial aspects of international trade: How are currencies of different nations exchanged when import and export transactions occur? Next, we analyze and interpret the international balance of payments: What is meant by a "favorable" or "unfavorable" balance of payments? Then we look at the two "pure" types of exchange-rate systems—flexible and fixed—which could be used to determine the worth of one currency in terms of another. After that, we examine the systems of exchange rates which major trading nations have actually used. Finally, we discuss the causes and consequences of the large trade deficits the United States has encountered during the past several years.

FINANCING INTERNATIONAL TRADE

One factor which makes international trade different from domestic trade is the involvement of different national currencies. When a U.S. firm exports goods to a South Korean firm, the U.S. exporter wants to be paid in dollars. But South Korean importers deal in won; they must exchange their wons for dollars to enable the U.S. export transaction to occur.

This problem is resolved in foreign exchange markets in which dollars can purchase South Korean wons, British pounds, Japanese yen, German marks, or any other currency, and vice versa. Sponsored by major banks in New York, London, Zurich, Tokyo, and elsewhere, foreign exchange markets facilitate exports and imports.

U.S. Export Transaction

Suppose a U.S. exporter agrees to sell $30,000 of computers to a British firm. Assume also that the rate of exchange—the rate at which pounds can be exchanged for, or converted into, dollars, and vice versa—is $2 for £1. This means the British importer must pay the equivalent of £15,000 to the U.S. exporter. Let's track what occurs in terms of the simple bank balance sheets in Figure 38-1. (A *balance sheet* is a statement showing a firm's *assets* and its *liabilities plus net worth*; the latter are claims on the assets by creditors and owners, respectively. Assets must always equal liabilities plus net worth because every asset of a firm is claimed by someone; those assets not claimed by creditors are claimed by owners.)

a. To pay for the computers, the British buyer draws a check for £15,000 on its checking account in a London bank. In Figure 38-1, this transaction (a) is shown by the −£15,000 checking account entry on the right side of the London bank's balance sheet.

b. The British firm sends this £15,000 check to the U.S. exporter. But the U.S. exporting firm must pay its bills in dollars, not pounds. Thus the exporter sells the £15,000 check on the London bank to its bank in, say, New York City, which is a dealer in foreign exchange. The bank adds $30,000 to the U.S. firm's checking account (b) for the £15,000 check. Note the new checking account entry of +$30,000 in the New York bank.

c. The New York bank deposits the £15,000 in a correspondent London bank for future sale. Thus, +£15,000 of deposits (c) appear in the liabilities column for the London bank. To simplify, we assume that the correspondent bank in London is the same bank from which the British importer obtained the £15,000 draft. This +£15,000 ($30,000) is an asset (c) as viewed by the New York bank, and it appears as such on that bank's balance sheet.

Note this important point: *U.S. exports create a foreign demand for dollars, and the fulfillment of this demand increases the supply of foreign currencies (pounds in this case) owned by U.S. banks and available to U.S. buyers.*

U.S. Import Transaction

Why would the New York bank be willing to buy pounds for dollars? As just indicated, the New York bank is a dealer in foreign exchange; it is in the business of buying (for a fee) and selling (also for a fee) one currency for another.

Let's now examine how the New York bank would sell pounds for dollars in financing a U.S. import (British export) transaction. Suppose a U.S. retail firm wants to import £15,000 of compact disks produced in Britain by a hot new rock group. Again, bank balance sheets, as shown in Figure 38-2, track what happens [as coded by (a), (b), and (c)].

a. Because the British exporting firm wants to be paid in pounds rather than dollars, the U.S. importer must exchange dollars for pounds, which it does by going to the New York bank and purchasing £15,000 for $30,000. (Perhaps the U.S.

LONDON BANK: Balance sheet 1	
Assets	Liabilities and net worth
	(a) Checking account of British importer: −£15,000
	(c) Deposit of New York bank: +£15,000

NEW YORK BANK: Balance sheet 1	
Assets	Liabilities and net worth
(c) Deposit in London bank: +£15,000 ($30,000)	(b) Checking account of U.S. exporter: +$30,000

FIGURE 38-1 Financing a U.S. export transaction In transaction (a), a British importer writes a check for £15,000 on its London bank account and uses it to pay for a U.S. import. In transaction (b), the U.S. exporter sells the £15,000 British check to its New York bank at the $1 = £2 exchange rate and deposits $30,000 in its New York checking account. In transaction (c), the New York bank deposits the £15,000 British check in its corresponding London bank for future use.

LONDON BANK: Balance sheet 2	
Assets	**Liabilities and net worth**
	(b) Demand deposit of British exporter: +£15,000
	(a) Deposit of New York bank: −£15,000

NEW YORK BANK: Balance sheet 2	
Assets	**Liabilities and net worth**
(a) Deposit in London bank: −£15,000 ($30,000)	(a) Checking account of U.S. importer: −$30,000

FIGURE 38-2 Financing a U.S. import transaction   In transaction (a), a U.S. importer purchases £15,000 at the $1 = £2 exchange rate by writing a check for $30,000 on its New York bank. This reduces the importer's New York checking account by $30,000 and reduces the New York bank's £15,000 deposit in its corresponding London bank. In transaction (b), the £15,000 payment goes to the British exporter, who deposits it in its checking account in its London bank.

----

importer purchases the same £15,000 which the New York bank acquired from the U.S. exporter.) In Figure 38-2, this purchase reduces the U.S. importer's checking account in the New York bank by $30,000, and the New York bank gives up its £15,000 deposit in the London bank.

b. The U.S. importer sends its newly purchased check for £15,000 to the British firm, which deposits it in the London bank; there, it is recorded as a +£15,000 deposit in the London bank.

Here you see that *U.S. imports create a domestic demand for foreign currencies (pounds, in this case), and the fulfillment of this demand reduces the supplies of foreign currencies held by U.S. banks and available for U.S. consumers.*

The combined export and import transactions bring one more point into focus. United States exports (the computers) make available, or "earn," a supply of foreign currencies for U.S. banks, and U.S. imports (the compact disks) create a demand for these currencies. In a broad sense, any nation's exports finance or "pay for" its imports. Exports provide the foreign currencies needed to pay for imports.

Postscript: Although our examples are confined to exporting and importing goods, demand for and supplies of pounds also arise from transactions involving services and the payment of interest and dividends on foreign investments. The United States demands pounds not only to buy imports but also to buy insurance and transportation services from the British, to vacation in London, to pay dividends and interest on British investments in the United States, and to make new financial and real investments in Britain. **(Key Question 2)**

THE BALANCE OF PAYMENTS

A nation's **balance of payments** is the sum of all transactions which take place between its residents and the residents of all foreign nations. These transactions include merchandise exports and imports, imports of goods and services, tourist expenditures, interest and dividends received or paid abroad, and purchases and sales of financial or real assets abroad. *The balance of payments statement shows all the payments a nation receives from foreign countries and all the payments it makes to them.* Table 38-1 is a simplified balance of payments statement for the United States in 1996. Let's take a close look at this accounting statement to see what it reveals about U.S. international trade and finance. To help our explanation, we divide the single balance of payments account into three components: the current account, the capital account, and the official reserves account.

Current Account

The top portion of Table 38-1 summarizes U.S. trade in currently produced goods and services and is called the **current account.** Items 1 and 2 show U.S. exports and imports of goods (merchandise) in 1996. U.S. exports have a *plus* (+) sign because they are a *credit;* they earn and make available foreign exchange in the United States. As you saw in the previous section, any export-type transaction which obligates foreigners to make "inpayments" to the United States generates supplies of foreign currencies in the U.S. banks.

TABLE 38-1   The U.S. balance of payments, 1996 (in billions)

Current account		
(1) U.S. goods exports..	$ +612	
(2) U.S. goods imports..	−803	
(3) *Balance of trade*		$−191
(4) U.S. exports of services	+237	
(5) U.S. imports of services	−157	
(6) *Balance on goods and services*		−111
(7) Net investment income	+3	
(8) Net transfers	−40	
(9) **Balance on current account**		**−148**
Capital account		
(10) Foreign purchases of assets in the United States ..	+517*	
(11) U.S. purchases of assets abroad	−376*	
(12) **Balance on capital account**		**+141**
Official reserves account		
(13) **Official reserves**		**+7**
		$ 0

*Includes one-half of a $37 billion statistical discrepancy which shows up in the balance of payments account.
Source: Survey of Current Business, September 1997.

U.S. imports have a *minus* (−) sign because they are a *debit;* they reduce the stock of foreign currencies in the United States. Our earlier discussion of trade financing indicated that U.S. imports obligate the United States to make "outpayments" to the rest of the world which reduce available supplies of foreign currencies held by U.S. banks.

Trade Balance   Items 1 and 2 in Table 38-1 reveal that in 1996 U.S. goods exports of $612 billion did not earn enough foreign currencies to finance U.S. goods imports of $803 billion. A country's goods balance of trade, or simply, its **trade balance,** is the difference between its exports and imports of goods. If exports exceed imports, the result is a trade surplus or "favorable balance of trade." If imports exceed exports, there is a trade deficit or "unfavorable balance of trade." We note in item 3 that in 1996 the United States incurred a trade deficit (of goods) of $191 billion. (Global Perspective 38-1 shows U.S. trade deficits and surpluses for selected nations or groups of nations.)

Balance on Goods and Services   Item 4 reveals that the United States not only exports goods, such as airplanes and computer software, but also services, such as insurance, consulting, travel, and brokerage

services, to residents of foreign nations. These service "exports" totaled $237 billion in 1996 and are a credit (thus the + sign). Item 5 indicates that the United States "imports" similar services from foreigners; these service imports were $157 billion in 1996 and are a debit (thus the − sign).

The **balance on goods and services,** shown as item 6, is the difference between U.S. exports of goods and services (items 1 and 4) and U.S. imports of goods and services (items 2 and 5). In 1996, U.S. imports of goods and services exceeded U.S. exports of goods and services by $111 billion.

Balance on Current Account   Item 7, *net investment income,* represents the excess of interest and dividend payments people abroad have paid the United States for the services of exported U.S. capital over what the United States paid in interest and dividends for the use of foreign capital invested in the United States. It shows that in 1996 U.S. net investment income was $3 billion worth of foreign currencies.

Item 8 shows net transfers, both public and private, between the United States and the rest of the world. Included here is foreign aid, pensions paid to citizens living abroad, and remittances by immigrants to relatives abroad. These $40 billion of transfers are net U.S. outpayments which decrease available supplies of for-

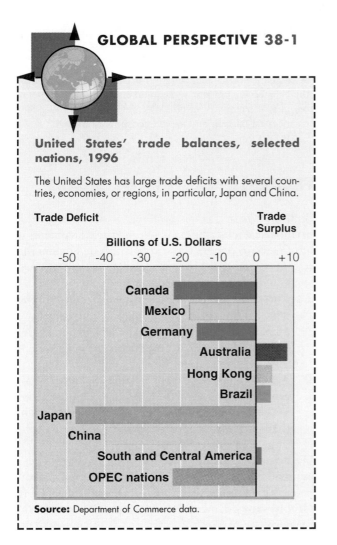

GLOBAL PERSPECTIVE 38-1

United States' trade balances, selected nations, 1996

The United States has large trade deficits with several countries, economies, or regions, in particular, Japan and China.

Source: Department of Commerce data.

eign exchange. They are, in a sense, the exporting of good will and the importing of "thank-you notes."

By adding all transactions in the current account, we obtain the **balance on current account** shown in item 9. In 1996 the United States had a current account deficit of $148 billion. This means that the U.S. current account transactions (items 2, 5, and 8) created a greater outpayment of foreign currencies from the United States than an inpayment of foreign currencies to the United States.

Capital Account

The second account within the overall balance of trade account is the **capital account,** which summarizes the flows of payments (money "capital") from the purchase or sale of real or financial assets. For ex-

ample, a foreign firm may buy a *real* asset, say, an office tower in the United States, or a financial asset, for instance, a U.S. government bond. Both kinds of transactions involve the "export" of the ownership of U.S. assets from the United States in return for inpayments of foreign currency (money "capital" inflows). As indicated in line 10, these "exports" of ownership of assets are designated *foreign purchases of assets in the United States.* They have a + sign because, like exports of U.S. goods and services, they represent an inpayment of foreign currencies.

Conversely, a U.S. firm may buy, say, a hotel chain (real asset) in a foreign country or common stock (financial asset) of a foreign firm. Both transactions involve "imports" of the ownership of real or financial assets to the United States and are paid for by outpayments (money "capital" outflows). These "imports" are designated U.S. *purchases of assets abroad* and, as shown in line 12, have a − sign; like U.S. imports of goods and services, they represent an outpayment of foreign currencies from the United States.

Items 10 and 11 combined yield a **balance on capital account** of +$141 billion in 1996 (line 12). In 1996 the United States "exported" $517 billion of ownership of its real and financial assets and "imported" $376 billion. This capital account *surplus* brought in $141 billion of foreign currencies to the United States.

Official Reserves Account

The third account in the overall balance of payments is the official reserves account. The central banks of nations hold quantities of foreign currencies called **official reserves.** These reserves can be drawn on to make up any net deficit in the combined current and capital accounts (much as you would draw on your savings to pay for a special purchase.) In 1996 the United States had a $7 billion deficit in the combined current and capital accounts (line 9 minus line 12). Balance in the U.S. international payments required the U.S. government to deplete its official reserves of foreign currencies by $7 billion (item 13). The + sign indicates that this drawdown of reserves is a credit— the inpayment from official reserves which was needed to balance the overall balance of payments account.

In some years, the current and capital accounts balances may be positive, meaning that the United States earned more foreign currencies than it needed. The surplus would create an outpayment, not to other countries, but to the stock of official reserves. As such, item 13 would have a − sign since it is a debit.

The three components of the balance of payments—the current account, the capital account, and the official reserves account—must together equal zero. Every unit of foreign exchange used (as reflected in a *minus* outpayment or debit transaction) must have a source (a *plus* inpayment or credit transaction).

Payments Deficits and Surpluses

Although the balance of payments *must always sum to zero,* economists and political officials speak of **balance of payment deficits and surpluses;** they are referring to imbalances between the current and capital accounts (line 9 minus line 12) which cause a drawing down or building up of foreign currencies. *A drawing down of official reserves (to create a positive official reserves entry in Table 38-1) measures a nation's balance of payments deficit; a building up of official reserves (which is shown as a negative official reserves entry) measures its balance of payments surplus.*

A balance of payments deficit is not necessarily bad, nor is a balance of payments surplus necessarily good. Both simply are realities. However, any nation's official reserves are limited. Persistent payments deficits, which must be financed by drawing down those reserves, would ultimately deplete the reserves. That nation would have to make policies to correct its balance of payments. These policies might require painful macroeconomic adjustments, trade barriers and similar restrictions, or a major depreciation of its currency. For this reason, nations seek to achieve payments balance, at least over several-year periods.

It is clear from Table 38-1 that in 1996 the United States had a large current account deficit, a large capital account surplus, and a relatively small payments deficit. Large current account deficits have been the pattern for the United States for several years. We need to examine the causes and consequences of trade deficits, but we will defer that discussion until later in this chapter. **(Key Question 3)**

QUICK REVIEW 38-1

■ U.S. exports create a foreign demand for dollars, and fulfillment of that demand increases the domestic supply of foreign currencies; U.S. imports create a domestic demand for foreign currencies, and fulfillment of that demand reduces the supplies of foreign currency held by U.S. banks.

■ The current account balance is a nation's exports of goods and services less its imports of goods and services plus its net investment income and net transfers.

■ The capital account balance is a nation's sale of real and financial assets to people living abroad less its purchases of real and financial assets from foreigners.

■ A balance of payments deficit occurs when the sum of the balances on current and capital accounts is negative; a balance of payments surplus arises when the sum of the balances on current and capital accounts is positive.

FLEXIBLE EXCHANGE RATES

Both the size and persistence of a nation's balance of payments deficits and surpluses and the adjustments it must make to correct these imbalances depend on the system of exchange rates being used. There are two "pure" types of exchange-rate systems:

1. A **flexible** or **floating exchange-rate system** by which the rates at which national currencies are exchanged for one another are determined by demand and supply and in which no government intervention occurs

2. A **fixed exchange-rate system** by which governments determine the rates at which currencies are exchanged and make necessary adjustments in their economies to ensure that these rates continue.

We being by looking at flexible exchange rates. Let's examine the rate, or price, at which U.S. dollars might be exchanged for British pounds. **Figure 38-3 (Key Graph)** shows demand D_1 and supply S_1 of pounds in the currency market.

The *demand for pounds curve* is downsloping because, if pounds become less expensive to the United States, then all British goods and services will be cheaper to the United States. That is, at lower dollar prices for pounds, the United States can get more pounds and therefore more British goods and services per dollar. To buy these cheaper British goods, U.S. consumers will increase the quantity of pounds they demand.

The *supply of pounds curve* is upsloping because, as the dollar price of pounds rises (that is, the pound price of dollars falls), the British will purchase more U.S. goods. When the British buy more U.S. goods, they supply a greater quantity of pounds to the foreign exchange market. In other words, they must exchange pounds for dollars to purchase U.S. goods.

The intersection of the supply curve and demand curve will determine the dollar price of pounds. Here, that price (exchange rate) is $2 for £1.

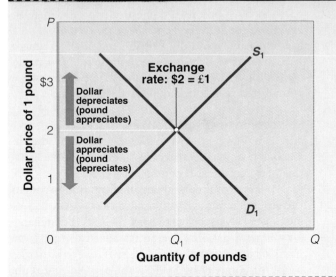

FIGURE 38-3 The market for foreign currency (pounds) The intersection of the demand for pounds D_1 and the supply of pounds S_1 determines the equilibrium dollar price of pounds, here, $2. That means that the exchange rate is $2 = £1. The upward green arrow is a reminder that a higher dollar price of pounds (say, $3 = £1) means that the dollar has depreciated (pound has appreciated). The downward green arrow tells us that a lower dollar price of pounds (say, $1 = £1) means that the dollar has appreciated (pound has depreciated). Such changes in equilibrium exchange rates would result from shifts of the supply and demand curves.

QUICK QUIZ 38-3

1. Which of the following is a true statement?
   a. The quantity of pounds demanded falls when the dollar appreciates.
   b. The quantity of pounds supplied declines as the dollar price of pounds rises.
   c. At the equilibrium exchange rate, the pound price of $1 is 1/2 pound.
   d. The dollar would appreciate if the demand for pounds increased.

2. At the price of $2 for 1 pound in this figure:
   a. the dollar-pound exchange rate is unstable.
   b. the quantity of pounds supplied equals the quantity demanded.
   c. the dollar price of 1 pound equals the pound price of $1.
   d. U.S. merchandise exports to Britain must equal U.S. merchandise imports from Britain.

3. All else equal, a leftward shift of the demand curve in this figure:
   a. would depreciate the dollar.

   b. creates a shortage of pounds at the previous price of $2 for 1 pound.
   c. might be caused by a major recession in the United States.
   d. might be caused by a significant rise of real interest rates in Britain.

4. All else equal, a rightward shift of the supply curve in this figure would:
   a. depreciate the dollar and might be caused by a significant rise of real interest rates in Britain.
   b. depreciate the dollar and might be caused by a significant fall of real interest rates in Britain.
   c. appreciate the dollar and might be caused by a significant rise of real interest rates in the United States.
   d. appreciate the dollar and might be caused by a significant fall of interest rates in the United States.

Answers: 1. c; 2. b; 3. c; 4. c

Depreciation and Appreciation

An exchange rate determined by market forces can, and often does, change daily, just as do stock and bond prices. When the dollar price of pounds increases, for example, from $2 for £1 to $3 for £1, the value of the dollar has depreciated relative to the pound. When a nation's currency depreciates, it takes more units of that nation's currency (dollars) to buy a single unit of some foreign currency (a pound).

When the dollar price of pounds decreases, say, from $2 for £1 to $1 for £1, the dollar has appreciated relative to the pound. When a nation's currency appreciates, it takes fewer units of that nation's currency (dollars) to buy a single unit of some foreign currency (pounds).

795

In our United States-Britain illustrations, depreciation of the dollar means an appreciation of the pound, and vice versa. A change in the exchange rate from $2 = £1 to $3 = £1 means that it takes more dollars to buy £1; the dollar has depreciated. But it now takes fewer pounds to buy $1. At the initial rate it took £½ to buy $1; at the new rate it takes only £⅓ to buy $1. The pound has appreciated relative to the dollar. If the dollar depreciates relative to the pound, the pound appreciates relative to the dollar. If the dollar appreciates relative to the pound, the pound depreciates relative to the dollar.

Determinants of Exchange Rates

So what factors would cause a nation's currency to appreciate or depreciate in the market for foreign exchange? Here are three generalizations:

1. If the demand for a nation's currency increases (all else equal), that currency will appreciate; if the demand declines, that currency will depreciate.
2. If the supply of a nation's currency increases, that currency will depreciate; if the supply decreases, that currency will appreciate.
3. If a nation's currency appreciates, some foreign currency depreciates relative to it.

With these generalizations in mind, let's examine the determinants of exchange rates, which are the factors that change either the demand for or supply of a nation's currency.

Changes in Tastes Any change in consumer tastes or preferences for the products of a foreign country may alter the demand for that nation's currency and change its exchange rate. If technological advances in U.S. cell phones make them more attractive to British consumers and businesses, then the British will supply more pounds in the exchange market in order to purchase more U.S. cell phones. The supply-of-pounds curve will shift rightward, the pound will depreciate, and the dollar will appreciate.

In contrast, if British woolen apparel becomes more fashionable in the United States, the U.S. demand for pounds will increase, the pound will appreciate, and the dollar will depreciate.

Relative Income Changes If the growth of a nation's income is more rapid than that of other countries', its currency is likely to depreciate. Here's why. A country's imports vary directly with its level of income. As total income rises in the United States, people there buy both more domestically produced goods *and* more foreign goods. If the U.S. economy is expanding rapidly and the British economy is stagnant, U.S. imports of British goods, and therefore U.S. demands for pounds, will increase. The dollar price of pounds will rise, so the dollar will depreciate.

Relative Price-Level Changes Changes in the relative price levels of two nations can change the demand and supply of currencies and alter the exchange rate between the two nations' currencies.

At the extreme, the **purchasing power parity theory** holds that exchange rates *equate* the purchasing power of various currencies. That is, the exchange rates among national currencies adjust to match the ratios of the nations' price levels: If a certain market basket of goods costs $100 in the United States and £50 in Great Britain, the exchange rate will be $2 = £1. In this theory, a dollar spent on goods sold in Britain, Japan, Turkey, and other nations will have equal purchasing power.

In practice, however, exchange rates depart from purchasing power parity, even over long periods. Nevertheless, changes in relative price levels are a determinant of exchange rates. If, for example, the domestic price level rises rapidly in the United States and remains constant in Great Britain, U.S. consumers will seek out low-priced British goods, increasing the demand for pounds. The British will purchase fewer U.S. goods, reducing the supply of pounds. This combination of demand and supply changes will cause the pound to appreciate and the dollar to depreciate.

Relative Interest Rates Changes in relative interest rates between two countries can alter their exchange rate. Suppose that real interest rates rise in the United States but stay constant in Great Britain. British citizens will then find the United States an attractive place in which to make financial investments. To undertake these investments, they will have to supply pounds in the foreign exchange market to obtain dollars. The increase in the supply of pounds results in depreciation of the pound and appreciation of the dollar.

Speculation *Currency speculators* are people who buy and sell currencies with an eye toward reselling or repurchasing them at a profit. Suppose speculators expect the U.S. economy to (1) grow more rapidly than the British economy and (2) experience a more rapid rise in its price level than Britain. These expectations translate to an anticipation that the pound will appreciate and the dollar will depreciate. Speculators who are holding dollars will therefore try to convert them into pounds. This effort will increase the demand for pounds and cause the dollar price of pounds to rise (that is, the dollar to depreciate). A self-fulfilling prophecy occurs: The pound appreciates and the dollar depreciates because speculators act on the belief that these changes will in fact take place. In this way, speculation can cause changes in exchange rates. (We deal with currency speculation in more detail in this chapter's Last Word.)

Table 38-2 has more illustrations of the determinants of exchange rates; we urge you to give the table a good look.

Flexible Rates and the Balance of Payments

Proponents argue that flexible exchange rates have an important feature: *They automatically adjust to eventually eliminate balance of payment deficits or surpluses.* We can explain this concept with S_1 and D_1 in Figure 38-4; they are the supply and demand curves for pounds from Figure 38-3. The equilibrium exchange rate of $2 = £1 means there is no balance of payments

TABLE 38-2   Determinants of exchange rates: factors which change the demand for or supply of a particular currency and thus alter the exchange rate

Determinant	Examples
Change in tastes	Japanese autos decline in popularity in the United States (Japanese yen depreciates; U.S. dollar appreciates)
	German tourists flock to the United States (U.S. dollar appreciates; German mark depreciates)
Change in relative incomes	England encounters a recession, reducing its imports, while U.S. real output and real income surge, increasing U.S. imports (British pound appreciates; U.S. dollar depreciates)
Change in relative prices	Germany experiences a 3% inflation rate compared to Canada's 10% rate (German mark appreciates; Canadian dollar depreciates)
Change in relative real interest rates	The Federal Reserve drives up interest rates in the United States, while the Bank of England takes no such action (U.S. dollar appreciates; British pound depreciates)
Speculation	Currency traders believe France will have much more rapid inflation than Sweden (French franc depreciates; Swedish krona appreciates)
	Currency traders think German interest rates will plummet relative to U.S. rates (German mark depreciates; U.S. dollar appreciates)

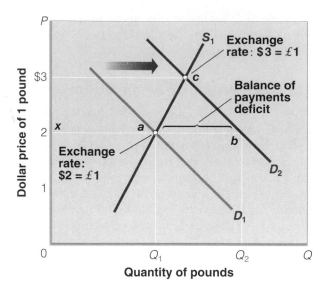

FIGURE 38-4 Adjustments under flexible exchange rates and fixed exchange rates Under flexible exchange rates, a shift in the demand for pounds from D_1 to D_2, other things equal, would cause a U.S. balance of payments deficit ab; it would be corrected by a change in the exchange rate from $2 = £1 to $3 = £1. Under fixed exchange rates, the United States would cover the shortage of pounds ab by using international monetary reserves, restricting trade, implementing exchange controls, or enacting a contractionary stabilization policy.

---

deficit or surplus between the United States and Britain. At the $2 = £1 exchange rate, the quantity of pounds demanded by U.S. consumers to import British goods, buy British transportation and insurance services, and pay interest and dividends on British investments in the United States equals the amount of pounds supplied by the British in buying U.S. exports, purchasing services from the United States, and making interest and dividend payments on U.S. investments in Britain. The United States would have no need to either draw down or build up its official reserves to balance its payments.

Suppose tastes change and U.S. consumers buy more British automobiles; the U.S. price level increases relative to Britain's; or interest rates fall in the United States compared to those in Britain. Any or all of these changes will cause the U.S. demand for British pounds to increase from D_1 to, say, D_2 in Figure 38-4.

If the exchange rate remains at the initial $2 = £1, a U.S. balance of payments deficit will be created in the amount of ab. That is, at the $2 = £1 rate, U.S. consumers will demand the quantity of pounds represented by point b, but Britain will supply the amount

represented by a; there will be a shortage of pounds. However, because this is a competitive market, the shortage will alter the exchange rate (the dollar price of pounds) from $2 = £1 to, say, $3 = £1; that is, the dollar will depreciate.

At this point we need to reemphasize that the exchange rate links all domestic (U.S.) prices with all foreign (British) prices. The dollar price of a foreign good is found by multiplying the foreign price by the exchange rate (in dollars per unit of the foreign currency). At an exchange rate of $2 = £1, a British automobile priced at £9000 will cost a U.S. consumer $18,000 (= 9000 × $2).

A change in the exchange rate alters the prices of all British goods to U.S. consumers and all U.S. goods to British buyers. The shift in the exchange rate (here from $2 = £1 to $3 = £1) changes the relative attractiveness of U.S. imports and exports and restores equilibrium in the U.S. (and British) balance of payments. From the U.S. point of view, as the dollar price of pounds changes from $2 to $3, the British auto priced at £9000, which formerly cost a U.S. consumer $18,000, now costs $27,000 (= 9000 × $3). Other British goods will also cost U.S. consumers more, and U.S. imports of British goods will decline. A movement from point b toward point c in Figure 38-4 graphically illustrates this concept.

From Britain's standpoint, the exchange rate (the pound price of dollars) has fallen (from £½ to £⅓ for $1). The international value of the pound has appreciated. The British previously got only $2 for £1; now they get $3 for £1. U.S. goods are therefore cheaper to the British, and U.S. exports to Britain will rise. In Figure 38-4, this is shown by a movement from point a toward point c.

The two adjustments—a decrease in U.S. imports from Britain and an increase in U.S. exports to Britain—are just what are needed to correct the U.S. balance of payments deficit. These changes end when, at point c, the quantities of British pounds demanded and supplied are equal. **(Key Questions 6 and 10)**

Disadvantages of Flexible Exchange Rates

Even though flexible exchange rates automatically work to eliminate payment imbalances, they may cause several significant problems.

Uncertainty and Diminished Trade The risks and uncertainties associated with flexible exchange rates may discourage the flow of trade. Suppose a U.S. automobile dealer contracts to purchase 10 British cars for £90,000. At the current exchange rate of, say, $2 for £1, the U.S. importer expects to pay $180,000 for these automobiles. But if in the 3-month delivery period the rate of exchange shifts to $3 for £1, the £90,000 payment contracted by the U.S. importer will now be $270,000.

This increase in the dollar price of pounds may thus turn the U.S. importer's anticipated profit into substantial losses. Aware of the possibility of an adverse change in the exchange rate, the U.S. importer may not be willing to assume the risks involved. The U.S. firm may confine its operations to domestic automobiles, with the result that international trade in this item does not occur.

The same thing can happen with investments. Assume that, when the exchange rate is $3 to £1, a U.S. firm invests $30,000 (or £10,000) in a British enterprise. It estimates a return of 10 percent; that is, it anticipates annual earnings of $3000 or £1000. Suppose these expectations prove correct in that the British firm earns £1000 in the first year on the £10,000 investment. But suppose that during the year, the value of the dollar appreciates to $2 = £1. The absolute return is now only $2000 (rather than $3000), and the rate of return falls from the anticipated 10 percent to only $6\frac{2}{3}$ percent (= $2000/$30,000). Investment is risky anyway. The added risk of changing exchange rates may persuade the U.S. investor to not venture overseas.[1]

Terms of Trade Changes

A nation's terms of trade will be worsened by a decline in the international value of its currency. For example, an increase in the dollar price of pounds will mean that the United States must export more goods and services to finance a specific level of imports from Britain.

Instability

Flexible exchange rates may have destabilizing effects on the domestic economy because wide fluctuations stimulate and then depress industries producing exported goods. If the U.S. economy is operating at full employment and its currency depreciates as in our illustration, the results will be inflationary, for two reasons. (1) Foreign demand for U.S. goods may increase, increasing total spending and pulling up U.S. prices. Also, the prices of all U.S. imports will increase. (2) Conversely, appreciation of the dollar will lower U.S. exports and increase imports, possibly causing unemployment.

Flexible or floating exchange rates may also complicate the use of domestic stabilization policies in seeking full employment and price stability. This is especially true for nations whose exports and imports are large relative to their total domestic output.

FIXED EXCHANGE RATES

To circumvent the disadvantages of flexible exchange rates, at times nations have fixed or "pegged" their exchange rates. For our analysis of fixed exchange rates, we assume the United States and Britain agree to maintain a $2 = £1 exchange rate.

The problem is that such a governmental agreement cannot keep from changing the demand for and supply of pounds. With the rate fixed, a shift in demand or supply will put pressure on the exchange rate system, and government must intervene if the exchange rate is to be maintained.

In Figure 38-4, suppose the U.S. demand for pounds increases from D_1 to D_2 and a U.S. payment deficit *ab* arises. This means that the U.S. government is committed to an exchange rate ($2 = £1) which is below the new equilibrium rate ($3 = £1). How can the United States prevent the shortage of pounds from driving the exchange rate up to the new equilibrium level? The answer is to alter market demand or market supply or alter both so that they will intersect at the $2 = £1 rate of exchange. There are several ways to do this.

Use of Reserves

One way to maintain a pegged exchange rate is to manipulate the market through the use of official reserves. By selling part of its reserves of pounds, the U.S. government could increase the supply of pounds, shifting supply curve S_1 to the right so that it intersects D_2 at *b* in Figure 38-4 and thereby maintains the exchange rate at $2 = £1.

How do official reserves originate? Perhaps in the past the opposite market conditions prevailed, so there was a surplus, rather than a shortage, of pounds. The U.S. government would have acquired that surplus.

---

[1]You will see in this chapter's Last Word, however, that a trader can circumvent part of the risk of unfavorable exchange rate fluctuations by "hedging" in the "futures market" or "forward market" for foreign exchange.

That is, at some earlier time the U.S. government may have spent dollars to buy surplus pounds which were threatening to reduce the $2 = £1 exchange rate to, say, $1 = £1. That condition would have built up the U.S. official reserves of pounds.

Nations have also used gold as "international money" to obtain official reserves. In our example, the U.S. government could sell some of the gold it owns to Britain for pounds. The pounds acquired could then be sold for dollars, as above, to shift the supply of pounds to the right so as to maintain the $2 = £1 exchange rate.

It is critical that the amount of reserves and gold be enough to accomplish the required increase in the supply of pounds. This is not a problem if deficits and surpluses occur more or less randomly and are about the same size. That is, last year's balance of payments surplus with Britain will increase the U.S. reserve of pounds, and that reserve can be used to "finance" this year's deficit. But if the United States encounters persistent and sizable deficits for an extended period, its reserves can become exhausted, forcing the United States to abandon fixed exchange rates. Or, at the least, a nation whose reserves are inadequate must use less appealing options to maintain exchange rates. Let's consider some of these options.

Trade Policies

To maintain fixed exchange rates, a nation can try to control the flow of trade and finance directly. The United States could try to maintain the $2 = £1 exchange rate in the face of a shortage of pounds by discouraging imports (thereby reducing the demand for pounds) and encouraging exports (thus increasing the supply of pounds). Imports can be reduced with new tariffs or import quotas; special taxes can be levied on the interest and dividends U.S. financial investors receive from foreign investments. Also, the U.S. government could subsidize certain U.S. exports to increase the supply of pounds.

The fundamental problem is that these policies reduce the volume of world trade and change its makeup from what is economically desirable. When we impose tariffs, quotas, and the like, we lose some of the economic benefits of a free flow of world trade. This loss should not be underestimated: Trade barriers by one nation lead to retaliatory responses from other nations, multiplying the loss.

Exchange Controls and Rationing

Another option is exchange controls and rationing. Under exchange controls, the U.S. government could handle the problem of a pound shortage by requiring that all pounds obtained by U.S. exporters be sold to the Federal government. Then the government would allocate or ration this short supply of pounds (represented by xa in Figure 38-4) among various U.S. importers, who actually demand the quantity xb. The effect of this policy is to restrict the value of U.S. imports to the amount of foreign exchange earned by U.S. exports. Assuming balance in the capital account, there is then no balance of payments deficit. U.S. demand for British imports with the value ab would simply not be fulfilled.

There are major objections to exchange controls:

1. **Distorted trade**   Like tariffs, quotas, and export subsidies (trade controls), exchange controls distort the pattern of international trade away from that suggested by comparative advantage.
2. **Favoritism**   The process of rationing scarce foreign exchange can lead to government favoritism toward selected importers (big contributors to reelection campaigns, for example).
3. **Restricted choice**   Controls limit freedom of consumer choice. The U.S. consumers who prefer Volkswagens may have to buy Chevrolets. The business opportunities for some U.S. importers may be impaired because government limits imports.
4. **Black markets**   There are likely to be enforcement problems. U.S. importers might want foreign exchange badly enough to pay more than the $2 = £1 official rate, setting the stage for black-market dealings between importers and illegal sellers of foreign exchange.

Domestic Macroeconomic Adjustments

A final way to maintain a stable exchange rate is to use domestic stabilization policies (monetary policy and fiscal policy) to eliminate the shortage of foreign currency. Tax hikes, reductions in government spending, and a high-interest-rate policy would reduce total spending in the U.S. economy and thus domestic income. Because imports vary directly with domestic income, demand for British goods, and therefore for pounds, would be restrained.

If these "contractionary" policies reduce the domestic price level relative to Britain's, U.S. buyers of consumer and capital goods would divert their demands from British goods to U.S. goods, also reducing the demand for pounds. Moreover, the high-interest-rate policy would lift U.S. interest rates relative to those in Britain.

Lower prices on U.S. goods and higher U.S. interest rates would increase British imports of U.S. goods and increase British financial investment in the United States. Both developments would increase the supply of pounds. The combination of a decrease in the demand for and an increase in the supply of pounds would reduce or eliminate the original U.S. balance of payments deficit. In Figure 38-4 the new supply and demand curves would intersect at some new equilibrium point on line *ab*, where the exchange rate remains at $2 = £1.

This way to maintain pegged exchange rates is hardly appealing. The "price" of exchange-rate stability for the United States would be falling output, employment, and price levels—in other words, a recession. Eliminating a balance of payments deficit and realizing domestic stability are both important national economic goals, but to sacrifice stability for payments balance is to let the tail wag the dog.

QUICK REVIEW 38-2

■ In a system in which exchange rates are flexible (meaning that they are free to float), the rates are determined by the demand for and supply of individual national currencies in the foreign exchange market.

■ Determinants of flexible exchange rates—factors which shift currency supply and demand curves—include changes in (a) tastes, (b) relative national incomes, (c) relative price levels, (d) real interest rates, and (e) speculation.

■ Under a system of fixed exchange rates, nations set their exchange rates and then maintain them by buying or selling reserves of currencies, establishing trade barriers, employing exchange controls, or incurring inflation or recession.

INTERNATIONAL EXCHANGE-RATE SYSTEMS

In recent times the world's nations have used three different exchange rate systems: a fixed rate system, a modified fixed rate system, and a modified flexible rate system.

The Gold Standard: Fixed Exchange Rates

Between 1879 and 1934 the major nations of the world adhered to a fixed-rate system called the **gold standard.** In this system, each nation must:

1. Define its currency in terms of a quantity of gold
2. Maintain a fixed relationship between its stock of gold and its money supply
3. Allow gold to be freely exported and imported

If each nation defines its currency in terms of gold, the various national currencies will have fixed relationships to one another. For example, if the United States defines $1 as worth 25 grains of gold, and Britain defines its pounds as worth 50 grains of gold, then a British pound is worth 2×25 grains, or $2. This exchange rate would be fixed; it would not change in response to changes in currency demand and supply.

Gold Flows If we ignore the costs of packing, insuring, and shipping gold between countries, under the gold standard the rate of exchange would not vary from this $2 = £1 rate. No one in the United States would pay more than $2 = £1 because 50 grains of gold could always be bought for $2 in the United States and sold for £1 in Britain. Nor would the British pay more than £1 for $2. Why should they when they could buy 50 grains of gold in Britain for £1 and sell it in the United States for $2?

Under the gold standard, the potential free flow of gold between nations would result in exchange rates which are fixed.

Domestic Macroeconomic Adjustments When the demand for, or supply of, currencies changes, the gold standard requires domestic macroeconomic adjustments for the fixed exchange rate to be maintained. To see why, suppose that U.S. tastes change such that U.S. consumers want to buy more British goods. The demand for pounds increases such that there is a shortage of pounds in the United States (recall Figure 38-4), implying a U.S. balance of payments deficit.

What will happen? Remember that the rules of the gold standard prohibit the exchange rate from moving from the fixed $2 = £1 rate; the rate cannot move to, say, a new equilibrium at $3 = £1 to correct the imbalance. Instead, gold will flow from the United States to Britain to remove the payments imbalance.

But recall that the gold standard required participants to maintain a fixed relationship between their domestic money supplies and their quantities of gold. The flow of gold from the United States to Britain will require a reduction of the money supply in the United States. Other things equal, this will reduce total spending in the United States and thereby lower U.S. real domestic output, employment, income, and perhaps, prices. Also, the decline in the money supply will boost U.S. interest rates.

The opposite will occur in Britain. The inflow of gold will increase the money supply, which will increase total spending in Britain. Domestic output, employment, income, and perhaps, prices will rise. The British interest rate will fall.

Declining U.S. incomes and prices will reduce U.S. demand for British goods and therefore reduce the U.S. demand for pounds. Lower interest rates in Britain will make it less attractive for U.S. investors to make financial investments there, also lessening the demand for pounds. For all these reasons, the demand for pounds in the United States will decline. In Britain, higher incomes, prices, and interest rates will make U.S. imports and U.S. financial investments more attractive. In buying these imports and making these financial investments, British citizens will supply more pounds in the exchange market.

In short, domestic macroeconomic adjustments in the United States and Britain, triggered by the international flow of gold, will produce new demand and supply conditions for pounds such that the $2 = £1 exchange rate is maintained. After all the adjustments are made, the United States will not have a payments deficit, and Britain will not have a payments surplus.

The gold standard thus has the advantage of stable exchange rates and automatic correction of balance of payments deficits and surpluses. However, its critical drawback is that nations must accept domestic adjustments in such distasteful forms as unemployment and falling incomes, on the one hand, or inflation, on the other hand. Under this system, a nation's money supply is altered by changes in supply and demand in currency markets. Under the gold standard, nations cannot set their own money supply in their own national interest. If the United States, for example, was experiencing declining output and incomes, the loss of gold under the gold system would reduce the U.S. money supply, which might cause higher interest rates, lower borrowing and spending, and cause further declines in output and income.

Demise of the Gold Standard The worldwide depression in the 1930s led to the collapse of the gold standard. As domestic outputs and employment fell worldwide, the restoration of prosperity became the primary goal of afflicted nations. These nations enacted protectionist measures to reduce imports. The idea was to expand consumption of domestically produced goods and get their economies moving again. To make their exports less expensive abroad, many nations redefined their currencies at lower levels in terms of gold. For example, a country previously defining the value of its currency at 1 unit = 25 ounces of gold might redefine it as 1 unit = 10 ounces of gold. Such redefining is an example of **devaluation**— a deliberate action by government to reduce the international value of its currency. A series of such devaluations in the 1930s meant that exchange rates were no longer fixed; a major tenet of the gold standard was violated, and the system broke down.

The Bretton Woods System

The Great Depression and World War II left world trade and the world monetary system in shambles. To lay the groundwork for a new international monetary system, an international conference of nations was held at Bretton Woods, New Hampshire, in 1944. The conference produced a commitment to a modified fixed exchange-rate system called an *adjustable-peg system*, or, simply, the **Bretton Woods system.** The new system sought to capture the advantages of the old gold standard (fixed exchange rate) while avoiding its disadvantages (painful domestic macroeconomic adjustments).

Furthermore, the conference created the **International Monetary Fund** (IMF) to make the new exchange-rate system feasible and workable. The new international monetary system managed through the IMF prevailed with modifications until 1971. (The IMF still plays a basic role in international finance; in recent years it has performed a major role in providing loans to developing countries and to economies making transitions to capitalism.)

IMF and Pegged Exchange Rates How did the adjustable-peg system of exchange rates work? First, as with the gold standard, each IMF member had to define its currency in terms of gold (or dollars), thus establishing rates of exchange between its currency and the currencies of all other members. In addition, each nation was obligated to keep its exchange rate stable with respect to every other currency. To do so, nations would have to use their official currency reserves to intervene in foreign exchange markets.

Assume again that the U.S. dollar and the British pound were "pegged" to each other at $2 = £1. Now again suppose that the demand for pounds temporarily increases so that a shortage of pounds occurs in the United States (the United States has a balance of payments deficit). How can the United States keep its pledge to maintain a $2 = £1 exchange rate when the new equilibrium rate is, say, $3 = £1? The United States can supply additional pounds to the exchange market, increasing the supply of pounds such that the equilibrium exchange rate falls back to $2 = £1.

Under the Bretton Woods system there were three main sources of the needed pounds:

1. **Official reserves** The United States might currently possess pounds in its official reserves, as the result of past actions against the opposite exchange-market condition (payments surplus).

2. **Gold sales** The U.S. government might sell some of its gold to Britain for pounds. The proceeds would then be offered in the exchange market to augment the supply of pounds.

3. **IMF borrowing** The needed pounds might be borrowed from the IMF. Nations participating in the Bretton Woods system were required to make contributions to the IMF based on the size of their national income, population, and volume of trade. If necessary, the United States could borrow pounds on a short-term basis from the IMF by supplying its own currency as collateral.

Fundamental Imbalances: Adjusting the Peg

The Bretton Woods system recognized that from time to time a nation may be confronted with persistent and sizable balance of payments problems which cannot be corrected through the means listed above. In these cases, the nation would eventually run out of official reserves and be unable to maintain its fixed exchange-rate system. The Bretton Woods remedy was correction by devaluation, that is, by an "orderly" reduction of the nation's pegged exchange rate. Also, the IMF allowed each member nation to alter the value of its currency by 10 percent, on its own, to correct a so-called fundamental (persistent and continuing) balance of payments deficit. Larger exchange-rate changes required the permission of the Fund's

board of directors. By requiring approval of significant rate changes, the Fund guarded against arbitrary and competitive currency devaluations by nations seeking only to boost output in their own countries at the expense of other countries. In our example, devaluation of the dollar would increase U.S. exports and lower U.S. imports, correcting its persistent payments deficit.

Demise of the Bretton Woods System Under this adjustable-peg system, gold and the dollar came to be accepted as international reserves. The acceptability of gold as an international medium of exchange derived from its earlier use under the gold standard. The dollar became accepted as international money because the United States had accumulated large quantities of gold, and between 1934 and 1971 it maintained a policy of buying gold from, and selling gold to, foreign governments at a fixed price of $35 per ounce. The dollar was convertible into gold on demand; thus the dollar came to be regarded as a substitute for gold, or "as good as gold." And, since the discovery of new gold was limited, the growing volume of dollars helped provide a medium of exchange for the expanding world trade.

But a major problem arose. The United States experienced persistent payments deficits throughout the 1950s and 1960s. These deficits were financed in part by U.S. gold reserves, but mostly by payment of U.S. dollars. As the amount of dollars held by foreigners soared and the U.S. gold reserves dwindled, other nations began to question whether the dollar was really "as good as gold." The U.S. ability to continue to convert dollars into gold at $35 per ounce became increasingly doubtful, as did the role of dollars as international monetary reserves. Thus the dilemma was: To maintain the dollar as a reserve medium, the U.S. payment deficit had to be eliminated. But elimination of the payments deficit would remove the source of additional dollar reserves and thus limit the growth of international trade and finance.

The problem came to a head in 1971 when the United States ended its 37-year-old policy of exchanging gold for dollars at $35 per ounce. It severed the link between gold and the international value of the dollar, thereby "floating" the dollar and letting its value be determined by market forces. The floating of the dollar in effect withdrew U.S. support from the Bretton Woods system of fixed exchange rates and sounded the system's death knell.

The Current System: The Managed Float

The current international exchange-rate system (1971–present) is an "almost" flexible system called **managed floating exchange rates.** Exchange rates among major currencies are free to float to their equilibrium market levels, but nations occasionally intervene in the foreign exchange market to stabilize or alter market exchange rates.

Normally, the major trading nations allow their exchange rates to float up or down to equilibrium levels based on supply and demand in the foreign exchange market. They recognize that changing economic conditions among nations require continuing changes in equilibrium exchange rates to avoid persistent payments deficits or surpluses. They rely on freely operating foreign exchange markets to accomplish the necessary adjustments. The result has been considerably more volatile exchange rates than during the Bretton Woods era (see Global Perspective 38-2).

But nations also recognize that some trends in the movement of equilibrium exchange rates may be at odds with national or international objectives. On occasion, nations therefore intervene in the foreign exchange market by buying or selling large amounts of specific currencies. This way, they can "manage" or stabilize exchange rates by influencing currency demand and supply.

For example, in 1987 the Group of Seven industrial nations (G-7 nations)—the United States, Germany, Japan, Britain, France, Italy, and Canada—

GLOBAL PERSPECTIVE 38-2

Changes in exchange rates relative to the dollar

The floating exchange rate system (managed float) introduced in 1971 has produced far more volatile exchange rates than those produced during the earlier Bretton Woods era. (Here, changes in the index show changes in each nation's dollar exchange rate relative to the dollar exchange rate which existed in 1948.)

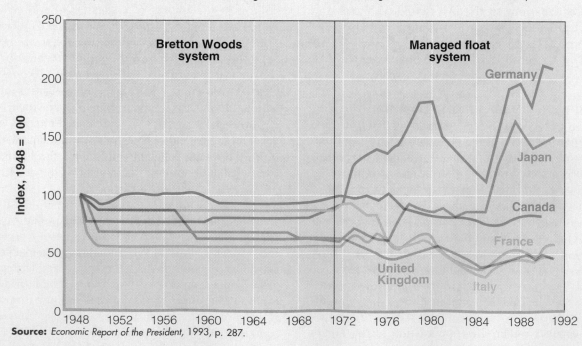

Source: *Economic Report of the President*, 1993, p. 287.

agreed to stabilize the values of the dollar. During the previous 2 years the dollar had declined rapidly because of large U.S. trade deficits. Although the U.S. trade deficits remained sizable, the G-7 nations concluded that further dollar depreciation might disrupt economic growth in member nations (other than the United States). The G-7 nations therefore purchased large amounts of dollars to boost the dollar's value. Since 1987 the G-7 nations (now G-8 with the addition of Russia) have periodically intervened in foreign exchange markets to stabilize currency values.

The current exchange-rate system is thus an "almost" flexible exchange-rate system. The "almost" mainly refers to the periodic currency interventions by governments; it also refers to the fact that the actual system is more complicated than described. While the major currencies—dollars, marks, pounds, yen, and the like—fluctuate in response to changing supply and demand, some of the European nations have tried to peg their currencies to one another. Also, many developing nations peg their currencies to the dollar and allow their currencies to fluctuate with it against other currencies. Finally, some nations peg the value of their currencies to a "basket" or group of other currencies.

How well has the managed float worked? It has both proponents and critics.

In Support of the Managed Float

Proponents argue that the managed float system has functioned well—far better than anticipated. Skeptics had predicted that fluctuating exchange rates would reduce world trade and finance. But in real terms world trade under the managed float has grown at about the same rate as during the 1960s under the Bretton Woods system of the fixed exchange rates. Moreover, as supporters are quick to point out, the currency crises in Mexico and Southeast Asia in the last half of the 1990s were not the result of the floating exchange-rate system itself. Rather, the abrupt currency devaluations and depreciations resulted from internal problems in those nations, in conjunction with the nations' tendency to peg their currencies to the dollar or to a basket of currencies. In some cases, flexible exchange rates would have made these adjustments far more gradual.

Proponents also point out that the managed float has weathered severe economic turbulence which might have caused a fixed-rate system to break down. Such events as extraordinary oil price increases in 1973–1974 and again in 1981–1983, inflationary recessions in several nations in the mid-1970s, major national recessions in the early 1980s, and large U.S.

budget deficits in the 1980s and the first half of the 1990s all caused substantial imbalances in international trade and finance. Flexible rates allowed the system to adjust to these developments, whereas the same events would have put unbearable pressures on a fixed-rate system.

Concerns with the Managed Float

There is still much sentiment in favor of greater exchange-rate stability. Those favoring stable exchange rates see problems with the current system. They argue that exchange rates have been excessively volatile under the managed float; this volatility threatens the continued expansion of international investment and trade. Moreover, some volatility has occurred even when underlying economic and financial conditions have been relatively stable, suggesting that speculation is playing too large a role in determining exchange rates. Perhaps more importantly, assert the critics, the managed float has not eliminated trade imbalances, as flexible rates are supposed to do. Thus, the United States has run persistent trade deficits for many years, while Germany and Japan have had persistent surpluses. Changes in exchange rates between dollars, marks, and yen have not yet corrected these imbalances, as is supposed to be the case under flexible exchange rates.

Skeptics say the managed float is basically a "nonsystem"; the guidelines concerning what each nation may or may not do with its exchange rates are not specific enough to keep the system working in the long run. Nations inevitably will be tempted to intervene in the foreign exchange market, not merely to smooth out short-term fluctuations in exchange rates but to prop up their currency if it is chronically weak or to manipulate the exchange rate to achieve domestic stabilization goals.

Flexible exchange rates have not worked perfectly, but they have not failed miserably. Thus far they have *survived*, and no doubt *eased*, several major shocks to the international trading system. Meanwhile, the "managed" part of the float has given nations some sense of control over their collective economic destinies. On balance, most economists favor continuation of the present system of "almost" flexible exchange rates.

QUICK REVIEW 38-3

■ Under the gold standard (1879–1934), nations fixed exchange rates by valuing their currencies in terms of gold, by tying their stocks of money to gold, and by allowing gold to flow between nations when balance of payments deficits and surpluses occurred.

■ The Bretton Woods exchange-rate system (1944–1971) fixed or pegged short-run exchange rates but permitted orderly long-run adjustments of the pegs.

■ The managed floating system of exchange rates (1971–present) relies on foreign exchange markets to establish equilibrium exchange rates. The system also permits nations to buy and sell foreign currency to stabilize short-term changes in exchange rates or to correct exchange-rate imbalances which are negatively affecting the world economy.

RECENT U.S. TRADE DEFICITS

Figure 38-5 reveals that U.S. trade and current account deficits in the 1990s have been large and persistent. For example, the goods trade deficit for 1997 was $199 billion. That year, the goods and services deficit was $114 billion, and the current account deficit was $166 billion.

Causes of the Trade Deficit

There are several reasons for these persistent trade deficits. First, since 1992 the U.S. economy has grown more rapidly than the economies of several major trading nations. This growth of income has boosted U.S. purchases of foreign goods (U.S. imports). In contrast, Japan, some European nations, and Canada have suffered recession or slow income growth during this period. Thus, their purchases of U.S. goods (U.S. exports) have not kept pace with the rise of U.S. imports. Persistent U.S. trade imbalances with Japan are particularly noteworthy.

Second, until recently the United States had large annual Federal budget deficits. These deficits required the Federal government to compete with the private sector for financing, which bid up real interest rates. The high real interest rates increased the foreign demand for dollars. The resulting high international value of the dollar made U.S. exports more expensive to foreigners and U.S. imports cheaper to consumers.

Finally, a declining saving rate in the United States has contributed to U.S. trade deficits. The saving rate (saving/total income) in the United States has declined at the same time the investment rate (investment/total income) has remained stable or even

(a) Balance of trade

(b) Balance on current account

FIGURE 38-5 Recent U.S. Trade Deficits U.S. trade deficits in (a) "goods" and "goods and services" and (b) the current account recently have been very large. (*Source:* U.S. Department of Commerce.)

increased. The gap has been met through foreign purchases of U.S. real and financial assets, creating a large capital account surplus. Because foreigners are financing more of U.S. investment, U.S. citizens are able to save less and consume more, including consumption of imported goods. That is, the capital account surplus may partly cause the trade deficit, not simply result from it.

Implications of U.S. Trade Deficits

Are large trade deficits something that should concern the United States? There is disagreement on this issue, but most economists see both benefits and costs to trade deficits.

Increased Current Consumption   At the time a trade or current account deficit is occurring, U.S. consumers benefit. A trade deficit means that the United States is receiving more goods and services as imports from abroad than it is sending out as exports. Taken alone, a trade deficit allows the United States to consume outside its production possibilities curve; a trade deficit augments the domestic standard of living. But as we will see next, there is a catch: The gain in present consumption comes at the expense of reduced future consumption.

Increased U.S. Indebtedness   A trade deficit is considered "unfavorable" because it must be financed by borrowing from the rest of the world, selling off assets, or dipping into foreign currency reserves. Recall that current account deficits are financed primarily by net inpayments of foreign currencies to the United States. When U.S. exports are insufficient to finance U.S. imports, the United States increases both its debt to people abroad and the value of foreign claims against assets in the United States. Financing of the U.S. trade deficit has resulted in a larger foreign accumulation of claims against U.S. financial and real assets than the U.S. claim against foreign assets. Today, the United States is the world's largest debtor nation. In 1996, foreigners owned $831 billion more of U.S. assets (corporations, land, stocks, bonds, loan notes) than the United States owned in foreign assets.

Just one implication is that the United States no longer has its once-large net inflow of dividend and interest payments (item 7 in Table 38-1) to help offset its trade deficits in its goods and services trade. That amount, as high as $30 billion in the early 1980s, is now approaching zero. Another implication is that if the United States wants to *regain* ownership of these domestic assets, at some future time it will have to export more than it imports. At that time, domestic consumption will be lower because the United States will need to send more of its output abroad than it receives as imports. Therefore, the current consumption gains delivered by U.S. trade deficits mean permanent debt, permanent foreign ownership, or large sacrifices of future consumption.

CHAPTER SUMMARY

1. U.S. exports create a foreign demand for dollars and make a supply of foreign exchange available to the United States. Conversely, U.S. imports create a demand for foreign exchange and make a supply of dollars available to foreigners. Generally, a nation's exports earn the foreign currencies needed to pay for its imports.

2. The balance of payments records all international trade and financial transactions taking place between a given nation and the rest of the world. The trade balance compares exports and imports of goods. The balance on goods and services compares exports and imports of both goods and services. The current account balance includes not only goods and services transactions but also net investment income and net transfers.

3. A deficit in the current account may be offset by a surplus in the capital account. Conversely, a surplus in the current account may be offset by a deficit in the capital account. A balance of payments deficit occurs when the sum of the current and capital accounts is negative. Such a deficit is financed with official reserves. A balance of payments surplus occurs when the sum of the current and capital accounts is positive. A payments surplus results in an increase in official reserves. The desirability of a balance of payments deficit or surplus depends on its size and its persistence.

4. Flexible or floating exchange rates between international currencies are determined by the demand for and supply of those currencies. Under floating rates a currency

Speculation in Currency Markets

Are speculators a negative or a positive influence in currency markets and international trade?

Most people buy foreign currency to facilitate the purchase of goods or services from another country. A U.S. importer buys Japanese yen to purchase Japanese autos. A Hong Kong financial investor purchases Australian dollars to invest in the Australian stock market. But there is another group of participants in the currency market—speculators—that buys and sells foreign currencies in the hope of reselling or rebuying them later at a profit.

1. Contributing to Exchange-Rate Fluctuations Speculators were much in the news in late 1997 and 1998 when they were widely accused of driving down the values of the South Korean won, Thailand baht, Malaysian ringgit, and Indonesian rupiah. The value of these currencies fell by as much as 50 percent within 1 month, and speculators undoubtedly contributed to the swiftness of these declines. The expectation of currency depreciation (or appreciation) can be self-fulfilling. If speculators, for example, expect the Indonesian rupiah to be devalued or to depreciate, they quickly sell rupiah and buy currencies which will increase in relative value. The sharp increase in the supply of rupiah indeed reduces its value; this reduction then may trigger further selling of rupiah in expectation of further declines in its value.

But changed economic realities, not speculation, are normally the *underlying* causes of changes in currency values. That was largely the case with the Southeast Asian countries in which actual and threatened bankruptcies in the financial and manufacturing sectors undermined confidence in the strength of the currencies. Anticipating the eventual declines in currency values, speculators simply hastened that decline. That is, the declines in value probably would have occurred with or without speculators.

Moreover, on a day-to-day basis, speculation clearly has positive effects in foreign exchange markets.

2. Smoothing Out Short-Term Fluctuations in Currency Prices When temporarily weak demand or strong supply reduces a currency's value, speculators quickly buy the currency, adding to its demand and strengthening its value. When temporary strong demand or weak supply increases a currency's value, speculators sell the currency. This selling increases the supply of the currency and reduces its value. In this way speculators smooth out supply and demand, and thus exchange rates, over short time periods. This day-to-day exchange-rate stabilization aids international trade.

3. Absorbing Risk Speculators also absorb risk which others do not want to bear. Because of potential adverse changes in exchange rates, international transactions are riskier than domestic transactions. Suppose AnyTime, a hypothetical retailer, signs a contract with a German manufacturer to buy 10,000 German clocks to be delivered in 3 months. The stipulated price is 75 marks per clock,

will depreciate or appreciate as a result of changes in tastes, relative income changes, relative price changes, relative changes in real interest rates, and speculation.

5. The maintenance of fixed exchange rates requires adequate reserves to accommodate periodic payments deficits. If reserves are inadequate, nations must invoke protectionist trade policies, engage in exchange controls, or endure undesirable domestic macroeconomic adjustments.

6. The gold standard, a fixed rate system, provided exchange-rate stability until its disintegration during the 1930s. Under this system, gold flows between nations precipitated sometimes painful changes in price, income, and employment levels in bringing about international equilibrium.

7. Under the Bretton Woods system, exchange rates were pegged to one another and were stable. Participating

nations were obligated to maintain these rates by using stabilization funds, gold, or loans from the IMF. Persistent or "fundamental" payments deficits could be resolved by IMF-sanctioned currency devaluations.

8. Since 1971 the world's major nations have used a system of managed floating exchange rates. Rates are generally set by market forces, although governments intervene with varying frequency to alter their exchange rates.

9. The United States has experienced large trade deficits in the 1990s. Causes include: **(a)** faster growth of U.S. income than in some European nations, Canada, and Japan, resulting in expanding U.S. imports; **(b)** until recently, large U.S. budget deficits, resulting in high real interest rates, a strong dollar, and expanding U.S. imports; and **(c)** a declining U.S. saving rate which has produced a large capital account surplus and freed U.S. income for spending on imports.

which in dollars is $50 per clock at the present exchange rate of $1 = 1.5 marks. AnyTime's total bill for the 10,000 clocks will be $500,000 (= 750,000 marks).

But if the German mark were to appreciate, say, to $1 = 1 mark, the dollar price per clock would rise from $50 to $75 and AnyTime would owe $750,000 for the clocks (= 750,000 marks). AnyTime may reduce the risk of such an unfavorable exchange-rate fluctuation by *hedging* in the *futures market*. Hedging is an action by a buyer or seller to protect against a change in future prices. The futures market is a market in which currencies are bought and sold at prices fixed now, for delivery at a specified date in the future.

AnyTime can purchase the needed 750,000 marks at the current $1 = 1.5 marks exchange rate, but with delivery in 3 months when the German clocks are delivered. And here is where speculators come in. For a price determined in the futures market, they agree to deliver the 750,000 marks to AnyTime in 3 months at the $1 = 1.5 marks exchange rate, regardless of the exchange rate then. The speculators need not own marks when the agreement is made. If the German mark *depreciates* to, say, $1 = 2 marks in this period, the speculators profit. They can

buy the 750,000 marks stipulated in the contract for $375,000, pocketing the difference between that amount and the $500,000 AnyTime has agreed to pay for the 750,000 marks. If the German mark *appreciates*, the speculators, but not AnyTime, suffer a loss.

The amount AnyTime must pay for this "exchange-rate insurance" will depend on how the market views the likelihood of the mark depreciating, appreciating, or staying constant over the 3-month period. As in all competitive markets, supply and demand determines the price of the futures contract.

The futures market thus eliminates much of the exchange-rate risk associated with buying foreign goods for future delivery. Without it, AnyTime might have decided against importing German clocks. But the futures market and currency speculators greatly increase the likelihood that the transaction will occur. Operating through the futures market, speculation promotes international trade.

In short, although speculators in currency markets occasionally contribute to swings in exchange rates, on a day-to-day basis they play a positive role in currency markets.

---

10. U.S. trade deficits have produced current increases in the living standards of U.S. consumers. However, these deficits have also increased U.S. debt to the rest of the world and have resulted in greater foreign ownership of assets in the United States.

TERMS AND CONCEPTS

balance of payments
current account
trade balance
balance on goods and
  services
balance on current
  account

capital account
balance on capital account
official reserves
balance of payments
  deficits and surpluses
flexible or floating
  exchange-rate system

fixed exchange-rate
  system
purchasing power parity
  theory
gold standard
devaluation

Bretton Woods system
International Monetary
  Fund
managed floating
  exchange rates

STUDY QUESTIONS

- -

1. Explain how a U.S. automobile importer might finance a shipment of Toyotas from Japan. Demonstrate how a U.S. export of machinery to Italy might be financed. Explain: "U.S. exports earn supplies of foreign currencies that Americans can use to finance imports."

2. KEY QUESTION Indicate whether each of the following creates a demand for, or a supply of, French francs in foreign exchange markets:
  a. A U.S. importer purchases a shipload of Bordeaux wine.
  b. A French automobile firm decides to build an assembly plant in Los Angeles.
  c. A U.S. college student decides to spend a year studying at the Sorbonne.
  d. A French manufacturer ships machinery from one French port to another on a Liberian freighter.
  e. The U.S. economy grows faster than the French economy.
  f. A U.S. government bond held by a French citizen matures and the loan amount is paid back to that person.
  g. It is widely believed that the international value of the franc will fall in the near future.

3. KEY QUESTION Alpha's balance of payments data for 1998 are shown below. All figures are in billions of dollars. What are **(a)** the balance of trade, **(b)** the balance on goods and services, **(c)** the balance on current account, and **(d)** the balance on capital account? Does Alpha have a balance of payments deficit or surplus? Explain.

Goods exports	+$40	Net transfers	+$10
Goods imports	− 30	Foreign purchases	
Service exports	+ 15	of assets in the	
Service imports	− 10	United States	+ 10
Net investment income	− 5	U.S. purchases of	
		assets abroad	− 40
		Official reserves	+ 10

4. "A rise in the dollar price of yen necessarily means a fall in the yen price of dollars." Do you agree? Illustrate and elaborate: "The critical thing about exchange rates is that they provide a direct link between the prices of goods and services produced in all trading nations of the world." Explain the purchasing power parity theory of exchange rates.

5. The Swedish auto company Saab imports car components from Germany and exports autos to the United States. In 1990 the dollar depreciated, and the German mark appreciated, relative to the Swedish krona. Speculate as to how this hurt Saab—twice.

6. KEY QUESTION Explain why the U.S. demand for Mexican pesos is downsloping and the supply of pesos to Americans is upsloping. Assuming a system of flexible exchange rates between Mexico and the United States, indicate whether each of the following would cause the Mexican peso to appreciate or depreciate:
  a. The United States unilaterally reduces tariffs on Mexican products.
  b. Mexico encounters severe inflation.
  c. Deteriorating political relations reduce American tourism in Mexico.
  d. The U.S. economy moves into a severe recession.
  e. The United States engages in a high-interest-rate monetary policy.
  f. Mexican products become more fashionable to U.S. consumers.
  g. The Mexican government encourages U.S. firms to invest in Mexican oil fields.
  h. The rate of productivity growth in the United States diminishes sharply.

7. Explain why you agree or disagree with the following statements:
  a. "A country which grows faster than its major trading partners can expect the international value of its currency to depreciate."
  b. "A nation whose interest rate is rising more rapidly than in other nations can expect the international value of its currency to appreciate."
  c. "A country's currency will appreciate if its inflation rate is less than that of the rest of the world."

8. "Exports pay for imports. Yet in 1996 the rest of the world exported about $111 billion more worth of goods and services to the United States than were imported from the United States." Resolve the apparent inconsistency of these two statements.

9. KEY QUESTION Diagram a market in which the equilibrium dollar price of one unit of fictitious currency Zee is $5 (the exchange rate is $5 = Z1). Then show on your diagram a decline in the demand for Zee.
  a. Referring to your diagram, discuss the adjustment options the United States would have in maintaining the exchange rate at $5 = Z1 under a fixed exchange-rate system.

b. How would the U.S. balance of payments surplus which is created (by the decline in demand) get resolved under a system of flexible exchange rates?

10. Compare and contrast the Bretton Woods system of exchange rates with that of the gold standard. What caused the demise of the gold standard? What caused the demise of the Bretton Woods system?

11. Describe what is meant by the term "managed float." Did the managed float system precede or follow the adjustable-peg system? Explain.

12. What have been the major causes of the large U.S. trade deficits since 1992? What are the major benefits and costs associated with trade deficits? Explain: "A trade deficit means that a nation is receiving more goods and services from abroad than it is sending abroad." How can that be called "unfavorable"?

13. (Last Word) Suppose Winter Sports—a French retailer of snowboards—wants to order 5000 snowboards made in the United States. The price per board is $200, the present exchange rate is 6 francs = $1, and payment is due in dollars when the boards are delivered in 3 months. Use a numerical example to explain why exchange-rate risk might make the French retailer hesitant to place the order. How might speculators absorb some of Winter Sports' risk?

14. WEB-BASED QUESTION   U.S. International Trade in Goods and Services—Latest Figures The U.S. Census http://www.census.gov/indicator/www/ustrade.html provides the latest data on U.S. trade in goods and services. Over the past year, has the trade balance in goods and services improved (that is, yielded a smaller deficit or larger surplus) or deteriorated? The major U.S. trade strength is in which category: goods or services? The largest increases in exports were in what products? The largest increases in imports were in what products?

15. WEB-BASED QUESTION   The Yen/Dollar Exchange Rate and Trade Deficits The Japanese yen/U.S.$ exchange rate is determined by market forces and changes frequently. A key determinant of exchange rates is a trade deficit or a trade surplus. Other things equal, if the United States has a trade deficit with Japan, the dollar should depreciate relative to the yen. The Federal Reserve Board of Governors http://www.bog.frb.fed.us/releases (Foreign Exchange Rates—Historical Data) provides yen/dollar exchange rates for the last decade. Trade data can be found at http://www.census.gov/indicator/www/ustrade.html under Exports, Imports, and Balance of Goods by Selected Countries. Select a time period, and compare the U.S. trade deficit with Japan with the yen/dollar exchange rate during that period. Do the data support the theory? What other factors might be influencing the yen/dollar rate?

39

The Economics of Developing Countries

It is difficult for those of us in the United States, where per capita (per person) GDP in 1997 was $27,571, to grasp the fact that some two-thirds of the world's population lives at, or perilously close to, the subsistence level. Hunger, squalor, and disease are common in many nations of the world. More than 1 billion people—about 20 percent of the world population—live on incomes of less than $2 per day.

Here we first identify the *developing countries* and discuss their characteristics. Then we discuss why these countries have such low standards of living: What obstacles have impeded their growth? Next, we examine the potentials and pitfalls of government's role in economic development. We also examine private money flows from the *advanced industrial countries* to the developing countries and assess the debt problem the developing countries face. Finally, we distill a list of possible policies which might help developing countries increase their growth rates.

THE RICH AND THE POOR

Just as there is considerable income inequality among individual families within a nation, so too is there great income inequality among the family of nations. Table 39-1 shows the remarkable degree of income differences in the world. The richest 20 percent of the world's population receive almost 83 percent of the world's income; the poorest 20 percent obtain less than 1.5 percent. The poorest 60 percent get less than 6 percent of the world's income.

Figure 39-1 helps us sort out the rich and poor by grouping high-income, middle-income, and low-income nations.

1. *Industrially advanced countries* The 26 high-income nations, shown in yellow, are known as the **industrially advanced countries (IACs);** they include the United States, Japan, Canada, Australia, New Zealand, and most of the nations of western Europe. These nations have well-developed market economies based on large stocks of capital goods, advanced production technologies, and well-educated workers. In 1995 these economies had a per capita output (or income) of $24,930.

2. *Developing countries* The remaining nations of the world, located mainly in Africa, Asia, and Latin America, are called **developing countries (DVCs).** These 107 nations have relatively low levels of industrialization. In general, literacy rates are low, unemployment is high, population growth

TABLE 39-1   Global income disparity

World population	Percentage of world income
Richest 20%	82.7
Second 20%	11.7
Third 20%	2.3
Fourth 20%	1.9
Poorest 20%	1.4

Source: United Nations Development Program, *Human Development Report 1992* (New York: Oxford University Press, 1992), p. 36.

is rapid, and exports consist largely of agricultural produce (such as cocoa, bananas, sugar, raw cotton) and raw materials (such as copper, iron ore, natural rubber). Capital equipment is minimal, production technologies are relatively simple, and labor productivity is very low. About three-fourths of the world's population live in these nations, all of which have widespread poverty.

Figure 39-1 breaks down these developing nations into *middle-income* and *low-income countries.* The first group of 58 middle-income DVCs (shown in purple) had an average per capita output of $2390 in 1995. Per capita output for this diverse group ranged from $766 to $9385. The other group is made up of 49 low-income DVCs (shown in red) with per capita outputs of $765 or less in 1995 and averaging only $430 that year. India, China, and the sub-Saharan nations of Africa dominate this group.

Several comparisons will bring global income differences into sharper focus.

1. In 1995, U.S. total output was approximately $6.9 trillion; the combined GDPs of the 107 DVCs in that year was only $5.5 trillion.

2. The United States, with only 5 percent of the world's population, produces one-fourth of the world's output.

3. The annual sales of the world's largest corporations exceed the GDPs of many of the DVCs. General Motors' annual world revenues are greater than the GDPs of all but 22 nations.

4. Per capita GDP in the United States is 337 times greater than in Mozambique, the world's poorest nation.

Growth, Decline, and Income Gaps

Two other things concerning Figure 39-1 should be noted. First, the various nations have demonstrated considerable differences in ability to improve their circumstances over time. On the one hand, DVCs such as China, Malaysia, Chile, and Thailand achieved high annual growth rates in their GDPs in recent decades. Consequently, their real output per capita rose several fold. Several previous DVCs such as South Korea, Singapore, and Hong Kong (now part of China) have achieved IAC-status. In contrast, many DVCs, such as those in sub-Saharan Africa, have experienced declining GDPs per capita during the past decade.

Second, the *absolute income gap* between rich and poor nations has been widening. To understand this point, suppose the per capita incomes of the advanced and developing countries were growing at about 2 percent per year. Because the income base in the advanced countries is initially much higher, the absolute income gap grows. If per capita income is $400 a year in a DVC, a 2 percent growth rate means an $8 increase in income. Where per capita income is $20,000 per year in an IAC, the same 2 percent growth rate translates into a $400 increase in income. Thus, the absolute income gap will have increased from $19,600 (= $20,000 − $400) to $19,992 (= $20,400 − $408). The DVCs must grow faster than the IACs to narrow the gap. **(Key Question 3)**

Implications

Mere statistics conceal the human implications of the extreme poverty characterizing so much of our planet:

. . . let us examine a typical "extended" family in rural Asia. The Asian household is likely to comprise ten or more people, including parents, five to seven children, two grandparents, and some aunts and uncles. They have a combined annual income, both in money and in "kind" (i.e., they consume a share of the food they grow), of from $250 to $300. Together they live in a poorly constructed one-room house as tenant farmers on a large agricultural estate owned by an absentee landlord who lives in the nearby city. The father, mother, uncle, and the older children must work all day on the land. None of the adults can read or write; of the five school-age children, only one attends school regularly; and he cannot expect to proceed beyond three or four years of primary education. There is only one meal a day; it rarely changes and it is rarely sufficient to alleviate the childrens' constant hunger pains. The house has no electricity, sanitation, or fresh water supply. There is much sickness, but qualified doctors and medical practitioners are far away in the cities attending to the needs of wealthier families. The work is

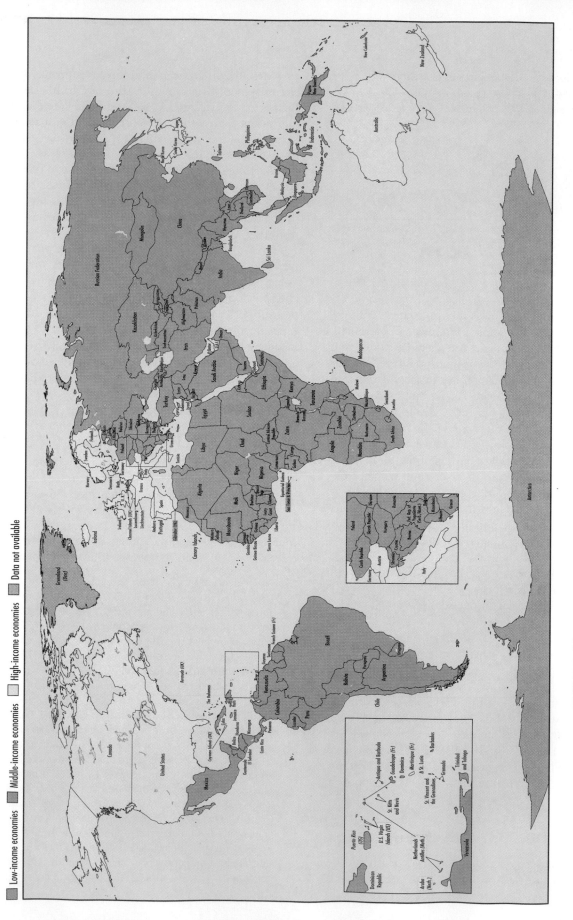

FIGURE 39-1 Groups of economies The world's nations are grouped into industrially advanced countries (IACs) and developing countries (DVCs). The IACs (shown in yellow) are high-income countries. The DVCs are middle-income and low-income countries (shown respectively in purple and in red.) (*Source:* World Bank data.)

Low-income economies   Middle-income economies   High-income economies   Data not available hard, the sun is hot and aspirations for a better life are constantly being snuffed out. In this part of the world the only relief from the daily struggle for physical survival lies in the spiritual traditions of the people.[1]

In Table 39-2 we contrast various socioeconomic indicators for selected DVCs with those for the United States and Japan. You will see that these data confirm the major points stressed in the quotation from Todaro.

OBSTACLES TO ECONOMIC DEVELOPMENT

The paths of economic development (economic growth) are essentially the same for developing countries as for the industrially advanced economies.

1. The DVCs must use their existing supplies of resources more efficiently. This means they must eliminate unemployment and underemployment and also combine labor and capital resources efficiently to achieve lowest-cost production. The DVCs must also direct their scarce resources such that they achieve allocative efficiency.

[1]Michael P. Todaro, *Economic Development in the Third World*, 5th ed. (New York: Longman, 1994), p. 4.

2. The DVCs must expand their available supplies of resources. Through greater supplies of raw materials, capital equipment, and productive labor, together with improved technological knowledge, a DVC can push its production possibilities curve outward.

All DVCs are aware of these two paths. Why then have some nations successfully traveled these paths while others have lagged far behind? The difference is in the physical, human, and socioeconomic environments of the various nations.

Natural Resources

There is no simple generalization as to the role of natural resources in the economic development of DVCs because the distribution of natural resources among them is very uneven. Some DVCs have valuable deposits of bauxite, tin, copper, tungsten, nitrates, and petroleum and have been able to use their natural resource endowments to achieve rapid growth and a significant redistribution of income from the rich to the poor nations. The Organization of Petroleum Exporting Countries (OPEC) is a standard example. In other instances, natural resources are owned or controlled by the multinational corporations of industrially advanced countries, with the economic benefits from these resources largely diverted

TABLE 39-2 Selected socioeconomic indicators of development

Country	(1) Per capita output, 1995	(2) Life expectancy at birth, 1995	(3) Infant mortality per 1000 live births, 1995	(4) Adult illiteracy rate, percent, 1995	(5) Percent of labor force in agriculture, 1990	(6) Per capita energy consumption, 1994*
Japan	$39,640	80 years	4	under 5	11	3,856
United States	26,980	77	8	under 5	3	7,819
Brazil	3,640	67	44	17	23	718
Mauritania	460	51	96	—	55	103
China	620	69	34	19	74	664
India	340	62	68	48	64	248
Bangladesh	240	58	79	62	64	64
Ethiopia	100	49	112	65	80	22
Mozambique	80	47	113	60	83	40

*Kilograms of oil equivalent.
Source: *World Development Report, 1997.*

abroad. Furthermore, world markets for many of the farm products and raw materials which the DVCs export are subject to large price fluctuations that contribute to instability in their economies.

Other DVCs lack mineral deposits, have little arable land, and have few sources of power. Also, most of the poor countries are in Central and South America, Africa, the Indian subcontinent, and Southeast Asia, where tropical climates prevail. The hot, humid climate hinders productive labor; human, crop, and livestock diseases are widespread; and weed and insect infestations plague agriculture.

A weak resource base can be a serious obstacle to growth. Real capital can be accumulated and the quality of the labor force improved through education and training. But it is difficult to augment the natural resource base. It may be unrealistic for many of the DVCs to envision an economic destiny comparable with that of, say, the United States and Canada. But we must be careful in generalizing: Switzerland and Japan, for example, have achieved high levels of living *despite* restrictive natural resource bases.

Human Resources

Three statements describe many of the DVCs circumstances with respect to human resources:
1. They are overpopulated.
2. Unemployment and underemployment are widespread.
3. Labor productivity is low.

Overpopulation Many of the DVCs with the most meager natural and capital resources have the largest populations to support. Table 39-3 shows the high population densities and population growth rates of a few selected nations compared with those of the United States and the world.

Most important for the long run is the contrast in growth rates. The middle- and low-income DVCs in Figure 39-1 currently are experiencing a 1.6 percent annual increase in population compared with a 0.7 percent annual rate for IACs. Since such a large percentage of the world's present population already resides in DVCs, this percentage difference in population growth rates is highly significant: 9 out of every 10 people added to the world population during the next 15 years will live in developing nations. (See Global Perspective 39-1.)

Population statistics help explain why the per capita income gap between the DVCs and IACs has

TABLE 39-3 Population statistics for selected countries

Country	Population per square mile, 1996	Annual rate of population increase, 1990–1995
United States	75	1.0%
Pakistan	430	2.9
Bangladesh	2380	1.6
Venezuela	65	2.3
India	829	1.8
China	336	1.1
Kenya	128	2.7
Philippines	647	2.2
World	**114**	**1.5%**

Sources: Statistical Abstract of the United States, 1996; World Development Report, 1997.

widened. In some of the poorest DVCs, rapid population growth actually presses on the food supply so much that per capita food consumption falls to or below the biological subsistence level. In the worst instances, only malnutrition and disease, and the high death rate they cause keep incomes near subsistence.

It would seem at first glance that, since

$$\frac{\text{Standard}}{\text{of living}} = \frac{\text{consumer goods (food) production}}{\text{population}}$$

the standard of living could be raised by boosting consumer goods—particularly food—production. But the problem is more complex because any increase in consumer goods production which initially raises the standard of living may induce a population increase. This increase, if sufficiently large, will dissipate the improvement in living standards, and subsistence living levels will again prevail.

But why might population growth in DVCs accompany increases in output? First, the nation's *death* or *mortality rate* will decline with initial increases in production. This decline is the result of (1) a higher level of per capita food consumption and (2) the basic medical and sanitation programs which accompany the initial phases of economic development.

Second, the *birthrate* will remain high or may increase, particularly as medical and sanitation programs cut infant mortality. The cliché that "the rich get richer and the poor get children" is uncomfortably accurate for many of the poorest DVCs. An in-

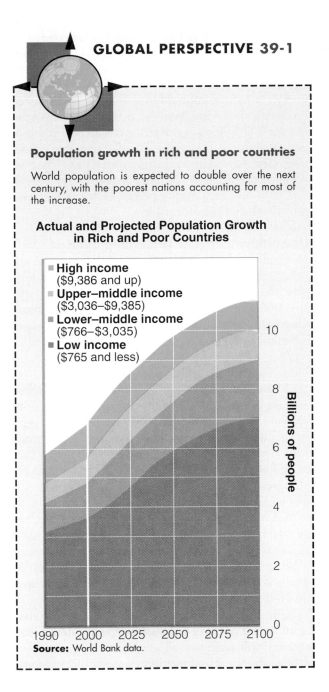

GLOBAL PERSPECTIVE 39-1

Population growth in rich and poor countries

World population is expected to double over the next century, with the poorest nations accounting for most of the increase.

Actual and Projected Population Growth in Rich and Poor Countries

- **High income** ($9,386 and up)
- **Upper–middle income** ($3,036–$9,385)
- **Lower–middle income** ($766–$3,035)
- **Low income** ($765 and less)

Billions of people

1990 2000 2025 2050 2075 2100

Source: World Bank data.

reasons why population expansion is often an obstacle to development.

Saving and Investment   Large families reduce the capacity of households to save, restricting the economy's ability to accumulate capital.

Productivity   As population grows, more investment is required to maintain the amount of real capital per person. If investment fails to keep pace, each worker will have fewer tools and equipment, reducing worker productivity (output per worker). Declining productivity implies stagnating or declining per capita incomes.

Resource Overuse   Because most developing countries are heavily dependent on agriculture, rapid population growth may result in overuse of limited natural resources such as land. The much-publicized African famines are partially the result of past overgrazing and overplanting of land caused by the pressing need to feed a growing population. (This chapter's Last Word is relevant.)

Urban Problems   Rapid population growth in the cities of the DVCs, accompanied by unprecedented flows of rural migrants, are generating massive urban problems. Substandard housing in impoverished slums, poor public services, congestion, pollution, and crime are all problems worsened by rapid population growth. The resolution or lessening of these difficulties necessitates a diversion of resources from growth-oriented uses.

Most authorities advocate birth control as the most effective means for breaking out of this dilemma. And breakthroughs in contraceptive technology in recent decades have made this solution increasingly relevant. But obstacles to population control are great. Low literacy rates make it difficult to disseminate information about contraceptive devices. In peasant agriculture, large families are a major source of labor. Adults may regard having many children as a kind of informal social security system: The more children, the greater the probability of having a relative to care for you during old age. Finally, many nations which stand to gain the most through birth control are often the least willing, for religious and sociocultural reasons, to embrace contraception programs. Population growth in Latin America, for example, is among the most rapid in the world.

China—with about one-fifth of the world's population—adopted a harsh "one-child" program in 1980.

crease in the per capita standard of living may lead to a population upsurge which will cease only when the standard of living has again been reduced to the level of bare subsistence.

In addition to the fact that rapid population growth can convert an expanding GDP into a stagnant or slow-growing GDP per capita, there are four other

The government advocated late marriages and one child per family. Couples having more than one child are fined or lose various social benefits. Even though the rate of population growth has diminished under this program, China's population continues to expand at about 100 million per decade. India, the world's second most populous nation, had a 242 million or 35 percent population increase in the 1980–1995 period. With a total population of 929 million, India has 16 percent of the world's population but less than 2.5 percent of its land mass.

Qualifications But our focus on population growth as a major cause of low incomes needs to be qualified in several ways.

As with natural resources, the relationship between population and economic growth is less clear than one might expect. A high population density and rapid population growth do not necessarily mean poverty. China and India have immense populations and are poor, but Japan and Hong Kong are densely populated and wealthy.

Also, population growth rates for the DVCs as a group have declined somewhat in recent decades. In the 1960s the annual population growth rate was about 2.0 percent; for the 1990s, it looks like it will be about 1.4 percent. Experts predict that this percentage will fall to about 1.2 percent by 2010.

Finally, there is a view contrary to the traditional one that reducing population growth is the key to increasing GDP per capita in developing countries. The **demographic transition view** holds that rising income first must be achieved; only then will slower population growth follow. This view observes there are both marginal benefits and marginal costs of having another child. In DVCs the marginal benefits are relatively large because the extra child becomes an extra worker who can help support the family. Extra children can provide financial support and security for their parents in their old age, so people in poor countries have high birthrates. But in wealthy IACs the marginal cost of children is much greater than in the DVCs. Care of children may require that one of the parents sacrifice high earnings, or there may be the need to purchase expensive childcare. Also, children require extended and expensive education for the highly skilled jobs characteristic of the IAC economies. Finally, the wealth of the IACs results in "social safety nets" which protect adults from the insecurity associated with old age and the inability to work. In this view, people in the IACs recognize that high birthrates are not in the family's short-term or long-term interest, so they choose to have fewer children.

Note the differences in causation the two views imply. The traditional view says that reduced birthrates must come first and then higher per capita income will follow; lower birthrates are the cause of per capita income growth. The demographic transition view says that higher incomes must first be achieved and then lower rates of population growth will follow; higher incomes cause slower population growth. **(Key Question 6)**

Unemployment and Underemployment Employment-related data for many DVCs either are nonexistent or highly unreliable. But observation suggests that *unemployment* is high; many people are unable to find jobs. There is also significant **underemployment,** which means that a large number of people are employed fewer hours per week than they want, work at jobs unrelated to their training, or spend much of the time on their jobs unproductively.

Many economists contend that unemployment may be as much as 15 to 20 percent in the rapidly growing urban areas of the DVCs. There has been substantial migration in most developing countries from rural to urban areas, motivated by the *expectation* of finding jobs with higher wage rates than are available in agricultural and other rural employments. But this huge migration reduces the chance of a migrant in fact obtaining a job. Migration to the cities has greatly exceeded the growth of urban job opportunities, resulting in very high urban unemployment rates. Thus, rapid rural-urban migration has given rise to urban unemployment rates which are two or three times as great as rural rates.

Underemployment is widespread and characteristic of most DVCs. In many of the poorer developing nations, rural agricultural labor may be so abundant relative to capital and natural resources that a significant percentage of this labor contributes little or nothing to agricultural output. Similarly, many DVC workers are self-employed as proprietors of small shops, in handicrafts, or as street vendors. A lack of demand means that small shop owners or vendors spend idle time in the shop or on the street. While they are not without jobs, these people are underemployed.

Low Labor Productivity Labor productivity tends to be low in DVCs. As we will see, the developing nations have found it difficult to invest in *physical capi-*

tal. As a result, their workers are underequipped with machinery and tools and hence are relatively unproductive. Keep in mind that rapid population growth tends to reduce the amount of physical capital available per worker, which decreases labor productivity and real incomes.

In addition, most poor countries have not been able to invest sufficiently in their *human capital* (see Table 39-2, columns 3 and 4); that is, expenditures on health and education have been meager. Low levels of literacy, malnutrition, lack of proper medical care, and insufficient educational facilities all contribute to populations which are ill-equipped for industrialization and economic expansion. Attitudes may also play a role: In some countries, hard work is associated with slavery, servitude, and inferiority, so people try to avoid it.

Particularly vital is the absence of a vigorous entrepreneurial class willing to bear risks, accumulate capital, and provide the organizational requisites essential to economic growth. Closely related is the lack of labor trained to handle the routine supervisory functions basic to any program of development. Ironically, the higher education systems of some DVCs are oriented toward the humanities and offer little work in business, engineering, and the sciences. Some DVCs are characterized by an authoritarian view of human relations—often fostered by repressive governments—which generates an environment hostile to independent thinking, taking initiatives, and assuming economic risks. Authoritarianism discourages experimentation and change—the essence of entrepreneurship.

An additional irony is that, while migration from the DVCs has modestly offset rapid population growth, it has also deprived some DVCs of highly productive workers. Often the best-trained and most highly motivated workers—physicians, engineers, teachers, and nurses—leave the DVCs to seek their fortunes in the IACs. This so-called **brain drain** contributes to the deterioration in the overall skill level and productivity of the labor force.

Capital Accumulation

An important focal point of economic development is the accumulation of capital goods, for several reasons:

1. All DVCs suffer from shortages of capital goods such as factories, machinery and equipment, and public utilities. Better-equipped labor forces would greatly enhance their productivity and help boost the per capita standard of living. There is a close relationship between output per worker (labor productivity) and real income per worker. A nation must produce more goods and services per worker to enjoy more goods and services per worker as income. One way of increasing labor productivity is to provide each worker with more tools and equipment. Indeed, studies for the DVCs confirm a positive relationship between investment and the growth of GDP. On the average, a 1 percentage point increase in the ratio of investment to GDP raises the overall growth rate by about one-tenth of 1 percentage point. Thus an increase in the investment-to-GDP ratio from 10 to 15 percent would increase the growth of real GDP by one-half of 1 percentage point.[2]

2. Increasing the stock of capital goods is crucial because of the very limited possibility of increasing the supply of arable land. If there is little likelihood of increasing agricultural output by increasing the supply of land, an alternative is to use more and better capital equipment with the available agricultural workforce.

3. Once initiated, the process of capital accumulation *may* be cumulative. If capital accumulation can increase output faster than population grows, a margin of saving may arise which permits further capital formation. In a sense, capital accumulation can feed on itself.

Let's first consider the prospects for developing nations to accumulate capital domestically. Then we will examine the possibility of foreign funds flowing into them to support expansion of capital.

Domestic Capital Formation A developing nation, as does any nation, accumulates capital through saving and investing. A nation must save (refrain from consumption) to release resources from production of consumer goods. Investment spending must then absorb these released resources in the production of capital goods. But impediments to saving and investing are much greater in a low-income nation than in an advanced economy.

Savings Potential Consider first the savings side of the picture. The situation here is mixed and varies

---

[2]International Monetary Fund, *World Economic Outlook* (Washington, 1988), p. 76.

greatly between countries. Some of the very poor countries, such as Ethiopia, Bangladesh, Uganda, Haiti, and Madagascar, save only 2 to 5 percent of their GDPs. The people are simply too poor to save a significant portion of their incomes. Interestingly, however, other developing countries save as large a percentage of their domestic outputs as do advanced industrial countries. In 1995 India and China saved 22 and 42 percent of their domestic outputs, respectively, compared to 29 percent for Japan, 23 percent for Germany, and 15 percent for the United States. The problem is that the domestic outputs of the DVCs are so low that even when saving rates are comparable to advanced nations, the total absolute volume of saving is not large.

Capital Flight   Some of the developing countries have suffered **capital flight,** the transfer of private DVC savings to accounts held in the IACs. (In this usage, "capital" is simply "money," "money capital," or "financial capital.") Many wealthy citizens of DVCs have used their savings to invest in the more economically advanced nations, allowing them to avoid the high investment risks at home, such as loss of saving or real capital from government expropriation, abrupt changes in taxation, potential hyperinflation, or high volatility of exchange rates. If a DVC's political climate is unsettled, savers may shift their funds overseas to a "safe haven" in fear that a new government might confiscate their wealth. Likewise, rapid or skyrocketing inflation in a DVC would have similar detrimental effects. The transfer of saving overseas may also be a means of evading high domestic taxes on interest income or capital gains. Finally, money capital may flow to the IACs, where there are higher interest rates or a greater variety of investment opportunities.

Whatever the motivation, the amount of capital flight from some nations is significant. This outflow of money capital offsets a considerable portion of the IACs' lending and giving of money capital to the developing nations.

Investment Obstacles   There are as many obstacles on the investment side of capital formation in DVCs as on the saving side. These investment obstacles involve a lack of investors and a lack of incentives to invest.

In some developing nations, the major obstacle to investment is the lack of entrepreneurs who are willing to assume the risks associated with investment.

This is a special case of the qualitative limitations of the labor force previously discussed.

But the incentive to invest may be weak even if substantial saving and a large number of willing entrepreneurs are present. Several factors may combine in a DVC to reduce investment incentives. In our discussion of capital flight we mentioned such factors as political instability and higher rates of inflation. Similarly, very low incomes in a DVC result in a limited domestic market, meaning a lack of buying power and thus weak demand for all but agricultural goods. This factor is crucial because the chances of successfully competing with mature industries in the IACs in the international market are slim. Then, too, lack of trained administrative personnel may be a factor in retarding DVC investment.

Finally, many DVCs simply do not have an adequate **infrastructure** (stock of public capital goods), which is necessary for achieving adequate returns on private investment. Poor roads and bridges, inadequate railways, little gas and electricity production, poor communications, unsatisfactory housing, and meager educational and public health facilities create an inhospitable environment for private investment. Much of any new private investment would have to be for the infrastructure needed by all firms. Rarely can firms provide such infrastructure themselves and still earn a positive return on their overall investment.

For all these reasons, investment incentives in many DVCs are lacking. It is significant that for multinational firms, about four-fifths of their overseas investments goes to IACs.

How then can developing nations build up the infrastructure necessary to attract investment? The higher-income DVCs may be able to accomplish this through taxation and public spending. But there is little income to tax in the poorest DVCs. Nevertheless, with leadership and a willingness to cooperate, a poor DVC can accumulate capital by transferring surplus agricultural labor to the improvement of the infrastructure. If each agricultural village allocated its surplus labor to the construction of irrigation canals, wells, schools, sanitary facilities, and roads, significant amounts of capital might be accumulated at no significant sacrifice of consumer goods production. Such investment simply bypasses the problems inherent in the financial aspects of the capital accumulation process. It does not require consumers to save portions of their money income, nor does it presume the presence of an entrepreneurial class anxious to invest. When leadership and cooperative spirit are present, this "in-kind" investment is a promising avenue for accumulation of basic capital goods. **(Key Question 7)**

Technological Advance

Technological advance and capital formation are frequently part of the same process. Yet there are advantages in treating technological advance and capital formation as separate processes.

The rudimentary state of technology in the DVCs leaves them far from the frontiers of technological advance. But there is an enormous body of technological knowledge accumulated by the advanced nations which developing countries *might* adopt and apply without expensive research. Crop rotation and contour plowing require no additional capital equipment and may contribute significantly to productivity. By raising grain storage bins a few inches aboveground, a large amount of grain spoilage can be avoided. Such changes may sound trivial to people of advanced nations. However, resulting gains in productivity can mean the difference between subsistence and starvation in some poverty-ridden nations.

In most instances application of either existing or new technological knowledge involves new and different capital goods. But, within limits, this capital can be obtained without an increase in the rate of capital formation. If the annual flow of replacement investment is rechanneled from technologically inferior to technologically superior capital equipment, productivity can be increased out of a constant level of investment spending. Actually, some technological advances may be **capital-saving technology** rather than **capital-using technology.** A new fertilizer, better adapted to a nation's topography and climate, might be cheaper than one currently employed. A seemingly high-priced metal plow which will last 10 years may be cheaper in the long run than an inexpensive but technologically inferior wooden plow which requires annual replacement.

To what extent have DVCs transferred and effectively used available IAC technological knowledge? The picture is mixed. There is no doubt that such technological borrowing has been instrumental in the rapid growth of such Pacific Rim countries as Japan, South Korea, Taiwan, and Singapore. Similarly, the OPEC nations benefitted greatly from IAC knowledge of oil exploration, production, and refining. Recently Russia, the nations of eastern Europe, and China have been using western technology to hasten their conversions to market-based economies.

At the same time, we must be realistic about the transferability of advanced technologies to the poorest developing countries. In industrially advanced nations technologies are usually predicated on relatively scarce, highly skilled labor and relatively abundant capital. Such technologies tend to be capital-using or, alternatively stated, labor-saving. In contrast, developing economies require technologies appropriate to *their* resource endowments—abundant unskilled labor and very limited quantities of capital goods. Labor-using and capital-saving technologies are appropriate to DVCs. But much of the highly advanced technology of advanced nations is inappropriate in the developing countries; they must develop their own technologies. Recall, too, that many DVCs still have "traditional economies" and are not highly receptive to change. This is particularly true in peasant agriculture, which dominates the economies of most poorer DVCs. A potential technological advance which fails can mean hunger and malnutrition; therefore, there is a strong tendency to retain traditional production techniques.

Sociocultural and Institutional Factors

Economic considerations alone do not explain why an economy does or does not grow. Substantial social and institutional readjustments are usually an integral part of the growth process. Economic development means not only changes in a nation's physical environment (new transportation and communications facilities, new schools, new housing, new plants and equipment) but also changes in the way people think, behave, and associate with one another. Emancipation from custom and tradition is frequently a prerequisite of economic development. A critical but intangible ingredient in economic development is **the will to develop.** Economic growth may hinge on what individuals within DVCs want for themselves and their children. Do they want more material abundance? If so, do they want it badly enough to make the necessary changes in their institutions and old ways of doing things?

Sociocultural Obstacles Sociocultural impediments to growth are numerous and varied:

1. Some of the very low income countries have failed to achieve the preconditions for a national economic unit. Tribal and ethnic allegiances take precedence over national identity. Warring tribes confine all economic activity to within the tribe, eliminating any possibility for production-increasing specialization and trade. The desperate economic circumstances in Somalia, Sudan, Liberia, Zaire, and other sub-Saharan nations of Africa are due in no small measure to martial and political conflicts among rival clans.

2. The existence of a formal or informal caste system causes labor to be allocated to occupations on the basis of status or tradition rather than on the basis of skill or merit. The result is a misallocation of human resources.

3. Religious beliefs and observances may seriously restrict the length of the workday and divert resources which might have been used for investment to ceremonial uses. Some religious and philosophical beliefs are dominated by the fatalistic **capricious universe view,** that is, the notion that there is little or no correlation between an individual's activities and endeavors and the outcomes or experiences which that person encounters.

> If the universe is deemed capricious, the individual will learn to expect little or no correlation between actions and results. This will result in a fatalistic attitude . . . .
>
> These attitudes impinge on all activities including saving, investment, long-range perspective, supply of effort, and family planning. If a higher standard of living and amassing of wealth is treated as the result of providence rather than springing from hard work and saving, there is little rationale for saving, hard work, innovations, and enterprise.[3]

Other attitudes and cultural factors may impede economic activity and growth: emphasis on the performance of duties rather than the exertion of individual initiative; the focus on group rather than individual achievement; the notion of a preordained and unalterable universe; the belief in reincarnation, which reduces the importance of one's present life.

Institutional Obstacles Political corruption and bribery are common in many DVCs. School systems and public service agencies are often ineptly administered and their functioning impaired by petty politics. Tax systems are frequently arbitrary, unjust, cumbersome, and detrimental to incentives to work and invest. Political decisions are often motivated by a desire to enhance the nation's international prestige rather than to foster development.

---

[3]Inder P. Nijhawan, "Socio-Political Institutions, Cultural Values, and Attitudes: Their Impact on Indian Economic Development," in J. S. Uppal (ed.), *India's Economic Problems* (New Delhi: Tata McGraw-Hill Publishing Company, Ltd., 1975), p. 33.

Because of the predominance of farming in DVCs, the problem of achieving an optimal institutional environment in agriculture is a vital consideration in any growth program. Specifically, the institutional problem of **land reform** demands attention in many DVCs. But needed reform may vary tremendously between specific nations. In some DVCs the problem is excessive concentration of land ownership in the hands of a few wealthy families. This situation is demoralizing for tenants, weakening their incentive to produce, and typically does not promote capital improvements. At the other extreme is the absurd arrangement whereby each family owns and farms a minute fragment of land far too small for the application of modern agricultural technology. An important complication to the problem of land reform is that political considerations sometimes push reform in that direction which is least defensible on economic grounds. For many nations, land reform may well be the most acute institutional problem to be resolved in initiating the process of economic development.

Examples: Land reform in South Korea undermined the political control of the landed aristocracy and made way for the development of strong commercial and industrial middle classes, all to the benefit of the country's economic development. In contrast, the prolonged dominance of the landed aristocracy in the Philippines has allegedly helped stifle the development of that economy.

QUICK REVIEW 39-1

■ About three-fourths of the world's population lives in the DVCs of Africa, Asia, and Latin America.

■ Natural resource scarcities and inhospitable climates restrict economic growth in many DVCs.

■ Most of the poorest DVCs are characterized by over-population, high unemployment rates, underemployment, and low labor productivity.

■ Low saving rates, capital flight, weak infrastructures, and lack of investors impair capital accumulation in many DVCs.

■ Sociocultural and institutional factors are often serious impediments to growth in DVCs.

THE VICIOUS CIRCLE

Many of the characteristics of DVCs just described are simultaneously *causes* and *consequences* of their poverty. These countries are caught in a **vicious cir-**

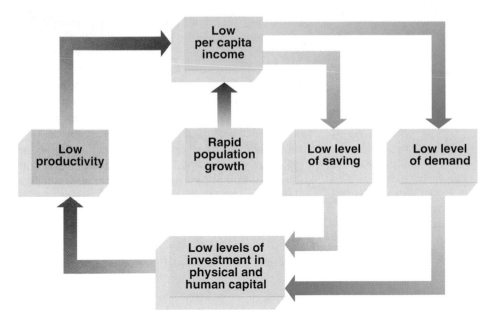

FIGURE 39-2 The vicious circle of poverty Low per capita incomes make it difficult for poor nations to save and invest, a condition which perpetuates low productivity and low incomes. Furthermore, rapid population growth may quickly absorb increases in per capita real income and thereby may negate the possibility of breaking out of the poverty circle.

----

cle of poverty. They *stay* poor because they *are* poor! Consider Figure 39-2. The fundamental feature of a DVC is low per capita income. Being poor, a family has little ability or incentive to save. Furthermore, low incomes means low levels of product demand. Thus, there are few available resources, on the one hand, and no strong incentives, on the other hand, for investment in physical or human capital, which means that labor productivity is low. And, since output per person is real income per person, it follows that per capita income is low.

Many economists think that the key to breaking out of this vicious circle is to increase the rate of capital accumulation, to achieve a level of investment of, say, 10 percent of the national income. But Figure 39-2 reminds us that rapid population growth may partially or entirely undo the potentially beneficial effects of this higher rate of capital accumulation. Suppose that initially a DVC is realizing no growth in its real GDP. But now it somehow manages to increase its saving and investment to 10 percent of its GDP. As a result, its real GDP begins to grow at, say 2.5 percent per year. With a stable population, real GDP per capita will also grow at 2.5 percent per year. If this growth persists, the standard of living will *double* in about 28 years. But what if population grows at the middle east and northern Africa rate of 2.5 percent per year? Then real income per person is unchanged and the vicious circle persists.

More optimistically, *if* population can be kept constant or constrained to some growth rate significantly below 2.5 percent, then real income per person will rise. This implies the possibility of still further enlargement in the flows of saving and investment, continued advances in productivity, and the continued growth of per capita real income. If a process of self-sustaining expansion of income, saving, investment, and productivity can be achieved, the self-perpetuating vicious circle of poverty can be transformed into a self-regenerating, beneficent circle of economic progress. The challenge is to make effective those policies and strategies which will accomplish this transition. **(Key Question 13)**

ROLE OF GOVERNMENT

Economists do not agree on the appropriate role of government in fostering DVC growth.

A Positive Role

One view is that, at least during initial stages of development, government should play a major role because of the character of the obstacles facing DVCs.

Law and Order Some of the poorest countries are plagued by banditry and intertribal warfare which divert both attention and resources from the task of development. A strong and stable national government is needed to establish domestic law and order and to achieve peace and unity. Research demonstrates that political instability (as measured by the number of revolutions and coups per decade) is associated with slow growth.

Lack of Entrepreneurship

The lack of a sizable and vigorous entrepreneurial class, ready and willing to accumulate capital and initiate production, indicates that in some DVCs, private enterprise is not capable of spearheading the growth process. Government may initially have to take the lead.

Infrastructure

Many obstacles to economic growth relate to an inadequate infrastructure. Sanitation and basic medical programs, education, irrigation and soil conservation projects, and construction of highways and transportation-communication facilities are all essentially nonmarketable goods and services yielding widespread spillover benefits. Government is the sole institution in a position to provide these public goods and services in required quantities.

Forced Saving and Investment

Government action may also be required to break through the saving-investment dilemma which impedes capital formation in DVCs.

It may be that only governmental fiscal action can provide a solution by forcing the economy to accumulate capital. There are two alternatives. One is to force the economy to save by increasing taxes. These tax revenues can then be channeled into priority investment projects. However, problems of honestly and efficiently administering the tax system and achieving a high degree of compliance with tax laws can be great.

The other alternative is to force the economy to save through inflation. Government can finance capital accumulation by creating and spending new money or by selling bonds to banks and spending the proceeds. The resulting inflation is the equivalent of an arbitrary tax on the economy.

There are serious arguments against public sector saving through inflation. First, inflation often distorts the composition of investment away from productive facilities to such items as luxury housing, precious metals and jewels, or foreign securities, which provide a better hedge against rising prices. Also, significant inflation may reduce voluntary private saving as potential savers become less willing to accumulate depreciating money or securities payable in money of declining value. Inflation also often induces capital flight. Internationally, inflation may boost the nation's imports and retard its flow of exports, creating balance of payments difficulties.

Social-Institutional Problems

Government is in the key position to deal effectively with the social-institutional obstacles to growth. Controlling population growth and land reform are problems which call for the broad approach only government can provide. And government is in a position to nurture the will to develop, to change a philosophy of "Heaven and faith will determine the course of events" to one of "God helps those who help themselves."

Public Sector Problems

But serious problems and disadvantages may exist with a governmentally directed development program. If entrepreneurial talent is lacking in the private sector, can we expect quality leaders in the ranks of government? Is there not a real danger that government bureaucracy will impede, not stimulate, much-needed social and economic change? And what of the tendency of some political leaders to favor spectacular "showpiece" projects at the expense of less showy but more productive programs? Might not political objectives take precedence over the economic goals of a governmentally directed development program?

Development experts are less enthusiastic about the role of government in the growth process than they were 30 years ago. Government maladministration and corruption are common in many DVCs. Government officials often line their own pockets with foreign aid funds. Similarly, political leaders frequently confer monopoly privileges on relatives, friends, and political supporters. A political leader may grant exclusive rights to relatives or friends to produce, import, or export certain products. These monopoly privileges lead to higher domestic prices for the relevant products and diminish the DVC's ability to compete in world markets. Similarly, managers of state-owned enterprises are often appointed on the basis of cronyism rather than competence. Many DVC governments, particularly in Africa, have created "marketing boards" as the sole purchaser of agricultural products from local farmers. The boards buy farm products at artificially low prices and sell the output at higher world prices; the "profit" ends up in the pockets of government officials. In recent years the perception of government has shifted from that of catalyst and promoter of growth to that of a potential impediment to development.

A Mixed Bag

It is possible to muster causal evidence on both sides of this question. Positive government contributions to development are evident in Japan, South Korea, and Taiwan. In comparison, Mobutu's Zaire, Somoza's Nicaragua, Marcos' Philippines, and Haiti under the Duvaliers are recognized examples of corrupt and inept governments which functioned as impediments to economic progress. Certainly the revolutionary transformations of the former Soviet Union and other eastern European nations away from communism and toward market-oriented economies make clear that central planning is no longer recognized as an effective mechanism for development. Many DVCs are belatedly recognizing that capitalism, with its focus on individual economic incentives and on competition, is the surest, most sustainable, avenue to economic growth.

ROLE OF ADVANCED NATIONS

How can industrially advanced nations help developing countries in their quest for growth? To what degree have IACs pursued these avenues of assistance?

Generally, developing nations can benefit from (1) an expanding volume of trade with advanced nations, (2) foreign aid in the form of grants and loans from governments of advanced nations, and (3) flows of private capital from the more affluent nations.

Expanding Trade

Some authorities maintain that the simplest and most effective way the United States and other industrially advanced nations can aid developing nations is by lowering international trade barriers. Such actions enable DVCs to expand their national incomes through increased trade.

Although there is some truth in this view, lowered trade barriers are not a panacea. Some poor nations do need only large foreign markets for their raw materials to achieve growth. But the problem for many poor nations is not one of obtaining markets to use existing production capacity or to sell relatively abundant raw materials but the more fundamental problem of getting the capital and technical assistance needed to produce something for export.

Moreover, close trade ties with advanced nations have some disadvantages. Dependence on import demand from the IACs leaves DVCs vulnerable to temporary declines in the IACs' production. By reducing the demand for resources, recessions in the IACs can have disastrous consequences for the prices of raw materials and the export earnings of the DVCs. For example, during the recession in the IACs in the early 1990s, the world price of zinc fell from $.82 per pound to $.46 per pound and the world price of tin fell from $5.20 per pound to $3.50 per pound. Because mineral exports are a major source of DVC income, stability and growth in IACs are important to economic progress in the developing nations.

Foreign Aid: Public Loans and Grants

Foreign capital—both public and private—can supplement an emerging country's saving and investment and play a crucial role in breaking the circle of poverty.

As previously noted, many DVCs are lacking in the infrastructure prerequisites for attracting either domestic or foreign private capital. Foreign public aid which increases infrastructure can thus enhance the flow of private capital to the DVCs.

Direct Aid The United States and other IACs have assisted DVCs directly through a variety of programs and through participating in international institutions designed to stimulate economic development. Over the past decade, U.S. aid to the DVCs in the forms of both loans and grants averaged $10–$14 billion per year. The bulk of this aid is administered by the U.S. Agency for International Development (USAID). Some aid, however, is in the form of grants of surplus food under the Food for Peace program. Other advanced nations also have substantial foreign aid programs. In recent years foreign aid from all IACs has been about $60 billion per year.

The IACs' aid programs merit several additional comments. First, aid is typically distributed on the basis of political and military rather than economic considerations. Israel, Turkey, Egypt, and Greece are major recipients of U.S. aid at the expense of Asian, Latin American, and African nations with much lower standards of living. Second, aid from the IACs amounts to only about one-third of 1 percent of the IAC's collective GDPs (see Global Perspective 39-2). Finally, the shift of Russia and eastern Europe toward more democratic, market-oriented systems has made these nations "new players" as foreign aid recipients. The DVCs worry that IAC aid which formerly flowed

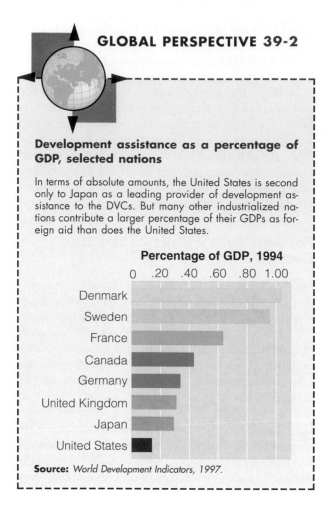

GLOBAL PERSPECTIVE 39-2

Development assistance as a percentage of GDP, selected nations

In terms of absolute amounts, the United States is second only to Japan as a leading provider of development assistance to the DVCs. But many other industrialized nations contribute a larger percentage of their GDPs as foreign aid than does the United States.

Percentage of GDP, 1994

Denmark
Sweden
France
Canada
Germany
United Kingdom
Japan
United States

Source: *World Development Indicators, 1997.*

to Latin America, Asia, and Africa is now redirected to, say, Poland, Hungary, and Russia. Similarly, there is the prospect of a substantially larger aid flow to the Middle East if the PLO-Israeli peace accord is durable.

The World Bank Group

The United States is a participant in the **World Bank,** whose major objective is helping DVCs achieve growth. [The World Bank was established in 1945, along with the International Monetary Fund (IMF).] Supported by nearly 180 member nations, the World Bank not only lends out of its capital funds, it also (1) sells bonds and lends the proceeds and (2) guarantees and insures private loans.

Several characteristics of the World Bank are noteworthy:

1. The World Bank is a "last resort" lending agency; its loans are limited to economic projects for which private funds are not readily available.

2. Because many World Bank loans have been for basic development projects—dams, irrigation projects, health and sanitation programs, communications and transportation facilities—the Bank's activities help provide the infrastructure needed to encourage flows of private capital.

3. The Bank has provided technical assistance to the LDCs by helping them discover what avenues of growth seem appropriate for their economic development.

The World Bank affiliates function in areas where the World Bank has been weak. The *International Finance Corporation (IFC)* has the primary function of investing in *private* enterprises in the DVCs. The *International Development Association (IDA)* makes "soft loans" (which may not be self-liquidating) to the poorest DVCs on more liberal terms than does the World Bank.

Foreign Harm?

However, foreign aid to the DVCs has been subject to several criticisms:

Dependency and Incentives A basic criticism is that, like domestic welfare programs, foreign aid may generate dependency rather than self-sustaining growth. It is argued that transfers of wealth from the IACs allow the DVCs to avoid the painful economic decisions, the institutional and cultural changes, and the alterations in attitudes regarding thrift, industry, hard work, and self-reliance which are needed for growth. Critics say that, after some five decades of foreign aid, the DVCs' demand for foreign aid has increased; if aid programs had been successful in promoting sustainable growth, demand should have fallen.

Bureaucracy and Centralized Government IAC aid is given, not directly to the residents and businesses of the LDCs, but to their governments. The consequence is that aid typically generates massive, relatively unproductive government bureaucracies and centralizes government power over the economy. The stagnation and collapse of the Soviet Union and eastern Europe is evidence that market-oriented economies are much more conducive to growth and development than are centrally planned economies. Furthermore, not only does the bureaucratization of the DVCs divert valuable human resources from the private to the public sector, it shifts the nation's focus from the *production* of output and income to its *redistribution.*

Corruption and Misuse Critics also allege that foreign aid is ineffectively used. Corruption is rampant in many DVCs, and some estimates suggest 10 to 20 percent of aid is diverted to government officials. Some of the wealthiest individuals in the world are rulers of DVCs. Foreign aid may create an ironic and perverse incentive for DVCs leaders to keep their populations poor so they continue to qualify for aid.

Also, IAC-based aid consultants and multinational corporations are major beneficiaries of aid programs. Some economists contend that as much as one-fourth or more of each year's aid is spent on expert consultants. Furthermore, because IAC corporations carry out most aid projects, they are major beneficiaries of, and lobbyists for, foreign aid.

The Decline of Foreign Aid

Foreign aid to developing countries is on the decline. In 1990 IACs provided $58 billion of foreign aid; by 1996 that aid had dropped to $40 billion. The criticisms of foreign aid just discussed are undoubtedly one reason for this decline. Another reason is the end of the Cold War, in which the United States and the former Soviet Union vied for the political and military allegiance of developing nations. Nations such as Cuba, Ethiopia, and North Korea which adhered to communist principles received substantial foreign aid from the Soviet Union. The United States, in turn, lavished foreign aid on developing nations such as Egypt, Mexico, Thailand, Turkey, and Chile, which tended to support U.S. policies. But with the disintegration of the former Soviet Union, the political-military rationale for foreign aid lost much of its force.

Private Capital Flows

The DVCs have also received substantial flows of *private* capital from the IACs. These private investors are corporations, commercial banks, and, more recently, financial investment companies. General Motors or Chrysler might finance construction of plants in Mexico or Brazil to assemble autos or produce auto parts. Citicorp or Bank of America might make loans to private firms operating in Argentina or China or directly to the governments of Thailand and Malaysia. And the financial investment companies Fidelity or Putnam might purchase stock of promising Hungarian and Chilean firms as part of their "emerging markets" mutual funds, which then could be purchased by individual investors in the IACs.

The DVCs' Debt Crisis of the 1980s

Private capital flows to the DVCs averaged $28 billion annually in the 1970s and increased throughout the period. Then in the 1980s several DVCs experienced a major *debt crisis:* They could not pay back their loans. This crisis was precipitated by a combination of factors:

1. Soaring prices of imported oil caused growing current account deficits in the DVCs, which financed these deficits largely through foreign borrowing.

2. In the early 1980s, a tight U.S. money policy (to control rapid inflation) had two detrimental effects on the DVCs. First, national income in the United States fell, causing a decline in U.S. imports from the DVCs. This decline sharply reduced DVC export earnings—earnings needed to pay interest and principal on their debts. Second, the high interest rates in the United States greatly increased the interest expense to the DVCs in refinancing loans from U.S. banks.

3. An appreciating dollar meant that DVCs had to pay more for their imports of U.S. goods. And because much DVC debt is denominated in dollars, it also meant that DVCs had to export a larger amount of their output to acquire each dollar needed to pay interest and principal on their debts.

4. Because of political corruption and economic mismanagement, DVC investment of loan funds was frequently unproductive. Returns on such investments were not sufficient to cover interest and principal payments, thereby generating loan defaults.

Actual defaults or near-defaults on existing loans in Mexico and several other DVCs brought an end to most of the flow of new and private foreign capital to the DVCs. A period of "muddling through" followed, in which creditor nations in cooperation with the International Monetary Fund tried to cope with the crisis on a nation-by-nation basis. The debts of many DVCs were rescheduled (stretched out over a longer period) to reduce the burden of annual interest and principal payments. And in some cases, commercial banks in the IACs had to "write off" much DVC debt as uncollectible, and thus as losses.

Reform and Revival in the 1990s

Although private capital flows to the DVCs virtually ceased in the 1980s, they have increased briskly in the 1990s. Specifically, they jumped from $50 billion in 1990 to

$250 billion in 1996. The major reason is that, as part of the debt renegotiations, heavily indebted DVCs agreed to reform their economies to promote growth and avert future debt crises. At the macro level, DVCs have made greater efforts to reduce budget deficits and control inflation. At the micro level, some governments have privatized state-owned businesses and deregulated industry. Some DVCs have reduced tariffs and adjusted unrealistically fixed exchange rates. In general, the DVCs have reduced the economic role of government and increased the role of free markets. These reforms have made the DVCs more attractive to foreign lenders.

The makeup of the revived private capital flows to the DVCs, however, is now different than before the debt crisis. First, private IAC firms and individuals, rather than commercial banks, are the primary lenders. Second, a greater proportion of the flows is now **direct foreign investment** in DVCs, rather than loans to DVC governments. Such direct investment includes the building of new factories by multinational firms in DVCs and the purchases of DVC firms (or parts of them). Whereas once DVCs viewed direct foreign investment as "exploitation," many of them now seek out direct foreign investment as a way to expand their capital stock and improve their citizen's job opportunities and wages. These wages are often very low by IAC standards but high by DVC standards. Another potential advantage of directly investing in DVCs is that management skills and technological knowledge often accompany such capital flows.

Two words of caution: The revived flow of capital is highly selective. Recently, most of the flow has been directed toward China, Mexico, Southeast Asian nations, and eastern European nations. Relatively little IAC capital is flowing toward extremely impoverished DVCs such as those in Africa.

Also, it is still premature to say that the DVC debt crisis has been totally resolved. Some developing nations still face staggering debt burdens, and there is no assurance that some combination of circumstances will not bring about future defaults. The DVC debt problem has been alleviated, not solved. For example, in 1995 the United States, other G-7 nations, and the IMF found it necessary to provide a $50 billion package of loan guarantees to offset the collapse of the Mexican peso. The immediate cause of the peso's dramatic fall was an expansion of Mexican debt in excess of export earnings. More recently, in late 1997 and early 1998 the currencies of Thailand, Malaysia, South

Korea, and Indonesia suddenly nose-dived in international value. Because most of these nations' debts are dollar-denominated, the depreciation of their currencies increased their expense of making interest and principal payments on their loans from the IACs. As in the earlier Mexican situation, the IMF coordinated multibillion dollar "financial rescue efforts" to help these countries cope with their domestic economic difficulties and to meet their financial obligations.

QUICK REVIEW 39-2

■ Governments of the DVCs may encourage growth by **(a)** providing law and order, **(b)** taking the lead in establishing enterprises, **(c)** improving the infrastructure, **(d)** forcing higher levels of saving and investing, and **(e)** resolving social-institutional problems.

■ The IACs can assist the DVCs through expanded trade, foreign aid, and private capital flows.

■ Many DVCs have large external debts which have become an additional obstacle to growth.

■ A decline in foreign aid to DVCs and an increase in private capital flows (particularly direct investment) have characterized the 1990s.

WHERE FROM HERE?

The developing nations face daunting tasks. There simply are no magic methods for quick economic development. Nevertheless, our discussion provided, or at least implied, several policies that DVCs and IACs might undertake to increase economic growth in the developing nations. We end this chapter by briefly summarizing these policies.

DVC Policies for Promoting Growth

Economists suggest that developing nations have several ways of enhancing their economic growth:

1. *Establishing the rule of law* Clearly defined and enforced property rights bolster economic growth by ensuring that individuals receive and retain the fruits of their labor. The rule of law also encourages direct foreign investments by firms from the IACs since legal protections reduce investment risk. Government itself must live by the law. The presence of government corruption in a sense sanctions criminality throughout the entire economic system. Such criminality undermines the growth of output because it diverts scarce resources toward activities which "transfer" income from others and away from activities which actually produce goods and services.

2. ***Opening economies to international trade*** Studies indicate that, other things equal, open economies grow as much as 1.2 percentage points per year faster than closed economies.

3. ***Controlling population growth*** Slower population growth converts increases in real output and income to increases in real output and income *per capita.* Fewer children reduce family consumption and enable family saving; smaller families also free up time for women to participate in the labor market.

4. ***Encouraging foreign direct investment*** DVCs which welcome and encourage direct foreign investment have had greater growth rates than nations which view such investment suspiciously and thus place severe obstacles in its way.

5. ***Building human capital*** Programs which increase basic literacy, education, and labor-market skills help enhance economic growth. Higher education loans and grants should contain strong incentives for recipients to remain in the home country (or return to the home country) after receiving their degrees.

6. ***Making peace with neighbors*** Countries at war or fear of war with neighboring nations divert scarce resources to armaments, rather than to, say, private capital or public infrastructure. Peace among neighboring nations can eventually lead to economic cooperation and integration, broadened markets, and enhanced growth.

7. ***Establishing independent central banks*** Hyperinflation is not conducive to economic investment and growth. DVCs can keep inflation in check by establishing independent central banks which maintain proper control over the nations' money supplies. Studies indicate that DVCs which control inflation have higher growth rates than those which do not.

8. ***Establishing realistic exchange-rate policies*** Exchange rates fixed at unrealistic levels invite balance of payments problems and speculative currency trading. Often, such trading forces a nation into abrupt revaluation of its currency, which shocks its economy. More flexible exchange rates enable more gradual adjustments and thus less susceptibility to major currency shocks and the domestic disruption they can cause.

9. ***Privatizing state industries*** Many DVCs could benefit by converting state enterprises into private firms. State enterprises often are inefficient; for example, they may be more concerned with appeasing labor unions than using modern technology and delivering goods and services at minimum per-unit cost. Also, relative to private firms, state enterprises are poor "incubators" for the development of profit-focused, entrepreneurial persons who may leave the firm to set up their own businesses.

IAC Policies for Fostering DVC Growth

What can the IACs do to improve living conditions and promote growth in the developing nations? While there is no consensus view, development economists offer a variety of suggestions, some of which we have already discussed:

1. ***Directing foreign aid to the poorest DVCs*** Much of the foreign aid from the IACs is strongly influenced by political and military considerations. Consequently, DVCs do not receive aid based on their economic needs or degree of destitution. Only one-fourth of foreign aid goes to those 10 countries whose population constitutes 70 percent of the world's poorest people. The most affluent 40 percent of the DVC population receives over twice as much aid as the poorest 40 percent. Many economists argue that the IACs should shift foreign aid away from the middle-income developing countries and toward the poorest group of DVCs.

2. ***Reducing tariffs and import quotas*** Trade barriers in the IACs are often highest for labor-intensive manufactured goods such as textiles, clothing, footwear, and processed agricultural products. These are precisely the types of goods in which DVCs have a comparative advantage. Also, many tariffs increase with the degree of product processing; for example, tariffs on chocolates are higher than on cocoa. This effectively denies the DVCs the opportunity to develop processing industries. One estimate suggests that trade barriers reduce the DVCs' gross domestic products by 3 percent, causing an annual loss of $75 billion in income. Thus, reducing such tariffs could greatly benefit the DVCs.

3. ***Providing debt relief to DVCs*** Development economists argue that, to the extent possible, the

Famine in Africa

The roots of Africa's persistent famines include both natural and human causes.

The early 1990s famine in Somalia—documented by shocking photos of fly-tormented, emaciated children with bloated bellies—is not uncommon in sub-Saharan Africa. Before U.S. armed forces and U.N. aid arrived in Somalia in late 1992, severe famine had caused an estimated 2000 deaths each day; 1 out of 4 Somali children under the age of 5—about 300,000—are believed to have died. Similarly, despite an outpouring of aid from the rich nations, the 1983–1984 Ethiopian famine caused 1 million deaths. A number of other African nations—including Ethiopia, Sudan, Angola, Liberia, Zaire, Mozambique, and Malawi—are persistently threatened by famine. Estimates put 5 to 20 million Africans at risk. This tragedy is ironic because most African countries were self-sufficient in food at the time they became independent nations; they are now heavily dependent on imported foodstuffs for survival.

The immediate cause of this catastrophe is drought. But the ultimate causes of Africa's declining ability to feed itself are more complex, an interplay of natural and human conditions. Lack of rainfall, chronic civil strife, rapid population growth, widespread soil erosion, and counterproductive public policies, all contribute to Africa's famines.

1. Civil Strife Regional rebellions and prolonged civil wars have devastated some African nations. Both Ethiopia and Sudan, for example, have been plagued by decades of civil strife. Not only do these conflicts divert precious resources from civilian uses, they also greatly complicate the ability of wealthy nations to provide famine and developmental aid. In the 1983–1984 famine the Ethiopian government denied food aid to areas occupied by rebel forces. Donated food is frequently diverted to the army and denied to starving civilians. During Ethiopia's 1973–1974 famine, Haile Selassie sold much of the donated food on world markets to enrich his regime! In Somalia, factional feuding destroyed most institutions—schools, factories, and government ministries—and reduced the country to anarchy. Armed gangs stole water pumps, tractors, and livestock from farms and looted ports of donated foodstuffs.

2. Population Growth In Africa population is growing more rapidly than is food production. Population is increasing about 3 percent per year while food output is growing only 2 percent per year. This grim arithmetic suggests declining living standards, hunger, and malnutrition. The World Bank reports that during the 1980s per capita incomes of the sub-Saharan nations fell to about three-quarters of the level reached by the end of the 1970s.

3. Ecological Degradation But apart from the simple numbers involved, population growth has contributed to the ecological degradation of Africa. With population pressures and the increasing need for food, marginal land has been deforested and put into crop production. In many

IACs should help the DVCs by stretching out payments of their debts. The present DVC debt is so large that it is a severe roadblock to DVC growth.

4. *Allowing in temporary workers while discouraging brain drains* Economists recognize that the IACs could help the DVCs by accepting more temporary workers from the DVCs. Temporary migration is not only an outlet for surplus DVC labor but also a source of income in the form of migrant remittance to their families in the home country. Also, IACs could discourage "brain drains" from the DVCs, in which the brightest and best-educated workers in the DVCs are recruited to the IACs. As you might imagine, these proposals have more support in the DVCs than in the IACs.

5. *Discouraging arms sales to the DVCs* Finally, the IACs should discourage sale of military equipment to the DVCs. Such purchases by the DVCs divert public expenditures from infrastructure and education.

cases trees which have served as a barrier to the encroachment of the desert have been cut for fuel, allowing the fragile topsoil to be blown away by desert winds. The scarcity of wood which has accompanied deforestation has forced the use of animal dung for fuel, thereby denying its traditional use as fertilizer. Furthermore, traditional fallow periods have been shortened, resulting in overplanting and overgrazing and a wearing out of the soil. Deforestation and land overuse have reduced the capacity of the land to absorb moisture, diminishing its productivity and its ability to resist drought. Some authorities feel that the diminished ability of the land to absorb water reduces the amount of moisture which evaporates into the clouds to return ultimately as rainfall. All this is complicated by the fact that there are few facilities for crop storage. Even when crops are good, it is difficult to accumulate a surplus for future lean years. A large percentage of domestic farm output in some parts of Africa is lost to rats, insects, and spoilage.

4. Public Policies and Debt Ill-advised public policies have contributed to Africa's famines. First, African governments generally have neglected investment in agriculture in favor of industrial development and military strength. It is estimated that African governments on the average spend four times as much on armaments as they do on agriculture. Second, many African governments have followed the policy of establishing the prices of agricultural commodities at low levels to provide cheap food for growing urban populations. This low-price policy has diminished farmers' incentives to increase productivity. While foreign aid has helped ease the effects of Africa's food-population problems, most experts reject aid as a long-term solution. Experience suggests that aid in the form of food can provide only temporary relief and may undermine the realization of long-run local self-sufficiency. Foreign food aid, it is contended, treats symptoms, not causes.

All this is made more complex by the fact that the sub-Saharan nations are burdened with large and growing external debts. The IMF reports that the aggregate debt of these nations rose from $84 billion in 1980 to $226 billion in 1995. As a condition of further aid, these nations have had to invoke austerity programs which have contributed to declines in their per capita incomes. One tragic consequence is that many of these nations have cut back on social service programs for children.

CHAPTER SUMMARY

1. The majority of the world's nations are developing countries (low- and middle-income nations) as opposed to high-income industrially advanced countries. While some DVCs have been realizing rapid growth rates in recent years, other have experienced little or no growth.

2. Initial scarcities of natural resources and the limited possibility of increasing existing supplies may limit a nation's ability to develop.

3. The large and rapidly growing populations in many DVCs contributes to low per capita incomes. Increases in per capita incomes frequently induce greater population growth, again reducing per capita incomes to near subsistence levels. The "demographic transition view," however, suggests that rising living standards must precede declining birthrates.

4. Most DVCs suffer from unemployment and underemployment. Labor productivity is low because of insufficient investment in physical and human capital.

5. In many DVCs, formidable obstacles impede both the saving and investment aspects of capital formation. In some of the poorest DVCs, the savings potential is very low. Many savers in DVCs transfer their funds to the IACs rather than invest domestically. The lack of a vigorous entrepreneurial class and the weakness of investment incentives also impede capital accumulation.

6. Appropriate social and institutional changes and, in particular, the presence of "the will to develop" are essential ingredients in economic development.

7. The vicious circle of poverty brings together many of the obstacles to growth, saying in effect that "poor countries stay poor because of their poverty." Low incomes inhibit saving and accumulation of physical and human capital, making it difficult to increase productivity and incomes. Rapid population growth can offset otherwise promising attempts to break the vicious circle.

8. The nature of the obstacles to growth—the absence of an entrepreneurial class, the dearth of infrastructure, the saving-investment dilemma, and the presence of social-institutional obstacles to growth—suggests a major role for government in initiating growth. However, the corruption and maladministration which are quite common to the public sectors of many DVCs suggest that government may not be very effective in instigating growth.

9. Advanced nations can assist in DVC development by reducing IAC trade barriers and by providing both public and private capital. Critics of foreign aid say that it **(a)** creates DVC dependency, **(b)** contributes to the growth of bureaucracies and centralized economic control, and **(c)** is ineffective because of corruption and mismanagement.

10. Rising energy prices, declining export prices, depreciation of the dollar, the unproductive use of borrowed funds, and concern about DVCs' creditworthiness combined to create a DVC debt crisis in the 1980s. External debt problems of many DVCs remain serious and hinder growth.

11. Economists suggest that DVCs can make future progress by establishing the rule of law, opening their economies to international trade, controlling population growth, encouraging foreign direct investment, building human capital, making peace with neighbors, establishing independent central banks, establishing realistic exchange rates, and privatizing state industries. The IACs can help in this process by directing foreign aid to the neediest nations, reducing tariffs and import quotas, providing debt relief, allowing more low-skilled immigration, and discouraging arms sales to the DVCs.

TERMS AND CONCEPTS

industrially advanced
  countries (IACs)
developing countries
  (DVCs)
demographic transition
  view

underemployment
brain drain
capital flight
infrastructure

capital-saving technology
capital-using technology
the will to develop
capricious universe view

land reform
vicious circle of poverty
World Bank
direct foreign investment

STUDY QUESTIONS

1. What are the characteristics of a developing nation? List the two basic avenues of economic growth available to such a nation. State and explain obstacles that DVCs face in breaking the poverty barrier. Use the "vicious circle of poverty" concept to outline steps a DVC might take to initiate economic development.

2. Explain how the absolute per capita income gap between rich and poor nations might increase, even though per capita income (or output) is growing faster in DVCs than in IACs.

3. KEY QUESTION Assume a DVC and an IAC presently have real per capita outputs of $500 and

$5000, respectively. If both nations have a 3 percent increase in their real per capita outputs, by how much will the per capita output gap change?

4. Discuss and evaluate:
  a. "The path to economic development has been clearly blazed by American capitalism. It is only for the DVCs to follow this trail."
  b. "The problem with the DVCs is that income is too equally distributed. Economic inequality promotes saving, and saving is prerequisite of investment. Therefore, greater inequality in the income distribution of the DVCs would be a spur to capital accumulation and growth."

c. "The core of economic development involves changing human beings more than it does altering a nation's physical environment."

d. "The U.S. 'foreign aid' program is a sham. In reality it represents neocolonialism—a means by which the DVCs can be nominally free in a political sense but remain totally subservient in an economic sense."

e. "The biggest obstacle facing poor nations in their quest for development is the lack of capital goods."

5. Studies indicate that, in general, landlocked countries tend to have lower per capita income levels than surrounding nations which are bordered by oceans and seas. Why do you think this is the case? Use Global Perspective 39-1 to identify a major exception to this generalization.

6. KEY QUESTION Contrast the "demographic transition view" of population growth with the traditional view that slower population growth is a prerequisite for rising living standards in the DVCs.

7. KEY QUESTION Because real capital is supposed to earn a higher return where it is scarce, how do you explain the fact that most international investment flows to the IACs (where capital is relatively abundant) rather than to the DVCs (where capital is very scarce)?

8. Do you think that the nature of the problems the DVCs face require governmentally directed as opposed to a private-enterprise-directed development process? Explain why or why not.

9. How did the DVC debt crisis of the 1980s come about? How did it get resolved?

10. What have been the trends relating to government-provided foreign aid versus private capital flows to the DVCs in the 1990s? Why do you think these trends are occurring?

11. What types of products do the DVCs typically export? How do these exports relate to the law of comparative advantage?

12. Do you think that IACs such as the United States should open their doors wider to immigration of low-skilled DVC workers to help the DVCs develop? Do you think that it is appropriate for students from DVC nations to stay in IAC nations to work and build careers?

13. KEY QUESTION Use Figure 39-2 (changing the box labels as necessary) to explain rapid economic growth in a country such as South Korea or Chile. What factors other than those contained in the figure might contribute to that growth?

14. (Last Word) Explain how civil wars, population growth, and public policy decisions have contributed to periodic famines in Africa.

15. WEB-BASED QUESTION Group of 77—**Promoting the Developing World** The Group of 77 (G-77) http://www.g77.org/ was established in 1964 by 77 developing countries. The Group of 77 promotes the collective economic interests of the developing world. What are the group's current developmental activities? What are the highlights in the latest *Group of 77 Journal* http://www.g77.org/Journal/message.htm?

16. WEB-BASED QUESTION **The World Bank Group—What's Hot in Development Economics** The major objective of the World Bank Group http://www.worldbank.org/ is to assist developing countries in achieving economic growth. What are three legs of the World Bank's development stool? What are the five agencies which make up the World Bank Group? Which one is the most influential? Go to the Development Economics section of the Topics in Development area and read the current research findings in What's Hot in Development Economics? What are the problems or opportunities, and what is the World Bank doing about them?

40

Transition Economies: Russia and China

Two of the most profound economic events of the past two decades are the collapse of communism in the Soviet Union and the rapid emergence of the market system in China. Russia (which emerged from the breakup of the Soviet Union) and China are perhaps the world's most significant developing economies: together they constitute 20 percent of the world's surface area and 24 percent of the world's population. (Global Perspective 40-1 compares salient facts about China, Russia, and the United States.)

In this final chapter, first we briefly look at the Marxian (communist) ideology which gave rise to the command economies. Then we examine the institutions and techniques of central planning common to both the Soviet Union and prereform China. Next, we discuss the coordination and incentive problems that central planning created. Finally, our attention turns to Russia and China's transitions to market economies.

IDEOLOGY AND INSTITUTIONS

To understand the command economies of the Soviet Union (prior to its collapse) and China (prior to market reforms), we must look back at the Marxian ideology which gave rise to central planning. Russia and China each have a unique history, but both nations established command economies following communist revolutions based on the ideas of Karl Marx. These revolutions established the Communist Party as the dominant force in political and economic life. The Russian revolution of 1917 resulted in a communist dictatorship under Vladimir Lenin and, later, Joseph Stalin and

others. The Chinese revolution of 1947 led to a communist dictatorship under Mao Zedong. At the heart of the communist ideology was belief in state (or communal) ownership of capital and land.

The Communist Party in the Soviet Union and China viewed itself as the representative of the *proletariat* (the working class) and the *peasantry*. Based on Marxist-Leninist and Marxist-Maoist doctrines, the communists envisioned their systems as the inevitable successor to capitalism, a system they believed was plagued by internal contradictions resulting from the private ownership of capital and land. To communists, the market system was chaotic, unstable, and inequitable. Markets bred infla-

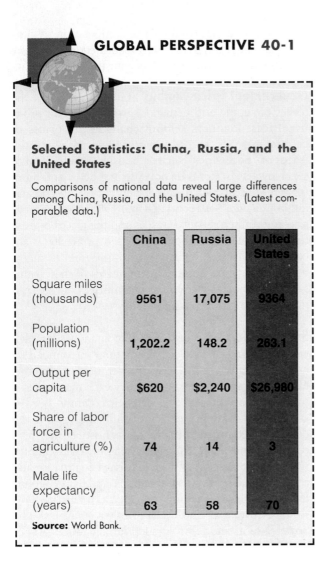

GLOBAL PERSPECTIVE 40-1

Selected Statistics: China, Russia, and the United States

Comparisons of national data reveal large differences among China, Russia, and the United States. (Latest comparable data.)

	China	Russia	United States
Square miles (thousands)	9561	17,075	9364
Population (millions)	1,202.2	148.2	263.1
Output per capita	$620	$2,240	$26,980
Share of labor force in agriculture (%)	74	14	3
Male life expectancy (years)	63	58	70

Source: World Bank.

tion, unemployment, discrimination, and an unfair distribution of income. In contrast, the communists viewed central planning of the economy as a way to rationally organize the economy's resources, meet basic human needs, achieve macroeconomic stability, provide greater equality, and end exploitation of labor by capitalists.

Marxists believed in a **labor theory of value,** which is the idea that the value of any good is determined solely by the amount of labor required for its production. Because of the capitalist institution of private property, Marxists argue, capitalists own the machinery and equipment necessary for production in an industrial society. The working class owns no such capital goods and therefore is dependent on capitalists for employment and its livelihood. Workers lack bargaining power because capitalists can dismiss labor agitators and replace them from the large "reserve army of the unemployed." Capitalists exploit workers by paying them a wage far below the value of workers' production. That is, capitalists can and will expropriate the remaining fruits of workers' labor as profit, or what Marx termed **surplus value.** While all value comes from labor, in the capitalist system labor does not receive all value. In the communist planned economic system, the state as an agency of the working class would extract surplus value and distribute it in large part through subsidies for public or quasi-public goods (for example, education, transportation, health care, and housing).

The function of communism was to overthrow capitalism and replace it with a classless society void of human exploitation. The Communist Party viewed itself as the vanguard of the working class and peasantry, and its actions were held to be in keeping with the goals of those groups. In reality, the Communist Party was a strong, one-party dictatorship which often pursued the interests of it party members.

STATE OWNERSHIP AND CENTRAL PLANNING

Two major institutional characteristics of the prereform and precollapse economies of Russia and China were (1) state (government) ownership of property resources and (2) authoritarian central planning.

State Ownership **State ownership** meant that the Soviet and Chinese governments owned all land, natural resources, transportation facilities, communication networks, the banking system, and virtually all industry. Most retail and wholesale enterprises and most urban housing were also government owned. Many farms were state-owned; most, however, were government collective farms, essentially cooperatives to which the state assigned land.

Central Economic Planning **Central economic planning** meant that the two nations had centralized "command" economies functioning according to a detailed economic plan. Both economies were government-directed rather than market-directed. Choices that are made through the market in the United States and other market economies were made by bureaucratic decisions in the Soviet Union and China. Through the central 5-year or 7-year plan (and its many subsets), the governments attempted to coordinate all economic activities of the economy as if they were parts of a large enterprise directed from their central headquarters.

Planning Goals and Techniques

Although central planning was far more complete in the Soviet Union than in China, each nation relied on direction from the central government. Several generalizations describe the functioning of central planning in both countries.

Industrialization (and Rural Development in China)

The former Soviet Union was dedicated to the task of rapid industrialization, economic growth, and military strength. These goals were achieved through extensive investment in heavy industry (such as steel, chemicals, and machine tools) and the allocation to the military of a large percentage of domestic output. In China, emphasis was also on rural development; for example, small-scale industries were scattered throughout the rural areas. But in both countries, the plans greatly neglected consumer goods industries and the distribution and service sectors.

Resource Overcommitment

In their efforts to increase total output (GDP), both the Soviet Union and China often overcommitted their economy's available resources. As a result, not every planning target could be achieved. In particular, the production of consumer goods suffered since planning priorities emphasized heavy industry, rural development, and the military.

Resource Mobilization

Both the Soviet Union and China initially achieved industrialization and economic growth through the mobilization of labor, capital, and raw materials. In the early years of planning there was substantial surplus labor in agriculture, which the central plans reallocated to industrial production. Similarly, both China and the Soviet Union induced or coerced a larger proportion of the population into the labor force. These countries achieved growth mainly by adding inputs rather than by using fixed amounts of inputs more productively. In the 1930s and again in the early post-World War II era, this strategy produced higher growth rates than those in the United States and other industrialized nations.

Allocation by Directives

Central planners directed the allocation of inputs among industries and firms, thereby determining the composition of output. Planning directives were substituted for the market system as an allocative mechanism.

Government Price Setting

Government, not the forces of supply and demand, set resource and product prices. Planners seldom changed the prices of consumer goods, and as a matter of social policy, the prices of "necessities" such as housing and food were set at low levels. Rents on housing in the Soviet Union, for example, averaged only 3 percent of income and did not change between 1928 and 1992. Government also determined resource prices and the prices of each firm's output. Such prices were used primarily as accounting devices to gauge a firm's progress in meeting its production goals. The emphases of the various 5- or 7-year plans were on the quantity of output, not on the cost or price of output.

Self-Sufficiency

The Soviet Union and China each viewed itself as a single socialist nation, surrounded by hostile capitalist countries. Moreover, neither communist country trusted the other. They each maintained a strong military presence along their common border, and they vied for supremacy of influence among the developing countries. Because of the hostility they perceived around them, the central plan in each country stressed economic self-sufficiency. Each country greatly restricted trade with western nations, and neither country established easy convertibility between their respective currencies and those of other countries. The Soviet Union and China traded largely among other communist nations such as East Germany, Poland, Hungary, Cuba, North Korea, and Vietnam.

Passive Macroeconomic Policies

Both the Soviet and prereform Chinese economies were quantity-directed systems in which money and prices played only a limited role in resource allocation. Monetary policy (changes in the money supply and interest rates) and fiscal policy (changes in government spending and taxes) were passive rather than active. Historically, unemployment—but not underemployment—was quite low, partly the result of ambitious planning targets and the various admonitions and "educational" campaigns to promote work. But low unemployment perhaps had more to do with overstaffing (managers could not fire redundant workers) and a lack of interest in cost-minimization (gross output was the overriding objective). It also had to do with the massive, highly labor-intensive, public works projects which both nations used to build infrastructure and glorify the socialist state.

Both countries primarily used direct government price setting as the primary device to control the price level. By simply not allowing prices to go up, both nations repressed any inflationary pressures. These price controls, however, created rising shortages of consumer goods.

PROBLEMS WITH CENTRAL PLANNING

Central planning was fraught with difficulties which ultimately led to the collapse of the Soviet economy and to the market reforms in China.

The Coordination Problem

As you have learned, the market system is a powerful organizing force which coordinates millions of individual decisions by consumers, resource suppliers, and businesses. In so doing, it promotes the efficient use of scarce resources. It is not easy to substitute central planning as a coordinating mechanism; such planning produces a significant **coordination problem.**

Example: Suppose that an enterprise in Moscow or Beijing is producing men's shoes. Planners must establish a realistic production target for that enterprise and then make available all the necessary inputs—labor, electric power, leather, rubber, thread, nails, appropriate machinery, transportation—for the production and delivery of that product. When the product is not as simple a one as shoes but a more complex one such as farm tractors, the planners' allocation problem are greatly compounded.

Because the outputs of many industries are inputs to other industries, the failure of any single industry to fulfill its output target will cause a chain reaction of adverse repercussions. If iron mines, for want of machinery or labor or transportation, do not supply the steel industry with the required inputs of iron ore, the steel mills will be unable to fulfill the input needs of the many industries dependent on steel. These steel-using industries (such as automobile, tractor, and transportation) will be unable to fulfill their planned production goals. Eventually the bottleneck chain reaction spreads to all firms using steel components as inputs.

The problem of centrally coordinating economic activity becomes more difficult as the economy grows.

Early planning under Stalin in the late 1930s and 1940s and Mao in China in the 1950s resembled the highly focused planning of capitalist nations in directing resources to the effort to fight World War II. The Communist Party established a few key production goals and directed resources toward fulfilling those goals regardless of costs or consumer welfare. But the past success of such "campaign planning" in the Soviet Union and China resulted in increasing complexity. Products and production processes became more sophisticated, and the number of industries for which to plan increased. Planning techniques which worked for a simple economy became inadequate and inefficient as these economies grew. Bottlenecks and production stoppages occurred with alarming regularity.

A lack of adequate success indicators adds to the coordination problem in central planning. Market economies have a single, comprehensive success indicator: profit. Profit or loss measures each firm's success or failure. Profit depends on consumer demand, production efficiency, and product quality. In contrast, the major success indicator of the Soviet and prereform China economies was a quantitative production target assigned by the central planners. Production costs, product quality, and product mix become secondary considerations. Managers and workers often sacrificed product quality since they were awarded bonuses for meeting quantitative, not qualitative, targets. If meeting production goals meant sloppy assembly work, so be it.

In fact, it is difficult at best for planners to assign quantitative production targets without unintentionally producing ridiculous distortions in output. If the production target for an enterprise manufacturing nails is specified in terms of weight (tons of nails), the producer will tend to produce all large nails. But if its target is a quantity (thousands of nails), it will be motivated to use available inputs to produce all small nails. The problem is that the economy needs *both* large and small nails.

The Incentive Problem

In the capitalist system, profits and losses not only signal success and failure, they also act as incentives for firms to increase or decrease production. If there is a product shortage, its price and profitability increase and producers are motivated to expand production. Conversely, a product surplus means falling prices and profits and a reduction in output. Improved product quality and better production techniques are sought because of their profitability. Improved job skills and greater work effort by labor mean higher money incomes which can be translated into a higher standard of living.

These actions and adjustments do not occur under central planning; there is an **incentive problem.** Central planners determined the output mix of the Soviet Union and the prereform China. When they misjudged how many automobiles, furniture, underwear, and chickens were wanted at the government-determined prices, there were persistent shortages and surpluses of those products. But since the managers who oversaw the production of these goods were rewarded for meeting their assigned production goals, they had no incentive to adjust production in response to product shortages or surpluses. And they did not have changes in prices and profitability to signal that more or less of certain products was desired. Thus, in the Soviet Union and China many products were unavailable or in short supply while other overproduced goods sat for months and years in warehouses.

The centrally planned system also lacked entrepreneurship. In market systems, the large potential monetary rewards to innovators is a stimulus to technological advancement. Moreover, firms which improve their products or production processes profit, while those which do not eventually suffer losses. Communist central planning does not allow the profit motive and does not reward innovation and enterprise.

The route for getting ahead in the centrally planned economies of the Soviet Union and China was by movement up the political hierarchy of the Communist Party. Moving up the hierarchy meant better housing, better access to health care, and the right to shop in special stores. Meeting planning targets and skillfully maneuvering through the minefields of party politics measured success in "business." But a definition of success based solely on political savvy is not conducive to technological advance, which is often disruptive to existing products, production methods, and organizational structures.

Indeed, in both the Soviet Union and prereform China, innovation was often resisted. Enterprises were essentially government-owned monopolies. As a result, there was no private gain to managers or workers for improving product quality or developing more efficient production techniques. Enterprise managers and workers actually resisted government-imposed innovations because higher and sometimes unrealistic production targets usually accompanied them.

Innovation also lagged because of a lack of competition. There were no new startup firms, driven by the profit motive, to introduce better products, superior managerial techniques, or more efficient production methods. Similarly, the goal of economic self-sufficiency isolated Soviet and Chinese enterprises from import competition. Over an extended period, enterprises produced the same products with the same techniques, even as both the products and techniques became increasingly obsolete by world standards.

Finally, individual workers lacked motivation to work hard because there were few material incentives. Because of the low priority assigned to consumer goods in the production plans, only a limited array of inferior products and services was available to consumers. While hard work might result in promotions and bonuses, the increase in money income did not translate into a proportionate increase in real income. Why work hard for additional money if there is nothing to buy with the money you earn? As a Soviet worker once lamented to a western journalist: "The government pretends to pay us and we pretend to work."

QUICK REVIEW 40-1

■ Marxian ideology is based on the labor theory of value and views capitalism as a system which expropriates surplus value from workers.

■ The main features of the former Soviet economy and the prereform Chinese economy were state ownership of property resources and central economic planning.

■ Central plans in the Soviet Union and China were characterized by **(a)** an emphasis on rapid industrialization, rural development (in China), and military power; **(b)** resource overcommitment; **(c)** growth through the use of more inputs rather than greater efficiency; **(d)** resource allocation by government directives rather than markets; **(e)** government price determination; **(f)** an emphasis on economic self-sufficiency; and **(g)** passive monetary and fiscal policies.

■ Two major problems of central planning are the **(a)** difficulty of coordinating inputs and outputs and **(b)** problem of fostering incentives, including those which cause technological advance.

COLLAPSE OF THE SOVIET ECONOMY

The general problems of central planning contributed to market reform in China and the collapse of the Soviet economy. Let's consider Russia first, then China.

In 1991, the Soviet Union broke into several newly independent states, the largest of which is the Russian Republic. The immediate reason for the collapse was political: a clumsy, failed attempt of old-line communists to wrest control of the government. (The failed military coupe led to the ascendancy of Boris Yeltsin in Russia and independence of the former republics of the Soviet Union). But behind the collapse of the Soviet Union were a number of economic problems, some stemming directly from the failures of central planning.

Declining Growth

Soviet economic growth in the 1950s and 1960s (at least as measured by questionable Soviet statistics) was quite impressive: The economy grew at roughly a 5 to 6 percent annual rate. But growth fell to 2 to 3 percent annually in the 1970s and declined to less than 2 percent in the mid-1980s. In the last year or two before the system broke down, real output was falling sharply.

Poor Product Quality

Further evidence of failure was the poor quality of Soviet goods. In such vital manufacturing sectors as computers and machine tools, Soviet technology lagged some 7 to 12 years behind the United States, Japan, and Germany.

It lagged even more in consumer goods, which were of notoriously poor quality and limited assortment. Durable goods such as automobiles, large household appliances, and consumer electronics were primitive by U.S. standards. Also, widespread shortages of basic goods, interminable shopper lines, black markets, and corruption in product distribution characterized the consumer sector.

Lack of Consumer Goods

Not only were consumer goods of poor quality, they were also in short supply. In the early decades of Soviet Communism, the government established a "social contract" with its citizens to the effect that, by enduring the consumer sacrifices associated with rapid industrialization and growth, the population would be rewarded with consumer abundance in the future. The failure of the system to meet such expectations contributed to frustration and deteriorating morale among consumers and workers. The rewards of past sacrifices simply never materialized.

Large Military Burden

Large Soviet military expenditures of 15 to 20 percent of domestic output, compared to 6 percent in the United States, absorbed great quantities of resources which otherwise would have been available for the development and production of consumer and capital goods. The government's policy during the Cold War era was to channel superior management and the best scientists and engineers to defense and space research, which adversely affected technological progress and the quality (and thus productivity) of capital in the civilian sector.

Agricultural Drag

By standards of the market economies, agriculture in the Soviet Union was a monument to inefficiency and a drag on economic growth. This sector used about 30 percent of the labor force and roughly one-fourth of annual investment. Furthermore, output per worker was only 10 to 25 percent of the U.S. level. The low productivity of Soviet agriculture was attributable to many factors: relative scarcity of good land, erratic weather patterns and growing seasons, serious errors in planning and administration, and perhaps most important, a lack of an effective incentive system.

Once a major exporter of grain and other agricultural products, the Soviet Union became one the world's largest importers of farm goods. This reliance on imports seriously drained the foreign currency reserves which the leadership might otherwise have used to import western capital goods and technology.

THE RUSSIAN TRANSITION TO A MARKET SYSTEM

The former Soviet republics, and particularly Russia, have committed themselves to making the transition to a market economy. There has been dramatic reform in the Russian economy since 1992, when Boris Yeltsin replaced Mikhail Gorbachev as Russia's leader.

Privatization

Private property rights have been established to encourage entrepreneurship. Much of the existing government property—housing, factories, machinery, equipment, and farmland—has been *privatized*, meaning transferred to private owners. Many new firms have formed and developed. Since 1992 more than two-thirds of former state-owned enterprises have been privatized: 90 percent of small companies are now privately owned, and 80 percent of service-sector companies are private.

The privatization process involved two phases. In the first phase, the government gave vouchers, each with a designated monetary value, to 40 million Russian citizens. Recipients could then pool these vouchers to purchase enterprises. The second phase, begun in 1994, allowed state enterprises to be purchased for cash. This enabled foreign investors to buy Russian enterprises and provided much-needed direct investment from abroad to those enterprises.

Land reform, on the other hand, has progressed more slowly. Although Boris Yeltsin decreed in 1996 that Russian peasants could buy and sell land, it will take many years to develop a functional market for farmland. Farmers, who have worked for decades on collective farms, in general fear the uncertainties and potential problems which might accompany privatization and free markets.

Price Reform

Unlike competitive market prices, the prices the Soviet government established bore no relationship to the economic value of either products or resources. In a competitive market system, the price of a product equals (at the margin) the value which consumers place on that good (the marginal benefit) and the value of the resources used in its production (the marginal cost). When free markets achieve this equality for all goods and services, the economy's scarce resources are being used efficiently to satisfy consumer wants.

But in the Soviet economy, government fixed both input and output prices and in many instances did not change those prices for many years. Because input prices did not measure the relative scarcities of resources, it was impossible for a firm to minimize real production costs. With fixed prices, it is impossible to produce a unit of a particular product in such a way as to minimize the sacrifice of alternative goods.

Example: High energy prices have caused firms in market economies to reduce energy use per unit of output. But the government underpriced such energy in the former Soviet Union (the world's largest producer of energy), so its industries used two or three times as much energy per unit of output as leading industrial countries.

Historically, not only was energy priced far below its true price, so too were many basic consumer goods. The Soviet rationale for these low prices was to ensure that everyone could afford such goods. As Figure 40-1 shows, this pricing policy helps explain the chronic product shortages and long lines which had frustrated Soviet consumers. The perfectly inelastic supply curve S_1 reflects the fixed output of, say, shoes which the central plan provided. The demand curve D_1 slope downward as it would in a market economy. In view of S_1, the equilibrium price would be P_a. But in an effort to make shoes accessible to those with lower incomes, the government fixed the price at P_f.

The result was that not everyone who wanted shoes at P_f could obtain them. At P_f the quantity demanded Q_f was substantially greater than the quantity supplied Q_a, so there was a shortage of shoes and other consumer goods priced below their market equilibrium. This explains the long lines of consumers and the empty shelves the rest of the world saw in television news clips. It also explains the black markets in which goods were sold at much higher prices than those fixed by government.

FIGURE 40-1 The effects of centrally planned prices
Central planners in the Soviet Union established below-equilibrium prices such as P_f on many basic consumer goods to allow low-income persons to buy them. But in fact, at such low prices quantity demanded (here Q_f) exceeded quantity supplied (set by planners at Q_a). This shortage meant that many consumers could not obtain such goods. The removal of government price setting at first increased price from P_f to P_a. But with privatization in Russia, the higher price stimulated greater output along supply curve S_2. Price therefore settled at P_e while output jumped from Q_a to Q_e.

The task, then, was to remove these price controls. In January 1992, the government decontrolled about 90 percent of all prices. The international value of the ruble (the Russian currency) also was decontrolled, that is, allowed to float to the value determined by demand and supply. As a result, domestic prices immediately surged and the international value of the Russian ruble sank.

The decontrol of prices, however, did have several positive effects. In terms of Figure 40-1, the decontrol at first raised prices rapidly, here from P_f to P_a. There simply was no mechanism for firms to expand the amount of output for sale in response to the price increases. But with privatization, the higher prices signaled profit opportunities to enterprises and thus a positive supply response. The relevant supply curve then took on its more familiar upward slope as in S_2, and equilibrium output increased from Q_a to Q_e. Equilibrium price moved downward from P_a to P_e. More generally, prices began to more closely reflect the marginal cost to the Russian economy of producing goods, which helped reallocate resources to where they were best suited to meet consumer wants.

Promotion of Competition

As we have seen, the industrial sector of the former Soviet Union consisted of large state-owned enterprises. Single firm "industries" produced about 30 to 40 percent of total industrial output. When several enterprises produced a product, the planning process coordinated their actions to create a cartel. In short, most production took place under monopoly or near-monopoly conditions.

Russian reformers realize that an efficient market economy requires the dismantling of these public monopolies and the creation of antitrust laws to sustain competition. But only limited "demonopolization" has accompanied privatization thus far. Private monopolies rather than public monopolies now reign in several industries. Joint ventures between Russia and foreign companies are one avenue for increasing competition, and Russian legislation has recently opened the door for foreign firms to invest directly in Russia. **(Key Question 5)**

Joining the World Economy

The Soviet economy was largely isolated from the world economy for 75 years. A key step in the transition to a market economy is to open the economy to international trade and finance. Russia has had some success in this endeavor; for example, it has made the ruble a fully convertible currency. This means that the ruble is acceptable in exchange for other currencies. The plunging value of the ruble (from 90 rubles = \$1 in 1992 to 5800 rubles = \$1 in 1997) was obviously detrimental to Russia's world trade. But recently the international value of the ruble has stabilized, which has helped Russia increase its volume of international trade and finance.

Price-Level Stabilization

The transition to free markets brought with it hyperinflation. The decontrol of prices in January 1992 tripled and quadrupled prices almost overnight. Also, Russian households had stored huge amounts of currency and deposits at saving banks during years of waiting for scarce consumer goods to become more abundant. This so-called "ruble overhang" helped fuel inflation once prices were decontrolled and privatization began to deliver consumer goods to the marketplace.

But the most important source of inflation was the large government deficits financed by increases in the money supply. The deficits in turn had many roots. Privatization of state enterprises caused the government to lose those profits, an important source of revenue. The uncertainties inherent in the transition led to general disorder and widespread tax evasion. To ease enterprise losses incurred during the transition, the government extended massive subsidy credits (financed by printing new money) to both industry and agriculture. Finally, the government also increased pensions and welfare benefits by printing money.

Russia's economic reforms, however, have created an independent central bank which has implemented an anti-inflationary monetary policy that has paid off in a swift decline in the rate of inflation. As shown in column 3 in Table 40-1, inflation declined from 1353 percent in 1992 to 14 percent in 1997. This decline has increased investor confidence in the stability of the Russian government and has been a major factor in the stabilization of the international value of the ruble. **(Key Question 6)**

Major Problems

Along with the successes and difficulties we just noted, the Russian transition to the market system has encountered two other significant problems:

TABLE 40-1   Real GDP growth and inflation in Russia, 1991–1997

(1) Year	(2) Growth of real GDP (percent)	(3) Rate of inflation (percent)
1991	−13	93
1992	−19	1353
1993	−12	896
1994	−15	302
1995	− 4	190
1996	− 6	22
1997	+ 1	14

Source: International Monetary Fund and Russian authorities.

Falling Output and Living Standards Thus far, the transition to capitalism in Russia has not paid off in rising real output and an improved standard of living for the great majority of Russians. Real output began to fall in the 1980s, but its decline accelerated during the reforms. Column 2 in Table 40-1 documents recent declines. Note, however, that the fall in real GDP bottomed out in 1992 at 19 percent. Declines of real output of this magnitude resemble those associated with the Great Depression in the United States.

Causes of these declines include the (1) rapid inflation, which created an uncertain environment for borrowing and investing, (2) unraveling of Russia's international trade relationships with former communist-bloc nations of eastern Europe, (3) bankruptcy and closing of many former state-owned enterprises which could not survive in a market environment, and (4) massive reallocation of resources required by the reforms and the major reduction in government spending on the military.

Because real output equals real income, declining real output has meant declines in Russian living standards. Farmers, government employees, and pensioners have been hard hit, and many workers have had to accept deep real wage cuts to keep their jobs. Some workers are owed large amounts of "back pay" because of the inability of their employers to make wage payments. At least 30,000 scientists have left Russia to work in other nations.

Russian authorities, however, believe that the decline in real output has reached an end. Real output increased by 1 percent in 1997 and is expected to rise by about that same amount in 1998.

Inequality and Social Costs Economic inequality has increased during the transition. While many people have become impoverished, a wealthy class of "new Russians" has emerged. Many of these people have gained their wealth through entrepreneurship. Others have prospered as executives, managers, and scientists in the newly privatized industries. Still others, however, have enriched themselves via corruption and illegal activities. The major disruptions, swift changes, and lack of regulatory oversight which accompanied the transition have created major opportunities for organized crime to expand and flourish.

Considerable friction between gainers and losers, the growth of organized crime, and "crony capitalism" fuels public doubts as to the desirability of a market economy. Greater economic freedom has also brought greater economic insecurity; medical and educational services have deteriorated, and school enrollments have declined. Alcoholism, historically high in Russia, has increased sharply, and life expectancy of Russian men declined from 65 in 1988 to 57 in 1997.

Future Prospects

A remaining concern about the transition to markets in Russia is the weakness of government in enforcing its laws, including the collection of taxes owed by enterprises and political subdivisions. Widespread tax evasion results in declining tax revenues, enlarged budget deficits, and the potential for financial instability. Declining tax revenues further weaken the government's ability to enforce tax laws, so a kind of vicious circle could continue until another political and economic collapse results. Declining tax revenues also cripple the central government's ability to perform other basic functions, such as maintaining law and order, providing regulatory oversight of banks and security markets, and providing a social safety net for its citizens. Pessimists point out that a government borrowing crisis, coupled with, say, a collapse of the Russia banking system, might plunge Russia into another depression. That could lead to the abandonment of capitalistic reforms and even an end to democracy.

The more likely scenario, however, is that Russia will eventually succeed in creating a vibrant market economy. The most severe economic dislocations in the form of inflation and a declining real output seem to have ended. Economists who closely monitor the progress of Russia believe that its transition from central planning to markets might span another decade or so but that the market reforms are now largely irreversible and that another economic collapse is highly unlikely. In this view, although Russia is still far from being an advanced market economy, the nation is on a path to achieving one of the truly amazing economic transitions in world history.

QUICK REVIEW 40-2

■ The former Soviet economy collapsed under pressure of declining economic growth, poor product quality, a lack of consumer goods, a large military burden, and agricultural inefficiency.

■ Russia has committed itself to becoming a capitalistic market economy. Ingredients in its transition from central planning to markets include **(a)** creating private property and property rights, **(b)** removing domestic price controls, **(c)** promoting competition, **(d)** opening the economy to international trade and finance, **(e)** ending inflation.

■ Russia's transition to markets has been accompanied by declining output and living standards, increasing income inequality, and social costs such as corruption, organized crime, increasing alcoholism, and reduced life expectancy.

■ Although Russia still faces difficult economic times, it has made substantial progress in its move from communism to capitalism.

MARKET REFORMS IN CHINA

China has taken a different path than Russia in its transition to a market economy. Russia pursued a "shock therapy" approach to reform in 1992, attempting to achieve "irreversibility" of its reforms through a rapid and radical transformation to private property and free markets. China's market reforms began far earlier—in 1978—in a piecemeal, experimental, and gradual manner. In 1992 Russia concluded that its political apparatus, the Communist Party in particular, was an obstacle to economic reform; political reform or democratization preceded economic reform. China, in contrast, has sought economic reform under the strong direction of its Communist Party. China's view is that the upsetting of the political system would generate endless debate, competition for power, and ultimate stagnation and failure for its economic reforms. Unlike Russia, China feels that communist dictatorship and markets are compatible. China has protected the existence and development of its state-owned enterprises while simultaneously encouraging the creation of competing private enterprises.

Although China's GDP per capita is only $620 compared to Russia's $2240, China has instituted its market reforms without suffering the economic depression which confronted Russia. In fact, China has achieved a 9 percent annual growth of real output over the past two decades (as compared to typical growth rates of 2 to 5 percent for most advanced economies).

Market reforms in China began in 1978 under the leadership of Deng Xiaoping, the successor to Mao Zedong. Deng did not share Mao's utopian vision of an eventual communist economy in which people would work for the glory of the community and monetary incentives would play only a minor role. Instead, Deng recognized that the profit incentives of a market economy could increase China's living standard. But he also realized that only a gradual transition to such an economy could preserve the Communist Party's political control over China. Many Chinese critics of Deng derisively called him "a capitalist roader," implying that he was setting China on the road toward capitalism. In retrospect, they were at least partly right.

Agricultural and Rural Reform

Market reform in China began in agriculture in 1978, at which time nearly 70 percent of the Chinese labor force was rural. The key elements of the 1978–1984 reforms were the leasing of land to individual farmers ("decollectivization") and the establishment of a *two-track price system*. For the first time, individual farmers were allowed to lease government-owned land (for 15-year periods). Under the dual price system, farmers had to sell a prescribed amount of farm output to the government at a set price but could sell any surplus in markets at market-determined prices. Farmers were eventually allowed to sell increasing portions of their output at market-determined prices rather than at lower government-determined prices. In 1978 farmers sold only 8 percent of their commodities in competitive markets, but by 1990 that share had increased to 80 percent.

Decollectivization and price reform greatly strengthened production incentives and swiftly moved the Chinese economy toward market-based agriculture. Responding to the profit motive, individual farmers boosted their productivity by substituting tools for labor, shifting crops toward more valuable commodities, and farming previously untilled land. Agricultural output in China rose dramatically throughout the

1980s. Equally important, the greater productivity in agriculture released labor resources to a growing number of privately owned rural manufacturing firms called **township and village enterprises.**

Reform of Urban Industries

The success of reforms in agriculture led the central government to extend the reforms to the **state-owned enterprises** (SOEs) in urban areas. These enterprises were granted more authority to determine the quantity and variety of their outputs, to make their own employment decisions, and to retain much of their profits. (Previously, they had to send the bulk of their profits to the central government.) The government also extended the two-track system of prices to nonagricultural products. SOEs were allowed to buy increasing portions of their inputs at market prices rather than at government-set prices. They were also allowed to sell increasing portions of their outputs at market prices as opposed to being forced to sell output to the government at fixed prices. The share of output sold at market prices rather than at government-set prices rose from 12 percent in 1980 to 66 percent in 1987.

Furthermore, the Chinese government encouraged the formation of nonstate enterprises called **urban collectives**—enterprises owned jointly by managers and their workforces. Like town and village enterprises, these nonstate firms were *not* subject to the directives of the central plan, so they were far more capable than SOEs of gauging and meeting consumer wants. The urban collectives experienced explosive growth of output and employment, some of it at the expense of SOEs. Also, the competition among these nonstate enterprises and the SOEs spurred productivity advance and innovation in many of the SOEs.

Special Economic Zones

In 1980 China created **special economic zones** (SEZs) open to foreign investment, private ownership, and international trade. Located in coastal regions, these special zones attracted increasing amounts of foreign capital (particularly from Hong Kong). They also significantly increased Chinese exports. As the successes of the SEZs became apparent, China increased their number and scope. The SEZs in China's southern provinces, in particular, became booming enclaves of "near-capitalism." The success of the

SEZs relative to other regions in China eventually undercut support for central planning.

Development of Supporting Institutions

The reforms in China also included the building of institutions to facilitate the market system and its macroeconomic control. Specific examples: First, the Chinese government established the Bank of China as the central bank and gave it the power to regulate the banking system and control the money supply to avoid inflation. Second, China replaced the system of "profit transfers" from state enterprises to the central government with an *enterprise tax system.* Third, it established a so-called "swap market" in which Chinese enterprises could trade foreign currency as needed to conduct international business. Finally, it developed a stock market for the exchange of the shares of newly created stockholder-owned corporations.

Transformation of the SOEs

In the 1990s Chinese reform turned to making state-owned enterprises more "corporate-like." The idea was to replace Communist Party operatives with professional managers who were independent of the central government. The government also redirected the goals of such enterprises away from social objectives (providing employment, housing, health care, and day care) and toward economic objectives (producing high-quality goods which people desire). This partial *"corporatization"* of state-enterprises, however, exposed the inefficiencies of the SOEs. In the competitive rather than state-directed environment, many SOEs found that they were producing the wrong goods, in the wrong amounts, using the wrong combinations of inputs. In short, thousands of SOEs simply were inefficient and unprofitable.

After Deng's death in the mid-1990s, leadership of China passed to Jiang Zemin. In 1997 Jiang and the Communist Party called for consolidation of the major SOEs into 1000 large enterprises. These SOEs will issue stock and become shareholder-owned corporations. The idea is to make the firms' management responsive to the shareholders. The government, however, will hold the controlling share of stock ownership in these 1000 corporations. All the other 300,000 state-owned enterprises will be sold to private individuals (or groups) or, if they have no value, will be allowed to go bankrupt.

OUTCOMES AND PROSPECTS

Economic reform in China has achieved impressive results, but is still incomplete.

Positive Outcomes of Reform

China's economic growth rate in the past two decades is among the highest recorded for any country during any period of world history; it has averaged nearly 9 percent annually since the beginning of reforms in 1978. That means that real output and real income have quadrupled in less than two decades. About 40 percent of this growth has resulted from increased capital. Expanded output and income has boosted domestic saving and investment. The expansion of capital goods has in turn further increased productivity, output, and income. The rising income has attracted more direct foreign investment. (Growth rates for recent years are shown in column 2, Table 40-2.)

A rapid expansion of China's international trade has accompanied the expansion of real output. Chinese exports rose from $5 billion in 1978 to more than $160 billion in 1996. These exports have provided the foreign currency needed to import consumer goods and capital goods. Imports of capital goods from industrially advanced countries have brought with them the highly advanced technology which is embodied within, for example, factory design, industrial machinery, office equipment, and telecommunications systems.

During the period of reform, China's real GDP and real income have grown much more rapidly than China's population. Per capita income has increased at a very high annual rate of 8 percent since 1980. This is noteworthy because China's population has expanded by 14 million a year (despite a policy which encourages "one-child" per family). Per capita income in China is now $620 annually based on exchange rates. But since the prices of many basic items in China are still low, Chinese per capita purchasing power is estimated to be nearly $3000.

The growth of per capita income in China has resulted from increased use of capital, improved technology, and shifts of labor away from lower-productivity toward higher-productivity uses. One such shift of employment has been from agriculture toward rural and urban manufacturing. Another such shift has been from state-owned enterprises toward private firms. Both shifts have raised the productivity of Chinese workers. And because these employment shifts have been gradual, they have not produced widespread unemployment. Currently, China's unemployment rate is about 7 percent, although there is substantial underemployment in many regions.

Problems

China still faces some significant economic problems in its transition to the market system.

Incomplete Property Rights After the initial surges in the 1980s, productivity growth in agriculture has stagnated. A possible reason may be that property rights are incomplete. The Communist Party has opposed privatization of farmland, fearing a reversion to the wealthy landlord system it fought to abolish. Instead, the government policy has been to lease land for 15-year periods. But without ownership rights, many farmers are reluctant to invest in farm equipment and capital improvements on the land. The return on such investment is dependent on the assurance of having land to farm. Thus, further capital investment in Chinese agriculture may be dependent on the right to buy and sell land.

Macroeconomic Instability At times investment booms in China have resulted in too much spending relative to production capacity. The result has been occasional periods of 15 to 25 percent annual rates of inflation. (See column 3 in Table 40-2 for recent Chinese inflation rates.) China is confronting this problem by giving its central bank more power so that when appropriate the bank can damp down

TABLE 40-2 Real GDP growth and inflation in China, 1991–1997

(1) Year	(2) Growth of real GDP (percent)	(3) Rate of inflation (percent)
1991	9	3
1992	14	5
1993	13	12
1994	12	22
1995	10	15
1996	9	5
1997	9	2

Source: International Monetary Fund and Chinese authorities.

I Think Everything Will Be OK.

A Russian baked-goods company is successfully making the difficult transition to capitalism.

MOSCOW (AP)—In Soviet times, a movie might have had a heroine much like Lyudmila Korilkova. She would be dressed in a white smock, her dark hair tufting out from behind a scarf, the tools of industrial production in her hands.

"I love my job very much," she would say. "Otherwise, I would not have stayed here for 40 years." Actually, Korilkova—in the smock and scarf, a pastry bag in her hand—said those words just the other day. More amazing still, she seemed to mean them. Maybe it had something to do with the fact that on January 1, her factory doubled her salary.

In today's Russian economy, Korilkova is a lucky woman. She works for a baked-goods company, Bolshevik, which has weathered the transition to a market economy and under new French management appears poised on the brink of success. Last year, Bolshevik's production increased for the first time in eight years. The improvement was modest—3 percent—but it comes close to mirroring national statistics that suggest the worst years of Russia's economic transition may be in the past.

You can see this at a company like Bolshevik, which has betrayed its name and wholeheartedly joined the capitalist mainstream. Siou and Company, as it was originally called, was founded by a French couple in Moscow in 1855. By the late 19th century, it was the biggest cookie baker in Russia. It acquired its current name in 1924, when it was nationalized by the new Bolshevik (communist) government. Even now, a statue of Bolshevik leader Vladimir Lenin stands watch over the courtyard of the landmark brick factory. By the late 1980s, Bolshevik was turning out 78,000 tons of cookies, cakes and other baked goods a year, as dictated by central planners. Quality was poor, factory workers now say, and production methods archaic.

In 1992, after the collapse of the Soviet Union, Bolshevik was privatized. In 1994, the French yogurt-maker Groupe Danone bought a 59 percent stake. In 1996, with sales slumping 14 percent a year, Danone brought in a Franco-Russian manager, Jacques Ioffe, to turn things around. A former physicist from St. Petersburg, Ioffe emigrated to France in 1977, went to business school and wound up managing a publishing company in Paris. Fluent in Russian, French and English, he had the credentials Danone was looking for.

---

investment spending by raising interest rates. Nevertheless, the financial and monetary control systems in China are still weak and inadequate. One potential problem is that many unprofitable SOEs owe colossal sums of money on loans made by the Chinese state-owned banks (a recent estimate is $96 billion). Because most of these loans are not collectable, there is a danger that China will need to bail out the banks to keep them in operation. If China (through its central bank) simply prints additional money to accomplish this bailout, renewed inflation could result.

Integration into the Global Economy China still has much work to do to fully integrate its economy into the world's system of international finance and trade. For example, China is not a member of the World Trade Organization, the successor to GATT, and it still has very high tariffs on many imported goods and restrictions on foreign ownership. In addition, China's record of protecting intellectual property rights such as copyrights, trademarks, and patents is very poor. Unauthorized copying of computer software, movie videos, and compact disks has been a major source of trade friction between China and the United States.

Geographically Uneven Development Finally, there is great regional unevenness in China's economic development. This fact is even more apparent now that the former British colony of Hong Kong is part of China. Hong Kong is a wealthy capitalist economy with per capita income of about $22,000. The standard of living is also relatively high in China's southern provinces and China's coastal cities, although not nearly as high as in Hong Kong. In fact, people living in these special economic zones have been the major beneficiaries of China's rapid growth. In contrast, the majority of people living elsewhere in China

"Danone said, 'Look, we've got a big company, we don't know what to do with it, we don't understand what they're saying,'" Ioffe recalled during an interview in his office, which is decorated with photos of Paris and little French and Russian flags. The biggest problem he found at Bolshevik was one of mentality. The Russian managers, while well meaning, simply couldn't grasp the idea of a market economy. There was no sales department, no marketing department, and the idea of basing production plans on sales was still foreign.

Today, all that is changing. The new marketing department recently unveiled its first billboard, just outside the factory gates. Television commercials will follow in June. And while Bolshevik now produces only half as much as it did a decade ago, it is producing what the market wants. Ioffe has set a goal of 20 percent growth for 1998. "Before, the quality lacked," said Svetlana Gritskova, who has worked at Bolshevik for 20 years and is in charge of assembling cakes for special orders. Now, she said, quality is much better. Plus, "our production is more versatile."

A few yards away, Korilkova decorated cakes, squeezing pink icing out of a pastry bag to form delicate flowers. Although her methods rely on classic—and simple—French tools, she pointed approvingly to modern mixers and refrigerators nearby. "We've become better technically equipped," she said. "Before, the state showed little concern for equipment to make our lives easier." Nor did it do what her current bosses have done: raise her monthly salary from $250 to $500. Others may fret, but Korilkova is now optimistic about the future of Russia.

"Yes," she said. "I think everything will be OK."

Source: "Russia's Economy May Be Past Worst," Associated Press, January 25, 1998. Printed by permission of the Associated Press.

have very low incomes. Despite its tremendous growth since 1978, China's per person income level, on average, suggests that it continues to be a relatively low-income developing country. **(Key Question 8)**

QUICK REVIEW 40-3

■ Market reform began earlier in China (1978) than in Russia (1992) and involves gradualism rather than "shock therapy."

■ Key elements of China's economic reform are decollectivization of agriculture, establishment of township and village enterprises, price reform, establishment of privately owned urban enterprises, creation of special economic zones, development of support and control institutions, and "corporatization" of state-owned enterprises.

■ Since the beginning of market reform in 1978, China's real output and per capita income have grown at average annual rates of 9 percent and 8 percent, respectively.

■ China's economy still faces problems of incomplete property rights, periodic inflation, lack of full integration with the world economy, and great unevenness in regional development.

CONCLUSION

Clearly, Russia and China have taken different paths in their transitions to market systems. It may seem that China's path of dictatorship and gradualism is superior economically (political realities aside) to Russia's path of democracy and swift transformation to capitalism. While Russia has suffered years of declining output and income, China has experienced very high rates of economic growth. But we must not be too hasty in reaching this conclusion. The disorder arising from Russia's abrupt transition to democracy and capitalism may be behind it, placing Russia in a stronger position than China to succeed in the future. The present "forced order" in China via the Communist Party may or may not last. History suggests that *economic* freedom usually creates demands for *political* freedom: free speech, freedom of peaceful assembly, freedom to organize political parties, free elections, and so on. Are China's communist leaders willing and able to design a gradual path toward political freedom? Or is China's period of disorder still to come? We have no answers for these questions. We simply note, in the words of a well-known sage: "the times they are a-changin."[1]

_____

[1]Bob Dylan song lyrics from *The Times They Are A-Changin'* (1963).

CHAPTER SUMMARY

1. The labor theory of value is a central principle of Marxian ideology. Capitalists, as property owners, allegedly expropriate most of labor's value as profits, or surplus value. The supposed solution was for the workers and peasants to take control of all production processes through their representative: the Communist Party.

2. Virtually complete state ownership of property resources, collective farming, and central planning were the major features of the Soviet economy and the prereform Chinese economy.

3. Characteristics of Soviet and Chinese central planning included **(a)** emphasis on industrialization, rural development (in China), and military strength; **(b)** overcommitment of resources through the central plans; **(c)** allocation of resources by bureaucracy rather than market decisions; **(d)** government price setting; **(e)** economic self-sufficiency; and **(f)** passive macroeconomic policies.

4. Central planners in the Soviet Union and China faced a coordination problem, which was the difficulty of achieving internal consistency in plans to avoid bottlenecks and the chain reaction of production failures which they cause. The more complex their economies became, the greater became the problem of coordinating inputs and outputs.

5. Central planners also faced a difficult incentive problem. Without private property, entrepreneurship, and availability of consumer goods, it proved difficult if not impossible to achieve efficiency, promote innovation, and induce hard work.

6. Along with the difficulties of central planning, the collapse of the Soviet economy resulted from a diminishing growth rate, limited and shoddy consumer goods, a large military burden, and stagnation of agriculture.

7. The key elements of the Russian transition to capitalism were privatizing firms, establishing market-based prices, promoting greater competition, liberalizing international trade and finance, and ending rapid inflation. Russia's transition to capitalism has not been easy. Output and income have declined, income inequality has increased, and social problems such as crime and alcoholism have worsened. Nevertheless, Russia has succeeded in making its reforms largely irreversible, and its output and income are now expected to rise.

8. Market reform in China has differed from reform in Russia in several ways: **(a)** it began earlier than in Russia (1978 compared to 1992); **(b)** it was not precipitated by collapse of the political system, as was true in Russia; **(c)** it has used a gradual approach, not "shock therapy"; **(d)** it has been directed by the Communist Party, not by anticommunist reformers; and **(e)** it only recently has begun the process of privatizing state-owned enterprises, whereas Russia has privatized most of its industry.

9. China's market reforms began with leasing of farmland and allowing farmers to sell increasing amounts of their output at market-determined rather than state-determined prices. Subsequent reforms included the establishment of township and village enterprises and urban collectives (both are types of private enterprises) and the setting up of special enterprise zones open to international trade and direct foreign investment. More recently, China's reforms have involved development of support and control institutions for the market system and the corporatization of state-owned enterprises, in some cases via issuance of stock.

10. China's reforms have generated two decades of rapid economic growth, with real GDP rising by 9 percent annually and per capita income rising by 8 percent annually. Nevertheless, this growth has been very uneven geographically and at times has been accompanied by rapid inflation. To continue its success, China may have to end prohibitions against ownership of land, integrate its economy more fully with the international system of trade and finance, and privatize state industries.

TERMS AND CONCEPTS

labor theory of value
surplus value
state ownership

central economic
   planning
coordination problem

incentive problem
township and village
   enterprises

state-owned enterprises
urban collectives
special economic zones

STUDY QUESTIONS

1. Compare the economic ideology of the former Soviet Union and prereform China with that of the capitalist economies as to the **(a)** source and role of profits, **(b)** ownership of capital, and **(c)** best method of allocating resources.

2. What does the term "central economic planning" mean? Describe the coordination problem which central planners in the Soviet Union and prereform China faced. Explain how a planning failure can cause a chain reaction of additional failures.

3. Why were new product introductions and the use of new methods of production so uncommon in the Soviet Union and prereform China compared to such capitalist economies as the United States?

4. What factors contributed to the collapse of the Soviet economy?

5. KEY QUESTION Use a supply and demand diagram to explain why persistent shortages of many consumer goods occurred under central planning in the Soviet Union and in prereform China. Why were black markets common in each country?

6. KEY QUESTION What are the major components of economic reform in Russia? What is meant when these reforms are described as "shock therapy"? How successful has Russia been thus far in its reforms?

7. In what general respects have Chinese economic reforms differed from those of Russia? Do you believe that these differences account for China's higher growth rate? Why?

8. KEY QUESTION Relate each of the following items to the success of market reform in China: **(a)** leasing farm land, **(b)** price reform, **(c)** private rural and urban enterprises, **(d)** special economic zones, and **(e)** corporatization of state-owned enterprises.

9. What progress has China achieved in its transition to a market economy? What problems remain?

10. Do you think that China's economic reforms will eventually result in the demise of the Communist Party in China? Explain your answer.

11. "Paradoxically, Russia's disorder may provide a firmer base for future growth than China's order." Do you agree or disagree? Explain.

12. (Last Word) Why was "marketing" a foreign concept to managers such as those of the baked-goods enterprise discussed in this chapter's Last Word? Why do you think the quality of the baked goods produced in this enterprise has increased?

13. WEB-BASED QUESTION **Russia's Transition to a Market Economy—Today's Business Headlines** Russia Today http://www.russiatoday.com/rtoday/business/business.html provides weekday business headlines about Russia. Review the Russian business headlines for the past 2 weeks. Identify which are related to its transition to a market economy (e.g., increased company profit) and which are nontransition-related (e.g., cold weather depletes heating-oil stocks). What portion of the transition-related headlines are reporting difficulties? What portion are describing success stories?

14. WEB-BASED QUESTION **China and Hong Kong—Beyond 1997** On July 1, 1997, Hong Kong, the world's fourth-largest trading entity, entered a new phase of its existence as Asia's business hub. After a 14-year transition period, its status changed from that of a Dependent Territory of Britain to that of a Special Administration Region of China. How is Hong Kong's capitalist system supposed to survive the control of China's Communist Party? Visit the Hong Kong 1997 Web Site http://www.hk1997.china.com/ and the South China Morning Post http://scmp.com/ for your answers.

Note: Terms in *italic* type are defined separately in this glossary.

A

Ability-to-pay principle The idea that those who have greater income (or wealth) should pay a greater proportion of it as taxes than those who have less income (or wealth).

Abstraction Elimination of irrelevant and noneconomic facts to obtain an *economic principle*.

Acreage allotment program A pre-1996 government program which determined the total number of acres to be used in producing (reduced amounts of) various agricultural products and allocated the acres among individual farmers; these farmers had to limit their plantings to the allotted number of acres to obtain *price supports* for their crops.

Actual budget A listing of amounts spent by the *Federal government* (to purchase goods and services and for *transfer payments*) and the amounts of tax revenue collected by it in any (fiscal) year.

Actual deficit The size of the Federal government's *budget deficit* actually recorded in any particular year.

Actual investment The amount which *firms* do invest; equal to *planned investment* plus *unplanned investment*.

Actual reserves The funds which a bank has on deposit at the *Federal Reserve Bank* of its district (plus its *vault cash*).

Adaptive expectations theory The idea that people determine their expectations about future events (for example, inflation) on the basis of past and present events (rates of inflation) and only change their expectations as events unfold.

Adjustable pegs The device used in the *Bretton Woods system* to alter *exchange rates* in an orderly way to eliminate persistent payments deficits and surpluses. Each nation defined its monetary unit in terms of (pegged it to) gold or the dollar, kept the *rate of exchange* for its money stable in the short run, and adjusted its rate in the long run when faced with international payments disequilibrium.

Adverse selection problem A problem arising when information known to one party to a contract is not known to the other party, causing the latter to incur major costs. Example: Individuals who have the poorest health are more likely to buy health insurance.

Advertising A seller's activities in communicating its message about its product to potential buyers.

AFDC (See *Aid to families with dependent children program*.)

Affirmative action Policies and programs which establish targets of increased employment and promotion for women and minorities.

AFL-CIO An acronym for the American Federation of Labor—Congress of Industrial Organizations; the largest federation of *labor unions* in the United States.

Aggregate demand A schedule or curve which shows the total quantity of goods and services demanded (purchased) at different *price levels*.

Aggregate demand–aggregate supply model The macroeconomic model which uses *aggregate demand* and *aggregate supply* to determine and explain the *price level* and the real *domestic output*.

Aggregate expenditures The total amount spent for final goods and services in the economy.

Aggregate expenditures–domestic output approach Determination of the *equilibrium gross domestic product* by finding the real GDP at which aggregate expenditures equal *domestic output*.

Aggregate expenditures schedule A schedule or curve showing the total amount spent for final goods and services at different levels of GDP.

Aggregate supply A schedule or curve showing the total quantity of goods and services supplied (produced) at different *price levels*.

Aggregation Combining individual units or data into one unit or number. For example, all prices of individual goods and services are combined into a *price level*, or all units of output are aggregated into *real gross domestic product*.

Aid to families with dependent children (AFDC) program A state-administered and partly federally funded program in the United States which provides aid to families in which dependent children do not have the support of a parent because of the parent's death, disability, or desertion.

Alcoa case A 1945 case in which the courts ruled that the possession of monopoly power, no matter how reasonably that power had been used, was a violation of the antitrust laws; temporarily overturned the *rule of reason* applied in the *U.S. Steel case*.

Allocative efficiency   The apportionment of resources among firms and industries to obtain the production of the products most wanted by society (consumers); the output of each product at which its *marginal cost* and *price* or *marginal benefit* are equal.

Annually balanced budget   A budget in which government expenditures and tax collections are equal each year.

Anticipated inflation   Increases in the price level (*inflation*) which occur at the expected rate.

Antitrust laws   Legislation (including the *Sherman Act* and *Clayton Act*) which prohibit anticompetitive business activities such as *price fixing*, bid rigging, monopolization, and *tying contracts*.

Antitrust policy   The use of the *antitrust laws* to promote *competition* and *economic efficiency*.

Applied economics   (See *Policy economics*.)

Appreciation (of the dollar)   An increase in the value of the dollar relative to the currency of another nation so that a dollar buys a larger amount of the foreign currency and thus of foreign goods.

"Asian tigers"   The newly industrialized and rapidly growing economies of Hong Kong, Singapore, South Korea, and Taiwan.

Asset   Anything of monetary value owned by a firm or individual.

Asset demand for money   The amount of *money* people want to hold as a *store of value;* this amount varies inversely with the *rate of interest*.

Asymmetric information   A situation in which one party to a market transaction has much more information about a product or service than the other; the result may be an under- or overallocation of resources.

Authoritarian capitalism   An economic system in which property resources are privately owned and government extensively directs and controls the economy.

Average fixed cost   A firm's total *fixed cost* divided by output (the quantity of product produced).

Average product   The total output produced per unit of a *resource* employed (*total product* divided by the quantity of that employed resource).

Average propensity to consume   Fraction (or percentage) of *disposable income* which households plan to spend for consumer goods and services; *consumption* divided by *disposable income*.

Average propensity to save   Fraction (or percentage) of *disposable income* which households save; *saving* divided by *disposable income*.

Average revenue   Total revenue from the sale of a product divided by the quantity of the product sold (demanded); equal to the price at which the product is sold when all units of the product are sold at the same price.

Average tax rate   Total tax paid divided by total (taxable) income, as a percentage.

Average total cost   A firm's *total cost* divided by output (the quantity of product produced); equal to *average fixed cost* plus *average variable cost*.

Average variable cost   A firm's total *variable cost* divided by output (the quantity of product produced).

B

Backflows   The return of workers to the countries from which they originally migrated.

Balanced-budget amendment   Proposed constitutional amendment that would require Congress to balance the Federal budget annually.

Balanced-budget multiplier   The extent to which an equal change in government spending and taxes changes *equilibrium gross domestic product;* always has a value of 1 since it is equal to the amount of the equal changes in *G* and *T*.

Balance of payments   (See *International balance of payments*.)

Balance of payments deficit   The amount by which the sum of the *balance on current account* and the *balance on the capital account* is negative in a year.

Balance of payments surplus   The amount by which the sum of the *balance on current account* and the *balance on the capital account* is positive in a year.

Balance on current account   The exports of goods and services of a nation less its imports of goods and services plus its *net investment income* and *net transfers* in a year.

Balance on goods and services   The exports of goods and services of a nation less its imports of goods and services in a year.

Balance on the capital account   The *capital inflows* of a nation less its *capital outflows*.

Balance sheet   A statement of the *assets, liabilities,* and *net worth* of a firm or individual at some given time.

Bank deposits   The deposits which individuals or firms have at banks (or thrifts) or which banks have at the *Federal Reserve Banks*.

Bankers' bank   A bank which accepts the deposits of and makes loans to *depository institutions;* in the United States, a *Federal Reserve Bank*.

Bank reserves   The deposits of commercial banks and thrifts at *Federal Reserve Banks* plus bank and thrift *vault cash*.

Barrier to entry   Anything which artificially prevents the entry of firms into an industry.

Barter   The exchange of one good or service for another good or service.

Base year   The year with which other years are compared when an index is constructed, for example, the base year for a *price index*.

Benefit-cost analysis   Comparing the *marginal benefits* of a government project or program with the *marginal costs* to decide whether or not to employ resources in that project or program and to what extent.

Benefit-reduction rate The percentage by which subsidy benefits in a *public assistance program* are reduced as earned income rises.

Benefits-received principle The idea that those who receive the benefits of goods and services provided by government should pay the taxes required to finance them.

Bilateral monopoly A market in which there is a single seller (*monopoly*) and a single buyer (*monopsony*).

Board of Governors The 7-member group which supervises and controls the money and banking system of the United States; the Board of Governors of the Federal Reserve System; the Federal Reserve Board.

Bond A financial device through which a borrower (a firm or government) is obligated to pay the principle and interest on a loan at a specific date in the future.

Brain drain The emigration of highly educated, highly skilled workers from a country.

Break-even income The level of *disposable income* at which *households* plan to consume (spend) all their income and to save none of it; also denotes that level of earned income at which subsidy payments become zero in an income transfer program.

Break-even output Any output at which a (competitive) firm's *total cost* and *total revenue* are equal; an output at which it has neither an *economic profit* nor a loss; at which it has only a *normal profit*.

Bretton Woods system The international monetary system developed after World War II in which *adjustable pegs* were employed, the *International Monetary Fund* helped to stabilize foreign exchange rates, and gold and the dollar were used as *international monetary reserves*.

Budget deficit The amount by which the expenditures of the Federal government exceed its revenues in any year.

Budget line A line which shows the different combinations of two products a consumer can purchase with a specific money income, given the products' prices.

Budget restraint The limit which the size of a consumer's income (and the prices which must be paid for goods and services) imposes on the ability of that consumer to obtain goods and services.

Budget surplus The amount by which the revenues of the Federal government exceed its expenditures in any year.

Built-in stabilizer A mechanism which increases government's budget deficit (or reduces its surplus) during a recession and increases government's budget surplus (or reduces its deficit) during inflation without any action by policymakers; the tax system is one such mechanism.

Business cycle Recurring increases and decreases in the level of economic activity over periods of years. Consists of peak, *recession*, trough, and recovery phases.

Business firm (See *Firm*.)

Business unionism Labor unionism which concerns itself with such practical and short-run objectives as higher wages, shorter hours, and improved working conditions.

C

Capital Human-made resources (buildings, machinery, and equipment) used to produce goods and services; goods which do not directly satisfy human wants; also called capital goods.

Capital account The section of a nation's *international balance of payments* statement in which the foreign purchases of assets in the United States (producing money *capital inflows*) and U.S. purchases of assets abroad (producing money *capital outflows* of that nation) are recorded.

Capital account deficit A negative *balance on the capital account*.

Capital account surplus A positive *balance on the capital account*.

Capital flight The transfer of savings from developing countries to industrially advanced countries to avoid government expropriation, taxation, and high rates of inflation or to realize better investment opportunities.

Capital gain The gain realized when securities or properties are sold for a price greater than the price paid for them.

Capital goods (See *Capital*.)

Capital inflow The expenditures made by the residents of foreign nations to purchase real and financial capital from the residents of a nation.

Capital-intensive commodity A product which requires a relatively large amount of *capital* to produce.

Capitalism (See *Pure capitalism*.)

Capital outflow The expenditures made by the residents of a nation to purchase real and financial capital from the residents of foreign nations.

Capital-saving technological advance An improvement in *technology* which permits a greater quantity of a product to be produced with a specific amount of *capital* (or permits the same amount of the product to be produced with a smaller amount of capital).

Capital stock The total available *capital* in a nation.

Capital-using technological advance An improvement in *technology* which requires the use of a greater amount of *capital* to produce a specific quantity of a product.

Cartel A formal agreement among firms in an industry to set the price of a product and the outputs of the individual firms or to divide the market for the product geographically.

Causation A relationship in which the occurrence of one or more events brings about another event.

CEA (See *Council of Economic Advisers*.)

Cease-and-desist order An order from a court or government agency to a corporation or individual to stop engaging in a specified practice.

Ceiling price (See *Price ceiling*.)

Celler-Kefauver Act The Federal act of 1950 that amended the *Clayton Act* by prohibiting the acquisition of the assets of one firm by another firm when the effect would be to lessen competition.

Central bank A bank whose chief function is the control of the nation's *money supply*; in the United States, the *Federal Reserve System*.

Central economic planning Government determination of the objectives of the economy and how resources will be directed to attain those objectives.

***Ceteris paribus* assumption** (See *"Other things equal" assumption.*)

Change in demand A change in the *quantity demanded* of a good or service at every price; a shift of the *demand curve* to the left or right.

Change in supply A change in the *quantity supplied* of a good or service at every price; a shift of the *supply curve* to the left or right.

Checkable deposit Any deposit in a *commercial bank* or *thrift institution* against which a check may be written; includes *demand deposits*.

Checking account A *checkable deposit* in a *commercial bank* or *thrift institution.*

Check clearing The process by which funds are transferred from the checking accounts of the writers of checks to the checking accounts of the recipients of the checks.

Circular flow model The flow of resources from *households* to *firms* and of products from firms to households. These flows are accompanied by reverse flows of money from firms to households and from households to firms.

Civil Rights Act of 1964 Title VII of this law outlaws discrimination based on race, color, religion, gender, or national origin in hiring, promoting, and compensating workers.

Classical economics The macroeconomic generalizations accepted by most economists before the 1930s which led to the conclusion that a capitalistic economy was self-regulating and therefore would usually employ its resources fully.

Clayton Act The Federal antitrust act of 1914 which strengthened the *Sherman Act* by making it illegal for firms to engage in certain specified practices.

Closed economy An economy which neither exports nor imports goods and services.

Closed shop A place of employment where only workers who are already members of a labor union may be hired.

Coase theorem The idea first stated by economist Ronald Coase that *spillover* problems may be resolved through private negotiations of the affected parties.

Coincidence of wants A situation in which the good or service which one trader desires to obtain is the same as that which another trader desires to give up, and an item which the second trader wishes to acquire is the same as that which the first trader desires to surrender.

COLA (See *Cost-of-living adjustment.*)

Collective bargaining The negotiation of labor contracts between *labor unions* and *firms* or government entities.

Collective voice The function a *labor union* performs for its members as a group when it communicates their prob-

lems and grievances to management and presses management for a satisfactory resolution.

Collusion A situation in which firms act together and in agreement (collude) to fix prices, divide a market, or otherwise restrict competition.

Command economy An economic system (method of organization) in which property resources are publicly owned and government uses *central economic planning* to direct and coordinate economic activities.

Commercial bank A firm which engages in the business of banking (accepts deposits, offers checking accounts, and makes loans).

Commercial banking system All *commercial banks* and *thrift institutions* as a group.

Communism (See *Command economy.*)

Comparative advantage A lower relative or comparative cost than another producer.

Compensating differences Differences in the *wages* received by workers in different jobs to compensate for nonmonetary differences in the jobs.

Compensation to employees *Wages* and salaries plus *wage and salary supplements* paid by employers to workers.

Competing goods (See *Substitute goods.*)

Competition The presence in a market of a large number of independent buyers and sellers competing with one another and the freedom of buyers and sellers to enter and leave the market.

Competitive industry's short-run supply curve The horizontal summation of the short-run supply curves of the *firms* in a purely competitive industry (see *Pure competition*); a curve which shows the total quantities offered for sale at various prices by the firms in an industry in the short run.

Competitive labor market A resource market in which a large number of (noncolluding) firms demand a particular type of labor supplied by a large number of nonunion workers.

Complementary goods Products and services which are used together; when the price of one falls the demand for the other increases (and conversely).

Complex multiplier The *multiplier* which exists when changes in the *gross domestic product* change *net taxes* and *imports*, as well as *saving*.

Concentration ratio The percentage of the total sales of an *industry* made by the four (or some other number) largest sellers in the industry.

Conglomerate combination A group of *plants* owned by a single *firm* and engaged at one or more stages in the production of different products (of products that do not compete with each other).

Conglomerate merger The merger of a *firm* in one *industry* with a firm in another industry or region (with a firm which is not a supplier, customer, or competitor).

Constant-cost industry An industry in which expansion by the entry of new firms has no effect on the prices firms in the industry must pay for resources and thus no effect on production costs.

Consumer goods   Products and services which satisfy human wants directly.

Consumer price index (CPI)   An index which measures the prices of a fixed "market basket" of some 300 goods and services bought by a "typical" consumer.

Consumer sovereignty   Determination by consumers of the types and quantities of goods and services which will be produced with the scarce resources of the economy; consumer direction of production through dollar votes.

Consumer surplus   The difference between what a consumer (or consumers) is willing to pay for an additional unit of a product or service and its market price; the triangular area below the demand curve and above the market price.

Consumption of fixed capital   Estimate of the amount of *capital* worn out or used up (consumed) in producing the *gross domestic product*; also called *depreciation*.

Consumption schedule   A schedule showing the amounts *households* plan to spend for *consumer goods* at different levels of *disposable income*.

Contractionary fiscal policy   A decrease in *government expenditures* for goods and services, an increase in *net taxes*, or some combination of the two, for the purpose of decreasing *aggregate demand* and thus controlling inflation.

Coordination failure   A situation in which people do not reach a mutually beneficial outcome because they lack some way to jointly coordinate their actions; a possible cause of macroeconomic instability.

Copayment   The percentage of (say, health care) costs which an insured individual pays while the insurer pays the remainder.

Copyright   A legal protection provided to developers and publishers of books, computer software, videos, and musical compositions against copying of their works by others.

Corporate income tax   A tax levied on the net income (profit) of corporations.

Corporation   A legal entity ("person") chartered by a state or the Federal government which is distinct and separate from the individuals who own it.

Correlation   A systematic and dependable association between two sets of data (two kinds of events); does not itself indicate causation.

Cost-of-living adjustment (COLA)   An automatic increase in the incomes (wages) of workers when inflation occurs; guaranteed by a collective bargaining contract between firms and workers.

Cost-push inflation   Increases in the price level (inflation) resulting from an increase in resource costs (for example, higher wage rates and raw material prices) and hence in *per-unit production costs*; inflation caused by reductions in *aggregate supply*.

Cost ratio   An equality showing the number of units of two products which can be produced with the same resources; the cost ratio 1 corn ≡ 3 olives shows that the re-

sources required to produce 3 units of olives must be shifted to corn production to produce 1 unit of corn.

Council of Economic Advisers   A group of three persons that advises and assists the President of the United States on economic matters (including the preparation of the annual *Economic Report of the President*).

Craft union   A labor union which limits its membership to workers with a particular skill (craft).

Creative destruction   The hypothesis that the creation of new products and production methods simultaneously destroys the market power of existing monopolies.

Credit   An accounting item which increases the value of an asset (such as the foreign money owned by the residents of a nation).

Credit union   An association of persons who have a common tie (such as being employees of the same firm or members of the same labor union) which sells shares to (accepts deposits from) its members and makes loans to them.

Cross elasticity of demand   The ratio of the percentage change in *quantity demanded* of one good to the percentage change in the price of some other good. A positive coefficient indicates the two products are *substitute goods*; a negative coefficient indicates they are *complementary goods*.

Crowding model of occupational discrimination   A model of labor markets suggesting that *occupational discrimination* has kept many women and minorities out of high-paying occupations and forced them into a limited number of low-paying occupations.

Crowding-out effect   A rise in interest rates and a resulting decrease in *planned investment* caused by the Federal government's increased borrowing in the money market.

Currency   Coins and paper money.

Currency appreciation   (See *Exchange rate appreciation*.)

Currency depreciation   (See *Exchange rate depreciation*.)

Current account   The section in a nation's *international balance of payments* which records its exports and imports of goods and services, its *net investment income*, and its *net transfers*.

Customary economy   (See *Traditional economy*.)

Cyclical deficit   A Federal *budget deficit* which is caused by a recession and the consequent decline in tax revenues.

Cyclical unemployment   A type of *unemployment* caused by insufficient total spending (or by insufficient *aggregate demand*).

Cyclically balanced budget   The equality of *government expenditures* and *net tax collections* over the course of a *business cycle*; deficits incurred during periods of recession are offset by surpluses obtained during periods of prosperity (inflation).

D

Debit   An accounting item which decreases the value of an asset (such as the foreign money owned by the residents of a nation).

Declining industry An industry in which *economic profits* are negative (losses are incurred) and which will, therefore, decrease its output as firms leave it.

Decreasing-cost industry An industry in which expansion through the entry of firms decreases the prices firms in the industry must pay for resources and therefore decreases their production costs.

Deductible The dollar sum of (for example, health care) costs which an insured individual must pay before the insurer begins to pay.

Deduction Reasoning from assumptions to conclusions; a method of reasoning which first develops a hypothesis (an assumption) and then tests the hypothesis with economic facts.

Deflating Finding the *real gross domestic product* by decreasing the dollar value of the GDP for a year in which prices were higher than in the *base year.*

Deflation A decline in the economy's *price level.*

Demand A schedule showing the amounts of a good or service buyers (or a buyer) wish to purchase at various prices during some time period.

Demand curve A curve illustrating *demand.*

Demand deposit A deposit in a *commercial bank* or *thrift* against which checks may be written; a *checkable deposit.*

Demand-deposit multiplier (See *Monetary multiplier.*)

Demand factor (in growth) The increase in the level of *aggregate demand* which brings about the *economic growth* made possible by an increase in the production potential of the economy.

Demand management The use of *fiscal policy* and *monetary policy* to increase or decrease *aggregate demand.*

Demand-pull inflation Increases in the price level (inflation) resulting from an excess of demand over output at the existing price level, caused by an increase in *aggregate demand.*

Dependent variable A variable which changes as a consequence of a change in some other (independent) variable; the "effect" or outcome.

Depository institutions Firms which accept the deposits of *money* of the public (businesses and persons); *commercial banks, savings and loan associations, mutual savings banks,* and *credit unions.*

Depreciation (See *Consumption of fixed capital.*)

Depreciation (of the dollar) A decrease in the value of the dollar relative to another currency so that a dollar buys a smaller amount of the foreign currency and therefore of foreign goods.

Derived demand The demand for a resource which depends on the demand for the products it can be used to produce.

Determinants of aggregate demand Factors such as consumption spending, *investment,* government spending, and *net exports* which, if they change, shift the *aggregate demand curve.*

Determinants of aggregate supply Factors such as input prices, *productivity,* and the legal-institutional environment which, if they change, shift the *aggregate supply curve.*

Determinants of demand Factors other than its price which determine the quantities demanded of a good or service.

Determinants of supply Factors other than its price which determine the quantities supplied of a good or service.

Devaluation A decrease in the governmentally defined value of a currency.

Developing countries Many countries of Africa, Asia, and Latin America which are characterized by a lack of capital goods, use of nonadvanced technologies, low literacy rates, high unemployment, rapid population growth, and labor forces heavily committed to agriculture.

Differentiated oligopoly An *oligopoly* in which the firms produce a *differentiated product.*

Differentiated product A product which differs physically or in some other way from the similar products produced by other firms; a product such that buyers are not indifferent to the seller when the price charged by all sellers is the same.

Diffusion The spread of an *innovation* through its widespread imitation.

Dilemma of regulation The tradeoff a *regulatory agency* faces in setting the maximum legal price a monopolist may charge: The *socially optimal price* is below *average total cost* (and either bankrupts the *firm* or requires that it be subsidized), while the higher *fair-return price* does not produce *allocative efficiency.*

Diminishing marginal returns (See *Law of diminishing returns.*)

Direct foreign investment The building of new factories (or the purchase of existing capital) in a particular nation by corporations of other nations.

Direct relationship The relationship between two variables which change in the same direction, for example, product price and quantity supplied.

Discount rate The interest rate which the *Federal Reserve Banks* charge on the loans they make to *commercial banks* and *thrift institutions.*

Discouraged workers Employees who have left the *labor force* because they have been unable to find employment.

Discrimination According individuals or groups inferior treatment in hiring, occupational access, education and training, promotion, wage rates, or working conditions, even though they have the same abilities, education and skills, and work experience as other workers.

Discrimination coefficient A measure of the cost or disutility of prejudice; the monetary amount an employer is willing to pay to hire a preferred worker rather than a nonpreferred worker.

Discretionary fiscal policy Deliberate changes in taxes (tax rates) and government spending by Congress to promote full-employment, price stability, and economic growth.

Diseconomies of scale   Increase in the *average total cost* of producing a product as the *firm* expands the size of its *plant* (its output) in the *long run*.

Disinflation   A reduction in the rate of *inflation*.

Disposable income   *Personal income* less personal taxes; income available for *personal consumption expenditures* and *personal saving*.

Dissaving   Spending for consumer goods and services in excess of *disposable income;* the amount by which *personal consumption expenditures* exceed disposable income.

Dividends   Payments by a corporation of all or part of its profit to its stockholders (the corporate owners).

Division of labor   Dividing the work required to produce a product into a number of different tasks which are performed by different workers; *specialization* of workers.

Dollar votes   The "votes" which consumers and entrepreneurs cast for the production of consumer and capital goods, respectively, when they purchase them in product and resource markets.

Domestic capital formation   Addition to a nation's stock of *capital* by saving and investing part of its own domestic output.

Domestic output   *Gross* (or net) *domestic product;* the total output of *final goods and services* produced in the economy.

Domestic price   The price of a good or service within a country, determined by domestic demand and supply.

Double taxation   The taxation of both corporate net income (profits) and the *dividends* paid from this net income when they become the personal income of households.

Dumping   The sale of products below cost in a foreign country or below the prices charged at home.

DuPont cellophane case   The antitrust case brought against DuPont in which the U.S. Supreme Court ruled (in 1956) that while DuPont had a monopoly in the narrowly defined market for cellophane, it did not monopolize the more broadly defined market for flexible packaging materials. It was thus not guilty of violating the *Sherman Act*.

Durable good   A consumer good with an expected life (use) of 3 or more years.

Dynamic efficiency   The development over time of less costly production techniques, improved products, and new products; technological progress.

E

E-cash   Electronic money; an entry (usable as money) stored in a computer or a stored-value card ("smart card").

Earned Income Tax Credit   A Federal tax credit for low-income working families designed to encourage labor force participation.

Earnings   The money income received by a worker; equal to the *wage* (rate) multiplied by the amount of time worked.

Easy money policy   Federal Reserve System actions to increase the *money supply* to lower interest rates and expand *real GDP*.

Economic analysis   Deriving *economic principles* from relevant economic facts.

Economic concentration   A description or measure of the degree to which an industry is monopolistic or competitive. (See *Concentration ratio*.)

Economic cost   A payment which must be made to obtain and retain the services of a *resource;* the income a firm must provide to a resource supplier to attract the resource away from an alternative use; equal to the quantity of other products which cannot be produced when resources are instead used to make a particular product.

Economic efficiency   Obtaining the socially optimal amounts of goods and services using minimum necessary resources; entails both *productive efficiency* and *allocative efficiency*.

Economic growth   (1) An outward shift in the *production possibilities curve* which results from an increase in resource quantity or quality or an improvement in *technology;* (2) an increase either in real output (*gross domestic product*) or in real output per capita.

Economic integration   Cooperation among and the complete or partial unification of the economies of different nations; the elimination of barriers to trade among these nations; the bringing together of the markets in each of the separate economies to form one large (a common) market.

Economic law   (See *Economic principle*.)

Economic model   A simplified picture of economic reality; an abstract generalization.

Economic perspective   A viewpoint which envisions individuals and institutions making rational decisions by comparing the marginal benefits and marginal costs associated with their actions.

Economic policy   A course of action intended to correct or avoid a problem.

Economic principle   A widely accepted generalization about the economic behavior of individuals and institutions.

Economic profit   The *total revenue* of a firm less all its *economic costs;* also called "pure profit" and "above normal profit."

Economic regulation   (See *Industrial regulation*.)

Economic rent   The price paid for the use of land and other natural resources, the supply of which is fixed (*perfectly inelastic*).

Economic resources   The *land, labor, capital,* and *entrepreneurial ability* which are used in the production of goods and services; productive agents; factors of production.

Economics   The social science dealing with the use of scarce resources to obtain the maximum satisfaction of society's virtually unlimited material wants.

Economic theory   Deriving *economic principles* from relevant economic facts; an *economic principle*.

Economic system   A particular set of institutional arrangements and a coordinating mechanism for solving the economizing problem; a method of organizing an economy; of which the *market economy, command economy,* and *traditional economy* are three general types.

Economies of scale   Reductions in the *average total cost* of producing a product as the firm expands the size of plant (its output) in the *long run;* the economies of mass production.

Economizing problem   The choices necessitated because society's material wants for goods and services are unlimited but the *resources* available to satisfy these wants are limited (scarce).

Efficiency factors (in growth)   The capacity of an economy to combine resources effectively to achieve growth of real output which the *supply factors* (of growth) make possible.

Efficiency loss of a tax   The loss of net benefits to society because a tax reduces the production and consumption of a taxed good below the level of allocative efficiency.

Efficient allocation of resources   That allocation of the resources of an economy among the production of different products which leads to the maximum satisfaction of the wants of consumers; producing the socially optimal mix of output with society's scarce resources.

Efficiency wage   A wage which minimizes wage costs per unit of output.

Elastic demand   Product or resource demand whose *price elasticity* is greater than 1; means the resulting change in *quantity demanded* is greater than the percentage change in *price.*

Elasticity coefficient   The number obtained when the percentage change in *quantity demanded* (or supplied) is divided by the percentage change in the *price* of the commodity.

Elasticity formula   (See *Price elasticity of demand.*)

Elastic supply   Product or resource supply whose price elasticity is greater than 1; means the resulting change in quantity supplied is greater than the percentage change in price.

Employment Act of 1946   Federal legislation that committed the Federal government to the maintenance of economic stability (a high level of employment, a stable price level, and economic growth); established the *Council of Economic Advisers* and the *Joint Economic Committee;* and required an annual economic report of the President to Congress.

Employment rate   The percentage of the *labor force* employed at any time.

Employment discrimination   Inferior treatment in hiring, promotions, work assignments, and such for a particular group of employees.

Entitlement programs   Government programs such as *social insurance, food stamps, Medicare,* and *Medicaid* which guarantee particular levels of *transfer payments* to all who fit the programs' criteria.

Entrepreneurial ability   The human resources which combine the other resources to produce a product, make nonroutine decisions, innovate, and bear risks.

Equality versus efficiency tradeoff   The decrease in *economic efficiency* which may accompany a decrease in *income inequality;* the presumption that some income inequality is required to achieve economic efficiency.

Equal Pay Act of 1963   Federal government legislation making it illegal to pay men and women different wage rates if they do equal work on jobs, the performance of which requires equal skill, effort, and responsibility, and which are performed under similar working conditions.

Equation of exchange $MV = PQ$, in which M is the supply of money, V is the *velocity of money, P* is the *price level,* and Q is the physical volume of *final goods and services* produced.

Equilibrium real domestic output   The *gross domestic product* at which the total quantity of final goods and services purchased (*aggregate expenditures*) is equal to the total quantity of final goods and services produced (the real domestic output); the real domestic output at which the *aggregate demand curve* intersects the *aggregate supply curve.*

Equilibrium price   The *price* in a competitive market at which the *quantity demanded* and the *quantity supplied* are equal; where there is neither a *shortage* nor a *surplus;* and where there is no tendency for price to rise or fall.

Equilibrium price level   The price level at which the *aggregate demand curve* intersects the *aggregate supply curve.*

Equilibrium quantity   (1) The quantity demanded and supplied at the equilibrium price in a competitive market; (2) the profit-maximizing output of a firm.

European Union (EU)   An association of European nations initiated in 1958 which has eliminated tariffs and import quotas that existed among them, established common tariffs for goods imported from outside the member nations, allowed the free movement of labor and capital among them, and created other common economic policies.

Excess capacity   Plant resources which are underused when imperfectly competitive firms produce less output than that associated with achieving minimum average total cost.

Excess reserves   The amount by which a bank or thrift's *actual reserves* exceed its *required reserves;* actual reserves minus required reserves.

Exchange control   (See *Foreign exchange control.*)

Exchange rate   The *rate of exchange* of one nation's currency for another nation's currency.

Exchange-rate appreciation   An increase in the value of a nation's currency in foreign exchange markets; an increase in the *rate of exchange* for foreign currencies.

Exchange-rate depreciation   A decrease in the value of a nation's currency in foreign exchange markets; a decrease in the *rate of exchange* for foreign currencies.

Exchange-rate determinant   Any factor other than the *rate of exchange* which determines a currency's demand and supply in the *foreign exchange market.*

Excise tax   A tax levied on the production of a specific product or on the quantity of the product purchased.

Exclusion principle   The ability to exclude those who do not pay for a product from receiving its benefits.

Exclusive unionism   The practice of a *labor union* of restricting the supply of skilled union labor to increase the wages received by union members; the policies typically employed by a *craft union*.

Exhaustive expenditure   An expenditure by government resulting directly in the employment of *economic resources* and in the absorption by government of the goods and services those resources produce; a *government purchase*.

Exit mechanism   The process of leaving a job and searching for another one as a means of improving one's working conditions.

Expanding industry   An industry whose firms earn *economic profits* and which experience an increase in output as new firms enter the industry.

Expansionary fiscal policy   An increase in *government expenditures* for goods and services, a decrease in *net taxes*, or some combination of the two for the purpose of increasing *aggregate demand* and expanding real output.

Expectations   The anticipations of consumers, firms, and others about future economic conditions.

Expected rate of return   The increase in profit a firm anticipates it will obtain by purchasing capital (or engaging in research and development), expressed as a percentage of the total cost of the investment (or R&D) activity.

Expenditures approach   The method which adds all expenditures made for *final goods and services* to measure the *gross domestic product*.

Expenditures-output approach   (See *Aggregate expenditures-domestic output approach*.)

Explicit cost   The monetary payment a *firm* must make to an outsider to obtain a *resource*.

Export controls   The limitation or prohibition of the export of certain products on the basis of foreign policy or national security objectives.

Export-Import Bank   A Federal institution which provides interest-rate subsidies to foreign borrowers who buy U.S. exports on credit.

Exports   Goods and services produced in a nation and sold to customers in other nations.

Export subsidies   Government payments to domestic producers to enable them to reduce the *price* of a good or service to foreign buyers.

Export supply curve   An upsloping curve showing the amount of a product domestic firms will export at each *world price* above the *domestic price*.

Export transactions   A sale of a good or service which increases the amount of foreign currency flowing to the citizens, firms, and governments of a nation.

External benefit   (See *Spillover benefit*.)

External cost   (See *Spillover cost*.)

External debt   Private or public debt owed to foreign citizens, firms, and institutions.

Externality   (See *Spillover*.)

F

Face value   The dollar or cents value stamped on a U.S. coin.

Factors of production   *Economic resources: land, capital, labor,* and *entrepreneurial ability*.

Fair-return price   The price of a product which enables its producer to obtain a *normal profit* and which is equal to the *average total cost* of producing it.

Fallacy of composition   Incorrectly reasoning that what is true for the individual (or part) is necessarily true for the group (or whole).

Fallacy of limited decisions   The false notion that there are a limited number of economic decisions to be made so that, if government makes more decisions, there will be fewer private decisions to render.

Farm problem   Technological advance, coupled with a price-inelastic and relatively constant demand, have made agriculture a *declining industry;* also, the tendency for farm income to fluctuate sharply from year to year.

FDIC   (See *Federal Deposit Insurance Corporation*.)

Federal Advisory Committee   The group of 12 commercial bankers that advises the Board of Governors on banking policy.

Federal Deposit Insurance Corporation (FDIC)   The Federally chartered corporation which insures the deposit liabilities of *commercial banks* and *thrift institutions*.

Federal funds rate   The interest rate banks and other depository institutions charge one another on overnight loans made out of their *excess reserves*.

Federal government   The government of the United States, as distinct from the state and local governments.

Federal Open Market Committee (FOMC)   The 12-member group that determines the purchase-and-sale policies of the *Federal Reserve Banks* in the market for U.S. government securities.

Federal Reserve Banks   The 12 banks chartered by the U.S. government to control the *money supply* and perform other functions. (See *Central bank, Quasipublic bank,* and *Banker's bank*.)

Federal Reserve Notes   Paper money issued by the *Federal Reserve Banks*.

Federal Trade Commission (FTC)   The commission of 5 members established by the *Federal Trade Commission Act* of 1914 to investigate unfair competitive practices of firms, to hold hearings on the complaints of such practices, and to issue *cease-and-desist orders* when firms were found to engage in such practices.

Federal Trade Commission Act   The Federal act of 1914 which established the *Federal Trade Commission*.

Feedback effects (of monetary policy)   The effects that a change in the money supply will have (because it affects the interest rate, planned investment, and the equilibrium GDP) on the demand for money, which is itself directly related to the GDP.

Fiat money   Anything which is *money* because government has decreed it to be money.

Final goods and services   Goods and services which have been purchased for final use and not for resale or further processing or manufacturing.

Financial capital   (See *Money capital*.)

Firm   An organization which employs resources to produce a good or service for profit and owns and operates one or more *plants*.

Fiscal federalism   The system of transfers (grants) by which the Federal government shares its revenues with state and local governments.

Fiscal policy   Changes in government spending and tax collections designed to achieve a full-employment and non-inflationary domestic output; also called *discretionary fiscal policy*.

Five fundamental economic questions   The 5 questions which every economy must answer: how much to produce, what to produce, how to produce it, how to divide the total output, and how to ensure economic flexibility.

Fixed cost   Any cost which in total does not change when the *firm* changes its output; the cost of *fixed resources*.

Fixed exchange rate   A *rate of exchange* which is set in some way and hence prevented from rising or falling with changes in currency supply and demand.

Fixed resource   Any resource whose quantity cannot be changed by a firm in the *short run*.

Flexible exchange rate   A *rate of exchange* determined by the international demand for and supply of a nation's money; a rate free to rise or fall (to float).

Floating exchange rate   (See *Flexible exchange rate*.)

Food stamp program   A program permitting low-income persons to purchase for less than their retail value, or to obtain without cost, coupons that can be exchanged for food items at retail stores.

Foreign competition   (See *Import competition*.)

Foreign exchange control   The control a government may exercise over the quantity of foreign currency demanded by its citizens and firms and over the *rates of exchange* in order to limit its *outpayments* to its *inpayments* (to eliminate a *payments deficit*).

Foreign exchange market   A market in which the money (currency) of one nation can be used to purchase (can be exchanged for) the money of another nation.

Foreign exchange rate   (See *Rate of exchange*.)

Foreign purchase effect   The inverse relationship between the *net exports* of an economy and its price level relative to foreign price levels.

45-degree line   A line along which the value of *GDP* (measured horizontally) is equal to the value of *aggregate expenditures* (measured vertically).

Fractional reserve   A *reserve ratio* that is less than 100 percent of the deposit liabilities of a *commercial bank* or *thrift institution*.

Freedom of choice   The freedom of owners of property resources to employ or dispose of them as they see fit, of workers to enter any line of work for which they are qualified, and of consumers to spend their incomes in a manner which they think is appropriate.

Freedom of enterprise   The freedom of *firms* to obtain economic resources, to use these resources to produce products of the firm's own choosing, and to sell their products in markets of their choice.

"Freedom to Farm" Act   A law passed in 1996 which revamped 60 years of U.S. farm policy by ending *price supports* and *acreage allotments* for wheat, corn, barley, oats, sorghum, rye, cotton, and rice.

Free-rider problem   The inability of potential providers of an economically desirable but indivisible good or service to obtain payment from those who benefit because the *exclusion principle* is not applicable.

Free trade   The absence of artificial (government-imposed) barriers to trade among individuals and firms in different nations.

Frictional unemployment   A type of unemployment caused by workers voluntarily changing jobs and by temporary layoffs; unemployed workers between jobs.

Fringe benefits   The rewards other than *wages* which employees receive from their employers; include pensions, medical and dental insurance, paid vacations, and sick leaves.

Full employment   (1) Use of all available resources to produce want-satisfying goods and services. (2) The situation when the *unemployment rate* is equal to the *full-employment unemployment rate* and there is *frictional* and *structural* but no *cyclical unemployment* (and the *real output* of the economy equals its *potential real output*).

Full-employment budget   A comparison of the government expenditures and tax collections which would occur if the economy operated at *full employment* throughout the year.

Full-employment unemployment rate   The *unemployment rate* at which there is no *cyclical unemployment* of the *labor force*; equal to about 5.5 percent in the United States because some *frictional* and *structural unemployment* are unavoidable.

Full production   Employment of available resources so that the maximum amount of (or total value of) goods and services is produced; occurs when both *productive efficiency* and *allocative efficiency* are realized.

Functional distribution of income   The manner in which *national income* is divided among the functions performed to earn it (or the kinds of resources provided to earn it); the division of national income into wages and salaries, proprietors' income, corporate profits, interest, and rent.

Functional finance The use of *fiscal policy* to achieve a noninflationary full employment *gross domestic product* without regard to the effect on the *public debt.*

G

G-7 Nations A group of seven major industrial nations (the United States, Japan, Germany, United Kingdom, France, Italy, and Canada) whose leaders meet regularly to discuss common economic problems and try to coordinate economic policies. (Recently has also included Russia, making it unofficially the G-8.)

Gains from trade The extra output which trading partners obtain through specialization of production and exchange of goods and services.

Game theory A means of analyzing the pricing behavior of oligopolists using the theory of strategy associated with games such as chess and bridge.

GDP (See *Gross domestic product.*)

GDP deflator The *price index* found by dividing *nominal GDP* by *real GDP;* a price index used to adjust money (or nominal) GDP to real GDP.

GDP gap The amount by which actual *gross domestic product* falls below *potential gross domestic product.*

General Agreement on Tariffs and Trade (GATT) The international agreement reached in 1947 in which 23 nations agreed to give equal and nondiscriminatory treatment to the other nations, to reduce tariff rates by multinational negotiations, and to eliminate *import quotas.* Now includes most nations and has become the *World Trade Organization.*

Generalization Statement of the nature of the relation between two or more sets of facts.

Gold standard A historical system of fixed exchange rates in which nations defined their currency in terms of gold, maintained a fixed relationship between their stock of gold and their money supplies, and allowed gold to be freely exported and imported.

Government purchases Disbursements of money by government for which government receives a currently produced good or service in return; the expenditures of all governments in the economy for *final goods and services.*

Government transfer payment The disbursement of money (or goods and services) by government for which government receives no currently produced good or service in return.

Grievance procedure The methods used by a *labor union* and a *firm* to settle disputes which arise during the life of the collective bargaining agreement between them.

Gross domestic product (GDP) The total market value of all *final goods and services* produced annually within the boundaries of the United States, whether by U.S. or foreign-supplied resources.

Gross private domestic investment Expenditures for newly produced *capital goods* (such as machinery, equipment, tools, and buildings) and for additions to inventories.

Guiding function of prices The ability of price changes to bring about changes in the quantities of products and resources demanded and supplied.

H

Health maintenance organization (HMO) Health care providers which contract with employers, insurance companies, labor unions, or governmental units to provide health care for their workers or others who are insured.

Herfindahl index A measure of the concentration and competitiveness of an industry; calculated as the sum of the squared percentage market shares of the individual firms.

Homogeneous oligopoly An *oligopoly* in which the firms produce a *standardized product.*

Horizontal axis The "left-right" or "west-east" axis on a graph or grid.

Horizontal combination A group of *plants* in the same stage of production which are owned by a single *firm.*

Horizontal merger The merger into a single *firm* of two firms producing the same product and selling it in the same geographical market.

Horizontal range The horizontal segment of the *aggregate-supply curve* along which the price level is constant as real domestic output changes.

Household An economic unit (of one or more persons) which provides the economy with resources and uses the income received to purchase goods and services that satisfy material wants.

Human capital The accumulation of prior investments in education, training, health, and other factors which increase productivity.

Human-capital discrimination The denial to members of particular groups of equal access to productivity-enhancing education and training.

Human-capital investment Any expenditure undertaken to improve the education, skills, health, or mobility of workers, with an expectation of greater productivity and thus a positive return on the investment.

Hyperinflation A very rapid rise in the price level.

Hypothesis A tentative, untested economic principle.

I

Illegal immigrant A person who enters a country without the country's permission for purpose of residing there.

IMF (See *International Monetary Fund.*)

Immobility The inability or unwillingness of a worker to move from one geographic area or occupation to another or from a lower-paying job to a higher-paying job.

Imperfect competition All market structures except *pure competition;* includes *monopoly, monopolistic competition,* and *oligopoly.*

Implicit cost The monetary income a *firm* sacrifices when it uses a resource it owns rather than supplying the resource in the market; equal to what the resource could have earned in the best-paying alternative employment.

Import competition The competition which domestic firms encounter from the products and services of foreign producers.

Import demand curve A downsloping curve showing the amount of a product which an economy will import at each *world price* below the *domestic price*.

Import quota A limit imposed by a nation on the quantity (or total value) of a good which may be imported during some period of time.

Imports Spending by individuals, *firms*, and governments for goods and services produced in foreign nations.

Import transaction The purchase of a good or service which decreases the amount of foreign money held by citizens, firms, and governments of a nation.

Incentive function of price The inducement which an increase in the price of a commodity gives to sellers to make more of it available (and conversely for a decrease in price); and the inducement which an increase in price offers to buyers to purchase smaller quantities (and conversely for a decrease in price).

Incentive pay plan A compensation structure which ties worker pay directly to performance. Such plans include piece rates, bonuses, commissions, and profit sharing.

Inclusive unionism The practice of a labor union of including as members all workers employed in an industry.

Income approach The method that adds all the income generated by the production of *final goods and services* to measure the *gross domestic product*.

Income effect A change in the price of a product changes a consumer's *real income* (*purchasing power*) and thus the quantity of the product purchased.

Income elasticity of demand The ratio of the percentage change in the *quantity demanded* of a good to a percentage change in consumer income; measures the responsiveness of consumer purchases to income changes.

Income inequality The unequal distribution of an economy's total income among persons or families.

Income-maintenance system Government programs designed to eliminate poverty and reduce inequality in the distribution of income.

Increase in demand An increase in the *quantity demanded* of a good or service at every price; a shift of the *demand curve* to the right.

Increase in supply An increase in the *quantity supplied* of a good or service at every price; a shift of the *supply curve* to the right.

Increasing-cost industry An *industry* in which expansion through the entry of new firms increases the prices *firms* in the industry must pay for resources and therefore increases their production costs.

Increasing marginal returns An increase in the *marginal product* of a resource as successive units of the resource are employed.

Independent goods Products or services for which there is no relationship between the price of one and the demand for the other; when the price of one rises or falls, the demand for the other remains constant.

Independent variable The variable causing a change in some other (dependent) variable.

Independent unions U.S. unions which are not affiliated with the AFL-CIO.

Indifference curve A curve showing the different combinations of two products which give a consumer the same satisfaction or *utility*.

Indifference map A set of *indifference curves*, each representing a different level of *utility*, and which together show the preferences of the consumer.

Indirect business taxes Such taxes as *sales*, *excise*, and business *property taxes*, license fees, and *tariffs* which firms treat as costs of producing a product and pass on (in whole or in part) to buyers by charging higher prices.

Individual demand The demand schedule or *demand curve* of a single buyer.

Individual supply The supply schedule or *supply curve* of a single seller.

Induction A method of reasoning which proceeds from facts to *generalization*.

Industrial concentration A situation in which a single firm or a small number of firms produces the major portion of an industry's output; fewness of producers within industries.

Industrially advanced countries High-income countries such as the United States, Canada, Japan, and the nations of western Europe which have highly developed *market economies* based on large stocks of technologically advanced capital goods and skilled labor forces.

Industrial policy Any policy by which government takes a direct and active role in promoting specific firms or industries for purposes of expanding their output and achieving economic growth; called "technology policy" when its goal is to promote *technological advance*.

Industrial regulation The older and more traditional type of regulation in which government is concerned with the prices charged and the services provided the public in specific industries: in contrast to *social regulation*.

Industrial union A *labor union* which accepts as members all workers employed in a particular industry (or by a particular firm).

Industry A group of (one or more) *firms* which produces identical or similar products.

Inelastic demand Product or resource demand for which the *price elasticity coefficient* is less than 1; means the resulting percentage change in *quantity demanded* is less than the percentage change in *price*.

Inelastic supply Product or resource supply for which the price elasticity coefficient is less than 1; the percentage change in *quantity supplied* is less than the percentage change in *price*.

Inferior good A good or service whose consumption declines as income rises (and conversely), price remaining constant.

Inflating Determining *real gross domestic product* by increasing the dollar value of the *nominal gross domestic product* produced in a year in which prices are lower than in a *base year*.

Inflation A rise in the general level of prices in an economy.

Inflation premium The component of the *nominal interest rate* which reflects anticipated inflation.

Inflationary expectations The belief of workers, firms, and consumers that substantial inflation will occur in the future.

Inflationary gap The amount by which the *aggregate expenditures schedule* must shift downward to decrease the *nominal GDP* to its full-employment noninflationary level.

Infrastructure The capital goods usually provided by the *public sector* for the use of its citizens and firms (for example, highways, bridges, transit systems, wastewater treatment facilities, municipal water systems, and airports).

Injection An addition of spending to the income-expenditure stream: *investment*, *government purchases*, and *net exports*.

Injunction A court order directing a person or organization not to perform a certain act because the act would do irreparable damage to some other person or persons; a restraining order.

In-kind investment (See *Nonfinancial investment.*)

In-kind transfer The distribution by government of goods and services to individuals and for which the government receives no currently produced good or service in return; a *government transfer payment* made in goods or services rather than in money; also called a noncash transfer.

Innovation The first commercially successful introduction of a new product, the use of a new method of production, or the creation of a new form of business organization.

Inpayments The receipts of its own or foreign money which individuals, firms, and governments of one nation obtain from the sale of goods and services abroad, or as investment income, *remittances*, and *capitals inflows* from abroad.

Insider-outsider theory The hypothesis that nominal wages are inflexible downward because firms are aware that workers ("insiders") who retain employment during recession may refuse to work cooperatively with previously unemployed workers ("outsiders") who offer to work for less than the current wage.

Insurable risk An event which would result in a loss but whose frequency of occurrence can be estimated with considerable accuracy; insurance companies are willing to sell insurance against such losses.

Interest The payment made for the use of money (of borrowed funds).

Interest income Payments of income to those who supply the economy with *capital*.

Interest rate The annual rate at which interest is paid; a percentage of the borrowed amount.

Interest-rate effect The tendency for increases in the *price level* to increase the demand for money, raise interest rates, and, as a result, reduce total spending in the economy (and the reverse for price level decreases).

Interindustry competition The competition for sales between the products of one industry and the products of another industry.

Interlocking directorate A situation in which one or more members of the board of directors of a *corporation* are also on the board of directors of a competing corporation; illegal under the *Clayton Act*.

Intermediate goods Products which are purchased for resale or further processing or manufacturing.

Intermediate range The upsloping segment of the *aggregate supply curve* lying between the *horizontal range* and the *vertical range*.

Internally held public debt *Public debt* owed to citizens, firms, and institutions of the same nation issuing the debt.

International balance of payments A summary of all the transactions which took place between the individuals, firms, and government unit of one nation and those in all other nations during a year.

International balance of payments deficit (See *Balance of payments deficit.*)

International balance of payments surplus (See *Balance of payments surplus.*)

International Bank for Reconstruction and Development (See *World Bank.*)

International gold standard (See *Gold standard.*)

International Monetary Fund (IMF) The international association of nations which was formed after World War II to make loans of foreign monies to nations with temporary *payments deficits* and, until the early 1970s, to administer the *adjustable pegs*; it now mainly makes loans to nations facing possible defaults on private and government loans.

International monetary reserves The foreign currencies and such assets as gold a nation may use to settle a *payments deficit*.

International value of the dollar The price which must be paid in foreign currency (money) to obtain one U.S. dollar.

Intrinsic value The market value of the metal within a coin.

Invention The first discovery of a product or process through the use of imagination, ingenious thinking, and experimentation and the first proof that it will work.

Inventories Goods which have been produced but are still unsold.

Inverse relationship The relationship between two variables which change in opposite directions, for example, product price and quantity demanded.

Inverted-U theory A theory saying that, other things equal, *R&D* expenditures as a percentage of sales rise with industry concentration, reach a peak at a *concentration ratio* of about 50 percent, and then fall as concentration further increases.

Investment Spending for the production and accumulation of *capital* and additions to inventories.

Investment goods Same as *capital.*

Investment schedule A curve or schedule which shows the amounts firms plan to invest at various possible values of *real gross domestic product.*

Investment-demand curve A curve which shows the amount of *investment* demanded by an economy at a series of *real interest rates.*

Investment in human capital (See *Human-capital investment.*)

Invisible hand The tendency of firms and resource suppliers seeking to further their own self-interests in competitive markets to also promote the interest of society as a whole.

J

Joint Economic Committee (JEC) Committee of Senators and Representatives which investigates economic problems of national interest.

K

Keynesian economics The macroeconomic generalizations which lead to the conclusion that a capitalistic economy is characterized by macroeconomic instability and that *fiscal policy* and *monetary policy* can be used to promote *full employment*, *price-level stability*, and *economic growth.*

Keynesianism The philosophical, ideological, and analytical views pertaining to *Keynesian economics.*

Kinked demand curve The demand curve for a noncollusive oligopolist, which is based on the assumption that rivals will follow a price decrease and will ignore a price increase.

L

Labor The physical and mental talents and efforts of people which are used to produce goods and services.

Labor force Persons 16 years of age and older who are not in institutions and who are employed or are unemployed (and seeking work).

Labor force participation rate The percentage of the working-age population which is actually in the *labor force.*

Labor-intensive commodity A product requiring a relatively large amount of *labor* to produce.

Labor productivity Total output divided by the quantity of labor employed to produce it; the *average product* of labor or output per worker per hour.

Labor theory of value The Marxian idea that the economic value of any commodity is determined solely by the amount of labor required to produce it.

Labor union A group of workers organized to advance the interests of the group (to increase wages, shorten the hours worked, improve working conditions, and so on.).

Laffer curve A curve showing the relationship between tax rates and the tax revenues of government and on which there is a tax rate (between 0 and 100 percent) where tax revenues are a maximum.

Laissez faire capitalism (See *Pure capitalism.*)

Land Natural resources ("free gifts of nature") used to produce goods and services.

Land-intensive commodity A product requiring a relatively large amount of land to produce.

Law of demand The principle that, other things equal, an increase in a product's price will reduce the quantity of it demanded; and conversely for a decrease in price.

Law of diminishing marginal utility As a consumer increases the consumption of a good or service, the *marginal utility* obtained from each additional unit of the good or service decreases.

Law of diminishing returns As successive increments of a *variable resource* are added to a *fixed resource*, the *marginal product* of the *variable resource* will eventually decrease.

Law of increasing opportunity costs As the production of a good increases, the *opportunity cost* of producing an additional unit rises.

Law of supply The principle that, other things equal, an increase in the price of a product will increase the quantity of it supplied; and conversely for a price decrease.

Leakage (1) A withdrawal of potential spending from the income-expenditures stream via *saving*, tax payments, or *imports*. (2) A withdrawal which reduces the lending potential of the banking system.

Leakages-injections approach Determination of the equilibrium *gross domestic product* by finding the real GDP at which *leakages* are equal to *injections.*

Least-cost combination of resources The quantity of each resource a firm must employ in order to produce a particular output at the lowest total cost; the combination at which the ratio of the *marginal product* of a resource to its *marginal resource cost* (to its *price* if the resource is employed in a competitive market) is the same for the last dollar spent on each resource employed.

Legal cartel theory of regulation The hypothesis that some industries seek regulation or want to maintain regulation so they may form or maintain a legal *cartel.*

Legal immigrant A person who lawfully enters a country for the purpose of residing there.

Legal reserves The minimum amount a *depository institution* must keep on deposit with the *Federal Reserve Bank* in its district, or in *vault cash*.

Legal tender Anything which government says must be accepted in payment of a debt.

Lending potential of an individual commercial bank The amount by which a single bank can safely increase the *money supply* by making new loans to (or buying securities from) the public; equal to the bank's excess reserves.

Lending potential of the banking system The amount by which the banking system can increase the money supply by making new loans to (or buying securities from) the public; equal to the *excess reserves* of the banking system multiplied by the *monetary multiplier*.

Liability A debt with a monetary value; an amount owed by a firm or an individual.

Limited liability Restriction of the maximum loss to a predetermined amount for the owners (stockholders) of a *corporation*; the maximum loss is the amount they paid for their shares of stock.

Limited-liability company An unincorporated business whose owners are protected by *limited liability*.

Line-item veto The presidential power to delete specific expenditure items from spending legislation passed by Congress.

Liquidity *Money* or things which can be quickly and easily converted into money with little or no loss of purchasing power.

Loanable funds *Money* available for lending and borrowing.

Loanable funds theory of interest The concept that the supply of and demand for *loanable funds* determine the equilibrium rate of interest.

Lockout An action by a firm which forbids workers to return to work until a new collective bargaining contract is signed; a means of imposing costs (lost wages) on union workers in a collective bargaining dispute.

Logrolling The trading of votes by legislators to secure favorable outcomes on decisions concerning the provision of *public goods* and *quasipublic goods*.

Long run (1) In *microeconomics*, a period of time long enough to enable producers of a product to change the quantities of all the resources they employ; period in which all resources and costs are variable and no resources or costs are fixed. (2) In *macroeconomics*, a period sufficiently long for *nominal wages* and other input prices to change in response to a change in the nation's *price level*.

Long-run aggregate supply curve The *aggregate supply curve* associated with a time period in which input prices (especially *nominal wages*) are fully responsive to changes in the *price level*.

Long-run competitive equilibrium The price at which firms in *pure competition* neither obtain *economic profit* nor suffer losses in the *long run* and the total quantity demanded and

supplied at that price are equal; a price equal to the minimum long-run *average total cost* of producing the product.

Long-run farm problem The tendency for agriculture to be a declining industry as technological progress increases supply relative to an inelastic and slowly increasing demand.

Long-run supply A schedule or curve showing the prices at which a *purely competitive industry* will make various quantities of the product available in the *long run*.

Lorenz curve A curve showing the distribution of income in an economy; the cumulated percentage of families (income receivers) is measured along the horizontal axis and cumulated percentage of income is measured along the vertical axis.

Lump-sum tax A tax which is a constant amount (the tax revenue of government is the same) at all levels of GDP.

M

M1 The most narrowly defined *money supply*; the *currency* and *checkable deposits* not owned by the *Federal government*, *Federal Reserve Banks*, or *depository institutions*.

M2 A more broadly defined money supply; equal to *M1* plus *noncheckable savings deposits, money market deposit accounts*, small *time deposits* (deposits of less than $100,000), and individual *money market mutual fund balances*.

M3 Very broadly defined *money supply*; equal to *M2* plus large *time deposits* (deposits of $100,000 or more).

Macroeconomics The part of economics concerned with the economy as a whole; with such major aggregates as the household, business, and governmental sectors; and with measures of the total economy.

Managed floating exchange rate An *exchange rate* which is allowed to change (float) as a result of changes in currency supply and demand but at times is altered (managed) by governments via their buying and selling of particular currencies.

Managerial-opposition hypothesis An explanation which attributes the relative decline of unionism in the United States to the increased and more aggressive opposition of management to unions.

Managerial prerogatives The decisions which management of the firm has the sole right to make; often enumerated in the labor contract (work agreement) between a *labor union* and a *firm*.

Marginal analysis The comparison of marginal ("extra" or "additional") benefits and marginal costs, usually for decision making.

Marginal benefit The extra (additional) benefit of consuming one more unit of some good or service; the change in total benefit when one more unit is consumed.

Marginal cost The extra (additional) cost of producing one more unit of output; equal to the change in *total cost* divided by the change in output (and in the short run to the change in total *variable cost* divided by the change in output).

Marginal labor cost The amount total labor cost increases when a *firm* employs one additional unit of labor (the quantity of other resources employed remaining constant); equal to the change in the total cost of labor divided by the change in the quantity of labor employed.

Marginal product   The additional output produced when one additional unit of a resource is employed (the quantity of all other resources employed remaining constant); equal to the change in total product divided by the change in the quantity of a resource employed.

Marginal productivity theory of income distribution   The contention that the distribution of income is equitable when each unit of each resource receives a money payment equal to its marginal contribution to the firm's revenue (its *marginal revenue product*).

Marginal propensity to consume   The fraction of any change in *disposable income* spent for *consumer goods*; equal to the change in consumption divided by the change in disposable income.

Marginal propensity to save   The fraction of any change in *disposable income* which households save; equal to the change in *saving* divided by the change in disposable income.

Marginal rate of substitution   The rate at which a consumer is prepared to substitute one good for another (from a given combination of goods) and remain equally satisfied (have the same *total utility*); equal to the slope of a consumer's *indifference curve* at each point on the curve.

Marginal resource cost   The amount the total cost of employing a *resource* increases when a firm employs one additional unit of the resource (the quantity of all other resource employed remaining constant); equal to the change in the *total cost* of the resource divided by the change in the quantity of the resource employed.

Marginal revenue   The change in *total revenue* which results from the sale of one additional unit of a firm's product; equal to the change in total revenue divided by the change in the quantity of the product sold.

Marginal-revenue—marginal-cost approach   A method of determining the total output at which *economic profit* is a maximum (or losses a minimum) by comparing the *marginal revenue* and the *marginal cost* of each additional unit of output.

Marginal revenue product   The change in a firm's *total revenue* when it employs one additional unit of a resource (the quantity of all other resources employed remaining constant); equal to the change in total revenue divided by the change in the quantity of the resource employed.

Marginal tax rate   The tax rate paid on each additional dollar of income.

Marginal utility   The extra *utility* a consumer obtains from the consumption of one additional unit of a good or service; equal to the change in total utility divided by the change in the quantity consumed.

Market   Any institution or mechanism which brings together buyers (demanders) and sellers (suppliers) of a particular good or service.

Market demand   (See *Total demand.*)

Market economy   An economy in which only the private decisions of consumers, resource suppliers, and firms determine how resources are allocated; the market system.

Market failure   The failure of a market to bring about the allocation of resources which best satisfies the wants of society. In particular, the over- or underallocation of resources to the production of a particular good or service because of *spillovers* or informational problems and because markets fail to provide desired *public goods*.

Market for externality rights   A market in which firms can buy rights to pollute the environment; the price of such rights is determined by the demand for the right to pollute and a *perfectly inelastic supply* of such rights (the latter determined by the quantity of pollution which the environment can assimilate).

Market period   A period in which producers of a product are unable to change the quantity produced in response to a change in its price; in which there is a *perfectly inelastic supply*.

Market socialism   An *economic system* (method of organization) in which property resources are publicly owned *and* markets and prices are used to direct and coordinate economic activities.

Market system   All the product and resource markets of a *market economy* and the relationships among them; a method which allows the prices determined in these markets to allocate the economy's scarce resources and to communicate and coordinate the decisions made by consumers, firms, and resource suppliers.

Median-voter model   The view that under majority rule the median (middle) voter will be in the dominant position to determine the outcome of an election.

Medicaid   A Federal program that helps finance the medical expenses of individuals covered by the *Supplemental Security Income* and *Aid to Families with Dependent Children* programs.

Medicare   A Federal program which is financed by *payroll taxes* and provides for (1) compulsory hospital insurance for senior citizens and (2) low-cost voluntary insurance to help older Americans pay physicians' fees.

Medium of exchange   Items sellers generally accept and buyers generally use to pay for a good or service; *money;* a convenient means of exchanging goods and services without engaging in *barter*.

Merger   The combination of two (or more) firms into a single firm.

Microeconomics   The part of economics concerned with such individual units as *industries, firms,* and *households;* and with individual markets, particular prices, and specific goods and services.

Minimum wage   The lowest *wage* employers may legally pay for an hour of work.

Mixed capitalism   An economy in which both government and private decisions determine how resources are allocated.

Monetarism   The macroeconomic view that the main cause of changes in aggregate output and the price level are fluctuations in the *money supply*; advocates of a *monetary rule*.

Monetary multiplier   The multiple of its *excess reserves* by which the banking system can expand *demand deposits* and thus the *money supply* by making new loans (or buying securities); and equal to 1 divided by the *required reserve ratio*.

Monetary policy   A central bank's changing of the *money supply* to influence interest rates and assist the economy in achieving a full-employment, noninflationary level of total output.

Monetary rule   The rule suggested by *monetarism*; the *money supply* should be expanded each year at the same annual rate as the potential rate of growth of the *real gross domestic product*; the supply of money should be increased steadily from 3 to 5 percent per year.

Money   Any item which generally is acceptable to sellers in exchange for goods and services.

Money capital   Money available to purchase *capital*.

Money income   (See *Nominal income*.)

Money interest rate   The *nominal interest rate*; the interest rate which includes an *inflationary premium* (if any).

Money market   The market in which the demand for and the supply of money determine the *interest rate* (or the level of interest rates) in the economy.

Money market deposit account (MMDA)   Interest-earning accounts at *banks* and *thrift institutions*, which pool the funds of depositors to buy various short-term securities.

Money market mutual funds (MMMF)   Interest-bearing accounts offered by investment companies, which pool depositors' funds for the purchase of short-term securities; depositors may write checks in minimum amounts or more against their accounts.

Money supply   Narrowly defined *M*1; more broadly defined, *M*2 and *M*3.

Money wage   (See *Nominal wage*.)

Money wage rate   (See *Nominal wage*.)

Monopolistic competition   A market structure in which many firms sell a *differentiated product*, into which entry is relatively easy, in which the firm has some control over its product price, and in which there is considerable *nonprice competition*.

Monopoly   A market structure in which the number of sellers is so small that each seller is able to influence the total supply and the price of the good or service. (Also see *Pure monopoly*.)

Monopsony   A market structure in which there is only a single buyer of a good, service, or resource.

Moral hazard problem   The possibility that individuals or institutions will change their behavior as the result of a contract or agreement; for example, a bank whose deposits are insured against loss may make riskier loans and investments.

Most-favored-nation (MFN) status   An agreement by the United States to allow some other nation's *exports* into the United States at the lowest tariff level levied by the United States, then or at any later time.

MR = MC rule   A firm will maximize its profit (or minimize its losses) by producing that output at which *marginal revenue* and *marginal cost* are equal, provided product price is equal to or greater than *average variable cost*.

MRP = MRC rule   To maximize profit (or minimize losses) a firm should employ that quantity of a resource at which its *marginal revenue product* (MRP) is equal to its *marginal resource cost* (MRC), the latter being the wage rate in pure competition.

Multinational corporation   A firm which owns production facilities in other countries and produces and sells its product abroad.

Multiple counting   Wrongly including the value of *intermediate goods* in the *gross domestic product*; counting the same good or service more than once.

Multiplier   The ratio of a change in the *equilibrium GDP* to the change in *investment* or in any other component of *aggregate expenditures* or *aggregate demand*; the number by which a change in any component of aggregate expenditures or aggregate demand must be multiplied to find the resulting change in the equilibrium GDP.

Multiplier effect   The effect on equilibrium GDP of a change in *aggregate expenditures* or *aggregate demand* (caused by a change in the *consumption schedule, investment, government expenditures*, or *net exports*).

Mutual interdependence   A situation in which a change in price strategy (or in some other strategy) by one firm will affect the sales and profits of another firm (or other firms); any firm which makes such a change can expect the other rivals to react to the change.

Mutual savings bank   A firm without stockholders which accepts deposits primarily from small individual savers and lends primarily to individuals to finance the purchases of autos and residences.

Mutually exclusive goals   Two or more goals which conflict and cannot be achieved simultaneously.

N

National bank   A *commercial bank* authorized to operate by the U.S. government.

National health insurance (NHI)   A proposed program in which the Federal government would provide a basic package of health care to all citizens at no direct charge or at a low cost-sharing level. Financing would be out of general tax revenues.

National income   Total income earned by resource suppliers for their contributions to *gross national product*; equal to the gross domestic product minus *nonincome charges*, minus *net foreign factor income*.

National income accounting   The techniques used to measure the overall production of the economy and other related variables for the nation as a whole.

National Labor Relations Act (Wagner Act of 1935) As amended, the basic labor-relations law in the United States; defines the legal rights of unions and management and identifies unfair union and management labor practices; established the *National Labor Relations Board.*

National Labor Relations Board (NLRB) The board established by the *National Labor Relations Act* of 1935 to investigate unfair labor practices, to issue *cease-and-desist orders,* and to conduct elections among employees to determine if they wish to be represented by a *labor union.*

Natural monopoly An industry in which *economies of scale* are so great the product can be produced by one firm at a lower average total cost than if the product were produced by more than one firm.

Natural rate hypothesis The idea that the economy is stable in the long run at the *natural rate of unemployment;* views the long-run *Phillips Curve* as vertical at the *natural rate of unemployment.*

Natural rate of unemployment The *full-employment unemployment rate;* the unemployment rate occurring when there is no *cyclical unemployment* and the economy is achieving its *potential output;* the unemployment rate at which actual inflation equals expected inflation.

Near-money Financial assets, the most important of which are *noncheckable savings accounts, time deposits,* and U.S. short-term securities and savings bonds, which are not a medium of exchange but can be readily converted into money.

Negative relationship (See *Inverse relationship.*)

Net domestic product *Gross domestic product* less the part of the year's output which is needed to replace the *capital goods* worn out in producing the output; the nation's total output available for consumption or additions to the *capital stock.*

Net export effect The idea that the impact of a change in *monetary policy* or *fiscal policy* will be strengthened or weakened by the consequent change in *net exports;* the change in net exports occurs because of changes in real interest rates, which affect exchange rates.

Net exports *Exports* minus *imports.*

Net foreign factor income Payments by a nation of resource income to the rest of the world minus receipts of resource income from the rest of the world.

Net investment income The interest and dividend income received by the residents of a nation from residents of other nations less the interest and dividend payments made by the residents of that nation to the residents of other nations.

Net private domestic investment *Gross private domestic investment* less *consumption of fixed capital;* the addition to the nation's stock of *capital* during a year.

Net taxes The taxes collected by government less *government transfer payments.*

Net transfers The personal and government transfer payments made by one nation to residents of foreign nations, less the personal and government transfer payments received from residents of foreign nations.

Net worth The total *assets* less the total *liabilities* of a firm or an individual; the claims of the owners of a firm against its total assets.

New classical economics The theory that, although unanticipated price level changes may create macroeconomic instability in the short run, the economy is stable at the full-employment level of domestic output in the long run because prices and wages adjust automatically to correct movements away from the full employment, noninflationary output.

NLRB (See *National Labor Relations Board.*)

Nominal gross domestic product (GDP) The *GDP* measured in terms of the price level at the time of measurement (unadjusted for *inflation*).

Nominal income The number of dollars received by an individual or group for its resources during some period of time.

Nominal interest rate The interest rate expressed in terms of annual amounts currently charged for interest and not adjusted for inflation.

Nominal wage The amount of money received by a worker per unit of time (hour, day, etc.); money wage.

Noncash transfer A *government transfer payment* in the form of goods and services rather than money, for example, housing assistance and job training; also called in-kind transfers.

Noncheckable savings account A *savings account* against which a check can *not* be written.

Noncollusive oligopoly An *oligopoly* in which the firms do not agree to act together in determining the price of the product and the output each firm will produce.

Noncompeting groups Groups of workers in the economy who do not compete with each other for employment because the skill and training of the workers in one group are substantially different from those in other groups.

Nondiscretionary fiscal policy (See *Built-in stabilizer*.)

Nondurable good A *consumer good* with an expected life (use) of less than 3 years.

Nonexhaustive expenditure An expenditure by government which does not result directly in the employment of economic resources or the production of goods and services; see *Government transfer payment.*

Nonfinancial investment An investment which does not require *households* to save a part of their money incomes; but which uses surplus (unproductive) labor to build *capital goods.*

Nonincome charges *Consumption of fixed capital* and *indirect business taxes;* amounts subtracted from *GDP* (along with *net foreign factor income*) in determining *national income.*

Nonincome determinants of consumption and saving All influences on *consumption* and *saving* other than the level of *GDP.*

Noninterest determinants of investment All influences on the level of investment spending other than the *interest rate.*

Noninvestment transaction An expenditure for stocks, bonds, or second-hand *capital goods.*

Nonmarket transactions The production of goods and services excluded in the measurement of the *gross domestic product* because they are not bought and sold.

Nonprice competition Distinguishing one's product by means of *product differentiation* and then *advertising* the distinguished product to consumers.

Nonproduction transaction The purchase and sale of any item which is not a currently produced good or service.

Nontariff barriers All barriers other than *protective tariffs* which nations erect to impede international trade: include *import quotas*, licensing requirements, unreasonable product-quality standards, and unnecessary red tape in customs procedures.

Normal good A good or service whose consumption increases when income increases and falls when income decreases, price remaining constant.

Normal profit The payment made by a firm to obtain and retain *entrepreneurial ability;* the minimum income which entrepreneurial ability must receive to induce it to perform entrepreneurial functions for a firm.

Normative economics That part of economics involving value judgments about what the economy should be like; concerned with identifying economic goals and promoting them via public policies.

North American Free Trade Agreement (NAFTA) A 1993 agreement establishing, over a 15-year period, a free trade zone composed of Canada, Mexico, and the United States.

O

OASDHI (See *Old Age, Survivors, and Disability Health Insurance.*)

Occupational discrimination Arbitrary restriction of particular groups from entering the more desirable higher-paying occupations.

Occupational licensure The laws of state or local governments which require a worker to satisfy certain specified requirements and obtain a license from a licensing board before engaging in a particular occupation.

Occupational segregation Crowding women or minorities into less desirable, lower-paying occupations.

Official reserves Foreign currencies owned by the central bank of a nation.

Okun's Law The generalization that any one percentage point rise in the *unemployment rate* above the *full-employment unemployment rate* will increase the GDP gap by 2 percent of the *potential output* (GDP) of the economy.

Old Age, Survivors, and Disability Health Insurance The social program in the United States financed by Federal *payroll taxes* on employers and employees and designed to replace some of the *earnings* lost when workers retire, die, or become unable to work.

Oligopoly A market structure in which a few firms sell either a *standardized* or *differentiated product*, into which entry is difficult, in which the firm has limited control over product price because of *mutual interdependence* (except when there is collusion among firms), and in which there is typically *nonprice competition.*

Oligopsony A market in which there are only a few buyers.

OPEC An acronym for the *Organization of Petroleum Exporting Countries.*

Open economy An economy which exports and imports goods and services.

Open-market operations The buying and selling of U.S. government securities by the *Federal Reserve Banks* for purposes of carrying out *monetary policy.*

Open shop A place of employment in which the employer may hire nonunion workers and in which the workers need not become members of a *labor union.*

Opportunity cost The amount of other products which must be forgone or sacrificed to produce a unit of a product.

Organization of Petroleum Exporting Nations (OPEC) The cartel formed in 1970 by 13 oil-producing countries to control the price and quantity of crude oil exported by its members, and which accounts for a large proportion of the world's export of oil.

Other things equal assumption The assumption that factors other than those being considered are held constant.

Outpayments The expenditures of its own or foreign currency which the individuals, firms, and governments of one nation make to purchase goods and services, for *remittances*, as investment income, and *capital outflows* abroad.

Output effect An increase in the price of one input will increase a firm's production costs and reduce its level of output, thus reducing the demand for other inputs; conversely for a decrease in the price of the input.

P

Paper money Pieces of paper used as a *medium of exchange*; in the United States, *Federal Reserve Notes.*

Paradox of voting A situation whereby paired-choice voting by majority rule fails to provide a consistent ranking of society's preferences for *public goods* or services.

Parity concept The idea that year after year a specific output of a farm product should enable a farmer to acquire a constant amount of nonagricultural goods and services.

Parity ratio The ratio of the price received by farmers from the sale of an agricultural commodity to the prices of other goods paid by them; usually expressed as a percentage; used as a rationale for *price supports.*

Partnership An unincorporated firm owned and operated by two or more persons.

Patent An exclusive right to inventors to produce and sell a new product or machine for a set period of time.

Payments deficit   (See *Balance of payments deficit.*)

Payments surplus   (See *Balance of payments surplus.*)

Payroll tax   A tax levied on employers of labor equal to a percentage of all or part of the wages and salaries paid by them; and on employees equal to a percentage of all or part of the wages and salaries received by them.

Per capita GDP   *Gross domestic product* (GDP) per person; the average GDP of a population.

Per capita income   A nation's total income per person; the average income of a population.

Perfectly elastic demand   Product or resource demand in which *quantity demanded* can be of any amount at a particular *price;* graphs as a horizontal *demand curve.*

Perfectly elastic supply   Product or resource supply in which *quantity supplied* can be of any amount at a particular *price;* graphs as a horizontal *supply curve.*

Perfectly inelastic demand   Product or resource demand in which *price* can be of any amount at a particular quantity of the product or resource demanded; *quantity demanded* does not respond to a change in price; graphs as a vertical *demand curve.*

Perfectly inelastic supply   Product or resource supply in which *price* can be of any amount at a particular quantity of the product or resource demanded; *quantity supplied* does not respond to a change in price; graphs as a vertical *supply curve.*

Per se violations   Collusive actions, such as attempts by firms to fix prices or divide a market, which are violations of the *antitrust laws* even if the actions are unsuccessful.

Personal consumption expenditures   The expenditures of *households* for *durable* and *nondurable consumer goods* and services.

Personal distribution of income   The manner in which the economy's *personal* or *disposable income* is divided among different income classes or different households.

Personal income   The earned and unearned income available to resource suppliers and others before the payment of *personal taxes.*

Personal income tax   A tax levied on the *taxable income* of individuals, households, and unincorporated firms.

Personal Responsibility Act   A 1996 law that eliminated the Federal government's 6-decade-long guarantee of cash assistance for poor families, whether adults in the family work or not; sets a limit of 5 years on receiving AFDC benefits and requires able-bodied adults to work after 2 years to continue to receive public assistance.

Personal saving   The *personal income* of households less *personal taxes* and *personal consumption expenditures; disposable income* not spent for *consumer goods.*

Per-unit production cost   The average production cost of a particular level of output; total input cost divided by units of output.

Phillips Curve   A curve showing the relationship between the *unemployment rate* (on the horizontal axis) and the annual rate of increase in the *price level* (on the vertical axis).

Planned economy   An economy in which government determines how resources are allocated.

Planned investment   The amount which *firms* plan or intend to invest.

Plant   A physical establishment which performs one or more functions in the production, fabrication, and distribution of goods and services.

"Play or pay"   A means of expanding health insurance coverage by requiring employers to either provide insurance for their workers or pay a special *payroll tax* to finance insurance for uncovered workers.

$P = MC$ **rule**   A purely competitive firm will maximize its profit or minimize its loss by producing that output at which the *price* of the product is equal to *marginal cost,* provided that price is equal to or greater than *average variable cost* in the short run and equal to or greater than *average total cost* in the long run.

Policy economics   The formulation of courses of action to bring about desired economic outcomes or to prevent undesired occurrences.

Political business cycle   The alleged tendency of Congress to destabilize the economy by reducing taxes and increasing government expenditures before elections and to raise taxes and lower expenditures after elections.

Positive economics   The analysis of facts or data to establish scientific generalizations about economic behavior.

Positive relationship   Direct relationship between two variables.

***Post hoc, ergo propter hoc* fallacy**   Incorrectly reasoning that when one event precedes another the first event must have caused the second event.

Potential competition   New competitors which may be induced to enter an industry if firms now in that industry are receiving large *economic profits.*

Potential output   The real output (*GDP*) an economy can produce when it fully employs its available resources.

Poverty   A situation in which the basic needs of an individual or family exceed the means to satisfy them.

Poverty rate   The percentage of the population with incomes below the official poverty income levels established by the Federal government.

Preferred provider organization (PPO)   The doctors and hospitals that agree to provide health care to insured individuals at rates negotiated with an insurer.

Premature inflation   A type of inflation which sometimes occurs before the economy has reached *full employment.*

Price   The amount of money needed to buy a particular good, service, or resource.

Price ceiling   A legally established maximum price for a good or service.

Price discrimination   The selling of a product to different buyers at different prices when the price differences are not justified by differences in cost.

Price elasticity of demand The ratio of the percentage change in *quantity demanded* of a product or resource to the percentage change in its *price;* a measure of the responsiveness of buyers to a change in the price of a product or resource.

Price elasticity of supply The ratio of the percentage change in *quantity supplied* of a product or resource to the percentage change in its *price;* the responsiveness of producers to a change in the price of a product or resource.

Price fixing The conspiring by two or more firms to set the price of their products; an illegal practice under the *Sherman Act.*

Price floor A legally determined price above the *equilibrium price.*

Price index An index number which shows how the weighted average price of a "market basket" of goods changes through time.

Price leadership An informal method which firms in an *oligopoly* may employ to set the price of their product: one firm (the leader) is the first to announce a change in price, and the other firms (the followers) soon announce identical or similar changes.

Price level The weighted average of the prices of all the final goods and services produced in an economy.

Price-level surprises Unanticipated changes in the price level.

Price maker A seller (or buyer) of a product or resource which is able to affect the product or resource price by changing the amount it sells (or buys).

Price-level stability A steadiness of the price level from one period to the next; zero or low annual inflation; also called "price stability."

Price support A minimum price which government allows sellers to receive for a good or service; a legally established or maintained minimum price.

Price taker A seller (or buyer) of a product or resource who is unable to affect the price at which a product or resource sells by changing the amount it sells (or buys).

Price-wage flexibility Changes in the *prices* of products and in the *wages* paid to workers; the ability of prices and wages to rise or fall.

Price war Successive and continued decreases in the prices charged by the firms in an oligopolistic industry; each firm lowers its price below rivals' prices, hoping to increase its sales and revenues at its rivals expense.

Prime interest rate The *interest rate* banks charge their most creditworthy borrowers, for example, large corporations with excellent financing credentials.

Principal-agent problem A conflict of interest which occurs when agents (workers or managers) pursue their own objectives to the detriment of the principals' (stockholders) goals.

Private good A good or service which is subject to the *exclusion principle* and which is provided by privately owned firms to consumers who are willing to pay for it.

Private property The right of private persons and firms to obtain, own, control, employ, dispose of, and bequeath *land, capital,* and other property.

Private sector The *households* and business *firms* of the economy.

Process innovation The development and use of a new or improved production or distribution method.

Product differentiation A strategy in which one firm's product is distinguished from competing products by means of its design, related services, quality, location, or other attributes (except price).

Product innovation The development and sale of a new or improved product (or service).

Production possibilities curve A curve showing the different combinations of two goods or services that can be produced in a *full-employment, full-production* economy in which the available supplies of resources and technology are fixed.

Productive efficiency The production of a good in the least costly way; occurs when production takes place at the output at which *average total cost* is a minimum and at which *marginal product* per dollar's worth of input is the same for all inputs.

Productivity A measure of average output or real output per unit of input. For example, the productivity of labor may be found by dividing real output by hours of work.

Productivity slowdown The decline in the rate at which *labor productivity* in the United States has increased in recent decades.

Product market A market in which products are sold by *firms* and bought by *households.*

Profit The return to the resource *entrepreneurial ability* (see *Normal profit*); *total revenue* minus *total cost* (see *Economic profit*).

Profit-maximizing combination of resources The quantity of each resource a firm must employ to maximize its profit or minimize its loss; the combination in which the *marginal revenue product* of each resource is equal to its *marginal resource cost* (to its *price* if the resource is employed in a competitive market).

Profit sharing plan A compensation device through which workers receive part of their pay in the form of a share of their employer's profit (if any).

Progressive tax A tax whose *average tax rate* increases as the taxpayer's income increases and decreases as the taxpayer's income decreases.

Property tax A tax on the value of property (*capital, land,* stocks and bonds, and other *assets*) owned by *firms* and *households.*

Proportional tax A tax whose *average tax rate* remains constant as the taxpayer's income increases or decreases.

Proprietor's income The net income of the owners of unincorporated firms (proprietorships and partnerships).

Protective tariff   A *tariff* designed to shield domestic producers of a good or service from the competition of foreign producers.

Public assistance programs   Government programs which pay benefits to those who are unable to earn income (because of permanent handicaps or because they have very low income and dependent children); financed by general tax revenues and viewed as public charity (rather than earned rights).

Public choice theory   The economic analysis of collective and government decision making, politics, and the democratic process.

Public debt   The total amount owed by the Federal government to the owners of government securities; equal to the sum of past government *budget deficits* less government *budget surpluses*.

Public finance   The branch of economics which analyzes government revenues and expenditures.

Public good   A good or service which is indivisible and to which the *exclusion principle* does not apply; a good or service with these characteristics provided by government.

Public interest theory of regulation   The presumption that the purpose of the regulation of an *industry* is to protect the public (consumers) from abuse of the power possessed by *natural monopolies*.

Public sector   The part of the economy which contains all government entities; government.

Public sector failure   Inefficiencies in resource allocation caused by problems in the operation of the public sector (government); occurs because of rent-seeking pressure by special-interest groups, short-sighted political behavior, limited and bundled choices, and bureaucratic inefficiencies.

Public utility   A firm which produces an essential good or service, has obtained from a government the right to be the sole supplier of the good or service in the area, and is regulated by that government to prevent the abuse of its monopoly power.

Purchasing power   The amount of goods and services which a monetary unit of income can buy.

Purchasing power parity   The idea that exchange rates between nations equate the purchasing power of various currencies; exchange rates between any two nations adjust to reflect the price-level differences between the countries.

Pure capitalism   An economic system in which property resources are privately owned and markets and prices are used to direct and coordinate economic activities.

Pure competition   A market structure in which a very large number of firms sell a *standardized product*, into which entry is very easy, in which the individual seller has no control over the product price, and in which there is no nonprice competition; a market characterized by a very large number of buyers and sellers.

Pure monopoly   A market structure in which one firm sells a unique product, into which entry is blocked, in which the single firm has considerable control over product price, and in which *nonprice competition* may or may not be found.

Pure profit   (See *Economic profit*.)

Pure rate of interest   An essentially risk-free, long-term interest rate which is free of the influence of market imperfections.

Q

Quantity demanded   The amount of a good or service buyers (or a buyer) desire to purchase at a particular price during some period.

Quantity supplied   The amount of a good or service producers (or a producer) offer to sell at a particular price during some period.

Quasipublic bank   A bank which is privately owned but governmently (publicly) controlled; each of the U.S. *Federal Reserve Banks*.

Quasipublic good   A good or service to which the *exclusion principle* could apply but which has such a large *spillover benefit* that government sponsors its production to prevent an underallocation of resources.

R

R&D   Research and development activities undertaken to bring about *technological progress*.

Ratchet effect   The tendency for the *price level* to rise when *aggregate demand* increases but not fall when aggregate demand declines.

Rate of exchange   The price paid in one's own money to acquire one unit of a foreign currency; the rate at which the money of one nation is exchanged for the money of another nation.

Rate of return   The gain in net revenue divided by the cost of an investment or a *R&D* expenditure; expressed as a percentage.

Rational expectations theory   The hypothesis that firms and households expect monetary and fiscal policies to have certain effects on the economy and (in pursuit of their own self-interests) take actions which make those policies ineffective.

Rationing function of prices   The ability of market forces in a competitive market to equalize *quantity demanded* and *quantity supplied* and to eliminate shortages and surpluses via changes in prices.

Real-balances effect   The tendency for increases in the price level to lower the real value (or purchasing power) of financial assets with fixed money value and, as a result, to reduce total spending; and conversely for decreases in the price level; also called the *wealth effect*.

Real business cycle theory   A theory that *business cycles* result from changes in technology and resource availability, which affect *productivity* and thus increase or decrease *long-run aggregate supply*.

Real capital   (See *Capital*.)

Real gross domestic product (GDP)   *Gross domestic product* adjusted for inflation; gross domestic product in a year divided by the *GDP deflator* for that year, expressed as a decimal.

Real GDP   (See *Real gross domestic product.*)

Real income   The amount of goods and services which can be purchased with *nominal income* during some period of time; nominal income adjusted for inflation.

Real interest rate   The interest rate expressed in dollars of constant value (adjusted for *inflation*); and equal to the *nominal interest rate* less the expected rate of inflation.

Real wage   The amount of goods and services a worker can purchase with his or her *nominal wage;* the purchasing power of the nominal wage.

Recession   A period of declining real GDP, accompanied by lower real income and higher unemployment.

Recessionary gap   The amount by which the *aggregate expenditures schedule* must shift upward to increase the *real GDP* to its full-employment, noninflationary level.

Reciprocal Trade Agreements Act   A 1934 Federal law which gave the President the authority to negotiate up to 50 percent lower tariffs with foreign nations that agreed to reduce their tariffs on U.S. goods (and which incorporated the *most-favored-nation clause*).

Refinancing the public debt   Paying owners of maturing government securities with money obtained by selling new securities or with new securities.

Regressive tax   A tax whose *average tax rate* decreases as the taxpayer's income increases, and increases as the taxpayer's income decreases.

Regulatory agency   An agency, commission, or board established by the Federal government or a state government to control the prices charged and the services offered by a natural monopoly.

Rental income   The payments (income) received by those who supply *land* to the economy.

Rent-seeking behavior   The actions by persons, firms, or unions to gain special benefits from government at the taxpayers' or someone else's expense.

Required reserves   The funds which banks and thrifts must deposit with the *Federal Reserve Bank* (or hold as *vault cash*) to meet the legal *reserve requirement;* a fixed percentage of the bank or thrift's checkable deposits.

Reserve requirement   The specified minimum percentage of its checkable deposits which a bank or thrift must keep on deposit at the Federal Reserve Bank in its district, or in *vault cash*.

Resource market   A market in which *households* sell and *firms* buy resources or the services of resources.

Retiring the public debt   Reducing the size of the *public debt* by paying money to owners of maturing U.S. government securities.

Revaluation   An increase in the governmentally defined value of its currency relative to other nations' currencies.

Revenue tariff   A *tariff* designed to produce income for the Federal government.

Reverse discrimination   The view that the preferential treatment associated with *affirmative action* efforts constitutes discrimination against other groups.

Right-to-work law   A state law (in about 20 states) which makes it illegal to require a worker to join a *labor union* in order to retain his or her job; laws which make *union shops* illegal.

Roundabout production   The construction and use of *capital* to aid in the production of *consumer goods*.

Rule of reason   The rule stated and applied in the *U.S. Steel case* that only combinations and contracts unreasonably restraining trade are subject to actions under the antitrust laws and that size and possession of monopoly power are not themselves illegal.

Rule of 70   A method for determining the number of years it will take for some measure to double, given its annual percentage increase. Example: To determine the number of years it will take for the *price level* to double; divide 70 by the annual rate of *inflation*.

S

Sales tax   A tax levied on the cost (at retail) of a broad group of products.

Saving   Disposable income not spent for consumer goods; equal to *disposable income* minus *personal consumption expenditures*.

Savings deposit   An interest-bearing deposit which normally can be withdrawn by the depositor at any time.

Savings and Loan association (S&L)   A firm which accepts deposits primarily from small individual savers and lends primarily to individuals to finance purchases such as autos and homes; now nearly indistinguishable from a *commercial bank*.

Saving schedule   A schedule which shows the amounts *households* plan to save (plan not to spend for *consumer goods*), at different levels of *disposable income*.

Savings institution   A *thrift institution*.

Say's law   The largely discredited macroeconomic generalization that the production of goods and service (supply) creates an equal *demand* for these goods and service.

Scarce resources   The limited quantities of *land, capital, labor,* and *entrepreneurial ability* which are never sufficient to satisfy the virtually unlimited material wants of humans.

Seasonal variations   Increases and decreases in the level of economic activity within a single year, caused by a change in the season.

Secular trend   Long-term tendency; change in some variable over a very long period of years.

Self-interest   That which each firm, property owner, worker, and consumer believes is best for itself and seeks to obtain.

Seniority   The length of time a worker has been employed absolutely or relative to other workers; may be used to determine which workers will be laid off when there is insufficient work for them all, and who will be rehired when more work becomes available.

Separation of ownership and control The fact that different groups of people own a *corporation* (the stockholders) and manage it (the directors and officers).

Service An (intangible) act or use for which a consumer, firm, or government is willing to pay.

Sherman Act The Federal antitrust act of 1890 which made monopoly and conspiracies to restrain trade criminal offenses.

Shirking Actions by workers to increase their *utility* or well-being by neglecting or evading work.

Shut-down case The circumstance in which a firm would experience a loss greater than its total *fixed cost* if it were to produce any output greater than zero; alternatively, a situation in which a firm would cease to operate when the *price* at which it can sell its product is less than its *average variable cost*.

Shortage The amount by which the *quantity demanded* of a product exceeds the *quantity supplied* at a particular (below-equilibrium) price.

Short run (1) In *microeconomics*, a period of time in which producers are able to change the quantity of some but not all of the resources they employ; a period in which some resources (usually plant) are fixed and some are variable. (2) In *macroeconomics*, a period in which nominal wages and other input prices do not change in response to a change in the price level.

Short-run aggregate supply curve An aggregate supply curve relevant to a time period in which input prices (particularly *nominal wages*) do not change in response to changes in the *price level*.

Short-run supply curve A supply curve which shows the quantity of a product a firm in a purely competitive industry will offer to sell at various prices in the *short run*; the portion of the firm's short-run marginal cost curve which lies above its *average variable cost* curve.

Short-run competitive equilibrium The price at which the total quantity of a product supplied in the *short run* in a purely competitive industry equals the total quantity of the product demanded and which is equal to or greater than *average variable cost*.

Short-run farm problem The sharp year-to-year changes in the prices of agricultural products and in the incomes of farmers.

Simple multiplier The *multiplier* in an economy in which government collects no *net taxes*, there are no *imports*, and *investment* is independent of the level of income; equal to 1 divided by the *marginal propensity to save*.

Slope of a line The ratio of the vertical change (the rise or fall) to the horizontal change (the run) between any two points on a line. The slope of an upward sloping line is positive, reflecting a direct relationship between two variables; the slope of a downward sloping line is negative, reflecting an inverse relationship between two variables.

Smoot-Hawley Tariff Act Legislation passed in 1930 which established very high tariffs. Its objective was to reduce imports and stimulate the domestic economy, but it only resulted in retaliatory tariffs by other nations.

Social accounting (See *National income accounting*.)

Social insurance programs The programs which replace some of the earnings lost when people retire or are temporarily unemployed, which are financed by *payroll taxes*, and which are viewed as earned rights (rather than charity).

Socially optimal price The price of a product which results in the most efficient allocation of an economy's resources and is equal to the *marginal cost* of the product.

Social regulation The regulation by which government is concerned with the conditions under which goods and services are produced, their physical characteristics, and the impact of their production on society; in contrast to *industrial regulation*.

Social security program (See *Old Age, Survivorship, and Disability Health Insurance* program.)

Sole proprietorship An unincorporated *firm* owned and operated by one person.

Special economic zones Regions of China open to foreign investment, private ownership, and relatively free international trade.

Special-interest effect Any result of government promotion of the interests (goals) of a small groups at the expense of a much larger group.

Specialization The use of the resources of an individual, a firm, a region, or a nation to produce one or a few goods and services.

Speculation The activity of buying or selling with the motive of later reselling or rebuying for profit.

Spillover A benefit or cost from production or consumption, accruing without compensation to nonbuyers and nonsellers of the product (see *Spillover benefit; Spillover costs*).

Spillover benefit A benefit obtained without compensation by third parties from the production or consumption of sellers or buyers. Example: A beekeeper benefits when a neighboring farmer plants clover.

Spillover cost A cost imposed without compensation on third parties by the production or consumption of sellers or buyers. Example: A manufacturer dumps toxic chemicals into a river, killing the fish sport fishers seek.

SSI (See *Supplemental Security Income*.)

Stagflation Inflation accompanied by stagnation in the rate of growth of output and an increase in unemployment in the economy; simultaneous increases in the *price level* and the *unemployment rate*.

Standardized product A product for which buyers are indifferent to the seller from whom they purchase it so long as the price charged by all sellers is the same; a product for which all units of the product are identical and thus perfect substitutes for each other.

Startup (firm)   A new firm focused on creating and introducing a particular new product or employing a specific new production or distribution method.

State bank   A *commercial bank* authorized by a state government to engage in the business of banking.

State-owned enterprises   Businesses which are owned by government; the major types of enterprises in Russia and China before their transitions to the market system.

Statistical discrimination   Judging an individual on the basis of the average characteristic of the group to which the person belongs rather than on personal characteristics.

Stock (corporate)   An ownership share in a corporation.

Store of value   An *asset* set aside for future use; one of the three functions of *money*.

Strategic trade policy   The use of trade barriers to reduce the risk inherent in product development by domestic firms, particularly that involving advanced technology.

Strike   The withholding of labor services by an organized group of workers (a *labor union*).

Structural-change hypothesis   The explanation which attributes the decline of unionism in the United States to changes in the structure of the economy and of the labor force.

Structural deficit   The extent to which the Federal government's expenditures exceed its tax revenues when the economy is at full employment (or the extent to which its current expenditures exceed the projected tax revenues which would accrue if the economy were at full employment); also known as a full-employment budget deficit.

Structural unemployment   Unemployment of workers whose skills are not demanded by employers, they lack sufficient skill to obtain employment, or they cannot easily move to locations where jobs are available.

Subsidy   A payment of funds (or goods and services) by a government, firm, or household for which it receives no good or service in return; when made by a government, it is a *government transfer payment*.

Substitute goods   Products or services which can be used in place of each other. When the price of one falls the demand for the other falls, and conversely with an increase of price.

Substitution effect   (1) A change in the price of a *consumer good* changes the relative expensiveness of that good and hence changes the consumer's willingness to buy it rather than other goods. (2) The effect of a change in the price of a *resource* on the quantity of the resource employed by a firm, assuming no change in its output.

Sunk cost   A cost which has been incurred and cannot be recovered.

Superfund Law   Federal legislation of 1980 which taxes manufacturers of toxic products and uses the revenues to finance the cleanup of toxic-waste sites; assigns liability for improperly dumped waste to the firms producing, transporting, and dumping that waste.

Superior good   (See *Normal good*.)

Supplementary Security Income program   A federally financed and administered program which provides a uniform nationwide minimum income for the aged, blind, and disabled who do not qualify for benefits under *the Old Age, Survivors, and Disability Health Insurance* or *unemployment insurance* program in the United States.

Supply   A schedule showing the amounts of a good or service sellers (or a seller) will offer at various prices during some period.

Supply curve   A curve illustrating *supply*.

Supply factor (in growth)   An increase in the availability of a resource, an improvement in its quality, or an expansion of technological knowledge which makes it possible for an economy to produce a greater output of goods and services.

Supply shock   An event which increases production costs, decreases *aggregate supply*, reduces *real GDP*, and increases *unemployment*.

Supply-side economics   A view of macroeconomics which emphasizes the role of costs and *aggregate supply* in explaining *inflation*, *unemployment*, and *economic growth*.

Surplus   The amount by which the *quantity supplied* of a product exceeds the *quantity demanded* at a specific (above-equilibrium) price.

Surplus payment   A payment to a resource which is not required to ensure the availability of the resource, for example, land rent.

Surplus value   A Marxian term; the amount by which the value of a worker's daily output exceeds the worker's daily wage; workers' output appropriated by capitalists as profit.

T

Tacit collusion   Any method by an oligopolist to set prices and outputs which does not involve outright (or overt) *collusion*; *price leadership* is an example.

Tariff   A tax imposed by a nation on an imported good.

Taste-for-discrimination model   A theory of discrimination which views discrimination as a preference for which an employer is willing to pay.

Tax   An involuntary payment of money (or goods and services) to a government by a *household* or *firm* for which the household or firm receives no good or service directly in return.

Tax incidence   The person or group who ends up paying a tax.

Tax subsidy   A grant in the form of reduced taxes through favorable tax treatment; for example, employer-paid health insurance is exempt from Federal income and payroll taxes.

Tax-transfer disincentives   Decreases in the incentives to work, save, invest, innovate, and take risks which allegedly result from high *marginal tax rates* and *transfer-payments*.

Technology The body of knowledge and techniques which can be used to produce goods and services from *economic resources.*

Technological advance New and better goods and services and new and better ways of producing or distributing them.

Terms of trade The rate at which units of one product can be exchanged for units of another product; the price of a good or service; the amount of one good or service which must be given up to obtain one unit of another good or service.

Theory of human capital Generalization that *wage differentials* are the result of differences in the amount of *human-capital investment*, and that the incomes of lower paid workers are increased by increasing the amount of such investment.

Thrift institution A *savings and loan association, mutual savings bank,* or *credit union.*

Tight money policy *Federal Reserve System* actions which contract, or restrict, the growth of the nation's *money supply* for the purpose of reducing or eliminating inflation.

Till money (See *Vault cash.*)

Time deposit An interest-earning deposit in a *commercial bank* or *thrift institution* which the depositor can withdraw without penalty after the end of a specified period.

Token money Coins having a *face value* greater than their *intrinsic value.*

Total cost The sum of *fixed cost* and *variable cost.*

Total demand The demand schedule or the *demand curve* of all buyers of a good or service; also called market demand.

Total demand for money The sum of the *transactions demand for money* and the *asset demand for money.*

Total product The total output of a particular good or service produced by a firm (or a group of firms or the entire economy).

Total revenue The total number of dollars received by a firm (or firms) from the sale of a product; equal to the total expenditures for the product produced by the firm (or firms); equal to the quantity sold (demanded) multiplied by the price at which it is sold.

Total-revenue test A test to determine elasticity of *demand* between any two prices: Demand is elastic if *total revenue* moves in the opposite direction as price; it is inelastic when it moves in the same direction as price; and it is of unitary elasticity when it does not change when price changes.

Total spending The total amount buyers of goods and services spend or plan to spend; also called *aggregate expenditures.*

Total supply The supply schedule or the supply curve of all sellers of a good or service; also called market supply.

Total utility The total amount of satisfaction derived from the consumption of a single product or a combination of products.

Township and village enterprises Privately owned rural manufacturing firms in China.

Trade balance The export of goods (or goods and services) of a nation less its imports of goods (or goods and services).

Trade bloc A group of nations which lowers or abolishes trade barriers among members. Examples include the *European Union* and the nations of the *North American Free Trade Agreement.*

Trade controls *Tariffs, export subsidies, import quotas,* and other means a nation may use to reduce *imports* and expand *exports.*

Trade deficit The amount by which a nation's *imports* of goods (or goods and services) exceed its *exports* of goods (or goods and services).

Trademark A legal protection which gives the originators of a product an exclusive right to use the brand name.

Tradeoffs The sacrifice of some or all of one economic goal, good, or service to achieve some other goal, good, or service.

Trade surplus The amount by which a nation's exports of goods (or goods and services) exceed its imports of goods (or goods and services).

Trading possibilities line A line which shows the different combinations of two products an economy is able to obtain (consume) when it specializes in the production of one product and trades (exports) it to obtain the other product.

Traditional economy An economic system in which traditions and customs determine how the economy will use its scarce resources.

Transactions demand for money The amount of money people want to hold for use as a *medium of exchange* (to make payments), and which varies directly with the *nominal GDP.*

Transfer payment A payment of *money* (or goods and services) by a government to a *household* or *firm* for which the payer receives no good or service directly in return.

Tying contract A promise made by a buyer when allowed to purchase a product from a seller that it will purchase certain other products from the same seller; a practice forbidden by the *Clayton Act.*

U

Unanticipated inflation Increases in the price level (*inflation*) at a rate greater than expected.

Underemployment (1) Failure to produce the maximum amount of goods and services which can be produced from the resources employed; failure to achieve *full production.* (2) A situation in which workers are employed in positions requiring less than the amount of education and skill than they have.

Undistributed corporate profits After-tax corporate profits not distributed as dividends to stockholders; corporate or business saving; also called retained earnings.

Unemployment Failure to use all available *economic resources* to produce goods and services; failure of the economy to fully employ its *labor force.*

Unemployment compensation (See *Unemployment insurance.*)

Unemployment insurance The social insurance program which in the United States is financed by state *payroll taxes* on employers and makes income available to workers who become unemployed and are unable to find jobs.

Unemployment rate The percentage of the *labor force* unemployed at any time.

Uninsurable risk An event which would result in a loss and whose occurrence is uncontrollable and unpredictable; insurance companies are not willing to sell insurance against such a loss.

Union shop A place of employment where the employer may hire either *labor union* members or nonmembers but where nonmembers must become members within a specified period of time or lose their jobs.

Unit elasticity Demand or supply for which the *elasticity coefficient* is equal to 1; means the percentage change in the quantity demanded or supplied is equal to the percentage change in price.

Unit labor cost Labor costs per unit of output; total labor cost divided by total output; also equal to the *nominal wage rate* divided by the *average product* of labor.

Unit of account A standard unit in which prices can be stated and the value of goods and services can be compared; one of the three functions of *money.*

Unlimited liability Absence of any limits on the maximum amount which an individual (usually a business owner) may become legally required to pay.

Unlimited wants The insatiable desire of consumers for goods and services which will give them satisfaction or *utility.*

Unplanned investment Actual investment less *planned investment;* increases or decreases in the *inventories* of firms resulting from production greater than sales.

Urban collectives Chinese enterprises jointly owned by their managers and their workforces, located in urban areas.

Uruguay Round The eighth and most recent round of trade negotiations under *GATT* (now the *World Trade Organization*).

U.S. Steel case The antitrust action brought by the Federal government against the U.S. Steel Corporation, in which the courts ruled (in 1920) that only unreasonable restraints of trade were illegal and that size and the possession of monopoly power were not violations of the antitrust laws.

Usury laws State laws which specify the maximum legal interest rate at which loans can be made.

Utility The want-satisfying power of a good or service; the satisfaction or pleasure a consumer obtains from the consumption of a good or service (or from the consumption of a collection of goods and services).

Utility-maximizing rule To obtain the greatest *utility* the consumer should allocate *money income* so that the last dollar spent on each good or service yields the same marginal utility.

V

Value added The value of the product sold by a *firm* less the value of the products (materials) purchased and used by the firm to produce the product.

Value-added tax A tax imposed on the difference between the value of the products sold by a firm and the value of the goods purchased from other firms to produce the product.

Value judgment Opinion of what is desirable or undesirable; belief regarding what ought or ought not to be (regarding what is right or just and wrong or unjust).

Value of money The quantity of goods and services for which a unit of money (a dollar) can be exchanged; the purchasing power of a unit of money; the reciprocal of the *price level.*

Variable cost A cost which in total increases when the firm increases its output and decreases when it reduces its output.

VAT (See *Value-added tax.*)

Vault cash The *currency* a bank has in its vault and cash drawers.

Velocity The number of times per year the average dollar in the *money supply* is spent for *final goods and services;* nominal GDP divided by the money supply.

Venture capital That part of household saving used to finance high-risk business ventures in exchange for shares of the profit if the business endeavors succeed.

Vertical axis The "up-down" or "north-south" axis on a graph or grid.

Vertical combination A group of *plants* engaged in different stages of the production of a final product and owned by a single *firm.*

Vertical intercept The point at which a line meets the vertical axis of a graph.

Vertical merger The merger of one or more *firms* engaged in different stages of the production of a final product.

Vertical range The vertical segment of the aggregate supply curve along which the economy is at full capacity.

Very long run A period in which *technology* can change and in which *firms* can introduce new products.

Vicious circle of poverty A problem common in some developing countries in which their low per capita incomes are an obstacle to realizing the levels of saving and investment requisite to acceptable rates of economic growth.

Voice mechanism Communication by workers through their union to resolve grievances with an employer.

Voluntary export restrictions Voluntary limitations by countries or firms of their exports to a particular foreign nation to avoid enactment of formal trade barriers by that nation.

W

Wage The price paid for the use or services of *labor* per unit of time (per hour, per day, and so on).

Wage differential The difference between the *wage* received by one worker or group of workers and that received by another worker or group of workers.

Wage discrimination The payment of a lower wage to members of particular groups than to preferred workers for the same work.

Wage rate (See *Wage*.)

Wages The income of those who supply the economy with *labor*.

Wealth effect (See *Real balances effect*.)

Welfare programs (See *Public assistance programs*.)

Wheeler-Lea Act The Federal act of 1938 which amended the *Federal Trade Commission Act* by prohibiting and giving the commission power to investigate unfair and deceptive acts or practices of commerce (such as false and misleading advertising and the misrepresentation of products).

"Will to develop" Wanting economic growth strongly enough to change from old to new ways of doing things.

World Bank A bank which lends (and guarantees loans) to developing nations to help them increase their *capital stock* and thus achieve *economic growth;* formally, the International Bank for Reconstruction and Development.

World price The international market price of a good or service, determined by world demand and supply.

World Trade Organization An organization established in 1994 to replace *GATT* to oversee the provisions of the *Uruguay round* and resolve any disputes stemming therefrom.

X

X-inefficiency Failure to produce any specific output at the lowest average (and total) cost possible.